S0-ECN-743

IMMIGRATION AND
NATIONALITY LAW

IMMIGRATION AND NATIONALITY LAW

Cases and Materials
Second Edition

Richard A. Boswell
Professor of Law
University of California
Hastings College of the Law

with

Gilbert Paul Carrasco
Professor of Law
Villanova University
School of Law

KF
4818
.B67
1992
West

To my parents, Dorothy E. Boswell and William P. Boswell, whose love and support for each other and their family have been an inspiration to me throughout my life.

and

To Karen, with love and appreciation for her constant support.

—R.A.B.

To my parents, Paul and Delia Carrasco.

—G.P.C.

The author acknowledges
WESTLAW
for allowing its use in the preparation of this book.

Copyright © 1992 by Richard Boswell
All Rights Reserved

International Standard Book Number: 0-89089-490-6
Library of Congress Card Catalog Number: 91-78016

Carolina Academic Press
700 Kent Street
Durham, North Carolina 27701
(919) 489-7486

Printed in the United States of America

Table of Contents

Acknowledgments

We have had occasion to note the striking resemblance between some of the laws we are called upon to interpret and King Minos's labyrinth in ancient Crete. The Tax Laws and the Immigration and Nationality Acts are examples we have cited of Congress's ingenuity in passing statutes certain to accelerate the aging process of judges. In this instance, Congress, pursuant to its virtually unfettered power to exclude or deport natives of other countries, and apparently confident of the aphorism that human skill, properly applied, can resolve any enigma that human inventiveness can create, has enacted a baffling skein of provisions for the I.N.S. and courts to disentangle.

These words, written by Chief Judge Irving R. Kaufman in *Lok v. INS*, 548 F.2d 37 (2d Cir. 1977), are an incredibly accurate description of U.S. immigration law. The undertaking to write this book came both from my realization of the wisdom of Judge Kaufman's observation and the challenge to make the law more understandable. This project started eight years ago when I began teaching immigration law at the George Washington University, National Law Center. Since the project first began, Congress has made several attempts at immigration reform. Indeed, at this writing the 101st Congress is considering even more changes to the law. No doubt, each amendment creates additional challenges for the teacher to make a little more sense of the resulting legislative chaos.

This book could not have been completed without the assistance and support of many friends and colleagues. Some of the people mentioned provided knowledgeable guidance and support without even knowing that their wisdom would find its way into this book. Others provided inspiration by example. Still others, commented on portions of the manuscript or answered questions on the finer points of immigration law.

I will be forever indebted to Charles Gordon, Ira Kurzban, Maurice Roberts and Marc Van der Hout and the late Jack Wasserman, lawyers and scholars who have been the driving forces for positive change in this country's immigration law and policy. Their continued commitment to principle and professionalism have been an inspiration to me as well as countless others in this field.

I give special thanks to Jerome A. Barron, C. Thomas Dienes, Harold P. Green and Eric S. Sirulnik of the National Law Center for their support and friendship while I was on the law faculty. There is no doubt in my mind that without the moral and financial support from the Notre Dame Law School's Deans David T. Link and Assistant Dean William O. McLean this project might never have been completed. Surely, without the help of Notre Dame Law School's fine library tour de force Associate Dean Roger Jacobs, Dwight King, Michael Slinger (presently, Librarian at Suffolk University Law School), Carmella Kinslow and Ken Kinslow I would still be in the stacks searching for sources. I especially thank Corinne Karlin of Notre Dame who endured with incredible patience and skill the typing and re-typing of the manuscript. I also wish to specially thank Gil Carrasco who appears on this book. While Gil joined in this project in its last year, he faced the difficult and challenging task of providing help by rounding out the book. Indeed, Gil provided the heart and substance of the entire Chapter on Immigrant's Rights in the Social Context (Chapter 14).

Chapter 4 (Asylum and Refugees) could not have been completed without the careful help of Karen Musalo of the University of San Francisco School of Law's Political Asylum Clinic who has dedicated herself to helping refugees and teaching her students the value of zealous and compassionate advocacy. I also wish to thank my many students at the George Washington University, National Law Center and Notre Dame Law School for their helpful comments and patience in dealing with photocopied paste-ups of this book. I will be forever indebted to, Michelle Aceto, Suzen Knell Bumbalo, Ali Farahmand, Daria Goggins, Nancy Hochman and Kimberly White for their comments, cite checks, edits, determination and good humor. In the final stage of putting this book together I was fortunate to find two dedicated and talented students, Betsy Johnsen and Hans Thomas of the University of California, Hastings College of the Law, who provided incredible assistance. I also thank Michael Olivas in more than one million ways. With all of these thanks, I assume full responsibility for any errors and omissions.

Over the course of my professional career I have had the privilege of representing people whose only crime was their desire to make a better life for themselves and their families. These often forgotten people are an inspiration to all of us to work for justice in this area of the law. For these reasons, I would like to give a special dedication to the immigrants of the world who struggle to survive, to avoid torture and death, and who seek a better life. But for these courageous human beings there would be little reason for this book.

—R.A.B.

Law students at Seton Hall University who have contributed to this effort are acknowledged with gratitude. Their names are Cecilia N. Anekwe, Dawn Dublin, Deborah J. Fennelly, Susan A. Halper, Vincenza Leonelli, and Randa Zagzoug.

It is also fitting that I acknowledge my colleagues on the faculty at Seton Hall (where I was a Visiting Professor of Law), particularly the Honorable William Strasser, the Honorable Peter W. Rodino, Jr., and Associate Dean Michael J. Zimmer for offering their constructive input and confidence, Dean Ronald J. Riccio and the Honorable Wilfredo Caraballo, then Associate Dean, for their financial support in providing research assistants to work with me, and Distinguished Professor Eugene Gressman for his ubiquitous inspiration and guidance. Professor Michael A. Olivas of the University of Houston, without whom this collaboration would not have come to fruition, is also extended my sincere thanks for his continuous encouragement. Lastly, I would like to thank my wife, Terri, for her patience.

—G.P.C.

To the Second Edition

Only one year has passed since the first edition of this book was completed. While the first edition was being printed, Congress enacted the Immigration Act of 1990. At this time, the executive branch is busily engaged in the process of issuing regulations interpreting the 1990 Act. The true impact and importance of the 1990 Act may not really be understood for years to come.

"Immigration reform" has been the subject of discussion for decades, and doubtless, the dramatic changes occurring throughout the world will continue to influence immigration law and policy in the future. If immigration policy is ever to amount to true reform, students of this subject must be willing to retain their idealism. One can hope that the reform efforts of the next century will reflect a greater appreciation of the human factors which are central to immigration law. Those who practice immigration law and others who work in this field see the human element each and every day. I mention this human element because understanding and feeling it is the challenge presented to anyone who embarks on learning this complex body of law. Without such an appreciation one cannot really understand the forces which effect immigration or what must be balanced.

In this second edition, I would like to express my gratitude to Deans Tom Read and Mary Kay Kane of Hastings for their continuing moral and financial support of this project through the Hastings faculty research fund. The work of editing the original text as well as incorporating the changes made by the 1990 Act could not have been completed without the diligent assistance of my research assistants: Joyce Alcantará, Rhonda Woo and David Wright. I also would like to thank everyone at Carolina Academic Press for their continuing support of this project. An author could not have a more responsive publisher. Most of all, I would like to thank my wife Karen, herself a luminary in refugee and human rights law. Without Karen's support, neither editions of this project could have been completed. Karen has always been there to edit, clarify and improve my work. She is and has been my constant support.

—R.A.B.

Foreword

During my 40 years in Congress, I was blessed with the opportunity to take part in the formation of numerous important legislative enactments affecting everything from anti-trust to civil rights. One of the lesser known, but, nevertheless, significant areas of personal and professional interest to me was the reform of United States immigration policies. I am proud of my contributions to the creation of more equitable immigration laws, particularly the abolition of the National Origin Quota system in 1965, the enactment of the 1980 Refugee Act, and culminating with the sponsorship and authorship of the Simpson-Rodino bill, the Immigration Reform and Control Act of 1986.

As the son of an Italian immigrant, I remain sensitive to the plight of the modern day undocumented workers who abound in my home city of Newark, New Jersey as well as in many other parts of the country. The discrimination and inequitable treatment suffered by modern immigrants continue, unfortunately, to play a part in the social·reality in which they must function. It is this concern that compelled me to initiate some of the modern reforms. The modern immigration laws were enacted with the hope that the United States could recapture the noble spirit of beneficence wherein we might embrace, support, and protect those foreign neighbors looking to this country for a new life.

The laws can be effectively applied, however, only if those charged with the task of upholding them are sufficiently enlightened. The best guarantee of equitable application and interpretation is education. This book will aid that goal immensely. It promises to be an invaluable teaching tool.

As a professor of law presently holding the Rodino Chair at Seton Hall University School of Law, I have begun to view materials from a teaching perspective. Boswell and Carrasco's book is the only text of which I am aware that is both instructively excellent and ideally suited to the actual practice of immigration law.

The authors have captured the spirit of the immigration laws as they have developed over time, from the early years of this country through the various political movements and events that have shaped the present day law. The book offers comprehensive treatment of all aspects of immigration law, making it an excellent resource for the immigration practitioner as well as an invaluable educational tool. In addition, the inclusion of relevant statutes and cases at the end of each chapter enhances the book's practical value to both practitioner and student.

The authors bring to the text their own personal commitment and professional expertise in the area of immigration law. The book communicates the longstanding ambivalence of the U.S. government toward immigration as well as the underlying nativism and xenophobia that have prompted various legislative actions in the area of immigration law.

I am delighted that the authors have combined their collective expertise, experience, and wisdom to create a text that promises to inspire as well as instruct. As one who has been deeply involved in the modern reform of our immigration policies, I can state with confidence that this book does those laws justice.

Peter W. Rodino Jr.

Peter W. Rodino, Jr. Distinguished Professor of Law
Seton Hall University School of Law

IMMIGRATION AND NATIONALITY LAW

Chapter 1

Introduction

These materials were designed to present a survey of the cases, statutes, and procedures in immigration and nationality law. It is fair to say that anyone who studies this subject matter will not become an immigration law expert in one semester. Seasoned practitioners in the field acknowledge that it takes many years to master the intricacies of immigration law.

This subject matter is considered by many to rival the complexity of tax and social security law. Indeed, immigration and tax law have developed in a similar manner in that one section is built upon another and each will have its own exceptions. For example, each of the deportation and exclusion provisions are complicated by other provisions which provide for their waiver. The result of this type of statutory scheme is that the immigration statutes have developed into a quilt-like patchwork of confusing rules.

In an effort to assist the reader, the important statutory and regulatory provisions have been reprinted and can be found at the end of each chapter. Where helpful, the pertinent agency's interpretations or operating instructions have also been provided.[1]

Immigration Reform

In recent years, Congress has endeavored to reform the Immigration and Nationality Act.[2] References to the changes enacted in 1986 will be referred to under a variety of headings: Simpson-Mazzoli, Simpson-Rodino, the Immigration Reform and

---

1. The operation instructions for the INS and Department of Labor are referred to as "OI's," those for the Department of State and used by consular officers are called the Foreign Affairs Manual or "FAM."

2. The Immigration and Nationality Act, as amended, will hereafter be referred to as the "Act."

The basic statute is commonly referred to as the McCarran-Walter Act of 1952, Pub. L. No. 82-414, 66 Stat. 163 (1952). The most important amendments to the basic statute since its enactment in 1952 include the Acts of Sept. 11, 1957, 7 Stat. 639; Oct. 3, 1965, 79 Stat. 911; Oct. 20, 1976, Pub. L. 94-571, 90 Stat. 2703; Oct. 5, 1978, Pub. L. 95-412, 92 Stat. 907; Refugee Act of 1980, enacted March 17, 1980, Pub. L. 96-212, 94 Stat. 102; Immigration and Nationality Amendments of 1981, enacted December 29, 1981, Pub. L. 97-116, 95 Stat. 1611. Immigration Reform and Control Act of 1986, enacted Nov. 6, 1986, Pub. L. 99-603, 100 Stat. 3359; Immigration Marriage Fraud Amendments of 1986, enacted Nov. 10, 1986, Pub. L. 99-639, 100 Stat. 3537; Immigration and Nationality Act Amendments of 1986, enacted Nov. 14, 1986, Pub. L. 99-653, 100 Stat. 3655; the United States Canada Free-Trade Agreement Implementation Act of 1988, enacted Sept. 28, 1988, Pub. L. 100-449, 102 Stat. 1851, and ratified by the Canadian government, effective Jan. 1, 1989; the Immigration Technical Corrections Act of 1988, enacted Oct. 24, 1988, Pub. L. 100-525, 102 Stat. 2609; the Anti-Drug Abuse Act of 1988, enacted Nov. 18, 1988, enacted Nov. 15, 1988, Pub. L. 100-658, 102 Stat. 3908; the Immigration Act of 1990, Pub. L. No. 101-649, 104 Stat. 4978.

Control Act of 1986, or simply "Reform Legislation." The legislation enacted in 1990 will be referred to as either the "1990 Act" or the "Immigration Act of 1990."

Notwithstanding the reforms of 1986 and 1990, the immigration statute enacted in 1952 comprises the greatest body of immigration law. A careful review of the immigration reform legislation reveals minimal changes to the overall policy objectives of U.S. immigration law. The basic concepts in immigration law revolving around exclusion, deportation, nonimmigrant visas, etc., and their underlying legal doctrines are not changed by the reform legislation. However, this does not mean that the changes are not important, as the reforms make changes with specific procedural and benefit provisions.

Toward a Global View of the "Immigration Problem"

Prior to commencing a survey of immigration law, the student should keep in mind that immigration is purely and simply the migration of people from one country to another. Migration has occurred since the beginning of civilization and will undoubtedly continue forever. There are many motivations behind an individual or a family making the critical decision to move from one place to another. One's reasons for migrating may include: fear of persecution or prosecution, civil war in one's homeland, the desire to join family in another country, or a simple desire to better one's economic status. At the same time, the policies underlying the immigration laws of virtually every nation are designed to frustrate this natural movement by placing specific controls on migration.

The charts which appear on the following pages provide information on the migration of refugees and those seeking work. The charts do not include data on the migration which is motivated by the desire for family reunification. Even a cursory review of these charts should lead the reader to the conclusion that the immigration problems of the rest of the world make the problems of the United States appear well under control. This does not mean, however, that illegal immigration is not a problem for this country. One should view the immigration problems of the United States from a global perspective and remember that those who migrate to this country have in all likelihood traveled through and/or stayed in other countries. The consequence of this extensive human movement is that all countries in the migrants, path will experience some level of upheaval.

Chart 1

Refugee Flow by Region
(1975–1987)

Source: M. Kidron & R. Segal, *The State of the World Atlas* 26 (1987)

Region	Numbers Admitted	Year	Source Country
U.S.A.	763,000	1975–87	Indochina, Haiti, Cuba, Middle East
Central America			
Guatemala			
(Displaced)	75,000	1982	El Salvador
Honduras, Costa Rica	750,000	1982–87	
Panama	49,000	1982	El Salvador
Nicaragua			
(Displaced)	500,000	1979–81	
South America			
Argentina, Chile, Venezuela and other countries	451,281	1975–87	Haiti, Chile and Vietnam
Mexico	190,000	1982–87	Guatemala and El Salvador
Asia			
Kampuchea			
(Displaced)	4,000,000	1980	
Vietnam	450,000	1980	Kampuchea
(Displaced)	3,500,000	1975–80	
Thailand	850,000	1979–80	Vietnam, Kampuchea
Other countries	2,800,000	1976–87	Vietnam, Laos, Kampuchea, India, Bangladesh, Burma, and Indoesia
Europe			
Portugal	320,000	1975	Mozambique, Angola
France, Germany and other countries	250,000	1975–87	Vietnam, Middle East
Middle East			
Syria, Jordan, Lebanon, Kuwait, Saudi Arabia	2,200,000	1982	Palestinians
Iran, Pakistan	3,900,000	1978–87	Afghanistan
Other countries	240,000		Palestinians and Cyprus (Displaced)
Africa			
Angola	390,000	1981–87	Namibia, South Africa
(Displaced)	700,000	1981–87	
Somalia	1,400,000	1977–87	Ethiopia
Ethiopia			
(Displaced)	1,500,000	1977–87	
Zaire	450,000	1975–87	Rwanda, Uganda and Angola
(Displaced)	235,000	1981	
Ghana	1,000,000	1983	Nigeria
Other countries	1,665,000	1978–87	Zambia, Nigeria, Central African Rep., South Africa, and Zimbabwe (Displaced)

Chart 2
Refugee Flow by Region
(1975–1979)

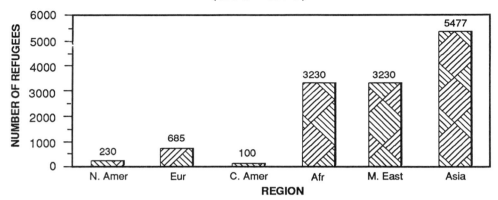

Source: M. Kidron & R. Segal, *The State of the World Atlas 32* (1981)

Chart 3
Percent of Foreign Workers in Labor Force

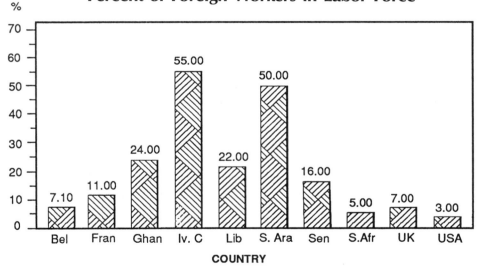

Note: Percentages represent percentage of the country's work force.

Source: M. Kidron & R. Segal, *The State of the World Atlas 32* (1981)

A Multitude of Government Agencies

The study of immigration law is more complicated than other areas of law because most immigration questions involve procedures of at least four agencies of the executive branch. These agencies are the Immigration and Naturalization Service (INS), Department of State, Department of Labor, and Public Health Service (PHS).[3]

Immigration and Naturalization Service (INS)

The responsibility of the INS Commissioner is to determine policy and overall management of the agency. The INS, an agency within the Department of Justice, is divided into four regions, each of which is headed by a regional commissioner. The regional commissioner, although previously responsible for certain administrative appeals, has a primarily managerial function.[4] In each of the four regions there is a district director whose major responsibility is the adjudication of petitions and the enforcement of the immigration laws within his jurisdiction. What follows is a recently revised organizational chart of the Immigration and Naturalization Service. (*See* Chart 4.)

Executive Office for Immigration Review (EOIR)

Separate from the Immigration and Naturalization Service is the Executive Office for Immigration Review (EOIR). The EOIR was created by the Attorney General in January 1983.[5] This office consists of immigration judges and the Board of Immigration Appeals (BIA). The immigration judges decide questions of deportability and excludability as well as certain cases involving the bonds on aliens seeking admission.[6] The BIA is the final administrative appellate body for cases under the immigration laws.[7]

Department of Labor

The Act provides that aliens who are coming to the United States to perform work must be first certified as not displacing U.S. workers or adversely affecting the

3. The Public Health Service (PHS) is within the Department of Health and Human Services (HHS). In labor certification cases which are discussed in Chapter 9, the employer seeking certification for temporary or permanent workers must apply first through a state employment training service office. Administrative review may involve the Executive Office for Immigration Review, a separate branch of the Department of Justice. *See* Chapter 5.

4. Changes in the administrative appeals process moved responsibility for most cases from the regional commissioner to the "Central Office" of the INS under the Associate Commissioner for Examinations. *See* 8 C.F.R. § 103.1

5. The separation of the immigration judges and Board of Immigration Appeals (BIA) from the INS became effective January 9, 1983. 60 Interpreter Releases 155 (1983). This separation was due to criticism by the private bar as well as the immigration judges who complained of pressures being imposed on them by the INS. [*See*, e.g., *Asylum Adjudication: Hearings before the Subcommittee on Immigration and Refugee Policy of the Senate Committee on the Judiciary*, 97th Cong., 1st Sess. 259-69 (1981) (statement of Ralph Farb, former member, Board of Immigration Appeals).]

6. The jurisdiction of the immigration judge will be discussed in more detail in Chapters 2, 3, 4 and 5.

7. The complexities of the administrative review scheme are discussed at greater length in Chapter 5.

Chart 4
Immigration and Naturalization Service

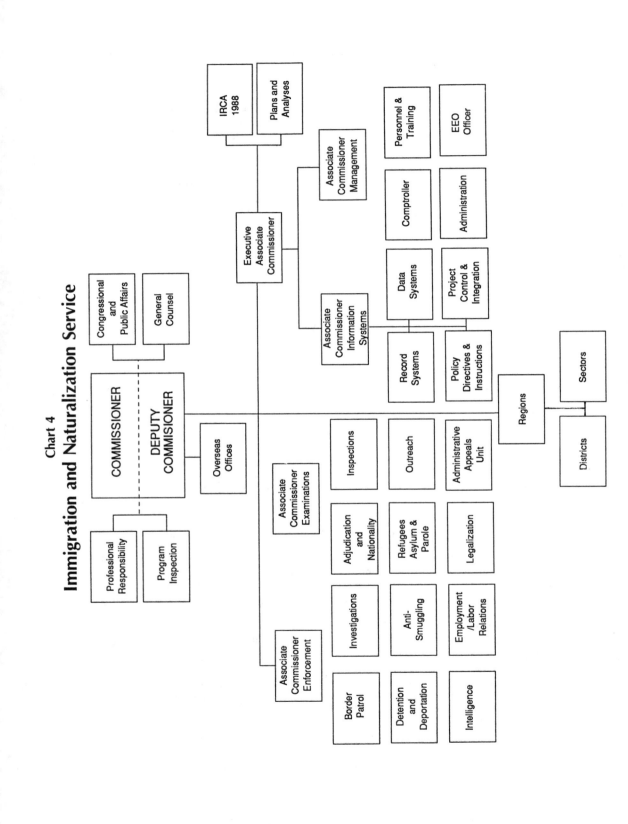

wages and working conditions of U.S. workers.[8] The Act also provides that temporary workers entering the U.S. must be similarly certified.[9] The statute delegates responsibility for this certification process to the Secretary of Labor. The procedures and requirements involved in temporary and permanent labor certifications will be discussed in Chapters 6 and 8.

It is important to know the underlying policy behind placing the labor certification requirement with the Secretary of Labor. Organized labor has a clear and obvious interest in protecting the jobs and working conditions of U.S. workers. The federal agency most likely to have the confidence of organized labor is the Department of Labor. Accordingly, the important labor certification function was assigned to this agency.

Part of the certification process places the initial recruitment in the hands of local or state employment training services where the job is or will be located. Accordingly, the alien and the employer or his attorney are required to deal with the state bureaucracy as well. The section within the Department of Labor responsible for providing the necessary information to the Secretary is the Employment Training Administration (E.T.A.). The country is divided into regions and each of the regions is headed by a regional certifying officer who bears the responsibility of assuring that the requirements of 8 U.S.C. § 1182(a)(5) are met. In the event that the labor certification application is denied by the regional certifying officer, the sponsoring employer may request a hearing before an administrative law judge.[10]

Department of State

The Act statutorily created the Bureau of Consular Affairs within the Department of State responsible for the department's role in administering the immigration laws.[11] U.S. consuls serving at embassies and consulates abroad are responsible for the issuance of immigrant and nonimmigrant visas to aliens who seeks permission to come to the United States.

Adverse decisions on visa applications by U.S. consuls are not appealable to the federal courts. The only recourse for an individual with an adverse decision is to seek an advisory opinion from the Bureau of Consular Affairs. As will be discussed later, these opinions are only advisory and do not bind the consular officers.[12]

Public Health Service

The immigration laws provide a number of ways to prevent persons who are or have been afflicted with certain psychological and medical problems from entering

---

8. 8 U.S.C. § 1182(a)(5), Sec. 212(a)(5) of the Act. It should also be noted that there is a statutory presumption that all persons coming to the U.S. are immigrants and therefore must be certified by the Department of Labor as not taking away jobs from U.S. workers. The exceptions from the labor certification requirement will be discussed in Chapter 7.

9. 8 U.S.C. § 1184(c), Sec. 214(c) of the Act. *See also* 8 C.F.R. § 214.2(h)(3).

10. The administrative appeal process within the Department of Labor will be discussed in the chapter on labor certifications (Chapter 9).

11. 8 U.S.C. § 1104, Sect. 104 of the Act.

12. The role of the consular officers in the immigrant and nonimmigrant visa issuing process is discussed in Chapters 6 and 7.

the United States.[13] It is the sole responsibility of the United States Public Health Service under the Department of Health and Human Services to make determinations regarding the medical and psychological conditions of these alien persons. These determinations are only reviewable by a panel of doctors under the Public Health Service.

A Historical Perspective

As noted earlier, U.S. immigration laws have a quilt-like design. The immigration laws have been called discriminatory on racial and national origin grounds.[14] As seen from the following discussion by the U.S. Civil Rights Commission, political, economic, and social factors bear heavily on the question of immigration reform.

The Tarnished Golden Door: Civil Rights Issues in Immigration
U.S. Commission on Civil Rights, 7-12 (1980)[1]

The Early Years

During the formative years of this country's growth, immigration was encouraged with little restraint. Any restrictions on immigration in the 1700s were the result of selection standards established by each colonial settlement. The only Federal regulation of immigration in this period lasted only 2 years and came from the Alien Act of 1798, which gave the President the authority to expel aliens who posed a threat to national security.[2]

Immigrants from northern and western Europe began to trickle into the country as a result of the faltering economic conditions within their own countries. In Germany, unfavorable economic prospects in industry and trade, combined with political unrest drove many of its nationals to seek opportunities to ply their trades here. In Ireland, the problems of the economy, compounded by several successive potato crop failures in the 1840s, sent thousands of Irish to seaports where ships bound for the United States were docked. For other European nationals, the emigration from their native countries received impetus not only from adverse economic conditions at home but also from favorable stories of free land and good wages in America.

The Nativist Movements

As a result of the large numbers of Catholics who emigrated from Europe, a nativist movement began in the 1830s. It advocated immigration restriction to prevent further arrivals of Catholics into this country. Anti-Catholicism was a very popular

---

13. 8 U.S.C. § 1224, Sect. 234 of the Act, deals with the authority of the Public Health Service in the "inspection" of aliens entering the United States. 8 U.S.C. § 1182 (a)(1), Secs. 212 (a)(1) are the statutory sections which prohibit the admission of certain persons with psychological and medical problems. These issues will be discussed further in Chapter 2.

14. Gordon, *The Need to Modernize our Immigration Laws*, 13 San Diego L. Rev. 1 (1975); Hing, *Racial Disparity: The Unaddressed Issue of the Simpson-Mazzoli Bill*, 1 La Raza L.J. 21 (1983).

1. Some footnotes have been removed.

2. Ch. 58, 1 Stat. 570 (1798).

theme, and many Catholics and Catholic institutions suffered violent attacks from nativist sympathizers. The movement, however, did not gain great political strength and its goal of curbing immigration did not materialize.

Immigrants in the mid-19th century did not come only from northern and western Europe. In China, political unrest and the decline in agricultural productivity spawned the immigration of Chinese to American shores. The numbers of Chinese immigrants steadily increased after the so-called Opium War, due not only to the Chinese economy, but also to the widespread stories of available employment, good wages, and the discovery of gold at Sutter's Mill, which filtered in through arrivals from the Western nations.

The nativist movement of the 1830s resurfaced in the late 1840s and developed into a political party, the Know-Nothing Party. Its western adherents added an anti-Chinese theme to the eastern anti-Catholic sentiment. But once again, the nativist movement, while acquiring local political strength, failed in its attempts to enact legislation curbing immigration. On the local level, however, the cry of "America for Americans" often led to discriminatory State statutes that penalized certain racially identifiable groups.[3] As an example, California adopted licensing statutes for foreign miners and fishermen, which were almost exclusively enforced against Chinese.

In the mid-1850s, the Know-Nothing Party lost steam as a result of a division over the question of slavery, the most important issue of that time. The nativist movement and anti-foreign sentiment receded because of the slavery issue and the Civil War. It maintained this secondary role until the Panic of 1873 struck.

Chinese Exclusion

The depression economy of the 1870s was blamed on aliens who were accused of driving wages to a substandard level as well as taking away jobs that "belonged" to white Americans. While the economic charges were not totally without basis, reality shows that most aliens did not compete with white labor for "desirable" white jobs. Instead, aliens usually were relegated to the most menial employment.[4]

The primary target was the Chinese, whose high racial visibility, coupled with cultural dissimilarity and lack of political power, made them more than an adequate scapegoat for the economic problems of the 1870s.[5] Newspapers adopted the exhortations of labor leaders, blaming the Chinese for the economic plight of the working class. Workers released their frustrations and anger on the Chinese, particularly in the West. Finally, politicians succumbed to the growing cry for exclusion of Chinese.

Congress responded by passing the Chinese Exclusion Act of 1882.[6] That act suspended immigration of Chinese laborers for 10 years, except for those who were

---

3. Mary Roberts Coolidge, *Chinese Immigration* (1909), pp. 69-82. Some municipalities also adopted ordinances that discriminated against Chinese. As an example, a San Francisco municipal ordinance, subsequently held unconstitutional in *Yick Wo v. Hopkins*, 118 U.S. 356 (1886), was enacted regulating the operation of public laundries but in practice was enforced almost exclusively against Chinese.

4. As one author noted, "[b]efore the late 1870's the Chinese engaged only in such work as white laborers refused to perform. Thus the Chinese not only were noninjurious competitors but in effect were benefactors to the white laborer." S.W. Kung, *Chinese in American Life: Some Aspects of Their History, Status, Problems and Contributions* (1962), p. 68.

5. Carey McWilliams, *Brothers Under the Skin* (rev. 1951), pp. 101-03.

6. Ch. 126, 22 Stat. 58 (1882).

in the country on November 17, 1880. Those who were not lawfully entitled to reside in the United States were subject to deportation. Chinese immigrants were also prohibited from obtaining United States citizenship after the effective date of the act.

The 1882 act was amended in 1884 to cover all subjects of China and Chinese who resided in any other foreign country.[7] Then in 1888, another act was enacted that extended the suspension of immigration for all Chinese except Chinese officials, merchants, students, teachers, and travelers for pleasure.[8] Supplemental legislation to that act also prohibited Chinese laborers from reentering the country, as provided for in the 1882 act, unless they reentered prior to the effective date of the legislation.[9]

Senator Matthew C. Butler of South Carolina summed up the congressional efforts to exclude Chinese by stating:

> [I]t seems to me that this whole Chinese business has been a matter of political advantage, and we have not been governed by that deliberation which it would seem to me the gravity of the question requires. In other words, there is a very important Presidential election pending. One House of Congress passes an act driving these poor devils into the Pacific Ocean, and the other House comes up and says, "Yes, we will drive them further into the Pacific Ocean, notwithstanding the treaties between the two governments."[10]

Nevertheless, the Chinese exclusion law was extended in 1892 and 1902, and in 1904 it was extended indefinitely.[11]

Although challenged by American residents of Chinese ancestry, the provisions of these exclusion acts were usually upheld by judicial decisions. For example, the 1892 act mandated that Chinese laborers obtain certificates of residency within 1 year after the passage of the act or face deportation.[12] In order to obtain the certificate, the testimony of one credible white witness was required to establish that the Chinese laborer was an American resident prior to the passage of the act. That requirement was upheld by the United States Supreme Court in *Fong Yue Ting v. United States*, 149 U.S. 698 (1893).

Literacy Tests and the Asiatic Barred Zone

The racial nature of immigration laws clearly manifested itself in further restrictions on prospective immigrants who were either from Asian countries or of Asian descent. In addition to extending the statutory life of the Chinese exclusion law, the 1902 act also applied that law to American territorial possessions, thereby prohibiting not only the immigration of noncitizen Chinese laborers from "such island territory to the mainland territory," but also "from one portion of the island territory of the United States to another portion of said island territory. Soon after, Japanese were restricted from free immigration to the United States by the "Gentleman's Agreement" negotiated between the respective governments in 1907. Additional evidence would

---

7. Ch. 220, 23 Stat. 115 (1884).

8. Ch. 1015, 25 Stat. 476 (1888).

9. Ch. 1064, 25 Stat. 504 (1888).

10. 19 Cong. Rec. 8218 (1888).

11. [*See* 27 Stat. 25 (1892), 32 Stat. 176 (1902), and 33 Stat. 428 (1904) respectively.]

12. Ch. 60, 27 Stat. 25 (1892).

be provided by the prohibition of immigration from countries in the Asia-Pacific Triangle as established by the Immigration Act of 1917.[13]

During this period, congressional attempts were also made to prevent blacks from immigrating to this country. In 1915 an amendment to exclude "all members of the African or black race" from admission to the United States was introduced in the Senate during its deliberations on a proposed immigration bill. The Senate approved the amendment on a 29 to 25 vote, but it was later defeated in the House by a 253 to 74 vote, after intensive lobbying by the NAACP.

In 1917 Congress codified existing immigration laws in the Immigration Act of that year.[14] That act retained all the prior grounds for inadmissibility and added illiterates to the list of those ineligible to immigrate, as a response to the influx of immigrants from southern and eastern Europe. Because of a fear that American standards would be lowered by these new immigrants who were believed to be racially "inassimilable" and illiterate, any alien who was over 16 and could not read was excluded. The other important feature of this statute was the creation of the Asia-Pacific Triangle, an Asiatic barred zone, designed to exclude Asians completely from immigration to the United States. The only exemptions from this zone were from an area that included Persia and parts of Afghanistan and Russia.

The 1917 immigration law reflected the movement of American immigration policy toward the curbing of free immigration. Free immigration, particularly from nations that were culturally dissimilar to the northern and western European background of most Americans, was popularly believed to be the root of both the economic problems and the social problems confronting this country.

The National Origins Quota System

Four years later, Congress created a temporary quota law that limited the number of aliens of any nationality who could immigrate to 3 percent of the United States residents of that nationality living in the country in 1910.[15] The total annual immigration allowable in any one year was set at 350,000. Western Hemisphere aliens were exempt from the quota if their country of origin was an independent national and the alien had resided there at least 1 year.

The clear intent of the 1921 quota law was to confine immigration as much as possible to western and northern European stock. As the minority report noted:

The obvious purpose of this discrimination is the adoption of an unfounded anthropological theory that the nations which are favored are the progeny of fictitious and hitherto unsuspected Nordic ancestors, while those discriminated against are not classified as belonging to that mythical ancestral stock. No scientific evidence worthy of consideration was introduced to substantiate this pseudoscientific proposition. It is pure fiction and the creation of a journalistic imagination....

The majority report insinuates that some of those who have come from foreign countries are non-assimilable or slow of assimilation. No facts are offered in

13. Ch. 29, 39 Stat. 874 (1917).
14. Ch. 29, 39 Stat. 874 (1917).
15. Ch. 8, 42 Stat. 5 (1921).

support of such a statement. The preponderance of testimony adduced before the committee is to the contrary.[16]

Notwithstanding these objections, Congress made the temporary quota a permanent one with the enactment of the 1924 National Origins Act.[17] A ceiling of 150,000 immigrants per year was imposed. Quotas for each nationality group were 2 percent of the total members of that nationality residing in the United States according to the 1889 census. Again, Western Hemisphere aliens were exempt from the quotas (thus, classified as "nonquota" immigrants). Any prospective immigrant was required to obtain a sponsor in this country and to obtain a visa from an American consulate office abroad. Entering the country without a visa and in violation of the law subjected the entrant to deportation without regard to the time of entry (no statute of limitation). Another provision, prohibiting the immigration of aliens ineligible for citizenship, completely closed the door on Japanese immigration, since the Supreme Court had ruled that Japanese were ineligible to become naturalized citizens. Prior to the 1924 act, Japanese immigration had been subjected to "voluntary" restraint by the Gentleman's Agreement negotiated between the Japanese Government and President Theodore Roosevelt.

In addition to its expressed discriminatory provisions, the 1924 law was also criticized as discriminatory against blacks in general and against black West Indians in particular.

The Mexican "Repatriation" Campaign

Although Mexican Americans have a long history of residence within present United States territory,[18] Mexican immigration to this country is of relatively recent vintage. Mexican citizens began immigrating to this country in significant numbers after 1909 because of economic conditions as well as the violence and political upheaval of the Mexican Revolution. These refugees were welcomed by Americans, for they helped to alleviate the labor shortage caused by the First World War. The spirit of acceptance lasted only a short time, however.

Spurred by the economic distress of the Great Depression, Federal immigration officials expelled hundreds of thousands of persons of Mexican descent from this country through increased Border Patrol raids and other immigration law enforcement techniques. To mollify public objection to the mass expulsions, this program was called the "repatriation" campaign. Approximately 500,000 persons were "repatriated" to Mexico, with more than half of them being United States citizens.

Erosion of Certain Discriminatory Patterns

Prior to the next recodification of the immigration laws, there were several congressional enactments that cut away at the discriminatory barriers established by the national origins system. In 1943 the Chinese Exclusion Act was repealed, allowing

---

16. As reprinted in the legislative history of the INA (1952) U.S. Code Cong. and Ad. News 1653, 1668.

17. Ch. 190, 43 Stat. 153 (1924).

18. Under the Treaty of Guadalupe Hidalgo, many Mexican citizens became United States citizens after the annexation of territory by the United States following the Mexican War. Leo Grebler, Joan W. Moore, and Ralph C. Guzman, *The Mexican American People*, pp. 40-41 (1970). The Treaty of Guadalupe Hidalgo is reprinted in Wayne Moquin, *A Documentary History of the Mexican Americans*, p. 183 (1971).

a quota of 105 Chinese to immigrate annually to this country and declaring Chinese eligible for naturalization.[19] The War Brides Act of 1945 permitted the immigration of 118,000 spouses and children of military servicemen. In 1946 Congress enacted legislation granting eligibility for naturalization to Filipinos and to races indigenous to India.[20] A Presidential proclamation in that same year increased the Filipino quota from 50 to 100. In 1948 the Displaced Persons Act provided for the entry of approximately 400,000 refugees from Germany, Italy, and Austria (an additional 214,000 refugees were later admitted to the United States).[21]

The McCarran-Walter Act of 1952

The McCarran-Walter Act of 1952, the basic law in effect today, codified the immigration laws under a single statute.[22] It established three principles for immigration policy: (1) the reunification of families, (2) the protection of the domestic labor force, and (3) the immigration of persons with needed skills. However, it retained the concept of the national origins system, as well as unrestricted immigration from the Western Hemisphere. An important provision of the statute removed the bar to immigration and citizenship for races that had been denied those privileges prior to that time. Asian countries, nevertheless, were still discriminated against, for prospective immigrants whose ancestry was one-half of any Far Eastern race were chargeable to minimal quotas for that nation, regardless of the birthplace of the immigrant.

"Operation Wetback"[23]

Soon after the repatriation campaigns of the 1930s, the United States entered the Second World War. Mobilization for the war effort produced a labor shortage that resulted in a shift in American attitudes toward immigration from Mexico. Once again Mexican nationals were welcomed with open arms. However, this "open arms" policy was just as short lived as before.

In the 1950s many Americans were alarmed by the number of immigrants from Mexico. As a result, then United States Attorney General Herbert Brownell, Jr., launched "Operation Wetback," to expel Mexicans from this country. Among those caught up in the expulsion campaign were American citizens of Mexican descent who were forced to leave the country of their birth. To ensure the effectiveness of the expulsion process, many of those apprehended were denied a hearing to assert their constitutional rights and to present evidence that would have prevented their deportation. More than 1 million persons of Mexican descent were expelled from this country in 1954 at the height of "Operation Wetback."

The 1965 Amendments

The national origins immigration quota system generated opposition from the time of its inception, condemned for its attempts to maintain the existing racial composition of the United States. Finally, in 1965, amendments to the McCarran-

---

19. Ch. 344, 57 Stat. 600 (1943).
20. *See* 59 Stat. 659 (1945), 60 Stat. 1353, and 60 Stat. 416 (1946) respectively.
21. Ch. 647, 62 Stat. 1009 (1948).
22. 66 Stat. 163 (1952).
23. [Authors Note:] The term "wetback" has become an extremely derogatory term.

Walter Act abolished the national origins systems as well as the Asiatic barred zone.[24] Nevertheless, numerical restrictions were still imposed to limit annual immigration. The Eastern Hemisphere was subject to an overall limitation of 170,000 and a limit of 20,000 per country. Further, colonial territories were limited to 1 percent of the total available to the mother country (later raised 3 percent or 600 immigrants in the 1976 amendments). The Western Hemisphere, for the first time, was subject to an overall limitation of 120,000 annually, although no individual per-country limits were imposed. In place of the national origins system, Congress created a seven category preference system giving immigration priority to relatives of United States residents and immigrants with needed talents or skills. The 20,000 limitation per country and the colonial limitations, as well as the preference for relatives of Americans preferred under the former selections process, have been referred to by critics as "the last vestiges of the national origins system" because they perpetuate the racial discrimination produced by the national origins system.

Restricting Mexican Immigration

After 1965 the economic conditions in the United States changed. With the economic crunch felt by many Americans, the cry for more restrictive immigration laws resurfaced. The difference from the 19th century situation is that the brunt of the attacks is now focused on Mexicans, not Chinese. High "guesstimates" of the number of undocumented Mexican aliens entering the United States, many of which originated from Immigration and Naturalization Service sources, have been the subject of press coverage.

As a partial response to the demand for "stemming the tide" of Mexican immigration, Congress amended the Immigration and Nationality Act in 1976, imposing the seven category preference system and the 20,000 numerical limitation per country on Western Hemisphere nations.[25] Legal immigration from Mexico, which had been more than 40,000 people per year, with a waiting list 2 years long, was thus cut by over 50 percent.

Recent Revisions of the Immigrant Quota System

Although the annual per-country limitations have remained intact, Congress did amend the Immigration and Nationality Act of 1978 to eliminate the hemispheric quotas of 170,000 for Eastern Hemisphere countries and 120,000 for Western Hemisphere countries. Those hemispheric ceilings were replaced with an overall annual worldwide ceiling of 290,000.

In 1980 the immigrant quota system was further revised by the enactment of the Refugee Act. In addition to broadening the definition of refugee, that statute eliminated the seventh preference visa category by establishing a separate worldwide ceiling for refugee admissions to this country. It also reduced the annual worldwide ceiling for the remaining six preference categories to 270,000 visas, and it increased the number of visas allocated to the second preference to 26 percent.[26]

---

24. Pub. L. No. 89-236, 79 Stat. 911 (1965).
25. Pub. L. No. 94-571, 90 Stat. 2703 (1976).
26. Refugee Act of 1980, Pub. L. No. 96-212.

The preceding article by the Civil Rights Commission concludes with a reference to the Refugee Act of 1980. Two major statutory changes, which will be presented in these materials, were later enacted. These amendments were the Immigration Reform and Control Act of 1986, and the Immigration Act of 1990. The former was designed to enhance the enforcement powers of the INS, and the latter was intended to increase the immigration quotas.[15]

Questions

1. The immigration laws only provide for the unification of families where the alien is the spouse, offspring, or sibling of a U.S. citizen or the spouse or unmarried child of a lawful permanent resident. These provisions have been criticized as attempting to prevent the influx of "too many" racial minorities. Is this criticism valid? Would this criticism be valid if it was established that during periods of previous immigration (when Europeans were immigrating in large numbers), the family relationship restrictions did not exist?

2. Since 1975 there has been extensive discussion about making changes in our laws to prevent illegal immigration. If anything, the trend seems to be moving toward making both legal and illegal immigration more difficult. Is it possible to place realistic controls on illegal immigration in a country with more than 6,000 miles of land borders on the north and south?

Glossary of Terms

There are many words, which, to the new reader of immigration law, will appear foreign. The following list is a short glossary which attempts to "loosely" define some of the more troublesome terms used in immigration. The terms of art will become clarified after one has reviewed the cases and materials.

Adjustment of Status. An immigration benefit accorded as a matter of discretion to certain aliens in the U.S. which allows them to have their status changed from that of a parolee or nonimmigrant to that of a lawful permanent resident. Adjustment of status is a term of art. Certain lawful permanent residents may have their status "adjusted" to that of a nonimmigrant. This benefit should be distinguished from "change of status," which generally applies to nonimmigrants moving from one nonimmigrant status to another. *See* 8 U.S.C. § 1255, Sec. 245.

Asylum. A discretionary benefit accorded to certain aliens inside the U.S. who are able to demonstrate that they are unable or unwilling to return to their country on account of persecution or a well-founded fear of persecution based on race, religion, nationality, membership in a particular social group, or political opinion. 8 U.S.C. § 1101(a)(42), Sec. 101(a)(42). One year after the receipt of asylum status the asylee may apply for lawful permanent residence. *See* Chapter 4.

Deportation. The removal, ejectment, or transfer of an alien from a country because her presence is deemed inconsistent with the public welfare. Deportation is not considered to be a form of punishment. Grounds for deportation are set out at 8 U.S.C. § 1251, Sec. 241 and are discussed in Chapter 3.

---

15. Some have described the 1986 amendments as controlling illegal immigration, and the 1990 Act as providing for increased legal immigration.

Immigrant.   Within the meaning of the Immigration and Nationality Act, as amended, "immigrant" means every alien except an alien who is within one of the classes of nonimmigrant aliens. *See* 8 U.S.C. § 1101(a)(15), Sec. 101(a)(15). Nonimmigrants are those with a residence abroad, who can prove that they will be coming for a temporary (short and definable) period of time, and fit into narrowly defined categories enumerated in the statute. Generally an immigrant is one who cannot establish her eligibility for status as a nonimmigrant. The inability to establish such eligibility will require the alien to meet the requirements of either having specific family ties with a U.S. citizen or lawful permanent resident (preference eligibility) or that she has a sponsoring employer in the U.S. and the job she will be taking does not displace or adversely effect U.S. workers. *See also* Labor Certification, Nonimmigrant and Preference Petition.

Immigrant Visa.   Permission obtained from a U.S. consul (abroad) to seek admission to the U.S. A visa is issued subsequent to establishing eligibility for admission on a permanent basis under the Immigration and Nationality Act, as amended. *See also* Preference Categories, Labor Certification, and Visa.

Immigration Judge.   Sometimes referred to in the statute and code of federal regulations as "Special Inquiry Officer," this person is responsible for deciding questions involving bond, exclusion and deportation. While in the past, immigration judges were employed by the INS, they are now employed by the Executive Office for Immigration Review (EOIR).

Labor Certification.   In order for most immigrants to come to the United States (other than those who qualify as immigrants based on their family ties with U.S. citizens or lawful permanent residents), they must establish the following: (1) an employer is willing to hire them in a job for which they are qualified; (2) there are no equally qualified U.S. workers for the job which is being offered; (3) the job will not adversely affect the wage rate or working conditions of U.S. workers (the employer must therefore be offering the job at the "prevailing wage" in the particular market). An employer's obtaining a labor certification does not entitle the alien to admission as she there is an annual quota on the numbers of foreign workers who may be admitted to the U.S. *See also* Preference Categories; *also see* Chapters 7 and 8.

Lawful Permanent Resident.   A person accorded the benefit of being able to reside in the U.S. on a permanent basis. Such a person may engage in employment but may not vote in U.S. elections. Lawful permanent resident status is the status gained by an alien who is admitted to the U.S. with an immigrant visa or has had her status adjusted to permanent residence after having first been admitted as a nonimmigrant. Lawful permanent resident status may be taken away for the commission of certain acts or through "abandonment."

Nonimmigrant.   A person who can establish that she has a residence abroad which she has no intention of abandoning, who is coming to the United States for a temporary period, and who fits into specifically defined categories under the Immigration and Nationality Act, as amended. *See* 8 U.S.C. § 1101(a)(15), Sec. 101(a)(15). Some of the nonimmigrant categories are students, tourists, treaty investors, foreign government officials, etc. *Also see* Immigrant.

Parole.   Permission granted by the Attorney General which allows an alien to physically enter the U.S. yet still be considered to have not legally entered the country.

Parole is a legal fiction. A person paroled into the U.S. is treated in a legal sense as if she were still at the border's edge seeking permission to enter. *See* 8 U.S.C. § 1182(d)(5), Sec. 212(d)(5).

Preference Categories.   Immigrant visas are allocated based under an annual quota. In order to qualify for admission the intending immigrant must show that (1) she is either married to a lawful permanent resident or is the unmarried son or daughter of a lawful permanent resident; (2) she is the son or daughter or sibling of a U.S. citizen (irrespective of marital status); (3) her employer has obtained a labor certification for her eventual employment in the U.S. Whether the alien meets the quota restriction will depend on her relationship as described above with a U.S. citizen or lawful permanent resident or whether the employment is of a skilled or unskilled nature. *See* Labor Certification; *also see* Chapters 7 and 8.

Preference Petition.   In order to determine the preference category to which a person is entitled, an application, or petition must first be submitted to the INS. The preference petition may be referred to as a family or employment-based preference petition. *See* Preference Categories.

Refugee.   A person outside of the U.S. and unable or unwilling to return to her country because of persecution or a well-founded fear of persecution on account of race, religion, nationality, membership in a particular social group, or political opinion. 8 U.S.C. § 1101(a)(42), Sec. 101(a)(42). Refugee admission to the U.S. is based upon annual quotas as established between the executive and legislative branches. A refugee, once admitted, may apply in one year for permanent resident status. *See* Chapter 4.

Visa.   Permission obtained from a U.S. consul (abroad) to seek admission to the U.S. at a designated port of entry. A visa may be either a nonimmigrant or immigrant visa. A visa is analogous to an airline ticket which may merely allow one to attempt to board the plane. A visa is an official endorsement upon a document or passport certifying that the bearer has been examined and is permitted to proceed.

Withholding of Deportation.   Upon a finding by the Attorney General that if returned to her country an alien's life or freedom would be threatened on account of race, religion, nationality, membership in a particular social group, or political opinion, the alien's return to that country is prohibited. 8 U.S.C. § 1253(h), Sec. 243(h). Receiving withholding of deportation does not confer on the person a right to stay in the United States as she may be returned to a hospitable country. *See* Chapter 4.

Readings on Immigration Law Reform

Boswell, *Immigration Reform Amendments of 1986: Reform or Rehash*, 14 J. Legis. 23 (1987)

Chiswick, *Guidelines for the Reform of Immigration Policy*, 36 U. Miami L. Rev. 36 (1982)

Corwin, *The Numbers Game: Estimates of Illegal Aliens in the U.S., 1970-1981*, 45 Law & Contemp. Probs. 223 (1982)

Fogel, *Illegal Aliens: Economic Aspects and Public Policy Alternatives*, 15 San Diego L. Rev. 63 (1977)

Fuchs, *Immigration Policy and the Rule of Law*, 44 U. Pitt. L. Rev. 433 (1983)

Gordon, *The Need to Modernize our Immigration Laws*, 13 San Diego L. Rev. 1, 3 (1975)

Hing, *Racial Disparity: The Unaddressed Issue of the Simpson-Mazzoli Bill*, 1 La Raza L.J. 21 (1983)

Hofstetter, *Economic Underdevelopment and the Population Explosion: Implications for U.S. Immigration Policy*, 45 Law & Contemp. Probs. 55 (1982)

Lopez, *Undocumented Mexican Migration: In Search of a Just Immigration Law and Policy*, 28 U.C.L.A. L. Rev. 615 (1981)

Martin & Houstoun, *European and American Immigration Policies*, 45 Law & Contemp. Probs. 29 (1982)

Note, *Select Commission on Immigration and Refugee Policy: Development of a Fundamental Legislative Policy*, 17 Willamette L. Rev. 141 (1983)

Sanger, *Immigration Reform and Control Act of 1986: the Undocumented Family*, 2 Geo. Imm. L. J. 295 (1988)

Schuck, *The Transformation of Immigration Law*, 84 Colum. L. Rev. 1 (1984)

Seller, *Historical Perspectives on American Immigration Policy: Case Studies and Current Implications*, 45 Law & Contemp. Probs. 137 (1982)

Travis, *Migration, Income Distribution and Welfare Under Alternative International Economic Policies*, 45 Law & Contemp. Probs. 81 (1982)

Whelan, *Principles of U.S. Immigration Policy*, 44 U. Pitt. L. Rev. 447 (1983)

Immigration and Nationality Act Conversion Table with Title 8 of the U.S. Code

The Immigration and Nationality Act, as amended (INA) [8 U.S.C. § 1101 *et seq.*], is most often cited in these materials to the corresponding section of the United States Code. Oftentimes cases will refer to sections of the INA. The table which appears below cross-references sections of the INA and the U.S. Code.

8 U.S.C. §	INA Section	Description
1101	101	Definitions
1102	102	
1103	103	Powers of the Atty Gen.
1104	104	Powers of the Sect'y of State
1105	105	
1105a	106	Judicial Review
1151	201	Immigrant Selection System
1152	202	Numerical Limitations
1153	203	Allocation of Imm. Visas
1154	204	Procedure for Granting Imm. Status
1155	205	Revocation of Petitions
1156	206	
1157	207	Refugee Admissions
1158	208	Asylum Procedures
1159	209	Adjustment for Refugees

8 U.S.C. §	INA Section	Description
1160	210	Special Agricultural Workers (SAW)
1161A	210A	Replenishment of SAW
1181	211	Documentary Requirements for Admission
1182	212	Classes of Exclusion and Waivers
1183	213	
1184	214	Nonimmigrants
1185	215	
1186a	216	Conditional Permanent Residence
1186	218	Admission of Temporary Agricult. Workers
1187	217	Visa Waiver Pilot Program
1201	221	
1202	222	
1203	223	
1204	224	
1221	231	
1222	232	
1223	233	Temporary Removal for Examination
1224	234	
1225	235	Inspection by Immigration Officers
1226	236	Exclusion of Aliens
1227	237	"Deportation" of Excluded Aliens
1228	238	
1229	239	
1230	240	Record of Admission
1251	241	Classes of Deportable Aliens
1252	242	Procedure for Deportation
1253	243	Country to Which Deported
1254	244	Suspension of Deportation, Vol. Depart
1254a	244A	Temporary Protected Status
1255	245	Adjustment of Status
1255a	245A	Amnesty Provisions
1256	246	Rescission of Adjustment
1257	247	
1258	248	Change of Nonimmigrant Classification

8 U.S.C. §	INA Section	Description
1259	 249	.... Registry
1260	 250	
1281	 251	
1282	 252	
1283	 253	
1284	 254	
1285	 255	
1286	 256	
1287	 257	
1301	 261	
1302	 262	
1303	 263	
1304	 264	
1305	 265	
1305	 266	
1321	 271	.... Unauthorized Landing of Aliens
1322	 272	
1323	 273	.... Unauthorized Bringing in of Aliens
1324	 274	.... Bringing in and Harboring
1324a	.... 274A	.... Unlawful Employment of Aliens
1324b	.... 274B	.... Unfair Immigration Related Employment Practices
1325	 275	
1326	 276	
1327	 277	
1328	 278	
1329	 279	.... Jurisdiction of District Courts
1330	 280	
1351	 281	
1352	 282	
1353	 283	
1354	 284	
1355	 285	
1356	 286	
1357	 287	.... Powers of Immigration Officers
1358	 288	.... Local Jurisdiction Over Imm. Stations

8 U.S.C. §	INA Section	Description
1443	 332	.... Procedural and Admin. Provisions
1444	 333	
1445	 334	
1446	 335	
1447	 336	
1448	 337	.... Oath of Renunciation and Allegiance
1449	 338	
1450	 339	
1451	 340	.... Revocation of Naturalization
1452	 341	
1453	 342	
1454	 343	
1455	 344	
1456	 345	
1457	 346	
1458	 347	
1459	 348	
1481	 349	.... Loss of Nationality
1482	 350	
1483	 351	.... Restrictions on Expatriation
1484	 352	
1485	 353	
1486	 354	
1487	 355	
1488	 356	
1489	 357	
1501	 358	
1502	 359	
1503	 360	

Chapter 2

Exclusion

On the Statue of Liberty is inscribed a verse which entreats the world to give the United States its "tired...poor...[and] huddled masses...."[1] As was seen in the discussion by the U.S. Civil Rights Commission, this verse is more appropriate to a much earlier period in our history. The exclusion and deportation provisions are the core of U.S. immigration law for they determine who is allowed to enter and who may remain. Those persons who may enter and remain in a nation reflect, in part, what the nation will be in the future, and hence has been the subject of much debate.[2] Participation in this debate requires a clear understanding of the exclusion provisions. Even upon careful review, the reader will find it difficult to see a cohesive pattern in the statute. Our discussion will therefore begin with an attempt to describe the statutory scheme which provides the foundation for understanding the provisions relating to exclusion.[3]

Substantive Grounds for Exclusion

A review of 8 U.S.C. § 1182 will certainly lead the reader to conclude that the grounds for exclusion encompass virtually every type of person. In an effort to make sense of the myriad grounds, our discussion will focus on six general categories.

- Economic
- Political
- Health
- Criminal
- Quasi-Criminal or Moral
- Miscellaneous

The grounds for exclusion are based upon a strong concern that certain people should not be allowed to come to this country. Persons without adequate financial resources have a greater potential for not being able to support themselves and there-

---

1. E. Lazarus, "The New Colossus" (1883).

2. One scholar has argued that the reason that the United States has had great difficulty in developing a coherent immigration policy is because the choices tug at the moral fabric of the nation. *See* Fuchs, *Immigration Policy and the Rule of Law*, 44 U. Pitt. L. Rev. 433, 433 (1983).

3. The substantive grounds for exclusion are found at 8 U.S.C. § 1182(a), Sec. 212(a) of the Act. The procedural requirements are found at 8 U.S.C. §§ 1221-30, Secs. 231-40 of the Act. [The corresponding federal regulations are included in the appendix to this chapter].

fore of becoming dependent on the government for support.[4] Persons that present a potential threat to this government or who have political ideologies counter to the interests of the United States (as deemed by Congress) are of concern to our government.[5] Persons having illnesses present the possibility of infecting healthy persons in this country or of becoming public charges.[6] Those with prior convictions are generally considered unsavory and therefore are not welcome.[7] Moreover, they present a potential threat in that they may commit such acts once again in this country. The quasi-criminal or moral grounds are designed to prevent entry of persons whose behavior is contrary to the norms of society as established by Congress when it passed the Act.[8] The miscellaneous grounds are designed to prevent the admission of persons whom Congress believed should not be allowed to come to this country and did not fall into the other categories.[9]

The grounds for exclusion should be viewed as an expression by this country of that which it does not like, abhors, or otherwise feels should not be allowed to become a part of this society. It is, by omission, an expression of the kind of people who might make up a perfect society. When studying these substantive grounds, it must be understood that from a legal standpoint, every nation has been recognized to have the absolute right to allow only those people whom it wishes to allow to enter the country.[10] It should also be remembered that these grounds for exclusion do not apply

---

4. Examples include persons likely to become public charges. *See* 8 U.S.C. § 1182(a)(4), Sec. 212(a)(4). Also included in this category are certain immigrants who will be entering the work force. Such persons are required to first obtain a "labor certification" and then wait in line, as there is a quota restricting the number who may be admitted. These issues will be discussed in Chapters 7 and 8.

5. Examples within this category include Communists [8 U.S.C. § 1182(a)(3)(D)(i)] or persons whose admission "the Secretary of State has reasonable grounds to believe would have potentially serious foreign policy consequences" [8 U.S.C. § 1182(a)(3)(C)]. In 1990 Congress expanded this category to include terrorists [8 U.S.C. § 1182(a)(3)(B), Sec. 212(a)(3)(B)].

6. Some examples include certain persons with mental disorders [8 U.S.C. § 1182(a)(1)(A)(ii)(I)] or who have a communicable disease of public health significance [8 U.S.C. § 1182(a)(1)(A)(ii)].

7. The criminal category includes persons who have been convicted of a crime involving moral turpitude [8 U.S.C. § 1182(a)(2)(A)(i)(I)], those convicted of more than one crime, irrespective of whether or not it involved moral turpitude [8 U.S.C. § 1182(a)(2)(B)], and persons who have been involved in the trafficking of narcotics [8 U.S.C. § 1182(a)(2)(C)].

8. Among these persons are polygamists [8 U.S.C. § 1182(a)(9)(A)] and prostitutes [8 U.S.C. § 1182(a)(2)(D)]. The Immigration Act of 1990 removed an exclusion ground for those entering to perform "immoral sex acts" [codified at 8 U.S.C. § 1182(a)(13)].

9. This designation has been used due to the fact that there appears to be no pattern to these areas of exclusion. Some examples of these other grounds for exclusion include the lack of documentation [8 U.S.C. § 1182(a)(7)], those accompanying excludable aliens [8 U.S.C. § 1182(a)(9)(B)], stowaways [8 U.S.C. § 1182(a)(6)(D)], and foreign medical school graduates [8 U.S.C. § 1182(a)(5)(B)]. An attempt to further define these patterns would only result in this description being equal in length to the exclusion statutes.

10. Scholars have criticized some of the cases which have upheld this absolutist rule. *See* Hart, *The Power of Congress to Limit the Jurisdiction of Federal Courts: An Exercise in Dialectic*, 66 Harv. L. Rev. 1362, 1392-96 (1953); Nafziger, *The General Admission of Aliens Under International Law*, 77 Am. J. Int'l L. 804, 823-29 (1983); Martin, *Due Process and Membership in the National Community: Political Asylum and Beyond*, 44 U. Pitt. L. Rev.

to U.S. citizens.[11] Moreover, as will be discussed in Chapter 12, many of these grounds for exclusion have been tempered by waiver provisions enacted by Congress. These provisions allow for the admission of excludable aliens upon their meeting certain conditions.

A clear understanding of the legal principles established in the exclusion cases which follow form a building block of mastering immigration law. Some examples of recent issues for which answers can only be given after exploring exclusion are the questions of testing aliens for AIDS, long-term or indefinite detention of aliens, banning the admission of controversial foreign political figures, controlling international terrorism, and the deportation of naturalized U.S. citizens found to have participated in Nazi activities during World War II.

The Exclusion Process

In order to understand the term "exclusion," one must first understand how a person can gain entry into the U.S. There are only two ways to come to this country. The first is by applying for a visa before a U.S. consul abroad.[12] Upon issuance of this visa, one is free to come to this country and attempt to gain entry. The second way would be to not apply for a visa but to attempt to gain entry without one. The person who goes to a U.S. consul will be questioned to make sure that she does not fit into one of the numerous grounds that would make her excludable. If all goes well, the person would be issued a visa and then would arrive at a port of entry by air, sea, or land and then would be questioned by the Immigration Service to determine again whether she was excludable or, alternatively, allowed to enter.[13] The person attempting to gain entry without a visa is faced with a very serious dilemma. When she arrives at the border (if she attempts to enter at a designated port), she will be prima facie excludable if without a visa.[14]

The Immigration Service's questioning of the alien at the border is called "inspection."[15] In most cases, this inspection process is done without the alien having the benefit of counsel. It has been clearly established that throughout this inspection process the applicant for entry has no constitutional protection as she is merely

---

165, 173-80 (1983); Boswell, *Rethinking Exclusion: The Rights of Cuban Refugees Facing Indefinite Detention in the United States*, 17 Vand. J. Transnt'l L. 925, 942-49 (1984).

11. *Gegiow v. Uhl*, 239 U.S. 3 (1915). A returning U.S. citizen unable to prove his citizenship could have problems.

12. The *only* way for a person to obtain a visa is by application before a U.S. consul abroad. The INS does not have any visa-issuing authority.

13. One change made by the 1990 Act is that all applicants who are denied a visa by a Consul or admission by an immigration officer must be presented with a written notice which states the determination and cites the specific provision under which the applicant is excludable, ineligible for entry or adjustment of status. *See* 8 U.S.C. § 1182(b), Sec. 212(b).

14. As will be discussed later in Chapter 3, a person who manages to gain entry notwithstanding his not having a visa will be subject to deportation.

15. Inspection is not defined in the statute, but is implicit within the statutory sections dealing with the procedure used by an INS officer in determining an alien's admissibility. It may include interrogation, perusal of documents, or other means of assuring that the applicant for entry is clearly entitled to land. *See* 1A C. Gordon & S. Mailman, Immigration Law & Procedure 1-12 (rev. ed. 1990) 8 U.S.C. § 1225(b), Sec. 235.

"knocking at the door," and therefore does not even have the rights afforded an alien already in the United States.[16]

Understandably, this process before both the United States consul and the immigration inspector at the border is a very quick one. The process is so fast that numerous people otherwise excludable manage to gain entry. The person arriving at the border has the burden of showing that she is "clearly and beyond a doubt entitled to land."[17] If the person is not entitled to land, or cannot establish to the satisfaction of the immigration inspector that she is admissible, she may be given the opportunity of withdrawing her application for entry, be bound over to the immigration judge for an exclusion hearing or paroled for completion of the inspection process at a local INS office.

The term "parole" is a legal fiction. Parole is a method of allowing a person to physically enter the U.S. while at the same time not allowing her to have the legal advantages of being "within" the U.S.[18]

Exclusion Hearing

The exclusion hearing is conducted by an immigration judge (sometimes referred to as a special inquiry officer). The judge's jurisdiction is defined at 8 C.F.R. § 235.1 and 8 U.S.C. § 1226(a).[19] As stated earlier, the alien has the burden of proving her admissibility to the United States. The alien is also permitted to have an attorney present and is given the opportunity to present evidence and to cross-examine witnesses.[20] In both deportation and exclusion hearings, strict rules of evidence are not followed, and it is the responsibility of the immigration judge to determine the admissibility and weight of evidence. At the conclusion of the hearing, the judge may immediately make an oral decision, whereupon the alien must state then and there whether she wishes to appeal. When the judge makes a written decision, the alien has 13 days in which to file the appeal.[21]

---

16. The term "knocking at the door" is used to illustrate that the right of an alien to enter the U.S. is analogous to the right of a stranger to enter one's home without permission.

17. 8 U.S.C. § 1225(b), Sec. 235 of the Act.

18. The legal advantages are discussed in Chapter 3. Briefly stated, they are primarily procedural. An alien who has "made an entry" will be accorded constitutional protection, will be entitled to judicial review of the deportation order, or may be entitled to suspension of deportation (*see* Chapter 11) or adjustment of status to that of a lawful permanent resident (*see* Chapter 9). An alien under parole will be allowed to stay in the U.S. despite the fact that she has no other legal basis to remain. In addition, at a later date she may be able to apply for lawful permanent residence.

19. Sec. 236 of the Act.

20. Although an alien has a right to counsel, the government will not provide an attorney. The right to counsel exists in exclusion and deportation proceedings under the statute. See 8 U.S.C. §§ 1252(b)(2), Sec. 242 and 1362, Sec. 292. While one may not have a constitutional right to counsel in exclusion proceedings, that right arguably exists for aliens in deportation. *See Castaneda-Delgado v. INS*, 525 F.2d 1295 (7th Cir. 1975); *Cheung v. INS*, 418 F.2d 460 (D.C. Cir. 1969); *but see Matter of Santos*, Interim Dec. 2969 (BIA 1984).

21. 8 C.F.R. § 236.7.

References

Aleinikoff, *Aliens, Due Process and Community Ties*, 44 U. Pitt. L. Rev. 237 (1983)

Boswell, *Rethinking Exclusion: The Rights of Cuban Refugees Facing Indefinite Detention in the U.S.*, 17 Vand. J. Transnt'l L. 925 (1984)

Carro, *From Constitutional Psychopathic Inferiority to AIDS: What is in the Future for Homosexual Aliens*, 7 Yale L. & Pol'y Rev. 201 (1989)

Comment, *Ideological Exclusions—Closing the Border to Political Dissidents*, 100 Harv. L. Rev. 930 (1987)

Gibney, *The Huddled Masses Myth*, 3 Geo. Imm. L. J. 361 (1989)

Henkin, *Essays Commemorating the One Hundredth Anniversary of the Harvard Law Review: The Constitution and United States Sovereignty: A Century of Chinese Exclusion and Its Progeny*, 100 Harv. L. Rev. 853 (1987)

E. Hull, Without Justice for All: The Constitutional Rights of Aliens (Greenwood Press, 1985)

Martin, *Due Process and Membership in the National Community*, 44 U. Pitt. L. Rev. 165, 173-80 (1983)

Nafziger, *The General Admission of Aliens Under International Law*, 77 Am. J. Int'l L. 804 (1983)

Note, *The Constitutional Rights of Excluded Aliens: Proposed Limitations on the Indefinite Detention of the Cuban Refugees*, 70 GEO. L. J. 1303 (1982)

Pedraza-Bailey, Political and Economic Migrants in America: Cubans and Mexicans 165-69 (1985)

Scanlan, *Aliens in the Marketplace of Ideas: The Government, the Academy and the McCarran-Walter Act*, 66 Tex. L. Rev. 1481 (1988)

Schuck, *The Transformation of Immigration Law*, 84 Colum. L. Rev. 1, 40 (1984)

A. The Exclusion Power

The Chinese Exclusion Case

130 U.S. 581 (1889) [*Chae Chan Ping v. United States*]

Mr. Justice FIELD delivered the opinion of the Court.

The appeal involves a consideration of the validity of the act of congress of October 1, 1888, prohibiting Chinese laborers from entering the United States who had departed before its passage, having a certificate issued under the act of 1882 as amended by the act of 1884, granting them permission to return. The validity of the act is assailed as being in effect an expulsion from the country of Chinese laborers, in violation of existing treaties between the United States and the government of China, and of rights vested in them under the laws of congress.

*   *   *

... That the government of the United States, through the action of the legislative department, can exclude aliens from its territory is a proposition which we do not think open to controversy. Jurisdiction over its own territory to that extent is an incident of every independent nation. It is a part of its independence. If it could not exclude aliens it would be to that extent subject to the control of another power. As said by this court in the case of *The Exchange*, 7 Cranch, 116, 136, speaking by Chief Justice Marshall:

> The jurisdiction of the nation within its own territory is necessarily exclusive and absolute. It is susceptible of no limitation not imposed by itself. Any restriction upon it, deriving validity from an external source, would imply a diminution of its sovereignty to the extent of the restriction, and an investment of that sovereignty to the same extent in that power which could impose such restriction. All exceptions, therefore, to the full and complete power of a nation within its own territories, must be traced up to the consent of the nation itself. They can flow from no other legitimate source.

> America has chosen to be in many respects, and to many purposes, a nation; and for all these purposes her government is complete; to all these objects, it is competent. The people have declared that in the exercise of all powers given for these objects it is supreme. It can, then, in effecting these objects, legitimately control all individuals or governments within the American territory. The constitution and laws of a state, so far as they are repugnant to the constitution and laws of the United States, are absolutely void. . . . It is invested with power over all the foreign relations of the country, war, peace, and negotiations and intercourse with other nations; all of which are forbidden to the state governments. . . .

*   *   *

> . . . To preserve its independence, and give security against foreign aggression and encroachment, is the highest duty of every nation, and to attain these ends nearly all other considerations are to be subordinated. It matters not in what form such aggression and encroachment come, whether from the foreign nation acting in its national character, or from vast hordes of its people crowding in upon us. The government, possessing the powers which are to be exercised for protection and security, is clothed with authority to determine the occasion on which the powers shall be called forth; and its determinations, so far as the subjects affected are concerned, are necessarily conclusive upon all its departments and officers. If, therefore, the government of the United States, through its legislative department, considers the presence of foreigners of a different race in this country, who will not assimilate with us, to be dangerous to its peace and security, their exclusion is not to be stayed because at the time there are no actual hostilities with the nation of which the foreigners are subjects. The existence of war would render the necessity of the proceeding only more obvious and pressing. The same necessity, in a less pressing degree, may arise when war does not exist, and the same authority which adjudges the necessity in one case must also determine it in the other. In both cases its determination is conclusive upon the judiciary. If the government of the country of which the foreigners excluded are subjects is dissatisfied with this action, it can make complaint to the executive head of our government, or resort to any other measure which, in its judgment, its interests or dignity may demand; and there lies its only remedy. The power of the government to exclude foreigners from the country whenever, in its judgment, the public interests require such exclusion, has been asserted in repeated instances, and never denied by the executive or legislative departments. . . .

The exclusion of paupers, criminals, and persons afflicted with incurable diseases, for which statutes have been passed, is only an application of the same power to particular classes of persons, whose presence is deemed injurious or a source of danger to the country. As applied to them, there has never been any question as to the power to exclude them. The power is constantly exercised; its existence is involved in the right of self-preservation. As to paupers, it makes no difference by whose aid they are brought to the country. As Mr. Fish, when secretary of state, wrote, in a communication under date of December 26, 1872, to Mr. James Moulding, of Liverpool, the government of the United States "is not willing and will not consent to receive the pauper class of any community who may be sent or may be assisted in their immigration at the expense of government or of municipal authorities." As to criminals, the power of exclusion has always been exercised, even in the absence of any statute on the subject. In a dispatch to Mr. Cramer, our minister to Switzerland, in December, 1881, Mr. Blaine, secretary of state under President Arthur, writes: "While, under the constitution and the laws, this country is open to the honest and the industrious immigrant, it has no room outside of its prisons or almshouses for deraved and incorrigible criminals or hopelessly dependent paupers who may have become a pest or burden, or both, to their own country." Wharton's Int. Law Dig., *supra*.

Notes

1. One of the issues which arose in *The Chinese Exclusion Case* was the extent to which the Chinese Exclusion Act affected a then-existing treaty between the U.S. and China. The Court noted a well-established principle when it stated

> It must be conceded that the act of 1888 is in contravention of express stipulations of the treaty of 1868, and of the supplemental treaty of 1880, but it is not on that account invalid, or to be restricted in its enforcement. The treaties were of no greater legal obligation than the act of congress. By the constitution, laws made in pursuance thereof, and treaties made under the authority of the United States, are both declared to be the supreme law of the land, and no paramount authority is given to one over the other. A treaty, it is true, is in its nature a contract between nations, and is often merely promissory in its character, requiring legislation to carry its stipulations into effect. Such legislation will be open to future repeal or amendment. If the treaty operates by its own force, and relates to a subject within the power of congress, it can be deemed in that particular only the equivalent of a legislative act, to be repealed or modified at the pleasure of congress. In either case the last expression of the sovereign will control.

For additional clarification on this point, *see Head-Money Cases*, 112 U.S. 580, 599 (1884); *Whitney v. Robertson*, 124 U.S. 190 (1888).

2. It cannot be presumed that Congress will lightly pass laws which are in conflict with the treaties. The courts will strain interpretation of a statute to avoid overturning a treaty unless there is a clear legislative directive otherwise.

Harisiades v. Shaughnessy
342 U.S. 580 (1952)

Justice JACKSON delivered the opinion of the Court.

The ultimate question in these three cases is whether the United States constitutionally may deport a legally resident alien because of membership in the Communist Party which terminated before enactment of the Alien Registration Act, 1940.

Harisiades, a Greek national, accompanied his father to the United States in 1916, when thirteen years of age, and has resided here since. He has taken a wife and sired two children, all citizens. He joined the Communist Party in 1925, when it was known as the Workers Party, and served as an organizer, Branch Executive Committeeman, secretary of its Greek Bureau, and editor of its paper "Empros." The party discontinued his membership, along with that of other aliens, in 1939, but he has continued association with members. He was familiar with the principles and philosophy of the Communist Party and says he still believes in them. He disclaims personal belief in use of force and violence and asserts that the party favored their use only in defense. A warrant for his deportation because of his membership was issued in 1930 but was not served until 1946. The delay was due to inability to locate him because of his use of a number of aliases. After hearings, he was ordered deported on the grounds that after entry he had been a member of an organization which advocates overthrow of the Government by force and violence and distributes printed matter so advocating. . . .

Mascitti, a citizen of Italy, came to this county in 1920, at the age of sixteen. He married a resident alien and has one American-born child. He was a member of the Young Workers Party, the Workers Party and the Communist Party between 1923 and 1929. His testimony was that he knew the party advocated a proletarian dictatorship, to be established by force and violence if the capitalist class resisted. He heard some speakers advocate violence, in which he says he did not personally believe, and he was not clear as to the party policy. He resigned in 1929, apparently because he lost sympathy with or interest in the party. A warrant for his deportation issued and was served in 1946. After the usual administrative hearings he was ordered deported on the same grounds as Harisiades.

* * *

Mrs. Coleman, a native of Russia, was admitted to the United States in 1914, when thirteen years of age. She married an American citizen and has three children, citizens by birth. She admits being a member of the Communist Party for about a year, beginning in 1919, and again from 1928 to 1930, and again from 1936 to 1937 or 1938. She held no office and her activities were not significant. She disavowed much knowledge of party principles and program, claiming she joined each time because of some injustice the party was then fighting. The reasons she gives for leaving the party are her health and the party's discontinuance of alien memberships. She has been ordered deported because after entry she became a member of an organization advocating overthrow of the Government by force and violence.

* * *

Validity of the hearing procedures is questioned for noncompliance with the Administrative Procedure Act, which we think is here inapplicable.[1] Admittedly, each of these deportations is authorized and required by the letter, spirit and intention of the statute. But the Act is assailed on three grounds: (1) that it deprives the aliens

---

1. Petitioner Harisiades and appellant Coleman contend that the proceedings against them must be nullified for failure to conform to the requirements of the Administrative Procedure Act, 60 Stat. 237, 5 U.S.C. 1001 *et seq*. However, § 12 of the Act, 60 Stat. 244, 5 U.S.C. § 1011, provides that ". . . no procedural requirement shall be mandatory as to any agency proceeding initiated prior to the effective date of such requirement." The proceedings against Harisiades and Coleman were instituted before the effective date of the Act.

of liberty without due process of law in violation of the Fifth Amendment; (2) that it abridges their freedoms of speech and assembly in contravention of the First Amendment; and (3) that it is an *ex post facto* law which Congress is forbidden to pass by Art. I, § 9, cl. 3 of the Constitution.

* * *

These aliens ask us to forbid their expulsion by a departure from the long-accepted application to such cases of the Fifth Amendment provision that no person shall be deprived of life, liberty or property without due process of law. Their basic contention is that admission for permanent residence confers a "vested right" on the alien, equal to that of the citizen, to remain within the country, and that the alien is entitled to constitutional protection in that matter to the same extent as the citizen.

* * *

So long as one thus perpetuates a dual status as an American inhabitant but foreign citizen, he may derive advantages from two sources of law—American and international. He may claim protection against our Government unavailable to the citizen. As an alien he retains a claim upon the state of his citizenship to diplomatic intervention on his behalf, a patronage often of considerable value. The state of origin of each of these aliens could presently enter diplomatic remonstrance against these deportations if they were inconsistent with international law, the prevailing custom among nations or their own practices.

The alien retains immunities from burdens which the citizen must shoulder. By withholding his allegiance from the United States, he leaves outstanding a foreign call on his loyalties which international law not only permits our Government to recognize but commands it to respect. In deference to it certain dispensations from conscription for any military service have been granted foreign nationals. They cannot, consistently with our international commitments, be compelled "to take part in the operations of war directed against their own country." In addition to such general immunities they may enjoy particular treaty privileges.

Under our law, the alien in several respects stands on an equal footing with citizens, but in others has never been conceded legal parity with the citizen. Most importantly, to protract this ambiguous status within the country is not his right but is a matter of permission and tolerance. The Government's power to terminate its hospitality has been asserted and sustained by this Court since the question first arose.

War, of course, is the most usual occasion for extensive resort to the power. Though the resident alien may be personally loyal to the United States, if his nation becomes our enemy his allegiance prevails over his personal preference and makes him also our enemy, liable to expulsion or internment, and his property becomes subject to seizure and perhaps confiscation. But it does not require war to bring the power of deportation into existence or to authorize its exercise. Congressional apprehension of foreign or internal dangers short of war may lead to its use. So long as the alien elects to continue the ambiguity of his allegiance his domicile here is held by a precarious tenure.

That aliens remain vulnerable to expulsion after long residence is a practice that bristles with severities. But it is a weapon of defense and reprisal confirmed by international law as a power inherent in every sovereign state.[2] Such is the traditional power of the Nation over the alien and we leave the law on the subject as we find it.

In historical context the Act before us stands out as an extreme application of the expulsion power. There is no denying that as world convulsions have driven us toward a closed society the expulsion power has been exercised with increasing severity, manifest in multiplication of grounds for deportation, in expanding the subject classes from illegal entrants to legal residents, and in greatly lengthening the period of residence after which one may be expelled.[3] This is said to have reached a point where it is the duty of this Court to call a halt upon the political branches of the Government.

It is pertinent to observe that any policy toward aliens is vitally and intricately interwoven with contemporaneous policies in regard to the conduct of foreign relations, the war power, and the maintenance of a republican form of government. Such matters are so exclusively entrusted to the political branches of government as to be largely immune from judicial inquiry or interference.

*   *   *

The First Amendment is invoked as a barrier against this enactment. The claim is that in joining an organization advocating overthrow of government by force and violence the alien has merely exercised freedoms of speech, press and assembly which that Amendment guarantees to him.

*   *   *

---

2. "... [I]n strict law, a State can expel even domiciled aliens without so much as giving the reasons, the refusal of the expelling State to supply the reasons for expulsion to the home State of the expelled alien does not constitute an illegal, but only a very unfriendly act." 1 Oppenheim, International Law (3d ed., Roxburgh, 1920), 498-502, at 499. But cf. 1 Oppenheim, International Law (7th ed., Lauterpacht, 1948), 630-634, at 631.

3. An open door to the immigrant was the early federal policy. It began to close in 1884 when Orientals were excluded. 23 Stat. 115. Thereafter, Congress has intermittently added to the excluded classes, and as rejections at the border multiplied illegal entries increased. To combat these, recourse was had to deportation in the Act of 1891, 26 Stat. 1086. However, that Act could be applied to an illegal entrant only within one year after his entry. Although that time limitation was subsequently extended, 32 Stat. 1218; 34 Stat. 904-905, until after the turn of the century expulsion was used only as an auxiliary remedy to enforce exclusion.

Congress, in 1907, provided for deportation of legally resident aliens, but the statute reached only women found engaging in prostitution, and deportation proceedings were authorized only within three years after entry.

From those early steps, the policy has been extended. In 1910, new classes of resident aliens were listed for deportation, including for the first time political offenders such as anarchists and those believing in or advocating the overthrow of the Government by force and violence. 36 Stat. 264. In 1917, aliens who were found after entry to be advocating anarchist doctrines or the overthrow of the Government by force and violence were made subject to deportation, a five-year time limit being retained. 39 Stat. 889. A year later, deportability because of membership in described subversive organizations was introduced. 40 Stat. 1012; 41 Stat. 1008. When this Court, in 1939, held that Act reached only aliens who were members when the proceedings against them were instituted, *Kessler v. Strecker*, 307 U.S. 22, Congress promptly enacted the statute before us, making deportation mandatory for all aliens who at any time past have been members of the proscribed organizations. In so doing it also eliminated the time limit for institution of proceedings thereunder. Alien Registration Act, 1940, 54 Stat. 670, 673.

True, it often is difficult to determine whether ambiguous speech is advocacy of political methods or subtly shades into a methodical but prudent incitement to violence. Communist Governments avoid the inquiry by suppressing everything distasteful. Some would have us avoid the difficulty by going to the opposite extreme of permitting incitement to violent overthrow at least unless it seems certain to succeed immediately. We apprehend that the Constitution enjoins upon us the duty, however difficult, of distinguishing between the two. Different formulae have been applied in different situations and the test applicable to the Communist Party has been stated too recently to make further discussion at this time profitable. We think the First Amendment does not prevent the deportation of these aliens.

The remaining claim is that this Act conflicts with Art. I, § 9, of the Constitution forbidding *ex post facto* enactments. An impression of retroactivity results from reading as a new and isolated enactment what is actually a continuation of prior legislation.

During all the years since 1920 Congress has maintained a standing admonition to aliens, on pain of deportation, not to become members of any organization that advocates overthrow of the United States Government by force and violence, a category repeatedly held to include the Communist Party. These aliens violated that prohibition and incurred liability to deportation. They were not caught unawares by a change of law. There can be no contention that they were not adequately forewarned both that their conduct was prohibited and of its consequences.

*   *   *

However, even if the Act were found to be retroactive, to strike it down would require us to overrule the construction of the *ex post facto* provision which has been followed by this Court from earliest times. It always has been considered that which it forbids is penal legislation which imposes or increases criminal punishment for conduct lawful previous to its enactment. Deportation, however severe its consequences, has been consistently classified as a civil rather than a criminal procedure. Both of these doctrines as original proposals might be debatable, but both have been considered closed for many years and a body of statute and decisional law has been built upon them. In *Bugajewitz v. Adams*, 228 U.S. 585, 591 (1913) Justice Holmes, for the Court, said

> It is thoroughly established that Congress has power to order the deportation of aliens whose presence in the country it deems hurtful. The determination by facts that might constitute a crime under local law is not a conviction of crime, nor is the deportation a punishment; it is simply a refusal by the government to harbor persons whom it does not want. The coincidence of the local penal law with the policy of Congress is an accident. . . . The prohibition of ex post facto laws in article 1, § 9, has no application . . . and with regard to the petitioner, it is not necessary to construe the statute as having any retrospective effect.

Later, the Court said, "It is well settled that deportation, while it may be burdensome and severe for the alien, is not a punishment. . . . The inhibition against the passage of an *ex post facto* law by Congress in section 9 of article 1˙of the Constitution applies only to criminal laws . . . and not to a deportation act like this. . . ." *Mahler v. Eby*, 264 U.S. 32, 39 (1924).

*   *   *

We find none of the constitutional objections to the Act well founded. The judgments accordingly are affirmed.

Justice Clark took no part in the consideration or decision of these cases.

Justice Frankfurter, concurring.

* * *

The Court's acknowledgment of the sole responsibility of Congress for these matters has been made possible by Justices whose cultural outlook, whose breadth of view and robust tolerance were not exceeded by those of Jefferson. In their personal views, libertarians like Justice Holmes and Justice Brandeis doubtless disapproved of some of these policies, departures as they were from the best traditions of this country and based as they have been in part on discredited racial theories or manipulation of figures in formulating what is known as the quota system. But whether immigration laws have been crude and cruel, whether they may have reflected xenophobia in general or anti-Semitism or anti-Catholicism, the responsibility belongs to Congress. Courts do enforce the requirements imposed by Congress upon officials in administering immigration laws, and the requirement of Due Process may entail certain procedural observances. But the underlying policies of what classes of aliens shall be allowed to enter and what classes of aliens shall be allowed to stay, are for Congress exclusively to determine even though such determination may be deemed to offend American traditions and may, as has been the case, jeopardize peace.

* * *

Justice Douglas, with whom Justice Black concurs, dissenting. There are two possible bases for sustaining this Act:

(1) A person who was once a Communist is tainted for all time and forever dangerous to our society; or

(2) Punishment through banishment from the country may be placed upon an alien not for what he did, but for what his political views once were. Each of these is foreign to our philosophy. We repudiate our traditions of tolerance and our articles of faith based upon the Bill of Rights when we bow to them by sustaining an Act of Congress which has them as a foundation. The view that the power of Congress to deport aliens is absolute and may be exercised for any reason which Congress deems appropriate rests on *Fong Yue Ting v. United States*, 149 U.S. 698, decided in 1893 by a six-to-three vote. That decision seems to me to be inconsistent with the philosophy of constitutional law which we have developed for the protection of resident aliens. We have long held that a resident alien is a "person" within the meaning of the Fifth and the Fourteenth Amendments. He therefore may not be deprived either by the National Government or by any state of life, liberty, or property without due process of law. Nor may he be denied the equal protection of the laws. A state was not allowed to exclude an alien from the laundry business because he was a Chinese, nor discharge him from employment because he was not a citizen, nor deprive him of the right to fish because he was a Japanese ineligible to citizenship. An alien's property [provided he is not an enemy alien], may not be taken without just compensation. He is entitled to habeas corpus to test the legality of his restraint, to the protection of the Fifth and Sixth Amendments in criminal trials, and to the right of free speech as guaranteed by the First Amendment.

* * *

The right to be immune from arbitrary decrees of banishment certainly may be more important to "liberty" than the civil rights which all aliens enjoy when they reside here. Unless they are free from arbitrary banishment, the "liberty" they enjoy while they live here is indeed illusory. Banishment is punishment in the practical sense. It may deprive a man and his family of all that makes life worth while. Those who have their roots here have an important stake in this country. Their plans for themselves and their hopes for their children all depend on their right to stay. If they are uprooted and sent to lands no longer known to them, no longer hospitable, they become displaced, homeless people condemned to bitterness and despair.

This drastic step may at times be necessary in order to protect the national interest. There may be occasions when the continued presence of an alien, no matter how long he may have been here, would be hostile to the safety or welfare of the Nation due to the nature of his conduct. But unless such condition is shown, I would stay the hand of the Government and let those to whom we have extended our hospitality and who have become members of our communities remain here and enjoy the life and liberty which the Constitution guarantees.

Congress has not proceeded by that standard. It has ordered these aliens deported not for what they are but for what they once were. Perhaps a hearing would show that they continue to be people dangerous and hostile to us. But the principle of forgiveness and the doctrine of redemption are too deep in our philosophy to admit that there is no return for those who have once erred.

Shaughnessy v. Mezei
345 U.S. 206 (1953)

Justice CLARK delivered the opinion of the Court.

This case concerns an alien immigrant permanently excluded from the United States on security grounds but stranded in his temporary haven on Ellis Island because other countries will not take him back. The issue is whether the Attorney General's continued exclusion of respondent without a hearing amounts to an unlawful detention, so that courts may admit him temporarily to the United States on bond until arrangements are made for his departure abroad. After a hearing on respondent's petition for a writ of habeas corpus, the District Court so held and authorized his temporary admission on $5,000 bond. The Court of Appeals affirmed that action, but directed reconsideration of the terms of the parole. Accordingly, the District Court entered a modified order reducing bond to $3,000 and permitting respondent to travel and reside in Buffalo, New York. Bond was posted and respondent released. Because of resultant serious problems in the enforcement of the immigration laws, we granted certiorari.

Respondent's present dilemma springs from these circumstances: Though, as the District Court observed, "[t]here is a certain vagueness about [his] history," respondent seemingly was born in Gibraltar of Hungarian or Rumanian parents and lived in the United States from 1923 to 1948. In May of that year he sailed for Europe, apparently to visit his dying mother in Rumania. Denied entry there, he remained in Hungary for some 19 months, due to "difficulty in securing an exit permit." Finally, armed with a quota immigration visa issued by the American Consul in Budapest, he proceeded to France and boarded the Ile de France in Le Havre bound for New

York. Upon arrival on February 9, 1950, he was temporarily excluded from the United States by an immigration inspector acting pursuant to the Passport Act as amended and regulations thereunder. Pending disposition of his case he was received at Ellis Island. After reviewing the evidence, the Attorney General on May 10, 1950, ordered the temporary exclusion to be made permanent without a hearing before a board of special inquiry, on the "basis of information of a confidential nature, the disclosure of which would be prejudicial to the public interest." That determination rested on a finding that respondent's entry would be prejudicial to the public interest for security reasons. But thus far all attempts to effect respondent's departure have failed: Twice he shipped out to return whence he came; France and Great Britain refused him permission to land. The State Department has unsuccessfully negotiated with Hungary for his readmission. Respondent personally applied for entry to about a dozen Latin American countries but all turned him down. So in June 1951 respondent advised the Immigration and Naturalization Service that he would exert no further efforts to depart. In short, respondent sat on Ellis Island because this country shut him out and others were unwilling to take him in.

Asserting unlawful confinement on Ellis Island, he sought relief through a series of habeas corpus proceedings. After four unsuccessful efforts on respondent's part, the United States District Court for the Southern District of New York on November 9, 1951, sustained the writ. The District Judge, vexed by the problem of "an alien who has no place to go," did not question the validity of the exclusion order but deemed further "detention" after 21 months excessive and justifiable only by affirmative proof of respondent's danger to the public safety. When the Government declined to divulge such evidence, even in camera, the District Court directed respondent's conditional parole on bond. By a divided vote, the Court of Appeals affirmed. Postulating that the power to hold could never be broader than the power to remove or shut out and that to "continue an alien's confinement beyond that moment when deportation becomes patently impossible is to deprive him of his liberty," the court found respondent's "confinement" no longer justifiable as a means of removal elsewhere, thus not authorized by statute, and in violation of due process. Judge Learned Hand, dissenting, took a different view: The Attorney General's order was one of "exclusion" and not "deportation"; respondent's transfer from ship to shore on Ellis Island conferred no additional rights; in fact, no alien so situated "can force us to admit him at all."

Courts have long recognized the power to expel or exclude aliens as a fundamental sovereign attribute exercised by the Government's political departments largely immune from judicial control. In the exercise of these powers, Congress expressly authorized the President to impose additional restrictions on aliens entering or leaving the United States during periods of international tension and strife. That authorization, originally enacted in the Passport Act of 1918, continues in effect during the present emergency. Under it, the Attorney General, acting for the President, may shut out aliens whose "entry would be prejudicial to the interest of the United States." And he may exclude without a hearing when the exclusion is based on confidential information the disclosure of which may be prejudicial to the public interest. The Attorney General in this case proceeded in accord with these provisions; he made the necessary determinations and barred the alien from entering the United States.

It is true that aliens who have once passed through our gates, even illegally, may be expelled only after proceedings conforming to traditional standards of fairness encompassed in due process of law. But an alien on the threshold of initial entry stands on a different footing: "Whatever the procedure authorized by Congress is, it is due process as far as an alien denied entry is concerned." *Knauf v. Shaughnessy*, 338 U.S. 537, 544 (1950). And because the action of the executive officer under such authority is final and conclusive, the Attorney General cannot be compelled to disclose the evidence underlying his determinations in an exclusion case; "it is not within the province of any court, unless expressly authorized by law, to review the determination of the political branch of the Government." In a case such as this, courts cannot retry the determination of the Attorney General.

Neither respondent's harborage on Ellis Island nor his prior residence here transforms this into something other than an exclusion proceeding. Concededly, his movements are restrained by authority of the United States, and he may by habeas corpus test the validity of his exclusion. But that is true whether he enjoys temporary refuge on land. In sum, harborage at Ellis Island is not an entry into the United States. *Kaplan v. Tod*, 267 U.S. 228, 230 (1925); *United States v. Ju Toy*, 198 U.S. 253, 263 (1905). For purposes of the immigration laws, moreover, the legal incidents of an alien's entry remain unaltered whether he has been here once before or not. He is an entering alien just the same, and may be excluded if unqualified for admission under existing immigration laws.

To be sure, a lawful resident alien may not captiously be deprived of his constitutional rights to procedural due process. *Kwong Hai Chew v. Colding*, 344 U.S. 590, 601 (1953). Only the other day we held that under some circumstances temporary absence from our shores cannot constitutionally deprive a returning lawfully resident alien of his right to be heard. *Kwong Hai Chew v. Colding*, *supra*. Chew, an alien seaman admitted by an Act of Congress to permanent residence in the United States, signed articles of maritime employment as chief steward on a vessel of American registry with home port in New York City. Though cleared by the Coast Guard for his voyage, on his return from four months at sea he was "excluded" without a hearing on security grounds. On the facts of that case, including reference to § 307(d)(2) of the Nationality Act of 1940, 8 U.S.C. § 707(d)(2), we felt justified in "assimilating" his status for constitutional purposes to that of continuously present alien residents entitled to hearings at least before an executive or administrative tribunal. *Id.*, 344 U.S. at pages 596, 599-601. Accordingly, to escape constitutional conflict we held the administrative regulations authorizing exclusion without hearing in certain security cases inapplicable to aliens so protected by the Fifth Amendment. *Id.* at 600.

But respondent's history here drastically differs from that disclosed in Chew's case. Unlike Chew who with full security clearance and documentation pursued his vocation for four months aboard an American ship, respondent, apparently without authorization or reentry papers, simply left the United States and remained behind the Iron Curtain for 19 months. Moreover, while § 307 of the 1940 Nationality Act regards maritime service such as Chew's to be continuous residence for naturalization purposes, that section deems protracted absence such as respondent's a clear break in an alien's continuous residence here. In such circumstances, we have no difficulty in holding respondent an entrant alien or "assimilated to [that] status" for constitutional purposes. *Id.* at 599. That being so, the Attorney General may lawfully exclude respondent without a hearing as authorized by the emergency regulations promulgated pursuant to the Passport Act. Nor need he disclose the evidence upon which that determination rests.

* * *

... While the Government might keep entrants by sea aboard the vessel pending determination of their admissibility, resulting hardships to the alien and inconvenience to the carrier persuaded Congress to adopt a more generous course. By statute it authorized, in cases such as this, aliens' temporary removal from ship to shore. But such temporary harborage, an act of legislative grace, bestows no additional rights. Congress meticulously specified that such shelter ashore "shall not be considered a landing" nor relieve the vessel of the duty to transport back the alien if ultimately excluded. And this Court has long considered such temporary arrangements as not affecting an alien's status; he is treated as if stopped at the border.

Thus we do not think that respondent's continued exclusion deprives him of any statutory or constitutional right. It is true that resident aliens temporarily detained pending expeditious consummation of deportation proceedings may be released on bond by the Attorney General whose discretion is subject to judicial review. *Carlson v. Landon*, 342 U.S. 524 (1952). By that procedure aliens uprooted from our midst may rejoin the community until the Government effects their leave. An exclusion proceeding grounded on danger to the national security, however, presents different considerations; neither the rationale nor the statutory authority for such release exists. Ordinarily to admit an alien barred from entry on security grounds nullifies the very purpose of the exclusion proceeding; Congress in 1950 declined to include such authority in the statute. That exclusion by the United States plus other nations inhospitality results in present hardship cannot be ignored. But, the times being what they are, Congress may well have felt that other countries ought not shift the onus to us; that an alien in respondent's position is no more ours than theirs. Whatever our individual estimate of that policy and the fears on which it rests, respondent's right to enter the United States depends on the congressional will, and courts cannot substitute their judgment for the legislative mandate.

Note

The provisions under which Shaughnessy was excluded have been modified by the *Immigration Act of 1990*. Under the heading "Security and Related Grounds"[22] the law provides that a person who a consular or immigration officer knows or has reasonable grounds to believe will engage in espionage, any unlawful activity, to overthrow the government of the U.S. by force or violence. The Act further divides those excludable for national security reasons under the headings of "terrorists," "foreign policy," "totalitarian party membership" and "nazi persecution." Terrorist activity is defined as any activity which is unlawful under the laws of the place where it is committed or would be unlawful if committed in the U.S. and involve any number of 6 activities listed in the subsection.[23] A person whose admission to the U.S. would

---

22. The security grounds can be found at 8 U.S.C. § 1182(a)(3), Sec. 212(a)(3).

23. *See* 8 U.S.C. § 1182(a)(3)(B)(ii), Sec. 212(a)(3)(B)(ii). The law specifically identifies the Palestine Liberation Organization as a terrorist group. 8 U.S.C. § 1182(a)(3)(B)(i)(II), Sec. 212(a)(3)(B)(i)(II).

have "potentially serious adverse foreign policy consequences for the U.S. is excludable."[24] However, persons who are officials or candidates for elected office cannot be excluded "solely because of their beliefs, statements or associations if their beliefs, statements or associations would be lawful in the U.S." The statute further provides protections for other aliens unless the Secretary of State personally determines that their admission would compromise a compelling foreign policy interest. Pursuant to this provision, the Secretary must notify the chairs of the House Judiciary and Foreign Affairs Committee and Senate Judiciary and Foreign Relations Committee. An immigrant (as opposed to a nonimmigrant) who has been or is affiliated with the Communist "or any other totalitarian party" are excludable, except that involuntary membership, and past membership where the membership was 2 years before the date of the application or 5 years before the date where the membership was with the controlling party in a foreign government. The Attorney General must be satisfied that the person poses no threat to the security of the U.S. Following longstanding national policy the law continues to bar the admission of persons who participated with the Nazis between March 23, 1933 and May 8, 1945 or has engaged in genocide under the definition established under the International Convention on the Prevention and Punishment of Genocide.

Parole of Aliens into the U.S.

In *Shaughnessy v. Mezei*, the Court referred to a procedure called "parole" whereby the person was allowed to be removed from the vessel pending the ultimate outcome of his case. Although parole was not statutorily authorized until 1952, it has been used by the executive branch since perhaps 1875, upon the implementation of the first exclusion statutes.

As was seen in *Mezei*, whether he was considered within or without the U.S. was of paramount significance. Although the parole power has not undergone serious scrutiny by the courts, its use by the executive has raised many issues as to the treatment of aliens seeking entry at the border. The effective parole statute is provided below and should be helpful prior to reviewing the following case.

1. The statutory authority for parole is contained in 8 U.S.C. § 1182(d)(5)(A) and provides that:

The Attorney General may, except as provided in subparagraph (B) or in [8 U.S.C. § 1184(f)], in his discretion parole into the United States temporarily under such conditions as he may prescribe for emergent reasons or for reasons deemed strictly in the public interest any alien applying for admission to the United States, but such parole of such alien shall not be regarded as an admission of the alien and when the purposes of such parole shall, in the opinion of the Attorney General, have been served the alien shall forthwith return or be returned to the custody from which he was paroled and thereafter his case shall continue to be dealt with in the same manner as that of any other applicant for admission to the United States.

(B) The Attorney General may not parole into the United States an alien who is a refugee unless the Attorney General determines that compelling reasons in the public interest with respect to that particular alien require that the alien be

24. 8 U.S.C. § 1182(a)(3)(C)(i), Sec. 212(a)(3)(C)(i)

paroled into the United States rather than be admitted as a refugee under section 1157 of this title.

2. Whether parole may be revoked and under what conditions is the subject of some debate. In *Paktorovics v. Murff*, 260 F.2d 610 (2d Cir. 1958), an appellate court held that due to the special circumstances under which Hungarian refugees were admitted as parolees the court would continue limits on the method used by the government in its revocation of the benefit. Notwithstanding this decision, *Paktorovics* has been viewed narrowly. *Ahrens v. Rojas*, 292 F.2d 406 (5th Cir. 1961); *Matter of Castellon*, 17 I. & N. Dec. 616 (BIA 1981). While a formal hearing is not required for the revocation of parole, the regulations require that written notice be given. *See* 8 C.F.R. § 212.5(d)(4). Of what value is this revocation notice if the parolee does not have a right to be heard by the INS?

3. A brief digression into some successful (or partially successful) challenges in parole cases may be helpful both in understanding parole and the importance of procedure in immigration cases. The agency's failure to follow its own regulations in the revocation of parole may amount to a violation of the rights conferred under the statute. *Moret v. Karn*, 746 F.2d 989 (3d Cir. 1984). Similarly, an allegation that the agency's action amounted to rulemaking in violation of the Administrative Procedure Act (APA) may be reviewed. *Louis v. Nelson*, 544 F. Supp. 973 (S.D. Fla. 1982), *rev'd in part aff'd in part sub nom. Jean v. Nelson*, 711 F.2d 1455 (11th Cir. 1983), *aff'd Jean v. Nelson*, 472 U.S. 846 (1985). Or where there is an allegation of a violation of an alien's other rights whether under statute or under the Constitution. *Nguyen Da Yen v. Kissinger*, 528 F.2d 1194 (9th Cir. 1975); *also see Gutierrez v. Ilchert*, 702 F. Supp. 787 (N.D. Ca. 1988).

4. As was noted earlier, one of the arguments that was successful in *Paktorovics* was that the Hungarian parolees had been invited to the U.S. In the case of the members of the Mariel boatlift, a similar argument was made and evidence was presented that the then President Carter had, in effect, invited the refugees to the U.S. This argument was rejected by an appellate court in *Garcia-Mir v. Meese*, 788 F.2d 1446 (11th Cir. 1986).

> The long-range implications of such a holding would be both profound and dangerous. It is a hallmark of our system of government that certain rights and liberties are enshrined in the social compact. These guarantees may be expanded or contracted through any of several constitutionally provided-for processes. But to give countenance to the notion that one of the political branches can simply wave a magic wand and "create" (and by implication extinguish) constitutional rights would be to undo completely the notion of limited government through separated, checked and balanced powers. This is a step we decline to take.

> * * *

> ...While in any event we decline to be bound by that holding, that case is inapposite because there is a critical distinction between the situation in Paktorovics and the instant case. While in both cases the President made public pronouncements to the effect that a certain ethnic group was welcome to come to America, in Paktorovics Congress [later] enacted legislation endorsing the extraordinary action of the President with respect to these Hungarian refugees.

In light of the cases noted above, is *Paktorovics* good law today?

B. Exclusion for Detention or Deportation

Rodriguez-Fernandez v. Wilkinson
654 F.2d 1382 (10th Cir. 1981)

[Note: This is an appeal from a decision of the district court granting a writ of habeas corpus. Rodriguez-Fernandez is a Cuban national who arrived in the U.S. on the Freedom Flotilla, which brought approximately 125,000 people from Cuba to Key West, Florida in the spring of 1980 seeking admission as refugees. Petitioner was detained pursuant to 8 U.S.C. § 1223(a). At the time that the petitioner arrived he was interrogated and admitted to having been convicted in 1959 and 1964 for theft and escaping prison. In 1973 he was convicted and received a four-year sentence for an attempted burglary. Petitioner denied being guilty for the attempted burglary for which he was tried in a military revolutionary court. Based on this record he was found excludable by an immigration judge and ordered deported pursuant to 8 U.S.C. § 1227(a). This hearing was conducted on July 21, 1980. On August 28, 1980 the INS requested the State Department to arrange for the acceptance by Cuba of this petitioner and other members of the Freedom Flotilla. The trial court found that despite repeated requests by the U.S. Department of State that Cuba refused to accept these people. No other country has been contacted about the possible acceptance. Upon receipt of this information the Attorney General ordered the petitioner's continued detention in the federal penitentiary at Leavenworth. *See Fernandez v. Wilkinson*, 505 F. Supp. 787 (D. Kan. 1980).]

LOGAN, Circuit Judge.

* * *

It is clear Rodriguez-Fernandez can invoke no constitutional protection against his exclusion from the United States. He may be excluded for considerations of race, politics, activities, or associations that would be constitutionally prohibited if he were a citizen. *See Kleindienst v. Mandel*, 408 U.S. 753 (1972); *The Chinese Exclusion Case*, 130 U.S. 581 (1889). He would fare no better if he were an alien resident in the United States. Note, *The Alien and the Constitution*, 20 U. Chi. L. Rev. 547, 549-550 (1953).

Under the theory that Congress' power in this area is plenary and that, in any case, a deportation is not penal in nature, it has been held that normal criminal rights are inapplicable. Thus, aliens may be arrested by administrative warrant issued without the order of a magistrate, *Abel v. United States*, 362 U.S. 217 (1960), and may thereafter be held without bail. *Carlson v. Landon*, 342 U.S. 524 (1952). Nevertheless, if an alien in Rodriguez-Fernandez' position should be accused of committing a crime against the laws of this country, he would be entitled to the constitutional protections of the Fifth and Fourteenth Amendments. *Yick Wo v. Hopkins*, 118 U.S. 356 (1886).

* * *

...In *Wong Wing v. United States*, 163 U.S. 228 (1896), the Court extended this concept.

Applying this reasoning to the 5th and 6th Amendments, it must be concluded that all persons within the territory of the United States are entitled to the protection guaranteed by those amendments, and that even aliens shall not be held to answer for a capital or other infamous crime, unless on a presentment or indictment of a grand jury, nor be deprived of life, liberty, or property without due process of law.

163 U.S. at 238.

*   *   *

[I]t would appear that an excluded alien in physical custody within the United States may not be "punished" without being accorded the substantive and procedural due process guarantees of the Fifth Amendment. Surely Congress could not order the killing of Rodriguez-Fernandez and others in his status on the ground that Cuba would not take them back and this country does not want them. Even petitioner's property cannot be taken without just compensation, absent the existence of a state of war between the United States and his country. *Russian Volunteer Fleet v. United States*, 282 U.S. 481 (1931). Certainly imprisonment in a federal prison of one who has been neither charged nor convicted of a criminal offense is a deprivation of liberty in violation of the Fifth Amendment, except for the fiction applied to these cases that detention is only a continuation of the exclusion. This euphemistic fiction was created to accommodate the necessary detention of excludable and deportable aliens while their cases are considered and arrangements for expulsion are made. Detention pending deportation seems properly analogized to incarceration pending trial or other disposition of a criminal charge, and is, thus, justifiable only as a necessary, temporary measure. Obviously detention pending trial assumes a different status if there is to be no trial. If, in this case, administrative officials ordered penitentiary confinement for life or a definite term because Cuba would not accept petitioner, it seems certain the courts would apply *Wong Wing* and hold that such imprisonment is impermissible punishment rather than detention pending deportation. Logic compels the same result when imprisonment is for an indefinite period, continued beyond reasonable efforts to expel the alien.

*   *   *

Federal circuit and district courts have long held deportable aliens in custody more than a few months must be released because such detention has become imprisonment. *See Petition of Brooks*, 5 F.2d 238, 239 (D. Mass. 1925).

*   *   *

The linchpin of the government's case is *Shaughnessy v. United States ex rel. Mezei*, 345 U.S. 206 (1953). There an alien was confined to Ellis Island for twenty-one months before his case was decided by the Supreme Court. The Court refused to require his release within the United States. It may be, as Judge McWilliams states in his dissent, that a fair reading of that case supports the view that no constitutional infirmity exists in the continuing incarceration of Rodriguez-Fernandez, who has been in custody only a year. Nevertheless, differences exist between that case and this one which we think are significant. First, the primary focus of *Mezei* was upon the excluded alien's right to a due process hearing concerning his right of reentry into this country. Also, he was excluded as a security risk and the Korean War was in progress; security risks and enemy aliens during wartime have always been treated specially. The conditions of Mezei's confinement on Ellis Island do not appear to be comparable to Rodriguez-Fernandez' imprisonment in two maximum security prisons. In Mezei there were continuing efforts to deport. Twice the alien was shipped out to other countries which refused to permit him to land; he applied for entry to other countries and thereafter voluntarily terminated his efforts to find a new home. His petition for relief sought not only release from confinement but also admission to the United States.

Even with these special facts Mezei has been criticized as the nadir of the law with which the opinion dealt. *See* Hart, *The Power of Congress to Limit the Jurisdiction of Federal Courts: An Exercise in Dialectic*, 66 Harv. L. Rev. 1362, 1387-1396 (1953). In more recent cases, the Supreme Court has expanded the constitutional protections owed aliens apart from the right to enter or stay in this country. *See e.g.,* *Hampton v. Mow Sun Wong*, 426 U.S. 88 (1976); *Graham v. Richardson*, 403 U.S. 365 (1971). Due process is not a static concept, it undergoes evolutionary change to take into account accepted current notions of fairness. Finally, we note that in upholding the plenary power of Congress over exclusion and deportation of aliens, the Supreme Court has sought support in international law principles.

*   *   *

Justice Tom Clark, who was Attorney General during the formation of the presently effective immigration laws, stated in *Leng May Ma v. Barber*, 357 U.S. 185, 190, "[p]hysical detention of aliens is now the exception, not the rule, and is generally employed only as to security risks or those likely to abscond."

... [S]ince the statute contemplates temporary detention, we hold that detention is permissible during proceedings to determine eligibility to enter and, thereafter, during a reasonable period of negotiations for their return to the country of origin or to the transporter that brought them here. After such a time, upon application of the incarcerated alien willing to risk the possible alternatives to continued detention, the alien would be entitled to release. This construction is consistent with accepted international law principles that individuals are entitled to be free of arbitrary imprisonment.

*   *   *

... Since our interpretation of the applicable law and the relief ordered differs somewhat from that of the district court, we give the government thirty days in which to effectuate his release in a manner consistent with this opinion.

C. The Reentry Doctrine

Landon v. Plasencia
459 U.S. 21 (1982)

Justice O'CONNOR delivered the opinion of the Court.

Respondent Maria Antonieta Plasencia, a citizen of El Salvador, entered the United States as a permanent resident alien in March, 1970. She established a home in Los Angeles with her husband, a United States citizen, and their minor children. On June 27, 1975, she and her husband travelled to Tijuana, Mexico. During their brief stay in Mexico, they met with several Mexican and Salvadoran nationals and made arrangements to assist their illegal entry into the United States. She agreed to transport the aliens to Los Angeles and furnished some of the aliens with alien registration receipt cards that belonged to her children. When she and her husband attempted to cross the international border at 9:27 on the evening of June 29, 1975, an INS officer at the port of entry found six nonresident aliens in the Plasencias' car. The INS detained the respondent for further inquiry pursuant to § 235(b) of the Immigration and Nationality Act of 1952, 66 Stat. 182, as amended, 8 U.S.C. § 1101 et seq. ["Act"]. In a notice dated June 30, 1975, the INS charged her under § 212(a)(31) of the Act, 8 U.S.C. § 1182(a)(31), which provides for the exclusion of any alien seeking admission "who at any time shall have, knowingly and for gain, encouraged, induced, assisted, abetted, or aided any other alien to enter or to try to enter the United States in violation of law," and gave notice that it would hold an exclusion hearing at 11:00 a.m. on June 30, 1975.

An immigration law judge conducted the scheduled exclusion hearing. After hearing testimony from the respondent, her husband, and three of the aliens found in the Plasencias' car, the judge found "clear, convincing and unequivocal" evidence that the respondent did "knowingly and for gain encourage, induce, assist, abet, or aid nonresident aliens" to enter or try to enter the United States in violation of law. He also found that the respondent's trip to Mexico was a "meaningful departure" from the United States and that her return to this country was therefore an "entry" within the meaning of § 101(a)(13), 8 U.S.C. § 1101(a)(13). On the basis of these findings, he ordered her "excluded and deported."

The respondent contends that she was entitled to have the question of her admissibility litigated in a deportation hearing, where she would be the beneficiary of the procedural protections and the substantive rights outlined above. Our analysis of whether she is entitled to a deportation rather than an exclusion hearing begins with the language of the Act. Section 235 of the Act, 8 U.S.C. § 1225, permits the INS to examine "[a]ll aliens" who seek "admission or readmission to" the United States and empowers immigration officers to take evidence concerning the privilege of any person suspected of being an alien "to enter, reenter, pass through, or reside" in the United States. *Ibid.* (emphasis added).

The language and history of the Act thus clearly reflect a congressional intent that, whether or not the alien is a permanent resident, admissibility shall be determined in an exclusion hearing. Nothing in the statutory language or the legislative history suggests that the respondent's status as a permanent resident entitles her to a suspension of the exclusion hearing or requires the INS to proceed only through a deportation hearing. Under the terms of the Act, the INS properly proceeded in an exclusion hearing to determine whether respondent was attempting to "enter" the United States and whether she was excludable.

To avoid the impact of the statute, the respondent contends, and the Court of Appeals agreed, that unless she was "entering," she was not subject to exclusion proceedings, and that prior decisions of this Court indicate that she is entitled to have the question of "entry" decided in deportation proceedings. The parties agree that only "entering" aliens are subject to exclusion. See Brief for Petitioner at 19. That view accords with the language of the statute, which describes the exclusion hearing as one to determine whether the applicant "shall be allowed to enter or shall be excluded and deported." Section 236(a), 8 U.S.C. § 1226(a) (emphasis added). But the respondent's contention that the question of entry can be determined only in deportation proceedings reflects a misconception of our decisions.

In *Rosenberg v. Fleuti*, 374 U.S. 449 (1963), we faced the question whether a resident alien's return from an afternoon trip across the border was an "entry" for immigration law purposes. The definition of that term was the same then as it is now: it means "any coming of an alien into the United States . . . except that an alien having a lawful permanent residence in the United States shall not be regarded as making an entry into the United States for the purposes of the immigration laws if the alien proves to the satisfaction of the Attorney General that his departure to a foreign port or place or to an outlying possession was not intended or reasonably to be expected by him. . . . " Section 101(a)(13), 8 U.S.C. § 1101(a)(13). We held in *Fleuti* that the "intent exception" refers to an intent to depart in a "manner which can be regarded as meaningfully interruptive of the alien's permanent residence." 374 U.S. at 462. Thus, an "innocent, casual, and brief excursion" by a resident alien outside this country's borders would not subject him to the consequences of an "entry" on his return. *Ibid.* If, however, "the purpose of leaving the country is to accomplish some object which is itself contrary to some policy reflected in our immigration laws, it would appear that the interruption of residence thereby occurring would properly be regarded as meaningful." *Ibid.* That distinction both protects resident aliens from "unsuspected risks and unintended consequences of . . . a wholly innocent action," *ibid.*, and gives effect to the language of § 101(a)(13).

The Court of Appeals viewed *Fleuti* as a deportation case rather than an exclusion case, and therefore not relevant in deciding whether the question of "entry" could be determined in exclusion proceedings. For guidance on that decision, the Court of Appeals turned to *Kwong Hai Colding*, 344 U.S. 590 (1953), which it read to hold that a resident alien returning from a brief trip "could not be excluded without the procedural due process to which he would have been entitled had he never left the country"—i.e., in this case, a deportation proceeding. 637 F.2d at 1288. The court concluded that Plasencia was entitled to litigate her admissibility in deportation proceedings. It would be "circular" and "unfair," thought the court, to allow the INS to litigate the question of "entry" in exclusion proceedings when that question also went to the merits of the respondent's admissibility. *Id.* at 1288-1289.

We disagree. The reasoning of *Chew* was only that a resident alien returning from a brief trip has a right to due process just as would a continuously present resident alien. It does not create a right to identical treatment for these two differently situated groups of aliens. As the Ninth Circuit seemed to recognize, if the respondent here was making an "entry," she would be subject to exclusion proceedings. It is no more "circular" to allow the immigration judge in the exclusion proceeding to determine whether the alien is making an entry than it is for any court to decide that it has jurisdiction when the facts relevant to the determination of jurisdiction are also relevant to the merits. Thus, in *United States v. Sing Tuck*, 194 U.S. 161 (1904), this Court held that an immigration inspector could make a determination whether an applicant for admission was an alien or a citizen, although only aliens were subject to exclusion. Nor is it in any way "unfair" to decide the question of entry in exclusion proceedings as long as those proceedings themselves are fair. Finally, the use of exclusion proceedings violates neither the "scope" nor the "spirit" of *Fleuti*. As the Court of Appeals held, that case only defined "entry" and did not designate the forum for deciding questions of entry. The statutory scheme is clear: Congress intended that the determinations of both "entry" and the existence of grounds for exclusion could be made at an exclusion hearing.

... Plasencia questions three aspects of the procedures that the government employed in depriving her of these interests. First, she contends that the immigration law judge placed the burden of proof upon her. In a later proceeding in *Chew*, the Court of Appeals for the District of Columbia Circuit held, without mention of the Due Process Clause, that, under the law of the case, *Chew* was entitled to a hearing at which the INS was the moving party and bore the burden of proof. *Kwong Hai Chew v. Rogers*, 257 F.2d 606 (D.C. Cir. 1958). The BIA has accepted that decision, and although the Act provides that the burden of proof is on the alien in an exclusion proceeding, § 291, 8 U.S.C. § 1361, the BIA has followed the practice of placing the burden on the government when the alien is a permanent resident alien. There is no explicit statement of the placement of the burden of proof in the Attorney General's regulations or in the immigration law judge's opinion in this case and no finding on the issue below.

Second, Plasencia contends that the notice provided her was inadequate. She apparently had less than eleven hours' notice of the charges and the hearing. The regulations do not require any advance notice of the charges against the alien in an exclusion hearing, and the BIA has held that it is sufficient that the alien have notice of the charges at the hearing. The United States has argued to us that Plasencia could have sought a continuance. It concedes, however, that there is no explicit statutory or regulatory authorization for a continuance.

*   *   *

If the exclusion hearing is to ensure fairness, it must provide Plasencia an opportunity to present her case effectively, though at the same time it cannot impose an undue burden on the government. It would not, however, be appropriate for us to decide now whether the new regulation on the right to notice of free legal services is of constitutional magnitude or whether the remaining procedures provided comport with the Due Process Clause. Before this Court, the parties have devoted their attention to the entitlement to a deportation hearing rather than to the sufficiency of the procedures in the exclusion hearing. Whether the several hours' notice gave Plasencia a realistic opportunity to prepare her case for effective presentation in the circumstances of an exclusion hearing without counsel is a question we are not now in a position to answer. Nor has the government explained the burdens that it might face in providing more elaborate procedures. Thus, although we recognize the gravity of Plasencia's interest, the other factors relevant to due process analysis—the risk of erroneous deprivation, the efficacy of additional procedural safeguards, and the government's interest in providing no further procedures—have not been adequately presented to permit us to assess the sufficiency of the hearing. We remand to the Court of Appeals to allow the parties to explore whether Plasencia was accorded due process under all of the circumstances.

Notes

1. Does the term "meaningfully interruptive," as used by the Court in *Rosenberg v. Fleuti*, 374 U.S. 449, 462 (1963) conform with the statutory language of a departure "not intended or reasonably expected" by him?

2. The Court in *Plasencia* recognized that Plasencia could claim protection under the due process clause. How does this conform with the established doctrine that

aliens in exclusion are not entitled to due process protection? *Knauf v. Shaughnessy*, 338 U.S. 537, 544 (1950).

3. The decisions which severally limited the rights of aliens in exclusion came about in cases of persons who were either excludable for membership in the Communist Party or for reasons of their being threats to the national security. Should the rights of aliens in exclusion be looked at differently where they pose no national security risk?

Entry Defined Under the Statute
Sec. 101(a)(13) [8 U.S.C. § 1101(a)(13)]

The term "entry" means any coming of an alien into the United States, from a foreign port or place or from an outlying possession, whether voluntarily or otherwise, except that an alien having a lawful permanent residence in the United States shall not be regarded as making an entry into the United States for the purposes of the immigration laws if the alien proves to the satisfaction of the Attorney General that his departure to a foreign port or place or to an outlying possession was not intended or reasonably to be expected by him or his presence in a foreign port or place or in an outlying possession was not voluntary: Provided, That no person whose departure from the United States was occasioned by deportation proceedings, extradition, or other legal process shall be held to be entitled to such exception.

D. Entry into the U.S.

Application of Phelisna
551 F. Supp. 960 (E.D. N.Y. 1982)

NICKERSON, District Judge.

Petitioner arrived without a visa in the United States on July 5, 1981, in a boat carrying some two hundred Haitians, who disembarked on a Florida beach near Miami. A report of the officers of the Public Safety Department of Dade County, Florida, shows that they apprehended the Haitians on Rickenbaker Causeway one quarter of a mile south of "Sundays Restaurant" and turned them over to the Service.

On July 28, 1981, the Service, claiming that petitioner had made no "entry" into the United States, instituted exclusion proceedings against her pursuant to 8 U.S.C. § 1226. When the hearing began on September 2, 1981, petitioner's counsel moved to convert it into one for "deportation"—technically, expulsion—on the ground that petitioner had "entered" the United States before being apprehended. Petitioner testified that she had arrived by boat, entered the United States on July 5, 1981, and did not know where she was. The immigration judge, who announced at the inception of the hearing that he would permit only "several questions" of petitioner and would limit "severely" the testimony, refused to subpoena the arresting officer, announced that "[t]he burden is on the applicant" to establish the impropriety of exclusion proceedings, and denied the motion to convert the hearing into one for deportation.

When the exclusion hearing was resumed on December 1, 1981, petitioner's counsel moved for reconsideration of the motion to change the proceeding to one for deportation and offered in evidence "a police report from Miami, Dade County." The immigration judge denied the motion for reconsideration, declined to accept the report in evidence, declined an offer of proof as to what the evidence would be, and found petitioner excludable under 8 U.S.C. § 1182(a)(20). After the hearing the immigration judge denied asylum and ordered petitioner excluded.

* * *

In order to put the issues in context it is useful to note that the immigration laws have long made a distinction between those aliens who have come to the United States seeking admission and those "in" the United States after an "entry," irrespective of its legality. *Leng May Ma v. Barber*, 357 U.S. 185, 187 (1958). The Immigration and Nationality Act preserves the distinction. Those seeking admission are subjected to "exclusion proceedings" to determine whether they "shall be allowed to enter or shall be excluded and deported." 8 U.S.C. § 1226(a), Section 236. Aliens once they have made an "entry" are subject to "expulsion" if they fall within those categories of aliens who may be "deported" by the Attorney General. 8 U.S.C. § 1251. Proceedings for expulsion are commonly referred to as "deportation proceedings." As will appear, Congress and the courts have conferred on aliens who have made an "entry" rights in addition to those accorded aliens who have not yet entered.

* * *

It may well make a difference to petitioner whether she is excluded or deported. If excluded, she can expect to be sent back to Haiti, since presumably she boarded the boat in that country. 8 U.S.C. § 1227. If deported, she must be deported to a country designated by her, provided it will accept her, unless the United States Attorney General concludes that deportation to that country would prejudice the United States. 8 U.S.C. § 1253(a). Moreover, if she is deportable, the Attorney General could, in his discretion, permit her to depart voluntarily. 8 U.S.C. § 1254(e).

* * *

Petitioner contends that she made an "entry," by "coming . . . into the United States" from a foreign place within the meaning of 8 U.S.C. 1101(a)(13). She urges that "entry" occurred when she was present in the United States free from restraint. Quite patently the statute cannot be read to mean that mere presence in the United States is enough to show an entry. The inspection stations at which the United States determines whether aliens are admissible are per force inside the nation's borders. Congress could not have meant that an alien had come "into" the United States when he arrived at one of the usual points where the government is prepared to process applications for admission.

But if the alien crosses the border where there are no inspection facilities, for example, somewhere along the Mexican or Canadian borders or the coast line of the United States, common sense suggests that ordinarily the alien has "entered" the United States. Even under those circumstances the cases have made an exception where the alien has established that he had an intent to be inspected. Thus, in Thack v. Zurbrick, 51 F.2d 634 (6th Cir. 1931), aliens, long time residents of the United States, returned to Poland for a visit without obtaining certificates entitling them to reentry here within a year. They came back across the Canadian border and headed for the nearest inspection station at Newport, Vermont. On arrival at the station they were arrested and charged with illegal entry. Later they were ordered deported. The court held that an alien who "merely follows the ordinary path from the international line to the nearest inspection point and presents himself for inspection" has not made an "entry" so as to be guilty of "an offense for which Congress intended he should be sent to his former foreign residence and forbidden ever to try to return to this country." 51 F.2d at 635. The court explained that had the aliens "not intended to go to an inspection point" or had they been apprehended "in the effort to evade doing so" the question would be different. Id. at 636. See also United States ex rel. Giacone v. Corsi, 64 F.2d 18 (2d Cir. 1933).

The government and the Board seize on these decisions to argue that petitioner, in order to prove that she had "entered," must demonstrate that when she arrived on the beach she had an intent to "evade" inspection. Aside from the question of burden of proof, this court does not believe that the above cases prescribe as an element of "entry" an intent to evade inspection. It would be enough that the alien had no intention, whether through ignorance or otherwise, to follow the usual path to an inspection station.

But in any event in this court's opinion the Board was not correct in imposing on petitioner more than the burden of proving that she came physically into the United States at some point not in the vicinity of an inspection station. If the government wishes to exclude an alien landing at a point far distant from such a station on the theory that the alien had the particular intent to submit himself to inspection and was on the way to doing so, the government must prove it.

*   *   *

The government contends that Congress intended to impose the burden on petitioner and points to language in 8 U.S.C. § 1361, providing that when a person "makes application for admission, or otherwise attempts to enter the United States, the burden of proof shall be upon such person to establish that he . . . is not subject to exclusion." The government asserts that petitioner was "obviously a person 'attempt[ing] to enter the United States.'" But that simply begs the question. The issue is whether "entry" was accomplished. One who is attempting to enter has by hypothesis not yet entered and must show he is entitled to do so. But one who has entered is no longer attempting to do so.

There is thus no express statutory provision allocating the burden of proving "entry," and the court must apply traditional criteria in deciding the question. . . .

*   *   *

Moreover, to impose on petitioner the burden of showing more than the time, place and manner in which she came within the borders of the United States on the beaches of Florida would hardly be the appropriate method of narrowing the issues for decision. If the government contends that an alien had a peculiar intent, not ordinarily inferable from the physical facts, it is not unfair to ask the government to assert that contention and to prove it.

———————

Notes

1. Consider the following: A arrives at LAX (Los Angeles International Airport); she is refused admission as a person traveling without a visa. The airline was directed

to detain A as she was from the People's Republic of China and traveling to Guatemala via Tokyo and Los Angeles. A escapes from the airline's custody. B arrives at LAX and is paroled for further inspection. B never appears for her interview with the immigration officer. C arrives at LAX and is first paroled and placed in a detention camp; she escapes from the detention camp and is paroled to a "half-way house." Three years pass and C disappears. Five years later, she is discovered by the INS. How should A, B, and C be treated? Should they be placed in exclusion or deportation proceedings? *See In re Tanahan*, 18 I. & N. Dec. 339 (BIA 1981).

2. The "political" grounds for exclusion prohibit Communists, persons prejudicial to the national interest or national security, or those presenting a danger to the United States from being allowed to enter the country. Also included in this category are anarchists or those who would like to overthrow by force or violence the government of the United States. What could be the reason for including the multitude of provisions found at 8 U.S.C. §§ 1182(a)(3)? Are these provisions overlapping and redundant? What would you submit as alternatives?

3. As noted earlier, the exclusion statute prohibits the entry of paupers, professional beggars, vagrants, and those likely to become public charges. The regulations provide that the U.S. consul may deny a visa if the alien is a pauper, professional beggar, or vagrant "at the time of the visa application." 22 C.F.R. § 42.91(a)(8). Are these provisions reconcilable?

4. The question of whether or not someone is likely to become a public charge is guided by the Department of Health and Human Services Poverty Income Guidelines. Obviously, "likelihood" of becoming a public charge is a vague term and some consuls do not feel bound by these guidelines. The poverty income guidelines are provided below. Also relevant to the question of likelihood of becoming a public charge is whether or not a person has a physical or mental affliction preventing her from working and being able to support herself. The Department of State's Foreign Affairs Manual (F.A.M.) provides the following guidance to U.S. consuls:

> An alien relying solely on personal income for support of self and dependent family members after admission should be presumed ineligible for an immigrant ...unless such income, including that to be derived from prearranged employment, will equal or exceed the poverty income guideline level for the alien's family size.... When considering this factor for the purpose of evaluating the prospective income against the poverty income guideline levels, consideration should be given to any other circumstances which indicate or suggest that the applicant will probably become a public charge.

[Note 3.4 of F.A.M. § 40.71(a)(15).]

55 Fed. Reg. 5,664 (1990)

1990—Poverty Income Guidelines for Alaska

Size of family unit	Poverty guideline
1	$ 7,840
2	10,520
3	13,200
4	15,880
5	18,560
6	21,240
7	23,920
8	26,600

For family units with more than 8 members, add $2,680 for each additional member.

1990—Poverty Income Guidelines for All States Except Alaska and Hawaii

Size of family unit	Poverty guideline
1	$ 6,280
2	8,420
3	10,560
4	12,700
5	14,840
6	16,980
7	19,120
8	21,260

For family units with more than 8 members, add $2,140 for each additional member.

1990—Poverty Income Guidelines for Hawaii

Size of family unit	Poverty guideline
1	$ 7,230
2	9,690
3	12,150
4	14,610
5	17,070
6	19,530
7	21,990
8	24,450

For family units with more than 8 members, add $2,460 for each additional member.

*   *   *

Given that the purpose of 8 U.S.C. § 1182(a)(4) is to prevent those likely to become public charges, how reasonable are the above guidelines?

5. The "health" grounds for exclusion prohibit the admission of the mentally retarded, the insane or those who have had one or more attacks of insanity, those afflicted with a psychopathic personality or sexual deviation, drug addicts or chronic alcoholics, or those having dangerous contagious diseases. There has been a great deal of controversy relating to the exclusion of homosexuals on grounds of being "afflicted" with psychopathic personality. The ability of Congress to exclude such persons has constitutional support. *Boutilier v. INS*, 387 U.S. 118 (1967). Since *Boutilier*, the Public Health Service, which is charged with defining what is and is not a "psychopathic personality disorder," has revised its medical interpretations so as not to include homosexuals within this disorder. Is this type of statutory delegation for purposes of defining a psychological personality disorder proper? If it is proper, could the Public Health Service later revise its determination to permit their exclusion? Would such a revision be proper?

6. For differences in treatment of this very controversial issue, *see Lesbian/Gay Freedom Day Comm. v. INS*, 541 F. Supp. 569 (N.D. Cal. 1982) *aff'd*, 714 F.2d 1470 (9th Cir. 1983); *Matter of Longstaff*, 716 F.2d 1439 (5th Cir. 1983). *See also* Carro, *From Constitutional Psychopathic Inferiority to AIDS: What is in the Future for Homosexual Aliens*, 7 Yale L. & Pol'y Rev. 201 (1989).

7. The criminal grounds for exclusion prohibit the admission of those persons who have been convicted of a crime involving moral turpitude (other than political offenses). [8 U.S.C. § 1182(a)(9), Sec. 212.] A crime involving moral turpitude is interpreted as that crime which is *malum in se* as opposed to a crime which is *malum prohibitum*. *Malum in se* is defined as an act or case involving illegality by the very nature of the transaction upon principle of the natural, moral, and public law. *See* Black's Law Dictionary 112 (5th ed. 1968).

The criminal grounds for exclusion are divided into five subcategories.[25] *Crimes generally*—Any person who has been convicted or who admits the commission of the essential elements of a crime involving moral turpitude or a violation or conspiracy to violate any law relating to a controlled substance. Excepted from this definition are persons who have committed one crime while under the age of 18, where the crime was committed more than 5 years prior to the application for admission *or* where the maximum possible penalty for the crime did not exceed 1 year and the applicant was not sentenced to more than 6 months. *Multiple convictions*—Any person convicted of 2 or more offenses, whether the conviction was in a single trial or whether the offenses arose from a single scheme of misconduct, irrespective of whether the offenses involved moral turpitude for which the aggregate sentence of confinement actually imposed was 5 years or more, is excludable. *Traffickers in controlled substances*—Where the consular or immigration officer knows or has reason to believe the applicant is or has been an illicit trafficker in a controlled substance is excludable. *Prostitutes or persons involved in commercialized vice*—A person who is coming to the U.S. principally or incidentally to engage in prostitution or has engaged in prostitution within 10 years from their application for admission (or adjustment of status) is excludable. This provision also provides for the exclusion of persons involved in "pimping" or even those who engage in "any other unlawful commercialized vice whether or not related to prostitution." *Persons involved in serious criminal activity and have asserted immunity from prosecution*—Any persons who have committed serious criminal offenses as defined in Section 101(h), who asserted immunity from criminal jurisdiction are excludable. Presumably, this provision applies to foreign diplomats asserting immunity from criminal prosecution.

8. The power to exclude rests solely with Congress and the courts cannot inquire into the constitutionality of the exclusion grounds. Would it be proper for Congress to establish a new ground for exclusion based upon the color of a person's eyes or skin? *See Fiallo v. Bell*, 430 U.S. 787 (1977), 1 C. Gordon & S. Mailman, Immigration Law & Procedure 1-10 (rev. ed. 1990); *see also* Wasserman, Immigration Law and Procedure 211 (1979).

9. In *Lennon v. INS*, 527 F.2d 187 (2d Cir. 1975), the court interpreted 8 U.S.C. § 1182(a)(23) [re-codified as 8 U.S.C. § 1182(a)(2)(C)] relating to the exclusion of persons convicted of possession or trafficking in narcotic drugs. The court held that the conviction for "possession" must have been a knowing possession. The *Lennon* case involved the Beatle, John Lennon, who had been convicted for possession of a small amount of marijuana under a British statute which treated "simple" possession as a minor offense, akin to a traffic violation.

Procedural Questions

1. What is the procedure for excluding someone who presents a threat to the national security?

2. Is there a procedure whereby a person in exclusion can obtain a bond in lieu of detention?

---

25. The criminal grounds for exclusion can be found generally at 8 U.S.C. § 1182(a)(2), Sec. 212(a)(2).

3. A applies abroad for a visa to enter the U.S. She is granted a (B-2) tourist visa. Upon arrival she is questioned by an INS inspector. The official does not advise A about any legal rights which she might have. Instead she verbally berates A. She then forces open A's luggage, searches through it and finds a letter which states a job offer with a business in the U.S. The inspector decides to exclude A. Was the INS oficer's actions proper? Does A have any cognizable legal defenses to the search or the exclusion?

4. B is paroled into the U.S. for humanitarian reasons. Four months later B receives a letter from a local district director stating that she must leave the U.S. because her parole has been revoked. No explanation is given for the parole revocation. What rights, if any, does B have? Upon revocation of her parole would B be placed in exclusion or deportation proceedings?

5. 8 C.F.R. § 236.1 provides that immigration judges "shall also exercise the discretion and authority... [of] the Attorney General... as is appropriate and necessary for the disposition of such cases." Does this mean what the immigration judge may adjudicate visa petitions and grant persons adjustment of status under 8 U.S.C. § 1255?

E. Exclusion Procedure Flow Chart

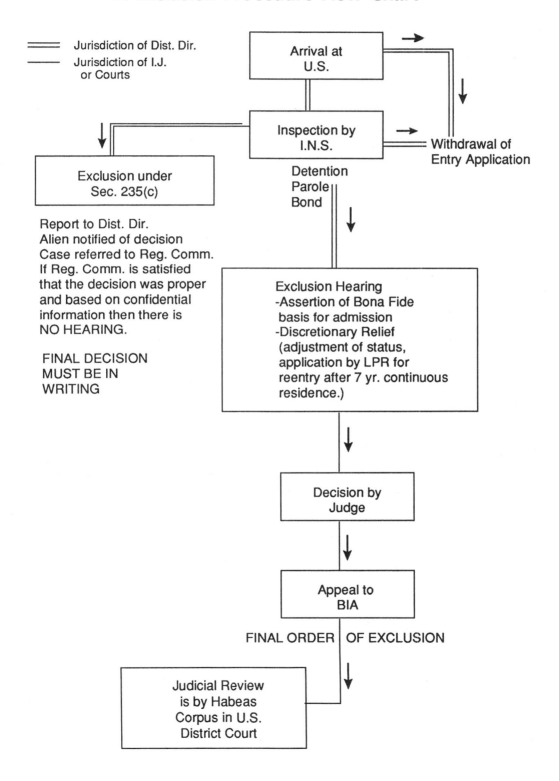

Jurisdiction of Dist. Dir.
Jurisdiction of I.J.
  or Courts

Arrival at
U.S.

Inspection by
I.N.S.

Withdrawal of
Entry Application

Exclusion under
Sec. 235(c)

Detention
Parole
Bond

Report to Dist. Dir.
Alien notified of decision
Case referred to Reg. Comm.
If Reg. Comm. is satisfied
that the decision was proper
and based on confidential
information then there is
NO HEARING.

FINAL DECISION
MUST BE IN
WRITING

Exclusion Hearing
-Assertion of Bona Fide
basis for admission
-Discretionary Relief
(adjustment of status,
application by LPR for
reentry after 7 yr. continuous
residence.)

Decision by
Judge

Appeal to
BIA

FINAL ORDER OF EXCLUSION

Judicial Review
is by Habeas
Corpus in U.S.
District Court

Index to Appendix

Qualification for Admission
Documentary Requirements
8 U.S.C. 1181, Sec. 211

(a) Except as provided in subsection (b) and subsection (c) no immigrant shall be admitted into the United States unless at the time of application for admission he (1) has a valid unexpired immigrant visa or was born subsequent to the issuance of such visa of the accompanying parent, and (2) presents a valid unexpired passport or other suitable travel document, or document of identity and nationality, if such document is required under the regulations issued by the Attorney General. With respect to immigrants to be admitted under quotas of quota areas prior to June 30, 1968, no immigrant visa shall be deemed valid unless the immigrant is properly chargeable to the quota area under the quota of which the visa is issued.

(b) Notwithstanding the provisions of section 212(a)(20) of this Act in such cases or in such classes of cases and under such conditions as may be by regulations prescribed, returning resident immigrants, defined in section 101(a)(27)(A), who are otherwise admissible may be readmitted to the United States by the Attorney General in his discretion without being required to obtain a passport, immigrant visa, reentry permit or other documentation.

(c) The provisions of subsection (a) shall not apply to an alien whom the Attorney General admits to the United States under section 207.

Substantive Grounds for Exclusion
8 U.S.C. § 1182(a), Sec. 212(a)

Except as otherwise provided in this Act, the following describes classes of excludable aliens who are ineligible to receive visas and who shall be excluded from admission into the United States:

(1) Health-Related Grounds.—

(A) In General.—Any alien—

(i) who is determined (in accordance with regulations prescribed by the Secretary of Health and Human Services) to have a communicable disease of public health significance,

(ii) who is determined (in accordance with regulations prescribed by the Secretary of Health and Human Services in consultation with the Attorney General)—

(I) to have a physical or mental disorder and behavior associated with the disorder that may pose, or has posed, a threat to the property, safety, or welfare of the alien or others, or

(II) to have had a physical or mental disorder and a history of behavior associated with the disorder, which behavior has posed a threat to the property, safety, or welfare of the alien or others and which behavior is likely to recur or to lead to other harmful behavior,

(iii) who is determined (in accordance with regulations prescribed by the Secretary of Health and Human Services) to be a drug abuser or addict, is excludable.

(B) Waiver Authorized.—For provision authorizing waiver of certain clauses of subparagraph (A), see subsection (g).

(2) Criminal and Related Grounds.—

(A) Conviction of Certain Crimes.—

(i) In General.—Except as provided in clause (ii), any alien convicted of, or who admits having committed, or who admits committing acts which constitute the essential elements of—

(I) a crime involving moral turpitude (other than a purely political offense), or

(II) a violation of (or a conspiracy to violate) any law or regulation of a State, the United States, or a foreign country relating to a controlled substance [as defined in section 102 of the Controlled Substances Act (21 U.S.C. 802)], is excludable.

(ii) Exception.—Clause (i)(I) shall not apply to an alien who committed only one crime if—

(I) the crime was committed when the alien was under 18 years of age, and the crime was committed (and the alien released from any confinement to a prison or correctional institution imposed for the crime) more than 5 years before the date of application for a visa or other documentation and the date of application for admission to the United States, or

(II) the maximum penalty possible for the crime of which the alien was convicted (or which the alien admits having committed or of which the acts that the alien admits having committed constituted the essential elements) did not exceed imprisonment for one year and, if the alien was convicted of such crime, the alien was not sentenced to a term of imprisonment in excess of 6 months (regardless of the extent to which the sentence was ultimately executed).

(B) Multiple Criminal Convictions.—Any alien convicted of 2 or more offenses (other than purely political offenses), regardless of whether the conviction was in a single trial or whether the offenses arose from a single scheme of misconduct and regardless of whether the offenses involved moral turpitude, for which the aggregate sentences to confinement actually imposed were 5 years or more is excludable.

(C) Controlled Substance Traffickers.—Any alien who the consular or immigration officer knows or has reason to believe is or has been an illicit trafficker in any such controlled substance or is or has been a knowing assister, abettor, conspirator, or colluder with others in the illicit trafficking in any such controlled substance, is excludable.

(D) Prostitution and Commercialized Vice.—Any alien who—

(i) is coming to the United States solely, principally, or incidentally to engage in prostitution, or has engaged in prostitution within 10 years of the date of application for a visa, entry, or adjustment of status,

(ii) directly or indirectly procures or attempts to procure, or (within 10 years of the date of application for a visa, entry, or adjustment of status) procured or attempted to procure or to import, prostitutes or persons for the purpose of prostitution, or receives or (within such 10-year period) received, in whole or in part, the proceeds of prostitution, or

(iii) is coming to the United States to engage in any other unlawful commercialized vice, whether or not related to prostitution, is excludable.

(E) Certain Aliens Involved in Serious Criminal Activity Who Have Asserted Immunity From Prosecution.—Any alien—

(i) who has committed in the United States at any time a serious criminal offense (as defined in section 101(h)),

(ii) for whom immunity from criminal jurisdiction was exercised with respect to that offense,

(iii) who as a consequence of the offense and exercise of immunity has departed from the United States, and

(iv) who has not subsequently submitted fully to the jurisdiction of the court in the United States having jurisdiction with respect to that offense, is excludable.

(F) Waiver Authorized.—For provision authorizing waiver of certain subparagraphs of this paragraph, see subsection (h).

(3) Security and Related Grounds.—

(A) In General.—Any alien who a consular officer or the Attorney General knows, or has reasonable ground to believe, seeks to enter the United States to engage solely, principally, or incidentally in—

(i) any activity to violate any law of the United States relating to espionage or sabotage or to violate or evade any law prohibiting the export from the United States of goods, technology, or sensitive information,

(ii) any other unlawful activity, or

(iii) any activity a purpose of which is the opposition to, or the control or overthrow of, the Government of the United States by force, violence, or other unlawful means, is excludable.

(B) Terrorist Activities.—

(i) In General.—Any alien who—

(I) has engaged in a terrorist activity, or

(II) a consular officer or the Attorney General knows, or has reasonable ground to believe, is likely to engage after entry in any terrorist activity (as defined in clause (iii)), is excludable. An alien who is an officer, official, representative, or spokesman of the Palestine Liberation Organization is considered, for purposes of this Act, to be engaged in a terrorist activity.

(ii) Terrorist Activity Defined.—As used in this Act, the term 'terrorist activity' means any activity which is unlawful under the laws of the place where it is committed (or which, if committed in the United States, would be unlawful under the laws of the United States or any State) and which involves any of the following:

(I) The highjacking or sabotage of any conveyance (including an aircraft, vessel, or vehicle).

(II) The seizing or detaining, and threatening to kill, injure, or continue to detain, another individual in order to compel a third person (including a governmental organization) to do or abstain from doing any act as an explicit or implicit condition for the release of the individual seized or detained.

(III) A violent attack upon an internationally protected person (as defined in section 1116(b)(4) of title 18, United States Code) or upon the liberty of such a person.

(IV) An assassination.

(V) The use of any—

(a) biological agent, chemical agent, or nuclear weapon or device, or

(b) explosive or firearm (other than for mere personal monetary gain), with intent to endanger, directly or indirectly, the safety of one or more individuals or to cause substantial damage to property.

(VI) A threat, attempt, or conspiracy to do any of the foregoing.

(iii) Engage In Terrorist Activity Defined.—As used in this Act, the term "engage in terrorist activity" means to commit, in an individual capacity or as a member of an organization, an act of terrorist activity or an act which the actor knows, or reasonably should know, affords material support to any individual, organization, or government in conducting a terrorist activity at any time, including any of the following acts:

(I) The preparation or planning of a terrorist activity.

(II) The gathering of information on potential targets for terrorist activity.

(III) The providing of any type of material support, including a safe house, transportation, communications, funds, false identification, weapons, explosives, or training, to any individual the actor knows or has reason to believe has committed or plans to commit an act of terrorist activity.

(IV) The soliciting of funds or other things of value for terrorist activity or for any terrorist organization.

(V) The solicitation of any individual for membership in a terrorist organization, terrorist government, or to engage in a terrorist activity.

(C) Foreign Policy.—

(i) In General.—An alien whose entry or proposed activities in the United States the Secretary of State has reasonable ground to believe would have potentially serious adverse foreign policy consequences for the United States is excludable.

(ii) Exception For Officials.—An alien who is an official of a foreign government or a purported government, or who is a candidate for election to a foreign government office during the period immediately preceding the election for that office, shall not be excludable or subject to restrictions or conditions on entry into the United States under clause (i) solely because of the alien's past, current, or expected beliefs, statements, or associations, if such beliefs, statements, or associations would be lawful within the United States.

(iii) Exception For Other Aliens.—An alien, not described in clause (ii), shall not be excludable or subject to restrictions or conditions on entry into the United States under clause (i) because of the alien's past, current, or expected beliefs, statements, or associations, if such beliefs, statements, or associations would be lawful within the United States, unless the Secretary of State personally determines that the alien's admission would compromise a compelling United States foreign policy interest.

(iv) Notification of Determinations.—If a determination is made under clause (iii) with respect to an alien, the Secretary of State must notify on a timely basis the chairmen of the Committees on the Judiciary and Foreign Affairs of the House of Representatives and of the Committees on the Judiciary and Foreign Relations of the Senate of the identities of the alien and the reasons for the determination.

(D) Immigrant Membership in Totalitarian Party.—

(i) In General.—Any immigrant who is or has been a member of or affiliated with the Communist or any other totalitarian party (or subdivision or affiliate thereof), domestic or foreign, is excludable.

(ii) Exception for Involuntary Membership.—Clause (i) shall not apply to an alien because of membership or affiliation if the alien establishes to the satisfaction of the consular officer when applying for a visa (or to the satisfaction of the Attorney General when applying for admission) that the membership or affiliation is or was involuntary, or is or was solely when under 16 years of age, by operation of law, or for purposes of obtaining employment, food rations, or other essentials of living and whether necessary for such purposes.

(iii) Exception for Past Membership.—Clause (i) shall not apply to an alien because of membership or affiliation if the alien establishes to the satisfaction of the consular officer when applying for a visa (or to the satisfaction of the Attorney General when applying for admission) that—

(I) the membership or affiliation terminated at least—

(a) 2 years before the date of such application, or

(b) 5 years before the date of such application, in the case of an alien whose membership or affiliation was with the party controlling the government of a foreign state that is a totalitarian dictatorship as of such date, and

(II) the alien is not a threat to the security of the United States.

(iv) Exception for Close Family Members.—The Attorney General may, in the Attorney General's discretion, waive the application of clause (i) in the case of an immigrant who is the parent, spouse, son, daughter, brother, or sister of a citizen of the United States or a spouse, son, or daughter of an alien lawfully admitted for permanent residence for humanitarian purposes, to assure family unity, or when it is otherwise in the public interest if the alien is not a threat to the security of the United States.

(E) Participants in Nazi Persecutions or Genocide.—

(i) Participation in Nazi Persecutions.—Any alien who, during the period beginning on March 23, 1933, and ending on May 8, 1945, under the direction of, or in association with—

(I) the Nazi government of Germany,

(II) any government in any area occupied by the military forces of the Nazi government of Germany,

(III) any government established with the assistance or cooperation of the Nazi government of Germany, or

(IV) any government which was an ally of the Nazi government of Germany, ordered, incited, assisted, or otherwise participated in the persecution of any person because of race, religion, national origin, or political opinion is excludable.

(ii) Participation in Genocide.—Any alien who has engaged in conduct that is defined as genocide for purposes of the International Convention on the Prevention and Punishment of Genocide is excludable.

(4) Public Charge.—Any alien who, in the opinion of the consular officer at the time of application for a visa, or in the opinion of the Attorney General at the time of application for admission or adjustment of status, is likely at any time to become a public charge is excludable.

(5) Labor Certification and Qualifications for Certain Immigrants.—

(A) Labor Certification.—

(i) In General.—Any alien who seeks admission or status as an immigrant under paragraph (2) or (3) of section 203(b) is excludable, unless the Secretary of Labor has determined and certified to the Secretary of State and the Attorney General that—

(I) there are not sufficient workers who are able, willing, qualified (or equally qualified in the case of an alien described in clause (ii)) and available at the time of application for a visa and admission to the United States and at the place where the alien is to perform such skilled or unskilled labor, and

(II) the employment of such alien will not adversely affect the wages and working conditions of workers in the United States similarly employed.

(ii) Certain Aliens Subject to Special Rule.—For purposes of clause (i)(I), an alien described in this clause is an alien who—

(I) is a member of the teaching profession, or

(II) has exceptional ability in the sciences or the arts.

(B) Unqualified Physicians.—An alien who seeks admission or status as an immigrant under paragraph (2) or (3) of section 203(b) who is a graduate of a medical school not accredited by a body or bodies approved for the purpose by the Secretary of Education (regardless of whether such school of medicine is in the United States) and who is coming to the United States principally to perform services as a member of the medical profession is excludable, unless the alien

(i) has passed parts I and II of the National Board of Medical Examiners Examination (or an equivalent examination as determined by the Secretary of Health and Human Services) and

(ii) is competent in oral and written English. For purposes of the previous sentence, an alien who is a graduate of a medical school shall be considered to have passed parts I and II of the National Board of Medical Examiners if the alien was fully and permanently licensed to practice medicine in a State on January 9, 1978, and was practicing medicine in a State on that date.

(6) Illegal Entrants and Immigration Violators.—

(A) Aliens Previously Deported.—Any alien who has been excluded from admission and deported and who again seeks admission within one year of the date of such deportation is excludable, unless prior to the alien's reembarkation at a place outside the United States or attempt to be admitted from foreign contiguous territory the Attorney General has consented to the alien's reapplying for admission.

(B) Certain Aliens Previously Removed.—Any alien who—

(i) has been arrested and deported,

(ii) has fallen into distress and has been removed pursuant to this or any prior Act,

(iii) has been removed as an alien enemy, or

(iv) has been removed at Government expense in lieu of deportation pursuant to section 242(b), and who seeks admission within 5 years of the date of such deportation or removal (or within 20 years in the case of an alien convicted of an aggravated felony) is excludable, unless before the date of the alien's embarkation or reembarkation at a place outside the United States or attempt to be admitted from foreign contiguous territory the Attorney General has consented to the alien's applying or reapplying for admission.

(C) Misrepresentation.—

(i) In General.—Any alien who, by fraud or willfully misrepresenting a material fact, seeks to procure (or has sought to procure or has procured) a visa, other documentation, or entry into the United States or other benefit provided under this Act is excludable.

(ii) Waiver Authorized.—For provision authorizing waiver of clause (i), see subsection (i).

(D) Stowaways.—Any alien who is a stowaway is excludable.

(E) Smugglers.—

(i) In General.—Any alien who at any time knowingly has encouraged, induced, assisted, abetted, or aided any other alien to enter or to try to enter the United States in violation of law is excludable.

(ii) Waiver Authorized.—For provision authorizing waiver of clause (i), see subsection (d)(11).

(F) Subject of Civil Penalty.—An alien who is the subject of a final order for violation of section 274C is excludable.

(7) Documentation Requirements.—

(A) Immigrants.—

(i) In General.—Except as otherwise specifically provided in this Act, any immigrant at the time of application for admission—

(I) who is not in possession of a valid unexpired immigrant visa, reentry permit, border crossing identification card, or other valid entry document required by this Act, and a valid unexpired passport, or other suitable travel document, or document of identity and nationality if such document is required under the regulations issued by the Attorney General under section 211(a), or

(II) whose visa has been issued without compliance with the provisions of section 203, is excludable.

(ii) Waiver Authorized.—For provision authorizing waiver of clause (i), see subsection (k).

(B) Nonimmigrants.—

(i) In General.—Any nonimmigrant who—

(I) is not in possession of a passport valid for a minimum of six months from the date of the expiration of the initial period of the alien's admission or contemplated initial period of stay authorizing the alien to return to the country from which the alien came or to proceed to and enter some other country during such period, or

(II) is not in possession of a valid nonimmigrant visa or border crossing identification card at the time of application for admission, is excludable.

(ii) General Waiver Authorized.—For provision authorizing waiver of clause (i), see subsection (d)(4).

(iii) Guam Visa Waiver.—For provision authorizing waiver of clause (i) in the case of visitors to Guam, see subsection (1).

(iv) Visa Waiver Pilot Program.—For authority to waive the requirement of clause (i) under a pilot program, see section 217.

(8) Ineligible for Citizenship.—

(A) In General.—Any immigrant who is permanently ineligible to citizenship is excludable.

(B) Draft Evaders.—Any alien who has departed from or who has remained outside the United States to avoid or evade training or service in the armed forces in time of war or a period declared by the President to be a national emergency is excludable, except that this subparagraph shall not apply to an alien who at the time of such departure was a nonimmigrant and who is seeking to reenter the United States as a nonimmigrant.

(9) Miscellaneous.—

(A) Practicing Polygamists.—Any immigrant who is coming to the United States to practice polygamy is excludable.

(B) Guardian Required to Accompany Excluded Alien.—Any alien accompanying another alien ordered to be excluded and deported and certified to be helpless from sickness or mental or physical disability or infancy pursuant to section 237(e), whose protection or guardianship is required by the alien ordered excluded and deported, is excludable.

(C) International Child Abduction.—

(i) In General.—Except as provided in clause (ii), any alien who, after entry of a court order granting custody to a citizen of the United States of a child having a lawful claim to United States citizenship, detains, retains, or withholds custody of the child outside the United States from the United States citizen granted custody, is excludable until the child is surrendered to such United States citizen.

(ii) Exception.—Clause (i) shall not apply to an alien who is a national of a foreign state that is a signatory to the Hague Convention on the Civil Aspects of International Child Abduction.

8 U.S.C. § 1182(b), Sec. 212(b)

Notices of Denials—If an alien's application for a visa, for admission to the United States, or for adjustment of status is denied by an immigration or consular officer because the officer determines the alien to be excludable under subsection (a), the officer shall provide the alien with a timely written notice that—

(1) states the determination, and

(2) lists the specific provision or provisions of law under which the alien is excludable or ineligible for entry or adjustment of status.

Procedure Governing Exclusion
8 U.S.C. § 1226, Sec. 236

(a) A special inquiry officer shall conduct proceedings under this section, administer oaths, present and receive evidence, and interrogate, examine, and cross-examine the alien or witnesses. He shall have authority in any case to determine whether an arriving alien who has been detained for further inquiry under section 235 shall be allowed to enter or shall be excluded and deported. The determination of such special inquiry officer shall be based only on the evidence produced at the inquiry. No special inquiry officer shall conduct a proceeding in any case under this section in which he shall have participated in investigative functions or in which he shall have participated (except as provided in this subsection) in prosecuting functions. Proceedings before a special inquiry officer under this section shall be conducted in accordance with this section, the applicable provisions of sections 235 and 287(b), and such regulations as the Attorney General shall prescribe, and shall be the sole and exclusive procedure for determining admissibility of a person to the United States under the provisions of this section. At such inquiry, which shall be kept separate and apart from the public, the alien may have one friend or relative present, under such conditions as may be prescribed by the Attorney General. A complete record of the proceedings and of all testimony and evidence produced at such inquiry shall be kept.

(b) From a decision of a special inquiry officer excluding an alien, such alien may take a timely appeal to the Attorney General, and any such alien shall be advised of his right to take such appeal. No appeal may be taken from a temporary exclusion under section 235(c). From a decision of the special inquiry officer to admit an alien, the immigration officer in charge at the port where the inquiry is held may take a timely appeal to the Attorney General. An appeal by the alien, or such officer in charge, shall operate to stay any final action with respect to any alien whose case is so appealed until the final decision of the Attorney General is made. Except as provided in section 235(c) such decision shall be rendered solely upon the evidence adduced before the special inquiry officer.

(c) Except as provided in subsections (b) or (d), in every case where an alien is excluded from admission into the United States, under this chapter or any other law or treaty now existing or hereafter made, the decision of a special inquiry officer shall be final unless reversed on appeal to the Attorney General.

(d) If a medical officer or civil surgeon or board of medical officers has certified under section 234 that an alien is afflicted with a disease specified in section 212(a)(6), or with any mental disease, defect, or disability which would bring such alien within any of the classes excluded from admission to the United States under paragraphs (1) to (4) or (5) of section 212(a), the decision of the special inquiry officer shall be based solely upon such certification. No alien shall have a right to appeal from such an excluding decision of a special inquiry officer. If an alien is excluded by a special inquiry officer because of the existence of a physical disease, defect, or disability, other than one specified in section 1182(a)(6) of this title, the alien may appeal from the excluding decision in accordance with subsection (b) of this section, and the provisions of section 213 may be invoked.

Regulations Governing Exclusion
8 C.F.R. § 236

§ 236.1 Authority of immigration judges

In determining cases referred for further inquiry as provided in section 235 of the Act, immigration judges shall have the powers and authority conferred upon them by the Act and this chapter. Subject to any specific limitation prescribed by the Act and this chapter, immigration judges shall also exercise the discretion and authority conferred upon the Attorney General by the Act as is appropriate and necessary for the disposition of such cases.

§ 236.2 Hearing

(a) Opening. Exclusion hearings shall be closed to the public, unless the alien at his own instance requests that the public, including the press, be permitted to attend; in that event, the hearing shall be open, provided that the alien states for the record that he is waiving the requirement in section 236 of the Act that the inquiry shall be kept separate and apart from the public. When the hearing is to be open, depending upon physical facilities, reasonable limitation may be placed upon the number in attendance at any one time, with priority being given to the press over the general public. The Immigration Judge shall ascertain whether the applicant for admission is the person to whom Form I-122 was previously delivered by the examining immigration officer as provided in Part 235 of this chapter; enter a copy of such form in evidence as an exhibit in the case; inform the applicant of the nature and purpose of the hearing; advise him of the privilege of being represented by an attorney of his own choice at no expense to the Government, and of the availability of free legal services programs qualified under Part 292a of this chapter and organizations recognized pursuant to § 292.2, of this chapter located in the district where his exclusion hearing is to be held; and shall ascertain that the applicant has received a list of such programs; and request him to ascertain then and there whether he desires representation; advise him that he will have a reasonable opportunity to present evidence in his own behalf, to examine and object to evidence against him, and to cross-examine witnesses presented by the Government; and place the applicant under oath.

(b) Procedure. The immigration judge shall receive and adduce material and relevant evidence, rule upon objections, and otherwise regulate the course of the hearing.

(c) General attorney. The district director shall direct the chief legal officer to assign a general attorney to each case in which an applicant's nationality is in issue. The district director may direct the chief legal officer to assign a general attorney to any case in which the district director deems such assignment necessary or advantageous. The duties of the general attorney include, but are not limited to, the presentation of evidence and the interrogation, examination, and cross-examination of the applicant and other witnesses. Nothing contained herein diminishes the authority of an immigration judge to conduct proceedings under this part.

(d) Depositions. The procedures specified in § 242.14(e) of this chapter shall apply.

(e) Record. The hearing before the immigration judge, including the testimony and exhibits, the immigration judge's decision, and all written orders, motions, appeals, and other papers filed in the proceeding shall constitute the record in the case. The hearing shall be recorded verbatim except for statements made off the record with the permission of the immigration judge.

[Note: §§ 236.3 and 236.4 are contained in the sections dealing with asylum applications and adjustment applications, respectively.]

§ 236.5 Decision of the immigration judge; notice to the applicant.

(a) Decision. The immigration judge shall inform the applicant of his or her decision in accordance with 8 C.F.R. § 3.35.

(b) Advice to alien ordered excluded. An alien ordered excluded shall be furnished with Form I-296, Notice to Alien Ordered Excluded by Immigration Judge, at the time of an oral decision by the immigration judge or upon service of a written decision.

(c) Holders of refugee travel documents. Aliens who are the holders of valid unexpired refugee travel documents may be ordered excluded only if they are found to be inadmissible under section 212(a)(9), (10), (12), (23), (27), (28), (29), or (31) of the Act, and it is determined that on the basis of the acts for which they are inadmissible there are compelling reasons of national security or public order for their exclusion. If the immigration judge finds that the alien is inadmissible but determines that there are no compelling reasons of national security or public order for exclusion, the immigration judge shall remand the case to the district director for parole.

§ 236.9 Visa Waiver Pilot Program

Pursuant to section 217(b)(4)(A) of the Act, an alien who applies for admission to the United States under the provisions of that section must waive any right to review or appeal an immigration officer's determination as to the admissibility of the alien at a port of entry, other than on the basis of an application for asylum. An alien applicant for admission under section 217 of the Act shall be removed from the United States upon a determination by an immigration officer (port director, officer-in-charge, or officer acting in either capacity) that the alien is inadmissible in accordance with procedures in § 217.4(b) of this chapter except that such an alien who applies for asylum in the United States shall be referred to an immigration judge for further inquiry as provided in section 235 of the Act and § 236.3 of this part.

Chapter 3

Deportation

Subsequent to a person's gaining entry into the U.S. the only way that she can be removed is through deportation.[1] As noted in the previous chapter, a person in exclusion has no rights other than those conferred by statute.[2] Someone in deportation proceedings is accorded constitutional protection as she is a person within the U.S.[3]

Substantive and Procedural Aspects of Deportation

The substantive grounds for deportation are much narrower than those for exclusion.[4] Although the grounds are narrower, it has been said that there are more than 700 separate grounds of deportation.[5] One example of the all-encompassing nature of the grounds for deportation can be found in the provision which makes deportable all aliens who gain entry into the U.S. who were "excludable at entry."[6] The following points provide additional framework within which the cases should be read:

    1. Even though a person manages to enter the U.S., each time she leaves the country, she is subject to the exclusion provisions when she returns.

    2. Even though a person becomes a lawful permanent resident of the U.S., she may still be subject to both the exclusion and the deportation statutes.[7]

    3. A person may be deportable for entering the U.S. without first having been inspected.[8]

---

    1. Obviously, if someone does not wish to stay in the U.S., she is free to depart voluntarily. Furthermore, the statute provides for voluntary departure either before or after a finding of deportability has been entered. *See* 8 U.S.C. § 1254(e), Sec. 244, 8 C.F.R. § 244.

    2. Since immigration laws are within Congress' plenary powers and the executive branch is merely an enforcement arm, new benefits cannot be set up without congressional action. This is not to say that the executive's policies do not often benefit certain groups of aliens.

    3. *Yick Wo v. Hopkins*, 118 U.S. 356 (1886); *Francis v. INS*, 532 F.2d 268 (2d Cir. 1976).

    4. The deportation provisions are found at 8 U.S.C. § 1251(a), Sec. 241(a) of the Act.

    5. *See* Wasserman, *The Undemocratic, Illogical and Arbitrary Laws of the United States*, 3 Int'l Law. 254 (1969). *See also* Gordon, *The Need to Modernize Our Immigration Laws*, 13 San Diego L. Rev. 1, 2 (1975).

    6. 8 U.S.C. § 1251(a)(1), Sec. 241(a)(1) of the Act.

    7. Exceptions are made for lawful permanent residents who may avail themselves of waivers for the grounds of deportability or excludability. These waivers are discussed in greater detail in Chapter 12.

    8. 8 U.S.C. § 1251(a)(1)(B), Sec. 241(a)(1)(B) of the Act.

4. Even if a person enters the U.S. properly, if she fails to "maintain" her status she will become deportable.[9]

5. A person may be deported for acts which follow her entry, irrespective of whether or not she has ever departed the U.S. These acts may postdate the person's admission for lawful permanent residence. Some examples include: a public charge,[10] committing certain criminal acts,[11] illegal possession of certain automatic or semi-automatic weapons.[12]

6. There is no statute of limitations for the grounds of exclusion or deportation.

Employer Sanctions— Extending the INS Enforcement Power

Congress' power to control which persons may enter or remain in the United States is extensive. However, once the foreigner gains entry, albeit surreptitiously, this power does not flow unfettered, for once the person is "within" the borders she receives a certain modicum of constitutional protection. The notion of Constitutional protection inuring once a person has gained entry provides an excellent backdrop for a discussion of the power of the enforcement arm of the immigration power (the INS) to search for and seize foreigners and ultimately deport them from the country.

The Supreme Court has noted in a number of cases that the United States had seemingly lost control of its borders.[13] The INS has long sought the authority to add to its enforcement power the ability to penalize employers for hiring undocumented aliens. The rationale for such sanctions is the belief that the great disparity between the economies of the "sending" nations and the United States is one of the primary motivations for illegal immigration to this country.[14]

In response to its frustration in controlling the flow of illegal migrants and what it perceived as a threat to the integrity of the system of legal migration, Congress enacted a system of "sanctions" to be imposed upon employers for hiring unauthorized workers.[15] It was thought that a system which penalized employers would deter the flow of unsanctioned migration to the United States. These employer sanctions, al-

---

9. 8 U.S.C. § 1251(a)(1)(C), Sec. 241(a)(1)(C) of the Act. The requirements for maintaining one's status are described in more detail in Chapter 6.

10. 8 U.S.C. § 1251(a)(5), Sec. 241(a)(5) of the Act.

11. 8 U.S.C. § 1251(a)(2), Sec. 241(a)(2) of the Act.

12. 8 U.S.C. § 1251(a)(2)(C), Sec. 241(a)(2)(C) of the Act.

13. *See, e.g., Plyler v. Doe,* 457 U.S. 202 (1982); *United States v. Brignoni-Ponce,* 422 U.S. 873 (1975); *Almeida-Sanchez v. U.S. INS,* 413 U.S. 266 (1973); *INS v. Errico,* 385 U.S. 214 (1966).

14. *See* Lopez, *Undocumented Mexican Migration: In Search of a Just Immigration Law and Policy,* 28 U.C.L.A. L. Rev. 615 (1981); J. Card, *Push and Pull Factors at Origin and Destination as Determinants of Migration* (Aug. 1980) (study prepared for the Select Commission on Immigration and Refugee Policy).

15. These sanctions are in the form of fines and/or criminal penalties. *See generally* Section Immigration Reform and Control Act of 1986, Pub. L. No. 99-603, 100 Stat. 3359, amending 8 U.S.C. § 1324.

though not retroactive, apply to all employers irrespective of the number of persons in their employ and to all job applicants irrespective of U.S. citizenship.[16]

The sanction provisions are intended to assist the INS in its enforcement of the immigration laws by imposing duties on the employer, which, when not followed, may expose her to civil or criminal penalties. The more important elements of the sanction provisions are described below.

Verification Requirements (8 C.F.R. § 274a.2(b))

1. Examination of documentation presented by the individual establishing *identity* and *employment eligibility*. These documents must be verified by the employer and the INS Form I-9 must be completed within three business days of the date the referred individual was hired by the employer.

2. The individual may present either an original document that establishes both employment authorization and identity, or an original document that establishes employment authorization and a separate original document that establishes identity.

a. One of the following documents are acceptable to establish identity only:

For individuals 18 years of age or older: (i) A state-issued driver's license or state-issued identification (with a photograph and identifying information such as: Name, date of birth, sex, height, color of eyes, and address). If the driver's license or identification card does not contain a photograph, the following documentation will satisfy the identification requirement: (ii) School identification card with a photograph; (iii) Voter's registration card; (iv) U.S. military card or draft record; (v) Identification card issued by federal, state, or local government agencies or entities; (vi) Military dependent's identification card; (vii) Native American tribal documents; (viii) United States Coast Guard Merchant Mariner Card; (ix) Driver's license issued by a Canadian government authority;

For individuals under the age of 18 unable to produce a document listed above: (i) School record or report card; (ii) Clinic doctor or hospital record; (iii) Day care or nursery school record.

Those under the age of 18 and unable to produce any of the documents listed above: The minor's parent or legal guardian completes the Form I-9 and writes, "minor under age 16."

b. Documents establishing employment eligibility only are:

A social security number card other than one which has printed on its face "not valid for employment purposes"; an unexpired reentry permit, INS Form I-327; an unexpired Refugee Travel document, INS Form I-571; a Certification

---

16. 8 U.S.C. § 1324a. While it remains to be seen how effective the sanctions will be, its provisions apply to all employers and job applicants, irrespective of U.S. citizenship or number of employees. While the regulations do not require the employers to review documentation of potential employees, it has been argued that because certain aliens are ineligible for employment and the antidiscrimination provisions require that *all* employees be verified, it behooves the employer to question all prospective employees.

The verification procedures are described at 8 C.F.R. § 274a.2(b).

of Birth issued by the Department of State, Form FS-545; a Certification of Birth Abroad issued by the Department of State, Form DS-1350; an original or certified copy of a birth certificate issued by a state, county, or municipal authority bearing a seal; an employment authorization document issued by the Immigration and Naturalization Service; Native American tribal document; United States Citizen Identification Card, INS Form I-197; Identification card for use of resident citizen in the United States, INS Form I-179.

c. Documents establishing identification and employment are:

A U.S. passport, certificate of U.S. citizenship (N-560 or N-561), Naturalization Certificate (N-550 or N-570), an unexpired foreign passport containing an unexpired stamp which reads, "Processed for I-551. Temporary Evidence of Lawful Admission for permanent residence. Valid until—. Employment authorized" or has attached an arrival-departure record (I-94) bearing the same name as the passport and contains an employment authorization stamp, Alien Registration Receipt Card (I-151), Temporary Resident Card (I-688), Employment Authorization Card (I-688A).

3. If an individual is unable to provide the required document or documents within three days, she must present a receipt for the application of the document or documents within three days of the hire and present the required document or documents within 21 days of the hire.

4. If an individual's employment eligibility document expires, the employer, recruiter, or referrer for a fee must update the I-9 to reflect that the individual is still authorized to work in the United States; otherwise the individual may no longer be employed, recruited, or referred. In order to update the Form I-9, the employee or referred individual must present a document that either shows continuing employment eligibility or a new grant of work authorization. The employer or the recruiter or referrer for a fee should review this document, and if it appears to be genuine and to relate to the individual, update the form by noting the document's identification number and expiration date on the Form I-9.

Sanctions (8 C.F.R. §§ 274a.3-10)

An employer who continues the employment of an employee hired after November 6, 1986, knowing that the employee is or has become an unauthorized alien with respect to that employment, is in violation of 8 U.S.C. §1324a(a)(2), Sec. 274. A respondent determined by the INS or by an administrative law judge (after a hearing)[17] to have failed to comply with the employment verification requirements shall be subject to a civil penalty in an amount of not less than $100 and not more than $1,000 for each individual with respect to whom such violation occurred.[18] In determining the

---

17. Decisions of the administrative law judge are reviewable in a court of appeals upon the filing of a petition for review within 45 days. The administrative law judges are granted subpoena powers to compel the appearance of witnesses and the production of witnesses.

18. The regulations also describe some of the civil sanctions according to the following schedule: first violation, not less than $250 and not more than $2,000 for each unauthorized alien; second violation, not less than $2,000 and not more than $5,000 for each unauthorized alien; more than two violations, not less than $3,000 and not more than $10,000 for each unauthorized alien. 8 C.F.R. § 274a.10(b)(1)(ii).

amount of the penalty, consideration shall be given to: (i) the size of the business of the employer being charged; (ii) the good faith of the employer; (iii) the seriousness of the violation; (iv) whether or not the individual was an unauthorized alien; and (v) the history of previous violations of the employer.

If the Attorney General has reasonable cause to believe that a person or entity is engaged in a pattern or practice of employment, recruitment, or referral violations, the Attorney General may bring civil action in the appropriate United States district court, requesting relief including a permanent or temporary injunction, restraining order, or other order against the person or entity, as the Attorney General deems necessary.[19] The Attorney General may also seek criminal penalties of not more than $3,000 for each unauthorized alien, or imprisonment for not more than six months for the entire pattern or practice, or both, notwithstanding the provisions of any other federal law relating to fine levels.[20]

Good faith defense (8 C.F.R. § 274a.4)

An employer, recruiter, or referrer for a fee who shows good faith compliance with the employment verification requirements shall have established a rebuttable affirmative defense that the person or entity has not violated 8 U.S.C. § 1324a(a)(1)(A) with respect to such hiring, recruiting, or referral.

Enforcement Procedures (8 C.F.R. § 274a.9)

Any person or entity having knowledge of a violation or potential violation may submit a signed, written complaint in person or by mail to the INS office having jurisdiction over the business or residence of the potential violator. The signed, written complaint must contain sufficient information to identify both the complainant and the potential violator, including their names and addresses. The complaint should also contain detailed factual allegations relating to the potential violation including the date, time, and place that the alleged violation occurred and the specific act or conduct of the employer alleged to constitute a violation of the Act. Written complaints may be delivered either by mail to the appropriate INS office or by personally appearing before any immigration officer at an INS office.

The INS may conduct investigations for violations on its own initiative and without having received a written complaint. When the INS receives a complaint from a third party, it shall investigate only those complaints which have a reasonable probability of validity. If it is determined after investigation that the person or entity has violated the sanction provisions, the INS will issue and serve upon the alleged violator a citation in the form of "Notice of Intent to Fine." INS officers are allowed reasonable access to examine any relevant evidence of any person or entity being investigated.

If after investigation the INS determines that a person or entity has committed a violation for the first time during the citation period (June 1, 1987 through May 31, 1988), the INS shall issue a citation. If after investigation the INS determines that a person or entity has violated the law for the second time during the citation period

19. 8 U.S.C. § 1324a(f)(2)
20. 8 U.S.C. § 1324a(f)(1)

or for the first time after May 31, 1988, the proceeding to assess administrative penalties is commenced by the INS by issuing a Notice of Intent to Fine. Notice is accomplished through service on the person or entity identified in the Notice of Intent to Fine which is issued by an INS officer after consultation with concurrence of the attorney for the INS or her designee.

The Notice of Intent to Fine should contain a concise statement of factual allegations informing the respondent (employer) of the act or conduct alleged to be in violation of law, a designation of the charge(s) against the respondent, the statutory provisions alleged to have been violated, and the penalty that will be imposed.

The Notice of Intent to Fine will provide the following notice to the respondent: (i) the person or entity has the right to representation by counsel of his or her own choice at no expense to the government; (ii) any statement given may be used against the person or entity; (iii) the person or entity has the right to request a hearing before an administrative law judge pursuant to 5 U.S.C. §§ 554-57, and that such request must be made within 30 days from the service of the Notice of Intent to Fine; (iv) the INS will issue a final order in 45 days if a written request for a hearing is not timely received and that there will be no appeal of the final order.

If a respondent contests the issuance of a Notice of Intent to Fine, she must, by mail, serve a written answer responding to each allegation listed in the notice and request a hearing within 30 days from the issuance of the notice. If the respondent does not file an answer within 30 days, the INS shall issue a final order to which there is no appeal.

References

Lopez & Lopez, *The Rights of Aliens in Deportation and Exclusion*, 20 Idaho L. Rev. 731 (1984)

Note, *Compromising Immigration Reform: The Creation of a Vulnerable Subclass*, 98 Yale L.J. 409 (1988)

Note, *Due Process and Deportation: A Critical Examination of the Plenary Power and the Fundamental Fairness Doctrine*, 8 Hastings Const. L.Q. 397 (1981)

Note, *Evidence in Deportation Proceedings*, 63 Tex. L. Rev. 1537 (1985)

Note, *Exclusionary Rule in Deportation Proceedings: A Time for Alternatives*, 14 J. Int'l L. & Econ. 349 (1980)

Note, *INS Factory Raids as Nondetentive Seizures*, 95 Yale L.J. 767 (1986)

Note, *Reexamining the Constitutionality of INS Workplace Raids After the Immigration Reform and Control Act of 1986*, 100 Harv. L. Rev. 1979 (1987)

Roberts & Yale-Loehr, *Employers as Junior Immigration Inspectors: The Impact of the 1986 Immigration Reform and Control Act*, 21 Int'l Law. 1013 (1987)

Rosenzweig, *Functional Equivalents of the Border, Sovereignty, and the Fourth Amendment*, 52 U. Chi. L. Rev. 1119 (1985)

Scharf & Hess, *What Process is Due? Unaccompanied Minors' Rights to Deportation Hearings*, 1988 Duke L.J. 114

Smith & Mendez, *Employer Sanctions and Other Labor Market Restrictions on Alien Employment: The "Scorched Earth Approach to Immigration Control*, 6 N.C. J. Int'l L. & Com. Reg. 19, 21 (1980)

Symposium, Implementation of IRCA, 2 Geo. Immigr. L.J. 447 (1988)

A. The Practice of Immigration Law

The author of the following article, the late Jack Wasserman, is considered to be one of the luminary figures in the practice of immigration law. Since the article was written, Title 8 of the Code of Federal Regulations was amended, adding a new section on proceedings before immigration judges and the Board of Immigration Appeals. Some of these regulations are reprinted and follow this article. In addition, in 1990 Congress enacted the Immigration Act of 1990, Pub. L. No. 101-649, 104 Stat. 4978. Notwithstanding these changes, the following article captures the practice of immigration law in the deportation hearing.

Practical Aspects of Representing an Alien at a Deportation Hearing
Wasserman, 14 San Diego L. Rev. 111 (1976)*

The Right to Counsel and Due Process in Deportation Proceedings

Although a deportation hearing is not a criminal proceeding, courts have recognized that an alien involved in deportation proceedings is entitled to procedural due process. Due process includes the right to the assistance of counsel. Congress has acknowledged the constitutional guarantee to counsel by enacting statutory provisions which have codified the right.

Sections 242(b)(2) and 292 of the Act provide that "the alien shall have the privilege of being represented by counsel." However, because deportation proceedings are civil in nature, there is no right to appointed counsel. The alien must be granted time to obtain counsel. The denial of a continuance in order to obtain counsel has been held violative of due process. Once counsel has been secured, the attorney representing the alien before the Service should ascertain the alien's registration number and file a notice of appearance on form G-28.

Deportation proceedings are instituted by the Service by serving the alien with an order to show cause on form I-221S. The order is combined with a notice of hearing and warrant for arrest of the alien. The order to show cause should contain a concise statement of the violation and a designation of charges. Due process requires that the alien be given a notice of charges and a hearing. To satisfy these constitutional standards, notice and an opportunity to be heard must be granted at a meaningful time and in a meaningful manner. Notice of the hearing should be given at least seven days prior to the hearing date, unless the public interest, safety or security requires a shorter period.

At the time the order to show cause is served the District Director will decide whether to utilize the warrant of arrest. If it is not utilized, the alien will be released upon his own recognizance. However, if the warrant of arrest is used, a custody determination will be made, setting the amount of bond. Aliens have a constitutional right to bail pending their deportation hearing, pending judicial review, and until they are required to report for actual deportation.

---

* Copyright 1976 San Diego Law Review Association. Reprinted with the permission of the San Diego Law Review. Footnotes have been omitted.

Prehearing Proceedings

The bond amount will appear on the reverse side of the order to show cause, form I-221S. Although bonds may range from $500.00 to $75,000.00, generally a bond will be either $1,000.00 or $2,500.00. Bond may be posted by a surety company, but usually a cashier's or certified check payable to Service is deposited. Form I-352 (Immigration Bond) and form I-305 (Collateral Receipt) are executed when the collateral is posted and copies of each form are given to the obligor. Form I-305 must be returned to obtain the collateral when the alien has departed from the United States or when he becomes a permanent resident.

A bond may contain conditions. The conditions are of a general nature, usually requiring the alien to report for hearing and deportation. However, the District Director may in certain situations impose a condition barring unauthorized employment. Any bond determination or decision by the District Director not to release an alien is reviewable by appeal to any immigration judge who is available in the region. Further appeal may be taken to the Board of Immigration Appeals. The bail or bond proceedings described are separate from the deportation hearing.

The Deportation Hearing

Location of the Hearing

The deportation is held in the district of the alien's arrest or residence. Preferably, it should be held at his place of residence. Counsel may request a change in the hearing location to the alien's place of residence. Generally, such a request will be granted, especially if the alien is released on bond or is released on his own recognizance. Hearings may be held in places other than the district of the alien's residence or in more than one district if required for the convenience of the alien, the alien's attorney, or witnesses.

Government Officials Present

The presiding officer at the deportation hearing is the special inquiry officer. He is often referred to as an immigration judge even though he is not subject to the Administrative Procedure Act. Although the immigration judge wears judicial robes and sits at a desk on a raised platform, the other aspects of the deportation hearing are less formal than are those of judicial proceedings. Witnesses, interpreters, and counsel sit around a conference table equipped with microphones. A recording device rather than a stenographer is used to preserve testimony adduced at the hearing.

The major functions of the immigration judge are to determine deportability, to grant certain forms of discretionary relief, to determine the country of the alien's deportation, and to certify a decision that involves an unusually complex or novel question of law or fact to the Board of Immigration Appeals. As the presiding officer, the immigration judge controls the conduct of the hearing, authorizes deposition testimony, grants continuances, and places both the interpreter and all witnesses under oath. He is required to advise the unrepresented alien of his right to counsel and to ask the alien to state his preference regarding such representation. The immigration judge is also required to advise the alien that he will have a reasonable opportunity to examine and object to adverse evidence and to cross-examine witnesses. He will have the factual allegations of the order to show cause read to the alien, explained in nontechnical language, and finally entered as an exhibit. The alien is required by the immigration judge to plead to the factual allegations of the order to show cause. After the hearing the judge will render an oral or written decision.

In some districts, a trial attorney is assigned in all deportation cases. Assignment by the District Director is required in all cases in which deportability is an issue, in cases of unrepresented incompetents or children under sixteen, in cases when requested by the immigration judge, or in cases after which nonrecorded, confidential information will be submitted to contest the grant of discretionary relief. Trial attorneys are generally members of the bar, but at times they may be immigration inspectors without law degrees.

The trial attorney is authorized to present evidence on behalf of the Government and to examine and cross-examine the alien and his witnesses. He is vested with authority to appeal a decision favorable to the alien and may move for reopening and reconsideration of decisions adverse to the Government's contentions. He may also file, in writing, additional charges of deportability. The document evidencing these additional charges will be entered as an exhibit and will serve as a basis for a continuance to allow the alien to meet the additional charges.

Courts have long perceived the importance of utilizing a competent interpreter. Some interpreters are highly skilled and efficient and have great experience and expertise in the art of translation. Others may not have acquired facility in the language. Inexperienced interpreters have problems transposing foreign sentences into English, a difficult task in any event because some languages have no literal counterpart for many English words. Thus, it is important for counsel to ascertain not only whether the interpreter speaks the same language as the alien but also whether the interpreter understands the same dialect.

At deportation hearings, unlike judicial proceedings, the Government furnishes all interpreters at its expense. The interpreter may be an employee of INS, of the State Department, or he may be a nongovernmental individual employed on a contract basis. In appropriate cases, an alien will be permitted to bring his own interpreter into the hearing to monitor the accuracy of the official translation.

*   *   *

Procedure in the Conduct of a Deportation Hearing

The immigration judge begins the hearing by turning on his recording machine. He then proceeds to call the case, identify the alien, counsel, the trial attorney, and the interpreter. The alien is asked whether he received the order to show cause which is entered as Exhibit 1. The alien or his attorney then pleads to the allegations of fact set forth in the order to show cause. If the alien has no attorney, he is advised of his rights. If deportability is contested, evidence is adduced on the issue.

Deportability and alienage must be established by substantial evidence—that is, by clear, convincing, and unequivocal evidence. Hearsay is admissible, but uncorroborated hearsay is not substantial evidence. The use of hearsay and guilt by association is considered erroneous. When hearsay is admitted, counsel for the alien should exercise his right to cross-examine by requesting a subpoena or depositions. The prior statements of adverse witnesses may be obtained under the Jencks rule by making a demand for them. An alien is entitled to equal treatment and nondiscriminatory rulings on evidentiary issues. Failure to accord the alien such treatment results in the hearing being deemed unfair.

Although oral argument is usually not encouraged before an immigration judge, it will be allowed in some cases. Briefs are not usually submitted but should be filed in complicated cases. The alien may decline to answer upon grounds of self-incrimination. If deportability is conceded, if it is established, or even when it remains disputed, consideration must be given to applications for discretionary relief. Such applications must be made during the hearing, and the burden of proof is upon the alien to establish that he is entitled to relief.

Designating the Place of Deportation

Prior to the conclusion of the hearing, the alien will be permitted to designate a place of deportation, if he is ordered deported. He may designate only one place of deportation, and this decision must be made in good faith. The alien may not designate contiguous territory or adjacent islands unless he has been a native, citizen, or resident of such places. The immigration judge may designate as an alternative place of deportation the alien's country of citizenship or last residence or any country willing to receive him.

The Immigration Judge's Decision

The immigration judge's decision may be oral or written. If deportability is contested, the decision contains a discussion of the evidence and findings concerning deportability. The decision also contains a discussion of evidence pertinent to discretionary relief and is concluded with an order granting or denying relief. The decision orders termination, grants permanent residence, orders voluntary departure with an alternate order of deportation, or deportation.

If deportability is determined on the pleadings and no discretionary relief other than voluntary departure is requested, the immigration judge enters an order of voluntary departure with an alternate order of deportation to a named country on form I-39 or an order of deportation on form I-38. These forms are served on the alien and his attorney at the conclusion of the hearing, and unless appeal is waived, service of the appeal form (I-290A) is required with advice about the appeal procedure.

When an oral decision is rendered, it is done in the presence of the alien, his counsel, and the trial attorney. Unless an appeal is waived, the appeal form and advice about appeal must be given. Upon request, the decision and a transcript will be provided without cost to enable the alien to pursue his appeal. If no appeal is taken, the immigration judge's decision is final. If the decision is favorable to the alien, the trial attorney has the right to appeal, and in appropriate cases, the case may be certified to the Board of Immigration Appeals for review by the immigration judge, by the Service, or by the Board.

Note

The 1990 Act created a significant procedural change in the way in which deportation cases are to be handled. This new section imposes severe limits on all persons in deportation proceedings. The statute specifies that the order to show cause must be served personally or by certified mail, that it advise the respondent of the time and place of the hearing. The most significant changes are statutorily imposed notice requirements and provisions enumerating the consequences of a respondent's failure to appear at her deportation hearing. Anyone who fails to appear at the deportation proceedings after having received notice pursuant to 8 U.S.C. § 1252b (a)(2), Sec. 242B(a)(2) may be deported *in absentia* and is ineligible for 5 years for most forms of discretionary relief such as voluntary departure, waivers of grounds of excludability under 212(c), suspension of deportation, adjustment of status and change of status.[21] In the event that the respondent fails to appear, the only way that she may be able to reopen her hearing is upon a showing of "exceptional circumstances."[22] In addition, a respondent who fails to depart pursuant to voluntary departure granted by an immigration judge is also precluded from certain discretionary relief.

8 C.F.R. §§ 3.12-3.37
Rules of Procedure in Cases
Before Immigration Judges

8 C.F.R. § 3.12 Scope of rules.

These rules are promulgated for the purpose of assisting in the expeditious, fair, and proper resolution of matters coming before Immigration Judges. Except where specifically stated, these rules apply to all matters before Immigration Judges, including deportation, exclusion, bond, and rescission proceedings. Specifically excluded from applicability under these rules are administrative proceedings involving the withdrawal of school approval under 8 C.F.R. 214 and departure-control hearings under 8 C.F.R. 215.

8 C.F.R. § 3.13 Definitions.

As used in this subpart:

Administrative Control—The term "administrative control" means custodial responsibility for the Record of Proceeding as specified in 8 C.F.R. 3.11.

Charging Document—The term "charging document" means the written instrument which initiates a proceeding before an Immigration Judge including an Order to Show Cause, a Notice to Applicant for Admission Detained for Hearing before Immigration Judge, and a Notice of Intention to Rescind and Request for hearing by Alien.

Filing—The term "filing" means the actual receipt of a document by the appropriate Office of the Immigration Judge.

Service—The term "service" means physically presenting or mailing a document to the appropriate party or parties.

---

21. *See* 8 U.S.C. § 1252b(e). The effective date of this provision is 6 months after the Attorney General has certified that a central address file system has been established. Sec. 545(g) of the Immigration Act of 1990, Pub. L. No. 101-649, 104 Stat. 4978. These forms of discretionary relief will be reviewed in greater detail in Chapters 9, 11 and 12.

22. *See* 8 U.S.C. § 1252b(e)(3)(A), Sec. 242b(e)(3)(A). The statute defines exceptional circumstances as "circumstances (such as serious illness of the alien or death of an immediate relative of the alien, but not including less compelling circumstances) beyond the control of the alien." 8 U.S.C. § 1252b(f)(2), Sec. 242b(f)(2).

8 C.F.R. § 3.14 Jurisdiction & commencement of proceedings.

(a) Jurisdiction vests and proceedings before an Immigration Judge commence when a charging document is filed with the Office of the Immigration Judge except for bond proceedings as provided in 8 C.F.R. 3.18 and 242.2(b).

(b) When the Immigration Judge has jurisdiction over the underlying proceeding, sole jurisdiction over applications for asylum shall lie with the Immigration Judge.

* * *

8 C.F.R. § 3.17 Scheduling of cases.

All cases shall be scheduled by the Office of the Immigration Judge. The Office of the Immigration Judge shall be responsible for providing notice of the time, place, and date of the hearing to the government and respondent/applicant.

8 C.F.R. § 3.18 Custody/bond.

(a) Custody and bond redeterminations made by the INS pursuant to 8 C.F.R. 242 may be reviewed by an Immigration Judge pursuant to 8 C.F.R. 242.

(b) Application for bond redetermination by a respondent, his or her attorney or representative may be made orally, in writing, in person, or in the discretion of the Immigration Judge, by telephone.

(c) Application for the exercise of such authority must be made in the following order:

(1) If the alien is detained, the Immigration Judge Office at or nearest the place of detention;

(2) The Immigration Judge Office having administrative control over the case;

(3) The Office of the Chief Immigration Judge for designation of an appropriate Office of the Immigration Judge.

(d) Consideration under this paragraph by the Immigration Judge of an application or request of an alien regarding custody or bond shall be separate and apart from any deportation hearing or proceeding, and shall form no part of such hearing or proceeding.

(e) The determination of an Immigration Judge in respect to custody status or bond redetermination shall be entered on the appropriate form at the time such decision is made and the parties shall be informed orally or in writing as to the reasons for the decision.

8 C.F.R. § 3.19 Change of venue.

(a) Except for bond proceedings as provided in §§ 3.18 and 242.2(b), venue shall lie at the Office of the Immigration Judge where the Service files a charging document.

(b) The Immigration Judge, for good cause, may change venue on motion by one of the parties, or upon his or her own authority after the charging document has been filed with the Office of the Immigration Judge.

(c) No change of venue shall be granted without identification of a fixed street address where the respondent/applicant may be reached for further hearing notification.

8 C.F.R. § 3.20 Pre-hearing conferences.

Pre-hearing conferences may be scheduled at the discretion of an Immigration Judge. The conference may be held to narrow issues, attain stipulations between the parties, voluntarily exchange information, and otherwise simplify and organize the proceeding.

* * *

8 C.F.R. § 3.22 Motions.

(a) Pre-Decision Motions. Unless otherwise permitted by the Immigration Judge, motions submitted prior to the final order of an Immigration Judge shall be in writing and shall state, with particularity the grounds therefore, the relief sought, and the jurisdiction. The Immigration Judge may set and extend time limits for the making of motions and replies thereto. A motion shall be deemed unopposed unless timely response is made.

(b) Reopening/Reconsideration.

(1) Motions to reopen or reconsider a decision of the Immigration Judge must be filed with the Office of the Immigration Judge having administrative control over the Record of Proceeding. Such motions shall comply with applicable provisions of 8 C.F.R. 208.11 and 242.22. Any motion to reopen for the purpose of acting on an application for relief must be accompanied by the appropriate application for relief and all supporting documents. The Immigration Judge may set and extend time limits for replies to motions to reopen or reconsider. A motion shall be deemed unopposed unless timely response is made.

(2) When requested in conjunction with a motion to reopen/reconsider, the Immigration Judge may stay the execution of a final order of deportation or exclusion.

8 C.F.R. § 3.23 Waivers of fees in Immigration Judge proceedings.

Any fees pertaining to a matter within the Immigration Judge's jurisdiction may be waived by the Immigration Judge upon a showing that the respondent/applicant is incapable of paying the fees because of indigency. A properly executed affidavit or unsworn declaration made pursuant to 28 U.S.C. 1746 by the respondent/applicant must accompany the request for waiver of fees and shall substantiate the indigency of the respondent/applicant.

8 C.F.R. § 3.24 Waiver of presence of respondent/applicant.

The Immigration Judge may, for good cause, waive the presence of a respondent/applicant at the hearing where the alien is represented or where the alien is a minor child whose parent(s) is present. In addition, in absentia hearings may be held pursuant to section 242(b) of the Act with or without representation.

8 C.F.R. § 3.25 Public access to hearings.

All hearings, other than exclusion hearings, shall be open to the public except that:

(a) Depending upon physical facilities, the Immigration Judge may place reasonable limitations upon the number in attendance at any one time with priority being given to the press over the general public;

(b) For the purpose of protecting witnesses, parties, or the public interest, the Immigration Judge may limit attendance or hold a closed hearing.

8 C.F.R. § 3.26 Recording equipment.

The only recording equipment permitted in the proceeding will be the equipment used by the Immigration Judge to create the official record. No other photographic, video, electronic, or similar recording device will be permitted to record any part of the proceeding.

*   *   *

8 C.F.R. § 3.29 Filing documents and applications.

All documents and applications to be considered in a proceeding before an Immigration Judge must be filed with the Office of the Immigration Judge having administrative control over the Record of Proceeding. Filing will be considered effective only after the payment of applicable fees or the waiver of fees pursuant to 8 C.F.R. 3.23. The Immigration Judge may set and extend time limits for the filing of applications and related documents and the responses thereto, if any. If an application or related document is not filed within the time set by the Immigration Judge, the opportunity to file that application shall be deemed waived.

*   *   *

8 C.F.R. § 3.33 Depositions.

(a) If an Immigration Judge is satisfied that a witness is not reasonably available at the place of hearing and that said witness' testimony or other evidence is essential, the Immigration Judge may order the taking of deposition either at his or her own instance or upon application of a party.

(b) Such order shall designate the official by whom the deposition shall be taken, may prescribe and limit the content, scope, or manner of taking the deposition, and may direct the production of documentary evidence. The Immigration Judge may also issue a subpoena in the event of the refusal or willful failure of a witness within the United States to appear, give testimony, or produce documentary evidence after due notice.

(c) The witness and all parties shall be notified as to the time and place of the deposition by the official designated to conduct the deposition.

(d) Testimony shall be given under oath or affirmation and shall be recorded verbatim.

(e) The official presiding at the taking of the deposition shall note but not rule upon objections, and shall not comment on the admissibility of evidence or on the credibility and demeanor of the witness.

*   *   *

8 C.F.R. § 3.36 Appeals.

(a) Decisions of Immigration Judges may be appealed to the Board of Immigration Appeals as authorized by 8 C.F.R. 3.1(b).

(b) The notice of appeal of the decision shall be filed with the Office of the Immigration Judge having administrative control over the Record of Proceeding within ten (10) calendar days after service of the decision. Time will be 13 days if mailed.

If the final date for filing falls on a Saturday, Sunday, or legal holiday, this appeal time shall be extended to the next business day.

(c) Briefs may be filed by both parties pursuant to 8 C.F.R. 3.3(c).

(d) In any proceeding before the Board wherein the respondent/applicant is represented, the attorney or representative shall file a notice of appearance on the appropriate form. Withdrawal or substitution of an attorney or representative may be permitted by the Board during proceedings only upon written motion submitted without fee.

8 C.F.R § 3.37 Finality of decision.

Except when certified to the Board, the decision of the Immigration Judge becomes final upon waiver of appeal or upon expiration of the time to appeal if no appeal is taken.

Detention or Release

Subsequent to a person's arrest, consideration is given to whether she will be detained or released. If the person is not released on her own recognizance, a bond will be set. There are three types of bonds or sureties commonly used in immigration cases: delivery, maintenance and public charge bonds. The delivery bonds are the most common, and may be forfeited if the person fails to appear at a scheduled appearance. Maintenance bonds are forfeited when a person admitted to the U.S. fails to maintain her status. Public charge are rarely imposed; the surety is forfeited upon the person admitted to the U.S. becoming a public charge. See 8 C.F.R. § 103.6(a)(2). Depending on the type of bond, the surety will be returned upon the person's death, departure or obtaining the status of a lawful permanent resident. 8 C.F.R. § 103.6(c).

While there is no absolute right to bond, it is generally granted unless an individual poses a threat to national security. The principal factors in setting the amount of the bond are: local family ties; prior arrest, convictions, and immigration history; employment status; membership in community organizations; manner of entry and length of stay in the U.S.; and financial ability to post bond. See *Matter of Daryoush*, 18 I. & N. Dec. 352 (BIA 1982); *Matter of Patel*, 15 I. & N. Dec. 666 (BIA 1976).

B. Burden of Proof in Deportation Proceedings

Woodby v. I.N.S.
385 U.S. 276 (1966)

Justice STEWART delivered the opinion of the Court.

The question presented by these cases is what burden of proof the Government must sustain in deportation proceedings. We have concluded that it is incumbent upon the Government in such proceedings to establish the facts supporting deportability by clear, unequivocal, and convincing evidence.

In Sherman (No. 80), the petitioner is a resident alien who entered this country from Poland in 1920 as a 14-year-old boy. In 1963 the Immigration and Naturalization Service instituted proceedings to deport him upon the ground that he had re-entered the United States in 1938, following a trip abroad, without inspection as an alien. After a hearing before a special inquiry officer, the petitioner was ordered to be deported, and the Board of Immigration Appeals dismissed his appeal.

The Government's evidence showed that the petitioner had obtained a passport in 1937 under the name of Samuel Levine, representing himself as a United States citizen. Someone using this passport sailed to France in June 1937, proceeded to Spain, returned to the United States in December 1938, aboard the S.S. Ausonia, and was admitted without being examined as an alien. To establish that it was the petitioner who had traveled under this passport, the Government introduced the testimony of Edward Morrow, an American citizen who had fought in the Spanish Civil War. Morrow was at first unable to remember the name Samuel Levine or identify the petitioner, but eventually stated that he thought he had known the petitioner as "Sam Levine," had seen him while fighting for the Loyalists in Spain during 1937 and 1938, and had returned with him to the United States aboard the S.S. Ausonia in December 1938. Morrow conceded that his recollection of events occurring 27 years earlier was imperfect, and admitted that his identification of the petitioner might be mistaken.

It is not clear what standard of proof the special inquiry officer and the Board of Immigration Appeals on de novo review applied in determining that it was the petitioner who had traveled to Spain and re-entered the United States under the Samuel Levine passport. At the outset of his opinion, the special inquiry officer stated that the Government must establish deportability "by reasonable, substantial and probative evidence," without discussing what the burden of proof was. Later he concluded that the Government had established its contentions "with a solidarity far greater than required," but did not further elucidate what was "required." The Board of Immigration Appeals stated that it was "established beyond any reasonable doubt" that the petitioner had obtained the Samuel Levine passport, and added that this established a "presumption" that the petitioner had used it to travel abroad. The Board further stated that it was a "most unlikely hypothesis" that someone other than the petitioner had obtained and used the passport, and asserted that "the Service has borne its burden of establishing" that the petitioner was deportable, without indicating what it considered the weight of that burden to be.

Upon petition for review, the Court of Appeals for the Second Circuit originally set aside the deportation order, upon the ground that the Government has the burden of proving the facts supporting deportability beyond a reasonable doubt. The court reversed itself, however, upon a rehearing en banc, holding that the Government need only prove its case with "reasonable, substantial, and probative evidence." We granted certiorari, 384 U.S. 904.

In Woodby (No. 40), the petitioner is a resident alien who was born in Hungary and entered the United States from Germany in 1956 as the wife of an American soldier. Deportation proceedings were instituted against her on the ground that she had engaged in prostitution after entry. A special inquiry officer and the Board of Immigration Appeals found that she was deportable upon the ground charged.

At the administrative hearing the petitioner admitted that she had engaged in prostitution for a brief period in 1957, some months after her husband had deserted her, but claimed that her conduct was the product of circumstances amounting to duress. Without reaching the validity of the duress defense, the special inquiry officer and the Board of Immigration Appeals concluded that the petitioner had continued to engage in prostitution after the alleged duress had terminated. The hearing officer and the Board did not discuss what burden of proof the Government was required to bear in establishing deportability, nor did either of them indicate the degree of certainty with which their factual conclusions were reached. The special inquiry officer merely asserted that the evidence demonstrated that the petitioner was deportable. The Board stated that the evidence made it "apparent" that the petitioner had engaged in prostitution after the alleged duress had ended, and announced that "it is concluded that the evidence establishes deportability. . . . "

In denying a petition for review, the Court of Appeals for the Sixth Circuit did not explicitly deal with the issue of what burden of persuasion was imposed upon the Government at the administrative level, finding only that "the Board's underlying order is 'supported by reasonable, substantial, and probative evidence on the record considered as a whole. . . . ' "

In the prevailing opinion in the Sherman case, the Court of Appeals for the Second Circuit stated that "[i]f the slate were clean," it "might well agree that the standard of persuasion for deportation should be similar to that in denaturalization, where the Supreme Court has insisted that the evidence must be 'clear, unequivocal, and convincing' and that the Government needs 'more than a bare preponderance of the evidence' to prevail. . . . But here," the court thought, "Congress has spoken. . . . " This view was based upon two provisions of the Immigration and Nationality Act which use the language "reasonable, substantial, and probative evidence" in connection with deportation orders. The provisions in question are § 106(a)(4) of the Act which states that a deportation order, "if supported by reasonable, substantial, and probative evidence on the record considered as a whole, shall be conclusive," and § 242(b)(4) of the Act which provides *inter alia* that "no decision of deportability shall be valid unless it is based upon reasonable, substantial, and probative evidence."

It seems clear, however, that these two statutory provisions are addressed not to the degree of proof required at the administrative level in deportation proceedings, but to quite a different subject—the scope of judicial review. The elementary but crucial difference between burden of proof and scope of review is, of course, a commonplace in the law. The difference is most graphically illustrated in a criminal case. There the prosecution is generally required to prove the elements of the offense beyond a reasonable doubt. But if the correct burden of proof was imposed at the trial, judicial review is generally limited to ascertaining whether the evidence relied upon by the trier of fact was of sufficient quality and substantiality to support the rationality of the judgment. In other words, an appellate court in a criminal case ordinarily does not ask itself whether it believes that the evidence at the trial established guilt beyond a reasonable doubt, but whether the judgment is supported by substantial evidence.

That § 106(a)(4) relates exclusively to judicial review is made abundantly clear by its language, its context, and its legislative history. Section 106 was added to the Act in 1961 in order "to create a single, separate, statutory form of judicial review of administrative orders for the deportation and exclusion of aliens from the United States." The section is entitled "Judicial Review of Orders of Deportation and Exclusion," and by its terms provides "the sole and exclusive procedure for" the "judicial review of all final orders of deportation." Subsection 106(a)(4) is a specific directive to the courts in which petitions for review are filed.

It is hardly less clear that the other provision upon which the Court of Appeals for the Second Circuit relied, § 242(b)(4) of the Act, is also addressed to reviewing courts, and, insofar as it represents a yardstick for the administrative factfinder, goes, not to the burden of proof, but rather to the quality and nature of the evidence upon which a deportation order must be based. The provision declares that "reasonable, substantial, and probative evidence" shall be the measure of whether a deportability decision is "valid"—a word that implies scrutiny by a reviewing tribunal of a decision already reached by the trier of the facts. The location of this provision in a section containing provisions dealing with procedures before the special inquiry officer has little significance when it is remembered that the original 1952 Act did not itself contain a framework for judicial review—although such review was, of course, available by habeas corpus or otherwise. And whatever ambiguity might be thought to lie in the location of this section is resolved by its legislative history. The Senate Report explained § 242(b)(4) as follows:

> The requirement that the decision of the special inquiry officer shall be based on reasonable, substantial and probative evidence means that, where the decision rests upon evidence of such a nature that it cannot be said that a reasonable person might not have reached the conclusion which was reached, the case may not be reversed because the judgment of the appellate body differs from that of the administrative body.

We conclude, therefore, that Congress has not addressed itself to the question of what degree of proof is required in deportation proceedings. It is the kind of question which has traditionally been left to the judiciary to resolve, and its resolution is necessary in the interest of the evenhanded administration of the Immigration and Nationality Act.

The petitioners urge that the appropriate burden of proof in deportation proceedings should be that which the law imposes in criminal cases—the duty of proving the essential facts beyond a reasonable doubt. The Government, on the other hand, points out that a deportation proceeding is not a criminal case, and that the appropriate burden of proof should consequently be the one generally imposed in civil cases and administrative proceedings—the duty of prevailing by a mere preponderance of the evidence.

To be sure, a deportation proceeding is not a criminal prosecution. *Harisiades v. Shaughnessy,* 342 U.S. 580. But it does not syllogistically follow that a person may be banished from this country upon no higher degree of proof than applies in a negligence case. This Court has not closed its eyes to the drastic deprivations that may follow when a resident of this country is compelled by our Government to forsake all the bonds formed here and go to a foreign land where he often has no contemporary identification. . . .

In denaturalization cases the Court has required the Government to establish its allegations by clear, unequivocal, and convincing evidence. The same burden has been imposed in expatriation cases. That standard of proof is no stranger to the civil law.

No less a burden of proof is appropriate in deportation proceedings. The immediate hardship of deportation is often greater than that inflicted by denaturalization, which does not, immediately at least, result in expulsion from our shores. And many resident aliens have lived in this country longer and established stronger family, social, and economic ties here than some who have become naturalized citizens.

We hold that no deportation order may be entered unless it is found by clear, unequivocal, and convincing evidence that the facts alleged as grounds for deportation are true.

Notes

1. The Immigration Act of 1990 removed 8 U.S.C. § 1252(b)(4) which providing that "no decision of deportability shall be valid unless it is based upon reasonable, substantial and probative evidence." If instead, Congress had replaced the word "substantial" in place of "reasonable, substantial and probative" what would be the result in light of *Woodby*? Is there any significance which can be attached to Congress' elimination of the "reasonable, substantial and probative" requirement? If Congress changed the burden of proof in deportation so as only to necessitate a preponderance of the evidence, would this be constitutional?

2. Although the burden of proof is on the government, deportability is usually easily and clearly established. As a result, in most cases deportability is generally conceded and the respondent seeks some form of discretionary relief such as asylum (Chapter 4), suspension of deportation (Chapter 11), or adjustment of status (Chapter 7).

3. **Voluntary departure.** The Court noted that Woodby had been granted voluntary departure. Voluntary departure is a benefit described in Section 244(e) of the Act, 8 U.S.C. § 1254(e) and requires that the applicant establish that she is a person of good moral character and is ready, willing, and able to leave the United States. *See also* 8 C.F.R. § 244.1. In effect, it allows the person protection from the adverse consequences of a deportation order. If a person is the subject of an order of deportation and does not have voluntary departure, she will not be allowed to return to the United States for five years unless she has first received permission from the Attorney General.[23] The usual period of voluntary departure is thirty days, although longer periods may be granted at the discretion of the immigration judge. *Matter of M—*, 4 I. & N. Dec. 626 (BIA 1969). For additional guidance on voluntary departure, *see* 8 C.F.R. §§ 244.1, 242.5, and 243.5.

C. The Burden of Proof Applied

Matter of Vivas
16 I. & N. Dec. 68 (BIA 1977)

The respondent appeals from an immigration judge's decision dated August 9, 1976. In this decision the respondent was found deportable under section 241(a)(1) of the Immigration and Nationality Act as excludable at entry under section 212(a)(14) and section 212(a)(20) of the Act and was granted the privilege of voluntary departure. The appeal will be dismissed.

---

23. *See also* discussion in Chapter 11 on relief from deportation.

The respondent is a 24-year-old native and citizen of Mexico. He entered the United States as an immigrant on August 31, 1974. At issue is whether the respondent's deportability has been established by clear, convincing and unequivocal evidence.

The record reveals that the respondent obtained his immigrant visa and his exemption from the labor certification on account of his marriage to a United States citizen. The Service must prove by the required degree of evidence that the respondent was not exempt at the time of entry from the labor certification and that the visa he presented to gain admission as a lawful permanent resident was invalid.

To prove its case, the Service presented as a witness a person claiming to be the individual referred to in the birth certificate used to establish the United States citizenship of the respondent's wife. The immigration judge concluded, on the basis of her testimony at the hearing and the other evidence in the record, that the birth certificate used to establish the citizenship of the respondent's wife belonged to the witness. The immigration judge's finding of fact carries great weight and will not ordinarily be set aside. Matter of T—, 7 I. & N. Dec. 417 (BIA 1957).

The witness testified that she has never gone through a marriage ceremony with the respondent, that she had never met him previously and that she is married to someone else presently. The respondent testified that he had not married the witness and that he had never seen her before. However, the respondent claimed that he married someone who was using the same name as the witness. The respondent presented no evidence to clarify his wife's identity or to prove that she is a United States citizen.

Since we have decided that the witness is the United States citizen referred to in the birth certificate, the question is, more concretely, whether the respondent's deportability as one who was excludable at entry under section 212(a)(14) of the Act is established by clear, convincing and unequivocal evidence when the Service establishes that the respondent is not married to the person whose birth certificate was used to establish the exemption from the labor certification and the respondent has not gone forward with evidence to establish the real identity of the person to whom he claims to have been married at the time he entered the United States. We hold in the affirmative for this proposition.

It is not a novel principle in immigration law that, notwithstanding the requirement of clear, convincing and unequivocal evidence to establish deportability, a respondent may properly be required to go forward with evidence to rebut prima facie showings by the Service. *See Matter of Tijerina-Villarreal*, 13 I. & N. Dec. 1 (BIA 1966). In the case at hand, the rule is justified.

In this situation, manifestly, the Service is under a serious practical handicap if it must prove the negative proposition: that the respondent did not marry a United States citizen when he married on June 9, 1973. The possibilities are of such magnitude as to defy inclusive rebuttal. On the other hand, the burden of affirmatively identifying the person whom he married is not an oppressive one for the respondent to undertake; the relevant facts to do that are peculiarly within his knowledge. He is only being called to identify properly the person; the Service still retains the obligation to prove by clear, convincing and unequivocal evidence that the respondent is deportable on the charges brought against him.

The rule that we are enunciating for this situation is not new to either criminal or civil proceedings. The burden of going forward with evidence can be placed on a party not bearing the burden of proof when the facts are within his particular knowledge or control. *See United States v. Fleischman*, 339 U.S. 349 (1950). The burden of going forward with evidence also arises under certain circumstances when a prima facie case is made by the opponent. And, more in line with the factual situation at hand, the burden of going forward with the evidence is placed on a party not having the burden of proof when he has better control or knowledge of the evidence and his adversary makes a prima facie showing of his case.

The Service has shown that the respondent has not married the person whose birth certificate was used to establish his exemption from the labor certification as the spouse of a United States citizen. The respondent has not gone forward with evidence to establish the identity of the person he married.

Counsel for the respondent argues on appeal that the respondent [is not deportable as excludable at entry under section 212(a)(14) because the record is silent as to the purpose of the respondent's entry. We reject counsel's contention.

The record shows that the respondent was employed in Chicago prior to his trek to Mexico to obtain his visa. The respondent when asked his occupation on the visa application said "Labores." The respondent was employed at the time of the hearing. There is an affidavit in the record from the purported wife of the respondent, dated June 24, 1974, stating that he was permanently employed by the Crane Company in Chicago. That evidence is sufficient to establish that his purpose to enter the United States was to perform skilled or unskilled labor. *Matter of Lee*, Interim Decision 2424 (BIA 1975). The respondent's deportability as one who was excludable at entry under section 212(a)(14) has been established clearly, convincingly, and unequivocally.

It is established that the birth certificate accompanying the documentation presented to the consul to prove the eligibility of the respondent for his immigrant visa did not refer to the respondent's wife. If that fact had been known to the consul at the time he issued the visa, he would not have issued it since there was no evidence before him that would establish the respondent's eligibility to receive the visa.

Where the true facts would have required a consul to rule that an applicant for a visa had not borne the burden of establishing eligibility, we must hold that concealment of those facts resulted in the procurement of a visa which was not valid. The fact that the applicant might have obtained a visa at a later date, establishing his full eligibility with evidence other than the one submitted at the time does not mean that the visa obtained on August 14, 1974 is a valid visa. *See Ablett v. Brownell*, 240 F.2d 625 (D.C. Cir. 1957). The respondent's inadmissibility under section 212(a)(20) of the Act at the time of entry has been established.

D. The Evolution of Search and Seizure Law

U.S. v. Brignoni-Ponce
422 U.S. 873 (1975)

Justice POWELL.

The Fourth Amendment applies to all seizures of the person, including seizures that involve only a brief detention short of traditional arrest. *Davis v. Mississippi*, 394 U.S. 721 (1969); *Terry v. Ohio*, 392 U.S. 1, 16-19 (1968). "[W]henever a police officer accosts an individual and restrains his freedom to walk away, he has 'seized' that person," id., at 16, and the Fourth Amendment requires that the seizure be "reasonable." As with other categories of police action subject to Fourth Amendment constraints, the reasonableness of such seizures depends on a balance between the public interest and the individual's right to personal security free from arbitrary interference by law officers. Id., at 20-21; *Camara v. Municipal Court*, 387 U.S. 523, 536-537 (1967).

The Government makes a convincing demonstration that the public interest demands effective measures to prevent the illegal entry of aliens at the Mexican border. Estimates of the number of illegal immigrants in the United States vary widely. A conservative estimate in 1972 produced a figure of about one million, but the INS now suggests there may be as many as 10 or 12 million aliens illegally in the country. Whatever the number, these aliens create significant economic and social problems, competing with citizens and legal resident aliens for jobs, and generating extra demand for social services. The aliens themselves are vulnerable to exploitation because they cannot complain of substandard working conditions without risking deportation. *See generally*, Hearings on Illegal Aliens before Subcommittee No. 1 of the *House Committee on the Judiciary*, 92d Cong., 1st and 2d Sess., ser. 13, pts. 1-5 (1971-1972).

The Government has estimated that 85% of the aliens illegally in the country are from Mexico. *United States v. Baca*, 368 F. Supp. 398, 402 (S.D. Cal. 1973). The Mexican border is almost 2,000 miles long, and even a vastly reinforced Border Patrol would find it impossible to prevent illegal border crossings. Many aliens cross the Mexican border on foot, miles away from patrolled areas, and then purchase transportation from the border area to inland cities, where they find jobs and elude the immigration authorities. Others gain entry on valid temporary border-crossing permits, but then violate the conditions of their entry. Most of these aliens leave the border area in private vehicles, often assisted by professional "alien smugglers." The Border Patrol's traffic-checking operations are designed to prevent this inland movement. They succeed in apprehending some illegal entrants and smugglers, and they deter the movement of others by threatening apprehension and increasing the cost of illegal transportation.

Against this valid public interest we must weigh the interference with individual liberty that results when an officer stops an automobile and questions its occupants. The intrusion is modest. The Government tells us that a stop by a roving patrol "usually consumes no more than a minute." There is no search of the vehicle or its occupants, and the visual inspection is limited to those parts of the vehicle that can be seen by anyone standing alongside. According to the Government, "[a]ll that is required of the vehicle's occupants is a response to a brief question or two and possibly the production of a document evidencing a right to be in the United States." Ibid.

Because of the limited nature of the intrusion, stops of this sort may be justified on facts that do not amount to the probable cause required for an arrest. In *Terry v. Ohio*, supra, the Court declined expressly to decide whether facts not amounting to probable cause could justify an "investigative 'seizure' " short of an arrest, 392 U.S., at 19 n. 16, but it approved a limited search—a pat-down for weapons—for the protection of an officer investigating suspicious behavior of persons he reasonably believed to be armed and dangerous. The Court approved such a search on facts that did not constitute probable cause to believe the suspects guilty of a crime, requiring only that "the police officer . . . be able to point to specific and articulable facts which, taken together with rational inferences from those facts, reasonably warrant" a belief that his safety or that of others is in danger. *Id.* at 21.

We are unwilling to let the Border Patrol dispense entirely with the requirement that officers must have a reasonable suspicion to justify roving-patrol stops. In the context of border area stops, the reasonableness requirement of the Fourth Amendment demands something more than the broad and unlimited discretion sought by the Government. Roads near the border carry not only aliens seeking to enter the country illegally, but a large volume of legitimate traffic as well. San Diego, with a metropolitan population of 1.4 million, is located on the border. Texas has two fairly large metropolitan areas directly on the border: El Paso, with a population of 360,000, and the Brownsville-McAllen area, with a combined population of 320,000. We are confident that substantially all of the traffic in these cities is lawful and that relatively few of their residents have any connection with the illegal entry and transportation of aliens. To approve roving-patrol stops of all vehicles in the border area, without any suspicion that a particular vehicle is carrying illegal immigrants, would subject the residents of these and other areas to potentially unlimited interference with their use of the highways, solely at the discretion of Border Patrol officers. The only formal limitation on that discretion appears to be the administrative regulation defining the term "reasonable distance" in § 287(a)(3) to mean within 100 air miles from the border. 8 C.F.R. § 287.1(a) (1975). Thus, if we approved the Government's position in this case, Border Patrol officers could stop motorists at random for questioning, day or night, anywhere within 100 air miles of the 2,000-mile border, on a city street, a busy highway, or a desert road, without any reason to suspect that they have violated any law.

We are not convinced that the legitimate needs of law enforcement require this degree of interference with lawful traffic.... [A] requirement of reasonable suspicion for stops allows the Government adequate means of guarding the public interest and also protects residents of the border areas from indiscriminate official interference.

* * *

The effect of our decision is to limit exercise of the authority granted by both § 287(a)(1) and § 287(a)(3). Except at the border and its functional equivalents, officers on roving patrol may stop vehicles only if they are aware of specific articulable facts, together with rational inferences from those facts, that reasonably warrant suspicion that the vehicles contain aliens who may be illegally in the country.

Note

In *Brignoni-Ponce*, the government argued that along the border, a person's Mexican ancestry satisfied the requirements of 8 U.S.C. § 1357. This argument was specifically rejected by the Court where they stated that "[t]he likelihood that any given person of Mexican ancestry is an alien is high enough to make Mexican appearance a relevant factor, but standing alone it does not justify stopping all Mexican-Americans to ask if they are aliens." 422 U.S. at 887. However, the BIA, in *Matter of King and Yang*, 16 I. & N. Dec. 502 (BIA 1978) held that the reasonable suspicion requirement was met where the person was of "oriental appearance," and worked at an establishment with a history of violations and the INS had received an anonymous tip. Would the fact that 8 U.S.C. § 1304(e) requires every adult alien to carry their certificate of alien registration or alien registration receipt card justify the INS officer's request for the document?

Smuggling Operations

What follows is an excerpt from the appendix to the concurring opinion by Chief Justice Burger in *Brignoni-Ponce*, citing from Judge Turrentine's opinion in *U.S. v. Baca*, 368 F. Supp. 398, 408 (S.D. Ca. 1973), which describes the *modus operandi* of smuggling operations:

1. Contact is made between the smuggler and the alien prior to the latter's leaving Mexico.

2. The aliens then make entry on foot, with possibly the aid of a "guide," or by use of temporary border passes. Then they enter vehicles approximately 2 or 20 miles inland after having passed through the Border Patrol's line watch activities.

3. To get through the traffic checkpoint they might use a "drop house," which acts as a staging area to keep the aliens awaiting inclement weather, or any event that might cause the checkpoint to close down temporarily. Or, they may use a "decoy" vehicle, which is a vehicle loaded with illegal aliens which it is anticipated will be stopped at the checkpoint and would therefore occupy the agents so that other vehicles could pass through without inspection. They even use "scout cars" to probe those roads where temporary checkpoints are maintained, so as to advise other vehicles whether it is safe to proceed.

4. The "load" vehicles themselves can be of any type of conveyance and the methods used to secrete aliens inside them are varied and often show some originality. Unfortunately, sometimes these are very dangerous to the aliens themselves. It has been reported, for example, that it is not at all unusual for an alien to die from asphyxiation while concealed in an automobile trunk or a tank car.

5. The cost of the transportation provided to the aliens is approximately $225 to $250 for each alien for the trip through the checkpoint on to the Los Angeles area. Since smuggling operations are almost exclusively "cash and carry" businesses and the average income among Mexican nationals who may wish to seek residence here illegally is quite small, this cost tends to act as a very significant deterrent in and of itself.

Blackie's House of Beef v. Castillo
659 F.2d 1211 (D.C. Cir. 1981), *cert. denied*, 455 U.S. 940 (1982)

McGOWAN, Circuit Judge.

In 1976, the INS began to receive information that illegal aliens were employed at Blackie's, a restaurant in the District of Columbia. One such indication was a sworn statement by an illegal alien who had been apprehended by the INS and was in the process of undergoing deportation hearings. This informant swore that he had worked at Blackie's and, furthermore, that he had personal knowledge that approximately 20 other illegal aliens were currently employed there. Another such affidavit was executed by an apprehended alien claiming to have worked at Blackie's. In addition to verifying the information provided in the first affidavit, the second informant indicated that "there were many Hispanics employed there and that the names of two illegal aliens who worked there were Rogelio and Pedro." Other information included three anonymous telephone calls in which informants notified the INS that Blackie's was employing illegal aliens. Finally, INS officers apprehended two illegal aliens who were carrying wage statements from Blackie's. The latter of the two swore by affidavit that Blackie's was employing illegal aliens from El Salvador and Africa, and supplied the first names of three such employees.

On the basis of this information, INS Agent Foster twice asked the owner and manager of Blackie's for permission to enter the restaurant and question suspected illegal aliens. Ulysses "Blackie" Auger twice refused such consent. After receiving the last of the above-described tips, Agent Foster again requested Auger's consent, which was again refused.

On March 17, 1978, Agent Foster presented the assembled evidence and accompanying affidavits to a federal magistrate, asking that "a search warrant be issued to any Agent of the Immigration and Naturalization Service authorizing him or them to enter with proper assistance ... [Blackie's] and there to search for and arrest the individuals subject to arrest pursuant to Title 8, United States Code, Section 1357." On March 27, 1978, the magistrate issued the requested warrant, which provided that INS agents might, within five days of the issuance of the warrant, search the "entire premises of Blackie's House of Beef" because "there is now being concealed certain persons namely Aliens who are believed to be in the United States in violation of ... Title 8, Section 1325 and Section 241(a)(2)." It was a standard form warrant, with the word "property" marked out and the word "persons" inserted in the above-quoted passage and in a subsequent passage providing that "there is probable cause to believe that the *persons* so described are being concealed on the person or premises above described." (emphasis added).

On March 30, 1978, INS agents executed the warrant, entering Blackie's Restaurant during the dinner hour. As noted on the return document, 15 employees were seized, at least 10 of whom proved to be illegal aliens subject to deportation.

Blackie's subsequently filed suit in the District Court for a declaratory judgment, injunctive relief, and damages, alleging that the search warrant was not supported by probable cause and thus violated the fourth amendment. In a memorandum opinion issued October 5, 1978, the District Court agreed that the warrant was invalid.

The INS continued to receive information that illegal aliens were being employed at Blackie's. The information—that upwards of 30 illegal aliens were currently employed at Blackie's—was supplied in an affidavit, dated October 27, 1978, by a previously reliable source. The affiant was quite specific, revealing names of suspected illegal aliens, explanations as to how he knew the suspects to be illegal aliens, and details as to the places in which such persons might be hiding.

To supplement this information, INS Agent Parry then surveyed Blackie's restaurant for several hours on October 23 and 24, 1978, and observed employees working both inside and outside the restaurant, eighteen of whom Parry believed to be aliens of Hispanic descent, principally because of their attire and seeming inability to speak any language but Spanish. In addition, Agent Riordan staked out Blackie's on October 27, and observed numerous persons of apparent Hispanic descent entering through the back doors of the restaurant.

Parry also stated that Blackie's was a known employer of illegal aliens. In support of this assertion, it was said that INS records showed that 48 illegal aliens employed by Blackie's have been apprehended by the Service since January 30, 1974. Further, attached to the affidavit was a recent Washington Post news story which reported the manager of Blackie's as having said that he hires foreign workers because of their reliability and that he does not demand to see their green cards (proof of legal immigrant status) except in Virginia.

*   *   *

On November 16, 1978, the magistrate issued a warrant, concluding that the INS had established probable cause to believe illegal aliens were present on Blackie's premises. Unlike the first warrant, this was not a form warrant, and Rule 41 was nowhere mentioned. Rather, the authority to search was premised upon sections 1357 and 1103 of the Immigration and Nationality Act, and the warrant was entitled "Order For Entry on Premises to Search for Aliens in the United States Without Legal Authority."

The warrant directed the INS to "enter the premises located on 22nd and M Streets, North West, Washington, D.C., in order to search for persons believed to be aliens in the United States without legal authority." The magistrate limited the INS's search to "the daylight hours and within 10 days of this order," and required a return within 10 days after completion of the search. The area for permissible search included "any locked rooms on the premises in order to locate aliens in the United States without legal authority."

On November 17, 1978, INS agents conducted a search of the public area, kitchen, and second-floor offices of Blackie's beginning at 11:12 A.M. and continuing for 23 minutes. During the 23-minute search, the INS removed 14 suspected illegal aliens from Blackie's, who were detained for an additional 10 minutes in an alley behind the restaurant while transportation to the local INS office was being arranged. The required warrant return was made on November 20, 1978, reciting the names and country of origin of 14 illegal aliens found on the premises. Ten patrons were observed in the restaurant during the search, and four more came in during the course of it.

Blackie's again filed suit for injunctive and declaratory relief, and for damages in the amount of $500,000, alleging that this second warrant violated the fourth amendment and that the search as executed was disruptive and exceeded all reasonable limits. Again the District Court, on defendants' motion to dismiss and cross-motions for summary judgment, held the warrant invalid, ruling that this second warrant failed to satisfy the fourth amendment requirement that "no Warrant shall issue, but upon probable cause, ... describing particularly ... the persons or things to be seized" because it failed to describe with particularity each alien sought. The court also objected to the magistrate's failure to signify, on the face of the warrant, that the magistrate had balanced the enforcement interests of the INS against the privacy interests of Blackie's, its employees, and its patrons. The district judge enjoined the INS from entering plaintiff's premises (except in exigent circumstances) without a warrant complying with the standards set forth in his second memorandum opinion. The plaintiff's actions against the defendants in their individual capacities were dismissed with prejudice.

*   *   *

The fourth amendment prohibits "unreasonable searches and seizures," requiring that "no Warrants shall issue, but upon probable cause, supported by Oath or affirmation, and particularly describing the place to be searched, and the persons or things to be seized." U.S. Const. Amend. IV. The warrant procedure contemplates that the necessity for every intrusion upon the privacy of an individual first be considered by a "neutral and detached magistrate instead of being judged by the officer engaged in the often competitive enterprise of ferreting out crime." *Johnson v. United States*, 333 U.S. 10, 14 (1948). This prior consideration must be more than pro forma: "[T]he magistrate must judge the reasonableness of every warrant in light of the circumstances of the particular case, carefully considering the description of the evidence sought, the situation of the premises, and the position and interests of the owner or occupant." *Zurcher v. Stanford Daily*, 436 U.S. at 570 (Powell, J., concurring). Our task in this case is to determine whether this warrant reflects careful and informed consideration by the magistrate, and reasonably "advise[s] the [subject] of the scope and objects of the search, beyond which limits the [officer] is not expected to proceed," *Marshall v. Barlow's, Inc.*, 436 U.S. 307, 323 (1978).

* * *

We think the District Court perceived correctly that the warrant at issue in this case was not comparable to the OSHA "routine inspection" warrant that the Supreme Court found to be constitutionally required in *Marshall v. Barlow's, Inc.*, 436 U.S. 307 (1978), because the nature of the two enforcement activities differs significantly. The INS sought to enter Blackie's to search for a particular violation, not to conduct a routine inspection of regulated industry premises, and therefore the "neutral standards" principle is inapposite.

The District Court erred, however, in failing to take this argument one step further and acknowledged that the situation also was not analogous to a criminal investigation. The Supreme Court has explicitly held that the detention and deportation of illegal aliens is not criminal law enforcement activity. *Harisiades v. Shaughnessy*, 342 U.S. 580, 594 (1952). There are no sanctions of any kind, criminal or otherwise, imposed by law upon a knowing employer of illegal aliens. This warrant in particular was issued to aid the agency in the enforcement of its statutory mandate, not to aid police in the enforcement of criminal laws.

We think that the District Court failed to recognize the unique aspects of an INS search, and thus erroneously concluded that Blackie's fourth amendment rights were violated by the second search warrant. Our decision rests on three determinations. First, we think that Congress, in passing the Immigration and Nationality Act, contemplated a vigorous enforcement program that might include INS entries onto private premises for the purpose of questioning "any alien or person believed to be an alien," and of detaining those aliens believed to be in this country illegally. Second, since an INS search is conducted pursuant to a civil administrative mandate, the warrant issued to permit such a search may therefore be evaluated under a standard of probable cause different from that applied to criminal warrants. *Marshall v. Barlow's, Inc.*, 436 U.S. 307 (1978). Last, we hold that the warrant in Blackie's II was properly tailored both to protect the fourth amendment rights of Blackie's and to aid the enforcement interests of the United States.

* * *

With the correct probable cause standard firmly in mind, we are forced to conclude that the District Court erred in striking down the warrant in Blackie's II. This warrant was as descriptive as was reasonably possible with respect to the persons sought, the place to be searched, and the time within which the search might take place. In our view, the warrant contained sufficient safeguards to assure that nothing impermissible would be left to the discretion of the INS agents. *Delaware v. Prouse*, 440 U.S. at 654.

The warrant was duly restricted to the location in which there was cause to believe aliens could be found: "the premises located at 22nd and M Streets, North West, Washington, D.C." It was also restricted as to the time within which the warrant could be executed, providing that execution must occur within 10 days of the order and during the daylight hours.

Furthermore, the INS was restricted as to how it could act once inside the premises. A search could only be conducted where aliens were likely to be hiding. Thus, the INS was proscribed from searching the files or books of Blackie's, and it is uncontroverted that they searched only those areas in which aliens were likely to be found. No private property of Blackie's within the premises was searched or seized.

*   *   *

Nor did the warrant leave impermissible discretion in the hands of the INS agents with respect to the persons sought to be questioned. The affidavits filed along with the application for search warrant suggested that numerous persons working in non-public areas of the restaurant were possibly illegal aliens, and gave credible reasons for the affiants' suspicions as well.

Taken in conjunction with the warrant, which authorized the INS to enter the premises and make a search "including, but not limited to, the search of any locked rooms on the premises in order to locate aliens in the United States without legal authority," these papers establish that the INS agents were empowered to enter Blackie's only for the purpose of questioning those employees whom the agents might reasonably suspect of being illegal aliens, on the basis of the information in the warrant and the standards set down for the questioning of suspected aliens in *Yam Sang Kwai v. INS*, 411 F.2d 683, 687 (D.C. Cir. 1969). As we noted above, some amount of questioning is always necessary in such a situation, as this court recognized when it held in *Yam Sang Kwai* that INS agents may question a person merely upon the articulable suspicion that the person is an alien. This warrant and accompanying affidavits narrowed down the field of potentially vulnerable persons to those employees whom INS agents might reasonably believe to be aliens. We think this was precisely within the contemplation of the Act, and "reasonable" within the meaning of the fourth amendment.

Our view as to the propriety of this warrant is also influenced by the significant amount of supporting evidence that accompanied the application for warrant. These included one affidavit summarizing two separate day-long surveillances of Blackie's, and a lengthy affidavit from an anonymous informant who claimed to have worked at Blackie's. The informant identified suspects by first names, described the layout of Blackie's Restaurant, and gave other indicia as to his credibility. The officers' surveillance of Blackie's corroborated the information set forth in the anonymous affiant's statement to the effect that Blackie's employed numerous persons of foreign appearance who were unable to speak English. On the basis of these three independent sources of information, it could be reasonably supposed that persons likely to be illegal aliens were being employed in Blackie's.

Note

As noted in the preceding case, the INS affidavits contained evidence as to Ulysses Auger's suspected employment of illegal aliens, including first names and descriptions of some suspected illegal aliens. The descriptions were provided by anonymous informants describing the suspects as persons dressed in "foreign-style apparel, who appeared to speak no English." What should an INS officer be required to show in order to be able to obtain a search warrant? Should the fact that criminal statutes are not being violated in any way change the standard?

I.N.S. v. Delgado
466 U.S. 210 (1984)

Justice REHNQUIST delivered the opinion of the Court.

In the course of enforcing the immigration laws, petitioner Immigration and Naturalization Service (INS) enters employers' worksites to determine whether any illegal aliens may be present as employees. The Court of Appeals for the Ninth Circuit held that the "factory surveys" involved in this case amounted to a seizure of the entire work forces, and further held that the INS could not question individual employees during any of these surveys unless its agents had a reasonable suspicion that the employee to be questioned was an illegal alien. *ILGWU v. Sureck*, 681 F.2d 624 (9th Cir. 1982). We conclude that these factory surveys did not result in the seizure of the entire work forces, and that the individual questioning of the respondents in this case by INS agents concerning their citizenship did not amount to a detention or seizure under the Fourth Amendment. Accordingly, we reverse the judgment of the Court of Appeals.

Acting pursuant to two warrants, in January and September, 1977, the INS conducted a survey of the work force at Southern California Davis Pleating Company (Davis Pleating) in search of illegal aliens. The warrants were issued on a showing of probable cause by the INS that numerous illegal aliens were employed at Davis Pleating, although neither of the search warrants identified any particular illegal aliens by name. A third factory survey was conducted with the employer's consent in October, 1977, at Mr. Pleat, another garment factory.

At the beginning of the surveys several agents positioned themselves near the buildings' exits, while other agents dispersed throughout the factory to question most, but not all, employees at their work stations. The agents displayed badges, carried walkie-talkies, and were armed, although at no point during any of the surveys was a weapon ever drawn. Moving systematically through the factory, the agents approached employees and, after identifying themselves, asked them from one to three questions relating to their citizenship. If the employee gave a credible reply that he was a United States citizen, the questioning ended, and the agent moved on to another employee. If the employee gave an unsatisfactory response or admitted that he was an alien, the employee was asked to produce his immigration papers. During the survey, employees continued with their work and were free to walk around within the factory.

*   *   *

The Fourth Amendment does not proscribe all contact between the police and citizens, but is designed "to prevent arbitrary and oppressive interference by law enforcement officials with the privacy and personal security of individuals." *United States v. Martinez-Fuerte*, 428 U.S. 543, 554 (1976). Given the diversity of encounters between police officers and citizens, however, the Court has been cautious in defining the limits imposed by the Fourth Amendment on encounters between the police and citizens. As we have noted elsewhere, "Obviously, not all personal intercourse between policemen and citizens involves 'seizures' of persons. Only when the officer, by means of physical force or show of authority, has restrained the liberty of a citizen may we conclude that a 'seizure' has occurred." *Terry v. Ohio*, 392 U.S. 1, 19, n.16 (1968). While applying such a test is relatively straightforward in a situation resembling a traditional arrest, the protection against unreasonable seizures also extends to "seizures that involve only a brief detention short of traditional arrest." *United States v. Brignoni-Ponce*, 422 U.S. 873, 878 (1975). What has evolved from our cases is a determination that an initially consensual encounter between a police officer and a citizen can be transformed into a seizure or detention within the meaning of the Fourth Amendment, "if, in view of all the circumstances surrounding the incident, a reasonable person would have believed that he was not free to leave." *Mendenhall*, 446 U.S. at 554 (footnote omitted).

Although we have yet to rule directly on whether mere questioning of an individual by a police official, without more, can amount to a seizure under the Fourth Amendment, our recent decision in *Royer*, plainly implies that interrogation relating to one's identity or a request for identification by the police does not, by itself, constitute a Fourth Amendment seizure. In *Royer*, when DEA agents found that the respondent matched a drug courier profile, the agents approached the defendant and asked him for his airplane ticket and driver's license, which the agents then examined. A majority of the Court believed that the request and examination of the documents was "permissible in themselves." *Id.* (plurality opinion), see *id.*, at 523, n.3 (opinion of Rehnquist, J.). In contrast, a much different situation prevailed in *Brown v. Texas*, 443 U.S. 47 (1979), when two policemen physically detained the defendant to determine his identity, after the defendant refused the officers' request to identify himself. The Court held that absent some reasonable suspicion of misconduct, the detention of the defendant to determine his identity violated the defendant's Fourth Amendment right to be free from an unreasonable seizure. *Id.*, at 52.

What is apparent from *Royer* and *Brown* is that police questioning, by itself, is unlikely to result in a Fourth Amendment violation. While most citizens will respond to a police request, the fact that people do so, and do so without being told they are free not to respond, hardly eliminates the consensual nature of the response. Unless the circumstances of the encounter are so intimidating as to demonstrate that a reasonable person would have believed he was not free to leave if he had not responded, one cannot say that the questioning resulted in a detention under the Fourth Amendment. But if the person refuses to answer and the police take additional steps—such as those taken in *Brown*—to obtain an answer, then the Fourth Amendment imposes some minimal level of objective justification to validate the detention or seizure.

The Court of Appeals held that "the manner in which the factory surveys were conducted in this case constituted a seizure of the workforce" under the Fourth Amendment. 681 F.2d, at 634. While the element of surprise and the systematic questioning of individual workers by several INS agents contributed to the court's holding, the pivotal factor in its decision was the stationing of INS agents near the exits of the factory buildings. According to the Court of Appeals, the stationing of agents near the doors meant that "departures were not to be contemplated," and thus, workers were "not free to leave." *Ibid.* In support of the decision below, respondents argue that the INS created an intimidating psychological environment when it intruded unexpectedly into the workplace with such a show of officers. Besides the stationing of agents near the exits, respondents add that the length of the survey and the failure to inform workers they were free to leave resulted in a Fourth Amendment seizure of the entire work force.

We reject the claim that the entire work forces of the two factories were seized for the duration of the surveys when the INS placed agents near the exits of the factory sites. Ordinarily, when people are at work their freedom to move about has been meaningfully restricted, not by the actions of law enforcement officials, but by the workers' voluntary obligations to their employers. The record indicates that when these surveys were initiated, the employees were about their ordinary business, operating machinery and performing other job assignments. While the surveys did cause some disruption, including the efforts of some workers to hide, the record also indicates that workers were not prevented by the agents from moving about the factories.

Respondents argue, however, that the stationing of agents near the factory doors showed the INS's intent to prevent people from leaving. But there is nothing in the record indicating that this is what the agents at the doors actually did. The obvious purpose of the agents' presence at the factory doors was to insure that all persons in the factories were questioned. The record indicates that the INS agents' conduct in this case consisted simply of questioning employees and arresting those they had probable cause to believe were unlawfully present in the factory. This conduct should have given respondents no reason to believe that they would be detained if they gave truthful answers to the questions put to them or if they simply refused to answer. If mere questioning does not constitute a seizure when it occurs inside the factory, it is no more a seizure when it occurs at the exits.

A similar conclusion holds true for all other citizens or aliens lawfully present inside the factory buildings during the surveys. The presence of agents by the exits posed no reasonable threat of detention to these workers while they walked throughout the factories on job assignments. Likewise, the mere possibility that they would be questioned if they sought to leave the buildings should not have resulted in any reasonable apprehension by any of them that they would be seized or detained in any meaningful way. Since most workers could have had no reasonable fear that they would be detained upon leaving, we conclude that the work forces as a whole were not seized.

The Court of Appeals also held that "detentive questioning" of individuals could be conducted only if INS agents could articulate "objective facts providing investigators with a reasonable suspicion that each questioned person, so detained, is an alien illegally in the country." 681 F.2d, at 638. Under our analysis, however, since there was no seizure of the work forces by virtue of the method of conducting the factory surveys, the only way the issue of individual questioning could be presented would be if one of the named respondents had in fact been seized or detained. Reviewing the deposition testimony of respondents, we conclude that none were.

The questioning of each respondent by INS agents seems to have been nothing more than a brief encounter. None of the three Davis Pleating employees were questioned during the January survey. During the September survey at Davis Pleating, respondent Delgado was discussing the survey with another employee when two INS agents approached him and asked him where he was from and from what city. When Delgado informed them that he came from Mayaguez, Puerto Rico, the agent made an innocuous observation to his partner and left. Respondent Correa's experience in the September survey was similar. Walking from one part of the factory to another, Correa was stopped by an INS agent and asked where she was born. When she replied "Huntington Park (California)," the agent walked away and Correa continued about her business. Respondent Labonte, the third Davis Pleating employee, was tapped on the shoulder and asked in Spanish, "Where are your papers?" Labonte responded that she had her papers and without any further request from the INS agents, showed the papers to the agents, who then left. Finally, respondent Miramontes, the sole Mr. Pleat employee involved in this case, encountered an agent en route from an office to her worksite. Questioned concerning her citizenship, Miramontes replied that she was a resident alien, and on the agent's request, produced her work permit. The agent then left.

Respondents argue that the manner in which the surveys were conducted and the attendant disruption caused by the surveys created a psychological environment which made them reasonably afraid they were not free to leave. Consequently, when respondents were approached by INS agents and questioned concerning their citizenship and right to work, they were effectively detained under the Fourth Amendment, since they reasonably feared that refusing to answer would have resulted in their arrest. But it was obvious from the beginning of the surveys that the INS agents were only questioning people. Persons such as respondents who simply went about their business in the workplace were not detained in any way; nothing more occurred than that a question was put to them. While persons who attempted to flee or evade the agents may eventually have been detained for questioning, respondents did not do so and were not in fact detained. The manner in which respondents were questioned, given its obvious purpose, could hardly result in a reasonable fear that respondents were not free to continue working or to move about the factory. Respondents may only litigate what happened to them, and our review of their description of the encounters with the INS agents satisfies us that the encounters were classic consensual encounters rather than Fourth Amendment seizures.

Accordingly, the judgment of the Court of Appeals is Reversed.

Justice BRENNAN, with whom Justice MARSHALL joins, concurring in part and dissenting in part.

As part of its ongoing efforts to enforce the immigration laws, the Immigration and Naturalization Service (INS) conducts "surveys" of those workplaces that it has reason to believe employ large numbers of undocumented aliens who may be subject to deportation. This case presents the question whether the INS's method of carrying out these "factory surveys" violates the rights of the affected factory workers to be secure against unreasonable seizures of one's person as guaranteed by the Fourth Amendment. Answering that question, the Court today holds, first, that the INS surveys involved here did not result in the seizure of the entire factory workforce for the complete duration of the surveys, and, second, that the individual questioning of respondents by INS agents concerning their citizenship did not constitute seizures within the meaning of the Fourth Amendment. Although I generally agree with the Court's first conclusion, I am convinced that a fair application of our prior decisions to the facts of this case compels the conclusion that respondents were unreasonably seized by INS agents in the course of these factory surveys.

* * *

Contrary to the Court's suggestion, we have repeatedly considered whether and, if so, under what circumstances questioning of an individual by law enforcement officers may amount to a seizure within the meaning of the Fourth Amendment. *See,* e.g., *Terry v. Ohio,* 392 U.S. 1 (1968); *Brown v. Texas,* 443 U.S. 47 (1979); *United States v. Mendenhall,* 446 U.S. 544 (1980); *Florida v. Royer,* 460 U.S. 491 (1983). Of course, as these decisions recognize, the question does not admit of any simple answer. The difficulty springs from the inherent tension between our commitment to safeguarding the precious, and all too fragile, right to go about one's business free from unwarranted government interference, and our recognition that the police must be allowed some latitude in gathering information from those individuals who are willing to cooperate. Given these difficulties, it is perhaps understandable that our efforts to strike an appropriate balance have not produced uniform results. Nevertheless, the outline of what appears to be the appropriate inquiry has been traced over the years with some clarity.

The Court launched its examination of this issue in *Terry v. Ohio, supra,* (1968), by explaining that "the Fourth Amendment governs 'seizures' of the person which do not eventuate in a trip to the station house and prosecution for crime—'arrests' in traditional terminology. *It must be recognized that whenever a police officer accosts an individual and restrains his freedom to walk away, he has "seized" that person."* *Id.* at 16 (emphasis added). Such a seizure, the Court noted, may be evidenced by either "physical force or a show of authority" indicating that the individual's liberty has been restrained. *Id.,* at 19, n.16. The essential teaching of the Court's decision in *Terry*—that an individual's right to personal security and freedom must be respected even in encounters with the police that fall short of full arrest—has been consistently reaffirmed. In *Davis v. Mississippi,* 394 U.S. 721, 726-727 (1969), for example, the Court confirmed that investigatory detentions implicate the protections of the Fourth Amendment and further explained that "while the police have the right to request citizens to answer voluntarily questions concerning unsolved crimes they have no right to compel them to answer." *Id.,* at 727, n.6. Similarly, in *Brown v. Texas,* 443 U.S. 47 (1979), we overturned a conviction for refusing to stop and identify oneself to police, because, in making the stop, the police lacked any "reasonable suspicion, based on objective facts, that the individual [was] involved in criminal activity." *Id.,* at 51. The animating principle underlying this unanimous decision was that the Fourth Amendment protects an individual's personal security and privacy from unreasonable interference by the police, even when that interference amounts to no more than a brief stop and questioning concerning one's identity.

Although it was joined at the time by only one other Member of this Court, Justice Stewart's plurality opinion in *United States v. Mendenhall,* 446 U.S. 544 (1980), offered a helpful, preliminary distillation of the lessons of these cases. Noting first that "as long as the person to whom questions are put remains free to disregard the questions and walk away, there has been no intrusion upon that person's liberty or privacy," Justice Stewart explained that "a person has been seized within the meaning of the Fourth Amendment only if, in view of all the circumstances surrounding the incident, a reasonable person would have believed that he was not free to leave." *Id.*, at 554. The opinion also suggested that such circumstances might include "the threatening presence of several officers, the display of a weapon by an officer, some physical touching of the person of the citizen, or the use of language or tone of voice indicating that compliance with the officer's request might be compelled." *Ibid.*

A majority of the Court has since adopted that formula as the appropriate standard for determining when inquiries made by the police cross the boundary separating merely consensual encounters from forcible stops to investigate a suspected crime. This rule properly looks not to the subjective impressions of the person questioned but rather to the objective characteristics of the encounter which may suggest whether or not a reasonable person would believe that he remained free during the course of the questioning to disregard the questions and walk away. *See*, 3 W. LaFave, *Search and Seizure*, § 9.2, p. 52 (1978). The governing principles that should guide us in this difficult area were summarized in the *Royer* plurality opinion:

> [L]aw enforcement officers do not violate the Fourth Amendment by merely approaching an individual on the street or in another public place, by asking him if he is willing to answer some questions, by putting questions to him if the person is willing to listen, or by offering in evidence in a criminal prosecution his voluntary answers to such questions. Nor would the fact that the officer identifies himself as a police officer, without more, convert the encounter into a seizure requiring some level of objective justification. The person approached, however, need not answer any question put to him; indeed, he may decline to listen to the questions at all and may go on his way. *He may not be detained even momentarily without reasonable, objective grounds for doing so; and his refusal to listen or to answer does not, without more, furnish those grounds.*

460 U.S. at 497-498 (citations omitted) (emphasis added).

Applying these principles to the facts of this case, I have no difficulty concluding that respondents were seized within the meaning of the Fourth Amendment when they were accosted by the INS agents and questioned concerning their right to remain in the United States. Although none of the respondents was physically restrained by the INS agents during the questioning, it is nonetheless plain beyond cavil that the manner in which the INS conducted these surveys demonstrated a "show of authority" of sufficient size and force to overbear the will of any reasonable person. Faced with such tactics, a reasonable person could not help but feel compelled to stop and provide answers to the INS agents' questions. The Court's efforts to avoid this conclusion are rooted more in fantasy than in the record of this case. The Court goes astray, in my view, chiefly because it insists upon considering each interrogation in isolation as if respondents had been questioned by the INS in a setting similar to an encounter between a single police officer and a lone passerby that might occur on a street corner. Obviously, once the Court begins with such an unrealistic view of the facts, it is only a short step to the equally fanciful conclusion that respondents acted voluntarily when they stopped and answered the agents' questions.

*   *   *

The Court's eagerness to conclude that these interrogations did not represent seizures is to some extent understandable, of course, because such a conclusion permits the Court to avoid the imposing task of justifying these seizures on the basis of reasonable, objective criteria as required by the Fourth Amendment.

The reasonableness requirement of the Fourth Amendment applies to all seizures of the person, including those that involve only a brief detention short of traditional arrest. But because the intrusion upon an individual's personal security and privacy is limited in cases of this sort, we have explained that brief detentions may be justified on "facts that do not amount to the probable cause required for an arrest." *United States v. Brignoni-Ponce*, 422 U.S. 873, 880 (1975). Nevertheless, our prior decisions also make clear that investigatory stops of the kind at issue here "must be justified by some objective manifestation that the person stopped is, or is about to be, engaged in criminal activity." *United States v. Cortez*, 449 U.S. 411, 417 (1981). As the Court stated in *Terry*, the "demand for specificity in the information upon which police action is predicated is the central teaching of this Court's Fourth Amendment jurisprudence." 392 U.S., at 21, n.18. Repeatedly, we have insisted that police may not detain and interrogate an individual unless they have reasonable grounds for suspecting that the person is involved in some unlawful activity. In *United States v. Brignoni-Ponce, supra,* for instance, the Court held that "[border patrol] officers on roving patrol may stop vehicles only if they are aware of specific articulable facts, together with rational inferences from those facts, that reasonably warrant suspicion that the vehicles contain aliens who may be illegally in the country." *Id.,* at 884. This requirement of particularized suspicion provides the chief protection of lawful citizens against unwarranted governmental interference with their personal security and privacy.

* * *

No one doubts that the presence of large numbers of undocumented aliens in this country creates law enforcement problems of titanic proportions for the INS. Nor does anyone question that this agency must be afforded considerable latitude in meeting its delegated enforcement responsibilities. I am afraid, however, that the Court has become so mesmerized by the magnitude of the problem that it has too easily allowed Fourth Amendment freedoms to be sacrificed. Before we discard all efforts to respect the commands of the Fourth Amendment in this troubling area, however, it is worth remembering that the difficulties faced by the INS today are partly of our own making.

The INS methods under review in this case are, in my view, more the product of expedience than of prudent law enforcement policy. The Immigration and Nationality Act establishes a quota-based system for regulating the admission of immigrants to this country which is designed to operate primarily at our borders. *See,* 8 U.S.C. §§ 1151-1153, 1221-1225 (1982). *See generally, Developments,* 96 Harv. L. Rev., at 1334-1369. With respect to Mexican immigration, however, this system has almost completely broken down. This breakdown is due in part, of course, to the considerable practical problems of patrolling a 2000-mile border; it is, however, also the result of our failure to commit sufficient resources to the border patrol effort. Furthermore, the Act expressly exempts American businesses that employ undocumented aliens from all criminal sanctions, 8 U.S.C. § 1324(a), thereby adding to the already powerful incentives for aliens to cross our borders illegally in search of employment.

[8 U.S.C. §§ 1357 (a) and (d) which appear below were
added by the Immigration Reform and Control Act of 1986,
Pub. L. No. 99-603, 100 Stat. 3359.]

(a) Any officer or employee of the Service authorized under regulations prescribed
by the Attorney General shall have power without warrant—

(1) to interrogate any alien or person believed to be an alien as to his right to
be or to remain in the United States;

(2) to arrest any alien who in his presence or view is entering or attempting to
enter the United States in violation of any law or regulation made in pursuance of
law regulating the admission, exclusion or expulsion of aliens, or to arrest any alien
in the United States in violation of any such law or regulation and is likely to escape
before a warrant can be obtained for his arrest, but the alien arrested shall be taken
without unnecessary delay for examination before an officer of the Service having
authority to examine aliens as to their right to enter or remain in the United States;

(3) within a reasonable distance from any external boundary of the United States,
to board and search for aliens any vessel within the territorial waters of the United
States and any railway car, aircraft, conveyance, or vehicle, and within a distance of
twenty-five miles from any such external boundary to have access to private lands,
but not dwellings for the purpose of patrolling the border to prevent the illegal entry
of aliens into the United States....

*   *   *

(d) Notwithstanding any other provision of this section other than paragraph (3) of
subsection (a), an officer or employee of the Service may not enter without the consent
of the owner [or agent thereof] or a properly executed warrant onto the premises of
a farm or other outdoor agricultural operation for the purpose of interrogating a
person believed to be an alien as to the person's right to be or to remain in the United
States.

Notes

1. Does 8 U.S.C. § 1357(e) which requires the INS to obtain a warrant or
permission of the farm owner prior to conducting a search create a justifiable disparity
in treatment between farmers and factory owners?

2. How can such distinctions be justified both in terms of national policy and
the Constitution?

E. The Exclusionary Rule

I.N.S. v. Lopez-Mendoza
468 U.S. 1032 (1984)

Justice O'CONNOR delivered the opinion of the Court.

This litigation requires us to decide whether an admission of unlawful presence
in this country made subsequent to an allegedly unlawful arrest must be excluded as

evidence in a civil deportation hearing. We hold that the exclusionary rule need not be applied in such a proceeding.

Respondents Adan Lopez-Mendoza and Elias Sandoval-Sanchez, both citizens of Mexico, were summoned to separate deportation proceedings in California and Washington, and both were ordered deported. They challenged the regularity of those proceedings on grounds related to the lawfulness of their respective arrests by officials of the Immigration and Naturalization Service (INS). On administrative appeal the Board of Immigration Appeals (BIA), an agency of the Department of Justice, affirmed the deportation orders.

The Court of Appeals for the Ninth Circuit, sitting en banc, reversed Sandoval's deportation order and vacated and remanded Lopez-Mendoza's deportation order. 705 F.2d 1059 (1983). It ruled that Sandoval's admission of his illegal presence in this country was the fruit of an unlawful arrest, and that the exclusionary rule applied in a deportation proceeding. Lopez-Mendoza's deportation order was vacated and his case remanded to the BIA to determine whether the Fourth Amendment had been violated in the course of his arrest.

Respondent Lopez-Mendoza was arrested in 1976 by INS agents at his place of employment, a transmission repair shop in San Mateo, Cal. Responding to a tip, INS investigators arrived at the shop shortly before 8 a.m. The agents had not sought a warrant to search the premises or to arrest any of its occupants. The proprietor of the shop firmly refused to allow the agents to interview his employees during working hours. Nevertheless, while one agent engaged the proprietor in conversation another entered the shop and approached Lopez-Mendoza. In response to the agent's questioning, Lopez-Mendoza gave his name and indicated that he was from Mexico with no close family ties in the United States. The agent then placed him under arrest. Lopez-Mendoza underwent further questioning at INS offices, where he admitted he was born in Mexico, was still a citizen of Mexico, and had entered this country without inspection by immigration authorities. Based on his answers, the agents prepared a "Record of Deportable Alien" (Form I-213), and an affidavit which Lopez-Mendoza executed, admitting his Mexican nationality and his illegal entry into this country.

A hearing was held before an Immigration Judge. Lopez-Mendoza's counsel moved to terminate the proceeding on the ground that Lopez-Mendoza had been arrested illegally. The judge ruled that the legality of the arrest was not relevant to the deportation proceeding and therefore declined to rule on the legality of Lopez-Mendoza's arrest. *Matter of Lopez-Mendoza*, No. A22 452 208 (INS, Dec. 21, 1977). The Form I-213 and the affidavit executed by Lopez-Mendoza were received into evidence without objection from Lopez-Mendoza. On the basis of this evidence the Immigration Judge found Lopez-Mendoza deportable. Lopez-Mendoza was granted the option of voluntary departure.

The BIA dismissed Lopez-Mendoza's appeal. It noted that "[t]he mere fact of an illegal arrest has no bearing on a subsequent deportation proceeding," and observed that Lopez-Mendoza had not objected to the admission into evidence of Form I-213 and the affidavit he had executed. The BIA also noted that the exclusionary rule is not applied to redress the injury to the privacy of the search victim, and that the BIA had previously concluded that application of the rule in deportation proceedings to deter unlawful INS conduct was inappropriate. *Matter of Sandoval*, 17 I. & N. Dec. 70 (BIA 1979).

The Court of Appeals vacated the order of deportation and remanded for a determination whether Lopez-Mendoza's Fourth Amendment rights had been violated when he was arrested.

Respondent Sandoval-Sanchez (who is not the same individual who was involved in *Matter of Sandoval*, supra) was arrested in 1977 at his place of employment, a potato processing plant in Pasco, Wash. INS Agent Bower and other officers went to the plant, with the permission of its personnel manager, to check for illegal aliens. During a change in shift officers stationed themselves at the exits while Bower and a uniformed Border Patrol agent entered the plant. They went to the lunchroom and identified themselves as immigration officers. Many people in the room rose and headed for the exits or milled around; others in the plant left their equipment and started running; still others who were entering the plant turned around and started walking back out. The two officers eventually stationed themselves at the main entrance to the plant and looked for passing employees who averted their heads, avoided eye contact, or tried to hide themselves in a group. Those individuals were addressed with innocuous questions in English. Any who could not respond in English and who otherwise aroused Agent Bower's suspicions were questioned in Spanish as to their right to be in the United States.

Respondent Sandoval-Sanchez was in a line of workers entering the plant. Sandoval-Sanchez testified that he did not realize that immigration officers were checking people entering the plant, but that he did see standing at the plant entrance a man in uniform who appeared to be a police officer. Agent Bower testified that it was probable that he, not his partner, had questioned Sandoval-Sanchez at the plant, but that he could not be absolutely positive. The employee he thought he remembered as Sandoval-Sanchez had been "very evasive," had averted his head, turned around, and walked away when he saw Agent Bower. Bower was certain that no one was questioned about his status unless his actions had given the agents reason to believe that he was an undocumented alien.

Thirty-seven employees, including Sandoval-Sanchez, were briefly detained at the plant and then taken to the county jail. About one-third immediately availed themselves of the option of voluntary departure and were put on a bus to Mexico. Sandoval-Sanchez exercised his right to a deportation hearing. Sandoval-Sanchez was then questioned further, and Agent Bower recorded Sandoval-Sanchez's admission of unlawful entry. Sandoval contends he was not aware that he had a right to remain silent.

At his deportation hearing Sandoval-Sanchez contended that the evidence offered by the INS should be suppressed as the fruit of an unlawful arrest. The Immigration Judge considered and rejected Sandoval-Sanchez's claim that he had been illegally arrested, but ruled in the alternative that the legality of the arrest was not relevant to the deportation hearing. *Matter of Sandoval-Sanchez*, No. A22 346 925 (INS, Oct. 7, 1977). Based on the written record of Sandoval-Sanchez's admissions the Immigration Judge found him deportable and granted him voluntary departure. The BIA dismissed Sandoval-Sanchez's appeal. *In re Sandoval-Sanchez*, No. A22 346 925 (BIA, Feb. 21, 1980). It concluded that the circumstances of the arrest had not affected the voluntariness of his recorded admission, and again declined to invoke the exclusionary rule, relying on its earlier decision in *Matter of Sandoval*, supra.

On appeal the Court of Appeals concluded that Sandoval-Sanchez's detention by the immigration officers violated the Fourth Amendment, that the statements he made were a product of that detention, and that the exclusionary rule barred their use in a deportation hearing. The deportation order against Sandoval-Sanchez was accordingly reversed.

A deportation proceeding is a purely civil action to determine eligibility to remain in this country, not to punish an unlawful entry, though entering or remaining unlawfully in this country is itself a crime. 8 U.S.C. §§ 1302, 1306, 1325. The deportation hearing looks prospectively, to the respondent's right to remain in this country in the future. Past conduct is relevant only insofar as it may shed light on the respondent's right to remain. See 8 U.S.C. §§ 1251, 1252(b); *Bugajewitz v. Adams*, 228 U.S. 585, 591 (1913); *Fong Yue Ting v. United States*, 149 U.S. 698, 730 (1893).

A deportation hearing is held before an immigration judge. The judge's sole power is to order deportation; the judge cannot adjudicate guilt or punish the respondent for any crime related to unlawful entry into or presence in this country. Consistent with the civil nature of the proceeding, various protections that apply in the context of a criminal trial do not apply in a deportation hearing. The respondent must be given "a reasonable opportunity to be present at [the] proceeding," but if the respondent fails to avail himself of that opportunity the hearing may proceed in his absence. 8 U.S.C. § 1252(b). In many deportation cases the INS must show only identity and alienage; the burden then shifts to the respondent to prove the time, place, and manner of his entry. See 8 U.S.C. § 1361; *Matter of Sandoval, supra*. A decision of deportability need be based only on "reasonable, substantial, and probative evidence," 8 U.S.C. § 1252(b)(4). The BIA for its part has required only "clear, unequivocal and convincing" evidence of the respondent's deportability, not proof beyond a reasonable doubt. 8 C.F.R. § 242.14(a) (1984). The Courts of Appeals have held, for example, that the absence of Miranda warnings does not render an otherwise voluntary statement by the respondent inadmissible in a deportation case. *Navia-Duran v. INS*, 568 F.2d 803, 808 (1st Cir. 1977); *Avila-Gallegos v. INS*, 525 F.2d 666, 667 (2d Cir. 1975); *Chavez-Raya v. INS*, 519 F.2d 397, 399-401 (7th Cir. 1975). *See also Abel v. United States*, 362 U.S. 217, 236-237 (1960) (search permitted incidental to an arrest pursuant to an administrative warrant issued by the INS); *Galvan v. Press*, 347 U.S. 522, 531, 911 (1954) (Ex Post Facto Clause has no application to deportation); *Carlson v. Landon*, 342 U.S. 524, 544-546 (1952) (Eighth Amendment does not require bail to be granted in certain deportation cases); *United States ex rel. Bilokumsky v. Tod*, 263 U.S. 149, 157 (1923) (involuntary confessions admissible at deportation hearing). In short, a deportation hearing is intended to provide a streamlined determination of eligibility to remain in this country, nothing more. The purpose of deportation is not to punish past transgressions but rather to put an end to a continuing violation of the immigration laws.

The "body" or identity of a defendant or respondent in a criminal or civil proceeding is never itself suppressible as a fruit of an unlawful arrest, even if it is conceded that an unlawful arrest, search, or interrogation occurred. A similar rule applies in forfeiture proceedings directed against contraband or forfeitable property. See, e.g., *United States v. Eighty-Eight Thousand, Five Hundred Dollars*, 671 F.2d 293 (8th Cir. 1982).

*   *   *

Respondent Sandoval has a more substantial claim. He objected not to his compelled presence at a deportation proceeding, but to evidence offered at that proceeding. The general rule in a criminal proceeding is that statements and other evidence obtained as a result of an unlawful, warrantless arrest are suppressible if the link between the evidence and the unlawful conduct is not too attenuated. *Wong Sun v. United States*, 371 U.S. 471 (1963). The reach of the exclusionary rule beyond the context of a criminal prosecution, however, is less clear. Although this Court has once stated in dictum that "[i]t may be assumed that evidence obtained by the [Labor] Department through an illegal search and seizure cannot be made the basis of a finding in deportation proceedings," *United States ex rel. Bilokumsky v. Tod, supra*, 263 U.S., at 155, the Court has never squarely addressed the question before. . . .

In *United States v. Janis*, 428 U.S. 433 (1976), this Court set forth a framework for deciding in what types of proceeding application of the exclusionary rule is appropriate. Imprecise as the exercise may be, the Court recognized in *Janis* that there is no choice but to weigh the likely social benefits of excluding unlawfully seized evidence against the likely costs. On the benefit side of the balance "the 'prime purpose' of the [exclusionary] rule, if not the sole one, 'is to deter future unlawful police conduct.' " *Id.*, at 446 citing *United States v. Calandra*, 414 U.S. 338, 347 (1974). On the cost side there is the loss of often probative evidence and all of the secondary costs that flow from the less accurate or more cumbersome adjudication that therefore occurs.

At stake in *Janis* was application of the exclusionary rule in a federal civil tax assessment proceeding following the unlawful seizure of evidence by state, not federal, officials. The Court noted at the outset that "[i]n the complex and turbulent history of the rule, the Court never has applied it to exclude evidence from a civil proceeding, federal or state." 428 U.S., at 447. Two factors in *Janis* suggested that the deterrence value of the exclusionary rule in the context of that case was slight. First, the state law enforcement officials were already "punished" by the exclusion of the evidence in the state criminal trial as a result of the same conduct. *Id.*, at 448. Second, the evidence was also excludable in any federal criminal trial that might be held. Both factors suggested that further application of the exclusionary rule in the federal civil proceeding would contribute little more to the deterrence of unlawful conduct by state officials. On the cost side of the balance, Janis focused simply on the loss of "concededly relevant and reliable evidence." *Id.*, at 447. The Court concluded that, on balance, this cost outweighed the likely social benefits achievable through application of the exclusionary rule in the federal civil proceeding.

While it seems likely that the deterrence value of applying the exclusionary rule in deportation proceedings would be higher than it was in *Janis*, it is also quite clear that the social costs would be very much greater as well. Applying the *Janis* balancing test to the benefits and costs of excluding concededly reliable evidence from a deportation proceeding, we therefore reach the same conclusion as in *Janis*.

The likely deterrence value of the exclusionary rule in deportation proceedings is difficult to assess. On the one hand, a civil deportation proceeding is a civil complement to a possible criminal prosecution, and to this extent it resembles the civil proceeding under review in *Janis*. The INS does not suggest that the exclusionary rule should not continue to apply in criminal proceedings against an alien who unlawfully enters or remains in this country, and the prospect of losing evidence that might otherwise be used in a criminal prosecution undoubtedly supplies some residual deterrent to unlawful conduct by INS officials. But it must be acknowledged that only a very small percentage of arrests of aliens are intended or expected to lead to criminal prosecutions. Thus the arresting officer's primary objective, in practice, will be to use evidence in the civil deportation proceeding. Moreover, here, in contrast to *Janis*, the agency officials who effect the unlawful arrest are the same officials who subsequently bring the deportation action. As recognized in *Janis*, the exclusionary rule is likely to be most effective when applied to such "intrasovereign" violations.

Nonetheless, several other factors significantly reduce the likely deterrent value of the exclusionary rule in a civil deportation proceeding. First, regardless of how the arrest is effected, deportation will still be possible when evidence not derived directly from the arrest is sufficient to support deportation. As the BIA has recognized, in many deportation proceedings "the sole matters necessary for the Government to establish are the respondent's identity and alienage—at which point the burden shifts to the respondent to prove the time, place and manner of entry." *Matter of Sandoval*, 17 I. & N. Dec., at 79. Since the person and identity of the respondent are not themselves suppressible, see *supra*, at 3485, the INS must prove only alienage, and that will sometimes be possible using evidence gathered independently of, or sufficiently attenuated from, the original arrest. The INS's task is simplified in this regard by the civil nature of the proceeding. As Justice Brandeis stated: "Silence is often evidence of the most persuasive character. . . . [T]here is no rule of law which prohibits officers charged with the administration of the immigration law from drawing an inference from the silence of one who is called upon to speak. . . . A person arrested on the preliminary warrant is not protected by a presumption of citizenship comparable to the presumption of innocence in a criminal case. There is no provision which forbids drawing an adverse inference from the fact of standing mute." *United States ex rel. Bilokumsky v. Tod*, 263 U.S., at 153-154.

The second factor is a practical one. In the course of a year the average INS agent arrests almost 500 illegal aliens. Over 97.5% apparently agree to voluntary deportation without a formal hearing. 705 F.2d, at 1071, n.17. Among the remainder who do request a formal hearing (apparently a dozen or so in all, per officer, per year) very few challenge the circumstances of their arrests. As noted by the Court of Appeals, "the BIA was able to find only two reported immigration cases since 1899 in which the [exclusionary] rule was applied to bar unlawfully seized evidence, only one other case in which the rule's application was specifically addressed, and fewer than fifty BIA proceedings since 1952 in which a Fourth Amendment challenge to the introduction of evidence was even raised." *Id.*, at 1071. Every INS agent knows, therefore, that it is highly unlikely that any particular arrestee will end up challenging the lawfulness of his arrest in a formal deportation proceeding. When an occasional challenge is brought, the consequences from the point of view of the officer's overall arrest and deportation record will be trivial. In these circumstances, the arresting officer is most unlikely to shape his conduct in anticipation of the exclusion of evidence at a formal deportation hearing.

Third, and perhaps most important, the INS has its own comprehensive scheme for deterring Fourth Amendment violations by its officers. Most arrests of illegal aliens away from the border occur during farm, factory, or other workplace surveys. Large numbers of illegal aliens are often arrested at one time, and conditions are understandably chaotic. To safeguard the rights of those who are lawfully present at inspected workplaces the INS has developed rules restricting stop, interrogation, and arrest practices. These regulations require that no one be detained without reasonable suspicion of illegal alienage, and that no one be arrested unless there is an admission of illegal alienage or other strong evidence thereof. New immigration officers receive instruction and examination in Fourth Amendment law, and others receive periodic refresher courses in law. Evidence seized through intentionally unlawful conduct is excluded by Department of Justice policy from the proceeding for which it was obtained. *See*, Memorandum from Benjamin R. Civiletti to Heads of Offices, Boards, Bureaus and Divisions, Violations of Search and Seizure Law (Jan. 16, 1981). The INS also has in place a procedure for investigating and punishing immigration officers who commit Fourth Amendment violations. *See* Office of General Counsel, INS, U.S. Dept. of Justice, The Law of Arrest, Search, and Seizure for Immigration Officers 35 (Jan. 1983). The INS's attention to Fourth Amendment interests cannot guarantee that constitutional violations will not occur, but it does reduce the likely deterrent value of the exclusionary rule. Deterrence must be measured at the margin.

Finally, the deterrent value of the exclusionary rule in deportation proceedings is undermined by the availability of alternative remedies for institutional practices by the INS that might violate Fourth Amendment rights. The INS is a single agency, under central federal control, and engaged in operations of broad scope but highly repetitive character. The possibility of declaratory relief against the agency thus offers a means for challenging the validity of INS practices, when standing requirements for bringing such an action can be met.

Respondents contend that retention of the exclusionary rule is necessary to safeguard the Fourth Amendment rights of ethnic Americans, particularly the Hispanic-Americans lawfully in this country. We recognize that respondents raise here legitimate and important concerns. But application of the exclusionary rule to civil deportation proceedings can be justified only if the rule is likely to add significant protection to these Fourth Amendment rights. The exclusionary rule provides no remedy for completed wrongs; those lawfully in this country can be interested in its application only insofar as it may serve as an effective deterrent to future INS misconduct. For the reasons we have discussed we conclude that application of the rule in INS civil deportation proceedings, as in the circumstances discussed in Janis, "is unlikely to provide significant, much less substantial, additional deterrence." 428 U.S., at 458. Important as it is to protect the Fourth Amendment rights of all persons, there is no convincing indication that application of the exclusionary rule in civil deportation proceedings will contribute materially to that end.

On the other side of the scale, the social costs of applying the exclusionary rule in deportation proceedings are both unusual and significant. The first cost is one that is unique to continuing violations of the law. Applying the exclusionary rule in proceedings that are intended not to punish past transgressions but to prevent their continuance or renewal would require the courts to close their eyes to ongoing violations of the law. This Court has never before accepted costs of this character in applying the exclusionary rule.

*   *   *

Other factors also weigh against applying the exclusionary rule in deportation proceedings. The INS currently operates a deliberately simple deportation hearing system, streamlined to permit the quick resolution of very large numbers of deportation actions, and it is against this backdrop that the costs of the exclusionary must be assessed. The costs of applying the exclusionary rule, like the benefits, must be measured at the margin.

The average immigration judge handles about six deportation hearings per day. Neither the hearing officers nor the attorneys participating in those hearings are likely to be well versed in the intricacies of Fourth Amendment law. The prospect of even occasional invocation of the exclusionary rule might significantly change and complicate the character of these proceedings.

* * *

The BIA's concerns are reinforced by the staggering dimension of the problem that the INS confronts. Immigration officers apprehend over one million deportable aliens in this country every year. *Id.*, at 85. A single agent may arrest many illegal aliens every day. Although the investigatory burden does not justify the commission of constitutional violations, the officers cannot be expected to compile elaborate, contemporaneous, written reports detailing the circumstances of every arrest. At present an officer simply completes a "Record of Deportable Alien" that is introduced to prove the INS's case at the deportation hearing; the officer rarely must attend the hearing. Fourth Amendment suppression hearings would undoubtedly require considerably more, and the likely burden on the administration of the immigration laws would be correspondingly severe.

Finally, the INS advances the credible argument that applying the exclusionary rule to deportation proceedings might well result in the suppression of large amounts of information that had been obtained entirely lawfully. INS arrests occur in crowded and confused circumstances. Though the INS agents are instructed to follow procedures that adequately protect Fourth Amendment interests, agents will usually be able to testify only to the fact that they followed INS rules. The demand for a precise account of exactly what happened in each particular arrest would plainly preclude mass arrests, even when the INS is confronted, as it often is, with massed numbers of ascertainably illegal aliens, and even when the arrests can be and are conducted in full compliance with all Fourth Amendment requirements.

In these circumstances we are persuaded that the Janis balance between costs and benefits comes out against applying the exclusionary rule in civil deportation hearings held by the INS. By all appearances the INS has already taken sensible and reasonable steps to deter Fourth Amendment violations by its officers, and this makes the likely additional deterrent value of the exclusionary rule small. The costs of applying the exclusionary rule in the context of civil deportation hearings are high. In particular, application of the exclusionary rule in cases such as Sandoval's would compel the courts to release from custody persons who would then immediately resume their commission of a crime through their continuing, unlawful presence in this country. "There comes a point at which courts, consistent with their duty to administer the law, cannot continue to create barriers to law enforcement in the pursuit of a supervisory role that is properly the duty of the Executive and Legislative Branches." *United States v. Janis*, 428 U.S., at 459. That point has been reached here.

We do not condone any violations of the Fourth Amendment that may have occurred in the arrests of respondents Lopez or Sandoval. Moreover, no challenge is raised here to the INS's own internal regulations. . . .

Notes

1. Amendments made to the immigration laws by the reform legislation now impose sanctions against certain employers for hiring undocumented aliens. In some

cases these sanctions are criminal sanctions. In addition the immigration statute in its present form imposes criminal penalties on aliens for avoiding inspection at the border. What considerations, if any, would you give to these provisions if you were deciding *Lopez-Mendoza*? What considerations would you give these factors if you were the Board of Immigration Appeals?

2. If there is no exclusionary rule, what remedies are there for an alien who has had her constitutional rights violated by an INS officer?

3. From a policy standpoint, what, if anything, should be done about INS officers, fourth amendment transgressions? Is this an important factor to be weighed by a court faced with an application of the exclusionary rule?

4. **Suppression of evidence.** While the Court refused to endorse an exclusionary rule in deportation proceedings, the BIA noted in one case that where the violation "prejudiced [the] interests of the alien . . . protected by the regulation" the evidence would be excluded. See *Matter of Garcia-Flores*, 17 I. & N. Dec. 325, 328 (BIA 1980). The validity of this case is not clear, given that the BIA was adopting a standard set by the Ninth circuit prior to *Lopez-Mendoza*. Suppression may still be possible where the Fifth Amendment is implicated. See *Wall v. INS*, 722 F.2d 1442 (9th Cir. 1984). Finally, when exclusion of evidence is not possible, injunction may be an alternative remedy. See e.g. *Int'l Moulders' & Allied Workers' Local Union 164 v. Nelson*, 799 F.2d 547 (9th Cir. 1986); *Pearl Meadows Mushroom Farm, Inc. v. Nelson*, 723 F. Supp. 432 (N.D. Ca. 1989).

F. Employer Sanctions

The following case presents the first court review of the employer sanction provisions of the Immigration Reform and Control Act of 1986 ("IRCA").

Mester Mfg. Co. v. INS
879 F.2d 561 (9th Cir. 1989)*

BEEZER, Circuit Judge.

*   *   *

Mester manufactures furniture at facilities in El Cajon, California, and Tijuana, Mexico. The El Cajon facility, employing about 70 people on the average, is at issue here. On July 2, 1987, agent Stephen A. Shanks of the INS Border Patrol made an initial educational visit to Mester. Shanks left a copy of the INS' "Handbook for Employers" and his business card for Mester's managers, none of whom was available at the time. No Mester official contacted Shanks, and Shanks did not make a return visit.

Shanks phoned Mester on August 7, 1987. He spoke with a senior official of Mester, James Saturley, who appeared satisfied with his present level of knowledge regarding IRCA. The owner of the company, Barry Mester, expressed no interest, at any time, in understanding and complying with the law. "Rarely in my experience,"

---

* Note: In editing this case the presentation has been rearranged for reasons of pedagogy.

said the ALJ, "has an employer demonstrated as did Barry Mester on the stand such a manifest lack of interest in the personnel practices of his own domain."

On August 26, 1987, the INS notified Mester of its intention to inspect the I-9's on file there, pursuant to 8 U.S.C. §§ 1324a(e)(1)(C) and (2)(A). On September 2, Shanks and three other Border Patrol agents inspected these documents. In response to Saturley's questions, the agents said they would get back to him.

The next day, Shanks and another agent returned to Mester to deliver the citation required by IRCA for a first violation. The citation alleged that Mester had violated "Section 274A(b)(1) of the Immigration and Nationality Act" (8 U.S.C. § 1324a(b)(1)) with respect to 11 named individuals. The citation thus alleged only paperwork violations. However, several counts contained statements that aliens were "still employed" after their work authorizations had expired, and others alleged that I-9's had not been completed for "illegal aliens," thus strongly suggesting that employment of these individuals, if continued, would violate 8 U.S.C. § 1324a(a)(2). The citation stated that no proceeding would result, and no penalties would be imposed.

In addition to the citation, Shanks gave Barry Mester a handwritten "interview list" containing, inter alia, the names of three employees whom the INS suspected of using false alien registration cards ("green cards"). The testimony regarding exactly what transpired between Shanks and Mester officials was confusing and contradictory. The ALJ found that Mester was put on notice that it should check the green card numbers of these employees and that, if the numbers matched those on the interview list that the INS had found in a computer search to belong to other aliens, they should be fired. Apparently, however, the Mester employee assigned to check the numbers operated under the false impression that if the numbers matched, the employees were authorized. Mester refused to allow the INS to interview the employees directly.

On September 8, Saturley wrote to the INS to complain that the four armed agents had intimidated Mester employees, and had not been forthcoming in responding to questions. On September 22, the INS announced a second inspection. That same day, Mester responded in writing to each allegation in the citation.

On September 25, Shanks and three agents again inspected Mester's I-9's. As a result of the inspection, the INS served a Notice of Intent to Fine ("NIF") on Mester on October 2, alleging that seven named employees had been continued in employment after Mester had learned on September 3, 1987 (presumably from the citation or the accompanying verbal information) that they were not authorized to work, all in violation of 8 U.S.C. § 1324a(a)(2) (the "employment violations"). The NIF also alleged nine paperwork violations for failure to present I-9's of specific employees for inspection on September 25. Mester requested a hearing. On November 16, 1987, the INS served a complaint asking that an ALJ conduct a hearing, issue a cease-and-desist order, and impose civil penalties on Mester. The complaint incorporated the NIF by reference.

Between February 9 and 12, 1988, ALJ Marvin H. Morse conducted an exhaustive hearing. The record extends to more than 2500 pages. The ALJ's written findings are extraordinarily detailed and thorough. The ALJ found in favor of the INS on counts 1-3 and 5-7, six of the employment violations. He dismissed count 4 because the evidence was not sufficient to find that Mester had employed that individual knowing of his unauthorized status, and dismissed all the paperwork violations, counts 8-17, because the NIF incorrectly stated which section of IRCA had been violated, and the error meant that Mester had insufficient notice of the charges.

On June 17, 1988, the ALJ issued a cease-and-desist order lasting one year, and penalized Mester $500 for each of the six violations. As the Chief Administrative Hearing Officer of the INS did not modify or vacate the ALJ's findings, the decision and order became final after 30 days. See 8 U.S.C. § 1324a(e)(7). Mester timely petitioned this court for review. See id. at § 1324a(e)(8). We have jurisdiction.

* * *

IRCA puts part of the burden of compliance upon employers. 8 U.S.C. § 1324a (Supp. V 1987). It is unlawful for an employer knowingly to hire an alien who is unauthorized to be employed in the United States, or to continue to employ an alien in the knowledge that his employment is unauthorized. Id. at § 1324a(a)(1), (2). The statute sets up an employment verification system under which an employer must execute a verification form ("I-9") attesting, under penalty of perjury, that it has verified that each employee (whether a U.S. citizen or an alien) is not an unauthorized alien by examining the requisite document, or documents, showing identity and employment authorization. Id. at § 1324a(b). The individual hired must also attest to his own eligibility. Id. at § 1324a(b)(2).

The attorney general is authorized to investigate violations of IRCA. Id. at § 1324a(e). That duty has been assigned to the Immigration and Naturalization Service ("INS"). 8 C.F.R. § 100, et seq. (1988). Persons charged with IRCA violations are entitled to notice, and to a hearing conducted by an ALJ in accordance with the Administrative Procedure Act. 8 U.S.C. § 1324a(e)(3); see 5 U.S.C. § 554 (1982).

The ALJ may require violators of IRCA's employment provisions to pay civil money penalties, and may issue a cease-and-desist order requiring future compliance with the statute. 8 U.S.C. § 1324a(e)(4). A "pattern or practice" of employment violations may lead to criminal penalties. Id. at § 1324a(f). A failure to adhere to the employment verification system, referred to as a "paperwork violation," will lead to a civil money penalty only, of a generally lesser amount than for an employment violation. Id. at § 1324a(e)(5). The ALJ's order becomes a final agency order 30 days after its issuance, if the agency does not modify or vacate it. Id. at § 1324a(e)(7). A party adversely affected by a final order may petition the Court of Appeals for review within 45 days after the order becomes final. Id. at § 1324a(e)(8).

Because of the burdens IRCA places upon employers, Congress provided for gradual implementation. The six-month period following enactment in November 1986 was a public information period; the appropriate agencies were to disseminate forms and information to employers during this period, and no enforcement action was to take place. Id. at § 1324a(i)(1). The subsequent twelve-month period, between June 1, 1987 and June 1, 1988, was the "first citation period." Id. at § 1324a(i)(2). "In the case of a person or entity, in the first instance in which the (INS) has reason to believe that the person or entity may have violated (IRCA) . . . the (INS) shall provide a citation to the person or entity indicating that such a violation or violations may have occurred and shall not conduct any proceeding, nor issue any order, under this section on the basis of such alleged violation or violations." Id. at § 1324a(i)(2). This case arose during the first citation period.

* * *

The INS correctly suggests that the APA standard of review should apply. See 5 U.S.C. § 706(2) (1982). IRCA requires that hearings be conducted in accordance with the Administrative Procedure Act. 5 U.S.C. § 554; 8 U.S.C. § 1324a(e)(3)(B). Therefore, we grant agency hearings under IRCA the same deference we give to other agency formal adjudications. We may only overturn agency findings of fact that are unsupported by substantial evidence. FTC v. Indiana Fed'n of Dentists, 476 U.S. 447, 454 (1986); 5 U.S.C. § 706(2)(E).

We apply a de novo standard of review to an agency's conclusions of law. See *Indiana Fed'n of Dentists*, 476 U.S. at 454; 5 U.S.C. § 706(2)....Within the de novo framework, however, we give a certain amount of deference to an agency's reasonable construction of a statute it is charged with administering. Indiana Fed'n of Dentists, 476 U.S. at 454 (agency's informed judgment applying applicable legal standard to facts entitled to "some deference")....If an agency's construction is reasonable, and consistent with congressional intent, we will accept it. Our deference to reasonable statutory interpretation extends to a new statute as well as to a longtime agency interpretation....

We reserve to ourselves, of course, the final authority to decide questions of statutory construction. See *California Energy Resources Conservation & Dev. Comm'n v. Johnson*, 807 F.2d 1456, 1461 (9th Cir. 1986). We consider the constitutionality of IRCA as a legal question of first impression.

Count 1 of the NIF alleged that "[o]n September 3, 1987 you (Mester) were informed that Francisco Estrada-Bahena had presented a false (green card) and was not an alien authorized to work in the United States. On September 25, 1987 Francisco Estrada-Bahena was still employed by you." The ALJ found that Estrada-Bahena's name was on the list of suspected unauthorized aliens, with green card numbers, given to Mester by Shanks on September 3. He further found that Mester received notice from Shanks that if the number on the list matched that on Estrada-Bahena's green card, Estrada-Bahena was unauthorized. Therefore, Mester was on notice as to Estrada-Bahena's suspect status. Mester made no inquiry of the INS, but unreasonably continued Estrada-Bahena's employment. The ALJ found Mester to have violated IRCA.

Mester argues that the evidence was insufficient for the INS to meet its burden of proof that in fact Estrada-Bahena was using a false green card. The INS relied on a computer search of its records system that revealed the false green card. Mester offered some evidence at the hearing that the system was prone to error, and offers this court other evidence outside the record in the form of a GAO report.

...Mester's general allegations of unreliability are accompanied by no specific contention, supported by facts, that the INS finding that Estrada-Bahena had a false green card is incorrect. The INS made a prima facie showing that the green card was false, and Mester failed to produce any evidence to the contrary. The ALJ's finding is supported by substantial evidence.

Counts 2 and 3 were very similar to count 1. They alleged that Mester was informed on September 3 that Santiago Mejia-Garcia and Jorge Maciel-Mejia had presented false green cards, but that on September 25 the two were still employed.

Mester contends, as a matter of law, that it did not have knowledge of the status of the aliens in counts 1-3 sufficient to find it liable because the form of notice was improper. Mester argues that unless it received official written notice from the INS that the green cards were false, it did not have knowledge.... The statutory scheme of citations and NIF's does not directly relate to the scienter element of the substantive offense. The INS must show, of course, by a preponderance of the evidence that the employer knowingly employed an unauthorized alien. 8 U.S.C. § 1324a(e)(3)(C).

... Mester received specific information that several of his employees were likely to be unauthorized. He made no further inquiry of the INS, and failed to take appropriate corrective action. The aliens turned out to be unauthorized. The knowledge element was satisfied; Mester had constructive knowledge, even if no Mester employee had actual specific knowledge of the employee's unauthorized status. Cf. *United States v. Jewell*, 532 F.2d 697 (9th Cir.) (en banc) (in criminal law, deliberate failure to investigate suspicious circumstances imputes knowledge), cert. denied, 426 U.S. 951 (1976).

Count 5 of the NIF alleged that Miguel Castel-Garcia had been retained in employment after Mester had learned on September 3 that he was unauthorized. The citation had previously alleged that no I-9 had been completed for Castel-Garcia, an "illegal alien." Thus, unlike counts 1-3, the written citation required by the statute later served as the proof for the knowledge element of the violation. Also unlike the aliens in counts 1-3, Castel-Garcia was fired on September 17, 1987, two weeks after the citation was issued.

Mester argues that it had a good-faith belief that Castel-Garcia was a legal "grandfathered" employee hired before the passage of IRCA. 8 C.F.R. § 274a.7 (1988). However, the ALJ found that Mester's records showed that Castel-Garcia had quit in December 1986, and had been rehired in April 1987, thus removing his authorization. He also found that Mester had not acted on its asserted belief by contacting the INS in a timely fashion to resolve the discrepancy.

Count 5 raises a troubling question: When must an employer terminate an employee upon learning that he or she is unauthorized to work in the United States? ... The statute does not answer these questions.

We interpret a statute "to avoid untenable distinctions and unreasonable results whenever possible." *American Tobacco Co. v. Patterson*, 456 U.S. 63, 71 (1982). Counsel for the INS conceded that a basic rule of reason would apply at some point to IRCA enforcement actions. It is apparent that the potential for unjust or capricious action exists.... The potential for abuse is heightened, in our view, by our recognition that employers are subject to a host of other federal and state laws affecting their right to terminate employees summarily.

Counsel for the INS recognized that employer sanctions for the five-minute violation would likely be unreasonable, but maintained that 21 or 30 days' continued employment would not be reasonable, especially in light of the allegedly transient and casual nature of much border employment. It appears that the INS wishes to proceed on an entirely ad hoc basis that will undoubtedly force this court to sketch out some standard of reasonableness in future litigation. Legislative or regulatory action that would set forth some reasonable time frame for termination acceptable to employers and the INS would seem appropriate.[1] Absent any such guidance, however, or any

---

1. In this case, the ALJ considered the steps taken, or not taken, by Mester to confirm the information provided by the INS on September 3 before terminating employees. It is apparent that an inquiry into a reasonable time frame for termination will include consideration, in certain cases, of factors other than the number of days alone—such as the certainty of the

independent reason to apply a different construction of the statute than that of the ALJ, we defer to the ALJ's conclusion, based on the relevant facts, that a two-week delay in firing Castel-Garcia amounted to an IRCA violation.

[Discussion regarding count 6 has been removed.]

*   *   *

Count 7 charged Mester with having continued the employment on September 17, 1987, of Juventino Barranca-Ballesteros, after having learned on September 3 that his "special rule status" had expired. . . . The ALJ again found that Mester had merely assumed that the citation was incorrect, rather than investigating the alien's status in a timely manner.

Mester contends that in fact Barranca-Ballesteros was not a special rule alien, and that he had submitted adequate documentation. A special rule alien is one who has applied for legalization under IRCA. See 8 C.F.R. §§ 274a.2(b)(i)(B); 274a.11 (1988). These aliens have conceded their unlawful presence in the United States. See 8 U.S.C. § 1255a. IRCA allowed them to work without authorization documents until September 1, 1987; after that date, they required such documentation, to be provided by the INS to legitimate legalization candidates. 8 U.S.C. § 1255a(e)(2)(B); 8 C.F.R. § 274a.11.

. . . It cannot seriously be contended that Mester was unaware of his unauthorized status after September 3. Confusion arose, however, over the documentation requirements. Contrary to the citation, Mester's I-9 on file for this alien was supported by adequate documentation—a social security card and a driver's license. See 8 U.S.C. § 1324a(b)(1)(C)(i), (D)(i). However, Mester confuses the violation charged, knowing employment of an unauthorized alien, with the paperwork violation that can result from an inadequate I-9. Even if the I-9 was entirely satisfactory, if the INS can show that Mester had knowledge of an employee's unauthorized status, and continued him in employment, that fact is of little assistance to Mester. The ALJ's findings that Mester had such knowledge, and failed to act on that notice promptly were supported by substantial evidence, and his conclusion that IRCA was violated is correct.

*   *   *

Mester argues that it was denied procedural due process because of the allegedly irregular and insufficient notice it received. . . . First, by arguing that the citation violated due process, Mester confuses the knowledge element of its offense with the notice constitutionally required to prosecute it. The citation did not lead to the final deprivation of property from Mester. The adjudicatory proceedings were initiated by the NIF. Although this document was not as clear as it could have been, as the ALJ noted, it gave adequate notice to Mester of the charges—at least, of those before us on appeal—and allowed Mester to defend itself. Mester does not challenge the adequacy of the hearing.

Mester's argument that it was deprived of substantive due process is wholly without merit. See, e.g., United States v. Salerno, 481 U.S. 739, 746 (1987)(substantive

_____

information providing the knowledge of unauthorized status, and steps taken by the employer to confirm it. In none of the situations at issue here do we conclude that the ALJ finding of an IRCA violation was an unreasonable application of the statute, based on our consideration of all the relevant facts.

due process prohibits only governmental conduct that shocks the conscience or interferes with rights implicit in the concept of ordered liberty).

Mester had a statutory right to receive a citation before any enforcement proceedings were initiated. But the citation was a predicate to the enforcement proceeding, not a part of it. Mester apparently believes that it had a right to a thorough briefing as to its violations of IRCA prior to enforcement. Mester's claimed ignorance of the statutory requirements is no defense to charges of IRCA violations. It is true that Congress provided for education of employers during the early period of IRCA. However, we do not read that accommodation to employers as in any way giving them an entitlement to the education, or prohibiting sanctions against an employer that can show that it has not received a handbook or other instruction, or (as here) that it has simply failed to pay attention to them.

. . . Section 1324a(i)(2) appears to require the INS to cite all suspected violations. It would violate the spirit, and likely the letter, of this section for the INS to cite one suspected violation only, thereby allowing others suspected at the time of the citation to be the subject of immediate enforcement proceedings. By citing only paperwork violations while orally notifying Mester of suspected false green cards, it can be argued that this is what the INS has done. It is an open question, of course, whether an INS error in issuing the citation can preclude a later enforcement action. But we need not reach the issue. The INS complied with the letter of the statute by citing only those violations—the paperwork violations—that actually were violations at that time. Because the knowledge element of the offenses of continuing to employ the three unauthorized aliens was not present on September 3, the offenses technically were not ripe, and thus not citable. They only became offenses after September 3, because the information conveyed by the INS on that date gave Mester the requisite knowledge.

Perhaps Mester would have complied better if the notice had been written. But since oral notice satisfied the knowledge element, we are unable to take Mester's advice and hold that the INS should institute better procedures. That is a matter of executive discretion.

[Mester argued further that IRCA was null and void, as unconstitutionally passed because Congress had presented the bill after it had adjourned sine die in violation of Article I, section 7, clause 2 of the Constitution. This argument was rejected by the court.]

*   *   *

Mester has failed to meet its burden of showing that the ALJ's findings of fact were not supported by substantial evidence, or that his construction of IRCA was legally incorrect. . . . The decision and order of the INS is therefore affirmed.

―――――――

Notes

1. If Mester came to you following the initial warnings received from the INS, what would you advise him?

2. What would you attempt to show at the hearing before the administrative law judge?

3. The court of appeals noted that employers have many obligations and may not be able to immediately dismiss an employee upon receipt of an allegation that

they do not have employment authorization. *See Patel v. Quality Inn South*, 846 F.2d 700, 704-05 (11th Cir. 1988) (Fair Labor Standards Act's coverage of undocumented aliens was not repealed by IRCA), *cert. denied*, U.S. (1989). Was the court's conclusion on this issue helpful for other employers who might be faced with this problem?

Procedural Questions

1. The respondent appears at her deportation hearing. She concedes deportability and requests discretionary relief of asylum or in the alternative, voluntary departure. What is the result if the alien departs the U.S. before she has fully presented her asylum claim and without requesting specific relief?

2. A, a foreigner, is arrested by local police for shoplifting. After posting bond in a local court, she is turned over to INS officials. The INS district director imposes a $5,000.00 bond. What remedies are available to A? How would A obtain this remedy and what, if anything, would have to be established?

3. What is the authority of the immigration judge to set the amount of bond after the respondent has been released? What can be done to reset the amount of bond? 8 C.F.R. § 242.2(d)

4. Is an application for voluntary departure or other discretionary relief a concession of deportability? 8 C.F.R. § 242.17(e)

G. Deportation Procedure

[The discussion which appears on this page is intended to accompany the chart on the following page.]

To initiate deportation proceedings, the INS serves an Order to Show Cause (including a Notice of Hearing) on the respondent. If the accompanying warrant for arrest is used, the person will be detained long enough for a custody determination and subsequent setting of bond. If she feels the bond amount is improper, she may appeal to an immigration judge for a redetermination of the amount. Should this new amount still be unsatisfactory, she may appeal to the Board of Immigration Appeals or, in very unusual circumstances, file a writ of habeas corpus. The serving officer may decide not to arrest her, in which case she could be released upon her own recognizance until the date of the deportation hearing.

At the hearing, the immigration judge is bound by a substantial evidence standard. She must make a determination of the respondent's status, deciding either to grant discretionary relief or to find her deportable. The respondent must, in good faith, designate a country of deportation. If found deportable, the respondent may request voluntary departure by a certain date, subject to extensions. This order is usually entered with an alternate order of deportation which becomes a final order if the respondent does not voluntarily leave the country by the date set. Complex questions may be certified to the BIA by the immigration judge; final orders may be appealed to the BIA either by the respondent or the INS trial attorney. Following a determination by the BIA, the case may be appealed to a federal court.

Deportation Procedure

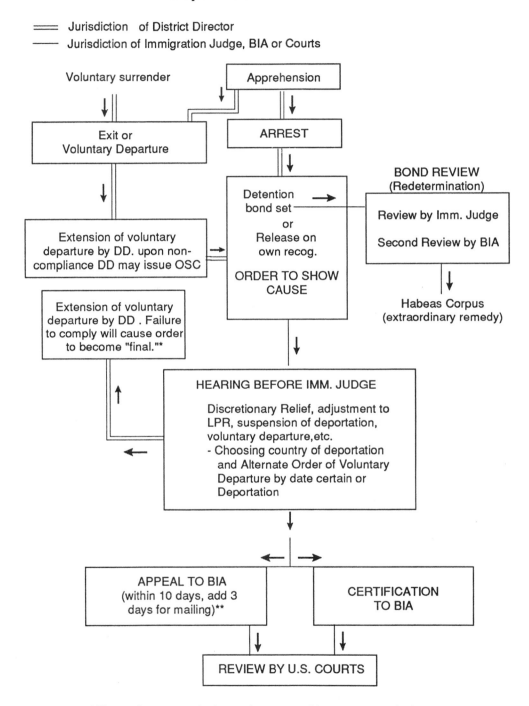

* The applicant may submit a motion to reconsider or reopen to the Immigration Judge for discretionary relief, etc., or apply for stay of deportation.

**If the decision is adverse the original period of voluntary departure may be reinstated.

Index to Appendix

Grounds for Deportation

8 U.S.C. § 1251(a), Sec. 241(a)—Classes of Deportable Aliens.

Any alien (including an alien crewman) in the United States shall, upon the order of the Attorney General, be deported if the alien is deportable as being within one or more of the following classes of aliens:

(1) Excludable at time of entry or of adjustment of status or violates status.—

(A) Excludable Aliens.—Any alien who at the time of entry or adjustment of status was within one or more of the classes of aliens excludable by the law existing at such time is deportable.

(B) Entered Without Inspection.—Any alien who entered the United States without inspection or at any time or place other than as designated by the Attorney General or is in the United States in violation of this Act or any other law of the United States is deportable.

(C) Violated Nonimmigrant Status or Condition of Entry.—

(i) Nonimmigrant Status Violators.—Any alien who was admitted as a nonimmigrant and who has failed to maintain the nonimmigrant status in which the alien was admitted or to which it was changed under section 248, or to comply with the conditions of any such status, is deportable.

(ii) Violators of Conditions of Entry.—Any alien whom the Secretary of Health and Human Services certifies has failed to comply with terms, conditions, and controls that were imposed under section 212(g) is deportable.

(D) Termination of Conditional Permanent Residence.—

(i) In General.—Any alien with permanent resident status on a conditional basis under section 216 (relating to conditional permanent resident status for certain alien spouses and sons and daughters) or under section 216A (relating to conditional permanent resident status for certain alien entrepreneurs, spouses, and children) who has had such status terminated under such section is deportable.

(ii) Exception.—Clause (i) shall not apply in the cases described in section 216(c)(4) (relating to certain hardship waivers).

(E) Smuggling.—

(i) In General.—Any alien who (prior to the date of entry, at the time of entry, or within 5 years of the date of entry) knowingly has encouraged, induced, assisted, abetted, or aided any other alien to enter or to try to enter the United States in violation of law is deportable.[24]

(ii) Waiver Authorized.—The Attorney General may, in his discretion for humanitarian purposes, to assure family unity, or when it is otherwise in the public interest, waive application of clause (i) in the case of any alien lawfully admitted for permanent residence if the alien has encouraged, induced, assisted, abetted, or aided only the alien's spouse, parent, son, or daughter (and no other individual) to enter the United States in violation of law.

(F) Failure to Maintain Employment.—Any alien who obtains the status of an alien lawfully admitted for temporary residence under section 210A who fails to meet the requirement of section 210A(d)(5)(A) by the end of the applicable period is deportable.

(G) Marriage Fraud.—An alien shall be considered to be deportable as having procured a visa or other documentation by fraud (within the meaning of section 212(a)(5)(C)(i)) and to be in the United States in violation of this Act (within the meaning of subparagraph (B)) if—

(i) the alien obtains any entry into the United States with an immigrant visa or other documentation procured on the basis of a marriage entered into less than 2 years prior to such entry of the alien and which, within 2 years subsequent to any entry of the alien in the United States, shall be judicially annulled or terminated, unless the alien establishes to the satisfaction of the Attorney General that such marriage was not contracted for the purpose of evading any provisions of the immigration laws, or

(ii) it appears to the satisfaction of the Attorney General that the alien has failed or refused to fulfill the alien's marital agreement which in the opinion of the Attorney General was made for the purpose of procuring the alien's entry as an immigrant.

(H) Waiver Authorized for Certain Misrepresentations.—The provisions of this paragraph relating to the deportation of aliens within the United States on the ground that they were excludable at the time of entry as aliens described in section 212(a)(6)(C)(i), whether willful or innocent, may, in the discretion of the Attorney General, be waived for any alien (other than an alien described in paragraph (6) or (7)) who—

(i) is the spouse, parent, son, or daughter of a citizen of the United States or of an alien lawfully admitted to the United States for permanent residence; and

---

24. The prior statute included a provision requiring that the smuggling be for "gain."

(ii) was in possession of an immigrant visa or equivalent document and was otherwise admissible to the United States at the time of such entry except for those grounds of inadmissibility specified under paragraphs (5)(A) and (7)(A) of section 212(a) which were a direct result of that fraud or misrepresentation. A waiver of deportation for fraud or misrepresentation granted under this subparagraph shall also operate to waive deportation based on the grounds of inadmissibility at entry directly resulting from such fraud or misrepresentation.

(2) Criminal Offenses.—

    (A) General Crimes.—

        (i) Crimes of Moral Turpitude.—Any alien who—

            (I) is convicted of a crime involving moral turpitude committed within five years after the date of entry, and

            (II) either is sentenced to confinement or is confined therefor in a prison or correctional institution for one year or longer, is deportable.

        (ii) Multiple Criminal Convictions.—Any alien who at any time after entry is convicted of two or more crimes involving moral turpitude, not arising out of a single scheme of criminal misconduct, regardless of whether confined therefor and regardless of whether the convictions were in a single trial, is deportable.

        (iii) Aggravated Felony.—Any alien who is convicted of an aggravated felony at any time after entry is deportable.

        (iv) Waiver Authorized.—Clauses (i), (ii), and (iii) shall not apply in the case of an alien with respect to a criminal conviction if the alien subsequent to the criminal conviction has been granted a full and unconditional pardon by the President of the United States or by the Governor of any of the several States.

    (B) Controlled Substances.—

        (i) Conviction.—Any alien who at any time after entry has been convicted of a violation of (or a conspiracy or attempt to violate) any law or regulation of a State, the United States, or a foreign country relating to a controlled substance (as defined in section 102 of the Controlled Substances Act (21 U.S.C. § 802)), other than a single offense involving possession for one's own use of 30 grams or less of marijuana, is deportable.

        (ii) Drug Abusers and Addicts.—Any alien who is, or at any time after entry has been, a drug abuser or addict is deportable.

    (C) Certain Firearm Offenses.—Any alien who at any time after entry is convicted under any law of purchasing, selling, offering for sale, exchanging, using, owning, possessing, or carrying in violation of any law, any weapon, part, or accessory which is a firearm or destructive device (as defined in section 921(a) of title 18, United States Code) is deportable.

    (D) Miscellaneous Crimes.—Any alien who at any time has been convicted (the judgment on such conviction becoming final) of, or has been so convicted of a conspiracy to violate—

        (i) any offense under chapter 37 (relating to espionage), chapter 105 (relating to sabotage), or chapter 115 (relating to treason and sedition) of title 18, United States Code, for which a term of imprisonment of five or more years may be imposed;

(ii) any offense under section 871 or 960 of title 18, United States Code;

(iii) a violation of any provision of the Military Selective Service Act (50 U.S.C. App. §§ 451 et seq.) or the Trading With the Enemy Act [50 U.S.C.App. §§ 1 et seq.]; or

(iv) a violation of section 215 or 278 of this Act, is deportable.

(3) Failure to Register And Falsification of Documents.—

(A) Change of Address.—An alien who has failed to comply with the provisions of section 265 is deportable, unless the alien establishes to the satisfaction of the Attorney General that such failure was reasonably excusable or was not willful.

(B) Failure to Register or Falsification of Documents.—Any alien who at any time has been convicted—

(i) under section 266(c) of this Act or under section 36(c) of the Alien Registration Act, 1940,

(ii) of a violation of, or a conspiracy to violate, any provision of the Foreign Agents Registration Act of 1938 [22 U.S.C. §§ 611 et seq.], or

(iii) of a violation of, or a conspiracy to violate, section 1546 of title 18, United States Code (relating to fraud and misuse of visas, permits, and other entry documents), is deportable.

(4) Security and Related Grounds.—

(A) In General.—Any alien who has engaged, is engaged, or at any time after entry has engaged in—

(i) any activity to violate any law of the United States relating to espionage or sabotage or to violate or evade any law prohibiting the export from the United States of goods, technology, or sensitive information,

(ii) any other criminal activity which endangers public safety or national security, or

(iii) any activity a purpose of which is the opposition to, or the control or overthrow of, the Government of the United States by force, violence, or other unlawful means, is deportable.

(B) Terrorist Activities.—Any alien who has engaged, is engaged, or at any time after entry has engaged in any terrorist activity (as defined in section 212(a)(3)(B)(iii)) is deportable.

(C) Foreign Policy.—

(i) In General.—An alien whose presence or activities in the United States the Secretary of State has reasonable ground to believe would have potentially serious adverse foreign policy consequences for the United States is deportable.

(ii) Exceptions.—The exceptions described in clauses (ii) and (iii) of section 212(a)(3)(C) shall apply to deportability under clause (i) in the same manner as they apply to excludability under section 212(a)(3)(C)(i).

(D) Assisted in Nazi Persecution or Engaged in Genocide.—Any alien described in clause (i) or (ii) of section 212(a)(3)(E) is deportable.

(5) Public Charge.—Any alien who, within five years after the date of entry, has become a public charge from causes not affirmatively shown to have arisen since entry is deportable.

8 U.S.C. § 1251(b), Sec. 241(b) Certain Provisions Inapplicable to Nonimmigrants

An alien, admitted as a nonimmigrant under the provision of either section 1101(a)(15)(A)(i) or 1101(a)(15)(G)(i) of this title, and who fails to maintain a status under either of those provisions, shall not be required to depart from the United States without the approval of the Secretary of State, unless such alien is subject to deportation under subsection (a)(4) of this section.

8 U.S.C. § 1251(d), Sec. 241(d)—Retroactive Application

Except as otherwise specifically provided in this section, the provisions of this section shall be applicable to all aliens belonging to any of the classes enumerated in subsection (a) of this section, notwithstanding (1) that any such alien entered the United States prior to June 27, 1952, or (2) that the facts, by reason of which any such alien belongs to any of the classes enumerated in subsection (a) of this section, occurred prior to June 27, 1952.

Deportation Procedure

8 U.S.C. § 1252, Sec. 242

(a)(1) Pending a determination of deportability in the case of any alien as provided in subsection (b) of this section, such alien may, upon warrant of the Attorney General, be arrested and taken into custody. Any such alien taken into custody may, in the discretion of the Attorney General and pending such final determination of deportability, (A) be continued in custody; or (B) be released under bond in the amount of not less than $500 with security approved by the Attorney General, containing such conditions as the Attorney General may prescribe; or (C) be released on conditional parole. But such bond or parole, whether heretofore or hereafter authorized, may be revoked at any time by the Attorney General, in his discretion, and the alien may be returned to custody under the warrant which initiated the proceedings against him and detained until final determination of his deportability. Any court of competent jurisdiction shall have authority to review or revise any determination of the Attorney General concerning detention, release on bond, or parole pending final decision of deportability upon a conclusive showing in habeas corpus proceedings that the Attorney General is not proceeding with such reasonable dispatch as may be warranted by the particular facts and circumstances in the case of any alien to determine deportability.

(2)(A) The Attorney General shall take into custody any alien convicted of an aggravated felony upon release of the alien (regardless of whether or note such release is on parole, supervised release, or probation, and regardless of the possibility of rearrest or further confinement in respect of the same offense). Notwithstanding paragraph (1) or subsections (c) and (d) but subject to subparagraph (B) the Attorney General shall not release such felon from custody. (B) The Attorney General shall release from custody an alien who is lawfully admitted for permanent residence on bond or such other conditions as the Attorney General may prescribe if the Attorney General determines that the alien is not a threat to the community and that the alien is likely to appear before any scheduled hearings.

(3)(A) The Attorney General shall devise and implement a system—

(i) to make available, daily (on a 24-hour basis), to Federal, State, and local authorities the investigative resources of the Service to determine whether individuals arrested by such authorities for aggravated felonies are aliens;

(ii) to designate and train officers and employees of the Service within each district to serve as a liaison to Federal, State, and local law enforcement and correctional agencies and courts with respect to the arrest, conviction, and release of any alien charged with an aggravated felony; and

(iii) which uses computer resources to maintain a current record of aliens who have been convicted of an aggravated felony and who have been deported; such record shall be made available to inspectors at ports of entry and to border patrol agents at sector headquarters for purposes of immediate identification of any such previously deported alien seeking to reenter the United States.

(B) The Attorney General shall submit reports to the Committees on the Judiciary of the House of Representatives and of the Senate at the end of the 6-month period and at the end of the 18-month period beginning on the effective date of this paragraph which describe in detail specific efforts made by the Attorney General to implement this paragraph.

(b) A special inquiry officer shall conduct proceedings under this section to determine the deportability of any alien, and shall administer oaths, present and receive evidence, interrogate, examine, and cross-examine the alien or witnesses, and, as authorized by the Attorney General, shall make determinations, including orders of deportation. Determination of deportability in any case shall be made only upon a record made in a proceeding before a special inquiry officer, at which the alien shall have reasonable opportunity to be present, unless by reason of the alien's mental incompetency it is impracticable for him to be present, in which case the Attorney General shall prescribe necessary and proper safeguards for the rights and privileges of such alien. If any alien has been given a reasonable opportunity to be present at a proceeding under this section, and without reasonable cause fails or refuses to attend or remain in attendance at such proceeding, the special inquiry officer may proceed to a determination in like manner as if the alien were present. In any case or class of cases in which the Attorney General believes that such procedure would be of aid in making a determination, he may require specifically or by regulation that an additional immigration officer shall be assigned to present the evidence on behalf of the United States and in such case such additional immigration officer shall have authority to present evidence, and to interrogate, examine and cross-examine the alien or other witnesses in the proceedings. Nothing in the preceding sentence shall be construed to diminish the authority conferred upon the special inquiry officer conducting such proceedings. No special inquiry officer shall conduct a proceeding in any case under this section in which he shall have participated in investigative functions or in which he shall have participated (except as provided in this subsection) in prosecuting functions. Proceedings before a special inquiry officer acting under the provisions of this section shall be in accordance with such regulations, not inconsistent with this chapter, as the Attorney General shall prescribe. Such regulations shall include requirements consistent with section 1252b.

The procedure so prescribed shall be the sole and exclusive procedure for determining the deportability of an alien under this section. In any case in which an alien is ordered deported from the United States under the provisions of this chapter, or of any other law or treaty, the decision of the Attorney General shall be final. In the discretion of the Attorney General, and under such regulations as he may prescribe, deportation proceedings, including issuance of a warrant of arrest, and a finding of deportability under this section need not be required in the case of any alien who admits to belonging to a class of aliens who are deportable under section 1251 of this title if such alien voluntarily departs from the United States at his own expense, or is removed at Government expense as hereinafter authorized, unless the Attorney General has reason to believe that such alien is deportable under paragraphs (4) to (2), (3), or (4) of section 1251(a) of this title. If any alien who is authorized to depart voluntarily under the preceding sentence is financially unable to depart at his own expense and the Attorney General deems his removal to be in the best interest of the United States, the expense of such removal may be paid from the appropriation for the enforcement of this chapter.

(c) When a final order of deportation under administrative processes is made against any alien, the Attorney General shall have a period of six months from the date of such order, or, if judicial review is had, then from the date of the final order of the court, within which to effect the alien's departure from the United States, during which period, at the Attorney General's discretion, the alien may be detained, released on bond in an amount and containing such conditions as the Attorney General may prescribe, or released on such other condition as the Attorney General may prescribe. Any court of competent jurisdiction shall have authority to review or revise any determination of the Attorney General concerning detention, release on bond, or other release during such six-month period upon a conclusive showing in habeas corpus proceedings that the Attorney General is not proceeding with such reasonable dispatch as may be warranted by the particular facts and circumstances in the case of any alien to effect such alien's departure from the United States within such six-month period. If deportation has not been practicable, advisable, or possible, or departure of the alien from the United States under the order of deportation has not been effected, within such six-month period, the alien shall become subject to such further supervision and detention pending eventual deportation as is authorized in this section. The Attorney General is authorized and directed to arrange for appropriate places of detention for those aliens whom he shall take into custody and detain under this section. Where no Federal buildings are available or buildings adapted or suitably located for the purpose are available for rental, the Attorney General is authorized, notwithstanding section 5 of title 41 or section 278a of title 40 to expend, from the appropriation provided for the administration and enforcement of the immigration laws, such amounts as may be necessary for the acquisition of land and the erection, acquisition, maintenance, operation, remodeling, or repair of buildings, sheds, and office quarters (including living quarters for officers where none are otherwise available), and adjunct facilities, necessary for the detention of aliens. For the purposes of this section an order of deportation heretofore or hereafter entered against an alien in legal detention or confinement, other than under an immigration process, shall be considered as being made as of the moment he is released from such detention or confinement, and not prior thereto.

(d) Any alien, against whom a final order of deportation as defined in subsection (c) of this section, heretofore or hereafter issued has been outstanding for more than six months, shall, pending eventual deportation, be subject to supervision under regulations prescribed by the Attorney General. Such regulations shall include provisions which will require any alien subject to supervision

(1) to appear from time to time before an immigration officer for identification;

(2) to submit, if necessary, to medical and psychiatric examination at the expense of the United States;

(3) to give information under oath as to his nationality, circumstances, habits, associations, and activities, and such other information, whether or not related to the foregoing, as the Attorney General may deem fit and proper; and

(4) to conform to such reasonable written restrictions on his conduct or activities as are prescribed by the Attorney General in his case. Any alien who shall willfully fail to comply with such regulations, or willfully fail to appear or to give information or submit to medical or psychiatric examination if required, or knowingly give false information in relation to the requirements of such regulations, or knowingly violate a reasonable restriction imposed upon his conduct or activity, shall be fined not more than $1,000 or shall be imprisoned not more than one year, or both.

(e) Any alien against whom a final order of deportation is outstanding by reason of being a member of any of the classes described in paragraphs (4) to (7), (11), (12), (2), (3), or (4) of section 1251(a) of this title, who shall willfully fail or refuse to depart from the United States within a period of six months from the date of the final order of deportation under administrative processes, or, if judicial review is had, then from the date of the final order of the court, or from September 23, 1950, whichever is the later, or shall willfully fail or refuse to make timely application in good faith for travel or other documents necessary to his departure, or who shall connive or conspire, or take any other action, designed to prevent or hamper or with the purpose of preventing or hampering his departure pursuant to such order of deportation, or who shall willfully fail or refuse to present himself for deportation at the time and place required by the Attorney General pursuant to such order of deportation, shall upon conviction be guilty of a felony, and shall be imprisoned not more than ten years: Provided, That this subsection shall not make it illegal for any alien to take any proper steps for the purpose of securing cancellation of or exemption from such order of deportation or for the purpose of securing his release from incarceration or custody: Provided further, That the court may for good cause suspend the sentence of such alien and order his release under such conditions as the court may prescribe. In determining whether good cause has been shown to justify releasing the alien, the court shall take into account such factors as

(1) the age, health, and period of detention of the alien;

(2) the effect of the alien's release upon the national security and public peace or safety;

(3) the likelihood of the alien's resuming or following a course of conduct which made or would make him deportable;

(4) the character of the efforts made by such alien himself and by representatives of the country or countries to which his deportation is directed to expedite the alien's departure from the United States;

(5) the reason for the inability of the Government of the United States to secure passports, other travel documents, or deportation facilities from the country or countries to which the alien has been ordered deported; and

(6) the eligibility of the alien for discretionary relief under the immigration laws.

(f) Should the Attorney General find that any alien has unlawfully reentered the United States after having previously departed or been deported pursuant to an order of deportation, whether before or after June 27, 1952, on any ground described in any of the paragraphs enumerated in subsection (e) of this section, the previous order of deportation shall be deemed to be reinstated from its original date and such alien shall be deported under such previous order at any time subsequent to such reentry. For the purposes of subsection (e) of this section the date on which the finding is made that such reinstatement is appropriate shall be deemed the date of the final order of deportation.

(g) If any alien, subject to supervision or detention under subsections (c) or (d) of this section, is able to depart from the United States under the order of deportation, except that he is financially unable to pay his passage, the Attorney General may in his discretion permit such alien to depart voluntarily, and the expense of such passage to the country to which he is destined may be paid from the appropriation for the enforcement of this chapter, unless such payment is otherwise provided for under this chapter.

(h) An alien sentenced to imprisonment shall not be deported until such imprisonment has been terminated by the release of the alien from confinement. Parole, supervised release, probation, or possibility of rearrest or further confinement in respect of the same offense shall not be a ground for deferral of deportation.

(i) In the case of an alien who is convicted of an offense which makes the alien subject to deportation, the Attorney General shall begin any deportation proceeding as expeditiously as possible after the date of the conviction.

8 U.S.C. § 1252b, Sec. 242B—Deportation Procedures; Required Notice of Deportation Hearing; Limitation on Discretionary Relief

(a) Notices.—

(1) Order to Show Cause.—In deportation proceedings under section 242, written notice (in this section referred to as an "order to show cause") shall be given in person to the alien (or, if personal service is not practicable, such notice shall be given by certified mail to the alien or to the alien's counsel of record, if any) specifying the following:

(A) The nature of the proceedings against the alien.

(B) The legal authority under which the proceedings are conducted.

(C) The acts or conduct alleged to be in violation of law.

(D) The charges against the alien and the statutory provisions alleged to have been violated.

(E) The alien may be represented by counsel and, upon request, the alien will be provided a list of counsel prepared under subsection (b)(2).

(F)(i) The requirement that the alien must immediately provide (or have provided) the Attorney General with a written record of an address and telephone number (if any) at which the alien may be contacted respecting proceedings under section 242.

(ii) The requirement that the alien must provide the Attorney General immediately with a written record of any change of the alien's address or telephone number.

(iii) The consequences under subsection (c)(2) of failure to provide address and telephone information pursuant to this subparagraph.

(2) Notice of Time and Place of Proceedings.—In deportation proceedings under section 242—

(A) written notice shall be given in person to the alien (or, if personal service is not practicable, written notice shall be given by certified mail to the alien or to the alien's counsel of record, if any), in the order to show cause or otherwise, of—

(i) the time and place at which the proceedings will be held, and

(ii) the consequences under subsection (c) of the failure to appear at such proceedings; and

(B) in the case of any change or postponement in the time and place of such proceedings, written notice shall be given in person to the alien (or, if personal service is not practicable, written notice shall be given by certified mail to the alien or to the alien's counsel of record, if any) of—

(i) the new time or place of the proceedings, and

(ii) the consequences under subsection (c) of failing, except under exceptional circumstances, to attend such proceedings.

(3) Form of Information.—Each order to show cause or other notice under this subsection—

(A) shall be in English and Spanish, and

(B) shall specify that the alien may be represented by an attorney in deportation proceedings under section 242 and will be provided, in accordance with subsection (b)(1), a period of time in order to obtain counsel and a current list described in subsection (b)(2).

(4) Central Address Files.—The Attorney General shall create a system to record and preserve on a timely basis notices of addresses and telephone numbers (and changes) provided under paragraph (1)(F).

(b) Securing of Counsel.—

(1) In General.—In order that an alien be permitted the opportunity to secure counsel before the first hearing date in proceedings under section 242, the hearing date shall not be scheduled earlier than 14 days after the service of the order to show cause.

(2) Current Lists Of counsel.—The Attorney General shall provide for lists (updated not less often than quarterly) of persons who have indicated their availability to represent aliens in proceedings under section 242.

(c) Consequences of Failure to Appear.—

(1) In General.—Any alien who, after written notice required under subsection (a)(2) has been provided to the alien or the alien's counsel of record, except as provided in paragraph (2), does not attend a proceeding under section 242, shall be ordered deported under section 242(b)(1) in absentia if the Service establishes by clear, une-

quivocal, and convincing evidence that, except as provided in paragraph (2), the written notice was so provided and that the alien is deportable.

(2) No Notice if Failure To Provide Address Information.—No written notice shall be required under paragraph (1) if the alien has failed to provide the address required under subsection (a)(1)(F). Such written notice shall be considered sufficient if provided at the most recent address provided under such subsection.

(3) Rescission of Order.—Such an order may be rescinded only—

(A) upon a motion to reopen filed within 180 days after the date of the order of deportation if the alien demonstrates that the failure to appear was because of exceptional circumstances (as defined in subsection (f)(2)), or

(B) upon a motion to reopen filed at any time if the alien demonstrates that the alien did not receive notice in accordance with subsection (a)(2) or the alien demonstrates that the alien was in Federal or State custody and did not appear through no fault of the alien. The filing of the motion to reopen described in subparagraph (A) or (B) shall stay the deportation of the alien pending disposition of the motion.

(4) Effect on Judicial Review.—Any petition for review under section 106 of an order entered in absentia under this subsection shall, notwithstanding such section, be filed not later than 60 days after the date of the final order of deportation and shall (except in cases described in section 106(a)(5)) be confined to the issues of the validity of the notice provided to the alien, to the reasons for the alien's not attending the proceeding, and to whether or not clear, convincing, and unequivocal evidence of deportability has been established.

(d) Treatment of Frivolous Behavior.—The Attorney General shall, by regulation—

(1) define in a proceeding before a special inquiry officer or before an appellate administrative body under this title, frivolous behavior for which attorneys may be sanctioned,

(2) specify the circumstances under which an administrative appeal of a decision or ruling will be considered frivolous and will be summarily dismissed, and

(3) impose appropriate sanctions (which may include suspension and disbarment) in the case of frivolous behavior. Nothing in this subsection shall be construed as limiting the authority of the Board to take actions with respect to inappropriate behavior.

(e) Limitation on Discretionary Relief for Failure to Appear.—

(1) At Deportation Proceedings.—Any alien against whom a final order of deportation is entered in absentia under this section and who, at the time of the notice described in subsection (a)(2), was provided oral notice, either in the alien's native language or in another language the alien understands, of the time and place of the proceedings and of the consequences under this paragraph of failing, other than because of exceptional circumstances (as defined in subsection (f)(2)) to attend a proceeding under section 242, shall not be eligible for relief described in paragraph (5) for a period of 5 years after the date of the entry of the final order of deportation.

(2) Voluntary Departure.—

(A) In General.—Subject to subparagraph (B), any alien allowed to depart voluntarily under section 244(e)(1) or who has agreed to depart voluntarily at his own expense under section 242(b)(1) who remains in the United States after the scheduled date of departure, other than because of exceptional circumstances, shall not be eligible for relief described in paragraph (5) for a period of 5 years after the scheduled date of departure or the date of unlawful reentry, respectively.

(B) Written and Oral Notice Required.—Subparagraph (A) shall not apply to an alien allowed to depart voluntarily unless, before such departure, the Attorney General has provided written notice to the alien in English and Spanish and oral notice either in the alien's native language or in another language the alien understands of the consequences under subparagraph (A) of the alien's remaining in the United States after the scheduled date of departure, other than because of exceptional circumstances.

(3) Failure to Appear Under Deportation Order.—

(A) In General.—Subject to subparagraph (B), any alien against whom a final order of deportation is entered under this section and who fails, other than because of exceptional circumstances, to appear for deportation at the time and place ordered shall not be eligible for relief described in paragraph (5) for a period of 5 years after the date the alien was required to appear for deportation.

(B) Written and Oral Notice Required.—Subparagraph (A) shall not apply to an alien against whom a deportation order is entered unless the Attorney General has provided, orally in the alien's native language or in another language the alien understands and in the final order of deportation under this section of the consequences under subparagraph (A) of the alien's failure, other than because of exceptional circumstances, to appear for deportation at the time and place ordered.

(4) Failure to Appear for Asylum Hearing.—

(A) In General.—Subject to subparagraph (B), any alien—

(i) whose period of authorized stay (if any) has expired through the passage of time,

(ii) who has filed an application for asylum, and

(iii) who fails, other than because of exceptional circumstances, to appear at the time and place specified for the asylum hearing, shall not be eligible for relief described in paragraph (5) for a period of 5 years after the date of the asylum hearing.

(B) Written and Oral Notice Required.—Subparagraph (A) shall not apply in the case of an alien with respect to failure to be present at a hearing unless—

(i) written notice in English and Spanish, and oral notice either in the alien's native language or in another language the alien understands, was provided to the alien of the time and place at which the asylum hearing will be held, and in the case of any change or postponement in such time or place, written notice in English and Spanish, and oral notice either in the alien's native language or in another language the alien understands, was provided to the alien of the new time or place of the hearing; and

(ii) notices under clause (i) specified the consequences under subparagraph (A) of failing, other than because of exceptional circumstances, to attend such hearing.

(5) Relief Covered.—The relief described in this paragraph is—

(A) relief under section 212(c),

(B) voluntary departure under section 242(b)(1),

(C) suspension of deportation or voluntary departure under section 244, and

(D) adjustment or change of status under section 245, 248, or 249.

(f) Definitions.—In this section:

(1) The term "certified mail" means certified mail, return receipt requested.

(2) The term "exceptional circumstances" refers to exceptional circumstances (such as serious illness of the alien or death of an immediate relative of the alien, but not including less compelling circumstances) beyond the control of the alien.

Voluntary Departure

8 U.S.C. § 1254(e), Sec. 244(e)

(e)(1) Except as provided in paragraph (2) the Attorney General may, in his discretion, permit any alien under deportation proceedings, other than an alien within the provisions of paragraph (2), (3), or (4) of section 1251(a) of this title (and also any alien within the purview of such paragraphs if he is also within the provisions of paragraph (2) of subsection (a) of this section), to depart voluntarily from the United States at his own expense in lieu of deportation if such alien shall establish to the satisfaction of the Attorney General that he is, and has been, a person of good moral character for at least five years immediately preceding his application for voluntary departure under this subsection.

(2) The authority contained in paragraph (1) shall not apply to any alien who is deportable because of a conviction for an aggravated felony.

---

8 C.F.R. § 242
Deportation Proceedings

§ 242.1 Order to Show Cause and Notice.

(a) Commencement. Every proceeding to determine the deportability of an alien in the United States is commenced by the filing of an Order to Show Cause with the Office of the Immigration Judge, except an alien who has been admitted to the United States under the provisions of section 217 of the Act and Part 217 of this chapter other than such an alien who has applied for asylum in the United States. In the proceeding the alien shall be known as the respondent. Orders to show cause may be issued by:

* * *

(b) Statement of Nature of Proceedings. The Order to Show Cause shall contain a statement of the nature of the proceeding, the legal authority under which the proceeding is conducted, a concise statement of factual allegations informing the respondent of the act or conduct alleged to be in violation of the law, and a designation of the charge against the respondent and of the statutory provisions alleged to have been violated. The Order shall require the respondent to show cause why he should not be deported. The Order shall call upon the respondent to appear before an Immigration Judge for a hearing at a time and place which shall be specified by the Office of the Immigration Judge.

(c) Service. Service of the order to show cause may be accomplished either by personal service or by routine service; however, when routine service is used and the respondent does not appear for hearing or acknowledge in writing that he has received the order to show cause, it shall be reserved by personal service. When personal delivery of an order to show cause is made by an immigration officer, the contents of the order to show cause shall be explained and the respondent shall be advised that any statement he makes may be used against him. He shall also be advised of his right to representation by counsel of his own choice at no expense to the Government. He shall also be advised of the availability of free legal services programs qualified under Part 292a of this chapter and organizations recognized pursuant to § 292.2 of this chapter, located in the district where his deportation hearing will be held. He shall be furnished with a list of such programs, and a copy of Form I-618, Written Notice of Appeal Rights, regardless of the manner in which the service of the order to show cause was accomplished. Service of these documents shall be noted on Form I-213.

(d) Visa Waiver Pilot Program. Pursuant to section 217(b)(4)(B) of the Act, an alien who has been admitted to the United States under the provisions of that section has waived any right to contest any action against him or her for deportation, other than on the basis of an application for asylum. An alien admitted to the United States under section 217 of the Act shall be taken into custody and removed from the United States upon a determination by an immigration officer (district director who has jurisdiction over the place where the alien is found) that the alien is deportable in accordance with procedures in § 217.4(c) of this chapter, and without commencement of a proceeding under this part, except that such an alien who applies for asylum in the United States shall be brought into proceedings as otherwise provided in this part.

§ 242.2 Apprehension, custody, and detention.

(a) Detainers in general.

(1) Only an immigration officer as defined in section 101(a)(18) of the Act, or § 103.1(q) of this chapter is authorized to issue a detainer. Detainers may only be issued in the case of an alien who is amenable to exclusion or deportation proceedings under any provision of law; however, no detainer shall be issued in the case of an alien who is in the United States without legal authority and is eligible to apply, or has applied, for legalization or special agricultural worker status under the provisions of section 245A or 210 of the Act, unless the Service has denied, or has issued a notice of intent to deny, the benefit applied for.

(2) Availability of records. In order for the Service to accurately determine the propriety of issuing a detainer, serving an order to show cause, or taking custody of an alien in accordance with this section, the criminal justice agency requesting such action or informing the Service of a conviction or act which renders an alien excludable or deportable under any provision of law shall provide the Service with all documentary records and information available from the agency which reasonably relates to the alien's status in the United States, or which may have an impact on conditions of release.

(3) Telephonic detainers. Issuance of a detainer in accordance with this section may be authorized telephonically, provided such authorizations are confirmed in writing on Form I-247, or by electronic communications transfer media (e.g., the National Law Enforcement Telecommunications System (NLETS)) within twenty-four

hours of the telephonic authorization. The contents of the electronic transfer shall contain substantially the same language as the Form I-247.

(4) Temporary detention at Service request. Upon a determination by the Service to issue a detainer for an alien not otherwise detained by a criminal justice agency, such agency shall maintain custody of the alien for a period not to exceed forty-eight hours, in order to permit assumption of custody by the Service.

(5) Financial responsibility for detention. No detainer issued as a result of a determination made under this chapter shall incur any fiscal obligation on the part of the Service, until actual assumption of custody by the Service, except as provided in paragraph (a)(4) of this section.

                                   *   *   *

(c) Warrant of arrest.

(1) At the time of issuance of the Order to Show Cause or at any time thereafter and up to the time the respondent becomes subject to supervision under the authority contained in section 242(d) of the Act, the respondent may be arrested and taken into custody under the authority of a warrant of arrest. However, such warrant may be issued by no other than a: (i) District director; (ii) Acting district director; (iii) Deputy district director; (iv) Assistant district director for investigations; (v) Assistant district director for deportation; (vi) Assistant district director for examinations; (vii) Assistant district director for anti-smuggling; (viii) Officer in charge (except foreign); (ix) Chief patrol agent; (x) Deputy chief patrol agent; (xi) Associate chief patrol agent; (xii) Assistant chief patrol agent; or (xiii) The Assistant Commissioner, Investigations.

(2) If, after the issuance of a warrant of arrest, a determination is made not to serve it, any officer authorized to issue such warrant may authorize its cancellation. When a warrant of arrest is served under this part, the respondent shall have explained to him/her the contents of the order to show cause, the reason for the arrest and the right to be represented by counsel of his/her own choice at no expense to the Government. He/she shall also be advised of the availability of free legal services programs qualified under Part 292a of this chapter and organizations recognized pursuant to § 292.2 of this chapter, located in the district where the deportation hearing will be held. The respondent shall be furnished with a list of such programs, and a copy of Form I-618, Written Notice of Appeal Rights. Service of these documents shall be noted on Form I-213. The respondent shall be advised that any statement made may be used against him/her. He/she shall also be informed whether custody is to be continued or, if release from custody has been authorized, of the amount and conditions of the bond or the conditions of release. A respondent on whom a warrant of arrest has been served may apply to any officer authorized by this section to issue such a warrant for release or for amelioration of the conditions under which he/she may be released. When serving the warrant of arrest and when determining any application pertaining thereto, the authorized officer shall furnish the respondent with a notice of decision, which may be on Form I-286, indicating whether custody will be continued or terminated, specifying any conditions under which release is permitted, and advising the respondent appropriately whether he/she may apply to an immigration judge pursuant to paragraph (d) of this section for release or modification of the conditions of release or whether he/she may appeal to the Board. A direct appeal to the Board from a determination by an officer authorized by this

section to issue warrants shall not be allowed except as authorized by paragraph (d) of this section.

(d) Authority of Immigration Judge; Appeals. After an initial determination pursuant to paragraph (c) of this section, and at any time before a deportation order becomes administratively final, upon application by the respondent for release from custody or for amelioration of the conditions under which he or she may be released, an Immigration Judge may exercise the authority contained in section 242 of the Act to continue to detain a respondent in, or release from custody, and to determine whether a respondent shall be released under bond, and the amount thereof, if any. Application for the exercise of such authority must be made in the following order: First, if the alien is detained, the Immigration Judge Office at or nearest the place of detention; second, the Immigration Judge Office having administrative control over the case; third, the Office of the Chief Immigration Judge for designation of an appropriate Office of the Immigration Judge. However, if the respondent has been released from custody, such application must be made within seven (7) days after the date of such release. Thereafter, application by a released respondent for modification of the terms release may be made only to the District Director. In connection with such application the Immigration Judge shall advise the respondent of his right to representation by counsel of his or her choice at no expense to the government. He or she shall also be advised of the availability of free legal services programs qualified under Part 292(a) of this chapter and organizations recognized pursuant to § 292.2 of this chapter, located in the district where his or her application is to be heard. The Immigration Judge shall ascertain that the respondent has received a list of such programs, and the receipt by the respondent of a copy of Form I-618, Written Notice of Appeal Rights. Upon rendering a decision on an application under this section, the Immigration Judge (or District Director if he renders the decision) shall advise the alien of his or her appeal rights under this section. The determination of the Immigration Judge in respect to custody status or bond redetermination shall be entered on the appropriate EOIR form at the time such decision is made, and the parties shall be promptly informed orally or in writing as to the reasons for the Judge's decision. Consideration under this paragraph by the Immigration Judge of an application or request of a alien regarding custody or bond shall be separate and apart from any deportation hearing or proceeding under this part, and shall form no part of such hearing or proceeding. The determination of the Immigration Judge as to custody status or bond may be based upon any information which is available to the Immigration Judge or which is presented to him by the alien or the Service. The alien and the Service may appeal to the Board of Immigration Appeals from any such determination. If the determination is appealed, a written memorandum shall be prepared by the Immigration Judge giving reasons for the decision. After a deportation order becomes administratively final, or if recourse to the Immigration Judge is no longer available because of the expiration of the seven-day period aforementioned, the respondent may appeal directly to the Board from a determination by the District Director, Acting District Director, Deputy District Director, Assistant District Director for Investigations, or Officer in Charge of an office enumerated in § 242.1(a), except that no appeal shall be allowed when the Service notifies the alien that it is ready to execute the order of deportation and takes him into custody for that purpose. An appeal to the Board shall be taken from a determination by an Immigration Judge pursuant to § 3.36 of this chapter. An appeal to the Board taken from an appealable determination by the District Director, Acting District Director, Deputy District Director, Assistant District Director for Investigations, or Officer in Charge of an office enumerated in § 242.1(a), shall be perfected by filing a notice of appeal with the District Director within 10 days after the date when written notification of the determination is served upon the respondent and the Service. Upon the filing of a notice of appeal from a District Director's determination, the District Director shall immediately transmit to the Board all records and information pertaining to that determination. The filing of an appeal from a determination of an Immigration Judge or a District Director shall not operate to delay compliance, during the pendency of the appeal, with the custody directive from which appeal is taken, or to stay the administrative proceedings or deportation.

(e) Revocation. When an alien who, having been arrested and taken into custody, has been released, such release may be revoked at any time in the discretion of the district director, acting district director, deputy district director, assistant district director for investigations, or officer in charge of an office enumerated in § 242.1(a), in which event the alien may be taken into physical custody and detained. If detained, unless a breach has occurred, any outstanding bond shall be revoked and cancelled. The provisions of paragraph (d) of this section shall govern availability to the respondent of recourse to other administrative authority for release from custody.

(f) Supervision. Until an alien against whom a final order of deportation has been outstanding for more than six months is deported, he shall be subject to supervision by a district director, acting district director, deputy district director, assistant district director for investigations, or officer in charge of an office enumerated in § 242.1(a), and required to comply with the provisions of section 242(d) of the Act relating to his availability for deportation.

(g) Privilege of communication. Every detained alien shall be notified that he may communicate with the consular or diplomatic officers of the country of his nationality in the United States. Existing treaties require immediate communication with appropriate consular or diplomatic officers whenever nationals of the following countries are detained in exclusion or expulsion proceedings, whether or not requested by the alien, and, in fact, even if the alien requests that no communication be undertaken in his behalf:

*   *   *

§ 242.5 Voluntary departure prior to commencement of hearing.

(a)(1) Authorized officers. The authority contained in section 242(b) of the act to permit aliens to depart voluntarily from the United States may be exercised by district directors, district officers who are in charge of investigations, officers in charge, and chief patrol agents.

(2) Authorization. Voluntary departure may be granted to any alien who is statutorily eligible:

(i) Who is a native of a foreign contiguous territory and not within the purview of class (vi) of this paragraph; or

(ii) whose application for extension of stay as a nonimmigrant is being denied; or

(iii) who has voluntarily surrendered himself to the Service; or

(iv) who presents a valid travel document and confirmed reservation for transportation out of the United States within 30 days; or

(v) who is an F-1, F-2, J-1, or J-2 nonimmigrant and who has lost such status solely because of a private bill introduced in his/her behalf; or

(vi) who is admissible to the United States as an immigrant and:

(A) Who is an immediate relative of a U.S. citizen, or

(B) is otherwise exempt from the numerical limitation on immigrant visa issuance, or

(C) has a priority date for an immigrant visa not more than 60 days later than the date shown in the latest Visa Office Bulletin and has applied for an immigrant visa at an American Consulate which has accepted jurisdiction over the case, or

(D) who is a third-preference alien with a priority date earlier than August 9, 1978, or

(E) who is the beneficiary of an approved sixth-preference petition who satisfies Examinations without another petition that he/she can qualify for third preference and who cannot obtain a visa solely because a visa number is unavailable, and who has a priority date earlier than August 9, 1978; or

(vii) who has been granted asylum and has not been granted parole status or a stay of deportation; or

(viii) in whose case the district director has determined there are compelling factors warranting grant of voluntary departure.

(3) Periods of time. Except for classes (v), (vi), (vii), and (viii) of paragraph (a)(2) of this section, any grant of voluntary departure shall contain a time limitation of usually not more than 30 days, and an extension of the original voluntary departure time shall not be authorized except under meritorious circumstances. Upon failure to depart, deportation proceedings will be pursued. Class (v) may be granted voluntary departure in increments of 1 year conditioned upon the F-1 or J-1 alien maintaining a full course of study at an approved institution of learning, or upon abiding by the terms and conditions of the exchange program within the limitations imposed by 22 CFR 514.23. Classes (vi) (A), (B), and (C) may be granted voluntary departure until the American consul is ready to issue an immigrant visa and, in the discretion of the district director, may be in increments of 30 days, conditioned upon continuing availability of an immigrant visa as shown in the latest Visa Office Bulletin and upon the alien's diligent pursuit of efforts to obtain the visa. Classes (vi) (D) and (E) may be granted voluntary departure, conditioned upon the approved third- or sixth-preference petition as appropriate, remaining valid as well as the alien's retention of the status established in the petition, for an indefinite period until an immigrant visa is available. Classes (vii) and (viii) may be granted voluntary departure in increments of time, not to exceed 1 year, as determined by the district director to be appropriate in the case. Form I-94 issued to an alien granted voluntary departure, who is within class (v), (vi), (vii), or (viii) of paragraph (a)(2) of this section may be stamped with the legend "Employment Authorized" if the alien seeks some indication from the Service that he is entitled to be employed.

(b) Application. Any alien who believes himself or herself to be eligible for voluntary departure under section 242(b) of the Act may apply therefore at any office of the Service any time prior to the commencement of deportation proceedings against him or her. The officers designated in paragraph (a) of this section may deny or grant the application and determine the conditions under which the alien's departure shall be effected. An appeal shall not lie from a denial of an application for voluntary departure under this section, but the denial shall be without prejudice to the alien's right to apply for relief from deportation under any provision of law.

(c) Revocation. If, subsequent to the granting of an application for voluntary departure under this section, it is ascertained that the application should not have been granted, that grant may be revoked without notice by any district director, district officer in charge of investigations, officer in charge, or chief patrol agent.

*　　*　　*

§ 242.7 Cancellation proceedings.

(a) Cancellation of an order to show cause. Any officer authorized by § 242.1 (a) of this part to issue an order to show cause may cancel an order to show cause prior to jurisdiction vesting with the Immigration Judge pursuant to § 3.14 of this chapter provided the officer is satisfied that:

(1) The respondent is a national of the United States;

(2) The respondent is not deportable under immigration laws;

(3) The respondent is deceased;

(4) The respondent is not in the United States; or

(5) The Order to Show Cause was improvidently issued.

(b) Motion to dismiss. After commencement of proceedings pursuant to § 3.14 of this chapter, any officer enumerated in paragraph (a) of this section may move for dismissal of the matter on the grounds set out under paragraph (a) of this section. Dismissal of the matter shall be without prejudice to the alien or the Service.

(c) Motion for remand. After commencement of the hearing, any officer enumerated in paragraph (a) of this section may move for remand of the matter to district jurisdiction on the ground that the foreign relations of the United States are involved and require further consideration. Remand of the matter shall be without prejudice to the alien or the Service.

(d) Warrant of arrest. When an order to show cause is cancelled or proceedings are terminated under this section any outstanding warrant of arrest is cancelled.

(e) Termination of deportation proceedings by immigration judge. An immigration judge may terminate deportation proceedings to permit the respondent to proceed to a final hearing on a pending application or petition for naturalization when the respondent has established prima facie eligibility for naturalization and the matter involves exceptionally appealing or humanitarian factors; in every other case, the deportation hearing shall be completed as promptly as possible notwithstanding the pendency of an application for naturalization during any state of the proceedings.

*　　*　　*

§ 242.8 Immigration judges.

(a) Authority. In any proceeding conducted under this part the immigration judge shall have the authority to determine deportability and to make decisions, including orders of deportation, as provided by section 242(b) of the Act; to reinstate orders of deportation as provided by section 242(f) of the Act; to determine applications under sections 208, 212(k), 241(a) (11), 241(f), 244, 245, and 249 of the Act; to determine the country to which an alien's deportation will be directed in accordance with section 243(a) of the Act; to order temporary withholding of deportation pursuant to section 243(h) of the Act; and to take any other action consistent with applicable law and regulations as may be appropriate. An immigration judge may certify his or her decision in any case to the Board of Immigration Appeals when it involves an unusually complex or novel question of law or fact. Nothing contained in this part shall be construed to diminish the authority conferred on immigration judges under section 103 of the Act.

(b) Withdrawal and substitution of special inquiry officers. The special inquiry officer assigned to conduct the hearing shall at any time withdraw if he deems himself disqualified. If a hearing has begun but no evidence has been adduced other than by the respondent's pleading pursuant to § 242.16(b), or if a special inquiry officer becomes unavailable to complete his duties within a reasonable time, or if at any time the respondent consents to a substitution, another special inquiry officer may be assigned to complete the case. The new special inquiry officer shall familiarize himself with the record in the case and shall state for the record that he has done so.

§ 242.9 Trial attorney.

(a) Authority. When an additional immigration officer is assigned to a proceeding under this part to perform the duties of a trial attorney, he shall present on behalf of the Government evidence material to the issues of deportability and any other issues which may require disposition by the special inquiry officer. The trial attorney is authorized to appeal from a decision of the special inquiry officer pursuant to § 242.21 and to move for reopening or reconsideration pursuant to § 242.22.

(b) Assignment. The district director shall direct the chief legal officer to assign a general attorney to each case within the provisions of § 242.16(c) of this part, and to each case in which an unrepresented respondent is incompetent or under 16 years of age, and is not accompanied by a guardian, relative or friend. A general attorney shall be assigned to every case in which the Commissioner approves the submission of nonrecord information under § 242.17(a) of this part. In his discretion, whenever he deems such assignment necessary or advantageous, the district director may direct the chief legal officer to assign a general attorney to any other case at any stage of the proceeding.

*   *   *

§ 242.12 Interpreter.

Any person acting as interpreter in a hearing before an Immigration Judge under this part shall be sworn to interpret and translate accurately, unless the interpreter is an employee of the United States Government, in which event no such oath shall be required.

§ 242.13 Postponement and adjournment of hearing.

After the commencement of the hearing, the Immigration Judge may grant a reasonable adjournment either at his or her own instance or, for good cause shown, upon application by the respondent or the Service.

§ 242.14 Evidence.

(a) Sufficiency. A determination of deportability shall not be valid unless it is found by clear, unequivocal and convincing evidence that the facts alleged as grounds for deportation are true.

(b) (Reserved)

(c) Use of prior statements. The special inquiry officer may receive in evidence any oral or written statement which is material and relevant to any issue in the case previously made by the respondent or any other person during any investigation, examination, hearing, or trial.

(d) Testimony. Testimony of witnesses appearing at the hearing shall be under oath or affirmation administered by the special inquiry officer.

(e) Depositions. The Immigration Judge may order the taking of depositions pursuant to § 3.33 of this chapter.

§ 242.15 Contents of record.

The hearing before the special inquiry officer, including the testimony, exhibits, applications and requests, the special inquiry officer's decision, and all written orders, motions, appeals, briefs, and other papers filed in the proceedings shall constitute the record in the case. The hearing shall be recorded verbatim except for statements made off the record with the permission of the special inquiry officer. In his discretion, the special inquiry officer may exclude from the record any arguments made in connection with motions, applications, requests, or objections, but in such event the person affected may submit a brief.

§ 242.16 Hearing.

(a) Opening. The Immigration Judge shall advise the respondent of his right to representation, at no expense to the Government, by counsel of his own choice authorized to practice in the proceedings and require him to state then and there whether he desires representation; advise the respondent of the availability of free legal services programs qualified under Part 292a of this chapter and organizations recognized pursuant to § 292.2 of this chapter, located in the district where the deportation hearing is being held; ascertain that the respondent has received a list of such programs, and a copy of Form I-618, Written Notice of Appeal Rights; advise the respondent that he will have a reasonable opportunity to examine and object to the evidence against him, to present evidence in his own behalf and to cross-examine witnesses presented by the Government; place the respondent under oath; read the factual allegations and the charges in the order to show cause to the respondent and explain them in nontechnical language; and enter the order to show cause as an exhibit in the record. Deportation hearings shall be open to the public, except that the Immigration Judge may, in his discretion and for the purpose of protecting witnesses, respondents, or the public interest, direct that the general public or particular individuals shall be excluded from the hearing in any specific case. Depending upon physical facilities, reasonable limitation may be placed upon the number in attendance at any one time, with priority being given to the press over the general public.

(b) Pleading by respondent. The special inquiry officer shall require the respondent to plead to the order to show cause by stating whether he admits or denies the factual allegations and his deportability under the charges contained therein. If the respondent admits the factual allegations and admits his deportability under the charges and the special inquiry officer is satisfied that no issues of law or fact remain, the special inquiry officer may determine that deportability as charged has been established by the admissions of the respondent. The special inquiry officer shall not accept an admission of deportability from an unrepresented respondent who is incompetent or under age 16 and is not accompanied by a guardian, relative, or friend; nor from an officer of an institution in which a respondent is an inmate or patient. When, pursuant to this paragraph, the special inquiry officer may not accept an admission of deportability, he shall direct a hearing on the issues.

(c) Issues of deportability. When deportability is not determined under the provisions of paragraph (b) of this section, the special inquiry officer shall request the assignment of a trial attorney, and shall receive evidence as to any unresolved issues, except that no further evidence need be received as to any facts admitted during the pleading.

(d) Additional charges. The Service may at any time during a hearing lodge additional charges of deportability, including factual allegations, against the respondent. Copies of the additional factual allegations and charges shall be submitted in writing for service on the respondent and entry as an exhibit in the record. The Immigration Judge shall read the additional factual allegations and charges to the respondent and explain them to him or her. The special inquiry officer shall read the additional factual allegations and charges to the respondent and explain them to him in nontechnical language. The special inquiry officer shall advise the respondent if he is not represented by counsel that he may be so represented and also that he may have a reasonable time within which to meet the additional factual allegations and charges. The respondent shall be required to state then and there whether he desires a continuance for either of these reasons. Thereafter, the provisions of paragraph (b) of this section shall apply to the additional factual allegations and lodged charges.

§ 242.17 Ancillary matters, applications.

(a) Creation of the status of an alien lawfully admitted for permanent residence. The respondent may apply to the special inquiry officer for suspension of deportation under section 244(a) of the Act, for adjustment of status under section 245 of the Act, or under section 1 of the Act of November 2, 1966, or under section 101 or 104 of the Act of October 28, 1977, or for creation of a record of lawful admission for permanent residence under section 214(d) or 249 of the Act; such application shall be subject to the requirements contained in Parts 244, 245, and 249 of this chapter. In conjunction with such applications, if the respondent is inadmissible under any provision of section 212(a) of the Act and believes he meets the eligibility requirements for a waiver of the ground of inadmissibility, he may apply to the special inquiry officer for such waiver. The special inquiry officer shall inform the respondent of his apparent eligibility to apply for any of the benefits enumerated in this paragraph and shall afford him an opportunity to make application therefor during the hearing. In exercising discretionary power when considering an application under this paragraph, the special inquiry officer may consider and base his decision on information not contained in the record and not made available for inspection by the respondent, provided the Commissioner has determined that such information is relevant and is classified under Executive Order No. 12356 (47 FR 14874; April 6, 1982) as requiring protection from unauthorized disclosure in the interest of national security. Whenever he believes he can do so consistently with safeguarding both the information and its source, the special inquiry officer should inform the respondent of the general nature of the information in order that the respondent may have an opportunity to offer opposing evidence. A decision based in whole or in part on such classified information shall state that the information is material to the decision.

(b) Voluntary departure. The respondent may apply to the special inquiry officer for voluntary departure in lieu of deportation pursuant to section 244(e) of the Act and Part 244 of this chapter.

(c) Temporary withholding of deportation. The special inquiry officer shall notify the respondent that if he is finally ordered deported his deportation will in the first instance be directed pursuant to section 243(a) of the Act to the country designated by him and shall afford the respondent an opportunity then and there to make such designation. The special inquiry officer shall then specify and state for the record the country, or countries in the alternate, to which respondent's deportation will be directed pursuant to section 243(a) of the Act if the country of his designation will not accept him into its territory, or fails to furnish timely notice of acceptance, or the respondent declines to designate a country. The respondent shall be advised that pursuant to section 243(h) of the Act he may apply for temporary withholding of deportation to the country or countries specified by the special inquiry officer and may be granted not more than ten days in which to submit his application. The application shall consist of respondent's statement setting forth the reasons in support of his request. The respondent shall be examined under oath on his application and may present such pertinent evidence or information as he has readily available. The respondent has the burden of satisfying the special inquiry officer that he would be subject to persecution on account of race, religion, or political opinion as claimed. The trial attorney may also present evidence or information for the record, and he may submit information not of record to be considered by the special inquiry officer provided that the special inquiry officer or the Board has determined that such information is relevant and is classified under Executive Order No. 12356 (47 FR 14874; April 6, 1982) as requiring protection from unauthorized disclosure in the interest of national security. When the special inquiry officer receives such non-record information he shall inform the respondent thereof and shall also inform him whether it concerns conditions generally in a specified country or the respondent himself. Whenever he believes he can do so consistently with safeguarding both the information and its source, the special inquiry officer should state more specifically the general nature of the information in order that the respondent may have an opportunity to offer opposing evidence. A decision based in whole or in part on such classified information shall state that such information is material to the decision.

(d) Application for relief under section 241(f). The respondent may apply to the immigration judge for relief from deportation under section 241(f) of the Act.

(e) General. An application under this section shall be made only during the hearing and shall not be held to constitute a concession of alienage or deportability in any case in which the respondent does not admit his alienage or deportability. The respondent shall have the burden of establishing that he is eligible for any requested benefit or privilege and that it should be granted in the exercise of discretion. The respondent shall not be required to pay a fee on more than one application within paragraphs (a) and (c) of this section, provided that the minimum fee imposed when more than one application is made shall be determined by the cost of the application with the highest fee. Nothing contained herein is intended to foreclose the respondent from applying for any benefit or privilege which he believes himself eligible to receive in proceedings under this part.

§ 242.18 Decision of special inquiry officer.

(a) Contents. The decision of the special inquiry officer may be oral or written. Except when deportability is determined on the pleadings pursuant to § 242.16(b), the decision of the special inquiry officer shall include a discussion of the evidence and findings as to deportability. The formal enumeration of findings is not required. The decision shall also contain a discussion of the evidence pertinent to any application made by the respondent under § 242.17 and the reasons for granting or denying the request. The decision shall be concluded with the order of the special inquiry officer.

(b) Summary decision. Notwithstanding the provisions of paragraph (a) of this section, in any case where deportability is determined on the pleadings pursuant to § 242.16(b) and the respondent does not make an application under 2.WL § 242.17, or the respondent applies for voluntary departure only and the special inquiry officer grants the application, the special inquiry officer may enter a summary decision on Form I-38, if deportation is ordered, or on Form I-39, if voluntary departure is granted with an alternate order of deportation.

(c) Order of the special inquiry officer. The order of the special inquiry officer shall direct the respondent's deportation, or the termination of the proceedings, or such other disposition of the case as may be appropriate. When deportation is ordered, the special inquiry officer shall specify the country, or countries in the alternate, to which respondent's deportation shall be directed. The special inquiry officer is authorized to issue orders in the alternative or in combination as he may deem necessary.

§ 242.19 Notice of decision.

(a) Written decision. A written decision shall be served upon the respondent and the trial attorney, together with the notice referred to in § 3.3 of this chapter. Service by mail is complete upon mailing.

(b) Oral decision. An oral decision shall be stated by the special inquiry officer in the presence of the respondent and the trial attorney, if any, at the conclusion of the hearing. Unless appeal from the decision is waived, the respondent shall be furnished with Notice of Appeal, Form I-290A, and advised of the provisions of § 242.21. A typewritten copy of the oral decision shall be furnished at the request of the respondent or the trial attorney.

(c) Summary decision. When the special inquiry officer renders a summary decision as provided in § 242.18(b), he shall serve a copy thereof upon the respondent at the conclusion of the hearing. Unless appeal from the decision is waived, the respondent shall be furnished with Notice of Appeal, Form I-290A, and advised of the provisions of § 242.21.

* * *

§ 242.23 Proceedings under section 242(f) of the Act.

(a) Order to show cause. In the case of an alien within the provisions of section 242(f) of the Act, the order to show cause shall charge him with deportability under section 242(f) of the Act. The prior order of deportation and evidence of the execution thereof, properly identified, shall constitute prima facie cause for deportability under this section.

(b) *Applicable procedure.* Except as otherwise provided in this section, proceedings under section 242(f) of the Act shall be conducted in general accordance with the rules prescribed in this part.

(c) *Deportability.* In determining the deportability of an alien alleged to be within the purview of paragraph (a) of this section, the issues shall be limited solely to a determination of the identity of the respondent, i.e., whether the respondent is in fact an alien who was previously deported, or who departed while an order of deportation was outstanding; whether the respondent was previously deported as a member of any of the classes described in paragraph (4), (5), (6), (7), (11), (12), (14), (15), (16), (17), or (18) of section 241(a) of the Act; and whether respondent has unlawfully reentered the United States.

(d) *Order.* If deportability as charged in the order to show cause is established, the special inquiry officer shall order that the respondent be deported under the previous order of deportation in accordance with section 242(f) of the Act.

(e) *Trial attorney; additional charges.* When a trial attorney is assigned to a proceeding under this section and additional charges are lodged against the respondent, the provisions of paragraphs (c) and (d) of this section shall cease to apply.

Voluntary Departure Incident to Deportation

8 C.F.R. § 244.1 Application.

Pursuant to Part 242 of this chapter and section 244 of the Act an immigration judge may authorize the suspension of an alien's deportation; or, if the alien establishes that he/she is willing and has the immediate means with which to depart promptly from the United States, an immigration judge may authorize the alien to depart voluntarily from the United States in lieu of deportation within such time as may be specified by the immigration judge when first authorizing voluntary departure, and under such conditions as the district director shall direct. An application for suspension of deportation shall be made on Form I-256A.

8 C.F.R. § 244.2 Extension of time to depart.

Authority to reinstate or extend the time within which to depart voluntarily specified initially by an immigration judge or the Board is within the sole jurisdiction of the district director, except that an immigration judge or the Board may reinstate voluntary departure in a deportation proceeding that has been reopened for a purpose other than solely making an application for voluntary departure. A request by an alien for reinstatement or an extension of time within which to depart voluntarily shall be filed with the district director having jurisdiction over the alien's place of residence. Written notice of the district director's decision shall be served upon the alien and no appeal may be taken therefrom.

8 C.F.R. § 243.5 Self-deportation.

A district director may permit an alien ordered deported to depart at his own expense to a destination of his own choice. Any alien who has departed from the United States while an order of deportation is outstanding shall be considered to have been deported in pursuance of law, except that an alien who departed before the expiration of the voluntary departure time granted in connection with an alternate order of deportation shall not be considered to have been so deported.

Chapter 4

Asylum and Refugee Status

The period following World War II has seen a tremendous growth in the international community's concern for the rights of refugees. The immigration laws of the United States originally did not recognize a right of asylum for persons seeking admission. Up until 1952, the only way that a person in fear of persecution could obtain refuge in this country was either through special legislation or through admission as a parolee.[1] As will be seen in the following discussion, the laws protecting refugees have followed a pattern of reacting to refugee crises rather than following a well-thought-out plan to assure the orderly admission of persons fleeing some type of upheaval.[2]

The post-World War II era presented enormous problems for the U.S., resulting in numerous legislative efforts to allow the admission of refugees. The first major legislative enactment was the Displaced Persons Act of 1948.[3] This statute allowed for the admission of more than 400,000 refugees as immigrants under the immigration quota system.[4] One writer has described the Displaced Persons Act as "mortgaging" of the regular immigration quotas into the future.[5] In short, the admission of these 400,000 refugees was at the expense of quotas normally allocated to immigrants.

The next important refugee provision, in effect from 1953 until 1956, was referred to as the Refugee Relief Act of 1953.[6] The Refugee Relief Act ameliorated some of the adverse impact of refugee admissions on the admission of other immigrants. This statute permitted the INS to admit 214,000 refugees without any effect on the quota system. The Hungarian revolt of 1956 brought confusion to the plans of the Refugee Relief Act as it occurred toward the end of 1956, coinciding with the expiration of the Refugee Relief Act. Ultimately, more than 38,000 Hungarian refugees were ad-

---

1. Though many refugees obtained sanctuary in the U.S., they came as immigrants, not asylees, under the general authorization of the immigration laws. The term "parolee" was discussed in Chapter 2.

2. One major distinction between the refugee and other persons coming to a country is that the refugee is fleeing some type of social or political upheaval. On the other hand many people do leave their country voluntarily: either for work (economic migrants) or to join family members (family unification).

3. Act of June 25, 1948, 62 Stat. 1009.

4. As will be discussed later, persons seeking permanent admission because of their family ties or due to the unavailability of U.S. workers are admitted in limited numbers under an immigrant quota system. *See* Chapter 7.

5. *See* 1 C. Gordon & S. Mailman, Immigration Law and Procedure 2-184 (rev. ed. 1990). This borrowing against future admissions was terminated in 1957. Act of Sept. 11, 1957, 71 Stat. 642.

6. Act of Aug. 7, 1953, 67 Stat. 400.

mitted to the United States. Only 6,000 were admitted under the Refugee Act and the remaining 32,000 had to be paroled into the country.

Protecting Refugees with Parole

The legislative approach used to respond to the refugee problems which followed World War II until 1956 became the model for refugee relief until the major statutory enactment in 1980. The pattern used to respond to refugees was one which reacted to crisis either by allowing the admission of the refugees through an act of grace by Congress or through the administrative grant of parole. The grant of parole would be followed within a short period by Congress' enactment of legislation adjusting the refugee's status to lawful permanent residence.[7] Prior to 1950, there was no special procedure for the protection of a person who feared persecution upon return to a particular country. The remedy available was either to admit the person under parole or defer her deportation.[8] In 1950, Section 243(h)[9] of the Act was amended to prevent the Attorney General from deporting a person to a country where she would be subjected to "physical" persecution.[10] Section 243(h) was modified in 1952 to emphasize the discretionary nature of the Attorney General's power to "withhold" deportation.[11] A 1965 amendment eliminated the requirement that persecution be physical.[12] The 1965 amendments also included a special provision for admitting a limited number of refugees through a procedure known as conditional entry status. This device was similar to the parole status discussed earlier. It provided for the admission and grant of permanent residence of certain groups fleeing persecution from Communist-dominated countries or Middle Eastern countries as well as persons fleeing a presidentially declared "natural calamity."[13]

---

7. *See* e.g., Cuban Adjustment Act of 1966, Pub. L. No. 89-732, 80 Stat. 1161; Indochina Refugee Adjustment Act of 1977, Pub. L. No. 95-145, 91 Stat. 1223.

8. *See* discussion of parole in Chapter 2. The administrative practice of deferred action or "deferral of prosecution" are discussed at Chapter 11.

9. 8 U.S.C. § 1253(h). This section of the statute deals with the deportation of persons from the United States.

10. *See* Sec. 20(a), Act of Feb. 5, 1917, 39 Stat. 890, as amended by Sec. 23, Internal Security Act of 1950, 64 Stat. 987.

11. Sec. 243(h), Act of 1952, 66 Stat. 214. This amendment provided that

The Attorney General is *authorized* to withhold deportation of any alien within the United States to any country in which *in his opinion* the alien would be subject to physical persecution and for such period of time as he deems to be necessary for such reason.

(Emphasis supplied.)

12. Sec. 11(f), Act of October 3, 1965, Pub. L. No. 89-236, 79 Stat. 918. This amendment added the words "persecution on account of race, religion, or political opinion" in place of "physical persecution."

13. *See* Sec. 20, Act of Oct. 3, 1965, Pub. L. No. 89-236, 79 Stat. 912. The Act defined the Middle East as the area

[B]etween and including (1) Libya on the west, (2) Turkey on the north, (3) Pakistan on the east, and (4) Saudi Arabia and Ethiopia on the south....

The statute also provided a similar benefit for those persons who were physically present in the U.S. In 1976 the Act was again amended to make the provisions for conditional entrants applicable to aliens from the Western Hemisphere quota. The requirements of flight from a Communist-dominated country or national calamity were preserved in the statute.

The most recent legislation affecting refugees was the Refugee Act of 1980.[14] The Refugee Act of 1980 was intended to bring U.S. law into compliance with the U.N. Protocol Relating to the Status of Refugees.[15] The definition of "refugee" in the Refugee Act directly tracked the language of the U.N. Protocol.[16] Passage of the Refugee Act was also intended to improve the cumbersome manner in which refugee admissions were previously handled and to stop the use of parole as a means for admitting refugee groups.[17] The 1980 Act established instead a separate annual allocation for the admission of refugees, fixed at 50,000 annually for 1980, 1981, and 1982. Admissions quotas for years following 1982 were established by the President after consultation with the Congress.

The Refugee Act eliminated the conditional entrant status which was created in the earlier amendments to the INA. Due to the elimination of the conditional entrant status,[18] the total annual quota allocation for *immigrants* was reduced from 290,000 to 270,000 and the percent allocated to the second preference immigrants was increased from 20% to 26% under the Act. In order to understand asylum and refugee law the following similarity and distinctions between the two should be noted.

1. The asylum and refugee applicant must show both that she has a "well-founded fear of persecution" and that the basis for the persecution is on account of her "race, religion, nationality, membership in a particular social group or political opinion."[19]

2. Applicants for asylum and refugee status must meet the same definition prescribed in the Refugee Act. One important difference between the two applicants is that there are annual quotas on the number of refugees admitted to this country, yet no limit on the number of asylum applications granted. These refugee quotas are set by the President in consultation with the Congress. Therefore, even if the refugee meets the statutory definition, she may not necessarily be allowed to enter the country. The applicant for asylum does not have this problem since there is no quota on the number of asylum applications to be granted. The control of the number of refugees admitted and their country of origin provides a mechanism for the injection of political

---

14. Act of March 17, 1980, Pub. L. No. 96-212, 93 Stat. 102. The full statute appears in the appendix to these materials.

15. The United Nations Convention Relating to the Status of Refugees was adopted in 1951 and was incorporated into U.S. law by the United Nations Protocol Relating to the Status of Refugees. 19 U.S.T. 6223, T.I.A.S. No. 6577 (entered into force with respect to the U.S. on November 1, 1968).

16. In tracking international standards, the Refugee Act eliminated the requirement that a person be fleeing persecution from a Communist government or the government of a specific geographical area. In so doing, the Refugee Act made the definition of refugee fact-specific and not ideologically based. On its face, this would enable a person in the U.S. seeking asylum from a nation friendly with the U.S. to also receive protection.

17. It should be noted that almost immediately after the enactment of the Refugee Act the United States was forced to parole approximately 125,000 Cuban refugees who came to the country in what became known as the Freedom Flotilla.

18. The conditional entrant status is sometimes referred to as the seventh preference category. The immigrant quota preference system will be discussed in Chapter 7.

19. *See* 8 U.S.C. § 1158. Certain persons are statutorily ineligible for asylum or refugee status. These include persons who engaged in the persecution of others and aggravated felons. *See* 8 U.S.C. §§ 1101(a)(42)(B) and 1158(d). The provision proscribing asylum for aggravated felons was added by the Immigration Act of 1990.

and foreign policy considerations into the decision-making process.[20] At the same time there is no annual quota on the number of asylum applicants who may be allowed to obtain protection.

3. An important distinction between asylum and refugee status is that of the physical location of the person when applying for protection from anticipated or experienced persecution. If the person is outside of her country and not inside the U.S. or at a port of entry when she applies, she must apply for refugee status. If the person is at a port of entry or inside the U.S., she must apply for asylum.

4. An important difference between refuge and asylum is its locus of decision. Refugee determinations are made overseas and the admission categories set by consultation between the executive and Congress, whereas asylum adjudications are without congressional involvement and are subject to judicial review.

5. While refugees admitted will be accorded lawful permanent residency in the U.S. one year after their admission, only 10,000 asylees per year are allowed to receive permanent residence due to quota restrictions.[21]

Asylum Procedure

Due in part to allegations of political bias on the part of the INS in the adjudication of asylum applications, the INS in 1990 established a corp of professional asylum officers who are to receive special training and are to adjudicate the applications in a non-adversarial setting.[22] These asylum officers, previously under the INS district director are now under the direction of the Assistant Commissioner, Office of Refugees, Asylum, and Parole and the Director of the Asylum Policy and Review Unit (APRU).[23]

---

20. There is some question as to the degree to which these quotas operate to reinstate the old geographical limitation on who could seek refuge. For example, in each of the fiscal years since enactment of the Refugee Act, the overwhelming majority of refugee admissions were from Asia with the fewest from Latin America and Africa. See, e.g., Presidential Determination No. 83-2, 47 Fed. Reg. 46,483 (1982); Presidential Determination No. 87-1, 51 Fed. Reg. 39,637 (1986); Presidential Determination No. 88-1, 52 Fed. Reg. 42,073 (1987).

21. See 8 U.S.C. § 1159(b). The quota on asylees who may adjust to permanent resident status created serious problems for those who had been granted asylum following enactment of the Refugee Act of 1980. In 1990, Congress removed the limitation on adjustment of status for those who had applied for permanent residence by June 1, 1990. See Sec. 104(c), Immigration Act of 1990, Pub. L. No. 101-649, 104 Stat. 4978. In addition, the number of future asylum applicants who may have their status adjusted to lawful permanent residency may not exceed the per country limits for annual immigration. See 8 U.S.C. § 1157(a)(4)(d)(2), Sec. 207(a)(4)(d)(2).

22. See 55 Fed. Reg. 30,674 (1990). The text of the asylum regulations appear at the end of this Chapter. The new procedures apply to asylum applications submitted on or after October 1, 1990. In addition, Guatemalan applicants who were in the United States prior to October 1, 1990 and El Salvadoran applicants who were in the United States prior to September 1, 1990 will have their cases adjudicated under the new regulation as the result of settlement reached in a class action alleging discrimination against Central American refugees seeking asylum in the United States. See American Baptist Churches v. Thornburgh, Civ. No. C-85-3255 RFP (N.D. Cal. Dec. 19, 1990); 67 Interpreter Releases 1480 (1990).

23. 8 C.F.R. § 208.1(b).

An applicant who is present in the U.S. or at a port of entry may apply for asylum if she qualifies as a refugee.[24] Asylum is not a right. Like most immigration benefits the applicant has the burden of proving that she qualifies for the relief.[25] It is granted at the discretion of the INS after first being filed at the INS district office where the person resides or enters the U.S.[26] The person must submit an application for asylum (I-589), along with biographic information (G-325A), photographs and fingerprint card. After receiving the asylum application, the asylum officer interviews the applicant to determine her credibility and to inquire as to whether there exists additional information to support the claim. After conducting this interview, the application is referred to the Department of State for an advisory opinion. At the time that the initial application is filed the applicant may apply for and receive employment authorization.[27] After receiving the Department of State's advisory opinion, the asylum officer makes her decision on the application. If it is approved and the applicant is granted asylum, she is free to stay in the country and apply for permanent residency after one year.[28] In the event of a denial of the application and commencement of deportation or exclusion proceedings, the applicant may renew the asylum request before an immigration judge.

Although asylum status is granted for one year, it may be terminated earlier by the asylum officer or an immigration judge if conditions improve in the person's country, thereby eliminating the need for asylum. After asylum status is terminated, the person is once again placed in exclusion or deportation proceedings.[29]

Refugee Procedure

Even if a person meets the definition of "refugee," the statute does not require her admission. Each year the President determines after consultation with the Congress the refugees to be admitted to the U.S. The INS is required to admit refugees in accordance with the presidential determination of special humanitarian concern.[30]

---

24. 8 U.S.C. § 1158. A refugee is defined at 8 U.S.C. § 1101(a)(42)(A) as:

[A]ny person who is outside any country of such person's nationality ... and is unable or unwilling to avail himself or herself of the protection of that country *because of persecution or a well-founded fear of persecution* on account of race, religion, nationality, membership in a political social group, or political opinion.

(Emphasis supplied.) It will be helpful for the reader's understanding of the asylum procedure to review the flow chart at the end of this chapter.

25. 8 C.F.R. §§ 208.13.

26. 8 C.F.R. §§ 208.2, 208.14.

27. 8 C.F.R. § 208.7.

28. There is an annual quota which restricts the numbers of asylees eligible for permanent residence status to 10,000. Recently, asylees in the U.S. applying for adjustment of status have had to wait for an extended period before receiving lawful permanent residence. See 64 Interpreter Releases 1372 (1987).

29. 8 C.F.R. § 208.24.

30. Although it is difficult to determine in advance and from year to year which refugees will be admitted, the following general guidelines have been used in the past: (1) past or present ties with the U.S.; (2) advancement of foreign policy objectives; (3) opportunities for resettlement in other countries; (4) ability of the U.S. to absorb the refugees; and (5) present or former political prisoners. *See* 8 C.F.R. § 207.1.

The refugee applicant must apply at a designated INS office overseas where she is interviewed by an INS officer and a determination is made as to her eligibility.[31] The decision by the officer, although reviewable informally within the INS, cannot be appealed. Although the person is required to be given a copy of the denial letter, it is not uncommon for the refugee to lack a clear understanding of why her application was denied. If the application is approved, the refugee is allowed to travel to the U.S.

References

Anker, *Discretionary Asylam: A Protection Remedy for Refugees Under the Refugee Act of 1980*, 28 Va. J. Int'l L. 1 (1987)

Anker & Posner, *The Forty Year Crisis: The Legislative History of the Refugee Act of 1980*, 19 San Diego L. Rev. 9 (1981)

Burke, Coliver, de la Vega & Rosenbaum, *Application of International Human Rights in State and Federal Courts*, 18 Tex. Int'l L.J. 291 (1983).

D'Amato, *The Concept of Human Rights in International Law*, 82 Colum. L. Rev. 1110, 1115 (1982)

G. Goodwin-Gill, The Refugee in International Law (1986)

Helton, *The Proper Role of Discretion in Political Asylum*, 22 San Diego L. Rev. 999 (1985)

Lillich, *The Role of Domestic Courts in Enforcing International Human Rights Law*, 74 Am. Soc. Int'l Proc. 20-25 (1980)

Martin, *Due Process and Membership in the National Community: Political Asylum and Beyond*, 44 U. Pitt. L. Rev. 165 (1983)

Musalo, *Swords to Ploughshares: Why the United States Should Provide Refuge to Young Men Who Refuse to Bear Arms for Reason of Conscience*, 26 San Diego L. Rev. 849 (1989)

Note, *A Refugee by any Other Name: An Examination of the Board of Immigration Appeals' Action in Asylum Claims*, 75 Va. L. Rev. 681 (1989)

Note, *Asylum Adjudication: No Place for the INS*, 20 Colum. Hum. Rts. L. Rev. 129 (1988)

Note, *Jean v. Nelson, A Stark Pattern of Discrimination*, 36 U. Miami L. Rev. 1005, 1024-28 (1982)

Note, *United States, Canadian and International Refugee Law: A Critical Comparison*, 12 Hastings Int'l & Comp. L. Rev. 261 (1988)

Note, *Women as a Social Group: Sex-Based Persecution as Grounds for Asylum*, 20 Colum. Hum. Rts. L. Rev. 203 (1988)

Scanlan, *Regulating Refugee Flow: Legal Alternatives and Obligations Under the Refugee Act of 1980*, 56 Notre Dame. L. Rev. 618 (1981)

Stepick, *Haitian Boat People: Both Political and Economic Refugees*, 45 Law & Contemp. Probs. 173 (1982)

Resources

American-Arab Anti-Discrimination Committee (Washington, D.C.)

American Council for Nationalities Services (New York, New York)

American Jewish Committee (New York, New York)

---

31. Under some circumstances the refugee applicant may be interviewed by a U.S. consul where there are no INS officers nearby.

Amnesty International, Reports on Human Rights Practices

Central American Resource Center (Austin, Tex.)

Department of State, Country Reports on Human Rights Practices

Haitian Refugee Center (Miami, Florida)

International Human Rights Law Group (Washington, D.C.)

Lawyers' Committee for Human Rights (New York, New York)

National Center for Immigrants' Rights (Los Angeles, Cal.)

National Immigration Project, National Lawyers Guild (Boston, Mass.)

U.N. High Comm'r for Refugees, Handbook on Procedures and Criteria for Determining Refugee Status (1979)

Washington Office on Latin America (Washington, D.C.)

A. The Burden of Proof (Withholding of Deportation)

8 U.S.C. § 1253(h), Sec. 243 Withholding of deportation.

(1) The Attorney General shall not deport or return any alien (other than an alien described in section 1251(a)(4)(D) of this title) to a country if the Attorney General determines that such alien's life or freedom would be threatened in such country on account of race, religion, nationality, membership in a particular social group, or political opinion.

(2) Paragraph (1) shall not apply to any alien if the Attorney General determines that—

(A) the alien ordered, incited, assisted, or otherwise participated in the persecution of any person on account of race, religion, nationality, membership in a particular social group, or political opinion;

(B) the alien, having been convicted by a final judgment of a particularly serious crime, constitutes a danger to the community of the United States;

(C) there are serious reasons for considering that the alien has committed a serious nonpolitical crime outside the United States prior to the arrival of the alien in the United States; or

(D) there are reasonable grounds for regarding the alien as a danger to the security of the United States. For purposes of subparagraph (B), an alien who has been convicted of an aggravated felony shall be considered to have committed a particularly serious crime.[32]

---

32. This provision applies to asylum applications filed on or after November 29, 1990.

I.N.S. v. Stevic
467 U.S. 407 (1984)

Justice STEVENS delivered the opinion of the Court.

Respondent, a Yugoslavian citizen, entered the United States in 1976 to visit his sister, an American citizen residing in Chicago. Petitioner, the Immigration and Naturalization Service (INS), instituted deportation proceedings against respondent when he overstayed his 6-week visa. Respondent admitted that he was deportable and agreed to depart voluntarily by February 1977. In January 1977, however, respondent married a United States citizen who obtained a new visa on his behalf. Shortly thereafter, respondent's wife died in an automobile accident. Respondent's new visa was automatically revoked, and petitioner ordered respondent to surrender for deportation to Yugoslavia.

Respondent moved to reopen the deportation proceedings in August 1977, seeking relief under § 243(h) of the Immigration and Naturalization Act.... Respondent's supporting affidavit stated that he had become active in an anti-Communist organization after his marriage in early 1977, that his father-in-law had been imprisoned in Yugoslavia because of membership in that organization, and that he feared imprisonment upon his return to Yugoslavia.

In October 1979, the Immigration Judge denied respondent's motion to reopen without conducting an evidentiary hearing. The Board of Immigration Appeals (BIA) upheld that action, explaining:

> A Motion to reopen based on a section 243(h) claim of persecution must contain prima facie evidence that there is a clear probability of persecution to be directed at the individual respondent. See *Cheng Kai Fu v. INS*, 386 F.2d 750 (2 Cir. 1967), cert. denied, 390 U.S. 1003 (1968). Although the applicant here claims to be eligible for withholding of deportation which was not available to him at the time of his deportation hearing, he has not presented any evidence which would indicate that he will be singled out for persecution.

Respondent did not seek judicial review of that decision.

After receiving notice to surrender for deportation in February 1981, respondent filed his second motion to reopen. He again sought relief pursuant to § 243(h) which then—because of its amendment in 1980—read as follows:

> The Attorney General shall not deport or return any alien ... to a country if the Attorney General determines that such alien's life or freedom would be threatened in such country on account of race, religion, nationality, membership in a particular social group, or political opinion.

Although additional written material was submitted in support of the second motion, like the first, it was denied without a hearing. The immigration judge held that respondent had not shown that the additional evidence was unavailable at the time his first motion had been filed and, further, that he had still failed to submit prima facie evidence that "there is a clear probability of persecution" directed at respondent individually. Thus, the Board of Immigration Appeals applied the same standard of proof it had applied regarding respondent's first motion to reopen, notwithstanding the intervening amendment of § 243(h) in 1980.

The United States Court of Appeals for the Second Circuit reversed and remanded for a plenary hearing under a different standard of proof. *Stevic v. Sava*, 678 F.2d 401 (2d Cir. 1982). Specifically, it held that respondent no longer had the burden of showing "a clear probability of persecution," but instead could avoid deportation by demonstrating a "well founded fear of persecution." . . .

Because of the importance of the question presented, and because of the conflict in the Circuits on the question, we granted certiorari, 460 U.S. 1010 (1983). We now reverse and hold that an alien must establish a clear probability of persecution to avoid deportation under § 243(h).

The basic contentions of the parties in this case may be summarized briefly. Petitioner contends that the words "clear probability of persecution" and "well-founded fear of persecution" are not self-explanatory and when read in the light of their usage by courts prior to adoption of the Refugee Act of 1980, it is obvious that there is no "significant" difference between them. If there is a "significant" difference between them, however, petitioner argues that Congress' clear intent in enacting the Refugee Act of 1980 was to maintain the status quo, which petitioner argues would mean continued application of the clear-probability-of-persecution standard to withholding of deportation claims. In this regard, petitioner maintains that our accession to the United Nations Protocol in 1968 was based on the express "understanding" that it would not alter the "substance" of our immigration laws.

Respondent argues that the standards are not coterminus and that the well-founded-fear-of-persecution standard turns almost entirely on the alien's state of mind. Respondent points out that the well-founded fear language was adopted in the definition of a refugee contained in the United Nations Protocol adhered to by the United States since 1968. Respondent basically contends that ever since 1968, the well-founded-fear standard should have applied to withholding of deportation claims, but Congress simply failed to honor the Protocol by failing to enact implementing legislation until adoption of the Refugee Act of 1980, which contains the Protocol definition of refugee.

Each party is plainly correct in one regard: in 1980 Congress intended to adopt a standard for withholding of deportation claims by reference to preexisting sources of law. We begin our analysis of this case by examining those sources of law.

United States Refugee Law prior to 1968

Legislation enacted by the Congress in 1950, 1952, and 1965 authorized the Attorney General to withhold deportation of an otherwise deportable alien if the alien would be subject to persecution upon deportation. At least before 1968, it was clear that an alien was required to demonstrate a "clear probability of persecution" or a "likelihood of persecution" in order to be eligible for withholding of deportation under § 243(h) of the Immigration and Nationality Act of 1952, 8 U.S.C. § 1253 (h) (1964 ed.). E.g., *Cheng Kai Fu v. INS*, 386 F.2d 750, 753 (2d Cir. 1967), cert. denied, 390 U.S. 1003 (1968). With certain exceptions, this relief was available to any alien who was already "within the United States," albeit unlawfully and subject to deportation.

The relief authorized by § 243(h) was not, however, available to aliens at the border seeking refuge in the United States due to persecution. See generally *Leng May Ma v. Barber*, 357 U.S. 185 (1958). Since 1947, relief to refugees at our borders has taken the form of an "immigration and naturalization policy which granted immigration preferences to 'displaced person,' 'refugees,' or persons who fled certain areas of the world because of 'persecution or fear of persecution on account of race, religion, or political opinion.'..." *Rosenberg v. Yee Chien Woo*, 402 U.S. 49, 52 (1971). Most significantly, the Attorney General was authorized under § 203(a)(7) of the Immigration and Nationality Act of 1952, 8 U.S.C. § 1153(a)(7)(A)(i) (1976 ed.), to permit "conditional entry" as immigrants for a number of refugees fleeing from a Communist-dominated area or the Middle East "because of persecution or fear of persecution on account of race, religion, or political opinion." See also § 212(d)(5) of the Act, 8 U.S.C. § 1182(d)(5) (granting Attorney General discretion to "parole" aliens into the United States temporarily for emergency reasons). An alien seeking admission under § 203(a)(7) was required to establish a good reason to fear persecution. Compare *In re Tan*, 12 I. & N. Dec. 564, 569-570 (BIA 1967) with *In re Ugricic*, 14 I. & N. Dec. 384, 385-386 (Dist. Dir. 1972).

The United Nations Protocol

In 1968 the United States acceded to the United Nations Protocol Relating to the Status of Refugees, Jan. 31, 1967, (1968) 19 U.S.T. 6223, T.I.A.S. No. 6577. The Protocol bound parties to comply with the substantive provisions of Articles 2 through 34 of the United Nations Convention Relating to the Status of Refugees, 189 U.N.T.S. 150 (July 28, 1951) with respect to "refugees" as defined in Article 1.2 of the Protocol.

Two of the substantive provisions of the Convention are germane to the issue before us. Article 33.1 of the Convention provides: "No Contracting State shall expel or return ('refouler') a refugee in any manner whatsoever to the frontiers of territories where his life or freedom would be threatened on account of his race, religion, nationality, membership of a particular social group or political opinion." 19 U.S.T. 6276 (1968). Article 34 provides in pertinent part: "The Contracting States shall as far as possible facilitate the assimilation and naturalization of refugees...." Ibid.

The President and the Senate believed that the Protocol was largely consistent with existing law.... And it was "absolutely clear" that the Protocol would not "requir(e) the United States to admit new categories or numbers of aliens." S. Exec. Rep. No. 14, 90th Cong., 2d Sess., 19 (1968). It was also believed that apparent differences between the Protocol and existing statutory law could be reconciled by the Attorney General in administration and did not require any modification of statutory language. See, e.g., S. Exec. K, 90th Cong., 2d Sess., VIII (1968).

United States Refugee Law: 1968-1980

Five years after our accession to the Protocol, the Board of Immigration Appeals was confronted with the same basic issue confronting us today in the case of *In re Dunar*, 14 I. & N. Dec. 310 (1973). The deportee argued that he was entitled to withholding of deportation upon a showing of a well-founded fear of persecution, and essentially maintained that a conjectural possibility of persecution would suffice to make the fear "well founded." The Board rejected that interpretation of "well founded," and stated that a likelihood of persecution was required for the fear to be "well founded." Id., at 319. It observed that neither § 243(h) nor Art. 33 used the term "well founded fear"....

The Board concluded that "Article 33 has effected no substantial changes in the application of section 243(h), either by way of burden of proof, coverage, or manner of arriving at decisions," id., at 323, and stated that Dunar had failed to establish "the likelihood that he would be persecuted. . . . Even if we apply the nomenclature of Articles 1 and 33, we are satisfied that respondent has failed to show a well-founded fear that his life or freedom will be threatened," id., at 324.

Although before In re Dunar, the Board and the courts had consistently used a clear probability or likelihood standard under § 243(h), after that case the phrase "well founded fear" was employed in some cases. The Court of Appeals for the Seventh Circuit, which had construed § 243(h) as applying only to "cases of clear probability of persecution" in a frequently cited case decided before 1968, Lena v. INS, 379 F.2d 536, 538 (7th Cir. 1967), reached the same conclusion in a case decided after our adherence to the Protocol. Kashani v. INS, 547 F.2d 376 (7th Cir. 1977). In that opinion Judge Swygert reasoned that the "well founded fear of persecution" language could "only be satisfied by objective evidence," and that it would "in practice converge" with the "clear probability" standard that the Seventh Circuit had previously "engrafted onto § 243(h)." Id., at 379. Other Courts of Appeals appeared to reach essentially the same conclusion. See e.g., Fleurinor v. INS, 585 F.2d 129, 132, 134 (5th Cir. 1978).

While the Protocol was the source of some controversy with respect to the standard for § 243(h) claims for withholding of deportation, our accession did not appear to raise any questions concerning the standard to be applied for § 203(a)(7) requests for admission. The "good reason to fear persecution" language was employed in such cases. See e.g., In re Ugricic, 14 I. & N. Dec., at 385-386.

Section 203(e) of the Refugee Act of 1980 amended the language of § 243(h), basically conforming it to the language of Art. 33 of the United Nations Protocol. The amendment made three changes in the text of § 243(h), but none of these three changes expressly governs the standard of proof an applicant must satisfy or implicitly changes that standard. The amended § 243(h), like Art. 33, makes no mention of a probability of persecution or a well-founded fear of persecution. In short, the text of the statute simply does not specify how great a possibility of persecution must exist to qualify the alien for withholding of deportation. To the extent such a standard can be inferred from the bare language of the provision, it appears that a likelihood of persecution is required. The section literally provides for withholding of deportation only if the alien's life or freedom "would" be threatened in the country to which he would be deported; it does not require withholding if the alien "might" or "could" be subject to persecution. Finally, § 243(h), both prior to and after amendment, makes no mention of the term "refugee;" rather, any alien within the United States is entitled to withholding if he meets the standard set forth.

Respondent understandably does not rely upon the specific textual changes in § 243(h) in support of his position that a well-founded fear of persecution entitles him to withholding of deportation. Instead, respondent points to the provision of the Refugee Act which eliminated the ideological and geographical restrictions on admission of refugees under § 203(a)(7) and adopted an expanded version of the United Nations Protocol definition of refugee. This definition contains the well-founded-fear language and now appears under § 101(a)(42)(A) of the Immigration and Nationality Act, 8 U.S.C. § 1101(a)(42)(A). Other provisions of the Immigration and Nationality Act, as amended, now provide preferential immigration status, within numerical limits, to those qualifying as refugees under the modified Protocol definition and renders a more limited class of refugees, though still a class broader than the Protocol definition, eligible for a discretionary grant of asylum.

Respondent, however, is not seeking discretionary relief under these provisions, which explicitly employ the well-founded-fear standard now appearing in § 101(a)(42)(A). Rather, he claims he is entitled to withholding of deportation under § 243(h) upon establishing a well-founded fear of persecution. Section 243(h), however, does not refer to § 101(a)(42)(A). Hence, there is no textual basis in the statute for concluding that the well-founded fear of persecution standard is relevant to a withholding of deportation claim under § 243(h).

*   *   *

The principal motivation for the enactment of the Refugee Act of 1980 was a desire to revise and regularize the procedures governing the admission of refugees into the United States. The primary substantive change Congress intended to make under the Refugee Act, and indeed in our view the only substantive change even relevant to this case, was to eliminate the piecemeal approach to admission of refugees previously existing under § 203(a)(7) and § 212(d)(5) of the Immigration and Nationality Act, and § 108 of the regulations, and to establish a systematic scheme for admission and resettlement of refugees. S. Rep. No. 96-256, p. 9.1 (1979), U.S. Code Cong. & Admin. News 1980, p. 141; H. Rep. No. 96-608, pp. 1-5 (1979). The Act adopted, and indeed, expanded upon, the Protocol definition of refugee, S. Rep., at 19; H. Rep., at 9-10, and intended that the definition would be construed consistently with the Protocol, S. Rep., at 9, 20. It was plainly recognized, however, that "merely because an individual or group of refugees comes within the definition will not guarantee resettlement in the United States. The Committee is of the opinion that the new definition does not create a new and expanded means of entry, but instead regularizes and formalizes the policies and practices that have been followed in recent years." H. Rep., at 10. The Congress distinguished between discretionary grants of refugee admission or asylum and the entitlement to a withholding of deportation if the § 243(h) standard was met. See id., at 17-18.

Elimination of the geographic and ideological restrictions under the former § 203(a)(7) was thought to bring our scheme into conformity with our obligations under the Protocol, see S. Rep., at 4, 15-16, and in our view these references are to our obligations under Art. 34 to facilitate the naturalization of refugees within the definition of the Protocol. There is, as always, some ambiguity in the legislative history—the term "asylum," in particular, seems to be used in various ways, see, e.g., S. Rep., at 9, 16—but that is understandable given that the same problem with nomenclature has been evident in case law as well. See *In re Lam*, Interim Dec. No. 2857 (BIA), Mar. 24, 1981). Going to the substance of the matter, however, it seems clear that Congress understood that refugee status alone did not require withholding of deportation, but rather, the alien had to satisfy the standard under § 243(h), S. Rep., at 16. The amendment of § 243(h) was explicitly recognized to be a mere conforming amendment, added "for the sake of clarity," and was plainly not intended to change the standard. H. Rep., at 1718.

The Court of Appeals' decision rests on the mistaken premise that every alien who qualifies as a "refugee" under the statutory definition is also entitled to a withholding of deportation under § 243(h). We find no support for this conclusion in either the language of § 243(h), the structure of the amended Act, or the legislative history.

We have deliberately avoided any attempt to state the governing standard beyond noting that it requires that an application be supported by evidence establishing that it is more likely than not that the alien would be subject to persecution on one of the specified grounds. This standard is a familiar one to immigration authorities and reviewing courts, and Congress did not intend to alter it in 1980. We observe that shortly after adoption of the Refugee Act, the Board explained: "As we have only quite recently acquired jurisdiction over asylum claims, we are only just now beginning to resolve some of the problems caused by this addition to our jurisdiction, including the problem of determining exactly how withholding of deportation and asylum are to fit together." *In re Lam*, Interim Dec. No. 2857 (BIA, Mar. 24, 1981). Today we resolve one of those problems by deciding that the "clear probability of persecution" standard remains applicable to § 243(h) withholding of deportation claims. We do not decide the meaning of the phrase "well-founded fear of persecution" which is applicable by the terms of the Act and regulations to requests for discretionary asylum. That issue is not presented by this case.

The Court of Appeals granted respondent relief based on its understanding of a standard which, even if properly understood, does not entitle an alien to withholding of deportation under § 243(h). Our holding does, of course, require the Court of Appeals to reexamine this record to determine whether the evidence submitted by respondent entitles him to a plenary hearing under the proper standard.

The judgment of the Court of Appeals is reversed, and the cause is remanded for further proceedings consistent with this opinion.

B. The Burden of Proof (Asylum)

Definition of Refugee: 8 U.S.C. § 1101(a)(42)(A), Sec. 101(a)(42)(A)

[A]ny person who is outside any country of such person's nationality . . . and is unable or unwilling to avail himself or herself of the protection of that country because of persecution or a well-founded fear of persecution on account of race, religion, nationality, membership in a particular social group, or political opinion.

INS v. Cardoza-Fonseca
480 U.S. 421 (1987)

[Justice STEVENS delivered the opinion of the Court, in which Justices Brennan, Marshall, Blackmun, and O'Connor joined. Justices Blackmun and Scalia filed separate concurring opinions. Justice Powell filed a dissenting opinion, in which Justices Rehnquist and White joined.]

* * *

Respondent is a 38-year-old Nicaraguan citizen who entered the United States in 1979 as a visitor. After she remained in the United States longer than permitted, and failed to take advantage of the Immigration and Naturalization Service's (INS) offer of voluntary departure, the INS commenced deportation proceedings against her. Respondent conceded that she was in the country illegally, but requested withholding of deportation pursuant to Section 243(h), and asylum as a refugee pursuant to Section 208(a).

To support her request under Section 243(h), respondent attempted to show that if she were returned to Nicaragua her "life or freedom would be threatened" on account of her political views; to support her request under Section 208(a), she attempted to show that she had a "well-founded fear of persecution" upon her return. The evidence supporting both claims related primarily to the activities of respondent's brother who had been tortured and imprisoned because of his political activities in Nicaragua. Both respondent and her brother testified that they believed the Sandinistas knew that the two of them had fled Nicaragua together and that even though she had not been active politically herself, she would be interrogated about her brother's whereabouts and activities. Respondent also testified that because of her brother's status, her own political opposition to the Sandinistas would be brought to that government's attention. Based on these facts, respondent claimed that she would be tortured if forced to return.

The Immigration Judge applied the same standard in evaluating respondent's claim for withholding of deportation under Section 243(h) as he did in evaluating her application for asylum under Section 208(a). He found that she had not established "a clear probability of persecution" and therefore was not entitled to either form of relief. On appeal, the Board of Immigration Appeals (BIA) agreed that the respondent had "failed to establish that she would suffer persecution within the meaning of section 208(a) or 243(h) of the Immigration and Nationality Act."

In the Court of Appeals for the Ninth Circuit, respondent did not challenge the BIA's decision that she was not entitled to withholding of deportation under Section 243(h), but argued that she was eligible for consideration for asylum under Section 208(a), and contended that the Immigration Judge and BIA erred in applying the "more likely than not" standard of proof from Section 243(h) to her Section 208(a) asylum claim. Instead, she asserted, they should have applied the "well-founded fear" standard, which she considered to be more generous. The court agreed. Relying on both the text and the structure of the Act, the court held that the "well-founded fear" standard which governs asylum proceedings is different, and in fact more generous, than the "clear probability" standard which governs withholding of deportation proceedings.... Agreeing with the Court of Appeals for the Seventh Circuit, the court interpreted the standard to require asylum applicants to present " 'specific facts' through objective evidence to prove either past persecution or 'good reason' to fear future persecution." [Citing *Carvajal-Munoz v. INS*, 743 F.2d 562, 574 (7th Cir. 1984).] The court remanded respondent's asylum claim to the BIA to evaluate under the proper legal standard. We granted certiorari to resolve a circuit conflict on this important question.

*   *   *

[E]ligibility for asylum depends entirely on the Attorney General's determination that an alien is a "refugee," as that term is defined in Section 101(a)(42), which was also added to the Act in 1980.

*   *   *

Thus, the "persecution or well-founded fear of persecution" standard governs the Attorney General's determination whether an alien is eligible for asylum.[1]

In addition to establishing a statutory asylum process, the 1980 Act amended the withholding of deportation provision, Section 243(h). *See Stevic*, 467 U.S., at 421, n.15. Prior to 1968, the Attorney General had discretion whether to grant withholding of deportation to aliens under Section 243(h). In 1968, however, the United States agreed to comply with the substantive provisions of Articles 2 thru 34 of the 1951 United Nations Convention Relating to the Status of Refugees. *See* 19 U.S.T. 6223, 6259, TIAS No. 6577 (1968). Article 33.1 of the Convention 189 U.N.T.S. 150, 176 (1954), reprinted in 19 U.S.T. 6259, 6276, which is the counterpart of Section 243(h) of our statute, imposed a mandatory duty on contracting States not to return an alien to a country where his "life or freedom would be threatened" on account of one of the enumerated reasons. Thus, although Section 243(h) itself did not constrain the Attorney General's discretion after 1968, presumably he honored the dictates of the United Nations Convention.[2] In any event, the 1980 Act removed the Attorney General's discretion in Section 243(h) proceedings.

In *Stevic* we considered it significant that in enacting the 1980 Act Congress did not amend the standard of eligibility for relief under Section 243(h). While the terms "refugee" and hence "well-founded fear" were made an integral part of the Section 208(a) procedure, they continued to play no part in Section 243(h). Thus we held that the prior consistent construction of Section 243(h) that required an applicant for withholding of deportation to demonstrate a "clear probability of persecution" upon deportation remained in force. Of course, this reasoning, based in large part on the plain language of Section 243(h), is of no avail here since Section 208(a) expressly provides that the "well founded fear" standard governs eligibility for asylum.

The Government argues, however, that even though the "well-founded fear" standard is applicable, there is no difference between it and the "would be threatened" test of Section 243(h). It asks us to hold that the only way an applicant can demonstrate a "well founded fear of persecution" is to prove a "clear probability of persecution." The statutory language does not lend itself to this reading.

To begin with, the language Congress used to describe the two standards conveys very different meanings. The "would be threatened" language of Section 243(h) has no subjective component, but instead requires the alien to establish by objective evidence that it is more likely than not that he or she will be subject to persecution upon deportation. In contrast, the reference to "fear" in the Section 208(a) standard obviously makes the eligibility determination turn to some extent on the subjective mental state of the alien. "The linguistic difference between the words 'well-founded fear' and 'clear probability' may be as striking as that between a subjective and an objective frame of reference.... We simply cannot conclude that the standards are

---

1. It is important to note that the Attorney General is not required to grant asylum to everyone who meets the definition of refugee. Instead, a finding that an alien is a refugee does no more than establish that "the alien may be granted asylum in the discretion of the Attorney General," Section 208(a). *See* Stevic, 467 U.S., at 423, n.18.

2. While the Protocol constrained the Attorney General with respect to Section 243(h) between 1968 and 1980, the Protocol does not require the granting of asylum to anyone, and hence does not subject the Attorney General to a similar constraint with respect to his discretion under Section 208(a).

identical." *Guevara Flores v. INS*, 786 F.2d 1242, 1250 (5th Cir. 1986) cert. pending, No. 86-388; see also *Carcamo-Flores v. INS*, 805 F.2d 60, 64 (2d Cir. 1986).

That the fear must be "well-founded" does not alter the obvious focus on the individual's subjective beliefs, nor does it transform the standard into a "more likely than not" one. One can certainly have a well-founded fear of an event happening when there is less than a 50% chance of the occurrence taking place. As one leading authority has pointed out:

> Let us . . . presume that it is known that in the applicant's country or origin every tenth adult male person is either put to death or sent to some remote labor camp. . . . In such a case it would be only too apparent that anyone who has managed to escape from the country in question will have "well-founded fear of being persecuted" upon his eventual return.

1 A. Grahl-Madsen, *The Status of Refugees in International Law* 180 (1966).

This ordinary and obvious meaning of the phrase is not to be lightly discounted. *See Russello v. United States*, 464 U.S. 16, 21 (1983). With regard to this very statutory scheme, we have considered ourselves bound to "assume 'that the legislative purpose is expressed by the ordinary meaning of the words used.' " *INS v. Phinpathya*, 464 U.S. 183, 189 (1984) (quoting *American Tobacco Co. v. Patterson*, 456 U.S. 63, 68 (1982), in turn quoting *Richards v. United States*, 369 U.S. 1, 9 (1962)).

The different emphasis of the two standards which is so clear on the face of the statute is significantly highlighted by the fact that the same Congress simultaneously drafted Section 208(a) and amended Section 243(h). In doing so, Congress chose to maintain the old standard in Section 243(h), but to incorporate a different standard in Section 208(a). "Where Congress includes particular language in one section of a statute but omits it in another section of the same Act, it is generally presumed that Congress acts intentionally and purposefully in the disparate inclusion or exclusion." *United States v. Wong Kim Bo*, 472 F.2d 720, 722 (5th Cir. 1972). The contrast between the language used in the two standards, and the fact that Congress used a new standard to define the term "refugee," certainly indicate that Congress intended the two standards to differ.

The message conveyed by the plain language of the Act is confirmed by an examination of its history.[3] Three aspects of that history are particularly compelling: The pre-1980 experience under Section 203(a)(7), the only prior statute dealing with asylum; the abundant evidence of an intent to conform the definition of "refugee" and our asylum law to the United Nation's Protocol to which the United States has been bound since 1968; and the fact that Congress declined to enact the Senate version of the bill that would have made a refugee ineligible for asylum unless "his deportation or return would be prohibited by Section 243(h)."

* * *

Section 203(a)(7) of the pre-1980 statute authorized the Attorney General to permit "conditional entry" to a certain number of refugees fleeing from communist-

---

3. As we have explained, the plain language of this statute appears to settle the question before us. Therefore, we look to the legislative history to determine only whether there is "clearly expressed legislative intention" contrary to that language, which would require us to question the strong presumption that Congress expresses its intent through the language it chooses.

dominated areas or the Middle East "because of persecution or fear of persecution on account of race, religion, or political opinion." 8 U.S.C. 1151. The standard that was applied to aliens seeking admission pursuant to Section 203(a)(7) was unquestionably more lenient than the "clear probability" standard applied in Section 243(h) proceedings. In *Matter of Tan*, 12 I. & N. Dec. 564, 569-570 (1967), for example, the BIA "found no support" for the argument that "an alien deportee is required to do no more than meet the standards applied under section 203(a)(7) of the Act when seeking relief under section 243(h)." Similarly, in *Matter of Adamska*, 12 I. & N. Dec. 201, 202 (1967), the Board held that an alien's inability to satisfy Section 243(h) was not determinative of her eligibility under the "substantially broader" standards of Section 203(a)(7).... In sum, it was repeatedly recognized that the standards were significantly different.

At first glance one might conclude that this wide practice under the old Section 203(a)(7) which spoke of "fear of persecution," is not probative of the meaning of the term, "well founded fear of persecution" which Congress adopted in 1980. Analysis of the legislative history, however, demonstrates that Congress added the "well founded" language only because that was the language incorporated by the United Nations Protocol to which Congress sought to conform. Congress was told that the extant asylum procedure for refugees outside of the United States was acceptable under the Protocol, except for the fact that it made various unacceptable geographic and political distinctions. The legislative history indicates that Congress in no way wished to modify the standard that had been used under Section 203(a)(7). Adoption of the Government's argument that the term "well founded fear" requires a showing of clear probability of persecution would clearly do violence to Congress' intent that the standard for admission under Section 207 be no different than the one previously applied under Section 203(a)(7).

*   *   *

If one thing is clear from the legislative history of the new definition of "refugee," and indeed the entire 1980 Act, it is that one of Congress' primary purposes was to bring United States refugee law into conformance with the 1967 United Nations Protocol Relating to the Status of Refugees, 19 U.S.T. 6223, TIAS No. 6577, to which the United States acceded in 1968. Not only did Congress adopt the Protocol's standard in the statute, but there were also many statements indicating Congress' intent that the new statutory definition of "refugee" be interpreted in conformance with the Protocol's definition. The Conference Committee Report, for example, stated that the definition was accepted "with the understanding that it is based directly upon the language of the Protocol and it is intended that the provision be construed consistent with the Protocol." S. Rep. No. 96-590, p. 20 (1980).

It is thus appropriate to consider what the phrase "well-founded fear" means with relation to the Protocol.... The [U.N.] Handbook explains that "[i]n general, the applicant's fear should be considered well-founded if he can establish, to a reasonable degree, that his continued stay in his country of origin has become intolerable to him for the reasons stated in the definition, or would for the same reasons be intolerable if he returned there."[4]

---

4. We do not suggest, of course, that the explanation in the U.N. Handbook has the force of law or in any way binds the INS with reference to the asylum provisions of Section 208(a). Indeed, the Handbook itself disclaims such force.

* * *

Both the House Bill, H.R. 2816, 96th Cong., 1st Sess. (1979), and the Senate Bill, S. 643, 96th Cong. 1st Sess. (1979), provided that an alien must be a "refugee" within the meaning of the Act in order to be eligible for asylum. The two bills differed, however, in that the House Bill authorized the Attorney General, in his discretion, to grant asylum to any refugee, whereas the Senate Bill imposed the additional requirement that a refugee could not obtain asylum unless "his deportation or return would be prohibited under section 243(h)." S. Rep. 26. Although this restriction, if adopted, would have curtailed the Attorney General's discretion to grant asylum to refugees pursuant to section 208(a), it would not have affected the standard used to determine whether an alien is a "refugee." Thus, the inclusion of this prohibition in the Senate bill indicates that the Senate recognized that there is a difference between the "well-founded fear" standard and the clear probability standard. The enactment of the House bill rather than the Senate bill in turn demonstrates that Congress eventually refused to restrict eligibility for asylum only to aliens meeting the stricter standard. "Few principles of statutory construction are more compelling than the proposition that Congress does not intend sub silentio to enact statutory language that it has earlier discarded in favor of other language." *Nachman Corp. v. Pension Benefit Guaranty Corp.*, 446 U.S. 359, 392-393. . . . [I]t is unrealistic to suggest that Congress did not realize that the well-founded fear standard was significantly different from the standard that has continuously been part of Section 243(h).

The Government makes two major arguments to support its contention that we should reverse the Court of Appeals and hold that an applicant can only show a "well-founded fear of persecution" by proving that it is more likely than not that he or she will be persecuted. We reject both of these arguments: the first ignores the structure of the Act; the second misconstrues the federal courts' role in reviewing an agency's statutory construction. First, the Government repeatedly argues that the structure of the Act dictates a decision in its favor, since it is anomalous for Section 208(a), which affords greater benefits than Section 243(h), see n. 6, supra, to have a less stringent standard of eligibility. This argument sorely fails because it does not take into account the fact that an alien who satisfies the applicable standard under Section 208(a) does not have a right to remain in the United States; he or she is simply eligible for asylum, if the Attorney General, in his discretion, chooses to grant it. An alien satisfying Section 243(h)'s stricter standard, in contrast, is automatically entitled to withholding of deportation. In *Matter of Salim*, 18 I. & N. Dec. 311 (1982), for example, the Board held that the alien was eligible for both asylum and withholding of deportation, but granted him the more limited remedy only, exercising its discretion to deny him asylum. We do not consider it at all anomalous that out of the entire class of "refugees," those who can show a clear probability of persecution are entitled to mandatory suspension of deportation and eligible for discretionary asylum, while those who can only show a well-founded fear of persecution are not entitled to anything, but are eligible for the discretionary relief of asylum. There is no basis for the Government's assertion that the discretionary/mandatory distinction has no practical significance. Decisions such as *Salim*, supra, and *Shirdel*, supra, clearly demonstrate the practical import of the distinction. Moreover, the 1980 Act amended Section 243(h) for the very purpose of changing it from a discretionary to a mandatory provision. *See* supra, at 1211-1212. Congress surely considered the discretionary/ mandatory distinction important then, as it did with respect to the very definition of "refugee" involved here. ... This vesting of discretion in the Attorney General is quite typical in the immigration area, *see, e.g., INS v. Jong Ha Wang*, 450 U.S. 139 (1981). If anything is anomalous, it is that the Government now asks us to restrict its discretion to a narrow class of aliens. Congress has assigned to the Attorney General and his delegates the task of making these hard individualized decisions; although Congress could have crafted a narrower definition, it chose to authorize the Attorney General to determine which, if any, eligible refugees should be denied asylum.

The Government's second principal argument in support of the proposition that the "well founded fear" and "clear probability" standard are equivalent is that the BIA so construes the two standards. The Government argues that the BIA's construction of the Refugee Act of 1980 is entitled to substantial deference, even if we conclude that the Court of Appeals' reading of the statutes is more in keeping with Congress' intent. This argument is unpersuasive.

*   *   *

The question of whether Congress intended the two standards to be identical is a pure question of statutory construction for the courts to decide. Employing traditional tools of statutory construction, we have concluded that Congress did not intend the two standards to be identical.[5]

The BIA has answered the question of the relationship between the objective Section 243(h) standard and the fear-based standard of Section 203(a)(7), Section 208, and the United Nations Protocol in at least three different ways. ... [T]he BIA concluded that the alien is not required to establish the likelihood of persecution to any "particular degree of certainty." There must be a "real chance" that the alien will become a victim of persecution, but it is not necessary to show "that persecution 'is more likely than not' to occur." ... [T]he long pattern of erratic treatment of this issue make it apparent that the BIA has not consistently agreed, and even today does not completely agree, with the Government's litigation position that the two standards are equivalent.

"The judiciary is the final authority on issues of statutory construction and courts must reject administrative constructions which are contrary to clear congressional intent. If a court, employing traditional tools of statutory construction, ascertains that Congress had an intention on the precise question at issue, that intention is the law and must be given effect."

*   *   *

Our analysis of the plain language of the Act, its symmetry with the United Nations Protocol, and its legislative history, lead inexorably to the conclusion that to show a "well-founded fear of persecution," an alien need not prove that it is more likely than not that he or she will be persecuted in his or her home country. We find these ordinary canons of statutory construction compelling, even without regard to the longstanding principle of construing any lingering ambiguities in deportation statutes in favor of the alien.

---

5. An additional reason for rejecting the Government's request for heightened deference to its position is the inconsistency of the positions the BIA has taken through the years. An agency interpretation of a relevant provision which conflicts with the agency's earlier interpretation is "entitled to considerably less deference" than a consistently held agency view.

Deportation is always a harsh measure; it is all the more replete with danger when the alien makes a claim that he or she will be subject to death or persecution if forced to return to his or her home country. In enacting the Refugee Act of 1980 Congress sought to "give the United States sufficient flexibility to respond to situations involving political or religious dissidents and detainees throughout the world." H.R. Rep. 9. Our holding today increases that flexibility by rejecting the Government's contention that the Attorney General may not even consider granting asylum to one who fails to satisfy the strict Section 243(h) standard. Whether or not a "refugee" is eventually granted asylum is a matter which Congress has left for the Attorney General to decide. But it is clear that Congress did not intend to restrict eligibility for that relief to those who could prove that it is more likely than not that they will be persecuted if deported.

The judgment of the Court of Appeals is Affirmed.

* * *

Justice Powell, with whom the Chief Justice and Justice White join, dissenting.

* * *

The Court's opinion seems to assume that the BIA has adopted a rigorous mathematical approach to asylum cases, requiring aliens to demonstrate an objectively quantifiable risk of persecution in their homeland that is more than 50%. The Court then argues that such a position is inconsistent with the language and history of the Act. But this has never been the BIA's position. Thus, it is useful to examine the BIA's approach in some detail before evaluating the Court's rejection of the BIA's approach.[6] After all, the BIA is the tribunal with the primary responsibility for applying the Act, and the greatest experience in doing so.

Under the BIA's analysis, an immigration judge evaluating an asylum application should begin by determining the underlying historical facts. The burden of persuasion rests on the applicant, who must establish the truth of these facts by a preponderance of the evidence. *See* 1A C. Gordon & H. Rosenfield, *Immigration Law & Procedure* § 5.10b (rev. ed. 1986).

* * *

[T]he requirement that the fear be "well-founded" rules out an apprehension which is purely subjective.... Some sort of showing must be made and this can ordinarily be done only by objective evidence. The claimant's own testimony as to the facts will sometimes be all that is available; but the crucial question is whether the testimony, if accepted as true, makes out a realistic likelihood that he will be persecuted.

Matter of Acosta (citation omitted), at 18-19 (quoting *Dunar*, supra, at 319). The Acosta Board went on to caution:

By use of such words [as "realistic likelihood"] we do not mean that "a well-founded fear of persecution" requires an alien to establish to a particular degree of certainty, such as a "probability" as opposed to a "possibility," that he will become a victim of persecution. Rather as a practical matter, what we mean can

---

6. The Court suggests that the BIA's interpretation of the "well-founded fear" standard has been "erratic." An examination of the relevant BIA decisions leads to a contrary conclusion.

best be described as follows: the evidence must demonstrate that (1) the alien possesses a belief or characteristic a persecutor seeks to overcome in others by means of punishment of some sort; (2) the persecutor is already aware, or could easily become aware, that the alien possesses this belief or characteristic; (3) the persecutor has the capability of punishing the alien; and (4) the persecutor has the inclination to punish the alien. *Acosta*, at 22.

* * *

One might conclude that "a well-founded fear of persecution," which requires a showing that persecution is likely to occur, refers to a standard that is different from "a clear probability of persecution," which requires a showing that persecution is "more likely than not" to occur. As a practical matter, however, the facts in asylum and withholding cases do not produce clear-cut instances in which such fine distinctions can be meaningfully made. Our inquiry in these cases, after all, is not quantitative, i.e., we do not examine a variety of statistics to discern to some theoretical degree the likelihood of persecution. Rather our inquiry is qualitative: we examine the alien's experiences and other external events to determine if they are of a kind that enable us to conclude the alien is likely to become the victim of persecution. In this context, we find no meaningful distinction between a standard requiring a showing that persecution is likely to occur and a standard requiring a showing that persecution is more likely than not to occur. *Acosta*, at 25.

In sum, contrary to the Court's apparent conclusion, the BIA does not contend that both the "well-founded fear" standard and the "clear probability" standard require proof of a 51% chance that the alien will suffer persecution if he is returned to his homeland.

* * *

... The critical question presented by this case is whether the objective basis required for a fear of persecution to be "well-founded" differs in practice from the objective basis required for there to be a "clear probability" of persecution. Because both standards necessarily contemplate some objective basis, I cannot agree with the Court's implicit conclusion that the statute resolves this question on its face. In my view, the character of evidence sufficient to meet these two standards is a question best answered by an entity familiar with the types of evidence and issues that arise in such cases.... That Board has examined more of these cases than any court ever has or ever can. It has made a considered judgment that the difference between the "well-founded" and the "clear probability" standards is of no practical import: that is, the evidence presented in asylum and withholding of deportation cases rarely, if ever, will meet one of these standards without meeting both.

* * *

Common sense and human experience support the BIA's conclusion. Governments rarely persecute people by the numbers. It is highly unlikely that the evidence presented at an asylum or withholding of deportation hearing will demonstrate the mathematically specific risk of persecution posited by the Court's hypothetical. Taking account of the types of evidence normally available in asylum cases, the BIA has chosen to make a qualitative evaluation of "realistic likelihoods." As I read the Acosta opinion, an individual who fled his country to avoid mass executions might be eligible for both withholding of deportation and asylum, whether or not he presented evidence of the numerical reach of the persecution. Nowhere does the Court consider whether the BIA's four-element interpretation of "well-founded" is unreasonable. Nor does the Court consider the BIA's view of the types of evidentiary presentations aliens generally make in asylum cases.

In sum, the words Congress has chosen—"well-founded" fear—are ambiguous. They contemplate some objective basis without specifying a particular evidentiary threshold. There is no reason to suppose this formulation is inconsistent with the analysis set forth in *Acosta.* . . . Based on the text of the Act alone, I can not conclude that this conclusion is unreasonable.

The Court bolsters its interpretation of the language of the Act by reference to three parts of the legislative history. A closer examination of these materials demonstrates that each of them is ambiguous. Nothing the Court relies on provides a positive basis for arguing that there is a material difference between the two standards.

*   *   *

In my view, the legislative history indicates that Congress' choice of the words "well-founded" fear as the standard of eligibility for asylum was intended to carry forward the practice of the Attorney General in adjudicating asylum applications. The Attorney General had concluded that the standard for asylum was substantially identical to the standard for withholding of deportation. His decision to interpret the language of Section 208 in the same way is entirely reasonable.

*   *   *

Even if I agreed with the Court's conclusion that there is a significant difference between the standards for asylum and withholding of deportation, I would reverse the decision of the Court of Appeals and uphold the decision of the BIA in this case. A careful reading of the decisions of the BIA and the Immigration Judge demonstrates that the BIA applied the lower asylum standard to this case.

Respondent's claim for asylum rested solely on testimony that her brother had experienced difficulties with the authorities in Nicaragua. The Immigration Judge rejected respondent's claim because he found "no evidence of any substance in the record other than her brother's claim to asylum."

I would reverse the decision of the Court of Appeals.

Notes

1. The asylum determination is discretionary. In *Matter of Pula,* Interim Dec. 3044 (BIA 1987), the Board modified a position which it had taken in an earlier case, *Matter of Salim,* 18 I. & N. Dec. 311 (BIA 1982), where it had denied asylum to an individual who had entered the U.S. with fraudulent documents thereby evading the normal refugee admission procedures. In *Pula* the Board held that an applicant's manner of entry or attempted entry is a proper and relevant discretionary factor to consider but that it should not automatically result in a denial of relief. The Board noted that the exercise of discretion requires a balancing of all of the countervailing equities. For an interesting discussion of discretion in the adjudication of asylum claims, *see* Anker, *Discretionary Asylum: A Protection Remedy for Refugees Under*

the Refugee Act of 1980, 28 Va. J. Int'l Law 1 (1987); Helton, *The Proper Role of Discretion in Political Asylum*, 22 San Diego L. Rev. 999 (1985).

2. In deciding *Cardoza-Fonseca* the Court noted that "[t]here is obviously some ambiguity in a term like 'well-founded fear' which can only be given concrete meaning through a process of case-by-case adjudication." *Cardoza-Fonseca* at 448. Following the Court's decision in *Cardoza-Fonseca*, the BIA elaborated on the well-founded fear standard, noting that the requirements were satisfied where "a reasonable person in his circumstances would fear persecution." *See Matter of Mogharrabi*, Interim Dec. 3028, slip op. at 8 (BIA 1987). This position taken by the Board is in harmony with decisions in a number of circuits. *See Guevara-Flores v. INS*, 786 F.2d 1242, 1249 (5th Cir. 1986), *cert. denied*, 480 U.S. 930 (1987); *Carcamo-Flores v. INS*, 805 F.2d 60 (2d Cir. 1986); *Ipina v. INS*, 868 F.2d 511, 514 (9th Cir. 1989).

3. A basic principle of administrative law and a matter which should be considered when analyzing INS policies applying the INA is that courts will defer to an agency's interpretation where the agency is formulating policy or is filling in gaps left by Congress in the legislation. *Morton v. Ruiz*, 415 U.S. 199 (1974). In cases where the statute or congressional intent is clear, the agency interpretation will not be followed if it conflicts with the statute. However, if the statute is not clear the courts will determine if the agency's interpretation is a "permissible construction of the statute." *See Chevron U.S.A. Inc. v. Natural Resources Defense Council, Inc.*, 467 U.S. 837 (1984). For excellent discussions of the issues raised by *Morton* and *Chevron*, see Anthony, *Which Agency Interpretations Should Bind Citizens and the Courts*, 7 Yale J. on Reg. 1 (1990); Breyer, *Judicial Review of Questions of Law*, 38 Admin. L. Rev. 363 (1986).

4. While *Mogharrabi* is good law today, the Board of Immigration Appeals acknowledged in its decision that it was merely a starting point in its "effort to formulate a workable and useful definition" of the standard. *Matter of Mogharrabi*, Interim Dec. 3028, slip op. at 5 (BIA 1987).

C. Firm Resettlement

8 C.F.R. § 207.1(b)

Firmly resettled. A refugee is considered to be "firmly resettled" if he/she has been offered resident status, citizenship, or some other type of permanent resettlement by a country other than the United States and has travelled to and entered that country as a consequence of his/her flight from persecution. Any applicant who has become firmly resettled in a foreign country is not eligible for refugee status under this chapter.

8 C.F.R. § 207.1(c)

Not firmly resettled. Any applicant who claims not to be firmly resettled in a foreign country must establish that the conditions of his/her residence in that country are so restrictive as to deny resettlement. In determining whether or not an applicant is firmly resettled in a foreign country, the officer reviewing the matter shall consider the conditions under which other residents of the country live:

(1) Whether permanent or temporary housing is available to the refugee in the foreign country;

(2) nature of employment available to the refugee in the foreign country; and

(3) other benefits offered or denied to the refugee by the foreign country which are available to other residents, such as (i) right to property ownership, (ii) travel documentation, (iii) education, (iv) public welfare, and (v) citizenship.

Matter of Lam

18 I. & N. Dec. 15 (BIA 1982)

In a decision dated September 24, 1979, an immigration judge found the respondent deportable as charged, granted his application for withholding of deportation from the People's Republic of China, pursuant to section 243(h) of the Immigration and Nationality Act, 8 U.S.C. 1253(h), denied a 243(h) application from Hong Kong, and denied asylum. The respondent's application for voluntary departure was also denied, and he was ordered deported to Hong Kong.[1] This appeal followed. Oral argument was heard before the Board on December 2, 1980. The record will be remanded.

The respondent is a 41-year-old native of the People's Republic of China, born in Foochow, China. According to his I-589 "Request for Asylum in the United States," he "fled from the Mainland of China to Macau and entered Hong Kong secretly in 1961." The application further reflects that his wife was born in and still lives in Foochow, China, and four children, born in 1960, 1964, 1966, and 1969, all were born in and now live in Foochow. The respondent entered the United States on June 15, 1974, as a non-immigrant crewman, with a Hong Kong seaman's book. He was authorized to remain in this country until his vessel departed, but in any event no longer than 29 days. An Order to Show Cause was issued against the respondent on June 20, 1977, charging him with deportability as an overstay under section 241(a)(2) of the Act, 8 U.S.C. 1251(a)(2).

At a deportation hearing held on September 21, 1979, the respondent, through counsel, admitted the allegations in the Order to Show Cause. He was found deportable based on these admissions. He declined to designate a country of deportation. The immigration judge named the People's Republic of China as the country of deportation, and the trial attorney for the Immigration and Naturalization Service designated Hong Kong. The respondent thereupon applied for withholding of deportation and for asylum. The Service did not oppose withholding of deportation from the People's Republic, and withholding from that country was accordingly granted by the immigration judge.[2] However, the immigration judge found no clear

---

1. The immigration judge's first order was an order of deportation to the People's Republic of China, the respondent's place of birth. However, as withholding from that country was granted, the effective order of deportation was to Hong Kong.

2. We have been informed by the Service that the government will now attempt to deport aliens to the People's Republic of China, and that applications for withholding of deportation from that country should not, under Service policy, be conceded by the Service trial attorneys.

probability of persecution in Hong Kong, so denied withholding from that place. The immigration judge's orders further reflect that the requests for political asylum as to both the People's Republic and Hong Kong were denied. The decision does not discuss the asylum applications, however.

By granting the respondent's application for withholding of deportation from the People's Republic of China, the immigration judge acknowledged that the respondent's "life or freedom would be threatened in such country on account of race, religion, nationality, membership in a particular social group, or political opinion." Section 243(h)(1) of the Act, as amended by Refugee Act of 1980. His application for asylum, for the same country, is therefore given stature as based on an apparent well-founded fear of persecution. The immigration judge's failure to set forth the reasons for denying asylum in this case leaves the Board without guidance as to his findings and makes even more essential our own careful analysis of the record. *See Dolenz v. Shaughnessy*, 206 F.2d 392 (2d Cir. 1953).

An alien may qualify for asylum under the Refugee Act of 1980 if it is determined that he is a "refugee" within the meaning of section 101(a)(42)(A) of the Immigration and Nationality Act, 8 U.S.C. 1101(a)(42)(A). That section defines a refugee as

> any person who is outside any country of such person's nationality or, in the case of a person having no nationality, is outside any country in such person last habitually resided, and who is unable or unwilling to return to, and is unable or unwilling to avail himself or herself of the protection of, that country because of persecution or a well-founded fear of persecution on account of race, religion, nationality, membership in a particular social group, or political opinion.

Thus, as a first step in establishing eligibility for relief, an alien must show persecution on account of one or more of these same five reasons, whether he is applying for asylum or for withholding. We note also that the form used to apply for asylum, the I-589, is often used for withholding applications as well. Moreover, the regulations provide that asylum requests made after the institution of exclusion or deportation proceedings "shall be considered as requests for withholding. . . . " 8 C.F.R. 208.3(b) (effective June 1, 1980). Given these considerations, we hold that where a finding has been made that an alien's life or freedom would be threatened in a given country, and that his deportation to that country should thus be withheld, then it should also be found that this alien has a well-founded fear of persecution in that country for asylum purposes.

This holding, however, does not mean that any alien who has been granted 243(h) relief will also be granted asylum. Despite the similarities between these two forms of relief, and despite the fact that the two terms have often been used interchangeably, there remain some differences between asylum and withholding of deportation.[3] For

---

A grant of section 243(h) relief is merely a stay of deportation. Should substantial changes occur in the country from which such relief is granted, or if, for other reasons, the grant should need to be reevaluated, the Service can move for reopening. A mere change of "policy," however, unsupported by a statement of reasons or supporting evidence, would not ordinarily warrant reopening. Were it not for other considerations, reopening of this case would not be warranted.

3. Prior to May 1979, neither immigration judges nor this Board were required to address asylum claims, as jurisdiction to adjudicate asylum applications then lay exclusively with the District Directors. Previously, then, we were not called upon to discuss the differences between asylum and 243(h) relief: we needed only to concern ourselves with applications for withholding

example, an alien granted asylum may after 1 year apply for adjustment of status under section 209 of the Immigration and Nationality Act, 8 U.S.C. 1159, whereas an alien who has only been granted withholding of deportation has no such means available for becoming a permanent resident.

A distinction which is very important in the present case is the fact that the concept of firm resettlement is a crucial issue with regard to asylum applications, but is not relevant to 243(h) applications. This is so because withholding of deportation is country-specific, barring deportation only to a single place. Thus, if there is any other place to which an alien may be deported under section 243(a), such deportation may be effected without regard to whether or not he may have resettled in that other place. Asylum will not even be granted, however, where the alien has been firmly resettled in a third place.

A showing that an alien will be persecuted in a given country will not necessarily result in his being granted asylum. There are several reasons why an alien with a valid persecution claim might be denied asylum. Asylum could be denied if the alien comes within one of the undesirable groups described in section 243(h)(2) and 8 C.F.R. 208.8(f)(1)(iii)(iv)(v)(vi). Or, as referred to above, an alien can be denied asylum if he has been firmly resettled in another country. *See* section 207(c)(1) of the Act; 8 C.F.R. 208.14.

"Firm resettlement," although not specifically provided for in the statutes prior to the 1980 Refugee Act, is a concept which has long been part of our laws relating to refugees. The predecessor statute, for instance, section 203(a)(7), 8 U.S.C. 1153(a)(7) repealed by section 203(c)(3) of the Refugee Act), failed to specifically mention the "firmly resettled" concept. The Supreme Court, however, when faced with the issue, found that this was a proper factor to consider in determining whether an alien was fleeing persecution and entitled to refugee status under section 203(a)(7). The Court noted that the doctrine of firm resettlement was inherent in the "central theme of 23 years of refugee legislation—the creation of a haven for the world's homeless people." *Rosenberg v. Yee Chien Woo*, 402 U.S. 49, 55 (1971). Thus, the inclusion in the new legislation of the firm resettlement doctrine is consistent with past recognition of the doctrine and its importance.

The question remaining, then, is whether the respondent in the present case has been firmly resettled in Hong Kong. The regulations give some guidance in this area. However, the question of firm resettlement is one of fact. The respondent has requested reopening so that he may litigate this issue before the immigration judge. His request has not been accompanied by any substantial offer of proof. However, despite his flight to Hong Kong in 1961 and his possession of a Hong Kong crewman book, his children were not born there, but were born in Mainland China, and his wife appears not to have joined him in Hong Kong. Thus, we are unable on the record before us to determine whether or not he has been firmly resettled in Hong Kong. The issue

---

of deportation. Effective May 19, 1979, however, the regulations gave authority to immigration judges and this Board to consider asylum applications made after the commencement or completion of deportation proceedings. *See* 8 C.F.R. 108.3. Interim regulations promulgated pursuant to the Refugee Act of 1980 similarly provide that asylum applications made after the institution of exclusion or deportation proceedings shall be considered by immigration judges. *See* 8 C.F.R. 208.3(h) (effective June 1, 1980). As we have only quite recently acquired jurisdiction, including the problem of determining exactly how withholding of deportation and asylum are to fit together.

does not appear to have been reached at the hearing below. A remand is therefore necessary to enable the respondent and the Service to present evidence on the question of firm resettlement. In addition to the guidelines provided by the regulations relating to the 1980 Refugee Act, there is a considerable body of case law regarding firm resettlement under previous statutes, which should be of some help in reaching a decision on this issue.

We note for the record that the immigration judge's denial of withholding of deportation from Hong Kong was correct. The respondent has apparently lived there off and on for a number of years, and there is nothing to show that he was ever in any way persecuted in Hong Kong. The respondent's asylum/withholding application reflects that he fears returning to Hong Kong only because, "I am afraid Hong Kong will be taken over by the Communists." This fear is purely speculative, and is insufficient to warrant a grant of 243(h) relief as to Hong Kong. If, therefore, it is found that the respondent has been firmly resettled in Hong Kong, there is nothing to prevent his return to that place.

For the reasons stated above, we will remand the record to the immigration judge for further proceedings.

Concurring and Dissenting Opinion: Irving A. Appleman, Board Member.

I dissent from that portion of the majority decision which holds that where a finding has been made that an alien's life or freedom would be threatened in a given country, so that deportation to that country should be withheld, it automatically follows that the alien has established a well-founded fear of persecution in that country for asylum purposes.

Experience has shown that with respect to deportation to Mainland China (PRC), it has been common practice for the Service to concede "persecution" under section 243(h) for purposes of disposing of a case, because the Government had neither the ability nor the intention at the time to deport to the People's Republic of China. *See also, Matter of Fwu*, Interim Decision 2787 (BIA 1980). This is precisely what happened in this case. There was no exposition or exploration whatsoever of the facts bearing on the relief. Under these circumstances, I would not give the finding of persecution the conclusive effect on this aspect of the asylum application it was accorded by the majority. While it obviously is entitled to some weight, it is conceivable that in another case, the evidence may clearly show the finding to have been unwarranted.

With respect to resettlement, if the record in a case were reasonably clear, I would not be disposed to remand solely for evidence on this issue, in the absence of at least an offer of proof of a useful purpose to be served by such a remand. However, if this respondent's children were born in Mainland China as a result of his visits there, it not only raises a question as to the reality of the threat to his life or freedom in the People's Republic of China, but also whether he was firmly settled in Hong Kong despite residence since 1961. Because of the obvious ambiguities of the record, I am willing to go along with the remand in this case.

———————

Notes

1. *Matter of Lam* was decided prior to the enactment of the Refugee Act. Can you find any statutory authority for precluding asylum to persons who have become firmly resettled? A non-statutory authority for denying asylum based on firm resettlement is 8 C.F.R. § 208.15. In view of the absence of statutory authority, is the INS justified in denying asylum to persons who have become firmly resettled? The position of the INS is that asylum may be denied as a matter of discretion if the alien is found to be firmly resettled. Do you see any problems with this analysis?

2. Even though a person has not been firmly resettled, may she be deported to the country of last residence? In *Matter of Salim*, Interim Dec. 2922 (BIA 1982), the BIA held that withholding of deportation was country specific. That is, it only protects the person from deportation to a country where her life or freedom would be threatened. In *Salim*, the Board, in denying the asylum application of an Afghan national, ordered the person deported to Pakistan instead of Afghanistan. The Board agreed with the applicant that his claim of persecution in Afghanistan had been proven but that such a claim could not be made as to conditions in Pakistan. Section 243(h) relief was granted only for Afghanistan. Assuming that the government could deport the person to another country, the person is entitled to assurances that the other country will not return them to the country where they would be persecuted. See *Amanullah v. Cobb*, 673 F. Supp. 28 (D. Mass. 1987), *aff'd* F.2d 362 (1st Cir. 1987), *vacated as moot*, 872 F.2d 11 (1st Cir. 1989).

3. Related to the issue of firm resettlement is that of "safe-haven." The issue of safe haven arises when an individual traveled through, or temporarily remained in, one or more countries en route to the United States. The INS has argued that even though the individual did not have any of the rights and benefits associated with firm resettlement, she should be denied asylum because these countries provided refuge. This developing position or argument is commonly referred to as "safe-haven." Is there a statutory basis for such a denial of an asylum application? Should such applications be denied refugee applicants waiting in third countries[33] for eventual admission to the United States where they have families? What, if any, differences do you see between the refugee and asylum applicant? The only case which even tangentially deals with the issue of safe-haven and firm resettlement as the basis for discretionary denial of asylum is *Diaz v. INS*, 648 F. Supp. 638 (E.D. Ca. 1986). In *Diaz*, the INS district director had denied work authorization because the asylum applicant had "failed" to apply for asylum in a third country prior to coming to the United States and the court in discussing the "safe-haven" basis for denial referred to the standards for firm resettlement. *Diaz* at 654. Cf. *Garcia-Ramos v. INS*, 775 F.2d 1370 (9th Cir. 1985).

D. Parsing Out the Asylum Claim

As was noted in the introduction to this chapter, it is not enough to establish a well-founded fear of persecution; the persecution must be "on account" of one or

---

33. The use of the term "third countries" is to describe the country of domicile as opposed to the applicant's country of nationality or in which she is seeking asylum.

more of the five enumerated statutory grounds. As courts review INS determinations on individual claims of persecution, they must interpret the meaning of each claim of persecution on account of "race, religion, nationality, membership in a particular social group, or political opinion." Below are excerpts from the U.N. High Commissioner for Refugees, United Nations Handbook on Procedures and Criteria for Determining Refugee Status (1979).[34]

Race

¶ 68 Race, in the present connexion, has to be understood in its widest sense to include all kinds of ethnic groups that are referred to as "races" in common usage. Frequently it will also entail membership of a specific social group of common descent forming a minority within a larger population. Discrimination for reasons of race has found world-wide condemnation as one of the most striking violations of human rights. Racial discrimination, therefore, represents an important element in determining the existence of persecution.

¶ 69 Discrimination on racial grounds will frequently amount to persecution in the sense of the 1951 Convention. This will be the case if, as a result of racial discrimination, a person's human dignity is affected to such an extent as to be incompatible with the most elementary and inalienable human rights, or where the disregard of racial barriers is subject to serous consequences.

¶ 70 The mere fact of belonging to a certain racial group will normally not be enough to substantiate a claim to refugee status. There may, however, be situations where, due to particular circumstances affecting the group, such membership will in itself be sufficient ground to fear persecution.

* * *

Religion

¶ 71 The Universal Declaration of Human Rights and the Human Rights Covenant proclaim the right to freedom of thought, conscience and religion, which right includes the freedom of a person to change his religion and his freedom to manifest it in public or private, in teaching, practice, worship and observance.

¶ 72 Persecution for "reasons of religion" may assume various forms, e.g., prohibition of membership of a religious community, of worship in private or in public, of religious instruction, or serous measures of discrimination imposed on persons because they practice their religion or belong to a particular religious community.

¶ 73 Mere membership of a particular religious community will normally not be enough to substantiate a claim to refugee status. There may, however, be special circumstances where mere membership can be a sufficient ground.

Nationality

¶ 74 The term "nationality" in this context is not to be understood only as "citizenship." It refers to membership of an ethnic or linguistic group and may occasionally

---

34. Hereinafter referred to as the "*Handbook*." The U.N. Handbook, while not carrying the force of law, is treated by courts as a significant interpretive guide to the U.N. Protocol to which Congress sought to conform. *See Stevic v. Sava,* 678 F.2d 401, 406 n.8, 409 (2d Cir. 1982), *rev'd on other grounds sub nom. INS v. Stevic,* 467 U.S. 407 (1984).

overlap with the term "race." Persecution for reasons of nationality may consist of adverse attitudes and measures directed against a national (ethnic, linguistic) minority may in itself give rise to well-founded fear of persecution.

¶ 75 The co-existence within the boundaries of a State of two or more national (ethnic, linguistic) groups may create situations of conflict and also situations of persecution or danger of persecution. It may not always be easy to distinguish between persecution for reasons of nationality and persecution for reasons of political opinion when a conflict between national groups is combined with political movements, particularly where a political movement is combined with political movements, particularly where a political movement is identified with a specific "nationality."

¶ 76 Whereas in most cases persecution for reason of nationality is feared by persons belonging to a national minority, there have been many cases in various continents where a person belonging to a majority group may fear persecution by a dominant minority.

Membership of a Particular Social Group

¶ 77 A "particular social group" normally comprises persons of similar background habits or social status. A claim to fear of persecution under this heading may frequently overlap with a claim to fear of persecution on other grounds, i.e., race, religion or nationality.

¶ 78 Membership of such a particular social group may be at the root of persecution because there is no confidence in the group's loyalty to the Government or because the political outlook, antecedents or economic activity of its members, or the very existence of the social group as such, is held to be an obstacle to the Government's policies.

¶ 79 Mere membership of a particular social group will not normally be enough to substantiate a claim to refugee status. There may, however, be special circumstances where mere membership can be a sufficient ground to fear persecution.

* * *

Deserters and Persons Avoiding Military Service

¶ 169 A deserter or draft-evader may also be considered a refugee if it can be shown that he would suffer disproportionately severe punishment for the military offence on account of his race, religion, nationality, membership of a particular social group or political opinion. The same would apply if it can be shown that he has well-founded fear of persecution on these grounds above and beyond the punishment for desertion.

¶ 170 There are, however, also cases where the necessity to perform military service may be the sole ground for a claim to refugee status, i.e., when a person can show that the performance of military service would have required his participation in military action contrary to his genuine political, religious or moral convictions, or to valid reasons of conscience.

¶ 171 Not every conviction, genuine though it may be, will constitute a sufficient reason for claiming refugee status after desertion or draft-evasion. It is not enough for a person to be in disagreement with his government regarding the political justification for a particular military action. Where, however, the type of military action, with which an individual does not wish to be associated is condemned by the international community as contrary to basic rules of human conduct, punishment for desertion or draft-evasion could, in the light of all other requirements of the definition, in itself be regarded as persecution.

¶ 172 Refusal to perform military service may also be based on religious convictions. If an applicant is able to show that his religious convictions are genuine, and that such convictions are not taken into account by the authorities of his country in requiring him to perform military service, he may be able to establish a claim to refugee status. Such a claim would, of course, be supported by any additional indications that the applicant or his family may have encountered difficulties due to their religious convictions.

¶ 173 The question as to whether objection to performing military service for reasons of conscience can give rise to a valid claim to refugee status should also be considered in the light of more recent developments in this field. An increasing number of States have introduced legislation or administrative regulations whereby persons who can invoke genuine reasons of conscience are exempted from military service, either entirely or subject to their performing alternative (i.e., civilian) service. The introduction of such legislation or administrative regulations has also been the subject of recommendations by international agencies. In the light of these developments, it would be open to Contracting States to grant refugee status to persons who object to performing military service for genuine reasons of conscience.

¶ 174 The genuineness of a person's political, religious or moral convictions, or of his reasons of conscience for objecting to performing military service, will of course need to be established by a thorough investigation of his personality and background. The fact that he may have manifested his views prior to being called to arms, or that he may already have encountered difficulties with the authorities because of his convictions, are relevant considerations. Whether he has been drafted into compulsory service or joined the army as a volunteer may also be indicative of the genuineness of his convictions.

[Provisions in the Handbook relating to political opinion have been omitted as these issues will be discussed in greater detail in the notes following the cases.]

Notes

1. **Social group persecution.** In *Ananeh-Firempong v. INS*, 766 F.2d 621 (1st Cir. 1985), the court of appeals reversed the BIA's denial of a motion to reopen the petitioner's deportation case to apply for withholding of deportation. The petitioner, a citizen of Ghana, had submitted extensive documentation alleging that she was subject to persecution based on membership in a social group. She argued that she was a member of three groups of people subject to persecution in her native country: (1) those associated with the former government; (2) members of the Ashanti tribe; and (3) professional business people and other highly educated individuals. In analyzing the claim, the court of appeals cited the Handbook and also noted that

> "[S]ocial group" persecution must be based on a "characteristic" that either is beyond the power of an individual to change or is so fundamental to individual identity or conscience that it ought not be required to be changed.

766 F.2d 621, 626 (citing) 1 A. Grahl-Madsen, *The Status of Refugees in International Law* 217 (1966).

2. In *Matter of Acosta*, Interim Dec. 2986 (BIA 1985), the Board described social group persecution as

> persecution that is directed toward an individual who is a member of a group of persons all of whom share a common, immutable characteristic. The shared characteristic might be an innate one such as sex, color, kinship ties, or in some circumstances it might be a shared experience such as former military leadership or landownership. The particular kind of group characteristic that will qualify under this construction remains to be determined on a case-by-case basis.

Matter of Acosta, Interim Dec. No. 2986, slip op. at 31 (BIA 1985). In this case the applicant was a member of a taxicab cooperative that was being persecuted by the guerillas for refusal to participate in work stoppages. The Board explained, in rejecting the claim that the characteristic was not immutable, that the applicant could quit being a cab driver or agree to participate and the problem would be resolved. Recalling *Rodriguez-Fernandez v. Wilkinson*, 654 F.2d 1381 (10th Cir. 1981), discussed in Chapter 2, could a person who came to the U.S. in early 1980 as a part of the Freedom Flotilla be considered a social group? What would you need to establish such a claim? *See Sanchez-Trujillo v. INS*, 801 F.2d 1371 (9th Cir. 1986).

3. **Combining grounds for persecution.** Asylum claims do not fall into neat packages conforming to the Protocol. As noted in the Handbook, the standards and interpretations have taken this into account. One example of persecution which can be characterized as falling into several categories is that of the individual who for reasons of conscience refuses to serve in the military. *Matter of Cañas*, Interim Dec. 3074 (BIA 1988), *petition for rev. filed*, 88-7444 (9th Cir., Nov. 7, 1988), presented the issue of whether religious conscientious objectors from El Salvador, a country with compulsory military service without the possibility of exemption, could qualify for asylum in the United States. The petitioners in *Cañas* argued that their refusal to serve in the military would result in prosecution and punishment, and that this punishment constituted persecution on account of their religion (Jehovah's Witness). In addition, they argued that their refusal to serve would be interpreted as a sign of disloyalty to the government, which would result in their torture or death. This feared persecution would be on account of their political opinion, the political opinion attributed to them by the Salvadoran government. In *Cañas* the Board had denied the claim of persecution based on political opinion, ruling that the evidence failed to establish that the applicants would be tortured or killed for their refusal to serve. The Board also held that punishment of religious conscientious objectors did not amount to persecution "on account of religion" unless it could be shown that the government's motive was to punish conscientious objectors for their religious beliefs rather than for their refusal to serve in the military. The Ninth Circuit rejected the Board's interpretation. *Cañas-Segovia v. INS*, 902 F.2d 717 (9th Cir. 1990) *petition for reh'g en banc filed*, 88-7444 (9th Cir., June 6, 1990).

4. A recognized principle of international law is that nations have the right to raise armies through conscription. In the absence of exemptions from military service for conscientious objectors, should the prosecution and punishment imposed for refusal to serve be considered as a form of persecution? Should it matter whether human rights abuses are attributable to the military and that this forms the basis for

objection. Should it matter that the military of a country is used to enforce a system, such as apartheid, which has been condemned by the community of nations? The *Handbook* notes that these factors should matter and recommends refugee status where the military action "is condemned by the international community as contrary to the basic rules of human conduct." *Handbook* at ¶ 171. In a Fourth Circuit *en banc* decision, the language of the *Handbook* regarding condemnation by the international community was interpreted to require an explicit U.N. resolution condemning the military action at issue. *M.A. v. INS*, 899 F.2d 304 (4th Cir. 1990). The *en banc* panel had rejected a prior ruling that did not require a U.N. resolution, but had held that proof of the violation of the Geneva Convention rules of war would be adequate to meet the *Handbook* requirement. *M.A. v. INS*, 858 F.2d 219 (4th Cir. 1988). Which is the better rule? During World War II should individuals who were asked to collaborate with the Nazis have waited for a U.N. resolution before refusing to participate?

5. **Neutrality as political opinion.** In *Maldonado-Cruz v. INS*, F.2d (9th Cir. 1989), the court of appeals extended a position taken earlier where it held that a person who refused to take sides in the civil war in El Salvador had established a well-founded fear of persecution on account of political opinion where the persecution was by non-governmental (guerrilla) forces. The court had earlier found that persecution by the government on account of neutrality could form the basis for asylum. *See Bolanos-Hernandez v. INS*, 767 F.2d 1277 (9th Cir. 1984); *Perlera-Escobar v. INS*, 894 F.2d 1292 (11th Cir. 1990).

6. **Past persecution.** In *Matter of Chen*, Interim Dec. 3104 (BIA 1989), the BIA held that past persecution or a well-founded fear of future persecution could be the basis for an asylum application. The existence of past persecution raises the rebuttable presumption of future persecution. The BIA also held that asylum could be denied where as a matter of discretion "there was little likelihood of future persecution." Is the BIA's use of discretion as a basis for denying asylum a proper exercise of its authority?

Matter of McMullen
17 I. & N. Dec. 542 (BIA 1980)

In a decision dated January 10, 1980, an immigration judge found the respondent deportable, but granted his applications for political asylum and for withholding of deportation. The Immigration and Naturalization Service appealed. Oral argument was heard before the Board on June 19, 1980. The appeal will be sustained.

The respondent, 32 years old, was born in Northern Ireland, and through this place of birth is a citizen of Great Britain. He also claims Irish citizenship through his grandmother's birth in Northern Ireland prior to 1921. He last entered the United States on April 29, 1978, as a nonimmigrant visitor, using a passport bearing the name of Kevin O'Shaughnessy. An Order to Show Cause was issued against him on May 19, 1978, charging him with deportability under section 241(a)(1) of the Immigration and Nationality Act, 8 U.S.C. 1251(1)(1), as an alien excludable at entry under section 212(a)(19), 8 U.S.C. 1182(a)(19), for having procured a visa by fraud or willful misrepresentation, and as an alien excludable at entry under section 212(a)(26), as a nonimmigrant not in possession of a valid nonimmigrant visa.

At a deportation hearing begun on May 22, 1978, and completed on October 28, 1979, the respondent admitted the allegations in the Order to Show Cause, and conceded deportability. He alleged, however, that he was formerly a member of the Provisional Irish Republican Army (hereinafter the PIRA), that in 1977 he refused to participate in a PIRA scheme to kidnap an American for ransom, and that, due to this refusal, he had been tried by the PIRA, and sentenced to death. He claims that if he is forced to return to Ireland, he will be killed by the PIRA, and the Irish government will be unable to prevent it. He also claims that he would be subject to persecution by the Irish government. The immigration judge did not address the claim of persecution by the government, but he accepted the claims of persecution by the PIRA. After some discussion, he found the respondent eligible for asylum and withholding, and, determining that he could not, under his interpretation of *Matter of Dunar*, 14 I & N Dec. 310 (BIA 1973), deny the applications on discretionary grounds, asylum and withholding were granted. We do not agree that the respondent has established that the government in Ireland will be unable or unwilling to protect the respondent from the PIRA. Nor do we believe that the respondent will suffer harm at the hands of the Irish government itself. The immigration judge's decision will accordingly be reversed.

An applicant for withholding of deportation under section 243(h) of the Act, 8 U.S.C. 1253(h), must show that, if deported, he would be subject to persecution based on his race, religion, nationality, membership in a particular social group, or political opinion. Section 243(h) of the Act, as amended by section 203(e) of the Refugee Act of 1980. To meet his burden of proof, an alien must demonstrate a clear probability that he will be persecuted if returned to his country. *Cheng Kai Fu v. INS*, 386 F.2d 750 (2d Cir. 1967, *cert. denied*, 390 U.S. 1003 (1968)). Under the Refugee Act, 243(h) relief is mandatory, not discretionary, once eligibility has been shown, unless an alien comes within one of the four exclusions now set forth in section 243(h). Similarly, to qualify for asylum, an alien must show that he would be persecuted for one or more of the same five reasons mentioned above in describing section 243(h). *See also* 8 C.F.R. 208.5 regarding the burden of proof in asylum cases (effective June 1, 1980). A grant of asylum is discretionary under the Refugee Act, however. *See* section 101(a)(42) of the Act, 8 U.S.C. 1101(a)(42).

Although in general 243(h) relief and asylum contemplate persecution of an alien by the government in the country to which he is returnable, the cases have held that a 243(h) claim can under certain circumstances be made where an alien claims that he will be persecuted not by a foreign government, but by an individual or an organization. In order to prevail with such a claim, there must be a showing that the government in power is either unable or unwilling to protect the alien. *Rosa v. INS*, 440 F.2d 100 (1st Cir. 1971); *Matter of Pierre*, 15 I & N Dec. 461 (BIA 1975); *Matter of Tan*, 12 I & N Dec. 564 (BIA 1967). While these cases were decided prior to the enactment of the Refugee Act of 1980, we believe they are applicable to an alien seeking 243(h) relief, or asylum, under the new Act.

The current language of 243(h) is broader than it was previously, in that it now speaks not specifically of "persecution," as did the old 243(h), but rather provides for withholding of deportation if the Attorney General determines that an "alien's life or freedom would be threatened" in a country to which he may be sent. There is nothing in the legislative history of the Refugee Act, however, to indicate that the new, broader language of 243(h) was intended to change the application of the section so as to provide relief to those who fear harm from a nongovernmental group or individual. Rather, the legislative history reflects that Congress' intent in substituting "life or freedom would be threatened" for "persecution," was simply to adopt, almost verbatim, the United Nations 1951 Convention and 1967 Protocol Relating to the Status of Refugees (United Nations Treaty Series, Vol. 189, p. 37 and Vol. 606, p. 267. *See* Article 1, section A(2) and F, and Article 33 of the Convention), and to insure that withholding under the Act be construed consistently with the Protocol. *See* S. Rep. No. 96-256, 9th Cong., 2nd Sess. 17, reprinted in April, 1980, *U.S. Code Cong. & Ad. News* 531; House Conference Rep. 96-781, Joint Explanatory Statement of the committee of Conference, 96th Cong., 2nd Sess. 20, reprinted in April 1980, *U.S. Code Cong. & Ad. News* 535. We will therefore require under the new Act, as we did under the old law, that an alien must show either persecution by the government in the country to which he is returnable, or persecution at the hands of an organization or person from which the government cannot or will not protect the alien.

In the present case, the immigration judge stated that, "I am satisfied from the evidence presented that the Government of the Republic of Ireland is unable to control the activities of the PIRA and that if the respondent were to be returned to that country he would suffer persecution within the meaning of the Convention, Protocol and section 243(h)." In making this determination, the immigration judge did not discuss the evidence in any meaningful manner; indeed he did not specifically discuss any evidence at all, so we cannot tell on what basis the immigration judge made his decision. Our own review of the evidence, however, does not persuade us that the respondent is likely to suffer persecution if returned to Ireland.

The respondent has submitted voluminous documents in support of his persecution claim. Most of the documents are of a general nature, describing such things as Irish history and the workings of the IRA and PIRA. Descriptions of numerous killings and violent incidents relating to the Irish conflict are given. There are also Amnesty International reports regarding allegations of brutality by the Irish police, and other documents relating to this alleged brutality. The vast majority of the documents relate either to conditions in Ireland and Northern Ireland generally, or to persons other than the respondent. Four documents, however, do relate specifically to the respondent. Two of these are articles from newspapers (the *Irish Times* on August 24, 1978, and the *San Francisco Examiner & Chronicle* on March 28, 1979) reporting on the respondent's extradition proceedings. Both articles refer briefly to the respondent's belief that the PIRA has a "contract" out on him to kill him. A third article, from the August 31, 1978, *Hibernia Review*, briefly describes the respondent's life, and indicates that he may have something to fear from the IRA. The final article, from the September 24, 1978, *San Francisco Sunday Examiner & Chronicle*, discusses the respondent's involvement in the 1972 bombing of a British army barracks and his subsequent break with the PIRA, but quotes several sources as saying that the IRA no longer has any interest in the respondent (these latter two articles speak of the respondent's involvement in the IRA, though in fact it was the PIRA in which the respondent was involved).

We do not give much weight to those articles submitted by the respondent which are of a general nature and do not in any way relate to the respondent himself. Such evidence is not probative on the issue of the likelihood of this alien being subject to persecution if deported to Ireland. *See generally Fleurinor v. INS*, 585 F.2d 129 (5th Cir. 1978); *Matter of Chumpitazi*, 15 I & N Dec. 629 (BIA 1978). Those articles which do relate to the respondent, together with his own statement and those of his mother, sister, and brother indicate that the respondent may be wanted, or may at one time have been wanted, by the PIRA. However, even accepting this possibility as fact, no adequate showing has been made that the government in Ireland cannot control the PIRA or protect the respondent from that organization. We recognize that the PIRA and the IRA have engaged in numerous acts of violence in recent years, and that the Irish government has not been able to wholly control this terrorism. However, the evidence presented by the respondent simply does not convince us that the respondent would be in imminent peril for his life or limb if returned to Ireland, and that the government there would be unable to protect him against harm from the PIRA. While the evidence submitted reflects the difficulty of controlling terrorism in Ireland, it does not show that the government there, which is a stable one, would not be able, if necessary, to protect the respondent.

We turn next to the respondent's claim of persecution by the Irish government itself. The immigration judge specifically limited his decision to anticipated persecution by the PIRA. However, as certain of the documents submitted by the respondent relate to alleged mistreatment of detainees and prisoners, especially those suspected of terrorist activity, by the Irish police (the "Garda"), and as the respondent has alleged on appeal that he would be persecuted by the Garda due to his former membership in the PIRA, it is appropriate to address this issue here.

We note at the outset that none of the evidence presented which relates to the actions of the Garda mentions the respondent specifically. Moreover, the evidence suggests that the Irish government has attempted to curb the abuses of the Garda. The respondent himself testified at his deportation hearing that when he was picked up and held by the Garda in 1974, he was not mistreated. He admits this again on appeal. However, the respondent argues that because he was a member of the PIRA and has knowledge of that organization, he will be questioned by the Garda if returned to Ireland. He further states that because of his fear of retaliation by the PIRA, he will refuse to give information to the Garda, as he did in 1974, and the Garda will therefore resort to physical and psychological coercion to force him to talk. These claims amount to no more than pure speculation. There is no evidence in the record, other than the respondent's own statements, to show that the Garda has any present interest in the respondent, or that, even if he were to be questioned, he would be mistreated or subject to undue coercion. The respondent has failed to meet his burden of establishing that he would be persecuted by the government of Ireland if deported to that country.

Much of the immigration judge's decision, as well as much of the discussion on appeal (at oral argument and in the briefs presented), related to the issue of whether the crimes committed by the respondent in Ireland were "political" crimes, and therefore not a bar to withholding of deportation or asylum. Because we have determined that the respondent has not established that he would be persecuted within the meaning of the law, we need not reach the intriguing question of whether his crimes were of such a nature that they would not prevent him from obtaining the relief he now seeks. We will state in this regard, however, that we do not consider ourselves bound by the United States Magistrate's decision in extradition proceedings, in which he found that the crimes committed by the respondent were political, and that they therefore barred his extradition.

Notes and Problems

1. It is extremely rare for the BIA to overturn a decision made by the immigration judge. What possible reasons could there have been for making such a determination in this case?

2. If you had been the immigration officer formulating the charges against McMullen, what would have been your approach to the case? What would have been your argument with respect to a claim of persecution in Northern Ireland or some other part of the United Kingdom?

3. In addition to its importance as an excellent factual presentation of the procedure involved in an asylum case, *McMullen* was the first published BIA decision which referred to the type of acceptable evidence allowed in assessing claims, e.g., Amnesty International Reports, newspaper articles, and other sources.

4. Following the BIA's decision in 1980 the Ninth Circuit reversed and remanded the case to the Board. See *McMullen v. INS*, 658 F.2d 1432 (9th Cir. 1981). On remand, the Board reviewed the case and denied asylum and withholding of deportation. On review in the court of appeals, the Ninth Circuit held that substantial evidence supported the Board's position that the PIRA, and hence McMullen, had committed serious non-political crimes rendering him ineligible for asylum and withholding of deportation. The issue of whether McMullen had engaged in serious non-political crimes was discussed earlier by a federal magistrate in McMullen's extradition hearings. There the magistrate determined that McMullen had engaged in political acts. See *McMullen v. INS*, 788 F.2d 591 (9th Cir. 1986). How is it that in the case before the BIA, McMullen's acts could be regarded as non-political, whereas in the extradition hearing the same acts were treated as political?

Compare the decisions in the two cases which follow [*Campos-Guardado v. I.N.S.*, 809 F.2d 285 (5th Cir. 1987) and *Lazo-Majano v. INS*, 813 F.2d 1432, 1435 (9th Cir. 1987)]. Consider the similarities between these cases.

Campos-Guardado v. I.N.S.
809 F.2d 285 (5th Cir. 1987), 814 F.2d 658, *reh'g denied*, 108 S.Ct. 92 (1987), *cert. denied*

GEE, Circuit Judge.

Sofia Campos-Guardado appeals the denial of her requests for withholding of deportation and asylum by the Board of Immigration Appeals. She also appeals the Board's grant of only twelve days in which to depart voluntarily....

*   *   *

Sofia Campos-Guardado, a native of El Salvador, illegally entered the United States in the fall of 1984. After conceding deportability, she applied for asylum and withholding of deportation. In support of her applications, Ms. Campos testified about incidents of violence in El Salvador, focusing on one particular episode. In early 1984, by her account, she took a two-hour bus trip to her uncle's home, to repay a debt owed by her father. Her uncle was the chairman of a local agricultural cooperative, one formed as a result of the controversial agrarian land reform movement instituted several years earlier. When she arrived, she found her uncle apprehensive; he explained that the day before two men had demanded money he held for the co-op and he had refused them. Although frightened, she remained to visit with her cousins. Later, an older woman and two young men with rifles arrived and knocked down the door. They dragged Ms. Campos, her uncle, a male cousin and three female cousins to the rim of the farm's waste pit. They tied all the victims' hands and feet and gagged the women. Forcing the women to watch, they hacked the flesh from the men's bodies with machetes, finally shooting them to death. The male attackers then raped the women, including Ms. Campos, while the woman who accompanied the attackers shouted political slogans. The assailants cut the victims loose, threatening to kill them unless they fled immediately. They ran and were taken to a hospital in San Salvador. Ms. Campos suffered a nervous breakdown and had to remain in the hospital 15 days.

Ms. Campos did not return to live with her parents, but remained to work in a factory in San Salvador. On her first visit home, two young men arrived at the door. Her mother introduced them as cousins who had recently fled from the guerillas and moved into the neighborhood. Ms. Campos immediately recognized one of them as one of her assailants. She testified that he later sought her out several times and threatened to kill her and her family if she revealed his identity. She did not disclose what she knew. After her workplace in San Salvador was burned down by guerillas, Ms. Campos did not want to return to live at her parents' home near her cousin-assailant. She came to this country. Affirming the immigration judge's decision, the Board held that Ms. Campos failed to meet her burden of proof to establish entitlement to withholding of deportation and statutory eligibility for asylum.

*   *   *

Ms. Campos bases her claim [for asylum and withholding of deportation] on two grounds, "political opinion" and "membership in a particular social group." She asserts she was persecuted in El Salvador for political opinions attributed to her by her assailants, on account of her family membership, and because of the concomitant association of the family with the agrarian land reform movement; as an eyewitness to the political assassination of her uncle and cousin, she is subject to future persecution if deported to El Salvador.

Because Ms. Campos's claim of persecution on account of "group membership" relies upon the attackers' alleged attribution of political opinions to the family group, we focus on the scope of the statutory term "political opinion." Ms. Campos contends the Board too narrowly construes this term in determining entitlement to withholding of deportation and eligibility for a discretionary grant of asylum. She asserts the Act contemplates persecution on the basis of political opinion imputed to the victim, whether rightly or wrongly, by the persecutor; the Board, she contends, impermissibly imposes as a prerequisite that the alien personally hold the political opinion that gives rise to the persecution.

Ms. Campos directs us to certain language in the Board's decision stating that a showing that a persecutor's conduct furthers his goal in a political controversy is insufficient to establish persecution on account of "political opinion" within the meaning of the Act. Instead, the alien must show that it is his own, individual political opinion that a persecutor seeks to overcome by infliction of harm or suffering.

Although the Board assumed the veracity of Ms. Campos's account of the events at her uncle's house, and that the attack resulted from her uncle's political views, it nevertheless concluded that Ms. Campos "had not shown that the attackers harmed her in order to overcome any of her own political opinions."

The Board further found it unlikely that the attackers had targeted Ms. Campos as a victim, because they could not have expected her to be present at her uncle's home that day....

Concerning Ms. Campos's fear of her assailant should she return to El Salvador, the Board concluded that these threats of reprisal were personally motivated—to prevent her from exposing his identity—and that there was "no indication he maintained an interest in her because of her political opinion or any other grounds specified in the Act."

Ms. Campos also contends this language indicates that the Board failed to consider all the relevant evidence. She argues the reasons motivating the persecutor are of greater importance than any opinion actually held by the victim. She asserts the record is replete with evidence that peasant leaders in the agrarian reform movement and their families are singled out for persecution; once she was in her uncle's home, his political views were attributed to her. Therefore, she argues, it was unreasonable for the Board to assume that the persecutors' reasons for victimizing her were different from their political motivations behind the torture, execution and rape of her family members. Further, as an eyewitness to the political assassination of her relatives, she contends that she is now a permanent target for future persecution.

Standards of Review

A denial of the withholding remedy must be sustained if supported by substantial evidence. 8 U.S.C. § 1105a(a)(4); *Young v. U.S. Dept. of Justice*, I.N.S., 759 F.2d 450, 455-56 n. 6 (5th Cir.), cert. denied, U.S. —— (1985). Because the decision whether to grant asylum is expressly at the discretion of the Attorney General, we cannot disturb the ultimate denial of asylum "absent a showing that such action was arbitrary, capricious, or an abuse of discretion." Id.

The Board's denial of relief is subject to review for errors of law. *Ka Fung Chan v. INS*, 634 F.2d 248, 252 (5th Cir. 1981).... Our review, however, is limited. The Supreme Court has noted that an administrator such as the Attorney General has considerable discretion in interpreting and implementing the statutory provisions of the Immigration and Naturalization Act. We accord deference to the Board's interpretation of immigration statutes unless there are compelling indications that the Board's interpretation is wrong. *Guevara-Flores v. INS*, 786 F.2d 1242, 1250 n.8 (5th Cir. 1986).

Statutory Construction

We first address Ms. Campos's contention that the Board misconstrues the scope of the "political opinion" grounds by requiring that the alien personally espouse the political belief that gives rise to the persecution. This Court has implied that a father's showing that he would be subject to harm because of his son's political activity is relevant evidence to show a well-founded fear of persecution. We have also implied that membership in a group that is singled out for persecution because of political beliefs is relevant to showing a likelihood of persecution should the alien be deported. *Bahramnia v. INS*, 782 F.2d 1243, 1248 (5th Cir. 1986). Under extreme circumstances, such as those obtaining under the former Duvalier regime in Haiti, the Service cannot presume that people without overt political activity, or lacking minority political opinions, will not be the victims of political persecution. *Coriolan v. INS, 559 F.2d at 1001, 1004.*

We do not, however, read the Board's decision as impermissibly resting on a single fatal flaw, i.e., that the alien failed to establish that she personally held the political beliefs in question. The Board specifically noted "the record does not establish that (Ms. Campos) was persecuted on account of any political opinion she herself possessed or was believed by the attackers to possess." Neither does the record reveal the sort of extraordinary circumstances existing in the Coriolan case, circumstances that require more latitude in assessing whether the persecution is on account of political opinion.

Ms. Campos asserts the Board did not consider the relevant evidence on the political implications underlying the attack at her uncle's home and the future harm she fears. To the contrary, we find the Board specifically acknowledged the evidence about the family relationship, of her uncle's role as a leader of the farm cooperative, and the documentary evidence discussing the agrarian reform movement and human rights violations in El Salvador. Contrary to Ms. Campos's contentions, the Board considered this evidence but concluded it was insufficient to establish that the harm Ms. Campos fears is based on political opinion, group membership, or a combination of the two.

We note that Congress chose not to define the reach of the term "political opinion." When Congress passed the Refugee Act of 1980, which amended the asylum provisions, it reiterated that it wished to "insure a fair and workable asylum policy which is consistent with this country's tradition of welcoming the oppressed of other nations." H.R. Rep. No. 608, 96th Cong., 1st Sess. 17 (1979). In passing the Act, however, the Congress specifically excluded the term "displaced persons" in its definition of refugee. An earlier version of the Senate bill had defined that term as including persons in their own country who have been displaced by military or civil disturbances or uprooted by arbitrary detention and are unable to return to their usual place of abode. Compare S. Rep. No. 256, 96th Cong., 1st Sess. 4 (1979) (accompanying S. 643) with H. Rep. No. 781, 96th Cong., 1st Sess. 19 (1979) (joint explanatory statement of the conference committee). Thus, we can infer that Congress did not intend to confer eligibility for asylum on all persons who suffer harm from civil disturbances—conditions that necessarily have political implications. The issue reduces to whether the political implications underlying an alien's fear of harm rise to the level of "political opinion" within the meaning of the statute or whether those conditions constitute the type of civil strife outside the intended reach of the statute. We have recognized that "a persuasive basis for vesting substantial discretion in the Service is that the evaluation of persecution claims involves the evaluation of the political conditions of a nation—a task for which courts are not well-suited."

Therefore, we cannot conclude as a matter of law that the Board erred in determining that Ms. Campos's predicament was not one of feared persecution "on account of political opinion." Reviewing the record as a whole, we conclude the Board's denial of the withholding claim is supported by substantial evidence, as is its determination that Ms. Campos is statutorily ineligible for a discretionary grant of asylum.

* * *

Finally, Ms. Campos contends that the Board abused its discretion in affirming the immigration judge's grant of only twelve days in which to depart voluntarily, instead of the customary thirty days. Ms. Campos, however, did not raise this as an issue in her appeal to the Board. This failure to exhaust her administrative remedies precludes our considering this issue on appeal. 8 U.S.C. § 1105a(c); *Young v. INS*, 759 F.2d at 454 n.2.

Lazo-Majano v. INS
813 F.2d 1432 (9th Cir. 1987)

NOONAN, Circuit Judge.

* * *

Olimpia Lazo-Majano is a thirty-four-year-old woman. She is the mother of three children. In 1981, when she was twenty-nine, her husband left El Salvador for political reasons: he had been in the rightist paramilitary group known as ORDEN; when he quit he was wanted by the guerrillas and distrusted by the government. Olimpia had always lived in the same small town. For five years she had been working as a domestic for another woman, getting a day off every fifteen days. In the middle of April 1982, she received a telephone call from Sergeant Rene Zuniga who had known her since childhood. He asked her to wash his clothes. Olimpia agreed.

On her day off during the next six weeks Olimpia worked for Zuniga at Zuniga's place. Zuniga then pointed out that Olimpia's husband was no longer in El Salvador and raped her. In Olimpia's words: "With a gun in his hand he made me be his." In the following months Olimpia accepted Zuniga's domination. She continued to wash for him on her days off. She accepted taunts, threats, and beatings from him. He broke her identity card in pieces and forced her to eat the pieces. He dragged her by the hair about a public restaurant. He pummeled her face, causing a blood clot to form in one eye; she thought that she had lost the eye. Olimpia became nervous, preoccupied, and depressed, ate little, and became thin and frail. She wanted to escape her tormentor but saw no way of doing so.

Central to the situation was the fact that Zuniga was a sergeant in the Fuerza Armada, the Armed Force which is the Salvadoran military. Zuniga used his gun in forcing Olimpia to submit the first time. On another occasion Zuniga held two hand grenades against her forehead. On another occasion he threatened to bomb her. When she referred to her husband, Zuniga said that if he returned Zuniga himself would cut him apart, kill both Olimpia and her husband and say that they were both subversives. Zuniga told Olimpia that it was his job to kill subversives.

Zuniga said to Olimpia that if she ever told on him he would have her tongue cut off, her nails removed one by one, her eyes pulled out, and she would then be killed. As Olimpia recalls his statement, he said: "And I can just say that you are contrary to us; subversive." When he was angry with her in the restaurant, he told a friend from the police "in front of all the other people in the restaurant" that she was a subversive and that was why her husband had left: "because she was a subversive."

Olimpia believed the Armed Force would let Zuniga carry out his threat. She believed that in 1979 a nineteen-year-old boy she knew by sight had been tied, tortured and killed by the Armed Force; that in 1981 the husband of a neighbor had been taken away in a truck at night with fifteen others and killed by the Armed Force; that the Armed Force had raped "young college girls," as had Zuniga himself. In her view there was nobody in El Salvador that could stop the Armed Force from doing such things. In her experience when Zuniga was dragging her by the hair in the restaurant no one helped because where the Armed Force is concerned, "no one will get involved."

In 1982 Olimpia escaped from Zuniga, left El Salvador and illegally entered the United States. In January 1983, Olimpia was ordered to show cause why she should not be deported for entry without inspection. She admitted deportability and applied for political asylum, claiming fear of persecution by Zuniga. Her request was denied by Immigration Judge William F. Nail on March 23, 1984. On May 9, 1985, the Board of Immigration Appeals upheld Judge Nail's decision and dismissed her appeal. It found that "the evidence attests to mistreatment of an individual, not persecution" and cited *In re Pierre*, 15 I & N Dec. 461 (BIA 1976) (a wife threatened with death by her husband, a high Haitian official, did not show persecution for a political opinion even though the government of Haiti would not restrain her husband). The Board declared as to the plight of Olimpia that it was "not unsympathetic with this deplorable situation" but "the fact remains that such strictly personal actions do not constitute persecution within the meaning of the Act."

*   *   *

Persecution is stamped on every page of this record. Olimpia has been singled out to be bullied, beaten, injured, raped, and enslaved. Olimpia's initial acquiescence does not alter the persecutory character of her treatment. That she continued to return to Zuniga's place after his initial attack upon her presents a pattern, all too familiar, of a victim identifying with the aggressor under conditions of terror.... The persecution has been conducted by a member of the Armed Force, a military power that exercises domination over much of El Salvador despite the staunchest efforts of the Duarte government to restrain it. Zuniga had his gun, his grenades, his bombs, his authority and his hold over Olimpia because he was a member of this powerful military group.

Uncontradicted evidence, then, pointed to both a clear probability of persecution and a well-founded fear of persecution. Olimpia relates that Zuniga said to her that if she ever left him, "(H)e would look for me, for my person, in all El Salvador." El Salvador is a small country. We take judicial notice of reports that persons being deported there from the United States have been tortured and have been killed. We are not in a position to verify these reports. We are in a position to say that they are sufficiently credible to show that Olimpia, the target of a police officer's persecution for her political opinion, would be in serious jeopardy if forced to return to her native land.

Was Olimpia, however, persecuted by an agent of the government because she had a political opinion, or was the relation of Olimpia and Zuniga purely personal? When "political opinion" in the sense used by the two statutes is analyzed, it must mean "the political opinion of the victim as seen by the persecutor." At times in the history of persecution the victims have been persons who did not share the prejudices and enthusiasms of their persecutors. Their opinions have been politically unaccept-able only because of the opposition and hostility the persecutors have read into their silence or noncommitment to the persecutors' opinions. So in this case, if the situation is seen in its social context, Zuniga is asserting the political opinion that a man has a right to dominate and he has persecuted Olimpia to force her to accept this opinion without rebellion. Zuniga told Olimpia that in his treatment of her he was seeking revenge. But Olimpia knew of no injury she had ever done Zuniga. His statement reflects a much more generalized animosity to the opposite sex, an assertion of a political aspiration and the desire to suppress opposition to it. Olimpia was not permitted by Zuniga to hold an opinion to the contrary. When by flight, she asserted one, she became exposed to persecution for her assertion. Persecution threatened her because of her political opinion. Olimpia has suffered persecution because of one specific political opinion Zuniga attributed to her. She is, she has been told by Zuniga, a subversive. Her husband left the country, a policeman has been told, because she is a subversive. If she complained of Zuniga, she was informed, she would be killed as a subversive. One cannot have a more compelling example of a political opinion generating political persecution than the opinion that is held by a subversive in opposition to the government. Zuniga viewed Olimpia as having such an opinion.

The opinion, it may be said, is not Olimpia's. It is only imputed to her by Zuniga. And it is imputed by Zuniga cynically. Zuniga knows that Olimpia is only a poor domestic and washerwoman. She does not participate in politics. Olimpia, however, does have a political opinion, camouflage it though she does. She believes that the Armed Force is responsible for lawlessness, rape, torture, and murder. Such views constitute a political opinion. And she has been persecuted for possessing it. Because she believes that no political control exists to restrain a brutal sergeant in the Armed Force she has been subjected to his brutality. Her subversive doubts about govern-mental law-abidingness have made her the prey of a hunter of subversives. Charac-terized as a subversive, she was forced to submit to Zuniga.

Even if she had no political opinion and was innocent of a single reflection on the government of her country, the cynical imputation of political opinion to her is what counts under both statutes. In deciding whether anyone has a well-founded fear of persecution or is in danger of losing life or liberty because of a political opinion, one must continue to look at the person from the perspective of the persecutor. If the persecutor thinks the person guilty of a political opinion, then the person is at risk. . . .

*   *   *

Here, when Zuniga manipulatively chooses to regard Olimpia as a subversive, he attributes to her the political opinion of a subversive, and she is being persecuted on account of a political opinion. The fact that Zuniga gave Olimpia the choice of being subjected to physical injury and rape or being killed as a subversive does not alter the significance of political opinion for Olimpia. Because of the status attributed to her by Zuniga and the political opinion that accompanied that status, Olimpia had to suffer the series of indignities that everyone sees as persecution.

Notes

1. Is there an explanation for the different decisions in *Capos-Guardado* and *Lazo-Majano* based on similar facts?

2.Was the court in *Campos-Guardado* correctly characterizing the facts when it stated that the BIA had not decided the case based upon the BIA's perception that the applicant should show actual and not imputed political opinion?

3. 8 U.S.C. § 1105a(a)(2) provides that venue for review of final orders of deportation may be in a jurisdiction where the respondent resides. If Campos-Guardado had moved to Los Angeles and filed her petition for review with the Ninth Circuit Court of Appeals, how might her case have been decided?

E. Interpreting the Statute by its "Plain Meaning"

Arauz v. Rivkind
834 F.2d 979 (11th Cir. 1987)

HATCHETT, Circuit Judge.

*   *   *

The appellee, Nemrod Jose Arauz, is a native and citizen of Nicaragua. In 1979, shortly after the fall of the Somoza government, Arauz decided to leave Nicaragua and sign on as a crewman with an American vessel. On November 1, 1979, after obtaining a non-immigrant crewman's visa, he departed Nicaragua and entered the United States. Upon entry, immigration officials inspected and admitted him as a crewman for a period not to exceed twenty-nine days.

Arauz did not leave the United States with the ship, and at some later time, his wife, mother, and five brothers joined him, all without immigration status in the United States. On August 12, 1983, the United States Coast Guard Cutter Sea Hawk intercepted Arauz at sea while he was aboard a United States fishing vessel. The Coast Guard officers intercepted the vessel in international waters and found in excess of 4,000 pounds of marijuana aboard. Consequently, the officers arrested Arauz, took him to Key West, Florida, and paroled him into the United States for prosecution pursuant to 8 C.F.R. § 212.5(a)(3).

On August 16, 1983, the government charged Arauz, along with the other crewmen arrested aboard the vessel, with conspiracy to distribute and with possession with intent to distribute a controlled substance while aboard an American vessel, in violation of 21 U.S.C. §§ 955a and 955c. After being indicted on the same charges, Arauz pleaded guilty to conspiracy to possess with intent to distribute marijuana, in violation of Section 955c, and the district court sentenced him to twenty months imprisonment.

On or about June 28, 1985, Arauz was released from prison into the custody of INS officials and served with a notice of referral to exclusion proceedings to determine whether he was entitled to enter the United States or would be excluded and deported. Following several appearances in court, the immigration judge determined that Arauz was properly in exclusion proceedings and that he was excludable pursuant to section 212(a)(23) of the Immigration and Nationality Act, 8 U.S.C. § 1182(a)(23). In addition, the immigration judge considered Arauz's application for political asylum. Pursuant to federal regulation, the immigration judge also considered application for political asylum as a request for withholding of exclusion or deportation under section 243(h) of the Immigration and Nationality Act, 8 U.S.C. § 1253(h).

Because Arauz's narcotics conviction was a "particularly serious crime, [which made him] a danger to the community of the United States," the immigration judge concluded that Arauz was statutorily ineligible for withholding of deportation under section 243(h) of the Immigration and Nationality Act. Additionally, the immigration judge refused to consider Arauz's request for political asylum, reasoning that Arauz did not warrant asylum in the exercise of the immigration judge's discretion based on his 1984 narcotics conviction. On appeal, the Board of Immigration Appeals (BIA) dismissed Arauz's appeal, and affirmed the immigration judge's denial of Arauz's request for asylum and withholding of deportation under sections 208(a) and 243(h) of the Immigration and Nationality Act, 8 U.S.C. §§ 1158(a) and 1253(h).

On January 27, 1986, immigration officials directed Arauz to appear at the INS offices for deportation to Nicaragua on February 10, 1986. Arauz then filed the present petition for habeas corpus in district court, seeking review of the BIA's order of exclusion. Finding that the immigration judge acted arbitrarily and capriciously by failing to conduct a full evidentiary hearing on the asylum application, the district court remanded the case to the INS for a full hearing on the asylum application. In all other respects, the BIA's decision was affirmed....

The sole issue involves the district court's remand for an evidentiary hearing on the asylum claim in light of the conviction for a serious crime.

Discussion

The Immigration and Nationality Act contains two provisions whereby an alien may resist deportation to a country where he believes his life or freedom would be threatened on account of his political opinion. One is 8 U.S.C. § 1158 (1982), governing asylum requests; the other is 8 U.S.C. § 1253(h) (1982), governing requests for withholding of deportation. While the distinction between political asylum and withholding of deportation has been somewhat muddled in this court's prior decisions, we note that sections 1253(h) and 1158 are separate and distinct provisions requiring different proceedings.

We agree with the district court that review of the record unequivocally shows that Arauz is statutorily ineligible for withholding of deportation. Title 8, U.S.C. § 1253(h)(2)(B) provides that withholding of deportation or return shall not apply if the Attorney General determines that the alien, "having been convicted by a final judgment of a particularly serious crime, constitutes a danger to the community of the United States...." As we said in *Crespo-Gomez v. Richard*, 780 F.2d 932 (11th Cir. 1986), "th[is] statute...does not connect its two clauses with a conjunction; rather the statute set forth a cause and effect relationship: the fact that the alien has committed a particularly serious crime makes the alien dangerous within the meaning of the statute." 780 F.2d at 934. Thus, we concluded then, as we do today, that "the only finding required by section 1253(h)(2)(B) is that the alien has been convicted of a 'particularly serious crime.'" 780 F.2d at 934-35.

The narcotics offense of which Arauz was convicted is clearly a serious crime which, in turn, makes him a danger to the United States within the meaning of 8 U.S.C. § 1253(h)(2)(B). Since Arauz's 1984 narcotics conviction was in the record, the immigration judge did not have to consider additional information concerning deportation, because no amount of evidence would have negated the fact of Arauz's statutory ineligibility for withholding of deportation. . . .

* * *

Arauz next contends that the Board of Immigration Appeals, as well as the immigration judge, abused its discretion in pretermitting his request for political asylum by failing to conduct a full evidentiary hearing on his asylum application. The government argues that while the right to request asylum generally carries with it the concomitant right to be heard on the application, the immigration judge acted well within his discretion. The government argues that no useful purpose would have been served by allowing the petitioner to introduce evidence because the immigration judge found in his discretion that Arauz did not warrant asylum.

. . . As stated previously, although the procedures are closely related, asylum applications are filed pursuant to 8 U.S.C. § 1158, while withholding petitions are filed pursuant to 8 U.S.C. § 1253(h). Significantly, the language of section 1158 does not provide that the granting of a withholding of deportation petition is a necessary prerequisite to the granting of an application for political asylum.

The government correctly notes that the district director of the Immigration and Naturalization Service may deny a request for asylum if he determines that "the alien, having been convicted by a final judgment of a particularly serious crime, constitutes a danger to the community of the United States. . . ." 8 C.F.R. § 208.8(f)(IV). We have previously acknowledged that "though the regulations do not specifically delineate the factors to be taken into account by the immigration judge in denying asylum requests, it can be assumed that they are identical to those applicable to district directors." *Zardui-Quintana*, 768 F.2d at 1218.

This is not to suggest, however, that an immigration judge is no longer obliged to entertain the merits of an asylum application once it has been determined that the alien has been convicted of a particularly serious offense. Even in that situation, the regulations still provide that the alien "may present evidence for the record in the exclusion or deportation proceedings." 8 C.F.R. § 208.10(c). In addition, the regulations provide that the immigration judge is to consider an advisory opinion submitted by the Bureau of Human Rights and Humanitarian Affairs. 8 C.F.R. § 208.10(b). We note that with regard to Arauz's application for political asylum, our standard of review is abuse of discretion. Given the unambiguous language of the aforementioned regulations, we hold that the immigration judge acted arbitrarily and capriciously in failing to conduct a full evidentiary hearing on the asylum application. Although the nature and gravity of Arauz's conviction of a narcotics offense is an adverse factor which would militate heavily against him in the review of his asylum application, it is clear that under the Attorney General's regulations, his conviction is not the only evidence to be considered by the immigration judge.

We are mindful that our disposition of this appeal seemingly turns upon a rather rigid application of the subtle nuances of the Attorney General's regulations. In reviewing the regulatory framework governing asylum requests, we note that the Attorney General has delegated to the district director jurisdiction to hear asylum requests which are made prior to the commencement of exclusion proceedings. 8 C.F.R. § 208.1(a). As mentioned previously, a district director may deny a request for asylum if he determines that "the alien, having been convicted by a final judgment of a particularly serious crime, constitutes a danger to the community of the United States...." 8 C.F.R. § 208.8(f)(IV).

The regulations further provide that where an asylum application is denied by the district director, the alien may renew his request for asylum before an immigration judge in exclusion or deportation proceedings. 8 C.F.R. § 208.9. Thus, at this point, what was previously a wholly administrative procedure takes on judicial overtones. Similarly, the regulations provide that once an alien has been served notice of exclusion or deportation proceedings, the immigration judge has exclusive jurisdiction to hear the asylum application. 8 C.F.R. § 208.1(b) (1987).

Note

The court's opinion in *Arauz* relating to the interpretation of 8 U.S.C. § 1253(h)(2)(B) in withholding cases has been followed in other circuits. *See Ramirez-Ramos v. INS*, 814 F.2d 1394 (9th Cir. 1987).

Does the plain meaning of 8 U.S.C. § 1253(h)(2)(B) [at pg. 148 of text] preclude withholding of deportation for persons convicted of serious crimes and are dangerous to the community, or does the conviction standing alone preclude withholding?

Refugee Procedure

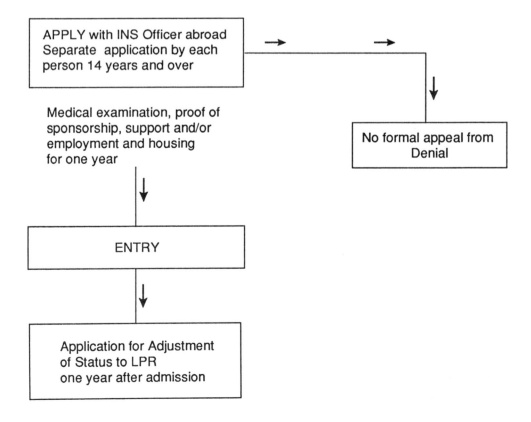

Asylum Procedures

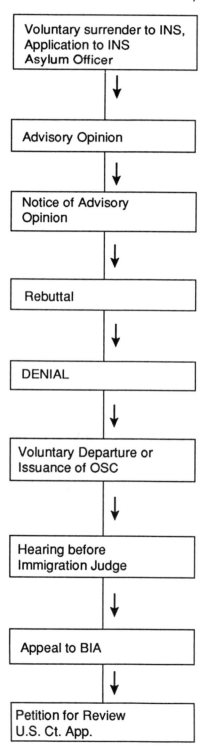

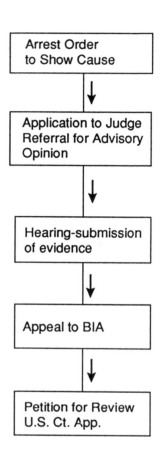

Index to Appendix

Admission of Refugees

8 U.S.C. § 1157, Sec. 207

(a) Maximum number of admissions; increases for humanitarian concerns; allocations

(1) Except as provided in subsection (b) of this section, the number of refugees who may be admitted under this section in fiscal year 1980, 1981, or 1982, may not exceed fifty thousand unless the President determines, before the beginning of the fiscal year and after appropriate consultation (as defined in subsection (e) of this section), that admission of a specific number of refugees in excess of such number is justified by humanitarian concern or is otherwise in the national interest.

(2) Except as provided in subsection (b) of this section, the number of refugees who may be admitted under this section in any fiscal year after fiscal year 1982 shall be such number as the President determines, before the beginning of the fiscal year and after appropriate consultation, is justified by humanitarian concerns or is otherwise in the national interest.

(3) Admissions under this subsection shall be allocated among refugees of special humanitarian concern to the United States in accordance with a determination made by the President after appropriate consultation.

(b) If the President determines, after appropriate consultation, that (1) an unforeseen emergency refugee situation exists, (2) the admission of certain refugees in response to the emergency refugee situation is justified by grave humanitarian concerns or is otherwise in the national interest, and (3) the admission to the United States of these refugees cannot be accomplished under subsection (a) of this section, the President may fix a number of refugees to be admitted to the United States during the succeeding period (not to exceed twelve months) in response to the emergency refugee situation and such admissions shall be allocated among refugees of special humanitarian concern to the United States in accordance with a determination made by the President after the appropriate consultation provided under this subsection.

(c) Admission by Attorney General of refugees; criteria; admission status of spouse or child; applicability of other statutory requirements; termination of refugee status of alien, spouse or child

(1) Subject to the numerical limitations established pursuant to subsections (a) and (b) of this section, the Attorney General may, in the Attorney General's discretion and pursuant to such regulations as the Attorney General may prescribe, admit any refugee who is not firmly resettled in any foreign country, is determined to be of special humanitarian concern to the United States, and is admissible (except as otherwise provided under paragraph (3)) as an immigrant under this chapter.

(2) A spouse or child (as defined in section 1101(b)(1)(A), (B), (C), (D), or (E) of this title) of any refugee who qualifies for admission under paragraph (1) shall, if not otherwise entitled to admission under paragraph (1) and if not a person described in the second sentence of section 1101(a)(42) of this title, be entitled to the same admission status as such refugee if accompanying, or following to join, such refugee and if the spouse or child is admissible (except as otherwise provided under paragraph (3)) as an immigrant under this chapter. Upon the spouse's or child's admission to the United States, such admission shall be charged against the numerical limitation established in accordance with the appropriate subsection under which the refugee's admission is charged.

(3) The provisions of paragraphs (14), (15), (20), (21), (25), and (32) of section 1182(a) of this title shall not be applicable to any alien seeking admission to the United States under this subsection, and the Attorney General may waive any other provision of such section (other than paragraph (27), (29), or (33) and other than so much of paragraph (23) as relates to trafficking in narcotics) with respect to such an alien for humanitarian purposes, to assure family unity, or when it is otherwise in the public interest. Any such waiver by the Attorney General shall be in writing and shall be granted only on an individual basis following an investigation. The Attorney General shall provide for the annual reporting to Congress of the number of waivers granted under this paragraph in the previous fiscal year and a summary of the reasons for granting such waivers.

(4) The refugee status of any alien (and of the spouse or child of the alien) may be terminated by the Attorney General pursuant to such regulations as the Attorney General may prescribe if the Attorney General determines that the alien was not in fact a refugee within the meaning of section 1101(a)(42) of this title at the time of the alien's admission.

(d) [Oversight reporting and consultative requirements have been omitted.]

Asylum Procedure

8 U.S.C. § 1158, Sec. 208

(a) The Attorney General shall establish a procedure for an alien physically present in the United states or at a land border or port of entry, irrespective of such alien's status, to apply for asylum, and the alien may be granted asylum in the discretion of the Attorney General if the Attorney General determines that such alien is a refugee within the meaning of section 1101(a)(42)(A) of this title.

(b) Asylum granted under subsection (a) of this section may be terminated if the Attorney General, pursuant to such regulations as the Attorney General may prescribe, determines that the alien is no longer a refugee within the meaning of section 1101(a)(42)(A) of this title owing to a change in circumstances in the alien's country of nationality or, in the case of an alien having no nationality, in the country in which the alien last habitually resided.

(c) A spouse or child (as defined in section 1101(b)(1)(A), (B), (C), (D), or (E) of this title) of an alien who is granted asylum under subsection (a) of this section may, if not otherwise eligible for asylum under such subsection, be granted the same status as the alien if accompanying, or following to join, such alien.

(d) An alien who has been convicted of an aggravated felony, notwithstanding subsection (a), may not apply for or be granted asylum.

Refugees and Asylees
Adjustment of Status

8 U.S.C. § 1159, Sec. 209

(a)(1) Any alien who has been admitted to the United States under section 1157 of this title—(A) whose admission has not been terminated by the Attorney General pursuant to such regulations as the Attorney General may prescribe, (B) who has been physically present in the United States for at least one year, and (C) who has not acquired permanent resident status, shall, at the end of such year period, return or be returned to the custody of the Service for inspection and examination for admission to the United States as an immigrant in accordance with the provisions of sections 1225, 1226, and 1227 of this title.

(2) Any alien who is found upon inspection and examination by an immigration officer pursuant to paragraph (1) or after a hearing before a special inquiry officer to be admissible (except as otherwise provided under subsection (c) of this section) as an immigrant under this chapter at the time of the alien's inspection and examination shall, notwithstanding any numerical limitation specified in this chapter, be regarded as lawfully admitted to the United States for permanent residence as of the date of such alien's arrival into the United States.

(b) Not more than ten thousand of the refugee admissions authorized under section 207(a) in any fiscal year may be made available by the Attorney General, in the Attorney General's discretion and under such regulations as the Attorney General may prescribe, to adjust to the status of an alien lawfully admitted for permanent residence the status of any alien granted asylum who—(1) applies for such adjustment, (2) has been physically present in the United States for at least one year after being granted asylum, (3) continues to be a refugee within the meaning of section 1101(a)(42)(A) of this title or a spouse or child of such a refugee, (4) is not firmly resettled in any foreign country, and (5) is admissible (except as otherwise provided under subsection (c) of this section) as an immigrant under this chapter at the time of examination for adjustment of such alien.

Upon approval of an application under this subsection, the Attorney General shall establish a record of the alien's admission for lawful permanent residence as of the date one year before the date of the approval of the application.

(c) Applicability of other federal statutory requirements. The provisions of paragraphs (4), (5), and (7)(A) of section 1182(a) of this title shall not be applicable to any alien seeking adjustment of status under this section, and the Attorney General may waive any other provision of such section [other than paragraph (2)(C) or subparagraph (A), (B), (C), or (E) of paragraph (3)] with respect to such an alien for humanitarian purposes, to assure family unity, or when it is otherwise in the public interest.

Asylum Procedures
8 C.F.R. § 208

§ 208.1 General.

(a) This part shall apply to all applications for asylum or withholding of deportation that are filed on or after October 1, 1990. No application for asylum or withholding of deportation that has been filed with a District Director or Immigration Judge prior to October 1, 1990, may be reopened or otherwise reconsidered under the provisions of this part except by motion granted in the exercise of discretion by the Board of Immigration Appeals, an Immigration Judge or an Asylum Officer for proper cause shown. Motions to reopen or reconsider must meet the requirements of 8 C.F.R. §§ 3.2, 3.8, 3.22, 103.5, and 242.22 where applicable. The provisions of this part shall not affect the finality or validity of any decision made by District Directors, Immigration Judges, or the Board of Immigration Appeals in any asylum or withholding of deportation case prior to October 1, 1990.

(b) There shall be attached to the Office of Refugees, Asylum, and Parole such number of employees as the Commissioner, upon recommendation from the Assistant Commissioner, shall direct. These shall include a corps of professional Asylum Officers who are to receive special training in international relations and international law under the joint direction of the Assistant Commissioner, Office of Refugees, Asylum, and Parole and the Director of the Asylum Policy and Review Unit of the Office of Policy Development of the Department of Justice. The Assistant Commissioner shall be further responsible for general supervision and direction in the conduct of the asylum program, including evaluation of the performance of the employees attached to the Office.

(c) As an ongoing component of the training required by paragraph (b) of this section, the Assistant Commissioner, Office of Refugees, Asylum and Parole, shall assist the Deputy Attorney General and the Director of the Asylum Policy and Review Unit, in coordination with the Department of State, and in cooperation with other appropriate sources, to compile and disseminate to Asylum Officers information concerning the persecution of persons in other countries on account of race, religion, nationality, membership in a particular social group, or political opinion, as well as other information relevant to asylum determinations, and shall maintain a documentation center with information on human rights conditions.

§ 208.2 Jurisdiction.

(a) Except as provided in paragraph (b) of this section, the Office of Refugees, Asylum, and Parole shall have initial jurisdiction over applications for asylum and withholding of deportation filed by an alien physically present in the United States or seeking admission at a port of entry. All such applications shall be decided in the first instance by Asylum Officers under this part.

(b) Immigration Judges shall have exclusive jurisdiction over asylum applications filed by an alien who has been served notice of referral to exclusion proceedings under part 236 of this chapter, or served an order to show cause under part 242 of this chapter, after a copy of the charging document has been filed with the Office of the Immigration Judge. The Immigration Judge shall make a determination on such claims de novo regardless of whether or not a previous application was filed and adjudicated by an Asylum Officer prior to the initiation of exclusion or deportation proceedings. Any previously filed but unadjudicated asylum application must be resubmitted by the alien to the Immigration Judge.

§ 208.3 Form of application.

(a) An application for asylum or withholding of deportation shall be made in quadruplicate on Form I-589 (Request for Asylum in the United States). The applicant's spouse and children as defined in section 101 of the Act may be included on the application if they are in the United States. An application shall be accompanied by one completed Form G-325A (Biographical Information) and one completed Form FD-258 (Fingerprint Card) for every individual included on the application who is fourteen years of age or older; additional supporting material may also accompany the application and, if so, must be provided in quadruplicate. Forms I-589, G-325A, and FD-258 shall be available from the Office of Refugees, Asylum, and Parole, each District Director, and the Offices of Immigration Judges.

(b) An application for asylum shall be deemed to constitute at the same time an application for withholding of deportation, pursuant to §§ 208.16, 236.3, and 242.17 of this chapter.

§ 208.4 Filing the application.

If no prior application for asylum or withholding of deportation has been filed, an applicant shall file any initial application according to the following procedures:

(a) With the District Director. Except as provided in paragraph (b) of this section, applications for asylum or withholding of deportation shall be filed with the District Director having jurisdiction over the place of the applicant's residence or over the port of entry from which the applicant seeks admission to the United States. The District Director shall immediately forward the application to an asylum Officer with jurisdiction in his district. The Asylum Officer shall notify the Asylum Policy and Review Unit of the Department of Justice and shall forward a copy of the completed application, including any supporting material subsequently received pursuant to § 208.9(e), to the Office of Refugees, Asylum and Parole and the Bureau of Human Rights and Humanitarian Affairs of the Department of State.

(b) With the Immigration Judge. Initial applications for asylum or withholding of deportation are to be filed with the Office of the Immigration Judge in the following circumstances (and shall be treated as provided in part 236 or 242 of this chapter):

(1) During exclusion or deportation proceedings. If exclusion or deportation proceedings have been commenced against an alien pursuant to part 236 or 242 of this chapter, an initial application for asylum or withholding of deportation from that alien shall be filed thereafter with the Office of the Immigration Judge.

(2) After completion of exclusion or deportation proceedings. If exclusion or deportation proceedings have been completed, an initial application for asylum or withholding of deportation shall be filed with the Office of the Immigration Judge having jurisdiction over the prior proceeding in conjunction with a motion to reopen pursuant to 8 C.F.R. §§ 3.8, 3.22 and 242.22 where applicable.

(3) Pursuant to appeal to the Board of Immigration Appeals. If jurisdiction over the proceedings is vested in the Board of Immigration Appeals under part 3 of this chapter, an initial application for asylum or withholding of deportation shall be filed with the Office of the Immigration Judge having jurisdiction over the prior proceeding in conjunction with a motion to remand or reopen pursuant to 8 C.F.R. §§ 3.2 and 3.8 where applicable.

(4) Any motion to reopen or remand accompanied by an initial application for asylum filed under paragraph (b) of this section must reasonably explain the failure to request asylum prior to the completion of the exclusion or deportation proceeding.

§ 208.5 Special duties toward aliens in custody of the Service.

(a) When an alien in the custody of the Service requests asylum or withholding of deportation or expresses fear of persecution or harm upon return to his country of origin or to agents thereof, the Service shall make available the appropriate application forms for asylum and withholding of deportation and shall provide the applicant with a list, if available, of persons or private agencies that can assist in preparation of the application.

(b) Where possible, expedited consideration shall be given to applications of aliens detained under 8 C.F.R. part 235 or 242. Except as provided in paragraph (c) of this section, such alien shall not be deported or excluded before a decision is rendered on his initial asylum or withholding of deportation application.

(c) A motion to reopen or an order to remand accompanied by an application for asylum or withholding of deportation pursuant to § 208.4(b) shall not stay execution of a final order of exclusion or deportation unless such a stay is specifically granted by the Board or the Immigration Judge having jurisdiction over the motion.

§ 208.6 Disclosure to third parties.

(a) An application for asylum or withholding of deportation shall not be disclosed, except as permitted by this section, or at the discretion of the Attorney General, without the written consent of the applicant. Names and other identifying details shall be deleted from copies of asylum or withholding of deportation decisions maintained in public reading rooms under § 103.9 of this chapter.

(b) The confidentiality of other records kept by the Service (including G-325A forms) that indicate that a specific alien has applied for asylum or withholding of deportation shall also be protected from disclosure. The Service will coordinate with the Department of State to ensure that the confidentiality of these records is maintained when they are transmitted to State Department offices in other countries.

(c) This section shall not apply to any disclosure to:

(1) Any United States Government official or contractor having a need to examine information in connection with:

(i) Adjudication of asylum or withholding of deportation applications;

(ii) The defense of any legal action arising from the adjudication of or failure to adjudicate the asylum or withholding of deportation application;

(iii) The defense of any legal action of which the asylum or withholding of deportation application is a part; or

(iv) Any United States Government investigation concerning any criminal or civil matter; or

(2) Any Federal, state, or local court in the United States considering any legal action:

(i) Arising from the adjudication of or failure to adjudicate the asylum or withholding of deportation application; or

(ii) Arising from the proceedings of which the asylum or withholding of deportation application is a part.

§ 208.7 Interim employment authorization.

(a) The Asylum Officer to whom an initial application for employment authorization (Form I-765) accompanying an application for asylum or withholding of deportation is referred shall authorize employment for a period not to exceed one year to aliens who are not in detention and whose applications for asylum or withholding of deportation the Asylum Officer determines are not frivolous. "Frivolous" is defined as manifestly unfounded or abusive.

(b) Employment authorization shall be renewable, in increments not to exceed one year, for the continuous period of time necessary for the Asylum Officer or Immigration Judge to decide the asylum application and, if necessary, for final adjudication of any administrative or judicial review.

(1) If the asylum application is denied by the Asylum Officer, the employment authorization shall terminate at the expiration of the employment authorization document or sixty days after the denial of asylum, whichever is longer.

(2) If the application is denied by the Immigration Judge, the Board of Immigration Appeals, or upon judicial review of the asylum denial, the employment authorization terminates upon the expiration of the employment authorization document.

(c) In order for employment authorization to be renewed under this section, the alien must provide the Asylum Officer, or District Director where appropriate, with a Form I-765 and proof that he has continued to pursue his application for asylum before an Immigration Judge or sought administrative or judicial review. Pursuit of an application for asylum, for purposes of employment authorization is established by presenting to the Asylum Officer one of the following, depending on the stage of the alien's immigration proceedings:

(1) If the alien's case is pending before the Immigration Judge, and the alien wishes to pursue an application for asylum, a copy of the asylum denial and the Order

to Show Cause (Form I-221/I-221S) or Notice to Applicant for Admission Detained for Hearing before Immigration Judge (Form I-122) placing the alien in proceedings after asylum has been denied;

(2) If the immigration judge has denied asylum a copy of the Notice of Appeal (EOIR-26) date stamped by the Office of the Immigration Judge to show that a timely appeal has been filed from a denial of the asylum application by the Immigration Judge; or

(3) If the Board has dismissed the alien's appeal of the denial of asylum, a copy of the petition for judicial review or for habeas corpus pursuant to section 106 of the Immigration and Nationality Act, date stamped by the appropriate court.

(d) In order for employment authorization to be renewed before its expiration, applications for renewal must be received by the Service sixty days prior to expiration of the employment authorization.

(e) Upon the denied applicant's request, the District Director, in his discretion, may grant further employment authorization pursuant to 8 C.F.R. § 274a.12(c)(12).

§ 208.8 Limitations on travel outside the United States.

An applicant who leaves the United States pursuant to advance parole granted under 8 C.F.R. § 212.5(e) shall be presumed to have abandoned his application under this section if he returns to the country of claimed persecution unless he is able to establish compelling reasons for having assumed the risk of persecution in so returning.

§ 208.9 Interview and procedure.

(a) For each application for asylum or withholding of deportation within the jurisdiction of an Asylum Officer, an interview shall be conducted by that Officer, either at the time of application or at a later date to be determined by the Officer in consultation with the applicant. Applications within the jurisdiction of an Immigration Judge are to be adjudicated under the rules of procedure established by the Executive Office for Immigration Review in parts 3, 236, and 242 of this chapter.

(b) The Asylum Officer shall conduct the interview in a nonadversarial manner and, at the request of the applicant, separate and apart from the general public. The purpose of the interview shall be to elicit all relevant and useful information bearing on the applicant's eligibility for the form of relief sought. The applicant may have counsel or a representative present and may submit affidavits of witnesses.

(c) The Asylum Officer shall have authority to administer oaths, present and receive evidence, and question the applicant and any witnesses, if necessary.

(d) Upon completion of the interview, the applicant or his representative shall have an opportunity to make a statement or comment on the evidence presented. The Asylum Officer, in his discretion, may limit the length of such comments or statement and may require their submission in writing.

(e) Following the interview the applicant may be given a period not to exceed 30 days to submit evidence in support of his application, unless, in the discretion of the Asylum Officer, a longer period is required.

(f) The application, all supporting information provided by the applicant, any comments submitted by the Bureau of Human Rights and Humanitarian Affairs of the Department of State, the Asylum Policy and Review Unit of the Department of

Justice, or by the Service, and any other information considered by the Asylum Officer shall comprise the record.

§ 208.10 Failure to appear.

The unexcused failure of an applicant to appear for a scheduled interview may be presumed an abandonment of the application. Failure to appear shall be excused if the notice of the interview was not mailed to the applicant's current address and such address had been provided to the Office of Refugees, Asylum, and Parole by the applicant prior to the date of mailing in accordance with section 265 of the Act and regulations promulgated thereunder, unless the Asylum Officer determines that the applicant received reasonable notice of the interview. Such failure to appear may be excused for other serious reasons in the discretion of the Asylum Officer.

§ 208.11 Comments from the Bureau of Human Rights and Humanitarian Affairs.

(a) At its option, the Bureau of Human Rights and Humanitarian Affairs (BHRHA) of the Department of State may comment on an application it receives pursuant to §§ 208.4(a), 236.3 or 242.17 of this chapter by providing:

(1) An assessment of the accuracy of the applicant's assertions about conditions in his country of nationality or habitual residence and his own experiences;

(2) An assessment of his likely treatment were he to return to his country of nationality or habitual residence;

(3) Information about whether persons who are similarly-situated to the applicant are persecuted in his country of nationality or habitual residence and the frequency of such persecution;

(4) Information about whether one of the grounds for denial specified in § 208.14 may apply; or

(5) Such other information or views as it deems relevant to deciding whether to grant or deny the application.

(b) In all cases, BHRHA shall respond within 45 days of receiving a completed application by either providing comments, requesting additional time in which to comment, or indicating that it does not wish to comment. If BHRHA requests additional time in which to provide comments, the Asylum Officer or Immigration Judge may grant BHRHA up to 30 additional days when necessary to gather information pertinent to the application or may proceed without BHRHA's comments. Failure to receive BHRHA's response shall not preclude final decision by the Asylum Officer or Immigration Judge if at least 60 days have elapsed since mailing the completed application to BHRHA. If the Deputy Attorney General determines that an expedited decision is necessary or appropriate, BHRHA shall provide its comments immediately.

(c) Any Department of State comments provided under this section shall be made a part of the asylum record. Unless the comments are classified under E.O. 12356 (3 C.F.R. § 1982 Comp., p. 166), the applicant shall be given a copy of such comments and be provided an opportunity to respond prior to the issuance of an adverse decision.

§ 208.12 Reliance on information compiled by other sources.

(a) In deciding applications for asylum or withholding of deportation, the Asylum Officer may rely on material provided by the Department of State, the Asylum Policy and Review Unit, the Office of Refugees, Asylum, and Parole, the District Director having jurisdiction over the place of the applicant's residence or the port of entry from which the applicant seeks admission to the United States, or other credible sources, such as international organizations, private voluntary agencies, or academic institutions. Prior to the issuance of an adverse decision made in reliance upon such material, that material must be identified and the applicant must be provided with an opportunity to inspect, explain, and rebut the material, unless the material is classified under E.O. 12356.

(b) Nothing in this part shall be construed to entitle the applicant to conduct discovery directed toward the records, officers, agents, or employees of the Service, the Department of Justice, or the Department of State.

§ 208.13 Establishing refugee status; burden of proof.

(a) The burden of proof is on the applicant for asylum to establish that he is a refugee as defined in section 101(a)(42) of the Act. The testimony of the applicant, if credible in light of general conditions in the applicant's country of nationality or last habitual residence, may be sufficient to sustain the burden of proof without corroboration.

(b) The applicant may qualify as a refugee either because he has suffered actual past persecution or because he has a well-founded fear of future persecution.

(1) Past persecution. An applicant shall be found to be a refugee on the basis of past persecution if he can establish that he has suffered persecution in the past in his country of nationality or last habitual residence on account of race, religion, nationality, membership in a particular social group, or political opinion, and that he is unable or unwilling to return to or avail himself of the protection of that country owing to such persecution.

(i) If it is determined that the applicant has established past persecution, he shall be presumed also to have a well-founded fear of persecution unless a preponderance of the evidence establishes that since the time the persecution occurred conditions in the applicant's country of nationality or last habitual residence have changed to such an extent that the applicant no longer has a well-founded fear of being persecuted if he were to return.

(ii) An application for asylum shall be denied if the applicant establishes past persecution under this paragraph but is determined not also to have a well-founded fear of future persecution under paragraph (b)(2) of this section, unless it is determined that the applicant has demonstrated compelling reasons for being unwilling to return to his country of nationality or last habitual residence arising out of the severity of the past persecution. If the applicant demonstrates such compelling reasons, he may be granted asylum unless such a grant is barred by paragraph (c) of this section or § 208.14(c).

(2) Well-founded fear of persecution. An applicant shall be found to have a well-founded fear of persecution if he can establish first, that he has a fear of persecution in his country of nationality or last habitual residence on account of race, religion, nationality, membership in a particular social group, or political opinion, second, that there is a reasonable possibility of actually suffering such persecution if he were to return to that country, and third, that he is unable or unwilling to return to or avail himself of the protection of that country because of such fear.

(i) In evaluating whether the applicant has sustained his burden of proving that he has a well-founded fear of persecution, the Asylum Officer or Immigration Judge shall not require the applicant to provide evidence that he would be singled out individually for persecution if:

(A) He establishes that there is a pattern or practice in his country of nationality or last habitual residence of persecution of groups of persons similarly situated to the applicant on account of race, religion, nationality, membership in a particular social group, or political opinion; and

(B) He establishes his own inclusion in and identification with such group of persons such that his fear of persecution upon return is reasonable.

(ii) The Asylum Officer or Immigration Judge shall give due consideration to evidence that the government of the applicant's country of nationality or last habitual residence persecutes its nationals or residents if they leave the country without authorization or seek asylum in another country.

(c) An applicant shall not qualify as a refugee if he ordered, incited, assisted, or otherwise participated in the persecution of any person on account of race, religion, nationality, membership in a particular social group, or political opinion. If the evidence indicates that the applicant engaged in such conduct, he shall have the burden of proving by a preponderance of the evidence that he did not so act.

§ 208.14 Approval or denial of application.

(a) An Immigration Judge or Asylum Officer may grant or deny asylum in the exercise of discretion to an applicant who qualifies as a refugee under section 101(a)(42) of the Act unless otherwise prohibited by paragraph (c) of this section.

(b) If the evidence indicates that one or more of the grounds for denial of asylum enumerated in paragraph (c) of this section may apply, the applicant shall have the burden of proving by a preponderance of the evidence that such grounds do not apply.

(c) Mandatory denials. An application for asylum shall be denied if:

(1) The alien, having been convicted by a final judgment of a particularly serious crime in the United States, constitutes a danger to the community;

(2) The applicant has been firmly resettled within the meaning of § 208.15; or

(3) There are reasonable grounds for regarding the alien as a danger to the security of the United States.

§ 208.15 Definition of "firm resettlement."

An alien is considered to be firmly resettled if, prior to arrival in the United States, he entered into another nation with, or while in that nation received, an offer of permanent resident status, citizenship, or some other type of permanent resettlement unless he establishes:

(a) That his entry into that nation was a necessary consequence of his flight from persecution, that he remained in that nation only as long as was necessary to arrange onward travel, and that he did not establish significant ties in that nation; or

(b) That the conditions of his residence in that nation were so substantially and consciously restricted by the authority of the country of refuge that he was not in fact resettled. In making his determination, the Asylum Officer or Immigration Judge shall consider the conditions under which other residents of the country live, the type of housing made available to the refugee, whether permanent or temporary, the types and extent of employment available to the refugee, and the extent to which the refugee received permission to hold property and to enjoy other rights and privileges, such as travel documentation including a right of entry and/or reentry, education, public relief, or naturalization, ordinarily available to others resident in the country.

§ 208.16 Entitlement to withholding of deportation.

(a) Consideration of application for withholding of deportation. If the Asylum Officer denies an alien's application for asylum, he shall also decide whether the alien is entitled to withholding of deportation under section 243(h) of the Act. If the application for asylum is granted, no decision on withholding of deportation will be made unless and until the grant of asylum is later revoked or terminated and deportation proceedings at which a new request for withholding of deportation is made are commenced. In such proceedings, an Immigration Judge may adjudicate both a renewed asylum claim and a request for withholding of deportation simultaneously whether or not asylum is granted.

(b) Eligibility for withholding of deportation; burden of proof. The burden of proof is on the applicant for withholding of deportation to establish that his life or freedom would be threatened in the proposed country of deportation on account of race, religion, nationality, membership in a particular social group, or political opinion. The testimony of the applicant, if credible in light of general conditions in the applicant's country of nationality or last habitual residence, may be sufficient to sustain the burden of proof without corroboration. The evidence shall be evaluated as follows:

(1) The applicant's life or freedom shall be found to be threatened if it is more likely than not that he would be persecuted on account of race, religion, nationality, membership in a particular social group, or political opinion.

(2) If the applicant is determined to have suffered persecution in the past such that his life or freedom was threatened in the proposed country of deportation on account of race, religion, nationality, membership in a particular social group, or political opinion, it shall be presumed that his life or freedom would be threatened on return to that country unless a preponderance of the evidence establishes that conditions in the country have changed to such an extent that it is no longer more likely than not that the applicant would be so persecuted there.

(3) In evaluating whether the applicant has sustained the burden of proving that his life or freedom would be threatened in a particular country on account of race, religion, nationality, membership in a particular social group, or political opinion, the Asylum Officer or Immigration Judge shall not require the applicant to provide evidence that he would be singled out individually for such persecution if:

(i) He establishes that there is a pattern or practice in the country of proposed deportation of persecution of groups of persons similarly situated to the applicant on account of race, religion, nationality, membership in a particular social group, or political opinion; and

(ii) He establishes his own inclusion in and identification with such group of persons such that it is more likely than not that his life or freedom would be threatened upon return.

(4) In addition, the Asylum Officer or Immigration Judge shall give due consideration to evidence that the life or freedom of nationals or residents of the country of claimed persecution is threatened if they leave the country without authorization or seek asylum in another country.

(c) Approval or denial of application. The following standards shall govern approval or denial of applications for withholding of deportation:

(1) Subject to paragraph (c)(2) of this section, an application for withholding of deportation to a country of proposed deportation shall be granted if the applicant's eligibility for withholding is established pursuant to paragraph (b) of this section.

(2) An application for withholding of deportation shall be denied if:

(i) The alien ordered, incited, assisted, or otherwise participated in the persecution of any person on account of race, religion, nationality, membership in a particular social group, or political opinion;

(ii) The alien, having been convicted by a final judgment of a particularly serious crime, constitutes a danger to the community of the United States;

(iii) There are serious reasons for considering that the alien has committed a serious nonpolitical crime outside the United States prior to arrival in the United States; or

(iv) There are reasonable grounds for regarding the alien as a danger to the security of the United States.

(3) If the evidence indicates that one or more of the grounds for denial of withholding of deportation enumerated in paragraph (c)(2) of this section apply, the applicant shall have the burden of proving by a preponderance of the evidence that such grounds do not apply.

(4) In the event that an applicant is denied asylum solely in the exercise of discretion, and the applicant is subsequently granted withholding of deportation under this section, thereby effectively precluding admission of the applicant's spouse or minor children following to join him, the denial of asylum shall be reconsidered. Factors to be so considered will include the reasons for the denial and reasonable alternatives available to the applicant such as reunification with his spouse or minor children in a third country.

§ 208.17 Decision.

The decision of an Asylum Officer to grant or deny asylum or withholding of deportation shall be communicated in writing to the applicant, the District Director having jurisdiction over the place of the applicant's residence or over the port of entry from which he sought admission to the United States, the Assistant Commissioner, Refugees, Asylum, and Parole, and the Director of the Asylum Policy and Review Unit of the Department of Justice. An adverse decision will state why asylum or withholding of deportation was denied and will contain an assessment of the applicant's credibility.

§ 208.18 Review of decisions and appeal.

(a) The Assistant Commissioner, Office of Refugees, Asylum, and Parole, shall have authority to review decisions by Asylum Officers, before they become effective, in any cases he shall designate. The Office of the Deputy Attorney General, assisted by the Asylum Policy and Review Unit, shall have authority to review decisions by

Asylum Officers, before they become effective, in any cases designated pursuant to 28 C.F.R. § 0.15(f)(3). There shall be no right of appeal to the Office of Refugees, Asylum, and Parole, to the Office of the Deputy Attorney General, or to the Asylum Policy and Review Unit, and parties shall have no right to appear before such offices in the course of such review.

(b) Except as provided in § 253.1(f) of this chapter, there shall be no appeal from a decision of an Asylum Officer. However, an application for asylum or withholding of deportation may be renewed before an Immigration Judge in exclusion or deportation proceedings. If exclusion or deportation proceedings have not been instituted against an applicant within 30 days of the Asylum Officer's final decision, the applicant may request in writing that the District Director having jurisdiction over the applicant's place of residence commence such proceedings. Absent exceptional circumstances, the District Director shall thereafter promptly institute proceedings against the applicant.

(c) A denial of asylum or withholding of deportation may only be reviewed by the Board of Immigration Appeals in conjunction with an appeal taken under 8 C.F.R. part 3.

§ 208.19 Motion to reopen or reconsider.

(a) A proceeding in which asylum or withholding of deportation was denied may be reopened or a decision from such a proceeding reconsidered for proper cause upon motion pursuant to the requirements of 8 C.F.R. §§ 3.2, 3.8, 3.22, 103.5, and 242.17 where applicable.

(b) A motion to reopen or reconsider shall be filed:

(1) With the District Director having jurisdiction over the location at which the prior determination was made who shall forward the motion immediately to an Asylum Officer; or

(2) With the Office of the Immigration Judge having jurisdiction over the prior proceeding.

§ 208.20 Approval and employment authorization.

When an alien's application for asylum is granted, he is granted asylum status for an indefinite period. Employment authorization is automatically granted or continued for persons granted asylum or withholding of deportation unless the alien is detained pending removal to a third country. Appropriate documentation showing employment authorization shall be provided by the INS.

§ 208.21 Admission of asylee's spouse and children.

(a) Eligibility. A spouse, as defined in section 101(a)(35) of the Act, or child, as defined in section 101(b)(1) (A), (B), (C), (D), or (E) of the Act, may also be granted asylum if accompanying or following to join the principal alien, unless it is determined that:

(1) The spouse or child ordered, incited, assisted, or otherwise participated in the persecution of any persons on account of race, religion, nationality, membership in a particular social group, or political opinion;

(2) The spouse or child, having been convicted by a final judgment of a particularly serious crime in the United States, constitutes a danger to the community of the United States; or

(3) There are reasonable grounds for regarding the spouse or child a danger to the security of the United States.

(b) Relationship. The relationship of spouse and child as defined in section 101(b)(1) of the Act must have existed at the time the principal alien's asylum application was approved, except for children born to or legally adopted by the principal alien and spouse after approval of the principal alien's asylum application.

(c) Spouse or child in the United States. When a spouse or child of an alien granted asylum is in the United States but was not included in the principal alien's application, the principal alien may request asylum for the spouse or child by filing Form I-730 with the District Director having jurisdiction over his place of residence, regardless of the status of that spouse or child in the United States.

(d) Spouse or child outside the United States. When a spouse or child of an alien granted asylum is outside the United States, the principal alien may request asylum for the spouse or child by filing form I-730 with the District Director, setting forth the full name, relationship, date and place of birth, and current location of each such person. Upon approval of the request, the District Director shall notify the Department of State, which will send an authorization cable to the American Embassy or Consulate having jurisdiction over the area in which the asylee's spouse or child is located.

(e) Denial. If the spouse or child is found to be ineligible for the status accorded under section 208(c) of the Act, a written notice explaining the basis for denial shall be forwarded to the principal alien. No appeal shall lie from this decision.

(f) Burden of proof. To establish the claim of relationship of spouse or child as defined in section 101(b)(1) of the Act, evidence must be submitted with the request as set forth in part 204 of this chapter. Where possible this will consist of the documents specified in 8 C.F.R. §§ 204.2(c)(2) and (c)(3). The burden of proof is on the principal alien to establish by a preponderance of the evidence that any person on whose behalf he is making a request under this section is an eligible spouse or child.

(g) Duration. The spouse or child qualifying under section 208(c) of the Act shall be granted asylum for an indefinite period unless the principal's status is revoked.

§ 208.22 Effect on deportation proceedings.

(a) An alien who has been granted asylum may not be excluded or deported unless his asylum status is revoked pursuant to § 208.24. An alien in exclusion or deportation proceedings who is granted withholding of deportation may not be deported to the country as to which his deportation is ordered withheld unless withholding of deportation is revoked pursuant to § 208.24.

(b) When an alien's asylum status or withholding of deportation is revoked under this chapter, he shall be placed in exclusion or deportation proceedings. Exclusion or deportation proceedings may be conducted concurrently with a revocation hearing scheduled under § 208.24.

* * *

§ 208.23 Restoration of status.

An alien who was maintaining his nonimmigrant status at the time of filing an application for asylum or withholding of deportation may continue or be restored to that status, if it has not expired, notwithstanding the denial of asylum or withholding of deportation.

§ 208.24 Revocation of asylum or withholding of deportation.

(a) Revocation of asylum by the Assistant Commissioner, Office of Refugees, Asylum, and Parole. Upon motion by the Assistant Commissioner and following a hearing before an Asylum Officer, the grant to an alien of asylum made under the jurisdiction of an Asylum Officer may be revoked if, by a preponderance of the evidence, the Service establishes that:

(1) The alien no longer has a well-founded fear of persecution upon return due to a change of conditions in the alien's country of nationality or habitual residence;

(2) There is a showing of fraud in the alien's application such that he was not eligible for asylum at the time it was granted; or

(3) The alien has committed any act that would have been grounds for denial of asylum under § 208.14(c).

(b) Revocation of withholding of deportation by the Assistant Commissioner, Office of Refugees, Asylum, and Parole. Upon motion by the Assistant Commissioner, and following a hearing before an Asylum Officer, the grant to an alien of withholding of deportation made under the jurisdiction of an Asylum Officer may be revoked if, by clear and convincing evidence, the Service establishes that:

(1) The alien is no longer entitled to withholding of deportation due to a change of conditions in the country to which deportation was withheld;

(2) There is a showing of fraud in the alien's application such that he was not eligible for withholding of deportation at the time it was granted;

(3) The alien has committed any other act that would have been grounds for denial of withholding of deportation under § 208.16(c)(2).

(c) Notice to applicant. Upon motion by the Assistant Commissioner to revoke asylum status or withholding of deportation, the alien shall be given notice of intent to revoke, with the reason therefore, at least thirty days before the hearing by the Asylum Officer. The alien shall be provided the opportunity to present evidence tending to show that he is still eligible for asylum or withholding of deportation. If the Asylum Officer determines that the alien is no longer eligible for asylum or withholding of deportation, the alien shall be given written notice that asylum status or withholding of deportation along with employment authorization are revoked.

(d) Revocation of derivative status. The termination of asylum status for a person who was the principal applicant shall result in termination of the asylum status of a spouse or child whose status was based on the asylum application of the principal.

(e) Reassertion of asylum claim. A revocation of asylum or withholding of deportation pursuant to paragraphs (a) or (b) of this section shall not preclude an applicant from reasserting an asylum or withholding of deportation claim in any subsequent exclusion or deportation proceeding.

(f) Review. The Office of the Deputy Attorney General, assisted by the Asylum Policy and Review Unit, shall have authority to review decisions to revoke asylum or withholding of deportation, before they become effective, in any cases designated pursuant to 28 C.F.R. § 0.15(f)(3). There shall be no right of appeal to the Office of the Deputy Attorney General or to the Asylum Policy and Review Unit and parties shall have no right to appear before such offices in the course of such review.

(g) Revocation of asylum or withholding of deportation by the Executive Office for Immigration Review. An Immigration Judge or the Board of Immigration Appeals may reopen a case pursuant to § 3.2 or § 242.22 of this chapter for the purpose of revoking a grant of asylum or withholding of deportation made under the exclusive jurisdiction of an Immigration Judge. In such a reopened proceeding, the Service must similarly establish by the appropriate standard of evidence one or more of the grounds set forth in paragraphs (a) or (b) of this section. Any revocation under this paragraph may occur in conjunction with an exclusion or deportation proceeding.

Asylum Procedures in Exclusion Cases
8 C.F.R. § 236

§ 236.3 Applications for asylum or withholding of deportation.

(a) If an alien expresses fear of persecution or harm upon return to his country of origin or to a country to which he may be deported after exclusion from the United States pursuant to part 237 of this chapter, the Immigration Judge shall:

(1) Advise the alien that he may apply for asylum in the United States or withholding of deportation to that other country; and

(2) Make available the appropriate application forms.

(b) An application for asylum or withholding of deportation must be filed with the Office of the Immigration Judge, pursuant to § 208.4(b) of this chapter. Upon receipt of the application, the Office of the Immigration Judge shall forward a copy to the Bureau of Human Rights and Humanitarian Affairs of the Department of State for their comments pursuant to § 208.11 of this chapter, and shall calendar the case for hearing, which shall be deferred pending receipt of the Department of State's comments. The reply, if any, from the Department of State, unless classified under E.O. 12356 (3 C.F.R. § 1982 Comp., p. 166), shall be given to both the applicant and to the Trial Attorney representing the government.

(c) Applications for asylum or withholding of deportation so filed will be decided by the Immigration Judge pursuant to the requirements and standards established in part 208 of this chapter after an evidentiary hearing that is necessary to resolve material factual issues in dispute. An evidentiary hearing extending beyond issues related to the basis for a mandatory denial of the application pursuant to 8 C.F.R. §§ 208.14 or 208.16 is not necessary once the Immigration Judge has determined that such a denial is required.

(1) Evidentiary hearings on applications for asylum or withholding of deportation will be closed to the public unless the applicant expressly requests that it be open pursuant to 8 C.F.R. § 236.2.

(2) Nothing in this section is intended to limit the authority of the Immigration Judge properly to control the scope of any evidentiary hearing.

(3) During the exclusion hearing, the applicant shall be examined under oath on his application and may present evidence and witnesses on his own behalf. The applicant has the burden of establishing that he is a refugee as defined in section 101(a)(42) of the Act pursuant to the standard set forth in § 208.13 of this chapter.

(4) The Trial Attorney for the government may call witnesses and present evidence for the record, including information classified under E.O. 12356 (3 C.F.R. § 1982 Comp., p. 166), provided the Immigration Judge or the Board has determined that such information is relevant to the hearing. When the Immigration Judge receives

such classified information he shall inform the applicant. The agency that provides the classified information to the Immigration Judge may provide an unclassified summary of the information for release to the applicant whenever it determines it can do so consistently with safeguarding both the classified nature of the information and its source. The summary should be as detailed as possible, in order that the applicant may have an opportunity to offer opposing evidence. A decision based in whole or in part on such classified information shall state that such information is material to the decision.

(d) The decision of an Immigration Judge to grant or deny asylum or withholding of deportation shall be communicated to the applicant and to the Trial Attorney for the government. An adverse decision will state why asylum or withholding of deportation was denied.

*   *   *

Refugee Regulations
8 C.F.R. § 207

§ 207.1

*   *   *

(d) Immediate relatives and special immigrants. Any applicant for refugee status who qualifies as an immediate relative or as a special immigrant shall not be processed as a refugee unless it is in the public interest. The alien shall be advised to obtain an immediate relative or special immigrant visa and shall be provided with the proper petition forms to send to any prospective petitioners. An applicant who may be eligible for classification under sections 203(a)(1), (2), (3), (4), (5), (6), or (7) of the Act, and for whom a visa number is now available, shall be advised of such eligibility but is not required to apply.

(e) Spouse and children. The spouse of child (as defined in section 101(b)(1)(A), (B), (C), (D), or (E) of the Act) of any refugee who qualifies for admission, shall if not otherwise entitled to admission and if not a person described in the second sentence of section 101(a)(42) of the Act, be entitled to the same status as such refugee if accompanying, or following to join such refugee. His/her entry shall be charged against the numerical limitation under which the refugee's entry is charged.

*   *   *

§ 207.3 Inadmissible applicants.

(a) Statutory exclusion. An applicant within the class of aliens excluded from admission to the United States under paragraphs (27), (29), (33), or so much of paragraph (23) as it relates to trafficking in narcotics of section 212(a) of the Act, shall not be admitted as a refugee under section 207 of the Act. However, an applicant seeking refugee status under section 207 is exempt by statute from the exclusionary provisions of paragraphs (14), (15), (20), (21), (25), and (32) of section 212(a) of the Act and a waiver of exclusion is not required.

(b) Waiver of exclusion. Except for the exclusionary and statutory exemption provisions noted in § 207.3(a) any other exclusionary provisions of section 212(a) of the Act may be waived for humanitarian purposes, to assure family unity, or when it is in the public interest. This authority is delegated to officers in charge who shall initiate the necessary investigations to establish the facts in each waiver application pending before them. Form I-602 (Application by Refugee for Waiver of Grounds of Excludability) may be filed with the officer in charge before whom the applicant's Form I-590 is pending. The burden is upon the applicant to show that the waiver should be granted based upon: (1) Humanitarian purposes, (2) family unity, or (3) public interest. The applicant shall be notified in writing regarding the application for waiver, including the reason for denial if the application is denied. There is no appeal from a waiver denial under this chapter.

*   *   *

§ 207.5 Waiting lists and priority of handling.

Waiting lists are maintained for each designated refugee group of special humanitarian concern. Each applicant whose application is accepted for filing by the Immigration and Naturalization Service shall be registered as of the date of filing. The date of filing is the priority date for purposes of case control. Refugees or groups of refugees may be selected from these lists in a manner that will best support the policies and interests of the United States. The Attorney General may adopt appropriate criteria for selecting the refugees and assignment of processing priorities for each designated group based upon such considerations as: Reuniting families, close association with the United States, compelling humanitarian concerns, and public interest factors.

*   *   *

§ 207.6 Control of approved refugee numbers.

Current numerical accounting of approved refugees is maintained for each special group designated by the President. As refugee status is authorized for each applicant, the total count is reduced correspondingly from the appropriate group so that information is readily available to indicate how many refugee numbers remain available for issuance.

*   *   *

§ 207.8 Termination of refugee status.

The refugee status of any alien (and of the spouse or child of the alien) admitted to the United States under section 207 of the Act shall be terminated by any district director in whose district the alien is found if the alien was not a refugee within the meaning of section 101(a)(42) of the Act at the time of admission. The district director shall notify the alien in writing of the Service's intent to terminate the alien's refugee status. The alien shall have 30 days from the date notice is served upon him/her or, delivered to his/her last known address, to present written or oral evidence to show why the alien's refugee status should not be terminated. There is no appeal under this chapter from the termination of refugee status by the district director. Upon termination of refugee status, the district director shall process the alien under sections 235, 236, and 237 of the Act.

Chapter 5

Administrative Appeals and Judicial Review

Understanding the regulatory and statutory scheme for administrative appeals and judicial review of immigration decisions presents a challenge to both the inexperienced and the seasoned practitioner. A careful inspection of the cases and statutes will reveal a number of important patterns which will help the student understand this difficult subject. The materials in this chapter are presented to enable the reader to first gain a clear understanding of the jurisdiction of each level of decision making within the immigration law.

The jurisdiction of both the federal courts and the administrative appeals bodies are governed by the locus of the original determination which gives rise to the appeal. Therefore our discussion will begin with a review of the jurisdiction of the four relevant federal agencies.[1] Since the most complicated area of administrative and judicial review revolves around the Immigration and Naturalization Service, most of our discussion will concentrate on the review of INS decisions.

The review of Department of State decisions is severely limited primarily for reasons of foreign policy and extraterritoriality. Courts have historically accorded the executive branch great deference in matters of foreign policy. In addition, adverse decisions made by officials of the Department of State are less likely to be appealed since they tend to occur when the alien is neither in the U.S. nor at the border.[2]

As noted in the introduction, the INA delegates some authority to the Secretary of Labor and to public health officials. The review of adverse decisions by the Secretary of Labor will be discussed in Chapter 9. The review of determinations by a public health officer regarding the excludability of aliens for psychological or health reasons are neither complicated nor routinely encountered and therefore will not be discussed here.[3]

---

1. The student should carefully review the regulations which limit the jurisdiction of each of these government agencies which can be found at the end of this chapter and are followed by "procedural" flow charts.

2. The limited procedures available for the review of adverse decisions made on visa application by U.S. consuls abroad will be discussed in Chapter 6.

3. The review of these determinations are conducted before a panel of three doctors of the Public Health Service. The alien has the right to counsel and to present medical evidence by an independent doctor of her choice (at her own expense). *See* 42 C.F.R. §§ 34.4 and 34.14. Judicial review of these decisions may be obtained through the normal procedure available in deportation and exclusion cases. *See* discussion *infra*.

Review by the Attorney General

Although the Attorney General is the primary official responsible for the enforcement of the immigration laws, much of his authority is delegated to other government officers. In addition, this extensive delegation precludes review before the Attorney General as a matter of right. At the same time cases may be reviewed by the Attorney General in some situations where the Attorney General directs.[4] The BIA chairperson, a majority of the BIA, or the Commissioner may also request referral of a case to the Attorney General.[5] Whether or not juducial review is available, and the manner of obtaining such, will depend on the nature of the decision and whether or not the decision is construed as a "final order of deportation."[6]

Review by the INS Central Office

The Attorney General's broad powers to review decisions under the immigration laws are rarely used. Most decisions within the INS are made initially by its district directors and appealable thereafter to its central office. In order to assure a greater nationwide uniformity of its decisions, the central office created an Administrative Appeals Unit (AAU). Most cases which are decided by the district directors may be appealed to the central office of the Immigration and Naturalization Service. The Administrative Appeals Unit has jurisdiction to review denials or revocations in the following cases:[7]

1. Breaching of bonds under 8 C.F.R. § 103.6(e);[8]

2. Employment-based preference petitions under 8 C.F.R. § 204.1(c), except when the denial of the petition is based upon lack of a certification by the Secretary of Labor under section 212(a)(5) of the Act.[9]

3. Indochinese refugee applications for adjustment of status under 8 C.F.R. § 245.2(a)(4) and (e).

4. Revocation of certain immigrant preference petitions under 8 C.F.R. § 205.2. Revocation of approval of certain nonimmigrant petitions as provided in 8 C.F.R. § 214.2.

---

4. Since the Attorney General is vested with the power of administering the immigrations, it would seem that informal contacts would not be precluded. However, such approaches certainly raise ethical questions and the public's right of access to equal access to governmental decision making.

5. 8 C.F.R. § 3.1(h).

6. "Final orders of deportation" are defined at 8 U.S.C. § 1105a, Sec. 106, and are discussed later in this chapter.

7. For a complete listing of the matters which are reviewable by the AAU, see 8 C.F.R. § 103.1.

8. As noted earlier, certain persons in deportation and exclusion proceedings may be required to post a cash bond in lieu of detention. When the conditions set out in the bond are violated, notice is given by the district director of the "breach" of the bond.

9. As will be discussed later, immigrants must establish entitlement to a "preference classification" in order to determine their position within the numerical quotas for persons seeking permanent residency in the U.S. A condition precedent to obtaining a third or sixth preference classification is approval of certification by the Secretary of Labor.

5. Applications for permission to reapply for admission to the United States after deportation or removal.[10]

6. Applications for waiver of certain grounds of excludability.

7. Applications for waiver of the two-year foreign residence requirement.[11]

8. Petitions for temporary workers or trainees and fiancees or fiances of U.S. citizens who are seeking admission to the United States as nonimmigrants.[12]

9. Adjustment of status of certain resident aliens to a nonimmigrant status under 8 C.F.R. § 247.12(b).

10. Applications to preserve residence for naturalization purposes under 8 C.F.R. § 316a.21(c).

11. Petitions to classify Amerasians as the children of United States citizens.

Review by the Board of Immigration Appeals

The Board of Immigration Appeals (BIA) is the body responsible for appeals from certain INS district director and immigration judge decisions. Prior to 1983 the BIA was part of the INS. Pursuant to amendments to the Code of Federal Regulations, the BIA and the immigration judges were placed in a separate part of the Department of Justice called the Executive Office for Immigration Review.[13] The jurisdiction of the BIA, defined at 8 C.F.R. § 3.1(b), includes the following:

1. Reviewing decisions of the immigration judge in exclusion and deportation proceedings.

2. Reviewing decisions on applications for waiver of inadmissability under 8 U.S.C. § 1182(c), Sec. 212(c), in deportation proceedings.[14]

3. Review of decisions involving the imposition of administrative fines and penalties.

4. Review of decisions on applications for the exercise of discretionary authority which permits the Attorney General to temporarily admit certain otherwise inadmissible nonimmigrants.

5. Review of certain decisions relating to bond or detention of aliens.

6. Review of decisions of immigration judges regarding rescission of adjustment of status.

---

10. Removal prohibits the alien's return for a period of one year (for exclusion) to five years (in the case of deportation). During this period an alien wishing to return to the U.S. must first obtain permission from the Attorney General. This permission to reapply for admission is discussed at Chapter 12.

11. One of the grounds prohibiting an alien's change or "adjustment" of status is when the alien was admitted into the U.S. with restrictions as an exchange alien (certain J-1 visas). In order to be eligible for "adjustment" of status or change in status, prior approval must be obtained from the Attorney General following a recommendation by the Secretary of State. The review process for the J-1 visa holder is discussed at Chapter 12.

12. *See* Chapter 6.

13. *See* 60 Interpreter Releases 155 (1983).

14. Previously, a direct appeal could be made to the BIA from a district director's adverse decision in a "212(c) waiver case." *See* 52 Fed. Reg. 2,942 (Jan. 29, 1987). The 212(c) waiver will be discussed in Chapter 12.

Some cases reach the BIA on its own certification of the case.[15] The commissioner or any other authorized officer of the INS may also certify cases to the BIA if the Board could have had jurisdiction under 8 C.F.R. § 3.1(b). A review of the above list demonstrates the difficulty in discerning a pattern for determining BIA reviewability. The cases in these materials begin with a case delineating the jurisdiction of the immigration judge. As will be seen delineating the judge's jurisdiction is a significant aid in defining the limits of the Board's jurisdiction.[16]

The Board is not limited, as are appellate courts, to a determination of whether there exists substantial evidence in the record to support the immigration judge's findings. Generally when the BIA reviews cases it may make a *de novo* review of the record. On questions of law and fact and in exercising discretion, the Board may make an independent evaluation and arrive at its own decision.[17] However, like most administrative and judicial review bodies, the Board will defer to the immigration judge on questions of fact.

Judicial Review of Final Orders

Section 106(a) [8 U.S.C. § 1105a] provides the exclusive procedure for judicial review of "final orders of deportation." The term "final order of deportation" has been interpreted as including all determinations and orders incidental to a deportation hearing by an immigration judge and reviewable by the Board of Immigration Appeals. A case which meets this definition can be reviewed in a federal appeals court by filing a petition for review before the court having jurisdiction where the alien resides or where the deportation order was entered. A condition precedent for obtaining review before a U.S. court of appeals is that the alien must have exhausted all administrative remedies. If the alien has left the United States after issuance of the order of deportation, her case cannot be reviewed as it is considered moot.[18]

Judicial Review of Exclusion Orders

Under Section 106(b) of the Act, 8 U.S.C. § 1105a(b), the exclusive remedy available to aliens against whom a final order of exclusion has been issued is a petition for a writ of habeas corpus. Just as in the case of the review of deportation orders, the alien must have exhausted her administrative remedies and not departed the U.S. after issuance of the exclusion order.[19] The courts will not make *de novo* findings but

---

15. *See* 8 C.F.R. § 3.1(c).

16. Conversely, decisions made by district directors and not reviewable before an immigration judge can only be challenged in the U.S. district court.

17. While a creature of regulation and not a statutory body, the BIA's jurisdiction is quite extensive. For example, 8 C.F.R. § 3.1(d) provides that the Board shall exercise the discretion and authority conferred upon the Attorney General "... as is appropriate and necessary for the disposition of the case." The Board reviews cases *de novo* and may even make new credibility findings or receive new evidence. *See, e.g., In Re Villanova-Gonzalez*, 13 I. & N. Dec. 399, 403 (BIA 1969); *Cañas-Segovia v. INS*, 902 F.2d 717, 727 (9th Cir. 1990); *Platero-Cortez v. INS*, 804 F.2d 1127 (9th Cir. 1986). While making new credibility findings and receiving new evidence are not the Board's preferred method of fact adjudication, they are within its authority. *See In Re Wong*, 12 I. & N. Dec. 417, 419 (BIA 1968).

18. *See* 8 U.S.C. § 1105(c).

19. *See* 8 U.S.C. § 1105a(c)

determine if there have been errors of law, whether the adverse decision was made after a fair hearing, and whether the final order of exclusion is supported by substantial evidence.

Declaratory Judgment Actions

The declaratory judgment remedy is a relatively recent development in the law.[20] The declaratory judgment, first recognized in 1919, was more commonly used in state courts than in the federal system.[21] The Supreme Court's decision in *Nashville, Chattanooga & St. Louis Ry. v. Wallace*[22] opened the door to the enactment of the Federal Declaratory Judgment Act of 1934.[23] The Declaratory Judgment Act was severely criticized because it was perceived as allowing the issuance of advisory opinions. This, of course, presented serious problems to the notion of separation of powers. It is from this tenet that an "actual controversy between real parties" is required in order that a court can have jurisdiction even under today's statute. Today, declaratory review can properly be sought in a wide variety of cases ranging from enforcing payment on promissory notes, contract matters, patent infringement cases and *sometimes* the review of an administrative agency's action.

The "sometimes" qualification exists because of the doctrine of sovereign immunity. Declaratory review was not originally contemplated as a tool for resolving disputes between persons and government but rather, between individuals and entities. The Declaratory Judgment Act does not constitute a waiver of sovereign immunity and should be viewed as a procedural, not jurisdictional, statute in the context of immigration law. Therefore, in order to successfully avoid a motion to dismiss, counsel must be able to identify an independent ground for jurisdiction.[24] Moreover, the answer to the jurisdictional question does not end the inquiry as there must still be an actual case in controversy,[25] venue must be proper, exhaustion of remedies must

---

20. The final adoption of the action in declaratory judgment in the federal system came about through the energies of Professors Borchard and Sunderland. *See* 10A Wright, Miller & Kane, *Federal Practice & Procedure* 728 (1983).

21. *See* The Declaratory Judgment Act of 1919 in Michigan. In 1922 the Commissioners on Uniform State Laws adopted the Uniform Declaratory Judgment Act.

22. 288 U.S. 249 (1933).

23. *See* 48 Stat. 955 (1934). The original enactment is largely intact and is now contained in 28 U.S.C. §§ 2201 and 2202.

§ 2201—Creation of Remedies. In a case of actual controversy within its jurisdiction, ... [except federal tax matters or proceedings under 11 U.S.C. §§ 505 or 1146] any court of the United States, upon the filing of an appropriate pleading, may declare the rights and other legal relations of any interested party seeking such declarations whether or not further relief is or could be sought. Any such declaration shall have the force and effect of a final judgment or decree and shall be reviewable as such.

§ 2202—Further Relief. Further necessary or proper relief based on a declaratory judgment or decree may be granted, after reasonable notice and hearing, against any adverse party whose rights have been determined by such judgment.

24. *See* 10A Wright, Miller & Kane, *Federal Practice & Procedure* 731-38 (1983).

25. For example, in *International Longshoremen's & Warehousemen's Union, Local 37 v. Boyd*, 347 U.S. 222 (1954), alien laborers challenged the constitutionality of a statute that would treat them as returning aliens upon their travel to Alaska to work in canneries—in this case the court refused to decide the case because it was "an inappropriate controversy."

not be a problem and the court must be willing to grant the relief in the sound exercise of its discretion.[26]

Administrative Procedure Act and Federal Question[27]

While it is clear that one can sue the government, the prevailing view is that the Administrative Procedure Act (APA) is not the proper basis for asserting jurisdiction in U.S. district court. Prior to 1976 the courts were divided on the question of whether the APA provided an independent basis for federal court jurisdiction.[28] Congress' amendment of the APA in 1976[29] and the later the Supreme Court's decision in *Califano v. Sanders*[30] made it clear that jurisdiction had not been conferred. Due to Congress' amendment of the federal question statute in 1980, the issue of whether the government could be sued has been eradicated.[31] No doubt, due to the confusion caused by the split in circuits (prior to 1977) counsel in immigration cases continue to cite every conceivable jurisdictional statute. While one could argue that the APA does provide jurisdiction the question is now academic. Perhaps an easier way of conceptualizing the relationship between the APA and federal question is to view the federal question statute as providing jurisdiction, and the APA as waiving sovereign immunity and controlling the scope of judicial review.

---

26. It should also be noted that a court may refuse declaratory relief if there is an alternative which is more effective (declaratory relief is discretionary). Borchard, *Discretion to Refuse Jurisdiction of Actions for Declaratory Judgments*, 26 Minn. L. Rev. 677 (1942); *Brillhart v. Excess Insurance Company of America*, 316 U.S. 491 (1942). At the same time, the court's perception that determination of the issue in controversy is being pursued in a piecemeal fashion could cause the dismissal of the action. 10A Wright, Miller & Kane, *Federal Practice & Procedure* 648 n.8 (1983).

27. The Administrative Procedure Act, 5 U.S.C. § 551 *et seq.* (hereinafter referred to as the "APA"). The federal question statute, 28 U.S.C. § 1331, although the subject of extensive discussion, is a short statute and provides that

The district courts shall have original jurisdiction of all civil actions arising under the Constitution, laws, or treaties of the United States.

28. *See Scanwell Labs, Inc. v. Thomas*, 521 F.2d 941 (D.C. Cir. 1975, *cert. denied*, 425 U.S. 910 (1975) (recognizing jurisdiction through the APA); *but see Chaudoin v. Atkinson*, 494 F.2d 1323 (3d Cir. 1983) (rejecting the claim that the APA granted jurisdiction).

29. *See* Pub. L. No. 94-574 (1976), amending 5 U.S.C. §§ 702 and 703.

30. 430 U.S. 99 (1977).

31. The 1980 amendments removed the minimum amount in controversy requirement of $10,000 in all cases. *See* 8 U.S.C. § 1331; *see also* 1980 U.S. Code Cong. & Admin. News 5063-69.

While the government can clearly be sued, it is *not* clear that the APA is the proper basis for jurisdiction. For example, in *Grumman Ohio Corp. v. Dole*, 776 F.2d 338 (D.C. Cir. 1985), the court sidestepped the jurisdictional issue since the plaintiff had asserted jurisdiction under the federal question statute. Other courts have specifically stated that the APA provides no independent basis for jurisdiction. *See, e.g., Choctaw Mfg. Co. v. U.S.*, 761 F.2d 609 (11th Cir. 1985).

The Immigration Jurisdictional Statute

8 U.S.C. § 1329[32] provides an important but limited basis for asserting jurisdiction of a declaratory nature. This provision places jurisdiction in the U.S. district courts, but is *limited* to provisions arising under Title II of the INA.[33] This jurisdictional provision, therefore, does not provide for review of matters such as the INS, DOS, or DOL compliance with the APA, review of DOL or another agency's actions, or INS compliance with the visa issuance process. However, the combination of 8 U.S.C. § 1329 and federal question jurisdiction (28 U.S.C. § 1331) provides jurisdictional basis with which to seek declaratory relief or judicial review of most agency action.

References

Barker, *A Critique of the Establishment of a Specialized Immigration Court*, 18 San Diego L. Rev. 25 (1980)

Gordon, *The Need to Modernize Our Immigration Laws*, 13 San Diego L. Rev. 1, 9 (1975)

Juceam & Jacobs, *Constitutional and Policy Considerations of an Article I Immigration Court*, 18 San Diego L. Rev. 29 (1980)

Legomsky, *Forum Choices for the Review of Agency Adjudication: A Study of the Immigration Process*, 71 Iowa L. Rev. 1297 (1986)

Levinson, *A Specialized Court for Immigration Hearings and Appeals*, 56 Notre Dame L. Rev. 644 (1981)

Note, *Jurisdiction to Review Prior Orders and Underlying Statutes in Deportation Appeals*, 65 Va. L. Rev. 403 (1979)

Roberts, *The Board of Immigration Appeals: A Critical Appraisal*, 15 San Diego L. Rev. 29 (1977)

Roberts, *Proposed: A Specialized Statutory Immigration Court*, 18 San Diego L. Rev. 1 (1980)

Verkuil, *A Study of Immigration Procedures*, 31 UCLA L. Rev. 1141 (1984)

Wildes, *The Need for a Specialized Immigration Court: A Practical Response*, 18 San Diego L. Rev. 53 (1980)

Wolff, *The Non-Reviewability of Consular Visa Decisions: An Unjustified Aberration from American Justice*, 5 N.Y.L. Sch. J. Int'l Comp. L. 341 (1984)

---

32. 8 U.S.C. § 1329, Sec. 279 provides that

The district courts of the United States shall have jurisdiction of all causes, civil and criminal, arising under any of the provisions of this title. It shall be the duty of the United States attorney of the proper district to prosecute every such suit when brought by the United States. Notwithstanding any other law, such prosecutions or suits may be instituted at any place in the United States at which the violation may occur or at which the person charged with a violation under section 1325 or 1326 of this title may be apprehended. No suit or proceeding for a violation of any of the provisions of this subchapter shall be settled, compromised, or discontinued without the consent of the court in which it is pending and any such settlement, compromise, or discontinuance shall be entered of record with the reasons therefor.

33. *See Ubiera v. Bell*, 463 F. Supp. 181 (C.D.N.Y. 1978); *Daneshvar v. Chauvin*, 644 F.2d 1248 (5th Cir. 1981). Title II includes 8 U.S.C. §§ 1151-1363 and issues such as immigrant visas, deportation, and adjustment.

A. Jurisdiction of the Immigration Judge

Matter of Roussis
18 I. & N. Dec. 256 (BIA 1982)

In a decision dated February 1, 1982, an immigration judge granted the respondent's motion to reopen his deportation proceedings and to remand his case to the District Director for consideration of his application for adjustment of status under section 245 of the Immigration and Nationality Act, 8 U.S.C. 1255. She then certified her decision to the Board for review pursuant to 8 C.F.R. 3.1(c) and 8 C.F.R. 242.8(a). The immigration judge's decision will be reversed.

The respondent, a 30-year-old native and citizen of Greece, was admitted to the United States on October 27, 1972, as a nonimmigrant student, authorized to remain until October 26, 1977. The respondent was found deportable as an overstay under section 241(a)(2) of the Act, 8 U.S.C. 1251(a)(2), but was granted the privilege of voluntary departure in lieu of deportation.

On February 1, 1982, the immigration judge ordered the deportation proceedings reopened on the basis of an immediate relative visa petition which had been filed on the respondent's behalf by his United States citizen spouse.[1] Over the objection of the Immigration and Naturalization Service, she further ordered that the case be remanded to the District Director for adjudication of the respondent's adjustment application. She then certified her decision to us for review.

The precise issue presented is whether an immigration judge is authorized to remand a case involving a section 245 application to the District Director for adjudication notwithstanding the fact that an Order to Show Cause has been issued, deportation proceedings have begun, and the District Director objects to the remand order.

The immigration judge concluded that an order of remand to permit consideration by the District Director of an adjustment application, coupled with an order of conditional termination of the deportation proceedings, is a permissible exercise of her authority. Such procedure, she submits, promotes efficiency and the savings of resources for the District, the Immigration Court, the aliens and their representatives and, at the same time, does not contravene the applicable regulations. Moreover, she contends that "to deny to an alien the ability to move for a remand [a procedure available to the Service in certain circumstances pursuant to 8 C.F.R. 242.7] would unfairly favor the Service...."

*   *   *

For resolution of this question, reference must be made to provisions within the Code of Federal Regulations. The pattern set out in the code to govern the adjudication of applications for adjustment of status is quite clear. Pursuant to 8 C.F.R. 245.2(a)(1), "after an alien has been served with an Order to Show Cause or warrant of arrest,

---

1. The respondent had already filed an earlier motion to reopen on August 27, 1977, in which he requested consideration of an adjustment application based upon a sixth preference petition. This motion was still pending when the immediate relative petition was substituted.

his application for adjustment of status under Section 245 of the Act shall be made and considered only in proceedings under Part 242 of this Chapter."[2] It is evident then that the immigration judge is charged by regulation, which has the force of law, with the responsibility of accepting and adjudicating an application for section 245 relief if that application is submitted by an alien in deportation proceedings.

The immigration judge acknowledges that 8 C.F.R. 245.2(a)(1) vests the immigration judge with exclusive jurisdiction to entertain adjustment applications, once an Order to Show Cause has been issued. It is her position, however, that nothing prevents the immigration judge from "ceding" that jurisdiction when practical and equitable considerations dictate. Thus, under the immigration judge's theory, the District Director could be forced to assume jurisdiction over a pending adjustment application simply because an immigration judge chooses to relinquish it. We do not believe that an issue as fundamental as jurisdiction is subject to *ad hoc* resolution, especially given the explicit mandate of the regulation in question.

Further, we agree with the Immigration and Naturalization Service that a *sua sponte* remand by an immigration judge impinges upon the District Director's exclusive authority to control the prosecution of deportable aliens. It has long been held that when enforcement officials of the Immigration and Naturalization Service choose to initiate proceedings against an alien and to prosecute those proceedings to a conclusion, the immigration judge is obligated to order deportation if the evidence supports a finding of deportability on the ground charged. Integral to a determination of whether an alien, although indisputably deportable, is to be ordered deported is whether or not he is eligible for any form of relief from deportation. *See* 8 C.F.R. 242.17. *See Lopez-Telles v. INS*, 564 F.2d 1302 (9th Cir. 1977).

Aside from 8 C.F.R. 242.7, which authorized the District Director, in certain specified instances, to cancel an Order to Show Cause and thereby terminate proceedings prior to their commencement or to request dismissal or remand of a case after proceedings have begun, there is no provision in the regulations which authorizes the termination, whether conditional or final, of deportation proceedings. On the contrary, the regulations emphatically require the prompt completion of the deportation hearing if no action to terminate or remand is taken by the District Director. *See* 8 C.F.R. 242.7.

In conclusion, we find that the immigration judge's decision to grant the respondent's motion to remand and thereby conditionally divest herself of jurisdiction over his adjustment application is in clear derogation of the carefully defined jurisdictional scheme set out in the regulations pertaining to section 245. Further, the immigration judge's concern that an alien just be allowed to move for a remand of his adjustment application if the Service and the alien are to stand before her as equals is misplaced. While an alien is given the right to submit an application for relief under section 245, no authority of which we are aware suggests that he also has the right to dictate the procedures whereby his application is adjudicated.

---

2. Section 242 governs the institution, conduct, and resolution of deportation proceedings.

B. Who Determines Venue?

Matter of Victorino
18 I. & N. 226 (BIA 1982)

The respondent appeals from a decision of the immigration judge dated January 15, 1982, denying her motion to change venue. The appeal will be sustained and the record will be remanded to the immigration judge.

As a general rule, the Board does not entertain appeals from interlocutory decisions rendered by immigration judges. *See Matter of Ruiz-Campuzano*, 17 I & N Dec. 108 (BIA 1979). However, where a significant issue is raised which affects the administration of the immigration laws, we have accepted jurisdiction over the matter. *See Matter of Alphonse*, Interim Decision 2892 (BIA 1981); *Matter of Wadas*, 17 I & N Dec. 346 (BIA 1980); *Matter of Seren*, 15 I & N Dec. 590 (BIA 1976). Inasmuch as an important question has been presented concerning the jurisdictional powers of the immigration judge and the District Director, we shall entertain this interlocutory appeal.

On September 21, 1981, the District Director in San Francisco issued an Order to Show Cause charging the respondent with deportability. The respondent, who had previously moved to the Los Angeles area, retained counsel in that location. The record reflects that the respondent's attorney first requested a change of venue prior to November 17, 1981, the date on which the respondent had been notified to appear for deportation proceedings. This request was denied by the District Director in a letter dated November 24, 1981, at which time the hearing was rescheduled for February 4, 1982. After further correspondence on the matter, the respondent filed a motion for change of venue to the immigration judge on December 10, 1981, arguing that the District Director had no jurisdiction to deny a change of venue after issuance of the Order to Show Cause.

The immigration judge denied the motion, concluding that he lacked jurisdiction to adjudicate the request to change venue because of the deportation hearing had not yet commenced. In reaching this decision, he distinguished the Board's ruling in *Matter of Seren*, *supra*, where we held that an immigration judge alone has authority to change venue. Noting that in *Matter of Seren* the motion was submitted at the hearing, the immigration judge determined that he did not have jurisdiction over venue questions until the hearing had commenced.

The immigration judge's interpretation of *Matter of Seren* is incorrect. In that case we stated that the District Director may determine venue prior to the commencement of deportation proceedings, but that once jurisdiction rests in the immigration judge, the District Director no longer has any authority to decide whether venue should be changed. The regulations clearly state that proceedings are commenced by the issuance and service of an Order to Show Cause by the Service. *See* 8 C.F.R. 242.1(a). Furthermore, as a practical matter, we see no reason to require the respondent to appear at a hearing in order to request a venue change, since the time and expense involved may be unnecessary if the request is granted. After the issuance of an Order to Show Cause, jurisdiction to change venue lies with the immigration judge, whether or not the respondent has appeared for a hearing. The letter from the District director of November 24, 1981, denying the respondent's request for change of venue, is of no effect since he lacked jurisdiction over the question of venue at that time. Consequently, the immigration judge should have heard the respondent's motion and ruled on the merits of the request for venue in the exercise of his discretion. Accordingly, we shall remand the record to the immigration judge for further proceedings consistent with this opinion.

Questions

1. What should counsel do in the event that her application for change of venue is denied?

2. Should interlocutory administrative appeals be allowed in deportation and exclusion proceedings? If so, what standards should be used in controlling interlocutory appeals?

C. Judicial Review

Before reading the case which follows, consider the following statute. How does the court's interpretation of the statute compare with the interpretation that you would have given?

8 U.S.C. § 1105a, Sec. 106

(a) The procedure prescribed by, and all the provisions of chapter 158 title 28, United States Code, shall apply to and shall be the sole and exclusive procedure for the judicial review of all final orders of deportation heretofore or hereafter made against aliens within the United States pursuant to administrative proceedings under section 1252(b) of this title or comparable provisions of any prior Act, except that—

(1) a petition for review may be filed not later than 90 days after the date of the issuance of the final deportation order, or in the case of an alien convicted of an aggravated felony, not later than 30 days after the issuance of such order;[34]

(2) the venue of any petition for review under this section shall be in the judicial circuit in which the administrative proceedings before a special inquiry officer were conducted in whole or in part, or in the judicial circuit wherein is the residence, as defined in this chapter, of the petitioner, but not in more than one circuit;

(3) the action shall be brought against the Immigration and Naturalization Service, as respondent. Service of the petition to review shall be made upon the Attorney General of the United States and upon the official of the Immigration and Naturalization Service in charge of the Service district in which the office of the clerk of the court is located. The service of the petition for review upon such official of the Service shall stay the deportation of the alien pending determination of the petition by the court, unless the court otherwise directs; or unless the alien is convicted of an aggravated felony, in which case the Service shall not stay the deportation of the alien pending determination of the petition of the court unless the court otherwise directs;[35]

---

34. The "90" and "30" day provisions are effective for final orders issued on or after January 1, 1991. The Anti-Drug Abuse Act of 1988, Pub. L. No. 100-690, 102 Stat. 4181 limited aggravated felons to 60 days in which to file their petition for review.

35. This last clause is effective 60 days after enactment of the Act, or January 28, 1991.

(4) except as provided in clause (B) of paragraph (5) of this subsection, the petition shall be determined solely upon the administrative record upon which the deportation order is based and the Attorney General's findings of fact, if supported by reasonable, substantial, and probative evidence on the record considered as a whole, shall be conclusive;

(5) whenever any petitioner, who seeks review of an order under this section, claims to be a national of the United States and makes a showing that his claim is not frivolous, the court shall (A) pass upon the issues presented when it appears from the pleadings and affidavits filed by the parties that no genuine issue of material fact is presented; or (B) where a genuine issue of material fact as to the petitioner's nationality is presented, transfer the proceedings to a United States district court for the district where the petitioner has his residence for hearing de novo of the nationality claim and determination as if such proceedings were originally initiated in the district court under the provisions of section 2201 of title 28. Any such petitioner shall not be entitled to have such issue determined under section 1503(a) of this title or otherwise;

(6) whenever a petitioner seeks review of an order under this section, any review sought with respect to a motion to reopen or reconsider such an order shall be consolidated with the review of the order;[36]

(7) if the validity of a deportation order has not been judicially determined, its validity may be challenged in a criminal proceeding against the alien for violation of subsection (d) or (e) of section 1252 of this title only by separate motion for judicial review before trial. Such motion shall be determined by the court without a jury and before the trial of the general issue. Whenever a claim to United States nationality is made in such motion, and in the opinion of the court, a genuine issue of material fact as to the alien's nationality is presented, the court shall accord him a hearing de novo on the nationality claim and determine that issue as if proceedings had been initiated under the provisions of section 2201 of title 28. Any such alien shall not be entitled to have such issue determined under section 1503(a) of this title or otherwise. If no such hearing de novo as to nationality is conducted, the determination shall be made solely upon the administrative record upon which the deportation order is based and the Attorney General's findings of fact, if supported by reasonable, substantial and probative evidence on the record considered as a whole, shall be conclusive. If the deportation order is held invalid, the court shall dismiss the indictment and the United States shall have the right to appeal to the court of appeals within thirty days. The procedure on such appeals shall be as provided in the Federal rules of criminal procedure. No petition for review under this section may be filed by any alien during the pendency of a criminal proceeding against such alien for violation of subsection (d) or (e) of section 1252 of this title;

(8) nothing in this section shall be construed to require the Attorney General to defer deportation of an alien after the issuance of a deportation order because of the right of judicial review of the order granted by this section, or to relieve any alien from compliance with subsections (d) and (e) of section 1252 of this title. Nothing contained in this section shall be construed to preclude the Attorney General from detaining or continuing to detain an alien or from taking him into custody pursuant

36. This provision affects final orders entered on or after January 1, 1991.

to subsection (c) of section 1252 of this title at any time after the issuance of a deportation order;

*   *   *

(9)(a) Any alien held in custody pursuant to an order of deportation may obtain judicial review thereof by habeas corpus proceedings; (b) Notwithstanding the provisions of any other law, any alien against whom a final order of exclusion has been made heretofore or hereafter under the provisions of section 1226 of this title or comparable provisions of any prior Act may obtain judicial review of such order by habeas corpus proceedings and not otherwise; (c) An order of deportation or of exclusion shall not be reviewed by any court if the alien has not exhausted the administrative remedies available to him as of right under the immigration laws and regulations or if he has departed from the United States after the issuance of the order. Every petition for review or for habeas corpus shall state whether the validity of the order has been upheld in any prior judicial proceeding, and, if so, the nature and date thereof, and the court in which such proceeding took place. No petition for review or for habeas corpus shall be entertained if the validity of the order has been previously determined in any civil or criminal proceeding, unless the petition presents grounds which the court finds could not have been presented in such prior proceeding, or the court finds that the remedy provided by such prior proceeding was inadequate or ineffective to test the validity of the order.

Cheng Fan Kwok v. I.N.S.
392 U.S. 206 (1968)

Justice HARLAN delivered the opinion of the Court.

It is useful first to summarize the relevant provisions of the Immigration and Nationality Act and of the regulations promulgated under the Act's authority. Section 242(b) provides a detailed administrative procedure for determining whether an alien may be deported. It permits the entry of an order of deportation only upon the basis of a record made in a proceeding before a special inquiry officer, at which the alien is assured rights to counsel, to a reasonable opportunity to examine the evidence against him, to cross-examine witnesses, and to present evidence in his own behalf. By regulation, various forms of discretionary relief may also be sought from the special inquiry officer in the course of the deportation proceeding; an alien may, for example, request that his deportation be temporarily withheld, on the ground that he might, in the country to which he is to be deported, "be subject to persecution. . . ." See 8 U.S.C. § 1253(h) (1964 ed., Supp. II); 8 CFR § 242.8(a).

Other forms of discretionary relief may be requested after termination of the deportation proceeding. The regulations thus provide that an alien "under a final administrative order of deportation" may apply to the district director "having jurisdiction over the place where the alien is at the time of filing" for a stay of deportation. 8 CFR § 243.4. The stay may be granted by the district director "in his discretion." *Ibid*. If the stay is denied, the denial "is not appealable" to the Board of Immigration Appeals. *Ibid*.

Section 106(a) provides that the procedures for judicial review prescribed by the Hobbs Act, 64 Stat. 1129, 68 Stat. 961, "shall apply to, and shall be the sole and exclusive procedure for, the judicial review of all final orders of deportation heretofore or hereafter made against aliens . . . pursuant to administrative proceedings under section 242(b) of this Act. . . . " These procedures vest in the courts of appeals exclusive jurisdiction to review final orders issued by specified federal agencies. In situations to which the provisions of § 106(a) are inapplicable, the alien's remedies would, of course, ordinarily lie first in an action brought in an appropriate district court.

The positions of the various parties may be summarized as follows. We are urged by both petitioner and the Immigration Service to hold that the provisions of § 106(a) are applicable to the circumstances presented by this case, and that judicial review thus is available only in the courts of appeals. The Immigration Service contends that § 106(a) should be understood to embrace all determinations "directly affecting the execution of the basic deportation order," whether those determinations have been reached prior to, during, or subsequent to the deportation proceeding. In contrast, *amicus* urges, as the Court of Appeals held, that § 106(a) encompasses only those orders made in the course of a proceeding conducted under § 242(b) or issued upon motions to reopen such proceedings.

*   *   *

This is the third case in which we have had occasion to examine the effect of § 106(a). In the first, [*Foti v. INS*, 375 U.S. 217 (1963)] the petitioner, in the course of a proceeding conducted under § 242(b), conceded his deportability but requested a suspension of deportation under § 244(a)(5). The special inquiry officer denied such a suspension, and petitioner's appeal from the denial was dismissed by the Board of Immigration Appeals. Petitioner commenced an action in the district court, but the action was dismissed on the ground that, under § 106(a), his exclusive remedy lay in the courts of appeals. He then petitioned for review to the Court of Appeals for the Second Circuit, but it dismissed for want of jurisdiction. A divided court held *en banc* that the procedures of § 106(a) were inapplicable to denials of discretionary relief under § 244(a)(5). 308 F.2d 779. On certiorari, we reversed, holding that "all determinations made during and incident to the administrative proceeding conducted by a special inquiry officer, and reviewable together by the Board of Immigration Appeals . . . are . . . included within the ambit of the exclusive jurisdiction of the Court of Appeals under § 106(a)." 375 U.S., at 229.

In the second case, *Giova v. Rosenberg*, 379 U.S. 18, petitioner moved before the Board of Immigration Appeals to reopen proceedings, previously conducted under § 242(b), that had terminated in an order for his deportation. The Board denied relief. The Court of Appeals for the Ninth Circuit concluded that the Board's denial was not embraced by § 106(a), and dismissed the petition for want of jurisdiction. 308 F.2d 347. On certiorari, this Court held, in a brief per curiam opinion, that such orders were within the exclusive jurisdiction of the courts of appeals.

Although *Foti* strongly suggests the result that we reach today, neither it nor *Giova* can properly be regarded as controlling in this situation. Unlike the order in *Foti*, the order in this case was not entered in the course of a proceeding conducted by a special inquiry officer under § 242(b); unlike the order in *Giova* the order here did not deny a motion to reopen such a proceeding. We regard the issue of statutory construction involved here as markedly closer than the questions presented in those cases; at the least, it is plainly an issue upon which differing views may readily be entertained. In these circumstances, it is imperative, if we are accurately to implement

Congress' purposes, to "seiz(e) everything from which aid can be derived." *Fisher v. Blight*, 2 Cranch 358, 386.

* * *

We cannot, upon close reading, easily reconcile the position urged by the Immigration Service with the terms of § 106(a). A denial by a district director of a stay of deportation is not literally a "final order of deportation," nor is it, as was the order in *Foti*, entered in the course of administrative proceedings conducted under § 242(b). Thus, the order in this case was issued more than three months after the entry of the final order of deportation, in proceedings entirely distinct from those conducted under § 242(b), by an officer other than the special inquiry officer who, as required by § 242(b), presided over the deportation proceeding. The order here did not involve the denial of a motion to reopen proceedings conducted under § 242(b), or to reconsider any final order of deportation.

* * *

The legislative history of § 106(a) does not strengthen the position of the Immigration Service. The "basic purpose" of the procedural portions of the 1961 legislation was, as we stated in *Foti*, evidently "to expedite the deportation of undesirable aliens by preventing successive dilatory appeals to various federal courts...." 375 U.S., at 226. Congress prescribed for this purpose several procedural innovations, among them the device of direct petitions for review to the courts of appeals. Although, as the Immigration Service has emphasized, the broad purposes of the legislation might have been expected to encompass orders denying discretionary relief entered outside § 242(b) proceedings, there is evidence that Congress deliberately restricted the application of § 106(a) to orders made in the course of proceedings conducted under § 242(b).

Thus, during a colloquy on the floor of the House of Representatives, to which we referred in *Foti*, Representative Moore, co-sponsor of the bill then under discussion, suggested that any difficulties resulting from the separate consideration of deportability and of discretionary relief could be overcome by "a change in the present administrative practice of considering the issues ... piecemeal. There is no reason why the Immigration Service could not change its regulations to permit contemporaneous court consideration of deportability and administrative application for relief." 105 Cong. Rec. 12728. In the same colloquy, Representative Walter, the chairman of the subcommittee that conducted the pertinent hearings, recognized that certain forms of discretionary relief may be requested in the course of a deportation proceeding, and stated that § 106(a) would apply to the disposition of such requests, "just as it would apply to any other issue *brought up in deportation proceedings*." 105 Cong. Rec. 12728 (emphasis added). Similarly, Representative Walter, in a subsequent debate, responded to a charge that judicial review under § 106(a) would prove inadequate because of the absence of a suitable record, by inviting "the gentleman's attention to the law in section 242, in which the procedure for the examiner is set forth in detail." 107 Cong. Rec. 12179.

We believe that, in combination with the terms of § 106(a) itself, these statements lead to the inference that Congress quite deliberately restricted the application of § 106(a) to orders entered during proceedings conducted under § 242(b), or directly challenging deportation orders themselves. This is concededly "a choice between uncertainties," but we are "content to choose the lesser." *Burnet v. Guggenheim*, 288 U.S. 280, 288.

We need not speculate as to Congress' purposes. Quite possibly, as Judge Browning has persuasively suggested, "Congress visualized a single administrative proceeding in which all questions relating to an alien's deportation would be raised and resolved, followed by a single petition in a court of appeals for judicial review. . . . " *Yamada v. Immigration & Naturalization Service*, 384 F.2d 214, 218. It may therefore be that Congress expected the Immigration Service to include within the § 242(b) proceeding "all issues which might affect deportation." *Ibid*. Possibly, as amicus cogently urges, Congress wished to limit petitions to the courts of appeals to situations in which quasi-judicial hearings had been conducted. It is enough to emphasize that neither of these purposes would be in any fashion impeded by the result we reach today. We hold that the judicial review provisions of § 106(a) embrace only those determinations made during a proceeding conducted under § 242(b), including those determinations made incident to a motion to reopen such proceedings.

*   *   *

The *per curiam* opinion in *Giova* did not take a wider view of § 106(a). The denial of an application to reopen a deportation proceeding is readily distinguishable from a denial of a stay of deportation, in which there is no attack upon the deportation order or upon the proceeding in which it was entered. Petitions to reopen, like motions for rehearing or reconsideration, are, as the Immigration Service urged in *Foti*, "intimately and immediately associated" with the final orders they seek to challenge. Thus, petitions to reopen deportation proceedings are governed by the regulations applicable to the deportation proceeding itself, and, indeed, are ordinarily presented for disposition to the special inquiry officer who entered the deportation order. The result in *Giova* was thus a logical concomitant of the construction of § 106(a) reached in *Foti*; it did not, explicitly or by implication, broaden that construction in any fashion that encompasses this situation.

The result we reach today will doubtless mean that, on occasion, the review of denials of discretionary relief will be conducted separately from the review of an order of deportation involving the same alien. Nonetheless, this does not seem an onerous burden, nor is it one that cannot be avoided, at least in large part, by appropriate action of the Immigration Service itself. More important, although "there is no table of logarithms for statutory construction," it is the result that we believe most consistent both with Congress' intentions and with the terms by which it has chosen to express those intentions.

Affirmed.

Justice White, dissenting.

If the special inquiry officer had possessed jurisdiction to issue a stay order pending petitioner's efforts to obtain discretionary relief from the District Director, I take it that his denial of the stay, like a refusal to re-open, would have been appealable to the Court of Appeals. But, as I understand it, no stay could have been granted by the hearing officer and it was sought from the District Director as an immediate consequence of there being outstanding a final order of deportation, which, if executed, might moot the underlying request for relief from the District Director. Section 106 does not limit judicial review in the Court of Appeals to orders entered "in the course of" § 242(b) proceedings, but extends it to all orders against aliens entered "pursuant" to such proceedings, that is, at least as Webster would have it, "acting or done in consequence" of the § 242(b) proceedings. Except for the order of deportation, there would have been no occasion of need to seek a stay. It hardly strains congressional intention to give the word "pursuant" its ordinary meaning in the English language. If there are reasons based on policy for the Court's contrary conclusion, they are not stated. I would reverse the judgment.

"A Rule of Thumb" Guide to Understanding the Scope of the Meaning of Final Orders

1. There is no simple guide to understanding the jurisdictional provisions discussed in *Cheng Fan Kwok*. However, one way to approach such questions is by first answering the question of whether the denied benefit was one which an immigration judge *could* have granted in the course of a deportation or exclusion hearing.[37] If the answer is in the affirmative then review should be sought by way of a "petition for review" only after the BIA has made a final determination.[38] If the challenge is to an irregularity in the conduct of the hearing, something clearly within the power of the immigration judge, injunctive relief may be sought only under rare circumstances.[39] Generally, decisions which are within the *exclusive* province of the district directors, Administrative Appeals Unit (AAU) or other agencies involved in deciding immigration cases may be reviewed by resorting to declaratory relief.[40] Utilizing the "rule of thumb" consider the following fact situation:

> A Nonimmigrant exchange visitor is seeking lawful permanent resident status in the U.S. In order to be eligible to apply for permanent residence exchange visitors are generally required to return and live in their native country for two years. This two year foreign residency requirement may be waived by the Attorney General in cases where the applicant can establish that exceptional hardship

---

37. The use of this "rule of thumb" is helpful for most cases, however there are situations where there may be an overlap in jurisdiction. For example, in asylum and adjustment cases the applicant may pursue the benefit initially before the district director and later with the immigration judge in deportation proceedings. However, the circuits are not in agreement on this issue. *See Galvez v. Howerton*, 503 F. Supp. 35 (D. Ca. 1980) (court found jurisdiction to review a denial of adjustment of status under 8 U.S.C. § 1254); *Chen Chaun-Fa v. Kiley*, 459 F. Supp. 762 (D. N.Y. 1978) (court found no jurisdiction to review a denial of asylum). However, it should be noted that when courts have dealt with this issue they have been more inclined to dismiss such cases on grounds that relief might be had in deportation proceedings. *See Kashani v. Nelson*, 793 F.2d 818 (7th Cir. 1986).

38. *See* 8 U.S.C. § 1105a.

39. Counsel will be required to show that all possibility of obtaining a fair hearing would be lost if the case is allowed to proceed as required by the immigration judge.

40. This was the approach that the court took in *Gurbisz v. INS*, 675 F. Supp. 436 (N.D. Ill. 1987) where the district court noted that

> [If] the issue is one over which the immigration judge lacks original jurisdiction, i.e., those decisions left solely to the district director, then § 279 gives the district court subject-matter jurisdiction over the issue.

675 F. Supp. at 439.

would be experienced by the exchange visitor's U.S. citizen spouse or children and receives a favorable recommendation from the Director of the U.S. Information Agency (USIA). In the event that the INS recommends in favor of the waiver and the Director of the USIA refuses, what is the proper forum for judicial review?

An action for declaratory relief may be brought in district court under the Administrative Procedure Act, 5 U.S.C. § 706(2)(A). However, the courts have refused to review the decision of the USIA because pursuant to 5 U.S.C. § 701(a) the decision is one committed to agency discretion by law and there is no meaningful standard of review to apply. *See Singh v. Moyer*, 867 F.2d 1035 (7th Cir. 1989); *Slyper v. Attorney General*, 827 F.2d 821 (D.C. Cir. 1987), *cert. denied sub nom. Slyper v. Meese*, ___U.S. ___, 108 S.Ct. 1121 (1988); *but see Chong v. Director, USIA*, 821 F.2d 171, 175 (3d Cir. 1987). The refusal by the USIA to favorably recommend a waiver presents an anomaly precluding review. Can you construct a constitutional challenge to the USIA decision or to the statute which does not provide for review?

2. **Standard of Review.** Part of understanding the standard of judicial review requires an understanding of the governmental power being exercised. In *Kleindienst v. Mandel*, 408 U.S. 753 (1972) the Court in reviewing a denial by the INS of a discretionary waiver of a particular ground of exclusion noted that the Attorney General, when acting pursuant to discretion committed to him by Congress, exercises some part of Congress' plenary power to make policies and rules in connection with the exclusion of aliens. The Court concluded that the exercise of this power should not be overturned if it rests on a "facially legitimate and bona fide reason." 408 U.S. at 408.

3. A survey of the cases reveals two standards for reviewing parole decisions. Some circuits review such decisions for an "abuse of discretion." *Moret v. Karn*, 746 F.2d 989 (3d Cir. 1984); *Ahrens v. Rojas*, 292 F.2d 406 (5th Cir. 1961). Other circuits apply a standard which accords greater deference amounting to a "facially legitimate and bona fide reason" for the decision, *Amanullah v. Nelson*, 811 F.2d 1, 10 (1st Cir. 1987); *Bertrand v. Sava*, 684 F.2d 204 (2d Cir. 1982). Is there a meaningful difference between these two standards?

4. **Frivolous behavior.** Congress, concerned about repeated attempts by lawyers pursuing legal remedies which act to prevent or delay their client's deportation, requires the Attorney General to take steps to curb what it refers to as "frivolous behavior." The statute calls for the Attorney General to establish what is "frivolous" and then to specify the manner in which a case should be handled (such as summary dismissal) or to discipline the lawyer.[41]

---

41. *See* 8 U.S.C. § 1252b(d), Sec. 242B(d). It is not clear whether the Attorney General will attempt to impose the full panoply of sanctions found in Rule 11 of the Federal Rules of Civil Procedure.

D. Practice Before the Board

Motions Practice Before the Board of Immigration Appeals
Hurwitz, 20 San Diego L. Rev. 79 (1982)*

* * *

The motion to reopen is, at base, a request to alter an earlier decision. It must present evidence which is "new" and was not available at the prior hearing. What constitutes "new evidence" is an often-litigated issue which is open to interpretation and depends upon the facts of each case.

The regulatory authority for motions to reopen is contained in sections 3.2 and 3.8 of title 8 of the Code of Federal Regulations. These sections provide the framework within which motions are adjudicated. A thorough understanding of these regulations is essential to a successful motion. Many motions to reopen that, if fully developed, might have been granted by the Board, have been denied merely because an essential element contained in the pertinent regulations was overlooked.

Filing

Generally, motions to reopen are directed to the administrative authority that last made a decision in the case. If the Board made the last decision, the motion should be directed there. All motions to reopen, however, are filed with the INS district office having control over the case.

Filing the motion to reopen with the proper INS district office cannot be over-emphasized. Too often, motions with applications and fees are received directly at the Board. These misfiled motions are returned to the local INS district office which controls the case, seriously delaying processing of the motion. Further, when filing a motion to reopen directed at the Board at an INS district office, it is useful to note prominently on the face of the motion that it is directly to the Board of Immigration Appeals. This can save considerable processing time.

Standing for filing motions to reopen must be considered in light of the underlying proceeding. Obviously, the Immigration and Naturalization Service, as a party in interest, has standing in most circumstances to file a motion to reopen. Aside from the government, it is apparent that in deportation proceedings, only the respondent may move to reopen, while in exclusion proceedings, the applicant may move to reopen. In visa petition proceedings, however, only the petitioner, and not the beneficiary, may move to reopen. Although this appears to be elementary, standing should be kept in mind, particularly in the visa petition context, where beneficiaries will often attempt to move to reopen a case.

The motion to reopen should be filed in triplicate. This facilitates review and allows all interested parties access to the motion.

Form and Content

The form of the motion to reopen varies with the type of motion filed. However, certain basic principles apply to almost all motions to reopen. Generally, a formal

---

* Copyright 1982 San Diego Law Review Association. Reprinted with the permission of the San Diego Law Review. Footnotes have been omitted.

written motion should be drafted and filed, and should include the following items: cover sheet, purpose of the motion, legal authority for the motion itself, any concurrent court litigation, supporting documentation, a brief, and a request for oral argument, if necessary. The motion should always contain a statement of the new facts to be proven if the case is reopened.

It is essential that the motion clearly state its goals and contents. Toward this end, the motion should contain a cover sheet, plainly outlining the thrust of the motion and summarizing the evidence that supports it. This cover sheet will serve to highlight the key elements of the motion, eliminating any possibility that some important item will be overlooked. In addition, the cover sheet adds a sense of organization to the motion, thus enhancing its chances for success.

The purpose of the motion should be clearly and succinctly stated. Motions are sometimes self-explanatory. Filing form I-485, for example, obviously means that the respondent is moving to reopen for adjustment of status to permanent resident. A respondent filing form I-256(a) is applying for suspension of deportation. There are other motions not designated by specific forms, such as motions for the granting of voluntary departure anew, motions for change of designation of country of deportation, and motions to reopen to consider recently acquired exculpatory evidence. The purpose of these motions is not patently obvious; consequently, it is critical to clearly state the purpose so as not to create confusion and delay at the Board.

*   *   *

A brief in support of the motion to reopen is sometimes essential. A routine motion may cite any necessary legal authority in the motion itself. As a general rule, briefs should accompany the motion where government opposition is expected or where a complex legal issue is perceived. The brief should be written as concisely as possible, in order to facilitate the Board's review.

The majority of motions are decided on the basis of the moving papers. However, motions regulations make oral argument discretionary with the Board. Oral argument must be specifically requested, and in practice, is not often heard on motions to reopen. Oral argument should be reserved for complex or novel cases only.

Prima Facie Case

The motion to reopen must present evidence which comprises a prima facie case for reopening as a matter of law. This issue has been extensively litigated over the years. The litigation usually revolves around the amount and quality of the evidence required to support each element of the motion. Perhaps the most effective way to review the necessary prima facie requirements is to examine several leading cases discussing the most common types of motions to reopen.

In Matter of Lam, respondent moved to reopen for suspension of deportation. A prima facie showing of the three statutory elements of suspension of deportation was required: seven years of continuous physical presence, good moral character and extreme hardship. In support of his claim of extreme hardship, the respondent submitted a conclusory affidavit that he would not be able to support himself in Hong Kong, he would be unable to obtain a job, he might starve to death, he feared the Communists in Hong Kong and he would become physically and emotionally ill if he had to leave the United States. His affidavit was found to be inadequate to support a prima facie case of extreme hardship, the claim was unsubstantiated by supporting evidence and the thrust of the claim appeared to be economic. The Board denied the motion, because the respondent failed to make out a prima facie case for suspension of deportation.

* * *

The recent *Matter of Martinez-Romero* illustrates the problem of what constitutes a prima facie case for reopening in asylum proceedings. Respondent, a native of El Salvador, received voluntary departure in a deportation proceeding. Subsequently, she filed a motion to reopen for political asylum under section 208 of the Immigration and Nationality Act. The motion was denied by the immigration judge and an appeal was taken to the Board of Immigration Appeals. The thrust of the motion was that she, as a student in United States schools, would be a prime target for political persecution in El Salvador. She openly criticized the oppression and killing caused by the El Salvador military. The Board dismissed the appeal, finding the general statements contained in the motion papers insufficient to establish a prima facie case for reopening. It noted that the respondent had not shown evidence that she would be singled out for persecution as the statute requires, and it stressed she had not given a satisfactory explanation as to why she did not apply for asylum at the original hearing.

Motions to Reconsider

Like motions to reopen, the procedure for motions to reconsider to the Board of Immigration Appeals is governed by sections 3.2 and 3.8 of title 8 of the Code of Federal Regulations. Attorneys sometimes confuse the two motions, referring to a motion to reopen as a motion to reconsider. However, they are separate types of motions, with key differences in purpose and form. To correctly prepare a motion to reconsider, these differences should be thoroughly understood.

The motion to reconsider is a request that the Board reexamine its decision in light of additional legal arguments, a change of law, or perhaps an argument or aspect of the case which was overlooked, while the motion to reopen is usually based upon new evidence or a change in factual circumstances. A motion to reconsider is generally made soon after the Board has rendered its decision but before further appeal to the courts. It requests a second look at a case.

Filing procedures are similar to those in a motion to reopen. The motion to reconsider is filed in triplicate in the INS district office having control over the case. It is not to be filed directly with the Board as that will result in delay.

Although similar in form to the motion to reopen, the motion to reconsider is based on legal argument and requires a full brief. The brief should fully discuss pertinent precedent and concisely set out the arguments to be considered by the Board. A deportation proceeding additionally requires discussion of any collateral civil or criminal court proceedings involving the respondent.

It must be remembered that it is very difficult to prevail on a motion to reconsider. The Board has already examined the record and made its decision. Having done that, it is not likely to reverse that decision. A mere reargument and rehash of the case is probably a waste of effort. If the potential moving party is convinced of the correctness of its legal position after an adverse Board decision, the better practice would be to take an appeal to the courts.

Motions to Remand

During the pendency of the appeal, circumstances such as new evidence or a new form of relief becoming available may give rise to a request that the case be remanded for consideration in light of the changed circumstances. This request is made in the form of a motion to remand.

The motion to remand is not expressly supported by any regulation or direct authority. However, it has developed as a practical procedure at the Board.

The form and substantive requirements of the motion to remand are similar to those of the motion to reopen. The motion to remand must, at a minimum, contain new evidence and a prima facie showing of eligibility as a matter of law and as a matter of discretion.

One major difference between the motion to remand and the motion to reopen is the place of filing. If the case file is physically at the Board, the motion to remand is sent directly to the Board. If the appeal has been filed but the record file is still physically at the INS district office awaiting completion of transcription or other processing, the motion to remand should be filed with the INS district office to be included in the record file for Board consideration.

Most of the same caveats apply to motions to remand as to motions to reopen. The evidence presented must be as complete as possible to properly support the emotion. Every key element must be covered. Briefs should be included when the legal questions are complex or opposition is expected. Care should be taken at every step to clearly inform the Board of all pertinent reasons for granting the motion.

Stays of Deportation

Section 3.6 of title 8 of the Code of Federal Regulations outlines procedure for stays. Direct appeals automatically stay deportation under section 3.6(a). Section 3.6(b) states, however, that motions to reopen or reconsider do not automatically stay the order of deportation. When an order of deportation is final, therefore, and a motion to reopen or reconsider is filed for the Board's consideration, it is often necessary to obtain a stay.

The motion for a stay should set out the reasons for the stay, stressing any hardships that might result from deportation and listing any equities that exist for the respondent. The motion should also include the scheduled date for deportation, if known, to inform the Board of the time remaining in which to decide the stay. Perhaps most crucial to the success of the stay is the strength of the underlying motion. As in most stay contexts, the Board tends to grant stays when the underlying motion appears meritorious.

[The author then discusses the factors necessary for the Board's consideration of an emergency (telephonic) stay of deportation.]

1. The alien must be in imminent danger of deportation. Generally, this means that the alien is (or is about to be) in INS custody and is to be deported within hours or days.

2. The Board must have proper jurisdiction over the case. The motion papers or appeal from a denial of a motion must already be filed with the local INS district office, vesting jurisdiction in the Board. A promise to file is not sufficient.

3. There must be no reasonable chance that a written stay request accompanying the main motion would reach the Board before deportation takes place.

4. All other administrative remedies for a stay should be exhausted. A stay should be requested of the District Director first, as s/he has the discretion to grant a stay. Also, in appropriate circumstances, a stay should be requested of the immigration judge. Only after these remedies have been unsuccessfully attempted should a stay request be made to the Board.

If the telephonic stay request is appropriate, the following procedure is employed, Counsel for the alien calls the Board directly in Falls Church, Virginia. A secretary of the Board is assigned to take counsel's statement over the telephone. The statements should set out brief biographical data on the alien, the reasons for the stay request, the nature and purpose of the underlying motion, any hardships or equities, any accompanying court proceedings, the custody status of the alien and the travel plans for deportation, if known. Counsel should also indicate the location of the INS office involved, whether the case has previously been before the Board, the date of filing the motion or appeal that vests jurisdiction with the Board and the names and telephone numbers of INS officers, particularly the deportation officer, involved in the case. The statement should be as clear and concise as possible because this is the only information for the alien that the Board will have when considering the stay request.

E. Motions to Reopen or for Reconsideration

Matter of Rodriguez-Vera

17 I. & N. Dec. 105 (BIA 1979)

In a decision dated January 31, 1978, the Board affirmed the October 6, 1977, decision of an immigration judge which found the respondent deportable as charged pursuant to section 241(a)(4) of the Immigration and Nationality Act, 8 U.S.C. 1251(a)(4), and denied his applications for a waiver of inadmissibility and for adjustment of status pursuant to sections 212(h) and 245 of the Act, respectively, 8 U.S.C. 1182(h) and 1255. The respondent thereafter submitted an application for discretionary relief under section 212(c) of the Act, 8 U.S.C. 1182(c), which we shall consider a motion to reopen the deportation proceedings, as did the District Director, with jurisdiction lying with the Board. See 8 C.F.R. 3.2. The service opposes the motion. The motion will be denied.

The respondent is a 39-year-old native and citizen of Mexico who was admitted to the United States for lawful permanent residence on March 18, 1971. Deportability is predicated upon the respondent's conviction in March of 1976 in the 92nd District Court of Hildalgo County, Texas, of the felony offense of murder. The respondent was sentenced to a prison term of 15 years and 6 months pursuant to that conviction and is presently serving his sentence.

Sentence 212(c) of the Act provides in essence that aliens lawfully admitted for permanent residence, who temporarily proceed abroad voluntarily and not under an order of deportation and who are returning to a lawful unrelinquished domicile of 7 consecutive years, may be admitted in the discretion of the Attorney General without regard to certain enumerated grounds for exclusion. The specified grounds include section 212(a)(9) of the Act, 8 U.S.C. 1182(a)(9), which renders excludable aliens convicted of a crime involving moral turpitude. Murder is such an offense. See *DeLucia v. Flagg*, 297 F.2d 58 (7th Cir. 1961), cert. denied, 369 U.S. 837 (1962). Pursuant to our decision in Matter of Silva, Interim Decision 2532 (BIA 1976), section 212(c) relief may be available to an alien in deportation proceedings notwithstanding the fact that he has not proceeded abroad subsequent to his admission for lawful permanent residence. *Francis v. INS*, 532 F.2d 268 (2d Cir. 1976).

The Service opposes the motion to reopen on the ground that the requested relief would surely be denied in the exercise of discretion and, therefore, no useful purpose would be served by granting the motion. We agree with the position of the Service.

Relief under section 212(c) is not available to all who are able to demonstrate statutory eligibility but, instead, requires the Attorney General or his delegate to determine as a matter of discretion whether an applicant merits the relief sought. The grant or denial of a motion to reopen is itself discretionary determination with the outcome dependent in part upon the likelihood that the applicant will be granted the relief sought if reopening is permitted. The proposition that reopening may be had, as of right, upon a bare showing of statutory eligibility has been rejected by the courts. See *Hibbert v. INS*, 554 F.2d 17 (2d Cir. 1977). The immigration judge and the Board are entitled, at a minimum, to factual allegations which indicate that the adverse factors of record may be overcome by the equities presented. In sum, it is incumbent upon the alien to make a prima facie showing both that the statutory requirements for the relief sought have been satisfied and that a grant of relief may be warranted as a matter of discretion.

In *Matter of Marin*, 16 I & N Dec. 581 (BIA 1978), we examined the principles to be applied in exercising discretion on section 212(c) applications and held that the immigration judge, in adjudicating such applications, "must balance the adverse factors evidencing an alien's undesirability as a permanent resident with the social and humane considerations presented in his behalf to determine whether the granting of section 212(c) relief appears in the best interests of this country." We noted that "[a]s the negative factors grow more serious, it becomes incumbent on the applicant to introduce additional offsetting favorable evidence, which in some cases may have to involve unusual or outstanding equities. Such a showing at time[s] may be required solely by virtue of the circumstances and nature of the exclusion ground sought [to be] waived." We further held that an applicant who has a criminal record will ordinarily be required to make a showing of rehabilitation before relief will be granted in the exercise of discretion.

*   *   *

Inasmuch as the evidence of record fails to demonstrate a reasonable likelihood that the relief sought would be granted at a reopened hearing, the respondent has not sustained his burden of establishing a prima facie case for reopening. The motion will accordingly be denied.

Notes

1. In *INS v. Abudu*, 485 U.S. 94 (1988) the court upheld the BIA's denial of a motion to reopen where the applicant had not applied for asylum at her deportation hearing and did not do so until three years later. The court noted that there were four bases for denying a motion to reopen: (1) the applicant failed to establish a

prima facie case for the underlying substantive relief sought; (2) the applicant did not show that the evidence which was not introduced earlier was previously unavailable; (3) the applicant failed to explain her failure to apply initially (where the reason for reopening is a benefit not previously requested); and (4) if the applicant is not deserving of a favorable exercise of discretion (where the benefit sought is discretionary). The appellate court, in determining whether a *prima facie* case had been presented, would have required the BIA to first treat the facts presented in the new application as true and then decide whether the case should be reopened. *See Abudu v. INS*, 802 F. 2d 1096, 1102 (9th Cir. 1986).

2. While the fourth basis presented in *Abudu* may not seem expansive, in actuality it covers almost every request to reopen because most immigration benefits are discretionary. Although, judicial deference to an agency's exercise of discretion is a well-settled principle of administrative law, can an argument be made in favor of less deference for the asylum applicant?

3. *Abudu* is seen by many as the death knell to a successful challenge from the denial of a motion to reopen. While abuse of discretion may be difficult to establish, it is essential that the application be presented with particularity on both the issue

Appeal Procedure Flow Chart

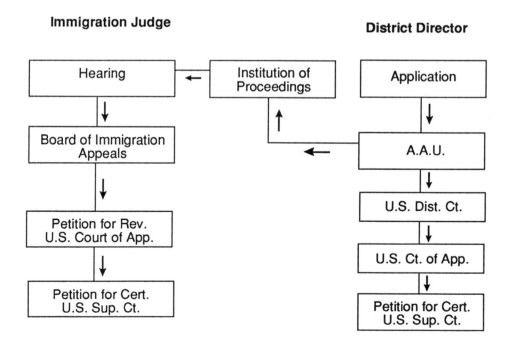

Flow Chart
Declaratory Review in Immigration Cases

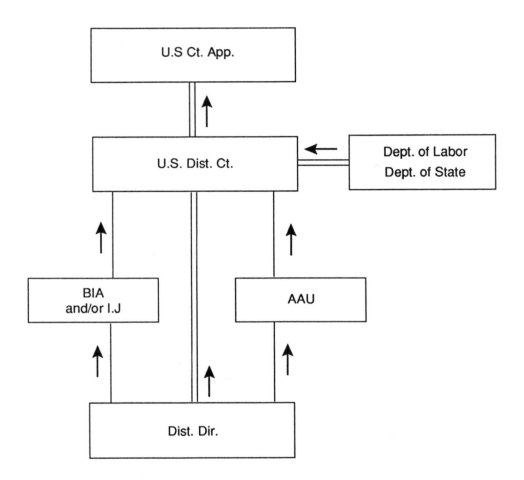

Flow Chart
Judicial Review of Final Orders
in Deportation and Exclusion Orders

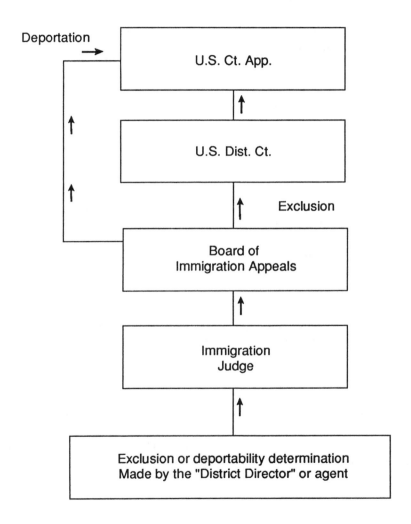

of eligibility, favorable exercise of discretion and an explanation for the failure to submit the application at the first hearing. For a review of other reopening cases with similar results, *see INS v. Wang*, 450 U.S. 139 (1981) (suspension of deportation); *INS v. Rios-Pineda*, 471 U.S. 444 (1985); *INS v. Bagamasbad*, 429 U.S. 24 (1976) (adjustment of status).

Some Final Points on Final Orders

1. The failure of a person to exhaust her available administrative remedies (such as filing a timely appeal to the BIA) will prohibit review by the court of appeals. However, a request to reopen proceedings before the BIA when the applicant has previously failed to file a timely appeal following the conclusion of her hearing can bring the new determination within the definition of "final order of deportation." *Rose v. Woolwine*, 344 F.2d 993 (1965).

2. Some examples of "final orders" are denial of discretionary relief, denial of motions to reopen, denial of suspension of deportation, and denial of withholding of deportation. What factors should be considered in determining whether an action is a final order?

3. Would a district director's denial of an application for extension of voluntary departure subsequent to deportation proceedings be reviewable as a final order? How might an alien attempt to have a decision reviewed if it is not treated as a "final order"?

4. Service of a petition for review acts as an automatic stay of the alien's deportation. *See* 8 U.S.C. § 1105a(3). First Circuit Rule 19 provides that

> The Clerk of this court shall file no petition for review under 8 U.S.C. § 1105a that has not been signed by a member of the Bar ... nor make service of the petition upon the Attorney General of the United States and upon the official of the Immigration and Naturalization Service until the said petition has been examined by the court, *and there will be no stay of deportation under* 8 U.S.C. § 1105a(3) until the court so directs

(emphasis supplied). Is the First Circuit's rule proper in light of the requirement that the filing of a petition for review acts as an automatic stay of deportation?

5. Generally when the government believes that the petition for review is frivolous, it may move for summary dismissal of the petition. This type of procedure is being used with increasing frequency and has been very successful.

Index to Appendix

Other Forms of Review

5 U.S.C. § 702 Right of review

A person suffering legal wrong because of agency action, or adversely affected or aggrieved by agency action within the meaning of a relevant statute, is entitled to judicial review thereof. An action in a court of the United States seeking relief other than money damages and stating a claim that an agency or an officer or employee thereof acted or failed to act in an official capacity or under color of legal authority shall not be dismissed nor relief therein be denied on the ground that it is against the United States or th   United States is an indispensable party. The United States may be named as a defendant in any such action, and a judgment or decree may be entered against the United States: Provided, That any mandatory or injunctive decree shall specify the Federal officer or officers (by name or by title), and their successors in office, personally responsible for compliance. Nothing herein (1) affects other limitations on judicial review or the power or duty of the court to dismiss any action or deny relief on any other appropriate legal or equitable ground; or (2) confers authority to grant relief if any other statute that grants consent to suit expressly or impliedly forbids the relief which is sought.

5 U.S.C. § 703 Form and venue of proceeding

The form of proceeding for judicial review is the special statutory review proceeding relevant to the subject matter in a court specified by statute or, in the absence or inadequacy thereof, any applicable form of legal action, including actions for declaratory judgments or writs of prohibitory or mandatory injunction or habeas corpus, in a court of competent jurisdiction. If no special statutory review proceeding is applicable, the action for judicial review may be brought against the United States, the agency by its official title, or the appropriate officer. Except to the extent that prior, adequate, and exclusive opportunity for judicial review is provided by law, agency action is subject to judicial review in civil or criminal proceedings for judicial enforcement.

5 U.S.C. § 706 Scope of review

To the extent necessary to decision and when presented, the reviewing court shall decide all relevant questions of law, interpret constitutional and statutory provisions, and determine the meaning or applicability of the terms of an agency action. The reviewing court shall

(1) compel agency action unlawfully withheld or unreasonably delayed; and

(2) hold unlawful and set aside agency action, findings, and conclusions found to be

(A) arbitrary, capricious, an abuse of discretion, or otherwise not in accordance with law;

(B) contrary to constitutional right, power, privilege, or immunity;

(C) in excess of statutory jurisdiction, authority, or limitations, or short of statutory right;

(D) without observance of procedure required by law;

(E) unsupported by substantial evidence in a case subject to sections 556 and 557 of this title or otherwise reviewed on the record of an agency hearing provided by statute; or

(F) unwarranted by the facts to the extent that the facts are subject to trial de novo by the reviewing court.

In making the foregoing determinations, the court shall review the whole record or those parts of it cited by a party, and due account shall be taken of the rule of prejudicial error.

Fed. R. Civ. P. 57 Declaratory judgments

The procedure for obtaining a declaratory judgment pursuant to Title 28, U.S.C. § 2201, shall be in accordance with these rules, and the right to trial by jury may be demanded under the circumstances and in the manner provided in Rules 38 and 39. The existence of another adequate remedy does not preclude a judgment for declaratory relief in cases where it is appropriate. The court may order a speedy hearing of an action for a declaratory judgment and may advance it on the calendar.

[NOTE: For review of certain decisions relating to questions of nationality, *see* Chapter 13.]

Regulations Governing Certain Administrative Appeals

8 C.F.R. § 3.1 General authorities. [Board of Immigration Appeals]

(a)(1) Organization. There shall be in the Department of Justice a Board of Immigration Appeals, subject to the general supervision of the Director, Executive Office for Immigration Review. The Board shall exercise so much of the immigration and nationality laws as he may delegate to it. The Board shall consist of a Chairman and four other members. A vacancy, or the absence or unavailability of a Board Member, shall not impair the right of the remaining members to exercise all the powers of the Board, and three members of the Board shall constitute a quorum of the Board. The Director may in his discretion designate immigration judges to act as temporary, additional Board members for whatever time the Director deems necessary. In the event that immigration judges are so designated, two panels of three members each may be designated by the Chairman. Each panel shall be empowered to review cases by majority vote. Each panel may exercise the appropriate authority of the Board as set out in Part 3 which is necessary to review cases before it. The permanent Board may, by majority vote on its own motion, reconsider en banc any case decided by a panel. The total number of Board members and temporary, additional Board members may not exceed seven individuals at any time. There shall also be attached to the Board such number of attorneys and other employees as the Deputy Attorney General, upon recommendation of the Director, shall from time to time direct.

(2) Chairman. The Chairman shall direct, supervise, and establish internal operating procedures and policies of the Board. He shall designate a member of the Board to act as Chairman in his absence or unavailability. The Chairman shall be assisted in the performance of his duties by a Chief Attorney Examiner, who shall be directly responsible to the Chairman. The Chief Attorney Examiner shall serve as an Alternate Board Member when, in the absence or unavailability of a Board Member or Members, his participation is deemed necessary by the Chairman. Once designated, his participation in a case shall continue to its normal conclusion.

(3) Board Members. Board Members shall perform the quasi-judicial function of adjudicating cases coming before the Board.

(b) Appellate jurisdiction. Appeals shall lie to the Board of Immigration Appeals from the following:

(1) Decisions of immigration judges in exclusion cases, as provided in Part 236 of this chapter.

(2) Decisions of immigration judges in deportation cases, as provided in Part 242 of this chapter, except that no appeal shall lie from an order of a immigration judge under § 244.1 of this chapter granting voluntary departure within a period of at least 30 days, if the sole ground of appeal is that a greater period of departure time should have been fixed.

(3) Decisions of immigration judges on applications for the exercise of the discretionary authority contained in section 212(c) of the Act as provided in Part 212 of this chapter.

(4) Decisions involving administrative fines and penalties, including mitigation thereof, as provided in Part 280 of this chapter.

(5) Decisions on petitions filed in accordance with section 204 of the act (except petitions to accord preference classifications under section 203(a)(3) or section 203(a)(6) of the act, or a petition on behalf of a child described in section 101(b)(1)(F) of the act), and decisions on requests for revalidation and decisions revoking the approval of such petitions, in accordance with section 205 of the act, as provided in Parts 204 and 205, respectively, of this chapter.

(6) Decisions on applications for the exercise of the discretionary authority contained in section 212(d)(3) of the act as provided in Part 212 of this chapter.

(7) Determinations relating to bond, parole, or detention of an alien as provided in Part 242 of this chapter.

(8) Decisions of immigration judges in rescission of adjustment of status cases, as provided in Part 246 of this chapter.

(c) Jurisdiction by certification. The Commissioner, or any other duly authorized officer of the Service, any Immigration Judge, or the Board may in any case arising under paragraph (b) of this section require certification of such case to the Board.

(d) Powers of the Board—

(1) Generally. Subject to any specific limitation prescribed by this chapter, in considering and determining cases before it as provided in this part the Board shall exercise such discretion and authority conferred upon the Attorney General by law as is appropriate and necessary for the disposition of the case.

(1-a) Summary dismissal of appeals. The Board may summarily dismiss any appeal in any case in which (i) the party concerned fails to specify the reasons for his appeal on Form I-290A (Notice of Appeal); (ii) the only reason specified by the party concerned for his appeal involves a finding of fact or a conclusion of law which was conceded by him at the deportation or exclusion hearing; (iii) the appeal is from an order that granted the party concerned the relief which he requested, or (iv) the Board is satisfied, from a review of the record, that the appeal is frivolous or filed solely for the purpose of delay.

(2) Finality of decision. The decision of the Board shall be final except in those cases reviewed by the Attorney General in accordance with paragraph (h) of this section. The Board may return a case to the Service or Immigration Judge for such further action as may be appropriate, without entering a final decision on the merits of the case.

(3) Rules of practices: Discipline of attorneys and representatives. The Board shall have authority, with the approval of the Director, EOIR, to prescribe rules governing proceedings before it. It shall also determine whether any organization desiring representation is of a kind described in § 1.1(j) of this chapter, and shall regulate the conduct of attorneys, representatives of organizations, and others who appear in a representative capacity before the Board or the Service or any special Inquiry Officer.

(e) Oral Argument. When an appeal has been taken, request for oral argument if desired shall be included in the Notice of Appeal. Oral argument shall be heard at the discretion of the Board at such date and time as the Board shall fix. The Service may be represented before the Board by an officer of the Service designated by the Service.

(f) Service of Board decisions. The decision of the Board shall be in writing and copies thereof shall be transmitted by the Board to the Service and a copy shall be served upon the alien or party affected as provided in Part 292 of this chapter.

(g) Decisions of the Board as precedents. Except as they may be modified or overruled by the Board or the Attorney General, decisions of the Board shall be binding on all officers and employees of the Service or Immigration Judges in the administration of the Act, and selected decisions designated by the Board shall serve as precedents in all proceedings involving the same issue or issues.

(h) Referral of cases to the Attorney General.

(1) The Board shall refer to the Attorney General for review of its decision all cases which:

(i) The Attorney General directs the Board to refer to him.

(ii) The Chairman or a majority of the Board believes should be referred to the Attorney General for review.

(iii) The Commissioner requests be referred to the Attorney General for review.

(2) In any case in which the Attorney General reviews the decision of the Board, the decision of the Attorney General shall be stated in writing and shall be transmitted to the Board for transmittal and service as provided in paragraph (f) of this section.

8 C.F.R. § 3.2 Reopening or reconsideration.

The Board may on its own motion reopen or reconsider any case in which it has rendered a decision. Reopening or reconsideration of any case in which a decision has been made by the Board, whether requested by the Commissioner or any other duly authorized officer of the Service, or by the party affected by the decision, shall be only upon written motion to the Board. Motions to reopen in deportation proceedings shall not be granted unless it appears to the Board that evidence sought to be offered is material and was not available and could not have been discovered or presented at the former hearing; nor shall any motion to reopen for the purpose of affording the alien an opportunity to apply for any form of discretionary relief be granted if it appears that the alien's right to apply for such relief was fully explained to him and an opportunity to apply therefor was afforded him at the former hearing unless the relief is sought on the basis of circumstances which have arisen subsequent to the hearing. A motion to reopen or a motion to reconsider shall not be made by or in behalf of a person who is the subject of deportation proceedings subsequent to his departure from the United States. Any departure from the United States of a person who is the subject of deportation proceedings occurring after the making of a motion to reopen or a motion to reconsider shall constitute a withdrawal of such motion. For the purpose of this section, any final decision made by the Commissioner prior to the effective date of the Act with respect to any case within the classes of cases enumerated in § 3.1(b)(1), (2), (3), (4), or (5) shall be regarded as a decision of the Board.

8 C.F.R. § 3.3 Notice of appeal.

(a) A party affected by a decision who is entitled under this chapter to appeal to the Board shall be given notice of his or her right to appeal. An appeal shall be taken by filing Notice of Appeal Form I-290A in triplicate with the Service office or Office of the Immigration Judge having administrative jurisdiction over the case, within the time specified in the governing sections of this chapter. The certification of a case as provided in this part shall not relieve the party affected from compliance with the provisions of this section in the event that he is entitled, and desires, to appeal from an initial decision, nor shall it serve to extend the time specified in the applicable parts of this chapter for the taking of an appeal. Departure from the United

States of a person under deportation proceedings prior to the taking of an appeal from a decision in his case shall constitute a waiver of his right to appeal.

(b) Fees. Except as otherwise provided in this section, a notice of appeal or a motion filed under this part by any person other than an officer of the Service shall be accompanied by the appropriate fee specified by, and remitted in accordance with, the provisions of § 103.7 of this chapter. In any case in which an alien or other party affected is unable to pay the fee fixed for an appeal or a motion, he or she shall file with the notice of appeal or the motion, his or her affidavit, or unsworn declaration made pursuant to 28 U.S.C. 1746, stating the nature of the motion or appeal and his or her belief that he or she is entitled to redress. Such document shall also establish his or her inability to pay the required fee, and shall request permission to prosecute the appeal or motion without prepayment of such fee. When such a document is filed with the officer of the Service or the Immigration Judge from whose decision the appeal is taken or with respect to whose decision the motion is addressed, such Service officer or Immigration Judge shall, if he or she believes that the appeal or motion is not taken or made in good faith, certify in writing his reasons for such belief for consideration by the Board. The Board may, in its discretion, authorize the prosecution of any appeal or motion without prepayment of fee. When such an affidavit is filed with the officer of the Service from whose decision the appeal is taken or with respect to whose decision the motion is addressed, such officer shall, if he believes that the appeal or motion is not taken or made in good faith, certify in writing his reasons for such belief for consideration by the Board. The Board may, in its discretion, authorize the prosecution of any appeal or motion without prepayment of fee.

(c) Briefs. Briefs in support of or in opposition to an appear shall be filed in triplicate with the officer of the Service having administrative jurisdiction over the case within the time fixed for appeal or within any other additional period designated by the Immigration Judge or Service Officer who made the decision. Such Special Inquiry Officer or the Board for good cause may extend the time for filing a brief or reply brief. The Board in its discretion may authorize the filing of briefs directly with it, in which event the opposing party shall be allowed a specified time to respond.

8 C.F.R. § 3.6 Stay of execution of decision.

(a) Except as provided in § 42.2 of this chapter and paragraph (b) of this section, the decision in any proceeding under this chapter from which an appeal to the Board may be taken shall not be executed during the time allowed for the filing of an appeal unless a waiver of the right to appeal is filed, nor shall such decision be executed while an appeal is pending or while a case is before the Board by way of certification.

(b) The provisions of paragraph (a) of this section shall not apply to an order of an immigration judge under § 242.22 of this chapter denying a motion to reopen or reconsider or to stay deportation, except when a stay pending appeal has been granted by the immigration judge. The Board may, in its discretion, stay deportation while an appeal is pending from any such order if no stay has been granted by the immigration judge.

(c) Saving clause. Notwithstanding the provisions of paragraph (b) of this section, any stay of execution of decision existing under paragraph (a) of this section when paragraph (b) of this section becomes effective shall continue until the Board has disposed of the appeal.

8 C.F.R. § 3.7 Notice of certification.

Whenever in accordance with the provisions of § 3.1(c), a case is required to be certified to the Board, the alien or other party affected shall be given notice of certification. A case shall be certified only after an initial decision has been made and before an appeal has been taken. If it is known at the time the initial decision is made that the case will be certified, the notice of certification shall be included in such decision and no further notice of certification shall be required. If it is not known until after the initial decision is made that the case will be certified, the Service office or Office of the Immigration Judge having administrative control over the Record of Proceeding shall cause a Notice of Certification (Form I-290C) to be served upon the party affected. In either case, the notice shall inform the party affected that the case is required to be certified to the Board and that he or she has the right to make representation before the Board, including the making of a request for oral argument and the submission of a brief. If the party affected desires to submit a brief, it shall be submitted to the Service office or Office of the Immigration Judge having administrative control over the Record of Proceeding for transmittal to the Board within ten (10) days from the date of receipt of the notice of certification, unless for good cause shown such Service office or Office of the Immigration Judge or the Board extends the time within which the brief may be submitted. The case shall be certified and forwarded to the Board by the Service office or Office of the Immigration Judge having administrative jurisdiction over the case upon receipt of the brief, or upon the expiration of the time within which the brief may be submitted, or upon receipt of a written waiver of the right to submit a brief.

8 C.F.R. § 3.8 Motion to reopen or motion to reconsider.

(a) Form. Motions to reopen and motions to reconsider shall be submitted in triplicate. A request for oral argument, if desired, shall be incorporated in the motion. The Board in its discretion may grant or deny oral argument. Motions to reopen shall state the new facts to be proved at the reopened hearing and shall be supported by affidavits or other evidentiary material. Motions to reconsider shall state the reasons upon which the motion is based and shall be supported by such precedent decisions as are pertinent. In any case in which a deportation order is in effect, there shall be included in the motion to reopen or reconsider such order a statement by or on behalf of the moving party declaring whether the subject of the deportation order is also the subject of any pending criminal proceeding under section 242(e) of the Act, and, if so, the current status of that proceeding. . . .

* * *

§ 242.21 Appeals. [From Immigration Judge's Decision in deportation proceeding]

(a) Pursuant to Part 3 of this chapter an appeal shall lie from a decision of a special inquiry officer under this part to the Board of Immigration Appeals. An appeal shall be taken within 10 days after the mailing of a written decision, or the stating of an oral decision, or the service of a summary decision on Form I-38 or Form I-39. The reasons for the appeal shall be stated briefly in the Notice of Appeal, Form I-290A; failure to do so may constitute a ground for dismissal of the appeal by the Board. When service of the decision is made by mail, as authorized by this section, 3 days shall be added to the period prescribed for the taking of an appeal.

(b) Prohibited appeals; legalization or applications. An alien respondent defined in § 245a.2(c) (5), (6), or (7) of this chapter who fails to file an application for adjustment of status to that of a temporary resident within the prescribed period(s), and who is thereafter found to be deportable by decision of an immigration judge, shall not be permitted to appeal the finding of deportability based solely on refusal by the immigration judge to entertain such an application in deportation proceedings.

§ 242.22 Reopening or reconsideration. [From Immigration Judge's Decision in deportation proceeding]

Except as otherwise provided in this section, a motion to reopen or reconsider shall be subject to the requirements of § 103.5 of this chapter. The immigration judge may upon his/her own motion, or upon motion of the trial attorney or the respondent, reopen or reconsider any case in which he/she had made a decision, unless jurisdiction in the case is vested in the Board of Immigration Appeals under Part 3 of this chapter. An order by the immigration judge granting a motion to reopen may be made on Form I-328. A motion to reopen will not be granted unless the immigration judge is satisfied that evidence sought to be offered is material and was not available and could not have been discovered or presented at the hearing; nor will any motion to reopen for the purpose of providing the respondent with an opportunity to make an application under § 242.17 be granted if respondent's rights to make such application were fully explained to him/her by the immigration judge and he/she was afforded an opportunity to do so at the hearing, unless circumstances have arisen thereafter on the basis of which the request is being made. The filing of a motion under this section with an immigration judge shall not serve to stay the execution of an outstanding decision; execution shall proceed unless the immigration judge who has jurisdiction over the motion specifically grants a stay of deportation. The immigration judge may stay deportation pending his/her determination of the motion and also pending the taking and disposition of an appeal from such determination.

* * *

8 C.F.R. § 103.1 (f)(2)
[Jurisdiction of the Administrative Appeals Unit.]

(i) Breaching of bonds under Section 103.6(e) of this part;

(ii) [Employment-based] preference petitions under Section 204.1(c) of this title except when the denial of the petition is based upon lack of a certification by the Secretary of Labor under section 212(a)(14) of the Act;

(iii) Indochinese refugee applications for adjustment of status under Section 245.2(a)(4) and (e) of this title;

(iv) Revoking approval of certain petitions under Section 205.2 of this title;

(v) Applications for permission to reapply for admission to the United States after deportation or removal under Section 212.2 of this title;

(vi) Applications for waiver of certain grounds of excludability under Section 212.7(a) of this title;

(vii) Applications for waiver of the two-year foreign residence requirement under Section 212.7(c) of this title;

(viii) Petitions for approval of schools under Section 214.3 of this title;

(ix) Proceedings by immigration judges to withdraw the approval of petitions by schools, as provided in Section 214.4(j) of this title;

(x) Petitions for temporary workers or trainees and fiancees or fiances of U.S. citizens under Section 214.2 of this title;

(xi) Applications for issuance of re-entry permits under Section 223.1 of this title;

(xii) Applications for refugee travel documents under Section 223a.4 of this title;

(xiii) Applications for benefits of section 13 of the Act of September 11, 1957, as amended, under Section 245.3 of this title;

(xiv) Adjustment of status of certain resident aliens to nonimmigrants under Section 247.12(b) of this title;

(xv) Applications to preserve residence for naturalization purposes under Section 316a.21(c) of this title;

(xvi) Applications for certificates of citizenship under Section 341.6 of this title;

(xvii) Administrative cancellation of certificates, documents, and records under Section 342.8 of this title;

(xviii) Applications for certificates of naturalization or repatriation under Section 343.1 of this title;

(xix) Applications for new naturalization or citizenship papers under Section 343a.1(c) of this title;

(xx) Applications for special certificates of naturalization under Section 343b.11(b) of this title;

(xxi) Applications by organizations to be listed on the Service listing of free legal services program and removal therefrom under Part 292a of this title;

(xxii) Petitions to classify Amerasians under Pub. L. 97-359 as the children of United States citizens;

(xxiii) Revoking approval of certain petitions, as provided in Section 214.2 of this title;

(xxiv) Orphan petitions under Section 204.1(b) of this title; and

(xxv) Applications for advance processing of orphan petitions under Section 204.1(b)(3) of this title.

*   *   *

Chapter 6

Nonimmigrant Visas

There are only three ways through which a non-citizen can legally enter the United States: (1) obtaining a visa from a U.S. consul abroad, (2) being granted parole by the INS, or (3) being granted asylum or refugee status by the INS. Since we have already discussed the subjects of parole and asylum in Chapter 4, our discussion here will be limited to nonimmigrant visas issued by U.S. consuls.[1]

It is easier to understand the role of the "visa" in the admission process by extending the analogy of the person "knocking at the door" discussed in the section on exclusion (Chapter 2). The person coming to the U.S. is merely applying for permission to seek admission, and is no different from someone who comes to your home and wishes to be allowed to stay for a period of time. The individual must obtain a visa as a condition precedent to seeking permission to enter the U.S. The issuance of a visa is therefore not a guarantee that the person will be admitted to the U.S.

Nonimmigrant visas are issued to persons outside the U.S. who wish to enter the U.S. temporarily for a specific purpose. There are thirteen general categories of nonimmigrant visas described at 8 U.S.C. § 1101(a)(15), Sec. 101(a)15). *See also* 8 C.F.R. § 214.2. In enacting the INA, Congress created a legal presumption that all visa applicants desire to come to the U.S. to stay permanently. This presumption places a heavy burden on the applicant to clearly show her eligibility for one of the nonimmigrant visa categories. The person's inability to meet this burden effectively precludes her from legal admission.[2] Below is a brief summary of the different types of nonimmigrant visas. It should be noted that these visas are commonly referred to by letter designation. These letter designations refer to the subparts of 8 U.S.C. § 1101(a)(15) to which that type of visa corresponds. For example, a tourist visa is called a "B" visa and is described in 8 U.S.C. § 1101(a)(15)(B).

Foreign Government Officials (diplomatic personnel): A visas

A-1: Ambassadors, public ministers, career diplomatic or consular officers, and members of their immediate families. A-2: Foreign government employees or officials

---

1. There are two types of visas which can be issued: immigrant visas and nonimmigrant visas. Nonimmigrant visas may be issued only to persons who meet the requirements of the statute and can show that they have a residence abroad to which they will return after completing their temporary stay in the U.S. Immigrant visas (for long-term residency) can only be issued to persons who establish the requisite family ties or a specific need for their work skills in the U.S. Immigrant visas are discussed in Chapter 7.

2. A person's ineligibility for a nonimmigrant visa does not act as a permanent bar to admission. While each visa application and denial are prejudicial to new requests, each application is a new opportunity to establish eligibility.

and their families. A-3: Personal employees, servants, etc., of persons holding A-1 and A-2 visas. A-1 and A-2 visas are valid as long as recognized by the Secretary of State. A-3 visas are valid for one year. [*See* 8 U.S.C. § 1101(a)(15)(A), Sec. 101(a)(15)(A); 8 C.F.R. § 214.2 (a); 22 C.F.R. §§ 41.21, 41.22, 41.26.]

Visitors: B visas

B-1: Visitor for business. May be admitted to U.S. to conduct business, attend conferences, etc., so long as it is on behalf of a foreign employer. She can be admitted for training and provided with room, board, and expenses, but her salary must be paid by the foreign employer. B-2: Visitor for pleasure. The prospective visitor for pleasure must demonstrate to the satisfaction of the U.S. consul abroad that residence is not being given up in the home country and that she has sufficient funds for self-support while in the U.S. [*See* 8 U.S.C. § 1101(a)(15)(B), Sec. 101(a)(15)(B); 8 C.F.R. §§ 214.1 and 214.2; 22 C.F.R. § 41.31.]

Crew Members: D visas

D-1: Crew members (including flight crew) remaining with their vessel. D-2: Those discharged from their vessel with intention to work on another vessel. Both D-1 and D-2 visas are valid for a maximum of 29 days. No change of status to any other classification is allowed. [*See* 8 U.S.C. § 1101(a)(15)(D), Sec. 101(a)(15)(D); 8 C.F.R. § 214.2 (2)(d); 22 C.F.R. § 41.41.]

Treaty Traders or Investors: E visas

E-1: Treaty Trader. E-2: Treaty Investor. Requirements: (1) a "treaty of commerce and navigation" must exist between the U.S. and the applicant's country, (2) the applicant must be a national of that country, and (3) the applicant must be coming to the U.S. solely to "carry on substantial trade" (E-1) or to "develop and direct an enterprise in which he has invested . . . a substantial amount of capital" (E-2). These visas are also available for the spouse and children of the holder of an E-1 or E-2 visa. Both visas are valid for one year, but unlimited extensions may be granted by INS in increments of up to two years. The requirement of temporariness of stay in the U.S. and unrelinquished domicile abroad are not as strict under this visa classification as for the B visa. [*See* 8 U.S.C. § 1101(a)(15)(E), Sec. 101(a)(15)(E); 8 C.F.R. § 214.2(e); 22 C.F.R. § 41.51.] Special reciprocal provisions exist for the entry of investors and traders from Canada. *See* The United States-Canada Free-Trade Agreement Implementation Act of 1988, Pub. L. No. 100-449, 102 Stat. 1851 (1988).

Students: F visas

F-1: Student visa. The visa applicants must be entering the U.S. temporarily solely to pursue a full course of study at an established elementary school, academic high school, college, university, seminary, conservatory, or language school recognized by the INS. A "full course of study" is defined in 8 C.F.R. § 214.2(f)(6). The prospective student visa applicant must satisfy the consular officer that she: (1) fits under the statutory definition of student, (2) the institution to be attended is approved by the Attorney General for attendance by foreign students,[3] (3) has sufficient funds to meet expenses for the entire period of anticipated study without having to resort to employment in the U.S., and (4) he has sufficient scholastic preparation and knowledge of the English language (unless English is not an essential requirement or arrangements have been made for tutoring).[4] F-2: Spouse and children of the student visa holder. [See 8 U.S.C. § 1101(a)(15)(F), Sec. 101(a)(15)(F); 8 C.F.R. § 214.2(f); 22 C.F.R. § 41.61.]

Work Authorization for Students: The 1990 Act created a three year experimental program allowing students to work off-campus in fields unrelated to the person's field of study. This work authorization is non-discretionary once the student meets the following 3 requirements: 1) she has completed at least 1 year in good academic standing as a nonimmigrant; 2) the employer provides an attestation that it has recruited for the position for at least 60 days and will pay the applicant at the rate for the occupation at that particular place of business or, if greater, at the market wage level; and 3) the student will not work for more than 20 hours per week during the school year but may work full-time during vacation periods.[5]

Vocational Students: M visas

M-1: Vocational or non-academic students who wish to enter the U.S. temporarily to pursue a course of study at a recognized vocational or non-academic institution. 8 U.S.C. § 1101(a)(15)(M), Sec. 101 (a)(15)(M). The period of stay is granted for up to one year or the period of study plus 30 days, whichever is less, and is renewable.

M-2: Family members who may stay as long as the M-1 visa holders. M visa holders ordinarily cannot accept employment but M-1 holders may work if the employment is part of their course of study. [See 8 C.F.R. § 214.2(M); 22 C.F.R. § 41.61.]

Representatives to or Employees of International Organizations: G visas

G-1: Principal representatives of governments recognized *de jure* by the U.S., or for representatives to an international organization and their family members. G-2: Other accredited representatives of foreign governments or international organizations and their family members. G-3: Persons (and their families) who would qualify for a G-1 or G-2 visa but their government is not recognized *de jure* by the U.S. G-4: Officers and employees of international organizations and their family members. G-5: Holders of C visas (persons who are entering to attend U.N. meetings). All G visas are issued for one year and are renewable. Only family members of G-4 visa holders

3. Presentation of Form I-20, a form filled out by the student's accepting school, is prima facie evidence of admission to an accredited institution. The I-20 is surrendered to the INS officer upon arrival at the U.S. border.

4. When a person enters the U.S. in one status (e.g., as a visitor for pleasure), then seeks to change to some other status (e.g., to that of student), unless a significant period of time has lapsed, it will be presumed by the INS that the person was attempting to evade the normal procedures for obtaining a visa abroad. The burden shifts to the applicant to prove that she really changed her intention after she entered the U.S. The denial of a change of status application is appealable to the INS Central Office. (*See* Administrative Appeals at Chapter 5.)

5. *See* Sec. 221, Immigration Act of 1990, Pub. L. No. 101-649, 104 Stat. 4978.

may accept employment in the U.S. Such employment must be approved by the INS. [*See* 8 U.S.C. § 1101(a)(15)(G); 8 C.F.R. § 214.2(g); 22 C.F.R. § 41.24, Sec. 101(a) (15)(G).]

Temporary Workers: H visas[6]

The unavailability of immigrant visas due to oversubscription under the quotas has caused increased usage of the temporary work visa.[7] The H (temporary work) visas often take less time to adjudicate and the requirements for documentation and evidence are less stringent than for immigrant visas. H visas are necessary if the job is temporary, as the Department of Labor will not grant a permanent labor certification (immigrant labor certification) for a temporary position.

H-1A: Persons coming temporarily to the U.S. as a licensed registered nurse. The employer must be able to attest to a number of requirements including the following: 1) the delivery of health care services would be disrupted, but for the admission of the H-1A nurse; 2) the employment of the foreigner would not adversely affect the wages and working conditions of U.S. workers; and 3) that the employer was taking significant steps to recruit and retain nurses who are U.S. citizens or permanent residents or"is subject to an approved State plan for the recruitment and retention of nurses."[8] H-1B: Persons coming to work in a "specialty occupation," defined as an occupation which requires the theoretical and practical application of a body of highly specialized knowledge and the attainment of a bachelors or higher degree as a minimum entry requirement for the position.[9] H-2A: Persons coming to "perform agricultural labor or services" of a "temporary or seasonal nature."[10] No skill or experience of the type necessary for an H-1 visa is required. A condition precedent for approval is that the prospective employer must obtain a certification

---

6. Historically, there has never been a limit imposed on the number of nonimmigrants admitted in a given year. One of the more dramatic policy shifts found in the 1990 Act was the quota imposed on the admission of nonimmigrants under the H-1B, H-2B, P-1 and P-3 categories. Under this amendment, the annual quota for H-1B workers is 65,000 and for H-2B workers, 66,000 (not counted within this annual quota are the derivative beneficiaries of the H workers and trainees).

7. This increased demand on the nonimmigrant visas is due to the fact that there is no limit on the number of visas that can be issued. Even though the applicant may be successful in obtaining her H visa, she may eventually be confronted with the denial of a request for adjustment of status due to the INS's determination that she had a "preconceived intent" to immigrate when she applied for the H visa. *See* Chapter 8.

8. These provisions were initially created by the Immigration Nursing Relief Act of 1989, Pub. L. No. 101-238, 103 Stat. 2099 and amended by Sec. 162 of the Immmigration Act of 1990, Pub. L. No. 101-649, 104 Stat. 4978. *See* 8 U.S.C. § 1182(m), Sec. 212(m). These provisions are effective until September 1, 1995 and may be extended based on the recommendations of an advisory group.

9. See, 8 U.S.C. § 1184(i)(1), Sec. 214(i)(1) for the definition of "specialty occupation." The 1990 Act removed artists, entertainers and athletes from the H visa category and created the O and P visas discussed below.

10. Amendments to the statute in 1986 created special procedures for the adjudication of these applications and broadly defined agricultural labor or services by incorporating definitions set out in the Internal Revenue Code of 1954 and the Fair Labor Standards Act of 1938.

which confirms that able, willing, and qualified domestic workers cannot be found at the time and place where they are needed, and that hiring the aliens will not adversely affect the wages and working conditions of similarly employed U.S. workers. H-2B: Persons coming to perform any other work of a temporary nature including seasonal work, if unemployed persons capable of performing such work cannot be found in the country. H-3: Persons coming to the U.S. to receive training not available in their home country; medical training is statutorily excluded. The person must apply for labor certification[11] and any extensions require re-certification by the Department of Labor. The applicant must also satisfy the consular officer that she will depart the U.S. at the end of her designated time and that the job is temporary. H-4: Spouse and children of H-1, H-2, and H-3 visa holders. The length of a person's authorized stay in the U.S. will depend on the type of H visa issued. H-4 visa holders cannot accept employment unless specifically approved by the INS. An employer who dismisses an H-1B or H-2B worker before the expiration of her visa must pay the reasonable cost of her return trip abroad. [*See* 8 U.S.C. § 1101(a)(15)(H), Sec. 101 (a)(15)(H); 8 C.F.R. § 214.2(h); 22 C.F.R. § 41.53.]

Exchange Visitors: J visas

J-1: Persons accepted to participate in exchange visitor programs designated by the U.S. Information Agency. J-2: The spouse and children of J-1 visa holders. The J-2 visa holder may obtain permission to work from the INS, provided it is work for her own support and not for the support of the principal exchange visitor. J visas are valid for up to one year and may be extended. J visa holders cannot change their status to any other visa classification except "A" (foreign government official) or "G" (representative to international organization). If the person is subject to the two-year foreign residency requirement, she must first return to her home country for two years prior to being eligible to return to the U.S. *See* 8 U.S.C. § 1258(3), Sec. 248(3). Whether or not a person is required to fulfill the residency requirement will depend on (1) whether the program sponsoring the applicant was funded in whole or in part by either the U.S. or the applicant's government, (2) whether the applicant's educational or skills training was designated as a skill which was in clear need by her country (as certified by the USIA), or (3) whether the applicant came to the U.S. in order to receive graduate medical training or education. [*See* 8 U.S.C. § 1101(a)(15)(J), Sec. 101(a)(15)(J); 8 U.S.C. § 1182(e), Sec. 212(e); 8 C.F.R. § 214.2(j); 22 C.F.R. §§ 41.65 514.]

Fiancees or Fiances of U.S. Citizen: K visas

This visa is designed to allow someone who intends to marry a U.S. citizen to enter the country. The person and the U.S. citizen must have met at least two years prior to filing the petition for the K visa. The person is allowed to enter the country for 90 days and must get married within that time. Holders of K visas may not change

---

11. This certification is different from the normal labor certification which is required of permanent resident applicants (schedule A—blanket labor certification) for which the Department of Labor must determine that the applicant is not displacing U.S. workers. See discussion in Chapter 8.

their nonimmigrant classification. [8 U.S.C. § 1101 (a)(15)(K), 101(a)(15)(K); 8 C.F.R. § 214.2(k); 22 C.F.R. § 41.81.]

Intracompany Transferees: L visas

This visa allows international corporations to transfer employees temporarily to the U.S. The person must have been continuously employed within the three preceding years for at least one year by the petitioning firm outside the U.S. The law further requires that the prospective employment in the U.S. be in a managerial or executive capacity or require specialized knowledge.[12]

L-1: Principal L visa holders. The L visa is generally issued for three years and may be renewed. The spouse and children of the L-1 recipient may be allowed to enter the country as L-2 visa holders, but may not work. Recent administrative decisions have established that L visas may be available to small, closely held companies as well as large, international corporations.[13]

Extraordinary Ability in Arts and Science: O visas

O-1: Persons of extraordinary ability in the sciences, arts, education, business, or athletics which has been demonstrated by "sustained national or international acclaim." In the case of persons in the motion picture or television industry they must have a "record of extraordinary achievement." O-2: Persons entering for the purpose of assisting in a performance where the beneficiary is "an integral part" of the performance. The issuance of this visa will require "consultation" with the appropriate union. O-3: Persons who are the spouse and minor children of the O visa recipient. The beneficiary of the O visa may be admitted at the discretion of the Attorney General for a sufficient period to attend the event for which she is admitted. [8 U.S.C. § 1101(a)(15)(O)(i).]

Athletes and Performing Artists: P visas [14]

P-1: Person who performs as an athlete, individually or as part of a group or team, at an internationally recognized level of performance, or who performs as part of an entertainment group that has been recognized internationally as being outstanding in the discipline for a sustained and substantial period of time. This visa designation is also for persons who are entering as an athlete or entertainer for a specific competition or performance. P-2: Persons coming to the U.S. as an artist or entertainer under a reciprocal exchange program. P-3: Persons entering the U.S. as an artist or entertainer individually or with a group "under a program which is culturally unique." P-4: Persons who are the spouse and children of the P visa recipient. In general, P visa recipients may remain in the U.S for as long as the Attorney General may specify

---

12. For additional guidance on the requirement of "specialized knowledge," *see* Campbell and Taggert, *The International Business Client and Nonimmigrant Visas*, 11 Colo. Law. 2545, 2550 (1982).

13. *See Matter of Aphrodite Investments, Ltd.*, 17 I. & N. Dec. 530 (Reg. Com. 1980).

14. The 1990 Act placed a limit of 25,000 per year for the P-1 and P-3 visas. *See* 8 U.S.C. 1184(g)(1)(C), Sec. 214(g)(1)(C).

in order to provide for the event for which the nonimmigrant is admitted. In the case of an individual athlete, she may be admitted for an initial period of up to 5 years which may be extended for an 5 additional years. A P-2 and a P-3 may not be readmitted in that status unless she has remained outside the U.S. for 3 months after the most recent admission (the Attorney General may waive this provision in cases of individual tours if undue hardship would result).[15] [*See* 8 U.S.C. §§ 1101(a)(15)(P) and 1184(a)(2)(B), Secs. 101(a)(15)(P) and 214(a)(2)(B).]

International Cultural Exchange Program: Q visas

Programs designated by the Attorney General to allow the person to obtain practical training, to share history, culture and traditions of her country, provided that the Q visa recipient will receive the same wage and be employed under the same working conditions of U.S. workers. The person entering with a Q visas is allowed to remain in the U.S. for a period not to exceed 15 months. [*See* 8 U.S.C. § 1101 (a)(15)(Q), Sec. 101(a)(15)(Q).]

Religious Occupations: R visas

Religious workers who have been members of a religious organization for 2 years preceding their application for admission to the U.S. may qualify for R visas. The religious organization must have a bona fide not for profit status in the U.S. These visa recipients may not stay in the U.S. for more than 5 years. [*See* 8 U.S.C. § 1101 (a)(15)(R), Sec. 101(a)(15)(R).][16]

Other Nonimmigrant Visas:[17] I visas

I visas are for representatives of foreign press, radio, film, television, or other media, provided that U.S. citizens are granted reciprocal privileges. C visas are issued to non-citizens in "immediate and continuous transit through the U.S."

In recent years increased attention has been focused on immigration law, particularly insofar as it affects our domestic economy. The public's perception that increases in the admission of foreign workers diminishes opportunities for U.S. workers has a significant impact on the formulation of a policy. This perception clashes with the traditional policy in our immigration law of encouraging family reunification and providing for refugees. Further strains are added to the formulation of a coherent immigration policy when the demands by industry for skilled and unskilled workers are not met by the available pool of U.S. workers.[18] Congress has thus far been unable

---

15. *See* 8 U.S.C. § 1184(a)(2), Sec. 214(a)(2).

16. The 1990 Act also revised the special immigrant provisions relating to religious workers. *See* Discussion infra at Chapter 7.

17. These nonimmigrant visas will not be discussed here. The reader should consult the appropriate section of the Code of Federal Regulations or Foreign Affairs Manual.

18. The provisions for temporary agricultural workers which were discussed earlier in these materials are an example of one of these clashes. The "temporary" agricultural worker provisions were designed to accommodate this important domestic industry, but these provisions conflict with the restrictions on nonimmigrant visas for persons coming to the U.S. for a short period of time. A strong argument could be made that if the rules applicable to other nonimmigrants were applied to agricultural workers they would be ineligible for the status.

to address most of these issues. The inability on the part of the executive and legislative branches to adequately resovle these issues may cause the INS to deal with the problems through regulations.[19]

An important point to remember when reading the following cases is that there is a much greater supply of foreign workers and willing employers in the U.S. than can be accommodated under the immigrant quota system. Since there are fewer limits on the number of nonimmigrant visas which may be issued, employers and foreigners are constantly searching for new methods of using the nonimmigrant visas to alleviate the labor supply problem.

References

Deluca, *Immigration Law: Entry of International Business Investors*, 17 Int'l Law. 535 (1983)

Evans, *Entry Formalities in the European Community*, 6 Eur. L. Rev. 3 (1981)

Fragomen & Robosson, *The Foreign Investor: Current Approaches Toward United States Immigration Law*, 18 Vand. J. Transnat'l L. 335 (1985)

Green, *The New F-1 Student Regulations: An Analysis*, 7 Immigr. J., June 1984 at 5 (1984)

Green, *The New F-1 Student Regulations: An Analysis Part II*, 7 Immigr. J., Dec. 1984 at 13

Green, *INS Issues F-1 Operation Instructions: An Overview*, 9 Immigr. J., March 1986 at 3

Gordon, *The Immigration Laws of the U.S. and the Employment of Foreign Personnel*, 9 N.C.J. Int'l L. & Comp. Reg. 397 (1984)

Immigration for Investors: A Comparative Analysis of U.S., Canadian and Australian Policies, 7 B.C. Int'l & Comp. L. Rev. 113 (1984)

Lichtman, *The New H-1 Regulations: Profession, Professionals and Prominence in Business*, 12 Immigr. J. 69 (1989)

Note, *Alien Students in the U.S.: Statutory Interpretation and the Problems of Control*, 5 Suffolk Transnat'l L.J. 235 (1981)

Note, *Intracompany Transferee Visas—The Labyrinth of Mobility for International Executives*, 19 N.Y.U. J. Int'l L. & Pol. 679 (1987)

Note, *The Treaty Investor Visa: Cure or Bandaid for the Ills of Foreign Investors?* 15 J. Legis. 45 (1988)

Voigt, *Visa Denials on Ideological Grounds and the First Amendment Right to Receive Information: The Case for Stricter Judicial Scrutiny*, 17 Cumb. L. Rev. 139 (1986)

Wolff, *The Nonreviewability of Consular Visa Decisions: An Unjustified Aberration from American Justice*, 5 N.Y.L. Sch. J. Int'l & Comp. L. 341 (1984)

---

19. The reader should compare the period nonimmigrants are generally permitted to stay in the U.S. with that allowed for holders of H, L, and E visas.

A. Visitors (B-1 and B-2)

Matter of Healy and Goodchild
17 I. & N. Dec. 22 (BIA 1979)

*   *   *

Mr. Healy, a native and citizen of Ireland and a resident of Australia, applied for a nonimmigrant visa at the United States Consulate General in Melbourne, Australia, for the stated purpose of visiting this country for a 1-month period. On September 7, 1977, he was issued a B-2 nonimmigrant visitor for pleasure visa, valid for multiple applications for admission to the United States within 3 months from the date of issuance. On that same date, Mr. Goodchild, a native and citizen of Great Britain, was issued a B-2 nonimmigrant visitor visa at the United States Embassy in London, England, which was valid for multiple applications for admission to this country within 6 months from the date of issuance.

In the course of inspection upon their respective arrivals in New York, each applicant was found to be in possession of a letter of acceptance for admission to a 9-month course of study at the Claymont School for Continuing Education, an institution which has not been approved for attendance by nonimmigrant students. The applicants were thereupon charged with excludability under section 212(a)(26) as nonimmigrant students not in possession of valid nonimmigrant student visas and under section 212(a)(19) as aliens who procured their visas by willfully misrepresenting material facts.

In the consolidated exclusion proceedings that ensued, the immigration judge found Mr. Goodchild excludable as charged under section 212(a)(26) but held that the charge under section 212(a)(19) could not be sustained in his case. As noted above, Mr. Healy was found excludable under both section 212(a)(26) and section 212(a)(19). The immigration judge's findings as to each charge will be examined in turn.

*   *   *

Under section 101(a)(15) of the Act, every alien is considered to be an immigrant unless he is able to establish that he is entitled to nonimmigrant status under one of the specified classes of nonimmigrants designated by Congress in section 101(a)(15)(A) through section 101(a)(15)(L). Section 214(b) of the Act, 8 U.S.C. 1184(b); 22 C.F.R. 41.10. Moreover, the burden is upon the alien to establish that he is entitled to the nonimmigrant classification and type of nonimmigrant visa for which he is an applicant. 22 C.F.R. 41.10; cf. section 291 of the Act, 8 U.S.C. 1361.

The applicants conceded that they are not entitled to status as nonimmigrant students under section 101(a)(15)(F) inasmuch as the Claymont School has not been approved by the Attorney General or his delegate.[1] Each applicant further acknowl-

---

1. The purpose and program of the basic course at the Claymont School are described as follows in excerpts from the institution's 1977-78 catalog:

The Claymont School for Continuous Education is founded on the principle that true education must include techniques of self-perfecting in mind, body, and spirit and must realize the potential latent in normal men and women. . . . The daily schedule normally begins at 6 a.m. All students and staff share in psychological and spiritual exercises until breakfast.

edged that the principal purpose of his visit was to participate in the basic course to which he was admitted at the Claymont School, that he had paid a deposit of $100 toward the $2,750 tuition for the course prior to seeking admission to the United States, and that he had been in attendance at the school since his parole into this country.

Counsel does not seriously contest the fact that the Claymont School is a school and that the applicants are students within the ordinary usage of those terms and we are satisfied that they are properly classifiable as such. Counsel argues instead that section 101(a)(15)(F) is solely concerned with alien students destined for approved schools. Since the Claymont School has not been accredited by the Service, he insists that the applicants are not subject to the provisions of section 101(a)(15)(F) of the Act but are admissible as visitors for pleasure. We disagree.

It is clear that absent Service approval of the school to which an alien student is destined, he may not establish eligibility for a nonimmigrant student visa under section 101(a)(15)(F). It does not follow ipso facto, however, that an alien bound for the United States for the primary purpose of pursuing a course of study at an un-approved school is entitled to status as a nonimmigrant visitor for pleasure under section 101(a)(15)(B). That such alien is not entitled to status as a nonimmigrant visitor is evident from the express terms of section 101(a)(15)(B) which includes among those classifiable as nonimmigrants:

an alien (other than one coming for the purpose of study or of performing skilled or unskilled labor or as a representative of foreign press, radio, film or other foreign information media coming to engage in such vocation) having a residence in a foreign country which he has no intention of abandoning and who is visiting the United States temporarily for business or temporarily for pleasure; ...

While the statutory term "pleasure" is not defined in the Act, State Department regulation 22 C.F.R. 41.25 provides the following definition:

(c) The term "pleasure," as used in section 101(a)(15)(B) of the Act, refers to legitimate activities of a recreational character, including tourism, amusement, visits with friends or relatives and rest; medical treatment, or activities of a fraternal, social or service nature.

* * *

It is thus apparent from the explicit language of section 101(a)(15)(B), as supplemented by the foregoing regulation, that the B-2, or visitor for pleasure, nonimmigrant category was not intended to be a "catch-all" classification available to all who wish to come to the United States temporarily for whatever purpose. Instead, as is the case with the other nonimmigrant classes enumerated by Congress in section 101(a)(15), section 101(a)(15)(B) was designed to encompass a specific, defined class of aliens; by the express terms of the statute, that class does not include aliens coming for the purpose of study. To accept counsel's theory would not only disregard the explicit language of section 101(a)(15)(B) but would undermine the requirements for

---

After breakfast, 4-5 hours are devoted to practical activities involving the acquisition of a wide variety of skills such as cooking, breadmaking, carpentry, housepainting, plumbing and electrical work, gardening, logging, animal and vegetable husbandry, repairs and special crafts and skills such as spinning, woodworking and pottery to meet particular needs....

entitlement to student status under section 101(a)(15)(F) and the detailed regulations which have been promulgated to implement that section.

We accordingly hold that an alien bound for the United States for the primary purpose of study is not admissible as a nonimmigrant visitor for pleasure as defined by section 101(a)(15)(B) but must instead establish his entitlement to nonimmigrant student status under section 101(a)(15)(F) and the pertinent regulations. We recognize that our decision in effect declares unapproved educational institutions such as the Claymont School to be unavailable to alien students. Our holding, however, is in keeping with the clear statutory scheme drawn by Congress which deems all aliens to be immigrants unless they can demonstrate that they qualify for status under one of the distinct nonimmigrant classes enumerated in section 101(a)(15). The dispositive fact is that Congress made no provision thereunder for aliens destined for the United States for the primary purpose of pursuing a course of study at an unapproved school.

* * *

The remaining issue before us concerns the finding of excludability under 212(a)(19) with respect to Mr. Healy. At the hearing, Mr. Goodchild testified that he had requested a visa valid for 9 months, telling the consul at the Embassy in London that he was "coming to a community where we practice all sorts of living." He conceded that he did not disclose to the consul that he intended to take an actual course of study here but accepted as accurate the immigration judge's summation that he had "more or less told them everything about the place except that it was a school." On the basis of this testimony, the immigration judge concluded, with the concurrence of the Service, that a charge under section 212(a)(19) had not been sustained with respect to Mr. Goodchild.

Mr. Healy testified that he had but one brief conversation with a State Department employee at the United States Consulate in Melbourne prior to obtaining his visa. He stated that he was told by that employee when he visited the Consulate to inquire about procedures for coming to the United States, that he need only fill out a visitor visa application form if he planned to remain here for 1 month or less but that he would have to produce documentary evidence of his intention to return to Australia if he contemplated a longer stay. He testified that he told the employee that he would apply for a 1-month visit but would probably seek an extension of his stay from the Service after his arrival in this country.

Mr. Healy maintained that his visa was issued on the basis of that single conversation, which involved no discussion as to the purpose of his trip, and of the visitor visa application form which he contemporaneously completed and returned to the Consulate employee. On his application form, Mr. Healy responded to Items 18 and 19 as follows:

18. What is the purpose of your trip? "to visit America"

19. How long do you plan to stay in the USA? "one month"

In response to the inquiry set forth in Item 20, "At what address will you reside in the USA?," Mr. Healy provided the address of the Claymont School.

At several points in the course of the hearing, Mr. Healy indicated that notwithstanding his acceptance at the Claymont School for a 9-month course of study and his payment of a $100 deposit to the school, he had not firmly decided to remain in this country for the duration of the course at the time he applied for his visa. He stated that he instead intended to visit the school and, if he found that course to be suitable, to apply to the Service for an extension of his stay. Mr. Healy explained that he would have requested additional time for his visit when he initially applied for a visa but felt he would have encountered difficulties in producing documentation to establish the requisite ties in Australia since he had terminated his employment in that country.

Mr. Healy stated that he believed that he was ineligible for a student visa since the Claymont School is not an approved educational institution and thought, as a consequence, that he could properly apply for a tourist visa. He further stated that while his acceptance at the Claymont School provided the primary impetus for seeking admission into the United States, he also wished to visit this country.

* * *

In determining whether an alien has procured his visa by fraud or willful mis-representation of a material fact within the meaning of section 212(a)(19), it is appropriate to examine the circumstances as they existed at the time the visa was issued. Under the rule of law announced herein, an alien's trip to the United States for the primary purpose of participating in a course of study at an educational institution that has not been approved by the Service may not be characterized as a "visit" of a nature which would qualify him for status as a visitor for pleasure under section 101(a)(15)(B). This precise issue, however, has not previously been addressed by the Board. Given the uncertain state of the law at the time Mr. Healy applied for his visa, it is not unlikely that he considered the declared purpose of his trip, "to visit America," to be an accurate statement of his intent.[2] Moreover, we find Mr. Healy's explanation with respect to his stated anticipated length of stay plausible, if not compelling.

In interpreting the term "willful" for purposes of section 212(a)(19), the Court of Appeals for the Third Circuit held in a recently decided cases that knowledge of the falsity of a representation satisfies the fraud and willfulness requirements of that section. *Suite v. INS*, 594 F.2d 972 (3d Cir. 1979). We are not persuaded that a finding of willfulness is warranted on the particular facts of this case, and we accordingly hold that Mr. Healy is not inadmissible under section 212(a)(19) of the Act for having procured his visa by fraud or by willfully misrepresenting a material fact.

In so holding, we recognize that the act places the burden on the alien to demonstrate that he is not inadmissible under one of the exclusionary grounds enumerated in section 212(a). Section 291 of the Act, 8 U.S.C. 1361. We believe, however, that given the harsh consequences of a finding of excludability under the first clause of section 212(a)(19), the factual basis of such finding should be subject to close scrutiny. This is particularly true where the alleged fraud or misrepresentation involves a disputed issue with respect to an alien's subjective intent.

In accordance with the foregoing discussion, we shall order each applicant excluded and deported solely on the ground of inadmissibility set forth in section 212(a)(20) of the Act.

———————

2. We note that unlike Mr. Goodchild, Mr. Healy apparently was not afforded an opportunity to fully discuss the purpose of his trip with a consular officer prior to the issuance of the visa.

B. Student Visas (F-1)

Matter of Yazdani

17 I. & N. Dec. 626 (BIA 1981)

The respondent is a 19-year-old native and citizen of Iran who entered the United States as a nonimmigrant student bound for a course of study at the University of Utah. She was admitted for the duration of her student status. Prior to her embarkation for this country, the respondent had been accepted for admission by both the University of Utah and the University of San Francisco and had obtained the requisite Form I-20, Certificate of Eligibility for Nonimmigrant "F-1" Student Status, from each institution. The Form I-20 from the University of San Francisco apparently arrived too late for the respondent to secure a visa to attend that school, however, and her visa was issued for attendance at the University of Utah.

The record reflects that upon her arrival in the United States, the respondent proceeded to the University of Utah, met with the Director of International Student Services there, and obtained that official's permission to transfer to the University of San Francisco together with his signature on her transfer request, Form I-538. The Form I-538 was submitted with the respondent's Form I-94 and her Form I-20 from the University of San Francisco to the Salt Lake City office of the Immigration and Naturalization Service. The respondent then enrolled at the University of San Francisco, beginning classes on September 24, 1979.

In December 1979, the respondent reported to the Service's San Francisco office pursuant to 8 C.F.R. 214.5. These deportation proceedings were thereafter instituted by the issuance of an Order to Show Cause charging the respondent with deportability for having violated the conditions of her status by transferring from the school which she was authorized to attend to another school without obtaining advance permission from the Service. At the deportation hearing that ensued on May 2, 1980, the immigration judge found the respondent deportable as charged. The District Director subsequently reviewed the respondent's file to determine whether she should be reinstated to student status and on October 17, 1980, decided against reinstatement.

Section 214(a) of the Act, 8 U.S.C. 1184(a), provides in pertinent part:

The admission to the United States of any alien as a nonimmigrant shall be for such time and under such conditions as the Attorney General may by regulations prescribe...

Under the regulations promulgated by the Attorney General, a nonimmigrant student must establish as a condition for admission that she is destined to and intends to attend the school specified in her visa. 8 C.F.R. 214.2(f)(2). She may not transfer to another school unless she submits a valid Form I-20 completed by that school and the Service grants her permission to transfer. 8 C.F.R. 214.2(f)(4). The regulations further provide that a nonimmigrant applying for admission must agree to abide by all the terms and conditions of her admission. 8 C.F.R. 214.1(a).

On appeal, the respondent through counsel argues (1) that advance permission to transfer is not required by the regulations, and (2) that the respondent is in any event not deportable because she substantially complied with the terms of her status in making application for a transfer. The respondent's arguments must be rejected.

In support of her first contention, the respondent points to language in Service Operations Instruction 214.2(f)(2) which she quotes as follows:

> ...if a school transfer has been effected, and the transfer request is submitted to the office having jurisdiction over the school to which he has transferred, the receiving office may adjudicate the request unless there is good reason not to do so."

The respondent maintains that the foregoing Operations Instruction casts doubt upon whether it is necessary for a student, in order to remain in status, to make application for permission to transfer prior to transferring schools. We disagree.

*   *   *

There is no question but that the District Director in charge of a Service office may through a retroactive grant of a transfer request reinstate an alien's student status, and Operations Instruction 214.2(f)(2) recognizes that power. The power, however, to reinstate student status or grant an extension of nonimmigrant stay lies within the exclusive jurisdiction of the District Director and neither the immigration judge nor the Board may review the propriety of the District Director's determinations. Matter of Teberen, 15 I & N Dec. 689 (BIA 1976); Matter of Hosseinpour, 15 I & N Dec. 191 (BIA 1975), aff'd, 520 F.2d 941 (5th Cir. 1975). In the instant case, the District Director considered and denied reinstatement.

We find the cases relied upon by the respondent as authority for her alternative argument to be inapposite. At issue in Mashi v. INS, 585 F.2d 1309 (5th Cir. 1978), was the proper interpretation to be given the statutory requirement that a nonimmigrant student "pursue a full course of study" (see 101(a)(15)(F)(i) of the Act, 8 U.S.C. 1101(a)(15)(i)) under superseded regulations which, unlike the present regulations, set forth no specific objective criteria for compliance with that requirement. Noting that the "12 credit" minimum requirement of the present regulations (8 C.F.R. 214.2(f)(1a)(ii)) did not apply to Mr. Mashi, the court found that he was in fact pursuing a full course of study and could not be deported for failure to comply with the conditions of his status simply because his academic load briefly dropped below 12 credits in the course of one semester.

Although the court in Mashi, id., suggested in dictum that the same result might be reached on the facts before it under the present regulations, there is room for interpretation in determining whether the "12 credit" rule of 8 C.F.R. 214.2(f)(1a)(ii) has been satisfied that does not exist in determining whether an alien has received permission from the Service to transfer as required by 8 C.F.R. 214.2(f)(4). The question is whether there has been compliance, not whether there has been substantial compliance, with the regulation in question.

We likewise find the respondent's reliance on the Board's decisions in Matter of Murat-Kahn, 14 I & N Dec. 465 (BIA 1973), and Matter of C—, 9 I & N Dec. 100 (BIA 1960), to be misplaced. We held in those cases that a student's conviction which does not interfere with her studies so as to meaningfully disrupt her education does not constitute a failure to maintain status. The instant case is concerned not with an alleged disruption of studies but rather with a separate, distinct violation of status—transferring schools without Service permission, a breach specifically defined by the regulations.

Finally, we cannot agree with the respondent's characterization of her failure to secure advance permission to transfer as a "minor, highly technical" violation of her status. The regulation in question, 8 C.F.R. 214.2(f)(4), like other regulations governing the activities of nonimmigrant students, is an essential tool in the administration of our immigration laws. The widespread disregard of those regulations which would likely result from lax enforcement thereof would severely hamper the Service in fulfilling its responsibilities of keeping track of the thousands of alien students within our borders and of enforcing the immigration laws with respect to those students.

We note that the respondent appears to have acted in good faith in all of her dealings with the Government. However, so long as the enforcement officials of the Service choose to initiate proceedings against an alien and to prosecute those proceedings to a conclusion, the immigration judge and the Board must order deportation if the evidence supports a finding of deportability on the ground charged. See Lopez-Telles v. INS, 564 F.2d 1302 (9th Cir. 1977).

... We find that deportability has been established by clear, unequivocal and convincing evidence on the basis of the respondent's concessions.

C. Treaty Investor/Trader (E-1 and E-2)

Matter of Nago
16 I. & N. Dec. 446 (BIA 1978)

The applicant is a 23-year-old single male alien who is a native and citizen of Japan. He arrived in the United States at Honolulu, Hawaii, on November 11, 1976. The applicant, at that time, was in possession of a valid passport issued by the Government of Japan and a nonimmigrant (E-2) visa. He applied for admission as a nonimmigrant treaty investor under section 101(a)(15)(E)(ii) of the Act.

The applicant was served by an immigration officer with a notice (Form I-122) informing him that he appeared to be an immigrant not in possession of a valid unexpired immigrant visa; that it did not appear that he was exempt from presentation of such a document; and that he may come within the exclusion provisions of section 212(a)(20) of the Act, 8 U.S.C. 1182(a)(20). He was also notified of the time and date of his hearing in exclusion proceedings. The hearing was conducted on February 14, 1977. The record reveals that the applicant is a Japanese specialty cook who is employed for a one-year period at "Yakiniku House Osaka," a Japanese restaurant located in Honolulu. The restaurant is owned by a Japanese nonimmigrant treaty investor who seeks the culinary services of the applicant who is apparently well versed in a specialized type of Japanese cooking known as "Nabemono." The applicant will cook in this form of cooking. It appears that "Nabemono" chefs are scarce in the United States and that the applicant's employer has been searching for such a chef for several years. The applicant's employer testified that the applicant is a graduate of a leading Japanese cooking school and experienced in the art of "Nabemono" cooking. The applicant's employer also testified that the applicant will teach other employees to carry on the "Nabemono" style of cooking, that the "Nabemono" process can be learned in one year, and that the applicant intends to return to Japan after one year. The immigration judge found that the "Nabemono" type of cooking "... requires a highly trained or specially qualified technical person for the preparation of the food and for the purpose of teaching others to perform the process."

*   *   *

In *Matter of Udagawa*, 14 I & N Dec. 578 (BIA 1974), we pointed out that a reasonable construction of section 101(a)(15)(E)(ii) is contained in 22 C.F.R. 41.41. The relevant portion of this Department of State regulation states:

> (a) An alien shall be classifiable as a nonimmigrant treaty investor if he establishes to the satisfaction of the consular officer that he qualifies under the provisions of section 101(a)(15)(E)(ii) of the Act and that: (1) He intends to depart from the United States upon the termination of his status; and (2) he is an alien who has invested or is investing capital in a bona fide enterprise and is not seeking to proceed to the United States in connection with the investment of a small amount of capital in a marginal enterprise solely for the purpose of earning a living; or that (3) he is employed by a treaty investor in a responsible capacity and the employer is a foreign person having the nationality of the treaty country who is maintaining the status of a nonimmigrant treaty investor, or an organization which is principally owned by a person or persons having the nationality of the treaty country, and if not residing abroad, maintaining nonimmigrant treaty investor status.

We construe the above regulation to mean that an alien such as the applicant will qualify as a "treaty investor" if he has the necessary intent to depart and if he meets the conditions imposed by subdivision (3) of the quoted portion of the regulation. Since the evidence adduced at the hearing indicates that the applicant's employer is a foreign person of the same nationality as the applicant and that the applicant possesses the requisite intent to return to Japan, the remaining issue in this case is whether he can be considered to be "employed ... in a responsible capacity. ..."

It is clear that the applicant is a highly trained chef who is engaged in a specialized form of Japanese cooking. The applicant has been brought to the United States to impart his knowledge and share his experiences with other employees of the treaty investor in order to enable them to become proficient in "Nabemono" cooking. We conclude that the applicant is employed by a treaty investor in a responsible capacity. Therefore, the applicant qualifies for admission as a nonimmigrant alien within the meaning of section 101(a)(15)(E)(ii) of the Act.

———————

Section 204(b) of the Immigration Act of 1990 expanded the potential beneficiaries of the E visa. In order to be effective, nationals of certain countries who have traditionally not provided large numbers of immigrants to the U.S. and who provide reciprocal treatment to U.S. citizens may be eligible to enter the U.S. with E visas.

D. Temporary Workers (H-1, H-2, and H-3)

Hong Kong T.V. Video Program, Inc. v. Ilchert
685 F. Supp. 712 (N.D. Ca. 1988)

SCHWARZER, District Judge.

... [P]laintiff Hong Kong T.V. Video Program, Inc., submitted a visa petition to the Immigration and Naturalization Service ("INS") to classify See Soo Chuan ("beneficiary") as a temporary worker of "distinguished merit and ability" pursuant to section 101(a)(15)(H)(i) of the Immigration and Nationality Act ("Act"), 8 U.S.C. § 1101(a)(15)(H)(i)....

The INS denied the petition on the grounds that a president and chief executive officer is not a member of a profession, that the beneficiary was not a professional because he did not have a university degree, that the person holding the position of president and chief executive officer of plaintiff was not required to be preeminent, and that the beneficiary was not preeminent in his field. The Administrative Appeals Unit ("AAU") dismissed plaintiff's appeal on July 8, 1986.

... [P]laintiff filed this action in federal court, seeking a declaration that the INS's denial of the petition was an abuse of discretion. Plaintiff moved for summary judgment, and defendant filed a cross-motion for summary judgment. A hearing on the motions was held on October 2, 1987. At the hearing, the Court stated that on the record as it then stood, the INS's denial appeared to be arbitrary and capricious and not supported by substantial evidence. However, the Court deferred ruling on the motions and gave the INS an opportunity to show cause why the plaintiff's nonimmigrant visa petition on behalf of the beneficiary should not be granted. The purpose of the deferral was to allow the INS to reconsider its decision.

The INS reopened plaintiff's visa petition proceedings for consideration of the factors set forth by the Court on the record... which again dismissed plaintiff's appeal and denied plaintiff's visa petition. That decision is now before the Court on the parties' previously filed and deferred cross-motions for summary judgment.

Plaintiff, a California corporation, imports and distributes motion picture and drama series foreign language video cassettes in Cantonese, Mandarin, Vietnamese, Cambodian, Thai, Korean, and Spanish languages. It is the largest Asian language video cassette distributor in the United States. It employs over seventy United States workers and has gross annual sales revenues of over eight million dollars.

Plaintiff seeks to employ the beneficiary as its president and chief executive officer. The beneficiary has twenty years of experience in business including temporary chief executive officer and president of plaintiff from 1981 to the present; special business advisor at Lumistar International Ltd. in Hong Kong from 1979 to the present; commission agent and coordinator for Lumistar International (Canada) Ltd. in Ontario from 1977 to 1980; joint venture in Dek's Corporation, an import/export business in Singapore from 1971 to 1976; sales manager with Star Trade Electronics Ltd. from 1969 to 1971; sales representative at Bright Office Equipment from 1964 to 1966; sales representative at Hageneyer Trading Co. Pte. Ltd. in Singapore from 1966 to 1969; sales executive with NCR Singapore, 1967-68; and special accounts sales representative for Olivetti in Singapore from 1967 to 1968.

As plaintiff's president, the beneficiary oversees monthly operating expenses of $150,000; controls a standard inventory of $500,000; is responsible for corporate, financial planning, marketing, and promotional strategy; negotiates contracts with United States licensees and Hong Kong HKTVB; supervises legal actions against video "pirates"; works on videotape anti-pirate technology; and makes high level decisions involving technical, legal and fiscal matters, capital improvements, and copyright infringement.

In support of the visa petition, plaintiff submitted a report from Oren Harari, a professor at McLaren College of Business, University of San Francisco. Professor Harari evaluates the professional experiences of students to determine whether their work experience may be translated into university credit. He found that the beneficiary was operating at a senior executive level of management and that his position, as president and chief executive officer, normally required an MBA. He also concluded that the beneficiary's record was "far more superior and impressive than the records which are ordinarily granted graduate credit" and that the beneficiary's work experience was equivalent to the content of a typical MBA program.

Professor Harari stated that the beneficiary could teach university level courses in Business Law (domestic and international, customs, copyright, trade, litigation), International Business (banking and currency exchange, capital budgeting, portfolio analysis, international strategic management and marketing), and Marketing Management (strategy, promotion, advertising, pricing, distribution, subcontracting, brokering and sales). He also stated that the beneficiary's impressive and extensive experience permitted him to be a guest lecturer in MBA courses dealing with marketing, sales, finance, operation, law, and personnel relations.

*   *   *

Section 101(a)(15)(H)(i) permits "an alien having a residence in a foreign country which he has no intention of abandoning . . . who is of distinguished merit and ability and who is coming temporarily to the United States to perform services of an exceptional nature requiring such merit and ability" to obtain an H-1 nonimmigrant visa.

The distinguished merit and ability test under this statute involves a two-step assessment. First, a person must occupy a position classifiable as a profession within the meaning of section 101(a)(32) to be classifiable as an alien of distinguished merit and ability. Secondly, the person must herself be a professional. *Matter of Gen. Atomic Co.*, 17 I. & N. Dec. 537 (Comm. 1980); *Matter of Essex Cryogenics Indus., Inc.*, 14 I. & N. Dec. 196 (Dep. Assoc. Comm. 1972). Alternatively, aliens of prominence, renown, or preeminence in their field may be classified as aliens of distinguished merit and ability.

*   *   *

The INS assumes that in order for an occupation to be a profession under section 101(a)(32), entrance into that occupation must, under the industry's standards, require at least a baccalaureate degree.

Examination of the occupations named in section 101(a)(32) of the Act indicates the following characteristics common to all: (1) recognition as a member of those professions normally requires the successful completion of a specified course of education on the college or university level, culminating in the attainment of a specific type of degree or diploma; and (2) the attainment of such a degree or diploma is usually the minimum requirement for entry into those occupations. *Matter of Asuncion*, 11 I. & N. Dec. 660 (Reg. Comm. 1966). In this case the INS maintains, therefore, that only occupations which have a degree requirement may be professions under 8 U.S.C. § 1011(a)(32).

Section 101(a)(32) of the Act states: "The term profession shall include but not be limited to architects, engineers, lawyers, physicians, surgeons, and teachers in elementary or secondary schools, colleges, academies, or seminaries." Thus the statute specifically states that the term "profession" is not limited to the occupations enumerated. The fact that certain professions are listed which usually require academic specialization as an entry level qualification does not preclude other kinds of professions or endeavors from being treated as professions within the meaning of subsection 32.

Subsection 32 covers a wide spectrum of "professions." It includes architects, engineers, physicians, surgeons and elementary teachers. Each listed profession requires different levels and types of higher education. Certainly the academic qualifications for an elementary school teacher cannot be considered equivalent to those of a surgeon or physician. Therefore, Congress clearly intended to permit a broad spectrum of occupations or positions with varying educational requirements to be treated as professions.

* * *

Moreover, the INS itself has not consistently required a degree as a prerequisite to classifying occupations as professions. *See Matter of Sun*, 12 I. & N. Dec. 535 (Reg. Comm. 1967). In *Matter of Sun*, the INS held that the vocation of hotel manager is a profession based on the complexity of the duties involved, not the existence of a degree. The INS concluded that the complex duties of personnel administration, establishing performance standards, allocating funds, planning budgets, authorizing expenditures, delegating authority, controlling and supervising performance of personnel, and insuring efficient and profitable operation of the hotel raised the occupation of hotel manager to a profession. The INS noted that as applied to the particular petitioner his degree supported his status as a professional. However, the INS did not consider the manager's degree in holding the occupation of hotel manager to be a profession.

The president of a multi-million dollar corporation, such as the plaintiff, performs all the duties performed by the hotel manager in Matter of Sun and numerous other duties including determining legal strategies and evaluating technical data. Therefore, like the hotel manager, the position of company president may be considered a profession based on the complexity of the duties alone.

The INS's determination in this case that the position of president and chief executive officer is not a profession simply because it does not require an academic degree is based on an erroneous interpretation of the statute and is in conflict with its own prior interpretation of the statute. For support of its determination, the INS relies on the Dictionary of Occupational Titles (4th ed. 1977). The Dictionary lists the occupation of president (DOT code 189.117-026) under the group of miscellaneous managers and officials not classified elsewhere. The classifications in the Dictionary include both professional and non-professional occupations and the locations do not purport to classify on the basis of whether an occupation is a profession. In any event president is listed in the Dictionary under the general heading of professional, technical and managerial occupations. Its worker function code, 117, which describes the responsibility level and functions of an occupation, is identical to that of a corporate lawyer (110.117-022), a patent lawyer (110.117-026), a hotel manager (187.117-038), and numerous other occupations which are classified as professions. Therefore, the location of the listing of president in the Dictionary of Occupational Titles contradicts rather than supports the INS's conclusion that president is not a profession. Accordingly, the INS's determination that the position of president and chief executive officer is not a profession is arbitrary and capricious and unsupported by substantial evidence.

* * *

Similarly, a person does not necessarily have to possess a degree to qualify as a professional under the statute. A university degree or its equivalent may demonstrate that the person is a member of a profession and a professional, but is not necessarily required. See Matter of Retino, 13 I. & N. Dec. 286 (R.C. 1969); Matter of Che, 12 I. & N. 146 (Dist. Dir. 1967).

The INS concluded that the beneficiary had neither a university degree nor its equivalent. While the beneficiary does not have an academic degree, substantial evidence supports the conclusion that he has the equivalent of a degree.

Professor Harari's opinion is the only evidence concerning the beneficiary's educational status. Professor Harari concluded that the beneficiary had at least the equivalent of an MBA. The INS did not question Professor Harari's qualifications to present this expert opinion during the initial determination, the first appeal or the Court's October 2, 1987 hearing. Nor has the INS presented any evidence to contradict Professor Harari's testimony. In its December 29, 1987 decision, the INS disregarded what it called Professor Harari's "allegedly advisory" opinion principally because he failed to specify "which aspects of the beneficiary's work experience may be equated to which courses and at which level." Decision at 5. However, after extensively discussing the beneficiary's past and present work experiences, Professor Harari specifically said that the beneficiary could "teach university courses in: Business Law (domestic and international, customs, copyright, trade, litigation), International Business (banking and currency exchange, capital budgeting, portfolio analysis . . .) and Market Management courses (strategy, promotion, advertising, . . .)," and be a guest lecturer in MBA courses covering marketing, sales, finance, operations, law, and personnel relations. Supplemental Administrative Record at 64. Obviously, if the beneficiary's experiences permit him to teach a course, those same experiences may be equated with the specific enumerated course he is qualified to teach.

The INS determination that the beneficiary is not a professional because he lacks the equivalent of a university degree is, therefore, arbitrary and capricious and unsupported by substantial evidence.

Notes

1. The situation presented in *Hong Kong Video*, where the only evidence available had been presented on behalf of the beneficiary, is common to most INS adjudications. From the advocate's perspective, *Hong Kong Video* teaches the importance of painstaking case preparation. As the representative of the INS's interest, how would you have presented the case differently?

2. *Hong Kong Video* demonstrates the nature of the disputes involving interpretations of the INA. The dispute in interpreting the statute can be characterized as a conflict between INS policy and legislative mandates. At what point should the courts become involved in such disputes?

3. Given the broad discretion delegated to the INS, should the agency also have discretion to interpret its statutes? Should Congress be more or less restrictive in what it delegates to the agency?

4. Given the INS's functions encompassing both enforcement and adjudication, is there an inherent conflict of interest within the INS? Should the INS's responsibilities be divided so that the enforcement officers are not involved in adjudications?

5. As noted earlier, H-1 visas are designated for persons of "distinguished merit and ability." *See* 8 U.S.C. § 1101(a)(15)(H)(i). Distinguished merit and ability may be established in two separate ways. First, a person may be a "professional" within the meaning of 8 U.S.C. § 1101(a)(32). *See Matter of General Atomic Co.*, 17 I. & N. Dec. 532 (Comm. 1980); *Matter of Essex Cryogenics Industries*, Inc., 14 I. & N. Dec. 196 (Dep. Assoc. Comm. 1972). Second, a person who is prominent or preeminent in their field may be classifiable as being of "distinguished merit and ability." *See Matter of Shaw*, 11 I. & N. Dec. 277 (Dist. Dir. 1966).

6. The traditional position of the INS has been that an occupation may be classifiable as "professional" where a baccalaureate degree is the minimal entrance requirement. See *Matter of Portugues Do Atlantico*, Interim Dec. 2982 (Comm. 1982). While this restrictive definition of professional has been modified it has been criticized by reviewing courts. See *Matter of Caron*, Interim Dec. 3085 (Comm. 1988) (recognizing substantial course work combined with experience as satisfactory of the requirement); 55 Fed. Reg. 2606, 2623 (1990) [to be codified at 8 C.F.R. § 214.2(h)(3)(ii)(A)]. For cases critical of the INS position, *see Augat v. Tovar*, 719 F. Supp. 1158 (D. Mass. 1989); *Hird/Blaker, Corp.*, 712 F. Supp. 1095 (S.D. N.Y. 1989).

7. Is the INS's interpretation of the statute which allows all persons classifiable as professionals to be eligible for H-1 status a reasonable interpretation?

8. It does not matter that the hiring of the foreign worker as an H-1 could displace a U.S. worker or that there might be an adverse effect on the wages and working conditions. In *Matter of Essex Cryogenics Industries, Inc.*, 14 I. & N. Dec. 196 (Dep. Assoc. Comm. 1972), where the INS district director had denied the employer's petition to classify an engineer as an H-1 employee, in part because it would grant foreign workers a benefit not available to U.S. workers, the claim was specifically rejected. Should this type of nonimmigrant visa include a requirement that the hiring of the foreign worker does not displace U.S. workers? If so, what type of procedure should be devised to accomplish this objective?

Matter of Artee Corporation
18 I. & N. Dec. 366 (Comm. 1982)

The sole issue in this case is the temporary need of the petitioner for the services of the beneficiary. In a situation involving a "temporary help" service, the Service has found that such a service is qualified to be and remains the actual employer of the beneficiary. *See Matter of Smith*, 12 I & N Dec. 774 (D.D. 1968). The petitioner in this case is a temporary help service and I agree with the Regional Commissioner that it qualifies as a petitioner and is the actual employer of the beneficiaries. The Regional Commissioner found that, because of the current wide-spread shortage of machinists in the United States, the nature of the employment offered must be viewed as permanent and not temporary. The decision examined the use of the beneficiaries' services by the customer of the help service in reaching this conclusion. I do not believe that this is the proper view of the employment situation involved. The test of the true nature of the temporary need for the position lies in examination of the temporary need of the temporary help service, not its customers.

Section 101(a)(15)(H)(ii) defines an H-2 temporary worker as an alien "who is coming temporarily to the United States to perform temporary services or labor, if unemployed persons capable of performing such services or labor cannot be found in this country...." As noted in *Matter of Contopoulos*, 10 I & N Dec. 654, 657 (Acting R.C. 1964), "... *both* the coming to the United States and the performance of service or labor must be *temporary*, the term 'temporary' being used twice." The nature of the duties to be performed were controlling, not the intent of the petitioner and the beneficiary concerning the time that the individual beneficiary would be employed in that position.

The Service now views this interpretation as incorrect. It is not the nature or the duties of the position which must be examined to determine the temporary need. It is the nature of the need for the duties to be performed which determines the temporariness of the position. Under this interpretation the key question in *Contopoulos* is: "Can the petitioner credibly establish that she has not employed a mother's helper in the past and that her need for a mother's helper will end in the near, definable future?" Likewise, in the instant case, the primary question becomes: "Can Artee establish that they have not employed machinists in the past and will not need the services of machinists in the near, definable future?" Here, as in *Contopoulos*, we are considering the second temporary requirement of the statute which concerns the position itself and not the first requirement which relates to the intent of the alien to enter for a temporary period. The function of a temporary help service is to provide for the fluctuating needs of other enterprises for specified services. In this case the petitioner provides technically-oriented personnel of a skilled nature to industries requiring such services. The customers of the petitioner do not have a steady need for a specific number of employees. Their business fluctuates and in so changing, their personnel needs change. To meet their needs, the customers of the petitioner turn to the petitioner to provide temporary help. While it is true that the temporary help may be needed for periods of 2 to 3 years, it is also true that shorter periods can be involved and that the need of the customer may not continue.

The situation of a temporary help service differs, however. The business of a temporary help service is to meet the temporary needs of its clients. To do this they must have a *permanent* cadre of employees available to refer their customers of the jobs for which there is frequently or generally a demand. By the very nature of this arrangement, it is obvious that a temporary help service will maintain on its payroll, more or less continuously, the types of skilled employee most in demand. This does not mean that a temporary help service can never offer employment of a temporary nature. If there is no demand for a particular type of skill, the temporary help service does not have a continuing and permanent need. Thus a temporary help service may be able to demonstrate that in addition to its regularly employed workers and permanent staff needs it also hires workers for temporary positions. For a temporary help service company, temporary positions would include positions requiring skill for which the company has a non-recurring demand or infrequent demand.

There is currently a wide-spread shortage of skilled machinists in the United States. Because of this shortage, the petitioner, as a prudent business measure, has ensured that it can supply machinists to its customers is ongoing. Therefore, as long as this universal shortage of machinists exists, the nature of the need for the position with the petitioner is such that the duties are not temporary and will persist as long as the shortage.

Matter of St. Pierre

18 I. & N. Dec. 308 (Reg. Comm. 1982)

This matter is before me on appeal from the District Director's decision of August 3, 1981, denying the petition to classify the beneficiary as a nonimmigrant trainee in accordance with section 101(a)(15)(H)(iii) of the Immigration and Nationality Act, as amended, 8 U.S.C. 1101(a)(15)(H)(iii). The appeal will be sustained.

The petitioner is an environmental consulting firm established in 1954 and located in Southfield, Michigan. Its business is to help industry and government identify and solve pollution problems. It has 65 employees and annual sales of $2.5 million. The beneficiary is a 44-year-old native and citizen of Canada. He is a professor of Chemical Engineering at the University of Windsor. He asked for and was granted an educational sabbatical with pay, of one year by his university in order to study industrial hygiene in the United States.

The beneficiary made application to the petitioner in 1980 for a one-year internship to learn survey and laboratory procedures in industrial hygiene such as:

- Evaluation of worker exposure to toxic chemicals such as lead, silica, benzene, and other potential cancer-causing chemicals.
- Evaluations and control of noise in the workplace.
- Evaluation and control of other physical stresses, such as radiation and heat and cold stress in industrial work environments.
- Development of new controls and procedures for minimizing/eliminating workplace hazards.

The petitioner accepted the beneficiary as an intern because of his superior credentials: Ph.D. from Northwestern University in Chemical Engineering (1965), engineering consultant and university professor since 1965. The beneficiary wanted to take his training with the petitioner in Southfield, Michigan because it was the only laboratory with facilities to provide industrial hygiene training close to Windsor.

The petitioner had five intern-trainees in the past and was training one at the time this petition was filed. The beneficiary will not receive any payment from the petitioner. Thus the suggestion of productive employment which would displace a resident worker which was noted in *Matter of Kraus Periodicals*, 11 I & N Dec. 63 (R.C. 1964), is absent. The beneficiary will continue to receive his professor's salary from the University of Windsor. He will return to his employment there at the end of one year's training. Thus the beneficiary is not being trained for eventual employment in the United States which was found impermissible in *Matter of Glencoe Press*, 11 I & N Dec. 764 (R.C. 1966).

Although the beneficiary's training is primarily on-the-job training, no productive labor will be involved because the beneficiary will be merely observing, not conducting field tests. The petitioner states that:

> Industrial hygiene, by its very nature, can only be learned in the work setting. It involves chemicals, noise, dust, gas and vapor measurement and testing done at the work site. Laboratory and office procedures involve research and evaluation of field tests and procedures. Thus it can only be learned by going into the field with trained professionally qualified regular company personnel.

However, the beneficiary will not be displacing a resident worker by his participation in this training program as required by *Matter of Treasure Craft of California*, 14 I & N Dec. 190 (R.C. 1972). The petitioner states that the beneficiary:

> ...will "tag along" on most field testing...he will perform little or no actual testing as most of the test procedures are performed under strict governmental reporting and sign-off requirements.... Obviously, the company could not jeopardize the credibility of its report by having [the beneficiary, an intern] do such work. The field work he would do is thus, in fact, extra or make-work for his use and benefit only. He would be the third man on a normal two man crew which would only need two men.

Thus the beneficiary will not, as required by *Matter of Miyaki Travel Agency, Inc.*, 10 I & N 644 (R.C. 1953), "be employed in a position which is in the normal operation of a business and in which citizens and resident aliens are regularly employed." (*Id.* at 645.)

* * *

I find that all the requirements of 8 C.F.R. 214.2(h)(2)(iii) (1981) and the precedent decisions relating to the H-3 classification have been met. The petitioner has specifically described a training program which will prepare the beneficiary to return to his position as Professor of Chemical Engineering with a sub-specialty in environmental engineering—a field just developing in Canada. The petitioner has demonstrated that this training is not available in Canada and must be taken here. The petitioner has established that the beneficiary will not be engaged in productive employment that might displace a resident worker.

E. Intracompany Transferees (L-1)

Matter of Chartier
16 I. & N. Dec. 284 (BIA 1977)

* * *

The respondent is a 52-year-old native and citizen of Canada. Immediately preceding the time of his application for admission to the United States, the respondent had been employed in Canada, as Canadian Manager of Technical Services, by Grow Chemical Company, a Michigan corporation.

Grow Chemical Company is a wholly owned subsidiary of Grow Chemical Corporation, headquartered in New York City. The parent corporation had sales of $92.8 million in 1975. The Michigan company forms part of the Automotive Group of the parent corporation. Other subsidiaries, which are part of this Automotive Group, are located in California and Belgium.

Grow Chemical Company manufactures and sells high efficiency thinners, solvents and specialty coatings for industrial applications. Its principal customers are manufacturers of automobiles, trucks and automotive parts in the United States, Canada and Western Europe.

Grow Chemical Company's sales to Canadian customers are approximately one million dollars a year. Despite this substantial Canadian business, the company has never established a Canadian subsidiary or even an office in Canada. Nor is the company officially licensed to do business in Canada. However, the company has stated that it intends to establish a Canadian sales and service subsidiary at some point, when market conditions and the supply of raw materials permit this.

When the respondent was employed by Grow in Canada, he worked out of his home. His job involved visiting automotive assembly plants on a regular basis to make sure that Grow's paint products were being applied properly.

In 1974, Grow decided to transfer the respondent to the United States, in order to perform similar services here.

The company filed a visa petition to classify the respondent as an intracompany transferee under section 101(a)(15)(L) of the Immigration and Nationality Act. The petition was approved by the District Director in Detroit, Michigan. The respondent entered the United States on June 14, 1974, with an L-1 nonimmigrant visa. He received extensions of stay, in the same status, until May 18, 1976. On September 17, 1974, the respondent brought his wife and four children from Etibicoke, Ontario, to Walled Lake, Michigan, to join him.

In July, 1975, the respondent filed an application for a labor certification from the Department of Labor. This event precipitated an investigation into the respondent's immigration status by the Immigration and Naturalization Service office in Detroit.

The District Director now decided that he had made a mistake in approving an L-1 visa petition in behalf of the respondent. The respondent was informed that he was not qualified for L-1 nonimmigrant status, and that he would be required to leave the United States. The respondent contested the District Director's interpretation of the law, and refused to leave the country voluntarily.

An Order to Show Cause was issued on November 14, 1975. In it, the Service charged that the respondent was not entitled to his L-1 visa classification because he was "not the representative of a foreign subsidiary or entity conducting business in Canada."

By this inartful language, what the Service meant to say was that the respondent's company did not have a subsidiary or affiliate in Canada, and that therefore he did not qualify as an intra-company transferee. The wording of the Order to Show Cause did not, however, cause any confusion.

Because he did not qualify as an intra-company transferee, continued the Order to Show Cause, the respondent was deportable under section 241(a)(1) of the Immigration and Nationality Act, in that, at the time of his entry he was within one or more of the classes of aliens excludable by the law, to wit, aliens who are nonimmigrant not in possession of a valid nonimmigrant visa, as described in section 212(a)(26) of the Act.

The Order to Show Cause also charged that the respondent was excludable under section 212(a)(2) of the Act as an immigrant not in possession of a valid, unexpired immigrant visa. In charging that the respondent entered the United States as an immigrant, the Service was alleging, somewhat redundantly, that, at the time of his entry, the respondent did not come within any of the defined classes of nonimmigrant set out in section 101(a)(15) of the Act. That same section of the Act defines the term "immigrant" as every alien who does not come within one of the defined classes of nonimmigrant.

The respondent denied deportability, claiming that, under a correct interpretation of section 101(a)(15)(L), he did qualify as an intra-company transferee. The respondent also argued that, even if the Service's interpretation of the Act was correct, it should be equitably estopped from deporting him, since it had approved his L-1 visa petition, and he had relied on that approval to his substantial detriment.

... Congress amended the Immigration and Nationality Act, to facilitate the entry of certain aliens into the United States, by creating additional categories of nonimmigrant. *See* Public Law 91-225.

※   ※   ※

The Service concedes that the express statutory language does not require the employer to have a subsidiary or other legal entity abroad. The Service argument is that such a requirement should be implied from the statutory requirement that the employment in the United States be temporary. The Service contends that if the corporation has not established foreign branch, there is no place for the alien to return to, and therefore his employment in the United States cannot be deemed temporary.

... [W]e are reluctant to read implied restrictions into the statute, particularly in the context of a deportation proceeding. It is settled doctrine that deportation statutes must be construed in favor of the alien. "Since the stakes are considerable for the individual, we will not assume that Congress meant to trench on his freedom beyond that which is required by the narrowest of several possible meanings of the words used." *Lennon v. INS*, 527 F.2d 187, 193 (2d Cir. 1975). *See Rosenberg v. Fleuti*, 374 U.S. 449, 459 (1963).

... [T]he Service has given us no reason to believe that its interpretation of the statute accords with Congress' intent. Section 101(a)(15)(L) was added to the Act in order to make it easier for corporations doing business in the United States to bring key foreign employees here to work.

The Service's interpretation of the statute would restrict the ability of companies such as Grow, which have not gone through the formalities of establishing subsidiaries or branch offices abroad, to bring their executives or technical specialists to the United States. We see no reason why a distinction should be made between United States companies with subsidiaries abroad and United States companies with employees abroad who work directly for the parent company.

The Service contends that this distinction is necessary to guarantee that the employee's stay in the United States be temporary. However, the Service ignores the possibility of sending the respondent back to his previous job in Canada. It also ignores the fact that Grow has an affiliate in Belgium to which the respondent could be sent after his sojourn in the United States.

Finally, the Service itself has consistently interpreted section 101(a)(15)(L) generously, so as to facilitate intra-company transfers.

The Service appears to be concerned by the fact that the respondent has applied for a labor certification, which may indicate that he intends to become a permanent resident if he can. However, there is nothing in the law which prevents the respondent from seeking to change his status to that of a lawful permanent resident. In fact, section 245 of the Act, which enables an alien to adjust his status to that of a lawful permanent resident without having to leave the United States to obtain an immigrant visa abroad, is designed to facilitate such changes of status.

F. Change and Maintenance of Status

Lun Kwai Tsui v. Attorney General
445 F. Supp. 832 (D.D.C. 1978)

FLANNERY, District Judge.

*   *   *

On February 13, 1976, plaintiffs were denied nonimmigrant visas by the United States Consul in La Paz, Bolivia. Plaintiffs reapplied for admission on May 28, 1976. In their application, they stated that they would be coming to the United States for a period of one month as tourists and would stay at the Surf Comber Hotel in Miami, Florida.

Plaintiffs were granted visas on July 2, 1976 in La Paz and entered this country on July 3. At that time, they requested and were granted a stay of six months in the United States and they represented to the inspector that they would be staying at an Annandale, Virginia address. On August 12, 1976, plaintiffs obtained certificates of eligibility for nonimmigrant student status from a private school in Falls Church, Virginia. On October 18, 1976, plaintiffs filed for a change of nonimmigrant status under 8 U.S.C. § 1258. In their applications, plaintiffs stated that their objective was to obtain an American education and that they did not apply for a student visa prior to entry because their parents decided that such an education was desirable after their arrival in the United States and consultation with school officials. They also submitted with their applications bank statements which indicated that each plaintiff had a bank account with a balance of $40,000.

The applications were rejected by the District Director of the Immigration and Naturalization Service (INS) on April 12, 1977. The basis for rejection was that at the time the applications for nonimmigrant visas were filed, plaintiffs had stated that they were entering for the purpose of tourism and that they would only stay one month before returning to China. In addition, the Director noted that they misrepresented the address at which they would be staying in their visa applications and promptly requested a six-month stay. He also pointed out that shortly after arriving they obtained the certificates of eligibility from the school and money was deposited in bank accounts for the plaintiffs. The Director concluded from these facts that the plaintiffs entered the United States with the intent of being students and therefore, denied the requested change.

Plaintiffs appealed to the Regional Commissioner of INS and submitted affidavits in support of their appeal. The Commissioner affirmed the Director's decision on August 17, 1977 and dismissed the appeal. The Commissioner held that plaintiffs were not bona fide visitors when they entered, but rather entered with the intent of becoming students. The Commissioner noted that the usual means for obtaining student visas was circumvented and that plaintiffs were excludable under 8 U.S.C. § 1182(a)(26), because they did not have proper documentation as nonimmigrants at that time. Therefore, the Commissioner held that plaintiffs were ineligible for a change of status under 8 U.S.C. § 1258.

*   *   *

Under 8 U.S.C. § 1258, a nonimmigrant alien may adjust his status from one classification to another subject to rules prescribed by the Attorney General provided that the alien has maintained his current nonimmigrant status. The burden of proof as to plaintiffs' eligibility for classification as nonimmigrant students is on them. *See* 8 U.S.C. § 2462; *Campos v. INS*, 402 F.2d 758, 760 (9th Cir. 1968). Thus, in this case at the administrative level the plaintiffs had to carry the burden of proof that they had maintained their status as nonimmigrant visitors for pleasure. The District Director and Regional Commissioner held that the plaintiffs do not possess valid nonimmigrant visas and therefore, they had not maintained their status. The basis for this conclusion was his opinion that the plaintiffs' obtaining visas as tourists was a pretext and that their original intent was to become students. Furthermore, they found that the plaintiffs were not properly documented as students at the time of entry and thus were inadmissible under 8 U.S.C. § 1182(a)(26). Thus, the Director and the Commissioner considered their present nonimmigrant visas invalid and the plaintiffs ineligible for a change of status under § 1258. See 8 U.S.C. § 1101(a)(15)(B).

The administrative record fully supports this finding with substantial evidence. The plaintiffs were issued visas as visitors for pleasure and gave the name of a hotel in Miami as their destination. Upon their arrival they obtained a six-month stay as temporary visitors and gave their destination as Annandale, Virginia. Prior to their arrival, their father transferred over $75,000 to a bank account in this country for their use. Within six weeks of their arrival, the plaintiffs obtained certificates of eligibility for nonimmigrant status as students from a private school in Virginia. On October 22, 1976, the plaintiffs filed applications for a change of status seeking student visas, including with the applications a bank certificate indicating that each plaintiff had a bank account of $40,000 to cover school expenses. Thus, it appears that the Director's and the Commissioner's conclusions that the plaintiffs' representations that they desired to enter this country for a brief visit were a pretext and that they actually intended to become students were not arbitrary, capricious, nor an abuse of discretion. Furthermore, the Commissioner and the Director properly understood and applied the relevant law in finding that the plaintiffs did not qualify for a change of status under § 1258. It is also apparent that the Commissioner and the

Director fully considered all of the relevant factors and the affidavits and the other evidence presented by the plaintiffs.

Plaintiffs' basic assertion is that INS has charged the plaintiffs with fraud and found their actions to have been fraudulent. Plaintiffs then present an extensive review of the law of fraud including the elements that must be established and the standards to be applied. It does not appear, however, that a determination of fraud is necessary in order to find that a nonimmigrant visa is invalid under 8 U.S.C. § 1182(a)(26). Although there has been no determination by the courts as to whether a finding of fraud is required by that section, it should be noted that there is another section specifically dealing with fraud and the government must prove that there were wilful, material misrepresentations under that section. 8 U.S.C. § 1182(a) (19); *Castaneda-Gonzalez v. INS*, 564 F.2d 417, 434 (D.C. Cir. 1977). In the present case, however, the government is not trying to deport the plaintiffs for misrepresentations under § 1182(a)(19). Therefore, it does not appear that a finding of fraud is necessary to a determination that a visa is invalid.

In any event, even if a finding of fraud is required by § 1182(a)(26), or the government is required to show wilful misrepresentations under § 1182(a)(19) to invalidate the visas, the grant of a change of nonimmigrant status is discretionary under § 1258. Thus, assuming *arguendo* that the facts in this case are insufficient to establish fraud by the plaintiffs, the questionable circumstances surrounding their entry certainly would warrant an exercise of discretion adverse to the plaintiffs. It was reasonable for the Commissioner and the Director to find that the plaintiffs were less than candid with immigration officials and therefore, a change in status from visitor to student was not warranted. It was not arbitrary, capricious, nor an abuse of discretion for these officials to decline to exercise their discretion in favor of the plaintiffs.

Plaintiffs also assert that the issuance of visas to them and their admission into this country preclude a challenge to the validity of their visas. Again, the exercise of discretion adverse to their applications can be upheld regardless of the validity of their visas. To address plaintiffs' point, however, it is evident that neither prior decisions of the State Department nor decisions of immigration inspectors are binding on the Attorney General and his delegates in subsequent proceedings.

Notes

1. Generally a nonimmigrant is not allowed to work while in the U.S. unless special permission is granted, or if employment is the basis for her visa. Unauthorized employment is a violation of the conditions of the person's status, thereby making her deportable.[20]

2. Once the person has obtained her nonimmigrant status, she must "maintain" this status. A person's failure or inability to maintain her nonimmigrant status will make her deportable.

3. An applicant's obtaining a nonimmigrant visa and entering the country with that visa is akin to entering into a contract. In this contract she is implicitly stating

---

20. Unauthorized employment, in addition to being a violation of the conditions of the alien's status, may cause the person to be ineligible for "adjustment of status," which will be discussed in greater detail in Chapter 7.

that she agrees to abide by all of the conditions relating to her nonimmigrant visa category. Violation of any one of those conditions can be grounds for deportation.

4. The most common grounds for violating one's nonimmigrant status are the following: (1) unauthorized employment, (2) failing to timely file for an extension of one's status, and (3) conviction for a crime of violence for which a sentence of more than 1 year could be imposed.

5. Most nonimmigrants (except those specifically prohibited from doing so by their nonimmigrant classification) may freely change from one nonimmigrant status to another.[21] A condition precedent to changing one's status is having properly maintained the status originally conferred upon entry. In addition, the applicant for a change of her classification must show that she qualifies for the new status. There is also the requirement described in *Lun Kwai Tsui v. Attorney General*, 445 F. Supp. 832 (D.D.C. 1978) that the applicant not have had a "preconceived intent" of obtaining the status in the first place.

6. **Extensions of status.** Invariably, many people with temporary work visas wish to remain in the U.S. Moreover, employers are also in need of their services. While E visas are indefinite, H and L visas may not be extended indefinitely. H-1 and L visas may be extended in increments of up to two years for a total of five years. This five year period can be extended for an additional year for extraordinary circumstances. H-2B visas may be extended for up to three years in one year increments. H-3 visas may be extended for up to two years in one year increments.

7. **Dual intent and permanent residency.** In recent years the unavailability of visas for immigrants has caused applicants to seek nonimmigrant visas and then later seek adjustment of their status to lawful permanent residency. This has raised conflicts as to whether the applicant is in fact a bona fide nonimmigrant. The INS promulgated regulations for H-1 and L visa holders which recognize the principal of "dual intent," the intention both to be a nonimmigrant as well as later to become a permanent resident. See 8 C.F.R. §§ 214.2(h)(16) and 214.2(l)((16); *see also Seihoon v. Levy*, 408 D. Supp. 1208, 1211 (M.D. La. 1976). Congress, through its enactment of the Immigration Act of 1990 removed the presumption of immigrant intent for H-1 and L visa applicants, making it much easier for these persons to sustain a claim of dual intent. *See* Sec. 205(b), Immigration Act of 1990, Pub. L. No. 101-649, 104 Stat. 4978 *amending* 8 U.S.C. §§ 1184(b) and (h), Sec. 214(b) and (h). Notwithstanding these changes, it should be noted that the INS determination to deny the application to change or adjust status is rarely overturned, as it is reviewed on an abuse of discretion standard. *See Patel v. Minnix*, 663 F.2d 1042 (5th Cir. 1981); *Mohammad v. Morris*, 477 F. Supp. 702 (E.D. Pa. 1979).

8. In order to qualify for a change or extension of status the applicant must have an unrelinquished domicile abroad which she has no intention of abandoning. How can this be reconciled with the provision allowing E visa holders to stay in the U.S indefinitely?

9. Assume that you are an immigration lawyer and a client comes to your office. During the course of your consultation the client tells you that she wishes to come to the U.S., yet gives you information which leads you to believe that she is ineligible

---

21. 8 U.S.C. § 1158 governs the requirements for change of nonimmigrant status. *See also* 8 C.F.R. § 248.

for any nonimmigrant visa. What advice will you give the client? Should she be advised to apply for the visa?

Nonimmigrant Visa Procedure

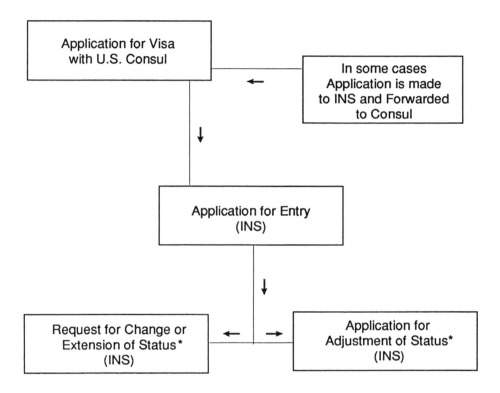

* Applicants for change and adjustment of status may be precluded from these benefits because of preconceived intent. *See* discussion in Chapter 9.

Index to Appendix

Nonimmigrants

8 U.S.C. § 1101(a)(15), Sec. 101

The term "immigrant" means every alien except an alien who is within one of the following classes of nonimmigrant aliens

(A)(i) an ambassador, public minister, or career diplomatic or consular officer who has been accredited by a foreign government, recognized *de jure* by the United States and who is accepted by the President or by the Secretary of State, and the members of the alien's immediate family; (ii) upon a basis of reciprocity, other officials

and employees who have been accredited by a foreign government recognized *de jure*
8 U.S.C. § 1101 by the United States, who are accepted by the Secretary of State, and
the members of their immediate families; and (iii) upon a basis of reciprocity, attendants, servants, personal employees, and members of their immediate families, of the
officials and employees who have a nonimmigrant status under (i) and (ii) above;

(B) an alien (other than one coming for the purpose of study or of performing
skilled or unskilled labor or as a representative of foreign press, radio, film, or other
foreign information media coming to engage in such vocation) having a residence in
a foreign country which he has no intention of abandoning and who is visiting the
United States temporarily for business or temporarily for pleasure;

(C) an alien in immediate and continuous transit through the United States, or
an alien who qualifies as a person entitled to pass in transit to and from the United
Nations Headquarters District and foreign countries, under the provisions of paragraphs (3), (4), and (5) of section 11 of the Headquarters Agreement with the United
Nations (61 Stat. 758);

(D)(i) an alien crewman serving in good faith as such in any capacity required
for normal operation and service on board a vessel (other than a fishing vessel having
its home port or an operating base in the United States) or aircraft, who intends to
land temporarily and solely in pursuit of his calling as a crewman and to depart from
the United States with the vessel or aircraft on which he arrived or some other vessel
or aircraft; (ii) an alien crewman serving in good faith as such in any capacity required
for normal operations and service aboard a fishing vessel having its home port or an
operating base in the United States who intends to land temporarily in Guam and
solely in pursuit of his calling as a crewman and to depart from Guam with the vessel
on which he arrived;

(E) an alien entitled to enter the United States under and in pursuance of the
provisions of a treaty of commerce and navigation between the United States and the
foreign state of which he is a national, and the spouse and children of any such alien
if accompanying or following to join him; (i) solely to carry on substantial trade,
including trade in services or trade in technology, principally between the United
States and the foreign state of which he is a national; or (ii) solely to develop and
direct the operations of an enterprise in which he has invested, or of an enterprise in
which he is actively in the process of investing, a substantial amount of capital;

(F)(i) an alien having a residence in a foreign country which he has no intention
of abandoning, who is a bona fide student qualified to pursue a full course of study
and who seeks to enter the United States temporarily and solely for the purpose of
pursuing such a course of study at an established college, university, seminary, conservatory, academic high school, elementary school, or other academic institution or
in a language training program in the United States, particularly designated by him
and approved by the Attorney General after consultation with the Secretary of Education, which institution or place of study shall have agreed to report to the Attorney
General the termination of attendance of each nonimmigrant student, and if any such
institution of learning or place of study fails to make reports promptly the approval
shall be withdrawn, and (ii) the alien spouse and minor children of any such alien if
accompanying him or following to join him;

(G)(i) a designated principal resident representative of a foreign government
recognized de jure by the United States, which foreign government is a member of

an international organization entitled to enjoy privileges, exemptions, and immunities as an international organization under the International Organizations Immunities Act (59 Stat. 669) [22 U.S.C. § 288 et seq.], accredited resident members of the staff of such representatives, and members of his or their immediate family; (ii) other accredited representatives of such a foreign government to such international organizations, and the members of their immediate families; (iii) an alien able to qualify under (i) or (ii) above except for the fact that the government of which such alien is an accredited representative is not recognized de jure by the United States, or that the government of which he is an accredited representative is not a member of such international organization; and the members of his immediate family; (iv) officers, or employees of such international organizations, and the members of their immediate families; (v) attendants, servants, and personal employees of any such representative, officer, or employee, and the members of the immediate families of such attendants, servants, and personal employees;

(H) an alien (i)(a)[22] who is coming temporarily to the United States to perform services as a registered nurse, who meets the qualifications described in section 212(m)(1) and with respect to whom the Secretary of Labor determines and certifies to the Attorney General that an unexpired attestation is on file and in effect under section 212(m)(2) for each facility (which facility shall include the petitioner and each worksite, other than a private household worksite, if the worksite is not the alien's employer or controlled by the employer) for which the alien will perform the services, or (b) who is coming temporarily to the United States to perform services (other than services described in subclause (a) during the period in which such subclause applies and other than services described in subclause (ii)(a) or in subparagraph (O) or (P)) in a specialty occupation described in section 214(i)(1), who meets the requirements for the occupation specified in section 214(i)(2), and with respect to whom the Secretary of Labor determines and certifies to the Attorney General that the intending employer has filed with, and had approved by, the Secretary an application under section 212(n)(1); or (ii) (a) having a residence in a foreign country which he has no intention of abandoning who is coming temporarily to the United States to perform agricultural labor or services, as defined by the Secretary of Labor in regulations and including agricultural labor defined in section 3121(g) of Title 26 and agriculture as defined in section 203(f) of Title 29, of a temporary or seasonal nature, or (b) having a residence in a foreign country which he has no intention of abandoning who is coming temporarily to the United States to perform other temporary service or labor if unemployed persons capable of performing such service or labor cannot be found in this country, but this clause shall not apply to graduates of medical schools coming to the United States to perform services as members of the medical profession; or (iii) having a residence in a foreign country which he has no intention of abandoning who is coming temporarily to the United States as a trainee, other than to receive graduate medical education or training; and the alien spouse and minor children of any such alien specified in this paragraph if accompanying him or following to join him in a training program that is not designed primarily to provide productive employment;

---

22. 8 U.S.C. § 1101(a)(15)(H)(i)(a), Sec. 101(a)(15)(H)(i)(a) was added by the Immigration Nursing Relief Act of 1989, Pub. L. No. 101-238, 103 Stat. 2099.

(I) upon a basis of reciprocity, an alien who is a bona fide representative of foreign press, radio, film, or other foreign information media, who seeks to enter the United States solely to engage in such vocation, and the spouse and children of such a representative, if accompanying or following to join him;

(J) an alien having a residence in a foreign country which he has no intention of abandoning who is a bona fide student, scholar, trainee, teacher, professor, research assistant, specialist, or leader in a field of specialized knowledge or skill, or other person of similar description, who is coming temporarily to the United States as a participant in a program designated by the Director of the United States Information Agency, for the purpose of teaching, instructing or lecturing, studying, observing, conducting research, consulting, demonstrating special skills, or receiving training and who, if he is coming to the United States to participate in a program under which he will receive graduate medical education or training, also meets the requirements of section 1182(j) of this title, and the alien spouse and minor children of any such alien if accompanying him or following to join him;

(K) an alien who is the fiancee or fiance of a citizen of the United States and who seeks to enter the United States solely to conclude a valid marriage with the petitioner within ninety days after entry, and the minor children of such fiancee or fiance accompanying him or following to join him;

(L) an alien who, within 3 years preceding the time of his application for admission into the United States, has been employed continuously for one year by a firm or corporation or other legal entity or an affiliate or subsidiary thereof and who seeks to enter the United States temporarily in order to continue to render his services to the same employer or a subsidiary or affiliate thereof in a capacity that is managerial, executive, or involves specialized knowledge, and the alien spouse and minor children of any such alien if accompanying him or following to join him;

(M)(i) an alien having a residence in a foreign country which he has no intention of abandoning who seeks to enter the United States temporarily and solely for the purpose of pursuing a full course of study at an established vocational or other recognized nonacademic institution (other than in a language training program) in the United States particularly designated by him and approved by the Attorney General, after consultation with the Secretary of Education, which institution shall have agreed to report to the Attorney General the termination of attendance of each nonimmigrant nonacademic student and if any such institution fails to make reports promptly the approval shall be withdrawn, and (ii) the alien spouse and minor children of any such alien if accompanying him or following to join him; or

(N)(i) the parent of an alien accorded the status of special immigrant under paragraph (27)(I)(i), but only if and while the alien is a child, or (ii) a child of such parent or of an alien accorded the status of a special immigrant under clause (ii), (iii), or (iv) of paragraph (27)(I).

(O)[23] An alien who—(i) has extraordinary ability in the sciences, arts, education, business, or athletics which has been demonstrated by sustained national or international acclaim or, with regard to motion picture and television productions a demonstrated record of extraordinary achievement, and whose achievements have

---

23. The entire subsections (O) through (R) of Title 8 of the United States Code were added by the Immigration Act of 1990.

been recognized in the field through extensive documentation, and seeks to enter the United States to continue work in the area of extraordinary ability, but only if the Attorney General determines that the alien's entry into the United States will substantially benefit prospectively the United States; or (ii)(I) seeks to enter the United States temporarily and solely for the purpose of accompanying and assisting in the artistic or athletic performance by an alien who is admitted under clause (i) for a specific event or events, (II) is an integral part of such actual performance, (III)(a) has critical skills and experience with such alien which are not of a general nature and which cannot be performed by other individuals, or (b) in the case of a motion picture or television production, has skills and experience with such alien which are not of a general nature and which are critical either based on a pre-existing long-standing working relationship or, with respect to the specific production, because significant principal photography will take place both inside and outside the United States and the continuing participation of the alien is essential to the successful completion of the production, and (IV) has a foreign residence which the alien has no intention of abandoning; or (iii) is the alien spouse or child of an alien described in clause (i) or (ii) and is accompanying, or following to join, the alien; or

(P) an alien having a foreign residence which the alien has no intention of abandoning who—(i)(I) performs as an athlete, individually or as part of a group or team, at an internationally recognized level of performance, or performs as part of an entertainment group that has been recognized internationally as being outstanding in the discipline for a sustained and substantial period of time and has had a sustained and substantial relationship with that group over a period of at least 1 year and provides functions integral to the performance of the group, and (II) seeks to enter the United States temporarily and solely for the purpose of performing as such an athlete or entertainer with respect to a specific athletic competition or performance; (ii)(I) performs as an artist or entertainer, individually or as part of a group, or is an integral part of the performance of such a group, and (II) seeks to enter the United States temporarily and solely for the purpose of performing as such an artist or entertainer or with such a group under a reciprocal exchange program which is between an organization or organizations in the United States and an organization in one or more foreign states and which provides for the temporary exchange of artists and entertainers, or groups of artists and entertainers, between the United States and the foreign states involved; (iii)(I) performs as an artist or entertainer, individually or as part of a group, or is an integral part of the performance of such a group, and (II) seeks to enter the United States temporarily and solely for the purpose of performing as such an artist or entertainer or with such a group under a program that is culturally unique; or (iv) is the spouse or child of an alien described in clause (i), (ii), or (iii) and is accompanying, or following to join, the alien;

(Q) an alien having a residence in a foreign country which he has no intention of abandoning who is coming temporarily (for a period not to exceed 15 months) to the United States as a participant in an international cultural exchange program designated by the Attorney General for the purpose of providing practical training, employment, and the sharing of the history, culture, and traditions of the country of the alien's nationality and who will be employed under the same wages and working conditions as domestic workers; or

(R) an alien, and the spouse and children of the alien if accompanying or following to join the alien, who—(i) for the 2 years immediately preceding the time of application for admission, has been a member of a religious denomination having a bona fide nonprofit, religious organization in the United States; and (ii) seeks to enter the United States for a period not to exceed 5 years to perform the work described in subclause (I), (II), or (III) of paragraph (27)(C)(ii).

*   *   *

8 U.S.C. § 1184(a), Sec. 214(a)—Admission of Nonimmigrants[24]

*   *   *

(2)(A) The period of authorized status as a nonimmigrant under section 101(a)(15)(O) shall be for such period as the Attorney General may specify in order to provide for the event for which the nonimmigrant is admitted.

    (B)(i) The period of authorized status as a nonimmigrant described in section 101(a)(15)(P) shall be for such period as the Attorney General may specify in order to provide for the competition, event, or performance for which the nonimmigrant is admitted. In the case of nonimmigrants admitted as individual athletes under section 101(a)(15)(P), the period of authorized status may be for an initial period (not to exceed 5 years) during which the nonimmigrant will perform as an athlete and such period may be extended by the Attorney General for an additional period of up to 5 years.

    (ii) An alien who is admitted as a nonimmigrant under clause (ii) or (iii) of section 101(a)(15)(P) may not be readmitted as such a nonimmigrant unless the alien has remained outside the United States for at least 3 months after the date of the most recent admission. The Attorney General may waive the application of the previous sentence in the case of individual tours in which the application would work an undue hardship; and

8 U.S.C. § 1184(b), Sec. 214. Presumption of status

(b) Every alien other than a nonimmigrant described in subparagraph (H)(i) or (L) of section 101(a)(15) shall be presumed to be an immigrant until he establishes to the satisfaction of the consular officer, at the time of application for a visa, and the immigration officers, at the time of application for admission, that he is entitled to a nonimmigrant status under section 1101(a)(15) of this title. An alien who is an officer or employee of any foreign government or of any international organization entitled to enjoy privileges, exemptions, and immunities under the International Organizations Immunities Act (22 U.S.C. § 288 et seq.), or an alien who is the attendant, servant, employee, or member of the immediate family of any such alien shall not be entitled to apply for or receive an immigrant visa, or to enter the United States as an immigrant unless he executes a written waiver in the same form and substance as is prescribed by section 1257(b) of this title.

8 U.S.C. § 1184(c)-(e), Sec. 214(c)-(e). Admission of certain nonimmigrant categories.

(c)(1) The question of importing any alien as a nonimmigrant under section 1101 (a)(15)(H), (L), (O), or (P)(i) of this title in any specific case or specific cases shall be determined by the Attorney General, after consultation with appropriate agencies

---

24. Added by the Sec. 207(b), Immigration Act of 1990, Pub. L. No. 101-649, 104 Stat. 4978.

of the Government, upon petition of the importing employer. Such petition shall be made and approved before the visa is granted. The petition shall be in such form and contain such information as the Attorney General shall prescribe. The approval of such a petition shall not, of itself, be construed as establishing that the alien is a nonimmigrant. For purposes of this subsection with respect to nonimmigrants described in section 1101(a)(15)(H)(ii)(a) of this title, the term "appropriate agencies of Government" means the Department of Labor and includes the Department of Agriculture. The provisions of section 1186 of this title shall apply to the question of importing any alien as a nonimmigrant under section 1101(a)(15)(H)(ii)(a) of this title.

(2)(A) The Attorney General shall provide for a procedure under which an importing employer which meets requirements established by the Attorney General may file a blanket petition to import aliens as nonimmigrants described in section 101(a)(15)(L) instead of filing individuals petitions under paragraph (1) to import such aliens. Such procedure shall permit the expedited processing of visas for entry of aliens covered under such a petition.

(B) For purposes of section 101(a)(15)(L), an alien is considered to be serving in a capacity involving specialized knowledge with respect to a company if the alien has a special knowledge of the company product and its application in international markets or has an advanced level of knowledge of processes and procedures of the company.

(C) The Attorney General shall provide a process for reviewing and acting upon petitions under this subsection with respect to nonimmigrants described in section 101(a)(15)(L) within 30 days after the date a completed petition has been filed.

(D) The period of authorized admission for—

(i) a nonimmigrant admitted to render services in a managerial or executive capacity under section 101(a)(15)(L) shall not exceed 7 years, or

(ii) a nonimmigrant admitted to render services in a capacity that involved specialized knowledge under section 101(a)(15)(L) shall not exceed 5 years.

(3) The Attorney General shall approve a petition—

(A) with respect to a nonimmigrant described in section 101(a)(15)(O)(i) only after consultation with peer groups in the area of the alien's ability or, with respect to aliens seeking entry for a motion picture or television production, after consultation with the appropriate union representing the alien's occupational peers and a management organization in the area of the alien's ability, or

(B) with respect to a nonimmigrant described in section 101(a)(15)(O)(ii) after consultation with labor organizations with expertise in the skill area involved. In the case of an alien seeking entry for a motion picture or television production, (i) any opinion under the previous sentence shall only be advisory, (ii) any such opinion that recommends denial must be in writing, (iii) in making the decision the Attorney General shall consider the exigencies and scheduling of the production, and (iv) the Attorney General shall append to the decision any such opinion.

(4)(A) A person may petition the Attorney General for classification of an alien as a nonimmigrant under clause (ii) of section 101(a)(15)(P).

(B) The Attorney General shall approve petitions under this subsection with respect to nonimmigrants described in clause (i) or (iii) of section 101(a)(15)(P) only after consultation with labor organizations with expertise in the specific field of athletics or entertainment involved.

(C) The Attorney General shall approve petitions under this subsection for nonimmigrants described in section 101(a)(15)(P)(ii) only after consultation with labor organizations representing artists and entertainers in the United States, in order to assure reciprocity in fact with foreign states.

(5) In the case of an alien who is provided nonimmigrant status under section 101(a)(15)(H)(i)(b) or 101(H)(ii)(b) and who is dismissed from employment by the employer before the end of the period of authorized admission, the employer shall be liable for the reasonable costs of return transportation of the alien abroad.

(6) If a petition is filed and denied under this subsection, the Attorney General shall notify the petitioner of the determination and the reasons for the denial and of the process by which the petitioner may appeal the determination.

(d) A visa shall not be issued under the provisions of section 1101(a)(15)(K) of this title until the consular officer has received a petition filed in the United States by the fiancee or fiance of the applying alien and approved by the Attorney General. The petition shall be in such form and contain such information as the Attorney General shall, by regulation, prescribe. It shall be approved only after satisfactory evidence is submitted by the petitioner to establish that the parties have previously met in person within 2 years before the date of filing the petition, have a bona fide intention to marry and are legally able and actually willing to conclude a valid marriage in the United States within a period of ninety days after the alien's arrival. In the event the marriage with the petitioner does not occur within three months after the entry of the said alien and minor children, they shall be required to depart from the United States and upon failure to do so shall be deported in accordance with sections 1252 and 1253 of this title except that the Attorney General in his discretion may waive the requirement that the parties have previously met in person.

(e)[25] Notwithstanding any other provisions of this Act, an alien who is a citizen of Canada and seeks to enter the United States under and pursuant to the provisions of Annex 1502.1 (United States of America), Part C—Professionals, of the United States-Canada Free-Trade Agreement to engage in business activities at a professional level as provided for therein may be admitted for such purpose under regulations of the Attorney General promulgated after consultation with the Secretaries of State and Labor.

8 U.S.C. § 1184(g), Sec. 214(g)—Limitation on Numbers of Temporary Workers and Trainees.[26]

(g)(1) The total number of aliens who may be issued visas or otherwise provided nonimmigrant status during any fiscal year (beginning with fiscal year 1992)—

(A) under section 101(a)(15)(H)(i)(b) may not exceed 65,000,

---

25. 8 U.S.C. § 1184(e), Sec. 214(e) was added by Section 307(b) of the United States-Canada Free-Trade Agreement Implementation Act of 1988, Pub. L. No. 100-449, 102 Stat. 1851 (1988).

26. Added by the Sec. 205(a), Immigration Act of 1990, Pub. L. No. 101-649, 104 Stat. 4978.

(B) under section 101(a)(15)(H)(ii)(b) may not exceed 66,000, or

(C) under section 101(a)(15)(P)(i) or section 101(a)(15)(P)(iii) may not exceed 25,000.

(2) The numerical limitations of paragraph (1) shall only apply to principal aliens and not to the spouses or children of such aliens.

(3) Aliens who are subject to the numerical limitations of paragraph (1) shall be issued visas (or otherwise provided nonimmigrant status) in the order in which petitions are filed for such visas or status.

(4) In the case of a nonimmigrant described in section 101(a)(15)(H)(i)(b), the period of authorized admission as such a nonimmigrant may not exceed 6 years.

8 U.S.C. § 1184(h), Sec. 214(h)—Construction Respecting Intent of Abandonment of Foreign Residence.[27]

(h) The fact that an alien is the beneficiary of an application for a preference status filed under section 204 or has otherwise sought permanent residence in the United States shall not constitute evidence of an intention to abandon a foreign residence for purposes of obtaining a visa as a nonimmigrant described in subparagraph (H)(i) or (L) of section 101(a)(15) or otherwise obtaining or maintaining the status of a nonimmigrant described in such subparagraph, if the alien had obtained a change of status under section 248 to a classification as such a nonimmigrant before the alien's most recent departure from the United States.

*   *   *

Change of Nonimmigrant Classification

8 U.S.C. § 1258, Sec. 248

The Attorney General may, under such conditions as he may prescribe, authorize a change from any nonimmigrant classification to any other nonimmigrant classification in the case of any alien lawfully admitted to the United States as a nonimmigrant who is continuing to maintain that status, except in the case of—

(1) an alien classified as a nonimmigrant under subparagraph (C), (D), or (K) of section 1101(a)(15) of this title,

(2) an alien classified as a nonimmigrant under subparagraph (J) of section 1101(a)(15) of this title who came to the United States or acquired such classification in order to receive graduate medical education or training,

(3) an alien (other than an alien described in paragraph (2)) classified as a nonimmigrant under subparagraph (J) of section 1101(a)(15) of this title who is subject to the two-year foreign residence requirement of section 1182(e) of this title and has not received a waiver thereof, unless such alien applies to have the alien's classification changed from classification under subparagraph (J) of section 1101(a)(15) of this title to a classification under subparagraph (A) or (G) of such section, and

(4) an alien admitted as a nonimmigrant visitor without a visa under section 212(l) or 217.

---

27. Added by Sec. 205(b)(2), Immigration Act of 1990, Pub. L. No. 101-649, 104 Stat. 4978.

Definitions

8 U.S.C. § 1101(a), Sec. 101(a)

(16) The term "immigrant visa" means an immigrant visa required by this chapter and properly issued by a consular officer at his office outside of the United States to an eligible immigrant under the provisions of this chapter.

(17) The term "immigration laws" includes this chapter and all laws, conventions, and treaties of the United States relating to the immigration, exclusion, deportation, or expulsion of aliens.

(18) The term "immigration officer" means any employee or class of employees of the Service or of the United States designated by the Attorney General, individually or by regulation, to perform the functions of an immigration officer specified by this chapter or any section of this title.

8 U.S.C. § 1184(i), Sec. 214(i)—Specialty Occupation Defined.[28]

(1) For purposes of section 101(a)(15)(H)(i)(b) and paragraph (2), the term "specialty occupation" means an occupation that requires—

(A) theoretical and practical application of a body of highly specialized knowledge, and

(B) attainment of a bachelor's or higher degree in the specific specialty (or its equivalent) as a minimum for entry into the occupation in the United States.

(2) For purposes of section 101(a)(15)(H)(i)(b), the requirements of this paragraph, with respect to a specialty occupation, are—

(A) full state licensure to practice in the occupation, if such licensure is required to practice in the occupation,

(B) completion of the degree described in paragraph (1)(B) for the occupation, or

(C)(i) experience in the specialty equivalent to the completion of such degree, and

(ii) recognition of expertise in the specialty through progressively responsible positions relating to the specialty.

Regulations Relating to Nonimmigrants

Extensions and Maintenance

8 C.F.R. § 214.1

Requirements for admission, extension, and maintenance of status.

(a) General. Every nonimmigrant alien who applies for admission to, or an extension of stay in, the United States, shall establish that he or she is admissible to the United States, or that any ground of inadmissibility has been waived under section 212(d)(3) of the Act. Upon application for admission, the alien shall present a valid passport and valid visa unless either or both documents have been waived. However, an alien applying for extension of stay shall present a passport only if requested to do so by

---

28. Added by Sec. 205(c)(2), Immigration Act of 1990, Pub. L. No. 101-649, 104 Stat. 4978.

the Service. The passport of an alien applying for admission shall be valid for a minimum of six months from the expiration date of the contemplated period of stay, unless otherwise provided in this chapter, and the alien shall agree to abide by the terms and conditions of his or her admission. The passport of an alien applying for extension of stay shall be valid at the time of application for extension, unless otherwise provided in this chapter, and the alien shall agree to maintain the validity of his or her passport and to abide by all the terms and conditions of his extension. The alien shall also agree to depart the United States at the expiration of his or her authorized period of admission or extension, or upon abandonment of his or her authorized nonimmigrant status. At the time a nonimmigrant alien applies for admission or extension of stay he or she shall post a bond on Form I-352 in the sum of not less than $500, to insure the maintenance of his or her nonimmigrant status and departure from the United States, if required to do so by the director, immigration judge, or Board of Immigration Appeals.

(b) Readmission of nonimmigrants under section 101(a)(15)(F), (J), or (M) to complete unexpired periods of previous admission or extension of stay.

(1) Section 101(a)(15)(F). The inspecting immigration officer shall readmit for duration of status as defined in § 214.2(f)(5)(iii), any nonimmigrant alien whose nonimmigrant visa is considered automatically revalidated pursuant to 22 CFR 41.125(f) and who is applying for readmission under section 101(a)(15)(F) of the Act, if the alien:

(i) Is admissible;

(ii) Is applying for readmission after an absence from the United States not exceeding thirty days solely in contiguous territory or adjacent islands;

(iii) Is in possession of a valid passport unless exempt from the requirement for presentation of a passport; and

(iv) Presents, or is the accompanying spouse or child of an alien who presents, an Arrival-Departure Record, Form I-94, issued to the alien in connection with the previous admission or stay, the alien's Form I-20 ID copy, and either: (A) A properly endorsed page 4 of Form I-20A-B if there has been no substantive change in the information on the student's most recent Form I-20A since the form was initially issued; or (B) A new Form I-20A-B if there has been any substantive change in the information on the student's most recent Form I-20A since the form was initially issued.

(2) Section 101(a)(15)(J). The inspecting immigration officer shall readmit for the unexpired period of stay authorized prior to the alien's departure, any nonimmigrant alien whose nonimmigrant visa is considered automatically revalidated pursuant to 22 CFR 41.125(f) and who is applying for readmission under section 101(a)(15)(J) of the Act, if the alien:

(i) Is admissible;

(ii) Is applying for readmission after an absence from the United States not exceeding thirty days solely in contiguous territory or adjacent islands;

(iii) Is in possession of a valid passport unless exempt from the requirement for presentation of a passport; and

(iv) Presents, or is the accompanying spouse or child of an alien who presents, Form I-94, issued to the alien in connection with the previous admission or stay or copy three of the last Form IAP-66 issued to the alien. Form I-94 or Form IAP-66 must show the unexpired period of the alien's stay endorsed by the Service.

(3) Section 101(a)(15)(M). The inspecting immigration officer shall readmit for the unexpired period of stay authorized prior to the alien's departure, any nonimmigrant alien whose nonimmigrant visa is considered automatically revalidated pursuant to 22 CFR 41.125(f) and who is applying for readmission under section 101(a)(15)(M) of the Act, if the alien:

(i) Is admissible;

(ii) Is applying for readmission after an absence not exceeding thirty days solely in contiguous territory;

(iii) Is in possession of valid passport unless exempt from the requirement for presentation of a passport; and

(iv) Presents, or is the accompanying spouse or child of an alien who presents, Form I-94, issued to the alien in connection with the previous admission or stay, the alien's Form I-20 ID copy, and a properly endorsed page 4 of Form I-20M-N.

(c) Extension of stay.—

(1) General. Any nonimmigrant alien defined in section 101(a)(15)(A)(i) or (ii) or (G)(i), (ii), (iii), or (iv) of the Act is to be admitted for, or granted a change of nonimmigrant classification for, as long as that alien continues to be recognized by the Secretary of State for that status. The alien need not apply for an extension of stay. Any nonimmigrant alien defined in section 101(a)(15)(C), (D), or (K) of the Act, or any alien admitted in transit without a visa, is ineligible for an extension of stay. A nonimmigrant defined in section 101(a)(15)(F) or (M) of the Act shall apply for an extension of stay on Form I-538. A nonimmigrant alien defined in section 101(a)(15)(J) of the Act shall apply for an extension of stay on Form IAP-66. An alien in any other nonimmigrant classification shall apply for an extension of stay on Form I-539. Except as provided in paragraph (c)(3) of this section, each alien seeking an extension of stay generally must execute and submit a separate application for extension of stay to the district office having jurisdiction over the alien's place of temporary residence in the United States.

(2) Time of filing application. The application must be submitted at least fifteen days but not more than sixty days before the expiration of the alien's currently authorized stay. If failure to file a timely application is found to be excusable, an extension of stay may be granted, but the extension must date from the time of expiration of the previously authorized stay.

(3) Family members of principal alien. Regardless of whether a principal nonimmigrant alien's spouse and minor unmarried children accompanied the principal alien to the United States, the spouse and children may be included in the principal alien's application for extension of stay without any additional fee. Extensions granted to members of a family group must be for the same period of time. If one member is eligible for only a six-month extension and another for a twelve-month extension, the shorter period will be granted to all members of the family.

(4) Decision on application for extension of stay. The district director shall notify the applicant of the decision and, if the application is denied, of the reason(s) for the denial. The applicant may not appeal the decision.

(5) Less than thirty days' additional time. When, because of conditions beyond an alien's control or other special circumstances, an alien needs an additional period of less than thirty days beyond the previously authorized stay within which to depart from the United States, the alien may present the alien's Form I-94 or, in the case of a nonimmigrant defined in section 101(a)(15)(F) or (M) of the Act, the alien's Form I-20 ID copy, at the district office having jurisdiction over the alien's place of temporary residence in the United States. The requested time may be granted without a formal application.

(6) Bonds. For procedures on cancelling and breaching bonds, see § 103.6(c) and (e) of this title.

(d) Termination of status. Within the period of initial admission or extension of stay, the nonimmigrant status of an alien shall be terminated by the revocation of a waiver previously authorized in his behalf under section 212(d)(3) or (4) of the Act; or by the introduction of a private bill to confer permanent resident status on such alien.

(e) Employment. A nonimmigrant in the United States in a class defined in section 101(a)(15)(B) of the Act as a temporary visitor for pleasure, or section 101(a)(15)(C) of the Act as an alien in transit through this country, may not engage in any employment. Any other nonimmigrant in the United States may not engage in any employment unless he has been accorded a nonimmigrant classification which authorizes employment or he has been granted permission to engage in employment in accordance with the provisions of this chapter. A nonimmigrant who is permitted to engage in employment may engage only in such employment as has been authorized. Any unauthorized employment by a nonimmigrant constitutes a failure to maintain status within the meaning of section 241(a)(9) of the Act.

(f) False information. A condition of a nonimmigrant's admission and continued stay in the United States is the full and truthful disclosure of all information requested by the Service. Willful failure by a nonimmigrant to provide full and truthful information requested by the Service (regardless of whether or not the information requested was material) constitutes a failure to maintain nonimmigrant status under Section 241(a)(9) of the Act.

(g) Criminal activity. A condition of a nonimmigrant's admission and continued stay in the United States is obedience to all laws of United States jurisdictions which prohibit the commission of crimes of violence and for which a sentence of more than one year imprisonment may be imposed. A nonimmigrant's conviction in a jurisdiction in the United States for a crime of violence for which a sentence of more than one year imprisonment may be imposed (regardless of whether such sentence is in fact imposed) constitutes a failure to maintain status under Section 241(a)(9) of the Act.

*   *   *

Tourists and Visitors for Business

8 C.F.R. § 214.2(b)

(1) General. Any B-1 visitor for business or B-2 visitor for pleasure may be admitted for not more than one year and may be granted an extension of a temporary

stay in increments of not more than 6 months each, except that alien members of a religious denomination coming temporarily and solely to do missionary work in behalf of that denomination may be granted an extension of stay in increments of not more than one year each, provided that such work does not involve the selling of articles or the solicitation or acceptance of donations. Those B-1 and B-2 visitors admitted pursuant to the waiver provided at § 212.1(e) of this Chapter may be admitted to and stay on Guam for a period not to exceed fifteen days and are not eligible for extension of stay.

(2) Minimum six month admissions. Any B-2 visitor who is found otherwise admissible and is issued a Form I-94, will be admitted for a minimum period of six months, regardless of whether less time is requested, provided, that any required passport is valid as specified in section 212(a) (26) of the Act. Exceptions to the minimum six month admission may be made only in individual cases upon the specific approval of the district director for good cause.

(3) Visa Waiver Pilot Program. Special requirements for admission and maintenance of status for visitors admitted to the United States under the Visa Waiver Pilot Program are set forth in section 217 of the Act and Part 217 of this chapter.

(4) Construction workers not admissible. Aliens seeking to enter the country to perform building or construction work, whether on-site or in-plant, are not eligible for classification or admission as B-1 nonimmigrants under section 101(a)(15)(B) of the Act. However, alien nonimmigrants otherwise qualified as B-1 nonimmigrants may be issued visas and may enter for the purpose of supervision or training of others engaged in building or construction work, but not for the purpose of actually performing any such building or construction work themselves.

Transits

8 C.F.R. § 214.2(c)

(1) Without visas. An applicant for admission under the transit without visa privilege must establish that he is admissable under the immigration laws; that he has confirmed and onward reservations to at least the next country beyond the United States, and that he will continue his journey on the same line or a connecting line within 8 hours after his arrival; however, if there is no scheduled transportation within that 8-hour period, continuation of the journey thereafter on the first available transport will be satisfactory. Transfers from the equipment on which an applicant arrives to other equipment of the same or a connecting line shall be limited to 2 in number, with the last transport departing foreign (but not necessarily nonstop foreign), and the total period of waiting time for connecting transportation shall not exceed 8 hours except as provided above. Notwithstanding the foregoing, an applicant, if seeking to join a vessel in the United States as a crewman, shall be in possession of a valid "D" visa and a letter from the owner or agent of the vessel he seeks to join, shall proceed directly to the vessel on the first available transportation and upon joining the vessel shall remain aboard at all times until it departs from the United States. Except for transit from one part of foreign contiguous territory to another part of the same territory, application for direct transit without a visa must be made at one of the following ports of entry: . . . . The privilege of transit without a visa may be authorized only under the conditions that the transportation line, without the prior consent of the Service, will not refund the ticket which was presented to the Service as evidence of the alien's confirmed and onward reservations; that the alien

will not apply for extension of temporary stay or for adjustment of status under section 245 of the Act; and that until his departure from the United States responsibility for his continuous actual custody will lie with the transportation line which brought him to the United States unless at the direction of the district director he is in the custody of this Service or other custody approved by the Commissioner.

(2) United Nations Headquarters District. An alien of the class defined in section 101(a)(15)(C) of the Act, whose visa is limited to transit to and from the United Nations Headquarters District, if otherwise admissible, shall be admitted on the additional conditions that he proceed directly to the immediate vicinity of the United Nations Headquarters District, and remain there continuously, departing therefrom only if required in connection with his departure from the United States, and that he have a document establishing his ability to enter some country other than the United States following his sojourn in the United Nations Headquarters District. The immediate vicinity of the United Nations Headquarters District is that area lying within a twenty-five mile radius of Columbus Circle, New York City, New York.

(3) Others. The period of admission of an alien admitted under section 101(a)(15)(C) of the Act shall not exceed 29 days.

Crewmen

8 C.F.R. § 214.2(d)

The provisions of Parts 252 and 253 of this chapter shall govern the landing of crewmen as nonimmigrants of the class defined in section 101(a)(15)(D) of the Act.

Treaty Traders and Investors

8 C.F.R. § 214.2(e)

An alien defined in section 101(a)(15)(E) of the Act may be admitted for an initial period of not more than one year and may be granted extensions of temporary stay in increments of not more than two years. A trader or investor and his or her spouse or child who accompanied or followed to join the trader or investor, who acquired nonimmigrant status on or after December 24, 1952 under section 101(a)(15)(E) (i) or (ii) of the Act shall submit to the district director having jurisdiction over the alien's place of residence properly executed Forms I-539 and I-126 to apply for an extension of the period of his or her temporary admission. A trader or investor may change from one employer to another after a written request for permission to do so has been approved by the district director having jurisdiction over the alien's residence. The request must be supported by evidence that the requester would still be classifiable as a trader or investor in the new employment. After the request is granted, Service offices shall make a notation on the reverse of the alien's Form I-94 reading "Employment by (name of new employer) authorized," followed by the date of the authorization. Any unauthorized change to a new employer will constitute a failure to maintain status within the meaning of section 241(a)(9) of the Act.

22 C.F.R. § 41.51

Treaty Trader or Investor.

(a) Treaty trader. An alien is classifiable as a nonimmigrant treaty trader (E-1) if the consular officer is satisfied that the alien qualifies under the provisions of INA 101(a)(15)(E)(i) and that the alien:

(1) Will be in the United States solely to carry on trade of a substantial nature, which is international in scope, either on the alien's behalf or as an agent of a foreign person or organization engaged in trade, principally between the United States and the foreign state of which the alien is a national, consideration being given to any conditions in the country of which the alien is a national which may affect the alien's ability to carry on such substantial trade; and

(2) Intends to depart from the United States upon the termination of E-1 status.

(b) Treaty investor. An alien is classifiable as a nonimmigrant treaty investor (E-2) if the consular officer is satisfied that the alien qualifies under the provisions of INA 101(a)(15)(E)(ii) and that the alien:

(1) Has invested or is actively in the process of investing a substantial amount of capital in a bona fide enterprise in the United States, as distinct from a relatively small amount of capital in a marginal enterprise solely for the purpose of earning a living; and

(2) Intends to depart from the United States upon the termination of E-2 status.

(c) Employee of treaty trader or investor. An alien employee of a treaty trader may be classified E-1 and an alien employee of a treaty investor may be classified E-2 if the employee is or will be engaged in duties of an executive or supervisory character, or, if employed in a minor capacity, the employee has special qualifications that make the services to be rendered essential to the efficient operation of the enterprise. The employer must be:

(1) A person having the nationality of the treaty country, who is maintaining the status of treaty trader or investor if in the United States; or

(2) An organization at least 50 percent owned by persons having the nationality of the treaty country who are maintaining nonimmigrant treaty trader or investor status if residing in the United States.

(d) Spouse and children of treaty alien. The spouse and children of a treaty alien accompanying or following to join the treaty alien are entitled to the same classification as the principal alien. The nationality of a spouse or child of a treaty alien is not material to the classification of the spouse or child under the provisions of INA 101(a)(15)(E).

Students

8 C.F.R. § 214.2(f)

(1) Admission of student.—

(i) Eligibility for admission. Except as provided in paragraph (f)(4) of this section, an alien seeking admission to the United States under section 101(a)(15)(F)(i) of the Act (as an F-1 student) and the student's accompanying F-2 spouse and minor children, if applicable, are not eligible for admission unless—(A) The student presents a Certificate of Eligibility for Nonimmigrant (F-1) Student Status, Form I-20A-B, properly and completely filled out by the student and by the designated official of the school to which the student is destined and the documentary evidence of the student's financial ability required by that form; and (B) It is established that the student is destined to and intends to attend the school specified in the student's visa, unless the student is exempt from the requirement for presentation of a visa.

(ii) Disposition of Form I-20A-B. When a student is admitted to the United States, the inspecting officer shall forward Form I-20A-B to the Service's processing center. The processing center shall forward the Form I-20B to the school which issued the form to notify the school of the student's admission.

(2) Form I-20 ID copy. The first time an F-1 student comes into contact with the Service for any reason, the student must present to the Service a Form I-20A-B properly and completely filled out by the student and by the designated official of the school the student is attending or intends to attend. The student will be issued a Form I-20 ID copy with his or her admission number. The student must have the Form I-20 ID copy with him or her at all times. If the student loses the Form I-20 ID copy, the student must request a new Form I-20 ID copy on Form I-102 from the Service office having jurisdiction over the school the student was last authorized to attend.

(3) Spouse and minor children following to join student. The F-2 spouse and minor children following to join an F-1 student are not eligible for admission to the United States unless they present, as evidence that the student is or will, within sixty days, be enrolled in a full course of study or is engaged in approved practical training, either—

(i) A properly endorsed page 4 of Form I-20A-B if there has been nonsubstantive change in the information on the student's most recent Form I-20A since the form was initially issued; or

(ii) A new Form I-20A-B if there has been any substantive change in the information on the student's most recent Form I-20A since the form was initially issued.

(4) Temporary absence.—

(i) General. An F-1 student returning to the United States from a temporary absence to attend the school which the student was previously authorized to attend must present either (A) A properly endorsed page 4 of Form I-20A-B if there has been no substantive change in the information on the student's most recent Form I-20A since the form was initially issued; or (B) A new Form I-20A-B if there has been any substantive change in the information on the student's most recent Form I-20A since the form was initially issued.

(ii) Student who intends to transfer or has transferred between schools. If an F-1 student has transferred or intends to transfer between schools and has been issued an I-20A-B by the school to which he or she has or intends to transfer, the name of the new school does not have to be specified on the student's visa to allow reentry into the United States after a temporary absence. If the student has not yet attended the new school, the inspecting officer will endorse Form I-20 ID Copy to indicate the new school, and will endorse Form I-20A-B and forward it to the Service's Data Processing Center.

(5) Duration of status—

(i) General. For purposes of this chapter, duration of status means the period during which the student is pursuing a full course of studies in any educational program (e.g., elementary or high school, bachelor's or master's degree, doctoral or post-doctoral program) and any periods of authorized practical training, plus sixty days within which to depart from the United States. An F-1 student who continues from one educational level to another is considered to remain in status, provided the transition to the new educational program is accomplished according to the transfer procedures outlined in paragraph (f)(8) of this section. An F-1 student at an academic institution is considered to be in status during the summer if the student is eligible, and intends to register for the next term. A student attending a school on a quarter or trimester calendar who takes only one vacation a year during any one of the quarters or trimesters instead of during the summer, is considered to be in status during that vacation provided the student is eligible, intends to register for the next term, and has completed the equivalent of an academic year prior to taking the vacation. A student who is compelled by illness or other medical condition to interrupt or reduce a course of study is considered in status during the illness or other medical condition. The student must resume a full course of study upon recovery.

(ii) Condition. Subject to the condition that the alien's passport is valid for at least six months at all times while in the United States, including any automatic revalidation accorded by the agreement between the United States and the country which issued the alien's passport (unless the alien is exempt from the requirement for presentation of a passport): (A) Any alien admitted to the United States as an F-1 student is to be admitted for duration of status as defined in paragraph (f)(5)(i) of this section except that a student may be admitted for 30 days with Form I-515; and (B) Any alien granted a change of nonimmigrant classification to that of an F-1 student is considered to be in status for duration of status as defined in paragraph (f)(5)(i) of this section.

(iii) Conversion to duration of status. Any F-1 student in college, university, seminary, conservatory, academic institution, or language training program who is pursuing a full course of study and is otherwise in status as a student, is automatically granted duration of status. The dependent spouse and children of the students are also automatically granted duration of status if they are maintaining F-2 status. Any alien converted to duration of status under this paragraph need not present Form I-94 to the Service. This paragraph constitutes official notification of conversion to duration of status. The Service will issue a new Form I-94 to the alien when the alien comes into contact with the Service.

(6) Full course of study. Successful completion of the course of study must lead to the attainment of a specific educational or professional objective. For purposes of this paragraph, a college or university is an institution of higher learning which awards recognized associate, bachelor's, master's, doctor's, or professional degree. Schools which devote themselves exclusively or primarily to vocational, business, or language instruction are not included in the category of colleges or universities. A "full course of study" as required by section 101(a)(15)(F)(i) of the Act means:

(i) Postgraduate study or postdoctoral study or research at a college or university, or undergraduate or postgraduate study at a conservatory or religious seminary, certified by a designated school official as a full course of study;

(ii) Undergraduate study at a college or university, certified by a school official to consist of at least twelve semester or quarter hours of instruction per academic term in those institutions using standard semester, trimester, or quarter hour systems, where all undergraduate students who are enrolled for a maximum of twelve semester or quarter hours are charged full-time tuition or are considered full-time for other administrative purposes, or its equivalent (as determined by the district director in the school approval process), except when the student needs a lesser course load to complete the course of study during the current term;

(iii) Study in a post-secondary language, liberal arts, fine arts or other non-vocational program at a school which confers upon its graduates recognized associate or other degrees or has established that its credits have been and are accepted unconditionally by at least three institutions of higher learning within category (1) or (2) of § 213.3(c), and which has been certified by a designated school official to consist of at least twelve clock hours of instruction a week, or its equivalent as determined by the district director in the school approval process;

(iv) Study in any other language, liberal arts, fine arts, or other nonvocational training program, certified by a designated school official to consist of at least eighteen clock hours of attendance a week provided that the dominant part of the course of study consists of classroom instruction, and twenty-two clock hours a week provided that the dominant part of the course of study consists of laboratory work; or

(v) Study in a primary or academic high school curriculum certified by a designated school official to consist of class attendance for not less than the minimum number of hours a week prescribed by the school for normal progress towards graduation.

(7) Extension of stay—

(i) Request after eight consecutive academic years. Any student who has been in student status for eight consecutive academic years must request an extension of stay from the Service. The application must be submitted to the Service on Form I-538. A student who has submitted an application for extension of stay may continue in student status until a decision is rendered by the Service. Departures from the United States of short duration during the academic year or during a vacation period do not break the continuity of a period of stay. Once a student has been granted an extension of stay, he or she does not have to request another extension until an additional eight-year period has elapsed.

(ii) Request after extended period in one academic level. Students who remain in one educational level for an extended period of time must request an extension of stay. The applicant must be submitted to the Service on Form I-538. The applicant must establish that there are valid academic reasons for going beyond the time limits. A student is required to request an extension of stay when according to the date on Form I-20A-B issued at the beginning of his or her program at the particular educational level:

(A) Studies are expected to be completed in two years or less, and the course is not completed within six months after the date studies are expected to be completed; or

(B) Studies are expected to be completed in more than two but within four years, but the course is not completed within one year after the date the studies are expected to be completed.

(C) Studies are expected to be completed in more than four years, but the course is not completed within eighteen months after the date the studies are expected to be completed.

(8) School transfer

(i) Eligibility. An F-1 student is eligible to transfer to another school if the student:

(A) Is a bona fide nonimmigrant student;

(B) Has been pursuing a full course of study at the school the student was last authorized to attend during the term immediately preceding the transfer (or the last term preceding a vacation as provided in paragraph (f)(5)(i) of this section);

(C) Intends to pursue a full course of study at the school to which the student intends to transfer; and

(D) Is financially able to attend the school to which the student intends to transfer.

(ii) Transfer procedure. The following procedures must be followed before a transfer will be considered to be completed:

(A) The F-1 student must obtain a properly completed Form I-20A-B from the school to which the student intends to transfer. The student must inform the designated school official at the school the student is currently attending of his or her intention to transfer;

(B) The student must enroll in the new school in the first term after leaving the previous school or the first term after vacation as provided in paragraph (f)(5)(i) of this section. The student must complete page 2 of Form I-20A-B as instructed and submit the Form I-20A-B to a designated school official of the new school within fifteen days after the date the student begins classes at the new school; and

(C) The designated school official receiving the Form I-20A-B must:

(1) Sign the reverse side of the Form I-20 ID Copy in the space provided for the designated school official's signature, thereby acknowledging the student's attendance in class;

(2) Return the Form I-20 ID Copy to the student;

(3) Add the name of the school from which the student has transferred to the front page of Form I-20A-B, item 2(C), and initial the addition;

(4) Submit the Form I-20A-B to the Service's Data Processing Center within thirty days of receipt from the student; and

(5) Submit a copy of Form I-20A-B to the school which the student was last authorized to attend.

(iii) Student not pursuing a full course of study. A student who wants to transfer to another school but has not pursued a full course of study at the school the student was last authorized to attend must apply for and be granted reinstatement to student status in accordance with the provisions of paragraph (f)(12) of this section before he or she may request a transfer. The student must include Form I-20A-B from the school which he or she intends to attend, if reinstated. If reinstatement is granted, the student is eligible to attend the new school without transfer.

(9) Employment.—

(i) On-campus employment. On-campus employment means employment performed on the school's premises. On-campus employment pursuant to the terms of a scholarship, fellowship, or assistantship is deemed to be part of the academic program of a student otherwise taking a full course of study. An F-1 student may, therefore, engage in this kind of on-campus employment or any other on-campus employment which will not displace a United States resident. Employment authorized under this paragraph must not exceed twenty hours a week while school is in session. An F-1 student authorized to work under this paragraph however, may work full-time when school is not in session (including during the student's vacation) if the student is eligible, and intends, to register for the next term or session. The student may not engage in on-campus employment after completion of the student's course or courses of study, except employment for practical training as authorized under paragraph (f)(10) of this section.

(ii) *Application for off-campus employment.* Off-campus employment is prohibited for students who remain in the United States in F-1 status for one year or less. Off-campus employment is also prohibited during the first year in the United States for students who remain in the United States in F-1 status for more than one year. It a student pursues more than one course of study, off-campus employment is prohibited only during the first year of study in the United States. The first year of study means the first full year in the United States in bona fide F-1 status. A temporary absence of five months or less from the United States during the first full year does not disqualify an F-1 student from being eligible for employment authorization. An F-1 student in a program longer than one year must apply for employment authorization on Form I-538 accompanied by the student's Form I-20 ID copy. The student must submit the application to the office of this Service having jurisdiction over the school the student was last authorized to attend. The designated school official must certify on Form I-538 that the student—

(A) Is in good standing as a student who is carrying a full course of study as defined in paragraph (f)(6) of this section;

(B) Has demonstrated economic necessity due to unforeseen circumstances arising subsequent to entry or subsequent to change to student classification;

(C) Has demonstrated that acceptance of employment will not interfere with the student's carrying a full course of study; and

(D) Has agreed not to work more than twenty hours a week when school is in session.

(iii) *Conditions for off-campus employment.* If off-campus employment is authorized, the adjudicating officer shall endorse the authorization on the student's Form I-20 ID copy and shall note the dates on which the employment authorization begins and ends. The employment authorization may be granted up to the expected date of completion of the student's current course of study. A student has permission to engage in off-campus employment only if the student receives his or her Form I-20 ID copy endorsed to that effect. Off-campus employment authorized under this section must not exceed twenty hours a week while school is in session. Any student authorized to work off-campus, however, may work full-time when school is not in session (including during the student's vacation) if the student is eligible, and intends, to register for the next term or session. Permission to engage in off-campus employment is terminated when the student transfers from one school to another or when the need for that employment ceases. Furthermore, a student may not engage in off-campus employment after completion of the student's course or courses of study except as authorized under paragraph (f)(10) of this section.

(iv) *Temporary absence of F-1 student granted off-campus employment authorization.* If a student who has been granted off-campus employment authorization departs from the United States temporarily and is readmitted to the United States during the period of time when employment is authorized, the student may resume the previously authorized employment. The student must be returning to attend the same school the student was authorized to attend when permission to accept off-campus employment was granted.

(v) Effect of strike or other labor dispute. Authorization for all employment, whether or not part of an academic program, is automatically suspended upon certification by the Secretary of Labor or the Secretary's designee to the Commissioner of Immigration and Naturalization or the Commissioner's designee that a strike or other labor dispute involving a work stoppage of workers is in progress in the occupation at the place of employment. As used in this paragraph, "place of employment" means wherever the employer or a joint employer does business.

(vi) Spouse and children of F-1 student. The F-2 spouse and children of an F-1 student may not accept employment.

(10) Practical training—

(i) Practical training prior to completion of studies—

(A) General. Temporary employment for practical training prior to completion of studies may be authorized only:

(1) After completion of all course requirements for the degree (excluding thesis or equivalent), if the student is in a bachelor's, master's or doctoral degree program;

(2) If the student is attending a high school, college, university, seminary, or conservatory which requires or makes optional practical training of candidates for a degree in that field or for a high school diploma; or

(3) During the student's annual vacation if the student is attending a college, university, seminary, or conservatory. A student may not be granted permission to accept practical training prior to completion of studies unless the student has been in student status for nine months. A student in a language training program may not be granted permission to accept practical training prior to completion of studies. A student may not be granted practical training exceeding twelve months in the aggregate prior to completion of studies.

(B) Making a request to accept practical training prior to completion of studies. A student must submit a request for practical training prior to completion of a course of study to the designated school official of the school the student is authorized to attend. The request must consist of:

(1) A completed request for practical training on Form I-538;

(2) Form I-20 ID Copy; and

(3) A certification from the head of the student's academic department or the professor who is the student's academic advisor stating that upon his or her information and belief, employment comparable to the proposed employment is not available to the student in the country of the student's foreign residence (unless the student is applying under paragraph (f)(10)(i)(A)(2) of this section).

(C) Action upon request to accept practical training prior to completion of studies. The designated school official must:

(1) Certify on Form I-538 that the proposed employment is for the purpose of practical training, that it is related to the student's course of study, and that upon the designated school official's information and belief, employment com-

parable to the proposed employment is not available to the student in the country of the student's foreign residence (unless the student is applying under paragraph (f)(10)(i)(A)(2) of this section);

(2) Endorse the Form I-538 to show that practical training from (date) to (date) has been authorized, and send the form to the Service's Data Processing Center; and

(3) Endorse Form I-20 ID Copy with the endorsement "practical training prior to completion of studies from (date) to (date) authorized," and return the form to the student.

(D) Curricular practical training programs. An F-1 student enrolled in a college, university, conservatory, or seminary having a curricular practical training program (such as alternate work/study, internship, or cooperative education) as part of the regular curriculum may participate in the program without obtaining a change of nonimmigrant status. Such programs shall be treated similar to practical training prior to completion of studies as defined in paragraph (f)(10)(i)(A)(2) of this section. Periods of actual off-campus employment in any such program which is full-time (no concurrent coursework) will be deducted from the total of twelve months practical training time before graduation for which the student is eligible. Periods of actual off-campus employment in any such program in which coursework and employment are engaged at the same time ("parallel programs") will be deducted from the total of twelve months' practical training time at the rate of 50% (one month deducted for every two months of parallel coursework and practical training). A student who participates in a curricular practical training experience for which six months or more of the practical training time prior to graduation is deducted is not eligible for practical training after completion of studies. A student may engage in practical training only after receiving the Form I-20 ID Copy endorsed to that effect.

(ii) Practical training after completion of studies—

(A) General. Temporary employment for practical training after completion of studies may be authorized only:

(1) After completion of the course of study, if the student intends to engage in only one course of study; or

(2) After completion of at least one course of study, if the student intends to engage in more than one course of study.

A student may not be granted permission to accept practical training after completion of studies unless the student has been in student status for nine months. After completion of studies, a student may not be granted practical training exceeding twelve months. A student in a language training program may not be granted permission to accept practical training after completion of studies.

(B) Request to accept a first period of practical training after completion of studies. A student must submit a request to accept a first period of practical training to the designated school official no more than sixty days prior to completion of the course of study, but less than thirty days after completion of the course of study. The request must consist of:

(1) A completed request for practical training on Form I-538;

(2) Form I-20 ID Copy; and

(3) A certification from the head of the student's academic department or the professor who is the student's academic advisor stating that upon his or her information and belief, employment comparable to the proposed employment is not available to the student in the country of the student's foreign residence.

(C) Action upon a request to accept a first period of practical training after completion of studies. The designated school official must:

(1) Certify on Form I-538 that the proposed employment is for the purposes of practical training, that it is related to the student's course of study, and that upon the designated school official's information and belief, employment comparable to the proposed employment is not available to the student in the country of the student's foreign residence;

(2) Endorse Form I-538 to show that practical training from (date) to (date) has been authorized, and send the form to the Service's Data Processing Center; and

(3) Endorse the Form I-20 ID Copy with the endorsement "First period of practical training authorized from (date) to (date)" and return the form to the student.

A student may engage in practical training only after receiving the Form I-20 ID Copy endorsed to that effect.

(D) Computation dates for practical training. For purposes of computation, the "beginning" date of the first period will be the date of completion of studies and the "ending" date will be a date six months after the date of completion of studies. The actual date of commencement of practical training will be determined by the Service at the time of application for a second period of practical training. The actual date of commencement of practical training will be the date the student begins employment, or a date sixty days after the date of completion of studies, whichever is earlier.

(iii) Second period to continue practical training after completion of studies—

(A) General. A second period to continue practical training after completion of studies may not be granted unless the student has actually begun qualified employment during the first authorized period. A student shall submit his or her application for a second period to continue practical training within 30 days after he or she begins qualified employment.

(B) Request for second period to continue practical training after completion of studies. A student must submit a request for a second period to continue practical training. The request must be submitted to the Service office having jurisdiction over the actual place of employment. The request must consist of:

(1) A completed request for practical training on Form I-538, properly certified by the designated school official;

(2) The Form I-20 ID Copy; and

(3) A letter from the applicant's employer stating the applicant's occupation, the exact date employment began, the date employment will terminate, and describing in detail the duties of the applicant in the employment.

The letter from the student's employer must be seen by the designated school official before the designated school official's certification is made. There is no requirement that the student re-establish to the Service that the employment engaged in is not available to the student in the country of the student's foreign residence.

(C) Action upon request for a second period to continue practical training after completion of studies. The district director must determine that the student began qualified employment during the first period of practical training, that the stated employment is related to the student's course of study, and that the student can complete practical training within the maximum time authorized. Upon approval of the student's request to continue practical training the district director must:

(1) Endorse Form I-538 with the approval stamp, show that practical training from (date) to (date) has been authorized, and send the Form I-538 to the Service's Data Processing Center; and

(2) Endorse the Form I-20 ID Copy with the endorsement "Second period of practical training authorized from (date) to (date)," and return the form to the student.

A student who has been authorized a first period of practical training may continue to be employed while the application for a second period of practical training is pending until he or she receives a decision from the Service. A student may in no case continue employment beyond twelve months.

(D) Computation dates for practical training. The actual "beginning" date of the second period of practical training will be the end date of the first period. The "end" date of the second period will be the date twelve months after the exact date employment began, or fourteen months after the date of completion of studies, whichever is earlier. The student therefore has a maximum of twelve months' work authorized.

(11) Decision on application for extension, permission to transfer to another school, or permission to accept or continue off-campus employment or practical training. The district director shall notify the applicant of the decision and, if the application is denied, of the reason or reasons for the denial. The applicant may not appeal the decision.

(12) Reinstatement to student status.—

(i) General. A district director may consider reinstating to F-1 student status an alien who was admitted to the United States as, or whose status was changed to that of, an F-1 student and who has overstayed the authorized period of stay or who has otherwise violated the conditions of his or her status only if the student—

(A) Establishes to the satisfaction of the district director that the violation of status resulted from circumstances beyond the student's control or that failure to receive reinstatement to lawful F-1 status would result in extreme hardship to the student;

(B) Makes a written request for reinstatement accompanied by a properly completed Form I-20A-B from the school the student is attending or intends to attend and the student's Form I-20 ID copy;

(C) Is currently pursuing, or intending to pursue, a full course of study at the school which issued the Form I-20A-B;

(D) Has not been employed off-campus without authorization, or, as a fulltime student, has continued on-campus employment pursuant to the terms of a scholarship, fellowship, or, assistantship or other on-campus employment which did not displace a United States resident after the expiration of the authorized period of stay; and

(E) Is not deportable on any ground other than section 241(a)(2) or (9) of the Act.

(ii) Decision. If the district director reinstates the student, the district director shall endorse Form I-20B and the student's Form I-20 ID copy to indicate that the student has been reinstated, return the Form I-20 ID copy to the student, and forward Form I-20B with Form I-20A to the Service's processing center for file updating. The processing center shall forward Form I-20B to the school which the student is attending or intends to attend to notify the school of the student's reinstatement. If the district director does not reinstate the student, the student may not appeal that decision.

(13) School code suffix on Form I-20A-B. Each school system, other than an elementary or secondary school system, approved prior to August 1, 1983 for attendance by F-1 students must assign permanent consecutive numbers to all schools within its system. The number of the school within the system which an F-1 student is attending or intends to attend must be added as a three-digit suffix following a decimal point after the school file number on Form I-20A-B (e.g. .001). If an F-1 student is attending or intends to attend an elementary or secondary school in a school system or a school which is not part of a school system, a suffix consisting of a decimal point followed by three zeros must be added after the school file number on Form I-20A-B. The Service will assign school code suffixes to those schools it approves beginning August 1, 1983. No Form I-20A-B will be accepted after August 1, 1983 without the appropriate three-digit suffix.

[Provisions relating to G visas (representatives of international organizations) have been omitted. *See* 8 C.F.R. § 214.2(g).]

* * *

Temporary Work Visas (H Visas)

8 C.F.R. § 214.2(h)

(1) Admission of temporary employees—General.

(i) Under section 101(a)(15)(H) of the Act, an alien having a residence in a foreign country which he or she has no intention of abandoning may be authorized to come to the United States temporarily to perform services or labor for or to receive training from an employer, if petitioned for by that employer. Under this nonimmigrant category, the alien may be classified under section 101(a)(15)(H)(i) as an alien of distinguished merit and ability, or under section 101(a)(15)(H)(ii)(a) as an alien who is coming to perform agricultural labor or services of a temporary or seasonal nature, or under section 101(a)(15)(H)(ii)(b) as an alien coming to perform other temporary services or labor, or under section 101(a)(15)(H)(iii) as an alien who is coming as a trainee. These classifications are commonly called H-1, H-2A, H-2B, and H-3, respectively. The employer must file a petition with the Service for review of the services or training and for determination of the alien's eligibility for classification as a temporary employee or trainee, before the alien may apply for a visa or seek admission to the United States. This paragraph sets forth the standards and procedures whereby these classifications may be applied for and granted, denied, extended, revoked, and appealed.

(ii) Description of classifications.

(A) An "H-1" classification applies to an alien who is of distinguished merit and ability and who is coming temporarily to the United States to perform services of an exceptional nature requiring such merit and ability. In the case of a graduate of a medical school coming to the United States to perform services as a member of the medical profession, the alien must be coming pursuant to an invitation from a public or nonprofit private educational research institution or agency in the United States to teach or conduct research, or both, at or for such institution or agency. Although the services to be pe[r]formed may be temporary or permanent in nature, it must be established that the employment is only for a temporary period.

(B) An "H-2A or H-2B" classification applies to an alien who is coming temporarily to the United States to:

(1) Perform agricultural labor or services of a temporary or seasonal nature, or

(2) Perform other temporary service or labor, if unemployed persons capable of performing such service or labor cannot be found in this country. This classification does not apply to graduates of medical schools coming to the United States to perform services as members of the medical profession. The temporary or permanent nature of the services or labor to be performed must be determined. This classification requires a temporary labor certification issued by the Secretary of Labor or the Governor of Guam or a notice from one of them that certification cannot be made prior to the filing of a petition with the Service.

(C) An "H-3" classification applies to an alien who is coming temporarily to the United States as a trainee, other than to receive graduate medical education or t[r]aining. The alien may receive training from an employer in any field other than graduate medical education. This classification may not be used when all of the training will be at an academic or vocational institution.

(2) Petitions—

(i) Filing of petitions—

(A) General—A United States employer (or foreign employer under the H-1 classification) seeking to classify an alien as an H-1, H-2A, H-2B, or H-3 temporary employee shall file a petition in duplicate on Form I-129H with the regional service center which has jurisdiction over I-129H, petitions in the area where the alien will perform services or receive training or as further prescribed in this section. A district director may, only in emergent circumstances, accept and adjudicate a clearly approvable I-129H petition for employment solely within his or her jurisdiction.

(B) Service or training in more than one location. A petition which requires services to be performed or training to be received in more than one location must include an itinerary with the dates and locations of the services or training and must be filed with the Service office which has jurisdiction over I-129H petitions in the area where the petitioner is located. The address which the petition specifies as its location on the I-129H petition shall be where the petitioner is located for purposes of this paragraph. If the petitioner is a foreign employer with no United States location, the petitioner shall be filed with the Service office that has jurisdiction over the area where the employment will begin.

(C) Services or training for more than one employer. If the beneficiary will perform nonagricultural services for, or receive training from, more than one employer, each employer must file a separate petition with the Service office that has jurisdiction over the area where the alien will perform services or receive training, unless an established agent files the petition. The alien may work part-time for multiple employers provided each has an approved petition for the alien.

(D) Change of employers. If the alien is in the United States and decides to change employers, the new employer must file a petition on Form I-129H. If the alien is accorded the same H classification, an extension of stay is not required until the alien's previously authorized stay is about to expire. If the new petition is accompanied by an application for extension of stay on Form I-539 and the new petition is approved, the extension of stay may be granted for the validity of the approved petition, but may not exceed the limits on the alien's temporary stay that are prescribed in paragraphs (h)(12) and (h)(14) of this section.

(E) Amended or new petition. The petitioner shall file an amended or new petition with the Service office where the original petition was filed to reflect any material changes in the terms and conditions of employment or training or the beneficiary's eligibility as specified in the original approved petition and obtain approval from the Service. An amended or new H-2A or B petition must be accompanied by an amended or new labor certification determination.

(F) Agents as petitioners. An established United States agent may file a petition in cases involving workers who traditionally are self-employed or use agents to arrange short-term employment in their behalf with numerous employers, and in cases where a foreign employer authorizes the agent to act in its behalf. A petition filed by a agent is subject to the following conditions:

(1) A person or company in business as an agent may file the H petition involving multiple employers as the representative of both the employers and the beneficiary(ies) if the supporting documentation includes a complete itinerary of services or engagements. The itinerary shall specify the dates of each service or engagement, the names and addresses of the actual employers, and the names and addresses of the establishments, venues, or locations where the services will be performed. In questionable cases, a contract between the employers and the beneficiary(ies) may be required. The burden is on the agent to explain the terms and conditions of the employment and to provide any required documentation.

(2) An agent performing the function of an employer must guarantee the wage offered and the other terms and conditions of employment by contractural (sic) agreement with the beneficiary(ies). The agent/employer must also provide an itinerary of definite employment and information on any other services planned for the period of time requested.

(ii) Multiple beneficiaries.—

(A) H-1 petitions. More than one beneficiary may be included in an H-1 petition if they are members of a group seeking classification based on the reputation of the group as an entity, or they are the accompanying aliens who derive H-1 classification from a principal H-1 beneficiary to whom their support is determined to be essential. The petition shall include the name and other identifying information required by Form I-129H for each beneficiary. If the beneficiaries will be applying for visas at more than one consulate, the petitioner shall submit a separate Form I-129H for each consulate. If the beneficiaries do not require visas and will be applying for admission at more than one port of entry, the petitioner shall submit a separate Form I-129H for each port of entry.

(B) H-2 and H-3 petitions. More than one beneficiary may be included in an H-2 or H-3 petition if the beneficiaries will be performing the same service or receiving the same training for the same period of time and in the same geographical area. If they will be applying for visas at more than one consulate, the petitioner shall submit a separate I-129H petition for each consulate. If the beneficiaries will be applying for admission at more than one port of entry, the petitioner shall submit a separate Form I-129H for each port of entry.

(iii) Named beneficiaries. Nonagricultural I-129H petitions must include the names of beneficiaries and other required information at the time of filing. Under the H-2B classification, exceptions may be granted in emergent situations involving multiple beneficiaries at the discretion of the director. If all of the beneficiaries covered by an H-2A or B labor certification have not been identified at the time a petition is filed, multiple petitions naming subsequent beneficiaries may be filed at different times with a copy of the same labor certification. Each petition must reference all previously filed petitions for that labor certification.

(iv) Substitution of beneficiaries. Beneficiaries may be substituted in H-1 and H-2B petitions that are approved for a group, if the qualifications of individual beneficiaries will not be or were not considered in according H classification. To request a substitution, the petitioner shall, by letter and a copy of the petition's approval notice, notify the consular office at which the alien will apply for a visa or the port of entry where the alien will apply for admission.

(v) H-2A Petitions. Special criteria for admission, extension, and maintenance of status apply to H-2A petitions and are specified in paragraph (h)(4) of this section. The other provisions of § 214.2(h) apply to H-2A only to the extent that they do not conflict with the special agricultural provisions in paragraph (h)(4) of this section.

(3) Petition for alien of distinguished merit and ability (H-1)—

(i) Types of H-1 classification—H-1 classification may be granted to an alien as an individual or as a member of a group, or to accompanying alien as defined in paragraph (h)(3)(ii)(D) of this section. The petition must indicate the capacity in which the alien is seeking H-1 classification at the time of filing.

(A) H-1 classification in individual capacity. H-1 classification may be granted to an alien who is of distinguished merit and ability. An alien of distinguished merit and ability is one who is a member of the professions or who is prominent in his or her field. The alien must be coming to the United States to perform services which require a member of the professions or person of prominence.

(B) H-1 classification as a member of a group. A group of distinguished merit and ability consists of two or more persons who function as a unit, such as an athletic team or performing ensemble. The group as a whole must be prominent in its field and must be coming to the United States to perform services which require a group of prominence. A person who is a member of a group of distinguished merit and ability may be granted H-1 classification based on that relationship, but may not perform services separate and apart from the group unless he or she is granted H-1 classification in an individual capacity.

(C) H-1 classification as an accompanying alien. A person who is an accompanying alien as defined in paragraph (h)(3)(ii)(D) of this section may be granted

H-1 classification based on a support relationship to an individual or group of distinguished merit and ability. The H-1 classification derived from the individual or group of distinguished merit and ability does not entitle an accompanying alien to perform services separate and apart from the individual or group of distinguished merit and ability.

(ii) Definitions.

(A) "Profession" means an occupation which requires theoretical and practical application of a body of highly specialized knowledge to fully perform the occupation in such fields of human endeavor as: architecture, engineering, mathematics, physical sciences, social sciences, medicine and health, education, business specialties, accounting, law, theology, and the arts. A profession requires completion of a specific course of education at an accredited college or university, culminating in a baccalaureate or higher degree in a specific occupational speciality (sic), where attainment of such degree or its equivalent is the minimum requirement for entry into the profession in the United States. There are two categories of persons who do not meet these requirements but are nevertheless regarded as members of a profession. They are: persons who, after passage of normal professional tests and requirements, are granted full state licenses to practice the profession; and persons who lack the required degree but, by virtue of a combination of education, specialized training and/or professional experience are recognized as members of a profession and are in fact lawfully practicing at a professional level.

(B) "Prominence" means a high level of achievement in a field evidenced by a degree of skill and recognition substantially above that ordinarily encountered to the extent that a person described as prominent is renowned, leading, or well-known in the field of endeavor.

(C) "Group" means two or more persons established as one entity to provide some form of service or activity. The reputation of the group, not that of individual members, is considered in according H classification.

(D) "Accompanying alien" means a support person such as a manager, trainer, musical accompanist, or other highly skilled, essential person determined by the director to be coming to the United States to perform support services which cannot be readily performed by a United States worker and which are essential to the successful performance of the services to be rendered by an H-1 individual or group in the arts, cultural, entertainment or professional sports field. Such alien must possess appropriate qualifications, significant prior experience with the H-1 individual or group, and critical knowledge of the specific type of services to be performed so as to render success of the services dependent upon his or her participation. A highly skilled alien meeting the above criteria may be accorded H-1 classification based on this relationship with the H-1 individual or group to whom his or her services are essential.

(E) "Recognized authority" means a person or an organization with expertise in a particular field, special skills or knowledge in that field, and the expertise to render the type of opinion requested. Such an opinion must state:

(1) The writer's qualifications as an expert;

(2) The writer's experience giving such opinions, citing specific instances where past opinions have been accepted as authoritative and by whom;

(3) How the conclusions were reached; and

(4) The basis for the conclusions, including copies or citations of any research material used.

(iii) Criteria and documentary requirements for a member of the professions. For H-1 classification as a member of the professions, the position offered to the alien must be in a profession and the alien must qualify as a member of the professions.

(A) Standards for a position in the professions. To qualify as a profession, the position must meet the following criteria:

(1) A baccalaureate or higher degree or its equivalent is normally the minimum requirement for entry into the particular profession;

(2) The degree requirement is common to the industry in parallel positions among similar organizations or, in the alternative, an employer may show that its particular position is so complex or unique that it can be performed only by a member of the profession;

(3) The employer normally requires a degree or its equivalent for the position;

(4) The nature of the specific duties are so specialized and complex that knowledge required to perform the duties is usually associated with the attainment of a baccalaureate or higher degree; and

(5) The position's level of responsibility and authority are commensurate with professional standing.

(B) Standards for a member of the professions. To qualify as a member of the professions, the alien must:

(1) Hold a United States baccalaureate or higher degree required by the profession from an accredited college or university; or

(2) Hold a foreign degree determined to be equivalent to a United States baccalaureate or higher degree required by the profession from an accredited college or university; or

(3) Hold an unrestricted State license, registration or certification which authorizes him or her to fully practice the profession and be immediately engaged in that profession in the state of intended employment; or

(4) Have education, specialized training, and/or professional-level experience that is equivalent to training acquired by the attainment of a United States baccalaureate or higher degree in the profession.

(C) Equivalence to training acquired by attainment of a college degree. For purposes of paragraph (h)(3)(iii)(B)(4) of this section, equivalence to training acquired by attainment of a United States baccalaureate or higher degree shall mean achievement of a level of knowledge, competence, and practice in the profession that has been determined to be equal to that of an individual who has a baccalaureate or higher degree in the profession; and shall be determined by one or more of the following:

(1) An evaluation from an official who has authority to grant college-level credit in the profession at an accredited college or university which has a program for granting such credit based on an individual's training and/or work experience; or

(2) The results of recognized college-level equivalency examinations or special credit programs, such as the College Level Examination Program (CLEP), or Program on Noncollegiate Sponsored Instruction (PONSI); or

(3) An evaluation of education by a reliable credentials evaluation service which specializes in evaluating foreign educational credentials; or

(4) Evidence of certification or registration from a nationally-recognized professional association or society for the profession that is known to grant certification or registration to members of the profession who have achieved a certain level of competence in the profession; or

(5) A determination by the Service that the equivalent of college-level training in the profession has been acquired through a combination of specialized training and progressively responsible work experience in areas related to the profession, and that the alien has achieved professional standing and recognition as a result of such training and experience. For purposes of determining equivalency to a baccalaureate or higher degree in the profession, three years of specialized training and/ or work experience must be demonstrated for each year of college-level training the alien lacks. It must be clearly demonstrated that the alien's training and/or work experience included the theoretical and practical application of specialized knowledge required at the professional level of the occupation; that the alien's experience was gained while working with peers, supervisors, or subordinates who are themselves professionals; and that the alien has professional standing and recognition evidenced by at least one type of documentation such as:

(i) Recognition of professional standing by at least two recognized authorities in the professional field,

(ii) Membership in a recognized foreign or United States association or society in the professional field,

(iii)Published material by or about the alien in professional publications, books, or major newspapers,

(iv) Licensure or registration to practice the profession in a foreign country, or

(v) Professional achievements which a recognized authority has determined to be significant contributions to the professional field.

(iv) Criteria and documentary requirements for prominence. Prominence in a field may be established by an individual alien or by a group. The reputation of the group as an entity, not the qualifications or accomplishments of individual members, shall be evaluated for H-1 classification. The work which a prominent alien or group is coming to the United States to perform must require the services of a prominent alien or group.

(A) Standards for a position requiring prominence. To qualify as a position requiring prominence, it must meet one of the following criteria:

(1) The position or services to be performed involve an event, production or activity which has a distinguished reputation;

(2) The services to be performed are as a lead or starring participant in a distinguished activity for an organization or establishment that has a distinguished reputation or record of employing prominent persons;

(3) The services primarily involve educational or cultural events sponsored by educational, cultural, or governmental organizations which promote international educational or cultural activities; or

(4) The position is with a business that requires the services of a prominent executive, manager, or highly technical person due to the complexity of the business activity or the broad range of responsibility required.

(B) Standards for prominent aliens. An alien or group may establish prominence in either one of the following categories. The alien(s) must:

(1) Have sustained national (foreign or U.S.) or international acclaim and recognition for achievements in the particular field, as evidenced by at least three different types of documentation showing that the alien or group:

(i) Has performed and will perform services as a lead or starring participant in productions or events which have a distinguished reputation as evidenced by critical reviews, advertisements, publicity releases, publications, or contracts;

(ii) Has been the recipient of significant national or international awards or prizes for services performed;

(iii) Has achieved national or international recognition for achievements evidenced by critical reviews or other published material by or about the individual or group in major newspapers, trade journals, or magazines;

(iv) Has performed and will perform services as a lead or starring participant for organizations and establishments that have a distinguished reputation;

(v) Has a record of major commercial or critically acclaimed successes, as evidenced by such indicators as title, rating, or standing in the field, box office receipts, credit for original research or product development, record sales, and other occupational achievements reported in trade journals, major newspapers, or other publications;

(vi) Has received significant recognition for achievements from organizations, critics, government agencies or other recognized experts in the field in which the alien or group is engaged. Such testimonials must be in a form that clearly indicates the author's authority, expertise, and knowledge of the alien's achievements; or

(vii) Has commanded and now commands a high salary or other substantial remuneration for services, evidenced by contracts or other reliable evidence.

(2) Be an artist who, or an artistic group that, is recognized by governmental agencies, cultural organizations, scholars, arts administrators, critics, or other experts in the particular field for excellence in developing, interpreting, or representing a unique or traditional ethnic, folk, cultural, musical, theatrical, or other artistic performance or presentation; be coming to the United States primarily for educational or cultural event(s) to further the understanding of or development of that art form; and be sponsored primarily by educational, cultural, or governmental organizations which promote such international cultural activities and exchanges. An artist or group which seeks H-1 classification under this provision must provide affidavits, testimonials, or letters from recognized experts attesting to the authenticity and excellence of the alien's or group's skills in performing, or presenting the unique

or traditional art form, explaining the level of recognition accorded the alien or group in the native country and the United States, and giving the credentials of the expert, including the basis of his or her knowledge of the alien's or group's skill and recognition. The alien or group must provide at a minimum:

(i) Evidence that most of the performances or presentations will be educational or cultural events sponsored by educational, cultural, or governmental agencies; and

(ii) Both an affidavit or testimonial from the Ministry of Culture, USIA Cultural Affairs Officer, the academy for the artistic discipline, a leading scholar, a cultural institution, or a major university in the alien's own country or from a third country, and a letter from a United States expert who has knowledge in the particular field, such as a scholar, arts administrator, critic, or representative of a cultural organization or government agency; or

(iii) A letter or certification from a U.S. Government cultural or arts agency such as the Smithsonian Institution, the National Endowment for the Arts, the National Endowment for the Humanities, or the Library of Congress.

(3) Have exceptional career achievement in business in executive, managerial, or highly technical positions, as evidenced by at least three significant factors such as:

(i) Managerial responsibility for an organization or a major subdivision of an organization which has a gross annual income of at least 10 million dollars;

(ii) At least 10 years of progressively responsible experience culminating in a high level executive, managerial, or technical position that involves a broad range of responsibilities;

(iii) A salary of at least $75,000 per year;

(iv) Responsibility for a sizeable work force which includes a significant number of professional, supervisory, or other managerial employees;

(v) Original development of a system or product which has major significance to the industry in which the alien is employed as reported in published materials or opinions of recognized experts in the field or industry; or

(vi) Recognition for achievements and significant contributions to an industry or field by recognized experts in the industry or field.

(v) Special H-1 requirements for certain groups—

(A) H-1 petitions for prominent aliens in the arts, cultural, or entertainment field—

(1) Adjudication of petition—

(i) In determining whether an alien in the arts, cultural, or entertainment field is prominent and whether the services require a person of prominence, the director shall consider, but not be limited to, evidence described in paragraph (h)(3)(iv) of this section, and where he or she deems necessary, may require further evidence on any of those or other appropriate factors.

(ii) The director may decide not to require full documentation of any of the factors in paragraph (h)(3)(iv) of this section, if the alien or group is of such distinguished merit and ability that the name or reputation standing by itself would be sufficient to establish without any question that the alien or group is of distinguished merit and ability and that the alien or group is coming to the United States to perform services which require such merit and ability. In such a case, the petitioner's statement which describes the beneficiary's standing and achievements in the field of endeavor may be accepted as sufficient for approval of the petition.

(iii) The director shall approve or deny the petition based on the information in the record when that information clearly establishes H-1 eligibility or ineligibility in accordance with paragraph (h)(3)(iv) of this section. In all other cases, before making a decision, the director shall consult with the appropriate union and a management organization, or recognized critics or experts in the appropriate field, for an advisory opinion regarding the qualifications of the alien and the nature of the services to be performed.

(2) Advisory opinions. An advisory opinion may be furnished orally by an appropriate official, subject to later confirmation in writing, when requested by the director. The written opinion shall be signed by a duly authorized and responsible official of the organization consulted. Advisory opinions shall be nonbinding upon the Service.

(3) Accompanying alien or member of a group. When an alien is entitled to H-1 classification as an accompanying alien or as a member of a group, the phrase "Accompanying Alien" or the name of the group shall be noted on the approved petition, the alien's travel documents, and arrival-departure record, Form I-94.

(B) H-1 petitions for physicians—

(1) Beneficiary requirements. An H-1 petition for a physician shall be accompanied by evidence that the physician:

(i) Has a license to practice medicine in the state of intended employment if the physician will perform direct patient care and the state requires the license, and

(ii) Has a full and unrestricted license to practice medicine in a foreign state or has graduated from a medical school in the United States or in a foreign state.

(2) H-1 classification for alien graduates of foreign medical schools—

(i) Petitioner requirements. If the alien graduated from a medical school in a foreign state, the petitioner must establish that the alien physician is coming to the United States primarily to teach or conduct research, or both, at or for a public or nonprofit private educational or research institution or agency at the invitation of that institution or agency, and that no patient care activities will be performed, except those that are incidental to the physician's teaching or research.

(ii) Exemption for physicians of national or international renown. A physician who graduated from a medical school in a foreign state and who is of national or international renown in the field of medicine is exempt from the requirements in paragraph (h)(3)(v)(B)(2)(i) of this section.

(3) H-1 classification for alien graduates of United States medical schools. An alien who graduated from a medical school in the United States and who is in all respects qualified for nonimmigrant classification under section 101(a)(15)(H)(i) of the Act is eligible for that classification in order to participate in a medical

residency in the United States and to perform any other services as a member of the medical profession, including services primarily involving direct patient care.

(C) H-1 Classification for a professional nurse—

(1) Beneficiary requirements. An H-1 petition for a professional nurse shall be accompanied by evidence that the nurse:

(i) Has obtained a full and unrestricted license to practice professional nursing in the country where the alien obtained nursing education, or has received nursing education in the United States or Canada;

(ii) Has passed the examination given by the Commission on Graduates of Foreign Nursing Schools, or has obtained a full and unrestricted (permanent) license under state law to practice professional nursing in the state of intended employment, or has obtained a full and unrestricted (permanent) license in any state or territory of the United States and received temporary authorization to practice professional nursing in the state of intended employment;

(iii) Is fully qualified and eligible under the laws (including such temporary or interim licensing requirements which authorize the nurse to be employed) governing the place of intended employment to engage in the practice of professional nursing as a registered nurse immediately upon admission to the United States, and is authorized under such laws to be employed by the employer; and

(iv) Otherwise meets the requirements of section 101(a)(15)(H)(i) of the Immigration and Nationality Act.

(2) Other. If the laws governing the place where the services will be performed place any limitations on the services to be performed by the beneficiary, a statement from the petitioner shall contain details as to the limitations. The director shall consider any limitations in determining whether the services which the beneficiary would perform are those of a professional nurse.

(vi) General documentary requirements for H-1 classification. An H-1 petition filed on Form I-129H shall be accompanied by:

(A) Documentation, certifications, affidavits, degrees, diplomas, writings, reviews, or any other required evidence sufficient to establish that the beneficiary is a person of distinguished merit and ability as described in paragraph (h)(3)(i) of this section, and that the services the beneficiary is to perform require a person of such merit and ability. The evidence shall conform to the following:

(1) School records, diplomas, degrees, affidavits, contracts, and similar documentation submitted must reflect periods of attendance, courses of study, and similar pertinent data, be executed by the person in charge of the records of the educational or other institution, firm, or establishment where education or training was acquired, and be an original document or a certified copy. Uncertified photocopies of documents such as advertisements, playbills, reviews, and other such published material may be submitted.

(2) Affidavits submitted by present or former employers or recognized experts certifying to the recognition and outstanding ability of the beneficiary shall specifically describe the beneficiary's recognition and ability in factual terms and must set forth the expertise of the affiant and the manner in which the affiant acquired such information.

(B) Copies of any written contracts between the petitioner and beneficiary, or a summary of the terms of the oral agreement under which the beneficiary will be employed, if there is no written contract.

(vii) Licensure for H classification—

(A) General. If an occupation requires a state or local license for an individual to fully perform the duties of the occupation, an alien (except a professional nurse) seeking H classification in that occupation must have that license prior to approval of the petition to be found qualified to enter the United States and immediately engage in employment in the occupation.

(B) Temporary licensure. If a temporary license is available and the alien is allowed to perform the duties of the occupation without a permanent license, the director shall examine the nature of the duties, the level at which the duties are performed, the degree of supervision received, and any limitations placed on the alien. If an analysis of the facts demonstrates that the alien under supervision is authorized to fully perform the duties of the occupation, H classification may be granted.

(C) Duties without licensure. In certain occupations which generally require licensure, a state may allow an individual to fully practice the occupation under the supervision of licensed senior or supervisory personnel in that occupation. In such cases, the director shall examine the nature of the duties and the level at which they are performed. If the facts demonstrate that the alien under supervision could fully perform the duties of the occupation, H classification may be granted.

(D) Professional nurses. In lieu of licensure, professional nurses may provide the evidence required in paragraph (h)(3)(v)(C) of this section.

(E) Limitation on approval of petition. Where licensure is required in any occupation, including professional nursing, the H petition may only be approved for a period of one year or for the period that the temporary license is valid, whichever is longer, unless the alien already has a permanent license to practice the occupation. An alien who is accorded H classification in an occupation which requires licensure may not be granted an extension of stay or accorded a new H classification after the one year unless he or she has obtained a permanent license in the state of intended employment or continues to hold a temporary license valid for the period of the requested extension.

* * *

(5) Petition for alien to perform temporary nonagricultural services or labor (H-2B)—

(i) General. An H-2B nonagricultural temporary worker is an alien who is coming temporarily to the United States to perform temporary services or labor, is not displacing United States workers capable of performing such services or labor, and whose employment is not adversely affecting the wages and working conditions of United States workers.

(ii) Temporary services or labor—

(A) Definition. Temporary services or labor under the H-2B classification refers to any job in which the petitioner's need for the duties to be performed by the employee(s) is temporary, whether or not the underlying job can be described as permanent or temporary.

(B) Nature of petitioner's need. As a general rule, the period of the petitioner's need must be a year or less, although there may be extraordinary circumstances where the temporary services or labor might last longer than one year. The petitioner's need for the services or labor shall be a one-time occurrence, a seasonal need, a peakload need, or an intermittent need:

(1) One-time occurence (sic). The petitioner must establish that it has not employed workers to perform the services or labor in the past and that it will not need workers to perform the services or labor in the future, or that it has an employment situation that is otherwise permanent, but a temporary event of short duration has created the need for a temporary worker.

(2) Seasonal need. The petitioner must establish that the services or labor is traditionally tied to a season of the year by an event or pattern and is of a recurring nature. The petitioner shall specify the period(s) of time during each year in which it does not need the services or labor. The employment is not seasonal if the period during which the services or labor is not needed is unpredictable or subject to change or is considered a vacation period for the petitioner's permanent employees.

(3) Peakload need. The petitioner must establish that it regularly employs permanent workers to perform the services or labor at the place of employment and that it needs to supplement its permanent staff at the place of employment on a temporary basis due to a seasonal or short-term demand and that the temporary additions to staff will not become a part of the petitioner's regular operation.

(4) Intermittent need. The petitioner must establish that it has not employed permanent or full-time workers to perform the services or labor, but occasionally or intermittently needs temporary workers to perform services or labor for short periods.

(iii) Procedures.

(A) Prior to filing a petition with the director to classify an alien as an H-2B worker, the petitioner shall apply for a temporary labor certification with the Secretary of Labor for all areas of the United States, except the Territory of Guam. In the Territory of Guam, the petitioning employer shall apply for a temporary labor certification with the Governor of Guam. The labor certification shall be advice to the director on whether or not United States workers capable of performing the temporary services or labor are available and whether or not the alien's employment will adversely affect the wages and working conditions of similarly employed United States workers.

(B) An H-2B petitioner shall be a United States employer, or the authorized representative of a foreign employer having a location in the United States. The petitioning employer shall consider available U.S. workers for the temporary services or labor, and shall offer terms and conditions of employment which are consistent with the nature of the occupation, activity, and industry in the United States.

(C) The petitioner may not file an H-2B petition unless the United States petitioner has applied for a labor certification with the Secretary of Labor or the Governor of Guam within the time limits prescribed or accepted by each, and has obtained a labor certification determination as required by paragraph (h)(5)(iv) or (h)(5)(v) of this section.

(D) The Secretary of Labor and the Governor of Guam shall separately establish procedures for administering the temporary labor certification program under his or her jurisdiction.

(E) After obtaining a determination from the Secretary of Labor or the Governor of Guam, as appropriate, the petitioner shall file a petition on I-129H, accompanied by the labor certification determination and supporting documents, with the director having jurisdiction for I-129Hs in the area of intended employment.

(iv) Labor certifications, except Guam—

(A) Secretary of Labor's determination. An H-2B petition for temporary employment in the United States, except for temporary employment on Guam, shall be accompanied by a labor certification determination that is either:

(1) A certification from the Secretary of Labor stating that qualified workers in the United States are not available and that the alien's employment will not adversely affect wages and working conditions of similarly employed United States workers; or

(2) A notice detailing the reasons why such certification cannot be made. Such notice shall address the availability of U.S. workers in the occupation and the prevailing wages and working conditions of U.S. workers in the occupation.

(B) Validity of the labor certification. The Secretary of Labor may issue a temporary labor certification for a period of up to one year.

(C) U.S. Virgin Islands. Temporary labor certifications filed under section 101(a)(15)(H)(ii)(b) of the Act for employment in the United States Virgin Islands may be approved only for entertainers and athletes and only for periods not to exceed 45 days.

(D) Attachment to petition. If the petitioner receives a notice from the Secretary of Labor that certification cannot be made, a petition containing counter-vailing evidence may be filed with the director. The evidence must show that qualified workers in the United States are not available, and that the terms and conditions of employment are consistent with the nature of the occupation, activity, and industry in the United States. All such evidence submitted will be considered in adjudicating the petition.

(E) Countervailing evidence. The countervailing evidence presented by the petitioner shall be in writing and shall address availability of U.S. workers, the prevailing wage rate for the occupation of the United States, and each of the reasons why the Secretary of Labor could not grant a labor certification. The petitioner may also submit other appropriate information in support of the petition. The director, at his or her discretion, may require additional supporting evidence.

(v) Labor certification for Guam—

(A) Governor of Guam's determination. An H-2B petition for temporary employment on Guam shall be accompanied by a labor certification determination that is either:

(1) A certification from the Governor of Guam stating that qualified workers in the United States are not available to perform the required services, and that the alien's employment will not adversely affect the wages and working conditions of United States resident workers who are similarly employed on Guam; or

(2) A notice detailing the reasons why such certification cannot be made. Such notice shall address the availability of U.S. workers in the occupation and/or the prevailing wages and working conditions of U.S. workers in the occupation.

(B) Validity of labor certification. The Governor of Guam may issue a temporary labor certification for a period up to one year.

(C) Attachments to petition. If the employer receives a notice from the Governor of Guam that certification cannot be made, a petition containing countervailing evidence may be filed with the director. The evidence must show that qualified workers in the United States are not available, and that the terms and conditions of employment are consistent with the nature of the occupation, activity, and industry in the United States. All such evidence submitted will be considered in adjudicating the petition.

(D) Countervailing evidence. The countervailing evidence presented by the petitioner shall be in writing and shall address availability of United States workers, the prevailing wage rate, and each of the reasons why the Governor of Guam could not make the required certification. The petitioner may also provide any other appropriate information in support of the petition. The director, at his or her discretion, may require additional supporting evidence.

(E) Criteria for Guam labor certifications. The Governor of Guam shall, in consultation with the Service, establish systematic methods for determining the prevailing wage rates and working conditions for individual occupations on Guam and for making determinations as to availability of qualified United States residents.

(1) Prevailing wage and working conditions. The system to determine wages and working conditions must provide for consideration of wage rates and employment conditions for occupations in both the private and public sectors, in Guam and/or in the United States (as defined in section 101(a)(38) of the Act), and may not consider wages and working conditions outside of the United States. If the system includes utilitzation (sic) of advisory opinions and consultations, the opinions must be provided by officially sanctioned groups which reflect a balance of the interests of the private and public sectors, government, unions and management.

(2) Availability of United States workers. The system for determining availability of qualified United States workers must require the prospective employer to:

(i) Advertise the availability of the position for a minimum of three consecutive days in the newspaper with the largest daily circulation on Guam;

(ii) Place a job offer with an appropriate agency of the Territorial Government which operates as a job referral service at least 30 days in advance of the need for the services to commence, except that for applications from the armed forces of the United States and those in the entertainment industry, the 30-day period may be reduced by the Governor to 10 days;

(iii) Conduct appropriate recruitment in other areas of the United and its territories if sufficient qualified United States construction workers are not available on Guam to fill a job. The Governor of Guam may require a job order to be placed more than 30 days in advance of need to accommodate such recruitment;

(iv) Report to the appropriate agency the names of all United States resident workers who applied for the position, indicating those hired and the job-related reasons for not hiring;

(v) Offer all special considerations, such as housing and transportation expenses, to all United States resident workers who applied for the position, indicating those hired and the job-related reasons for not hiring;

(vi) Meet the prevailing wage rates and working conditions determined under the wages and working conditions system by the Governor; and

(vii) Agree to meet all Federal and Territorial requirements relating to employment, such as nondiscrimination, occupational safety, and minimum wage requirements.

(F) Approval and publication of employment systems on Guam—

(1) Systems. The Commissioner of Immigration and Naturalization must approve the system to determine prevailing wages and working conditions and the system to determine availability of United States resident workers and any future modifications of the systems prior to implementation. If the Commissioner, in consultation with the Secretary of Labor, finds that the systems or modified systems meet the requirements of this section, the Commissioner shall publish them as a notice in the Federal Register and the Governor shall publish them as a public record in Guam.

(2) Approval of construction wage rates. The Commissioner must approve specific wage data and rates used for construction occupations on Guam prior to implementation of new rates. The Governor shall submit new wage survey data and proposed rates to the Commissioner for approval at least eight weeks before authority to use existing rates expires. Surveys shall be conducted at least every two years, unless the Commissioner prescribes a lesser period.

(G) Reporting. The Governor shall provide the Commissioner statistical data on temporary labor certification workload and determinations. This information shall be submitted quarterly no later than 30 days after the quarter ends.

(H) Invalidation of temporary labor certification issued by the Governor of Guam—

(1) General. A temporary labor certification issued by the Governor of Guam may be invalidated by a director if it is determined by the director or a court of law that the certification request involved fraud or willful misrepresentation. A temporary labor certification may also be invalidated if the director determines that the certification involved gross error.

(2) Notice of intent to invalidate. If the director intends to invalidate a temporary labor certification, a notice of intent shall be served upon the employer, detailing the reasons for the intended invalidation. The employer shall have 30 days in which to file a written response in rebuttal to the notice of intent. The director shall consider all evidence submitted upon rebuttal in reaching a decision.

(3) Appeal of invalidation. An employer may appeal the invalidation of a temporary labor certification in accordance with Part 103 of this chapter.

(vi) Evidence for H-2B petitions. An H-2B petition filed on Form I-129H shall be accompanied by:

(A) Labor certification or notice. A temporary labor certification or a notice that certification cannot be made, issued by the Secretary of Labor or the Governor of Guam, as appropriate;

(B) Countervailing evidence. Evidence to rebut the Secretary of Labor's or the Governor of Guam's notice that certification cannot be made, if appropriate;

(C) Alien's qualifications. Documentation that the alien qualifies for the job offer as specified in the application for labor certification, except in petitions where the labor certification application requires no education, training, experience, or special requirements of the beneficiary; and

(D) Statement of need. A statement describing in detail the temporary situation or conditions which make it necessary to bring the alien to the United States and whether the need is a one-time occurrence, seasonal, peakload, or intermittent. If the need is seasonal, peakload, or intermittent, the statement shall indicate whether the situation or conditions are expected to be recurrent.

(6) Petition for alien trainee (H-3)—

(i) General. The H-3 trainee is a nonimmigrant who seeks to enter the United States at the invitation of an organization or individual for the purpose of receiving instruction in any field of endeavor, such as agriculture, commerce, communications, finance, government, transportation, or the professions, as well as training in a purely industrial establishment. This category shall not apply to physicians, who are statutorily ineligible to use H-3 classification in order to receive any type of graduate medical education or training.

(A) Externs. A hospital approved by the American Medical Association or the American Osteopathic Association for either an internship or residency program may petition to classify as an H-3 trainee a medical student attending a medical school abroad, if the alien will engage in employment as an extern during his/her medical school vacation.

(B) Nurses. A petitioner may seek H-3 classification for a nurse who is not H-1 if it can be established that there is a genuine need for the nurse to receive a brief period of training that is unavailable in the alien's native country and such training is designed to benefit the nurse and the overseas employer upon the nurse's return to the country of origin, if:

(1) The beneficiary has obtained a full and unrestricted license to practice professional nursing in the country where the beneficiary obtained a nursing education, or such education was obtained in the United States or Canada; and

(2) The petitioner provides a statement certifying that the beneficiary is fully qualified under the laws governing the place where the training will be received to engage in such training, and that under those laws the petitioner is authorized to give the beneficiary the desired training.

(ii) Evidence—

(A) Conditions. The petitioner is required to demonstrate that:

(1) The proposed training is not available in the alien's own country;

(2) The beneficiary will not be placed in a position which is in the normal operation of the business and in which citizens and resident workers are regularly employed;

(3) The beneficiary will not engage in productive employment unless such employment is incidental and necessary to the training; and

(4) The training will benefit the beneficiary in pursuing a career outside the United States.

(B) Description of training program. Each petition for a trainee must include a statement which:

(1) Describes the type of training and supervision to be given, and the structure of the training program;

(2) Sets forth the proportion of time that will be devoted to productive employment;

(3) Shows the number of hours that will be spent, respectively, in classroom instruction and in on-the-job training;

(4) Describes the career abroad for which the training will prepare the alien;

(5) Indicates the reasons why such training cannot be obtained in the alien's country and why it is necessary for the alien to be trained in the United States; and

(6) Indicates the source of any remuneration received by the trainee and any benefit which will accrue to the petitioner for providing the training.

(iii) Restrictions. A training program may not be approved which:

(A) Deals in generalities with no fixed schedule, objectives, or means of evaluation;

(B) Is incompatible with the nature of the petitioner's business or enterprise;

(C) Is on behalf of a beneficiary who already possesses substantial training and expertise in the proposed field of training;

(D) Is in a field in which it is unlikely that the knowledge or skill will be used outside the United States;

(E) Will result in productive employment beyond that which is incidental and necessary to the training;

(F) Is designed to recruit and train aliens for the ultimate staffing of domestic operations in the United States;

(G) Does not establish that the petitioner has the physical plant and sufficiently trained manpower to provide the training specified; or

(H) Is designed to extend the total allowable period of practical training previously authorized a nonimmigrant student.

(7) Certification of documents. A copy of a document submitted in support of a visa petition filed pursuant to section 214(c) of the Act and section 214.2(h) of this part may be accepted without the original, if the copy bears a certification by an attorney or by a voluntary agency in accordance with section 204.2(j) of this chapter or by a United States immigration or consular officer. However, the original document shall be submitted if requested by the director.

(8) Approval and validity of petition—

(i) Approval. The director shall consider all the evidence submitted and such other evidence as he or she may independently require to assist his or her adjudication. The director shall notify the petitioner of the approval of the petition on Form I-171C, Notice of Approval or Form I-797, Notice of Action. The approval shall be as follows:

(A) The approval notice shall include the beneficiary's(ies') name(s) and classification and the petition's period of validity. A petition for more than one beneficiary and/or multiple services may be approved in whole or in part. The approval notice shall cover only those beneficiaries approved for classification under section 101(a)(15)(H) of the Act.

(B) The petition may not be filed or approved earlier than six months before the date of actual need for the beneficiary's services or training.

(ii) Recording the validity of petitions. Procedures for recording the validity period of petitions are:

(A) If a new H petition is approved before the date the petitioner indicates that the services or training will begin, the approved petition and approval notice shall show the actual dates requested by the petitioner as the validity period, not to exceed the limits specified by paragraph (h)(8)(iii) of this section or other Service policy.

(B) If a new H petition is approved after the date the petitioner indicates that the services or training will begin, the approved petition and approval notice shall show a validity period commencing with the date of approval and ending with the date requested by the petitioner, as long as that date does not exceed either the limits specified by paragraph (h)(8)(iii) of this section or other Service policy.

(C) If the period of services or training requested by the petitioner exceeds the limit specified in paragraph (h)(8)(iii) of this section, the petition shall be approved only up to the limit specified in that paragraph.

(iii) Validity. The initial approval period of an H petition shall conform to the limits prescribed as follows:

(A) H-1 petition. An approved petition for an alien classified under section 101(a)(15)(H)(i) of the Act shall be valid for a period of up to three years.

(B) H-2B petition—

(1) Labor certification attached. If a certification by the Secretary of Labor or the Governor of Guam is attached to a petition to accord an alien a classification under section 101(a)(15)(H)(ii)(B) of the Act, the approval of the petition shall be valid for a period of up to one year.

(2) Notice that certification cannot be made attached—

(i) Countervailing evidence. If a petition is submitted containing a notice from the Secretary of Labor or the Governor of Guam that certification cannot be made, and is not accompanied by countervailing evidence, the petitioner shall be informed that he or she may submit the countervailing evidence in accordance with paragraphs (h)(5)(iii)(E) and (h)(5)(iv)(D) of this section.

(ii) Approval. In any case where the director decides that approval of the H-2B petition is warranted despite the issuance of a notice by the Secretary of Labor or the Governor of Guam that certification cannot be made, the approval shall be certified by the Director to the Commissioner pursuant to 8 CFR 103.4. In emergent situations, the certification may be presented by telephone to the Chief of the Administrative Appeals Unit, Central Office. If approved, the petition is valid for the period of established need not to exceed one year. There is no appeal from a decision which has been certified to the Commissioner.

(C) H-3 petition. An approved petition for an alien classified under section 101(a)(15)(H)(iii) of the Act shall be valid for a period of up to two years.

(iv) Spouse and dependents. The spouse and unmarried minor children of the beneficiary are entitled to H nonimmigrant classification, subject to the same period of admission and limitations as the beneficiary, if they are accompanying or following to join the beneficiary in the United States. Neither the spouse nor a child of the beneficiary may accept employment unless he or she is the beneficiary of an approved petition filed in his or her behalf and has been granted a nonimmigrant classification authorizing his or her employment.

(9) Denial of petition—

(i) Multiple beneficiaries. A petition for multiple beneficiaries may be denied in whole or in part.

(ii) Notice of intent of deny. When an adverse decision is proposed on the basis of evidence not submitted by the petitioner, the director shall notify the petitioner of the intent to deny the petition and the basis for the denial. The petitioner may inspect and rebut the evidence and will be granted a period of 30 days from the date of the notice in which to do so. All relevant rebuttal material will be considered in making a final decision.

(iii) Notice of denial. The petitioner shall be notified on Form I-292 of the decision, the reasons for the denial, and the right to appeal the denial under section 103 of this chapter.

(10) Revocation of approval of petition—

(i) General. The petitioner shall immediately notify the Service of any changes in the employment of a beneficiary which would affect eligibility under 101(a)(15)(H) of the Act and paragraph (h) of this section.

(ii) Automatic revocation. The approval of any petition is automatically revoked if the petitioner goes out of business or files a written withdrawal of the petition.

(iii) Revocation on notice—

(A) Grounds for revocation. The director shall send to the petitioner a notice of intent to revoke the petition in relevant part if he or she finds that:

(1) The beneficiary is no longer employed by the petitioner in the capacity specified in the petition, or if the beneficiary is no longer receiving training as specified in the petition; or

(2) The statement of facts contained in the petition was not true and correct; or

(3) The petitioner violated terms and conditions of the approved petition; or

(4) The petitioner violated requirements of section 101(a)(15)(H) of the Act or paragraph (h) of this section; or

(5) The approval of the petition violated paragraph (h) of this section or involved gross error.

(B) Notice and decision. The notice of intent to revoke shall contain a detailed statement of the grounds for the revocation and the time period allowed for the petitioner's rebuttal. The petitioner may submit evidence in rebuttal within 30 days of receipt of the notice. The director shall consider all relevant evidence presented in deciding whether to revoke the petition in whole or in part. If the petition is revoked in part, the remainder of the petition shall remain approved and a revised approval notice shall be sent to the petitioner with the revocation notice.

(11) Appeal of a denial or a revocation of a petition—

(i) Denial. A petition denied in whole or in part may be appealed under Part 103 of this chapter.

(ii) Revocation. A petition that has been revoked on notice in whole or in part may be appealed under Part 103 of this chapter. Automatic revocations may not be appealed.

(12) Admission.—

(i) General. A beneficiary may be admitted to the United States for the validity period of the petition, plus a period of up to 10 days before the validity period begins and 10 days after the validity period ends. The authorized period of the beneficiary's admission shall not exceed the above limits. The beneficiary may not work except during the validity period of the petition.

(ii) H-1 limitation on admission. An alien who has spent five, or in certain extraordinary circumstances, six years in the United States under section 101(a) (15)(H)(i) and or (L) of the Act may not seek extension, change status, or be readmitted to the United States under the H or L visa classification, unless the alien has resided and been physically present outside the United States, except for brief trips for pleasure or business, for the immediate prior year. In view of this restriction, a new petition shall not be approved for an alien who has spent five or six years in the United States under section 101(a)(15)(H)(i) and/or (L) of the Act, unless the alien has resided and been physically present outside the United States for the immediate prior year. Brief trips for pleasure or business to the United States during the immediate prior year are not interruptive of the one-year requirement, but do not count towards fulfillment of that requirement. The petitioner shall provide information about the alien's employment, place of residence, and the dates and purposes of any trips to the United States for the previous year.

(iii) H-2B and H-3 limitation on admission. An alien who has spent three years in the United States under section 101(a)(15)(H)(ii) or two years under section 101 (a)(15)(H)
(iii) of the Act may not seek extension, change status, or be readmitted to the United States under the H or L visa classification unless the alien has resided and been physically present outside the United States for the immediate prior six months. In view of this restriction, a new petition shall not be approved for an alien who has spent three years in the United States under section 101(a)(15)(H)(ii) or two years under section 101(a)(15)(H)(iii) of the Act unless the alien has resided and been physically present outside the United States, except for brief trips for business or pleasure, for the immediate prior six months. The petitioner shall provide information about the alien's employment, place of residence, and the dates and purpose of any trips to the United States for the previous six months. Brief trips for business or pleasure to the United States during the immediate prior six months are not interruptive of the six-month requirement, but do not count towards fulfillment of that requirement.

(iv) Exceptions. The limitations in paragraph (h)(12(ii) and (h)(12)(iii) of this section shall not apply to H-1, H-2B, and H-3 aliens who did not reside continually in the United States and whose employment in the United States was seasonal or intermittent or an aggregate of six months or less per year. In addition, the limitations shall not apply to aliens who reside abroad and regularly commute to the United States to engage in part-time employment. To qualify for this exception, the petitioner and the alien must provide clear and convincing proof that the alien qualifies for an exception. Such proof shall consist of evidence such as arrival and departure records, copies of tax returns, and records of employment abroad.

(13) Extension of visa petition validity.—

(i) Approval. A visa petition under section 101(a)(15)(H) of the Act shall be automatically extended, without the filing of Form I-129H, if the director extends the stay of the alien beneficiary(ies) in accordance with paragraph (h)(14) of this section. A new approval notice shall be issued to the petitioner at the same time that the beneficiary is notified that his or her extension of stay application has been approved. The dates of extension shall be the same for the petition and the beneficiary's extension of stay. No action shall be taken on the visa petition if the alien's application for extension of stay is denied.

(ii) Denial. Although an application for extension of stay under the H classification does not require the filing of a petition extension, the director may consider information relating to the petition in adjudicating the beneficiary's extension of stay. If the director determines that there are grounds to readjudicate the petition before granting or denying the extension, the director shall move to reopen or reconsider the original petition in accordance with 8 CFR 103.5. If the petition is denied, the alien's extension of stay shall be denied for lack of an approved supporting petition.

(14) Extension of stay.—

(i) Procedure—

(A) H-1 and H-3 beneficiaries. If maintaining status, the beneficiary of an H-1 or H-3 petition may apply for an extension of stay by submitting an application for extension of stay, a copy of the original petition's approval notice, and a letter from the petitioner which describes the beneficiary's current duties, hours of work, and salary; indicates whether any terms and conditions of the original petition have changed, gives the reasons for the extension, gives the dates of the alien's periods of stay in the United States for the previous six years under H-1 or the previous three years under H-3, and specifies the new dates of employment or training requested.

(B) H-2B beneficiaries. The petitioner must obtain a new labor certification or a notice that certification cannot be made in order for the H-2B beneficiary to apply for an extension of stay. If maintaining status, the H-2B beneficiary may apply for an extension of stay by submitting an application for extension of stay, a copy of the original petition's approval notice, a statement which gives the dates of the alien's periods of stay in the United States for the previous three years, and the new labor certification or notice with countervailing evidence.

(C) Multiple beneficiaries. An application for extension of stay on behalf of multiple beneficiaries covered by the same original petition must be filed by each individual alien, except that in the case of an extension of stay for members of a group as defined in paragraph (h)(3)(i)(B) of this section, one application for extension of stay is required with an attached list of beneficiaries.

(ii) Extension periods—

(A) H-1 extension of stay. An extension of stay may be authorized for a period of up to two years for a beneficiary of an H-1 petition. The alien's total period of stay may not exceed five years, except in extraordinary circumstances. Beyond five years, an extension of stay not to exceed one year may be granted under extraordinary circumstances. Extraordinary circumstances shall exist when the director finds that termination of the alien's services will impose extreme hardship on the petitioner's business operation or that the alien's services are required in the national welfare, safety, or security interests of the United States. No further extensions may be granted.

If the director decides that approval of the one-year extension is warranted because of extraordinary circumstances, the decision shall be certified to the Administrative Appeals Unit.

(B) H-2B extension of stay. An extension of stay for the beneficiary of an H-2 petition may be authorized for the validity of the labor certification or for a period of up to one year. The alien's total period of stay as an H-2B worker may not exceed three years, except that in the Virgin Islands, the alien's total period of stay may not exceed 45 days.

(C) H-3 extension of stay. An extension of stay may be authorized for a period of up to one year for the beneficiary of an H-3 petition. The alien's total period of stay as an H-3 trainee, however, may not exceed two years.

(iii) Denial of extension of stay. If an H beneficiary's request for extension of stay is denied, the alien shall be notified of the reasons for the denial. There is no appeal from the denial of an alien's application for an extension of stay.

(15) Effect of approval of a permanent labor certification or filing of a preference petition on H classification—

(i) H-1 classification.—

(A) Petitioner—

(1) Conditions. The approval of a permanent labor certification or the filing of a preference petition for an alien is not by itself a ground to deny an H-1 petition if the director, in his/her judgment, determines that the following conditions are met:

(i) The dates of employment must be within the time limit for which an H-1 petition may be authorized, and

(ii) The petitioner must establish that temporary classification is not being requested for the principal purpose of enabling the employee to enter the United States permanently in advance of the availability of a visa number.

(2) Evidence. In deciding whether or not the foregoing conditions have been met, the director will consider evidence provided by the petitioner of factors such as, but not limited to the following, as appropriate:

(i) Petitioner's prior history of use of aliens in temporary and permanent capacities and extent to which petitioner has employed aliens without lawful authorization, and

(ii) Whether the employment appears to be an accommodation rather than a bona fide employer/employee relationship.

(B) Beneficiary—

(1) Conditions. The approval of a labor certification or the filing of a preference petition is not by itself a ground to deny an H-1 beneficiary's application for admission, change of status, or extension of stay if the director, in his or her judgment, determines that the following conditions are met:

(i) The alien must demonstrate that he or she has not abandoned residence abroad; and

(ii) The alien must establish that he or she intends to enter and remain in the United States only in accordance with any authorized stay and to return abroad voluntarily at or before termination of that authorization, unless he or she has become a permanent resident of the United States in the meantime.

(2) Evidence. In determining whether the alien meets these conditions, the director shall consider evidence provided by the alien that establishes factors such as, but not limited to, the following:

(i) Evidence of a residence abroad, such as home, bank accounts, or prospects of a job abroad at the end of the authorized stay;

(ii) Close family ties abroad;

(iii) History of previous visa classifications and stays in the United States, and evidence that the alien has not entered or remained in the United States in violation of United States immigration laws; and

(iv) Employment history within and outside the United States.

(ii) H-2B and H-3 classification. The approval of a permanent labor certification or the filing of a preference petition for an alien in the same or a different job or training position and for the same petitioner shall be a ground to deny the alien's request for extension of stay.

(16) Effect of a strike. If the Secretary of Labor certifies to the Commissioner of Immigration and Naturalization that a strike or other labor dispute involving a work stoppage of workers is in progress in the occupation at the place where the beneficiary is to be employed or trained, and that the employment or training of the beneficiary would adversely affect the wages and working conditions of U.S. citizens and lawful resident workers:

(i) A petition to classify an alien as a nonimmigrant as defined in section 101 (a)(15)(H) of the Act shall be denied.

(ii) If a petition has been approved, but the alien has not yet entered the United States, or has entered the United States but has not commenced the employment, the approval of the petition is automatically suspended, and the application for admission on the basis of the petition shall be denied.

(iii) If the alien has already commenced employment in the United States under an approved petition and is participating in a strike or labor dispute involving a work stoppage of workers, the alien:

(A) Is failing to maintain his or her nonimmigrant status, and

(B) Remains subject to the time limits on a temporary stay which apply to his or her classification.

(17) Use of approval notice, Form I-171C or Form I-797. The Service shall notify the petitioner on Form I-171C or Form I-797 whenever a visa petition or an extension of a visa petition is approved under the H classification. The beneficiary of an H petition who does not require a nonimmigrant visa may present a copy of the approval notice at a port of entry to facilitate entry into the United States. A beneficiary who is required to present a visa for admission and whose visa will have expired before the date of his or her intended return may use an original Form I-171C or Form I-797 to apply for a new or revalidated visa during the validity period of the petition. The copy of Form I-171C or Form I-797 shall be retained by the beneficiary and presented during the validity of the petition when reentering the United States to resume the same employment with the same petitioner and when applying for an extension of stay.

Information Media

(i) Representatives of information media. The admission of an alien of the class defined in section 101(a)(15)(I) of the Act constitutes an agreement by the alien not to change the information medium or his or her employer until he or she obtains permission to do so from the district director having jurisdiction over his or her residence. An alien classified as an information media nonimmigrant (I) may be authorized admission for the duration of employment.

Exchange Aliens

§ 214.2(j)

(1) General.—

(i) "Exchange alien" means a nonimmigrant admitted under a section 101(a)(15)(J) of the Act or who acquired such status, or who acquired exchange-visitor status under the United States Information and Education Exchange Act. Any exchange alien coming to the United States as a participant in a program designated under section 101(a)(15)(J) of the Act and accompanying spouse and minor children shall not be admitted without submitting a completely executed Form IAP-66. The spouse and minor children following to join the participant shall not be admitted without a copy of current Form IAP-66 endorsed by the program sponsor indicating the expiration of stay date as shown on Form I-94. Any alien seeking to change nonimmigrant status to exchange visitor status shall file Form I-506 and attach a valid Form IAP-66.

(ii) Admission. The initial admission of an exchange alien, spouse, and children may not exceed the period specified on Form IAP-66, plus a period of 30 days for the purpose of travel. Regulations of the United States Information Agency published at 22 CFR 514.23 give general limitations on the length of stay of the various classes of exchange visitors. A spouse or child (J-2) may not be admitted for longer than the principal exchange alien (J-1).

(iii) Readmission. An exchange alien may be readmitted to the United States for the remainder of the time authorized on Form I-94, without presenting Form IAP-66, if the alien is returning from a visit solely to foreign contiguous territory or adjacent islands after an absence of less than 30 days and if the original Form I-94 is presented. All other exchange aliens must present a valid Form IAP-66. An original Form IAP-66 or copy three (the pink copy) of a previously issued form presented by an exchange alien returning from a temporary absence shall be retained by the exchange alien for re-entries during the balance of the alien's stay.

(iv) Extensions of Stay. If an exchange alien requires an extension beyond the initial admission period, the alien shall apply by submitting a new Form IAP-66 which indicates the date to which the alien's program is extended. The extension may not exceed the period specified on Form IAP-66, plus a period of 30 days for the purpose of travel. Extensions of stay for the alien's spouse and children require, as an attachment to Form IAP-66, Form I-94 for each dependent, and a list containing the names of the applicants, dates and places of birth, passport numbers, issuing countries, and expiration dates. An accompanying spouse or child may not be granted an extension of stay for longer than the principal exchange alien.

(v) Employment. The accompanying spouse and minor children of a participant may accept employment for support (including, but not limited to, customary rec-

reational and cultural activities and related travel) of the accompanying nonpartici-
pating spouse and minor children in the United States if authorized by the Service.
Employment shall not be authorized if this income is needed to support the participant.
Application to accept employment must be made to the district director having jurisdiction over the place where the participant is residing temporarily. The application
for employment does not have to be in writing.

(2) Special Reporting Requirement. Each exchange alien participating in a program
of graduate medical education or training shall file Form I-644 (Supplementary Statement for Graduate Medical Trainees) annually with the Service attesting to the conditions as specified on the form. The exchange alien shall also submit Form I-644 as
an attachment to a completed Form IAP-66 when applying for an extension of stay.

(3) Alien in Cancelled Programs. When the approval of an exchange visitor program
is withdrawn by the Director of the United States Information Agency, the district
director shall send a notice of the withdrawal to each participant in the program and
a copy of each such notice shall be sent to the program sponsor. If the exchange
visitor is currently engaged in activities authorized by the cancelled program, the
participant is authorized to remain in the United States to engage in those activities
until expiration of the period of stay previously authorized. The district director shall
notify participants in cancelled programs that permission to remain in the United
States as an exchange visitor, or extension of stay may be obtained if the participant
is accepted in another approved program and a Form IAP-66, executed by the new
program sponsor, is submitted. In this case, a release from the sponsor of the program
would result from not permitting the alien to participate in the program: Provided
that the exemption will not increase the total number of aliens then participating in
such programs to a level greater than that participating on January 10, 1978.

Fiances

§ 214.2(k) Fiancees and fiances of United States citizens.

(1) Petition and supporting documents. To be classified as a fiance or fiancee as
defined in section 101(a)(15)(k) of the Act, and alien must be the beneficiary of an
approved visa petition filed on Form I-129F. The petition with supporting documents
shall be filed by the petitioner with the district director having administrative jurisdiction over the place where the petitioner is residing in the United States. A copy of
a document submitted in support of a visa petition filed pursuant to section 214(d)
of the Act and this paragraph may be accepted, though unaccompanied by the original,
if the copy bears a certification by an attorney, typed or rubber-stamped in the
language set forth in § 204.2(j) of this chapter. However, the original document shall
be submitted, if submittal is requested by the Service.

(2) Requirement that petitioner and beneficiary have met. The petitioner shall
establish to the satisfaction of the director that the petitioner and beneficiary have
met in person within the two years immediately preceding the filing of the petition.
As a matter of discretion, the director may exempt the petitioner from this requirement
only if it is established that compliance would result in extreme hardship to the
petitioner or that compliance would violate strict and long-established customs of the
beneficiary's foreign culture or social practice, as where marriages are traditionally
arranged by the parents of the contracting parties and the prospective bride and
groom are prohibited from meeting subsequent to the arrangement and prior to the

wedding day. In addition to establishing that the required meeting would be a violation of custom or practice, the petitioner must also establish that any and all other aspects of the traditional arrangements have been or will be met in accordance with the custom or practice. Failure to establish that the petitioner and beneficiary have met within the required period or that compliance with the requirement should be waived shall result in the denial of the petition. Such denial shall be without prejudice to the filing of a new petition once the petitioner and beneficiary have met in person.

(3) Children of beneficiary. Without the approval of a separate petition on his or her behalf, a child of the beneficiary [as defined in section 101(b)(1)(A), (B), (C), (D), or (E) of the Act] may be accorded the same nonimmigrant classification as the beneficiary if accompanying or following to join him or her.

(4) Notification. The petitioner shall be notified of the decision and, if the petition is denied, of the reasons therefor and of the right to appeal in accordance with the provisions of Part 103 of this chapter.

(5) Validity. The approval of a petition under this paragraph shall be valid for a period of four months. A petition which has expired due to the passage of time may be revalidated by a director or a consular officer for a period of four months from the date of revalidation upon a finding that the petitioner and beneficiary are free to marry and intend to marry each other within 90 days of the beneficiary's entry into the United States. The approval of any petition is automatically terminated when the petitioner dies or files a written withdrawal of the petition before the beneficiary arrives in the United States.

(6) Adjustment of status from nonimmigrant to immigrant—

(i) Nonimmigrant visa issued prior to November 10, 1986. If the beneficiary contracts a valid marriage with the petitioner within 90 days of his or her admission to the United States pursuant to a valid K-1 visa issued prior to November 10, 1986, and the beneficiary and his or her minor children are otherwise admissible, the director shall record their lawful admission for permanent residence as of the date of their filing of an application for adjustment of status to lawful permanent resident (Form I-485). Such residence shall be granted under section 214(d) of the Act as in effect prior to November 10, 1986 and shall not be subject to the conditions of section 216 of the Act.

(ii) Nonimmigrant visa issued on or after November 10, 1986. Upon contracting a valid marriage to the petitioner within 90 days of his or her admission as a nonimmigrant pursuant to a valid K visa issued on or after November 10, 1986, the beneficiary and his or her minor children may apply for adjustment of status to lawful permanent resident under section 245 of the Act. Upon approval of the application the director shall record their lawful admission for permanent residence in accordance with that section and subject to the conditions prescribed in section 216 of the Act.

Intracompany Transferees

§ 214.2(l)

(1) Admission of intracompany transferees—

(i) General. Under section 101(a)(15)(L) of the Act, an alien employee of a qualifying organization may be admitted temporarily to the United States to continue employment with a branch of his/her same employer or a parent, affiliate, or subsidiary of that employer in a managerial, executive, or specialized knowledge capacity. An alien transferred to the United States under this nonimmigrant classification is referred to as an intracompany transferee, and the organization which seeks the classification of an alien as an intracompany transferee is referred to as the petitioner. The Service has responsibility for determining whether the alien is eligible for admission and whether the petitioner is a qualifying organization. These regulations set forth the procedures whereby these benefits may be applied for and granted, denied, extended, or revoked. They also set forth procedures for appeal of adverse decisions and admission of intracompany transferees. Certain petitioners seeking the classification of aliens as intracompany transferees may file blanket petitions with the Service. Under the blanket petition process, the Service is responsible for determining whether the petitioner and its parent, branches, subsidiaries, and affiliates specified are qualifying organizations. The Department of State or, in certain cases, the Service is responsible for determining the classification of the alien.

(ii) Definitions.

(A) "Intracompany transferee" means an alien who, immediately preceding the time of his/her application for admission into the United States, has been employed abroad continuously for the immediate prior year by a firm or corporation or other legal entity or parent, branch, affiliate, or subsidiary thereof, and who seeks to enter the United States temporarily in order to continue to render his/her services to a branch of the same employer or a parent, subsidiary, or affiliate thereof in a capacity that is managerial, executive, or involves specialized knowledge. Periods spent in the United States in lawful status for a branch of the same employer or a parent, subsidiary, or affiliate thereof shall not be interruptive of the one year of continuous employment abroad, but such periods shall not be counted toward fulfillment of that requirement.

(B) "Managerial capacity" means an assignment within an organization in which the employee primarily directs the organization or a department or subdivision of the organization, supervises and controls the work of other supervisory, professional, or managerial employees, has the authority to hire and fire or recommend those as well as other personnel actions (such as promotion and leave authorization), and exercises discretionary authority over day-to-day operations. The term manager does not include a first-line supervisor, unless the employees supervised are professional, nor does it include an employee who primarily performs the tasks necessary to produce the product and/or to provide the service(s) of the organization. See paragraph (1)(3)(v) of this section for application of this definition to aliens who are coming to the United States to open a new office.

(C) "Executive capacity" means an assignment within an organization in which the employee primarily directs the management of an organization or a major component or function of that organization, establishes the goals and policies of the organization, component or function, exercises wide latitude in discretionary decision-making, and receives only general supervision or direction from higher level executives, the board of directors, or stockholders of the business. This definition does not include an employee who primarily performs the tasks necessary to produce the product and/or to provide the service(s) of the organization. See paragraph (1)(3)(v) of this section for application of this definition to aliens who are coming to the United States to open a new office.

(D) "Specialized knowledge" means knowledge possessed by an individual whose advanced level of expertise and proprietary knowledge of the organization's product, service, research, equipment, techniques, management, or other interests of the employer are not readily available in the United States labor market. This definition does not apply to persons who have general knowledge or expertise which enables them merely to produce a product or provide a service.

(E) "Specialized knowledge professional" means an individual who has specialized knowledge as defined in paragraph (l)(1)(ii)(D) of this section and is a member of the professions as defined in section 101(a)(32) of the Immigration and Nationality Act.

(F) "New office" means an office that has been doing business for less than one year.

(G) "Qualifying organization" means a United States or foreign firm, corporation, or other legal entity which, for the duration of the alien's stay in the United States as an intracompany transferee, directly or through a parent, branch, affiliate, or subsidiary, is or will be doing business as an employer in the United States and in at least one other country and which otherwise meets the requirements of section 101(a)(15)(L). A qualifying organization is not required to engage in international trade.

(H) "Doing business" means the regular, systematic, and continuous provision of goods and/or services by a qualifying organization which has employees and does not include the mere presence of an agent or office of the qualifying organization in the United States or abroad.

(I) "Parent" means a firm, corporation, or other legal entity which has subsidiaries.

(J) "Branch" means an operating division or office of the same organization housed in a different location.

(K) "Subsidiary" means a firm, corporation, or other legal entity of which a parent owns, directly or indirectly, more than half of the entity and controls the entity; or owns, directly or indirectly, 50% of a 50-50 joint venture and has equal control and veto power; or owns, directly or indirectly, less than half of the entity, but in fact controls the entity.

(L) "Affiliate" means one of two subsidiaries both of which are owned and controlled by the same parent or individual or one of two legal entities owned and controlled by the same group of individuals, each individual owning and controlling approximately the same share or proportion of each entity.

(M) "Director" means a district director or Regional Service Center director with delegated authority at 8 CFR 103.1.

(2) Filing of petitions—

(i) Except as provided in paragraph (l)(2)(ii) of this section, a petitioner seeking to classify an alien as an intracompany transferee shall file a petition in duplicate on Form I-129L with the director having jurisdiction over the area where the alien will be employed. The petitioner shall advise the Service whether it has filed a petition for the same beneficiary with another office and certify that it will not file a petition for the same beneficiary with another office, unless the circumstances and conditions in this petition have changed. Failure to make a full disclosure of previous petitions filed will result in denial of this petition.

(ii) A United States petitioner which meets the requirements of paragraph (l)(4) of this section and seeks continuing approval of itself and its parent, branches, specified subsidiaries and affiliates as qualifying organizations and, later, classification under section 101(a)(15)(L) of multiple numbers of aliens employed by itself, its parent, or those branches, subsidiaries, or affiliates may file a blanket petition on Form I-129L with the director having jurisdiction over the area where the petitioner is located. The blanket petition shall be adjudicated and maintained at the appropriate Regional Service Center. Approved blanket petition files shall be maintained indefinitely by that Regional Service Center. The petitioner shall be the single representative for the qualifying organizations with which the Service will deal regarding the blanket petition.

§ 214.2(l)(3)(v)(C)

(3) Evidence for individual petitions. An individual petition filed on Form I-129L shall be accompanied by:

(i) Evidence that the petitioner and the organization which employed or will employ the alien are qualifying organizations as defined in paragraph (l)(1)(ii)(G) of this section.

(ii) Evidence that the alien will be employed in an executive, managerial, or specialized knowledge capacity, including a detailed description of the services to be performed.

(iii) Evidence that the alien has at least one continuous year of full-time employment abroad with a qualifying organization immediately preceding the filing of the petition.

(iv) Evidence that the alien's prior year of employment abroad was in a position that was managerial, executive, or involved specialized knowledge and that the alien's prior education, training, and employment qualifies him/her to perform the intended services in the United States; however, the work in the United States need not be the same work which the alien performed abroad.

(v) If the petition indicates that the beneficiary is coming to open or to be employed in a new office in the United States, the petitioner shall submit evidence that:

(A) Sufficient physical premises to house the new office have been secured;

(B) The beneficiary's prior year abroad was in an executive or managerial capacity and the proposed employment involves executive or managerial authority over the new operation;

(C) The intended United States operation, within one year of approval of the petition, will support an executive or managerial position as defined in paragraphs (l)(ii) (A) or (B) of this section, supported by information regarding:

(1) The proposed number of employees and the types of positions they will hold;

(2) The size of the United States investment and the financial ability of the foreign entity to remunerate the beneficiary and to commence doing business in the United States; and

(3) The size and staffing levels of the foreign entity.

(vi) If the beneficiary is an owner or major stockholder of the company, the petition must be accompanied by evidence that the beneficiary's services are to be used for a temporary period and evidence that the beneficiary will be transferred to an assignment abroad upon the completion of the temporary services in the United States.

(vii) Such other evidence as the director, in his or her discretion, may deem necessary.

(4) Blanket petitions—

(i) A petitioner which meets the following requirements may file a blanket petition seeking continuing approval of itself and some or all of its parent, branches, subsidiaries, and affiliates as qualifying organizations if:

(A) The petitioner and each of those entities are engaged in commercial trade or services;

(B) The petitioner has an office in the United States that has been doing business for one year or more;

(C) The petitioner has three or more domestic and foreign branches, subsidiaries, or affiliates; and

(D) The petitioner and the other qualifying organizations have obtained approval of petitions for at least ten "L" managers, executives, or specialized knowledge professionals during the previous 12 months; or have U.S. subsidiaries or affiliates with combined annual sales of at least $25 million; or have a United States work force of at least 1,000 employees.

(ii) Managers, executives, and specialized knowledge professionals employed by firms, corporations, or other entities which have been found to be qualifying organizations pursuant to an approved blanket petition may be classified as intracompany transferees and admitted to the United States as provided in paragraphs (l)(5) and (11) of this section.

(iii) When applying for a blanket petition, the petitioner shall include in the blanket petition all of its branches, subsidiaries, and affiliates which plan to seek to transfer aliens to the United States under the blanket petition. An individual petition may be filed by the petitioner or organizations in lieu of using the blanket petition procedure. However, the petitioner and other qualifying organizations may not seek L classification for the same alien under both procedures, unless a consular officer first denies eligibility. Whenever a petitioner which has blanket L approval files an individual petition to seek L classification for a manager, executive, or specialized knowledge professional, the petitioner shall advise the Service that it has blanket L approval and certify that the beneficiary has not and will not apply to a consular officer for L classification under the approved blanket petition.

(iv) Evidence. A blanket petition filed on Form I-129L shall be accompanied by:

(A) Evidence that the petitioner meets the requirements of paragraph (l)(4)(i) of this section.

(B) Evidence that all entities for which approval is sought are qualifying organizations as defined in subparagraph (l)(1)(ii)(G) of this section.

(C) Such other evidence as the director, in his or her discretion, deems necessary in a particular case.

(5) Certification and admission procedures for beneficiaries under blanket petition.

(i) Jurisdiction. United States consular officers shall have authority to determine eligibility of individual beneficiaries outside the United States seeking L classification under blanket petitions, except for visa-exempt nonimmigrants. An application for a visa-exempt nonimmigrant seeking L classification under a blanket petition or by an alien in the United States applying for change of status to L classification under a blanket petition shall be filed with the Service office at which the blanket petition was filed.

(ii) Procedures—

(A) When one qualifying organization listed in an approved blanket petition wishes to transfer an alien outside the United States to a qualifying organization in the United States and the alien requires a visa to enter the United States, that organization shall complete Form I-129S, Certificate of Eligibility for Intracompany transferee under a Blanket Petition, in an original and three copies. The qualifying organization shall retain one copy for its records and send the original and two copies to the alien. A copy of the approved Form I-171C must be attached to the original and each copy of Form I-129S.

(B) After receipt of Form I-171C and Form I-129S, a qualified employee who is being transferred to the United States may use these documents to apply for visa issuance with the consular officer within six months of the date on Form I-129S.

(C) When the alien is a visa-exempt nonimmigrant seeking L classification under a blanket petition or when the alien is in the United States and is seeking a change of status from another nonimmigrant classification to L classification under a blanket petition, the petitioner shall submit Form I-129S, a copy of the approved Form I-171C, and, as appropriate, Form I-506 (Application for Change of Nonimmigrant Status) completed by the alien beneficiary to the Service office with which the blanket petition was filed.

Nonimmigrant Visas—Denial

22 C.F.R. § 41.121 Refusal of individual visas

*   *   *

(b) Refusal procedure. If a consular officer knows or has reason to believe that an alien is ineligible to receive a visa on grounds of ineligibility which cannot be overcome by the presentation of additional evidence, the officer shall refuse the visa and, if practicable, shall require a nonimmigrant visa application to be executed before the refusal is recorded. In the case of a visa refusal the consular officer shall inform the applicant of the provision of law or regulations upon which the refusal is based. If the alien fails to execute a visa application after being informed by the consular officer of a ground of ineligibility to receive a nonimmigrant visa, the visa shall be considered refused. The officer shall then insert the pertinent data on the visa application, noting the reasons for the refusal, and the application form shall be filed in the consular office. Upon refusing a nonimmigrant visa, the consular officer shall retain the original or a copy of each document upon which the refusal was based as well as each document indicating a possible ground of ineligibility and may return all other supporting documents supplied by the applicant.

(c) Review of refusal at consular office. If the ground(s) of ineligibility upon which the visa was refused cannot be overcome by the presentation of additional evidence, the principal consular officer, or a specifically designated alternate, shall review the case without delay, record the review decision, and sign and date the prescribed form. If the ground(s) of ineligibility may be overcome by the presentation of additional evidence, and the applicant has indicated the intention to submit such evidence, a review of the refusal may be deferred for not more than 120 days. If the principal consular officer or alternate does not concur in the refusal, that officer shall either

(1) Refer the case to the Department for an advisory opinion, or

(2) Assume responsibility for the case by reversing the refusal.

(d) Review of refusal by Department. The Department may request a consular officer in a specific case or in specified classes of cases to submit a report if a visa has been refused. The Department will review each report and may furnish an advisory opinion to the consular officer for assistance in considering the case further. If the officer believes that action contrary to an advisory opinion should be taken, the case shall be resubmitted to the Department with an explanation of the proposed action. Rulings of the Department concerning an interpretation of law, as distinguished from an application of the law to the facts, shall be binding upon consular officers.

Change of Nonimmigrant Classification

8 C.F.R. § 248.1

(a) General. Except for those classes enumerated in § 248.2, any alien lawfully admitted to the United States as a nonimmigrant, including an alien who acquired such status pursuant to section 247 of the Act, who is continuing to maintain his nonimmigrant status, may apply to have his nonimmigrant classification changed to any nonimmigrant classification other than that of a fiancee or fiance under section 101(a)(15)(K) of the Act.

(b) Maintenance of status. In determining whether an applicant has continued to maintain nonimmigrant status, the district director shall consider whether the alien has remained in the United States for a longer period than that authorized by the Service. The district director shall consider any conduct by the applicant relating to the maintenance of the status from which the applicant is seeking a change. An applicant may not be considered as having maintained nonimmigrant status within the meaning of this section if the applicant failed to submit an application for change of nonimmigrant classification before the applicant's authorized temporary stay in the United States expired, unless the district director determines that—

(1) The failure to file a timely application is excusable;

(2) The alien has not otherwise violated the nonimmigrant status;

(3) The alien is a bona fide nonimmigrant; and

(4) The alien is not the subject of deportation proceedings under Part 242 of this chapter.

(c) Change of nonimmigrant classification to that of a nonimmigrant student. A nonimmigrant applying for a change to classification as a student under sections 101(a)(15)(F)(i) or 101(a)(15)(M)(i) of the Act is not considered ineligible for such a change solely because the applicant may have started attendance at school before the application was submitted. The district director shall deny an application for a change to classification as a student under section 101(a)(15)(M)(i) of the Act if the applicant intends to pursue the course of study solely in order to qualify for a subsequent change of nonimmigrant classification to that of an alien temporary worker under section 101(a)(15)(H) of the Act. Furthermore, an alien may not change from classification as a student under section 101(a)(15)(M)(i) of the Act to that of a student under section 101(a)(15)(F)(i) of the Act.

(d) Application for change of nonimmigrant classification from that of a student under section 101(a)(15)(M)(i) to that described in section 101(a)(15)(H). A district director shall deny an application for change of nonimmigrant classification from that of an M-1 student to that of an alien temporary worker under section 101 (a)(15)(H) of the Act if the education or training which the student received while an M-1 student enables the student to meet the qualifications for temporary worker classification under section 101(a)(15(H) of the Act.

(e) Change of nonimmigrant classification to that as described in section 101 (a)(15)(N). An application for change to N status shall not be denied on the grounds the applicant is an intending immigrant. Change of status shall be granted for three years not to exceed termination of eligibility under section 101(a)(15)(N) of the Act. Employment authorization pursuant to section 274(A) of the Act may be granted to an alien accorded nonimmigrant status under section 101(a)(15)(N) of the Act.

Employment authorization is automatically terminated when the alien changes status or is no longer eligible for classification under section 101(a)(15)(N) of the Act.

*   *   *

§ 248.3 Application

(a) General. A nonimmigrant alien who seeks to change the visa classification under which he or she was admitted to the United States shall apply for a change of nonimmigrant classification on Form I-506, Applicant for Change of Nonimmigrant Status. The applicant shall submit documentary evidence establishing eligibility for the change of classification being requested. Form I-506 must be filed with the district director having jurisdiction over the applicant's place of temporary residence in the United States, except for change of status to classification under section 101(a)(15) (H) or (L) of the Act.

(b) Change to H or L. An applicant for change of nonimmigrant classification to H or L shall submit Form I-506 accompanied by either Form I-129B, Petition to Classify Nonimmigrant as Temporary Worker or Trainee, or a copy of the Form I-171C, Notice of Approval or Extension of Nonimmigrant Visa Petition of H or L Alien, to the district director having jurisdiction over the place of employment. If the services will be performed or the training will be received in more than one location in the United States, the petition and application shall be filed with a Service office having jurisdictions over at least one of those areas. In the case of a "blanket L" applicant, the I-506 may be filed with the district director having jurisdiction over at least one of the areas where the services will be performed, or may be filed with the district director where the blanket petition was filed.

(c) Application and fee not required. For a change of nonimmigrant classification to a classification under section 101(a)(15)(A) or 101(a)(15)(G) of the Act, the Department of State must send a letter to the district director. For all other changes of nonimmigrant classification as described below, the applicant must submit a letter to the district director requesting the change of nonimmigrant classification. Neither an application nor a fee is required for the following changes of nonimmigrant classification:

(1) A change to classification under section 101(a)(15)(A) or (G) of the Act.

(2) A change to classification under sections 101(a)(15)(A) or (G) of the Act for an immediate family member, as defined in 22 C.F.R. 41.1, of a principal alien whose status has been changed to such a classification.

(3) A change to the appropriate classification for the nonimmigrant spouse or child of an alien whose status has been changed to a classification under sections 101(a)(15)(E), (F), (H), (I), (J), (L), or (M) of the Act.

(4) A change of classification from that of a visitor for pleasure under section 101(a)(15)(B) of the Act to that of a visitor for business under the same section.

(5) A change of classification from that of a student under section 101(a)(15)(F)(i) of the Act to that of an accompanying spouse or minor child under section 101(a)(15)(F)(ii) of the Act or vice versa.

(6) A change from any classification within section 101(a)(15)(H) of the Act to any other classification within section 101(a)(15)(H) of the Act provided that the requisite Form I-129B visa petition has been filed and approved.

(7) A change from classification as a participant under section 101(a)(15)(J) of the Act to classification as an accompanying spouse or minor child under that section or vice versa.

(8) A change from classification as an intra-company transferee under section 101(a)(15)(L) of the Act to classification as an accompanying spouse or minor child under that section or vice versa.

(9) A change of classification from that of a student under section 101(a)(15)(M)(i) of the Act to that of an accompanying spouse or minor child under section 101(a)(15)(M)(ii) of the Act or vice versa.

(d) Fee not required. No fee is required for a request for change to exchange alien classification under section 101(a)(15)(J) of the Act made by an agency of the United States Government. In such a case, the agency may submit Form IAP-66, Certificate of Eligibility for Exchange-Visitor (J-1) Status, together with its request in lieu of Form I-506, Application for Change of Nonimmigrant Status.

(e) Change of classification not required. The following do not need to request a change of classification:

(1) An alien classified as a visitor for business under section 101(a)(15)(B) of the Act who intends to remain in the United States temporarily as a visitor for pleasure during the period of authorized admission; or

(2) An alien classified under sections 101(a)(15)(A) or 101(a)(15)(G) of the Act as a member of the immediate family of a principal alien classified under the same section, or an alien classified under section 101(a)(15)(E), (F), (H), (I), (J), (L), or (M) of the Act as the spouse or child who accompanied or followed to join a principal alien who is classified under the same section, to attend school in the United States, as long as the immediate family member, spouse or child continues to be qualified for and maintains the status under which the family member, spouse or child is classified.

(f) Approval of application. If the application is granted, the applicant shall be notified of the decision and granted a new period of time to remain in the United States without the requirement of filing a separate application and paying a separate fee for an extension of stay. The applicant's nonimmigrant status under his new classification shall be subject to the terms and conditions applicable generally to such classification and to such other additional terms and conditions, including exaction of bond, which the district director deems appropriate to the case.

(g) Denial of Application. When the application is denied, the applicant shall be notified of the decision and the reasons for the denial. There is no appeal from the denial of the application under this chapter.

Chapter 7

Immigrant Visas

During the early history of America, few restrictions were placed on immigration. Any action that was taken by the federal government in the area of immigration law was designed to protect and encourage migration to this country. For instance, when Congress enacted the Act of March 2, 1819 its primary concern was the safety and health of the immigrants embarked on vessels bound for the United States.[1]

In the late 1800s the official policy toward immigration began to become more restrictive. It initially took the form of health and welfare standards imposed on prospective citizens. Excluded were so-called "idiots, lunatics, convicts and persons likely to become a public charge,"[2] "persons suffering from a loathsome or dangerous contagious disease...paupers and polygamists,"[3] and people convicted of certain criminal offenses. These restrictions sought to limit legal immigration to physically healthy and law-abiding applicants.

Less rationally based, and more controversial, restrictions were later imposed. The first of these was a restriction on the grounds of national origin in the Chinese Exclusion Act of 1882.[4] The Chinese exclusion statutes were later expanded into the creation of what was called the Asiatic Barred Zone.[5] The zone rendered inadmissible natives of China, India, Burma, Siam, Polynesia, parts of Russia, Afghanistan, and the countries of the Middle East.[6] The admission of Japanese and other Asian people not specifically barred by this 1917 Act was restricted by an informal undertaking to limit their emigration, which became known as "the Gentleman's Agreement."

In addition to the racial exclusion provisions, the 1917 Act imposed literacy requirements for aliens over the age of sixteen.[7] Interestingly, the literacy test did not require the ability to read English but rather excluded people "who could not read the English language or some other language or dialect." Each person could designate the particular language or dialect in which she desired the examination to be given.

These restrictions, and the value judgments inherent in them, were perhaps attributable to the historically large influx of immigrants during the strongly isolationist period which immediately preceded World War I. The two types of restrictions, a preference for people who were related to or ethnically similar to citizens already

---

1. 3 Stat. 488.

2. Act of August 3, 1882, 22 Stat. 214.

3. Act of March 3, 1891, 26 Stat. 1084.

4. Act of May 6, 1882, 22 Stat. 58.

5. Act of Feb. 5, 1917, 39 Stat. 874 (1917).

6. Like a number of later immigration statutes, the 1917 Act was enacted over the President's veto.

7. Section 3 of the Act of Feb. 5, 1917, 39 Stat. 874.

here, plus achievement of a certain level of education, have developed into recurring themes of our immigration laws.

The general preference for people with closer (cultural) ties with the dominant groups in the U.S. was reflected in the Quota Law of 1921.[8] The 1921 enactment attempted to freeze in place the then-existing national features of the United States. The freeze was accomplished by limiting the number of persons of any nationality admitted into the United States in any year to 3% of the foreign-born persons of that nationality who lived in this country in 1910. The McCarran-Walter Act continued the quota system and is the foundation of present immigration law.

These "national origin" quota provisions, though often modified, were eventually repealed by the Immigration and Nationality Act Amendments of 1965.[9] The 1965 amendment reflected two basic values. The first was a desire to promote the unification of families by issuing visas to close relatives of U.S. citizens and permanent residents. The second objective was a desire to promote the immigration of educated, skilled aliens who would enrich the community.[10]

In 1986, due in part to the existence of millions of undocumented aliens, and in an effort to stem the flow of illegal migration, legislation was enacted to "legalize" or grant "amnesty" to these persons.[11] While the effect of the 1986 amendments on the immigrant quota system cannot be predicted, that legislation did not alter the allocation of immigrant visas. In 1990, as the culmination in the process of immigration reform begun by the 1986 legislation, Congress modified the system of allocating immigrant visas.[12] This reform legislation expanded the number of immigrants permitted to enter the United States each year, and at the same time shifted the allocation of visas as between the family unification and employment-based visas.

Under our laws, an immigrant is a person who seeks admission for the purpose of staying permanently. If admitted as such she may reside in this country indefinitely and is eligible to apply for naturalization within either 3 or 5 years.[13] All immigrants must meet certain personal qualitative standards[14] and must complete the required

---

8. Act of May 19, 1921, 42 Stat. 5.

9. Pub. L. No. 89-236, 79 Stat. 911 (1965). For an excellent historical study of the legislation up to and including the 1952 Act, see 1952 U.S. Code Cong. & Admin. News 1680, 1692. The repeal of the national origin quota did not change the immigrant quota system or the racial biases reflected under the prior immigration statutes. Scholars have argued that because most immigration is based on close family ties, the closing out of racial minorities in the past was not remedied by the removal of the national origin quotas. Moreover, U.S. immigration laws continue to prohibit the immigration of more than 20,000 persons per year per country. See 8 U.S.C. § 1152(a), Sec. 202(a).

10. Immigration and Nationality Act Amendments of 1965, Pub. L. No. 89-236, 1965 U.S. Code Cong. & Admin. News 3329.

11. The Immigration Reform and Control Act of 1986, Pub. L. No. 99-603, § 201, 100 Stat. 3359 (adding 8 U.S.C. § 1255a Sec. 245A).

12. See Sections 111, 121, 131 and 132 Immigration Act of 1990, Pub. L. No. 101-649, 104 Stat. 4978.

13. The time within which a person can apply for citizenship varies, depending on how she obtained her permanent residency. Generally, if permanent residency was obtained through marriage to a U.S. citizen, the residency period is shorter. See Chapter 13.

14. These "personal qualitative standards" deal with the health, economic, and criminal

administrative formalities prior to entry.[15] A person who is excludable from the U.S. and cannot obtain a waiver of the grounds of excludability will not receive an immigrant visa. As noted earlier, there is a statutory presumption that every person coming to the U.S. is an immigrant unless she proves otherwise to a U.S. consul and INS officer.

The statute requires that the arriving person be excluded unless she fits into one of the specified immigrant visa categories (or otherwise establishes entitlement to a bona fide nonimmigrant visa). In addition to requiring that foreigners meet specific criteria of the immigrant visa categories, the immigration laws also limit their entry through an annual numerical quota. During the period from October 1991 through October 1994, the quota will be 700,000 and in the following years 675,000.[16] The statute precludes the admission of more than approximately 26,000 immigrants in any year from any one country. The statute further limits the immigration of persons from colonies to approximately 7,300.

What follows is a brief description of the various immigrant visa categories:

Immigrants Admitted Without Numerical Limits[17]

1. *Immediate Relatives.* There is no quota for this category, which includes spouses, parents, and children of U.S. citizens. In the case of parents, of U.S. citizens, the petitioning "child" must be over the age of 21 in order to qualify the parents for admission.

2. *Special Immigrants.*[18] This category includes persons such as ministers of religions,[19] returning lawful permanent residents, former U.S. government employees abroad, certain employees of the Panama Canal Company, certain employees of the U.S. Consulate General in Hong Kong,[20] and certain retired employees of international organizations or family members of present or former employees of these international organizations.[21]

---

grounds of exclusion which were not altered by the 1986 amendments. *See generally* 8 U.S.C. § 1182, Sec. 212.

15. *See generally* 8 U.S.C. § 1181(a), Sec. 211(a).

16. *See* Sec. 101, Immigration Act of 1990, Pub. L. No. 101-649, 104 Stat. 4978.

17. While the admission of immigrants under this category is not restricted by an annual quota, approximately 254,000 of the first visas issued to immediate relatives are counted against the quota allocation for the family-based immigrants. *See* 8 U.S.C. § 1151(c), Sec. 203(c).

18. 8 U.S.C. § 1101(a)(27), Sec. 101(a)(27).

19. These visas will phase out by October 1994 and apply to persons who have been members of a religious denomination for at least two years prior to their application for admission to the U.S. under the following conditions: 1) the sole purpose of their coming to the U.S. is to carry on the vocation of minister in the religion; 2) the person seeks to enter the U.S. before October 1994 to work for an organization in a professional capacity in a "religious vocation or occupation;" or 3) seeks to enter the U.S. before October 1, 1994 to work for the organization or an organization which is affiliated with the religious organization. After 1994 religious workers will only be allowed to enter as R nonimmigrants unless they can qualify as employment-based immigrants.

20. *See* 8 U.S.C. § 1101(a)(27)(D), Sec. 101(a)(27)(D), Sec. 152 of the Immigration Act of 1990, Pub. L. No. 101-649, 104 Stat. 4978.

21. The special immigrant provision relating to retired or present employees of interna-

Immigrants Subject to Numerical Limits

The most significant changes made to the immigration laws by the 1990 Act related to the issuance of immigrant visas. The most significant of these changes for immigrant visas was in the immigrant selection system. Under prior law, "quota" visas were allocated to persons under six preference categories with a "catch-all" non-preference category. Changes made by the 1990 Act to the "quota" visas created the "family-based," "employment-based" and "diversity and transition" immigrant categories.[22] Our discussion of the employment-based immigrants will be covered in Chapter 8. The family-based immigrants are divided into four preferences:

1. *First Preference.* Unmarried sons and daughters of U.S. citizens. This preference is limited to 23,400 visas plus any unused visas from the fourth preference visas.

2. *Second Preference.* Spouse and unmarried sons and daughters of lawful permanent residents. This category, is allocated 114,200 visas plus the unused portion for family immigration not used by immediate relatives and whatever visas are not used under the first preference category; not less than 77% of the visas in this preference category is allocated for the spouse and minor children of lawful permanent residents.

3. *Third Preference.* Married sons and daughters of U.S. citizens. This preference is allotted 23,400 plus whatever visas are not used by the first and second preferences.

4. *Fourth Preference.* Brothers and sisters of U.S. citizens. This preference is allocated 65,000 plus whatever is not used by the first, second and third preferences.

A separate category of immigrant visas termed *diversity and transition immigrants*,[23] because they are not based on exclusively on the familial or employment relation normally required for immigration to the the U.S. The 1990 Act allocated 95,000 visas each year for the period from October 1, 1991 through September 30, 1994 for visas for the spouse and minor children of persons legalized under the Immigration Reform and Control Act of 1986 (55,000) and for persons from countries who have traditionally immigrated in fewer numbers (40,000). For diversity purposes Northern Ireland is treated as a "diversity state." Forty percent (40%) of these visas are to go to persons from the country receiving most of the NP-5 visas under IRCA (Ireland). The visas issued during the period from 1991 to 1994 are designated as transition visas. Beginning in October, 1994 the legislation calls for creation of a permanent program for "diversity" visas in the amount of 55,000.

Due to the extremely heavy demand for immigrant visas, most of the preference categories require that the applicant wait a lengthy period of time before actually obtaining a visa and becoming eligible for admission. A practitioner must fully understand each of the different preference categories and their relationship with the nonimmigrant categories in order to assure a client the most speedy admission possible

---

tional organizations was added by Section 312(1) of the Immigration Reform and Control Act, Pub. L. No. 99-603, 100 Stat. 3359 (1986).

22. Diversity and transition are further described below. The complicated formula for determining the diversity immigrants is described at 8 U.S.C. § 1153(c), Sec. 203(c).

23. The diversity visas are described at 8 U.S.C. § 1153(c), Sec. 203(c). The transition visas are not codified in the United States Code, but are temporary provisions covered under the Act. *See* Sections 112, 132 and 133 of the Immigration Act of 1990, Pub. L. No. 101-649, 104 Stat. 4978 (1990).

into the U.S. The cases which follow concentrate on the familial relationships which must be established in order for the person to qualify for the applicable immigrant visa category.

It should be remembered that qualification for a preference category does not insure receipt of an immigrant visa. The person must additionally establish before the U.S. consul (or the INS, in the case of an application for adjustment of status under 8 U.S.C. § 1255) that she is not excludable from the U.S. Inability to overcome this hurdle will make the applicant ineligible for the visa.

References

Boswell, *The Immigration Reform Amendments of 1986: Reform or Rehash?*, 14 J. Legis. 23 (1987)

P. Ehrlich, L. Bilderback & A. Ehrlich, *The Golden Door: International Migration, Mexico and the United States* (1981)

Fragomen & Del Rey, *The Immigration Selection System: A Proposal for Reform*, 17 San Diego L. Rev. 1 (1979)

Gordon, *The Need to Modernize Our Immigration Laws*, 13 San Diego L. Rev. 1, 3 (1975)

Hing, *Racial Disparity: The Unaddressed Issue of the Simpson-Mazzoli Bill*, 1 La Raza L.J. 21, 22-31 (1983)

Hofstetter, *Economic Underdevelopment and the Population Explosion: Implications for U.S. Immigration Policy*, 45 Law & Contemp. Probs. 55 (1982)

Note, *The Immigration System: Need to Eliminate Discrimination and Delay*, 8 U.C. Davis L. Rev. 191 (1975)

Scanlan, *Immigration Law and the Illusion of Numerical Control*, 36 U. Miami L. Rev. 819, 827 (1982)

J. Simon, *The Economic Consequences of Immigration* (1989)

Study, *Consular Discretion in the Immigrant Visa-Issuing Process* 16 San Diego L. Rev. 87 (1978)

Wolff, *The Non-Reviewability of Consular Visa Decisions: An Unjustified Aberration from American Justice*, 5 N.Y.L. Sch. J. Int'l Comp. L. 341 (1984)

A. Constitutional Issues

Fiallo v. Bell

430 U.S. 787 (1976)

Justice POWELL delivered the opinion of the Court.

This case brings before us a constitutional challenge to §§ 101(b)(1)(D) and 101(b)(2) of the Immigration and Nationality Act of 1952 (Act), 66 Stat. 182, as amended, 8 U.S.C. §§ 1101(b)(1)(D) and 1101(b)(2).

The Act grants special preference immigration status to aliens who qualify as the "children" or "parents" of United States citizens or lawful permanent residents. Under § 101(b)(1), a "child" is defined as an unmarried person under 21 years of age who is a legitimate or legitimated child, a stepchild, an adopted child, or an illegitimate child seeking preference by virtue of his relationship with his natural mother. The definition does not extend to an illegitimate child seeking preference by virtue of his relationship with his natural father. Moreover, under § 101(b)(2), a person qualifies as a "parent" for purposes of the Act solely on the basis of the person's relationship with a "child." As a result, the natural father of an illegitimate child who is either a United States citizen or permanent resident alien is not entitled to preferential treatment as a "parent."

The special preference immigration status provided for those who satisfy the statutory "parent-child" relationship depends on whether the immigrant's relative is a United States citizen or permanent resident alien. A United States citizen is allowed the entry of his "parent" or "child" without regard to either an applicable numerical quota or the labor certification requirement. 8 U.S.C. §§ 1151(a), (b), 1182(a)(14). On the other hand, a United States permanent resident alien is allowed the entry of the "parent" or "child" subject to numerical limitations but without regard to the labor certification requirement. 8 U.S.C. § 1182(a)(14).

Appellants are three sets of unwed natural fathers and their illegitimate offspring who sought, either as an alien father or an alien child, a special immigration preference by virtue of a relationship to a citizen or resident alien child or parent. In each instance the applicant was informed that he was ineligible for an immigrant visa unless he qualified for admission under the general numerical limitations and, in the case of the alien parents, received the requisite labor certification.[1]

Appellants filed this action in July 1974 in the United States District Court for the Eastern District of New York challenging the constitutionality of §§ 101(b)(1) and 101(b)(2) of the Act under the First, Fifth, and Ninth Amendments. Appellants alleged that the statutory provisions (i) denied them equal protection by discriminating against natural fathers and their illegitimate children "on the basis of the father's marital status, the illegitimacy of the child and the sex of the parent without either compelling or rational justification"; (ii) denied them due process of law to the extent that there was established "an unwarranted conclusive presumption of the absence of strong psychological and economic ties between natural fathers and their children born out of wedlock and not legitimated"; and (iii) "seriously burden[ed] and infringe[d] upon the rights of natural fathers and their children, born out of wedlock and not legitimated, to mutual association, to privacy, to establish a home, to raise natural children and to be raised by the natural father." Appellants sought to enjoin

---

1. Appellant Ramon Martin Fiallo, a United States citizen by birth, currently resides in the Dominican Republic with his natural father, appellant Ramon Fiallo-Sone, a citizen of that country. The father initiated procedures to obtain an immigrant visa as the "parent" of his illegitimate son, but the United States consul for the Dominican Republic informed appellant Fiallo-Sone that he could not qualify for the preferential status accorded to "parents" unless he legitimated Ramon Fiallo.

Appellant Cleophus Warner, a naturalized United States citizen, is the unwed father of appellant Serge Warner, who was born in 1960 in the French West Indies. In 1972 Cleophus Warner petitioned the Immigration and Naturalization Service to classify Serge as Warner's "child" for purposes of obtaining an immigrant visa, but the petition was denied on the ground that there was no evidence that Serge was Warner's legitimate or legitimated offspring.

Appellants Trevor Wilson and Earl Wilson, permanent resident aliens, are the illegitimate children of appellant Arthur Wilson, a citizen of Jamaica. Following the death of their mother in 1974, Trevor and Earl sought to obtain an immigrant visa for their father. We are informed by the appellees that although the application has not yet been rejected, denial is certain since the children are neither legitimate nor legitimated offspring of Arthur Wilson.

permanently enforcement of the challenged statutory provisions to the extent that the statute precluded them from qualifying for the special preference accorded other "parents" and "children."

*   *   *

At the outset, it is important to underscore the limited scope of judicial inquiry into immigration legislation. This Court has repeatedly emphasized that "over no conceivable subject is the legislative power of Congress more complete than it is over" the admission of aliens. *Oceanic Navigation Co. v. Stranahan*, 214 U.S. 320, 339 (1909); *accord, Kleindienst v. Mandel*, 408 U.S. 753, 766 (1972). Our cases "have long recognized the power to expel or exclude aliens as a fundamental sovereign attribute exercised by the Government's political departments largely immune from judicial control." . . . Just last Term, for example, the Court had occasion to note that "the power over aliens is of a political character and therefore subject only to narrow judicial review." *Hampton v. Mow Sun Wong*, 426 U.S. 88, 101 n.21 (1976). And we observed recently that in the exercise of its broad power over immigration and naturalization, "Congress regularly makes rules that would be unacceptable if applied to citizens."

*   *   *

Appellants . . . argue that none of the prior immigration cases of this Court involved "double-barreled" discrimination based on sex and illegitimacy, infringed upon the due process rights of citizens and legal permanent residents, or implicated "the fundamental constitutional interests of United States citizens and permanent residents in a familial relationship." But this Court has resolved similar challenges to immigration legislation based on other constitutional rights of citizens, and has rejected the suggestion that more searching judicial scrutiny is required. In *Kleindienst v. Mandel*, for example, United States citizens challenged the power of the Attorney General to deny a visa to an alien who, as a proponent of "the economic, international, and governmental doctrines of World communism," was ineligible to receive a visa under 8 U.S.C. § 1182(a)(28)(D) absent a waiver by the Attorney General. The citizen-appellees in that case conceded that Congress could prohibit entry of all aliens falling into the class defined by § 1182(a)(28)(D). They contended, however, that the Attorney General's statutory discretion to approve a waiver was limited by the Constitution and that their First Amendment rights were abridged by the denial of Mandel's request for a visa. The Court held that "when the Executive exercises this (delegated) power negatively on the basis of a facially legitimate and bona fide reason, the courts will neither look behind the exercise of that discretion, nor test it by balancing its justification against the First Amendment interests of those who seek personal communication with the applicant." We can see no reason to review the broad congressional policy choice at issue here under a more exacting standard than was applied in *Kleindienst v. Mandel*, a First Amendment case.[2]

---

2. The thoughtful dissenting opinion of our Brother Marshall would be persuasive if its basic premise were accepted. The dissent is grounded on the assumption that the relevant portions of the Act grant a "fundamental right" to American citizens, a right "given only to the citizen" and not to the putative immigrant. The assumption is facially plausible in that the families of putative immigrants certainly have an interest in their admission. But the fallacy of the assumption is rooted deeply in fundamental principles of sovereignty. . . . [T]here are widely varying relationships and degrees of kinship, and it is appropriate for Congress to consider not only the nature of these relationships but also problems of identification, administration, and the potential for fraud.

*   *   *

Finally, appellants characterize our prior immigration cases as involving foreign policy matters and congressional choices to exclude or expel groups of aliens that were "specifically and clearly perceived to pose a grave threat to the national security," citing *Harisiades v. Shaughnessy*, 342 U.S. 580 (1952), "or to the general welfare of this country," . . . .We find no indication in our prior cases that the scope of judicial review is a function of the nature of the policy choice at issue. To the contrary, "[s]ince decisions in these matters may implicate our relations with foreign powers, and since a wide variety of classifications must be defined in the light of changing political and economic circumstances, such decisions are frequently of a character more appropriate to either the Legislature or the Executive than to the Judiciary," and "[t]he reasons that preclude judicial review of political questions also dictate a narrow standard of review of decisions made by the Congress or the President in the area of immigration and naturalization." As Mr. Justice Frankfurter observed in his concurrence in *Harisiades v. Shaughnessy*:

> The conditions of entry for every alien, the particular classes of aliens that shall be denied entry altogether, the basis for determining such classification, the right to terminate hospitality to aliens, the grounds on which such determination shall be based, have been recognized as matters solely for the responsibility of the Congress and wholly outside the power of this Court to control."

342 U.S., at 596-597.

As originally enacted in 1952, § 101(b)(1) of the Act defined a "child" as an unmarried legitimate or legitimated child or stepchild under 21 years of age. The Board of Immigration Appeals and the Attorney General subsequently concluded that the failure of this definition to refer to illegitimate children rendered ineligible for preferential nonquota status both the illegitimate alien child of a citizen mother, *Matter of A*, 5 I. & N. Dec. 272, 283-284 (A.G. 1953), and the alien mother of a citizen born out of wedlock, *Matter of F*, 7 I. & N. Dec. 448 (B.I.A. 1957). The Attorney General recommended that the matter be brought to the attention of Congress, Matter of A, supra, at 284, and the Act was amended in 1957 to include what is now 8 U.S.C. § 1101(b)(1)(D). Congress was specifically concerned with the relationship between a child born out of wedlock and his or her natural mother, and the legislative history of the 1957 amendment reflects an intentional choice not to provide preferential immigration status by virtue of the relationship between an illegitimate child and his or her natural father.

This distinction is just one of many drawn by Congress pursuant to its determination to provide some but not all families with relief from various immigration restrictions that would otherwise hinder reunification of the family in this country. In addition to the distinction at issue here, Congress has decided that children, whether legitimate or not, cannot qualify for preferential status if they are married or are over 21 years of age. 8 U.S.C. § 1101(b)(1). Legitimated children are ineligible for preferential status unless their legitimation occurred prior to their 18th birthday and at a time when they were in the legal custody of the legitimating parent or parents. § 1101(b)(1)(C). Adopted children are not entitled to preferential status unless they were adopted before the age of 14 and have thereafter lived in the custody of their adopting or adopted parents for at least two years, § 1101(b)(1)(E). And stepchildren cannot qualify unless they were under 18 at the time of the marriage creating the stepchild relationship. § 1101(b)(1)(B).

*   *   *

Appellants suggest that the distinction drawn in § 101(b)(1)(D) is unconstitutional under any standard of review since it infringes upon the constitutional rights of citizens and legal permanent residents without furthering legitimate governmental interests. Appellants note in this regard that the statute makes it more difficult for illegitimate children and their natural fathers to be reunited in this country than for legitimate or legitimated children and their parents, or for illegitimate children and their natural mothers. And appellants also note that the statute fails to establish a procedure under which illegitimate children and their natural fathers could prove the existence and strength of their family relationship. Those are admittedly the consequences of the congressional decision not to accord preferential status to this particular class of aliens, but the decision nonetheless remains one "solely for the responsibility of the Congress and wholly outside the power of this Court to control." Harisiades v. Shaughnessy, 342 U.S., at 597, 72 S.Ct., at 522 (Frankfurter, J., concurring). Congress obviously has determined that preferential status is not warranted for illegitimate children and their natural fathers, perhaps because of a perceived absence in most cases of close family ties as well as a concern with the serious problems of proof that usually lurk in paternity determinations. In any event, it is not the judicial role in cases of this sort to probe and test the justifications for the legislative decision.

Note

The 1986 legislation removed the disparity between the rights of petitioning fathers and mothers under the INA. The statute was changed to allow a petition by the natural father "if the father has or had a bona fide parent-child relationship." *See* 8 U.S.C. § 1101(b)(1)(D), Sec. 101(b)(1)(D).

As will be seen in the following cases, determining who is a "child" is the foundation to establishing other relationships required of the petitioner under the family reunification provisions. These determinations apply to all INS adjudications involving statutory benefits. It is for this reason that we will explore family relationships at length.

Definition of "Child"
8 U.S.C. § 1101(b), Sec. 101(b)

(1) The term "child" means an unmarried person under twenty-one years of age who is—

(A) a legitimate child;

(B) a stepchild, whether or not born out of wedlock, provided the child had not reached the age of eighteen years at the time the marriage creating the status of stepchild occurred;

(C) a child legitimated under the law of the child's residence or domicile, or under the law of the father's residence or domicile, whether in or outside the United

States, if such legitimation takes place before the child reaches the age of eighteen years and the child is in the legal custody of the legitimating parent or parents at the time of such legitimation;

(D) an illegitimate child, by, through whom, or on whose behalf a status, privilege, or benefit is sought by virtue of the relationship of the child to its natural mother or to its natural father if the father has or had a bona fide parent-child relationship with the person;

(E) a child adopted while under the age of sixteen years if the child has been in the legal custody of, and has resided with, the adopting parent or parents for at least two years: Provided, That no natural parent of any such adopted child shall thereafter, by virtue of such parentage, be accorded any right, privilege, or status under this chapter; or

(F) a child, under the age of sixteen at the time a petition is filed in his behalf to accord a classification as an immediate relative under section 1151(b) of this title, who is an orphan because of the death or disappearance of, abandonment or desertion by, or separation or loss from, both parents, or for whom the sole or surviving parent is incapable of providing the proper care and has in writing irrevocably released the child for emigration and adoption; who has been adopted abroad by a United States citizen and spouse jointly, or by an unmarried United States citizen at least twenty-five years of age, who personally saw and observed the child prior to or during the adoption proceedings; or who is coming to the United States for adoption by a United States citizen and spouse jointly, or by an unmarried United States citizen at least twenty-five years of age, who have or has complied with the preadoption requirements, if any, of the child's proposed residence; Provided, That the Attorney General is satisfied that proper care will be furnished the child if admitted to the United States; Provided further, That no natural parent or prior adoptive parent of any such child shall thereafter, by virtue of such parentage, be accorded any right, privilege, or status under this chapter.

(2) The terms "parent," "father," or "mother" mean a parent, father, or mother only where the relationship exists by reason of any of the circumstances set forth in subdivision (1) of this subsection.

B. Adoption

Matter of Garcia-Rodriquez
16 I. & N. Dec. 438 (BIA 1978)

The United States citizen petitioner applied for immediate relative status for the beneficiary as her adopted daughter under section 201(b) of the Immigration and Nationality Act, 8 U.S.C. 1151(b). In a decision dated October 5, 1976, the District Director denied the petition. The petitioner has appealed. The appeal will be dismissed.

The beneficiary, a 15-year-old native and citizen of Mexico, was "adopted" by the petitioner and her husband in H. Matamoros, State of Tamaulipas, Mexico, on August 6, 1974. The couple had natural children of their own living at the time of this "adoption." A visa petition was submitted on behalf of the beneficiary on August 16, 1976.

Certain adopted children of United States citizen parents can qualify for "immediate relative status" under section 201(b) of the act. The District Director, however, denied this petition based on his finding that the petitioner failed to establish that the beneficiary had been lawfully adopted. Noting that article 400 of the Civil Code of Tamaulipas authorizes only persons "who do not have natural descendants" to adopt minor children, he concluded that the beneficiary's adoption was not in compliance with controlling law as the petitioner and her spouse had other natural children living in August 1974.

On appeal, the petitioner submits that the District Director erred by looking only to article 400 of the Civil Code of Tamaulipas. She states that article 400 governs only adoptions by single persons and that article 401 authorizes a "married couple [to] adopt if both agree to consider the adopted one as their son." The petitioner maintains that the adoption of the beneficiary was in compliance with the requirements of the Civil Code of Tamaulipas and that her daughter should, therefore, be recognized as her "immediate relative."

The burden of establishing both controlling foreign law (Matter of Annang, 14 I & N Dec. 502 (BIA 1973)) and eligibility for the benefit sought (Matter of Brantigan, 11 I & N Dec. 493 (BIA 1966)) rests with the petitioner. We conclude that the petitioner has failed to sustain either burden.

Article 400 of the Civil Code of Tamaulipas provides:

Persons over 30 years of age, in the full exercise of their rights and who have no descendants, may adopt a minor or an incompetent even if he is of legal age, provided the adopter is 17 years older than the person adopted, and that the adoption is beneficial to the latter.

Article 401 of the Code states:

The man and wife can adopt when both are in accord in considering the adopted child as their own son or daughter.

It seems evident that the former article is a general provision governing all adoptions, while the latter article sets forth an additional requirement to be imposed upon married couples. Thus, it would appear that the petitioner and her spouse were subject to the restrictions in article 400 at the time they attempted to adopt the beneficiary.

The petitioner would have us conclude that article 400 applies only to single persons. On its face, however, no such limitation appears. Moreover, to accept such an interpretation would be to conclude that the age differential and "welfare of the child" provisions of article 400 do not apply to adoptions by married couples. We decline to so conclude, and find that the petitioner has failed to establish that her reading of articles 400 and 401 of the Civil Code of Tamaulipas is correct.

Matter of Palelei
16 I. & N. Dec. 716 (BIA 1979)

*   *   *

On June 16, 1976, the lawful permanent resident petitioner applied for second-preference benefits for the beneficiary as her adopted daughter under section 203(a)(2) of the Immigration and Nationality Act, 8 U.S.C. 1153(a)(2). The petition was initially approved on June 18, 1976, but on August 30, 1976, the District Director advised the petitioner of his intent to revoke the petition on the ground that the adoption was not recognized under Tongan Civil Law and because the petitioner had failed to establish that the beneficiary was under 14 years of age at the time of the adoption. The District Director revoked approval of the petition on September 30, 1976. On appeal, the petitioner submitted additional evidence suggesting that her adoption of the beneficiary was in accordance with the customs of Tonga and was recognized under the law of Tonga. We remanded the record to the District Director for consideration of the additional evidence and entry of a new decision. On March 8, 1978, the District Director reaffirmed his revocation of approval of the petition on the basis that an adoption under Tongan law had not been established. The petitioner has appealed from that decision. The appeal will be dismissed.

The beneficiary, a native and citizen of Tonga, was born legitimate on January 18, 1951. Shortly after her birth he was given over onto the care of her uncle. In 1956 the beneficiary was taken into the home of the uncle's natural daughter, the petitioner in this case, and her husband. The beneficiary resided with this couple until their departure for the United States in 1975. The petitioner argues that we should find a valid adoption pursuant to the customary and tribal law of Tonga.

*   *   *

In order to qualify as a "daughter" for preference purposes, a beneficiary must once have qualified as a "child" of the petitioner under section 101(b)(1) of the Act. *Nazareno v. Attorney General*, 512 F.2d 936 (D.C. Cir. 1975), *cert. denied*, 423 U.S. 832 (1975). The relevant provision in this case is section 101(b)(1)(E), which includes in the definition of child:

> [A] child adopted while under the age of fourteen years if the child has thereafter been in the legal custody of, and has resided with, the adopting parent or parents for at least two years. . . .

We have held that an adoption, to be valid for immigration purposes, must create a legal status or relationship. *Matter of Benjamin*, Interim Decision 2505 (BIA 1976). A relationship in the nature of charitable help to a needy child is not an adoption under our immigration laws. To determine whether the requisite relationship exists, we look to the law of the country in which the adoption took place. *Matter of Garcia-Rodriquez*, Interim Decision 2630 (BIA 1978). If the civil law of a country does not recognize adoptions, no benefits accrue under the United States immigration laws based on adoptions allegedly occurring in that country. *Matter of Ashree, Ahmed and Ahmed*, 14 I. & N. Dec. 305 (BIA 1973).

In Matter of B—, supra, we discussed customary adoptions:

> [I]n the absence of a statutory procedure of adoption, the petitioner must establish that a custom existed . . . which was recognized officially as resulting in a legal adoption, legally binding upon the parties concerned, and that it was necessary to establish that the adoption of the beneficiary by the petitioner conformed with these customs and resulted in a legal adoption.

This Board has accepted as valid customary adoptions which are recognized as legally valid by the country in which the adoption occurred. *Matter of Yue*, 12 I & N Dec. 747 (BIA 1968); *Matter of Ng*, 14 I & N Dec. 135 (BIA 1972).

* * *

Before making his decision in this case, the District Director requested assistance from the Library of Congress. The Library of Congress consulted the Crown solicitor of Tonga who advised that the law of Tonga provides for the adoption of illegitimate children under certain circumstances, but that:

There is no provision in our law for the adoption of children born legitimately. Nevertheless, it has been a common practice in Tonga for relatives to raise and maintain children, including legitimate children, as part of the family and to treat them in all respects as if they were legally adopted. Such "adoption" does not give the child any legal right in the estate of the foster parent and is not recognized as legally valid under Tongan law.

The petitioner argues that inasmuch as the Crown Solicitor acknowledges the existence of customary adoptions, his opinion is deficient because it appears to conclude that such customary adoptions are not legally recognized because the adopted child has no right in the estate of the adoptive parent. We disagree. In our view, the Crown Solicitor merely acknowledges the fact that there are customary adoptions in his country, but in his opinion, such adoptions are not recognized as legally valid under Tongan law. His statement that the adoption does not give the child any right in the estate of the foster parent is merely a prelude to his conclusion; it points to one of the attributes of a natural parent-child relationship which does not accrue to a child adopted pursuant to Tongan custom.

C. Stepchildren

Matter of Moreira
17 I. & N. Dec. 370 (BIA 1980)

This is the second time this case has been before us. In a prior decision, dated July 16, 1979, we remanded that record to the District Director to give the petitioner an opportunity to show that the beneficiary qualified as her "stepchild" under the Immigration and Nationality Act, as that term was defined in our prior decision, which was designated as a precedent. *Matter of Moreira*, Interim Decision 2720 (BIA 1979). The District Director, in a decision dated October 30, 1979, determined that the beneficiary did not qualify as the petitioner's stepchild as we had interpreted that term. In accordance with our previous order, the District Director then certified his decision back to this Board for review. Oral argument was heard before this Board on February 21, 1980. The decision of the District Director is reversed.

The petitioner in this case is a 52-year-old native of Argentina and citizen of the United States. The beneficiary is a 25-year-old native and citizen of Argentina who was born out of wedlock to the petitioner's husband and a woman he never married. The petitioner married the beneficiary's father in 1972, when the beneficiary was 17 years old. Thus, a purely technical steprelationship came into existence prior to the beneficiary's eighteenth birthday. However, in our prior precedent decision in this case, we held that more than a merely technical relationship was required in order to establish a steprelationship under the Act. After a careful review of the legislative history of the stepchild provision, as well as of the case law, both from this Board and from the courts, we held that a steprelationship exists for immigration purposes where the stepparent has, prior to the child's eighteenth birthday, evinced an active concern for the stepchild's support, instruction, and general welfare. While such an interest can be demonstrated by taking the child into the home and caring for him as a parent, it can also be shown, we held, by a stepparent's continuing and genuine interest in the well-being of a stepchild who may, due to distance, immigration restrictions, or national boundaries, be unable to actually live with the stepparent.

The petitioner in the present case has submitted an affidavit which indicates that she knew of and accepted the existence of the beneficiary from the time she first met her husband, approximately one year before they were married. She states that because the beneficiary had always been a great concern of her husband's, he became a concern of her's also, and that she and her husband sent money to the beneficiary and the beneficiary's sister would become her children "as fully and completely as if they were mine by blood. . . . " She acknowledges twice in the affidavit that she has an "obligation" to the beneficiary.

The special problem presented by this case lies in the fact that the petitioner's marriage to the beneficiary's father occurred only 4 months before the beneficiary reached his eighteenth birthday. The Immigration and Naturalization Service argues, and counsel for the petitioner has all but conceded, that the requirements of our precedent decision could not have been, and were not, met in those 4 months. We believe that the interpretation given to our decision by both counsel and by the Service is too narrow. What we sought in our prior decision was to encourage and preserve relationships where genuine familial bonds existed, but also to recognize the fact that a simple marriage ceremony will not in every case serve to create such genuine bonds between persons who have become steprelatives. . . .

The fact that the marriage creating a relationship occurs shortly before a stepchild's eighteenth birthday should not be fatal to a finding that the Moreira standards have been satisfied. Each case must be decided on its own facts. If, as in the present case, there is very little time between the marriage and the birthday, it is not improper to inquire into what occurred between the stepchild and stepparent before the marriage, or to inquire into what occurred after the child reached the age of 18. In both *Nation v. Esperdy*, 239 F. Supp. 531 (S.D.N.Y.) 1965) and *Andrade v. Esperdy*, 270 F. Supp. 516 (S.D.N.Y. 1967), for example, the Court emphasized that the stepmothers evinced an active parental interest in their future stepchildren even before they married the children's fathers. In the present case, the record indicates that the petitioner showed concern for the beneficiary prior to her marriage to the beneficiary's father, and it is quite clear that this interest continued, even grew, up until the beneficiary reached his eighteenth birthday, and beyond. As we do not consider our inquiry into the relationship to be strictly limited to the time between the marriage and the time of the child's eighteenth birthday, we are able to find that the requirements set forth for a steprelationship have been satisfied in this case. We are convinced that the timely parental interest the petitioner showed in the beneficiary was "active" in the particular circumstances of this case.

We do not by our decision today write out *Moreira*'s requirement that the bona fide steprelationship be established prior to the stepchild's eighteenth birthday. It would not be sufficient, for example, if the marriage creating the relationship occurred prior to the child's eighteenth birthday, but the stepparent either did not know of, or accept a genuine and continuing parental interest in, the child in any way before the child turned 18, even if afterwards great concern for the child was shown. We emphasize that each case must be decided on its own facts, and the key question must always be whether a bona fide parent-child relationship exists.

In his brief on appeal, and at oral argument, counsel strongly objected to the criteria set forth in *Matter of Moreira*, supra, and argued that the proper standard should be that set forth in *Andrade*, supra. He argues that to apply *Andrade* only in the Southern District of New York is a denial of equal protection to persons who live outside that judicial district. In the first place, it is not a denial of equal protection to have differing rules in different judicial districts. See *Castillo-Felix v. INS*, 601 F.2d 459 (9th Cir. 1979). More important, in our decision in Moreira, supra, we did not reject Andrade, supra, but rather we interpreted that decision to mean that while a "close family unit" need not be shown in order to establish a steprelationship for immigration purposes, some evidence of genuine family bonds did need to be shown. We expect our decision in Moreira to be applied nationwide, including in the Southern District of New York.

As we find that the petitioner in this case has sufficiently exhibited the requisite parental concern for the support, instruction and welfare of the beneficiary, we will reverse the District Director's decision, and grant the visa petition.

Matter of McMillan
17 I. & N. Dec. 605 (BIA 1981)

In a decision dated July 23, 1980, the Acting District Director denied the visa petitions filed by the United States citizen petitioner to accord the beneficiaries immediate relative status as her stepsons pursuant to section 201(b) of the Immigration and Nationality Act, 8 U.S.C. 1151(b). The petitioner has appealed from that decision. The appeal will be sustained and the visa petitions will be approved.

The record reflects that the beneficiaries, twin brothers, were born in London, England, on July 26, 1962, to the petitioner's husband and a woman who was not then and never became his wife. The beneficiaries' natural mother abandoned them when they were infants and they have since resided with their paternal grandmother in Grenada, West Indies. The petitioner and the beneficiaries' father married in March 1964. The Acting District Director determined that the beneficiaries do not qualify as stepchildren of the petitioner within the meaning of the Act (see section 101(b)(1), 8 U.S.C. 1101(b)(1)) inasmuch as the petitioner failed to establish the existence of a close family relationship between herself, her husband, and the beneficiaries.

Section 101(b)(1)(B) of the Act includes within the definition of the term "child" "... a stepchild, whether or not born in wedlock, provided the child had not reached the age of eighteen years at the time the marriage creating the status of stepchild occurred...." In construing section 101(b)(1)(B), we have long adhered to the view that given the underlying Congressional policy of reuniting families, the mere fact of a marriage which technically creates a steprelationship does not in itself establish a stepparent-stepchild relationship for purposes of the immigration laws. We had until recent date imposed the additional requirement, apparently applied by the Acting District Director in the instant case, that a close family unit be shown to exist between the stepparent, the stepchild, and the natural parent. *See Nation v. Esperdy*, 239 F. Supp. 531 (S.D.N.Y. 1965).

We recently reexamined that position in *Matter of Moreira*, Interim Decisions 2720 and 2792 (BIA 1979 and 1980), and established a new standard that modified to some extent the close family unit test. After careful review of relevant legislative history and pertinent Board and court decisions, we held that a steprelationship exists for immigration purposes where, prior to the stepchild's eighteenth birthday, the stepparent not only married the child's natural parent but evinced an active parental interest in the child's support, instruction and general welfare.

In *Palmer v. Reddy*, 622 F.2d 463 (9th Cir. 1980), the United States Court of Appeals for the Ninth Circuit specifically rejected both the Moreira "active parental interest" test and its predecessor, the "close family unit" rule, concluding that persons who become stepchildren through the marriage of a natural parent prior to their eighteenth birthday are entitled to visa preference as a class under section 101(b)(1)(B) without further qualification. We found ourselves bound to follow *Palmer v. Reddy*, id., in *Matter of Bonnette*, Interim Decision 2840 (BIA 1980), a subsequent case arising in the Ninth Circuit.

We have now determined, with some reluctance, to retreat from our position in *Matter of Moreira*, supra, and to apply the holding in *Palmer v. Reddy*, supra, nationwide. The difficulties inherent in the literal interpretation given section 101(b)(1)(B) by the Ninth Circuit are manifest. See generally concurring opinion of Board Member Appleman in *Matter of Bonnette*, supra. However, the Ninth Circuit is the only Circuit Court of Appeals to have construed the stepchild provision thus far. The Government appears to have acquiesced in the Ninth Circuit's interpretation of section 101(b)(1)(B). We shall accordingly adopt that interpretation as controlling outside as well as within the Ninth Circuit.

The record establishes that the petitioner married the beneficiaries' natural father when the beneficiaries were 20 months of age. Under the rule of *Palmer v. Reddy*, the beneficiaries thereupon qualified as stepchildren of the petitioner within the meaning of section 101(b)(1)(B) and are entitled to immediate relative status as the children of a United States citizen. The visa petitions will be approved.

———

Notes

1. In those cases where there is a determination that a marriage was entered into "fraudulently for the purpose of obtaining an immigration benefit," the stepchild relationship will not be recognized. *Matter of Teng*, 15 I. & N. Dec. 516 (BIA 1975).

2. When a visa petition was filed on behalf of a "second" wife by the child of the "first" wife and her husband, the relationship between the child and "second" wife was not recognized. *Matter of Man*, 16 I. & N. Dec. 543 (BIA 1978). The reasoning for not recognizing the relationship was that the BIA was of the view that Congress did not intend to accord preference classification on the basis of polygamous relationships. 16 I. & N. Dec. at 546.

3. The BIA has held that it will recognize the stepchild relationship between the first wife and the child of the "second" wife. In this case the BIA also approved the petition by the child for his natural mother. *Matter of Fong*, 17 I. & N. Dec. 212 (BIA 1980). As long as there is no polygamy, the relationship will be recognized.

4. The Attorney General also recognized a stepchild relationship as existing between the child conceived as a result of an extramarital adulterous relationship and the "new" wife of the natural father. *Matter of Stultz*, 15 I. & N. Dec. 362 (A.G. 1975).

D. Brothers and Sisters

Matter of Mahal
12 I. & N. Dec. 409 (BIA 1967)

The cases come forward pursuant to certification by the District director of his orders dated October 28, 1966 denying the visa petitions for the reason that the beneficiaries are the offspring of a second polygamous marriage, which while valid where performed in Pakistan, cannot be considered as valid for immigration purposes; and that the issue of such a marriage do not enjoy a brother-sister relationship with the issue of the original and recognized marriage and are not entitled to status as the brother and/or sister of a citizen of the United States.

The petitioner, a native of Pakistan, a citizen of the United States by naturalization on December 12, 1960, seeks preference status under section 203(a)(5) of the Immigration and Nationality Act on behalf of the beneficiaries as his half brother and half sister, respectively. The beneficiaries are both married. The male beneficiary was born December 3, 1929 in Pakistan and the female beneficiary was born October 17, 1936 in India.

The information submitted in support of the visa petitions established that the petitioner is the legitimate son of Udham Singh Mahal and Anpar Piram Kaur Mahal, who were married June 1917 in India accordance to the Hindu Rites. The beneficiaries, the half brother and half sister of the petitioner, are the offspring of a second marriage of the same father to Aupar Kaur Mahal in October 1928 also under the Hindu Rites. According to information from the Consulate General of India at San Francisco dated September 7, 1966, before the enactment of the Hindu Code Bill in 1955/1956, a man could legally marry more than one wife in India. It is established then that the petitioner and the beneficiaries are the children of polygamous marriage. It has been ascertained from the Indian Embassy at Washington, D.C. that the children of these polygamous marriages, which, it must be remembered, were legal in both India and Pakistan until 1953/1956, under the Hindu law are legitimate in every sense of the word.

The case therefore falls squarely within the decision in *Matter of K— W— S—*, 9 I & N Dec. 396 (A.G. 1961). In that case the parties were a sister and her half brother who were the offspring of a wife and a concubine, respectively, in China. Under Chinese law the child of a concubine who is acknowledged by the father was equally as legitimate as the child of his lawful wife. In affirming the Board's order that these children, who were legitimated under the law of China, should be regarded as brother and sister, the Attorney General pointed out that neither the decision nor the 1952 Act implies any approval of the institution of concubinage or polygamy, which constitutes a class excluded from entry into the United States under section 212(a)(11) of the Immigration and Nationality Act. However, in the 1952 Act, Congress deemed it more in accordance with humanitarian principles to try to keep together those offspring of a common parent who have lived together as a family unit in accordance with the established laws and institutions of their place of residence, regardless of whether or not those laws are in conformity with the long social and family institutions.

In the instant case the polygamous marriage of the father to two wives in India or Pakistan was legal under Hindu law prevailing at that time and the children of such polygamous marriages were under the law then prevailing considered legitimate. *Matter of K— W— S—*, (supra), is considered dispositive of the case to accord recognition of a brother and sister relationship such as will support a petition for preference status.

ORDER: It is ordered that the visa petitions be approved for fifth preference quota status on behalf of the beneficiaries.

E. Spouse

Matter of McKee
17 I. & N. Dec. 332 (BIA 1980)

The petitioner has appealed from the decision of a District Director, dated December 12, 1978, denying the visa petition filed on behalf of the beneficiary as his spouse under section 201(b) of the Immigration and Nationality Act, 8 U.S.C. 1151(b). The record will be remanded.

The petitioner, a 24-year-old native and citizen of Australia, on August 12, 1977 in Pensacola, Florida. On October 12, 1977, the petitioner filed a visa petition on the beneficiary's behalf seeking to accord her immediate relative status. In his decision, the District Director found that the parties had separated, and, on that basis, he denied the petition. On appeal, the petitioner has raised several arguments in support of his claim that the District Director erred in considering the unsworn statement of the beneficiary that she and the petitioner had separated, in not affording the petitioner an opportunity to rebut this adverse evidence, and in considering the separation of the parties as a valid basis upon which to deny the petition.

In connection with the petitioner's last argument, we requested the position of the Immigration and Naturalization Service on April 24, 1979. In a memorandum dated June 22, 1979, the Service indicated their agreement with the rationale of the recent decision of *Chan v. Bell*, 464 F. Supp. 125 (D.D.C. 1978), thereby accepting the court's ruling that, where the parties to a marriage were living apart, but there was no contention that the marriage was a sham at its inception in that it had been entered into for the purpose of evading the immigration laws, the Service could not deny the visa petition solely because the parties were no longer living together.

* * *

Chan v. Bell, supra, involved an appeal from the denial of a visa petition filed by a United States citizen petitioner on behalf of her husband. The parties in that case had known each other for several years prior to their marriage on January 10, 1975. The couple lived together for several months subsequent to their marriage during which time they jointly purchased property. In July 1975, they separated but continued an amicable relationship and their joint property ownership. In May 1976, the petitioner informed the District Director by letter that she and her husband had separated. Based upon this separation, the District Director denied the visa petition on June 14, 1976. A subsequent appeal to the Board was denied on November 9, 1977.

In its decision, the Chan court characterized the Attorney General's role in the adjudication of immediate relative visa petitions under section 201(b) of the Act as "limited: he is required to approve any true petition of a spouse of an American citizen in order that such spouse may secure immediate relative status." Id. at 127. The court noted that, at the time the visa petition was filed, the parties were lawfully married and that no divorce or legal separation had taken place, nor had any proceedings for divorce or legal separation been instituted. The court then went on to state its reasons for rejection of our decision affirming the District Director's denial of the visa petition based upon our characterization of the Chans' marriage as "nonviable."

The Chan court addressed the distinction between a sham and a nonviable marriage, recognizing that the Service is not precluded "from refusing to recognize fraudulent marriages." Id. at n.8. However, the court found no support in the statute or regulations for our refusal to approve a visa petition based on a finding that the parties to a valid marriage did not have a subsisting relationship. We find the reasoning of the court's decision in this regard persuasive.

In the present case, the District Director denied the visa petition based upon his determination that—

> [I]t must be established that a viable marriage exists both at the time of filing of the petition and at this time. On October 16, 1978, the beneficiary of the petition related to an officer of this Service that you and she were no longer residing together as man and wife.

He, therefore, based his denial of the petition on the sole basis that the parties were not residing together. The record indicates that the parties entered into a marriage valid under the laws of Florida, the place of celebration; there is no evidence that they have since obtained a legal separation or dissolution of that marriage under the laws of any state. Accordingly, we find that it was error for the District Director to deny the instant visa petition based solely on the separation of the parties. To the extent the Matter of Mintah, supra, indicates otherwise, it is hereby modified.

However, it is important to recognize that, although a separation in and of itself is no longer a valid basis for denial of a visa petition based upon a determination that the marriage is not viable, it is a relevant factor in determining the parties' intent at the time of their marriage, i.e., whether the marriage is a sham. . . . [A] marriage [is] a "sham" if "the bride and groom did not intend to establish a life together at the time they were married." 511 F.2d at 1201. . . . [T]he duration of a separation is relevant, but not dispositive, on the issue of intent—

> Conduct of the parties after marriage is relevant only to the extent that it bears upon their subjective state of mind at the time they were married. Evidence that the parties separated after their wedding is relevant in ascertaining whether they intended to establish a life together when they exchanged marriage vows. But

evidence of separation, standing alone, cannot support a finding that a marriage was not bona fide when it was entered.... Of course, the time and extent of separation, combined with other facts and circumstances, can and have adequately supported the conclusion that a marriage was not bona fide.

511 F.2d at 1202 (citations omitted).

In the present case, no determination has been made regarding the parties' intent at the time of their marriage.... Additionally, there is no evidence concerning the present status of the petitioner's marriage, i.e., whether the parties are legally separated or have dissolved their marriage, nor has there been compliance with the regulation requiring the Service to give the petitioner an opportunity to rebut any adverse evidence before rendering a decision. See 8 C.F.R. 103.2(b)(2); Matter of Holmes, 14 I & N Dec. 647 (BIA 1974). Accordingly, we will remand the record for further consideration and the entry of a new decision. See generally Matter of To, 14 I & N Dec. 679 (BIA 1974). The petitioner should be given an opportunity on remand to submit any additional evidence he may have in support of the petition.

Notes

1. While the INS may not be able to challenge the viability of a marriage, other restrictions may apply to a person's ability to obtain an immigrant visa based on the marriage. The Immigration Marriage Fraud Amendments, [Act of November 10, 1986, Pub. L. No. 99-639, 100 Stat. 3537], provided that an immigrant visa cannot be accorded when based upon a marriage entered into during "the period ... [in] which administrative or judicial proceedings are pending regarding the person's right to enter or remain in the United States" until the beneficiary has resided outside the U.S. for two years.

2. The Marriage Fraud Amendments also modified 8 U.S.C. § 1255, Sec. 245 by restricting the right of aliens who were attempting to adjust their status to that of a lawful permanent resident when it was based upon a marriage entered into during the proscribed period. *See* discussion in Chapter 9.

F. When Is a Relationship Not Really a Relationship?

As was mentioned in the notes which followed *McKee*, in 1986 Congress enacted legislation which significantly changed the way that marriages are treated under the immigration laws. This legislation is referred to as the Immigration Marriage Fraud Amendments [Act of November 10, 1986, Pub. L. No. 99-639, 100 Stat. 3537], or "IMFA." The case which follows was the first major case interpreting the IMFA, and was decided prior to the changes which were made to 8 U.S.C. §§ 1154(g) and 1255(e), Sections 204(g) and 245(3). This case is instructive, as it shows the approach taken by the courts in interpreting legislation designed to curb marriage fraud.

Immigration and Marriage Fraud
8 U.S.C. § 1154(g), Sec. 204(g)
as amended by the 1990 Act[24]

Notwithstanding subsection (a) except as provided in section 1255(e)(3),[25] a petition may not be approved to grant an alien immediate relative status or preference status by reason of a marriage which was entered into during the period described in section 1255(e)(2) of this title, until the alien has resided outside the United States for a 2-year period beginning after the date of the marriage.

Immigration and Marriage Fraud
8 U.S.C. § 1255(e), Sec. 245(e)
as amended by the 1990 Act

(1) Except as provided in paragraph (3), an alien who is seeking to receive an immigrant visa on the basis of a marriage which was entered into during the period described in paragraph (2) may not have the alien's status adjusted under subsection (a) of this section.

(2) The period described in this paragraph is the period during which administrative or judicial proceedings are pending regarding the alien's right to enter or remain in the United States.

(3) Paragraph (1) and section 204(h) shall not apply with respect to a marriage if the alien establishes by clear and convincing evidence to the satisfaction of the Attorney General that the marriage was entered into in good faith and in accordance with the laws of the place where the marriage took place and the marriage was not entered into for the purpose of procuring the alien's entry as an immigrant and no fee or other consideration was given (other than a fee or other consideration to an attorney for assistance in preparation of a lawful petition) for the filing of a petition under section 204(a) or 214(d) with respect to the alien spouse or alien son or daughter. In accordance with regulations, there shall be only one level of administrative appellate review for each alien under the previous sentence.

Anetekhai v. INS
876 F.2d 1218 (5th Cir. 1989)

* * *

Prior to the enactment of the IMFA [Immigration Marriage Fraud Amendments] in 1986, any United States citizen claiming that his or her alien spouse was entitled

---

24. This provision was added by Sec. 702(b), Immigration Act of 1990, Pub. L. No. 101-649, 104 Stat. 4978.

25. Sec. 702(c) of the Immigration Act of 1990 provides that "[t]he amendments made by this section shall apply to marriages entered into before, on, or after the date of the enactment of this Act."

to immediate relative status could seek an adjustment in status for the alien spouse simply by "[f]iling a petition with the Attorney General for such classification." 8 U.S.C. § 1154(a). If, after an investigation, the Attorney General determined that the facts stated in the petition were true—in other words, if the Attorney General concluded that the marriage was bona fide—then the status of the alien spouse was adjusted to that of permanent resident alien. 8 U.S.C. § 1154(b). If, on the other hand, the Attorney General determined that the marriage had been entered into fraudulently for the purpose of obtaining immigration benefits, no adjustment in status was made.

Perceived abuses of this process and the difficulty of ferreting out sham marriages prompted Congress to enact the IMFA. Under the IMFA, an alien who marries a United States citizen while no deportation proceedings are pending against him receives a two-year conditional adjustment of status so long as the investigation into the facts surrounding the marriage reveal that it is bona fide. See generally 8 U.S.C. § 1186a. In order for the conditional status to be removed at the end of the two-year period, the couple must submit a joint petition to the Attorney General in accordance with statutory requirements and must appear for a personal interview. 8 U.S.C. § 1186a(c)(1). If the Attorney General concludes that the facts and information provided by the couple are true, the condition is removed and the alien spouse obtains full permanent resident status. 8 U.S.C. § 1186a(c)(3)(B).

The procedure that a couple must follow in order for the alien spouse to obtain preferential status is different if, at the time of the marriage, the alien is involved in deportation proceedings. In that case the alien spouse is required to reside outside the United States for a two-year period before he or she may obtain an adjustment in status based on the marriage. 8 U.S.C. § 1154(h) and § 1255(e). It is this aspect of the IMFA which is at issue here.

In January 1982, Paul Anetekhai, a Nigerian citizen, entered the United States on a nonimmigrant student visa. In February 1986, the INS, having discovered that Paul was employed without authorization, commenced deportation proceedings against him. Also in early 1986, Paul met and began dating Mona Morris; they married in January 1987. Believing that his marriage to a United States citizen would entitle him to an immediate adjustment in status and thus make the deportation proceedings unnecessary, Paul moved to dismiss the proceedings. The immigration judge denied the motion and, finding Paul deportable, granted him until January 31, 1988, to depart voluntarily from the United States. The INS later extended the date for departure to February 28, 1988.

*   *   *

In addressing the constitutionality of an immigration provision, "it is important to underscore the limited scope of judicial inquiry into immigration legislation." *Fiallo*, 430 U.S. at 792. The broad power that Congress possesses to decide not only which classes of aliens may enter the United States but also the terms and conditions of their entry cannot be disputed. *See Oceanic Steam Navigation Co. v. Stranahan*, 214 U.S. 320, 339. . . .

*   *   *

. . . The Court also has recognized that, in exercising its broad discretion over immigration, "Congress regularly makes rules that would be unacceptable if applied to citizens." *Mathews v. Diaz*, 426 U.S. 67, 80 (1976). The Anetekhais do not deny that, ordinarily, courts should be highly deferential in reviewing congressional enactments in the areas of immigration and naturalization. They argue, however, that we should apply strict scrutiny in analyzing the immigration provision at issue here since § 1154(h) "affects Mona's fundamental rights in the domestic area." The Supreme Court rejected this very argument in Fiallo. . . .

Of prime importance in the Court's decision to review the INA provisions challenged in Fiallo with such deference was its conclusion that at issue there were the rights of the alien children, not the rights of United States citizens. Indeed, it was this very point which divided the majority from the dissent. Fiallo, 430 U.S. at 795 n.6. Similarly, in this case we are concerned with whatever rights Mr. Anetekhai, the alien spouse, may possess—not the rights of Mrs. Anetekhai.[1] That Mrs. Anetekhai asserts her fundamental right to marry here does not alter our analysis.[2] In Fiallo, the Supreme Court, too, was dealing with the citizens' fundamental interests in familial relationships.

Applying the deferential standard of review articulated in Fiallo to the case before us, we have no difficulty in concluding that § 1154(h) passes constitutional muster.[3] The Anetekhais admit that Congress has a strong and legitimate interest in deterring marriages which are entered into for the purpose of obtaining immigration benefits. We, like the other courts that have considered this issue, believe that Congress logically could have concluded that aliens who are engaged in deportation proceedings are more likely than aliens not so situated to enter into fraudulent marriages as a means of avoiding expulsion from the United States. "Since marriage to a United States citizen will no longer allow an alien engaged in deportation proceedings to remain in this country, it is rational to conclude that the two-year non-residency requirement will have some effect in reducing the incidence of marriage fraud" within this class of aliens. Smith, 684 F. Supp. at 1117.

In its amicus brief, the American Civil Liberties Union ("ACLU") attempts to distinguish Fiallo from this case. It argues that the issue in Fiallo was the validity of a statute establishing classes of admissible aliens. The ACLU concedes that Congress has virtually unlimited power in making such policy decisions. It argues that in this case, however, no policy decision is at issue. Instead, according to the ACLU, "the statute recognizes that aliens who marry citizens are admissible and then establishes a procedure designed to deny immigrant visas to aliens who base their claims on a fraudulent marriage." The ACLU contends that, because the procedure does not afford couples the opportunity to demonstrate that their marriages are not fraudulent, the statute violates their rights to procedural due process. We disagree. As an initial

---

1. Obviously our decision will have a significant impact on Mrs. Anetekhai's interests. We note, however, that Mrs. Anetekhai has no constitutional right to have her alien spouse remain in the United States. *See Burrafato v. United States Department of State,* 523 F.2d 554, 555 (2d Cir. 1975), cert. denied, 424 U.S. 910 (1976).

2. Nor does the fact that Mrs. Anetekhai asserts her "First Amendment rights to privacy and association" affect the outcome here. The Supreme Court made clear in *Fiallo* that, in ruling on the constitutionality of a provision, we are to apply the same standard regardless of whether Fifth Amendment or First Amendment rights are asserted.

3. The INS argues that the test for determining the constitutionality of an immigration provision is whether it is based upon a "facially legitimate and bona fide reason." *See Fiallo,* 430 U.S. at 794-95 (citing Kleindienst, 408 U.S. at 770). Because we conclude that § 1154(h) easily passes a rational basis test, we need not decide whether some lesser standard might be appropriate.

matter, we reject the ACLU's attempt to characterize § 1154(h) as a matter of procedure only. Inherent in Congress' broad policy making power in the area of immigration law is the power to prescribe reasonable procedures by which that policy may be implemented. Congress made a policy decision to distinguish aliens who marry while involved in deportation proceedings from aliens who marry at other times. This decision, in effect, created two classes of alien spouses. The first class, those aliens who marry United States citizens at a time when no deportation proceedings are pending against them, follows track one. Their citizen spouses may petition on their behalf for an adjustment in status at any time after they are married; if the petition is approved, the alien is granted preferred status on a conditional basis for a two-year period. The second class, those aliens who marry after deportation proceedings are initiated against them, follow track two. In order for these aliens to obtain immediate relative status, they must reside outside the United States for a two-year period before they may obtain an adjustment in status. We believe that Congress acted well within its power in establishing this policy and procedure.

In addition, we disagree with the ACLU's suggestion that § 1154(h) deprives alien spouses of any protected interests in "immigrant visas." Far from being a provision designed to deprive aliens of benefits to which they are entitled, § 1154(h) is part and parcel of the statutory scheme under which those benefits are conferred in the first instance. The section title itself states: "Procedure for granting immigrant status." 8 U.S.C. § 1154 (emphasis added). Procedural due process guarantees attach only when the government deprives a citizen or alien of life, liberty or property. *Plyler v. Doe*, 457 U.S. 202 (1982). In concluding that § 1154(h) does not deprive Mr. Anetekhai of a protected interest, we do not mean to suggest that he is entitled to absolutely no due process under that provision. We simply hold that the process which he is due is limited to fair procedures to determine whether § 1154(h) was invoked properly. In other words, if the Anetekhais had married before the INS initiated deportation proceedings against Mr. Anetekhai, he would be entitled to demonstrate that fact.

The Anetekhais argue, however, that § 1154(h) violates their due process rights by creating an irrebuttable presumption that their marriage, and every other marriage entered into during deportation proceedings, is fraudulent; they maintain that, before this conclusion can be reached, they must be afforded the opportunity to present contrary evidence. Certainly, if Congress had conditioned an alien's eligibility for a status adjustment on the existence of a bona fide marriage, procedural due process would require that the couple be given an opportunity to establish that fact before an adjustment could be denied. See *Smith*, 684 F. Supp. at 1118. That is not what Congress did here, however. Section 1154(h) does not require a two-year nonresidency because it presumes that the marriage is fraudulent. Instead, the statute requires an alien in Mr. Anetekhai's position to leave the United States for a two year period simply because the timing of his marriage places him in that class of aliens for whom a two-year nonresidency is required. Again, Congress rationally could conclude that this provision would deter those who are faced with imminent deportation from entering into fraudulent marriages for the purpose of gaining immigration benefits.

The Anetekhais also argue that, because there are several ways in which § 1154(h) can be avoided, it is not rationally related to the government's interest in deterring marriage fraud. We recognize that there are several ways in which a couple could avoid the seemingly harsh results of this provision, and that there may be better ways for Congress to accomplish its objective of deterring marriage fraud. However, we cannot conclude that because there might be a better way to write the statute, the statute as it exists is irrational.

Nor do we agree with the ACLU that § 1154(h) "suffers from precisely the same defect" that *Francis v. INS*, 532 F.2d 268 (2d Cir. 1976), held to be irrational. In *Guan Chow Tok v. INS*, 538 F.2d 36, 38-39 (2d Cir. 1976), the Second Circuit explained that "[i]n Francis, we held it irrational to distinguish between two categories of narcotic offenders on the basis of a brief visit out of the country. Here, the distinction is between narcotic offenders and other offenders, a distinction that has a rational basis." Similarly, in this case, the distinction is between aliens who marry while involved in deportation proceedings and aliens who marry at other times. This distinction, too, has a rational basis. Section 1154(h) withstands constitutional challenge under the Fifth and First Amendments.

The Anetekhais also challenge § 1154(h) under the Ninth and Tenth Amendments. They claim that, in enacting § 1154(h), "Congress overstepped its authority by purporting to regulate Louisiana marriages." This argument is without merit. The two-year nonresidency requirement of § 1154(h), by itself, does not in any way affect the legal status of the Anetekhais' marriage under state law. See La. Civ. Code Ann. art. 138 (West Supp. 1989); La. Rev. Stat. Ann. § 9:301 (West Supp. 1989).

Notes

1. In *Anetekhai*, the court noted with regard to the IMFA that "... Congress rationally could conclude that this provision would deter those who are faced with imminent deportation from entering into fraudulent marriages for the purpose of gaining immigration benefits." Is this a legitimate exercise of the congressional power? Does this mean that Congress can do whatever it wishes as long as it has as its goal the control of immigration?

2. The IMFA precludes preference or immediate relative status to persons involved in deportation proceedings. Do deportation proceedings commence at the time that the order to show cause is served or at the time that the case is presented to an immigration judge? In *Matter of Enriquez*, Interim Dec. 3045 (BIA 1988), the Board, citing 8 C.F.R. § 3.14(a), noted that the case begins with the filing of the order to show cause with the office of the immigration judge. The INS's position is that deportation proceedings commence upon the service of the order to show cause. See 8 C.F.R. § 242.1(2)(iii).

3. Can the two-year foreign residency requirement for persons described in 8 U.S.C. § 1154(h) be construed more broadly than applying to deportation or exclusion proceedings? Does the period following the INS's denial of a request for change of status?

4. What would happen if the Anetekhais had divorced and then remarried after Paul had left the U.S. under voluntary departure?

5. The IMFA has been challenged as unconstitutional with little success. See *Manwani v. U.S. DOJ*, 736 F. Supp. 1367 (W.D. N.C. 1990) (holding the provisions unconstitutional); *Almario v. Attorney General*, 872 F.2d 147 (6th Cir. 1989) (upholding the constitutionality of the provisions); *Smith v. INS*, 684 F. Supp. 1113, 1117 (D. Mass. 1988) (rejecting an equal protection and due process challenge); *compare Blancada v. Turnage*, 891 F.2d 688, 690 (9th Cir. 1989) (without deciding consti-

tutional claims court reversed the denial of a stay of deportation request and motion to reopen to raise challenge to the IMFA).

Presumptions of Fraud
8 U.S.C. § 1154(a)(2)(A), Sec. 204(a)(2)(A)

The Attorney General may not approve a spousal second preference petition filed by an alien who, by virtue of a prior marriage, has been accorded the status of an alien lawfully admitted for permanent residence as the spouse of a citizen of the United States or as the spouse of an alien lawfully admitted for permanent residence, unless—

(i) a period of 5 years has elapsed after the date the alien acquired the status of an alien lawfully admitted for permanent residence, or

(ii) the alien establishes to the satisfaction of the Attorney General by clear and convincing evidence that the prior marriage (on the basis of which the alien obtained the status of an alien lawfully admitted for permanent residence) was not entered into for the purpose of evading any provision of the immigration laws.

Matter of Patel
Interim Dec. 3083 (BIA 1988)

*   *   *

The petitioner is a 30-year-old native of Kenya. He acquired lawful permanent resident status in the United States on February 3, 1985, as the spouse of a lawful permanent resident whom he had married on June 23, 1983. The petitioner and his first wife were divorced on November 25, 1985. The beneficiary is a 29-year-old native and citizen of India. The petitioner and the beneficiary were married on March 6, 1986. On June 12, 1986, the petitioner filed a visa petition on behalf of the beneficiary as his spouse. On February 9, 1987, the district director denied the petition on the ground that the petitioner had failed to comply with section 204(a)(2)(A) of the Act, 8 U.S.C. § 1154(a)(2)(A) (Supp. IV 1986), which requires that the petitioner establish by clear and convincing evidence that his prior marriage was not entered into for the purpose of evading any provision of the immigration laws.

At the time he filed his appeal to the Board, the petitioner also filed a motion to reopen and/or reconsider with the district director. He argued that he had failed to comply with section 204(a)(2)(A) of the Act because that provision did not exist at the time he filed his visa petition. He pointed out that section 204(a)(2)(A) of the Act was not enacted into law until November 10, 1986, with the signing of the Immigration Marriage Fraud Amendments of 1986, Pub. L. No. 99-639, 100 Stat. 3537 ("Amendments"), 5 months after the filing of his visa petition. With his motion, the petitioner attached documentary evidence in an attempt to show that his marriage to his first wife was bona fide.

*   *   *

In a decision dated March 25, 1987, the district director denied the petitioner's motion to reopen and/or reconsider. He nonetheless proceeded to consider each document submitted by the petitioner individually. He characterized the petitioner's affidavit as "self-serving" and offering no evidence which was not available to the petitioner previously and, citing *Seihoon v. Levy*, 408 F. Supp. 1208 (M.D. La. 1976), asserted that the relatively short period of time between the petitioner's acquisition of lawful permanent resident status and his divorce from his first wife indicated a fraudulent intent. The district director discounted the other affidavits on the various grounds that they contained evidence which was known at the time of the original filing of the visa petition, that they provided no new meaningful evidence, and that the affiants could not attest to the intentions of the petitioner when he entered into his first marriage. In addition, he stated that he was not considering the untranslated document, the unidentified photographs, and the undated copies of Christmas cards. The district director did acknowledge that the copies of the tax returns, the corporate bond, and the financial statements lent credence to the marriage, but he noted that these documents, as well as the divorce decree and the property settlement agreement, were available to the petitioner at the time of the original filing of his visa petition. The district director further observed that the petitioner had not supplied evidence of any insurance policies, property leases, or bank accounts naming his first wife, and that she had gained nothing upon her divorce from the petitioner. He concluded by finding that the petitioner's evidence failed to sustain his burden of proof.

On appeal, the petitioner contends that he has shown by clear and convincing evidence that his first marriage was bona fide. He maintains that the district director erred in requiring his motion to reopen and/or reconsider to be accompanied only by evidence which was not known at the time he filed his visa petition. He also asserts that the district director's decision reflects a predisposition to deny the petition, overlooking the fact that the Amendments provide for a presumption of fraud which is rebuttable. He claims in this regard that while the district director considers his intent at the time of his marriage to be critical, it is impossible for him to prove that his intent was bona fide when the district director dismisses his affidavit as "self-serving" and refuses to give any weight to the affidavits of his first wife and of people who observed them during their marriage. Finally, the petitioner argues that the 5-year rule of section 204(a)(2)(A) of the Act is unconstitutional because it violates his right of privacy. With his brief on appeal, the petitioner submitted documents in an attempt to cure defects noted by the district director in his decision denying his motion. These documents include an affidavit from one of the petitioner's older male relatives, who states that he has reviewed the photographs submitted with the motion and recognizes them as having been taken at the wedding of the petitioner and his first wife, and a translation of the greeting card submitted with the motion which reveals that it is a wedding invitation for the wedding ceremony of the petitioner and his first wife.

* * *

... [T]he petitioner's right to petition for a second-preference visa beneficiary has only been restricted by section 204(a)(2)(A) of the Act, not eliminated. After a lawful permanent resident has been in lawful permanent resident status for 5 years, he may apply for a second-preference visa for a new spouse without being subject to the requirement that he establish by clear and convincing evidence that his prior marriage was not entered into for the purpose of evading any provision of the immigration laws. The regulations provide that a denial of a second-preference visa petition for failure to meet the clear and convincing evidentiary requirement will be without prejudice to the filing of a new petition once the petitioner has acquired 5 years of lawful permanent residence. 8 C.F.R. § 204.1(a)(2)(ii) (1988). Thus, even if a petitioner cannot meet the new evidentiary requirement of section 204(a)(2)(A) of the Act, that section still makes provision for the granting of a second-preference visa petition for a new spouse, albeit after a delay of up to 5 years....

... [W]e will apply that section to the visa petition before us and determine whether the petitioner has met his burden of establishing by clear and convincing evidence that his prior marriage was not entered into for the purpose of evading any provision of the immigration laws.

... The burden on the petitioner in visa petition proceedings is usually that of a preponderance of the evidence. *Matter of Soo Hoo*, 11 I & N Dec. 151 (BIA 1965). Section 204(a)(2)(A) of the Act, however, sets forth a presumption of a fraudulent prior marriage in any visa petition in which fewer than 5 years will have elapsed between the time a petitioner acquired his lawful permanent resident status based on that prior marriage and the time his visa petition for a subsequent spouse is adjudicated. In order to rebut this presumption, the petitioner has the burden of establishing by the standard of clear and convincing evidence that the prior marriage was not entered into for the purpose of evading any provision of the immigration laws.

Clear and convincing evidence is a standard of proof which requires more than the preponderance of the evidence standard applied in most civil cases, but less than the beyond a reasonable doubt standard used in criminal proceedings. The clear and convincing standard imposes a lower burden than the clear, unequivocal, and convincing standard applied in deportation and denaturalization proceedings because it does not require that the evidence be unequivocal or of such a quality as to dispel all doubt. We have defined clear and convincing evidence as "that degree of proof though not necessarily conclusive, which will produce in the mind of the court a firm belief or conviction, or as that degree of proof which is more than a preponderance but less than beyond a reasonable doubt." *Matter of Carrubba*, 11 I & N Dec. 914, 917 (BIA 1966).

In attempting to show by clear and convincing evidence that his prior marriage was not entered into for the purpose of evading any provision of the immigration laws, a petitioner should submit evidence which includes that considered in any visa petition where the validity of a marital relationship is in issue. The issue of whether a marriage is bona fide has typically arisen in visa petition proceedings in cases of suspected fraudulent or "sham" marriages. Such marriages, entered into for the primary purpose of circumventing the immigration laws, have not been recognized as enabling an alien spouse to obtain immigration benefits. The central question in such cases is whether the bride and groom intended to establish a life together at the time they were married. The conduct of the parties after marriage is relevant to their intent at the time of marriage. Evidence to establish intent could take many forms, including, but not limited to, proof that the beneficiary has been listed as the petitioner's spouse on insurance policies, property leases, income tax forms, or bank accounts, and testimony or other evidence regarding courtship, wedding ceremony, shared residence, and experiences together. *Matter of Phillis*, 15 I & N Dec. 385 (BIA 1975).

Two significant distinctions exist between the typical sham marriage visa petition case and a case in which section 204(a)(2)(A) of the Act applies, however. The first is that the typical sham marriage visa petition case involves an assessment of the validity of a petitioner's present marriage to his beneficiary, while the inquiry under section 204(a)(2)(A) of the Act is directed exclusively towards marriages which have already been terminated. Thus, in addition to the forms of evidence suggested in *Matter of Phillis, supra,* in a visa petition proceeding under section 204(a)(2)(A) of the Act, evidence regarding such matters as the length of time the petitioner and the prior spouse resided together and the reasons for the termination of their marriage is also relevant. See 8 C.F.R. § 204.1(a)(2)(ii) (1988).

The second evidentiary distinction between the typical sham marriage visa petition case and a case in which section 204(a)(2)(A) of the Act applies is that the burdens of proof differ. The clear and convincing evidence standard in section 204(a)(2)(A) of the Act imposes a greater evidentiary burden on the petitioner than the preponderance of the evidence standard ordinarily applied in visa petition proceedings. As a result, while the petitioner in a case in which section 204(a)(2)(A) of the Act applies may be submitting evidence similar to that considered in a typical sham marriage visa petition case, his evidence must be stronger and more persuasive before his petition may be granted.

Further, it should be pointed out that Congress designed the presumption of fraud in a prior marriage in section 204(a)(2)(A) of the Act to be rebuttable by clear and convincing evidence. In order to have any possibility of rebutting the presumption by that high standard, a petitioner in a case under section 204(a)(2)(A) of the Act must be accorded the same fair and reasonable evaluation of his evidence and factual situation as that given to any petitioner in visa petition proceedings. Simply because there is a statutory presumption that a petitioner's prior marriage was fraudulent, it should not be presumed that the petitioner's evidence is false or contrived or that any possible adverse inference which may be drawn applies to the sequence of events surrounding the prior marriage....

We turn now to the evidence considered by the district director with regard to the petitioner's prior marriage. This evidence was submitted by the petitioner with his motion to reopen and/or reconsider. The district director denied the motion on the dual grounds that the evidence could have been submitted at the time of the filing of the visa petition and that it failed to show by clear and convincing evidence that the petitioner's prior marriage was not entered into for the purpose of evading any provision of the immigration laws. Although the petitioner appealed from the district director's original decision rather than from the decision on the motion, we note that we disagree with both grounds relied on by the district director in denying the petitioner's motion. First of all, at the time the petitioner filed his petition, section 204(a)(2)(A) of the Act had not yet become law; the petitioner was not then directed by the regulations or the statute to submit evidence with his petition to establish the bona fides of his prior marriage. It was therefore illogical and unreasonable to penalize the petitioner and reject his documents because he failed to submit with his visa petition evidence which was neither requested nor required to be submitted at that time.

* * *

The evidence submitted by the petitioner to the district director includes affidavits from relatives and business acquaintances. We find the affidavits to be credible and worthy of considerable weight because they are detailed, internally consistent, and plausible; they include explanations of how the affiants acquired knowledge of the facts set forth; and they are corroborated by historical evidence. These sworn statements by people who attended the elaborate wedding ceremony of the petitioner and his first wife and observed them sharing a residence, visiting relatives together, and entertaining guests in their home, provide objective evidence of the conduct of the petitioner and his first wife which is supportive of their subjective bona fide intent at the time of their marriage. Conduct of the petitioner and his first wife supportive of a bona fide intent is further shown by evidence which documents joint financial dealings, such as their filing of joint state and federal income tax returns and their joint ownership of a Daily Passport Cash Trust account and a $5,000 corporate bond.

In addition, the petitioner submitted affidavits from himself and his first wife which indicate that they originally intended to have a lasting marriage, but that the petitioner's first wife eventually filed for divorce because she had become lonely living apart from her family and friends in a town where there were no other Indian nationals with whom they could socialize. Their account is corroborated by the actions of two of the affiants, relatives of the petitioner who traveled to LaFayette to try to help the couple reconcile. Obviously these relatives would not have made these efforts had they not regarded the marriage as a bona fide relationship worthy of salvaging. Further, unlike the district director, we do not find the failure of the petitioner's first wife to exact any financial advantage in the property settlement to be remarkable, as she was the one who wanted the divorce, there were no children from the marriage to provide for, and the only asset of considerable value, the motel operated by the petitioner, was purchased by the petitioner before the marriage and constituted the means by which he earned his livelihood.

Therefore, based on the evidence submitted to the district director with the motion to reopen and/or reconsider, we find that the petitioner has met his evidentiary burden under section 204(a)(2)(A) of the Act . . .

Notes

1. How much must a visa applicant be required to show in order to overcome the presumption of fraud? When do the requirements violate due process rights? Will the rights be different depending on whether the applicant is applying from within or from outside the U.S.?

2. Would it be proper for Congress to have created an irrebuttable presumption of fraud? Could Congress have provided, as it did in 8 U.S.C. § 1255(e)(2), that persons who were divorced within five years of their marriage were ineligible to receive immigrant visas for five years? Could Congress have made persons who divorced within five years of their marriage ineligible for any immigration benefits?

3. In *Matter of Patel*, Interim Dec. 3083 (BIA 1988), the Board held that the IMFA applied retroactively to a spousal second-preference petition which was pending adjudication when the IMFA was enacted. In articulating the basis for reaching this conclusion, the Board stated that:

Generally, a new statute applies to cases pending on the date of its enactment unless manifest injustice would result or there is a statutory directive or legislative history to the contrary. *Bradley v. Richmond School Board*, 416 U.S. 696 (1974). In determining whether a retroactive application would cause manifest injustice, three factors must be assessed: "(a) the nature and identity of the parties, (b) the nature of their rights, and (c) the nature of the impact of the change in law upon those rights."

Interim Dec. 3083, slip op. at 14. On balance, the Board concluded that the legislative history was silent on the question of retroactivity. It reasoned that Congress was so concerned about the possibility of benefits being obtained through fraudulent marriage that the Board sought to apply the statute as quickly and strictly as possible. In light of this reasoning, should the two-year residency requirement be applicable to persons who had not received their permanent residency before the statute was passed?

Priority Dates

In addition to the substantive requirement for immigrant visas, the applicant must wait until there are visas available. 8 U.S.C. §§ 1152 and 1153 provide for the allocation of visas based upon an annual quota with allocations for individual countries. The determination of whether an individual may be issued a visa (or receive permanent residence through "adjustment of status") will be controlled by the person's "priority date." In the case of a relative preference petition, the priority date is the date on which the petition was filed with the INS. In the case of a person who is immigrating based on her employment, the priority date is the date the labor certification was filed with the State employment office, or in the case of schedule A petitions, the date the petitions were filed with the INS.

The following case demonstrates how complicated the visa allocation process can be and some of the consequences of error.

Silva v. Bell
605 F.2d 978 (7th Cir. 1989)

TONE, Circuit Judge.

During the period from 1968 to 1976, 144,999 Cuban refugees were granted permanent resident status pursuant to the Cuban Adjustment Act of 1966, Pub. L. No. 89-732, 80 Stat. 1161. The visa numbers assigned to them were charged against the Western Hemisphere immigration quota, thereby making those visa numbers unavailable to applicants from Western Hemisphere countries other than Cuba. In 1976 it was determined that the Cuban charging was in error. The question in this case is how the erroneously charged visa numbers should be allocated among the Western Hemisphere applicants on the waiting list, chronologically without regard to national origin, as plaintiffs contend and the district court ordered, or in accordance with the historical immigration patterns for the countries involved, as the defendants contend. Also in issue are the standing of class members who are non-resident aliens, the proper composition of the plaintiff class, and the need for subclasses.

Plaintiffs sue on behalf of themselves and a class of visa applicants from Western Hemisphere countries whose applications were filed between July 1, 1968, and December 31, 1976, but have not yet been processed. Defendants are the Attorney General of the United States, other federal officials responsible for the implementation of the immigration laws, the Immigration and Naturalization Service (INS), and the Department of State.

*   *   *

When Congress enacted the present Immigration and Nationality Act in 1952, Pub. L. No. 82-414, 66 Stat. 163, See 8 U.S.C. §§ 1101 et seq., it placed no restriction on the number of Western Hemisphere[1] immigrants who could obtain permanent residence visas. 8 U.S.C. § 1101(a)(27)(C) (1964). In the 1965 amendment of the Act, Pub. L. No. 89-236, 79 Stat. 911, Congress created a select commission to study the problems of Western Hemisphere immigration and to recommend appropriate changes in the immigration laws, Id. at §§ 21(a) through (d), 79 Stat. 920-921. Western Hemisphere immigrants were classified as "special immigrants," Id. at § 8, 79 Stat. 916, but were not immediately subject to any quota. Congress did, however, provide that unless it enacted legislation to the contrary in the intervening time period, a numerical limitation on Western Hemisphere immigrants of 120,000 per fiscal year would become effective on July 1, 1968. Id. at § 21(e), 79 Stat. 921.

After the adoption of the 1965 Amendment but before the effective date of the § 21(e) quota on Western Hemisphere immigration, Congress enacted the Cuban Adjustment Act, Pub. L. No. 89-732, 80 Stat. 1161 (1966), to alleviate the barrier to permanent residence that immigration laws interposed for Cuban political refugees who had fled from Cuba to the United States after the revolution in that country. Admitted to the United States by the Attorney General pursuant to his discretionary parole power, 8 U.S.C. § 1182(d)(5), these refugees did not have visas granting them permanent residence status. Because, as § 1182(d)(5) prescribes, parole admittance is temporary and a paroled alien must eventually either secure a visa through regular procedures or return to his country of origin, these refugees sought visas. Regular procedures for visa application required contact with a consular post abroad.[2] Most refugees, however, could not establish this necessary contact. The United States consulate in Cuba had been closed since 1961, making it impossible for Cubans to obtain visas in their native land. Many of the refugees arrived in this country in an impoverished state and were unable to pay for a trip outside the United States to visit a consulate. The closest consulates, those in Mexico and Canada, had lengthy waiting lists, which exacerbated the problem. Adjustment of status, the only avenue by which visa applicants already present in the United States could avoid the trip to a foreign country, 8 U.S.C. § 1255 (1970), was unavailable to natives of Cuba, 8 U.S.C. §§ 1255(c) and 1101(b)(5) (1970). In the Cuban Adjustment Act, Congress granted the Attorney General authority to adjust the status of any Cuban native or citizen who had been lawfully physically present in the United States for at least two years to that of permanent resident alien.

---

1. The Western Hemisphere consists of "Canada, the Republic of Mexico, the Republic of Cuba, the Republic of Haiti, the Dominican Republic, the Canal Zone, [and the] independent countr[ies] of Central [and] South America." Pub. L. No. 82-414, § 101(a)(27)(C), 66 Stat. 169 (1952), superseded effective December 1, 1965, by 22 C.F.R. § 42.1.

2. An alien seeking a visa initiated the application process by submitting, or having submitted on his behalf, to a consular officer or the INS certain required documentation relevant to eligibility. After this filing the applicant was placed on the waiting list, his "priority date" on that list being the date on which the requisite filing was completed. 22 C.F.R. § 42.62 (1967). Applications were processed in chronological order based on priority dates, without regard to an applicant's country of origin. Id. When an applicant's priority date was reached he was scheduled for a final interview at a consular post for the purpose of establishing his eligibility. Applicants successfully bearing their burden of proof at the interview received visas granting entry into the United States as lawful permanent resident aliens.

As the conditionally effective date of the § 21(e) Western Hemisphere quota approached, it became apparent that Congress would not enact countermanding legislation. Because the Cuban Adjustment Act did not expressly address the issue, defendants had to determine whether Congress had intended that Cuban "adjustees" be charged against the Western Hemisphere quota. Without formally explaining its reasons for doing so, the INS adopted the policy of charging the Cubans against the quota; apparently with some reluctance, the Department of State acquiesced in this decision.

The charging commenced on July 1, 1968, and continued for over eight years. In 1975 and 1976 several individual actions were filed by visa applicants challenging the charging policy. While these actions were pending the Attorney General re-examined the policy. The Justice Department's Office of Legal Counsel concluded in a memorandum that "Cuban refugees whose status is adjusted to that of alien admitted for permanent residence are not to be counted against the Western Hemisphere quota." Thereupon, on August 31, 1976, the Attorney General ordered the INS to alter its policy to conform with the position stated in the memorandum. The INS complied with this order on October 1, 1976. By that time, however, 144,999 Cuban adjustees had been charged against Western Hemisphere quotas. During the period the Cuban charging took place, each Cuban adjustee was charged against the Western Hemisphere quota for the year in which his status was adjusted.

On October 20, 1976, before the 144,999 erroneously charged visa numbers could be reclaimed and allocated to waiting applicants, Congress again amended the Immigration and Nationality Act, Pub. L. No. 94-571, 90 Stat. 2703. The 1976 Amendment retained the 120,000 person per year quota on total Western Hemisphere immigration, see 8 U.S.C. § 1151(a), and, in addition, imposed a limit of 20,000 on the total number of immigrant visas available in a fiscal year to natives of any single Western Hemisphere state. That limit became effective on January 1, 1977. Pub. L. No. 94-571, § 3(2), 90 Stat. 2703. This new quota reduced Mexican immigration to this country by as much as 50 per cent and thus "made room" for increased non-Mexican immigration under the total Western Hemisphere immigration quota. Because only Mexicans have sought visas in numbers exceeding 20,000, the length of time Mexicans must wait to have their applications processed has increased, and concomitantly, the percentage of Mexicans on the waiting list has grown since January 1, 1977. The 1976 Amendment also extended the preference system, formerly applicable only to Eastern Hemisphere immigration, to Western Hemisphere immigration, but that feature of the Amendment does not concern us. The new 20,000-per-country quotas established by the 1976 Amendment, although they did not become effective until three months after the Cuban charging ceased and one and one-half months after this action was filed, are the major cause of difficulty in shaping appropriate relief in this case, as we shall explain later.

Plaintiffs filed this action on November 18, 1976, contending that defendants' charging policy violated the Immigration and Nationality Act and the due process clause of the Fifth Amendment, and seeking, inter alia, to compel defendants to "recapture" the visa numbers assigned to Cuban refugees and reissue those numbers to members of the proposed plaintiff class. On January 12, 1977, the district court certified the plaintiff class, defined as follows: All natives from independent countries of the Western Hemisphere who have been assigned priority dates for the issuance of immigrant visas between July 1, 1968 and December 31, 1976, and those priority dates have not yet been reached for processing and who have not been called for final immigrant visa interviews.

Insofar as is relevant here, the next significant event occurred on June 21, 1977, when defendants entered into a stipulation with the plaintiffs in *Zambrano v. Levi*, 76-C-1456, a related individual action pending before the trial judge to whom the instant case was assigned. In that stipulation defendants conceded that the challenged charging policy was in error; the court ordered defendants to recapture two of the wrongfully issued visa numbers and reissue them to the *Zambrano* plaintiffs. Remaining before the district court in this case after defendants' concession of liability was the question of relief, i.e., how to distribute the wrongfully issued visa numbers. Shortly after the *Zambrano* order was entered, defendants took it upon themselves to design a program to recapture and reissue the remaining wrongfully issued visa numbers, and by August, 1977, had commenced redistribution of these numbers without having consulted with plaintiffs or obtained the permission of the court.

In designing their original recapture and reissuance program, defendants relied on estimates of the size of the plaintiff class made from the annual statistical reports submitted by the Western Hemisphere consular posts. Based on these reports, defendants assumed, first, that only Mexican class members would require recaptured visa numbers because there would be enough unused numbers for non-Mexican class members under the quotas instituted by the 1965 and 1976 Amendments, and second, that the recaptured visa numbers would suffice to satisfy the needs of all Mexican class members. Hence defendants issued recaptured visa numbers only to Mexican class members, despite opposition from counsel for plaintiffs, who warned that defendants' estimates were inaccurate. The manner in which defendants reissued the visa numbers to Mexican class members was also contrary to the demand of plaintiffs' counsel that reissuance be conducted in strict chronological order, without regard to national origin. Mexican class members who could and did qualify for preference classification under the 1976 Amendment received preferential treatment in the issuance of recaptured visa numbers.

In February 1978, it became apparent from the annual report submitted by the Western Hemisphere consular posts that defendants had significantly underestimated the numbers of both Mexican and non-Mexican class members. Defendants thereupon began processing Mexican class members who established preference status for current visa numbers under the annual 20,000 person quota and nonpreference Mexican class members for recaptured visa numbers in strict chronological order. Although defendants admit in their brief that they then realized that non-Mexican class members would also need recaptured visa numbers, they apparently did not alter their program to accommodate this need at that time.

Finally, in May 1978, defendants performed a major restructuring of their program, adopting what they term a "historical approach" to recapture and reissuance. This approach is an attempt to factor out the effects of the 20,000-per-country quotas introduced by the 1976 Amendment, effects which are not properly remediable, and to issue recaptured visa numbers based solely on the harm resulting from the charging policy. Defendants' historical approach embodied the following procedure for issuing the recaptured visa numbers: first, determine how many visa numbers were charged to Cuban adjustees in each of the relevant fiscal years; second, determine what percentage of the properly issued visa numbers was awarded to applicants from each of the Western Hemisphere nations in each of the relevant fiscal years; third, issue the visa numbers recaptured from each year so that they are apportioned among plaintiff class members from each nation in the same percentage that immigrants from that nation received properly issued visa numbers in that fiscal year.[3] We assume, although the record does not show, that within each national group recaptured visa numbers were issued to applicants on a chronological basis.

Plaintiffs, as we have said, did not approve of defendants' original recapture program, and in February 1978 they moved to enjoin further visa issuance pursuant to it. In responding to the motion, defendants notified plaintiffs of the subsequent restructuring of the program; plaintiffs also disapproved of the restructured program and moved to halt its implementation. The district court denied plaintiffs' motion for injunctive relief on June 7, 1978, but, following additional discovery and a hearing, the court approved plaintiffs' proposed plan of relief and ordered the processing of the current waiting list of class members in strict chronological order.[4] The district court stayed, during the pendency of this appeal, the portion of its judgment requiring that visa applications for the recaptured numbers be processed in strict chronological order.

* * *

Stated simply, the Cuban charging injured plaintiff class members by delaying the processing of their visa applications. Visa numbers were available in limited quantities, 120,000 per fiscal year. Demand exceeded supply. Each visa number issued to a Cuban adjustee therefore not only reduced by one the number of Western Hemisphere natives admitted to the United States in the year of its issuance but also prevented persons on the waiting list from advancing to the positions on the list they would have occupied but for the wrongful visa number issuance.

* * *

[The court discussed the issue of whether the plaintiffs had standing to maintain the action, holding in this case that they all did.]

---

3. For example, assume that in the first fiscal year in which unlawful charging occurred, visa numbers were erroneously allocated to 1,000 Cuban adjustees; assume further that the remaining visa numbers were assigned to applicants from the following Western Hemisphere nations in the following percentages: Mexico, 45%; Canada, 15%; Brazil, 10%; Venezuela, 10%; Peru, 10%; Bolivia, 10%. The 1,000 recaptured visa numbers would be distributed to plaintiff class members native to these countries in the same percentages, resulting in the following pattern of distribution: Mexico, 450; Canada, 150; Brazil, 100; Venezuela, 100; Peru, 100; Bolivia, 100. The same procedure would be repeated for each fiscal year in which unlawful charging occurred.

4. Congress enacted the most recent major amendment to the Immigration and Nationality Act on October 5, 1978, Pub. L. No. 95-412, 92 Stat. 907 (the One World Amendment). The 1978 Amendment combined the former Eastern and Western Hemisphere quotas into one quota for immigrants from both areas. Defendants asserted that this legislation would have the effect of reducing the number of Western Hemisphere nonpreference immigrants granted visas and would consequently slow the rate at which plaintiff class members would receive visas through normal procedures. Assuming this to be true, the 1978 Amendment does not in any event impose any selective factors on the order in which visa applications are processed, as did the 1976 Amendment; rather, it would appear to slow the application processing for all nonpreference applicants regardless of national origin. Because the 1978 Amendment has no new differential effects on the processing of visa applications of natives of the Western Hemisphere countries, it poses no additional obstacles to the shaping of relief.

Defendants also contend that the district court erred in holding that the charging policy violated plaintiffs' due process rights. Regardless of the merits of that holding, it was unnecessary in light of the court's holding that the charging policy violated the Immigration and Nationality Act. Constitutional questions should not be decided unnecessarily. *Rescue Army v. Municipal Court of Los Angeles*, 331 U.S. 549, 568-574 (1947). The recital of this holding in the judgment is stricken.

* * *

Absent the effects of the 20,000-per-country quota imposed by the 1976 Amendment, shaping relief to restore plaintiff class members to the approximate positions they should have occupied would have been a simple task. As the parties agreed at oral argument, if it had been possible to effect complete relief as soon as the entitlement of each of the plaintiff class members was established and before January 1, 1977, the effective date of the 1976 Amendment, the proper procedure would have been to process the applicants in strict chronological order based on their priority dates, i.e., in their order on the waiting list, until defendants had either issued all the visa numbers or processed the applications of all plaintiff class members. This action would have had the effect of advancing each of the plaintiff class members on the list approximately as many places as he or she had lost through the Cuban charging policy. This was the relief each applicant on the list was entitled to at that time, and that relief should not be denied because of either lapse of time or an extraneous event.

The 1976 Amendment complicated matters by adding country of origin as a factor affecting the order in which defendants processed applications. As we explained in Part I of this opinion, the application of this selective factor in the ongoing processing of visa applications during the pendency of this suit has caused many applications of Mexicans to be passed over in favor of applications of non-Mexicans with later priority dates. Hence the percentage of Mexican class members has continuously increased, and the top of the current Western Hemisphere waiting list consists almost exclusively of Mexicans.

In order to achieve, as near as may be, the result that would have been obtained had it been possible to give relief before the effective date of the 1976 Amendment, the effects of the amendment must be factored out.

[The court went on to elaborate upon an intricate plan to provide relief to the plaintiffs.]

* * *

For purposes of simplicity we also have assumed the following:

(1) that Mexican immigration in each of the relevant years constituted 50 per cent of the total Western Hemisphere immigration, and the waiting list on January 1, 1977 reflected that pattern, every second person on the list being Mexican;

(2) that two full years of application processing have passed since January 1, 1977, during which four Mexican class members and twenty non-Mexican class members have received visas through normal processing and during which defendants issued none of the recaptured visa numbers; and

(3) that all class members are qualified to receive visas.

* * *

. . . It is apparent . . . that the proper object of relief is better served by defendants' historical plan than by the strict chronological plan ordered by the district court and advocated by plaintiffs. We recognize that in actual implementation the historical approach will not produce a perfect replication of the ideal, because the result will be affected by the sequence in which Mexican and other applicants' names happen to appear on the list, and because death and other causes have removed names from the list, thus advancing other names. The replication will, however, when corrected as provided below, be as accurate as the circumstances permit.

Plaintiffs have two objections to defendants' historical approach to the reissuance of recaptured visa numbers. First, they contend that the historical approach, by using national origin as a criterion for determining the order in which applications are processed, is inconsistent with the Congressional policy during the relevant period, viz., that visa applications were to be processed chronologically without regard to national origin. Ignoring the effect of the 20,000-per-country quotas of the 1976 Amendment, however, as plaintiffs propose, would have the practical effect of skewing the results in favor of one national group, which is hardly consistent with pre-1976 Congressional policy. Congressional policy is not offended, and justice to all parties is best served, by achieving the result, as near as may be, that would have been achieved by a grant of the proper relief at the time plaintiffs became entitled thereto.

Plaintiffs also object to defendants' historical approach on the ground that it will not result in reissuance of all recaptured visa numbers, even though some class members might remain unprocessed. As defendants concede, plaintiffs are correct in stating this would be the result. Because relief granted when plaintiffs' rights were established and before December 31, 1976, would have included reissuance of all the recaptured visa numbers or processing of all class members and issuance of as many recaptured visa numbers as there were qualified applicants, plaintiffs are entitled to that relief now. Fortuitous delay should not result in curtailment of the remedy.

* * *

The court will adopt, as the basic format for reissuance, defendants' historical approach . . . . Two modifications of that plan are necessary, however, to insure maximum approximation of the pre-1977 ideal. First, the new plan must account for those recaptured visa numbers, between 68,000 and 69,000 in number, which had already been reissued by defendants before the district court entered its judgment. Fortunately, factoring out the effects of the unauthorized reissuance should not prove too difficult. The district court should first determine how many of the recaptured visa numbers issued before October 10, 1978, were given to natives of each of the Western Hemisphere countries. In implementing what we have described in the text accompanying note 5, supra, as the third step of their historical plan, defendants should reduce the number of recaptured visa numbers to be issued to plaintiff class members from each country by the number of recaptured visa numbers previously issued to natives of the respective countries.

The second modification is necessary to remedy the failure of defendants' plan to provide for the reissuance of all recaptured visa numbers. It involves adding a redistribution process to the distribution process already adopted by the government in its historical approach. Visa numbers shall continue to be allocated to each country according to its historical share computed on the basis of the eight-year cumulative totals from 1968 to 1976. Those visa numbers already issued pursuant to the unauthorized recapture program shall be credited against each country's total historical share. Should a country exhaust its total historical share of visa numbers, no further visa numbers would be allocated to it except under the redistribution process as described below.

Under the redistribution process, those historical share visa numbers which are unused shall be redistributed to countries with qualified visa demand in excess of their total historical share. These unused visa numbers shall be redistributed to such countries in proportions equal to their relative historical use of visa numbers between 1968 and 1976. For example, assume Mexico, Colombia, and Jamaica are the only countries for which redistribution is required. Then, if Mexico received 75 per cent of the visa numbers issued to these three countries between 1968 and 1976, Mexico would receive 75% of the unused visa numbers. The redistribution percentages shall be recomputed, as necessary, to permit the addition or deletion of countries from the redistribution process.

The parties advise the court that it is highly probable that some countries will not exhaust their shares, with the result that other countries will necessarily participate in the redistribution of the unused numbers. Accordingly, as soon as practicable, the district court shall permit redistribution during the historical share distribution process, and require periodic recomputation of the quantity of unused visa numbers for redistribution to reflect the actual issuances. It is recognized that, even though unused visa numbers from a country have already been identified as available for redistribution, late qualifying applicants from that country may appear; if this occurs, the supply of unused visa numbers for redistribution will be correspondingly reduced. These late applicants, who may have encountered delays in gathering their visa paperwork, shall be eligible to participate in the recapture program until all recaptured visa numbers are exhausted.

Within each national group, recaptured visa numbers shall be made available to visa applicants in the chronological order in which they qualify. The processing of applications should not cease until all recaptured visa numbers are reissued or all plaintiff class members have been processed.

The district court shall require the entire recapture program to be completed within two years of the entry of the order on remand. This timetable may not be altered unless deemed necessary by the parties or upon a compelling showing that the interests of justice so require or that subsequent circumstances impose an unduly heavy burden on the defendants so as to justify a short extension of time to complete the processing. The district court may exercise its discretion, when necessary, to effect this court's order by adopting procedures reasonably calculated to facilitate the recapture program.

Notes

1. Priority dates are essentially the manifestation of intent to immigrate coupled with a prima facie eligibility for the preference category. It is for this reason that an applicant is considered to have a priority date based on the date on which the preference petition was filed on her behalf (in the case of relative visa petitions) or the filing date of the labor certification application. The use of priority dates establishes a uniform method for determining the order of processing of visa applications. Review the statute and consider what changes the INS could make to the existing rules on

priority dates. *See* 8 U.S.C. § 1153(c), Sec. 203(c). Could the INS require that a priority date would not be accorded where it was later determined that the beneficiary was in the United States when the application was filed? Could the INS ignore a person's priority date where it was later determined that the applicant had been working illegally in the United States and her whereabouts were not disclosed in the application?

2. **Chargeability.** Throughout the *Silva* case, the court referred to "charging" visa numbers. The immigrant visa statutory scheme allocates visa numbers to beneficiaries based on eligibility for preference classification, order of application, and country of birth. Since the number of immigrants who may be admitted to the United States is limited to 20,000 per year, the visas must, in effect, be charged to the country's allotment. As a general rule, immigrant visas are charged to the person's country of birth. *See* 8 U.S.C. § 1152(b), Sec. 202(b). Exceptions have been provided in the interest of family unity, enabling a child or spouse to be chargeable to the visa allocation from the parent or spouse's country of birth. 8 U.S.C. §§ 1152(b)(1) and (2), Sec. 202(b)(1) and (2). The charging of visas to the country of one's parent or spouse is referred to as "cross chargeability."

3. The table which appears on the following page is used by lawyers in determining how long it might take for an applicant to proceed from establishing eligibility for a visa to actually receiving the visa. The vertical column at the left margin represents the preference categories. The horizontal row across the top represents the beneficiary's country of nationality. The dates which appear in the columns represent the priority date which is being processed for immigrant visas during the month of the bulletin. The letter "C" signifies that visas may be issued to persons having priority dates up to and including the month of the bulletin. The letter "U" signifies that no visas may be issued under that preference category for persons from the country in the horizontal column. For example: assume that A is the beneficiary of a third preference family application submitted on 12/1/90 and that A was born in India. Even though A was eligible for third preference classification, she will not be issued an immigrant visa in December 1991, but she might be eligible in June 1992.

4. In the event that a visa application is denied by the U.S. consul, the applicant may have her case reviewed by the Bureau of Consular Affairs, Advisory Opinions Office, which will issue its view as to whether the application was properly denied. 22 C.F.R. §§ 42.81(c) and (d) (1989). These opinions are advisory to the consul and assume the facts in the case are as determined by the consul. *See* Wolff, *The Non-Reviewability of Consular Visa Decisions: An Unjustified Aberration from American Justice*, 5 N.Y.L. Sch. J. Int'l Comp. L. 341, 347-50 (1984).

Visa Preference Numbers for December 1991

Preferences Family-based	All Chargeability Areas Except Those Listed	Dominican Republic	India	Mexico	Philippines
1st	C	C	C	2-1-91	2-22-85
2A (Exempt)	1-1-89	1-1-89	1-1-89	1-1-89	1-1-89
2A (Subject)	7-1-89	U	7-1-89	U	U
2B	6-8-89	6-1-87	6-8-89	11-1-84	9-22-94
3rd	8-1-90	8-1-90	8-1-90	7-15-83	5-12-82
4th	1-1-83	1-1-83	8-5-82	7-8-79	3-26-77
Preferences Employment-based					
1st	C	C	C	C	C
2nd	C	C	7-1-90	C	C
3rd	C	C	C	C	2-22-87
(Other workers)	7-15-87	7-15-87	7-15-87	7-15-87	2-22-87
4th	C	C	C	C	C
Certain other workers	C	C	C	C	C
5th	C	jC	C	C	C
(Targeted employment areas)	C	C	C	C	C

Source: U.S. Department of State—Visa Office Bulletin, Dec. 1991

"Exempt" means exempt from the per country limits. "Subject" means subject to the per country limits. 8 U.S.C. § 1152(a)(4), Sec. 202(a)(4) provides that 75% of the visas allocated for the spouse and children of lawful permanent residents are to be issued without regard to the per-country limits, the remaining 25% are subject to the annual per country limitation.

Family-based Preferences:

1st Preference—unmarried sons and daughters of U.S. citizens; 2nd Preference (A)—spouse and children of lawful permanent residents; 2nd Preference (B)—unmarried sons and daughters of permanent residents; 3rd Preference—married sons and daughters of U.S. citizens; 4th Preference—brothers and sisters of U.S. citizens.

Employment-based Preferences (*see* Chapter 8):

1st Preference—(priority workers) persons of extraordinary ability, outstanding professors and certain multinational executives; 2nd Preference—members of the professions with advanced degrees and persons of exceptional ability; 3rd Preference—skilled workers and professionals with baccalaureate degrees; 3rd Preference (other workers)—unskilled workers; 4th Preference—special immigrants (with the exception of religious workers) described under 8 U.S.C. § 1101(a)(27); 4th Preference (certain other workers)—special immigrants who are religious workers; 5th Preference—investors of $1,000,000; 5th Preference (targeted employment areas)—investors of $1,000,000 in certain designated rural areas or areas of higher unemployment.

Immigrant Visa Flow Chart

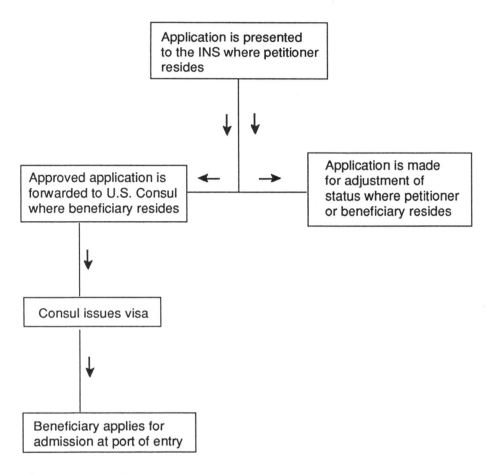

Index to Appendix

Statutes

Special Immigrant Provisions

8 U.S.C. § 1101(a)(27), Sec. 101(a)(27)

The term "special immigrant" means—

(A) an immigrant, lawfully admitted for permanent residence, who is returning from a temporary visit abroad;

(B) an immigrant who was a citizen of the United States and may, under section 1435(a) or 1438 of this title, apply for reacquisition of citizenship;

(C)[26] an immigrant, and the immigrant's spouse and children if accompanying or following to join the immigrant, who—(i) for at least 2 years immediately preceding the time of application for admission, has been a member of a religious denomination having a bona fide nonprofit, religious organization in the United States; (ii) seeks to enter the United States—(I) solely for the purpose of carrying on the vocation of a minister of that religious denomination, (II) before October 1, 1994, in order to work for the organization at the request of the organization in a professional capacity in a religious vocation or occupation, or (III) before October 1, 1994, in order to work for the organization (or for a bona fide organization which is affiliated with the religious denomination and is exempt from taxation as an organization described in section 501(c)(3) of the Internal Revenue Code of 1986) at the request of the organization in a religious vocation or occupation; and (iii) has been carrying on such vocation, professional work, or other work continuously for at least the 2-year period described in clause (i);

---

26. *See* 8 U.S.C. § 1101(a)(15)(R), Sec. 101(a)(15)(R) for provisions establishing a new nonimmigrant classification for religious workers.

(D) an immigrant who is an employee, or an honorably retired former employee, of the United States Government abroad, and who has performed faithful service for a total of fifteen years, or more, and his accompanying spouse and children: Provided, That the principal officer of a Foreign Service establishment, in his discretion, shall have recommended the granting of special immigrant status to such alien in exceptional circumstances and the Secretary of State approves such recommendation and finds that it is in the national interest to grant such status;

(E) an immigrant, and his accompanying spouse and children, who is or has been an employee of the Panama Canal Company or Canal Zone Government before the date on which the Panama Canal Treaty of 1977 (as described in section 3602(a)(1) of title 22) enters into force (October 1, 1979), who was resident in the Canal Zone on the effective date of the exchange of instruments of ratification of such Treaty (April 1, 1979), and who has performed faithful service as such an employee for one year or more;

(F) an immigrant, and his accompanying spouse and children, who is a Panamanian national and (i) who, before the date on which such Panama Canal Treaty of 1977 enters into force (October 1, 1979), has been honorably retired from United States Government employment in the Canal Zone with a total of 15 years or more of faithful service, or (ii) who, on the date on which such Treaty enters into force, has been employed by the United States Government in the Canal Zone with a total of 15 years or more of faithful service and who subsequently is honorably retired from such employment;

(G) an immigrant, and his accompanying spouse and children, who was an employee of the Panama Canal Company or Canal Zone Government on the effective date of the exchange of instruments of ratification of such Panama Canal Treaty of 1977 (April 1, 1979), who has performed faithful service for five years or more as such an employee, and whose personal safety, or the personal safety of whose spouse or children, as a direct result of such Treaty, is reasonably placed in danger because of the special nature of any of that employment;

(H) an immigrant, and his accompanying spouse and children, who (i) has graduated from a medical school or has qualified to practice medicine in a foreign state, (ii) was fully and permanently licensed to practice medicine in a State on January 9, 1978, and was practicing medicine in a State on that date, (iii) entered the United States as a nonimmigrant under subsection (a)(15)(H) or (a)(15)(J) of this section before January 10, 1978, and (iv) has been continuously present in the United States in the practice or study of medicine since the date of such entry; or

(I)(i) an immigrant who is the unmarried son or daughter of an officer or employee, or of a former officer or employee, of an international organization described in paragraph (15)(G)(i), and who (I) while maintaining the status of a nonimmigrant under paragraph (15)(G)(iv) or paragraph (15)(N), has resided and been physically present in the United States for periods totaling at least one-half of the seven years before the date of application for a visa or for adjustment of status to a status under this subparagraph and for a period or periods aggregating at least seven years between the ages of five and 21 years, and (II) applies for admission under this subparagraph no later than his twenty-fifth birthday or six months after November 6, 1986, whichever is later; (ii) an immigrant who is the surviving spouse of a deceased officer or employee of such an international organization, and who (I) while maintaining the status of a nonimmigrant under paragraph (15)(G)(iv) or paragraph (15)(N), has resided and been physically present in the United States for periods totaling at least one-half of the seven years before the date of application for a visa or for adjustment of status to a status under this subparagraph and for a period or periods aggregating at least 15 years before the date of the death of such officer or employee, and (II) applies for admission under this subparagraph no later than six months after the date of such death or six months after November 6, 1986, whichever is later; (iii) an immigrant who is a retired officer or employee of such an international organization, and who (I) while maintaining the status of a nonimmigrant under paragraph (15)(G)(iv), has resided and been physically present in the United States for periods totaling at least one-half of the seven years before the date of application for a visa or for adjustment of status to a status under this subparagraph and for a period or periods aggregating at least 15 years before the date of the officer or employee's retirement from any such international organization, and (II) applies for admission under this subparagraph before January 1, 1993, and no later than six months after the date of such retirement or six months after November 6, 1986, whichever is later; or (iv) an immigrant who is the spouse of a retired officer or employee accorded the status of special immigrant under clause (iii), accompanying or following to join such retired officer or employee as a member of his immediate family.

Immigrant Selection System

8 U.S.C. § 1151, Sec. 201. Numerical limitations

(a) In General.—Exclusive of aliens described in subsection (b), aliens born in a foreign state or dependent area who may be issued immigrant visas or who may otherwise acquire the status of an alien lawfully admitted to the United States for permanent residence are limited to—

(1) family-sponsored immigrants described in section 203(a) (or who are admitted under section 211(a) on the basis of a prior issuance of a visa to their accompanying parent under section 203(a)) in a number not to exceed in any fiscal year the number specified in subsection (c) for that year, and not to exceed in any of the first 3 quarters of any fiscal year 27 percent of the worldwide level under such subsection for all of such fiscal year;

(2) employment-based immigrants described in section 203(b) (or who are admitted under section 211(a) on the basis of a prior issuance of a visa to their accompanying parent under section 203(b)), in a number not to exceed in any fiscal year the number specified in subsection (d) for that year, and not to exceed in any of the first 3 quarters of any fiscal year 27 percent of the worldwide level under such subsection for all of such fiscal year; and

(3) for fiscal years beginning with fiscal year 1995, diversity immigrants described in section 203(c) (or who are admitted under section 211(a) on the basis of a prior issuance of a visa to their accompanying parent under section 203(c)) in a number not to exceed in any fiscal year the number specified in subsection (e) for that year, and not to exceed in any of the first 3 quarters of any fiscal year 27 percent of the worldwide level under such subsection for all of such fiscal year.

(b) Aliens Not Subject to Direct Numerical Limitations.—Aliens described in this subsection, who are not subject to the worldwide levels or numerical limitations of subsection (a), are as follows:

(1)(A) Special immigrants described in subparagraph (A) or (B) of section 101(a)(27).

(B) Aliens who are admitted under section 207 or whose status is adjusted under section 209.

(C) Aliens whose status is adjusted to permanent residence under section 210, 210A, or 245A.

(D) Aliens whose deportation is suspended under section 244(a).

(E) Aliens provided permanent resident status under section 249.

(2)(A)(i) Immediate Relatives.—For purposes of this subsection, the term "immediate relatives" means the children, spouses, and parents of a citizen of the United States, except that, in the case of parents, such citizens shall be at least 21 years of age. In the case of an alien who was the spouse of a citizen of the United States for at least 2 years at the time of the citizen's death and was not legally separated from the citizen at the time of the citizen's death, the alien shall be considered, for purposes of this subsection, to remain an immediate relative after the date of the citizen's death but only if the spouse files a petition under section 204(a)(1)(A) within 2 years after such date and only until the date the spouse remarries.

(ii) Aliens admitted under section 211(a) on the basis of a prior issuance of a visa to their accompanying parent who is such an immediate relative.

(B) Aliens born to an alien lawfully admitted for permanent residence during a temporary visit abroad.

(c) Worldwide Level of Family-Sponsored Immigrants.—

(1)(A) The worldwide level of family-sponsored immigrants under this subsection for a fiscal year is, subject to subparagraph (B), equal to—

(i) 480,000, minus

(ii) the number computed under paragraph (2), plus

(iii) the number (if any) computed under paragraph (3).

(B)(i) For each of fiscal years 1992, 1993, and 1994, 465,000 shall be substituted for 480,000 in subparagraph (A)(i).

(ii) In no case shall the number computed under subparagraph (A) be less than 226,000.

(2) The number computed under this paragraph for a fiscal year is the sum of the number of aliens described in subparagraphs (A) and (B) of subsection (b)(2) who were issued immigrant visas or who otherwise acquired the status of aliens lawfully admitted to the United States for permanent residence in the previous fiscal year.

(3) The number computed under this paragraph for a fiscal year is the difference (if any) between the maximum number of visas which may be issued under section 203(b) (relating to employment-based immigrants) during the previous fiscal year and the number of visas issued under that section during that year.

(d) Worldwide Level of Employment-Based Immigrants.—

(1) The worldwide level of employment-based immigrants under this subsection for a fiscal year is equal to—

(A) 140,000, plus

(B) the number computed under paragraph (2).

(2) The number computed under this paragraph for a fiscal year is the difference (if any) between the maximum number of visas which may be issued under section 203(a) (relating to family-sponsored immigrants) during the previous fiscal year and the number of visas issued under that section during that year.

(e) Worldwide Level of Diversity Immigrants.—The worldwide level of diversity immigrants is equal to 55,000 for each fiscal year.

Allocation of Immigrant Visas

8 U.S.C. § 1152, Sec. 202. Country Limitations

(a) Per Country Level.—

(1) Nondiscrimination.—Except as specifically provided in paragraph (2) and in sections 101(a)(27), 201(b)(2)(A)(i), and 203, no person shall receive any preference or priority or be discriminated against in the issuance of an immigrant visa because of the person's race, sex, nationality, place of birth, or place of residence.

(2) Per Country Levels for Family-Sponsored and Employment-Based Immigrants.—Subject to paragraphs (3) and (4), the total number of immigrant visas made available to natives of any single foreign state or dependent area under subsections (a) and (b) of section 203 in any fiscal year may not exceed 7 percent (in the case of a single foreign state) or 2 percent (in the case of a dependent area) of the total number of such visas made available under such subsections in that fiscal year.

(3) Exception if Additional Visas Available.—If because of the application of paragraph (2) with respect to one or more foreign states or dependent areas, the total number of visas available under both subsections (a) and (b) of section 203 for a calendar quarter exceeds the number of qualified immigrants who otherwise may be issued such a visa, paragraph (2) shall not apply to visas made available to such states or areas during the remainder of such calendar quarter.

(4) Special Rules for Spouses and Children of Lawful Permanent Resident Aliens.—

(A) 75 Percent of Minimum 2nd Preference Set-Aside for Spouses and Children Not Subject to Per Country Limitation.—

(i) In General.—Of the visa numbers made available under section 203(a) to immigrants described in section 203(a)(2)(A) in any fiscal year, 75 percent of the 2-A floor (as defined in clause (ii)) shall be issued without regard to the numerical limitation under paragraph (2).

(ii) 2-A Floor Defined.—In this paragraph, the term "2-A floor" means, for a fiscal year, 77 percent of the total number of visas made available under section 203(a) to immigrants described in section 203(a)(2) in the fiscal year.

(B) Treatment of Remaining 25 Percent for Countries Subject to Subsection (e).—

(i) In General.—Of the visa numbers made available under section 203(a) to immigrants described in section 203(a)(2)(A) in any fiscal year, the remaining 25 percent of the 2-A floor shall be available in the case of a state or area that is subject to subsection (e) only to the extent that the total number of visas issued in accordance with subparagraph (A) to natives of the foreign state or area is less than the subsection (e) ceiling (as defined in clause (ii)).

(ii) Subsection (e) Ceiling Defined.—In clause (i), the term "subsection (e) ceiling" means, for a foreign state or dependent area, 77 percent of the maximum number of visas that may be made available under section 203(a) to immigrants who are natives of the state or area under section 203(a)(2) consistent with subsection (e).

(C) Treatment of Unmarried Sons and Daughters in Countries Subject to Subsection (e).—In the case of a foreign state or dependent area to which subsection (e) applies, the number of immigrant visas that may be made available to natives of the state or area under section 203(a)(2)(B) may not exceed—

(i) 23 percent of the maximum number of visas that may be made available under section 203(a) to immigrants of the state or area described in section 203(a)(2) consistent with subsection (e), or

(ii) the number (if any) by which the maximum number of visas that may be made available under section 203(a) to immigrants of the state or area described in section 203(a)(2) consistent with subsection (e) exceeds the number of visas issued under section 203(a)(2)(A), whichever is greater.

(D) Limiting Pass Down for Certain Countries Subject to Subsection (e).—In the case of a foreign state or dependent area to which subsection (e) applies, if the total number of visas issued under section 203(a)(2) exceeds the maximum number of visas that may be made available to immigrants of the state or area under section 203(a)(2) consistent with subsection (e) (determined without regard to this paragraph), in applying paragraphs (3) and (4) of section 203(a) under subsection (e)(2) all visas shall be deemed to have been required for the classes specified in paragraphs (1) and (2) of such section.;"

(b) *Rules for Chargeability.* Each independent country, self-governing dominion, mandated territory, and territory under the international trusteeship system of the United Nations, other than the United States and its outlying possessions, shall be treated as a separate foreign state for the purposes of a numerical level established under subsection (a)(2) when approved by the Secretary of State. All other inhabited lands shall be attributed to a foreign state specified by the Secretary of State. For the purposes of this chapter the foreign state to which an immigrant is chargeable shall be determined by birth within such foreign state except that (1) an alien child, when accompanied by or following to join his alien accompanying parent or parents, may be charged to the foreign state of either parent if such parent has received or would be qualified for an immigrant visa, if necessary to prevent the separation of the child from the parent or parents, and if immigration charged to the foreign state to which such parent has been or would be chargeable has not reached a numerical level established under subsection (a)(2) for that fiscal year; (2) if an alien is chargeable to a different foreign state from that of his spouse, the foreign state to which such alien is chargeable may, if necessary to prevent the separation of husband and wife, be determined by the foreign state of the spouse he is accompanying or following to join, if such spouse has received or would be qualified for an immigrant visa and if immigration charged to the foreign state to which such spouse has been or would be chargeable has not reached a numerical level established under subsection (a)(2) for that fiscal year; (3) an alien born in the United States shall be considered as having been born in the country of which he is a citizen or subject, or, if he is not a citizen or subject of any country, in the last foreign country in which he had his residence as determined by the consular officer; (4) an alien born within any foreign state in which neither of his parents was born and in which neither of his parents had a residence at the time of such alien's birth may be charged to the foreign state of either parent.

(c) Chargeability for Dependent Areas.—Any immigrant born in a colony or other component or dependent area of a foreign state overseas from the foreign state, other than an alien described in section 201(b), of this title shall be chargeable for the purpose of the limitation set forth in subsection (a) of this section, to the foreign state.

(d) Changes in Territory.—In the case of any change in the territorial limits of foreign states, the Secretary of State shall, upon recognition of such change issue appropriate instructions to all diplomatic and consular offices.

(e) Special Rules for Countries at Ceiling.—If it is determined that the total number of immigrant visas made available under subsections (a) and (b) of section 203 to natives of any single foreign state or dependent area will exceed the numerical limitation specified in subsection (a)(2) in any fiscal year, in determining the allotment of immigrant visa numbers to natives under subsections (a) and (b) of section 203, visa numbers with respect to natives of that state or area shall be allocated (to the extent practicable and otherwise consistent with this section and section 203) in a manner so that—

(1) the ratio of the visa numbers made available under section 203(a) to the visa numbers made available under section 203(b) is equal to the ratio of the worldwide level of immigration under section 201(c) to such level under section 201(d);

(2) except as provided in subsection (a)(4), the proportion of the visa numbers made available under each of paragraphs (1) through (4) of section 203(a) is equal to the ratio of the total number of visas made available under the respective paragraph to the total number of visas made available under section 203(a), and

(3) the proportion of the visa numbers made available under each of paragraphs (1) through (5) of section 203(b) is equal to the ratio of the total number of visas made available under the respective paragraph to the total number of visas made available under section 203(b). Nothing in this subsection shall be construed as limiting the number of visas that may be issued to natives of a foreign state or dependent area under section 203(a) or 203(b) if there is insufficient demand for visas for such natives under section 203(b) or 203(a), respectively, or as limiting the number of visas that may be issued under section 203(a)(2)(A) pursuant to subsection (a)(4)(A).

8 U.S.C. § 1153, Sec. 203. Preference System

(a) Preference Allocation for Family-Sponsored Immigrants.—Aliens subject to the worldwide level specified in section 201(c) for family-sponsored immigrants shall be allotted visas as follows:

(1) Unmarried Sons and Daughters of Citizens.—Qualified immigrants who are the unmarried sons or daughters of citizens of the United States shall be allocated visas in a number not to exceed 23,400, plus any visas not required for the class specified in paragraph (4).

(2) Spouses and Unmarried Sons and Unmarried Daughters of Permanent Resident Aliens.—Qualified immigrants—

(A) who are the spouses or children of an alien lawfully admitted for permanent residence, or

(B) who are the unmarried sons or unmarried daughters (but are not the children) of an alien lawfully admitted for permanent residence, shall be allocated visas in a number not to exceed 114,200, plus the number (if any) by which such worldwide level exceeds 226,000, plus any visas not required for the class specified in paragraph (1); except that not less than 77 percent of such visa numbers shall be allocated to aliens described in subparagraph (A).

(3) Married Sons and Daughters of Citizens.—Qualified immigrants who are the married sons or married daughters of citizens of the United States shall be allocated visas in a number not to exceed 23,400, plus any visas not required for the classes specified in paragraphs (1) and (2).

(4) Brothers and Sisters of Citizens.—Qualified immigrants who are the brothers or sisters of citizens of the United States, if such citizens are at least 21 years of age, shall be allocated visas in a number not to exceed 65,000, plus any visas not required for the classes specified in paragraphs (1) through (3).

(b) [See p. 443 for provisions relating to "Employment-Based Immigrants]

(c) Diversity Immigrants.—(1) In general.—Except as provided in paragraph (2), aliens subject to the worldwide level specified in section 1151(e) of this title for diversity immigrants shall be allotted visas each fiscal year as follows:

(A) Determination of preference immigration.—The Attorney General shall determine for the most recent previous 5 fiscal-year period for which data are available, the total number of aliens who are natives of each foreign state and who

(i) were admitted or otherwise provided lawful permanent resident status (other than under this subsection) and

(ii) were subject to the numerical limitations of section 1151(a) of this title (other than paragraph (3) thereof) or who were admitted or otherwise provided lawful permanent resident status as an immediate relative or other alien described in section 1151(b)(2) of this title.

(B) Identification of high-admission and low-admission regions and high-admission and low-admission states.—The Attorney General—

(i) shall identify—

(I) each region (each in this paragraph referred to as a "high-admission region") for which the total of the numbers determined under subparagraph (A) for states in the region is greater than 1/6 of the total of all such numbers, and

(II) each other region (each in this paragraph referred to as a "low-admission region"); and

(ii) shall identify—

(I) each foreign state for which the number determined under subparagraph (A) is greater than 50,000 (each such state in this paragraph referred to as a "high-admission state"), and

(II) each other foreign state (each such state in this paragraph referred to as a "low-admission state").

(C) Determination of percentage of worldwide immigration attributable to high-admission regions.—The Attorney General shall determine the percentage of the total of the numbers determined under subparagraph (A) that are numbers for foreign states in high-admission regions.

(D) Determination of regional populations excluding high-admission states and ratios of populations of regions within low-admission regions and high-admission regions.—The Attorney General shall determine—

(i) based on available estimates for each region, the total population of each region not including the population of any high-admission state;

(ii) for each low-admission region, the ratio of the population of the region determined under clause (i) to the total of the populations determined under such clause for all the low-admission regions; and

(iii) for each high-admission region, the ratio of the population of the region determined under clause (i) to the total of the populations determined under such clause for all the high-admission regions.

(E) Distribution of visas.—

(i) No visas for natives of high-admission states.—The percentage of visas made available under this paragraph to natives of a high-admission state is 0.

(ii) For low-admission states in low-admission regions.—Subject to clauses (iv) and (v), the percentage of visas made available under this paragraph to natives (other than natives of a high-admission state) in a low-admission region is the product of—

(I) the percentage determined under subparagraph (C), and

(II) the population ratio for that region determined under subparagraph (D)(ii).

(iii) For low-admission states in high-admission regions.—Subject to clauses (iv) and (v), the percentage of visas made available under this paragraph to natives (other than natives of a high-admission state) in a high-admission region is the product of—

(I) 100 percent minus the percentage determined under subparagraph (C), and

(II) the population ratio for that region determined under subparagraph (D)(iii).

(iv) Redistribution of unused visa numbers.—If the Secretary of State estimates that the number of immigrant visas to be issued to natives in any region for a fiscal year under this paragraph is less than the number of immigrant visas made available to such natives under this paragraph for the fiscal year, subject to clause (v), the excess visa numbers shall be made available to natives (other than natives of a high-admission state) of the other regions in proportion to the percentages otherwise specified in clauses (ii) and (iii).

(v) Limitation on visas for natives of a single foreign state.—The percentage of visas made available under this paragraph to natives of any single foreign state for any fiscal year shall not exceed 7 percent.

(F) Region defined.—Only for purposes of administering the diversity program under this subsection, Northern Ireland shall be treated as a separate foreign state, each colony or other component or dependent area of a foreign state overseas from the foreign state shall be treated as part of the foreign state, and the areas described in each of the following clauses shall be considered to be a separate region:

(i) Africa.

(ii) Asia.

(iii) Europe.

(iv) North America (other than Mexico).

(v) Oceania.

(vi) South America, Mexico, Central America, and the Caribbean.

(2) Requirement of education or work experience.—An alien is not eligible for a visa under this subsection unless the alien—

(A) has at least a high school education or its equivalent, or

(B) has, within 5 years of the date of application for a visa under this subsection, at least 2 years of work experience in an occupation which requires at least 2 years of training or experience.

(3) Maintenance of information.—The Secretary of State shall maintain information on the age, occupation, education level, and other relevant characteristics of immigrants issued visas under this subsection.

(d) Treatment of Family Members.—A spouse or child as defined in subparagraph (A), (B), (C), (D), or (E) of section 101(b)(1) shall, if not otherwise entitled to an immigrant status and the immediate issuance of a visa under subsection (a), (b), or (c), be entitled to the same status, and the same order of consideration provided in the respective subsection, if accompanying or following to join, the spouse or parent.

(e) Order of Consideration.—

(1) Immigrant visas made available under subsection (a) or (b) shall be issued to eligible immigrants in the order in which a petition in behalf of each such immigrant is filed with the Attorney General (or in the case of special immigrants under section 101(a)(27)(D), with the Secretary of State) as provided in section 204(a).

(2) Immigrant visa numbers made available under subsection (c) (relating to diversity immigrants) shall be issued to eligible qualified immigrants strictly in a random order established by the Secretary of State for the fiscal year involved.

(3) Waiting lists of applicants for visas under this section shall be maintained in accordance with regulations prescribed by the Secretary of State.

(f) Presumption.—Every immigrant shall be presumed not to be described in subsection (a) or (b) of this section, section 101(a)(27), or section 201(b)(2), until the immigrant establishes to the satisfaction of the consular officer and the immigration officer that the immigrant is so described. In the case of any alien claiming in his application for an immigrant visa to be described in section 201(b)(1) or in subsection (a) or (b) of this section, the consular officer shall not grant such status until he has been authorized to do so as provided by section 204.

(g) Lists.—For purposes of carrying out the Secretary's responsibilities in the orderly administration of this section, the Secretary of State may make reasonable estimates of the anticipated numbers of visas to be issued during any quarter of any fiscal year within each of the categories under subsections (a), (b), and (c) and to rely upon such estimates in authorizing the issuance of visas. The Secretary of State shall terminate the registration of any alien who fails to apply for an immigrant visa within one year following notification to the alien of the availability of such visa, but the Secretary shall reinstate the registration of any such alien who establishes within 2 years following the date of notification of the availability of such visa that such failure to apply was due to circumstances beyond the alien's control.

8 U.S.C. § 1154, Sec. 204. Procedure

(a)(1)(A) Any citizen of the United States claiming that an alien is entitled to classification by reason of a relationship described in paragraph (1), (3), or (4) of section 203(a) or to an immediate relative status under section 201(b)(2)(A)(i) may file a petition with the Attorney General for such classification.

(B) Any alien lawfully admitted for permanent residence claiming that an alien is entitled to a classification by reason of the relationship described in section 203(a)(2) may file a petition with the Attorney General for such classification.

(C) Any alien desiring to be classified under section 203(b)(1)(A), or any person on behalf of such an alien, may file a petition with the Attorney General for such classification.

(D) Any employer desiring and intending to employ within the United States an alien entitled to classification under section 203(b)(1)(B), 203(b)(1)(C), 203(b)(2), or 203(b)(3) may file a petition with the Attorney General for such classification.

(E)(i) Any alien (other than a special immigrant under section 101(a)(27)(D)) desiring to be classified under section 203(b)(4), or any person on behalf of such an alien, may file a petition with the Attorney General for such classification.

(ii) Aliens claiming status as a special immigrant under section 101(a)(27)(D) may file a petition only with the Secretary of State and only after notification by the Secretary that such status has been recommended and approved pursuant to such section.

(F) Any alien desiring to be classified under section 203(b)(5) may file a petition with the Secretary of State for such classification.

(G)(i) Any alien desiring to be provided an immigrant visa under section 203(c) may file a petition at the place and time determined by the Secretary of State by regulation. Only one such petition may be filed by an alien with respect to any petitioning period established. If more than one petition is submitted all such petitions submitted for such period by the alien shall be voided.

(ii)(I) The Secretary of State shall designate a period for the filing of petitions with respect to visas which may be issued under section 203(c) for the fiscal year beginning after the end of the period.

(II) Aliens who qualify, through random selection, for a visa under section 203(c) shall remain eligible to receive such visa only through the end of the specific fiscal year for which they were selected.

(III) The Secretary of State shall prescribe such regulations as may be necessary to carry out this clause.

(iii) A petition or registration under this subparagraph shall be in such form as the Secretary of State may by regulation prescribe and shall contain such information and be supported by such documentary evidence as the Secretary of State may require.

(2)(A) The Attorney General may not approve a spousal second preference petition filed by an alien who, by virtue of a prior marriage, has been accorded the status of an alien lawfully admitted for permanent residence as the spouse of a citizen of the United States or as the spouse of an alien lawfully admitted for permanent residence, unless—

(i) a period of 5 years has elapsed the date the alien acquired the status of an alien lawfully admitted for permanent residence, or

(ii) the alien establishes to the satisfaction of the Attorney General by clear and convincing evidence that the prior marriage (on the basis of which the alien obtained the status of an alien lawfully admitted for permanent residence) was not entered into for the purpose of evading any provision of the immigration laws. (A) In this subparagraph, the term "spousal second preference petition" refers to a petition, seeking preference status under section 1153(a)(2) of this title, for an alien as a spouse of an alien lawfully admitted for permanent residence. (B) Subparagraph shall not apply to a petition filed by an alien whose prior marriage was terminated by the death of his or her spouse.

(b) After an investigation of the facts in each case, and after consultation with the Secretary of Labor with respect to petitions to accord a status under section or 203(b)(3) of this title, the Attorney General shall, if he determines that the facts stated in the petition are true and that the alien in behalf of whom the petition is made is an immediate relative specified in section 1151(b) of this title, or is eligible for a preference under subsection (a) or (b) of 203, approve the petition and forward one copy thereof to the Department of State. The Secretary of State shall then authorize the consular officer concerned to grant the preference status.

(c) Notwithstanding the provisions of subsection (b) no petition shall be approved if (1) the alien has previously been accorded, or has sought to be accorded, an immediate relative or preference status as the spouse of a citizen of the United States or the spouse of an alien lawfully admitted for permanent residence, by reason of a marriage determined by the Attorney General to have been entered into for the purpose of evading the immigration laws, or (2) the Attorney General has determined that the alien has attempted or conspired to enter into a marriage for the purpose of evading the immigration laws.

(d) Notwithstanding the provisions of subsections (a) and (b) no petition may be approved on behalf of a child defined in section 1011(b)(1)(F) of this title unless a valid home-study has been favorably recommended by an agency of the State of the child's proposed residence, or by an agency authorized by that State to conduct such a study, or, in the case of a child adopted abroad, by an appropriate public or private adoption agency which is licensed in the United States.

(e) Nothing in this section shall be construed to entitle an immigrant, in behalf of whom a petition under this section is approved, to enter the United States as a[n] immigrant under subsection (a), (b), or (c) of section 203 or as an immediate relative under section 1151(b) of this title if upon his arrival at a port of entry in the United States he is found not to be entitled to such classification.

(f) [Subsection (f) which provides for the immigration of Amerasian children has been omitted]

(g) [Subsection (g) appears at p. 365 of the text]

Immigrant Visa Regulations

8 C.F.R. § 204

§ 204.1 Petitions

(a) Relative—

(1) Filing petition. A petition to accord preference classification under section 203(a)(1), (2), (4), or (5) of the Act or classification as an immediate relative under section 201(b) of the Act, other than for a child as defined in section 101(b)(1)(F) of the Act or a Pub. L. 97-359 Amerasian, must be filed on a separate Form I-130 for each beneficiary and must be accompanied by the fee required under § 103.7(b) of this chapter.

(2) Jurisdiction—

(i) Petitioner residing in the United States. The petition must be filed in the office of the Service having jurisdiction over the place where the petitioner is residing in the United States, except that when accompanied by an application for adjustment of status, a petition may be filed and a decision made in the Service office having jurisdiction over the place where the beneficiary is residing.

(ii) Petitioner residing abroad. Except as provided in paragraph (a)(2)(iii) of this section, when the petitioner resides outside of the United States, the petition must be filed with the overseas office of the Service designated to act on the petition. This may be ascertained by consulting an American consul.

(iii) Jurisdiction assumed by American consular officers. American consular officers assigned to visa-issuing posts abroad except those in Austria, Germany, Greece, Hong Kong, India, Italy, Korea, Mexico, the Philippines, Republic of Panama, Singapore, and Thailand are authorized to approve I-130 petitions only if the petitioner is residing in the area over which these consular officers have jurisdiction. While these consular officers are authorized to approve petitions, they must refer any petition which is not clearly approvable to the appropriate Service office outside the United States for a decision.

(3) Decision. The petitioner will be notified of the decision, and, if the petition is denied, of the reasons for the denial, and of the petitioner's right to appeal to the Board within 15 days after mailing the notification of the decision in accordance with the provisions of Part 3 of this chapter.

(4) Derivative beneficiaries. Under section 203(a)(8) of the Act, a child or spouse accompanying or following to join an alien may be accorded the same preference as the alien without the approval of a separate petition if the immediate issuance of a visa is not otherwise available under section 203(a) (1) through (7) of the Act. However, no alien may be classified as an immediate relative as defined in section 201(b) of the Act unless he or she is the direct beneficiary of that classification. Therefore, a child or spouse of an alien who is classified as an immediate relative is not eligible for benefits under section 203(a)(8) and must file a separate petition.

(b) Orphan

 (1) Jurisdiction—

(i) Petitioner residing in the United States. A petitioner residing in the United States shall file a petition in behalf of a child defined in section 101(b)(1)(F) of the Act or an application for advance processing the petition with the Service office having jurisdiction over the place where the petitioner resides.

(ii) Petitioner residing abroad—

(A) General. A petitioner residing outside of the United States shall file an orphan petition or advance processing application with the overseas or stateside office of the Service designated to act on the petition or application. This can be ascertained by consulting an American consul.

(B) Petitioner residing in Canada. Since no Service office in Canada is designated to process orphan cases, a petitioner residing in that country shall file an orphan petition or advance processing application with the office of the Service having jurisdiction over the place of the child's intended residence in the United States.

(iii) Petitioner proceeding abroad when a district director at a stateside office has made a favorable determination concerning an advance processing application—

(A) Jurisdiction retained by stateside office. When a district director at a stateside office has made a favorable determination concerning an advance processing application and an unmarried petitioner or either a married petitioner or spouse or both are traveling abroad to locate a child, or are traveling abroad to adopt a child, the petition in behalf of the child may be filed at the stateside office if it will facilitate processing the petition.

(B) Jurisdiction assumed by American consulate or embassy. In an advance processing case where the petitioner does not wish to have the jurisdiction retained by the stateside Service office as provided in paragraph 204.1(b)(1)(iii)(A) of this section, the orphan petition may be filed at the American consulate or embassy having jurisdiction over the place where the child is residing unless the child is residing in Austria, Germany, Greece, Italy, Korea, the Philippines, Hong Kong, Mexico, Singapore, Republic of Panama, or Thailand.

(C) Authority of consular officers. An American consular officer is authorized to approve an orphan petition when the district director at a stateside Service office has made a favorable determination concerning an advance processing application and the unmarried petitioner or either the married petitioner or spouse or both have traveled abroad to locate or adopt a child or facilitate the adoption in the United States of a known child who resides in a country with no Service office. Consular officers, however, shall refer any petition which is not clearly approvable for a decision by the Service office having jurisdiction over the place where the child is residing. The consular officer's adjudication includes all aspects of eligibility for classification as an orphan under section 101(b)(1)(F) of the Act other than the ability of the prospective adoptive parent or parents to furnish proper care to the beneficiary orphan.

(D) Jurisdiction assumed by overseas Service office. If the child is residing in Austria, Germany, Greece, Italy, Korea, the Philippines, Hong Kong, Mexico, Singapore, Uruguay, or Thailand, the orphan petition may be filed at the overseas Service office having jurisdiction over the child's place of residence.

(2) Petition—

(i) Filing the petition. A petition for a child as defined in § 101(b)(1)(F) of the Act must be filed on Form I-600 by a United States citizen. It must identify the child and must be accompanied by the fee required under § 103.7(b)(1) of this chapter. If the petitioner is married, the Form I-600 must also be signed by the petitioner's spouse. If unmarried, the petitioner must be at least twenty-five years of age at the time of the adoption and when the petition is filed.

(ii) Decision. The petitioner shall be notified of the decision. If the petition is denied, the petitioner shall be advised of the reasons for the denial and of the right to appeal in accordance with the provisions of Part 103 of this chapter. When the petition is denied, the fee will not be refunded.

(iii) Child in the United States. A child who is in parole status and who has not been adopted in the United States is eligible for the benefits of an orphan petition and adjustment of status to permanent residence when all the requirements of §§ 101(b)(1)(F) and 204(e) of the Act have been met. A child in the United States either illegally or as a nonimmigrant, however, is ineligible for the benefits of an orphan petition and adjustment of status on that basis.

(3) Advance processing application—

(i) Circumstances when advance processing application may be filed. A prospective petitioner may file an Application for Advance Processing of Orphan Petition, Form I-600A, when—

(A) A child has not been located and identified;

(B) The prospective petitioner, and/or spouse if married, is traveling abroad to locate a child for adoption in the United States or to adopt while abroad; or

(C) The prospective petitioner, and/or spouse if married, is traveling abroad to a country with no Service office to adopt a known child while abroad or facilitate the adoption of a known child in the United States and wants to file a petition, Form I-600, at the American consulate or embassy having jurisdiction over the child's place of residence.

(ii) Filing the application. A United States citizen may file Form I-600A. The certification of prospective petitioner must be completed. The form must be accompanied by the fee specified in § 103.7(b)(1) of this chapter. If the petitioner is married, the petitioner's spouse shall also sign the Form I-600A. If unmarried, the petitioner must be at least twenty-four years of age at the time of filing Form

I-600A and at least twenty-five years of age at the time of the child's adoption and the filing of a petition, Form I-600, in behalf of the child. . . .

(iii) Disposition of advance processing application—

(A) Favorable determination. If the district director or officer in charge makes a favorable determination concerning the ability of the prospective adoptive parent or parents to furnish proper care to a beneficiary orphan if admitted to the United States, the district director or officer in charge shall advise the petitioner of the action taken. The district director or officer in charge shall also advise the petitioner that the advance processing application will be retained for one year from the date of completion of all advance processing, that if a child is not identified to this Service within that year, the application will be considered abandoned, and that any further proceedings will require the filing of a new advance processing application or an orphan petition.

(B) Unfavorable determination. When adverse information about the prospective adoptive parent or parents is developed which indicates that an orphan petition should not be approved because the prospective adoptive parent or parents are unable to furnish proper care to a beneficiary orphan, the district director or officer in charge shall render an unfavorable determination concerning the advance processing application. The district director or officer in charge shall advise the petitioner of the reasons for the unfavorable determination and of the right of appeal in accordance with the provisions of Part 103 of this chapter. When an unfavorable determination is made concerning an advance processing application, the fee will not be refunded.

(iv) When a child is identified—

(A) Pending advance processing application. When a child is identified while an advance processing application is pending, the petitioner shall submit a completed Form I-600 with all documentary evidence relating to the child. A new fee is not required.

(B) Completed advance processing application—favorable determination. When a child is identified after there has been a favorable determination concerning an advance processing application, the petitioner shall submit a completed Form I-600 with all documentary evidence relating to the child. A new fee is not required if the petitioner submits the Form I-600 within one year from the date of completion of all advance processing.

(C) Completed advance processing application—unfavorable determination. If the petitioner submits a petition, Form I-600, in behalf of a child when there has been an unfavorable determination concerning an advance processing application, the fee specified in § 103.7(b)(1) of this chapter must be submitted. If the grounds for the unfavorable determination have not been overcome, the district director or officer in charge shall deny the petition.

§ 204.1(c) Amerasians

(1) Eligibility. An alien is eligible for classification under section 201(b), 203(a)(1) or 203(a)(4) of the Act as the Amerasian child, son, or daughter of a United States citizen pursuant to section 204(g) of the Act if there is reason to believe that the alien—

(i) Was born in Korea, Vietnam, Laos, Kampuchea, or Thailand after December 31, 1950 and before October 22, 1982; and

(ii) Was fathered by a United States citizen.

(2) Filing petition. Any alien claiming to be eligible for benefits as a Pub. L. 97-359 Amerasian, or any person on the alien's behalf, may file a petition, Form I-360, Petition to Classify Pub. L. 97-359 Amerasian as the Child, Son, or Daughter of a United States Citizen, without fee. A natural person filing the petition must be eighteen years of age or older or an emancipated minor. In addition, a corporation incorporated in the United States may file the petition. The petition must be filed with the office of the Service having jurisdiction over the place of the alien's intended residence in the United States or with the overseas Service office having jurisdiction over the alien's residence abroad.

(3) (i) Preliminary processing. Upon initial submission of a petition with the documentary evidence required by § 204.2(g)(1)(i), the district director or officer-in-charge shall adjudicate the petition to determine whether there is reason to believe the beneficiary was fathered by a United States citizen. If the preliminary processing is completed in a satisfactory manner, the district director or officer-in-charge shall advise the petitioner to submit the documentary evidence required by § 204.2(g)(1)(ii) and (iii) and the fingerprints of the sponsor on Form FD-258 as required by § 204.2(g)(1)(iv) if they have not already been submitted. The petitioner must submit all requested documents within one year of the date of the request or the petition will be considered abandoned. To reactivate an abandoned petition, the petitioner must submit a new petition, Form I-360, without the previously submitted documentation, to the Service office having jurisdiction over the prior petition.

(ii) Final processing. Upon submission of the documentary evidence required by § 204.2(g)(1)(ii) and (iii) and, if applicable, § 204.2(g)(1)(iv), the district director or officer-in-charge shall complete the adjudication of the petition.

(4) One-stage processing of petition. If all documentary evidence required by § 204.2(g)(1)(ii), (iii), and (iv) is available when the petition is initially filed, the petitioner may submit it at that time. In that case, the district director of officer-in-charge shall consider all evidence without using the two-stage processing procedure under paragraph (c)(3) of this section.

(5) Decision—

(i) General. The district director or officer-in-charge shall notify the petitioner of the decision and, if the petition is denied, of the reasons for the denial.

(ii) Denial upon completion of preliminary processing. The district director or officer-in-charge may deny the petition upon completion of the preliminary processing under paragraph (c)(3) of this section for—

(A) Failure to establish that there is reason to believe the alien was fathered by a United States citizen; or

(B) Failure to meet the sponsorship requirements if the fingerprints of the sponsor, required by § 204.2(g)(1)(iv), were submitted during the preliminary processing and the completed background check of the sponsor discloses adverse information resulting in a finding that the sponsor is not of good moral character.

(iii) Denial upon completion of final processing. The district director or officer-in-charge may deny the petition upon completion of the final processing for failure to establish that the sponsorship requirements or one or more of the other applicable requirements have been met.

(iv) Denial upon completion of one-stage processing. The district director or officer-in-charge may deny the petition upon completion of all processing for failure to meet any of the applicable requirements in a case being processed under the one-stage processing described in paragraph (c)(4) of this section.

(v) Appeal. If the petition is denied, the petitioner may appeal the decision under Part 103 of this chapter.

(6) Classification of Pub. L. 97-359 Amerasian. If the petition is approved the beneficiary is classified as follows:

(i) An unmarried beneficiary under the age of twenty-one is classified as the child of a United States citizen under section 201(b) of the Act.

(ii) An unmarried beneficiary twenty-one years of age or older is classified as the unmarried son or daughter of a United States citizen under section 203(a)(1) of the Act.

(iii) A married beneficiary is classified as the married son or daughter of a United States citizen under section 203(a)(4) of the Act.

8 C.F.R. § 204.4

(a) Relative petitions. Unless revoked pursuant to section 203(e) of the Act or Part 205 of this chapter, the approval of a petition to classify an alien as a preference immigrant under section 203(a)(1), (2), (4), or (5) of the Act, or as an immediate relative under section 201(b) of the Act, shall remain valid for the duration of the relationship to the petitioner, and status, as established in the petition.

(b) Petitions under sections 203(a)(3) and (6). Unless revoked pursuant to section 203(e) of the Act or Part 205 of this chapter, the approval of a petition to classify an alien as a preference immigrant under section 203(a)(3) or (6) of the Act shall remain valid for as long as the supporting labor certification is valid and unexpired, provided there is no change in the respective intentions of the prospective employer and the beneficiary that the beneficiary will be employed by the employer in the capacity indicated in the supporting job offer. The approval of a petition to classify an alien under section 203(a)(3) or (6) of the Act which had heretofore become invalid solely because of expiration of the period of validity, is hereby reinstated provided the conditions of this paragraph are met.

(c) Subsequent petition by same petitioner for same beneficiary. When a visa petition has been approved, and subsequently a new petition by the same petitioner is approved for the same preference classification in behalf of the same beneficiary, the latter approval shall be regarded as a reaffirmation or reinstatement of the validity of the original petition, except when the original petition has been revoked under section 203(e) of the Act.

(d) Petitions for natives of former Western Hemisphere dependent areas. An approved visa petition which previous to January 1, 1977 granted a preference classification to a beneficiary who was at the time of approval a native of a dependent area in the Western Hemisphere, and which thereafter became inoperative solely because that area became an independent country, shall on and after January 1, 1977 be considered reinstated provided the status and relationship on the basis of which the petition was originally approved continue unchanged and provided any necessary labor certification remains valid.

(e) Revocation. The validity of any petition under this section may be revoked pursuant to the provisions of Part 205 of this chapter prior to the time limitations set forth herein.

(f) Exception to revalidation. Any petition approved under Section 204(b) of the Act ceases to convey a priority date or visa classification, and cannot be restored after it has been used by a beneficiary to obtain either an adjustment of status to lawful permanent residence or admission as an immigrant to lawful residence based upon a consular immigrant visa.

Conversion of Classification

8 C.F.R. § 204.5

(a) By change in beneficiary's marital status.

(1) A currently valid petition previously approved to classify the beneficiary as the unmarried son or daughter of a United States citizen under section 203(a)(1) of the Act shall be regarded as approved for preference status under section 203(a)(4) of the Act as of the date the beneficiary marries. The beneficiary's priority date is the same as the date the petition for classification under section 203(a)(1) was properly filed.

(2) A currently valid petition previously approved to classify a child of a United States citizen an immediate relative under section 201(b) of the Act shall be regarded as approved for preference status under section 203(a)(4) of the Act as of the date the beneficiary marries. The beneficiary's priority date is the same as the date the petition for 201(b) classification was properly filed.

(3) A currently valid petition classifying the married son or married daughter of a United States citizen for preference status under section 203(a)(4) of the Act shall, upon legal termination of the beneficiary's marriage, be regarded as approved under section 203(a)(1) of the Act. The beneficiary's priority date is the same as the date the petition for classification under section 203(a)(4) was properly filed. If the beneficiary is under 21 years of age, the petition is considered approved for status as an immediate relative under section 201(b) of the Act as of the date of termination of the marriage.

(b) By beneficiary's attainment of the age of 21 years. A currently valid petition classifying the child of a United States citizen as an immediate relative under section 201(b) of the Act shall be regarded as approved for preference status under section 203(a)(1) of the Act as of the beneficiary's twenty-first birthday. The beneficiary's priority date is the same as the date the petition for 201(b) classification was filed.

(c) By petitioner's naturalization. Effective upon the date of naturalization of a petitioner who had been lawfully admitted for permanent residence, a currently valid petition according preference status under section 203(a)(2) of the Act to the petitioner's spouse, unmarried children under 21 years of age, or unmarried son or unmarried daughter over 21 years of age shall be regarded as approved for immediate relative status under section 201(b) of the Act, for the spouse and unmarried children under 21 years of age, and for the unmarried son or unmarried daughter shall be regarded as approved under section 203(a)(1) of the Act. In any case of conversion to classification under section 203(a)(1), the beneficiary's priority date is the same as the date the petition for classification under section 203(a)(2) was properly filed.

Priority Dates

22 C.F.R. § 42.53 Priority date of individual applicants.

(a) Preference applicant. The priority date of a first, second, fourth or fifth preference visa applicant shall be the filing date of the approved petition that accorded preference. In the case of a third or sixth preference petition the filing date of the petition within the meaning of INA 203(c) shall be determined by the INS in accordance with INS regulations.

(b) Nonpreference applicant and certain special immigrants. The priority date of other applicants shall be:

(1) The date that an individual labor certification under INA 212(a)(14) has been granted for the applicant, or

(2) The date of submission to the consular officer, or to INS in appropriate cases, of evidence to establish:

(i) That the applicant is within one of the professional or occupational groups listed by the Department of Labor in Schedule A,

(ii) That circumstances specified in 22 CFR 40.7(a)(14)(iii) are applicable to the applicant and therefore the applicant is not within the purview of INA 212(a)(14), or

(iii) That the applicant is entitled to classification as a special immigrant under INA 101(27)(E), (F), or (G).

(c) Former Western Hemisphere applicant with priority date prior to January 1, 1977. Notwithstanding the provisions of paragraphs (a) and (b) of this section, an alien who prior to January 1, 1977, was subject to the numerical limitation specified in section 21(e) of the Act of October 3, 1965, and who was registered as a Western Hemisphere immigrant with a priority date prior to January 1, 1977, shall retain that priority date as a nonpreference immigrant under INA 203(a)(7) or as a preference immigrant upon approval of a petition according status under INA 203(a)(1)-(6).

(d) Derivative priority date for spouse or child of principal alien. Notwithstanding the provisions of paragraphs (a) and (b) of this section, a spouse or child of an INA 203(a) principal alien acquired prior to the principal alien's admission into the United States shall be entitled to the priority date of the principal alien, whether or not named in the immigrant visa application of the principal alien. A child born of a marriage which existed at the time of an INA 203(a) principal alien's admission to the United States is considered to have been acquired prior to the principal alien's admission.

Consular Processing

22 C.F.R. § 42.61 Place of application.

(a) Alien to apply in consular district of residence. Under ordinary circumstances, an alien seeking an immigrant visa shall have the case processed in the consular district in which the alien resides. The consular officer shall accept the case of an alien having no residence in the consular district, however, if the alien is physically present and expects to remain therein for the period required for processing the case. An immigrant visa case may, in the discretion of the consular officer, or shall, at the direction of the Department, be accepted from an alien who is neither a resident of, nor physically present in, the consular district. An alien residing temporarily in the United States is considered to be a resident of the consular district of last residence abroad.

(b) Transfer of immigrant visa cases.

(1) All documents, papers, and other evidence relating to an applicant whose case is pending or has been refused at one post may be transferred to another post at the applicant's request and risk when there is reasonable justification for the transfer and the transferring post has no reason to believe that the alien will be unable to appear at the receiving post.

(2) Any approved petition granting immediate relative or preference status should be included among the documents when a case is transferred from one post to another.

(3) In no case may a visa number be transferred from one post to another. A visa number which cannot be used as a result of the transfer must be returned to the Department immediately.

Chargeability

22 C.F.R. § 42.12 Rules of chargeability.

(a) Applicability. An immigrant shall be charged to the numerical limitation for the foreign state or dependent area of birth, unless—(1) Classifiable as an immediate relative under INA 201(b), or (2) Classifiable as a special immigrant under INA 101(a)(27), or (3) The case falls within one of the exceptions to the general rule of chargeability provided by INA 202(b) and paragraphs (b) through (e) of this section to prevent the separation of families.

(b) Exception for child. If necessary to prevent the separation of a child from the alien parent or parents, an immigrant child, including a child born in a dependent area, may be charged to the same foreign state to which a parent is chargeable if the child is accompanying or following to join the parent, in accordance with INA 202(b)(1).

(c) Exception for spouse. If necessary to prevent the separation of husband and wife, an immigrant spouse, including a spouse born in a dependent area, may be charged to a foreign state to which a spouse is chargeable if accompanying or following to join the spouse, in accordance with INA 202(b)(2).

(d) Exception for alien born in the United States. An immigrant who was born in the United States shall be charged to the foreign state of which the immigrant is a citizen or subject. If not a citizen or subject of any country, the alien shall be charged to the foreign state of last residence as determined by the consular officer, in accordance with INA 202(b)(3).

(e) Exception for alien born in foreign state in which neither parent was born or had residence at time of alien's birth. An alien who was born in a foreign state, as defined in § 40.1, in which neither parent was born, and in which neither parent had a residence at the time of the applicant's birth, may be charged to the foreign state of either parent as provided in INA 202(b)(4). The parents of such an alien are not considered as having acquired a residence within the meaning of INA 202(b)(4), if, at the time of the alien's birth within the foreign state, the parents were visiting temporarily or were stationed there in connection with the business or profession and under orders or instructions of an employer, principal, or superior authority foreign to such foreign state.

Refusal of Application

22 C.F.R. § 40.6 Basis for refusal.

A visa can be refused only upon a ground specifically set out in the law or implementing regulations. The term "reason to believe," as used in INA 221(g), shall be considered to require a determination based upon facts or circumstances which would lead a reasonable person to conclude that the applicant is ineligible to receive a visa as provided in INA and as implemented by the regulations. Consideration shall be given to any evidence submitted indicating that the ground for a prior refusal of a visa may no longer exist. The burden of proof is upon the applicant to establish eligibility to receive a visa under INA 212 or any other provision of law or regulation.

22 C.F.R. § 42.81 Procedure in refusing individual visas.

(a) Issuance or refusal mandatory. When a visa application has been properly completed and executed before a consular officer in accordance with the provisions of INA and the implementing regulations, the consular officer shall either issue or refuse the visa. Every refusal shall be in conformance with the provisions of 22 C.F.R. § 40.6.

(b) Refusal procedure. A consular officer may not refuse an immigrant visa until Form OF-230, Application for Immigrant Visa and Alien Registration, has been executed by the applicant. When an immigrant visa is refused, an appropriate record shall be made in duplicate on a form prescribed by the Department. The form shall be signed and dated by the consular officer. Each document related to the refusal shall then be attached to Form OF-230 for retention in the refusal files. Any document not related to the refusal shall be returned to the applicant. If the grounds of ineligibility may be overcome by the presentation of additional evidence and the applicant indicates an intention to submit such evidence, all documents may, with the consent of the alien, be retained in the consular files for a period not to exceed one year. If the refusal has not been overcome within one year, any documents not relating to the refusal shall be removed from the file and returned to the alien. The consular officer shall inform the applicant of the provision of law or implementing regulation on which the refusal is based and of any statutory provisions under which administrative relief is available.

(c) Review of refusal at consular office. If the grounds of ineligibility upon which the visa was refused cannot be overcome by the presentation of additional evidence, the principal consular officer at a post, or a specifically designated alternate, shall review the case without delay, record the review decision, and sign and date the prescribed form. If the grounds of ineligibility may be overcome by the presentation of additional evidence and the applicant indicates the intention to submit such evidence, a review of the refusal may be deferred. If the principal consular officer or alternate does not concur in the refusal, that officer shall either (1) refer the case to the Department for an advisory opinion, or (2) assume responsibility for final action on the case.

(d) Review of refusal by Department. The Department may request a consular officer in an individual case or in specified classes of cases to submit a report if an immigrant visa has been refused. The Department will review each report and may furnish an advisory opinion to the consular officer for assistance in considering the case further. If the officer believes that action contrary to an advisory opinion should be taken, the case shall be resubmitted to the Department with an explanation of the proposed action. Rulings of the Department concerning an interpretation of law, as distinguished from an application of the law to the facts, are binding upon consular officers.

(e) Reconsideration of refusal. If a visa is refused, and the applicant within one year from the date of refusal adduces further evidence tending to overcome the ground of ineligibility on which the refusal was based, the case shall be reconsidered. In such circumstance, an additional application fee shall not be required.

Chapter 8

Labor Certification

Our earlier discussion focused on the presumption that all foreigners coming to the U.S. were immigrants. This presumption is coupled with a requirement that most of these immigrants must establish that their employment in the U.S. will not displace or adversely affect U.S. workers.[1]

The concerns reflected in the labor certification requirements of U.S. immigration laws are common to most countries and are reflected in foreign immigration laws. For example, Austria requires aliens to obtain a labor permit or certificate of exemption prior to seeking employment.[2] Austria also utilizes a quota system, but, unlike the U.S., provides for exceeding the quota in extraordinary circumstances.[3]

In both the certificate of exemption and flexible quota systems, Austria seems to focus on macroeconomic and public interest concerns in issuing work permits.[4]

The United Arab Emirates applies a stricter limitation on the entry of foreign workers. Those brought in to work for the government as diplomats or as domestics are the only aliens exempted from obtaining an entry permit.[5] Under special circumstances, an employer may apply on behalf of individuals or collective immigrants. In order to accomplish this, the employer must:

1. Submit written evidence that his business requires the particular worker(s),

2. Enter into an agreement with the Ministry of Labor and Social Affairs assuming responsibility for the workers,

3. Enter into written work contracts with the immigrants, and guarantee the return of the workers to the sending country.[6]

Such agreements place a heavy burden on the employers, making it less likely that the employer will "import" foreign labor unless it is essential for the continued maintenance of the business. According to one scholar, similar policy is reflected in

---

1. 8 U.S.C. § 1182(a)(5), Sec. 212(a)(5). This proscription does not apply to immigrants coming to the U.S. under the family reunification provisions of the statute; immigrants entering as immediate relatives and under the first, second, fourth, and fifth preferences need not obtain labor certification. In addition, persons entering as derivative beneficiaries under any of the preference categories need not obtain labor certifications.

2. W. R. Bohring, *Studies in International Labour Migration* 36 (1984).

3. *Id.* at 37. In contrast, the United States does not provide for flexibility in the immigration of workers even when the need is urgent.

4. *Id.*

5. *Id.* at 38.

6. *Id.* at 38.

the reform legislation. Placing more of the burden on employers results from the belief that an employer has more to lose (in the way of reputation, financial losses, etc.) and hence can be more effectively sanctioned.[7]

While many countries do enact laws which attempt to severely restrict the immigration of foreign workers, these laws are often selectively enforced or officially circumvented by regional agreements. Hence the European Economic Community[8] exempts member countries from each country's labor certification requirements.[9] Similarly, Iraq and the Syrian Arab Republic treat all citizens of Arab States as nationals for purposes of immigration and employment.[10] Finally, the Scandinavian countries[11] have done the same since 1954.[12] Such agreements are clear evidence of the sense of identity these nations share. A valuable side effect is the relief from the bureaucratic red tape involved in admitting the foreign worker into a state.

Our labor certification requirements have been roundly criticized by virtually every political group. Those who believe in a more liberal immigration policy criticize the procedures as requiring an inordinate amount of paperwork without providing effective protection for U.S. workers. Those who believe in stronger restrictions criticize the strong emphasis on family reunification. As these critics point out, although there is great public concern to limit the influx of immigrant workers, present U.S. policy permits entry of 80% of its immigrants under the family reunification program which carries no restrictions on employment and does not require labor certification.[13] At the same time, agricultural interests desirous of bringing in workers point to the severe shortage of U.S. workers willing to harvest crops and note that if significantly higher wages were paid to farmworkers, U.S. farmers could not compete in the world market.

---

7. Liebowitz, *The Immigration Challenge and the Congressional Response*, 1 La Raza L.J. 1(1983).

8. The members of the European Economic Community or "EEC" are Belgium, France, Italy, Ireland, the United Kingdom, Luxembourg, the Netherlands, and the Federal Republic of Germany. *See* Bohring, *supra*, at 41.

9. *Id.*

10. *Id.*

11. Denmark, Finland, Norway, and Sweden comprise this group. *Id.*

12. *Id.*

13. *Id.* at 44. Some critics argue that this country should adopt a policy similar to Germany, which has the most compromised policy between the competing interests of protecting native workers and reuniting families. Families of gainfully employed foreign workers are permitted to enter the country under the family reunification program but are restricted from the labor market for several years. While this may be perceived as a hardship to those immigrating, it is argued that this more restrictive approach protects the interests of German workers while recognizing some of the needs of immigrants residing in Germany.

While some of the criticism of immigration policy has been blunted by the Immigration Act of 1990, a careful analysis will show that only a relatively small number of people are actually required to meet the labor certification requirement. Under the 1990 Act, of the approximately 700,000 immigrant visas which will be issued each year from 1991-1994, 140,000 are allocated for employment-based immigrants. Of those 140,000 visas, only 100,000 are in "certification preference categories," many of which will be filled by accompanying spouse and children, none of whom will be required to obtain certification.

In 1990, as part of a reform package, legislation was enacted that attempted to deal with some of the problems of bringing in foreign workers.[14] The 1990 Act increased the number of employment-related immigrants who may enter the U.S. from 54,000 to 140,000.[15] The 1990 legislation retained the requirement that most employment-based immigrants must obtain certification from the Secretary of Labor that "there are not sufficient workers able, willing and qualified" to take the position to be filled by the foreigner. These employment-based visas are set out into the categories as follows:

1. *First Preference—Priority Workers.* Forty thousand visas are set aside for persons of "extraordinary ability," "outstanding professor and researchers" and certain executives and managers of multinational corporations. The 40,000 visas here will be augmented by any visas not used by the 4th and 5th categories below. These persons will not have to establish that there are insufficient U.S. workers able, willing, and qualified to fill the position of the foreign worker.[16]

2. *Second Preference—Professionals and Persons of "Exceptional Ability."* Forty thousand visas are set aside for these applicants who must hold advanced degrees and are members of the professions. The 40,000 visas here will be augmented by any visas not used by the 1st category above. Exceptional ability is defined in terms of the benefit to the "national economy, cultural or educational interests."[17] In those cases where the Attorney General deems that the immigration of the person is in the "national interest" the job offer requirement may be waived.[18] It is contemplated that these applicants will still be required to satisfy the labor certification requirement.[19]

3. *Third Preference—Skilled Workers, Professionals and Other Workers*: Forty thousand visas are set aside for these applicants. The 40,000 visas here will be augmented by any visas not used by the 1st and 2nd categories above. Thirty thousand of these visas are set aside for skilled workers, persons with baccalaureate degrees and members of the professions. The remaining 10,000 visas are set aside for unskilled

---

14. *See* Sections 121 and 122, Immigration Act of 1990, Pub. L. No. 101-649, 104 Stat. 4978 (1990).

15. The increase in the employment-based immigrants was founded on the conclusion that U.S. workers will not be sufficiently trained to meet the demands on the U.S. to compete in the global economy. *See* C. Gordon & S. Mailman, Immigration Law and Procedure § 39A.01 (rev. ed. 1991).

16. 8 U.S.C. § 1153(b)(1), Sec. 203(b)(1). Employment-based immigrants must have a sponsoring employer, this is not required of those who meet the "extraordinary ability" requirement. Even though the "extraordinary ability immigrant must be coming to work in the U.S. The exemption from the labor certification requirement is a significant procedural advantage as the applicant does not have to proceed through the bureaucratic labyrinth of yet another government agency.

17. 8 U.S.C. § 1153(b)(2)(A), Sec. 203(b)(2)(A).

18. 8 U.S.C. § 1153(b)(2)(B), Sec. 203(b)(2)(B).

19. There is some question as to whether all of these immigrants are subject to the labor certification requirement. A plain reading of the statute indicates that the certification is applicable to professionals with exceptional ability. *See* 8 U.S.C. § 1182(a)(5)(A). Compare 8 U.S.C. § 1153(b)(2) (does not include language requiring certification) with 8 U.S.C. § 1153(b)(3)(C) (requires certification for skilled workers, professionals and other workers).

workers. All workers under this category must satisfy the labor certification requirement.[20]

4. *Fifth Preference—Employment Creation (Investors)*. [Fourth preference are special immigrant religious workers.] Persons who have invested or are actively in the process of investing at least $1,000,000 in capital and employ ten or more U.S. workers have been allocated 10,000 visas. Of the 10,000 visas, 3,000 are set aside for investment in "targetted" employment areas. Investors are termed "entrepreneurs" and are admitted to permanent residence on a conditional basis for 2 years, whereupon their status is made permanent upon a timely petition. The status may be terminated for failure to file within the prescribed period, failure to invest or maintain the enterprise, or fraud. The purpose of the conditional status was the deterrence of "immigration-related entrepreneurship fraud."[21]

The cases and notes which follow the discussion below will focus on the labor certification requirement and its relation to the preference petitions.

Labor Certification Requirements

8 U.S.C. § 1182(a)(5)[22] provides that persons other than those immigrants seeking admission under a family preference category must first be certified by the Secretary of Labor as not displacing U.S. workers. The statute further requires that the Secretary also certify that the employment of the foreign worker will not adversely affect the wages and working conditions of U.S. workers. In the vast majority of cases this certification can only be obtained after the employer has, in effect, surveyed the market to determine whether there are qualified, willing, and able U.S. workers.[23] The employer (applicant for certification) must show the following:

1. The position has been advertised describing the job opportunity with particularity. The documentation must include a copy of at least one advertisement placed by the employer.

2. Notice of the availability of the position must be posted at the worksite and if there is a bargaining representative, the representative must be notified at the time the application is filed.

3. The employer's advertising has produced no satisfactory results.[24]

If the certifying officer determines that the applicant has not met the requirements of 20 C.F.R. § 656.21 or that there is a United States worker who is "able, willing,

---

20. *See* 8 U.S.C. §§ 1182(a)(5)(A) and 1153(b)(3)(C), Sec. 212(a)(5)(A) and 203(b)(3)(C).

21. 8 U.S.C. § 1186a(b), Sec. 216A(b).

22. Section 212(a)(5) of the Immigration and Nationality Act, as amended.

23. For this reason, if the employer has provided training to the person on whose behalf she is seeking certification, she must be willing to provide training to U.S. worker applicants.

24. The regulations require the certifying officer, in judging whether a United States worker is "willing" to take the job opportunity, to examine the results of the employer's recruitment efforts and determine if there are other appropriate sources of workers from which the employer should have or might be able to recruit U.S. workers. Failure by the employer to comply with the application procedures constitutes a separate ground for denying certification.

qualified, and available" for the job, the officer issues a Notice of Findings setting forth the specific basis for the decision.[25]

The procedures described above may appear to be simple, however the certification process is time consuming. Given that there is a widespread perception that foreigners take work from U.S. citizens the INS and Department of Labor have increased the problems faced by employers through narrow interpretations of 8 U.S.C. § 1182(a)(5). One should also remember that even if certification is obtained, the foreign worker may not immigrate until there are visas available under the quota system.

References

Flores, *The Impact of Undocumented Migration on the U.S. Labor Market*, 5 Hous. J. Int'l L. 287 (1983)

Rubin & Mancini, *An Overview of the Labor Certification Requirement for Intending Immigrants*, 14 San Diego L. Rev. 76 (1976)

J. Simon, *The Economic Consequences of Immigration* (1989)

Steel, *In Defense of the Permanent Resident: Alleged Defects Relating to Alien Labor Certifications*, 19 San Diego L. Rev. 119 (1981)

Production Tool v. Employment Training Administration
688 F.2d 1161 (7th Cir. 1982)

WOOD, Jr., Circuit Judge.

Production Tool Corp. and Kenall Manufacturing Co. appeal from separate orders affirming final decisions of the United States Department of Labor denying their applications for permanent alien labor as provided for by the Immigration and Nationality Act, § 212(a)(14), 8 U.S.C. § 1182(a)(14) (as amended), and the regulations promulgated thereunder, 20 C.F.R. 656 (1980). Appellants challenge the validity and application of those regulations. For the following reasons, we affirm.

*   *   *

On May 3, 1977, Production Tool filed an application for labor certification on behalf of its employee Manuel Aguilar. The certifying officer denied that application in part for the stated reason that Production Tool "elected not to comply" with the advertising requirements of 20 C.F.R. § 656.21(b)(9). The hearing officer affirmed and the district court denied relief on the same ground. Production Tool admits that it did not comply with that regulation.

On June 13, 1977, Kenall filed an application on behalf of Blanca Fabian. Kenall had advertised the position in the Reader at a wage rate of $4.00. The Certifying

---

25. The employer may then submit rebuttal evidence which the certifying officer must review. A final determination to grant or deny is then made, and if certification is denied, the employer may request administrative review by the Board of Alien Labor Certification Appeals (BALCA). *See* 20 C.F.R. §§ 656.25–656.27. The case can be taken to federal court through a declaratory judgment action.

Officer, after receiving Kenall's rebuttal evidence, denied certification on the ground, inter alia, that Kenall's newspaper advertisements did not satisfy 20 C.F.R. § 656.21(b)(9) because they did not offer the prevailing wage of $4.70 and were not placed in a newspaper of "general circulation." The Hearing Officer affirmed, noting that counsel for Kenall had conceded, and the record showed, that the advertising did not fully comply with the regulations: "This undisputed fact together with the unacceptable advertising in the Reader establishes a sufficient basis for affirming the denial." The district court entered summary judgment for appellees.

Production Tool and Kenall contend that the Secretary of Labor was without statutory authority to promulgate the regulations at issue and that, even if authorized, the regulations are invalid because they are inconsistent with the command and purpose of § 212(a)(14). Kenall separately argues that the denial of labor certification constituted an abuse of discretion because 1) it had offered to pay and advertise the prevailing wage and 2) the Reader, under Illinois law, is considered a newspaper of general circulation.

The validity of the advertising regulation, according to appellants, turns on the distinction between "legislative" and "interpretive" rules. Appellants assert that the regulation at issue is legislative because it "creates or changes existing rights and obligations" and, as such, "require[s] specific statutory authorization." . . . After examining the relevant case law, we believe that the distinction between legislative and interpretive rules is of little, if any, value in determining whether the Secretary must have a specific grant of rule making authority to promulgate the regulation at issue. That distinction nonetheless becomes important when reviewing the regulation to determine whether it constitutes a proper exercise of rule making authority.

*   *   *

. . . In an area where the Secretary has considerable power under general statutory standards and must decide numerous cases in a routine fashion, the clarification of policy through rules or published pronouncements would protect against arbitrary action. The absence of an express delegation of legislative power does not itself render the advertising regulation void.[1]

Appellants also contend that the advertising regulation shifts the burden of proving unavailability of domestic workers to the employer-applicant. This, they say, is contrary to the intent of Congress and to the greater weight of judicial decisions construing § 212(a)(14). Appellants' argument is not without merit, but we agree with the district court that the regulation constitutes a valid exercise of the Secretary's inherent authority to promulgate rules governing the administration of § 212(a)(14). The interpretation of a statute by the agency charged with enforcement or administration is entitled to great deference provided it is consistent with the congressional purpose. "[W]e need not find that [the agency's] construction is the only reasonable one, or even that it is the result we would have reached had the question arisen in the first instance in judicial proceedings." *Udall v. Tallman*, 380 U.S. 1, 16 (1965). "[T]he rulings, interpretations and opinions [of the agency], while not controlling

---

1. We decide only that promulgation of the advertising requirement was a valid exercise of the Secretary's inherent rule making power. We therefore need not determine whether Congress intended to delegate "legislative" authority under § 212(a)(14), though other courts apparently have assumed such a grant. See, e.g., Lewis-Mota v. Secretary of Labor, 469 F.2d 478 (2d Cir. 1972).

upon the courts by reason of their authority, do constitute a body of experience and informed judgment to which courts and litigants may properly resort for guidance." *Skidmore*, 323 U.S. at 140. Deference is especially appropriate where, as here, the rule was adopted only after all interested persons were given notice and an opportunity to comment pursuant to § 553 procedures.

Congress enacted § 212(a)(14) to protect the domestic labor force from job competition and adverse working conditions as a result of foreign workers entering the labor market. H.R. Rep. No. 1365, 82d Cong., 2d Sess. (1952), *reprinted in*, 1952 U.S. Code Cong. & Ad. News 1653, 1705; S. Rep. No. 748, 89th Cong., 1st Sess. (1965), *reprinted in*, 1965 U.S. Code Cong. & Ad. News 3328, 3329, 3333-34. The labor market findings the Secretary must make are designed to effectuate that purpose. The 1952 version of § 212(a)(14) provided that aliens will not be permitted to enter to perform work "if the Secretary of Labor has determined and certified ... that (A) sufficient workers in the United States who are able, willing, and qualified are available ... or (B) the employment of such aliens will adversely affect the wages and working conditions...." § 212(a)(14), 66 Stat. 183. In 1965 Congress sought to strengthen the protection of United States workers by amending § 212(a)(14) to require exclusion unless the Secretary affirmatively finds that there are not sufficient domestic workers available and that entry of the foreign worker will not adversely affect working conditions. Pub. L. No. 89-236, § 10(a), 79 Stat. 917. As the Senate Report stated, "Under the instant bill, [the present] procedure is substantially changed. The primary responsibility is placed upon the intending immigrant to obtain the Secretary of Labor's clearance prior to issuance of a visa establishing" the two statutory prerequisites. Whereas the 1952 Act opened the door to immigrant workers unless the Secretary acted to exclude them, the 1965 amendment closed that door and placed direct responsibility on the alien to petition the Secretary to open it.

Appellees rely on *Pesikoff v. Secretary of Labor*, 501 F.2d 757 (D.C. Cir.), cert. denied, 419 U.S. 1038 (1974), wherein the D.C. Circuit found that, based on its assessment of the statutory language and legislative history, § 212(a)(14) sets up a presumption that aliens may not enter the United States for permanent employment. Thus the court held:

> if the Secretary's consultation of the general labor market data readily available to him suggests that there is a pool of potential workers available to perform the job which the alien seeks, the burden should be placed on the alien or his putative employer to prove that it is not possible for the employer to find a qualified American worker.

To support its conclusion the court cited the language change by the 1965 amendment and Senator Kennedy's remark on the Senate floor that the amendment "places the burden of proving no adverse effect on the applying alien." Id. at 762, citing 111 Cong. Rec. 24227 (1965).

Judge MacKinnon, in a strong dissent, commented that "[a]lthough this is consistent with the statutory structure, it does present some problems not considered in the majority opinion." Id. at 771. He noted that by bearing the "ultimate burden of persuasion," the employer is required to "prove the existence of the nonexistent, a sometimes difficult proposition." Id. Instead, he suggested that it would be reasonable and sufficient for the employer to bear the "burden of production" by documenting his efforts to find domestic workers "through newspaper advertisements, employment agencies and the assistance of friends." Id. If those efforts are shown to be unsuccessful, "[t]he Secretary then must introduce sufficient competent evidence to overcome that adduced by the employer, failing which certification must issue." As appellants point out, however, *Pesikoff* does not represent the law of this circuit. Several decisions of this court have held that it constitutes an abuse of discretion to deny labor certification on the basis of evidence which was challenged and not shown to be reliable. *Stenographic Machines, Inc. v. Regional Administrator for Employment & Training*, 577 F.2d 521 (7th Cir. 1978); *Shuk Yee Chan v. Regional Manpower Administrator*, 521 F.2d 592 (7th Cir. 1975). The rationale for this circuit's position . . . is the basic principle of administrative law that a finding unsupported by reliable record evidence cannot be sustained . . . . Thus [the government's position was rejected in a case where the] . . . reviewing officer . . . had relied exclusively on raw ISES (Illinois State Employment Service) "availability data" which did not show "that the persons listed were in fact qualified, were still available for employment, or were willing to work for an employer such as plaintiff, as specified in the provisions of 8 U.S.C. § 1182(a)(14)." 361 F. Supp. at 1340. Implicit in this court's reasoning is the premise that labor certification must be granted under § 212(a)(14) unless the Secretary affirmatively determines that able, qualified, and willing United States workers are available or that employment of the alien will have an adverse effect. Appellants therefore contend that, under the law of this circuit, the burden of proof rests with the Secretary.

While this court has never addressed the statutory basis for that unstated assumption, we need not defend it here,[2] for we believe that the advertising rule, as written, is not inconsistent with Seventh Circuit precedent. In promulgating 20 C.F.R. § 656.21, the Secretary in effect adopted Judge MacKinnon's position in Pesikoff. An applicant-employer does not bear the ultimate burden of persuasion. The regulations require the certifying officer to look to various sources in determining whether a United States worker is available, able, and qualified and whether employment of the alien will have an adverse effect on wages and working conditions. 20 C.F.R. §§ 656.24 (b)(2)(ii)-(iv), (b)(3). The documented results of the employer's recruitment efforts are considered only to determine whether a United States worker is willing to take the job opportunity. Id. § 656.24(b)(2)(1). Even on that inquiry, the certifying officer must also look to the Employment Service Office's recruitment efforts and, presumably, may consider any other sources that may be appropriate. Moreover, the regulations parallel this circuit's position that certification may be denied only upon an affirmative finding of availability and adverse effect.

We believe that Seventh Circuit precedent does not preclude the imposition of a "burden of production" that is well-defined, very specific, and not unduly burdensome. Rather, documentation of the employer's recruitment efforts will enable the Secretary

---

2. Senator Kennedy's reference to the alien's "burden of proof," to which the Pesikoff court attributed great weight, is somewhat ambiguous when viewed in light of his . . . remark that "there will be cases where the Secretary will be expected to ascertain in some detail the need for the immigrant in this country under the provisions of the law." 111 Cong. Rec. 24227 (1965) . . . . "The remarks of a single legislator, even the sponsor, are not controlling in analyzing legislative history. [Any] statement must be considered with the Reports of both Houses and the statements of other Congressmen. . . . " The change in the wording of § 212(a)(14) may be explained, in view of remarks by other Congressmen and even the Senate Report, as a device which would ensure that certification decisions are made "on an individual case basis." See 111 Cong. Rec. 21579 (remarks of Rep. Madden) . . . .

to make an informed decision on the basis of reliable evidence....Indeed, the regulations may be viewed as a reaction to strong criticism by this and other circuits of the data upon which determinations had been made and the failure to determine the subsidiary questions of whether the available worker is able, qualified, and willing. In particular, the Secretary has found it a difficult task to establish that an available worker is "willing." *See, e.g., Ratnayake v. Mack*, 499 F.2d 1207, 1213 (8th Cir. 1974). These regulations seem reasonably designed to gather the most reliable information on that requirement. Finally, by specifying the information to be relied upon in determining whether a worker is willing, the regulations reduce the potential for arbitrariness, a major point of criticism under the prior regulations. Given the strong congressional intent to protect American workers and the statutory duty of the Secretary to determine worker availability and labor conditions, we find the Secretary's advertising regulation to be a reasonable exercise of rule making authority.

Having determined the advertising requirement to be a valid rule, it follows that the Secretary must be permitted to give effect to that rule by making substantial compliance[3] a prerequisite to approval of an application. Production Tool admits that it did not comply. Kenall, however, argues in the alternative that the certifying officer abused his discretion by ruling that the Reader is not a newspaper of general circulation.

An agency's interpretation of its own regulation is controlling unless "plainly erroneous or inconsistent." We agree with the district court that the certifying officer's construction must stand. Under the regulations, an employer must advertise the job opportunity "in such media as newspapers of general circulation, and ethnic and professional publications." 20 C.F.R. § 656.21(b)(9)(i). The obvious purpose of that requirement is, as the hearing officer noted, to test adequately the labor market in the area of intended employment. See id. §§ 656.24(b)(2)(i), (iv). The statute itself refers to workers who are available "at the place" of the job opportunity. 8 U.S.C. § 1182(a)(14). The hearing officer, however, found Kenall's advertisement deficient under the regulation since the Reader is a neighborhood weekly with a circulation of 92,000 in only a limited area of Chicago.

The Tenth Circuit upheld a requirement that a Denver employer advertise in the eastern edition of the Wall Street Journal for a foreign investment representative. In view of the sophisticated nature of the job sought, the court concluded that "[a] requirement that does not involve a significant expenditure of money which is likely to reach the pool of U.S. citizen prospects, is not inconsistent with the law or the regulations promulgated thereunder." Here, the job opportunity-quality control inspector—is centrally located in the city of Chicago. It is entirely reasonable for the Secretary to require advertisement for such a job to be run in one of the two major Chicago newspapers which circulate in the entire metropolitan area. The Illinois cases Kenall cites define "newspaper of general circulation" only for the purpose of publishing legal notices and have very little bearing on whether a job advertisement in the Reader adequately tests the relevant labor market. What constitutes the relevant labor market is a question that falls squarely within the Secretary's realm of expertise. Thus we are especially hesitant to second guess that judgment.

---

3. The current regulations specify that the certifying officer may grant certification if he determines that the employer has committed "harmless error." 20 C.F.R. § 656.24(b)(1) (1981).

Failure on the part of appellants substantially to comply with the Secretary of Labor's valid advertising regulation precluded the certifying officer from being able to determine whether any available United States worker was "willing" to take the job opportunities which appellants sought to fill with alien labor. The decisions of the district courts therefore are Affirmed.

A. Business Necessity

Pancho Villa Restaurant, Inc. v. U.S. Dept. of Labor
796 F.2d 596 (2d Cir. 1986)

OAKES, Circuit Judge.

Conflicting determinations of the United States District Court for the Eastern District of New York relating to applications for alien labor certification filed by Pancho Villa Restaurant, Inc. ("Pancho Villa"), which, not surprisingly, serves Mexican food, are appealed here. Judge Sifton, in ("Pancho Villa I"), held that the decision of the Secretary of Labor to deny two applications for alien labor certification pursuant to § 212(a)(14) of the Immigration and Nationality Act, as amended, 8 U.S.C. § 1182(a)(14) (1982), "appears arbitrary and without rational basis." In the second case, ("Pancho Villa II"), then Judge Altimari upheld the denial of another such application. We agree with Judge Altimari that the Secretary did not act arbitrarily or capriciously or abuse his discretion in finding that a one-year minimum experience requirement for a Mexican specialty cook was unnecessary and that the restaurant had failed to show that it was unable to train a cook who lacked any experience. Indeed, the restaurant hired and trained the three aliens whose applications are at issue here when they had no experience as Mexican specialty cooks.

In 1983 Pancho Villa filed three applications seeking certification for three alien employees as specialty cooks for Mexican foods such as "Tacos, Enchiladas, Burritos, etc." The applications show that the aliens were paid $250 per week for a forty-hour week. Pancho Villa also informed the Department of Labor ("DOL") that it had employed two cooks and had sales of $337,560 in 1982, while in 1983 it had employed three cooks and had annual sales totalling $488,175.

In February 1984 the DOL certifying officer issued a "Notice of Findings" in each case that Pancho Villa had not documented that its requirements for the job opportunity were the minimum necessary for the performance of the job and that it had not hired or it was not feasible for it to hire workers with less training or experience as mandated by 20 C.F.R. § 656.21(b)(6) (1986). In each case the certifying officer found that the alien had no prior experience before his employment and insisted that Pancho Villa document why it was not now feasible to train a United States worker. In response to these Notices of Findings, the restaurant argued that in 1977 when it opened for business in Huntington, Long Island, it had time to train inexperienced cooks, but business had increased to a point where it was no longer feasible to train someone without at least one year of experience. It also resubmitted its 1981/82 and 1982/83 annual sales data, arguing from these figures that it no longer had the time to train inexperienced cooks. In April, 1984, the certifying officer issued final determinations that Pancho Villa had not "adequately document[ed] why it is not feasible for [it] to train a U.S. worker at this time."

These decisions were affirmed by two administrative law judges. In a "Decision and Order" involving one of the aliens in Pancho Villa I, the ALJ found [that the], "Employer has not shown why it cannot train a new person with a staff of the three cooks when it was able to do so with a staff of two" and that "employer has not demonstrated that its business would suffer if an inexperienced cook were to join the staff." He made almost identical findings as to the other alien in Pancho Villa I. The ALJ in Pancho Villa II stated,

> If it is assumed that all of the cooks are responsible equally for the preparation and cooking of all the food which is sold by the Employer, then an analysis of the figures presented by the Employer shows that each cook who is currently working for the Employer is responsible for the preparation and cooking of approximately the same amount of food as was his counterpart in 1981.

Subsequently, the restaurant filed complaints in the United States District Court for the Eastern District of New York seeking review of the final decisions of the Secretary based upon the ALJs' conclusions.

*   *   *

By virtue of § 212(a)(14), Congress sought to exclude aliens competing for jobs that American workers could fill. The DOL has adopted regulations requiring an employer to conduct a systematic recruitment of domestic workers. See 20 C.F.R. § 656.21 (1986). Failure to comply with these regulations may result in a denial of the labor certification. See 20 C.F.R. § 656.24(b)(1) (1986). We agree with the United States Court of Appeals for the District of Columbia that the scope of review of a denial of an alien labor certification is limited to a determination under § 706(2)(A) of the Administrative Procedure Act, 5 U.S.C. § 706(2)(A) (1982), as to whether the decision was "arbitrary, capricious, an abuse of discretion, or otherwise not in accordance with law." In making this determination, we examine only the administrative record. We agree with the Secretary that Judge Sifton erred in finding the ALJ's decision "appear[ed]" to be arbitrary; Pancho Villa simply did not meet its burden of proving its entitlement to an exemption. The restaurant's own figures indicate that each cook in 1983 had less work per sales volume than in the previous year. Thus, the employer presented insufficient evidence of a change in circumstances such that it could not train an inexperienced cook with three experienced cooks in 1983. Even if we interpret Judge Sifton's questionable use of the word "appears" to mean "is" arbitrary, we think the Secretary's finding that the employer has not shown that its business would suffer if an inexperienced cook joined the staff was rational and not an abuse of discretion. Judge Sifton also found the Secretary's determination that one year's experience was unnecessary to be "arbitrary and unconvincing." Because all three aliens were hired with no experience and because the employer failed to show that inexperienced cooks could not be trained, the Secretary acted rationally in concluding that one year's experience was not the employer's actual minimum requirement. Judge Sifton in effect impermissibly substituted his judgment for that of the Secretary by making his own factual determinations based upon a reevaluation of the record. Judge Altimari, on the other hand, correctly upheld the ALJ's determination. Appellant's contention that the DOL lacks authority to promulgate regulations pursuant to § 212(a)(14) is wholly without merit.

Actual Minimum Job Requirements in Labor Certifications: Application of Title 20, Section 656.21(b)(6) of the Code of Federal Regulations to Experience or Training Gained with the Employer

Burgess, 23 San Diego L. Rev. 375 (1986)*

Not infrequently a United States employer seeks labor certification for an alien who has worked for the employer previously. In such circumstances, it may be reasonable to require that the amount of experience the alien has gained be included in the application. Labor Department regulations preclude application requirements other than the actual minimum requirements of the employer. In addition, the employer must not have hired workers with less training or experience for a job similar to that in which the labor certification is sought. Departmental interpretation indicates that it is possible to require experience which the alien has gained working for the employer in a different occupation. Inconsistent application of this interpretation by the Department of Labor adjudicators leaves an employer at peril of losing a labor certification whenever an alien has been previously employed in a position with the petitioning employer even though the position is different than the one for which certification is sought.

Introduction

The Immigration and Nationality Act provides for the exclusion of aliens seeking to enter the United States for the purpose of performing skilled or unskilled labor, unless the Secretary of Labor has granted them certification. In order to obtain a labor certification, the alien's prospective employer must demonstrate that it has attempted to recruit United States workers for the position which it desires the alien to fill. Furthermore, the employer must show that hiring the alien would not adversely affect the wages and working conditions of similarly employed United States workers. The procedure and requirements for this certification are set forth in title 20, section 656 of the Code of Federal Regulations.

*   *   *

Application of the Regulations

The general rule which accounts for the resolution of numerous cases is that a labor certification will be denied under section 656.21(b)(6) when the alien has been employed in the position for which certification is sought and has gained experience which is required by the job offer while working for the employer in that position. This rule is supported by the explanation in TAG [Technical Assistance Guide] and the language of the regulation itself. The rationale behind this basis for denial is that

---

* Copyright 1986 San Diego Law Review Association. Reprinted with the permission of the San Diego Law Review. Footnotes have been omitted.

since the employer was willing to hire the alien without the experience, the experience must not be an actual minimum requirement for performance of the job.

This principle has been applied even though the alien gained the experience while working for the employer abroad. In *In re Speedent USA Corp.*, the employer contended that the alien gained the experience in China and that the Chinese employer was a different entity. The A.L.J. affirmed denial, however, because the names of the American and Chinese companies were similar, and insufficient documentation of their separateness had been provided.

*   *   *

In a situation in which the alien has on the job experience in the position for which certification is sought, and that experience is required in the application for labor certification, section 656.2(b)(6) requires proof that it is infeasible to hire workers with less training or experience than listed in the application for labor certification. In many cases, where the alien has acquired training and experience while working for the employer, the employer has attempted to show compliance with section 656.21(b)(6) by demonstrating that it is infeasible to hire workers with less training or experience.

Changed Business Conditions

A common approach to establishing infeasibility is through documentation that business conditions have changed since the alien was hired. Although at the time the alien was hired the business entity had been able to train an inexperienced worker on the job, it may no longer be feasible to train an employee because of changed business conditions. This exception was suggested in *In re Gartenhausfurs, Inc.*, where the A.L.J. found it 'highly unrealistic' to interpret the regulations in a way that failed to take change of business conditions over a six year period into consideration. 'Surely that is not the intent of the Regulation.'

In *In re McAliece Paper Co.*, a decrease in business scale justified a finding of infeasibility. The employer was able to show that since hiring the alien, his volume of business and labor force were so reduced as to preclude hiring an applicant in need of extensive training. The A.L.J. found this to be sufficient evidence of infeasibility since the 'employer no longer enjoys the sufficient manpower nor the economic resources to conduct such instruction.' A contrary result, however, was reached in In re Lancer II, Restaurant Corp. The A.L.J. held that documentation of a decrease in sales did not demonstrate infeasibility without a showing of the time needed to train, or evidence that the training would interfere with other workers. An increase in business has also justified infeasibility. In In re Veselka Coffee Shop, the employer adequately documented that expansion of business precluded hiring an inexperienced person as a cook. The A.L.J. observed that a good cook was indispensable to a successful restaurant and that the greater the pressure, the greater the gamble that an inexperienced cook would destroy the reputation of the restaurant.

In other cases, an increase in business was not sufficient evidence of infeasibility, because the employer either failed to document the business increase or failed to show why the business increase limited training capacity. In *In re Giulio Cesare Restorante, Inc.*, increased volume was not sufficient to show infeasibility of training when the job was not that of chief cook. Moreover, in *In re Ace Grinding Co.*, the A.L.J. suggested expansion of business should make it easier to provide training. In *In re Pancho Villa Restaurant*, infeasibility to train due to a dramatic business increase was not substantiated. As a result of the increased sales, the A.L.J. concluded that the employer appeared more prosperous: "Employer has not shown why it cannot train a new person with a staff of three cooks when it was able to do so with a staff of two.... [He saw] no reason why the firing of an inexperienced cook would necessitate reducing the number of experienced cooks...," one of whom was the alien himself. Even when training has been shown to involve additional expenses and a slowing down in production, some A.L.J.s have found these grounds insufficient to show infeasibility.

These cases suggest that although it is a recognized principle that changed business conditions may constitute infeasibility to hire an inexperienced employee, many labor certifications are denied because the employer has not provided sufficient objective evidence of why the changed conditions limit the ability to train an inexperienced worker on the job.

B. The Recruitment Process

Industrial Holographics, Inc. v. Donovan
722 F.2d 1362 (7th Cir. 1983)

CUDAHY, Circuit Judge.

This case presents a challenge to a refusal by the Department of Labor to certify an alien for lawful employment in the United States. Specifically, the appellants challenge the Department's regulations equating an employer's offer of "prevailing wages and working conditions" with terms which "will not adversely affect the wages and working conditions" of American workers. The appellants also object to the prevailing wage determination in this case. The district court upheld the Secretary's action and we affirm.

Under § 212(a)(14) of the Immigration and Nationality Act, 8 U.S.C. § 1182 (a)(14), the State Department may not issue an alien a visa for admission to the United States for purposes of employment unless the Secretary of Labor certifies that American workers are not "able, willing, qualified..., and available" for the work, and that the employment of the alien "will not adversely affect the wages and working conditions" of similarly employed Americans. The Secretary of Labor has promulgated regulations which establish standards and procedures for the certification of alien workers under § 212(a)(14). See 20 C.F.R. §§ 656.20 et seq. (1983). If an employer wishes to hire an alien for work in the United States, these regulations require the employer first to recruit among American workers offering the "prevailing wage" and "prevailing working conditions" to determine whether any American workers are "able, willing, qualified, and available" for the job. See 20 C.F.R. § 656.21(b)(1), (3) and (9) (1980). If an employer submits documentation showing it has been unable to recruit American workers on these terms, then the Secretary of Labor may certify the alien to enter the country and perform the work.

*　　*　　*

Plaintiff Industrial Holographics, Inc. (the "employer") manufactures and tests machinery used to make rubber tires. Plaintiff Roger K. Yu is an alien whom Industrial

Holographics has sought to employ in Michigan as an export manager. The record indicates that Yu has never been in the United States. In June 1979, Industrial Holographics applied for labor certification on behalf of Yu. Industrial Holographics followed the various provisions in 20 C.F.R. § 656.21 (1980), requiring it to post the job for internal recruitment, to advertise the job in newspapers and to post the job with the state employment service. On August 24, 1979, the employer submitted to the certifying officer[1] documentation showing that it had complied with the requirements of § 656.21.

The employer, however, had advertised that the salary for the job of export manager was $1,000 per month. § 656.21 requires the employer to advertise and post the job at the "prevailing wage" and "prevailing working conditions" in order to obtain certification. 20 C.F.R. § 656.21(b)(3) and (9) (1980). The Michigan Employment Security Commission (the "MESC") was responsible for determining the prevailing wage in this case, see 20 C.F.R. § 656.21(f) (1980), and it determined that the prevailing wage for export managers in the area was $1,666 per month. Therefore, the certifying officer issued to the employer a Notice of Findings proposing to deny labor certification for Yu because the employer had failed to advertise the job at the prevailing wage.

After receiving the Notice of Findings, the employer agreed to repeat the advertising and recruiting process at the higher salary of $1,666 per month. The employer advertised the job at the higher salary, but it failed to comply with all of the requirements of § 656.21. Specifically, the employer did not show it had posted the job for internal recruitment at the higher salary, § 656.21(b)(10), did not document the results of its recruitment efforts, § 656.21(b)(15), and did not recruit for thirty days through the state employment service, § 656.21(g)(1). Because the employer had failed to comply with the strict advertising requirements within the relevant time limits, the certifying officer denied the certification for Yu.[2] On review within the Department of Labor, the administrative law judge concluded that the employer had failed to comply with the regulations and that certification was properly denied.

*   *   *

Plaintiffs now appeal presenting three issues. First, they contend that the Secretary of Labor exceeded his statutory authority when he promulgated regulations requiring the employer to advertise the job at the "prevailing wage." Second, they argue that the prevailing wage determination in this case was incorrect. Finally, they argue that they substantially complied with the regulations and that they are therefore entitled to certification. . . .

. . . The applicable statutory language says that the Secretary shall certify the alien only if his or her employment "will not adversely affect the wages and working conditions" of similarly employed workers in the United States. 8 U.S.C. § 1182(a)(14)(B).

---

1. The certifying officer is the regional official of the Employment and Training Administration who decides whether to grant or deny labor certification. The certifying officer's decision is then subject to review by an administrative law judge and later by the courts.

2. The employer had sought and received two written extensions of time to complete advertising at the higher wage. In the administrative hearings, the employer claimed that it had received a third oral extension and that it fulfilled the requirements within the time allowed by the third extension, but the administrative law judge rejected this claim. Appellants do not challenge the law judge's finding here, so we assume that appellants did not comply with the relevant time limits.

The district court relied upon our decision in *Production Tool Corp. v. Employment and Training Admin.*, 688 F.2d 1161 (7th Cir. 1982), in holding that the Secretary had statutory authority to issue the prevailing wage standard. In *Production Tool*, the employers argued that the Immigration and Nationality Act did not authorize the Secretary to issue any interpretative regulations under § 212(a)(14), and that the regulations could not properly impose on the employer the burden of producing evidence showing that United States workers were not "able, willing, qualified, and available." This court held that the Secretary had inherent authority to issue the regulations requiring an employer to advertise positions among American workers and imposing on an employer the burden of producing evidence showing it had complied with the advertising procedures. On this appeal, appellants present us with a narrower challenge to the same regulations. They argue only that the regulations improperly equate the statute's standard of adverse effects with the payment of wages below "prevailing wages." This precise issue was not before the court in *Production Tool*, so we must go beyond that decision in considering the Secretary's authority to issue the prevailing wage requirement. However, the court's reasoning in *Production Tool* is highly relevant to this issue of statutory authority; hence, we believe that the *Production Tool* reasoning extends to the prevailing wage requirement.

In *Production Tool* this court clarified the authority under which the labor certification regulations were promulgated. The Immigration and Nationality Act does not expressly authorize the Secretary to issue regulations. However, the standards of § 212(a)(14) are quite broad. The Secretary must decide whether there are sufficient American workers who are "able, willing, qualified, and available," and whether the alien's employment would "adversely affect the wages and working conditions" of American workers. The statute leaves to the Department a broad area for the exercise of its discretion in issuing labor certificates. Where the agency must make a large number of individual discretionary decisions, it is entirely appropriate for it to issue regulations informing the public about the standards and procedures the agency intends to apply. Those regulations simplify the administrative task and help guard against arbitrary agency action. *See Silva v. Secretary of Labor*, 518 F.2d 301, 310 (1st Cir. 1975) (criticizing absence of regulations for certifying alien agricultural workers). As the court held in *Production Tool*, the labor certification regulations promote these ends, and the Secretary has inherent authority to issue them.

Because the Secretary did not act beyond his authority in issuing the advertising regulations, the only substantial reason appellants offer for finding the prevailing wage regulations invalid is that they are inconsistent with the language and underlying purpose of § 212(a)(14). In our view, the regulations as applied in this case are consistent with the statute and thus are not arbitrary, capricious or an abuse of discretion. The Secretary has exercised appropriately his inherent power to develop standards and procedures for achieving the statute's goals.

* * *

The language of § 212(a)(14) does little more than identify Congressional goals: aliens should not take jobs from "able, willing, qualified, and available" American workers, and an alien's employment should not "adversely affect" the wages and working conditions of American workers. The statute leaves to the Secretary the task of developing operational standards to effect the Congressional purpose. The breadth of the statutory language and the volume of decisions virtually require the Secretary to develop systematic standards and procedures for deciding upon labor certification applications. Each year the Department of Labor receives a large number of applications for permanent labor certification.[3] A complete and thorough analysis of all relevant factors affecting the impact of each individual alien's employment on the labor market is clearly out of the question. Sound administration and concern for consistency and fairness require simplified rules of general application for imposing the statutory standards.

The regulations here assume, as a general proposition, that the employment of an alien at wages below the prevailing wage will tend to affect adversely the wages and working conditions of American workers. Appellants have provided no evidence to persuade us that this general assumption is arbitrary or capricious.[4] While it may be possible to conceive of cases in which the prevailing wage standard would be inconsistent with the statute's purpose, that is not the case here.

*　*　*

In *Naporano Metal & Iron*, 529 F.2d 537 (3d Cir. 1976), the Secretary denied labor certification for an alien working in the United States as a welder and scrap metal cutter. The alien was paid a wage under a collective bargaining agreement, but the Secretary found that the union wage was below the "prevailing wage" required by the predecessor regulation of § 656.21. The Third Circuit held that payment of a union wage negotiated to cover both alien and United States workers could not, as a matter of law, adversely affect the wages and working conditions of similarly employed American workers. 529 F.2d at 541.[5] The court also described the "adverse effect" standard of the statute as "substantially different" from the "prevailing wage" requirement of the regulation, but the court did not consider whether the regulation was consistent with the statute. We agree that the statutory standard differs from the regulation's standard, but the standards are not necessarily inconsistent. The regulation simply gives operational meaning to the statute's expression of Congressional purpose. The Secretary clearly has authority to issue clarifying regulations, and, as applied in this case, the regulations are not inconsistent with the statute.

Ozbirman v. Regional Manpower Adm'r, 335 F. Supp. 467 (S.D.N.Y. 1971) provides appellants more direct support. There an alien was denied labor certification as an auto mechanic. The wage he was offered matched the union negotiated wage in the area, but the Secretary found the wage to be below the "prevailing wage" as required by the predecessor regulation of § 656.21. The district court remanded the matter to the Secretary on two alternative grounds. First, the court held that the "prevailing wage" standard improperly construed the term "adverse effect" and did not implement the statutory purpose. Second, the court held that the denial was an

---

3. In fiscal year 1981, the Department of Labor received approximately 33,000 applications for permanent labor certification, and it granted certification in 25,763 cases. Employment and Training Report of the President 51 (1982). In fiscal year 1980, the Department received 32,800 applications and granted certification in 29,000 cases. Employment and Training Report of the President 49 (1981).

4. The regulations were adopted after appropriate notice and comment procedures. See 42 Fed. Reg. 3440 (1977).

5. The Secretary amended the definition of "prevailing wage" in 1977 to reflect the Naporano Metal & Iron holding regarding union wages. See 20 C.F.R. § 656.40(a)(2)(ii) (1983); 42 Fed. Reg. 3450 (1977). Because there is no union wage involved here, that provision does not apply to this case.

abuse of discretion because the alien's wage would have been equal to that of his co-workers and was union negotiated. The court discussed at length the complexity of a thorough determination of whether a particular package of wages and other benefits and working conditions would adversely affect American wages and working conditions. It concluded that the "prevailing wage" standard did not adequately take into account the other relevant variables. We agree with the *Ozbirman* court that a truly thorough analysis of adverse effects involves factors other than wages. However, we do not agree that the Secretary of Labor is without authority to issue regulations simplifying the inquiry so that decisions will be less arbitrary and more consistent.

We conclude that the Secretary acted reasonably in giving operational content to the language of § 212(a)(14) by applying the prevailing wage standard in this case. Therefore, the Secretary acted within his legal authority in relying on the prevailing wage standard of § 656.21(b) to deny labor certification in this case.

The second issue on appeal is whether the agency's determination of the prevailing wage was correct in this case. The employer contends that the agency did not properly calculate the prevailing wage for export managers in Michigan, and that the error was arbitrary, capricious or an abuse of discretion. See 5 U.S.C. § 706(2)(A)....

The Department of Labor has promulgated regulations describing the calculation of the "prevailing wage" for labor certification. 20 C.F.R. § 656.40 (1983). The section applicable to this case provides that the "prevailing wage" shall be:

> The average rate of wages, that is, the rate of wages to be determined, to the extent feasible, by adding the wage paid to workers similarly employed in the area of intended employment and dividing the total by the number of such workers. Since it is not always feasible to determine such an average rate of wages with exact precision, the wage set forth in the application shall be considered as meeting the prevailing wage standard if it is within 5 percent of the average rate of wages....

20 C.F.R. § 656.40(a)(2)(i) (1983). In this case the MESC contacted five Michigan employers to determine the salary each paid its export manager.[6] From answers received from these inquiries, the MESC calculated that the average wage of export managers in Michigan was $1,666 per month.

Appellants argue that this calculation was improper because the MESC surveyed employers in industries other than the rubber tire machinery business. They contend that the export managers for the other employers are not "similarly employed" as the regulations require. 20 C.F.R. § 656.40(a)(2)(i) (1983). However, we do not believe that the agency acted arbitrarily and capriciously in surveying the other five employers. The agency concluded that jobs with similar functions in other industries were sufficiently comparable for purposes of determining a prevailing wage. Appellants have provided no evidence showing that the other jobs are not comparable.

Appellants rely on cases which are not apposite here. It is true that the prevailing wage calculation may be improper if the agency simply uses the wrong occupational category, *see Reddy, Inc. v. Department of Labor*, 492 F.2d 538, 544-45 (5th Cir.

---

6. The Secretary has delegated to local employment services the task of determining the prevailing wage according to federal standards. 20 C.F.R. § 656.21(e) (1983); 20 C.F.R. § 656.21(f) (1980).

1974) (rate calculated for civil engineer where alien was mechanical engineer), but appellants have not shown that the job category used in this case was improper.[7] Therefore, we conclude that the agency's calculation of the prevailing wage in this case was not arbitrary, capricious or an abuse of discretion.

Finally, appellants contend that they are entitled to labor certification because they substantially complied with the advertising regulations when they recruited at the higher salary level. After the certifying officer issued the Notice of Findings informing the employer that it was not offering the prevailing wage, the employer tried to recruit American workers at the higher wage level. The employer sought and received two extensions of time to complete its second round of advertising. The employer submitted documents to show its compliance with the regulations. However, the certifying officer found that the employer failed to show it had posted the job at the higher salary level inside its own organization, 20 C.F.R. § 656.21(b)(10) (1980), that it failed to document the results of its recruitment efforts among American workers, 20 C.F.R. § 656.21(b)(15) (1980), and that it failed to show it had posted the job with the local employment service for thirty days, 20 C.F.R. § 656.21(g)(1) (1980). The administrative law judge also concluded that the employer failed to comply with (b)(10), (b)(15), and (g)(1) . . . . The employer here argues that its efforts amount to substantial compliance. Appellants have not shown that the agency erred in finding that appellants did not comply with (b)(10), (b)(15) and (g)(1).[8] Therefore, we need only consider whether appellants are entitled to certification despite these failures.

We find no abuse of discretion in the agency's denial of certification where the employer failed to comply with the internal posting requirement of § 656.21(b)(10), the documentation requirement of § 626.21(b)(15) and the employment service posting requirement of § 656.21(g)(1). The internal posting requirement insures that an employer's current employees—who are already familiar with the employer's products and organization—have an opportunity to apply for the job. The requirements that the employer advertise through the local employment service and document the results of its domestic recruitment efforts provide the agency with a means for monitoring the results of the employer's recruitment efforts. Therefore, we conclude that the Department of Labor did not abuse its discretion by denying labor certification because the employer failed to comply with the advertising regulations.

---

7. Appellants' reliance on two cases involving Montessori school teachers is misplaced. See Ratnayake v. Mack, 499 F.2d 1207, 1213-14 (8th Cir. 1974); Montessori Children's House and School, Inc. v. Secretary of Labor, 443 F. Supp. 599, 608 (N.D. Tex. 1977). In both cases the employers had introduced evidence showing that the jobs of Montessori teachers differed substantially from those of public school teachers. By contrast, appellants in this case have made no attempt to show that the job offered to Yu differs from those surveyed by the MESC. The prevailing wage inquiry should be reasonably specific, but there is no reason to conclude a priori that it is improper to compare similar jobs in other industries.

8. Appellants correctly argue that the agency has the discretionary power to waive some defects in compliance; however, this argument does not establish that the agency abused its discretion when it chose not to waive the defects here.

C. Qualifying Experience

Matter of Lam
16 I. & N. Dec. 432 (BIA 1978)

This is an appeal from the immigration judge's denial of the relief of adjustment of status in a decision entered on February 3, 1977, in which the immigration judge granted to the respondent the privilege of voluntary departure. The appeal will be sustained.

The record relates to a married male alien, 40 years of age, who is a native and citizen of China. He was admitted to the United States on February 6, 1973, as a nonimmigrant visitor. He was originally found deportable in an earlier decision by the immigration judge on January 12, 1976. The finding of deportability rested on the respondent's admissions. The respondent did not appeal from that decision. He thereafter obtained reopening of the proceedings in order to apply for adjustment of status. This appeal is brought from the immigration judge's subsequent denial of that relief.

The respondent is a specialty cook of Chinese style food. He has been employed as a Chinese cook by the China Shoppe Restaurant in Maryland from May 1976 to the present time. He was previously employed by the Red Blazer Restaurant from January 1976 to April 1976 in New York, by the Horse River Restaurant in Maryland from May 1974 to December 1975, and by the Oriental Garden Restaurant in Virginia from April 1973 to April 1974. The China Shoppe Restaurant filed a labor certification application on behalf of the respondent, which was approved on April 15, 1976. A sixth-preference petition filed by the China Shoppe Restaurant on behalf of the respondent was approved on June 30, 1976.

On the labor certification the China Shoppe Restaurant specified that two years experience was required for the position offered. All of the qualifying experience shown by the respondent in support of the labor certification was gained in the United States as listed above. At his deportation hearing the respondent testified that his sole experience as a cook prior to coming to the United States consisted of part-time work of about ten hours a week for several months during 1970. Inasmuch as that experience did not amount to the two years of experience required by the United States employer, the respondent's eligibility for a labor certification must necessarily depend upon the experience he gained while in the United States.

Because the respondent's qualifying employment experience was gained while he was here as a nonimmigrant visitor and later as an overstay, the immigration judge declined to exercise his discretion favorably to the respondent and denied him adjustment of status. The issue posed is whether the fact that qualifying experience for a labor certification was gained by employment which was not authorized under the immigration laws constitutes a factor adverse to the exercise of discretion, when considering an application for adjustment of status.

We have previously considered the general issue in the case of *Matter of Arai*, 13 I. & N. Dec. 494 (BIA 1970). Arai, like the present respondent, sought adjustment of status on the basis of an approved labor certification as a specialty cook. In that case, as in this, no finding was made by the immigration judge that the respondent was other than a bona fide visitor when he first arrived in the United States. The immigration judge, however, considered Arai's taking of employment as an adverse factor. We reversed the immigration judge and held that the case presented no adverse factors affecting the respondent's application. We characterized the employment as a potential benefit to the United States inasmuch as there was a shortage of United States workers in his field of employment . . . .

In the case before us the immigration judge, in declining to exercise discretion favorably, focused on the fact that the unauthorized employment was crucial to eligibility for the labor certification, rather than on the fact that the employment was unauthorized. While the focus is thus somewhat different from Arai's case, the immigration judge's consideration of the employment as an adverse factor is nonetheless inconsistent with the decision in *Matter of Arai*, supra. Inasmuch as the recitation of facts in Arai did not specify to the contrary, we must assume that Arai's work experience in the United States was crucial to his labor certification. . . . The immigration judge's decision below that approval of a labor certification should be disregarded in the exercise of discretion when the experience was gained in the United States by means of unauthorized employment cannot, therefore, be reconciled with the decision in *Matter of Arai*, supra.

When a labor certification has been granted concerning employment, it has been determined that the employment is not detrimental to the United States labor market. An important concern of our immigration laws is the protection of our domestic economy. Taking unauthorized employment in violation of law may be an adverse discretionary factor. However, this is offset when unauthorized employment is not detrimental, and is in fact of potential benefit to our country, in view of the shortage of United States workers. In this case not only has a labor certification been granted for the employment, but a sixth-preference petition as well.

D. Certification versus "Work Authorization"

Matter of Raol
16 I. & N. Dec. 466 (BIA 1978)

The respondent has appealed from a May 16, 1977, decision of an immigration judge denying a motion to reopen deportation proceedings for the purpose of applying for adjustment of status under section 245 of the Immigration and Nationality Act, 8 U.S.C. 1255, and also denying a request for reinstatement of voluntary departure. Oral argument was held on October 12, 1977. The appeal will be dismissed in part and sustained in part.

The record reflects the following facts. The respondent is a 27-year-old native and citizen of India who entered the United States as a nonimmigrant student on March 29, 1972. He graduated from Texas A&M University in December of 1974 with a B.S. degree in chemical engineering. The respondent was employed by the Louisiana Air Control Commission (hereinafter referred to as the LACC), with the permission of the Immigration and Naturalization Service, as an "on-the-job trainee" in connection with his student visa. This employment commenced in March of 1975 and the authorization of employment by the Immigration and Naturalization Service expired on March 13, 1976.

The record further indicates that a labor certification application was filed by the LACC on the respondent's behalf in early 1976. This application was denied on June 14, 1976, and on June 23, 1976, the District Director denied an application for adjustment of status filed by the respondent. The respondent was subsequently found deportable at a hearing held on October 14, 1976. He was granted voluntary departure until January 14, 1977, and this period was extended by the District Director through February 25, 1977. On January 24, 1977, a second application for a labor certification was filed by the LACC. This application was approved and a labor certification was issued on February 24, 1977. On March 1, 1977, the respondent filed a motion to reopen deportation proceedings for the purpose of applying for adjustment of status and a petition to classify the respondent for sixth-preference status, accompanied by the labor certification.

The motion to reopen was denied by the immigration judge for the reason that the respondent was precluded from adjusting his status under section 245(c) of the Act, 8 U.S.C. 1255(c). This provision was added to the Immigration and Nationality Act by the 1976 Amendments, Public Law 94-571, 90 Stat. 2703, effective January 1, 1977. It provides in pertinent part, that the benefits of section 245 are inapplicable to:

> an alien (other than an immediate relative as defined in section 201(b)) who hereafter continues in or accepts unauthorized employment prior to filing an application for adjustment of status. . . .

The respondent admits that he has continued his employment with the LACC as a chemical engineer beyond March 13, 1976, when the permission to work as an "on-the-job trainee" granted by the Service expired. He contends, however, that approval of a labor certification application by the Secretary of Labor for that position removes him from the unauthorized employment bar of section 245(c).

While sympathizing with the respondent's predicament, we disagree with his position that a labor certification issued pursuant to section 212(a)(14) of the Act, 8 U.S.C. 1182(a)(14), operates to authorize one's employment within the meaning of section 245(c). By issuing a labor certification, the Department of Labor, in conjunction with its regional divisions and local state employment offices, confirms that the employment of an alien in a particular job or profession will not displace a qualified American worker. An individual or blanket labor certification is a prerequisite for obtaining an approved third- or sixth-preference visa petition. See 8 C.F.R. 204.2 (c)(4); 20 C.F.R. 656.1 et seq. However, the Immigration and Naturalization Service is the entity that approves a third- or sixth-preference visa petition and issues an immigrant visa to an alien already in this country. See 8 C.F.R. 204.2(c)(1); 8 C.F.R. 245.1(d).

The proposition that an alien's employment is unauthorized unless the Service has given specific approval has been affirmed in numerous administrative and Federal court decisions. See, e.g., Ahmed v. United States, 480 F.2d 531 (2d Cir. 1973) (maintenance of status and departure bond); Matter of Yarden, Interim Decision 2513 (R.C. 1976) (adjustment of status); Matter of Boroumand, 13 I. & N. Dec. 306 (BIA 1969) (deportation). Although Congress did not define the term "unauthorized employment" when it enacted section 245(c), we do not believe that a labor certification, standing alone, would shield an applicant for adjustment of status from the operation of that section.

Had the respondent obtained permission from the Service to continue his employment after January 1, 1977, his case would be on a different footing. Pursuant to the Service's Operations Instruction 245.9, an applicant for adjustment may be granted permission to work during the time his application for status as a permanent resident is pending. However, there is no evidence that the respondent's permission to work extended beyond March 13, 1976. Consequently, we must agree with the immigration judge that the respondent is statutorily precluded from adjusting his status due to his continuing in unauthorized employment after January 1, 1977, and at the time of applying for adjustment of status.

Issues Involving Labor Certifications

Business Necessity. In determining whether the job offer in the labor certification application has been tailor-made for the foreign worker-beneficiary, an argument available to the U.S. employer is that the requirements are dictated by business necessity. According to 20 C.F.R. § 656.21(b)(2)(i) the requirements must "bear a reasonable relationship to the occupation in the context of the employer's business and are essential to perform" the job. Whether there is such a reasonable relationship or are "unduly restrictive" will be guided, in part by the *Dictionary of Occupational Titles* (DOT) and the *Selected Characteristics of Occupations Defined in the Dictionary of Occupational Titles* (Selected Characteristics) which describe the skills, experience and educational requirements for occupations in the DOT. In essence, compliance with the DOT and Selected Characteristics make out a prima facie case.

The reasonable job requirements, including those militated by business necessity, may form the basis for rejecting U.S. workers who apply for the advertised position. See *Ashbrook-Simon-Hartley v. McLaughlin, 863 F.2d 410 (5th Cir. 1989); 20 C.F.R. § 656.24(a)(2)(ii)*.

Ability to Pay the Prevailing Wage. Within the "job offer" of the labor certification is the advertisement of the job at a particular wage. Both *Production Tool* and *Industrial Holographic* explore the meaning of the "prevailing wage." A corollary issue often arises after the certification has been approved and prior to the beneficiary's being accorded lawful permanent residence (which can take a number of years) is whether the employer has the ability to pay the wages offered. The INS takes the position that the employer must show that she is able to pay the wages at the time the certification is filed. See *Matter of Great Wall*, 16 I. & N. Dec. 142 (Reg. Comm. 1977); *Matter of Dial Auto Repair Shop, Inc.*, Interim Decision No. 3035 (Comm. 1986). While courts have upheld INS' power to investigate the ability of the employer to pay the wages offered, the imposition of unrealistic requirements of proof on the employer have been rejected. *Masonry Masters v. Thornburgh*, 875 F.2d 898 (D.C. Cir. 1989). The problem occurs, in part because of the 20 C.F.R. § 656.20(c)(2) is prospective (when the foreign worker will begin working) and the INS interpretation is retrospective (when the certification was filed). The problem is further compounded by the two step process for permanent residency. The employer must obtain a certification from the Department of Labor and the INS does not become involved until the preference petition is filed, which is often years later.

Status of the Employer.   A major issue arises when the petitioner and beneficiary of the labor certification are one and the same. While the Department of Labor (DOL) recognizes corporate identity, if the foreign worker is a major shareholder in a closely held corporation, she may not be the beneficiary of a labor certification. One appellate court has upheld the certifying officers's denial of a labor certification on grounds that there was no job opportunity clearly open to U.S. workers as there was no true employer-employee relationship. See *Hall v. McLaughlin*, 864 F.2d 868 (D.C. Cir. 1989). DOL does not take an absolute position that such that these applications cannot be certified. Indeed, the issue is presented as a burden of proof problem. See 20 C.F.R. §§ 656.20(c)(8) and 656.21(b).

Special Handling Applications.   College and university teachers, aliens of exceptional ability in the arts and sheepherders are treated differently from other labor certification beneficiaries. See 20 C.F.R. § 656.21a. These applications are denoted as "special handling" primarily because the normal procedures are dispensed with. The central difference with these applications is that the employer need only show that a U.S. "as qualified" as the foreign worker could not be found. See Hopper, *Special Handling Labor Certifications for College and Teachers* 12 Imm. J. 77 (1989). Notice that the measure for the job qualifications are those of the foreign worker, whereas in the normal labor certification, the position as defined in the *DOT* and *Selected Characteristics* determine the necessary qualifications. With regards to college or university teachers the application for certification need not be filed until 18 months after the candidate has been selected as long as it can be shown that there was a "competitive recruitment process" which should have included a national search. For persons in the performing arts of exceptional ability the employer must document that the person's renown in the field as well as the nature of the work which will be performed in the U.S. In the case of sheepherders, special handling is allowed where she has worked as a nonimmigrant sheepherder for at least thirty three of the preceding thirty six months.

Schedule A Applications.   While many occupations require that the foreigner seeking an immigrant visa first obtain a labor certification, some occupations have been designated by the Secretary as being *prima facie* certifiable. These "pre-certified" positions are referred to as "Schedule A occupations," not requiring a market survey.[26] These applications are filed directly with the INS for the employment preference petition. The largest group of persons who fall within Schedule A are nurses, therapists, persons of exceptional ability in the arts and sciences (with the exception of performing artists), certain religious workers and physical therapists.[27] The 1990 Act directs the Secretary of Labor to designate up to ten occupational classifications for

---

26. This section of the statute was poorly drafted. Depending on how one reads the new law, it either requires or waives the labor certification requirement for persons in the teaching profession or who have exceptional ability in the sciences. *See* 8 U.S.C. § 1182(a)(5)(ii), Sec. 212(a)(5)(ii).

27. Proposed regulations published by the Department of Labor in July, 1991 indicate that the Secretary intends to remove persons of exceptional ability in the arts and science, religious workers and those holding a managerial or executive position from Schedule A precertification. Apparently, the Secretary's decision was predicated on the 1990 Act's creation of employment-based preference categories. *See*, Proposed Rulemaking on the Labor Certification Process, 56 Fed. Reg. 32,244 (July 15, 1991).

testing shortages and surpluses for setting aside as pre-certified positions.[28] If a shortage is designated the certification is deemed to have been issued, essentially having the same effect as Schedule A. If there is a surplus the Secretary may only certify the position upon a showing that the position cannot be filled notwithstanding "extensive recruitment efforts."[29] According to the 1990 Act, this program is authorized for a three year period beginning in October, 1991.

Thus far, our discussion has focused on the labor certification application which is filed with the Department of Labor. This is only a small part of the process. There are two approaches that can be taken in employment immigration cases: (1) after the labor certification has been approved an application for a preference petition is filed with the INS; (2) if the foreign worker is eligible for Schedule A, the labor certification and preference application may be submitted directly to the INS. In any event, upon approval, the result is the same the beneficiary may apply for lawful permanent residence. The case which follows explores the relationship between the DOL and the INS in adjudicating the labor certification and preference petition.

E. Labor Certifications and Preference Petitions

Madany v. Smith
696 F.2d 1008 (D.C. Cir. 1983)

MIKVA, Circuit Judge.

* * *

Madany, a native citizen of Afghanistan, has successfully completed a three-year professional nursing course in India and is a member of the nursing profession for the purposes of the Immigration and Nationality Act, §§ 101-360, 8 U.S.C. §§ 1101-1503 (1976 & Supp. V 1981) (Act). Madany entered the United States on July 3, 1979 as a business visitor, with authority to remain until February 20, 1980. In December 1979, Clinch Valley Community Hospital (Clinch Valley) submitted an application to DOL on Madany's behalf, seeking a labor certification as a nurse. The labor certification job description included the requirement that the prospective employee be able to obtain, or already have, a Virginia nursing license. In her statement of qualifications, appellant claimed she had the "ability to obtain (a) nursing license in the State of Virginia" and that she "will obtain (a) Virginia R.N. license." DOL granted the labor certification based on this claim.

Subsequently, on December 21, 1979, Clinch Valley filed with INS a petition, which included the DOL-issued labor certification, to obtain a third preference visa classification for appellant. Approximately nine months later, on September 10, 1980, the INS District Director denied the petition, finding that Clinch Valley had not met its burden of establishing that Madany met the "specific requirements of the individual

---

28. *See* Sec. 122, Immigration Act of 1990, Pub. L. No. 101-649, 104 Stat. 4978 (1990).

29. Sec. 122(a)(2)(B), Immigration Act of 1990, Pub. L. No. 101-649, 104 Stat. 4978 (1990).

labor certification"—in particular, that she was able to obtain a nursing license. The only evidence presented on this issue was her eligibility to take a nursing license exam and her registration to take the July 1980 registered nurse's exam for the District of Columbia. INS concluded that this evidence was insufficient to sustain appellant's burden of proof, especially when coupled with the low 20% passing rate for foreign nurse candidates on licensing exams. On appeal, the INS Regional Commissioner upheld the District Director's decision. Appellant then filed this action for declaratory relief in the district court, arguing that INS' review of her ability to obtain a Virginia license was outside its statutory authority; that she had, in fact, demonstrated an ability to obtain a license; and that, having met the relevant statutory criteria, she was entitled to a third preference visa classification. In a memorandum opinion, the district court granted summary judgment in favor of INS. The court found that INS properly may review whether a particular alien meets the specific qualifications of the labor certification under its general power to determine whether the alien qualifies for the preference classification sought. The court also held that INS' conclusion in this case was supported by substantial evidence and did not constitute an abuse of discretion.

*   *   *

II. The Visa Preference Classification Design

Section 203(a)(3) of the Act establishes the criteria for the grant of a third preference visa classification. The alien must be a "qualified immigrant" who possesses membership in a profession or an exceptional ability in the arts or sciences, and whose services in the professions, arts, or sciences are sought by an employer. 8 U.S.C. § 1153(a)(3) (Supp. V 1981). Section 212(a)(14) of the Act additionally preconditions third preference classifications on the receipt of a labor certification from DOL. The purpose and content of the labor certification are explicit. The Secretary of Labor must certify that:

> (A) there are not sufficient workers who are able, willing, qualified (or equally qualified in the case of aliens who are members of the teaching profession or who have exceptional ability in the sciences or the arts), and available at the time of application for a visa and admission to the United States and at the place where the alien is to perform such skilled or unskilled labor, and (B) the employment of such aliens will not adversely affect the wages and working conditions of the workers in the United States similarly employed.

8 U.S.C. § 1182(a)(14) (Supp. V 1981). The purpose of the third preference classification petition, therefore, is to show that the alien is a member of a profession, has been offered employment in that profession, and has been issued a labor certification.

The Act also sets forth the procedure for granting the petition:

> After an investigation of the facts in each case, and after consultation with the Secretary of Labor with respect to petitions to accord a status under section 1153(a)(3) or 1153(a)(6) of this title, the Attorney General shall, if he determines that the facts stated in the petition are true and that the alien . . . is eligible for a preference status under section 1153(a) of this title, approve the petition. . . .

Act § 204(b), 8 U.S.C. § 1154(b) (1976); *cf.* 8 C.F.R. § 2.1 (1980) (delegating all powers of the Attorney General relating to the immigration and naturalization of aliens to INS). In addition to this broad mandate to investigate alien eligibility, the Act endows INS with the specific authority to reject a petition upon a finding that the alien procured any document offered in support of the petition through fraud or willful misrepresentation of a material fact, Act § 212(a)(19), 8 U.S.C. § 1182(a)(19) (1976), and to revoke a previously granted petition at any time for "good or sufficient cause," Act § 205, 8 U.S.C. § 1155 (1976). The failure to acquire a job qualification that was critical to the initial grant of the petition may constitute such sufficient cause. *See Navarro v. District Director*, 574 F.2d 379 (7th Cir.), *cert. denied*, 439 U.S. 861 (1978) (failure to acquire nursing license in two years is sufficient cause to permit revocation of a third preference classification); *see also* 8 C.F.R. § 204.4(b) (1980).

III. The Division of Authority

The essence of appellant's argument is that the content of the labor certification and the findings implicit therein are the product of DOL in performance of its statutory functions under section 212(a)(14). The grant of the labor certification, then, constitutes a final determination by DOL and, as such, is not the proper subject of review by INS. To the extent that the actions of DOL and INS interface, because a labor certification is a prerequisite to the preference classification, appellant urges that the scope of INS inquiry is limited to the fact of certification and nothing more.

It is true that determinations vested by statute with one agency are not normally subject to horizontal review by a sister entity, absent congressional authorization to that effect. But this case does not present an instance of INS trespass onto DOL territory. Appellant misreads the nature of DOL's findings and the arrangement that is implicitly, if not explicitly, set up by the Act. Although the Act allocates a limited role to DOL, it vests primary responsibility for implementation with INS.

* * *

The review here in question concerns the alien's skills or qualifications and is not one of the inquiries expressly allocated to DOL by section 212(a)(14). This does not mean that DOL cannot, or does not, undertake analysis of an alien's qualifications as it performs its statutory functions. Indeed, DOL may gauge an alien's skill level in evaluating the effect of the alien's employment on United States workers. The fact that DOL may find such an analysis useful, however, does not foreclose INS from considering alien qualifications in the preference classification decision.

* * *

We are aware that at least one district court addressed the identical issue in the context of a sixth preference classification petition. *See Singh v. Attorney General*, 510 F. Supp. 351 (D.D.C. 1980), *aff'd on other grounds*, 672 F.2d 894 (D.C. Cir. 1981). Sixth preference classifications are granted to "qualified immigrants who are capable of performing specified skilled or unskilled labor ... for which a shortage of employable and willing persons exists in the United States," Act § 203(a)(6), 8 U.S.C. § 1153(a)(6) (Supp. V 1981), and also are prefaced upon the receipt of a labor certification. The *Singh* court read the legislative history of the Act to signify that DOL is vested with primary authority to review alien qualifications, relying in part on the following statement by Senator Philip Hart:

It is my understanding that when an immigrant seeks admission under these categories as special immigrants or preference immigrants and a determination by the Secretary of Labor is required, the Secretary will make a certification in the case of the individual immigrant. He must ascertain the prospective immigrant's skill and will match those skills with the employment and manpower reports he has available from the labor market area where the immigrant expects to reside. On the basis of such an analysis, the Secretary will be in a position to meet the requirement of the law, and provide the type of employment safeguards sought in this legislation.

* * *

Given the language of the Act, the totality of the legislative history, and the agencies' own interpretations of their duties under the Act, we must conclude that Congress did not intend DOL to have primary authority to make any determinations other than the two stated in section 212(a)(14). If DOL is to analyze alien qualifications, it is for the purpose of "matching" them with those of corresponding United States workers so that it will then be "in a position to meet the requirement of the law," namely the section 212(a)(14) determinations. We therefore do not follow the ruling in *Singh* to the extent it suggests that INS does not have primary authority for preference classification decisions.

IV. The License Requirement

Given that review of Madany's qualifications was within the discretionary authority of INS, its decision must be sustained if based on substantial evidence and not an abuse of discretion. *Wing Ding Chan v. INS*, 631 F.2d 978, 980-81 (D.C. Cir. 1980), *cert. denied*, 450 U.S. 921 (1981). Appellant maintains that INS abused its discretion by imposing a job requirement on her beyond that contemplated by DOL.

The language at issue states that appellant "must be able to obtain Virginia nursing license or have Virginia nursing license." A.R. 40. Because appellant did not already possess a Virginia nursing license, the controversy focuses on the significance of the words "able to obtain." Appellant argues that this language means "eligible to sit" for the examination, and that she satisfies such a requirement through her foreign nursing education. In support of this interpretation, appellant cites to a letter solicited from DOL clarifying the requirement's purposes. This letter indicates that the requirement was designed to serve two purposes. First, it was intended to protect similarly situated United States workers who did not currently possess a Virginia license but who could sit for the exam. The second and primary purpose, however, was to ensure compliance with the state law requiring that professional nurses possess a license in order to be legally employed. Va. Code § 54-367.17 (1982); *see* 20 C.F.R. § 656.21(b)(16) (1979) (terms of job opportunity offered to alien must conform to the requirements of federal, state, and local law).

* * *

The next inquiry must be whether appellant sustained this burden. Appellant presented evidence of her nursing education, her registration to take the District of Columbia nursing exam, and possible reciprocity between the District of Columbia and Virginia. INS found this evidence to be insufficient, and the district court agreed.

We are wary of jumping too quickly to the conclusion that the evidence, because it did not show that appellant in fact would obtain the license, was thereby insufficient to sustain her burden. Insofar as it speaks to appellant's future potential, the "able to obtain" requirement is something that cannot, except in rare instances, be concretely proved or disproved now. In evaluating an individual alien's satisfaction of such a requirement, INS cannot require that the alien already have acquired the skill or met the qualification, thereby eliminating the grace period contained within the requirement when it states that future compliance is sufficient. Such a burden would effectively permit INS to impose an additional or different job requirement, something which it has no authority to do. Between those two extremes, mere eligibility to sit for the examination and current possession of the license, lies the level of proof that balances the alien's ability to show a future qualification and INS' responsibility to ensure that, at some point, the alien will be able to perform the certified job. INS may require a preliminary showing that the alien intends to acquire and is reasonably likely to acquire the qualification in question within a reasonable period of time. This reasonable period of time should vary according to the nature of the qualification, the usual time period it takes to acquire the qualification, and the prospective employer's needs and expectations. But once this preliminary showing is made, the alien has satisfied her burden of demonstrating compliance with this type of job requirement. Thereafter, INS can deny the preference classification on that basis only if there is a finding, supported by substantial evidence, that the *particular* alien actually will not be able to acquire the specified qualification. For this reason, INS cannot rely on the low passing rate of foreign nurse candidates in general as the basis for rejecting appellant's petition once a preliminary showing is made.

* * *

We recognize that the statutory division of authority between DOL's labor certification determination and INS' preference classification decision can lead to some discontinuity insofar as DOL-imposed job requirements are subject to interpretation by INS in its review of the alien's qualifications. Accordingly, INS will need the sensitivity to coordinate DOL and INS interpretations and to follow the Act's directive to consult with DOL when correctable discrepancies between the alien's qualifications and the labor certification job requirements appear. INS must also recognize that DOL bears the authority for setting the content of the labor certification and that it cannot impose job qualifications beyond those contemplated therein. However delicate that task may be in future cases, we have no reason to upset the decision of INS in this case.

Notes

1. The INS has considered membership in the "professions" to be where the attainment of a baccalaureate degree is the minimum requirement for entry into the occupation. *Matter of Asuncion*, 11 I. & N. Dec. 660 (Reg. Comm. 1966) *Matter of Caron*, Interim Decision No. 3085 (Comm. 1988). This rigid approach in defining professional workers has been rejected by the courts in favor of a standard which takes into account the nature of the work and experience required for the position. See e.g. *Hong Kong T.V. Video Program, Inc. v. Ilchert*, 685 F. Supp. 712, 716 (N.D. Ca. 1988); *Augat v. Tovar*, 719 F. Supp. 1158 (N.D. Mass. 1989).

The Immigration Act of 1990, for the first time, defined "managerial" and "executive." *Managerial* is loosely defined as a person with the power: 1) to manage an organization, function or component of an organization; 2) to supervise and control the work of other supervisory personnel or to supervise an essential function of the organization; 3) to hire and fire; and 4) to exercise discretion in the day-to-

Labor Certification Flow Chart
Non-Schedule A Occupations

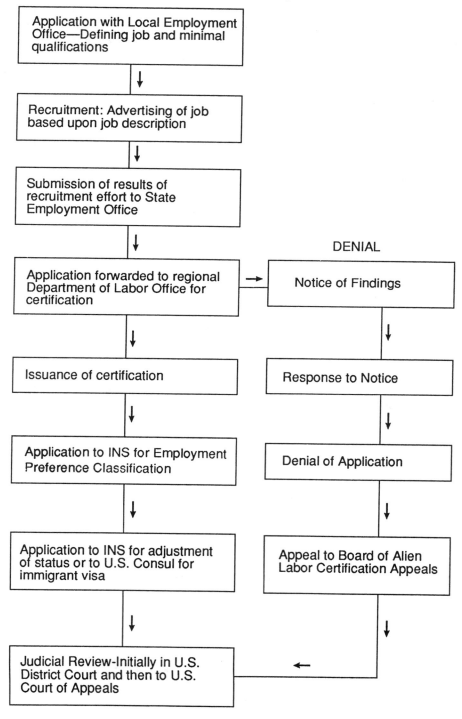

Schedule A Occupations

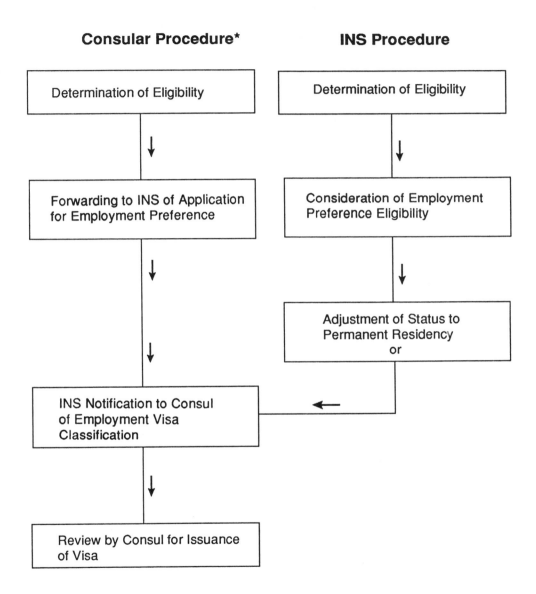

Consular Procedure*

Determination of Eligibility

↓

Forwarding to INS of Application for Employment Preference

↓

↓

INS Notification to Consul of Employment Visa Classification

↓

Review by Consul for Issuance of Visa

INS Procedure

Determination of Eligibility

↓

Consideration of Employment Preference Eligibility

↓

Adjustment of Status to Permanent Residency or

←

*The direct filing for "Schedule A" with the Consul is rare. Normally, the application will be submitted directly to the INS by the employer and applicant.

day operations. *Executive* is defined as a person with the power: 1) to direct the management or a function or component of the organization; 2) to set goals and policies of the organization; 3) to exercise a wide range of discretion in the decision-making process while receiving only general supervision from superiors.[30]

2. Prior to the 1990 Act, nonimmigrant H-1 visas were issued to "persons of distinguished merit and ability." In analyzing an individual's qualifications and determining whether she qualifies for one of the employment-based preferences requiring extraordinary, or exceptional ability, or is a member of the professions reference should be made to the discussion in Chapter 6 and the notes following *Matter of Artee Corporation.*

The job descriptions which follow illustrate the importance of how the definition of an occupation can affect whether a job may or may not be certified. It may also be instructive to compare your own impression of the job with these definitions which were extracted from the *Dictionary of Occupational Titles.*

Examples of Certifiable and Non-Certifiable Occupations

Non-Certifiable
Schedule B Occupations

(15) Clerk Typists. Perform general clerical work which, for the majority of duties, requires the use of typewriters: perform such activities as typing reports, bills, application forms, shipping tickets, and other matters from clerical records, filing records and reports, posting information to records, sorting and distributing mail, answering phones and similar duties.

(26) Household Domestic Service Workers. Perform a variety of tasks in private households, such as cleaning, dusting, washing, ironing, making beds, maintaining clothes, marketing, cooking, serving food, and caring for children or disabled persons. This definition, however, applies only to workers who have had less than one year of documented full-time paid experience in the tasks to be performed, working on a live-in or live-out basis in private households or in public or private institutions or establishments where the worker has performed tasks equivalent to tasks normally associated with the maintenance of a private household. This definition does not include household workers who primarily provide health or instructional services.

(30) "Kitchen Workers" perform routine tasks in the kitchens of restaurants. Their primary responsibility is to maintain work areas and equipment in a clean and orderly fashion by performing such tasks as mopping floors, removing trash, washing pots and pans, transferring supplies and equipment, and washing and peeling vegetables.

Certifiable Occupations

201.362-030 Secretary (Clerical) secretarial stenographer.

Schedules appointments, gives information to callers, takes dictation, and otherwise relieves officials of clerical work and minor administrative and business detail. Reads and routes incoming mail. Locates and attaches appropriate file to correspondence to be answered by employer. Takes dictation in shorthand or by machine [Stenotype Operator (clerical)] and transcribes notes on typewriter, or transcribes from

---

30. 8 U.S.C. § 1101(a)(44), Sec. 101(a)(44).

voice recordings [Transcribing-Machine Operator (clerical)]. Composes and types routine correspondence and other records. Answers telephone and gives information to callers or routes call to appropriate official and places outgoing calls. Schedules appointments for employer. Greets visitors, ascertains nature of business....

Note: A live-in or live-out household domestic may be certified if the alien has 1 year or more experience. *See* 20 C.F.R. § 656.11(b)(26).

313.361-034 Garde Manger cold meat chef; cook.

Prepares such dishes as meat loaves. Consults with supervisory staff to determine dishes that will use greatest amount of leftovers. Prepares appetizers, relishes, and hors d'oeuvres. Chops, dices, and grinds meats and vegetables. Slices cold meat dishes....

Index to Appendix

Statutory Provisions Relating to Labor Certifications

8 U.S.C. § 1182(a)(5), Sec. 212(a)(5)—Labor Certification Requirement[31]

(A) Labor Certification.—

(i) In General.—Any alien who seeks admission or status as an immigrant under paragraph (2) or (3) of section 203(b) is excludable, unless the Secretary of Labor has determined and certified to the Secretary of State and the Attorney General that—

(I) there are not sufficient workers who are able, willing, qualified (or equally qualified in the case of an alien described in clause (ii)) and available at the time of application for a visa and admission to the United States and at the place where the alien is to perform such skilled or unskilled labor, and

(II) the employment of such alien will not adversely affect the wages and working conditions of workers in the United States similarly employed.

(ii) Certain Aliens Subject to Special Rule.—For purposes of clause (i)(I), an alien described in this clause is an alien who—

(I) is a member of the teaching profession, or

(II) has exceptional ability in the sciences or the arts.

(B) Unqualified Physicians.—An alien who seeks admission or status as an immigrant under paragraph (2) or (3) of section 203(b) who is a graduate of a medical school not accredited by a body or bodies approved for the purpose by the Secretary of Education (regardless of whether such school of medicine is in the United States) and who is coming to the United States principally to perform services as a member of the medical profession is excludable, unless the alien

(i) has passed parts I and II of the National Board of Medical Examiners Examination (or an equivalent examination as determined by the Secretary of Health and Human Services) and

(ii) is competent in oral and written English. For purposes of the previous sentence, an alien who is a graduate of a medical school shall be considered to have passed parts I and II of the National Board of Medical Examiners if the alien was fully and permanently licensed to practice medicine in a State on January 9, 1978, and was practicing medicine in a State on that date.

8 U.S.C. § 1101(a)(32) Definition of "Profession"

The term "profession" shall include but not be limited to architects, engineers, lawyers, physicians, surgeons, and teachers in elementary or secondary schools, colleges, academies, or seminaries.

8 U.S.C. § 1101(a)(44), Sec. 101(a)(44)—Definition of "Managerial" and "Executive"[32]

(A) The term "managerial capacity" means an assignment within an organization in which the employee primarily—

(i) manages the organization, or a department, subdivision, function, or component of the organization;

---

31. This provision was added by Sec. 162 and 601 of the Immigration Act of 1990, Pub. L. No. 101-649, 104 Stat. 4978.

32. This section was added by Sec. 123 of the Immigration Act of 1990, Pub. L. No. 101-649, 104 Stat. 4978.

(ii) supervises and controls the work of other supervisory, professional, or managerial employees, or manages an essential function within the organization, or a department or subdivision of the organization;

(iii) if another employee or other employees are directly supervised, has the authority to hire and fire or recommend those as well as other personnel actions (such as promotion and leave authorization) or, if no other employee is directly supervised, functions at a senior level within the organizational hierarchy or with respect to the function managed; and

(iv) exercises discretion over the day-to-day operations of the activity or function for which the employee has authority. A first-line supervisor is not considered to be acting in a managerial capacity merely by virtue of the supervisor's supervisory duties unless the employees supervised are professional.

(B) The term "executive capacity" means an assignment within an organization in which the employee primarily—

(i) directs the management of the organization or a major component or function of the organization;

(ii) establishes the goals and policies of the organization, component, or function;

(iii) exercises wide latitude in discretionary decision-making; and

(iv) receives only general supervision or direction from higher level executives, the board of directors, or stockholders of the organization.

(C) If staffing levels are used as a factor in determining whether an individual is acting in a managerial or executive capacity, the Attorney General shall take into account the reasonable needs of the organization, component, or function in light of the overall purpose and stage of development of the organization, component, or function. An individual shall not be considered to be acting in a managerial or executive capacity (as previously defined) merely on the basis of the number of employees that the individual supervises or has supervised or directs or has directed."

8 U.S.C. § 1153(b)—Employment-Based Immigrants[33]

Aliens subject to the worldwide level specified in section 1151(d) of this title for employment-based immigrants in a fiscal year shall be allotted visas as follows:

(1) Priority workers.—Visas shall first be made available in a number not to exceed 40,000, plus any visas not required for the classes specified in paragraphs (4) and (5), to qualified immigrants who are aliens described in any of the following subparagraphs (A) through (C):

(A) Aliens with extraordinary ability.—An alien is described in this subparagraph if—

(i) the alien has extraordinary ability in the sciences, arts, education, business, or athletics which has been demonstrated by sustained national or international acclaim and whose achievements have been recognized in the field through extensive documentation,

(ii) the alien seeks to enter the United States to continue work in the area of extraordinary ability, and

---

33. 8 U.S.C. § 1153, Sec. 203 was reorganized into preferences for "Family-Sponsored" immigrants at subsection (a) and for "Employment-Based" immigrants at subsection (b).

(iii) the alien's entry into the United States will substantially benefit prospectively the United States.

(B) Outstanding professors and researchers.—An alien is described in this subparagraph if—

(i) the alien is recognized internationally as outstanding in a specific academic area,

(ii) the alien has at least 3 years of experience in teaching or research in the academic area, and

(iii) the alien seeks to enter the United States—

(I) for a tenured position (or tenure-track position) within a university or institution of higher education to teach in the academic area,

(II) for a comparable position with a university or institution of higher education to conduct research in the area, or

(III) for a comparable position to conduct research in the area with a department, division, or institute of a private employer, if the department, division, or institute employs at least 3 persons full-time in research activities and has achieved documented accomplishments in an academic field.

(C) Certain multinational executives and managers.—An alien is described in this subparagraph if the alien, in the 3 years preceding the time of the alien's application for classification and admission into the United States under this subparagraph, has been employed for at least 1 year by a firm or corporation or other legal entity or an affiliate or subsidiary thereof and who seeks to enter the United States in order to continue to render services to the same employer or to a subsidiary or affiliate thereof in a capacity that is managerial or executive.

(2) Aliens who are members of the professions holding advanced degrees or aliens of exceptional ability.—

(A) In general.—Visas shall be made available, in a number not to exceed 40,000, plus any visas not required for the classes specified in paragraph (1), to qualified immigrants who are members of the professions holding advanced degrees or their equivalent or who because of their exceptional ability in the sciences, arts, or business, will substantially benefit prospectively the national economy, cultural or educational interests, or welfare of the United States, and whose services in the sciences, arts, professions, or business are sought by an employer in the United States.

(B) Waiver of job offer.—The Attorney General may, when he deems it to be in the national interest, waive the requirement of subparagraph (A) that an alien's services in the sciences, arts, or business be sought by an employer in the United States.

(C) Determination of exceptional ability.—In determining under subparagraph (A) whether an immigrant has exceptional ability, the possession of a degree, diploma, certificate, or similar award from a college, university, school, or other institution of learning or a license to practice or certification for a particular profession or occupation shall not by itself be considered sufficient evidence of such exceptional ability.

(3) Skilled workers, professionals, and other workers.—

(A) In general.—Visas shall be made available, in a number not to exceed 40,000, plus any visas not required for the classes specified in paragraphs (1) and (2), to the following classes of aliens who are not described in paragraph (2):

(i) Skilled workers.—Qualified immigrants who are capable, at the time of petitioning for classification under this paragraph, of performing skilled labor (requiring at least 2 years training or experience), not of a temporary or seasonal nature, for which qualified workers are not available in the United States.

(ii) Professionals.—Qualified immigrants who hold baccalaureate degrees and who are members of the professions.

(iii) Other workers.—Other qualified immigrants who are capable, at the time of petitioning for classification under this paragraph, of performing unskilled labor, not of a temporary or seasonal nature, for which qualified workers are not available in the United States.

(B) Limitation on other workers.—Not more than 10,000 of the visas made available under this paragraph in any fiscal year may be available for qualified immigrants described in subparagraph (A)(iii).

(C) Labor certification required.—An immigrant visa may not be issued to an immigrant under subparagraph (A) until the consular officer is in receipt of a determination made by the Secretary of Labor pursuant to the provisions of section 1182(a)(5)(A) of this title.

(4) Certain special immigrants.—Visas shall be made available, in a number not to exceed 10,000, to qualified special immigrants described in section 1101(a)(27) of this title (other than those described in subparagraph (A) or (B) thereof), of which not more than 5,000 may be made available in any fiscal year to special immigrants described in subclause (II) or (III) of section 1101(a)(27)(C)(ii) of this title.

(5) Employment creation.—

(A) In general.—Visas shall be made available, in a number not to exceed 10,000, to qualified immigrants seeking to enter the United States for the purpose of engaging in a new commercial enterprise—

(i) which the alien has established,

(ii) in which such alien has invested (after November 29, 1990) or, is actively in the process of investing, capital in an amount not less than the amount specified in subparagraph (C), and

(iii) which will benefit the United States economy and create full-time employment for not fewer than 10 United States citizens or aliens lawfully admitted for permanent residence or other immigrants lawfully authorized to be employed in the United States (other than the immigrant and the immigrant's spouse, sons, or daughters).

(B) Set-aside for targetted employment areas.—

(i) In general.—Not less than 3,000 of the visas made available under this paragraph in each fiscal year shall be reserved for qualified immigrants who establish a new commercial enterprise described in subparagraph (A) which will create employment in a targetted employment area.

(ii) Targetted employment area defined.—In this paragraph, the term "targetted employment area" means, at the time of the investment, a rural area or an area which has experienced high unemployment (of at least 150 percent of the national average rate).

(iii) Rural area defined.—In this paragraph, the term "rural area" means any area other than an area within a metropolitan statistical area or within the outer boundary of any city or town having a population of 20,000 or more (based on the most recent decennial census of the United States).

(C) Amount of capital required.—

(i) In general.—Except as otherwise provided in this subparagraph, the amount of capital required under subparagraph (A) shall be $1,000,000. The Attorney General, in consultation with the Secretary of Labor and the Secretary of State, may from time to time prescribe regulations increasing the dollar amount specified under the previous sentence.

(ii) Adjustment for targetted employment areas.—The Attorney General may, in the case of investment made in a targetted employment area, specify an amount of capital required under subparagraph (A) that is less than (but not less than 1/2 of) the amount specified in clause (i).

(iii) Adjustment for high employment areas.—In the case of an investment made in a part of a metropolitan statistical area that at the time of the investment—

(I) is not a targetted employment area, and

(II) is an area with an unemployment rate significantly below the national average unemployment rate, the Attorney General may specify an amount of capital required under subparagraph (A) that is greater than (but not greater than 3 times) the amount specified in clause (i).

Labor Certification Regulations

20 C.F.R. § 656.10 Schedule A

The Administrator, United States Employment Service (Administrator), has determined that there are not sufficient United States workers who are able, willing, qualified, and available for the occupations listed below on Schedule A and that the wages and working conditions of United States workers similarly employed will not be adversely affected by the employment of aliens in Schedule A occupations. An alien seeking a labor certification for an occupation listed on Schedule A may apply for that labor certification pursuant to § 656.22.

Schedule A

(a) Group I:

(1) Persons who will be employed as physical therapists, and who possess all the qualifications necessary to take the physical therapist licensing examination in the State in which they propose to practice physical therapy.

(2) Aliens who will be employed as professional nurses; and (i) who have passed the Commission on Graduates of Foreign Nursing Schools (CGFNS) Examination; or (ii) who hold a full and unrestricted license to practice professional nursing in the State of intended employment.

(3) Definitions of Group I occupations:

(i) "Physical therapist" means a person who applies the art and science of physical therapy to the treatment of patients with disabilities, disorders and injuries to relieve pain, develop or restore function, and maintain performance, using physical means, such as exercise, massage, heat, water, light, and electricity, as prescribed by a physician (or surgeon). (ii) "Professional nurse" is defined in § 656.50.

(b) Group II:

Aliens (except for aliens in the performing arts) of exceptional ability in the sciences or arts including college and university teachers of exceptional ability who have been practicing their science or art during the year prior to application and who intend to practice the same science or art in the United States. For purposes of this group, the term "science or art" means any field of knowledge and/or skill with respect to which colleges and universities commonly offer specialized courses leading to a degree in the knowledge and/or skill. An alien, however, need not have studied at a college or university in order to qualify for the Group II occupation.

(c) Group III:

(1) Aliens who seek admission to the United States in order to perform a religious occupation, such as the preaching or teaching of religion; and (2) Aliens with a religious commitment who seek admission into the United States in order to work for a nonprofit religious organization.

(d) Group IV:

(1) Aliens who have been admitted to the United States in order to work in, and who are currently working in, managerial or executive positions with the same international corporations or organizations with which they were continuously employed as managers or executives outside the United States for one year before they were admitted.

(2) Aliens outside the United States who will be engaged in the United States in managerial or executive positions with the same international corporations or organizations with which they have been continuously employed as managers or executives outside the United States for the immediately prior year.

(3) For the purposes of this paragraph (d), the international corporation or organization must have been established and doing business in the United States for a period of at least one year prior to the submission of the application for the alien to qualify under Schedule A, Group IV. For the purposes of this paragraph (d), "doing business" shall mean a regular, systematic, and continuous course of conduct, including both the offer of and the provision of goods and/or services by the employer, and shall not be limited to the mere presence in the United States of an agent or office of the international corporation or organization.

*   *   *

20 C.F.R. § 656.22 Procedure for Schedule A Occupations.

(a) An alien or agent of an alien shall apply for a labor certification for a Schedule A occupation by filing an Application for Alien Employment Certification form in duplicate with a U.S. Consular office abroad or with an INS office in the United States, not with the Department of Labor or a State job service local office.

(b) An alien whose occupation is on Schedule A and who is seeking a third or sixth preference, as described in § 656.2(d)(1)(ii) and (iii), shall show evidence of prearranged employment by having an employer complete, and sign, the job offer description portion of the Application for Alien Employment Certification form. There is, however, no need for the employer to provide the other documentation required under this Part for non-Schedule A occupations.

(c) Aliens seeking labor certifications under Group I of Schedule A shall file as part of their labor certification applications documentary evidence of the following:

(1) Aliens seeking Schedule A labor certifications as physical therapists (§ 656.10(a)(1)) shall file as part of their labor certification applications a letter or statement signed by an authorized State physical therapy licensing official in the State of intended employment, stating that the alien is qualified to take that State's written licensing examination for physical therapists. Application for certification of permanent employment as a physical therapist may be made only pursuant to this section, and not pursuant to §§ 656.21, 656.21a, or § 656.23.

(2) Aliens seeking Schedule A labor certifications as professional nurses (§ 656.10(a)(3)) shall file as part of their labor certification applications, documentation that the alien has passed the Commission on Graduates of Foreign Nursing Schools (CGFNS) Examination; or that the alien holds a full and unrestricted license to practice professional nursing in the State of intended employment. Application for certification of employment as a professional nurse may be made only pursuant to paragraph (a)(3) of this section, and not pursuant to §§ 656.21, 656.21a, or § 656.23.

→ (d) Aliens seeking labor certifications under Group II of Schedule A shall file as part of their labor certification applications documentary evidence testifying to the current widespread acclaim and international recognition accorded them by recognized experts in their field; and documentation showing that their work in that field during the past year did, and their intended work in the United States will, require exceptional ability. In addition, the aliens must file, as part of their labor certification applications, documentation from at least two of the following seven groups:

(1) Documentation of the alien's receipt of internationally recognized prizes or awards for excellence in the field for which certification is sought;

(2) Documentation of the alien's membership in international associations, in the field for which certification is sought, which require outstanding achievements of their members, as judged by recognized international experts in their disciplines or fields;

(3) Published material in professional publications about the alien, relating to the alien's work in the field for which certification is sought, which shall include the title, date, and author of such published material;

(4) Evidence of the alien's participation on a panel, or individually, as a judge of the work of others in the same or in an allied field of specialization to that for which certification is sought;

(5) Evidence of the alien's original scientific or scholarly research contributions of major significance in the field for which certification is sought;

(6) Evidence of the alien's authorship of published scientific or scholarly articles in the field for which certification is sought, in international professional journals or professional journals with an international circulation; and/or

(7) Evidence of the display of alien's work, in the field for which certification is sought, at artistic exhibitions in more than one country.

(e) Aliens seeking a labor certification under Group III of Schedule A shall file as part of their labor certification applications documentary evidence showing that they have been primarily engaged in the religious occupation or in working for the nonprofit religious organization for the previous two years, and they will be principally engaged (more than 50 percent of working time) in the United States in performing the religious occupation or working for the nonprofit religious organization.

(f)(1) Aliens seeking labor certifications under Group IV of Schedule A shall meet, at the time of filing the application, the eligibility requirements of the Immigration and Nationality Act for an L-1 nonimmigrant visa classification as a manager or an executive. See 8 U.S.C. 1101(a)(15)(L); and 8 CFR 214.2(1). However, persons who are eligible for an L-1 visa on the basis of specialized knowledge, but not managerial or executive experience, do not meet the requirements for Group IV of Schedule A. The actual filing of an L-1 visa petition is not required.

(2) Aliens seeking labor certifications under Group IV of Schedule A shall file as part of their labor certification applications a written verification of employment statement, signed by an authorized officer of the international corporation or organization which will employ the alien in the United States. The written verification of employment statement shall set forth:

(i) The dates of the alien's employment with the international corporation or organization;

(ii) The name(s) of the components of that employer for which the alien has been and/or is being employed, inside and outside the United States;

(iii) Unless such information has been entered on the Application for Alien Employment Certification form, a description of the positions held by the alien within the international corporation or organization, and the dates the alien held each position; and

(iv) The dates the international corporation or organization was established and has been doing business in the United States prior to the submission of the application. The term "doing business" is defined in paragraph (d)(3) of Schedule A (§ 656.10(d)(3)).

(g) If the alien is requesting a preference described at § 656.2(d) and if the alien has filed an Application for Alien Employment Certification form at a Consular office, the Consular Officer shall review the form as appropriate and shall then forward the application to the INS in accordance with the procedures of the Department of State and the INS.

(h) An Immigration Officer, or Consular Officer (except as provided in paragraph (g) of this section), shall determine whether the alien has met the applicable requirements of this section and of Schedule A (§ 656.10), shall review the application and shall determine whether or not the alien is qualified for and intends to pursue the Schedule A occupation.

(1) The Immigration or Consular Officer may request an advisory opinion as to whether the alien is qualified for the Schedule A occupation from the Division of Labor Certifications, United States Employment Service, 601 D Street, NW, Washington, D.C. 20213.

(2) The Schedule A determination of the INS or Department of State shall be conclusive and final. The alien, therefore, may not make use of the review procedures set forth at § 656.26.

(i) If the alien qualifies for the occupation, the Immigration or Consular Officer shall indicate the occupation on the Application for Alien Employment Certification form. The Consular or Immigration Officer shall then promptly forward a copy of the Application for Alien Employment Certification form, without attachments, to the Administrator, indicating thereon the occupation, the Immigration or Consular office which made the Schedule A determination and the date of the determination (see § 656.30 for the significance of this date).

Non-Certifiable Occupations[18]

20 C.F.R. § 656.11 Schedule B.
(1) Assemblers
(2) Attendants, Parking Lot
(3) Attendants (Service Workers such as Personal Service Attendants, Amusement and Recreation Service Attendants)
(4) Automobile Service Station Attendants
(5) Bartenders
(6) Bookkeepers II
(7) Caretakers
(8) Cashiers
(9) Charworkers and Cleaners
(10) Chauffeurs and Taxicab Drivers
(11) Cleaners, Hotel and Motel
(12) Clerks, General
(13) Clerks, Hotel
(14) Clerks and Checkers, Grocery Stores
(15) Clerk Typists
(16) Cooks, Short Order
(17) Counter and Fountain Workers
(18) Dining Room Attendants
(19) Electric Truck Operators
(20) Elevator Operators
(21) Floorworkers
(22) Groundskeepers
(23) Guards
(24) Helpers, any industry
(25) Hotel Cleaners
(26) Household Domestic Service Workers
(27) Housekeepers
(28) Janitors
(29) Key Punch Operators
(30) Kitchen Workers
(31) Laborers, Common

---

18. There is a strong presumption that the positions noted are not certifiable. However, an employer may obtain a waiver of this provision. *See* 20 C.F.R. § 656.23.

(32) Laborers, Farm

(33) Laborers, Mine

(34) Loopers and Toppers

(35) Material Handlers

(36) Nurses' Aides and Orderlies

(37) Packers, Markers, Bottlers and Related

(38) Porters

(39) Receptionists

(40) Sailors and Deck Hands

(41) Sales Clerks, General

(42) Sewing Machine Operators and Handstitchers

(43) Stock Room and Warehouse Workers

(44) Streetcar and Bus Conductors

(45) Telephone Operators

(46) Truck Drivers and Tractor Drivers

(47) Typists, Lesser Skilled

(48) Ushers, Recreation and Amusement

(49) Yard Workers

*   *   *

8 C.F.R. § 656.20 General Filing Instructions.

(a) A request for a labor certification on behalf of any alien who is required by the Act to become a beneficiary of a labor certification in order to obtain permanent resident status in the United States may be filed as follows:

(1) Except as provided in paragraphs (a)(2) through (4) of this section, an application for a labor certification shall be filed pursuant to this section and § 656.21.

(2) An employer seeking a labor certification for an occupation designated for special handling shall apply for a labor certification pursuant to this section and § 656.21a.

(3) An alien seeking labor certification for an occupation listed on Schedule A may apply for a labor certification pursuant to this section and § 656.22.

(4) An employer seeking a labor certification for an occupation listed on Schedule B shall apply for a waiver and a labor certification pursuant to this section and §§ 656.21 and 656.23.

(b)(1) Aliens and employers may have agents represent them throughout the labor certification process. If an alien and/or an employer intends to be represented by an agent, the alien and/or the employer shall sign the statement set forth on the Application for Alien Employment Certification form: That the agent is representing the alien and/or employer and that the alien and/or employer takes full responsibility for the accuracy of any representations made by the agent.

(2) Aliens and employers may have attorneys represent them. Each attorney shall file a notice of appearance on Immigration and Naturalization Service (INS) Form G-28, naming the attorney's client or clients. Whenever, under this Part, any notice or other document is required to be sent to an employer or alien, the document shall be sent to their attorney or attorneys who have filed notices of appearance on INS Form G-28, if they have such an attorney or attorneys.

(3)(i) It is contrary to the best interests of U.S. workers to have the alien and/or agents or attorneys for the alien participate in interviewing or considering U.S. workers for the job offered the alien. As the beneficiary of a labor certification application, the alien cannot represent the best interests of U.S. workers in the job opportunity. The alien's agent and/or attorney cannot represent the alien effectively and at the same time truly be seeking U.S. workers for the job opportunity. Therefore, the alien and/or the alien's agent and/or attorney may not interview or consider U.S. workers for the job offered to the alien, unless the agent and/or attorney is the employer's representative as described in paragraph (b)(3)(ii) of this section.

(ii) The employer's representative who interviews or considers U.S. workers for the job offered to the alien shall be the person who normally interviews or considers, on behalf of the employer, applicants for job opportunities such as that offered the alien, but which do not involve labor certifications.

(4) No person under suspension or disbarment from practice before the United States Department of Justice's Board of Immigration Appeals pursuant to 8 CFR 292.3 shall be permitted to act as an agent, representative, or attorney for an employer and/or alien under this part.

(c) Job offers filed on behalf of aliens on the Application for Alien Employment Certification form must clearly show that:

(1) The employer has enough funds available to pay the wage or salary offered the alien;

(2) The wage offered equals or exceeds the prevailing wage determined pursuant to § 656.40, and the wage the employer will pay to the alien when the alien begins work will equal or exceed the prevailing wage which is applicable at the time the alien begins work;

(3) The wage offered is not based on commissions, bonuses or other incentives, unless the employer guarantees a wage paid on a weekly, bi-weekly, or monthly basis;

(4) The employer will be able to place the alien on the payroll on or before the date of the alien's proposed entrance into the United States;

(5) The job opportunity does not involve unlawful discrimination by race, creed, color, national origin, age, sex, religion, handicap, or citizenship;

(6) The employer's job opportunity is not:

(i) Vacant because the former occupant is on strike or is being locked out in the course of a labor dispute involving a work stoppage; or

(ii) At issue in a labor dispute involving a work stoppage;

(7) The employer's job opportunity's terms, conditions and occupational environment are not contrary to Federal, State or local law; and

(8) The job opportunity has been and is clearly open to any qualified U.S. worker.

(9) The conditions of employment listed in paragraphs (c)(1) through (8) of this section shall be sworn (or affirmed) to, under penalty of perjury pursuant to 28 U.S.C. 1746, on the Application for Alien Employment Certification form.

(d) If the application involves labor certification as a physician (or surgeon)(except a physician (or surgeon) of international renown), the labor certification application shall include the following documentation:

(1)(i) Documentation which shows clearly that the alien has passed Parts I and II of the National Board of Medical Examiners Examination (NBMEE), or the Visa Qualifying Examination (VQE) offered by the Educational Commission for Foreign Medical Graduates (ECFMG); or

(ii) Documentation which shows clearly that:

(A) The alien was on January 9, 1977, a doctor of medicine fully and permanently licensed to practice medicine in a State within the United States;

(B) The alien held on January 9, 1977, a valid specialty certificate issued by a constituent board of the American Board of Medical Specialties; and

(C) The alien was on January 9, 1977, practicing medicine in a State within the United States; or

(iii) The alien is a graduate of a school of medicine accredited by a body or bodies approved for the purpose by the Secretary of Education or that Secretary's designee (regardless of whether such school of medicine is in the United States).

(e) Whenever any document is submitted to a State or Federal agency pursuant to this part, the document either shall be in the English language or shall be accompanied by a written translation into the English language, certified by the translator as to the accuracy of the translation and his/her competency to translate.

(f) The forms required under this part for applications for labor certification are available at U.S. Consular offices abroad, at INS offices in the United States, and at local offices of the State; job service agencies. The forms will contain instructions on how to comply with the documentation requirements for applying for a labor certification under this part. OMB Control No. 1205-0015.

20 C.F.R. § 656.21 Basic Labor Certification Process.

(a) Except as otherwise provided by §§ 656.21a and 656.22, an employer who desires to apply for a labor certification on behalf of an alien shall file, signed by hand and in duplicate, a Department of Labor Application for Alien Employment Certification form and any attachments required by this part with the local Job Service office serving the area where the alien proposes to be employed. The employer shall set forth on the Application for Alien Employment Certification form, as appropriate, or in attachments:

(1) A statement of the qualifications of the alien, signed by the alien;

(2) A description of the job offer for the alien employment, including the items required by paragraph (b) of this section; and

(3) If the application involves a job offer as a live-in household domestic service worker:

(i) A statement describing the household living accommodations;

(ii) Two copies of the employment contract, each signed and dated by both the employer and the alien (not by their agents). The contract shall clearly state:

(A) The wages to be paid on an hourly and weekly basis;

(B) Total hours of employment per week, and exact hours of daily employment;

(C) That the alien is free to leave the employer's premises during all non-work hours except that the alien may work overtime if paid for the overtime at no less than the legally required hourly rate;

(D) That the alien will reside on the employer's premises;

(E) Complete details of the duties to be performed by the alien;

(F) The total amount of any money to be advanced by the employer with details of specific items, and the terms of repayment by the alien of any such advance by the employer;

(G) That in no event shall the alien be required to give more than two weeks' notice of intent to leave the employment contracted for and that the employer must give the alien at least two weeks' notice before terminating employment;

(H) That a duplicate contract has been furnished to the alien;

(I) That a private room and board will be provided at no cost to the worker; and

(J) Any other agreement or conditions not specified on the Application for Alien Employment Certification form; and

(iii)(A) Documentation of the alien's paid experience in the form of statements from past or present employers setting forth the dates (month and year) employment started and ended, hours of work per day, number of days worked per week, place where the alien worked, detailed statement of duties performed on the job, equipment and appliances used, and the amount of wages paid per week or month. The total paid experience must be equal to one full year's employment on a full-time basis. For example, two year's experience working half-days is the equivalent of one year's full time experience. Time spent in a household domestic service training course cannot be included in the required one year of paid experience.

(B) Each statement must contain the name and address of the person who signed it and show the date on which the statement was signed. A statement not in the English language shall be accompanied by a written translation into the English language certified by the translator as to the accuracy of the translation, and as to the translator's competency to translate.

(b) Except for labor certification applications involving occupations designated for special handling (see § 656.21a) and Schedule A occupations (see §§ 656.10 and 656.22), the employer shall submit, as a part of every labor certification application, on the Application for Alien Employment Certification form or in attachments, as appropriate, the following clear documentation:

(1) If the employer has attempted to recruit U.S. workers prior to filing the application for certification, the employer shall document the employer's reasonable good faith efforts to recruit U.S. workers without success through the Job Service System and/or through other labor referral and recruitment sources normal to the occupation:

(i) this documentation shall include documentation of the employer's recruitment efforts for the job opportunity which shall:

(A) List the sources the employer may have used for recruitment, including, but not limited to, advertising; public and/or private employment agencies; colleges or universities; vocational, trade, or technical schools; labor unions; and/or development or promotion from within the employer's organization;

(B) Identify each recruitment source by name;

(C) Give the number of U.S. workers responding to the employer's recruitment;

(D) Give the number of interviews conducted with U.S. workers;

(E) Specify the lawful job-related reasons for not hiring each U.S. worker interviewed; and

(F) Specify the wages and working conditions offered to the U.S. workers; and

(ii) If the employer advertised the job opportunity prior to filing the application for certification, the employer shall include also a copy of at least one such advertisement.

(2) The employer shall document that the job opportunity has been and is being described without unduly restrictive job requirements:

(i) The job opportunity's requirements, unless adequately documented as arising from business necessity:

(A) Shall be those normally required for the job in the United States;

(B) Shall be those defined for the job in the Dictionary of Occupational Titles (D.O.T.) including those for subclasses of jobs;

(C) Shall not include requirements for a language other than English.

(ii) If the job opportunity involves a combination of duties, for example engineer-pilot, the employer must document that it has normally employed persons for that combination of duties and/or workers customarily perform the combination of duties in the area of intended employment, and or the combination job opportunity is based on a business necessity.

(iii) If the job opportunity involves a requirement that the worker live on the employer's premises, the employer shall document adequately that the requirement is a business necessity.

(iv) If the job opportunity has been or is being described with an employer preference, the employer preference shall be deemed to be a job requirement for purposes of this paragraph (b)(2).

(3) Except for job opportunities for private households, the employer shall document that it has posted notices of the job opportunity at its place of business:

(i) Notices of the job opportunity posted by the employer shall contain the information required for advertisements by paragraph (g)(3) through (g)(8) of this section, except that they shall direct applicants to report to the employer, not the local employment service office;

(ii) Notices of the job opportunity shall be posted by the employer for at least 10 consecutive business days; shall be clearly visible and unobstructed while posted; and shall be posted in conspicuous places, where the employer's U.S. workers readily can read the posted notice on the way to or from their place of employment. Appropriate locations for posting notices of the job opportunity include, but are not limited to, locations in the immediate proximity of wage and hour notices required by 29 CFR 516.4 or occupational safety and health notices required by 29 CFR 1903.2(a).

(4) The employer shall document that its other efforts to locate and employ U.S. workers for the job opportunity, such as recruitment efforts by means of private employment agencies, labor unions, advertisements placed with radio or TV stations, recruitment at trade schools, colleges, and universities or attempts to fill the job opportunity by development or promotion from among its present employees, have been and continue to be unsuccessful. Such efforts may be required after the filing of an application if appropriate to the occupation.

(5) If unions are customarily used as a recruitment source in the area or industry, the employer shall document that they were unable to refer U.S. workers.

(6) The employer shall document that its requirements for the job opportunity, as described, represent the employer's actual minimum requirements for the job opportunity, and the employer has not hired workers with less training or experience for jobs similar to that involved in the job opportunity or that it is not feasible to hire workers with less training or experience than that required by the employer's job offer.

(7) If U.S. workers have applied for the job opportunity, the employer shall document that they were rejected solely for lawful job-related reasons.

(c) The local job service office shall determine if the application is for a labor certification involving Schedule A. If the application is for a Schedule A labor certification, the local job service office shall advise the employer that the forms must be filed with an INS or Consular Office pursuant to § 656.22, and shall explain that the Administrator has determined that U.S. workers in the occupation are unavailable throughout the United States (unless a geographic limitation is applicable) and that the employment of the alien in the occupation will not adversely affect U.S. workers similarly employed.

(d) The local office shall date stamp the application (see § 656.30 for the significance of this date), and shall make sure that the Application for Alien Employment Certification form is complete. If it is not complete the local office shall return it to the employer and shall advise the employer to refile it when it is completed.

(e) The local Job Service office shall calculate, to the extent of its expertise using wage information available to it, the prevailing wage for the job opportunity pursuant to § 656.40 and shall put its finding into writing. If the local office finds that the rate of wages offered is below the prevailing wage, it shall advise the employer in writing to increase the amount offered. If the employer refuses to do so, the local office shall advise the employer that the refusal is a ground for denial of the application by the Certifying Officer; and that if the denial becomes final, the application will have to be refiled at the local office as a new application.

(f) The local Job Service office, using the information on [the] job offer portion of the Application for Alien Employment Certification form, shall prepare and process a Job Service job order:

(1) If the job offer is acceptable, the local office, in cooperation with the employer, then shall attempt to recruit United States workers for the job opportunity for a period of thirty days, by placing the job order into the regular Job Service recruitment system.

(2) If the employer's job offer is discriminatory or otherwise unacceptable as a job order under the Job Service (JS) Regulations (as defined at § 651.7 of this chapter), the local office, as appropriate, either shall contact the employer to try to remedy the defect or shall return the Application for Alien Employment Certification form to the employer with instructions on how to remedy the defect. If the employer refuses to remedy the defect, the local office shall advise the employer that it is unable to recruit U.S. workers for the job opportunity and that the application will be transmitted to the Certifying Officer for determination.

(g) In conjunction with the recruitment efforts under paragraph (f) of this section, the employer shall place an advertisement for the job opportunity in a newspaper of general circulation or in a professional, trade, or ethnic publication, whichever is appropriate to the occupation and most likely to bring responses from able, willing, qualified, and available U.S. workers. The employer may request the local office's assistance in drafting the text. The advertisement shall:

(1) Direct applicants to report or send resumes, as appropriate for the occupation to the local Job Service office for referral to the employer;

(2) Include a local office identification number and the complete address or telephone number of the local office, but shall not identify the employer;

(3) Describe the job opportunity with particularity;

(4) State the rate of pay, which shall not be below the prevailing wage for the occupation, as calculated pursuant to § 656.40;

(5) Offer prevailing working conditions;

(6) State the employer's minimum job requirements;

(7) Offer training if the job opportunity is the type for which employers normally provide training;

(8) Offer wages, terms, and conditions of employment which are no less favorable than those offered to the alien; and

(9) If published in a newspaper of general circulation, be published for at least three consecutive days; or, if published in a professional, trade, or ethnic publication, be published in the next published edition.

(h) The employer shall supply the local office with required documentation or requested information in a timely manner. If documentation or requested information is not received within 45 calendar days of the date of the request the local office shall return the Application for Alien Employment Certification form, and any supporting documents submitted by the employer and/or the alien, to the employer to be filed as a new application.

(i) The Certifying Officer may reduce the employer's recruitment efforts required by paragraphs (b)(3), (f), and/or (g) of this section if the employer satisfactorily documents that the employer has adequately tested the labor market with no success at least at the prevailing wage and working conditions; but no such reduction may be granted for job offers involving occupations listed on Schedule B.

(1) To request a reduction of recruitment efforts pursuant to this paragraph (i), the employer shall file a written request along with the Application for Alien Employment Certification form at the appropriate local Job Service office. The request shall contain:

(i) Documentary evidence that within the immediately preceding six months the employer has made good faith efforts to recruit U.S. workers for the job opportunity, at least at the prevailing wage and working conditions, through sources normal to the occupation; and

(ii) Any other information which the employer believes will support the contention that further recruitment will be unsuccessful.

(2) Upon receipt of a written request for a reduction in recruitment efforts pursuant to this paragraph (i), the local office shall date stamp the request and the application form and shall review and process the application pursuant to this § 656.21, but without regard to paragraphs (b)(3), (f), and (g), and (j)(1) of this section (i.e., the internal notice, advertisement, and job order; and the wait for results).

(3) After reviewing and processing the application pursuant to paragraph (i)(2) of this section, the local office (and the State Job Service office) shall process the application pursuant to paragraphs (j)(2) and (k) of this section.

(4) The Certifying Officer shall review the documentation submitted by the employer and the comments of the local office. The Certifying Officer shall notify the employer and the local (or State employment service) office of the Certifying Officer's decision on the request to reduce partially or completely the recruitment efforts required of the employer.

(5) Unless the Certifying Officer decides to reduce completely the recruitment efforts required of the employer, the Certifying Officer shall return the application to the local (or State) office so that the employer might recruit workers to the extent required in the Certifying Officer's decision, and in the manner required by paragraphs (b)(3), (f), (g), and (j)(1) of this section (i.e., by internal notice, employment service job order, and advertising; and a wait for results). If the Certifying Officer decides to reduce completely the recruitment efforts required of the employer, the Certifying Officer then shall determine, pursuant to § 656.24 whether to grant or to deny the application.

(j)(1) The employer shall provide to the local office a written report of the results of all the employer's post-application recruitment efforts during the 30-day recruitment period; except that for job opportunities advertised in professional and trade, or ethnic publications, the written report shall be provided no less than 30 calendar days from the date of the publication of the employer's advertisement. The report of recruitment results shall:

(i) Identify each recruitment source by name;

(ii) State the number of U.S. workers responding to the employer's recruitment;

(iii) State the names, addresses, and provide resumes (if any) of the U.S. workers interviewed for the job opportunity and job title of the person who interviewed each worker; and

(iv) Explain, with specificity, the lawful job-related reasons for not hiring each U.S. worker interviewed.

(2) If, after the required recruitment period, the recruitment is not successful, the local office shall send the application, its prevailing wage finding, copies of all documents in the particular application file, and any additional appropriate information (such as local labor market data), to the Job Service agency's State office or, if authorized, to the regional Certifying Officer.

(k) A Job Service agency's State office which receives an application pursuant to paragraph (j)(2) of this section may add appropriate data or comments, and shall transmit the application promptly to the appropriate Certifying Officer.

20 C.F.R.§ 656.21a Applications for labor certifications for occupations designated for special handling.

(a) An employer shall apply for a labor certification to employ an alien as a college or university teacher or an alien represented to be of exceptional ability in the performing arts by filing, in duplicate, an Application for Alien Employment Certification form, and any attachments required by this Part, with the local Job Service office serving the area where the alien proposes to be employed.

(1) The employer shall set forth the following on the Application for Alien Employment Certification form, as appropriate, or in attachments:

(i) The employer shall submit a statement of the qualifications of the alien, signed by the alien.

(ii) The employer shall submit a full description of the job offer for the alien employment.

(iii) If the application involves a job offer as a college or university teacher, the employer shall submit documentation to show clearly that the employer selected the alien for the job opportunity pursuant to a competitive recruitment and selection process, through which the alien was found to be more qualified than any of the United States workers who applied for the job. For purposes of this paragraph (a)(1)(iii), evidence of the "competitive recruitment and selection process" shall include:

(A) A statement, signed by an official who has actual hiring authority, from the employer outlining in detail the complete recruitment procedure undertaken; and which shall set forth:

(1) The total number of applicants for the job opportunity;

(2) The specific lawful job-related reasons why the alien is more qualified than each U.S. worker who applied for the job; and

(3) A final report of the faculty, student, and/or administrative body making the recommendation or selection of the alien, at the completion of the competitive recruitment and selection process;

(B) A copy of at least one advertisement for the job opportunity placed in a national professional journal, giving the name and the date(s) of publication; and which states the job title, duties, and requirements;

(C) Evidence of all other recruitment sources utilized; and

(D) A written statement attesting to the degree of the alien's educational or professional qualifications and academic achievements.

(E) Applications for permanent alien labor certification which are filed after December 31, 1981, for job opportunities as college and university teachers, shall be filed within 18 months after a selection is made pursuant to a competitive recruitment and selection process.

(iv) If the application is for an alien represented to have exceptional ability in the performing arts, the employer shall document that the alien's work experience during the past twelve months did require, and the alien's intended work in the United States will require, exceptional ability; and shall submit:

(A) Documentation to show this exceptional ability, such as:

(1) Documents attesting to the current widespread acclaim and international recognition accorded to the alien, and receipt of internationally recognized prizes or awards for excellence;

(2) Published material by or about the alien, such as critical reviews or articles in major newspapers, periodicals, and/or trade journals (the title, date, and author of such material shall be indicated);

(3) Documentary evidence of earnings commensurate with the claimed level of ability;

(4) Playbills and star billings;

(5) Documents attesting to the outstanding reputation of theaters, concert halls, night clubs, and other establishments in which the alien has appeared, or is scheduled to appear; and/or

(6) Documents attesting to the outstanding reputation of repertory companies, ballet troupes, orchestras, or other organizations in which or with which the alien has performed during the past year in a leading or starring capacity; and

(B) A copy of at least one advertisement placed in a national publication appropriate to the occupation (and a statement of the results of that recruitment) which shall:

(1) Identify the employer's name, address, and the location of the employment, if other than the employer's location;

(2) Describe the job opportunity with particularity;

(3) State the rate of pay, which shall not be below the prevailing wage for the occupation, as calculated pursuant to § 656.40;

(4) Offer prevailing working conditions;

(5) State the employer's minimum job requirements;

(6) Offer training if the job opportunity is the type for which employers normally provide training; and

(7) Offer wages, terms, and conditions of employment which are no less favorable than those offered to the alien; and

(C) Documentation that unions, if customarily used as a recruitment source in the area or industry, were unable to refer equally qualified U.S. workers.

(2) The local Job Service office, upon receipt of an application for a college or university teacher or an alien represented to have exceptional ability in the performing

arts, shall follow the application processing and prevailing wage determination procedures set forth in §§ 656.21 (d) and (e), and shall transmit a file containing the application, the local office's prevailing wage findings, and any other information it determines is appropriate, to the State Job Service agency office, or if authorized by the State office, to the appropriate Certifying Officer.

(3) If the local Job Service office transmits the file described in paragraph (a)(3) of this section to the State office, the State office shall follow the procedures set forth at § 656.21(k).

(b)(1) An employer shall apply for a labor certification to employ an alien (who has been employed legally as a nonimmigrant sheepherder in the United States for at least 33 of the preceding 36 months) as a sheepherder by filing an Application for Alien Employment Certification form, and any attachments required by this paragraph (b), directly with a Department of State Consular Officer or with a District Office of INS, not with a local or State office of a State Job Service agency, and not with an office of DOL. The documentation for such an application shall include:

(i) A completed Application for Alien Employment Certification form, including the Job Offer for Alien Employment, and the Statement of Qualification of Alien; and

(ii) A signed letter or letters from all U.S. employers who have employed the alien as a sheepherder during the immediately preceding 36 months, attesting that the alien has been employed in the United States lawfully and continuously as a sheepherder, for at least 33 of the immediately preceding 36 months.

(2) An Immigration Officer, or a Consular Officer, shall review the application and the letters attesting to the alien's previous employment as a sheepherder in the United States, and shall determine whether or not the alien and the employer(s) have met the requirements of this paragraph (b).

(i) The determination of the Immigration or Consular Officer pursuant to this paragraph (b) shall be conclusive and final. The employer(s) and the alien, therefore, may not make use of the review procedures set forth at §§ 656.26 and 656.27.

(ii) If the alien and the employer(s) have met the requirements of this paragraph (b), the Immigration or Consular Officer shall indicate on the Application for Alien Employment Certification form the occupation, the immigration or consular office which made the determination pursuant to this paragraph (b), and the date of the determination (see § 656.30 for the significance of this date). The Immigration or Consular Officer then shall forward promptly to the Administrator copies of the Application for Alien Employment Certification form, without the attachments.

(c) If an application for a college or university teacher, an alien represented to be of exceptional ability in the performing arts, or a sheepherder does not meet the requirements for an occupation designated for special handling under this section, the application may be filed pursuant to § 656.21.

Employment Preference Classification

8 C.F.R. § 204.1(d)

(1) General. A petition to classify the status of an alien under section 203(a) (3) or (6) of the Act shall be filed on Form I-140. For each beneficiary a separate Form

I-140 must be submitted, accompanied by the fee required under § 103.7(b) of this chapter. Before the petition may be accepted and considered properly filed, the petitioner or authorized representative shall sign the visa petition (under penalty of perjury) in the block provided on the form. The petition must be accompanied by a completed Labor Department Form ETA 750, Application for Alien Employment Certification, including Part A, Offer of Employment, and Part B, Statement of Qualifications of Alien. The certification under section 212(a)(14) of the Act must be affixed to Part A of this form by the Secretary of Labor or the Secretary's designated representative, except that such certification may be omitted if the beneficiary is qualified for and will be engaged in an occupation currently listed in the Department of Labor's Schedule A (20 CFR Part 656). The petition shall be filed in the office of the Service having jurisdiction over the place of intended employment, except that when accompanied by an application for adjustment of status, a petition may be filed and a decision thereon made in the Service office having jurisdiction over the place where the beneficiary is residing.

* * *

(3) Filing date. In the case of a third- or sixth-preference petition (except for an occupation listed in Schedule A), the filing date of the petition within the meaning of section 203(c) of the Act will be the date the request for certification was accepted for processing by any office within the employment service system of the Department of Labor. If a third- or sixth-preference petition for an occupation listed in Schedule A is approved, the filing date of the petition shall be the date it is properly filed with the appropriate Service office. If a third- or sixth-preference petition for an occupation listed in Schedule A is not approved, no priority date shall be established.

(4) Sixth-preference petition for member of the professions or person having exceptional ability in the sciences or arts. Nothing contained in this part shall preclude an employer who desires and intends to employ an alien who is a member of the professions or a person having exceptional ability in the sciences or the arts from filing a petition for a sixth-preference classification; however, any such petition shall be subject to the requirements of this part governing sixth-preference petitions.

(5) Interview and decision. Prior to decision by the district director, the beneficiary and the petitioner may be required as a matter of discretion to appear in person before an immigration or consular officer and be interrogated under oath concerning the allegations in the petition. The petitioner shall be notified of the decision and, if the petition is denied, of the reasons therefor and of his right to appeal in accordance with the provisions of Part 103 of this chapter. However, no appeal shall lie from a decision denying a petition for lack of a certification by the Secretary of Labor pursuant to section 212(a)(14) of the Act.

Priority Dates

8 C.F.R. § 204.6. Effect of changed employment on priority dates.

(a) Petition for third preference classification. When the beneficiary of an approved third preference petition no longer intends to accept employment with the prospective employer or the offer of employment is withdrawn, the petition shall be deemed invalid and the beneficiary shall no longer be entitled to a priority date as of the date of filing of the petition. However, upon submission of a new Job Offer for Alien Employment form, and an individual labor certification under section 212(a)(14) in the case of an occupation not listed in Schedule A, the petition shall be deemed reinstated with the original priority date. The provisions of the paragraph shall not apply when the original petition has been revoked under section 203(e) of the Act.

(b) Petition for sixth-preference classification. When a new petition by another employer is approved in behalf of the beneficiary of a previously approved sixth-preference petition, and the beneficiary has accepted or intends to accept employment with the new petitioner, the beneficiary shall no longer be entitled to a priority date as of the date of filing of the original petition and that petition shall be deemed invalid. Instead, his priority date shall be the date of filing of the subsequently approved petition for sixth-preference classification. However, the original petition shall be deemed reinstated and the original priority date shall be restored if the beneficiary returns to the original petitioner's employment or established that he intends upon arrival in the United States to be employed by the original employer as specified in the original petition. The provisions of this paragraph shall not apply when the original petition has been revoked under section 203(e) of the Act.

Chapter 9

Adjustment of Status

It has been said that obtaining lawful permanent resident status is one of the most important steps in a foreigner's effort to stay in this country. While obtaining lawful permanent residence may not be the goal of all aliens arriving at our shores, it is certainly the objective of a substantial number of them.

In addition to severely limiting the numbers of foreigners who may remain in the U.S. for more than just a short period of time, the immigration laws were designed to allow only a limited number of persons to change their status to that of a permanent resident while remaining in the U.S. This is distinguished from the case of someone who is outside of the United States and seeking to immigrate based on a family relationship or a petitioning employer in this country.[1] Our discussion in this section will concentrate on the person who has already entered and wishes to obtain permanent residency, without first having to return to her country.[2]

The procedure of "adjustment of status," when favorable, results in the granting of permanent residence. Adjustment of status is a procedural benefit made available to a narrow group who meet specific criteria as set out in the statute. The statute which governs this area is 8 U.S.C. § 1254, Sec. 245 of the Act.[3] A condition precedent to qualifying for adjustment of status is establishment of the requisite familial relationship with a permanent resident or U.S. citizen,[4] or the offer of a job in the U.S. which will not displace a qualified, willing, and able U.S. worker. Once the person establishes the requisite familial relationship or job offer, she has only met the first step in a rather difficult process. At this point she must also establish the following:

    1. That she was "inspected and admitted or paroled into the United States."[5]

    2. That there is an immigrant visa "immediately available" to her at the time that the application for adjustment of status is filed.[6]

---

    1. A person applying for permanent residence from *outside* the U.S. is an applicant for an immigrant visa, which upon obtaining the visa and passing inspection converts her to lawful permanent resident (LPR) status. Immigrant visas are discussed in Chapter 7.

    2. As will be seen later, the fact that a person cannot "adjust" her status to that of a lawful permanent resident does not necessarily mean that he cannot eventually enter the country with an immigrant visa.

    3. This most particular statutory provision precludes the admission of most aliens who lack what is referred to as a labor certification. *See* 8 U.S.C. § 1182(a)(5), Sec. 212(a)(5) of the INA. The major exceptions to this certification requirement are persons fleeing persecution and those seeking admission as family-based immigrants. *See* 8 U.S.C. § 1153(a), 203(a). For a more detailed discussion of the labor certification requirement, *see* Chapter 8.

    4. The familial relationship must meet the requirements that were discussed in the section on immigrant visas. *See* Chapter 7.

    5. 8 U.S.C. § 1255(a), Sec. 245(a).

    6. 8 U.S.C. § 1255(a)(2), Sec. 245(a)(2).

3. That she was lawfully in status at the time of filing the application, except in the case of persons who are immediate relatives of U.S. citizens.[7]

4. That she is otherwise eligible for admission to the U.S.: the person must not be excludable, or if she is excludable she must be eligible for a waiver of the grounds of excludability.[8]

5. That the person, other than those applying as immediate relatives of U.S. citizens, has not engaged in unauthorized employment after January 1, 1977.

After meeting these requirements the applicant must also convince the Attorney General (immigration officer) that the "discretionary relief" or benefit of adjustment of status should be granted.

Conditional and Temporary Residence

As was noted in our discussion of family-based preference petitions (Chapter 7), the Immigration Marriage Fraud Amendments (IMFA) restrict the accordance of immigration benefits including adjustment of status to persons who marry while they are in deportation proceedings. The IMFA was amended in 1990 as follows: 1) where the applicant can establish by "clear and convincing evidence" satisfactory to the INS that the marriage was entered into "in good faith" she will not be precluded from adjustment because she was married after the commencement of deportation proceedings and 2) where the alien beneficiary (spouse or child) was the victim of cruelty caused by the U.S. citizen or lawful permanent resident spouse, the fact that the marriage no longer exists will not preclude the person from adjustment of status. *See* Section 702, of the Immigration Act of 1990, Pub. L. No. 101-649, 104 Stat. 4978 [amending 8 U.S.C. § 1255(e), Sec. 245(e)]; 8 U.S.C. § 1186(c)(4)(C), Sec. 216(c) (4)(C). The statute has general language allowing for a discretionary hardship waiver for the beneficiary spouse who has entered into a bona fide marriage and can show that extreme hardship would result due to the denial of the permanent residency petition. In addition, the statute provides that an applicant will receive conditional residence for two years and later permanent residence where the benefit being sought is on account of her marriage. *See* 8 U.S.C. § 1186a, Sec. 216. This conditional residence is also imposed on the children of the beneficiary. Congress' creation of a conditional residence status was an anomaly in immigration law. In the past, persons would move from a nonimmigrant status to full permanent residency without passing through this intermediate step. As will be seen in our later discussion, this temporary or conditional status was also created for persons illegally in the United States who received the benefit of "legalization."

Registry

In 1986 Congress enacted amendments to the immigration law which allowed millions of undocumented persons, otherwise illegally in the country, to legalize their

---

7. Prior to enactment of the Immigration Reform and Control Act of 1986, Pub. L. No. 99-603, 100 Stat. 3359 (1986), an applicant could adjust her status even when her permission to stay in the U.S. had expired. The requirement of maintaining one's status does not apply if the person is out of status "through no fault of her own" or for technical reasons.

8. *Id.* Waivers of excludability are discussed in Chapter 12.

status. The amnesty or "legalization" was accomplished through amendments to the adjustment of status provisions of the 1952 Act. Amnesty is very similar to the long-standing immigration benefit known as "registry," which from time to time has been used to legalize the immigration status of those with long-term residency in the U.S.[9] Registry provides that those persons who have resided continuously in the U.S. since January 1, 1972 may apply to have their status adjusted to that of a lawful permanent resident.[10] The essential requirements for qualifying for registry are: continuous residency, good moral character, and not being inadmissible on grounds of criminal conviction/s, narcotics or subversive grounds, or being otherwise ineligible for U.S. citizenship.[11]

Amnesty or Legalization

There were two legalization programs, one for non-agricultural workers and the other for agricultural workers. Both of these programs provide for a two-tiered resident status for its beneficiaries.[12] Both legalization plans included cut-off dates for eligibility as well as residency requirements. The primary difference between the plans is that the cut-off date covering when the applicant must have entered the U.S. in order to qualify is more generous in the agricultural worker program.

Upon qualification, the applicant received only a temporary or conditional status which can be converted in two or more years to full lawful permanent residency. In order to obtain *temporary resident* status, the applicant must have resided unlawfully in the U.S. since before January 1, 1982. The unlawful status must have been continuous, and the applicant must have shown that she had resided in this country since that date to the present. The application must be filed within a 12-month period (beginning not later than six months after enactment of the amendments). The rules governing the applications were as follows:

1. Persons upon whom a show cause order had been issued during the first 11 months of the amnesty must have applied for temporary resident status not later than 30 days after the implementation of rules regarding the application procedure or within 30 days from the issuance of the order to show cause.

2. In establishing residence, although the applicant must have established that she had been physically present since January 1, 1982, "brief, casual, and innocent absences" did not break the continuity of residence.[13]

---

9. The registry provisions are found at 8 U.S.C. § 1259, Sec. 249. Like all adjustment applications, a registry application is subject to a favorable exercise of discretion by the INS district director.

10. In addition to granting amnesty, the 1986 amendments changed the registry date from June 30, 1948 to January 1, 1972.

11. The original purpose of registry was to allow long-term residents to obtain citizenship and thus ineligibility for citizenship would preclude an alien's receiving the benefit. As will be seen later in Chapter 12, certain grounds of ineligibility may be waived by the Attorney General.

12. For discussion of the legalization program for agricultural workers, see the discussion which follows under that heading.

13. *See* amendment to 8 U.S.C. § 1255a(a)(3)(B), Sec. 245A.

3. Exchange visitors subject to the foreign residency requirement and ineligible for its waiver were not eligible for the amnesty.[14]

4. The applicant must also have established that she was otherwise admissible as an immigrant and had not been convicted of a felony or three or more misdemeanors committed in the U.S. All grounds of exclusion were either disregarded or waived except the following:

a. 8 U.S.C. §§ 1182 (a)(14), (20), (21), (25), and (32) are inapplicable.[15]

b. All grounds except 8 U.S.C. §§ 1182 (a)(9), (10), (15), (23), (27)-(29), and (33) are waivable.[16]

5. Temporary residents may not petition for their family members to join them in the U.S. although they may travel abroad for "brief, casual trips as reflect an intention" to become a lawful permanent resident.[17]

In order to qualify for *permanent residence*, the applicant must first have been granted temporary residence and must have remained lawfully in that status for at least one year. The requirements are as follows:

1. The alien *must* apply during the one-year period beginning with the nineteenth month after she was granted temporary residence.

2. She must show that she has continuously resided in the U.S. since obtaining temporary residence status. A break in the continuity of residence will be treated the same as it would if the person were applying for temporary residence.

3. The applicant must continue to be admissible as an immigrant under the same provisions as when she applied for temporary residence.

4. The applicant must demonstrate that she has certain "basic citizenship skills" described as: a minimal understanding of ordinary English, and knowledge of history and government of the U.S. as required of applicants for naturalization. Alternatively, the applicant may be "satisfactorily" pursuing a course of study to satisfy the language and history requirement. Meeting this requirement satisfies the language and civic knowledge requirement which would normally be required of applicants for U.S. citizenship.[18]

A person will lose her temporary resident status if it appears to the Attorney General that she was not entitled to it in the first place; if she commits an act rendering her inadmissible; or if by the end of the forty-third month after the date upon which

---

14. For further explanation of the foreign residency requirement, *see* 8 U.S.C. § 1101 (a)(15)(J) 101(a)(15)(J); Chapter 6.

15. These provisions deal with the exclusion grounds barring most immigrants without labor certification, prohibiting the admission of illiterates, and prohibiting the admission of foreign medical school graduates.

16. These provisions deal with persons who are excludable because they are likely to become public charges, have been convicted of drug offenses (except for possession of small amounts of marihuana), are Communists, national security risks, or Nazis.

17. It appears that the trips contemplated under the statute are those involving family obligations such as death or illness of a close relative or for another type of family need. *See* amendments to 8 U.S.C. § 1255a(b)(3)(A), Sec. 245A(b)(3)(A).

18. Persons 65 years or older may have the language and history requirements waived.

she obtained temporary residence she has not filed an application for permanent residence under this bill.

Unlike the farmworker provisions, the reform statute does not provide for amnesty applications to be made before U.S. consuls abroad. The only possible options for an otherwise qualified applicant who has left the U.S. for a short period would be to request parole (or enter the country surreptitiously) and then apply for amnesty.[19] The residency application may be filed with the Attorney General, or with a "designated entity"[20] (if the applicant consents to the forwarding of the application to the Attorney General).

Residence and physical presence must be "established" through documents and "independent corroboration," yet it is not clear from the legislation what specific documentation is required. The amendments clearly evidence a preference for "employment related documentation" whenever possible. Whatever the level of proof that is required of the applicant, it appears from the language of the statute that Congress wished to leave the decision to the discretion of the INS adjudicators. This documentation provision must be viewed in light of the section requiring the alien to establish residency and employment by a "preponderance of the evidence" test. It appears only reasonable, given the tremendous benefit being granted to the farm worker for such a short period of residency, that a more rigorous test would be called for.

Special Agricultural Workers

Agricultural workers who meet the following requirements are eligible to become "alien[s] lawfully admitted for temporary residence."

1. The person must apply within a period of 18 months, beginning 7 months after the enactment of the amendment.

2. The person must be able to show that she has worked for at least 90 man-days during the 12-month period ending May 1, 1986.

3. She must be otherwise admissible as an immigrant. (This provision is the same as that for other persons applying under the amnesty provisions.)

4. Following the granting of temporary residence the Attorney General will accord "lawful permanent resident" status at the following times:

Group 1 consisting of the first 350,000 applicants who have established eligibility. They will become lawful permanent residents 1 year after the date upon which they became "lawful temporary residents."

---

19. Absences caused by a person's having been on "advance parole" are specifically treated as not constituting a break in the period of continuous residence. Section 201, amending, 8 U.S.C. § 1254a(g)(2)(B)(ii), Sec. 245A(g)(2)(B)(ii). Advance parole is parole issued to a person prior to her departure from the U.S., authorizing her return in the status.

20. The statute provides for voluntary organizations to assist the government in the processing of applications under both the agricultural and non-agricultural workers' programs. The designated agency is not authorized to adjudicate the application but acts as a screener. In order to make an amnesty program work, it is very important that the applicant believe that the adjudication system is fair. Given the great distrust of the INS, the voluntary agencies (organizations such as those involved in refugee resettlement) played a critical role in the legalization process.

Group 2 will consist of the remainder of persons qualified to become lawful permanent residents over the 350,000 accorded temporary residence. Members of this group will become lawful permanent residents 1 year after the end of the application period for temporary status.

In addition, a person's status as a temporary resident shall be terminated upon a determination that she has become deportable. The temporary resident may travel abroad and shall be granted employment authorization in the form of a document issued by the INS.

The person applying for the farm labor benefit has the burden of establishing eligibility by a "preponderance of the evidence" test. The burden may be met by showing the employer's records. The applicant may also show that she in fact was employed by producing sufficient evidence to show the extent of the employment as a matter of just and reasonable inference. In these cases the burden then shifts to the Attorney General to negate the reasonableness of the inference.

There are no numerical limitations on the number of persons who may become permanent residents under the amendment other than those described above in the special agricultural workers section. Moreover, most of the grounds for exclusion are inapplicable and others are waived.[21]

An anomaly was created by the amnesty provisions of the Immigration Reform and Control Act of 1986. The spouse and children of these legalized persons were not eligible for legalization unless they could show that they had entered the United States prior to January 1, 1982 or had worked for the requisite period on a farm before May 1, 1986. Congress enacted the family unity provisions in the 1990 Act which provide some of these people with protection from deportation and employment authorization.[22] In addition, the 1990 Act provides the spouse and minor children of legalized persons with the possibility of obtaining permanent residence outside of the traditional statutory scheme. In fiscal years 1992-1994, 55,000 immigrant visas will be made available to the spouse and children of legalized persons under both amnesty programs.[23] The family unity provisions do not enable otherwise unqualified persons to adjust their status, but instead allows them to stay in the U.S. until they can have their immigrant visa petition processed.[24]

---

21. The applicability of the exclusion provisions are the same as those relating to the "general" amnesty. The primary difference is that 8 U.S.C. § 1182(a)(15), Sec. 212(a)(15) (public charge provision) is to be interpreted liberally by the INS, where the applicant's employment history evidences self-support.

22. *See* Sec. 301, Immigration Act of 1990, Pub. L. No. 101-649, 104 Stat. 4978. The protected group includes those who are the spouse or unmarried child of a legalized person or beneficiary of a permanent resident under the legalization program. Unprotected members are those who have been convicted of a felony or three or more misdemeanors, who participated in the persecution of others, who present a threat to the security of the United States or who have been convicted of a particularly serious crime constituting a danger to the community. Sec. 301(e), Immigration Act of 1990, Pub. L. No. 101-649, 104 Stat. 4978 (1990).

23. These visas will be reduced by the number of visas issued to immediate relatives and aliens born to lawfully admitted aliens, calculated as of the prior fiscal year, which exceeds 239,000. *See* Sec. 112(a)(1), Immigration Act of 1990, Pub. L. No. 101-649, 104 Stat. 4978.

24. This is the same program referred to as "transition immigrants" in Chapter 7.

References

Carrasco, *The Golden Moment of Legalization*, X In Defense of the Alien 32 (1987)

Carrasco, *The Implementation of the American Legalization Experiment in Recent Retrospect*, XI In Defense of the Alien 30 (1988)

Guendelsberger, *Implementing Family Unification Rights in American Immigration Law*, 25 San Diego L. Rev. 227 (1988)

The Proverbial Catch-22: Unconstitutionality of Section Five of the Immigration Marriage Fraud Amendments of 1986, 25 Cal. W. L. Rev. 1 (1988)

Sanger, *Immigration Reform and Control of the Undocumented Family*, 2 Geo. Imm. L. J. 295 (1987)

Tucker, *Assimilation to the United States: A Study of the Adjustment of Status and the Immigration Marriage Fraud Statutes*, 7 Yale L. & Pol'y Rev. 20, 82-100 (1989)

A. "[I]nspected and [A]dmitted . . ."

8 U.S.C. § 1255, Sec. 245

(a) The status of an alien who was inspected and admitted or paroled into the United States may be adjusted by the Attorney General, in his discretion and under such regulations as he may prescribe, to that of an alien lawfully admitted for permanent residence if (1) the alien makes an application for such adjustment, (2) the alien is eligible to receive an immigrant visa and is admissible to the United States for permanent residence, and (3) an immigrant visa is immediately available to him at the time his application is filed.

(b) Upon the approval of an application for adjustment made under subsection (a) of this section, the Attorney General shall record the alien's lawful admission for permanent residence as of the date the order of the Attorney General approving the application for the adjustment of status is made, and the Secretary of State shall reduce by one the number of the preference or nonpreference visas authorized to be issued under sections 1152(e) or 1153(a) of this title within the class to which the alien is chargeable for the fiscal year then current.

Matter of Areguillin

17 I. & N. Dec. 308 (BIA 1980)

In a decision dated January 25, 1978, an immigration judge found the respondent deportable as charged on the basis of her concessions at the hearing, denied her application for adjustment of status pursuant to section 245 of the Immigration and Nationality Act, 8 U.S.C. 1255, but granted her the privilege of voluntary departure in lieu of deportation. The respondent has appealed from the denial of relief under section 245. The appeal will be sustained and the record remanded for further proceedings before the immigration judge.

The respondent, a 45-year-old native and citizen of Mexico, claims eligibility for adjustment on the basis of her status as the beneficiary of an approved immediate relative visa petition which had been filed on her behalf by her United States citizen spouse. The immigration judge found that the respondent had not been inspected and admitted at the time of her last entry into the United States and therefore has not satisfied the statutory requirements for the relief sought under section 245 of the Act.

The respondent offered the following account with respect to the entry in issue. The respondent testified that she crossed the Mexican-United States border in a car with two couples and another woman. She had no travel or entry documents in her possession at the time. The respondent stated that the immigration officer at the port of entry looked inside the car, asked the driver a question, then permitted the car and its occupants to proceed into the United States. She testified that she personally was asked no questions by the immigration officer; she apparently volunteered no information.

The immigration judge concluded as a matter of law that the manner of entry described by the respondent does not establish an inspection and admission for purposes of section 245 inasmuch as the respondent was in fact inadmissible for lack of documentation at the time she presented herself for inspection. The immigration judge sought to distinguish the well-established line of cases which holds that an alien who physically presents himself for questioning is "inspected" even though he volunteers no information and is asked no questions by the immigration authorities. *See Matter of F—*, 1 I&N Dec. 90 (BIA 1941; A.G. 1941); *Matter of F—*, 1 I&N Dec. 343 (BIA 1942); *Matter of G—*, 3 I&N Dec. 136 (BIA 1948). He noted that the burden was on the Government in the foregoing cases to show, as part of its burden of establishing deportability, that inspection had not occurred while in the present case, the respondent bears the burden of proving she had been inspected as an element of establishing her eligibility for adjustment.

We agree with the respondent that the immigration judge's distinction is without a difference in determining what constitutes "inspection and admission." We find no basis for concluding that Congress, in first imposing the requirement that an alien be "inspected and admitted" or paroled into the United States as a condition for establishing eligibility for relief under section 245, intended to depart from the long-settled construction of that term in favor of the interpretation adopted by the immigration judge, i.e., that only an alien who has been "lawfully or legally" admitted to the United States may qualify for adjustment of status as one who has been inspected and admitted. Regardless of which party bears the burden of establishing the presence or absence of an inspection and admission, that which must be proved remains unchanged. The rule that an alien has not entered without inspection when he presented himself for inspection and made no knowing false claim to citizenship applies in determining whether an alien has satisfied the inspection and admission requirement of section 245 of the Act.

We are satisfied that if the facts are found to be as claimed by the respondent, she was inspected and admitted within the contemplation of the law. The respondent, however, bears the burden of proving that she did, in fact, present herself for inspection. Inasmuch as the immigration judge found the respondent ineligible as a matter of law for adjustment under section 245, he made no finding with respect to the credibility or sufficiency of the evidence offered, which at present consists of the respondent's uncorroborated testimony. We shall accordingly remand the record to the immigration judge for further proceedings, during which the respondent should be accorded an opportunity to offer any additional evidence she may be able to produce in support of her assertions, and for the entry of a new decision. In the event the decision on remand is again adverse to the respondent, we direct that the case be certified back to the Board for review.

Finally, the respondent for the first time on appeal argues that termination of these proceedings is required by the Temporary Restraining Order entered in *Silva v. Levi*, No. 76-C4268 (N.D. Ill. March 22, 1977; as amended April 1, 1977), which enjoins the Service from initiating, continuing, or concluding any effort to expel an alien within the plaintiff class, and further enjoins the Board from dismissing an alien's appeal or sustaining a Service appeal in a deportation case involving such alien, unless it has been determined that the alien is ineligible to receive an immigrant visa or that his continued presence in this country is contrary to the national interest or security. We find no merit in her contention.

The class of aliens protected by the Silva injunction is defined as follows:

> ... natives of independent countries of the Western Hemisphere who have priority dates for the issuance of immigrant visas between July 1, 1986 and December 31, 1976, whose priority dates have not been reached for processing or who have not been called for final views.

Silva v. Bell, supra, "Findings of Fact," Para. 9. The protected class is comprised of aliens who should have been issued one of 144,999 visa numbers which were assigned to Cuban refugees and wrongfully charged against the annual Western Hemisphere quota between July 1968 and October 1976. The respondent, as an immediate relative not subject to the numerical limitations of the Act, did not receive a priority date for the allocation of a visa number and was in no manner affected by the unlawful charging policy which the Silva order seeks to remedy. We conclude that immediate relatives and other aliens exempted from the numerical limitations of the Act are not within the purview of the Silva injunction.

B. "Unauthorized Employment"

8 U.S.C. § 1255(c), Sec. 245(c)

Subsection (a) of this section shall not be applicable to (1) an alien crewman; (2) an alien (other than an immediate relative as defined in section 1151(b) of this title or a special immigrant described in section 1101(a)(27)(H) of this title) who hereafter continues in or accepts unauthorized employment prior to filing an application for adjustment of status; or who is not in legal immigration status on the date of filing the application for adjustment of status or who has failed (other than through no fault of his own for technical reasons) to maintain continuously a legal status since entry into the United States; or (3) any alien admitted in transit without visa under section 1182(d)(4)(C) of this title; or (5)* an alien (other than an immediate relative as defined in section 1151(b) of this title) who was admitted as a nonimmigrant visitor without a visa under section 1182(l) or section 1187 of this title.

---

* No clause (4) has been enacted.

Matter of Hall

8 I. & N. Dec. 203 (BIA 1982)

At a deportation hearing conducted on December 19, 1978, an immigration judge found the respondent deportable as an overstayed nonimmigrant pursuant to section 241(a)(2) of the Immigration and Nationality Act, 8 U.S.C. 1251(a)(2), and statutorily ineligible for adjustment of status under section 245 of the Act, 8 U.S.C. 1255, by reason of the unauthorized employment bar of section 245(c)(2), 8 U.S.C. 1255(c)(2), but granted him the privilege of voluntary departure in lieu of deportation. The respondent concedes deportability but contests the denial of section 245 relief.

At the conclusion of the deportation hearing, as the immigration judge was stating his decision, the respondent through counsel made an oral motion to reopen the proceedings to permit further development of the record with respect to his eligibility for adjustment of status. The immigration judge declared the hearing closed and refused to entertain the respondent's motion to reopen. Subsequent to the hearing, on December 26, 1978, the respondent submitted a formal, written motion to reopen which the immigration judge denied in a decision dated February 14, 1979. The respondent appealed from that decision and oral argument in the case was heard by the Board on May 1, 1980.

In seeking to reopen deportation proceedings, it is incumbent upon the alien to make a prima facie showing of eligibility for the relief sought. *Matter of Rodriguez*, 17 I & N Dec. 105 (BIA 1979). The respondent has not sustained his burden. Upon careful consideration of the arguments advanced by the respondent since the hearing, we are satisfied that section 245(c)(2) operates to bar adjustment in his case. As no purpose would be served by reopening, the respondent's appeal from the denial of his motion to reopen will be dismissed.

The record reflects that the respondent, a 36-year-old single male, a native and citizen of Guyana, entered the United States at New York in May 1976 upon presentation of a nonimmigrant visitor visa. He came to the United States for the purpose of attending a rally sponsored by the Unification Church at Yankee Stadium. In July 1976, the respondent departed New York for Puerto Rico to "work . . . as a missionary" for the Unification Church (Tr. p. 9), a pursuit in which he is apparently still engaged.

According to the respondent, his duties as a missionary consist of holding and attending seminars, witnessing, visiting houses and teaching people on the street the word of God, distributing literature, helping people financially under Church auspices, and visiting churches. Those duties also include selling toys, jewelry and trinkets as a means of raising funds for the Church. The respondent estimates that he spends from one-third to one-half of his time fund-raising.

The respondent testified that the proceeds of his fund-raising efforts are turned over to the Director of the Church in Puerto Rico with whom he shares a rented house. In return, the respondent receives full support from the Church which includes housing, food, clothing, medical expenses, transportation, entertainment, toiletries, and other personal expenses. In addition, the respondent is given approximately $25 in cash each month for "walking around" money, enough to ensure that he has $10 in pocket money at all times.

The unauthorized employment bar of section of 245(c)(2), added by the 1976 Amendments to the Act, renders ineligible for adjustment of status aliens (other than immediate relatives) who, after the effective date of the bar, continued in or accepted unauthorized employment prior to filing an adjustment application. The respondent continued his activities on behalf of the Unification Church, which he does not contend were authorized by the Service, after the January 1, 1977, effective date of the bar. His adjustment application, based upon his status as the beneficiary of an approved second-preference visa petition submitted by his lawful permanent resident mother, was not filed under May 1977. The dispositive question, then, is whether those activities constitute "employment" within the contemplation of section 245(c)(2). The immigration judge answered that question in the affirmative, concluding that the respondent was employed as a fund-raiser for the Church.

The respondent contends that the activities in question may not properly be characterized as employment so as to bar him from the benefits of section 245. He describes his position with the Church as an unpaid volunteer, not an employee, arguing that he labors for no salary. He submits that his service as a missionary is not the type of pursuit Congress contemplated in enacting section 245(c)(2). Finally, the respondent argues that his fund-raising efforts and his teaching, proselytizing, and other religious duties are integral, indivisible parts of his missionary work and that it is not within the province of the Immigration and Naturalization Service or the immigration judge to determine what constitutes missionary work for any particular church.

The respondent's contention that he is an unpaid volunteer in the service of the Church is not persuasive. He clearly receives compensation in return for his efforts on behalf of the Church. By his own account, he is provided the wherewithal to cover both necessary and nonessential expenses, such as entertainment, and recreation. He is, in addition, given discretionary funds as needed. The respondent's relationship with the Church in effect guarantees him a standard of living similar to that of many moderate-income wage earners. The fact that he receives no fixed salary or remuneration in an amount proportional to his success as a fund-raiser is, in our view, immaterial.

The respondent insists that his work on behalf of the Unification Church is not the sort of undertaking Congress intended to discourage with the imposition of the unauthorized employment bar inasmuch as his activities have no adverse impact on the United States labor force. As the respondent acknowledges, however, the legislative history of section 245(c)(2) provides little guidance as to the specific end or ends sought to be served by the bar. Congress' sole statement of purpose, contained in the House judiciary Committee report to the 1976 Amendments, reads as follows:

> ... [under the proposed legislation,] aliens who are not defined as immediate relatives and who accept unauthorized employment prior to filing their adjustment application would be ineligible for adjustment of status. The Committee believes that this provision would deter many nonimmigrants from violating the conditions of their admission by obtaining unauthorized employment. Similar provisions were included in legislation which was passed by the House of Representatives during the 92d and 93d Congresses.

(Emphasis added.)

Concern over the impact of a nonimmigrant's unauthorized employment upon the American labor force may well have been a motivating factor underlying the enactment of section 245(c)(2). However, Congress did not so indicate, either indirectly in the legislative history of the proposal ultimately enacted or directly in the express language of the statute. Absent a clear expression of legislative intent, we are unwilling to conclude that detriment to American labor was Congress' sole or, for that matter, primary concern.

Manifest in the report language quoted above is Congress' substantial interest— apart from its arguable interest in protecting the domestic labor market—in the enforcement of our immigration laws with respect to nonimmigrant aliens within our borders. Cf. *Matter of Yazdani*, 17 I & N Dec. 626 (BIA 1981). Correlatively, by penalizing nonimmigrants who work in violation of the terms of their admission, Congress may well have sought to discourage aliens admitted to the United States for a temporary purpose from acquiring a source of funds to support a prolonged unlawful stay in this country.

In any event, we are not persuaded that the respondent's activities as a fund-raiser are without adverse impact on the United States labor market. Unlike the purely ministerial duties carried on by the respondent, we consider the raising of funds a secular function which could successfully be performed by persons or business enterprises outside the Church. We note, moreover, that the respondent does not merely solicit donations in the name of the Unification Church but engages in the sale of goods, an entrepreneurial undertaking which places the Church in competition with other sellers of such goods.

Under the circumstances here presented, were the institution or organization for which the respondent performs his fund-raising services not a church, we would have no difficulty in finding the section 245(c)(2) bar applicable. We find no basis in the language or history of the statute for carving out an exception to the bar in the case of a church, at least with respect to the secular activities of its adherents.

We reject the respondent's suggestion that the Government, by isolating his fund-raising activities, improperly seeks to dictate to the Unification Church the permissible scope of its missionaries' duties. Determining the status or the duties of an individual within a religious organization is one thing; determining whether that individual qualifies for status or benefits under our immigration laws is another. Authority over the latter determination lies not with the Unification Church or any other ecclesiastical body but with the secular authorities of the United States. See *Matter of Rhee*, 16 I & N Dec. 607 (BIA 1978).

In sum, we conclude that the respondent, through his fund-raising activities, engaged in employment without Service permission in contravention of section 245(c)(2) and consequently is not eligible to adjust his status in this country to that of a lawful permanent resident. His motion to reopen the proceedings to permit consideration of his application for adjustment of status under section 245 was, therefore, properly denied. The appeal will be dismissed.

Notes

1. As was noted in our discussion on fraudulent marriages in Chapter VII, the INS has been plagued by "fraudulent" marriages entered into with the purpose of helping intending immigrants to remain in the United States. When Congress enacted

the reform legislation in 1986, it also enacted the Marriage Fraud Amendments, Act of November 10, 1986, Pub. L. No. 99-639, 100 Stat. 3537. One section of the Marriage Fraud Amendments modified 8 U.S.C. § 1255(e), Sec. 245(e) by restricting adjustment of status of persons who marry *while* they are in deportation or exclusion proceedings. The 1990 Act attempts to ameliorate the consequences of a marriage entered into during the pendency of deportation proceedings. Consider 8 U.S.C. § 1255(e), Sec. 245(e) as amended in 1990, [a copy of which appears at p. 365 in Chapter 7]. Is this statute constitutional? How would you challenge this statute? What problems do you think will continue to plague persons in deportation proceedings because of this bar to adjustment? For an excellent exploration of the constitutional implications of IMFA, *see* Tucker, *Assimilation to the United States: A Study of the Adjustment of Status and the Immigration Marriage Fraud Statutes*, 7 Yale L. & Pol'y Rev. 20, 82–100 (1989): *Manwani v. U.S. DOJ*, 736 F. Supp. 1367 (W.D. N.C. 1990) (holding the provisions unconstitutional); *Almario v. Attorney General*, 872 F. 2d 147 (6th Cir. 1989) (upholding the constitutionality of the provisions).

2. The preclusion from becoming a lawful permanent resident also requires the would-be immigrant who marries to reside outside of the United States for a period of two years beginning after the date of the marriage before she can become a permanent resident.

3. The statute precludes from adjustment of status, beneficiaries other than immediate relatives who are not in a legal status at the time that the application is filed. *See* 8 U.S.C. § 1255(c)(2). The preclusion is inapplicable to those who are not in "legal status...through no fault of his own for technical reasons." *See* 8 C.F.R. § 245.1(c)(2). How should the term "legal immigration status" be interpreted? What standard should be applied in determining who was not in status? What should be the standard applied by the courts in reviewing INS interpretation of this statutory language?

C. Employment Authorization

Lawful permanent resident status, whether obtained through adjustment or the immigrant visa procedure, accords the beneficiary the right to engage in employment and travel in and out of the United States. Employment authorization is a benefit which is also of importance to those who may not be permanent residents. For example, an alien seeking asylum or who is married to a U.S. citizen may need to work pending the adjudication of her application.

The employer sanction provisions coupled with the employee verification procedures which were discussed earlier[25] make it particularly difficult for persons in the U.S. who do not have permanent residence to be employed. Moreover, the preclusion against "unauthorized employment" contained in 8 U.S.C. § 1255(c), Sec. 245(c) requires that the alien take great pain not to violate the proscription. The following regulations control the INS power to grant employment authorization.

---

25. *See* Chapter 3.

Authorized Incident to Status
8 C.F.R. § 274a.12(a)

... [T]he following classes of aliens are authorized to be employed in the United States without restrictions as to location or type of employment as a condition of their admission or subsequent change to one of the indicated classes, and specific employment authorization need not be requested:

(1) An alien who is a lawful permanent resident (with or without conditions pursuant to section 216 of the Act), as evidenced by Form I-151 or Form I-551 issued by the Service;

(2) An alien admitted to the United States as a lawful temporary resident pursuant to section 245A or 210 of the Act, as evidenced by an employment authorization document issued by the Service;

(3) An alien admitted to the United States as a refugee pursuant to section 207 of the Act for the period of time in that status, as evidenced by an employment authorization document issued by the Service;

(4) An alien paroled into the United States as a refugee for the period of time in that status, as evidenced by an employment authorization document issued by the Service;

(5) An alien granted asylum under section 208 of the Act for the period of time in that status, as evidenced by an employment authorization document issued by the Service;

(6) An alien admitted to the United States as a nonimmigrant fiance or fiancee pursuant to section 101(a)(15)(K) of the Act, or an alien admitted as the child of such alien, for the period of admission of the United States, as evidenced by an employment authorization document issued by the Service;

(7) An alien admitted as a parent (N-8) or dependent child (N-9) of an alien granted permanent residence under section 101(a)(27)(I) of the Act, as evidenced by an employment authorization document issued by the Service;

(8) An alien admitted to the United States as a citizen of the Federated States of Micronesia (CFA/FSM) or of the Marshall Islands (CFA/MIS) pursuant to agreements between the United States and the former trust territories, as evidenced by an employment authorization document issued by the Service;

(9) An alien granted suspension of deportation under section 244(a) of the Act for the period of time in that status, as evidenced by an employment authorization document issued by the Service;

(10) An alien granted withholding of deportation under section 243(h) of the Act for the period of time in that status, as evidenced by an employment authorization document issued by the Service; or

(11) An alien who has been granted extended voluntary departure by the Attorney General as a member of a nationality group pursuant to a request by the Secretary of State. Employment is authorized for the period of time in that status as evidenced by an employment authorization document issued by the Service.

Authorized for Specific Employer
8 C.F.R. § 274a.12(b)

(1) A foreign government official (A-1 or A-2), pursuant to § 214.2(a) of this chapter. An alien in this status may be employed only by the foreign government entity;

(2) An employee of a foreign government official (A-3), pursuant to § 214.2(a) of this chapter. An alien in this status may be employed only by the foreign government official;

(3) A foreign government official in transit (C-2 or C-3), pursuant to § 214.2(c) of this chapter. An alien in this status may be employed only by the foreign government entity;

(4) A nonimmigrant crewman (D-1 or D-2) pursuant to § 214.2(d), and Parts 252 and 253, of this chapter. An alien in this status may be employed only in a crewman capacity on the vessel or aircraft of arrival, or on a vessel or aircraft of the same transportation company, and may not be employed in connection with domestic flights or movements of a vessel or aircraft;

(5) A nonimmigrant treaty trader (E-1) or treaty investor (E-2), pursuant to § 214.2(e) of this chapter. An alien in this status may be employed only by the treaty-qualifying company through which the alien attained the status. Employment authorization does not extend to the dependents of the principal treaty trader or treaty investor (also designated "E-1" or "E-2"), other than those specified in paragraph (c)(2) of this section;

(6) A nonimmigrant student (F-1) who is in valid nonimmigrant student status and pursuant to 8 C.F.R. § 214.2(f) is seeking on-campus employment for not more than twenty hours per week while school is in session or full time when school is not in session if the student intends and is eligible to register for the next term or session. Part-time on campus employment is authorized by the school and no specific endorsement by a school official or Service officer is necessary;

(7) A representative of an international organization (G-1, G-2, G-3, or G-4), pursuant to § 214.2(g) of this chapter. An alien in this status may be employed only by the foreign government entity or the international organization;

(8) A personal employee of an official or representative of an international organization (G-5), pursuant to § 214.2(g) of this chapter. An alien in this status may be employed only by the official or representative of the international organization;

(9) A temporary worker or trainee (H-1, H-2A, H-2B, or H-3), pursuant to § 214.2(h) of this chapter. An alien in this status may be employed only by the petitioner through whom the status was obtained;

(10) An information MEDIA representative (I), pursuant to § 214.2(i) of this chapter. An alien in this status may be employed only for the sponsoring foreign news agency or bureau. Employment authorization does not extend to the dependents of an information MEDIA representative (also designated "I");

(11) An exchange visitor (J-1), pursuant to § 214.2(j) of this chapter and 22 C.F.R. § 514.24. An alien in this status may be employed only by the exchange visitor program sponsor or appropriate designee and within the guidelines of the program approved by the United States Information Agency as set forth in the Certificate of Eligibility (Form IAP-66) issued by the program sponsor;

(12) An intra-company transferee (L-1), pursuant to § 214.2(1) of this chapter. An alien in this status may be employed only by the petitioner through whom the status was obtained;

(13) Officers and personnel of the armed services of nations of the North Atlantic Treaty Organization, and representatives, officials, and staff employees of NATO

(NATO-1, NATO-2, NATO-3, NATO-4, NATO-5, and NATO-6), pursuant to § 214.2(o) of this chapter. An alien in this status may be employed only by NATO;

(14) An attendant, servant or personal employee (NATO-7) of an alien admitted as a NATO-1, NATO-2, NATO-3, NATO-4, NATO-5, or NATO-6, pursuant to § 214.2(o) of this chapter. An alien admitted under this classification may be employed only by the NATO alien through whom the status was obtained; or

(15) A nonimmigrant alien within the class of aliens described in paragraphs (b)(2), (5), (8), (9), (10), (11), and (12) of this section whose status has expired but who has filed a timely application for an extension of such status pursuant to § 214.2 of this chapter. These aliens are authorized to continue employment with the same employer for a period not to exceed 120 days beginning on the date of the expiration of the authorized period of stay. If the alien's application for extension of stay has not been adjudicated within this period, the alien may apply to the district director for employment authorization pursuant to paragraph (c)(15) of this section.

Aliens Who Must Apply
8 C.F.R. § 274a.12(c)

. . . If authorized, such an alien may accept employment subject to any restrictions indicated in the regulations or cited on the employment authorization document:

(1) An alien spouse or unmarried dependent son or daughter of a foreign government official (A-1 or A-2) pursuant to § 214.2(a)(2) of this chapter;

(2) An alien spouse or unmarried dependent son or daughter of an alien employee of the Coordination Council for North American Affairs (E-1) pursuant to § 214.2(e) of this chapter;

(3) A nonimmigrant (F-1) student who:

(i) Is seeking off-campus employment authorization due to economic necessity pursuant to § 214.2(f) of this chapter. A student authorized employment under this section may use a properly endorsed I-20 ID issued to the student to establish employment authorization pursuant to 8 C.F.R. § 274a.2(b)(1)(v)(C)(7). To constitute a proper endorsement for this section, the Form I-20 ID must contain the date until which employment is authorized; a statement that the hours authorized per week while school is in session may not exceed 20 hours weekly; the identifying number of the Service officer; and the date and location of the endorsement.

(ii) Is seeking employment for purposes of practical training (including curricular practical training) pursuant to § 214.2(f) of this chapter, provided the alien will be employed only in an occupation which is directly related to his or her course of studies. A student authorized employment under this section may use a properly endorsed I-20 ID issued to the student, to establish employment authorization pursuant to 8 C.F.R. 274a.2(b)(1)(v)(C)(7). A properly endorsed Form I-20 ID must contain the date until which employment is authorized; the occupation or field in which employment is authorized; the name, title and signature of the designated school official or the identifying number of the Service officer; and the date and location of the endorsement; or

(iii) Has been offered employment under the sponsorship of an international organization within the meaning of the International Organization Immunities Act (59 Stat. 669), if such international organization provides written certification to the district director having jurisdiction over the intended place of employment that the proposed employment is within the scope of the organization's sponsorship;

(4) An alien spouse or unmarried dependent son or daughter of an officer or employee of an international organization (G-4) pursuant to § 214.2(g) of this chapter;

(5) An alien spouse or minor child of an exchange visitor (J-2) pursuant to § 214.2(j) of this chapter;

(6) A nonimmigrant (M-1) student seeking employment for practical training pursuant to § 214.2(m) of this chapter following completion of studies if such employment is directly related to the student's course of study;

(7) A dependent of an alien classified as NATO-1 through NATO-7 pursuant to § 214.2(n) of this chapter;

(8) Any alien who has filed a non-frivolous application for asylum pursuant to Part 208 of this chapter. Employment authorization shall be granted in increments not exceeding one year during the period the application is pending (including any period when an administrative appeal or judicial review is pending) and shall expire on a specified date;

(9) Any alien who has filed an application for adjustment of status to lawful permanent resident pursuant to Part 245 of this chapter. Employment authorization shall be granted in increments not exceeding one year during the period the application is pending (including any period when an administrative appeal or judicial review is pending) and shall expire on a specified date;

(10) Any alien who has filed an application for suspension of deportation pursuant to Part 244 of this chapter, if the alien establishes an economic need to work. Employment authorization shall be granted in increments not exceeding one year during the period the application is pending (including any period when an administrative appeal or judicial review is pending) and shall expire on a specified date;

(11) Any alien paroled into the United States temporarily for emergent reasons or reasons deemed strictly in the public interest pursuant to § 212.5 of this chapter;

(12) Any deportable alien granted voluntary departure, either prior to or after hearing, for reasons set forth in § 242.5(a)(2)(v), (vi), or (viii) of this chapter may be granted permission to be employed for that period of time prior to the date set for voluntary departure including any extension granted beyond such date. Factors which may be considered in adjudicating the employment application of an alien who has been granted voluntary departure are the following:

(i) The length of voluntary departure granted;

(ii) The existence of a dependent spouse and/or children in the United States who rely on the alien for support;

(iii) Whether there is a reasonable chance that legal status may ensue in the near future; and

(iv) Whether there is a reasonable basis for consideration of discretionary relief;

(13) Any alien against whom exclusion or deportation proceedings have been instituted, who does not have a final order of deportation or exclusion, and who is not detained may be granted temporary employment authorization if the district

director determines that employment is appropriate. Factors which may be considered by the district director in adjudicating the employment application of such an alien are the following:

(i) The existence of the economic necessity to be employed;

(ii) The existence of a dependent spouse and/or children in the United States who rely on the alien for support;

(iii) Whether there is a reasonable chance that legal status may ensue in the near future; and

(iv) Whether there is a reasonable basis for consideration of discretionary relief;

(14) An alien who has been granted deferred action, an act of administrative convenience to the government which gives some cases lower priority, if the alien establishes an economic necessity for employment;

(15) A nonimmigrant alien within the class of aliens described in paragraphs (b)(2), (5), (8), (9), (10), (11), and (12) of this section whose application for extension of stay has not been adjudicated within the 120-day period as set forth in paragraph (b)(15) of this section.

Establishing "Economic Necessity"
8 C.F.R. § 274a.12(d)

Title 45—Public Welfare, Poverty Guidelines, 45 C.F.R. 1060.2 should be used as the basic criteria to establish eligibility for employment authorization when the alien's economic necessity is identified as a factor. The alien shall submit an application for employee authorization listing his or her assets, income, and expenses as evidence of his or her economic need to work. Permission to work granted on the basis of the alien's application for employment authorization may be revoked under § 274a.14 of this chapter upon a showing that the information contained in the statement was not true and correct.

Application for Employment Authorization
8 C.F.R. § 274a.13

(a) General. An application (in the form of a written request) for employment authorization by an alien under § 274a.12(c) and Part 214 of this chapter shall be filed with the district director having jurisdiction over the applicant's residence. Except for paragraph (c)(8) of this section, the approval of an application for employment authorization shall be within the discretion of the district director. Where economic necessity is identified as a factor, the alien must provide information regarding his or her assets, income, and expenses on the application for employment authorization.

(b) Approval of application. If the application is granted, the alien shall be notified of the decision and issued employment authorization for a specific period of time. Such authorization shall be subject to any conditions noted on the employment authorization document.

(c) Denial of application. If the application is denied, the applicant shall be notified in writing of the decision and the reasons for the denial. There shall be no appeal from the denial of the application.

(d) Interim employment authorization. The district director shall adjudicate the application for employment authorization within 60 days from the date of receipt of the application by the Service or the date of receipt of a returned application by the Service. Failure to complete the adjudication within 60 days will result in the grant of interim employment authorization for a period not to exceed 120 days. Such authorization shall be subject to any conditions noted on the employment authorization document. However, if the district director adjudicates the application prior to the expiration date of the interim employment authorization and denies the individual's employment authorization application, the employment authorization granted under this section shall automatically terminate.

Notes

1. Are the definitions which appear above understandable to the average person (employer)? What would you suggest as alternatives to the above regulations?

2. Employer sanctions for hiring persons who are not eligible to work under the immigration laws require that employers be particularly careful when making the hiring decision. In enacting the sanction provisions the Congress also directed that the INS study the implementation of a verifiable identification system. Given that the identification card would have to be used by all persons seeking work, how would you allay the concerns of those wishing to prevent the abuse of such a system?

3. In *Ramos v. Thornburgh*, 732 F. Supp. 696 (E.D. Tex. 1989); 66 *Interpreter Releases* 840 (1989), a district court held that the INS had been misapplying the test for granting work authorization. In 1987 the INS had instructed its field offices that a frivolous application for asylum (which constituted a basis for denial of employment authorization) was where the asylum application was "patently without substance" and cautioned INS officers not to consider the merits of the application. 64 *Interpreter Releases* 873, 886-87 (1987). The district court held that the INS had violated its regulations by considering the merits of the asylum applications. In adjudicating requests for employment authorization, the INS had been conducting interviews of asylum applicants. The court also required the INS to immediately adjudicate requests for employment authorization in accordance with 8 C.F.R. § 274a.13(d)

D. Preconceived Intent

Matter of Cavazos
17 I. & N. Dec. 215 (BIA 1980)

This case is before us on appeal from the December 21, 1977, decision of an immigration judge, rendered in reopened deportation proceedings, which denied the respondent's application for adjustment of status pursuant to section 245 of the Immigration and Nationality Act, 8 U.S.C. 1255. The appeal will be sustained.

The respondent, a 26-year-old native and citizen of Mexico, entered the United States as a nonimmigrant visitor for pleasure on July 1, 1976, upon presentation of a border crossing card, Form I-186, issued to him in 1972. On that same date, he married his United States citizen spouse whom he had known for a considerable period of time prior to their marriage; a child was born in the United States in 1974 as a result of that relationship.

At the initial deportation hearing, the respondent conceded deportability as a nonimmigrant who remained longer than permitted and was granted the privilege of voluntary departure in lieu of deportation. Prior to the expiration of the authorized period of voluntary departure, the respondent filed the present motion to reopen for consideration of his application for section 245 relief predicated upon his status as the beneficiary of an approved immediate relative visa petition. The immigration judge granted the respondent's motion to reopen the deportation proceedings, found him statutorily eligible for adjustment at the reopened hearing that ensured, but denied him the relief sought in the exercise of discretion on the ground that he had entered the United States in July of 1976 with a preconceived intent to remain permanently.

We find that the record, while providing some support for the immigration judge's findings, is ambiguous at best with respect to the respondent's actual intentions at the time of his entry. We need not dwell on that question, however, in light of our conclusion that the adverse factor of preconceived intent, if it existed, has been overcome by the equities presented.

We note with approval present Immigration and Naturalization Service policy, as reflected in Service Operations Instruction 245.3(b), regarding the discretionary grant or denial of an adjustment application. Operations Instruction 245.3(b) provides that notwithstanding evidence establishing an intent on the part of a nonimmigrant to circumvent the normal visa process, i.e., a preconceived intent to remain permanently at the time of entry as a nonimmigrant, an adjustment application should not be denied in the exercise of discretion where substantial equities are present in the case. Under that Instruction, substantial equities are considered to exist if the facts are such that the alien would be granted voluntary departure until he is invited to appear at a United States consulate to apply for an immigrant visa. The Code of Federal Regulations, 8 C.F.R. 242.5(a)(1)(vi)(A) and 24.5(a)(c), authorizes the District Director in his discretion, to grant voluntary departure to an immediate relative of a United States citizen, prior to the commencement of his deportation hearing, until such time as the United States consul abroad is ready to issue an immigrant visa.

The Service's internal Operations Instruction 245.3(b) binds neither the immigration judge nor the Board; moreover, under the express terms of the regulation which gives effect to the Instruction, whether an alien may benefit from the Instruction as one who would be granted extended voluntary departure is a discretionary determination to be made by the District Director prior to the commencement of the hearing. We believe, however, that the policy manifest in the Instruction, i.e., to favor immediately relatives seeking a grant of adjustment of status by essentially negating preconceived intent as an adverse factor in meritorious cases, may appropriately be adopted by the immigration judge and the Board in exercising discretion on applications for relief under section 245.

The finding of preconceived intent was the only negative factor cited by the immigration judge in denying the respondent's adjustment application and no additional adverse matters are apparent in the record. A significant equity is presented by the respondent's United States citizen wife and child. We conclude that a grant of adjustment of status is warranted in this case and will accordingly sustain the appeal and remand the record to the immigration judge for further processing of the application for adjustment of status filed by the respondent and for the entry of an order not inconsistent with this opinion. In light of our holding, we need not reach the alternative arguments advanced by the respondent on appeal.

Problem

The following fact situation and questions should serve as a useful vehicle for discussing the interrelationship between a person's proper admission to the U.S. in a nonimmigrant status and her eventual obtaining of lawful permanent residence.

In August (year 3) Smith went to the U.S. embassy in country A to apply for a student visa. Her sole means of *support* was her Uncle Ted who owned an auto repair shop on the outskirts of the capital city. Smith was interviewed by the U.S. vice-consul, and was asked whether or not she was married. Smith told the vice-consul that she was married and that she did not have proof of the marriage because there had only been a tribal ceremony. Smith's statement to the vice-consul was not true as she was not married to anyone.

Smith was issued a nonimmigrant student (F-1) visa. She traveled to the U.S. and was inspected and admitted to the U.S. as a student pursuant to the visa issued to her by the consular officer in country A. At the time of her admission Smith was allowed to remain in the U.S. for the *"duration of her status."* Smith attended ABC University where she studied accounting. During the time that Smith was in school she was an excellent student. She dedicated all of her time to her studies as she was receiving full financial support from her Uncle Ted from her country. In August (year 1), Smith received news from her family that her uncle had died as a result of a massive heart attack. She also learned that she would not be receiving any money for some time to support her in school. Apparently, even though Smith was the sole heir of her Uncle Ted's estate, it would take a long time before she would be able to receive any money from the sizable estate.

After hearing this bad news Smith applied to her school for permission to take on part-time employment while she continued her studies. She was informed by the foreign student advisor's office that they were not sure what to do and that they would be checking with the INS on the application. After waiting for eight (8) months on her work permit (March, year 0), Smith in frustration went to the local INS office and was told that someone was looking into the problem and that she should "cool her jets." After waiting until April (year 0), Smith ran out of money and took on a part-time job as a night guard. The INS contacted Smith in June (year 0) by mail and requested that she provide them with a copy of her uncle's death certificate. Smith wrote home and received the certificate in August (year 0) and submitted the paper to both her foreign student advisor's office and the INS. In September (year 0) the INS in a routine check of Smith's employer's records discovered that Smith and five other people were working without the proper documentation. Smith and the five other people were arrested, served with OSCs (orders to show cause) for deportation and scheduled for hearings before an immigration judge. This all occurred notwithstanding Smith's protestations about her earlier attempts to properly obtain employment authorization.

Questions

1. If you were the arresting immigration officer, how would you justify the issuance of the order to show cause in this case? What allegations would you set forth in the order to show cause?

2. If you were the INS trial attorney, what would be your arguments and what facts would you need to establish at the deportation hearing?

3. If you were representing Smith, what would you advise her and what would you argue before the immigration judge?

4. If you were the immigration judge, what would be your ruling on the question of whether Smith had properly maintained her nonimmigrant status?

5. Did Smith follow the correct procedure for obtaining employment authorization?

Assume that when you interviewed Smith she informed you that she has known a wonderful person for at least one year and that they have been planning on getting married for some time.

6. What would you advise Smith about what she should do?

7. Did Smith's representations about her *marital status* to the vice-consul when she applied for her student visa jeopardize any future applications that might be filed with the INS?

8. Why would the vice-consul ask Smith if she was married?

9. Would the INS be justified in having Smith prove that she had not been married in her home country before adjudicating an application for lawful permanent residence?

10. Does Smith have a reasonable likelihood of obtaining lawful permanent residence in the future if she marries her friend? What additional information would you need to have before answering this question?

E. Adjudicating Petitions

Matter of Kotte
16 I. & N. Dec. 449 (BIA 1978)

In a decision dated April 18, 1977, the respondent was found deportable by the immigration judge under section 241(a)(9) of the Immigration and Nationality Act [8 U.S.C. 1251(a)(9)]. The respondent was granted the privilege of voluntary departure on or before July 18, 1977. On April 28, 1977, he filed a notice of appeal. The appeal will be dismissed.

The respondent, a native and citizen of India, entered the United States on January 3, 1975, as a nonimmigrant student, who was authorized to remain in the United States until January 2, 1976. He subsequently received an extension of stay until January 2, 1977. An Order to Show Cause issued on January 31, 1977, alleged that since October 25, 1976, the respondent was employed as a machine operator for a private corporation and that, therefore, he was subject to section 241(a)(9) of the Act as an alien who failed to comply with the conditions of his nonimmigrant status under which he was admitted. At his hearing, he admitted, through counsel, the factual allegations contained in the Order to Show Cause and conceded deportability. We conclude that deportability has been established by clear, convincing, and unequivocal evidence.

The facts of this case show that on December 30, 1976, the respondent petitioned the District Director for classification as a third-preference immigrant. An application for adjustment of status was filed on the same day. On April 5, 1977, the respondent filed a "notice of intent" with the District Director, stating his desire that his application as a third-preference immigrant and his application for adjustment of status be considered simultaneously under amended regulation 8 C.F.R. 245.2(a)(2).

At his hearing in deportation proceedings on March 8, 1977, the respondent applied for adjustment of status under section 245 of the Immigration and Nationality Act (8 U.S.C. 1255). He requested that the immigration judge continue the hearing and defer consideration of his application for adjustment of status until the District Director adjudicated his visa petition. An adjournment was granted until April 18, 1977. On reconvening, the third-preference petition had not yet been approved. The immigration judge denied respondent's request for further continuance and for relief on the ground that the respondent did not have an approved visa petition and that, therefore, respondent's adjustment of status application could not be approved.

On appeal, the respondent argues that the immigration judge erred by not granting the continuance request. The respondent argues that unless the deportation proceedings are continued until the District Director adjudicates his visa petition, the amendment to 8 C.F.R. 245.2(a)(2) is rendered meaningless and serves no purpose. It also appears that by filing his "notice of intent" after January 1, 1977, the effective date of the new regulation, the respondent is claiming that his application for adjustment of status lies within the ambit of the amendment to 8 C.F.R. 245.2(a)(2).

The amendment to 8 C.F.R. 245.2(a)(2) which became effective on January 1, 1977, provides in pertinent part that:

> Before an application for adjustment of status under section 245 of the Act may be considered properly filed, a visa must be immediately available. If a visa would be available only upon approval of a visa petition, the application will not be considered properly filed unless such petition has first been approved. If a visa petition is submitted simultaneously with the adjustment application, the adjustment application shall be retained for processing only if approval of the petition when reached for adjudication would make a visa immediately available at the time of filing of the adjustment application. If such petition is subsequently approved, the date of filing the adjustment application shall be deemed the date on which the accompanying petition was filed.

The regulatory history reveals that this amendment and other amendments to the regulations were made necessary by the enactment into law of the Immigration and Nationality Act Amendments of 1976 (Pub. L. 94-571) on October 20, 1976. Under this law, section 245(a) of the Act was amended to provide that:

> The status of an alien ... who was inspected and admitted or paroled into the United States may be adjusted by the Attorney General, in his discretion and under such regulations as he may prescribe, to that of an alien lawfully admitted

for permanent residence if (1) the alien makes an application for such adjustment, (2) the alien is eligible to receive an immigrant visa and is admissible to the United States for permanent residence, and (3) an immigrant visa is immediately available to him at the time his application is filed.

The legislative history of this statute shows that, under the amendment to section 245(a) of the Act, the date that the application for adjustment of status is filed is designated as the date used in determining availability of a visa number rather than the date that the application is approved. We note that the legislative history is silent as to the reason for this amendment to section 245(a) of the Act.

The issue before us is whether or not the immigration judge is required to continue a hearing in deportation proceedings pending the adjudication of respondent's visa petition by a District Director in light of the aforementioned amendments. It is probable that the amendment to section 245.2(a)(2) of the regulations was predicated upon the amendment to section 245(a) of the Act. We find that the legislative and regulatory histories do not express the reason for the amendment.

The respondent submits that the effect of amended regulation, 8 C.F.R. 245.2(a)(2) is that, once the immigration judge in a deportation proceeding becomes aware that the respondent has pending before the District Director a petition for classification as a preference immigrant filed simultaneously with an application for adjustment of status, he must adjourn the deportation proceedings until such time as the visa petition is adjudicated. We disagree that amended regulation 8 C.F.R. 245.2(a)(2) was intended to have this effect upon deportation proceedings.

We find no provision of law or regulation that gives an alien an absolute right to an adjournment of a deportation hearing in order to have his application for adjustment of status disposed of *Matter of Finalora*, 11 I. & N. Dec. 592 (BIA 1966); *Matter of M—*, 5 I. & N. Dec. 622 (BIA 1954).

8 C.F.R. 245.1(d) provides that an applicant for preference status such as this respondent is not eligible for the benefits of section 245 of the Act unless he is the beneficiary of a valid unexpired visa petition filed in accordance with 8 C.F.R. 204 and approved to accord him such status. 8 C.F.R. 103.1(m)(2) and (n) places the determination of whether or not an alien possesses the qualifications for third-preference status solely within the jurisdiction of the appropriate District Director and Regional Commissioner. 8 C.F.R. 242.8 does not vest in the immigration judge authority over such a question; and 8 C.F.R. 3.1(b)(5) specifically excepts appellate jurisdiction of such a question from this Board.

The respondent does not possess an approved visa petition for a third preference. Therefore, he is statutorily ineligible for adjustment of status under section 245 of the Act. Respondent's remedy lies with the District Director. There is no merit to respondent's contention that the immigration judge was required to continue deportation proceedings. The respondent has available to him the remedy of a motion to reopen should future events in connection with his visa petition render such action appropriate. *See Matter of Ching*, Interim Decision 2518 (BIA 1976); *Matter of Finalora, supra*. The immigration judge's decision was correct. Accordingly, the appeal will be dismissed.

Notes

1. Immigration law is steeped in procedure and issues such as the ones which occurred in the *Kotte* case can appear frequently.

2. The statute has changed since the *Kotte* case was decided. Why did the Board not reject the appeal because the adjustment applicant had worked without authorization. *See* 8 U.S.C. § 1255(c). What additional reasons might there be for the BIA to dismiss the appeal if the case were before it today?

3. As counsel in the *Kotte* case, what would you advise your client with respect to the adjudication of the third-preference petition?

Matter of Garcia
16 I. & N. Dec. 653 (BIA 1978)

* * *

In *Matter of Kotte*, a case which dealt with the same issue in a different procedural context, we held that notwithstanding the foregoing changes in the statute and the regulations, an alien does not have an absolute right to an adjournment of a deportation hearing until such time as the visa petition upon which his adjustment application is predicated has been adjudicated. Implicit in our holding, however, is the corollary proposition that an immigration judge may, in his discretion, grant a continuance or reopen a deportation hearing pending final adjudication of the petition. For the reasons that led us to our conclusion that a motion to reopen for consideration of adjustment application should not be denied solely because the accompanying visa petition has not yet been approved, we believe that discretion should, as a general rule, be favorably exercised where a prima facie approvable visa petition and adjustment application have been submitted in the course of a deportation hearing or upon a motion to reopen. To the extent that our decision in *Matter of Kotte*, supra, may have been misinterpreted to require a contrary disposition in such cases, Kotte is herewith clarified.

We do not intend, by our holding, to establish an inflexible rule requiring the immigration judge in all cases to continue the deportation proceedings at the initial hearing or on remand or, in another procedural context, to reopen the proceedings pending final adjudication by the District Director of the visa petition. It clearly would not be an abuse of discretion for the immigration judge to summarily deny a request for a continuance or a motion to reopen upon his determination that the visa petition is frivolous or that the adjustment application would be denied on statutory grounds or in the exercise of discretion notwithstanding the approval of the petition. We are satisfied that the breadth of the immigration judge's discretion, together with continuing efforts by the Service to expedite the processing of visa petitions submitted simultaneously with applications for adjustment of status, should serve to alleviate concerns that the policy announced herein will result in unduly delaying the entry of final orders of deportation in unmeritorious cases.

Notes

1. One of the biggest complaints about the INS are the delays experienced by applicants when seeking the adjudication of their claims before the agency. Does *Garcia* really clarify the issues?

2. Are *Kotte* and *Garcia* irrelevant today, given that the law after November 1986 provided that in order for the applicant to be eligible for adjustment she must be in status?

3. The problems presented in these cases illustrate the difficulties encountered by immigration judges. Since the judge has the authority to adjudicate the adjustment application but not the visa petition what can she do to resolve the case?

4. In addition, the system overload experienced by the INS leads the agency to view deportation hearings as an impediment to its job, thereby encouraging efforts at limiting the jurisdiction of the immigration judge.

5. Should the adjudication of visa petitions be shared by the district directors and the judges? If so, what kind of constitutional issues arise? For an extensive discussion of the some of these issues, *see* Legomsky, *Forum Choices for the Review of Agency Adjudication: A Study of the Immigration Process*, 71 Iowa L. Rev. 1297 (1986).

Adjustment of Status Procedure

> Submission of Application to INS
> or an Immigration Judge in
> Deportation proceedings. The
> requirements are as follows:

1. Did applicant enter U.S. and was s/he inspected?   ] If not, ineligible

2. If applicant is not the spouse or child of U.S. citizen, did applicant work without permission after January 1, 1982?   ] If so, ineligible

3. If applicant is not applying as spouse or child of U.S. citizen, is s/he still in lawful status?   ] If not, ineligible

4. If applicant is applying as a spouse, did the marriage take place while the beneficiary was in deportation proceedings?   ] If so, must show that marriage is bona fide

5. Can applicant be approved for a preference classification?   ] If not, ineligible

6. Does applicant fit any of the grounds of exclusion under 8 U.S.C. §1182? If so, does the applicant qualify for a waiver of the exclusion ground?   ] Must qualify for waiver in order to be eligible

7. If so, are there immigrant visas available immediately for issuance to the applicant?   ] If not, ineligible

If application is approved and applicant is applying based on marriage to U.S. citizen or permanent resident, lawful temporary residence is accorded. Otherwise applicant receives permanent residence.

Index to Appendix

Adjustment to Nonimmigrant Status

8 U.S.C. § 1257, Sec. 247

(a) The status of an alien lawfully admitted for permanent residence shall be adjusted by the Attorney General, under such regulations as he may prescribe, to that of a nonimmigrant under paragraph (15)(A), (E), or (G) of section 1101(a) of this title, if such alien had at the time of entry or subsequently acquires an occupational status which would, if he were seeking admission to the United States, entitle him to a nonimmigrant status under such paragraphs. As of the date of the Attorney General's order making such adjustment of status, the Attorney General shall cancel the record of the alien's admission for permanent residence, and the immigrant status of such alien shall thereby be terminated.

(b) The adjustment of status required by subsection (a) of this section shall not be applicable in the case of any alien who requests that he be permitted to retain his status as an immigrant and who, in such form as the Attorney General may require, executes and files with the Attorney General a written waiver of all rights, privileges, exemptions, and immunities under any law or any executive order which would otherwise accrue to him because of the acquisition of an occupational status entitling him to a nonimmigrant status under paragraph (15)(A), (E), or (G) of section 1101(a) of this title.

* * *

Conditional Permanent Residence— Alien Spouse and Sons and Daughters

8 U.S.C. § 1186, Sec. 216

(a) In general

(1) Notwithstanding any other provision of this chapter, an alien spouse (as defined in subsection (g)(1) of this section) and an alien son or daughter (as defined in subsection (g)(2) of this section) shall be considered, at the time of obtaining the status of an alien lawfully admitted for permanent residence, to have obtained such status on a conditional basis subject to the provisions of this section.

(2) Notice of requirements

(A) At the time an alien spouse or alien son or daughter obtains permanent resident status on a conditional basis under paragraph (1), the Attorney General shall provide for notice to such a spouse, son, or daughter respecting the provisions of this section and the requirements of subsection (c)(1) of this section to have the conditional basis of such status removed.

(B) In addition, the Attorney General shall attempt to provide notice to such a spouse, son, or daughter, at or about the beginning of the 90-day period described in subsection (d)(2)(A) of this section, of the requirements of subsections (c)(1) of this section.

(C) The failure of the Attorney General to provide a notice under this paragraph shall not affect the enforcement of the provisions of this section with respect to such a spouse, son, or daughter.

(b) Termination of status if finding that qualifying marriage improper

(1) In the case of an alien with permanent resident status on a conditional basis under subsection (a), if the Attorney General determines, before the second anniversary of the alien's obtaining the status of lawful admission for permanent residence, that—

(A) the qualifying marriage—

(i) was entered into for the purpose of procuring an alien's entry as an immigrant, or

(ii) has been judicially annulled or terminated, other than through the death of a spouse; or

(B) a fee or other consideration was given (other than a fee or other consideration to an attorney for assistance in preparation of a lawful petition) for the filing of a petition under section 1154(a) of this title or 1184(d) of this title with respect to the alien; the Attorney General shall so notify the parties involved and, subject to paragraph (2), shall terminate the permanent resident status of the alien (or aliens) involved as of the date of the determination.

(2) Any alien whose permanent resident status is terminated under paragraph (1) may request a review of such determination in a proceeding to deport the alien. In such proceeding, the burden of proof shall be on the Attorney General to establish, by a preponderance of the evidence, that a condition described in paragraph (1) is met.

(c) Requirements of timely petition and interview for removal of condition.

(1) In order for the conditional basis established under subsection (a) of this section for an alien spouse or an alien son or daughter to be removed—

(A) the alien spouse and the petitioning spouse (if not deceased) jointly must submit to the Attorney General, during the period described in subsection (d)(2) of this section, a petition which requests the removal of such conditional basis and which states, under penalty of perjury, the facts and information described in subsection (d)(1) of this section, and

(B) in accordance with subsection (d)(3) of this section, the alien spouse and the petitioning spouse (if not deceased) must appear for a personal interview before an officer or employee of the Service respecting the facts and information described in subsection (d)(1) of this section.

(2) Termination of permanent resident status for failure to file petition or have personal interview.

(A) In the case of an alien with permanent resident status on a conditional basis under subsection (a) of this section, if—

(i) no petition is filed with respect to the alien in accordance with the provisions of paragraph (1)(A), or

(ii) unless there is good cause shown, the alien spouse and petitioning spouse fail to appear at the interview described in paragraph (1)(B), the Attorney General shall terminate the permanent resident status of the alien as of the second anniversary of the alien's lawful admission for permanent residence.

(B) In any deportation proceeding with respect to an alien whose permanent resident status is terminated under subparagraph (A), the burden of proof shall be on the alien to establish compliance with the conditions of paragraphs (1)(A) and (1)(B).

(3) Determination after petition and interview

(A) In general, if—

(i) a petition is filed in accordance with the provisions of paragraph (1)(A), and

(ii) the alien spouse and petitioning spouse appear at the interview described in paragraph (1)(B), the Attorney General shall make a determination, within 90 days of the date of the interview, as to whether the facts and information described in subsection (d)(1) of this section and alleged in the petition are true with respect to the qualifying marriage.

(B) If the Attorney General determines that such facts and information are true, the Attorney General shall so notify the parties involved and shall remove the conditional basis of the parties effective as of the second anniversary of the alien's obtaining the status of lawful admission for permanent residence.

(C) If the Attorney General determines that such facts and information are not true, the Attorney General shall so notify the parties involved and, subject to subparagraph (D), shall terminate the permanent resident status of an alien spouse or an alien son or daughter as of the date of the determination.

(D) Any alien whose permanent resident status is terminated under subparagraph (C) may request a review of such determination in a proceeding to deport the alien. In such proceeding, the burden of proof shall be on the Attorney General to establish, by a preponderance of the evidence, that the facts and information described in subsection (d)(1) of this section and alleged in the petition are not true with respect to the qualifying marriage.

(4) Hardship waiver. The Attorney General, in the Attorney General's discretion, may remove the conditional basis of the permanent resident status for an alien who fails to meet the requirements of paragraph (1) if the alien demonstrates that—

(A) extreme hardship would result if such alien is deported, or

(B) the qualifying marriage was entered into in good faith by the alien spouse, but the qualifying marriage has been terminated (other than through the death of the spouse) by the alien spouse for good cause and the alien was not at fault in failing to meet the requirements of paragraph (1). In determining extreme hardship, the Attorney General shall consider circumstances occurring only during the period that the alien was admitted for permanent residence on a conditional basis.

(C) the qualifying marriage was entered into in good faith by the alien spouse and during the marriage the alien spouse or child was battered by or was the subject of extreme cruelty perpetrated by his or her spouse or citizen or permanent resident parent and the alien was not at fault in failing to meet the requirements of paragraph (1).

In determining extreme hardship, the Attorney General shall consider circumstances occurring only during the period that the alien was admitted for permanent residence on a conditional basis. The Attorney General shall, by regulation, establish measures to protect the confidentiality of information concerning any abused alien spouse or child, including information regarding the whereabouts of such spouse or child.

(d) Details of petition and interview

(1) Each petition under subsection (c)(1)(A) of this section shall contain the following facts and information:

(A) Statement of proper marriage and petitioning process. The facts are that—

(i) the qualifying marriage—

(I) was entered into in accordance with the laws of the place where the marriage took place,

(II) has not been judicially annulled or terminated, other than through the death of a spouse, and

(III) was not entered into for the purpose of procuring an alien's entry as an immigrant; and

(ii) no fee or other consideration was given (other than a fee or other consideration to an attorney for assistance in preparation of a lawful petition) for the filing of a petition under section 1154(a) of this title or 1184(d) of this title with respect to the alien spouse or alien son or daughter.

(C) under section 1153(a)(2) of this title as the spouse of an alien lawfully admitted for permanent residence, by virtue of a marriage which was entered into less than 24 months before the date the alien obtains such status by virtue of such marriage, but does not include such an alien who only obtains such status as a result of section 1153(a)(8) of this title.

(2) The term "alien son or daughter" means an alien who obtains the status of an alien lawfully admitted for permanent residence (whether on a conditional basis or otherwise) by virtue of being the son or daughter of an individual through a qualifying marriage.

(3) The term "qualifying marriage" means the marriage described to in paragraph (1).

(4) The term "petitioning spouse" means the spouse of a qualifying marriage, other than the alien.

* * *

Registry

8 U.S.C. § 1259, Sec. 249

A record of lawful admission for permanent residence may, in the discretion of the Attorney General and under such regulations as he may prescribe, be made in the case of any alien, as of the date of the approval of his application or, if entry occurred prior to July 1, 1924, as of the date of such entry, if no such record is otherwise available and such alien shall satisfy the Attorney General that he is not inadmissible under section 1182(a) of this title insofar as it relates to criminals, procurers and other immoral persons, subversives, violators of the narcotic laws or smugglers of aliens, and he establishes that he—

(a) entered the United States prior to January 1, 1972;

(b) has had his residence in the United States continuously since such entry;

(c) is a person of good moral character; and

(d) is not ineligible to citizenship.

Sec. 301, Immigration Act of 1990, Pub. L. No. 101-649, 104 Stat. 4978— Family Unity Provisions

(a) Temporary Stay of Deportation and Work Authorizaton for Certain Eligible Immigrants.—The Attorney General shall provide that in the case of an alien who is an eligible immigrant (as defined in subsection (b)(1)) as of May 5, 1988, who has entered the United States before such date, who resided in the United States on such date, and who is not lawfully admitted for permanent residence, the alien—

(1) may not be deported or otherwise required to depart from the United States on a ground specified in paragraph (1), (2), (5), (9), or (12) of section 241(a) of the Immigration and Nationality Act (other than so much of section 241(a)(1) of such Act as relates to a ground of exclusion described in paragraph (9), (10), (23), (27), (28), (29), or (33) of section 212(a) of such Act), and

(2) shall be granted authorization to engage in employment in the United States and be provided an "employment authorized" endorsement or other appropriate work permit.

(b) Eligible Immigrant and Legalized Alien Defined.—In this section:

(1) The term "eligible immigrant" means a qualified immigrant who is the spouse or unmarried child of a legalized alien.

(2) The term "legalized alien" means an alien lawfully admitted for temporary or permanent residence who was provided—

(A) temporary or permanent residence status under section 210 of the Immigration and Nationality Act,

(B) temporary or permanent residence status under section 245A of the Immigration and Nationality Act, or

(C) permanent residence status under section 202 of the Immigration Reform and Control Act of 1986.

(c) Application of Definitions.—Except as otherwise specifically provided in this section, the definitions contained in the Immigration and Nationality Act shall apply in the administration of this section.

(d) Temporary Disqualification from Certain Public Welfare Assistance.—Aliens provided the benefits of this section by virtue of their relation to a legalized alien described in subsection (b)(2)(A) or (b)(2)(B) shall be ineligible for public welfare assistance in the same manner and for the same period as the legalized alien is ineligible for such assistance under section 245A(h) or 210(f), respectively, of the Immigration and Nationality Act.

(e) Exception for Certain Aliens.—An alien is not eligible for the benefits of this section if the Attorney General finds that—

(1) the alien has been convicted of a felony or 3 or more misdemeanors in the United States, or

(2) the alien is described in section 243(h)(2) of the Immigration and Nationality Act.

(f) Construction.—Nothing in this section shall be construed as authorizing an alien to apply for admission to, or to be admitted to, the United States in order to obtain benefits under this section.

(g) Effective Date.—This section shall take effect on October 1, 1991; except that the delay in effectiveness of this section shall not be construed as reflecting a Congressional belief that the existing family fairness program should be modified in any way before such date.

Adjustment of Status Regulations

8 C.F.R. § 245.1 Eligibility

(a) General

Any alien who was inspected and admitted or paroled into the United States, except an alien who is ineligible to apply for adjustment of status as noted in paragraph (b) of this section, may apply for adjustment of status to permanent resident if the applicant is eligible to receive an immigrant visa and an immigrant visa is immediately available at the time of filing of the application.

(b) Ineligible aliens

The following categories of aliens are ineligible to apply for adjustment of status to permanent residence under section 245 of the Act:

(1) Any alien who entered the United States in transit without a visa;

(2) Any alien who, on arrival in the United States, was serving in any capacity on board a vessel or aircraft or was destined to join a vessel or aircraft in the United States to serve in any capacity thereon;

(3) Any alien who was not admitted or paroled following inspection by an immigration officer;

(4) Any alien who on or after January 1, 1977 was employed in the United States without authorization prior to filing an application for adjustment of status, except an applicant who is an immediate relative as defined in section 201(b) of the Act or a special immigrant as defined in section 101(a)(27)(H) of the Act;

(5) Any alien who on or after November 6, 1986 is not in legal immigration status on the date of filing his or her application for adjustment of status, except an applicant who is an immediate relative as defined in section 201(b) or a special immigrant as defined in section 101(a)(27)(H);

(6) Any alien who files an application for adjustment of status on or after November 6, 1986, who has failed (other than through no fault of his or her own for technical reasons) to maintain continuously a legal status since entry into the United States, except an applicant who is an immediate relative as defined in section 201(b) of the Act or a special immigrant as defined in section 101(a)(27)(H) of the Act;

(7) Any nonpreference alien who is seeking or engaging in gainful employment in the United States who is not the beneficiary of a valid individual or blanket labor certification issued by the Secretary of Labor or who is not exempt from certification requirements under § 212.8(b) of this chapter;

(8) Any alien who has or had the status of an exchange visitor under section 101(a)(15)(J) of the Act and who is subject to the foreign residence requirement of section 212(e) of the Act, unless the alien has complied with the foreign residence requirement or has been granted a waiver of that requirement, under that section;

(9) Any alien who has nonimmigrant status under paragraph (15)(A), (15)(E), or (15)(G) of section 101(a) of the Act, or has an occupational status which would, if the alien were seeking admission to the United States, entitle the alien to nonimmigrant status under those paragraphs, unless the alien first executes and submits the written waiver required by section 247(b) of the Act and Part 247 of this chapter; and

(10) Any alien who claims immediate relative status under section 201(b) or preference status under sections 203(a)(1) through 203(a)(6) of the Act, unless the applicant is the beneficiary of a valid unexpired visa petition filed in accordance with Part 204 of this chapter.

(11) Any alien admitted as a visitor under the visa waiver provisions of § 212.1(e) of this chapter.

* * *

(15) Any alien admitted as a Visa Waiver Pilot Program visitor under the provisions of section 217 of the Act and Part 217 of this chapter other than an immediate relative as defined in section 201(b) of the Act.

(c) Definitions—

(1) Legal Immigration Status. For purposes of section 245(c)(2) of the Act, the term "legal immigration status" is limited to individuals who are:

(i) In lawful permanent resident status;

(ii) Admitted in nonimmigrant status as defined in section 101(a)(15) of the Act, or whose nonimmigrant status has been extended in accordance with Part 214 of this chapter;

(iii) In refugee status under section 207 of the Act, such status not having been revoked;

(iv) In asylee status under section 208 of the Act, such status not having been revoked; or

(v) In parole status which has not expired.

(2) No fault of the applicant for technical reasons. The parenthetical phrase "other than through no fault of his or her own for technical reasons" shall be limited to: (i) Inaction of another individual or organization designated by regulation to act on behalf of an individual and over whose actions the individual has no control, if the inaction is acknowledged by that individual or organization (as, for example, where a designated school official certified under § 214.2(f) of this chapter or an exchange program sponsor under § 214.2(j) of this chapter did not provide required notification to the Service of continuation of status, or did not forward a request for continuation of status to the Service); or (ii) A technical violation resulting from inaction of the Service (as, for example, where an applicant establishes that he or she properly filed a timely request to maintain status and the Service has not yet acted on that request). An individual whose refugee status or asylee status has expired through passage of time, but whose status has not been revoked, will be considered to have gone out of status "through no fault of his or her own for technical reasons." (iii) A technical violation caused by the physical inability of the applicant to request an extension of nonimmigrant stay from the Service either in person or by mail (as, for example, an individual who is hospitalized with an illness at the time nonimmigrant stay expires). The explanation of such a technical violation shall be accompanied by a letter explaining the circumstances from the hospital or attending physician.

(3) Effect of departure. The departure and subsequent reentry of an individual who was employed without authorization in the United States after January 1, 1977 does not erase the bar to adjustment of status in section 245(c)(2) of the Act. Similarly, the departure and subsequent reentry of an individual who has not maintained a legal immigration status on any previous entry into the United States does not erase the bar to adjustment of status in section 245(c)(2) of the Act for any application filed on or after November 6, 1986.

(d) Special categories—

(1) Alien medical graduates. Any alien who is a medical graduate qualified for special immigrant classification under section 101(a)(27)(H) of the Act is eligible for adjustment of status. An accompanying spouse and children also may apply for adjustment of status under this section. Temporary absences from the United States of 30 days or less do not interrupt the continuous presence requirement during which the applicant was practicing or studying medicine. Temporary absences authorized

under the Service's advance parole procedures will not be considered interruptive of continuous presence when the alien applies for adjustment of status.

(2) Nonpreference investors—

(i) Any alien investor, if otherwise qualified, is eligible for adjustment of status if: (A) The applicant was present in the United States on or before June 1, 1978; (B) The applicant qualified as a non-preference immigrant under section 203(a)(8) of the Act as in effect on or before June 1, 1978; (C) The applicant applied for adjustment of status on or before June 1, 1978; (D) The applicant was determined to be exempt from the labor certification requirement of section 212(a)(14) of the Act because the applicant had actually invested capital in an enterprise in the United States before that date; (E) The applicant was a principal manager of that enterprise; and (F) That enterprise employed one or more U.S. citizens or permanent residents other than a spouse or child of the applicant.

(ii) The employment of the U.S. citizen or permanent resident may have occurred at any time and for any period of time in the enterprise or any subsequent enterprise.

(iii) Any applicant under this section may qualify with an investment in an enterprise other than that used to establish the applicant's priority date, or may qualify without a present investment.

(iv) Any applicant will have qualified as a nonpreference immigrant on or before June 1, 1978 for purposes of this section, if the application for investor status was actually approved on or before that date, or the application was subsequently approved with a priority date on or before June 1, 1978.

(v) Any alien qualified under this subsection is exempt from the restrictions of sections 212(a)(14) and 245(c)(2) of the Act.

(vi) A spouse or children of an investor qualified under this section may also apply for adjustment of status.

(e) Concurrent applications to overcome exclusionary grounds.

Except as provided in Parts 235 and 249 of this chapter, an application under this part shall be the sole method of requesting the exercise of discretion under section 212(g), (h), (i), and (k) of the Act, as they relate to the excludability of an alien in the United States. Any applicant for adjustment under this part may also apply for the benefits of section 212(c) of the Act, for permission to reapply after deportation or removal under section 212(a)(17) of the Act, and for the benefits of section 212(a)(28)(I)(ii) of the Act. No fee is required for filing an application to overcome the exclusionary grounds of the Act if filed concurrently with an application for adjustment of status under the provisions of the Act of October 28, 1977, and of this part.

(f) Availability of immigrant visas under section 245 and priority dates—

(1) Availability of immigrant visas under section 245. An alien is ineligible for the benefits of section 245 of the Act unless an immigrant visa is immediately available to him at the time the application is filed. If the applicant is a preference or nonpreference alien, the current Department of State Visa Office Bulletin on Availability of Immigrant Visa Numbers will be consulted to determine whether an immigrant visa is immediately available. An immigrant visa is considered available for accepting and

processing the application Form I-485 if the preference or nonpreference category applicant has a priority date on the waiting list which is no later than the date shown in the Bulletin or the Bulletin shows that numbers for visa applicants in his category are current. Information as to the immediate availability of an immigrant visa may be obtained at any Service office.

(2) Priority dates. The priority date of an applicant who is seeking the allotment of an immigrant visa number under one of the first six preference classes specified in section 203(a) of the Act by virtue of a valid visa petition approved in his behalf shall be fixed by the date on which such approved petition was filed. The priority date of an applicant who is seeking the allotment of a nonpreference immigrant visa number shall be fixed by the following factors, whichever is the earliest:

(i) The priority date accorded the applicant by the consular officer as a nonpreference immigrant;

(ii) the date on which Form I-485 is filed if the applicant establishes that he is qualified for and will be engaged in an occupation currently listed in Schedule A (20 CFR Part 656), or that the provisions of section 212(a)(14) of the Act do not apply to him; or

(iii) the date on which an approved valid third- or sixth-preference visa petition in his behalf was filed; or

(iv) the date an application for certification based on a job offer was accepted for processing by any office within the employment service system of the Department of Labor, provided the certification applied for was issued. A nonpreference priority date, once established, is retained by the alien even though at the time a visa number becomes available and he is allotted a nonpreference visa number he meets the provisions of section 212(a)(14) of the Act by some means other than that by which he originally established entitlement to the nonpreference priority date.

(g) Indochinese refugee.

An alien who ordered, assisted, or otherwise participated in the persecution of any person because of race, religion, or political opinion is not eligible for the benefits under any provisions of the Act of October 28, 1977. An alien is not eligible for the benefits of any provisions of the Act of October 28, 1977, unless he has been physically present in the United States for at least one year subsequent to March 31, 1975 and prior to the date of filing the application for adjustment of status. An alien is not eligible for the benefits of section 101 or 103 of the Act of October 28, 1977, unless he is a native or citizen of Vietnam, Laos, or Cambodia who was paroled into the United States as a refugee from those countries under section 212(d)(5) of the Immigration and Nationality Act subsequent to March 31, 1975, but prior to January 1, 1979; or who was inspected and admitted or paroled into the United States on or before March 31, 1975, and was physically present in the United States on March 31, 1975.

8 C.F.R. § 245.2 Applications

(a) General.

(1) Jurisdiction. An alien who believes he meets the eligibility requirements of section 245 of the Act or section 1 of the Act of November 2, 1966, or section 101 or 104 of the Act of October 28, 1977, and § 245.1 of this chapter shall apply to the

district director having jurisdiction over his place of residence. After an alien has been served with an order to show cause or warrant of arrest, his application for adjustment of status under section 245 of the Act or section 1 of the Act of November 2, 1966 or section 101 or 104 of the Act of October 28, 1977, shall be made and considered only in proceedings under Part 242 of this chapter. An adjustment application by an alien paroled under section 212(d)(5) of the Act, which has been denied by the district director, may be renewed in exclusion proceedings under section 236 of the Act only under the following two conditions: First, the denied application must have been properly filed subsequent to the applicant's earlier inspection and admission to the United States; second, the applicant's later absence from and return to the United States must have been under the terms of an advance parole authorization on Form I-512 granted to permit the applicant's absence and return to pursue the previously filed adjustment application.

(2) Proper filing of application—

(i) General. An applicant shall not be considered eligible for the benefits of section 245, the Act of October 28, 1977 (Adjustment of Status of Indochina Refugees), or the Act of November 2, 1966 (Cuban Refugee Adjustment Act), unless he or she has properly filed an application.

(ii) Under section 245. Before an application for adjustment of status under section 245 of the Act may be considered properly filed, a visa must be immediately available. If a visa would be immediately available upon approval of a visa petition, the application will not be considered properly filed unless such petition has first been approved. If a visa petition is submitted simultaneously with the adjustment application, the adjustment application shall be retained for processing only if approval of the visa petition would make a visa immediately available at the time of filing the adjustment application. If the visa petition is subsequently approved, the date of filing the adjustment application shall be deemed to be the date on which the accompanying petition was filed. If the applicant is claiming that the provisions of section 212(a)(14) of the Act do not apply to him or her because he or she is within the exemption described in § 212.8(b)(4) of this chapter, the application shall not be considered properly filed unless it is accompanied by Form I-526, Request for Determination that Prospective Immigrant is an Investor. An application for adjustment of status under section 245 of the Act as a nonpreference alien shall not be considered properly filed unless the applicant establishes that he or she is entitled to a priority date for allotment of a nonpreference visa number in accordance with § 245.1 (e)(2) and that a visa is immediately available within the contemplation of § 245.1 (e)(1). A nonpreference alien for whom a visa is not immediately available may not file an application for adjustment of status, but may seek to establish a nonpreference priority date through an application for an immigrant visa at a United States consular office.

(iii) Under the Act of October 28, 1977. An application for the benefits of section 101 or 104 of the Act of October 28, 1977 was not properly filed unless submitted on or before October 28, 1983. An applicant was ineligible for the benefits of the Act of October 28, 1977 unless he or she had been physically present in the United States for at least one year (amended from two years by the Refugee Act of 1980). The physical presence requirement was met only if the applicant had been actually physically present in the United States for a period or periods in the aggregate of at least one year subsequent to March 31, 1975 and prior to the date of filing the application. An application submitted by a spouse or child of a native or citizen of Vietnam, Laos, or Cambodia was not properly filed under the Act of October 28, 1977 unless the applicant was ineligible for the provisions of section 101 of the Act in his or her own right.

(iv) Under the Act of November 2, 1966. An application for the benefits of section 1 of the Act of November 2, 1966 is not properly filed unless the applicant was inspected and admitted or paroled into the United States subsequent to January 1, 1959. An applicant is ineligible for the benefits of the Act of November 2, 1966 unless he or she has been physically present in the United States for one year (amended from two years by the Refugee Act of 1980).

(3) Submission of documents

(i) General. A separate application shall be filed by each applicant for benefits under section 245, the Act of October 28, 1977, or the Act of November 2, 1966. Each application shall be accompanied by an executed Form G-325A, if the applicant has reached his or her 14th birthday. Form G-325A shall be considered part of the application. An application under this part shall be accompanied by the document specified in the instructions which are attached to the application.

(ii) Under section 245. An application for adjustment of status is submitted on Form I-485, Application for Permanent Residence. The application must be accompanied by the appropriate fee as explained in the instructions to the application.

(iii) Under the Act of October 28, 1977. An application for adjustment of status was made on Form I-485C. There was no fee required in an application for benefits of this Act.

(iv) Under the Act of November 2, 1966. An application for adjustment of status is made on Form I-485A. There is no fee required in the application for the benefits of this Act. The application must be accompanied by Form I-643, Health and Human Services Statistical Data Sheet. The application must include a clearance from the local police jurisdiction for any area in the United States when the applicant has lived for six months or more since his or her 14th birthday.

(4) Effect of departure—

(i) General. The effect of a departure from the United States is dependent upon the law under which the applicant is applying for adjustment.

(ii) Under section 245. The departure from the United States of an applicant who is under deportation proceedings shall be deemed an abandonment of the application constituting grounds for termination of the deportation proceeding by reason of the departure. The departure of an applicant who is not under deportation proceedings shall be deemed an abandonment of his or her application constituting grounds for termination, unless the applicant was previously granted advance parole by the Service for such absence, and was inspected upon returning to the United States. If the application of an individual granted advance parole is subsequently denied, the applicant will be subject to the exclusion provisions of section 236 of the Act. No alien granted advance parole and inspected upon return shall be entitled to a deportation hearing.

(iii) Under the Act of October 28, 1977. If an applicant for adjustment temporarily departed the United States after March 31, 1975, but prior to January 1, 1979, had no intention of abandoning his or her residence, and was readmitted or paroled upon return, the temporary absence shall be disregarded for purpose of the applicant's "arrival" into the United States in regard to section 102.

(iv) Under the Act of November 2, 1966. If an applicant who was admitted or paroled subsequent to January 1, 1959, later departs from the United States temporarily with no intention of abandoning his or her residence, and is readmitted or paroled upon return, the temporary absence shall be disregarded for purposes of the applicant's "last arrival" into the United States in regard to cases filed under section 1 of the Act of November 2, 1966.

(5) Decision—

(i) General. The applicant shall be notified of the decision of the district director and, if the application is denied, the reasons for the denial.

(ii) Under section 245. If the application is approved, the applicant's permanent residence shall be recorded as of the date of the order approving the adjustment of status. An application for adjustment of status as a preference or nonpreference alien shall not be approved until an immigrant visa number has been allocated by the Department of State. No appeal lies from the denial of an application by the district director, but the applicant retains the right to renew his or her application in proceedings under Part 242 of this chapter, or under Part 236 if the applicant is a parolee and meets the two conditions outlined in § 245.2(a)(1).

(iii) Under the Act of October 28, 1977. If the application is approved under section 101, the applicant's permanent residence shall be recorded in accordance with the provisions of section 102. If an application is approved under section 104, the applicant's date of permanent residence shall be the same date accorded the permanent resident through whom the applicant derives eligibility or the date of the applicant's arrival in the United States, whichever is later. If the application is denied, the applicant shall be advised of his or her right to appeal in accordance with the provisions of Part 103 of this chapter. There is no fee for the appeal.

(iv) Under the Act of November 2, 1966. If the application is approved, the applicant's permanent residence shall be recorded in accordance with the provisions of section 1. No appeal lies from the denial of an application by the district director, but the applicant retains the right to renew his or her application in proceedings under Part 242 of this chapter, or under Part 236, if the applicant is a parolee and meets the two conditions outlined in paragraph 1 of § 245.2(a)(1).

(b) Application by nonpreference alien seeking adjustment of status for purpose of engaging in gainful employment—

(1) Alien whose occupation is included in Schedule A (20 CFR Part 656). An applicant for adjustment of status as a nonpreference alien under section 245 of the Act who is subject to the labor certification requirement of section 212(a)(14) of the Act must submit a Statement of Qualifications of Alien form with his application, if he is qualified for and will be engaged in an occupation currently listed in Schedule A (20 CFR Part 656). The Statement of Qualifications of Alien form must be executed

in accordance with the instructions for completion of that form, and must be accompanied by the evidence of the applicant's qualifications specified in the instructions attached to the application for adjustment of status. The other documents specified in § 245.2(a) must also be submitted in support of the application for adjustment of status. Determination concerning certification under section 212(a)(14) of the Act will be made in accordance with the pertinent provisions of § 204.2(e)(4) of this chapter.

(2) Other nonpreference aliens who will engage in gainful employment. An applicant for adjustment of status as a nonpreference alien under section 245 of the Act, who is subject to the labor certification requirement of section 212(a)(14) of the Act and whose occupation is not listed in Schedule A, must submit the certification with his application. In such case the applicant's employer or prospective employer makes the application for the certification to the local State Employment Service.

(c) Application under section 2 of the Act of November 2, 1966.

An application by a native or citizen of Cuba or by his spouse or child residing in the United States with him, who was lawfully admitted to the United States for permanent residence prior to November 2, 1966, and who desires such admission to be recorded as of an earlier date pursuant to section 2 of the Act of November 2, 1966, shall be made on Form I-485A. The application shall be accompanied by the Alien Registration Receipt Card, Form I-151 or I-551, issued to the applicant in connection with his lawful admission for permanent residence, and shall be submitted to the district director having jurisdiction over the applicant's place of residence in the United States. The decision on the application shall be made by the district director. No appeal shall lie from his decision. If the application is approved, the applicant will be furnished with a replacement of his Form I-151 or I-551 bearing the new date as of which the lawful admission for permanent residence has been recorded.

(d) Application under section 214(d).

An application for permanent resident status pursuant to section 214(d) of the Act shall be filed on Form I-485 with the district director having jurisdiction over the applicant's place of residence. A separate application shall be filed by each applicant. If the application is approved, the district director shall record the lawful admission of the applicant as of the date of approval. The fee previously paid for filing the application shall be considered payment of the required visa fees, as of the date of the approval of the application. The applicant shall be notified of the decision and, if the application is denied, of the reasons therefor. No appeal shall lie from the denial of an application by the district director but such denial shall be without prejudice to the alien's right to renew his application in proceedings under Part 242 of this chapter.

(e) Application under section 103 of the Act of October 28, 1977.

An application by a native or citizen of Vietnam, Laos, or Cambodia who was lawfully admitted to the United States for permanent residence under the provisions of the Immigration and Nationality Act subsequent to March 31, 1975 but prior to October 28, 1977, and who desires such admission to be recorded as of an earlier date pursuant to section 103 of the Act of October 28, 1977, shall be made on Form I-485C. The application shall be submitted to the district director having jurisdiction over the applicant's place of residence in the United States. The decision on the application shall be made by the district director. The applicant shall be notified of the decision and, if the application is denied, of the reasons therefor and of his right to appeal in accordance with the provisions of Part 103 of this chapter. No fee shall be required either for the filing of the application or for the filing of the appeal. If the application is approved, the applicant, upon surrender of his Form I-551, will be furnished with a replacement thereof bearing the new date as of which the lawful admission for permanent residence has been recorded.

8 C.F.R. § 245.3 Adjustment of status under section 13 of the Act of September 11, 1957, as amended.

Any application for benefits under section 13 of the Act of September 11, 1957, as amended, must be filed on Form I-485 with the district director having jurisdiction over the applicant's place of residence. The benefits under section 13 are limited to aliens who were admitted into the United States under section 101, paragraphs (a)(15)(A)(i), (a)(15)(A)(ii), (a)(15)(G)(i), or (a)(15)(G)(ii) of the Immigration and Nationality Act who performed diplomatic or semi-diplomatic duties and to their immediate families, and who establish that there are compelling reasons why the applicant or the member of the applicant's immediate family is unable to return to the country represented by the government which accredited the applicant and that adjustment of the applicant's status to that of an alien lawfully admitted for permanent residence would be in the national interest. Aliens whose duties were of a custodial, clerical, or menial nature, and members of their immediate families, are not eligible for benefits under section 13. In view of the annual limitation of 50 on the number of aliens whose status may be adjusted under section 13, any alien who is prima facie eligible for adjustment of status to that of a lawful permanent resident under another provision of law shall be advised to apply for adjustment pursuant to such other provision of law. An applicant for the benefits of section 13 shall not be subject to the labor certification requirement of section 212(a)(14) of the Immigration and Nationality Act. The applicant shall be notified of the decision and, if the application is denied, of the reasons for the denial and of the right to appeal under the provisions of Part 103 of this chapter. Any applications pending with the Service before December 29, 1981 must be resubmitted to comply with the requirements of this section.

8 C.F.R. § 245a.3 Application for adjustment from temporary to permanent resident status.

(a) Application period for permanent residence.

(1) An alien may submit an application for lawful permanent resident status, with fee, immediately subsequent to the granting of lawful temporary resident status. Any application received prior to the alien's becoming eligible for adjustment to permanent resident status will be administratively processed and held by the INS, but will not be considered filed until the beginning of the nineteenth month after the date the alien was granted temporary resident status as defined in § 245a.2(s) of this chapter.

(2) No application shall be denied for failure to timely apply before the end of 30 months from the date of actual approval of the temporary resident application.

(b) Eligibility. Any alien who has been lawfully admitted for temporary resident status under section 245A(a) of the Act, such status not having been terminated, may apply for adjustment of status of that of an alien lawfully admitted for permanent residence if the alien:

(1) Applies for such adjustment anytime subsequent to the granting of temporary resident status but on or before the end of 30 months from the date of actual approval of the temporary resident application. The alien need not be physically present in the United States at the time of application; however, the alien must establish continuous residence in the United States in accordance with the provisions of paragraph (b)(2) of this section and must be physically present in the United States at the time of interview and/or processing for permanent resident status (ADIT processing);

(2) Establishes continuous residence in the United States since the date the alien was granted such temporary residence status. An alien shall be regarded as having resided continuously in the United States for the purpose of this part if, at the time of applying for adjustment from temporary to permanent resident status, or as of the date of eligibility for permanent residence, whichever is later, no single absence from the United States has exceeded thirty (30) days, and the aggregate of all absences has not exceeded ninety (90) days between the date of approval of the temporary resident application, Form I-687 (not the "roll-back" date) and the date the alien applied or became eligible for permanent resident status, whichever is later, unless the alien can establish that due to emergent reasons or circumstances beyond his or her control, the return to the United States could not be accomplished within the time period(s) allowed. A single absence from the United States of more than 30 days, and aggregate absences of more than 90 days during the period for which continuous residence is required for adjustment to permanent residence, shall break the continuity of such residence, unless the temporary resident can establish to the satisfaction of the district director or the Director of the Regional Processing Facility that he or she did not, in fact, abandon his or her residence in the United States during such period;

(3) Is admissible to the United States as an immigrant, except as otherwise provided in paragraph (g) of this section; and has not been convicted of any felony, or three or more misdemeanors; and

(4)(i)(A) Can demonstrate that the alien meets the requirements of section 312 of the Immigration and Nationality Act, as amended (relating to minimal understanding of ordinary English and a knowledge and understanding of the history and government of the United States); or

(B) Is satisfactorily pursuing a course of study recognized by the Attorney General to achieve such an understanding of English and such a knowledge and understanding of the history and government of the United States.

(ii) The requirements of paragraph (b)(4)(i) of this section must be met by each applicant. However, these requirements shall be waived without formal application for persons who, as of the date of application or the date of eligibility for permanent residence under this part, whichever date is later, are:

(A) Under 16 years of age; or

(B) 65 years of age or older; or

(C) Over 50 years of age who have resided in the United States for at least 20 years and submit evidence establishing the 20-year qualification requirement. Such evidence must be submitted pursuant to the requirements contained in Section 245a.2(d)(3) of this chapter; or

(D) Developmentally disabled as defined at § 245a.1(v) of this chapter. Such persons must submit medical evidence concerning their developmental disability; or

(E) Physically unable to comply. The physical disability must be of a nature which renders the applicant unable to acquire the four language skills of speaking, understanding, reading, and writing English in accordance with the criteria and precedence established in OI 312.1(a)(2)(iii) (Interpretations). Such persons must submit medical evidence concerning their physical disability.

(iii)(A) Literacy and basic citizenship skills may be demonstrated for purposes of complying with paragraph (b)(4)(i)(A) of this section by:

(1) Speaking and understanding English during the course of the interview for permanent resident status. An applicant's ability to read and write English shall be tested by excerpts from one or more parts of the Federal Textbooks on Citizenship at the elementary literacy level. The test of an applicant's knowledge and understanding of the history and form of government of the United States shall be given in the English language. The scope of the testing shall be limited to subject matter covered in the revised (1987) Federal Textbooks on Citizenship or other approved training material. The test questions shall be selected from a list of 100 standardized questions developed by the Service. In choosing the subject matter and in phrasing questions, due consideration shall be given to the extent of the applicant's education, background, age, length of residence in the United States, opportunities available and efforts made to acquire the requisite knowledge, and any other elements or factors relevant to an appraisal of the adequacy of his or her knowledge and understanding; or

(2) By passing a standardized section 312 test (effective retroactively as of November 7, 1988) such test being given in the English language by the Legalization Assistance Board with the Educational Testing Service (ETS) or the California State Department of Education with the Comprehensive Adult Student Assessment System (CASAS). The scope of the test is based on the 1987 edition of the Federal Textbooks on Citizenship series written at the elementary literacy level. An applicant may evidence passing of the standardized section 312 test by submitting the approved testing organization's standard notice of passing test results at the time of filing Form I-698, subsequent to filing the application but prior to the interview, or at the time of the interview. The test results may be independently verified by INS, if necessary.

(B) An applicant who fails to pass the English literacy and/or the U.S. history and government tests at the time of the interview, shall be afforded a second opportunity after six (6) months (or earlier, at the request of the applicant) to pass the tests, submit evidence of passing an INS approved section 312 standardized examination or submit evidence of fulfillment of any one of the "satisfactorily pursuing" alternatives listed at § 245a.1(s) of this chapter. The second interview shall be conducted prior to the denial of the application for permanent residence and may be based solely on the failure to pass the basic citizenship skills requirements. An applicant whose period of eligibility expires prior to the end of the six-month re-test period, shall still be accorded the entire six months within which to be re-tested.

(iv) To satisfy the English language and basic citizenship skills requirements under the "satisfactorily pursuing" standard as defined at § 245a.1(s) of this chapter the applicant must submit evidence of such satisfactory pursuit in the form of a "Certificate of Satisfactory Pursuit" (Form I-699) issued by the designated school or program official attesting to the applicant's satisfactory pursuit of the course of study as defined at § 245a.1(s) (1) and (4) of this chapter; or a high school diploma or general educational development diploma (GED) under § 245a.1(s)(2) of this chapter;

or certification on letterhead stationery from a state recognized, accredited learning institution under § 245a.1(s)(3) of this chapter; or evidence of having passed the IRCA Test for Permanent Residency under § 245a.1(s)(5) of this chapter. Such applicants shall not then be required to demonstrate that they meet the requirements of § 245a.3(b)(4)(i)(A) of this chapter in order to be granted lawful permanent residence provided they are otherwise eligible. Evidence of "Satisfactory Pursuit" may be submitted at the time of filing Form I-698, subsequent to filing the application but prior to the interview, or at the time of the interview (the applicant's name and A90M number must appear on any such evidence submitted). An applicant need not necessarily be enrolled in a recognized course of study at the time of application for permanent residency.

(v) Enrollment in a recognized course of study as defined in § 245a.3(b)(5) and issuance of a "Certificate of Satisfactory Pursuit" must occur subsequent to May 1, 1987.

(5) A course of study in the English language and in the history and government of the United States shall satisfy the requirement of paragraph (b)(4)(i) of this section if the course materials for such instruction include textbooks published under the authority of section 346 of the Act, and it is

(i) Sponsored or conducted by:

(A) An established public or private institution of learning recognized as such by a qualified state certifying agency;

(B) An institution of learning approved to issue Forms I-20 in accordance with § 214.3 of this chapter;

(C) A qualified designated entity within the meaning of section 245A(c)(2) of the Act, in good-standing with the Service; or

(D) Is certified by the district director in whose jurisdiction the program is conducted, or is certified by the Director of the Outreach Program nationally.

(ii) A program seeking certification as a course of study recognized by the Attorney General under paragraph (b)(5)(i)(D) of this section shall file Form I-803, Petition for Attorney General Recognition to Provide Course of Study for Legalization: Phase II, with the Director of Outreach for national level programs or with the district director having jurisdiction over the area in which the school or program is located. In the case of local programs, a separate petition must be filed with each district director when a parent organization has schools or programs in more than one INS district. A petition must identify by name and address those schools or programs included in the petition. No fee shall be required to file Form I-803;

(A) The Director of Outreach and the district directors may approve a petition where they have determined that (1) a need exists for a course of study in addition to those already certified under § 245a.3(b)(5)(i) (A), (B), or (C); and/or (2) of this chapter the petitioner has historically provided educational services in English and U.S. history and government but is not already certified under § 245a.3(b)(5)(i) (A), (B), or (C); and (3) of this chapter the petitioner is otherwise qualified to provide such course of study;

(B) Upon approval of the petition the Director of Outreach and district directors shall issue a Certificate of Attorney General Recognition on Form I-804 to the petitioner. If the petition is denied, the petitioner shall be notified in writing of the decision therefor. No appeal shall lie from a denial of Form I-803, except that in such case where the petitions of a local, cross-district program are approved in one district and denied in another within the same State, the petitioner may request review of the denied petition by the appropriate Regional Commissioner. The Regional Commissioner shall then make a determination in this case;

(C) Each district director shall compile and maintain lists of programs approved under paragraph (b)(5)(i)(D) of this section within his or her jurisdiction. The Director of Outreach shall compile and maintain lists of approved national level programs.

* * *

(13) Courses of study recognized by the Attorney General as defined at § 245a.3(b)(5) of this chapter shall provide certain standards for the selection of teachers. Since some programs may be in locations where selection of qualified staff is limited, or where budget constraints restrict options, the following list of qualities for teacher selection is provided as guidance. Teacher selections should include as many of the following qualities as possible:

(i) Specific training in Teaching English to Speakers of Other Languages (TESOL);

(ii) Experience as a classroom teacher with adults;

(iii) Cultural sensitivity and openness;

(iv) Familiarity with competency-based education;

(v) Knowledge of curriculum and materials adaptation;

(vi) Knowledge of a second language.

(c) Ineligible aliens.

(1) An alien who has been convicted of a felony, or three or more misdemeanors in the United States.

(2) An alien who is inadmissible to the United States as an immigrant, except as provided in § 245a.3(g)(1).

(3) An alien who was previously granted temporary resident status pursuant to section 245A(a) of the Act who has not filed an application for permanent resident status under section 245A(b)(1) of the Act by the end of 30 months from the date of actual approval of the temporary resident application.

(4) An alien who was not previously granted temporary resident status under section 245A(a) of the Act.

(5) An alien whose temporary resident status has been terminated under § 245a.2(u) of this chapter

(d) Filing the application. The provisions of Part 211 of this chapter relating to the documentary requirements for immigrants shall not apply to an applicant under this part.

(1) The application must be filed on Form I-698. The application will be mailed to the designated Regional Processing Facility having jurisdiction over the applicant's residence. Form I-698 must be accompanied by the correct fee and documents specified in the instructions.

(2) Certification of documents. The submission of original documents is not required at the time of filing Form I-698. A copy of a document submitted in support

of Form I-698 filed pursuant to section 245A(b) of the Act and this part may be accepted, though unaccompanied by the original, if the copy is certified as true and complete by

(i) An attorney in the format prescribed in § 204.2(j)(1) of this chapter; or

(ii) An alien's representative in the format prescribed in § 204.2(j)(2) of this chapter; or

(iii) A qualified designated entity (QDE) in good standing as defined in § 245a.1(r) of this chapter, if the copy bears a certification by the QDE in good-standing, typed or rubber-stamped in the following language:

(I certify that I have compared this copy with its original and it is a true and complete copy.

Signed: _____

Name: _____

QDE in good-standing representative

Name of QDE in good-standing: _____

Address of QDE in good-standing: _____

INS-QDE Cooperative Agreement Number: _____

(iv) Authentication. Certification of documents must be authenticated by an original signature. A facsimile signature on a rubber stamp will not be acceptable.

(v) Original documents. Original documents must be presented when requested by the Service. Official government records, employment or employment-related records maintained by employers, unions, or collective bargaining organizations, medical records, school records maintained by a school or school board or other records maintained by a party other than the applicant which are submitted in evidence must be certified as true and complete by such parties and must bear their seal or signature or the signature and title of persons authorized to act in their behalf. At the discretion of the district director and/or the Regional Processing Facility director, original documents may be kept for forensic examination.

(3) A separate application (I-698) must be filed by each eligible applicant. All fees required by 103.7(b)(1) of this chapter must be submitted in the exact amount in the form of a money order, cashier's check or certified bank check. No personal checks or currency will be accepted. Fees will not be waived or refunded under any circumstances.

(4) Applicants who filed for temporary resident status prior to December 1, 1987, are required to submit the results of a serologic test for HIV virus on Form I-693, "Medical Examination of Aliens Seeking Adjustment of Status", completed by a designated civil surgeon, unless the serologic test for HIV was performed and the results were submitted on Form I-693 when the applicant filed for temporary resident status. Applicants who did submit an I-693 reflecting a serologic test for HIV was performed prior to December 1, 1987, must submit evidence of this fact when filing the I-698 application in order to be relieved from the requirement of submitting another I-693. If such evidence is not available, applicants may note on their I-698 application their prior submission of the results of the serologic test for HIV. This information shall then be verified at the Regional Processing Facility. Applicants having to submit an I-693 pursuant to this section are not required to have a complete

medical examination. All HIV-positive applicants shall be advised that a waiver of the ground of excludability under section 212(a)(6) of the Act is available and shall be provided the opportunity to apply for the waiver. To be eligible for the waiver, the applicant must establish that:

(i) The danger to the public health of the United States created by the alien's admission to the United States is minimal,

(ii) The possibility of the spread of the infection created by the alien's admission to the United States is minimal, and

(iii) There will be no cost incurred by any government agency without prior consent of that agency. Provided these criteria are met, the waiver may be granted only for humanitarian purposes, to assure family unity, or when the granting of such a waiver is in the public interest in accordance with § 245a.3(g)(2) of this chapter.

(5) If necessary, the validity of an alien's temporary resident card (I-688) will be extended in increments of one (1) year until such time as the decision on an alien's properly filed application for permanent residence becomes final.

(6) An application lacking the proper fee or incomplete in any way shall be returned to the applicant with request for the proper fee, correction, additional information, and/or documentation. Once an application has been accepted by the Service and additional information and/or documentation is required, the applicant shall be sent a notice to submit such information and/or documentation. In such case the application Form I-698 shall be retained at the RPF. If a response to this request is not received within 60 days, a second request for correction, additional information, and/or documentation shall be made. If the second request is not complied with by the end of 30 months from the date the application for temporary residence, Form I-687, was approved the application for permanent residence will be adjudicated on the basis of the existing record.

(e) Interview. Each applicant regardless of age, must appear at the appropriate Service office and must be fingerprinted for the purpose of issuance of Form I-551. Each applicant shall be interviewed by an immigration officer, except that the adjudicative interview may be waived for a child under 14, or when it is impractical because of the health or advanced age of the applicant. An applicant failing to appear for the scheduled interview may, for good cause, be afforded another interview. Where an applicant fails to appear for two scheduled interviews, his or her application shall be held in abeyance until the end of 30 months from the date the application for temporary residence was approved and adjudicated on the basis of the existing record.

(f) Numerical limitations. The numerical limitations of sections 201 and 202 of the Act do not apply to the adjustment of aliens to lawful permanent resident status under section 245A(b) of the Act.

(g) Applicability of exclusion grounds.

(1) Grounds of exclusion not to be applied. The following paragraphs of section 212(a) of the Act shall not apply to applicants for adjustment of status from temporary resident to permanent resident status: (14) workers entering without labor certification; (20) immigrants not in possession of valid entry documents; (21) visas issued without compliance of section 203; (25) illiterates; and (32) graduates of non-accredited medical schools.

(2) Waiver of grounds of excludability. Except as provided in paragraph (g)(3) of this section, the Service may waive any provision of section 212(a) of the Act only

in the case of individual aliens for humanitarian purposes, to assure family unity, or when the granting of such a waiver is otherwise in the public interest. In any case where a provision of section 212(a) of the Act has been waived in connection with an alien's application for lawful temporary resident status under section 245A(a) of the Act, no additional waiver of the same ground of excludability will be required when the alien applies for permanent resident status under section 245A(b)(1) of the Act. In the event that the alien was excludable under any provision of section 212(a) of the Act at the time of temporary residency and failed to apply for a waiver in connection with the application for temporary resident status, or becomes excludable subsequent to the date temporary residence was granted, a waiver of the ground of excludability, if available, will be required before permanent resident status may be granted.

(3) Grounds of exclusion that may not be waived. Notwithstanding any other provisions of the Act the following provisions of section 212(a) of the Act may not be waived by the Attorney General under paragraph (g)(2) of this section:

(i) Paragraphs (9) and (10) (criminals);

(ii) Paragraph (15) (public charge) except for an alien who is or was an aged, blind, or disabled individual (as defined in section 1614(a)(1) of the Social Security Act);

(iii) Paragraph (23) (narcotics), except for a single offense of simple possession of thirty grams or less of marijuana;

(iv) Paragraphs (27) (prejudicial to the public interest), (28) (communists), and (29) (subversives);

(v) Paragraph (33) (participated in Nazi persecution).

(4) Determination of "Likely to become a public charge" and Special Rule. Prior to use of the special rule for determination of public charge, paragraph (g)(4)(iii) of this section, an alien must first be determined to be excludable under section 212(a)(15) of the Act. If the applicant is determined to be "likely to become a public charge," he or she may still be admissible under the terms of the Special Rule.

(i) In determining whether an alien is "likely to become a public charge" financial responsibility of the alien is to be established by examining the totality of the alien's circumstances at the time of his or her application for legalization. The existence or absence of a particular factor should never be the sole criteria for determining if an alien is likely to become a public charge. The determination of financial responsibility should be a prospective evaluation based on the alien's age, health, income, and vocation.

(ii) The Special Rule for determination of public charge, paragraph (g)(4)(iii) of this section, is to be applied only after an initial determination that the alien is inadmissible under the provisions of section 212(a)(15) of the act.

(iii) Special Rule. An alien who has a consistent employment history which shows the ability to support himself or herself even though his or her income may be below the poverty level is not excludable under paragraph (g)(3)(ii) of this section. The alien's employment history need not be continuous in that it is uninterrupted. It should be continuous in the sense that the alien shall be regularly attached to the workforce, has an income over a substantial period of the applicable time, and has demonstrated the capacity to exist on his or her income without recourse to public cash assistance. The Special Rule is prospective in that the Service shall determine, based on the alien's history, whether he or she is likely to become a public charge. Past acceptance of public cash assistance within a history of consistent employment will enter into this decision. The weight given in considering applicability of the public charge provisions will depend on many factors, but the length of time an applicant has received public cash assistance will constitute a significant factor. It is not necessary to file a waiver in order to apply the Special Rule for Determination of Public Charge.

(5) Public cash assistance and criminal history verification. Declarations by an applicant that he or she has not been the recipient of public cash assistance and/or has not had a criminal record are subject to a verification of facts by the Service. The applicant must agree to fully cooperate in the verification process. Failure to assist the Service in verifying information necessary for proper adjudication may result in denial of the application.

(h) Departure. An applicant for adjustment to lawful permanent resident status under section 245A(b)(1) of the Act who was granted lawful temporary resident status under section 245A(a) of the Act, shall be permitted to return to the United States after such brief and casual trips abroad, as long as the alien reflects a continuing intention to adjust to lawful permanent resident status. However, such absences from the United States must not exceed the periods of time specified in § 245a.3(b)(2) of this chapter in order for the alien to maintain continuous residence as specified in the Act.

(i) Decision. The applicant shall be notified in writing of the decision, and, if the application is denied, of the reason therefor. Applications for permanent residence under this chapter will not be denied at local INS offices (districts, suboffices, and legalization offices) until the entire record of proceeding has been reviewed. An application will not be denied if the denial is based on adverse information not previously furnished to the Service by the alien without providing the alien an opportunity to rebut the adverse information and to present evidence in his or her behalf. If inconsistencies are found between information submitted with the adjustment application and information previously furnished to the Service, the applicant shall be afforded the opportunity to explain discrepancies or rebut any adverse information. A party affected under this part by an adverse decision is entitled to file an appeal on Form I-694. If an application is denied, work authorization will be granted until a final decision has been rendered on an appeal or until the end of the appeal period if no appeal is filed. An applicant whose appeal period has ended is no longer considered to be an Eligible Legalized Alien for the purposes of the administration of State Legalization Impact Assistance Grants (SLIAG) funding. An alien whose application is denied will not be required to surrender his or her temporary resident card (I-688) until such time as the appeal period has tolled, or until expiration date of the I-688, whichever date is later. After exhaustion of an appeal, an applicant who believes that the grounds for denial have been overcome may submit another application with fee, provided that the application is submitted within his or her eligibility period.

(j) Appeal process. An adverse decision under this part may be appealed to the Associate Commissioner, Examinations (Administrative Appeals Unit) the appellate authority designated in 103.1(f)(2). Any appeal shall be submitted to the Regional Processing Facility with the required fee within thirty (30) days after service of the Notice of Denial in accordance with the procedures of 103.3(a) of this chapter. An appeal received after the thirty (30) day period has tolled will not be accepted. The thirty (30) day period for submitting an appeal begins three days after the notice of denial is mailed. If a review of the Record of Proceeding (ROP) is requested by the alien or his or her legal representative and an appeal has been properly filed, an additional thirty (30) days will be allowed for this review from the time the Record of Proceeding is photocopied and mailed. A brief may be submitted with the appeal form or submitted up to thirty (30) calendar days from the date of receipt of the appeal form at the Regional Processing Facility. Briefs filed after submission of the appeal should be mailed directly to the Regional Processing Facility. For good cause shown, the time within which a brief supporting an appeal may be submitted may be extended by the Director of the Regional Processing Facility.

(k) Motions. The Regional Processing Facility director may reopen and reconsider any adverse decision sua sponte. When an appeal to the Associate Commissioner, Examinations (Administrative Appeals Unit) has been filed, the INS director of the Regional Processing Facility may issue a new decision that will grant the benefit which has been requested. The director's new decision must be served on the appealing party within forty-five (45) days of receipt of any briefs and/or new evidence, or upon expiration of the time allowed for the submission of any briefs.

(l) Certifications. The Regional Processing Facility director or district director may, in accordance with 103.4 of this chapter, certify a decision to the Associate Commissioner, Examinations (Administrative Appeals Unit) when the case involves an unusually complex or novel question of law or fact. The decision on an appealed case subsequently remanded back to either the Regional Processing Facility director or the district director will be certified to the Administrative Appeals Unit.

(m) Date of adjustment to permanent residence. The status of an alien whose application for permanent resident status is approved shall be adjusted to that of a lawful permanent resident as of the date of filing of the application for permanent residence or the eligibility date, whichever is later. For purposes of making application to petition for naturalization, the continuous residence requirements for naturalization shall begin as of the date the alien's status is adjusted to that of a person lawfully admitted for permanent residence under this part.

(n) Limitation on access to information and confidentiality.

(1) No person other than a sworn officer or employee of the Department of Justice or bureau or agency thereof, will be permitted to examine individual applications. For purposes of this part, any individual employed under contract by the Service to work in connection with the Legalization Program shall be considered an "employee of the Department of Justice or bureau or agency thereof."

(2) No information furnished pursuant to an application for permanent resident status under this section shall be used for any purpose except:

(i) To make a determination on the application; or

(ii) for the enforcement of the provisions encompassed in section 245A(c)(6) of the Act, except as provided in paragraph (n)(3) of this section.

(3) If a determination is made by the Service that the alien has, in connection with his or her application, engaged in fraud or willful misrepresentation or concealment of a material fact, knowingly provided a false writing or document in making his or her application, knowingly made a false statement or representation, or engaged in any other activity prohibited by section 245A(c)(6) of the Act, the Service shall

refer the matter to the United States Attorney for prosecution of the alien and/or of any person who created or supplied a false writing or document for use in an application for adjustment of status under this part.

(4) Information contained in granted legalization files may be used by the Service at a later date to make a decision

(i) On an immigrant visa petition or other status filed by the applicant under section 204(a) of the Act;

(ii) On a naturalization application submitted by the applicant;

(iii) For the preparation of reports to Congress under section 404 of IRCA, or;

(iv) For the furnishing of information, at the discretion of the Attorney General, in the same manner and circumstances as census information may be disclosed by the Secretary of Commerce under section 8 of Title 13, Unites States Code.

(o) Rescission. Rescission of adjustment of status under 245a shall occur under the guidelines established in section 246 of the Act.

* * *

§ 236.4 Renewal of Application in Exclusion Proceedings.

An adjustment application by an alien paroled under section 212(d)(5) of the Act, which has been denied by the district director, may be renewed in exclusion proceedings under section 236 of the Act before an immigration judge under the following two conditions: First, the denied application must have been properly filed subsequent to the applicant's earlier inspection and admission to the United States; second, the applicant's later absence from and return to the United States must have been under the terms of an advance parole authorization on Form I-512 granted to permit the applicant's absence and return to pursue the previously filed adjustment application.

Registry

8 C.F.R. § 249.2 Application.

(a) Jurisdiction. An application by an alien who has been served with an order to show cause or warrant of arrest shall be considered only in proceedings under Part 242 of this chapter. In any other case, an alien who believes he or she meets the eligibility requirements of section 249 of the Act shall apply to the district director having jurisdiction over his or her place of residence. The application shall be made on Form I-485 and shall be accompanied by Form G-325A, which shall be considered part of the application. The application shall also be accompanied by documentary evidence establishing continuous residence in the United States since prior to January 1, 1972, or since entry and prior to July 1, 1924. All documents must be submitted in accordance with § 103.2(b) of this chapter. Documentary evidence may include any records of official or personal transactions or recordings of events occurring during the period of claimed residence. Affidavits of credible witnesses may also be accepted. Persons unemployed and unable to furnish evidence in their own names may furnish evidence in the names of parents or other persons with whom they have been living, if affidavits of the parents or other persons are submitted attesting to the residence. The numerical limitations of sections 201 and 202 of the Act shall not apply.

(b) Decision. The applicant shall be notified of the decision and, if the application is denied, of the reasons therefor. If the application is granted, a Form I-551, showing that the applicant has acquired the status of an alien lawfully admitted for permanent residence, shall not be issued until the applicant surrenders any other document in his or her possession evidencing compliance with the alien registration requirements of former or existing law. No appeal shall lie from the denial of an application by the district director, but such denial shall be without prejudice to the alien's right to renew the application in proceedings under Part 242 of this chapter.

Chapter 10

Revocation of Visas and Rescission of Adjustment

A. Revocation of Nonimmigrant Visas

The immigration laws provide a mechanism for the multilayered review of persons coming to the United States. As noted earlier, an applicant who receives a visa is subsequently subjected to inspection at the border. In order to assure that those who are ineligible but who have nevertheless managed to obtain a visa for which they are ineligible, the INA provides a mechanism for visa revocation. The ultimate effect of a visa revocation when completed is to render the person without a legal basis for remaining in the United States.[1]

The first case in this chapter deals with the issue of the revocation of a non-immigrant visa by the Secretary of State after a person has entered the U.S. Is a person who has entered the United States entitled to notice of the grounds for issuance of an intent to revoke her visa? Should she have an opportunity to refute the charges spelled out in the notice of intent? What should be the standards for judicial review of a revocation? Consider these questions while reading the following case.

---

8 U.S.C. § 1201(i), Sec. 221

After the issuance of a visa or other documentation to any alien, the consular officer or the Secretary of State may at any time, in his discretion, revoke such visa or other documentation. Notice of such revocation shall be communicated to the Attorney General, and such revocation shall invalidate the visa or other documentation from the date of issuance: Provided, that carriers or transportation companies, and masters, commanding officers, agents, owners, charterers, or consignees, shall not be penalized under section 1323(b) of this title for action taken in reliance on such visas or other documentation, unless they received due notice of such revocation prior to the alien's embarkation.

---

1. Visa revocation may not necessarily preclude the person from receiving some other immigration benefit (such as asylum) allowing her to remain in the United States.

Knoetze v. Dep't of State
634 F.2d 207 (5th Cir. 1981), cert. denied,
454 U.S. 823 (1981)

* * *

Knoetze, a world-class boxer and former policeman from South Africa, came to the United States on a non-immigrant visa to take part in a prize fight. Knoetze then discovered through the news media that his visa had been revoked. The Secretary of State revoked his visa after concluding that Knoetze was convicted in South Africa of a crime corresponding to an American felony involving moral turpitude. The Immigration and Nationality Act renders such foreign convicts ineligible for a visa of entry into our country. 8 U.S.C. § 1182(a)(9).

Knoetze received a preliminary injunction against deportation and competed in the prize fight. He also applied for an H-class visa, which would have permitted him to work in this country. The Immigration and Na[tur]alization Service (INS) denied this application because of the Secretary's act of revocation.

The trial court refused to grant a permanent injunction against the revocation of Knoetze's visa. The court agreed with Knoetze that the Secretary's act of revocation was subject to judicial review. The court also considered Knoetze's charge that civil rights leaders had exerted such intense political pressure upon the executive branch as to constitute impermissible levels of "political interference." Yet the court accepted the position of the Secretary that Knoetze's visa was lawfully revoked because of an admitted conviction in South Africa for a crime which the Secretary reasonably viewed as equivalent to an American felony involving moral turpitude.

This South African crime is entitled "Attempting to Obstruct or Impede the Process of Justice." The indictment to which Knoetze pled guilty alleged that he made several false statements while serving as a policeman in order to persuade citizens of his country to drop assault charges against a fellow police officer. The trial court accepted the conclusion of the Secretary that Knoetze's criminal conduct corresponded to the United States felony of "Influencing or Injuring an Officer, Juror or Witness," 18 U.S.C. § 1503, a felony involving moral turpitude. The trial court therefore upheld the Secretary's act of revocation.

* * *

We agree with the trial court that the judiciary may review a decision by the Secretary of State to revoke the visa of an alien within our country. On appeal, the government has dropped its argument of non-reviewability. The proper standard of judicial review is expressed in the Administrative Procedure Act, 5 U.S.C. § 706(2). This is the limited standard of review applicable in the analogous context of deportation proceedings. *Wong Yang Sung v. McGrath*, 339 U.S. 33 (1950); *Jarecha v. INS*, 417 F.2d 220 (5th Cir. 1969).

* * *

Under this limited standard of review, we can enjoin the revocation of Knoetze's visa only if the Secretary has violated the law or committed a clear error of judgment. *Bowman Transportation, Inc. v. Arkansas-Best Freight Systems, Inc.*, 419 F.2d 281 (1974); *Refrigerated Transport Co. v. ICC*, 616 F.2d 748 (5th Cir. 1980). Our standard of review is the same as that of the trial court.

Congress has conferred upon the Secretary the power to revoke a visa in the following language: "After the issuance of a visa or other documentation to any alien, the consular officer, or the Secretary of State may at any time, in his discretion, revoke such visa or other documentation." 8 U.S.C. § 1201(i). No court has been called upon to decide whether this broad language confers authority upon the Secretary to revoke the visa of an alien after his entry into our country.

Knoetze argues that § 1201(i) merely confers revocation power prior to an alien's entry into the United States. He makes three supporting arguments. First, the overall statute to which this section belongs addresses the procedures for the issuance of visas to foreigners seeking initial entry. 8 U.S.C. § 1151-1230. The language of § 1201(i) itself, after authorizing visa revocation, goes on to treat the liabilities of a transportation company that brings aliens into the country after the revocation of their visas.

Second, Congress entrusted major responsibility over aliens within the country to the Attorney General, rather than the Secretary of State, under a wholly different statutory scheme. 8 U.S.C. §§ 1251-60.

Third, Knoetze argues that the provision of due process safeguards in the Attorney General's deportation authorization, § 1252(b), coupled with the absence of any such safeguards in the Secretary's visa revocation authorization, § 1201(i), indicates a legislative intention of assigning responsibility for handling aliens within our country to the Attorney General, rather than the Secretary of State. Knoetze bolsters this argument by noting that aliens within the country are constitutionally entitled to procedural due process, while those outside the country receive no constitutional protection. He contends that in recognition of this distinction, Congress provided procedural safeguards in the Attorney General's deportation authorization because Congress intended the Attorney General to have responsibility over aliens after their arrival. We disagree.

We accept the argument of the government that § 1201(i) means exactly what it says: the Secretary may revoke an alien's visa "at any time." We reject Knoetze's invitation to limit this clear and broad language. We must assume that Congress used the unambiguous words "at any time" as they are commonly understood, even if a different interpretation would yield a result we would prefer. *U.S. v. Stewart*, 311 U.S. 60 (1940). Moreover, we accord considerable deference to the interpretation of § 1201(i) by the Department of State, the agency empowered by Congress to administer the issuance and revocation of visas. We hold that Congress has conferred upon the Secretary the authority to revoke the visa of an alien "at any time," even after he has entered our country.

We must now consider the substantive and procedural limitations upon the power conferred by § 1201(i). These limitations are implicit in the standard of review expressed in the Administrative Procedure Act, 5 U.S.C. § 706(2): (a) the Secretary must comply with any statutory procedures for the revocation of a visa; (b) the Secretary's act of revocation must not exceed his statutory authority; (c) the Secretary may not abuse his discretion by acting capriciously in revoking a visa; and (d) the Secretary must respect the constitutional rights enjoyed by visa holders within our borders. The Secretary's method of revoking Knoetze's visa violated no statutory procedural requirements because the authorizing statute contains no procedural requisites. 8 U.S.C. § 1201(i). The Secretary acted within the bounds of his statutory authority because § 1201(i), as interpreted above, permitted the Secretary to revoke Knoetze's visa even after Knoetze had fully entered our country.

We further find that the Secretary lawfully acted within his discretion in revoking Knoetze's visa. The trial court determined that the Secretary revoked Knoetze's visa not because of impermissible "political interference," but because of Knoetze's conviction for a South African crime reasonably believed to correspond to an American felony involving moral turpitude.

Strong evidence of the politicalization of an otherwise routine, bureaucratic decision might raise a suspicion of discriminatory agency action. In this case, however, it is undisputed that Knoetze pled guilty to the South African crime of "Attempting to Obstruct or Impede the Process of Justice."

*　　*　　*

The American consul in South Africa issued Knoetze a visa because it believed that his offense fell within the misdemeanor petty offense exception of this Act. 8 U.S.C. § 1182(a)(9). The Secretary later concluded that Knoetze's conviction corresponded to a conviction for a felony involving moral turpitude. Because South African law differs greatly from American law, the Secretary compared the South African crime of "Attempting to Obstruct or Impede the Process of Justice" to the federal crime of "Influencing or Injuring an Officer, Juror or Witness," 18 U.S.C. § 1503. The acts prohibited by § 1503 constitute a felony. See 18 U.S.C. § 1(1). The misdemeanor petty offense exception is therefore inapplicable. The fraudulent acts prohibited by § 1503 also indicate moral turpitude: "fraud has consistently been regarded as such a contaminating component in any crime that American courts have, without exception, included such crimes within the scope of moral turpitude." *Jordan v. DeGeorge*, 341 U.S. 223, 229 (1951). The Secretary thus concluded that Knoetze was ineligible for a visa under 8 U.S.C. § 1182(a)(9).

... The conclusion reached by the Secretary in this case does not appear to be arbitrary or capricious or otherwise abusive of the discretion conferred upon him by § 1201(i). Even if experts differ as to whether Knoetze's foreign conviction corresponds to a felony involving moral turpitude, and even if hindsight shows that the Secretary has erred, his methods and conclusions appear entirely reasonable.

We must now determine whether the revocation of Knoetze's visa without notice complied with the due process rights guaranteed by the Constitution. The fifth amendment to the Constitution provides that "[n]o person shall be ... deprived of life, liberty, or property, without due process of law." ... [F]ifth amendment protection attaches only when the federal government seeks to deny a liberty or property interest. *Perry v. Sinderman*, 408 U.S. 593 (1972).

Knoetze argues that he has such a protected interest in the retention of his entry visa. He points out that he was denied a working visa by INS because of the revocation of his entry visa by the State Department. He contends that by denying him the opportunity to work in our country, the government effectively denied him the ability to remain here. Knoetze therefore urges us to recognize the constitutionally protected liberty and property interest in the retention of his visa. We decline.

We accept the position of the government that the revocation of an entry visa issued to an alien already within our country has no effect upon the alien's liberty or property interests. Revocation of an entry visa by the Secretary does not automatically lead to deportation of the alien. Congress has entrusted deportation to a different department of government, the Attorney General, and established different criteria for deportation than those for visa issuance and revocation. 8 U.S.C. § 1251 (Deportable Aliens—General Classes). Moreover, Congress has provided extensive procedural safeguards to those subject to deportation, including the right to reasonable notice, a fair hearing, opportunity for cross-examination and legal representation. 8 U.S.C. § 1252(b). Since deportation does not automatically follow visa revocation and any resulting deportation proceeding includes significant procedural safeguards, we hold that the revocation of an alien's visa jeopardizes no liberty or property interest entitled to constitutional protection.

Notes

1. Is the Court's conclusion that Knoetze has a liberty interest reasonable? What counter-arguments would you have made to this point?

2. Is the court's statement that revocation of a visa is not necessarily followed by deportation proceedings a fair characterization of the procedural posture in which Knoetze found himself? Does this make any difference to the underlying constitutional question?

3. If Knoetze had been denied a visa by the U.S. consul in South Africa, his case could not have been reviewed under the doctrine of non-reviewability of consular decisions. *See Kleindienst v. Mandel*, 408 U.S. 753, 766 (1972) and discussion at Chapter 6. However, litigants have been able to obtain review of visa revocations. *See Wong v. Dep't of State*, 789 F.2d 1380 (9th Cir. 1986). How would Knoetze have obtained review if his visa had been revoked prior to his arrival in the U.S.? Recently, a district court held that it had jurisdiction to review an overseas visa revocation where the litigant was in the U.S. Apparently, the consul had granted the applicant a B-1 visa to allow him to tidy his affairs. *Shimizu v. Dep't of State*, CV 89-2741 (C.D. Cal. May 31, 1990).

4. The procedures governing visa revocation are found at 22 C.F.R. § 41.122. The notes to the Foreign Affairs Manual instruct consular officers not to revoke the visa if the person is "believed to be in the U.S. or has begun an uninterrupted journey to the U.S." 9 FAM 41.122, note 2. The procedure to be followed in such cases is for the consul to notify the Department of State which will then determine whether revocation and notification of the INS is appropriate. 9 FAM 41.122, procedural note 3.2.

B. Revocation of Immigrant Visas and Section 204(c)

As we have seen, marriage fraud has been a recurring problem in immigration cases. Getting permanent residency based on a marriage to a citizen or permanent resident is difficult enough. Those who are later discovered to have fraudulently obtained their immigration benefits face severe consequences.

In 1961 Congress enacted 8 U.S.C. § 1154(c), Sec. 204(c) in an effort to curb what it perceived as a serious problem of sham marriages designed to obtain permanent residence.[2] As can be seen, the legal consequences of marriage fraud have always been quite severe. Read the following Section 204(c) cases and consider how the Board dealt with its statutory mandate.

---

8 U.S.C. § 1154(c), Sec. 204

Notwithstanding the provisions of subsection (b) of this section no petition shall be approved if (1) the alien has previously been accorded, or has sought to be accorded, immediate relative or preference status as the spouse of a citizen of the United States or the spouse of an alien lawfully admitted for permanent residence, by reason of a marriage determined by the Attorney General to have been entered into for the purpose of evading the immigration laws, or (2) the Attorney General has determined that the alien has attempted or conspired to enter into a marriage for the purpose of evading the immigration laws.

Matter of Rahmati
16 I. & N. Dec. 538 (BIA 1978)

The United States citizen petitioner applied for immediate relative status for the beneficiary as her spouse under section 201(b) of the Immigration and Nationality Act, 8 U.S.C. 1151(b). The petition was approved on October 20, 1977. In a decision dated February 15, 1978, the District Director revoked approval of the petition on the ground that the beneficiary had previously been accorded immediate relative status as the spouse of a United States citizen by reason of a marriage determined by the Attorney General to have been entered into for the purpose of evading the immigration laws. The petitioner has appealed. The appeal will be sustained.

The beneficiary, a 36-year-old native and citizen of Iran, married the petitioner in 1973. The record reflects that this was his second marriage to a United States citizen. The first occurred in 1967.

On the basis of the 1967 marriage, the beneficiary was granted immediate relative status under section 201(b) of the Act as the spouse of a United States citizen, and his status was adjusted to that of a lawful permanent resident under section 245 of the Act, 8 U.S.C. 1255.

On April 27, 1971, after proceedings under section 246(a) of the Act, 8 U.S.C. 1256(a), an immigration judge ordered the beneficiary's grant of status as a lawful permanent resident rescinded on the ground that the 1967 marriage was no longer viable when it was used as a basis for adjusting the beneficiary's status. Although the beneficiary and his spouse had lived together, and a child had been born to them, they had not lived together continuously for more than a few months at a time and she had left him before his status was adjusted. The record reflects that she obtained a divorce on November 19, 1968.

The District Director based his decision on section 204(c) of the Act, 8 U.S.C. 1154(c), which states that " . . . no petition shall be approved if the alien has previously

---

2. Act of Sept. 26, 1961, Pub. L. No. 87-301, 35 Stat. 654. Efforts to curb marriage fraud were extended further when Congress enacted the Immigration Marriage Fraud Amendments, Pub. L. No. 99-639, 100 Stat. 3537 (1986). See discussion *infra* at Chapters 6 and 9.

been accorded a nonquota or preference status as the spouse of a citizen of the United States . . . by reason of a marriage determined by the Attorney General to have been entered into for the purpose of evading the immigration laws." The District Director apparently considered the prior decision of the immigration judge in the rescission proceedings to be a conclusive determination that the beneficiary's prior marriage to a United States citizen was entered into for the purpose of evading the immigration laws. This conclusion was erroneous.

The section 204(c) decision is to be made on behalf of the Attorney General by the District Director in the course of his adjudication of the subsequent visa petition. *Matter of Samsen*, Interim Decision 2305 (BIA 1974). In making that adjudication, he may rely on any relevant evidence, including evidence having its origin in prior Service proceedings involving the beneficiary. This determination, however, is for the District Director to make, and he shall not ordinarily give conclusive effect to the determinations made in the prior collateral proceedings. He should reach his own independent conclusion based on the evidence actually before him. See *Matter of F—*, 9 I. & N. Dec. 684 (BIA 1962).

The record in this case does not support the District Director's conclusion that the beneficiary's prior marriage was entered into for the purpose of evading the immigration laws. The rescission determination dealt only with the viability of the marriage at the time when adjustment of status was granted. Section 204(c), however, goes to the underlying purpose of the marriage. *Matter of Samsen, supra.* We note, moreover, that the beneficiary and his spouse of that marriage apparently lived together as man and wife and had a child together. Thus, it does not appear that the marriage was entered into for the purpose of evading the immigration laws.

We conclude, therefore, that the District Director's determination regarding the beneficiary's previous marriage is erroneous. Accordingly, the petitioner's appeal will be sustained, and the District Director's decision will be reversed.

ORDER: The appeal is sustained, and the approval of the visa petition is reinstated.

Matter of Anselmo
16 I. & N. Dec. 152 (BIA 1977)

The lawful permanent resident petitioner applied for preference status for the beneficiary as his spouse under section 203(a)(2) of the Immigration and Nationality Act. In a decision dated March 29, 1976, the District Director denied the petition and the petitioner has appealed from that denial. The record will be remanded to the District Director for further proceedings.

Both the petitioner and the beneficiary are natives and citizens of the Philippine Islands. The beneficiary had previously been accorded immediate relative status as the spouse of a United States citizen and had entered the United States as a lawful permanent resident on July 14, 1973. In a sworn statement to the Service, dated October 31, 1974, the beneficiary admitted that the marriage upon which the first visa petition had been based was a fiction and that she had neither met nor married the man listed as her spouse. On February 22, 1975, the beneficiary married the present petitioner who subsequently filed another visa petition in her behalf. The

District Director concluded that the beneficiary had previously been accorded immediate relative status as the spouse of a United States citizen by reason of a marriage entered into in order to circumvent the immigration laws. Relying on section 204(c) of the Act, the District Director denied the petition.

Section 204(c) states, in pertinent part, that—

...no petition shall be approved if the alien has previously been accorded a nonquota or preference status as the spouse of a citizen of the United States..., by reason of a *marriage* determined by the Attorney General to have been *entered into* for the purpose of evading the immigration laws. (Emphasis supplied.)

The beneficiary has previously been accorded immediate relative status as the spouse of a United States citizen. However, she was accorded that status, according to her sworn statement, on the basis of falsified documents, not on the basis of a marriage *entered into* for the purpose of evading the immigration laws. Although the beneficiary benefited from the Service determination that a valid marriage existed, a marriage did not in fact exist. In the absence of an actual marriage, section 204(c) does not apply. *Matter of Concepcion*, Interim Decision 2529 (BIA September 8, 1976).

We note from the record that, at present, the beneficiary apparently possesses the very status that ultimately would be accorded her should the visa petition be approved. Although she has admitted that her present lawful permanent resident status was fraudulently obtained, the record is silent as to whether the Service has as yet instituted deportation or rescission proceedings. Should the Service take such action, the beneficiary would then be eligible, as an "alien" within the meaning of section 245 of the Act, to seek to adjust her status to that of a permanent resident alien. See *Matter of Calilao*, Interim Decision 2555 (BIA February 7, 1977). Under 8 C.F.R. 245.1(d), an applicant for preference status is not eligible for adjustment of status unless he or she is the beneficiary of a valid unexpired visa petition filed in accordance with 8 C.F.R. 204 and approved to accord such status. Accordingly, while the need for this visa petition has not been conclusively demonstrated, in view of the beneficiary's apparent deportable status, and the possibility that approval may be needed as a prerequisite for adjustment, we would normally entertain the petition on its merits.

However, the District Director based his decision on section 204(c), and it does not appear that he considered whether the beneficiary's present marriage is bona fide. Therefore, on remand, the District Director may determine whether the marriage between the petitioner and the beneficiary is bona fide. See *Matter of Phillis*, Interim Decision 2407 (BIA 1975).

Warren R. Torrington, Member, Dissenting:

* * *

In my view, the language of section 204(c) of the Immigration and Nationality Act is broad enough to encompass the situations encountered in *Concepcion* and in the case now before us. A person who has not even bothered to go to the trouble of entering into a sham marriage (that is, a marriage entered into for the purposes of evading the immigration laws), but has merely pretended to be married, and has presented false documents as evidence of a marriage, should not, on what appears to me to be specious reasoning, be considered outside the provisions of section 204(c) of the Act. In my view, he is less entitled to approval of a second visa petition than the person who has previously gone through the formalities of a (sham) marriage; and a holding which treats him better than it does a person who has gone through the motions of a sham marriage does not make good sense. *Concepcion* permits aliens to avoid the clear provisions of section 204(c) of the Act by not even going to the trouble of entering into actual sham marriages. I cannot consider that a commendable outcome.

This is strictly a visa petition matter. The matter of possible future adjustment of the beneficiary's status is not before us. I therefore fail to see the relevance of the references, in the majority opinion, to a possible future application for adjustment of the beneficiary status, and to the fact that the record does not reveal whether rescission or deportation proceedings are pending.

As I read the Second Circuit's decision in *Tibke v. INS*, 335 F.2d 42 (2d Cir. 1964), which the majority opinion does not mention, but which was relied on in the here cited decision in *Matter of Calilao*, Interim Decision 2555 (BIA February 7, 1977), *Tibke* does not make rescission or deportation proceedings a prerequisite for approval of visa petitions filed for potentially deportable permanent resident aliens. All we have now before us in such a visa petition.

Matter of Oseguera
17 I. & N. Dec. 386 (BIA 1980)

The United States citizen petitioner filed a visa petition on behalf of the beneficiary to accord her immediate relative status as his mother under section 201(b) of the Immigration and Nationality Act, 8 U.S.C. 1151(b). In a decision dated September 11, 1978, the District Director denied the petition. The petitioner has appealed from that decision. The appeal will be sustained and the record will be remanded to the District Director.

The petitioner is a 24-year-old native of Mexico and naturalized citizen of the United States. The beneficiary is a 47-year-old native and citizen of Mexico.

The record reflects that the beneficiary entered the United States as an immigrant on January 7, 1960, with a visa indicating that she was classified as an O-1 nonquota immigrant. Subsequent to her entry, the beneficiary admitted to immigration officials that, on the advice of a notary public, she had entered into a sham marriage with a person whom she believed to be Francisco Calderon-Ramirez, a lawful permanent resident of the United States, in order to facilitate her acquisition of permanent resident status.[1]

* * *

---

1. The beneficiary, in fact, unwittingly married someone posing as Francisco Calderon-Ramirez, whose immigration documents had been borrowed by the notary public for use, without his knowledge, in obtaining a visa for the beneficiary. The scheme was discovered by the Service when Mr. Calderon-Ramirez reported that he had received visas in the mail for the beneficiary and the petitioner, whom he did not know. Having admitted the fraudulent marriage, the beneficiary was apparently permitted to leave the country voluntarily. We note that the record contains documents relative to her subsequent immigration history which need not be discussed since they are not relevant to the issue on appeal.

In our previous discussion, we explored the treatment of persons who were seeking status in the U.S. Now we shall consider how the statute deals with persons who are lawful permanent residents.

The Board has previously determined that the language of section 204(c) is unrestricted, barring approval not only of new "spouse" petitions but of all subsequent visa petitions, and that its mandatory provisions do not permit the exercise of any discretion. See *Matter of La Grotta*, 14 I & N Dec. 110 (BIA 1972); *Matter of Cabeliza*, 11 I & N Dec. 812 (BIA 1966). However, before approval of a visa petition can be denied pursuant to section 204(c), it must be established that a fraudulent marriage was entered into and that the beneficiary was issued a visa as a nonquota or preference immigrant on the basis of that marriage. See *Amarante v. Rosenberg*, 326 F.2d 58 (9th Cir. 1964); *Matter of Rubino*, 15 I & N Dec. 194 (BIA 1975); *Matter of Pisciotta*, 10 I & N Dec. 685 (BIA 1964); *Matter of F—*, 9 I & N Dec. 684 (BIA 1962).

In the instant case, the record clearly indicates that the beneficiary fraudulently entered into a marriage for the purpose of obtaining immigration benefits. However, it is equally apparent from the O-1 classification on her visa that she was accorded nonquota status as a native of Mexico, not as the spouse of a lawful permanent resident of the United States. Therefore, we conclude that approval of the visa petition filed by her son on her behalf is not precluded by section 204(c). Cf. *Matter of Villagomez*, 15 I & N Dec. 528 (BIA 1975). Accordingly, the appeal will be sustained.

Notes

1. What would have been the effect had the petition been denied under 204(c)? What action would the INS have taken had they approved the petition and discovered the alleged fraudulent act prior to the admission of the beneficiary? What would have been the procedure used had the beneficiary been admitted and the fraud had been discovered later?

2. **Immigrant visa revocation.** Unlike the treatment of marriages under 204(c), immigrant visas once approved are considered valid as long as the relationship exists between the petitioner and the beneficiary. The procedures for immigrant visa revocation are prescribed at 8 C.F.R. § 205 *et seq*. Where the applicant has not yet been admitted to the U.S., or the consul or the INS learn of the termination of the relationship, then she will be subject to exclusion. In the event that the INS or the consul learn of the termination of the relationship subsequent to the applicant's admission to the U.S., she may be subject to deportation. The critical issue will be whether the relationship was terminated prior to or following the applicant's admission to the United States.

3. It should be noted that *Rahmati*, *Oseguera*, and *Anselmo* were decided prior to the enactment of the Immigration Marriage Fraud Amendments which changed Section 204(c) to include the language "or has sought to procure" in place of "previously been accorded."

4. After reading these cases, are you able to draw any conclusions as to why the Board interpreted Section 204(c) narrowly rather than broadly?

5. Was the dissent in *Anselmo* correct in the statement that 204(c) was broad enough to encompass a fictitious marriage used to obtain immigration benefits?

6. In *Anselmo*, the Board referred to the possibility of the petitioner's applying for adjustment of status. Who would adjudicate this application? How do you think the application would be decided?

C. Rescission of Adjustment

Earlier, we explored the treatment afforded to persons who were seeking permanent residency status in the United States. Now we shall consider how the statute deals with persons who have been admitted to lawful permanent residence and are later found to have been ineligible for that status. As can be seen from the cases which follow, there has been some confusion on how these people should be treated.

---

8 U.S.C. § 1256, Sec. 246

(a) If, at any time within five years after the status of a person has been adjusted under the provisions of section 1254 of this title or under section 19(c) of the Immigration Act of February 5, 1917, to that of an alien lawfully admitted for permanent residence, it shall appear to the satisfaction of the Attorney General that the person was not in fact eligible for such adjustment of status, the Attorney General shall submit to the Congress a complete and detailed statement of the facts and pertinent provisions of law in the case. Such reports shall be submitted on the first and fifteenth day of each calendar month in which Congress is in session. If during the session of the Congress at which a case is reported, or prior to the close of the session of the Congress next following the session at which a case is reported, the Congress passes a concurrent resolution withdrawing suspension of deportation, the person shall thereupon be subject to all provisions of this chapter to the same extent as if the adjustment of status had not been made. If, at any time within five years after the status of a person has been otherwise adjusted under the provisions of section 1255 or 1259 of this title or any other provision of law to that of an alien lawfully admitted for permanent residence, it shall appear to the satisfaction of the Attorney General that the person was not in fact eligible for such adjustment of status, the Attorney General shall rescind the action taken granting an adjustment of status to such person and cancelling deportation in the case of such person if that occurred and the person shall thereupon be subject to all provisions of this chapter to the same extent as if the adjustment of status had not been made.

(b) Any person who has become a naturalized citizen of the United States upon the basis of a record of a lawful admission for permanent residence, created as a result of an adjustment of status for which such person was not in fact eligible, and which is subsequently rescinded under subsection (a) of this section, shall be subject to the provisions of section 1451 of this title as a person whose naturalization was procured by concealment of a material fact or by willful misrepresentation.

* * *

Matter of Saunders

16 I. & N. Dec. 326 (BIA 1977)

Before the Board, January 27, 1977

In a decision dated January 30, 1976, the immigration judge found the respondent deportable as charged and ordered his deportation to Great Britain. The respondent has appealed from that decision. The appeal will be sustained.

The respondent, a native and citizen of Great Britain, was convicted in England for possession of marihuana in 1969 and 1971. He entered the United States as a nonimmigrant visitor for pleasure in 1973 and subsequently married a United States citizen. The respondent thereafter made an application for adjustment of status to that of a lawful permanent resident under section 245 of the Immigration and Nationality Act. In connection with this application the respondent disclosed the fact of his convictions. The Immigration and Naturalization Service granted the application on October 1, 1974, and the respondent's status was adjusted to that of a lawful permanent resident.

Shortly thereafter, on November 13, 1974, the Acting District Director sent a letter to the respondent notifying him of his intention to rescind the respondent's permanent resident status pursuant to the provisions of section 246 of the Act and informing him of his opportunity to answer within 30 days. The letter, which is in the record before us, states that the respondent was ineligible for adjustment of status under sections 212(a)(23) and 212(a)(19) of the Act. It contains the following statements:

> (1) You have been found ineligible under Section 212(a)(23) for two convictions of illegal possession of narcotic drugs or marihuana to receive a visa for entry into the United States.

> (2) You have been found ineligible under Section 212(a)(19), for obtaining or procuring a visa or other documentation to enter the United States by fraud or by wilfully misrepresenting a material fact, by not revealing the prior arrests and convictions, at the time you obtained your nonimmigrant visa at the American Embassy in London.

The respondent, who did not receive the letter of November 13, 1974, but learned of the action against him from a friend who received the letter, wrote the Service from Mexico requesting a six-month period within which to depart from the United States. In his letter he stated that he did not deny allegations made against him. On December 23, 1974 the District Director notified the respondent that his permanent resident status had been rescinded. This letter was returned undelivered to the Service. These deportation proceedings were subsequently instituted against the respondent under section 241(a)(11) of the Act which provides that any alien who has been convicted of a violation of any law relating to the illicit possession of marihuana shall be deported.

*   *   *

In those cases in which section 246 is applicable, its provisions must be complied with before deportation proceedings may be instituted. *Matter of V—*, 7 I. & N. Dec. 363 (BIA 1956). If, within five years of the alien's adjustment of status under section 245, it appears that the alien was ineligible for that adjustment, his permanent resident status must be rescinded pursuant to section 246 before deportation proceedings can be instituted against him.

In the present case, rescission proceedings were instituted against the respondent prior to these proceedings. Counsel, however, has raised a question as to whether the respondent had notice of the procedural safeguards guaranteed him in those proceedings. See generally 8 C.F.R. 246. In this case defenses that would have been available to the respondent in rescission proceedings may have been lost for failure to raise them. Under these circumstances, we shall terminate deportation proceedings. The District Director, of course, may determine to reinstitute rescission proceedings against the respondent. That decision lies generally within his discretion. See *Matter of Quan*, 12 I. & N. Dec. 487 (Deputy Assoc. Comm'r. 1967).

In view of the above opinion, we need not address the issue of estoppel.

ORDER: The appeal is sustained; the proceedings are terminated.

Before the Board August 25, 1977

The Service has moved that we reconsider our decision dated January 27, 1977 sustaining the respondent's appeal and terminating the proceedings. The motion will be denied.

In our decision we held that, because five years had not passed since the respondent had his status adjusted to that of a lawful permanent resident under section 245 of the Immigration and Nationality Act, his permanent resident status must be rescinded pursuant to section 246 before deportation proceedings could be instituted against him. Because it appeared that the respondent did not have adequate notice of the procedural safeguards guaranteed him in the rescission proceedings which had been brought against him, we ordered that the deportation proceedings be terminated. We pointed out in our opinion that the decision whether to reinstitute rescission proceedings against him lies within the discretion of the District Director. In view of our decision to terminate, we did not reach the issue of estoppel which was raised by the respondent.

The Service presents two issues in its Motion to Reconsider. First, it contends that the respondent had adequate notice of the rescission proceedings against him. With respect to this issue, the respondent testified that, while he was on vacation, the notice of intention to rescind was mailed to him. The person living in the respondent's home signed the return receipt and informed the respondent by telephone of the contents of the letter. The notice dated December 23, 1974, advising the respondent that his status had been rescinded was not received by the respondent and was returned to the Service undelivered.

Ordinarily, the notice of intention to rescind provided the respondent would be sufficient under section 246. See 8 C.F.R. 246.1. However, this case presents unusual circumstances, in particular, an intention by the Service to rescind the adjustment on the basis of evidence which was provided by the alien at the time his status was adjusted. Moreover, the respondent was on vacation at the time of the proceedings, and there is evidence that the Service knew it. The respondent also contends that another Service office informed him that his adjustment could be rescinded only after the commission of a felony. Under these circumstances, we conclude that the notice of intention to rescind provided the respondent was insufficient. The respondent did not have an adequate opportunity to be heard—a safeguard provided him under the law.

With respect to the first contention of the Service, it is also argued that *Matter of Quan*, 12 I. & N. Dec. 487 (Dep. Assoc. Comm'r. 1967), a case cited in our January 27, 1977, decision, is distinguishable. Reference to our decision will show that *Matter of Quan* was cited as support for the point that the District Director is not compelled to institute rescission proceedings in every case. His decision is a matter for the exercise of discretion.

The Service also contends that an alien whose status is adjusted under section 245 is not thereby exempt from the exclusion and deportation provisions of the Act. We agree. Relying on *Matter of V*, 7 I. & N. Dec. 363 (BIA 1956), we merely held that, during the five years subsequent to the alien's adjustment, the adjustment must be rescinded where it appears that the alien was not in fact eligible for the adjustment before deportation proceedings can be instituted against him on the basis of his ineligibility. It is the Service's contention that the holding in *Matter of V* is inapplicable because in the present case, unlike in *Matter of V*, the ground of ineligibility could have subjected the respondent to deportation prior to the adjustment. We disagree. We are of the opinion that the distinction is not material.

The Service also claims that our holding with respect to the necessity of first rescinding the adjustment before deportation proceeding can be instituted is erroneous in view of the Attorney General's decision in *Matter of S—*, 9 I. & N. Dec. 548 (BIA 1961; Attorney General 1962; BIA 1962). In *Matter of S—*, the Attorney General was presented with a case in which the five year period had passed and the alien was claiming that, as a consequence, he was saved from deportation on grounds which existed prior to the adjustment. In the present case, five years have not passed, since the respondent's status was adjusted. Therefore, *Matter of S—*, is inapposite.

Our decision of January 27, 1977, is correct. The Motion to Reconsider will be denied.

Irving A. Appleman, Member, Concurring:

*   *   *

In our decision of February 4, 1977, sustaining the appeal and terminating proceedings, we noted that the respondent had raised three contentions. The first of these, relating to the Second Circuit decision in *Lennon v. INS*, 527 F.2d 187 (1975), was ruled on adversely to the respondent, because we are concerned with a different statute than in *Lennon*. As to the second, we found merit, in the somewhat unusual facts of the case, to the argument that there was doubt whether the respondent had adequate notice of the procedural safeguards guaranteed him under section 246 of the Act (8 U.S.C. 1256), and 8 C.F.R. 246.

It will be noted that this alien, adjudicated a lawful permanent resident in 1974, would have defenses available to him in a rescission proceeding which are not available to him in these deportation proceedings. An initial consideration would be whether the institution of rescission proceedings was warranted. While rescission may occur, in the literal language of the statute, for "lack of eligibility" alone (Section 246, 8 U.S.C. 1256), it is, in the experience of this Member, most unusual to attempt rescission where some element of fraud or concealment was not involved in the adjustment. Respondent could certainly argue that the congressional intent of the rescission provision did not cover one in his position. Alternatively, he would urge that as a matter of prosecutive judgment, quite apart from estoppel, having fully disclosed a relatively minor arrest record, and having effected complete rehabilitation (so far as the record before us reveals) the Service should not pursue rescission. More importantly, in rescission proceedings, the alien could raise the estoppel issue in the direct framework of the claimed prejudicial action, with appropriate appeals and review if decision were adverse.

In contrast, in deportation proceedings, if rescission is viewed as a *fait accompli*, the respondent has lost his favored status as a lawful permanent resident, and the inquiry is limited to the lawfulness of his status before the adjustment occurred—in this case, whether in 1974 he had remained longer as a nonimmigrant than authorized. (Section 246 8 U.S.C. 1256.)

There is no question that the respondent was seriously prejudiced by the failure to have a hearing in the rescission proceedings. The vigor with which the Service resists affording him that opportunity is somewhat startling, given the somewhat unusual facts of the case. It is a fact that the respondent did not receive the letter advising of an intention to rescind. There is considerable question, from this record, what was read to him during the long distance telephone call by his "friend." Respondent's letter of December 9, 1974, from Mexico (Ex. 5) says that he has "heard of the allegations." Was he also fully aware of his rights to a hearing and to make a defense? His letter does not indicate it. On the contrary it reveals a woeful ignorance of his position. Far from reflecting an understanding that the Service letter was a *Notice of Intention to Rescind*, only; he appears to have accepted the letter as a determination of deportability, something which may or may not occur *after* rescission takes place and which usually requires the institution of separate proceedings, as this case illustrates. Nowhere does Exhibit 5 reflect respondent's understanding of his rights under the law. On the contrary he asks for "compassion" and "understanding," and for a few months to put his affairs in order before leaving. He states his intention to contact the Service on arrival in the United States. Two weeks later, after an *in absentia* determination, the letter advising of the fact of rescission went out.

One cannot help question the "compassion" and "understanding" received by this lawful permanent resident, married to a United States citizen, with a United States citizen child, who, after complete disclosure of his "crimes," suddenly gets word, as he erroneously understands it, that his permanent residence has already been taken away and he must leave the country forthwith. In these circumstances I completely concur in that portion of the majority decision which rejects the Service argument that there was adequate compliance with procedural due process requirements in the rescission action. In this connection it is worth noting that the burden the United States bears in a rescission proceeding is the same clear, convincing and unequivocal burden borne in deportation, *Waziri v. INS*, 392 F.2d 55 (9th Cir. 1968).

It is further contention of the Service that this alien is subject to deportation proceedings in any event, and even without the institution of rescission proceedings, since the ground for deportation existed prior to the adjustment of status. As to this I am in agreement with the majority that the interpretation given the statute by the Attorney General in *Matter of S—*, 9 I. & N. Dec. 548 (BIA 1962), does not warrant the conclusion the Service urges, but I reach that result for somewhat different reasons.

Matter of S— was an exclusion proceeding. The alien fraudulently obtained an adjustment of status in April 1955, concealing the fact that he had obtained a visa by fraud in 1949. No rescission occurred within five years. Instead, the facts came to light when he attempted to reenter the United States in August 1960, as a lawfully returning resident alien after a visit abroad. The Board held that the passing of the five years operated as a statute of limitation barring exclusion on any ground which existed prior to the adjustment. Pointing to the Congressional history, the Attorney General noted that adjustment under section 245 was never intended to confer greater rights than those enjoyed by a permanent resident who gained his status through entry with an immigrant visa. Since there exists no statute of limitation as to the latter, and he may be deported or excluded at any time, for proper cause, the same treatment must be accorded the alien adjusted under section 245,. . . .

What then is the effect and meaning of the five-year limitation in section 246, on rescission of permanent resident status? In this area *Matter of S—* is somewhat vague, and one can readily appreciate the Service difficulty in applying the provision. The solution the Service offers here, however, is, for all practical purposes, to read section 246 out of the statute altogether. I cannot agree that Congress intended section 246 to be that meaningless.

The majority decision points to one instance where section 246 should be applicable, i.e., where deportation (or exclusion) is sought, as here, *within* the five-year period. This has the virtue of reconciling *Matter of S—*, as the Attorney General pointed out, with the earlier decision of this Board in *Matter of V—*, 7 I. & N. Dec. 363 (BIA 1956). In the Attorney General's language, in *Matter of V—* (as here) the rescission procedure, specifically provided to determine the issue of the alien's ineligibility for the record of lawful admission, was "available," the five years not yet having elapsed; whereas in *Matter of S—* this was not the case. The majority decision thus finds some support in *Matter of S—*. However, the implication which flows from this is that *within* the five years a deportation or exclusion proceeding based on a ground rendering the alien ineligible for the adjustment must be preceded by rescission, but that *after* the five years there need be no compliance with section 246. The difficulty with this is the lack of any reason for such a distinction. On the contrary, why should the alien who had been a lawful permanent resident for more than five years, with correspondingly greater equities, be in a far worse position than one who has resided here for a shorter period of time?

In my opinion section 246 does permit of another interpretation. As to any ground of deportation or exclusion, known and embraced by the grant of adjustment of status, the five-year rule should apply with full force, and operate as a full statute of limitations. As to any ground arising before the grant of adjustment, and not known at the time of adjustment, deportation or exclusion proceedings should lie without regard to rescission and the five-year rule. In short, section 245 should be read as a waiver and adjustment of known grounds of disability. As to these, if the Service is to deport or exclude, it must first rescind under section 246, and must do so within five years. As to all other grounds the alien is no different from any other permanent resident. With this interpretation the Congressional intent is given meaning and the existing case law reconciled.

Applied here, this interpretation clearly dictates the necessity of a rescission proceeding, and for this reason I have concurred in the result reached by the majority. For the reasons set forth in part I of this opinion, this case is best resolved by a swift and merciful termination of the deportation proceedings.

Matter of Belenzo

17 I. & N. Dec. 374 (BIA 1980, A.G. 1981)

The respondent is a native and citizen of the Philippines who initially entered the United States as a visitor in August 1971. He last entered the United States in May 1976 as a returning resident alien. He obtained permanent resident status in March 1972, by virtue of his marriage to a United States citizen 2 months after his arrival here. He was therefore exempt from the requirement of an alien labor certification. The respondent, however, concealed from the Service a prior marriage to a native and citizen of the Philippines in 1964, which was never terminated. The respondent stated at the hearing that he still supported his first wife and their four children and wanted to bring them to this country from the Philippines. He further stated that he and his second spouse never lived together as husband and wife and that their marriage was entered into so that he could adjust his immigration status. The marriage ended in divorce in 1973.

* * *

The immigration judge found that more than 5 years had elapsed since the respondent's status was adjusted under section 245 of the Act, 8 U.S.C. 1255, and that the time in which rescission proceedings could have been brought under section 246 of the Act had expired. In ordering these proceedings terminated, the immigration judge noted that the respondent was last admitted to the United States upon presentation of his alien registration receipt card (Form I-151) and that rescission proceedings under section 246 of the Act have never been instituted against him. The immigration judge further noted that deportation proceedings were not instituted within the 5 year period during which rescission proceedings could have been brought and found that the Service apparently commenced the instant proceedings on the theory that such action is permissible under the Attorney General's decision in *Matter of S—*, 9 I & N 548 (BIA 1961; A.G. 1962; BIA 1962). The immigration judge concluded that none of the deportation charges in the instant case would have been "appropriate prior to the grant of 245 relief" even if the permanent resident status of the respondent could have been voided. A fortiori, he found that if the grant of the respondent's permanent resident status cannot now be rescinded, such charges would not lie.

On appeal, and at oral argument, the Service contended that the mere fact that an alien has had his status adjusted within the United States to that of a lawful permanent resident pursuant to section 245 of the Act does not preclude the subsequent deportation of the alien although his status as a lawful permanent resident was not rescinded nor an action begun within the statutory 5 year period pursuant to section 246 of the Act. In support of its position, the Service cites *Matter of S—*, *supra*.

Upon review of the record, we adopt the rationale of the immigration judge. We conclude that since the Service cannot now rescind the respondent's adjustment of status solely on eligibility grounds because of the specified time limitation in section 246 of the Act, the qualitative charges stated in the Order to Show Cause, which did not exist independently of the procurement of adjustment, cannot be supported in deportation proceedings. Accordingly, the appeal by the Service will be dismissed.

Irving A. Appleman, Member, Concurring:

This respondent obtained an adjustment of status in March 1972, by claiming a fraudulent marriage to a United States citizen at a time when he was already married to someone else. He last entered in 1976 as a returning resident. No rescission proceedings were ever brought under section 246 of the Act to take away the lawful permanent residence acquired in 1972. Instead, on October 31, 1977, an Order to Show Cause was issued, charging him with deportability (1) under section 241(a)(1) of the Immigration and Nationality Act, in that at time of entry in 1976 he did not have the required labor certification (section 212(a)(14)) and (2) under section 241(a)(1) in that at time of entry in 1976 he had obtained documentation by fraud (section 212(a)(19)). The immigration judge terminated since the respondent's lawful permanent residence had never been revoked. The Service appealed.

The Service appeal is predicated on language in *Matter of S—*, 9 I & N Dec. 548 (BIA 1961; A.G. 1962; BIA 1962), which, it is argued, permits a deportation action notwithstanding the fact that the 5 year rescission period authorized in section 246 has run. As the immigration judge correctly noted in his excellent decision below, we had addressed this issue in *Matter of Saunders*, 16 I & N Dec. 326 (BIA 1977). In that case I took issue, in a separate opinion, with what I regarded as the aberrated reasoning that rescission *must* take place if the 5 years have not yet run, but is not required if the 5 years have run.

The present ruling comes much closer to the position I urged in *Saunders*, and I have no difficulty in concurring. In this case the claimed deportable grounds stem entirely from the "fraud" perpetrated at the time of the adjustment. There are no deportable grounds preceding the adjustment, that have independent existence outside of that "fraudulent" adjustment. So long as the adjustment exists, and is a fact, the alien cannot be deported. In this respect the case differs factually from *Matter of S—*, supra, but is the same as *Matter of V—*, 7 I & N Dec. 363 (BIA 1956).

Since the adjustment can no longer be rescinded, and there is no deportable ground preceding the adjustment and independent of it, the proceeding must be terminated.

This is the thrust of the decision, and, while the majority does not labor the point, the majority position in *Saunders* now appears to be overruled.

BEFORE THE BOARD
(December 2, 1980)

The Service has moved for reconsideration of our decision of May 6, 1980, in which we affirmed a decision of the immigration judge terminating the proceedings, and dismissed the Service appeal. Execution of our order has been deferred pending disposition of the instant motion. The motion to reconsider will be denied.

The Service contends that "both case law and legislative history support the view that an adjustment can be successfully attacked in deportation proceedings" and that section 246 was not meant to be a statute of limitations; that "an adjustee was never intended to gain additional benefits by virtue of his adjustment." The Service has cited *Matter of S—*, 9 I & N Dec. 548 (BIA 1961; A.G. 1962; BIA 1962), as well as *Ubiera v. Bell*, 463 F. Supp. 181 (S.D.N.Y. 1978), *aff'd*, without opinion *Ubiera v. Bell*, 594 F.2d 853 (2d Cir. 1978), as support.

The motion further argues that rescission was originally intended as a summary procedure to take away permanent residence "without all the complex, due process requirements of the deportation proceedings"; that the 5 years can be read as a "simple time limit" in which this "summary" procedure could be used, but that after 5 years, because of greater equities, the alien's status could only be taken away by a deportation proceeding.

We find this reading of the statute unacceptable. The statute says that after rescission, the alien may or may not be deported—*i.e.*, he shall be treated as any other alien. Deportation does not necessarily follow after rescission, *e.g.*—the case may receive nonpriority treatment, the alien may again adjust, etc. If deportation is to occur, another proceeding must be initiated after rescission—*i.e.*, there must be two proceedings instead of the one which the Service argues can take place any time after 5 years. Rather than being "summary" the procedure is more cumbersome. As an argument for the Service's position it must be rejected.

In addition, we note that whatever the 5 year time limit on rescission means for section 245 adjustment, it means the same thing for section 244 (suspension of deportation) and for section 249 (registry). If rescission of adjustment of status under section 245 can be bypassed after the 5 years, then so to can rescission of adjustment under section 249 or section 244. Yet section 246 requires a concurrent resolution of the Congress for withdrawal of a grant of suspension of deportation. Obviously, this is a mandate not lightly to be ignored, nor is it consistent with the "summary" vs. "expeditious" argument of the Service.

Such judicial expressions as exist also afford no comfort to the Service position. The courts have been uniformly solicitous to preserve lawful permanent residence, once acquired from procedurally improper encroachment; *see generally Chew v. Colding*, 344 U.S. 590 (1953); *Waziri v. INS*, 392 F.2d 55 (9th Cir. 1968); *Fulgencio v. INS*, 573 F.2d 596 (9th Cir. 1978). Those courts which have dealt specifically with the 5-year limitation have tended to view it as an absolute statute of limitations, to be ignored only upon a tolling of its running. *See Quintana v. Holland*, 255 F.2d 161 (3d Cir. 1958); *Singh v. INS*, 456 F.2d 1092 (9th Cir. 1972); *cert. denied*, 409 U.S. 847 (1972); *Zaoutis v. Kiley*, 558 F.2d 1096 (2d Cir. 1977). Nowhere in these cases is there an intimation the Service would have the choice of proceeding alternatively in deportation.

In *Fulgencio v. INS, supra*, the government attempted to urge a somewhat analogous position to that presented here. *Fulgencio* had been granted adjustment of status "conditioned upon the absence of any derogatory information" upon later record checks. The Service subsequently sought to reopen the deportation proceedings when derogatory information developed. Pointing to fundamental unfairness in reopening the deportation case, the court pointed out that rescission was preferable because of its procedural safeguards. The conditional grant in deportation proceedings, according to the court, "undermined the security which ought to attend permanent resident status," whereas "a rescission proceeding is governed by a 5 year statute of limitations." *Id.* at 598. Citing *Quintana v. Holland, supra*, with approval, the court held the conditional grant improper.

It is true that in *Matter of S—, supra*, the Attorney General ruled that an adjusted alien was not intended to be favored over other permanent resident aliens with respect to deportability. In that case the ground of deportation, a fraud at time of original entry, existed *dehors* the adjustment and independently of it. Rescission was not necessary to reach the deportable ground. Both *Matter of S—* and *Ubiera v. Bell, supra,* are consistent with our holding in this case.

This "deportation" proceeding is in effect a rescission proceeding under a different name. The alleged fraud and labor certification violation occurred at the time of adjustment. When perceived as to what it really is, the necessity for compliance with the 5 year limit becomes apparent. The accident of reentry after adjustment, which the motion for reconsideration notes as establishing the deportation charge, does not affect the rule of law involved. It is doubtful that the Service is advocating that the respondent is deportable only because he effected a reentry, and that if he had not done so, he would not be deportable. Rather, the motion is addressed to all aliens in the respondent's category, and would presumably hold true whether the alien had departed or not, *cf. Francis v. INS,* 532 F.2d 268 (2d Cir. 1976). In any case, we take the same position whether or not reentry is involved. The grounds of deportability arising from the reentry all relate to the claimed illegal procurement of adjustment. This is to mask a rescission proceeding under the guise of a deportation proceeding, and if it is a rescission proceeding it must be initiated within the 5 years.

The motion erroneously states (Tr. p. 5) that the Board has set up an absolute bar to deportation. The bar exists only where deportation is based on an attack on the adjustment itself, as here. If the adjustment is thus attacked, it must be attacked directly and within the 5 years. If deportation is predicated on something outside the adjustment, there is no bar.

The respondent is presently a lawful permanent resident of the United States and until his lawful permanent residence is revoked or rescinded, he is not deportable. In this respect he differs from the alien in *Matter of S—, supra,* who was deportable, whether or not rescission took place, because of a fraud which was not related to the adjustment. *See also Matter of V—,* 7 I & N Dec. 363 (BIA 1956). We know of no deportation charge in this case which can exist independently of the alleged impropriety in achieving adjustment, nor does the Service allege any. Since the adjustment can no longer be revoked, the motion must be denied.

ORDER: The motion for reconsideration is denied.

Before the Attorney General
April 28, 1981

* * *

Analysis of the issue presented in this case must begin with the Attorney General's opinion in *Matter of S—.* In that case the INS sought in 1960 to exclude applicant on the ground that he procured his initial entry into the United States, in 1949, by fraud or wilful misrepresentation of a material fact. In April 1955 the applicant's status had been adjusted to that of a permanent resident. The immigration judge and BIA concluded that exclusion or deportation proceedings based on grounds that would also have supported rescission were indirect attacks on the adjustment of status, and that Congress, in barring rescission of adjustment status after 5 years, also intended to bar indirect attacks on that adjustment.

The Attorney General disagreed. He noted that the exclusion and deportation provisions of the Immigration and Nationality Act, unlike the rescission provisions, contain no statutes of limitations. Congress did not, in his view, intend to give special immunity from deportation to those who acquired permanent resident status. The

Attorney General found no "basis for believing that the 5-year limitation . . . on the Attorney General's rescission authority has the effect of broadening the benefits conferred by [an] . . . adjustment so as to place nonimmigrants who thereby acquire the status of aliens lawfully admitted for permanent residence in a better position than those who have initially entered as permanent residents." *Id.* at 552. *Accord Ubiera v. Bell*, 463 F. Supp. 181, 186 (S.D.N.Y. 1978), *aff'd without opinion, Ubiera v. Bell*, 594 F.2d 853 (2d Cir. 1978). On the contrary, he concluded that "the effect of the 5-year limitation on rescission is simply to bar the Attorney General from returning an alien with adjusted status to the category of nonimmigrant." *Id.* at 554. So "narrow" a provision was not "intended to be read as qualifying the express authority provided by the Act to deport or exclude aliens without time limitation." *Id.* at 555.

In a passage of particular relevance to the present matter, the Attorney General recognized that, under his construction, "the time limitation in section 246 . . . may be of little practical value to the alien." But as he understood it, the purpose of the limitation was merely to "cut off the availability of a procedure which, although to all intents and purposes would establish deportability, *permitted* the Attorney General to act more informally and expeditiously than he could in a deportation proceeding." In the Attorney General's view, the rescission procedures might provide a more informal and expeditious means of correcting mistakes made in granting permanent residence status through adjustment. The Attorney General concluded:

> Congress must have been aware that rescission by returning the alien to nonimmigrant status, in fact, established his deportability on the ground that he had overstayed the period of his admission. The 5-year limitation would thus seem to be a recognition that it would be unfair to permit indefinitely such serious consequences to be effected through a somewhat informal procedure. After 5 years, the Attorney General is, therefore, required to correct mistakes in granting permanent resident status to those initially admitted as nonimmigrants in the same manner as in the case of other aliens, i.e., through deportation.

Id. at 555-56 n.8. Under this view of the purpose underlying the 5-year limitations period for rescission, the Attorney General concluded that the limitations period was inapplicable to deportation proceedings, which were governed by different statutory provisions and which, by statute, furnished generous procedural safeguards.

In my view, *Matter of S—* was correctly decided, and the Attorney General's reasoning in that case leads to rejection of the BIA's position here. Under the plain terms of the Act, there is no statute of limitations for deportation and the 5-year period of §1256 is, by its own terms, applicable only to rescission. The BIA's approach would have the anomalous consequence of favoring those who gained permanent resident status through adjustment over those who initially entered as permanent residents. For these reasons, I believe that the deportation proceeding at issue here is not barred.

I acknowledge that this conclusion, based on the text of the Act, might be avoided if it were plainly inconsistent with the intent underlying the 5-year limitations period. The BIA purported to find such an inconsistency, contending that the period would have no function if it did not insulate the alien from all claims arising from improprieties in the alien's conduct in obtaining permanent resident status. This position, however, was squarely rejected in *Matter of S—*. As the Attorney General there explained, the limitations period is designed to assure that, if no action to obtain rescission is taken within 5 years, the Attorney General may not use the procedural mechanism for rescission, but must instead seek deportation, a route that offers special statutory safeguards to the alien. The underlying purpose of the limitation period for rescission does not, therefore, justify its application to deportation proceedings.

The BIA suggested in this case that *Matter of S—* might be distinguished because the grounds for deportation in that case were entirely separate from the procurement of permanent resident status. Here, by contrast, alleged misconduct in the adjustment is the asserted grounds for deportation. I see no basis, however, for the conclusion that the 5-year limitations period for rescission becomes applicable to deportation proceedings simply because those proceedings are based on conduct in obtaining the adjustment. There is no ground for such a conclusion in the language, history, or structure of the Act, and the proposition advanced by the BIA is certainly not self-evident. I believe that the BIA's distinction is unpersuasive.

The BIA also takes the position that the limitations period is applicable because, in substance, the current proceeding is one for rescission. I disagree. The INS seeks deportation, not rescission. The respondent is entitled to the safeguards accompanying deportation, not those applicable to rescission. To be sure, the allegations on which deportation was sought could also have formed the basis for an action for rescission if the 5-year limitations provisions were satisfied. That fact does not, however, alter the fundamental nature of the proceeding. Since this proceeding is one for deportation, the limitations period applicable to rescission is not applicable here.

I conclude that under the terms of the Act, the 5-year limitations period in § 1256 is not applicable to a deportation proceeding, and that nothing in the underlying purposes of the relevant statutes requires a contrary result. Accordingly, I disapprove the BIA's decision, and the case is remanded for further proceedings consistent with this opinion.

Notes

1. In *Matter of Saunders*, the Board cited *Matter of Quan*, 12 I. & N. Dec. 487 (Dep. Assoc. Comm'r 1967), which held that whether the government chose to pursue rescission was a matter within the exercise of its discretion. Understanding the distinction between *Saunders* and *Quan* requires a review of the INS and BIA's jurisdictional authority. *Quan* was decided by the Deputy Associate Commissioner (of the INS) who determined that under the circumstances rescission would not be sought. In *Saunders* the INS had already decided to institute proceedings and therefore the Board was without authority to reverse the exercise of *prosecutorial* discretion. How would you attempt to seek judicial review of the INS decision to institute rescission proceedings? Assuming that you could have the issue reviewed, what would you have to prove?

2. Under current rescission regulations, the "statute of limitations" for the institution of rescission prescribed in Section 246(A), 8 U.S.C. § 1256(a), is tolled by the issuance of a Notice of Intent to Rescind within 5 years of the respondent's adjustment of status. *See* 8 C.F.R. § 246.1; *see also Zaoutis v. Kiley*, 558 F.2d 1096 (2d Cir. 1977); *Singh v. INS*, 456 F.2d 1092 (9th Cir.), *cert. denied*, 409 U.S. 847 (1972); *Matter of Pereira*, Interim Dec. 2978 (BIA 1984); *but see Quintana v. Holland*, 255 F.2d 161 (3d Cir. 1958). Should the calculation of the tolling of the time within which rescission must be brought be a matter of regulatory or statutory interpretation?

D. Rescission—Deportation and Exclusion

Matter of Anwal

Interim Dec. 3056 (BIA 1988)

This is an appeal from a decision of the immigration judge, dated October 4, 1983, rescinding the respondent's prior grant of adjustment of status. Oral argument was heard before the Board on August 21, 1985. The appeal will be dismissed.

The respondent is a 25-year-old native and citizen of Bangladesh. He apparently was paroled into the United States on September 9, 1972. On July 15, 1974, his status was adjusted to that of a lawful permanent resident of the United States. His adjustment was based on his status as the stepchild of his mother's United States citizen husband. See section 101(b)(1)(B) of the Immigration and Nationality Act, 8 U.S.C. § 1101(b)(1)(B) (1982). On August 18, 1975, a notice of intent to rescind was sent to the respondent. The notice alleged that the respondent's mother was separated from her husband at the time his adjustment was granted, and that the respondent therefore did not qualify as the stepchild of a United States citizen at that time. A similar notice was sent to the respondent's mother. Prior counsel of both the respondent and his mother apparently responded to the notices and requested a hearing. A rescission hearing relating only to the respondent's mother was held, and her adjustment was ordered rescinded on the ground that her marriage was a sham entered into in order to procure immigration benefits. This Board ultimately upheld the mother's rescission on August 15, 1979.

On March 5, 1981, the respondent's parole was terminated, and he was placed in exclusion proceedings, charged with excludability under section 212(a)(20) of the Act, 8 U.S.C. § 1182(a)(20) (1982), as an immigrant not in possession of a valid immigrant visa. Counsel for the respondent filed a trial brief in which it was argued, inter alia, that there was no jurisdiction to hold an exclusion hearing because the respondent's lawful permanent resident status had never been rescinded. The respondent noted that in rescission proceedings the Government bears the burden of proving ineligibility for adjustment by clear, unequivocal, and convincing evidence. See, e.g., *Waziri v. INS*, 392 F.2d 55 (9th Cir. 1968); *Matter of Suleiman*, 15 I & N Dec. 784 (BIA 1974). At a hearing held on May 18, 1982, counsel reiterated his contention that exclusion proceedings were improper because there had been no rescission proceedings. Because of the complex issues involved, the case was continued by the immigration judge.

A further hearing was held on October 4, 1983. On that date, the immigration judge stated that he was conducting a rescission hearing. Counsel made a motion to terminate the exclusion proceedings because the respondent had not had his lawful permanent resident status rescinded. The immigration judge again noted that he was conducting rescission, not exclusion, proceedings, so the motion was found to be premature. Counsel appeared to accede to this. However, counsel then moved for termination of the rescission proceedings because 8 years had passed since the notice of intent to rescind was served.

It was argued that it would be "inappropriate and unjust" to proceed with rescission after such a long delay. The immigration judge denied this motion, finding no affirmative misconduct on the part of the Government. See generally *INS v. Hibi*, 414 U.S. 5 (1973). The rescission hearing went forward.

Following the hearing, the immigration judge issued an oral decision rescinding the respondent's adjustment of status. He found the respondent to be a truthful witness and to be innocent of any wrongdoing. He further found that the respondent and his ex-stepfather had a familial relationship during and for some time after the marriage. However, he concluded that because the underlying marriage had been found to be a sham, there had never been a valid marriage under the immigration laws and thus the respondent could not obtain immigration benefits through that marriage. He relied for this holding on our decision in *Matter of Teng*, 15 I & N Dec. 516 (BIA 1975).

On appeal, the respondent first makes two arguments regarding the propriety of the proceedings. He argues that these are exclusion proceedings and the immigration judge was without authority to conduct a rescission hearing in exclusion proceedings. It is alternatively argued that, because the Immigration and Naturalization Service "abandoned" the rescission proceedings for 8 years, it would be fundamentally unfair and excessively harsh to rescind the respondent's adjustment of status now. The primary focus of the respondent's appeal, however, is on the proper interpretation of Matter of Teng, supra. He contends that under that decision immigration benefits are available through a stepparent-stepchild relationship even where the underlying marriage was a sham, so long as there has been active parental interest shown by the stepparent in the stepchild.

* * *

Preliminarily, we find that these rescission proceedings are proper. As pointed out by Appellate Counsel for the Service, the respondent argued that he should be in rescission, not exclusion, proceedings. The immigration judge agreed with the respondent and a rescission hearing was held. The respondent cannot now complain that a rescission hearing should not have been held. We note that counsel pled to the allegations set forth in the notice of intent to rescind and did not protest that he was not prepared for rescission proceedings. Nor has there been a showing that the respondent was prejudiced by the holding of these rescission proceedings, or by the delay in holding them. Moreover, even if we were to hold that, because of the delay, the proceedings were in some way unfair and should be terminated, that would not result in the end of all proceedings against the respondent. Exclusion proceedings could still be brought. See generally *Matter of Belenzo*, 17 I & N Dec. 374 (BIA 1980, 1981; A.G. 1981). While the delay in this case is unfortunate, we conclude that the rescission proceedings were properly held.[1]

* * *

---

1. The respondent cites Matter of Quan, 12 I & N Dec. 487 (D.A.C. 1967), for his contention that the Service should not have instituted rescission proceedings in this case because of the excessively harsh consequences that could result. . . . In fact, what is complained of here is not the institution of rescission proceedings, but the delay in holding the rescission hearing. In any event, Matter of Quan can be of no help to the respondent since neither the immigration judge nor this Board has any authority to terminate proceedings as improvidently begun. The decision whether or not to institute proceedings is a matter of prosecutorial discretion, and once the Service, in the exercise of that discretion, institutes proceedings, we are required to go forward to determine whether the evidence warrants a decision to rescind.

The respondent's eligibility for immigration benefits depended entirely on his mother's marriage to a United States citizen. That marriage has been found to have been a sham, and the mother's own adjustment of status was rescinded because of the fraudulent marriage. Based on our discussion above, that marriage cannot form the basis for the respondent's adjustment of status. His adjustment was therefore properly ordered rescinded, and his appeal must accordingly be dismissed.

Notes

1. *Anwal* presents in stark terms the footing held by a person who has had her status rescinded. She is, in effect, deprived of permanent residency and placed back into the position held at the time that she was applying for permanent residency. The creation of a statute of limitations has been proposed by law reformers for some time; thus far it has not been placed into the statute. *See*, e.g., *Whom We Shall Welcome*, Report of the President's Commission on Immigration and Naturalization (1953); Maslow, *Recasting our Deportation Laws: Proposals for Reform*, 56 Colum L. Rev. 309 (1956); Gordon, *The Need to Modernize Our Immigration Laws*, 13 San Diego L. Rev. 1 (1975).

2. Assume that you were Anwal's lawyer. What would you do after the BIA had rejected your appeal? What information would you need to have from your client before answering this question?

3. Assume that Anwal had entered the U.S. with a nonimmigrant visa and his status had been rescinded. Procedurally, what would be the next step to be taken by the INS? *See Matter of Pereira*, Interim Dec. 2978 (BIA 1984).

Index to Appendix

Revocation

8 U.S.C. § 1155, Sec. 205

The Attorney General may, at any time, for what he deems to be good and sufficient cause, revoke the approval of any petition approved by him under section 1154 of this title. Such revocation shall be effective as of the date of approval of any such petition. In no case, however, shall such revocation have effect unless there is mailed to the petitioner's last known address a notice of the revocation and unless notice of the revocation is communicated through the Secretary of State to the beneficiary of the petition before such beneficiary commences his journey to the United States. If notice of revocation is not so given, and the beneficiary applies for admission to the United States, his admissibility shall be determined in the manner provided for by sections 1225 and 1226 of this title.

Regulations

Revocation of Nonimmigrant Visa by Consular Officer
22 C.F.R. § 41.122

(a) Grounds for revocation by consular officers. A consular officer is authorized to revoke a nonimmigrant visa issued to an alien if:

(1) The officer finds that the alien was not, or has ceased to be, entitled to the nonimmigrant classification under INA 101(a)(15) specified in the visa or that the alien was at the time the visa was issued, or has since become, ineligible under INA 212(a) to receive a visa;

(2) The visa has been physically removed from the passport in which it was issued prior to the alien's embarkation upon a continuous voyage to the United States; or

(3) For any of the reasons specified in paragraph (h) of this section if the visa has not been revoked by an immigration officer as authorized in that paragraph.

(b) Notice of proposed revocation. When consideration is being given to the revocation of a nonimmigrant visa under paragraph (a)(1) or (2) of this section, the consular officer considering that action shall, if practicable, notify the alien to whom the visa was issued of intention to revoke the visa. The alien shall also be given an opportunity to show why the visa should not be revoked and requested to present the travel document in which the visa was originally issued.

(c) Procedure for physically canceling visas. A nonimmigrant visa which is revoked shall be canceled by writing or stamping the word "REVOKED" plainly across the face of the visa. The cancellation shall be dated and signed by the officer taking the action. The failure of the alien to present the visa for cancellation does not affect the validity of action taken to revoke it.

(d) Notice to carriers. Notice of revocation shall be given to the master, aircraft captain, agent, owner, charterer, or consignee of the carrier or transportation line on which it is believed the alien intends to travel to the United States, unless the visa has been physically canceled as provided in paragraph (c) of this section.

(e) Notice to Department. When a visa is revoked under paragraph (a)(1) or (2) of this section, the consular officer shall promptly submit notice of the revocation, including a full report on the facts in the case, to the Department for transmission to INS. A report is not required if the visa is physically canceled prior to the alien's departure for the United States except in cases involving A, G, C-2, C-3, NATO, diplomatic or official visas.

(f) Record of action. Upon revocation of a nonimmigrant visa under paragraph (a)(1) or (2) of this section, the consular officer shall complete for the post files a Certificate of Revocation by Consular Officer which includes a statement of the reasons for the revocation. If the revocation is effected at other than the issuing office, a copy of the Certificate of Revocation shall be sent to that office.

(g) Reconsideration of revocation

(1) The consular office shall consider any evidence submitted by the alien or the alien's attorney or representative in connection with a request that the revocation be reconsidered. If the officer finds that the evidence is sufficient to overcome the basis for the revocation, a new visa shall be issued. A memorandum regarding the action taken and the reasons therefor shall be placed in the consular files and appropriate notification shall be made promptly to the carriers concerned, the Department, and the issuing office if notice of revocation has been given in accordance with paragraphs (d), (e), and (f) of this section.

(2) In view of the provisions of § 41.107(d) providing for the refund of fees when a visa has not been used as a result of action by the U.S. Government, a fee shall not be charged in connection with a reinstated visa.

(h) Revocation of visa by immigration officer. An immigration officer is authorized to revoke a valid visa by physically canceling it in accordance with the procedure prescribed in paragraph (c) of this section if:

(1) The alien obtains an immigrant visa or an adjustment of status to that of permanent resident;

(2) The alien is ordered excluded from the United States pursuant to INA 235(c) or 236;

(3) The alien is notified pursuant to INA 235(b) by an immigration officer at a port of entry that the alien appears to be inadmissible to the United States and the alien requests and is granted permission to withdraw the application for admission;

(4) A final order of deportation or a final order granting voluntary departure with an alternate order of deportation is entered against the alien pursuant to INS regulations;

(5) The alien has been permitted by INS to depart voluntarily from the United States pursuant to INS regulations;

(6) A waiver of ineligibility pursuant to INA 212(d)(3)(A) on the basis of which the visa was issued to the alien is revoked by INS;

(7) The visa is presented in connection with an application for admission to the United States by a person other than the alien to whom it was issued; or

(8) The visa has been physically removed from the passport in which it was issued.

Revocation of Immigrant Visas by Consular Officer
22 C.F.R. § 42.82

(a) Grounds for revocation. Consular officers are authorized to revoke an immigrant visa under the following circumstances:

(1) The consular officer knows, or after investigation is satisfied, that the visa was procured by fraud, a willfully false or misleading representation, the willful concealment of a material fact, or other unlawful means;

(2) The consular officer obtains information establishing that the alien was otherwise ineligible to receive the particular visa at the time it was issued; or

(3) The consular officer obtains information establishing that, subsequent to the issuance of the visa, a ground of ineligibility has arisen in the alien's case.

(b) Notice of proposed revocation. The bearer of an immigrant visa which is being considered for revocation shall, if practicable, be notified of the proposed action, given an opportunity to show cause why the visa should not be revoked, and requested to present the visa to the consular office indicated in the notification of proposed cancellation.

(c) Procedure in revoking visas. An immigrant visa which is revoked shall be canceled by writing the word "REVOKED" plainly across the face of the visa. The cancellation shall be dated and signed by the consular officer taking the action. The failure of an alien to present the visa for cancellation does not affect the validity of any action taken to revoke it.

(d) Notice to carriers. Notice of revocation of a visa shall be given to the master, commanding officer, agent, owner, charterer, or consignee of the carrier or transportation line on which it is believed the alien intends to travel to the United States, unless the visa has been canceled as provided in paragraph (c) of this section.

(e) Notice to Department. The consular officer shall promptly submit notice of the revocation, including a full report of the facts in the case, to the Department for transmission to the INS. A report is not required if the visa has been physically canceled prior to the alien's departure for the United States.

(f) Record of action. Upon the revocation of an immigrant visa, the consular officer shall make appropriate notation for the post file of the action taken, including a statement of the reasons therefor, and if the revocation of the visa is effected at other than the issuing office, a report of the action taken shall be sent to that office.

(g) Reconsideration of revocation.

(1) The consular officer shall consider any evidence submitted by the alien or the alien's attorney or representative in connection with a request that the revocation of the visa be reconsidered. If the officer finds that the evidence is sufficient to overcome the basis for the revocation, a new visa shall be issued. A memorandum regarding the action taken and the reasons therefore shall be placed in the consular files and appropriate notification made promptly to the carriers concerned, the Department, and the issuing office if notice of revocation has been given in accordance with paragraphs (d), (e), and (f) of this section.

(2) In view of the provisions of § 42.71(b) providing for the refund of fees when the visa has not been used as a result of action by the U.S. Government, no fees shall be collected in connection with the application for or issuance of such a reinstated visa.

Revocation of Visa Petition by INS
8 C.F.R. § 205.1 Automatic revocation

The approval of a petition made under section 204 of the Act and in accordance with Part 204 of this chapter is revoked as of the date of approval if the Secretary of State shall terminate the registration of any beneficiary pursuant to the provisions of section 203(e) of the Act or if any of the following circumstances occur before the beneficiary's journey to the United States commences, or if the beneficiary is an applicant for adjustment of status to that of a permanent resident before the decision on his application becomes final:

(a) Relative petitions

(1) Upon written notice of withdrawal filed by the petitioner with any officer of the Service who is authorized to grant or deny petitions.

(2) Upon the death of the petitioner or beneficiary.

(3) Upon the death of the petitioner unless the Attorney General in his discretion determines that for humanitarian reasons revocation would be inappropriate.

(4) Upon the legal termination of the relationship of husband and wife when a petition has accorded status as the spouse of a citizen or lawful resident alien, respectively, under section 201(b), or section 203(a)(2) of the Act.

(5) Upon a child beneficiary reaching the age of 21, when he has been accorded immediate relative status under section 201(b) of the Act; however, such petition is valid for the duration of the relationship to accord preference status under section 203(a)(1) of the Act if the beneficiary remains unmarried, or to accord preference status under section 203(a)(4) of the Act if he marries.

(6) Upon the marriage of a beneficiary accorded status as the child of a United States citizen under section 201(b) of the Act; however, such petition is valid for the duration of the relationship to accord preference status under section 203(a)(4) of the Act.

(7) Upon the marriage of a beneficiary accorded preference status as a son or daughter of a United States citizen under section 203(a)(1) of the Act; however, such petition is valid for the duration of the relationship to accord preference status under section 203(a)(4) of the Act.

(8) Upon the marriage of a beneficiary accorded a status as a son or daughter of a lawful resident alien under section 203(a)(2) of the Act.

(9) Upon the legal termination of the petitioner's status as an alien admitted for lawful permanent residence in the United States; unless the petitioner became a United States citizen, then § 204.5(c) of this title applies.

(b) Petition for Pub. L. 97-359 Amerasian—

(1) Upon formal notice of withdrawal filed by the petitioner with the officer who approved the petition.

(2) Upon the death of the beneficiary.

(3) Upon the death or bankruptcy of the sponsor who executed Form I-361, Affidavit of Financial Support and Intent to Petition for Legal Custody for Pub. L. 97-359 Amerasian. In that event, a new petition may be filed in the beneficiary's behalf with the documentary evidence relating to sponsorship and, in the case of a

beneficiary under eighteen years of age, placement. If the new petition is approved, it will be given the priority date of the previously approved petition.

(4) Upon the death or substitution of the petitioner if other than the beneficiary or sponsor. However, if the petitioner dies or no longer desires or is able to proceed with the petition, and another person eighteen years of age or older, an emancipated minor, or a corporation incorporated in the United States desires to be substituted for the deceased or original petitioner, a written request may be submitted to the Service or American consular office where the petition is located to reinstate the petition and restore the original priority date.

(5) Upon the beneficiary's reaching the age of twenty-one when the beneficiary has been accorded classification under section 201(b) of the Act. Provided that all requirements of section 204(g) of the Act continue to be met, however, the petition is to be considered valid for purposes of according the beneficiary preference classification under section 203(a)(1) of the Act if the beneficiary remains unmarried or under section 203(a)(4) if the beneficiary marries.

(6) Upon the beneficiary's marriage when the beneficiary has been accorded classification under section 201(b) or section 203(a)(1) of the Act. Provided that all requirements of section 204(g) of the Act continue to be met, however, the petition is to be considered valid for purposes of according the beneficiary preference classification under section 203(a)(4) of the Act.

(c) Petitions under section 203(a)(3) or (6)

(1) Upon invalidation pursuant to 20 CFR Part 656 of the labor certification in support of the petition.

(2) Upon the death of the petitioner or beneficiary.

(3) Upon written notice of withdrawal filed by the petitioner, in third preference cases, with any officer of the Service who is authorized to grant or deny petitions.

(4) Upon written notice of withdrawal filed by the petitioner, in sixth-preference cases, with any officer of the Service who is authorized to grant or deny petitions.

(5) Upon termination of the employer's business in a sixth-preference case.

(d) Notice. When it shall appear to the district director that the approval of a petition has been automatically revoked, he shall cause a notice of such revocation to be sent promptly to the consular office having jurisdiction over the visa application and a copy of such notice to be mailed to the petitioner's last known address.

8 C.F.R. 205.2 Revocation on notice

(a) General. Any Service officer authorized to approve a petition under section 204 of the Act may revoke the approval of that petition upon notice to the petitioner on any ground other than those specified in § 204.1 when the necessity for the revocation comes to the attention of this Service.

(b) Revocation of the approval of a petition under paragraph (a) of this section will be made only on notice to the petitioner who must be given an opportunity to offer evidence in support of the petition and in opposition to the grounds alleged for revocation of the approval. If, upon reconsideration, the approval previously granted is revoked, the district director shall notify the petitioner of the decision and of the reasons for the revocation. The petitioner may appeal the decision within fifteen days after the service of notice. Except in the case of a petition filed under section 204(g) of the Act, if the petition was approved for a preference under section 203(a)(1), (2), (4), or (5) of the Act or for immediate relative classification under section 201(b) of the Act other than for a child as defined in section 101(b)(1)(F) of the Act, the petitioner must file the appeal as provided in Part 3 of this chapter. If the petition was approved for a preference under section 203(a)(3) or (6) of the Act, for a child as defined in section 101(b)(1)(F) of the Act, or for a Pub. L. 97-359 Amerasian, the petitioner must file the appeal as provided in Part 103 of this Chapter. The district director shall notify the consular officer having jurisdiction over the visa application, if applicable, of the revocation of an approval.

Rescission of Adjustment of Status

8 C.F.R. § 246.1 Notice

If it appears to a district director that a person residing in his district was not in fact eligible for the adjustment of status made in his case, a proceeding shall be commenced by the personal service upon such person of a notice of intention to rescind which shall inform him of the allegations upon which it is intended to rescind the adjustment of his status. In such a proceeding the person shall be known as the respondent. The notice shall also inform the respondent that he may submit, within thirty days from the date of service of the notice, an answer in writing under oath setting forth reasons why such rescission shall not be made, and that he may, within such period, request a hearing before a special inquiry officer in support of, or in lieu of, his written answer. The respondent shall further be informed that he may have the assistance of or be represented by counsel or representative of his choice qualified under Part 292 of this chapter, without expense of the Government, in the preparation of his answer or in connection with his hearing, and that he may present such evidence in his behalf as may be relevant to the rescission.

8 C.F.R. § 246.2 Procedure

If the answer admits all the allegations in the notice, or if no answer is filed within the thirty-day period, or if no hearing is requested within such period, and the status of that of a permanent resident was acquired through suspension of deportation under section 19(c) of the Immigration Act of February 5, 1917, or under section 244 of the Immigration and Nationality Act, the district director shall forward the respondent's file containing a copy of the notice and the answer, if any, to the regional commissioner for further action in accordance with section 246 of the Immigration and Nationality Act. If the answer admits the allegations in the notice, or if no answer is filed within the thirty-day period, or if no hearing is requested within such period, and the status of that of a permanent resident was acquired through adjustment of status under section 245 or 249 of the Immigration and Nationality Act, the district director shall rescind the adjustment of status previously granted, and no appeal shall lie from his decision.

8 C.F.R. § 246.3 Allegations contested or denied

If, within the prescribed time following service of the notice pursuant to § 246.1, the respondent has filed an answer which contests or denies any allegation in the notice, or a hearing is requested, a hearing pursuant to § 246.5 shall be conducted by a special inquiry officer and the procedures specified in §§ 242.10, 242.11, 242.12, 242.13, 242.14 (c), (d) and (e), and 242.15 of this chapter shall apply.

8 C.F.R. § 246.4 Authority of Special Inquiry Officer

In any proceeding conducted under this part, the special inquiry officer shall have authority to interrogate, examine, and cross-examine the respondent and other witnesses, to present and receive evidence, to determine whether adjustment of status shall be rescinded, to make decisions thereon, including an appropriate order, and to take any other action consistent with applicable provisions of law and regulations as may be appropriate to the disposition of the case. Nothing contained in this part shall be construed to diminish the authority conferred on special inquiry officers by the Act. The special inquiry officer assigned to conduct a hearing shall, at any time, withdraw if he deems himself disqualified. If a hearing has begun but no evidence has been adduced other than the notice and answer, if any, pursuant to §§ 246.1 and 246.2, or if a special inquiry officer becomes unavailable to complete his duties within a reasonable time, or if at any time the respondent consents to a substitution, another special inquiry officer may be assigned to complete the case. The new special inquiry officer shall familiarize himself with the record in the case and shall state for the record that he has done so.

8 C.F.R. § 246.9 Surrender of Form I-151 or I-551[3]

A respondent whose status as a permanent resident has been rescinded in accordance with section 246 of the Immigration and Nationality Act and this part shall, upon demand, promptly surrender to the district director having administrative jurisdiction over the office in which the action under this part was taken, the Form I-151 or I-551 issued to him at the time of the grant of permanent resident status.

---

3. The I-151 or I-551 is commonly known as a "green card" and is evidence of a person's status as a lawful permanent resident.

Chapter 11
Relief from Deportation

As we have seen there are numerous grounds under which a person may be found to be either deportable or excludable. What relief from deportation is available to the person who has managed to gain entry and is faced with the prospect of being deported? How can she avoid deportation? In this section we will attempt to explore some of the defenses which can be raised to prevent deportation.

Earlier, we discussed asylum, withholding of deportation, and adjustment of status, remedies which can be sought at the deportation hearing. Four additional benefits which merit special attention due to their importance in immigration law and discretionary nature are: voluntary departure [8 U.S.C. 1254(e)], temporary protected status,[1] deferred action,[2] and suspension of deportation.

Like other immigration benefits, relief from deportation is discretionary, requiring that the applicant establish why discretion should be favorably exercised on her behalf. In all of these cases the exercise of discretion amounts to a balancing of equities, requiring the fact finder to weigh the social and humane considerations presented in her application against the adverse factors evidencing her undesirability for the benefit being requested.[3] Other cases such as suspension of deportation require the fact finder to also assess the amount of hardship which will be inflicted on the applicant and her family should she be required to depart the U.S. In cases involving deferred action and other benefits without clear statutory origins, the exercise of discretion has been almost without parameters.

A. Voluntary Departure

The INA provides at 8 U.S.C. § 1254(e), Sec. 244(e) that the Attorney General may permit a person otherwise deportable to "depart voluntarily from the United States at her own expense in lieu of deportation" if the person can establish that she

---

1. Temporary Protected Status or TPS, was created by Congress in the *Immigration Act of 1990*. *See* 8 U.S.C. § 1254a, Sec. 244A. Until the enactment of the 1990 Act, the only corollary was an unclear benefit which was referred to as "extended voluntary departure" or EVD. The government's position had been that EVD was really a benefit of prosecutorial discretion.

2. The benefit of deferred action is similar to EVD. One difference between the two is that deferred action is usually granted on a case-by-case basis, while EVD is generally granted to a class of individuals. For additional information on the deferred action program, *see* Wildes, *The Nonpriority Program of the Immigration and Naturalization Service Goes Public: The Litigative Use of the Freedom of Information Act*, 14 San Diego L. Rev. 42 (1976).

3. *See Matter of Edwards*, Interim Dec. 3134 (BIA 1990); *Matter of Marin*, 16 I & N Dec. 581 (BIA 1978)

is and has been a person of good moral character for at least five years preceding the time of the application and merits a favorable exercise of discretion.[4]

Voluntary departure assures that the person who leaves the country (notwithstanding the fact that she has been found to be deportable by an immigration judge) may return to the United States, if admissible, without having to seek the special permission from the Attorney General that is required of persons returning within five years of their deportation.

B. Temporary Protected Status

As noted earlier, TPS is a newly created statutory remedy. The remedy allows some persons who are otherwise deportable to remain in the U.S. for a temporary period of time. Up until 1990, when asylum was not possible, some foreigners in the U.S. could only hope for extended voluntary departure (EVD) in order to remain in the United States. This relief, while providing the person with temporary protection was totally discretionary and was granted only by the Attorney General after consultation with the Secretary of State. It was unlike the statutory voluntary departure described earlier in that the person was not contemplating departure within a relatively short period. If the person departed the U.S., she could not return. In short, the benefit was one of a humanitarian nature due to compelling circumstances in one's home country.

TPS has all of the indicia of EVD except that it is codified. The basic requirements of TPS are as follows: 1) while the status is available for nationals of a particular country in an area of conflict, the eligible person is not required to apply for the status, but must be provided notice of eligibility;[5] 2) the status may be terminated upon the review and determination made by the Attorney General; such determinations must be published in the Federal Register;[6] 3) the determination to terminate TPS is not subject to judicial review, however applicants for TPS are entitled to some type of administrative review including assertion of relief in deportation proceedings;[7] 4) those who receive TPS may not use the period while they are in TPS status to count towards other forms of discretionary relief such as suspension of deportation, unless the Attorney General determines that extreme hardship exists;[8] 5) applicants may be required to pay a registration fee not to exceed $50 to obtain the benefit;[9] 6) persons who are excludable on grounds of criminal offenses are ineligible for this

---

4. The statute precludes granting voluntary departure to persons who are deportable under 8 U.S.C. §§ 1251(a)(2)-(4) [persons deportable due to criminal convictions, failure to register per section 36(c) of the Alien Registration Act of 1940, falsification of immigration documents and security grounds] or if they are aggravated felons.

5. 8 U.S.C. § 1254a(a)(3), Sec. 244A(a)(3).

6. 8 U.S.C. § 1254a(b)(3)(A), Sec. 244A(b)(3)(A).

7. 8 U.S.C. § 1254a(b)(5), Sec. 244A(b)(5).

8. 8 U.S.C. § 1254a(e), Sec. 244A(e).

9. The TPS program for El Salvadoran nationals provided for a fee in "amount sufficient to cover the costs of administration." *See* Sec. 303(b)(2), Immigration Act of 1990, Pub. L. No. 101-649, 104 Stat. 4978.

benefit;[10] and 7) beneficiaries of TPS may not be granted adjustment of status under a special statutory provision except upon passage by a super majority of three-fifths.[11]

It remains to be seen whether TPS will be viewed as being wholly discretionary by the courts or how its statutory language will be interpreted, if at all. The case which follows shows how one court dealt with the EVD remedy.

Hotel & Rest. Employees Union, Local 25 v. Smith
594 F. Supp. 502 (D.D.C. 1984)[1]

RICHEY, J.

Before the Court are defendants' two motions for partial summary judgment, along with memoranda in support thereof and in opposition thereto. This case involves two distinct issues relating to the status of the estimated hundreds of thousands of El Salvadoran nationals currently residing illegally in the United States. Defendants' first summary judgment motion involves a decision by the Attorney General not to grant the El Salvadoran nationals "Extended Voluntary Departure," hereinafter "EVD," status, which, according to Count I of plaintiff's Complaint, would have had the effect of a blanket insulation from deportation procedures for all Salvadoran nationals now in the United States until such time as the turmoil in that country subsides. The second of defendants' motions for partial summary judgment relates to Count II of plaintiffs' Complaint and the procedures utilized by the Immigration and Naturalization Service (INS), after considering advisory opinions from the Department of State, in reviewing applications for asylum made by Salvadoran nationals now illegally in the United States.

Plaintiffs in this case are the Hotel and Restaurant Workers Union, whose membership is largely made up of Salvadoran nationals, and a plaintiff/intervenor, Mauro Hernandez, himself a Salvadoran national, currently residing in this country. They have brought this suit seeking both declaratory judgments and injunctive relief on both the EVD and asylum issues.

Plaintiffs claim that Salvadoran nationals are entitled to be granted blanket EVD status. They base this assertion on what they perceive as the controlling "humanitarian" standard for such action, which would require the Attorney General to extend EVD status to Salvadorans. Plaintiffs allege that the result of the Attorney General's denial of EVD is to deprive Salvadoran nationals of the protection of the Due Process Clause of the 5th Amendment to the U.S. Constitution. Defendant argues that this is a matter of the Attorney General's absolute discretion on issues of foreign and prosecutorial policy, and as such finds no basis for judicial review under the Administrative Procedure Act or the Constitution beyond whether the decision was rationally

---

10. 8 U.S.C. § 1254a(c)(2), Sec. 244A(c)(2). Those persons with drug convictions involving simple possession of less than 30 grams of marijuana are excepted.

11. *See* 8 U.S.C. § 244a(h), Sec. 244A(h).

1. The full case history is *Hotel & Rest. Employees Union, Local 25 v. Smith*, 563 F. Supp. 157 (D.D.C. 1983) (denial of motion to dismiss), 594 F. Supp. 502 (granting of summary judgment for defendants), 804 F.2d 1256 (reversing in part and affirming in part), 808 F.2d 847 (rehearing granted judgment vacated), 846 F.2d 1499 (en banc panel evenly divided).

based. The Court agrees. Defendants further argue that EVD is extra-statutory, and as such is not a right or privilege to which due process considerations attach, an argument with which the Court also is in agreement.

[The court then discussed the second issue involving the procedures for processing and acting upon applications for asylum submitted by Salvadoran nationals.]

. . . [T]he Court, while especially sympathetic to the plight of Salvadoran nationals and conscious of the tumultuous situation in that country, feels it is compelled by applicable law to grant the defendants' motions for summary judgment, . . . and as hereinafter provided, the case will be dismissed.

. . . Initially, it must be noted that the issue presented in this case, that of judicial review of the Attorney General's determination regarding a grant of EVD, is one of first impression in the Courts. EVD is an extra-statutory form of discretionary relief from the deportation provisions of the Immigration and Nationality Act of 1952, as amended. It is granted to an entire class of persons, usually based upon nationality. It is a term not found anywhere in the Immigration and Nationality Act or in the applicable regulations. Rather, the term Extended Voluntary Departure describes the Attorney General's discretion in determining the circumstances of both foreign and domestic policy which may give rise to a discretionary decision to grant a temporary suspension of deportation proceedings to members of a particular class of illegal aliens. As such, EVD is based on the prosecutorial discretion of the Attorney General after consultation or advice received from the State Department.

The Constitutional foundation for grants of EVD derives from the Executive's express and inherent authority in the areas of both foreign and prosecutorial policy. The Constitution places responsibility for the conduct of foreign affairs with the Executive branch. U.S. Const. art. II, § 2. *United States v. Pink*, 315 U.S. 203 (1942). "Intricately interwoven" with this plenary authority over foreign relations are actions taken in the regulation of aliens. *Harisiades v. Shaughnessy*, 342 U.S. 580, 588-89 (1952). Regulation of immigration is an "inherent executive power." United States ex rel. Knauff v. Shaughnessy, 338 U.S. 537, 542 (1950).

The Attorney General's prosecutorial discretion finds its Constitutional basis under Article III, sections 1 and 3, which the Supreme Court has interpreted to mean that discretionary matters, such as in the immigration area, belong to the plenary, if not exclusive authority of the Executive. Specifically, it has been held that a determination "to commence a deportation proceeding or not to do so" is a matter of "prosecutorial discretion." *Johns v. Department of Justice*, 653 F.2d 884, 893 (5th Cir. 1981). This Constitutional authority to determine when or on what basis to prosecute a case is strongest when, as here, the matter involves enforcement of immigration laws. Further, grants of EVD do not relieve the aliens of individual adjudication and deportation procedures prescribed by the Act and regulations, but merely act to postpone those proceedings. Thus, EVD is an exercise of the Executives "pure enforcement power."

The statutory basis for the Attorney General's discretionary power to grant or deny EVD is found in the Immigration and Nationality Act of 1952, as amended by the Refugee Act of 1980. 8 U.S.C. § 1101 et seq. The Act provides the framework for the Attorney General's authority over aliens seeking residence or refuge in the United States. The statute charges the Attorney General "with the administration and enforcement of the Act," and empowers him to "establish such regulations . . . and perform such other acts as he deems necessary for carrying out his authority ... ". 8 U.S.C. § 1103(a). See *Jean v. Nelson*, 727 F.2d 957, 964-65 (11th Cir. 1984) (en banc). Thus, the Attorney General is vested with discretionary power to take actions and to "develop standards, principles and rules" so long as his actions are based upon "considerations rationally related to the statute he is administering." This Circuit has held that the Act "need not specifically authorize each and every action taken by the Attorney General, so long as his action is reasonably related to the duties imposed upon him." *Narenji v. Civiletti*, 617 F.2d 745, 747 (D.C. Cir. 1979), cert. denied, 446 U.S. 957, 100 (1980). Thus, the fact that EVD is extra-statutory in no way affects its validity as a discretionary action under the Act. "The Attorney General may govern the exercise of his discretion by written or unwritten rules." Mak, 435 F.2d at 731. Similarly, there can be no question that EVD is "rationally related to the statute (the Attorney General) is administering." Id. EVD is a tool utilized by the Attorney General, after consultation with the State Department, to respond to emergency situations which might require broad application of his authority under the Act, and which demand a speedy response.... There is no basis for the plaintiffs' blanket claims except for an abuse of discretion, which in this case cannot be said to exist.

*   *   *

The first step in the analysis is the Administrative Procedure Act, 5 U.S.C. § 701 et seq. Under § 704 of that title, an agency action may only be subject to review if it is "made reviewable by statute or if it is a final agency action for which there is no other adequate remedy in a court." 5 U.S.C. § 704. The Attorney General's decision to deny EVD status to El Salvadorans is not made reviewable by any statute. Nor does the decision denying EVD status to Salvadorans in any way affect their remedies of appeal to the United States Courts of Appeal after exhausting the administrative process in deportation proceedings. The Salvadorans' "adequate remedy in a court" is found in the regulations under the Immigration and Nationality Act. Salvadorans subject to deportation, irrespective of the denial of EVD, retain the right to a hearing should such deportation proceedings be instituted. 8 C.F.R. Part 242 (1984). Nor does the Attorney General's decision not to grant EVD to Salvadoran nationals affect their right to appeal an adverse result in such a deportation hearing, both to the Board of Immigration Appeals and to the United States Court of Appeals. 8 C.F.R. Part 3 and 8 U.S.C. § 1105(a). Therefore, judicial review of the Attorney General's decision, in this broad claim under the Administrative Procedure Act, is precluded.

In addition, judicial review of agency actions is precluded when such action is "committed to agency discretion by law." 5 U.S.C. § 701(a)(2). The legislative history of the Administrative Procedure Act indicates that this is applicable where "statutes are drawn in such broad terms that in a given case there is no law to apply." S. Rep. No. 752, 79th Cong., 1st Sess., 26 (1945). *Citizens To Preserve Overton Park, Inc. v. Volpe*, 401 U.S. 402, 410 (1971). In the case of EVD, there is indeed "no law to apply" because of its extra-statutory nature, and these aliens at the case at bar have an adequate remedy in deportation proceedings....

The factors involved in determining the propriety of judicial review of an agency's exercise of discretion are the breadth of the discretionary power, the administrative expertise as balanced against judicial competence to evaluate the action at issue, whether there exists meaningful criteria by which a court may evaluate the action, and whether the decision is one based on policies to which a court must defer to the political branches. Upon weighing these factors, the Court is faced with the inescapable conclusion that the Attorney General's decision is not subject to judicial review.

It is clear from the discussion, supra, of the Constitutional basis for EVD that the decision here at issue is clearly a matter of the Attorney General's prosecutorial discretion, after his review of the evidence, to suspend, or, as here, not to suspend enforcement of the immigration laws in a specific case. It is well settled that the Executive has "exclusive authority and absolute discretion to decide whether to pros-ecute a case." *United States v. Nixon*, 418 U.S. 683, 693 (1974). The Attorney General was acting in this prosecutorial discretionary capacity when he made his decision in the case at bar, and, therefore, judicial review is inappropriate under this thread of the analysis.

There is no question that, under our system of separation of powers, matters involving an area such as foreign, military, or diplomatic policy, which has been entrusted exclusively to the Executive or Legislative branches, are subject, at most, to limited judicial review. *Baker v. Carr*, 369 U.S. 186 (1962). It is also well settled that "any policy toward aliens is vitally and intricately interwoven" with the conduct of this country's foreign affairs. Harisiades v. Shaughnessy, supra, 342 U.S. at 589-90 (1952). The Supreme Court has recently affirmed that "matters relating to the conduct of foreign relations . . . are so exclusively entrusted to the political branches of government as to be largely immune from judicial inquiry or interference." *Regan v. Wald*, U.S. ___, 104 S. Ct. 3026, 3039 (1984). . . . Only in the case of a clear abuse of discretion may a Court impose its judgment over that of the Executive in a case such as the one at bar.

Before a Court can be assured that an abuse has occurred, there must first exist some kind of a standard by which to measure the Executive's action. In this case the plaintiffs would have us impose upon the Attorney General a "humanitarian" standard based upon what plaintiff perceives as a pattern or practice of past EVD grants in individual cases. While agreeing that such considerations may be a factor in EVD decisions, the Court does not agree that humanitarian concerns are, or can be, the sole or overriding factor in an EVD determination. The plaintiff points out that humanitarian concerns have been a part of such decisions in the past. However, this does not mean that a standard based solely on such concerns has evolved. There is nothing in the Immigration and Nationality Act that would establish such a standard. Indeed, such a standard would be difficult to define and enforce. Humanitarianism is a vague concept, and by its terms overbroad. For a Court to order EVD in this case would set a far-reaching precedent, wholly within the prerogatives of Congress, and might then apply to all situations of widespread fighting, destruction and the breakdown of public services and order throughout the world. Also, such situations as famine, drought, or other natural disasters might at any time also raise "human-itarian" concerns, wherever they might occur. To require the Attorney General to grant blanket EVD status to all such nationals would be to open up irresponsibly the floodgates to illegal aliens, without regard to foreign policy and internal immigration concerns, or, of equal importance, to the concerns of American working men and women in the United States and our taxpayers generally.

The only remaining question concerning judicial review of the Attorney General's decision is whether the decision was rationally based. This requires that the Attorney General exhibit some facially legitimate reason for his decision. The Court is satisfied that the Attorney General acted rationally in making his decision. Besides foreign policy considerations, the Attorney General advances several other factors. These include (i) the number of illegal Salvadoran aliens currently in the United States, (ii) the current crisis in generally controlling the "floodtide" of illegal immigration, (iii) the prospect of encouraging further illegal immigration, (iv) the effect of such illegal immigration upon this country's limited law enforcement capabilities, social services and economic resources, and (v) the availability under the Immigration and Nationality Act of alternate avenues of relief, such as asylum. The aggregate of these factors is that the Attorney General did fashion his decision in a considered and rational manner....

Plaintiffs also claim that this decision acts to deprive Salvadoran nationals of their Constitutional right to due process under the 5th Amendment of the U.S. Constitution. The Court holds that it does not. Again, EVD is extra-statutory in nature. In addition, it is clear that aliens have no Constitutional right to enter or remain in the United States. Therefore, no right or privilege is involved. There has been no denial of due process since the decision leaves unaffected the right to existing INS procedures, including hearing and appeal rights. There is no Equal Protection issue here, either. Historically, nationality-based distinctions have been seen as inevitable in the immigration field. Moreover, the Attorney General, acting for the Executive, has the authority to make such distinctions based upon nationality. *Narenji v. Civiletti*, 617 F.2d 745, 747 (D.C. Cir. 1979). Therefore, the Court concludes that there was no violation of due process involved in the EVD decision, particularly since the plaintiffs may invoke whatever rights they have in individual deportation proceedings including the right to appeal.

Notes

1. In lieu of answering the complaint in *Local 25*, the government moved to dismiss, and the district court in denying the defendant's motion to dismiss noted that:

> ... [T]he Court finds that the grant or denial of extended voluntary departure is not a nonjusticiable political question. As defendants admit, the control of immigration is not directly committed by the text of the Constitution to a coordinate federal branch. It is true that the political branches have been allowed broad leeway to regulate the flow of immigrants, but the Supreme Court has expressly left room for a "narrow standard of (judicial) review of decisions made by the Congress or the President in the area of immigration and naturalization." *Mathews v. Diaz*, 426 U.S. 67, 82 (1976).... Such review has long been exercised, as for instance in cases alleging a due process violation in immigration decisions. [*Hotel & Restaurant Workers Union, Local 25 v. Smith*, 563 F. Supp. 157, 159 (D.D.C. 1983)]

*   *   *

> ... [T]he Court does not lack a standard or the resources to decide the issues presented in this case. As plaintiff points out, defendants themselves have in the past articulated a cognizable standard for the grant of extended voluntary departure to a group of aliens—"wide-spread fighting, destruction and breakdown of public services and order" in the aliens' country of origin. 128 Cong. Rec. 5832 (daily ed. Feb. 11, 1982). At least one court has made findings as to

the serious conditions that exist in El Salvador. *Orantes-Hernandez v. Smith*, 541 F. Supp. 351, 359 (C.D. Cal. 1982). [*Hotel & Restaurant Workers Union, Local 25 v. Smith*, 563 F. Supp. 157, 160 (D.D.C. 1983).]

In another case which raised some of the same issues brought in *Local 25*, a district court was willing to consider the claims raised by the litigants that the failure to accord EVD to El Salvadorans and Guatemalans could be subject to judicial review. *See American Baptist Churches v. Thornburgh*, 712 F. Supp. 756 (N.D. Ca. 1989). Subsequently, this case was settled, allowing Guatemalan asylum applicants who were in the United States prior to October 1, 1990 and El Salvadoran applicants who were in the United States prior to September 1, 1990 to have their cases re-adjudicated under new asylum regulations. El Salvadorans present in the U.S. were able to take advantage of "TPS" which was granted by Congress in the 1990 Act. *See American Baptist Churches v. Thornburgh*, 760 F. Supp. 796 (N.D. Ca. 1991); 67 Interpreter Releases 1480 (1990).

2. **Voluntary departure and EVD.** 8 U.S.C. § 1254(e) authorizes the Attorney General to grant voluntary departure to persons of good moral character who are ready, willing, and able to depart the U.S. Can an individual apply for a prolonged period of voluntary departure in lieu of requesting "extended voluntary departure"? *See Matter of Quintero*, 18 I. & N. Dec. 348 (BIA 1982)(rejecting indefinite voluntary departure, yet acknowledging authority of judge to grant voluntary departure, in this case for five months). For additional discussion of voluntary departure, *see* Chapter 3.

3. Is asylum really an "alternative" to EVD thereby providing a legitimate reason to justify the denial of the benefit?

4. Following the *Local 25* case, the BIA has dealt with the question of individualized requests for relief. In *Matter of Medina*, Interim Dec. 3078 (BIA 1988), the Board rejected arguments that either the Geneva Convention Relative to the Protection of Civilian Persons in Time of War or customary international law created a remedy from deportation akin to EVD. The Board held that the exclusive remedies were provided for in the asylum and withholding statute and that neither EVD nor deferred action were statutory remedies.

5. Below is a list of the many times when the Attorney General has conferred EVD status on certain aliens based on their nationality and the conditions existing in their home countries.[12]

Cuba	granted effective November 29, 1960, terminated effective November 2, 1966 (*see* Public Law No. 89-732)
Dominican Republic	granted effective October 18, 1966 (for arrivals between April 24, 1965 and June 3, 1966), terminated effective April 26, 1978

---

12. This list was extracted from the defendants' June 13, 1983, response to plaintiff's First Set of Interrogatories [No. 1(d)]. *See Hotel & Restaurant Employees Union, Local 25 v. Smith*, 563 F. Supp. 157 (D.D.C. 1983). This list was updated to conform with present EVD policies. *See* B. Hing, *Handling Immigration Cases*, § 6.36 (Supp. 1988), *citing EVD Update*, 65 Interpreter Releases 964 (1988). For INS policy regarding the handling of persons who are recipients of EVD, *see* O.I. 242.10e(3).

"Western Hemisphere"	granted July 1, 1968 [for certain individuals with visa preference dates from July 1, 1968 to December 31, 1976, inclusive, in response to the order entered in *Silva v. Levi*, Civil Action No. 76-C-4268 (N.D. Ill.)], terminated effective December 31, 1976; second grant effective August 1982, second grant terminated effective January 31, 1983
Czechoslovakia	granted effective August 21, 1968, terminated effective December 30, 1977
Chile	granted effective April 9, 1971, terminated effective December 30, 1977
Cambodia	granted effective April 4, 1975, terminated effective October 28, 1977 (*see* Public Law No. 95-145)
Vietnam	granted effective April 4, 1975, terminated effective October 28, 1977 (*see* Public Law No. 95-145)
Laos	granted effective July 9, 1975, terminated effective October 28, 1977 (*see* Public Law No. 95-145)
Ethiopia	granted effective July 12, 1977 (for arrivals prior to June 30, 1980), expired March 1, 1989
Uganda	granted effective June 8, 1978, terminated effective September 30, 1986
Iran	granted effective April 16, 1975, renewed effective August 9, 1979, terminated effective December 13, 1979
Nicaragua	granted effective July 3, 1979, renewed effective August 29, 1979, and January 4 and July 1, 1980, terminated effective September 28, 1980
Mexico	granted effective December 31, 1979 [for certain second preference visa holders, *in* response to the order entered in *Contreras v. Bell*, Civil Action No. 80-1590 (N.D. Ill.)], terminated effective August 25, 1981
Afghanistan	granted effective December 2, 1980 (for arrivals prior to June 30, 1980), expired March 1, 1989
Poland	granted effective December 23, 1981 (for arrivals prior to December 24, 1981), renewed effective March 25, June 21, and December 20, 1982, and June 30, 1983, expired March 1, 1989
People's Republic of China	granted effective April 11, 1990 to January 1, 1994 (for arrivals between June 5, 1989 to April 11, 1990). (Exec. Order No. 12,711)

Additionally, since February 12, 1976, it has been the policy to view sympathetically requests by Lebanese nationals for extensions of the time permitted for voluntary departure where an individual's request is based on compelling humanitarian circumstances. Because such policy does not include the cessation of expulsion proceedings and provides only for the extension of grants of voluntary departure in individual cases, it differs significantly from the grants listed above. *Cf.* 8 U.S.C. § 1254(e) and 8 C.F.R. § 244.2.

In 1987, Congress passed special legislation to provide for the legalization (adjustment of status) for nationals of Poland, Afghanistan, Ethiopia and Uganda who had been eligible for EVD status prior to July 21, 1984 and resided continuously since that time. This legalization program ended on December 22, 1989. See Foreign Relations Authorization Act of 1987, Pub. L. No. 100–204, 101 Stat. 1331 (1987).

C. Deferred Action

Deferred action is different from TPS or EVD in that, first, it is usually applied on a case-by-case basis while TPS and EVD are generally granted to a class of individuals, and, second, there is a definite procedure enumerated in the INS operating instructions with respect to the criteria and procedure to be used in granting the benefit. It has been said that both EVD and deferred action are the exercise of prosecutorial discretion. In both cases, the ultimate benefit to the person is that she is allowed to stay in the U.S. and is given permission to work. If, however, the person should ever depart the U.S., she may not be allowed to return.[13] The following description is from the INS operating instruction which describes deferred action.

Deferred Action[14]
O.I. 103.1a(1)(ii)

(ii) Deferred action. The district director may, in his discretion, recommend consideration of deferred action, an act of administrative choice to give some cases lower priority and in no way an entitlement, in appropriate cases.

The deferred action category recognizes that the Service has limited enforcement resources and that every attempt should be made administratively to utilize these resources in a manner which will achieve the greatest impact under the immigration laws. In making deferred action determinations, the following factors, among others, should be considered:

(A) the likelihood of ultimately removing the alien, including:

(1) likelihood that the alien will depart without formal proceedings (e.g., minor child who will accompany deportable parents);

(2) age or physical condition affecting ability to travel;

(3) likelihood that another country will accept the alien;

(4) the likelihood that the alien will be able to qualify for some form of relief which would prevent or indefinitely delay deportation;

---

13. It should also be noted that EVD is effective in exclusion cases. For example many Afghans in the U.S. who were denied asylum and found excludable were not "deported" due to the policy of EVD for Afghans.

14. For an interesting discussion of the deferred action program and how it was discovered, see Wildes, *The Nonpriority Program of the Immigration and Naturalization Service Goes Public: The Litigative Use of the Freedom of Information Act*, 14 San Diego L. Rev. 42 (1976).

(B) the presence of sympathetic factors which, while not legally precluding deportation, could lead to unduly protracted deportation proceedings, and which, because of a desire on the part of the administrative authorities or the courts to reach a favorable result, could result in a distortion of the law with unfavorable implications for future cases;

(C) the likelihood that because of the sympathetic factors in the case, a large amount of adverse publicity will be generated which will result in a disproportionate amount of Service time being spent in responding to such publicity or justifying actions;

(D) whether or not the individual is a member of a class of deportable aliens whose removal has been given a high enforcement priority (e.g., dangerous criminals, large-scale alien smugglers, narcotic drug traffickers, terrorists, war criminals, habitual immigration violators).

References

Coles, *Temporary Refuge and the Large Scale Influx of Refugees*, 8 Austl. Y.B. Int'l L. 189 (1983)

Note, *The Agony and the Exodus: Deporting Salvadorans in Violation of the Fourth Geneva Convention*, 18 N.Y.U. J. Int'l L. & Pol. 703 (1986)

Note, *Extended Voluntary Departure: Limiting the Attorney General's Discretion in Immigration Matters*, 85 Mich. L. Rev. 152 (1986)

Note, *Temporary Safe-Haven for De Facto Refugees from War, Violence and Disasters*, 28 Va. J. Int'l L. 509 (1988)

Perluss & Hartman, *Temporary Refuge: Emergence of a Customary Norm*, Va. J. Int'l L. 551 (1986)

Sultan, *Ronald Reagan on Human Rights: The Gulag vs. the Death Squads*, 10 U. Dayton L. Rev. 245 (1985)

D. Suspension of Deportation

8 U.S.C. §§ 1254(a)(1) and (2), Sec. 244(a)(1) and (2) provides discretionary relief to persons in deportation proceedings which, when favorably exercised, accords them lawful permanent resident status. The applicant must prove continuous residency of seven years, good moral character during the statutory period, and that the deportation of the applicant would cause extreme hardship to the applicant, her spouse, parent, or child who is a citizen or lawful permanent resident. As will be seen in the following discussion, suspension of deportation is rarely exercised and has been the subject of much litigation.

Whether an individual can qualify for suspension relief will depend on the basis for the applicant's deportability. The previously described form of suspension of deportation applies to persons who are *not* deportable on criminal misconduct or political grounds.[15] Otherwise, she may be eligible for suspension if she can prove

---

15. Prior to 1986 former Nazis (persons deportable under 8 U.S.C. § 1251(a)(19)) were eligible for suspension of deportation under this broad category.

ten years of residency following the act which made her deportable, good moral character during the ten-year period, and that her deportation would result in "exceptional and extremely unusual hardship" to the applicant or her spouse, parent, or child, who is a citizen or lawful permanent resident.

---

8 U.S.C. § 1254, Sec. 244

(a) As hereinafter prescribed in this section, the Attorney General may, in his discretion, suspend deportation and adjust the status to that of an alien lawfully admitted for permanent residence, in the case of an alien (other than an alien described in section 1251(a)(19) of this title) who applies to the Attorney General for suspension of deportation and—

> (1) is deportable under any law of the United States except the provisions specified in paragraph (2) of this subsection; has been physically present in the United States for a continuous period of not less than seven years immediately preceding the date of such application, and proves that during all of such period he was and is a person of good moral character; and is a person whose deportation would, in the opinion of the Attorney General, result in extreme hardship to the alien or to his spouse, parent, or child, who is a citizen of the United States or an alien lawfully admitted for permanent residence; or

> (2) is deportable under paragraphs (4), (5), (6), (7), (11), (12), (14), (15), (16), (17), or (18) of section 1251(a) of this title; has been physically present in the United States for a continuous period of not less than ten years immediately following the commission of an act, or the assumption of a status, constituting a ground for deportation, and proves that during all of such period he has been and is a person of good moral character; and is a person whose deportation would, in the opinion of the Attorney General, result in exceptional and extremely unusual hardship to the alien or to his spouse, parent, or child, who is a citizen of the United States or an alien lawfully admitted for permanent residence.

(b)(1) The requirement of continuous physical presence in the United States specified in paragraphs (1) and (2) of subsection (a) of this section shall not be applicable to an alien who (A) has served for a minimum period of twenty-four months in an active-duty status in the Armed Forces of the United States and, if separated from such service, was separated under honorable conditions, and (B) at the time of his enlistment or induction was in the United States; and

> (2)[16] An alien shall not be considered to have failed to maintain continuous physical presence in the United States under paragraphs (1) and (2) of subsection (a) if the absence from the United States was brief, casual, and innocent and did not meaningfully interrupt the continuous physical presence.

(c) Fulfillment of requirements of subsection (a); report to Congress

> (1) Upon application by any alien who is found by the Attorney General to meet the requirements of subsection (a) of this section the Attorney General may in his discretion suspend deportation of such alien.

---

16. This section was amended after *Phinpathya*, the case which follows this statute.

(d) Upon the cancellation of deportation in the case of any alien under this section, the Attorney General shall record the alien's lawful admission for permanent residence as of the date the cancellation of deportation of such alien is made.

* * *

I.N.S. v. Phinpathya
464 U.S. 183 (1984)

Justice O'CONNOR delivered the opinion of the Court.

* * *

Respondent, a native and citizen of Thailand, first entered the United States as a nonimmigrant student in October, 1969. Respondent's husband, also a native and citizen of Thailand, entered the country in August, 1968. Respondent and her husband were authorized to remain in the United States until July, 1971. However, when their visas expired, they chose to stay without securing permission from the immigration authorities.

In January, 1977, petitioner, the Immigration and Naturalization Service (INS), commenced deportation proceedings against respondent and her husband pursuant to § 241(a)(2) of the Act. See 8 U.S.C. § 1251(a)(2). Respondent and her husband conceded deportability and applied for suspension pursuant to § 244(a)(1). 8 U.S.C. § 1254(a)(1). An immigration judge found that respondent's husband had satisfied § 244(a)(1)'s eligibility requirements and suspended his deportation. But respondent's own testimony showed that she had left the country during January, 1974, and that she had improperly obtained a nonimmigrant visa from the United States consular officer in Thailand to aid her reentry three months later. On the basis of this evidence, the immigration judge concluded that respondent had failed to meet the seven year "continuous physical presence" requirement of the Act:

> [Respondent's] absence was not brief, innocent, or casual. The absence would have been longer than three months if she had not obtained the [visa as the spouse of a student] as fast as she did obtain it. It was not casual because she had to obtain a new Tha[i] passport, as well as a nonimmigrant visa from the American Consul, to return to the United States. It was not innocent because she failed to inform the American Consul that she was the wife of a student who had been out of status for three years [and therefore not entitled to the nonimmigrant visa she received].

Accordingly, he denied respondent's application for suspension.

The Board of Immigration Appeals (BIA) affirmed the immigration judge's decision on the "continuous physical presence" issue. BIA observed that respondent was illegally in the United States at the time she left for Thailand and that she was able to return only by misrepresenting her status as the wife of a foreign student. Based on these observations, BIA concluded that respondent's absence was meaningfully interruptive of her continuous physical presence in the United States.

The Court of Appeals reversed. It noted that, although respondent traveled to Thailand for three months, "she intended, at all times, to return to the United States."

Phinpathya v. INS, 673 F.2d 1013, 1017 (9th Cir. 1982). The Court held that BIA had placed too much emphasis on respondent's illegal presence prior to her departure and on the increased risk of deportation that her departure had engendered. Id. at 1017-1018. Finding BIA's approach legally erroneous, it concluded that:

> an absence cannot be "meaningfully interruptive" if two factors are present: (1) the hardships would be as severe if the absence had not occurred, and (2) there would not be an increase in the risk of deportation as a result of the absence.

Since BIA "failed to view the circumstances in their totality and [analyze those circumstances] in light of the underlying Congressional purpose," the Court remanded for further proceedings on the "continuous physical presence" issue.

We granted certiorari to review the meaning of § 244(a)(1)'s requirement that an otherwise deportable alien have been "physically present in the United States for a continuous period of not less than seven years...." 8 U.S.C. § 1254(a)(1). We find that the Court of Appeals' interpretation of this statutory requirement departs from the plain meaning of the Act.

This Court has noted on numerous occasions that "in all cases involving statutory construction, 'our starting point must be the language employed by Congress,' ... and we assume 'that the legislative purpose is expressed by the ordinary meaning of the words used.' " *American Tobacco Co. v. Patterson*, 456 U.S. 63, 68 (1982), quoting *Reiter v. Sonotone Corp.*, 442 U.S. 330, 337 (1979). The language of § 244(a) requires certain threshold criteria to be met before the Attorney General or his delegates, in their discretion, may suspend proceedings against an otherwise deportable alien. This language plainly narrows the class of aliens who may obtain suspension by requiring each applicant for such extraordinary relief to prove that he:

> has been physically present in the United States for a continuous period of not less than seven years immediately preceding the date of such application, ... that during all such period he was and is a person of good moral character; and is a person whose deportation would, in the opinion of the Attorney General, result in extreme hardship to the alien or to his spouse, parent, or child, who is a citizen of the United States or an alien lawfully admitted for permanent residence...."

8 U.S.C. § 1254(a)(1). The ordinary meaning of these words does not readily admit any "exception[s] to the requirement of seven years of 'continuous physical presence' in the United States to be eligible for suspension of deportation."

By contrast, when Congress in the past has intended for a "continuous physical presence" requirement to be flexibly administered, it has provided the authority for doing so. For example, former § 301(b) of the Act, which required two years of "continuou(s) physical presen(ce)" for maintenance of status as a United States national or citizen, provided that "absence from the United States of less than sixty days in the aggregate during the period for which continuous physical presence in the United States is required shall not break the continuity of such physical presence." 86 Stat. 1289, repealing 71 Stat. 644 (12-month aggregate absence does not break continuity of physical presence). The deliberate omission of a similar moderating provision in § 244(a)(1) compels the conclusion that Congress meant this "continuous physical presence" requirement to be administered as written.

Indeed, the evolution of the deportation provision itself shows that Congress knew how to distinguish between actual "continuous physical presence" and some irreducible minimum of "non-intermittent" presence. Prior to 1940, the Attorney General had no discretion in ordering deportation, and an alien's sole remedy was to obtain a private bill from Congress. *See INS v. Wang*, 450 U.S. 139 (1981). In 1940, Congress authorized the Attorney General to suspend deportation of aliens of good moral character whose deportation "would result in serious economic detriment" to the aliens or their families. *See* 54 Stat. 672. Then, in 1948, Congress amended the statute again to make the suspension process available to aliens who "resided continuously in the United States for seven years or more" and who could show good moral character for the preceding five years, regardless of family ties. 62 Stat. 1206. Finally, in 1952, "in an attempt to discontinue lax practices and discourage abuses," Congress replaced the seven year "continuous residence" requirement with the current seven year "continuous physical presence" requirement. H.R. Rep. No. 1365, 82d Cong., 2d Sess., 31 (1952), U.S. Code Cong. & Admin. News 1952, p. 1653. It made the criteria for suspension of deportation more stringent both to restrict the opportunity for discretionary action, see id., and to exclude:

> aliens [who] are deliberately flouting our immigration laws by the processes of gaining admission into the United States illegally or ostensibly as nonimmigrants but with the intention of establishing themselves in a situation in which they may subsequently have access to some administrative remedy to adjust their status to that of permanent residents.

S. Rep. No. 1137, 82d Cong., 2d Sess., pt. 1, 25 (1952).

Had Congress been concerned only with "non-intermittent" presence or with the mere maintenance of a domicile or general abode, it could have retained the "continuous residence" requirement. Instead, Congress expressly opted for the seven year "continuous physical presence" requirement.

* * *

Respondent contends that we should approve the Court of Appeals' "generous" and "liberal" construction of the "continuous physical presence" requirement notwithstanding the statute's plain language and history. She argues that the Court of Appeals' construction is in keeping both with our decision in *Rosenberg v. Fleuti*, 374 U.S. 449 (1963), and with the equitable and ameliorative nature of the suspension remedy. We disagree.

In *Fleuti*, this Court held that a lawful permanent resident alien's return to the United States after an afternoon trip to Mexico did not constitute an "entry" within the meaning of § 101(a)(13) of the Act. We construed the term "intended" in the statutory exception to the definition of "entry" to mean an "intent to depart in a manner which can be regarded as meaningfully interruptive of the alien's permanent residence." *Id.* at 462. We interpreted the statute not to allow a lawful resident alien like *Fleuti* to be excluded "for a condition for which he could not have been deported had he remained in the country . . ." because it would subject the alien to "unsuspected risks and unintended consequences of . . . wholly innocent action." Id. at 460. Since Fleuti had gone to Mexico, without travel documents, for only a few hours, we remanded for a determination whether his departure had been "innocent, casual, and brief," and so "meaningfully interruptive" of his permanent residence. Ibid.

Fleuti is essentially irrelevant to the adjudication of respondent's § 244(a)(1) suspension application. *Fleuti* dealt with a statutory exception enacted precisely to ameliorate the harsh effects of prior judicial construction of the "entry" doctrine. See *id*. at 457-462. By contrast, this case deals with a threshold requirement added to the statute specifically to limit the discretionary availability of the suspension remedy. Thus, whereas a flexible approach to statutory construction was consistent with the congressional purpose underlying § 101(a)(13), such an approach would not be consistent with the congressional purpose underlying the "continuous physical presence" requirement.

In *Fleuti*, the Court believed that Congress had not considered the "meaningless and irrational hazards" that a strict application of the "entry" provision could create. Thus, it inferred that Congress would not have approved of the otherwise harsh consequences that would have resulted to *Fleuti*. See 374 U.S., at 460-462. Here, by contrast, we have every reason to believe that Congress considered the harsh consequences of its actions. Congress expressly provided a mechanism for factoring "extreme hardship" into suspension of deportation decisions. We would have to ignore the clear Congressional mandate and the plain meaning of the statute to find that Fleuti is applicable to the determination whether an otherwise deportable alien has been "physically present in the United States for a continuous period of not less than seven years . . . ." 8 U.S.C. § 1254(a) (1). We refuse to do so.

We also note, though it is not essential to our decision, that *Fleuti* involved the departure of a lawful resident alien who, but for his departure, otherwise had a statutory right to remain in this country. This case, by contrast, deals with the departure of an unlawful alien who could have been deported even had she remained in this country. Such an alien has no basis for expecting the Government to permit her to remain in the United States or to readmit her upon her return from foreign soil. Thus, respondent simply is not being excluded "for a condition for which (she) could not have been deported had [she] remained in the country. . . ." 374 U.S., at 460.

* * *

It is also clear that Congress intended strict threshold criteria to be met before the Attorney General could exercise his discretion to suspend deportation proceedings. Congress drafted § 244(a)(1)'s provisions specifically to restrict the opportunity for discretionary administrative action. Respondent's suggestion that we construe the Act to broaden the Attorney General's discretion is fundamentally inconsistent with this intent. In *INS v. Wang*, we rejected a relaxed standard for evaluating the "extreme hardship" requirement as impermissibly shifting discretionary authority from INS to the courts. 450 U.S. 139, 146 (1981). Respondent's suggestion that we construe the Act to broaden the Attorney General's discretion analogously would shift authority to relax the "continuous physical presence" requirement from Congress to INS and, eventually, as is evident from the experience in this case, to the courts. We must therefore reject respondent's suggestion as impermissible in our tripartite scheme of government. Congress designs the immigration laws, and it is up to Congress to temper the laws' rigidity if it so desires.

The Court of Appeals' approach ignores the plain meaning of § 244(a)(1) and extends eligibility to aliens whom Congress clearly did not intend to be eligible for suspension of deportation. Congress meant what it said: otherwise deportable aliens must show that they have been physically present in the United States for a continuous period of seven years before they are eligible for suspension of deportation. The judgment of the Court of Appeals therefore is reversed.

Notes

1. The reform legislation contained a provision which replaced the more liberal interpretation of the statute, allowing for departures which are meaningful interruptions of residency. Should the fact that Congress so quickly rejected the Court's interpretation have any bearing on future statutory interpretations?

2. The Court's approach to the suspension statute is not unlike the manner in which it has dealt with other statutes. Are there other provisions of the INA which have been interpreted more "loosely," which you believe could be overturned?

3. Although the Court did not specifically overturn its decision in *Rosenberg v. Fleuti*, 374 U.S. 449 (1963), how do you believe that it might deal with the cases if it was presented with the issue today?

What Went Wrong with Wang?: An Examination of INS v. Wang
Loue, 20 San Diego L. Rev. 59 (1982)*

Until 1940 deportation was mandatory for aliens illegally in the United States. This strict rule produced harsh results in many cases. Congress responded to requests for reform by enacting into law in 1940 provisions authorizing the legalization of an alien's status where he could demonstrate both five years' good moral character and that deportation would result in serious economic detriment to a permanent resident or citizen spouse, parent, or minor child. Congress extended the law in 1948 to authorize suspension of deportation for those without family ties who had resided in the United States for a period of seven years.

Section 244(a)(1) of the Immigration and National Act of 1952 authorized suspension of deportation only where the alien could demonstrate "exceptional and extremely unusual hardship" to himself or to a lawful permanent resident or citizen spouse, parent, or child. Congress intended that this relief be available only where the hardship was unusual and where deportation would be unconscionable. In determining whether or not to grant relief under this provision, the Board of Immigration Appeals (Board) considered various factors: 1) the length of the alien's residence, including the means and purpose of entry; 2) the alien's family ties in the United States and overseas; 3) the possibility of the alien's obtaining a visa overseas; 4) the financial difficulty the alien would face in traveling overseas to obtain the visa; and 5) the alien's health and age. Hardship could be established by the presence of several of these factors.

In 1962 Congress changed the requirement of "exceptional and extremely unusual hardship" to the current requirement of "extreme hardship," presumably to

---

* Copyright 1982 San Diego Law Review Association. Reprinted with the permission of the *San Diego Law Review*.

lessen the degree of hardship required for suspension of deportation. In 1975, the House Judiciary Committee recommended that in addition to the factors previously considered for section 244(a)(1) relief, the Board consider several additional factors: 1) the economic and political conditions of the country to which the alien would be returnable; 2) the alien's business and occupation; 3) the possibility of other means of adjustment of status; 4) whether the alien was of special assistance to the United States or to the community; 5) the alien's immigration history; and 6) the alien's position in the community.

The issue of suspension of deportation generally arises in the context of deportation proceedings, during which the alien may apply to the immigration judge for such relief. If circumstances change following the deportation proceeding, the alien may move to reopen the proceeding where "the evidence sought to be offered is material and was not available and could not have been discovered or presented at the hearing. . . . "

Through the Adjudicative Looking Glass: Extreme Hardship Defined

Various courts have acknowledged the difficulty in any attempt to define the term "extreme hardship," recognizing that "[t]hese words are not self-explanatory and reasonable men could easily differ as to their construction." Although the House Judiciary Committee suggested various factors to be considered by the Board in making such determinations, ultimately the Board and the courts must weigh the variables in each individual case. The task confronting an alien attempting to establish extreme hardship before these adjudicative bodies may well appear herculean.

The alien may base a claim of extreme hardship on hardship to himself or "his spouse, parent, or child, who is a citizen of the United States or an alien lawfully admitted for permanent residence." However, the presence of a single factor will not by itself warrant a finding of extreme hardship. The courts and the Board have consistently refused to find extreme hardship present where the alien premised his claim primarily upon economic detriment or upon the existence of United States citizen children. Even these two factors taken together will not necessarily trigger a finding of extreme hardship. Indeed, the presence of additional factors will guarantee the alien neither a pronouncement of extreme hardship nor a result consistent with prior decisions.

The courts differ, too, in the extent to which they are willing to infer additional factors from the presentation of a single consideration. Most aliens would experience some degree of financial loss upon deportation. Few courts, though, have recognized as worthy of consideration the personal consequences which emanate naturally from this one source, including decreased health care, a loss of educational opportunities, and possible malnutrition. Where an alien asserts hardship to a United States citizen child departing with the deportable parent(s), the courts will not infer particular consequences from the fact of the relocation. Rather, the alien must not only allege any educational deprivation, emotional difficulty, or lack of medical care which would ensue upon the child's departure with the deportable parent(s), but will also be required to demonstrate that such benefits are unavailable in the country to which the family would relocate.

The Board and the courts have thus visited their struggles with "extreme hardship" upon the aliens appearing before them. Even when presented with the most compelling circumstances, the adjudicative body often finds that the alien has failed to demonstrate "extreme hardship." The criteria are nebulous and difficult to establish. The unsuccessful alien's only additional recourse may be a change of circumstances allowing the presentation of new evidence in support of a motion to reopen.

The alien moving to reopen deportation proceedings must establish a prima facie case of eligibility before addressing extreme hardship. While this appears upon preliminary examination to be a lesser burden than the establishment of extreme hardship, the task confronting the alien may actually be substantial. Although the alien may appeal a Board denial of his motion to the court of appeals, Wang has seriously curtailed the parameters of the appellate court's authority with respect to such motions.

Immigration and Naturalization Service v. Wang

Wang involved a husband and wife, citizens of Korea, who entered the United States as "treaty traders" in 1970. They were found deportable in 1974 as individuals who had overstayed their authorized visit and were granted voluntary departure. In 1975 they moved to reopen their deportation proceedings to apply for adjustment of status. Following a finding of ineligibility, they appealed to the Board. The Board dismissed their appeal and they subsequently moved to reopen to apply for suspension of deportation. The Board denied the motion, finding that the Wangs had failed to establish a prima facie case of eligibility to justify suspension.

The court of appeals reversed, finding that the Wangs had established a prima facie case in support of the motion. The court addressed at length the requirements of a successful motion to reopen and the standard applicable to Board rulings on such motions. The alien must allege new facts supported by affidavits or other evidentiary material. Conclusory allegations were deemed insufficient to require a reopening and afford the alien a hearing. The facts had to be such as to establish eligibility and potentially affect the outcome of the proceedings. The court required the Board to include in its decision a discussion of the evidence upon which it based its decision to grant or to deny the alien's request.

The Ninth Circuit also found that, contrary to the opinion of the Board, the Wangs had established the existence of extreme hardship. The court found that the alien need allege extreme hardship to only one of the persons enumerated in the statute, but admonished the Board to consider as well the aggregate effect of deportation on all individuals alleged by the alien to suffer extreme hardship as a result. The court further noted that the determination of the existence of a prima facie showing of extreme hardship was to be based upon the facts of each individual case.

The Wangs had claimed that their children would encounter serious economic, educational, and cultural deficiencies if they were forced to leave the United States with their parents. The Board found that this consideration did not constitute the degree of hardship contemplated by the statute. The court noted that both children had always lived in the United States and that neither spoke Korean. The court acknowledged that the existence of a United States citizen child would not confer favored status on an alien nor validate an invalid claim of extreme hardship or automatically establish extreme hardship to the child. The court found, however, that the Board had failed altogether to consider whether the parents' deportation would, in fact, cause the child extreme hardship.

The Wangs further alleged that deportation would force them to liquidate their United States-held assets to their detriment. The Board found that a mere showing of economic hardship was equally insufficient to establish extreme hardship within the meaning of the statute. The court noted that economic hardship need not be totally eliminated from consideration, but could be considered in conjunction with additional factors present to determine the existence of extreme hardship.

The United States Supreme Court reversed the decision of the Ninth Circuit, holding that the court of appeals had erred in granting the motion to reopen. The Court acknowledged the difficulty involved in construing the term "extreme hardship" but refused to adopt a liberal construction of its meaning. It found instead that the Immigration and Nationality Act committed the definition and construction of "extreme hardship" to the Attorney General and his delegates. It further noted that the Attorney General acted within his authority to adopt a narrow interpretation of "extreme hardship."

Despite the fears voiced by several courts, suspension of deportation has not been a readily available remedy for aliens illegally present in the United States. Even where the alien has fulfilled the good moral character and physical presence requirements, the establishment of extreme hardship may remain an unattainable vision. With the exception of the Ninth Circuit, the Supreme Court's decision in Wang effectively curtailed whatever liberality the courts of appeals had been demonstrating in ruling upon motions to reopen. The courts have been increasingly reluctant since Wang to fund an abuse of discretion in the denials of motions to reopen, and the Board has vehemently reasserted its authority to deny such motions in the exercise of its discretion. In light of the often harsh consequences of deportation and the ameliorative purposes underlying the relevant legislation, this narrowing construction is unfortunate and ill-advised.

As currently construed, the suspension provision and related regulations allow the Attorney General to exercise discretion at three levels: 1) in finding the existence of extreme hardship as a result of the individual's deportation; 2) in suspending deportation; and 3) in ruling upon a motion to reopen. In Wang, the Supreme Court effectively cut off judicial review of the definition and determination of "extreme hardship," thereby allowing instances of injustice to remain uncorrected. There currently are no guidelines to aid the Attorney General and his delegates in defining that term. With severely limited judicial review of this decision, the need for regulations has become all the more critical in order to provide a standard and to promote consistency. The commonality of the factors presented for consideration in determining extreme hardship provide a foundation for the formulation of such guidelines. The regulations must further provide, as courts are now demanding with respect to motions to reopen, that the Board in its determinations regarding extreme hardship discuss each factor separately and in conjunction with all other factors presented. This requirement would result in greater attention to each case on its own merits and greater consistency between cases, as well as facilitate judicial review.

The Board routinely denies suspension of deportation when the allegation of extreme hardship is economic in nature. Adjudicative bodies have been reluctant to draw a distinction between "mere economic detriment" and economic hardship so severe as to constitute "extreme hardship." One court has deemed the loss of one's investment and difficulty in finding employment in one's profession as "mere economic detriment" insufficient to rise to the level of "extreme hardship." The same court noted, however, that there exists "a qualitative difference between 'mere economic detriment' and the complete inability to find employment." The complete inability to find employment in the country of deportation may indeed constitute extreme hardship if taken together with its attendant consequences of decreased health care, malnutrition, and possible starvation. Although the Board has expressed a willingness to consider economic detriment together with advanced age and/or severe illness to find the extreme hardship necessary for suspension of deportation, it has, in fact, not done so. The regulations must reflect the realities of existence and distinguish between those factors which constitute "mere economic detriment" and those which, either taken separately or in conjunction with each other, rise to the level of "extreme hardship." Extreme hardship must necessarily encompass, as a sole consideration, the alien's total inability to find employment where the alien has no other demonstrable means of support.

Note

Following the *Wang* decision, courts have been extremely reluctant to overturn denials of suspension applications by the BIA based on its exercise of discretion. However, some courts have been willing to look more closely at the factors considered by the Board in assessing extreme hardship. These courts appear willing to reverse the decision where the BIA has failed to give consideration to a proferred hardship factor. *See Ravancho V. INS*, 658 F.2d 169 (3d Cir. 1981); *Santana-Figueroa v. INS*, 644 F.2d 1354 (9th Cir. 1981); *Antoine-Dorcelli v. INS*, 703 F.2d 19 (1st Cir. 1983); *Carrete-Michel v. INS*, 749 F.2d 490 (8th Cir. 1984).

On review, the individual applicant is entitled first to have her case decided on its own facts and the weighing of these facts must be evident from the decision. In one case, a Ninth Circuit *en banc* panel criticized the BIA for its summary approach to a review of the evidence and for having invoked a floodgates argument in denying the applicant's claim. *See Prapavat v. INS*, 638 F.2d 87 (9th Cir. 1980), *aff'd en banc*, 662 F.2d 561 (1981). For an interesting discussion of judicial review of suspension cases, *see* Note, *Judicial Review of "Extreme Hardship" in Suspension of Deportation Cases*, 34 Am. U. L. Rev. 175 (1984).

E. Extreme Hardship

Matter of Anderson
16 I. & N. Dec. 596 (BIA 1978)

In a decision dated November 4, 1977, an immigration judge found the respondent deportable as charged, denied his application for suspension of deportation under section 244(a), but granted him the privilege of voluntary departure in lieu of deportation. The respondent has appealed. The appeal will be dismissed.

The respondent, a 55-year-old native and citizen of the Dominican Republic, entered the United States on August 3, 1969, as a nonimmigrant visitor. He has conceded deportability as a visitor who has remained here beyond the period authorized. The finding we are asked to review on appeal concerns the denial of suspension of deportation.

In order to establish eligibility for section 244(a)(1) relief, an alien must prove that he has been physically present in the United States for the last seven years, that he has been a person of good moral character for the same period, and that his deportation will result in extreme hardship to himself or to his United States citizen or permanent resident spouse, children, or parents.

The immigration judge appears to have found that the respondent failed to establish two of the three statutory criteria, continuous physical presence and extreme hardship. The issue of the respondent's good moral character was not challenged by the Immigration and Naturalization Service. In view of our conclusion on the hardship issue, we find it unnecessary to reach the question of continuous physical presence.

In testimony given at the hearing, the respondent contended that the economy of the Dominican Republic is so severely depressed that he will find it difficult to support himself and his wife, who is also in the United States illegally. Medical treatment for her psychological maladjustments could not be afforded, according to the respondent. The immigration judge concluded that the thrust of the respondent's argument was that he would suffer economic detriment if deported. The judge correctly noted that under the prevailing interpretation of the extreme hardship requirement, financial hardship in the absence of substantial additional equities has not been a persuasive factor. See Matter of Uy, 11 I. & N. Dec. 159 (BIA 1965); *Matter of Sangster*, 11 I. & N. Dec. 309 (BIA 1965); *Matter of Gibson*, Interim Decision 2541 (BIA 1976).

At oral argument, counsel for the respondent directed our attention to recent comments by the House Judiciary Committee on the issue of extreme hardship. Counsel was referring to a report by the committee in the 94th Congress on §4 of H.R. 8713, a bill which provided for discretionary adjustment of status for certain aliens whose deportation would result in "unusual hardship." The committee report contains the following discussion:

> With respect to determining hardship under section 4 of this bill the Attorney General is expected to apply similar criteria to that which is currently utilized in granting suspension of deportation and consider the following facts and circumstances among others: age of the subject; family ties in the United States and abroad; length of residence in the United States; condition of health; conditions in the country to which the alien is returnable—economic and political; financial status—business and occupation; the possibility of other means of adjustment of status; whether of special assistance to the United States or community; immigration history; position in the community.

In light of these statements, counsel contends that the impoverished economy of the Dominican Republic should be a dispositive factor in this suspension application.

Conditions in an alien's homeland are relevant in determining hardship, as the Committee pointed out. It is obvious, however, that laying critical emphasis on the economic and political situation would mandate a grant of relief in most cases for it is a demonstrable fact that despite the beleaguered state of our own economy, the United States enjoys a standard of living higher than that in most of the other countries of the world. For this reason, most deported aliens will likely suffer some degree of financial hardship. Nonetheless, we do not believe that Congress intended to remedy this situation by suspending the deportation of all those who will be unable to maintain the standard of living at home which they have managed to achieve in this country. Clearly, it is only when other factors such as advanced age, severe illness, family ties, etc. combine with economic detriment to make deportation extremely hard on the alien or the citizen or permanent resident members of his family that Congress has authorized suspension of the deportation order.

We do not dispute the respondent's characterization of the Dominican economy. However, we cannot find a sufficient number of other adverse factors to conclude that deportation will result in the degree of hardship that section 244(a)(1) was designed to alleviate. The respondent has spent most of his eight years in the United States as a self-employed carpenter. Prior to his arrival, he also worked as a carpenter for the Dominican Government where his ability was apparently highly regarded. While he has several cousins who live in the United States, his brothers, sisters, and ten children all live in the Dominican Republic. Treatment of his wife's emotional difficulties can surely be obtained at home, albeit with economic sacrifices. Despite the sympathetic facts in this case, we are not persuaded that the respondent warrants the extraordinary relief authorized in section 244(a)(1) of the Act.

Notes

1. The statute also provides for a special suspension of deportation which requires a showing of *"exceptional and extremely unusual hardship"* in the case of persons who are deportable for most criminal convictions, drug addiction [Sec. 241, 8 U.S.C. §§ 1251(a)(2) and (3)], or because of security grounds [Sec. 241(a)(4), 8 U.S.C. §§ 1251(a)(4)].[17] This form of suspension requires that the applicant has been present in the U.S. for ten years.

2. Under both the normal and special forms of suspension relief, the applicant must show the requisite hardship and good moral character in the period following the commission of the act rendering her deportable.

3. Very few cases have elaborated on the definition of exceptional and extremely unusual hardship. One court described it as when deportation would be unconscionable. *Asikese v. Brownell*, 230 F.2d 34 (D.C. Cir. 1956).

4. The concept that the factor of hardship should be used to ameliorate the consequences of deportation has been a constant theme in immigration law. You will recall that in our discussion of adjustment of status, the concept of "balancing of equities" was introduced. In suspension cases, the analysis is focused more on the degree of hardship than in weighing positive and negative factors of the applicant's conduct. Therefore, the challenge for the immigration judge is to consider all of the factors in the aggregate. *See Santana-Figueroa v. INS*, 644 F.2d 635 (7th Cir. 1981); *Barrera-Leyva v. INS*, 637 F.2d 640 (9th Cir. 1980); *Ramos v. INS*, 695 F.2d 181 (5th Cir. 1983).

5. Prior to 1978, suspension of deportation was available to persons who had assisted or participated with the Nazis during World War II; in 1981 all forms of suspension for these persons were removed. *See* Immigration Amendments of 1978, Pub. L. No. 95-549, subsection (e); Immigration Amendments of 1981, Pub. L. No. 97-116, § 18(h)(2). For a discussion of the application of these two INA amendments, *see Matter of Fedorenko*, Interim Dec. 2963 (BIA 1984).

---

17. This suspension of deportation is contained in 8 U.S.C. § 1254(a)(2), Sec. 244.

F. The Difficulties in Suspension of Cases

Matter of Louie

10 I. & N. Dec. 223 (BIA 1963)

The respondent was born on the mainland of China and lived there until 1949. He stated that at that time he fled to Hong Kong because the Communists were taking control of China. He left Hong Kong for Central America in 1950. He was married in 1950 while still in Hong Kong, and one child was born there of the marriage on March 5, 1951. The respondent's wife and child still reside in Hong Kong and she is employed there as a nursemaid in an orphanage. The respondent contributes to their support by sending $50 to $100 monthly. He has been employed in the United States as a waiter and now earns about $85 weekly. In his application for suspension of deportation, he stated that his assets amounted to $2,350.

The respondent's statement of November 6, 1961 (Ex. 8, p. 2) contains information verifying his admission as a nonimmigrant on August 21, 1951, and he has testified that he has not been absent on any occasion since that date. The special inquiry officer concluded that the respondent had been physically present in the United States for a continuous period of at least ten years, and we are also satisfied from the record as to the respondent's continuous physical presence in this country since August 21, 1951. It follows that he meets the requirement of section 244(a)(1), as amended, concerning physical presence in the United States for a continuous period of not less than seven years.

The special inquiry officer also concluded that the respondent had established good moral character during the statutory period. The respondent testified that he had never been arrested or convicted of any crime. A search of the local police records and a report received from the Identification Division of the Federal Bureau of Investigation indicate that the respondent has no criminal record. An independent investigation conducted by the Service was favorable to the respondent. We conclude that the respondent has established his good moral character during the seven years preceding his application.

Prior to the amendment of October 24, 1962, the five paragraphs of section 244(a) required an applicant to establish that his deportation would result "in exceptional and extremely unusual hardship" to the alien or to his citizen or legally resident spouse, parent or child. This same language was retained in amended section 244(a)(2), but in amended section 244(a)(1), which is involved here, the language was changed to require the alien to establish that his deportation would result "in extreme hardship" to him or to his citizen or legally resident spouse, parent or child. Although the special inquiry officer held that extreme hardship meant something less than exceptional and extremely unusual hardship, he was not satisfied that the respondent's case met this statutory requirement.

The respondent asserts that his deportation would result in extreme hardship to him and to his father. The latter has lived in this country since his lawful admission on September 20, 1922, and he was naturalized as a United States citizen on June 27, 1958. On November 6, 1961 the respondent testified that his father was partially paralyzed, and the record contains a certificate (Ex. 10) from a physician indicating that the respondent's father has been under his medical care since March 8, 1960 and is permanently disabled. From 1952 until recently, the respondent lived with his father in Los Angeles but the latter, who is 72 years old, is now in the International Guest Home in that city. The respondent testified that the cost of his father's maintenance is about $125 per month; that this is paid by Los Angeles County; that his father has no income; that he receives an old age pension of $125 which he returns to the International Guest Home; that (the respondent) contributes about $50 monthly toward his father's support and care; and that he takes his father to the doctor each week (pp. 13-15). Apparently the respondent and his father have no close relatives in the United States. In view of the father's advanced age and physical condition, we believe it would be extremely harsh, both to the respondent and his father, to deport this alien from the United States.

The respondent states that he desires to bring his wife and son to the United States from Hong Kong. He testified that he has never been a member of the Communist Party of any country and has not been a member of any organization affiliated with the Party, and there is nothing to indicate such membership. He testified that he fears physical persecution if returned to Communist China because he is opposed to communism and fled China for that reason. However, the special inquiry officer did not direct deportation to Communist China but to the Republic of China on Formosa or to Hong Kong. The respondent also stated that he cannot return to Hong Kong because he never established residence there. The respondent has lived continuously in Los Angeles since March 1952—a period of 11 years. If the respondent were deported to Formosa or Hong Kong, we believe he would experience great difficulty in obtaining employment or in adjusting to life in a new country, particularly since he is now 42 years of age.

Notes

1. The result of a successful application for suspension of deportation is that the applicant receives lawful permanent residency. Although the applicant may obtain permanent residence by passing through the bureaucratic labyrinth required to establish extreme hardship, suspension of deportation is a difficult benefit for the alien to obtain. *See Suspension of Deportation: Illusory Relief,* 14 San Diego L. Rev. 229 (1976); *but see Suspension of Deportation: A Revitalized Relief for the Alien,* 18 San Diego L. Rev. 65 (1980).

2. In fashioning an argument for extreme hardship, a lawyer must use creative approaches. In *Matter of Anderson* the BIA outlined the criteria to be used in assessing the extreme hardship claim. What argument might be presented where the individual simultaneously applied for asylum *and* suspension of deportation? What should be the burden of proof in such a claim?

3. *Procedural Note:* The INS district director does not decide suspension of deportation cases. A suspension of deportation application is made to an immigration judge because the statute requires that the person first be found deportable.[18] The reader will recall that only the immigration judge may make a determination of whether or not a person can be deported. Once the deportation hearing has com-

---

18. The suspension of deportation application is more commonly used as a defense to the INS effort to deport. It is rarely sought by the alien as a means of obtaining permanent residence.

menced, jurisdiction lies with the immigration judge. In the event that a determination is made by the judge to deny the application, the applicant may appeal the decision to the BIA.

Due to the peculiar nature of the procedure in these cases, suspension cases are brought in the following manner: (a) if the applicant is in custody or an order to show cause (OSC) has been issued, the application is presented before the judge at the commencement of the hearing; and (b) if the person's identity and location is not known, the "prospective" suspension applicant must present herself to the INS and request an OSC so that the application can be presented to the judge. The attorney therefore must be cautious before deciding to "turn the client in" to proceed with a suspension of deportation application.

4. Proving the claim of hardship requires a careful presentation of the facts initiated by the submission of the application form I-256A, affidavits, letters, other documents, and witnesses. In order to make out the strongest case, the presentation will include all of these elements. Assume, for example, that you were attempting to show that an infirmity coupled with advanced age and sick children constituted sufficient hardship. You would first present the application, affidavits attesting to good moral character, police reports reflecting no derogatory information, copies of income tax returns and pay receipts, the birth certificates of the children, medical reports on the applicant and children, and live testimony from experts such as treating physicians, psychiatrists, and persons knowledgable of conditions in the applicant's country. Can you think of additional information which you would present at the hearing? Would it make any difference if you were submitting the evidence as part of a motion to reopen?

5. Although the INS district director does not decide suspension cases, the applicant's ability to present strong evidence can occasionally have the effect of creating an uncontested suspension case.

6. The BIA has stated that an alien's "difficulty in eventually being able to obtain an immigrant visa" should be a favorable factor in assessing "extreme hardship." *See In Re S—*, 5 I. & N. Dec. 409 (BIA 1953); *In Re U—*, 5 I. & N. Dec. 413 (BIA 1953).

In many cases the attorney will be seeking a preference status at the same time that she is filing for suspension. In these cases the applicant may be eligible to obtain permanent residency due to the availability of immigrant visas in the not too distant future.

Should the fact that the person will be able to obtain an immigrant visa in the future be a favorable factor in assessing extreme hardship? What arguments would you present in support of this position? What might be the rationale behind the BIA's rulings in *In Re S—* and *In Re U—*, *supra*?

7. In a motion to reopen for purposes of applying for suspension of deportation, the immigration judge will apply less weight to extreme hardship equities acquired after a deportation order has been issued than to those acquired before an alien has been found deportable. *See Matter of Correa*, Interim Dec. 2973 (BIA 1984).

Procedure for Obtaining Relief from Deportation

Relief Prior to Institution of Proceedings

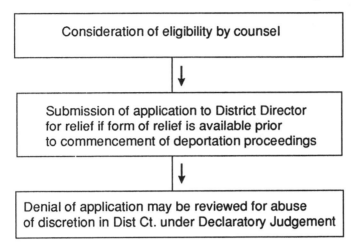

Consideration of eligibility by counsel

↓

Submission of application to District Director
for relief if form of relief is available prior
to commencement of deportation proceedings

↓

Denial of application may be reviewed for abuse
of discretion in Dist Ct. under Declaratory Judgement

Relief After Deportation Proceedings Have Commenced

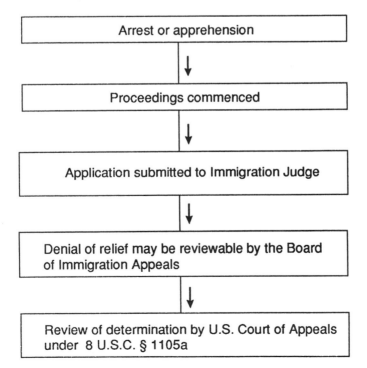

Arrest or apprehension

↓

Proceedings commenced

↓

Application submitted to Immigration Judge

↓

Denial of relief may be reviewable by the Board
of Immigration Appeals

↓

Review of determination by U.S. Court of Appeals
under 8 U.S.C. § 1105a

Chapter 12

Amelioration of Grounds of Excludability and Deportability

As we discussed in Chapters 2 and 3, the grounds under which a person may be excluded or deported are extensive. These bases for exclusion and deportation represent the congressional intent to exclude foreigners, using their plenary power. As we will see, most of the grounds for exclusion and deportation include waiver provisions which may be obtained depending on the applicant's length of residency, relationship to U.S. citizens or lawful permanent residents, and degree of hardship.[1] The grounds for exclusion and the waivers which are provided in the statute can be compared to the angry person who decides that she does not want to allow certain people into her home and then learns later that the broad categories would cause her to exclude people who she otherwise might like to invite. Similarly, there are certain circumstances where a criminal conviction may not be treated as such for purposes of deportation and exclusion.

With the passage of the Anti-Drug Abuse Act in 1988, Pub. L. No. 100-690 102 Stat. 4181 (1988) and the Immigration Act of 1990, Pub. L. No. 101-649, 104 Stat. 4978 the available ameliorative devices for foreigners with criminal convictions have become more restricted. For example, until November, 28, 1990 sentencing judges could grant a person a judicial recommendation against deportation, thereby precluding its use in a subsequent deportation proceeding. It remains to be seen what affect, if any, the limiting of discretionary ameliorative devices will have on criminal and immigration proceedings. In addition, the multiple grounds under which a person could be charged with deportability coupled with the haste with which Congress proceeded could well cause the modification of some of the provisions discussed here.[2] The discussion and cases which follow, attempt to present the various mechanisms which can be used to protect the person from the many grounds of exclusion and deportation.

Pardons

In order to avoid the immigration consequences of a criminal conviction, a pardon must be made by the President of the United States or by the supreme authority of

---

1. In most cases which require hardship, the applicant will be required to show the degree of hardship which will be inflicted on herself or her family.

2. For example, Section 505 of the 1990 Act eliminated the judicial recommendation provision and eliminated the benefits of pardons for foreigners who had been convicted of aggravated felonies. Also, Section 602 eliminated all of 8 U.S.C. § 1251(b). See Sec. 602(b), Immigration Act of 1990, Pub. L. No. 101-649, 104 Stat. 4978. The result of these changes caused some commentators to speculate about whether pardons were eliminated along with the judicial recommendation against deportation. See e.g. UNDERSTANDING THE IMMIGRATION ACT OF 1990, at 231 (P. Schmidt ed. 1991)

the state which is empowered to extend pardons.[3] The pardon can only be used to waive the immigration consequences of crimes involving moral turpitude, multiple criminal convictions and aggravated felonies, i.e., those situations where the person is found deportable under 8 U.S.C. § 1251(a)(2)(A)(iv). The pardon may also protect the person from the INS's use of the criminal conviction to negate an assertion of lack of good moral character which would be required to obtain voluntary departure, registry, and U.S. citizenship.[4]

Petty Offense and Juvenile Exceptions

A "petty crime"[5] is one in which the maximum possible penalty does not exceed imprisonment for one year and where the person's prison sentence did not exceed six months.[6]

8 U.S.C. § 1182(a)(2), which provides for excludability based on criminal acts, specifically exempts persons who would be excludable because of a conviction for a petty crime.[7]

> An alien who would be excludable because of the conviction of an offense for which the sentence actually imposed did not exceed a term of imprisonment in excess of six months, or who would be excludable as one who admits the commission of an offense for which a sentence not to exceed one year's imprisonment might have been imposed may be granted a visa and admitted to the United States if otherwise admissible: Provided. That the alien has committed only one such offense, or admits the commission of acts which constitute the essential elements of only one such offense.

In the case of foreign convictions, one must look to the sentence imposed by the foreign court. In the absence of a crime with a classification comparable to U.S. law (i.e., misdemeanor versus felony), one may look to the U.S. Code to find a similar crime. If no authority is found, the D.C. Code should be consulted. In addition, the exclusion provisions relating to criminal acts by minors (juveniles) may be inapplicable.[8] In the event that the minor is treated as an adult offender and the trial court expressly forgoes the juvenile proceeding, she will be subject to deportation under 8

---

3. *See* 8 U.S.C. § 1251(a)(2)(A)(iv), Sec. 241(a)(2)(A)(iv). This is so, even though the statute specifically limits its coverage to pardons issued by the President or a governor. *See Matter of Tajer*, 15 I. & N. Dec. 125 (BIA 1974) (pardon issued by the parole board and recognized for immigration purposes where the parole board was the final authority in the state to issue pardons); 22 C.F.R. § 42.91 (a)(9)(vii).

4. *See Giambanco v. INS*, 531 F.2d 141 (3d Cir. 1976).

5. The term "petty crime" crime does not appear in the statute.

6. *See* 8 U.S.C. § 1182(a)(2)(A)(ii)(II), Sec. 212(a)(2)(A)(ii)(II). The statute allows the commission of only one petty crime.

7. 8 U.S.C. § 1182(a)(2) was amended retroactively effective November 1, 1986, by the Omnibus Crime Control Act of October 12, 1984, 98 Stat. 1837. The earlier statute required that the crime be a misdemeanor and petty offense under section 1(3) of 18 U.S.C. and the punishment *imposed* must have been within the statutory definition of six months.

8. *See Matter of C.M.*, 5 I. & N. Dec. 327 (BIA 1953); *Matter of Ramirez-Rivero*, 18 I. & N. Dec. 135 (BIA 1981). For references relating to the treatment of juveniles, consult the Federal Juvenile Delinquency Act (18 U.S.C. § 1 *et seq.*)

U.S.C. § 1182(a)(2).[9] If the person was convicted under a foreign statute, the conviction will be viewed according to the standards of the Federal Juvenile Delinquency Act.[10]

Waivers

Waivers of grounds of excludability or deportability are both an admission of the grounds of exclusion or deportation and an affirmative request for an exercise of discretion.[11] To understand the waiver provisions, one must first revisit the exclusion grounds discussed earlier.[12] Nonimmigrants have traditionally been accorded greater latitude with respect to the various grounds of exclusion. For example, nonimmigrants entering the United States for employment, with the exception of certain H visa applicants, need not obtain labor certifications as required under 8 U.S.C. § 1182(a)(5). In addition, applicants to the U.S. who are graduates of foreign medical schools are allowed admission in certain nonimmigrant classifications notwithstanding the foreign residency requirement of 8 U.S.C. § 1182(e). This difference in the treatment of nonimmigrants is attributable to the fact that they are not perceived as becoming a part of American society.[13]

Insofar as waivers are concerned, certain categories of persons are viewed with disfavor irrespective of the length or purpose of their stay or visit in the United States. These include persons whose activities would have potentially serious adverse foreign policy consequences,[14] those likely to engage in espionage or overthrow the government of the United States,[15] and those associated with Nazi Germany or who have persecuted others.[16]

What follows is a list of the various grounds of exclusion and the bases for obtaining their waiver.

    1. Lack of proper documents—Waiver may be available in certain cases for returning lawful permanent residents. *See* 8 U.S.C. §§ 1181(b) and (k). Nonimmigrants may otherwise be admitted based on an unforeseen emergency or a reciprocity agreement with their country of nationality.

---

    9. Juveniles convicted of violent crimes and tried as adults will be subject to exclusion under 8 U.S.C. § 1182(a)(9). *See* 18 U.S.C. § 1(1) and (16).

    10. *See Matter of Ramirez-Rivero, supra.*

    11. Waivers, as distinguished from pardons, recommendations against deportation, petty and juvenile offense exceptions, are discretionary.

    12. *See* discussion *infra* Chapter 2.

    13. An example of an exclusion ground inapplicable to nonimmigrants is the provisions dealing with polygamists. *See* 8 U.S.C. § 1182(a)(9), Sec. 212(a)(9). Diplomats are also protected from the ideological exclusion provisions. *Id.* The general nonimmigrant waiver provision is described at 8 U.S.C. § 1182(d)(3), Sec. 212.

    14. *See* 8 U.S.C. § 1182(a)(3)(C), Sec. 212(a)(3)(C).

    15. 8 U.S.C. § 1182(a)(3)(A), Sec. 212(a)(3)(A).

    16. 8 U.S.C. § 1182(a)(3)(E), Sec. 212(a)(3)(E). Another category of persons coming into this group are those involved in the trafficking of narcotics and terrorists. *See* Anti-Drug Abuse Act of 1988 Pub. L. No. 100-690, 102 Stat. 4181; 8 U.S.C. § 1182(a)(3)(B), Sec. 212(a)(3)(B).

2. Exchange visitors subject to the 2-year foreign residency requirement and who have not fulfilled the requirement—The applicant must establish that her return would cause extreme hardship upon her U.S. citizen or lawful permanent resident spouse or child. The applicant may also qualify if she can show that she would be subject to persecution on account of race, religion, or political opinion. A waiver may also be obtained involving diplomatic notes, where the Attorney General has received a "no objection" diplomatic note from the applicant's country. In all cases involving diplomatic notes, the USIA must favorably recommend granting such a waiver. *See* 8 U.S.C. § 1182(e).

3. Persons with a communicable disease of public health significance or who have a physical or mental disorder—In the case of a person with a communicable disease she must be the spouse, parent, unmarried son/daughter of a U.S. citizen or lawful permanent resident or person who has been issued an immigrant visa. Such a waiver is discretionary. In the case of a person excludable due to a physical or mental disorder, she may be admitted under terms and conditions set by the Attorney General after consultation with the Secretary of Health and Human Services. *See* 8 U.S.C. § 1182(g), Sec. 212(g).

4. Prostitutes or criminals, not including narcotics traffickers or murderers or torturers[17]—In order to obtain the waiver, the applicant must satisfy the Attorney General that the acts occurred 15 years prior to the application for the waiver, the admission of the person is not contrary to the national welfare or security and the person has been rehabilitated. *See* 8 U.S.C. § 1182(h).

5. Fraud or misrepresentation—In order to obtain the waiver, the applicant must establish that she is the spouse, parent, or child of a U.S. citizen or LPR.[18]

Long-term Permanent Residents

For obvious reasons, lawful long-term permanent residents have been accorded special protection. Persons who have been permanent residents for at least seven consecutive years may be eligible for waiver of most grounds of exclusion including the aggravated felons provision.[19] This waiver, commonly referred to as the "212(c) waiver," does not waive excludability for Nazis, persons coming to the U.S. to engage in activities which present a danger to national security, persons who are likely to engage in espionage or overthrow the government of the U.S., or persons excluded on politically based grounds. This waiver may be requested in deportation as well as in exclusion proceedings, notwithstanding the clear language of the statute providing the relief only to returning permanent residents.[20]

---

17. This ground of exclusion applies to persons who have been convicted of crimes as well as those who admit to the commission of acts which would be crimes.

18. *See Matter of Lopez-Monzon*, 17 I. & N. Dec. 280 (Comm. 1979); *Matter of Alonzo*, 17 I. & N. Dec. 292 (Comm. 1979); *Matter of DaSilva*, 17 I. & N. Dec. 292 (Comm. 1979); 8 U.S.C. § 1182(i).

19. 8 U.S.C. § 1182(c). *Tapia-Acuna v. INS*, 640 F.2d 223 (9th Cir. 1981). The provision relating to aggravated felons applies only to those aggravated felons who have been imprisoned for five years or less. 8 U.S.C. § 1182(c), Sec. 212(c).

20. *See Francis v. INS*, 532 F.2d 268 (2d Cir. 1976); *Matter of Silva*, 16 I. & N. Dec. (BIA 1976). For developing issues in 212(c) waivers, consult the following cases: *Wall v. INS*,

In the cases and notes which follow, we will explore some of the important issues involved in ameliorating or waiving grounds for exclusion and deportation.

References

Comment, *The Right of the Alien to be Informed of Deportation Consequences Before Entering a Plea of Guilty or Nolo Contendre*, 21 San Diego L. Rev. 195 (1983)

Exclusion or Deportation of Aliens for the Conviction of Crimes Involving Moral Turpitude: The Petty Offence Exception, 14 Cornell Int'l L.J. 135 (1981)

Gordon, *The Need to Modernize Our Immigration Laws*, 13 San Diego L. Rev. 1 (1975)

Griffith, *Exclusion and Deportation—Waivers Under Section 212(c) and Section 244(a)(1) of the Immigration and Nationality Act*, 32 De Paul L. Rev. 523 (1983)

D. Kesselbrenner & L. Rosenberg, Immigration Law and Crimes (1989)

Lawful Domicile under Section 212(c) of the Immigration and Nationality Act, 47 U. Chi. L. Rev. 771 (1982)

Musto & Ruffo, *Are the Borders Closing? Errico to Reid: A New Court and An Aging Frontier*, 31 U. Miami L. Rev. 1 (1976)

Note, *Section 212(c) of the Immigration and Nationality Act in the Federal Courts*, 24 Colum. J. Trannat'l L. 623 (1986)

A. When Is a Conviction a "Conviction"?

Matter of Ozkok
Interim Dec. 3044 (BIA 1988)

In a decision dated September 13, 1985, the immigration judge found the respondent deportable under section 241(a)(11) of the Immigration and Nationality Act, 8 U.S.C. § 1251(a)(11) (1982), as an alien convicted of a narcotics violation, and ordered him deported from the United States. On October 18, 1985, the immigration judge certified his decision for our review.[1]

* * *

The respondent is a 32-year-old native and citizen of Turkey who was admitted to the United States as a lawful permanent resident on October 9, 1967. . . . [H]e pleaded guilty on August 20, 1981, to unlawful possession with intent to distribute cocaine in the Circuit Court for Baltimore County, Maryland. On October 23, 1981, the court stayed judgment and placed the respondent on probation for 3 years pursuant

---

722 F.2d 1442 (9th Cir. 1984); *Tim Lok v. INS (Lok I)*, 548 F.2d 37 (2d Cir. 1977); *Tim Lok v. INS (Lok II)*, 681 F.2d 107 (2d Cir. 1982); *Marti-Xique v. INS*, 713 F.2d 1511 (11th Cir. 1983), *rev'd on rehearing*, 741 F.2d 350 (11th Cir. 1984).

1. Subsequent to the issuance of the immigration judge's decision and his certification thereof to the Board, the respondent requested that the immigration judge render a supplemental order in view of the fact that an application for a waiver of inadmissibility under section 212(c) of the Act, 8 U.S.C. §1182(c) (1982), which had been filed on November 17, 1983, was still pending. On October 31, 1985, the immigration judge issued a supplemental order vacating the order of deportation subject to the presentation of the respondent's waiver request. That order has also been certified to the Board. Inasmuch as the immigration judge no longer retained jurisdiction over the case following his certification of the order of deportation dated September 13, 1985, his supplemental order is of no effect. However, in view of our decision to remand the record for consideration of the respondent's waiver application, the issue is moot.

to the provisions of Article 27, section 641 of the Annotated Code of Maryland. The judge further ordered the respondent to perform 100 hours of volunteer community service and to pay a fine of $1,500 plus court costs.

On October 8, 1982, the Immigration and Naturalization Service issued an Order to Show Cause and Notice of Hearing (Form I-221) charging the respondent with deportability under section 241(a)(11) of the Act [8 U.S.C. §1251(a)(11)]. The record reflects that the respondent denied deportability and sought termination of the proceedings on the ground that the action of the criminal court did not constitute a conviction for immigration purposes under the standards set forth by the Board. The Service opposed termination, arguing that a conviction existed. . . .

. . . As early as 1942, we considered the effect of a state expunction statute on the status of a conviction for immigration purposes. Matter of F—, 1 I & N Dec. 343 (BIA 1942). In 1955 the United States Supreme Court addressed the conviction issue in a per curiam decision, stating only that the alien's conviction under a Massachusetts procedure, which permitted the sentence to be revoked and the case to be put "on file," had not "attained such finality as to support an order of deportation." Pino v. Landon, 349 U.S. 901 (1955). Recognizing the need for a federal standard for a final conviction . . . [w]e concluded there that a final conviction existed where, after a finding of guilt was made, a fine or sentence to imprisonment was imposed or either the execution or imposition of a sentence was suspended. We also found that if the court postponed further consideration of the case so that it was still pending for imposition of some sentence, an examination under Pino would be necessary to determine if the conviction had achieved sufficient finality to support a deportation order.

A few years later the Board enunciated the three-pronged test which has been the standard we have applied since then to determine whether a conviction exists for immigration purposes. Matter of L—R—, 8 I & N Dec. 269 (BIA 1959).[2] During this same period, the Attorney General also examined the effect of expunction procedures on convictions for narcotics offenses, concluding that Congress did not intend for a narcotics violator to escape deportation as a result of a technical erasure of his conviction by a state. Matter of A—F—, 8 I & N Dec. 429 (BIA, A.G. 1959). In so finding, the Attorney General noted the federal policy to treat narcotics offenses seriously and determined that it would be inappropriate for an alien's deportability for criminal activity to be dependent upon "the vagaries of state law." Id. at 446. He further pointed out that in 1959, when his decision was rendered, only a few states had expunction procedures, concluding that it was unfair to give preferential treatment to only a few aliens who were convicted in those jurisdictions.

It is apparent from a review of our decisions that most states now employ some method of ameliorating the consequences of a conviction. The procedures vary from

---

2. According to our definition as set forth in Matter of L—R—, supra, a conviction exists for immigration purposes where all of the following elements are present:

(1) there has been a judicial finding of guilt;

(2) the court takes action which removes the case from the category of those which are (actually, or in theory) pending for consideration by the court—the court orders the defendant fined, or incarcerated or the court suspends sentence, or the court suspends the imposition of sentence;

(3) the action of the court is considered a conviction by the state for at least some purpose.

state to state and include provisions for annulling or setting aside the conviction, permitting withdrawal of the plea, sealing the records after completion of a sentence or probation, and deferring adjudication of guilt with dismissal of proceedings following a probationary period. Many states have more than one ameliorative provision, some applying only to youthful or first offenders, and others being available to the convicted population at large.

In keeping with the opinions of the Supreme Court and the Attorney General, the Board has attempted over the years to reconcile its definition of a final conviction with the evolving criminal procedures created by the various states. Having reviewed our decisions in this regard, we must acknowledge that the standard which we have applied to the many variations in state procedure may permit anomalous and unfair results in determining which aliens are considered convicted for immigration purposes. For example, alien A, who has been found guilty of a narcotics violation by a jury or judge, but against whom no formal judgment has been entered by the judge, and who was placed on probation, fined, and even incarcerated as a special condition of probation, but who has no right to appeal and is subject to automatic entry of a judgment upon violation of probation, would not be considered 'convicted' under our three-pronged test because there has been no judicial adjudication of guilt. On the other hand, we would find a conviction in the case of alien B, who pleaded nolo contendere to the same charge and against whom a formal judgment was entered by the court, but whose sentence was deferred with no other penalty imposed, so long as the state also considered him convicted for some purpose.

*   *   *

... [W]e shall consider a person convicted if the court has adjudicated him guilty or has entered a formal judgment of guilt. Since such a judicial action is generally deemed a final conviction in both federal and state jurisdictions, it will be sufficient to constitute a conviction for immigration purposes without consideration of the other two factors of our former test.

... As a general rule, a conviction will be found for immigration purposes where all of the following elements are present:

(1) a judge or jury has found the alien guilty or he has entered a plea of guilty or nolo contendere or has admitted sufficient facts to warrant a finding of guilty;

(2) the judge has ordered some form of punishment, penalty, or restraint on the person's liberty to be imposed (including but not limited to incarceration, probation, a fine or restitution, or community-based sanctions such as a rehabilitation program, a work-release or study-release program, revocation or suspension of a driver's license, deprivation of nonessential activities or privileges, or community service); and

(3) a judgment or adjudication of guilt may be entered if the person violates the terms of his probation or fails to comply with the requirements of the court's order, without availability of further proceedings regarding the person's guilt or innocence of the original charge.

*   *   *

We note that a conviction for a crime involving moral turpitude may not support an order of deportation if it has been expunged. We shall continue in this regard to follow the rule which was set forth by the Attorney General in *Matter of G—*, supra, and subsequently reaffirmed in *Matter of Ibarra-Obando*, 12 I & N Dec. 576 (BIA 1966; A.G. 1967), and *Matter of Gutnick*, 13 I & N Dec. 672 (BIA 1971). Furthermore, it is the policy of the Service to defer institution of deportation proceedings until an alien who is eligible to have his conviction for a crime involving moral turpitude expunged has had a reasonable opportunity to apply for expunction. *Matter of Tinajero*, 17 I & N Dec. 424 (BIA 1980); Immigration and Naturalization Service Operations Instructions 242.1(a)(29). However, pursuant to the Attorney General's determination in *Matter of A—F—, supra*, a conviction for a narcotics or marihuana violation is final regardless of the possibility of expunction.

Applying our new standard to the respondent's case, we look first to the record of conviction, which indicates that the respondent pleaded guilty to unlawful possession of cocaine in sufficient quantity to reasonably indicate an intent to distribute the drug. It further reflects that the judge stayed entry of the judgment pursuant to Article 27, section 641 of the Annotated Code of Maryland and placed the respondent on probation for 3 years. In addition, he ordered the respondent to donate 100 hours of volunteer community service and to pay a $1,500 fine plus court costs. Since the respondent entered a plea of guilty and the judge imposed several forms of punishment, the first two parts of our test for a conviction have been met.

We must next examine the statutory authority under which the judge acted to determine whether the third element is satisfied. According to subsection (b) of section 641, the court may enter judgment and proceed with disposition of the person upon violation of probation as if the person had not been placed on probation. It is clear from the statute that, if a violation of probation occurs, judgment may be automatically entered without further review of the question of guilt. This third requirement of our test having been met, we conclude that the respondent's conviction is sufficiently final to support an order of deportation. Accordingly, we shall affirm the September 13, 1985, decision of the immigration judge to the extent that the respondent was found deportable on the basis of his conviction. However, inasmuch as the respondent had an application for section 212(c) relief pending at the time of the immigration judge's decision, we find that a remand of the record for consideration of his waiver request is appropriate.

ORDER: The September 13, 1985, decision of the immigration judge is affirmed in part . . . . The record is remanded to the immigration judge for consideration of the respondent's application for section 212(c) relief and the entry of a new decision.

Notes

1. A conviction does not exist for immigration purposes where a person's criminal charges were dismissed without prejudice following his successful completion of a pretrial intervention program. *Matter of Grullon*, Interim Dec. 3103 (BIA 1989).

2. *Matter of Ozkok* has been severely criticized for its inconsistency with the Board's prior holdings as well as its harsh effect. *See* B. Hing, *Handling Immigration Cases* 113-14 (1988 Supp.) (noting that the BIA's position may be rejected when challenged in court. *Cf. Rehman v. INS*, 544 F.2d 71 (2d Cir. 1976).

3. In *Matter of Derris*, Interim Dec. 3102 (BIA 1989), the Board extended its holding in *Ozkok* beyond drug cases. It stated that[21]

> Our holding in this regard applies not only to more serious drug offenses, but also to any crime not related to possession of drugs. In *Matter of Ozkok*, Interim Decision 3044 (BIA 1988), we pointed out that there exists in the various states a myriad of provisions for ameliorating the effects of a conviction. We further noted that, as a result, aliens who have clearly been guilty of criminal behavior and whom Congress intended to be considered "convicted" have escaped the immigration consequences normally attendant upon a conviction. We accordingly revised our standard for determining what constitutes a final conviction for immigration purposes in order to avoid any continued dependency on "the vagaries of state law."
>
> Congress restricted first offender treatment to those it believed might be rehabilitated from drug abuse. This congressional policy of leniency was not extended to persons guilty of any other crime. We therefore find that Congress intended that aliens who have been sentenced under state first offender statutes of general applicability for violations of law unrelated to drug possession should be considered "convicted" and should not be exempt from the immigration consequences of their crime.

4. **Petty Offenses.** The "petty offense" exception of 8 U.S.C. § 1182(a)(2)(ii)(II) has gone through a number of changes. In accordance with changes made in 1984 the critical question was more on the actual sentence imposed and not on the sentence which the person could have received. According to the statute as revised by the 1990 Act one must look to both the possible sentence as well as the sentence which was actually imposed. In analyzing the sentence which was actually imposed it is important to know whether the sentence received was a suspended sentence or whether the trial court has suspended imposition of the sentence. Where the person has received a suspended sentence for the requisite time period she could be excluded. *See* Matter of Patel, 15 I. & N. Dec. 212 (BIA 1975). Where the imposition of the sentence has been suspended, she could not yet be excluded. *See* Matter of Castro, Interim Dec. 3073 (BIA 1988).

5. **Refugees and Asylees.** As with youthful and petty offenders, special treatment has been accorded to refugees and asylees. All grounds of excludability may be waived for refugees and asylees for humanitarian purposes or to assure family unity except where the person was: convicted of drug-related crimes or engaged in activities which are a danger to national security, likely to engage in espionage or to overthrow the government of the U.S., or excludable on politically based grounds.[22]

---

21. *Matter of Derris*, Interim Dec. 3102, ft. 7 (BIA 1989).

22. *See* 8 U.S.C. § 1157(c)(3) which provides that:

The provisions of paragraphs (14), (15), (20), (21), (25), and (32) of section 1182(a) of this title shall not be applicable to any alien seeking admission to the United States under this subsection, and the Attorney General may waive any other provision of such section (other than paragraph (27), (29), or (33) and other than so much of paragraph (23) as relates to trafficking in narcotics) with respect to such an alien for humanitarian purposes, to assure family unity, or when it is otherwise in the public interest.

6. **Anti-Drug Abuse Act of 1988, Pub. L. No. 100–690 102 Stat. 4181 (1988).** In 1988 Congress enacted the Anti-Drug Abuse Act which was intended to expedite the deportation of persons convicted of crimes involving drugs as well as other "aggravated felonies." The statute which amended 8 U.S.C. § 1251(a)(2), Sec. 241(a)(2) creates a presumption of deportability for these convicted persons and requires the person to appeal their deportation order within thirty days.

In 1990, Congress once again redefined the aggravated felony provisions. Aggravated felonies now include illicit trafficking in controlled substances, money laundering and crimes of violence for which the sentence imposed is at least 5 years. The actual text of the statute appears below with new provisions italicized.[23]

> The term "aggravated felony" means murder, *any illicit trafficking in any controlled substance, (as defined in section 102 of the Controlled Substances Act) including* any drug trafficking crime as defined in section 924(c)(2) of title 18, United States Code, or any illicit trafficking in any firearms or destructive devices as defined in section 921 of such title, *any offense described in section 1956 of title 18, United States Code (relating to laundering of monetary instruments), or any crime of violence (as defined in section 16 of title 18, United States Code, not including a purely political offense) for which the term of imprisonment imposed (regardless of any suspension of such imprisonment) is at least 5 years,* or any attempt or conspiracy to commit any such act. *Such term applies to offenses described in the previous sentence whether in violation of Federal or State law, and also applies to offenses described in the previous sentence in violation of foreign law for which the imprisonment was completed within the previous 15 years.*

The new definition of aggravated felony goes into effect on 2 different dates, depending on the deportable act. If the person was convicted for illicit trafficking it is effective as of the enactment of section 7342 of the Anti-Drug Abuse Act of 1988.[24] If the conviction involved a sentence of imprisonment of at least 5 years it is effective as of November 29, 1990. The new provision includes federal and state crimes and foreign offenses where the term of imprisonment was completed after 1975.

7. **Pardons.** In order for a pardon to be effective in preventing deportation, it must be full and unconditional. *Matter of Nolan,* Interim Dec. 3043 (BIA 1988). The pardon, if granted by a foreign government, will not be effective. *Matter of M—,* 9 I. & N. Dec. 132 (1960). The statute restricts the pardon's protection from deportability under 8 U.S.C. § 1251(a)(4), Sec. 241(a)(4). Therefore there are many instances where a person may still be deportable notwithstanding the fact that a pardon has been granted. Some examples are prostitution, smuggling of "aliens," and narcotics law violations which are separate grounds of deportability.

---

23. 8 U.S.C. § 1101(a)(43), Sec. 101(a)(43).

24. Sec. 501(b), Immigration Act of 1990, Pub. L. No. 101-649, 104 Stat. 4978 (1990).

B. Section 212(a)(6)(A) and (B) Waiver [Persons Previously Deported][25]

Matter of Lee
17 I. & N. Dec. 275 (Comm'r. 1978)

The applicant is a 39-year-old native and citizen of China residing in Hong Kong. He first came to Service attention as a crewman on board the M/V Easter Star applying for permission to land temporarily in pursuit of his calling on June 1, 1965. His application was refused and he was ordered detained on board as a mala fide crewman. On a subsequent arrival on the same vessel on November 9, 1965, at Port Angeles, Washington, he was granted permission to land temporarily as a crewman. On November 18, 1965, the applicant, accompanied by two other crewmembers, left the vessel at Port Angeles, Washington, and traveled by bus to Seattle, Washington, despite a standing order issued by the Captain of the M/V Easter Star that shore leave for all crewmembers was restricted to the immediate area of Port Angeles. The applicant and his two companions were taken into custody at the bus station in Seattle by immigration officers. They were charged with attempting to desert the vessel on which they arrived, permission to land was revoked, and they were ordered deported pursuant to section 252(b) of the Immigration and Nationality Act of 1952, as amended, 8 U.S.C. 1282(b). The applicant was returned to his vessel at Port Angeles on November 20, 1965, and ordered detained on board in custody of the Master. His deportation from the United States was effected on November 24, 1965, upon the vessel's departure from the United States. The applicant was refused landing privileges as a crewman on five subsequent occasions of arrival on foreign-registered vessels in the United States. On the fifth occasion of arrival (July 3, 1969), he deserted his vessel, the M/V Deganya, at Newark, New Jersey. Efforts by the Service to locate the applicant were unsuccessful. On July 21, 1975, a sixth-preference petition was submitted by the China Garden Restaurant, Incorporated, Raynham, Massachusetts, on the applicant's behalf. This petition was approved on May 21, 1976. At the request of this Service, the applicant surrendered himself to this Service at Boston, Massachusetts, and was granted the privilege of departing voluntarily from the United States. The record contains verification of departure on August 21, 1976, from Anchorage, Alaska, to Tokyo, Japan.

The applicant made application for an immigrant visa at the United States Consulate in Hong Kong and was informed on October 22, 1976, that he needed permission to reapply for admission into the United States after deportation. The instant application was then filed on October 29, 1976, at Boston and subsequently transferred to the Seattle office, which had jurisdiction in the matter pursuant to 8 C.F.R. 212.2(c).

The District Director denied the application as a matter of discretion and cited *Matter of Tin*, 14 I & N Dec. 371 (R.C. 1973), and *Matter of Chim*, 14 I & N Dec. 357 (R.C. 1973), as justification for his action. The Regional Commissioner affirmed the District Director's decision and dismissed the appeal.

---

25. Prior to the passage of the Immigration Act of 1990, these provisions were cited as 8 U.S.C. § 1182(a)(16) and (17).

Section 212(a)(17) of the Immigration and Nationality Act of 1952, as amended, 8 U.S.C. 1182(a)(17), has its roots in section 3 of the Act of 1917. Section 3 made prostitutes and other immoral classes who had been previously debarred or deported from the United States excludable unless they had received permission from the Secretary of Labor to reapply for admission. The Act of March 2, 1929, extended this provision, making it a felony to reenter the United States after having been deported unless the Secretary had granted permission to reapply for admission.

Section 212(a)(17) of the Immigration and Nationality Act of 1952, as amended, 8 U.S.C. 1182(a)(17), has its roots in section 3 of the Act of 1917. Section 3 made prostitutes and other immoral classes who had been previously debarred or deported from the United States excludable unless they had received permission from the Secretary of Labor to reapply for admission. The Act of March 2, 1929, extended this provision, making it a felony to reenter the United States after having been deported unless the Secretary had granted permission to reapply for admission after deportation.

The Immigration and Nationality Act of 1952, as amended, incorporated the same language but made a distinction between those previously excluded (section 212(a)(16) and those who had been deported (section 212(a)(17) of the Act). Those previously excluded require permission of the Attorney General to reapply for admission if that application was to be made within 1 year of the date of exclusion and deportation. Those previously deported require the permission of the Attorney General to reapply for admission at any time after deportation.

The intent of Congress in enacting section 212(a)(16) and (17) can best be found in the conclusions and recommendations of the Senate Committee on the Judiciary in their report (S. Rep. No. 1515, 81st Cong. 2nd Sess. (1950)) concerning the effectiveness and necessity of retaining the various laws affecting immigration. A study was conducted pursuant to S. Res. 137, 80th Cong., 1st Sess., for the purpose of bringing all laws pertaining to immigration and nationality under one composite heading. (The Immigration and Nationality Act of 1952 was the fruit of these labors.) The Committee report issuing from this study addressed the subject of previously deported or excluded aliens and made the following conclusions and recommendations.

Speaking of section 3 of the 1917 Act, the Committee stated:

The subcommittee finds that the law as it is now written is adequate to prevent the abuse of the exclusion and deportation laws by aliens who attempt to reapply for admission to the United States soon after their exclusion or deportation, as well as to allow reconsideration when the alien is able to overcome the handicaps which brought about the original exclusion and deportation. Page 365. (Underscoring supplied.)

The second clause of these conclusions and recommendations directly concerns the instant application. The import of these words is to give a previously deported alien a second chance and connotes a remedial relief rather than a punitive provision of statute. In this regard, I find the several decisions affecting permission to reapply after deportation lacking this attitude. *Matter of H—R—*, 5 I & N Dec. 769 (C.O. 1954), and *Matter of Chim, supra*, convey a punitive attitude and attach conditions beyond anything I believe Congress intended in granting the Attorney General authority to allow previously deported or excluded aliens to reapply for entry into the

United States. The discussion of the issues raised in the instant case will be made with the foregoing in mind.

1. Moral character of the applicant:

In a recent case before me on certification, the Regional Commissioner also held that a record of immigration violations denoted poor moral character and cited this finding as one of the adverse factors considered. In that case, I ruled that contention was without merit, and reaffirmed *Matter of T—*, 1 I & N Dec. 158 (BIA 1941), in that a record of immigration violations standing alone will not conclusively support a finding of a lack of good moral character. In the instant case, I will likewise dismiss the contention that the applicant is a person lacking good moral character.

2. Recency of the deportation:

The recency of the deportation is mentioned as a factor to be considered in *Matter of Tin, supra*. However, there is but a passing reference to this factor. ("As a further example, an alien who was deported many years ago solely for a minor immigration violation and who has a bona fide reason for wanting to immigrate to the United States, may be granted permission to reapply....")

I believe that the recency of the deportation can only be considered when there is a finding of poor moral character based on moral turpitude in the conduct and attitude of a person which evinces a callous conscience. In such circumstances, there must be a measurable reformation of character over a period of time in order to properly assess an applicant's ability to integrate into our society. In all other instances when the cause of deportation has been removed and the person now appears eligible for issuance of a visa, the time factor should not be considered.

3. Need for applicant's services in the United States:

The Regional Commissioner considered the need for the services of the applicant in the United States and dismissed this as a favorable factor. However, I find there is merit in counsel's contention that where the applicant will provide services to the public in a job category where sufficient workers in the United States are not available, this is a favorable factor in behalf of the applicant.

4. Applicant's contention that he did not know he was deported:

This contention will be dismissed without discussion. The record clearly shows he was deported pursuant to section 252(b) of the Act and does need permission of the Attorney General to apply for admission to the United States.

5. Length of time applicant had been in the United States:

I can only relate a positive factor of residence in the United States where that residence is pursuant to a legal admission or adjustment of status as a permanent resident.

If we were to reward a person for remaining in the United States in violation of law, the structure of all laws pertaining to immigration would be seriously threatened. Therefore, I will dismiss counsel's contention that this should be considered a favorable factor.

In applying the principles set forth in this discussion and weighing all factors present, I find that the applicant should be granted permission to reapply for admission into the United States after deportation and will set aside the order of the District Director denying the application and the Regional Commissioner's dismissal of the appeal. *Matter of Chim, supra*, and *Matter of Tin, supra*, are modified insofar as the weight given to adverse factors is inconsistent with the weight accorded the adverse factors in this decision.

Note

The 1990 Act extended the exclusion ground for previously deported aggravated felons to 20 years.

C. Section 212(i) Waivers

Matter of Lopez-Monzon
17 I. & N. Dec. 280 (Comm'r. 1979)

The applicant is an unmarried female citizen of Guatemala, born June 11, 1939, in Ratelhuleu, Guatemala. She is a resident of Guatemala, as are her three older children who are citizens of Guatemala and one illegitimate child who is a citizen of the United States by birth in Brooklyn, New York, on August 16, 1969. The three Guatemalan citizen children reside apart from the applicant and the United States citizen child resides with his natural father, also a citizen and resident of Guatemala, who is responsible for the child's care. The applicant's former husband, who is the father of the three older children, died February 14, 1973. The applicant was found excludable under section 212(a)(19)[26], by a United States Consular Officer in Guatemala City, Guatemala, because she obtained a nonimmigrant visa by fraud on February 26, 1968, and thereafter entered the United States where she remained and secured unauthorized employment. Although the record is not clear as to the number of entries the applicant has made into the United States nor the duration of her stays in this country, it appears that he last departure was in February 1978, when she returned to Guatemala.

The Acting District Director in his decision of July 14, 1978, has pointed out that the United States citizen child of the applicant lives with his father in Guatemala and would not accompany the applicant to the United States. He concludes therefrom that no economic or emotional hardship would be caused to the child by the applicant remaining outside the United States. In view of this, and in the absence of any persuasive humanitarian consideration, favorable exercise of discretion was not warranted in this case.

In the applicant's appeal, she has stated that she obtained the nonimmigrant visa in question legally; her behavior has been good; she has always thought of bringing her child to the United States; and her former employers in the United States want her to return to her former employment with them. Attached to the appeal are letters from her former employers stating their need for her services and from a minister in the United States which attests to the applicant's high moral standards.

Eligibility to apply under section 212(i) of the Immigration and Nationality Act, 8 U.S.C. 1182(i), for a waiver of the grounds of excludability specified in section

---

26. Section 212(a)(19) was recodified as 8 U.S.C. § 1182(a)(6)(C), Sec. 212(a)(6)(C).

212(a)(19) of the Immigration and Nationality Act, 8 U.S.C. 1182(a)(19), is limited to aliens who are spouses, parents, or children of United States citizens or lawful permanent residents of the United States. This provision of law was not contained in the original Act, but was added by the Act of September 26, 1961 (75 Stat. 655). The intent of Congress in adding this provision of law, which is evident from its language, was to provide for the unification of families, thereby avoiding the hardship of separation.

In the instant case this is not the situation. The applicant's child, upon whom eligibility to apply for the waiver is based, does not live in the United States nor is the evidence persuasive that the applicant intends to bring him with her or live with him here in the future. The past record indicates otherwise and her statement upon appeal merely shows that she has been thinking of doing so. There is no evidence that she has legal custody or would be able to legally obtain custody of the child from his natural father even if she wished to do so.

In view of the factors in this case, it is evident that the applicant wants to return to employment which would benefit her economically, as well as fill a need for her prospective employers. While this is an understandable desire, it would not unite or reunite a family and the intent of the law would not be satisfied. Upon careful consideration, it is concluded that the favorable exercise of the Attorney General's discretion is not warranted in this case, and the Acting District Director's decision will be affirmed and the appeal dismissed.

D. The Controversy over Section 212(c) [Seven-year Unrelinquished Domicile]

The following cases present the controversy over a provision of the immigration laws which provide a broad form of relief for deportable persons who have been long-term permanent residents of the United States. Consider whether the Board's interpretation of 8 U.S.C. § 1182(c), Sec. 212(c) is reasonable in light of the statute's language.

8 U.S.C. § 1182(c), Sec. 212(c)

Aliens lawfully admitted for permanent residence who temporarily proceeded abroad voluntarily and not under an order of deportation, and who are returning to a lawful unrelinquished domicile of seven consecutive years, may be admitted in the discretion of the Attorney General without regard to the provisions of paragraphs (1) to (25), (30), and (31) of subsection (a) of this section. Nothing contained in this subsection shall limit the authority of the Attorney General to exercise the discretion vested in him under section 1181(b) of this title. The first sentence of this subsection shall not apply to an alien who has been convicted of aggravated felony and has served a term of imprisonment of at least 5 years.

Matter of Bowe

17 I. & N. Dec. 488 (BIA 1980)

Previously, on February 14, 1978, this Board denied the respondent's 212(c) application as a matter of discretion. The United States Court of Appeals for the Ninth Circuit, on April 23, 1979, affirmed the Board on the ground that 212(c) relief is unavailable to an alien who is deportable for a drug offense under section 241(a)(11) of the Act, 8 U.S.C. 1251(a)(11). *Bowe v. INS*, 597 F.2d 1158 (9th Cir. 1979). The respondent argues that he can obtain the relief now sought, despite the ruling of the Ninth Circuit, because the 212(c) application previously before the Board and the Court was not made in conjunction with an adjustment application. The Service, in its memorandum supporting the motion, urges the Board to disregard the Ninth Circuit precedent decisions cited in Bowe and to adhere to the Board's decision in *Matter of Silva*, 16 I & N Dec. 26 (BIA 1976). We stated there, following *Francis v. INS*, 532 F.2d 268 (2d Cir. 1976), that an alien convicted of a crime which renders him excludable is eligible to apply in deportation proceedings for the benefits of section 212(c) if he has the requisite lawful unrelinquished domicile, even if he is not an applicant for readmission from outside the United States, and has not been such an applicant since the act which rendered him excludable.

We do not accept the Service's suggestion that *Matter of Mangabat*, 14 I & N Dec. 75 (BIA 1972), *aff'd*, 477 F.2d 108 (9th Cir. 1973), *cert. denied*, 414 U.S. 841 (1973), allows us to reject Ninth Circuit precedents regarding section 212(c) in the case now before us. In *Matter of Mangabat*, the Board declined to apply a Ninth Circuit precedent in a case arising in that circuit. It was emphasized, however, that the position taken by the Ninth Circuit on the issue involved there (the availability of section 241(f) relief) had been expressly disapproved by the Attorney General, and the Solicitor General had challenged the Court's position in a petition for certiorari filed in the Supreme Court. In the present case, no representation has been made that the Attorney General agrees with the Service's position that the Ninth Circuit has erred in its interpretation of section 212(c), and that he is willing to support a petition for certiorari to the Supreme Court in an appropriate case. The fact that the respondent's 212(c) application is now made in conjunction with a 245 application does not change the fact that in Bowe, the Court flatly stated that 212(c) relief is unavailable to aliens facing deportation under section 241(a)(11) for drug offenses. Furthermore, we disagree that we are free to decline to follow the Ninth Circuit's decision in Bowe, supra, in Bowe's own case. We believe that the Court's decision in Bowe is res judicata and binding on this Board.

Although the Court cites in *Bowe*, *id.*, a series of Ninth Circuit decisions as if they consistently provided the same legal interpretation, analysis reveals variations which leave us confused. This line of cases began with *Arias-Uribe v. INS*, 466 F.2d 1198 (9th Cir. 1972). *Arias-Uribe* involved an alien who was deportable under section 241(a)(11) section 212(c). The Court discussed certain Board decisions regarding the availability of 212(c) relief in deportation proceedings, but distinguished them from the case before it because the aliens in the Board cases had been excludable at the time they last entered the United States. Of these cases, the Court wrote,

> The Board held that discretionary relief was available and might be granted to effect a retroactive waiver of the ground of excludability existing at the time of

the subject's entry and that if such relief was granted, then the basis for his deportation was entirely eliminated. Petitioner, however, is in a different situation. His deportation is sought, not because he was excludable at the time he last entered the United States, but because he was convicted of a narcotics offense after entering the United States. The Attorney General is not given discretion by the immigration laws to waive or suspend deportation for narcotics of fenders, nor is he authorized, once proceedings under §241(a) are begun, to allow such persons to leave the country voluntarily in lieu of deportation. See 8 U.S.C. §1254(a), (e). Id. at 1199. (Emphasis added.)

The actual holding in this case is somewhat unclear, especially given the last sentence in the quoted passage, but we read the decision to mean that the respondent could not obtain a 212(c) waiver because he had not departed from the United States since the commission of the act which rendered him excludable. A nunc pro tunc waiver of excludability could thus not be used, as it had been in the Board cases cited. The headnote in Arias-Uribe, id., appear to say that ineligibility for 212(c) relief arises from the drug related nature of the ground of deportability, but that is not our understanding of what the decision itself says. We believe the case is more properly read to stand for the proposition that 212(c) relief was unavailable because the respondent had not departed from the United States since the time of his conviction.

Our interpretation of Arias-Uribe, id., is supported by the next Ninth Circuit case to address section 212(c), *Dunn v. INS*, 499 F.2d 856 (9th Cir. 1974), *cert. denied*, 419 U.S. 1106 (1975). This case, like *Arias-Uribe*, involved an alien who was deportable under section 241(a)(11) of the Act. *Dunn* did not discuss 212(c) at any length; rather, it quickly disposed of the respondent's 212(c) claim....

*   *   *

The next two cases of interest are *Nicholas v. INS*, 590 F.2d 802 (9th Cir. 1979), and *Bowe, supra*. In *Nicholas*, the Court addressed several issues, but with respect to 212(c) it had only this to say: "Relief under issues, but with respect to 212(c) had been held to be unavailable to an alien facing deportation for conviction of a drug-related crime, pursuant to 8 U.S.C. 1251(a)(11)." The authority it cites for this rule..., cited this exact language in finding this respondent ineligible for 212(c) relief. It simply added *Nicholas, supra* to its list of authority. No further discussion of the issue was offered.

Another Ninth Circuit case to mention section 212(c), *Castillo Felix v. INS*, 601 F.2d 459 (9th Cir. 1979), did not involve alien drug offender, and did not directly address the problems at issue here. In an interesting footnote, however, the Court mentioned "an apparent conflict between this circuit and the Second Circuit," noting that the Second Circuit in *Francis v. INS, supra*, held that the denial of section 212(c) relief to aliens who had not fortuitously departed from the United States after committing an excludable offense, while granting it to those who had, was a violation of equal protection. The Second Circuit therefore held 212(c) to be available whether or not the "actual departure" requirement of that section had been met. The Ninth Circuit, after describing Francis, and adding that the INS [sic] had "acquiesced" in the *Francis* holding (in *Matter of Silva, supra*) (in fact it was this Board, not the Service, which determined to apply *Francis, supra*, nationwide), stated, "This circuit, however, continues to recognize the actual departure requirement." *Castillo-Felix* at 462, n.6. It cited for this comment its prior decisions in *Arias-Uribe, supra*, and

Dunn, supra. Castillo-Felix thus lends support to our analysis of the line of Ninth Circuit 212(c) cases, and to our belief that *Nicholas* and *Bowe, supra,* misinterpreted *Arias-Uribe* and *Dunn, supra,* inasmuch as the latter two cases appear to us to turn on the lack of a departure, not on the drug-related nature of the offense.

*   *   *

None of the Ninth Circuit cases discussed above has explained why section 212(c) should be unavailable to drug offenders, particularly in deportation proceedings. That section in fact includes drug offenders within its stated terms. To be sure, it specifies that the waiver is available to aliens who are excludable as drug offenders under section 212(a)(23), and does not mention aliens who are deportable as persons convicted of drug related crimes under section 241(a)(11). So far the Court has not explained how the apparently anomalous results the line of cases discussed above may produce would be reconcilable with the legislative intent that excludability of some narcotic offenders may be waived.

We are not persuaded by the respondent's argument that reopening is warranted because his case is now presented in a wholly different posture in that his 212(c) application is now made in conjunction with a section 245 application. He claims that the actual departure requirement of *Arias-Uribe, Dunn,* and *Castillo-Felix, supra,* is met because he, as an applicant for adjustment, is now in the position of one seeking to make a new entry. . . .

*   *   *

Concurring Opinion: Mary P. Maguire, Board Member

While I concur in the result, I would deny the motion to reopen and hold that an applicant for adjustment of status under section 245 of the Act is not eligible for section 212(c) relief.

This case illustrates the problems which result from strained interpretations of the Immigration and Nationality Act. The language of section 212(c) of the Immigration and Nationality Act is clear; an alien is eligible for a waiver of certain grounds of inadmissibility, including a narcotics conviction, if he is a lawful permanent resident who temporarily and voluntarily departed the United States and who is returning to a lawful unrelinquished domicile in the United States for seven consecutive years prior to reentry.

This Board began diluting such requirements in a line of cases which prompted the Second Circuit to hold in *Francis v. INS,* 532 F.2d 268 (2d Cir. 1976), that a lawful permanent resident who became deportable after entry was eligible for section 212(c) relief even though he had never made a temporary departure and reentry. The Francis decision was adopted by this Board and applied on a nationwide basis in *Matter of Silva,* 16 I & N Dec. 26 (BIA 1976).

In my opinion, the majority erroneously reads the Ninth Circuit decisions as holding that section 212(c) relief is unavailable to drug offenders. Such a reading does not go far enough. I read Ninth Circuit decisions to hold that section 212(c) relief is available to a drug offender only if he voluntarily departs the United States and is inadmissible under 212(a)(23) as a convicted drug offender upon his return. Since this respondent never departed the United States after his drug conviction, he is not entitled to section 212(c) relief.

*   *   *

Such a conclusion is based on an erroneous premise which indicates a lack of understanding of the Ninth Circuit position with respect to the actual departure requirement and a failure to recognize the nature of adjustment of status under section 245 of the Act. The majority, therefore, does not address fully the impact of Smith on this case. If one were to apply the holding in *Smith* to this respondent, he would be prima facie eligible to apply for section 245 adjustment of status since he is the beneficiary of an approved visa petition, has an immigrant visa immediately available to him, was inspected on his last admission, and has submitted a section 212(c) application. But *Smith* creates a fictional remedy for the non-departing alien who has become deportable after entry. It oversimplifies completely, in my opinion, the nature of adjustment of status. In *Smith*, the Board reasoned that an applicant for adjustment of status under section 245 stands in the same position as an applicant who is seeking entry into the United States with an immigrant visa for permanent residence. With that premise I have no quarrel. The Board then went on to state that an applicant for section 245 adjustment of status is subject to all of the exclusion provisions of section 212(a). Again, I have no quarrel with that statement.

However, I cannot make the leap from those two premises to the Board's conclusion in *Smith* that since the section 245 applicant is subject to all of the 212(a) exclusion provisions there is no valid reason to deny him the benefits of section 212(c) on the "technical ground" that he is not returning to the United States after a voluntary departure. The logical extension of such reasoning is to find all applicants for admission entitled to apply for the benefits of section 212(c) relief. Section 245 applicants are presumably not lawful permanent residents—they would have no need to apply for adjustment of status if they were permanent residents. Since they are not permanent residents, they cannot be found to be assimilated to the status of a returning resident alien who seeks relief under section 212(c) for the purpose of returning to his lawful unrelinquished 7-years' continuous domicile in the United States. I would, therefore, overrule *Matter of Smith, supra*, and deny the motion to reopen on the ground that an applicant for adjustment of status under section 245 is not eligible for the benefits of section 212(c).

Dissenting Opinion: Irving A. Appleman, Board Member

I cannot accept the majority conclusions (a) that the Ninth Circuit precedents bar any possibility of a section 212(c) waiver in conjunction with an adjustment of status under section 245 since the respondent is a narcotic offender and (b) that the prior holding in *Bowe v. INS*, 597 F.2d 1158 (9th Cir. 1979), has created an estoppel by judgment to granting the present motion.

In *Matter of Arias-Uribe*, 13 I & N Dec. 696 (BIA 1971), this Board held that an alien convicted of a narcotics offense after entry and therefore deportable under section 241(a)(11) was statutorily ineligible for a section 212(c) waiver, inasmuch as he was not an alien returning to the United States to resume a lawful domicile of 7 years after a temporary and voluntary absence subsequent to his conviction. We distinguished such a case from other cases in which the relief had been granted (1) *nunc pro tunc* to cure a ground of deportability originating in inadmissibility at the time of a previous entry, when the alien was eligible for the relief, *Matter of G—A—*, 7 I & N Dec. 274 (BIA 1956), or, (2) to an applicant for adjustment of status under section 245(a), 8 U.S.C. 1255(a), who, in order to meet the requirement of section 245(a)(2) that he is "eligible to receive an immigrant visa and is admissible . . . ," had coupled his adjustment application with a request for a waiver under section

212(c), of a ground of inadmissibility which would otherwise have barred the adjustment. *Matter of Smith*, 11 I & N Dec. 325 (BIA 1965).

In both (1) and (2), notwithstanding the application was made during a deportation proceeding relief under section 212(c) derived authority from the words "may be admitted" in that section, and the waivers were of specific grounds of excludability specified in that section. See *Matter of Silva*, 16 I & N Dec. 26, 30 (BIA 1976). It is the second type of request which is before us today, namely, for a waiver under section 212(c) in conjunction with an application for adjustment of status.

In noting our authority to rule on such application, in *Matter of Smith, supra*, we assimilated an applicant for section 245 adjustment of status (the Immigration and Nationality Act replacement for the cumbersome and expensive "preexamination" procedure which had evolved under prior legislation) to an applicant seeking to enter the United States with an immigration visa.

The Ninth Circuit has repeatedly held that an alien seeking adjustment under section 245 is assimilated to an alien seeking to enter the United States for permanent residence. Thus, in *Amarante v. Rosenberg*, 326 F.2d 58 (9th Cir. 1964), the Court held that the Attorney General's action in adjusting an alien's status to that of a permanent resident "is equivalent to the issuance of a visa by a United States Consul outside the United States." Id. at 61. Final authority "rests with the consular office (or Attorney under section 245) who grants the alien's application and actually accords the nonquota status." Id. at 62 (emphasis supplied). *See also Campos v. INS*, 402 F.2d 758 (9th Cir. 1968); *Hamid v. INS*, 538 F.2d 1389, 1390 (9th Cir. 1976). Cf. *Khadjenouri v. INS*, 460 F.2d 461 (9th Cir. 1972).

It is against this background that *Arias-Uribe v. INS*, 466 F.2d 1198 (9th Cir. 1972), and succeeding cases of the Ninth Circuit, should be read. Rather than reflecting inconsistency, the Ninth Circuit decisions have uniformly required compliance with the express terms of section 212(c). The relief cannot be considered unless it involves a waiver of a specified ground of excludability which would prevent an otherwise lawful permanent resident from resuming a lawful domicile here. In *Arias-Uribe v. INS*, the Court pointed out that the alien's deportation was not sought because he was excludable at the time he last entered the United States, but because he was convicted of a narcotics offense after entering the United States, and hence he did not come within the language of 212(c).

Significantly, in a footnote, the Court said as to the Board's holding in *Matter of Smith, supra*, respecting the availability of section 212(c) in conjunction with an adjustment of status, "We need not decide whether this interpretation is correct since adjustment of status is unavailable to natives of any country in the Western Hemisphere." *Arias-Uribe v. INS*, at 1199, n.3.

*   *   *

I am equally unable to go along with the majority's additional basis for denial, that relief is barred merely because Bowe is deportable under section 241(a)(11). In *Arias-Uribe v. INS, supra*, the Court accepted the reasoning of the Board, that the relief was unavailable because deportability arose from circumstances occurring after the alien's entry. Whereas section 212(c), by its literal language, pertains only to inadmissibility at the time an entry either occurred, or will occur. The Court's further comments in *Arias-Uribe* respecting deportability arising from a narcotics offense are dicta, which only emphasize the distinction between an exclusion ground and a deportation ground, in the exercise of this particular relief. The reference to drug offenders in succeeding decisions which rely on *Arias-Uribe* would seem to be largely a fortuitous circumstance, stemming from the nature of the deportation charge in each of those cases. *See Dunn v. INS*, 499 F.2d 856 (9th Cir. 1974), *cert. denied*, 419 U.S. 1106 (1975); *Nicholas v. INS*, 590 F.2d 802 (9th Cir. 1979); *Bowe v. INS, supra*. There is no legal basis for distinguishing drug offenders from other deportable aliens in these circumstances.

That the result would have been the same for any deportation charge not tied to an entry gains some support from *Castillo-Felix v. INS*, a recent Ninth Circuit decision where the deportation charge was not drug related, but in which the Court rejected the relief. In *Castillo-Felix* also, the Court, in noting its apparent conflict with the Second Circuit decision in *Francis v. INS*, stated, "This circuit, however, continues to recognize the actual departure requirement," citing *Arias-Uribe*, supra—language which one may interpret as meaning the relief is available only in connection with reentry after a departure (real or assimilated), and then only for waiver of a ground of excludability specified in section 212(c). I therefore differ with so much of the majority decision as would find the respondent automatically barred from the relief merely because he is a drug offender. There is a substantial difference between a waiver of a ground of deportation under section 241(a)(110), which was rejected in Bowe v. INS, supra, and a waiver of an exclusion ground under section 212(a)(23), which he now seeks, and which is included in the specified grounds of section 212(c).

Clearly the Ninth Circuit is unwilling to accept section 212(c) as an alternate deportation relief standing by itself. Its rejection of Francis, supra, makes this clear once again. It has consistently held to this position. *Mondragon v. Ilchert, supra*, cited by the majority, is but another example of this. *Mondragon* was charged under section 241(a)(2) of the Act, 8 U.S.C. 1251(a)(2), with having entered without inspection. There is no provision in section 212(c), as a matter of law, for a waiver of such a charge. It is not a specified ground of exclusion, nor is there even an exclusion ground comparable to the deportation ground. *Matter of Granados*, 16 I & N Dec. 726 (BIA 1979). However, it does not follow that section 212(c) relief, when it concerns a waiver of a ground of excludability that is within the express language of the section, and is coupled with the safeguards written into the adjustment procedure by the statute and implementing regulations, would not be acceptable to that Court. In any event, I am unwilling to reach that conclusion in the present state of the law and am unwilling to accept what I regard as an over simplistic analysis of *Bowe v. INS, supra*, and related cases.

Before the Board, December 17, 1980

The Immigration and Naturalization Service has filed a motion for reconsideration of our decision, dated August 28, 1980, in the above-named case. In our prior decision, we denied the respondent's unopposed motion to reopen his deportation proceedings to enable him to apply for a waiver under section 212(c) of the Immigration and Nationality Act, 8 U.S.C. 1182(c), in conjunction with an adjustment of status application under section 245 of the Act, 8 U.S.C. 1255. *Matter of Bowe*, Interim Decision 2819 (BIA 1980). The motion to reconsider will be denied.

*   *   *

In its present motion to reconsider, the Service argues that this Board is not bound by Ninth Circuit precedents in the section 212(c) area. It now bolsters this argument by pointing out that, subsequent to our decision in *Matter of Bowe, supra*, the Solicitor General on October 2, 1980, filed a brief with the Supreme Court in support of its petition for a writ of certiorari in the case of *Tapia-Acuna v. INS*, No. 80-74, U.S.L.W. 3165. The petition for writ of certiorari was filed with the Supreme Court on July 17, 1980, but neither the petition, nor the reason for it, was made known to this Board prior to our decision in *Matter of Bowe, supra*. The brief urged the Court to remand the case to the Ninth Circuit for reconsideration of that Court's prior decision denying the alien 212(c) relief. The Government requested that the Ninth Circuit be given the opportunity to reconsider its decision in light of the present government position that 212(c) should be available to drug-offenders in deportation proceedings even in the Ninth Circuit, and that the Ninth Circuit decisions holding the relief to be unavailable to such aliens are incorrect.

Although the Solicitor General in his brief before the Supreme Court specifically stated that it was the Government's position that *Bowe v. INS, supra* and *Nicholas, supra*, "are erroneous and should be overruled," and although there exists a clear conflict among the circuits regarding the availability of 212(c) relief, thus paving the way for the Supreme Court to make a ruling on the merits of the issue. Rather, he specifically sought a remand of the case to enable the Ninth Circuit to reconsider in view of the present government position. As the Ninth Circuit has for 4 years been aware of the *Francis* decision, *supra*, and of this Board's decision to apply Francis everywhere except in the Ninth Circuit, but has in dictum expressed its disapproval of those decision, it is interesting that the Solicitor General sought the opportunity to ask the Court of Appeals to change its prior decisions, instead of seeking to litigate the basic question before the Supreme Court, and obtain a definitive decision there. In any event, the Supreme Court on November 3, 1980, granted the writ of certiorari, and granted the Government's request that the case be remanded to the Ninth Circuit "for further consideration in light of the position presently asserted by the Solicitor General in his brief filed October 3, 1980." *Tapia-Acuna v. INS*, 101 S. Ct. 344 (1980).

* * *

[The Board stated that it would not make any decision before the Ninth Circuit made its own decision in *Tapia-Acuna, supra*.]

BEFORE THE BOARD
April 23, 1981

By: Milhollan, Chairman; Maniatis, Appleman, and Maguire, Board Members

In our decision of August 28, 1980, we denied the respondent's unopposed motion to reopen his deportation proceedings to enable him to apply for a waiver under section 212(c) of the Immigration and Nationality Act, 8 U.S.C. 1182(c), in conjunction with an adjustment of status application under section 245 of the Act, 8 U.S.C. 1255. Subsequently, the Immigration and Naturalization Service filed a motion for reconsideration of that decision. In our decision dated December 17, 1980, we concluded that the United States Supreme Court's decision in *Tapia-Acuna v. INS*, 101 S. Ct. 344 (1980), made it inappropriate for us to grant the Service's motion. Accordingly, the motion to reconsider was denied.

On February 20, 1981, in accordance with the request of the Acting Commissioner of the Service, our decision of December 17, 1980 was certified to the Attorney General for review pursuant to 8 C.F.R. 3.1(h)(1)(iii). The request for certification was withdrawn by the Service in a memorandum dated March 25, 1981, and the record of proceedings was returned to us for appropriate action.

In light of the above chronology of events and the decision of the United States Court of Appeals for the Ninth Circuit in *Tapia-Acuna v. INS*, 640 F.2d 223 (9th Cir. 1981), we shall reopen these proceedings on our own motion and remand the record to enable the respondent to fully present his application for relief under section 212(c) of the Act, predicated upon the present facts, before an immigration judge.

Notes

1. A condition precedent to eligibility for 212(c) relief is that the applicant must have been a lawful permanent resident for the requisite time period. Therefore, an applicant who has been in the U.S. as a nonimmigrant cannot apply for the waiver even though she has been in the country for seven years. *Matter of Lok*, 15 I. & N. Dec. 720 (BIA 1981).

2. The outcome in *Bowe* was the nationwide application by the INS of *Francis* and *Tapia-Acuna*. Given the Supreme Court's deference in immigration matters to the dictates of the statutory language, can an argument be made that *Francis* and *Tapia-Acuna* should be overturned? On the other hand, can one interpret the Supreme Court's remand of *Tapia-Acuna* to consider the Solicitor General's position a tacit acceptance of the rule in *Francis*? What would happen if the INS reversed its position outside of the Second and Ninth Circuits? How would the INS justify its changed position? How would courts deal with this (hypothetically) new interpretation of 212(c)?

In January 1990, the BIA decided *Matter of Hernandez*, Interim Dec. (BIA 1990). The INS Commissioner requested that the Board refer the case to the Attorney General for review to consider the question of whether 212(c) relief should be available only to those seeking readmission. *See 67 Interpreter Releases* 244 (1990).

Matter of Duarte
18 I. & N. Dec. 329 (BIA 1982)

In a decision dated April 15, 1981, an immigration judge found the applicant excludable under section 212(a)(23) of the Immigration and Nationality Act, 8 U.S.C. 1182(a)(23), denied as a matter of law his application for relief under section 212(c) of the Act, 8 U.S.C. 1182(c), and ordered him excluded and deported from the United States. The applicant has appealed from that decision.

The applicant, a 32-year-old native and citizen of Mexico, was admitted to the United States for lawful permanent residence on July 25, 1969. In the spring of 1970, he returned to Mexico where he resided until August 1974, crossing the border regularly to work in this country as a migrant farm worker. The applicant married a Mexican citizen in 1971 and has two sons by that marriage who are also citizens of Mexico. The applicant's wife and children never immigrated to the United States.

On August 14, 1974, approximately 79 pounds of marijuana were discovered in the applicant's automobile as he sought to reenter the United States. He was paroled into the United States for prosecution and on November 4, 1974, was convicted of a violation of 21 U.S.C. 841(a)(1), to wit, possession of a controlled substance with intent to distribute. The applicant was sentenced to serve 120 days of a 3-year term of imprisonment pursuant to that conviction, the balance of the term suspended with probation conditioned upon his returning forthwith to Mexico and not entering the United States without permission. Upon his release from confinement, the applicant was met by officers of the Immigration and Naturalization Service who returned him to Mexico without instituting exclusion proceedings.

According to his testimony, the applicant returned to the United States in January 1975, entering without inspection, and remained in this country to the time of his exclusion hearing. He visited Mexico about four times a year, reentering the United States without inspection on each occasion. In December 1979, after his criminal probation had expired, the applicant applied for admission to the United States. These exclusion proceedings ensued. On appeal, the applicant does not challenge the immigration judge's finding of excludability but appeals solely from the denial of section 212(c) relief.

Section 212(c) of the Act provides in pertinent part:

> Aliens lawfully admitted for permanent residence who temporarily proceeded abroad voluntarily and not under an order of deportation, and who are returning to a lawful unrelinquished domicile of seven consecutive years, may be admitted in the discretion of the Attorney General without regard to the provisions of paragraph (1) through (25) and paragraphs (30) and (31) of subsection (a)....

The immigration judge found that the applicant had lost his lawful permanent resident status prior to the hearing and, hence, could not establish statutory eligibility for section 212(c) relief. He cited alternative rationales for his holding: (1) that the applicant's lawful permanent resident status ended when he entered without inspection (*see Matter of M—*, 5 I & N Dec. 642 (BIA 1954) and (2) that such status terminated when the applicant departed and reentered the United States within the first 7 years of acquiring lawful permanent residence subsequent to an act or event that rendered him excludable (*see Matter of M—*, 7 I & N Dec. 34 (BIA 1979) and 17 I & N Dec. 322 (BIA 1980)).

In a recently published case, *Matter of Gunaydin*, Interim Decision 2925 (BIA 1982), we retreated from our decision in *Matter of M—*, 5 I & N Dec. 642 (BIA 1954), to the extent that decision has been understood to hold that an entry without inspection automatically terminates an alien's lawful permanent resident status. We found that proposition inconsistent with and superseded by subsequent Board precedents which held that an act or event which provides a basis for an alien's deportation does not in itself terminate his lawful permanent resident status but, rather, that such status ends as a result of his commission of a deportable offense only upon the entry of a final administrative order of deportation. *See Matter of Lok*, Interim Decision 2878 (BIA 1981), *aff'd, Lok v. INS*, 681 F.2d 107 (2d Cir. 1982); *Matter of Gunaydin, supra.*

We turn now to the alternative basis for the immigration judge's decision. *Matter of Hinojosa*, 17 I & N Dec. 34 (BIA 1979) and 17 I & N Dec. 322 (BIA 1980), the only precedent decisions which discussed *Matter of M—*, 7 I & N Dec. 140 (BIA 1956), in its 26-year history, distinguished the case on the facts. The holding in *Matter of M—, id.*, is now squarely before us. As we find the present *Matter of M—*, like the Volume 5 case of the same name, incompatible with subsequent case law, we shall withdraw from our holding therein and from the dicta in *Matter of Hinojosa, supra.*

In *Matter of M—*, the Board held that a lawful permanent resident who departed and reentered the United States while in the state of being inadmissible had no "lawful domicile" in this country from the date of that entry and could not thereafter accumulate time toward the satisfaction of the 7-year "lawful unrelinquished domicile" requirement of section 212(c). Thus, an alien who had not completed 7 years as a lawful permanent resident at the time of an entry made subsequent to an act or event giving rise to excludability, and hence could not qualify for a section 212(c) waiver at the time of such entry, was forever barred from establishing eligibility for relief under section 212(c). That result followed notwithstanding the fact that there had been no adjudication of the alien's excludability until after the 7-year period had elapsed.

In *Matter of Lok, supra*, the Board observed that the United States domicile of one who retains his lawful permanent resident status must be considered lawful. We then proceeded to consider the point in the deportation proceedings at which the status of an alien lawfully admitted for permanent residence comes to an end by reason of the act or event that rendered him deportable. We concluded that the alien retains his lawful status until a final administrative order of deportation has been entered in his case. The rule in *Lok*, announced in the context of deportation proceedings, applies as well to an alien in exclusion proceedings. As the applicant in the instant case is not now under a final administrative order of exclusion and deportation and does not appear to have been otherwise divested of his lawful permanent resident status, we find that such status continued to exist to the present time, as does the lawfulness of his domicile if he in fact is domiciled in the United States. Our contrary holding in *Matter of M—*, *i.e.*, that an alien who enters while in an excludable class prior to accruing 7 years of lawful permanent residence thereby loses his lawful status and his eligibility for section 212(c) relief, is herewith overruled.

We note parenthetically the critical significance *Matter of M—* attached to an "entry." Such emphasis on the comings and goings of a lawful permanent resident would appear inappropriate in light of *Francis v. INS*, 532 F.2d, 268 (2d Cir. 1976), a decision adopted by the Board in *Matter of Silva*, 16 I & N Dec. 26 (BIA 1976). *See Matter of Hinojosa*, 17 I & N Dec. 322, 324 (BIA 1980).

Deciding that the applicant retains his lawful permanent resident status and thus is not precluded by its termination from establishing statutory eligibility for a section 212(c) waiver does not dispose of the case. A question remains whether the applicant was domiciled in the United States for the requisite period. It is clear that the applicant was a commuter prior to his arrest in August 1974 and that his domicile until that time was in Mexico, not the United States. *See generally Matter of Sanchez*, 17 I & N Dec. 218 (BIA 1980); *Matter of Hoffman-Arvayo*, 13 I & N Dec. 750 (BIA 1971). The location of his domicile since his reentry in January 1975 is not, however, discernible from the record presently before us. Inasmuch as we conclude that a favorable exercise of discretion is not warranted in this case, it will not be necessary to remand the record for further development of the question. *See generally INS v. Bagamasbad*, 429 U.S. 24 (1976).

We regard the applicant's crime, which involved trafficking in a large quantity of marijuana, to be an extremely serious negative factor that has not been overcome by a showing of unusual or outstanding countervailing equities. *See generally Matter of Marin*, 16 I. & N. Dec. 581 (BIA 1978). The presence in the United States of the applicant's mother and brother is not in itself sufficient to outweigh the serious adverse factor militating against a grant of relief. The applicant has failed to demonstrate any other substantial equities. His wife and children reside in Mexico. The applicant himself has spent a considerable amount of time in his native country since his admission to the United States.

Notes

1. Should the rendering by the Board of its decision be treated as the termination of a person's permanent residence? Should permanent residence be treated as terminated as of the issuance or service of the Order to Show Cause or the decision by the appellate court? The position of the BIA, which has been followed in four circuits, is that lawful permanent residence is terminated when the BIA renders its decision. *See Variamparambil v. INS*, 831 F.2d 1362 (7th Cir. 1987); *Rivera v. INS*, 810 F.2d 540 (5th Cir. 1987); *Reid v. INS*, 756 F.2d 7 (3d Cir. 1985). The position in the Ninth Circuit is that lawful permanent residence is lost when the case is decided by the court of appeals unless deportability was conceded at the deportation hearing. *Wall v. INS*, 722 F.2d (9th Cir. 1984); *Avila-Murrieta v. INS*, 762 F.2d 733 (9th Cir. 1985). The Eleventh Circuit has taken the position that the time is tolled upon the issuance of the Order to Show Cause. *Marti-Xiques v. INS*, 741 F.2d 340 (11th Cir. 1984); *Balbe v. INS*, 886 F.2d 306 (11th Cir. 1989), *cert. denied* 110 S. Ct. 2166 (1990). Which of the above positions is most reasonable? *See also* 8 C.F.R. §§ 242.1(a), 3.14(a).

2. The Board cited *Matter of Marin*, 16 I. & N. Dec. 581 (BIA 1978), as authority for denying the waiver in this case. *Marin* presented the important factors to be weighed in 212(c) cases, some of which are: rehabilitation, length of residence in the United States, family ties, employment record, job skills, criminal history, ties to the country of deportation, and hardship to the family or applicant caused by deportation. Given the changes in the public's attitude toward persons involved with drugs, is it reasonable for the Board to also change its approach in 212(c) cases? How far can the Board go before it contravenes the congressional intent in enacting the waiver provision.

3. While 212(c) relief is broad, it is not all-encompassing. For example, it is not available for a conviction for firearms possession because there is no comparable exclusion provision. *See Matter of Waddud*, Interim Dec. 2980 (BIA 1980). Therefore, even though one can apply for a 212(c) waiver in deportation proceedings, there must be an equivalent exclusion provision to prevent the deportation.

E. Section 241(a)(1)(H) Waivers [Deportability for Fraud or Misrepresentation]

Matter of Raqueño
17 I. & N. Dec. 10 (BIA 1979)

The record relates to a married female alien, 33 years of age, who is a native and citizen of the Philippines. She was admitted to the United States on September

4, 1975, in possession of an immigrant visa classifying her in the second preference as the unmarried daughter of a lawful permanent resident. An approved visa petition so classifying her was attached to the visa. In fact, the respondent had married before she was issued the visa. She was interviewed and issued the visa on August 11, 1975. Her marriage date was July 19, 1975.

In her motion to reconsider, the respondent raises two legal arguments, neither of which was advanced at the time of her hearing below or during the previous appeal. First, the respondent argues that she is eligible for relief from deportation under section 241(f) of the Immigration and Nationality Act, 8 U.S.C. 1251(f). That provision saves from deportation those aliens who were excludable at the time of their entry on the basis of having procured a visa or other documentation or entry into the United States by fraud or misrepresentation if they are the spouse, parent, or a child of a United States' citizen or lawful permanent resident alien. In *Matter of Da Lomba*, 16 I & N Dec. 616 (BIA 1978), we held that section 241(f) forgives deportability under sections 241(a)(1) of the Act, 8 U.S.C. 1251(a)(1), and 212(a)(20) of the Act, 8 U.S.C. 1182(a)(20), where there has been compliance with the immigrant visa requirements and the entry document is invalid because of a fraud. We regard our decision in *Matter of Da Lomba*, *id.*, that a fraudulent misrepresentation is necessary to qualify an alien for section 241(f) relief from deportation as a rejection of our previous cases that held that an "innocent" misrepresentation was sufficient for such relief. *See Matter of Ideis*, 14 I & N Dec. 701 (BIA 1974); *Matter of Louie*, 14 I & N Dec. 421 (BIA 1973); *Matter of Torbergsen*, 13 I & N Dec. 432 (BIA 1969); *Matter of Lim*, 13 I & N Dec. 169 (BIA 1969); *cf. Matter of Gabouriel*, 13 I & N Dec. 742 (BIA 1971); *Matter of Koryzma*, 13 I & N Dec. 514 (BIA 1970). These cases followed the decision in *In re Yuen Lan Ham*, 289 F. Supp. 204 (S.D.N.Y. 1968), in which the court held that section 241(f) would be applicable in a case where an alien innocently claimed to be the spouse of a United States citizen upon her entry. We have decided to follow the dictum in *Reid v. INS*, 420 U.S. 619 (1975), disapproving of the holding in *In re Yuen Lan Ham*, *supra*, *see* 420 U.S. at 629, and, accordingly, we regard this line of cases as overruled.

In the present case, the respondent has consistently denied fraud in the obtainment of her immigrant visa. At a deportation hearing held on May 14, 1976, the respondent testified that she signed a Form FS-548 on August 11, 1972, attesting that she knew she would lose her immigrant status if she married before her entry into the United States. She stated further that she did not read the form because it was late in the day and she was "tired and hungry." On June 10, 1976, at the continued deportation hearing, the respondent again indicated that she did not know what she was signing because no one explained the form to her. Counsel for the respondent argued at the June 10 hearing that the visa application signed by the respondent, which indicated her marital status to be "single" (Ex. 2), was unclear as to whether the respondent's status at the time the visa petition was filed on her behalf was to be controlling, at which time (February 1, 1975) she was in fact single, or whether the time of the completion of the visa application was to control, at which time she was married. The implication is that, rather than fraudulently concealing her true marital status, the respondent innocently indicated that she was single because she believed that the query as to her marital status referred to the date on which her mother filed a visa petition on her behalf. The respondent has not established, therefore, eligibility for section 241(f) relief within the meaning of our decision in *Matter of Da Lomba, id.*, as she has not shown that her visa is invalid as fraudulently obtained. We believe that our finding in this regard is supported by the position taken by the Trial Attorney that the Government was not "alleging any fraud whatsoever," and also the statement of the immigration judge that the respondent "did not intentionally defraud the American Consul."

The second argument raised by the respondent is that the proceedings were technically defective because the Service never alleged that the respondent was ineligible for any other numerical classification. She relies for this proposition on our decision in *Matter of Suleiman*, 15 I & N Dec. 784 (BIA 1974), in which we held that, in rescission proceedings based on non-entitlement to the numerical classification accorded, it is essential that the Notice of Intention to Rescind allege ineligibility for any other numerical classification.

The respondent is charged with entry without a valid document in violation of section 212(a)(20) of the Act. Regardless of eligibility for another preference classification, the fact is that the respondent entered the United States as a second-preference immigrant when she was not entitled to that classification because she was married at the time of her entry. *See, generally, Hendrix v. INS*, 583 F.2d 1102 (9th Cir. 1978).

Matter of Agustin

17 I. & N. Dec. 14 (BIA 1979)

The respondent is a 23-year-old native and citizen of the Philippines who was admitted to the United States as a lawful permanent resident on January 29, 1971. She obtained an immigrant visa as the unmarried daughter of an alien lawfully admitted for permanent residence under section 203(a)(2) of the Immigration and Nationality Act, 8 U.S.C. 1153(a)(2). On June 9, 1976, an Order to Show Cause was issued, charging the respondent with deportability under section 241(a)(1) of the Act, 8 U.S.C. 1251(a)(1), as an alien excludable at entry under section 212(a)(20) of the Act, 8 U.S.C. 1182(a)(20), as an immigrant not in possession of a valid unexpired immigrant visa or other valid entry document.

At a deportation hearing held on June 23, 1976, the Service introduced into evidence a statement of the respondent, dated June 23, 1976, in which she stated that, in December 1970, prior to her admission into the United States, she married Francisco Ignacio. The Service also introduced an excerpt from the Civil Register of Marriages in the Philippines which indicates that a marriage between Lydia N. Carino and Francisco Ignacio was registered on January 6, 1971. However, on January 22, 1971, the respondent completed an application for an immigrant visa in which she stated her marital status as single (Ex. 2). The respondent conceded deportability, and the immigration judge found her deportable in a decision dated June 23, 1976, but granted her the privilege of voluntary departure in lieu of deportation.

On April 19, 1978, the respondent moved to reopen her deportation proceedings, asking that the immigration judge reconsider his decision and also allow the respondent to apply for relief from deportation under Section 241(f) of the Act, 8 U.S.C. 1251(f). On July 3, 1978, the immigration judge denied the respondent's motion. The respondent has appealed from that denial.

* * *

... [W]e find that the proceedings should be reopened to enable the respondent to apply for relief from deportation under section 241(f) of the Act. Concerning nondeportability under section 241(f), we determined, subsequent to the immigration judge's decision herein, that an alien was not precluded from 241(f) relief merely because the deportation charge was brought under sections 241(a)(1) and 212(a)(20) of the Act. *Matter of Da Lomba*, 16 I & N Dec. 616 (BIA 1978). In *Da Lomba*, we held that it is not necessary that a deportation charge be brought under section 212(a)(19) of the Act, 8 U.S.C. 1182(a)(19), in order for section 241(f) to be operative, if, in fact, immigration documentation was obtained by fraud. In the present case, the respondent admitted that she entered as an unmarried child and that she was actually married at the time. Her defense to deportation that, as a matter of law, she was unmarried at the time her visa was issued is not probative on the issue of her mental processes at that time. Accordingly, we shall remand the record for receipt of evidence on the issue of whether there was fraudulent intent when the respondent represented herself as single in her visa application.

The Trial Attorney has argued extensively in his brief on appeal that, even assuming the respondent is eligible to apply for relief from deportation under section 241(f), she was not "otherwise admissible" at the time of her entry as required by that section. In *Matter of Gonzalez*, 16 I & N Dec. 564 (BIA 1978), we held that section 241(f) was not operative where the alien seeking relief was not "otherwise admissible" at the time of entry for lack of a valid labor certification and was not exempt therefrom. However, we find that the respondent in the present case was exempt from the labor certification requirements of section 212(a)(14) due to her age. Volume 9 of the Foreign Affairs Manual, note 1.1 under 22 C.F.R. 42.91(a)(14), provides:

> Any alien under the age of sixteen when a visa is issued ... would not require a labor certification even though such alien might become employed upon attaining working age ....

The respondent was issued her visa on January 22, 1971, while she was under the age of sixteen (Ex. 2). We find, therefore, that she may not be precluded from establishing that she was otherwise admissible at the time of her entry within the meaning of section 241(f) for lack of a labor certification.

Note

The 1990 Act provided for waiver of certain misrepresentations for persons excludable at entry and described under the revised 8 U.S.C. § 1182(a)(6)(C)(i), Sec. 212(a)(6)(C)(i). The waiver is discretionary and available to the spouse, parent, son or daughter of a U.S. citizen or lawful permanent resident and is in possession of an immigrant visa. *See* Sec. 602(a)(1)(H) of the Immigration Act of 1990.

F. J Visa Waivers
[Foreign Residency Requirement]

Al-Khayyal v. INS
818 F.2d 827 (11th Cir. 1987)

HILL, Circuit Judge:

*   *   *

Faiz Al-Khayyal is a native of Saudi Arabia. He received his undergraduate and graduate degrees during a previous stay in the United States. Towards the end of his stay, in 1979, Al-Khayyal married Riccarda Heising, an American citizen. After their marriage, Al-Khayyal and his new bride moved to Saudi Arabia, where they resided for about one and one-half years. Both were employed by the Arabian American Oil Company. In 1980, Al-Khayyal accepted a faculty position at the Georgia Institute of Technology School of Industrial and Systems Engineering. Based on his proposed temporary employment as a visiting professor at Georgia Tech, Georgia Tech determined that appellant could enter the United States on a "J-1" visa. See 8 U.S.C. § 1101(a)(15)(J) (1982). The University then sent Al-Khayyal a copy of form IAP-66, the form used to secure a J-1 visa.

According to Al-Khayyal's affidavit, he reviewed the form, filled out the necessary sections, and sent it, along with his passport, to the U.S. Consulate in Dhahran, Saudi Arabia for issuance of the visa. He returned a few days later to pick up the visa, and was given a sealed envelope which he was instructed to give to an immigration officer at his port of entry in the United States. In December of 1980, when appellant arrived at Hartsfield International Airport in Atlanta, Georgia, an immigration official opened the sealed envelope, processed the IAP-66 form, and gave the appellant a copy. Appellant then noticed that Part III of the form had been filled out. The form clearly stated that he would be subject to a two-year home country residence requirement. According to appellant's affidavit, he did not "fully understand" the meaning of this, but decided for himself that it could not develop into any "serious complications" because his wife was a United States citizen.

After his arrival in the United States, Al-Khayyal began his teaching duties at Georgia Tech. He requested and received two one-year extensions of his visa from the INS. In 1982, his wife entered law school at Georgetown University. During her tenure at law school the two remained geographically separate, but saw each other once a month and during holidays.

In August of 1983, Al-Khayyal sought to change his visa classification from nonimmigrant exchange visitor (J-1 visa) to a nonimmigrant temporary worker (H-1). See 8 U.S.C. § 1101(a)(15)(H) (1982). The INS district director denied his application on the grounds that Al-Khayyal was subject to the home country residence requirement attached to certain J-1 visas, and that Al-Khayyal had neither complied with that requirement nor secured a waiver as permitted by law. See 8 U.S.C. § 1182(e) (1982). In September of 1983, the appellant submitted an application for a waiver of the foreign residence requirement to the INS. After the INS denied his application, Al-Khayyal appealed to the INS Administrative Appeals Unit, which dismissed his appeal and his subsequent request for reconsideration. Al-Khayyal next filed a complaint in federal district court, seeking judicial review of the INS's administrative decision. He now appeals the district court's order, 630 F. Supp. 1162, granting summary judgment in favor of the INS.

J-1 visas are issued to residents of a foreign country, "which (they) have no intention of abandoning," for the purpose of studying, teaching, or obtaining a specialized skill. See 8 U.S.C. § 1101(a)(15)(J) (1982). Three categories of persons admitted under J-1 visas are required to reside in their home country for two years before they are eligible for an immigrant visa, certain less restrictive nonimmigrant visas, or for permanent residence. The three categories are: persons whose activities in the United States were financed by the United States government or the government of their home country; persons possessing "specialized knowledge or skill" needed in their home country; and persons receiving graduate medical education or training in the United States. 8 U.S.C. § 1182(e) (1982). It is undisputed that appellant was eligible for a J-1 visa, and that he is covered by the second category above in light of his industrial engineering skills.

Aliens who must meet two-year foreign residence requirements, such as the appellant, may obtain a waiver of that requirement under section 212(e) of the Act. The relevant portion of that section provides:

Provided, that upon the favorable recommendation of the Director of the United States Information Agency, pursuant to a request of an interested United States government agency, or of the Commissioner of Immigration and Naturalization after he has determined that departure from the United States would impose exceptional hardship upon the alien's spouse or child (if such spouse or child is a citizen of the United States or a lawfully admitted resident alien),... the Attorney General may waive the requirement of such two-year foreign residence abroad in the case of any alien whose admission to the United States is found by the Attorney General to be in the public interest....

8 U.S.C. § 1182(e).

*   *   *

The term "exceptional hardship" as used in the waiver provision is not defined by the statute; however, the legislative history behind the 1961 amendment strongly supports stringent enforcement of the two-year home country residence requirement. See H.R. Rep. No. 721, 87th Cong. 1st Sess. 121 (1961). The INS has broad discretion in determining whether exceptional hardship exists.

The relevant[1] factors cited by the appellant in support of his claim of extraordinary hardship include the interruption of his wife's legal education and career. He claims that it is unlikely that she will be able to find a position as an attorney in Saudi Arabia.[2] Should she therefore decide to stay in the United States, maintaining two households will create a financial and emotional strain upon the marriage.

---

1. Appellant also contended that factors related to hardship imposed upon the appellant, such as the fact that he has a close relationship with a niece and nephew in this country, and is working on an engineering treatise, militate in favor of granting the waiver. However, the waiver is granted for hardship imposed upon the spouse or child. 8 U.S.C. § 1182(e) (emphasis supplied). The INS official did not abuse his discretion by determining that these factors do not affect appellant's spouse or child such that they constitute grounds for a waiver.

2. This factor should now be moot because Al-Khayyal's wife was scheduled to graduate

*   *   *

In granting the INS's motion for summary judgment, the district court noted that the supposedly similar precedents offered by Al-Khayyal in support of his application for a waiver were "of limited value in reviewing an agency determination which is as fact-specific as the judgment of exceptional hardship." The district court explained that Al-Khayyal's situation varied from each of the cases cited, and in light of the broad discretion given the agency in granting a waiver, the court was unable to find that the INS's decision in Al-Khayyal's case varied so significantly from earlier decisions as to constitute an abuse of that discretion.

Next, Al-Khayyal argued that the INS erred in failing to apply a more lenient standard for exceptional hardship to his case due to the fact that he was a teacher and not a student. The district court noted that some of the legislative history of the waiver provision does suggest that a more liberal attitude might be taken toward hardship applications from teachers. However, it did not establish that the teachers had a right to a lower standard for hardship, much less a right to a waiver. Moreover, the district court noted that the associate commissioner did take this factor into account, noting that Al-Khayyal's status as a teacher was an "ameliorative factor."
. . .

Next, Al-Khayyal argued to the district court that he was not told that he was subject to the two-year foreign residence requirement as is required by INS regulations. The district court found that despite the fact that Al-Khayyal claimed that he had no knowledge of the two-year requirement, the record as a whole demonstrated that he should have known that he was subject to the two-year foreign residence requirement. His original J-1 form clearly showed that such a requirement might be applied. He stated that he did read the form instructions. Moreover, the form showed Al-Khayyal's signature below a statement which indicated that a consulate or immigration officer would determine whether appellant was subject to the "two-year home country physical presence requirement," and that if such officer determined that he was subject to it, Al-Khayyal would comply. Finally, Al-Khayyal conceded in his affidavit that he saw the consul's determination that he would be subject to the requirement when he received a copy of his visa at Hartsfield airport. The district court determined that, "plaintiff therefore should have been aware of the residence requirement, not from pouring over the Immigration Act but from the plain language of the form he signed." In light of all of the above facts, the district court concluded that it could not find an abuse of discretion in the INS's refusal to grant a waiver of the residence requirement.

*   *   *

. . . The standard of review applicable to this case is a very restrictive one. As the district court correctly noted, the Act commits the definition of "extraordinary hardship" to the Commissioner of INS and his delegates, "and their construction and application of the standard should not be overturned by a reviewing court simply because it may prefer another interpretation of this statute." *Immigration & Naturalization Serv. v. Wang*, 450 U.S. 139, 144 (1981) (holding that determining "extreme hardship" as used in 8 U.S.C. § 1254(a)(1), a similar statute, was committed to the

---

from law school in May of 1985. Thus, her only career-related hardship would be a potential two-year interruption in the beginning of her legal career, should she be unable to find legal employment in Saudi Arabia.

attorney general and his delegates); *Chokloikaew v. Immigration and Naturalization Service*, 601 F.2d 216, 218 (5th Cir. 1979). Further, the legislative history of the amendment allowing waiver of the residence requirement at the discretion of the Attorney General suggests that the hardship requirement must be strictly enforced. Despite appellant's protestations to the contrary, the INS was not required to apply a more lenient standard of hardship to his case. H.R. Rep. No. 721, 87th Cong. 1st Sess. 121 (1961).[4] An examination of the administrative decision denying appellant's request for a waiver clearly indicates that all relative factors were considered. There was no abuse of discretion.

Finally, the district court did not err in determining that the circumstances surrounding the issuance of appellant's visa do not, as a matter of law, require that he be granted the hardship waiver. Appellant claims that his case is controlled by two prior cases, in which an alien relied upon a government official's misinformation. In *Slyper v. The Attorney General*, 576 F. Supp. 559 (D.D.C. 1983), an alien applying for a J-1 visa was verbally told, before the issuance of the visa, that he would not be subject to the two-year residence requirement. He was not married at the time that the visa was issued, and his American spouse had relied upon the fact that he would not have to return to his home country in deciding whether or not to marry him. When it was determined that the J-1 residence requirement did in fact apply to Mr. Slyper, he applied for a waiver. The waiver was granted because the hardship was created, in part, by the affirmative misinformation given to Mr. Slyper.

Here, appellant was informed in writing of the U.S. Consul's determination that the two-year residence requirement would apply to him at the time that he was issued his visa. The fact that he did not pay sufficient attention to this does not mean that any hardship caused by an imposition of the residence requirement was due to affirmative misinformation being given to appellant by the U.S. Consul. In fact, appellant and his wife were married before the visa was issued, and were already living in Saudi Arabia.

Appellant also contends that this case is controlled by *Corniel Rodriguez v. The Immigration and Naturalization Service*, 532 F.2d 301 (2d Cir. 1976). There, an alien who had applied for entry into the United States (under special circumstances not presented here) was not told by consulate officials that if she were married at the time she tried to enter the United States, the visa she had been issued would be invalidated. Just before entering the United States she married her childhood sweetheart. When she arrived, she was refused entry. Had she married her spouse immediately after entering the United States, she would have complied with her visa requirements. The Court of Appeals for the Second Circuit determined that this was a typical "trap for the unwary," and found that, under the circumstances, she should have been allowed into the country.

---

4. The legislative history did suggest that a more lenient policy could be applied by the attorney general to teachers; however, no such distinction was formally adopted in the implementing regulations, and consideration of this factor is not necessary, although it may be considered, in the exercise of the attorney general's discretion. Here, the INS official reviewing appellant's appeal did note that the fact that Al-Khayyal was a teacher and not a student was "an ameliorative factor in determining whether exceptional hardship exists." But the INS officer correctly noted that this "does not mean that a waiver may be granted where exceptional hardship is not found."

This is a far cry from what occurred in this case. Appellant was informed of the two-year residence requirement. The fact that he made long term plans to stay in the United States does not mean that the Attorney General must grant him the waiver that he seeks. This case concerns an exercise of statutorily granted discretion, and the appellant has not shown that this discretion was abused. Accordingly, we affirm the district court decision.

Notes

1. J waivers are rarely successful since the courts interpret the statute as granting a great deal of discretion to the Attorney General. Moreover, Congress, in enacting the statute, contemplated that exchange visitors would return to their countries except under rare circumstances. Therefore, the challenge for the advocate is to clearly lay out and document each element of hardship, which in the aggregate may engender sympathy from the INS or reviewing court.

2. One of the peculiarities of the J waiver is that even where the INS erroneously approves it without a recommendation from the Department of State, the waiver is invalid because the recommendation is necessary. *See Matter of Tayabji*, Interim Dec. 2994 (BIA 1985).

3. One statutory basis for obtaining the waiver is the fear of persecution based on political, religious, or other reasons. Consider whether the burden of proof should be the same as it is for asylum. *See Almirol v. INS*, 550 F. Supp. 253 (N.D. Ca. 1982).

G. Judicial Recommendation Against Deportation

Matter of Parodi
17 I. & N. Dec. 608 (BIA 1980)

*   *   *

The respondent is a 30-year-old native and citizen of Ecuador who entered the United States on March 19, 1974, as a lawful permanent resident. On August 2, 1977, he was convicted in United States District Court for the Southern District of Illinois, for the offense of passing counterfeit $20 Federal Reserve notes, in violation of 18 U.S.C. 472. He was sentenced to 6 years' imprisonment for this crime, and served over 2 years before being released on probation. On June 30, 1978, he was convicted, for the same acts, in the District Court for the Northern District of Illinois, of the crime of conspiring to commit offenses against the United States, in violation of 18 U.S.C. 371. The presiding judge in the Northern District granted the respondent's request for a recommendation against deportation, pursuant to section 241(b)(2) of the Immigration and Nationality Act, 8 U.S.C. 1251(b)(2). In an Order to Show Cause issued on May 18, 1979, the respondent was charged with deportability based only on his 1977 conviction; the 1978 conviction was not mentioned. At a deportation hearing begun on August 27, 1979, and completed on February 22, 1980, the respondent admitted the allegations in the Order to Show Cause, but denied deportability. He argued at the hearing, as he argues on appeal, that the recommendation against deportation issued by the Court for the Northern District bars his deportation altogether because both the 1977 and the 1978 convictions arose out of a single scheme of misconduct.

* * *

The real issue here is a narrow one: whether an alien who is granted a recommendation against deportation by a judge in one criminal proceeding is protected by that recommendation when he is convicted in another, separate criminal proceeding, in a different court and under a different charge, for the same underlying criminal misconduct, and the second court does not recommend against deportation. Although this question appears to be one of first impression, we have little trouble in resolving it. The section of the Act relating to recommendations against deportation provides that the provisions of section 241(a)(4) shall not apply "if the court sentencing such alien for such crime shall make . . . a recommendation . . . that such alien not be deported . . . ." Section 241(b)(2) of the Act. The respondent urges us to construe section 241(b)(2) liberally, and emphasizes Congress' ameliorative purpose in enacting the section, as well as the general rule that doubts in interpretation of the Act are to be resolved in favor of the alien. See Fong Haw Tan v. Phelan, 333 U.S. 6, 10 (1948). The respondent also recognizes, however, that acts of Congress must, where possible, be given their plain meaning; this is a basic rule of statutory construction. *See e.g. Ernst & Ernst v. Hochfelder*, 425 U.S. 185 (1976); *Burns v. Alcala*, 420 U.S. 575 (1975); *Kelly v. United States*, 531 F.2d 1144 (2d Cir. 1976).

Despite Congress' liberal intent, we believe that the plain meaning of section 241(b)(2) requires us to find that a judicial recommendation against deportation is effective to protect against deportation only for the crime or crimes for which an alien is convicted before that judicial tribunal.

* * *

The immigration judge also properly found the respondent ineligible for voluntary departure. See section 244(e) of the Act, 8 U.S.C. 1254(e). However, we note that the respondent may qualify for other discretionary relief. The fact that he has been a lawful permanent resident does not preclude him from applying for adjustment of status under section 245 of the Act, 8 U.S.C. 1255. *Tibke v. INS*, 335 F.2d 42 (2d Cir. 1964); *Matter of Loo*, 15 I & N Dec. 307 (BIA 1975); *Matter of Krastman*, 11 I & N Dec. 720 (BIA 1966). As he has a lawful permanent resident wife, he may be able to obtain that relief. In order to qualify for adjustment of status, an alien must be admissible to the United States. Section 345 of the Act. The respondent here is presently inadmissible under section 212(a)(9), 8 U.S.C. 1182 (a)(9), because of his convictions. He may, however, be able to receive a waiver of such excludability under section 212(h). An alien deportable under section 241(a)(4) is eligible to receive this waiver nunc pro tunc. Matter of Sanchez, Interim Decision 2751 (BIA 1980). Although the respondent in this case has not departed from the United States since the time of his excludable act, and thus cannot obtain nunc pro tunc relief, he could obtain the relief as an applicant for adjustment. Applicants for this relief have been held to be in the same position as aliens presenting themselves at the border, seeking entry as lawful permanent residents. *See Hamid v. INS*, 538 F.2d 1389 (9th Cir. 1976); *Campos v. INS*, 402 F.2d 758 (9th Cir. 1968); *Matter of Smith*, 11 I & N Dec. 325 (BIA

1965). Such aliens are therefore both subject to the exclusion provisions of section 212(a) and eligible for waivers of excludability. *See Matter of Smith, id.* Recognizing this, we have held that a 212(h) waiver may be obtained in deportation proceedings if it is granted in conjunction with adjustment of status. *See Matter of Bernabella,* 13 I & N Dec. 42 (BIA 1968).

We note that the respondent has a United States citizen child by his first wife, whom he helps to support, and also that his present wife testified at the hearing as to the hardship she might suffer if her husband is forced to leave the United States. These would of course be factors to consider should the respondent apply for a 212(h) waiver and section 245 relief. As no steps have as yet been taken to seek such relief, however, and as we have rejected the respondent's arguments regarding his deportability, this appeal must be dismissed.

As was noted earlier, the 1990 Act eliminated the judicial recommendation against deportation. The Act provided further that it applied to all "convictions entered before, on, or after" the enactment of the statute (November 29, 1990)[26] As counsel for a client who has pleaded guilty prior to November 29, 1990, relying on the existence of the judicial recommendation, what would you do for your client?

H. 212(h) Waivers
[Crimes Involving Moral Turpitude and
Multiple Criminal Convictions]

Matter of Ngai
Interim Dec. 2989 (Comm'r 1984)

*   *   *

The applicant is a Chinese national born in 1927. She is an applicant for an immigrant visa based on an approved visa petition filed by her husband, a permanent resident of the United States. She has been found to be excludable from the United States pursuant to section 212(a)(9) of the Immigration and Nationality Act, 8 U.S.C. § 1182(a)(9), which provides, in part, for the exclusion of aliens who have been convicted of crimes involving moral turpitude. The applicant was found so excludable as a result of a 1974 conviction in Hong Kong of obtaining property by deception in that she was an accomplice to defrauding money from persons by promising to introduce them to United States citizens for the purpose of arranging marriages and immigration to the United States.

The applicant filed the instant application, seeking that this permanent bar to her admission be waived as provided in section 212(h) of the Act, 8 U.S.C. § 1182(h), which provides:

Any alien, who is excludable from the United States under paragraphs (9), (10), or (12) of this section, who (A) is the spouse or child, including a minor unmarried

---

26. Sec. 505, Immigration Act of 1990, Pub. L. No. 101-649, 104 Stat. 4978 (1990).

adopted child, of a United States citizen, or of an alien lawfully admitted for permanent residence . . . shall, if otherwise admissible, be issued a visa and admitted to the United States for permanent residence (1) if it shall be established to the satisfaction of the Attorney General that (A) the alien's exclusion would result in extreme hardship to the United States citizen or lawfully resident spouse, parent, or son or daughter of such alien, and (B) the admission to the United States of such alien would not be contrary to the national welfare, safety or security of the United States; and (2) if the Attorney General, in his discretion, and pursuant to such terms, conditions, and procedures as he may by regulations prescribe, has consented to the alien's applying or reapplying for a visa and for admission to the United States.

In this application she cited the fact that her husband and three daughters were permanent residents in the United States while she has one son remaining with her. She asserted that the bar to her admission imposed a hardship on her husband due to the fact of their imposed separation and the financial strain of his having to maintain two households.

The district director denied this application, concluding that there was in fact no hardship of any kind as a result of the bar. He found the applicant to be self-supporting in Hong Kong rather than financially supported by her husband. He further found, based on that husband's statement, that husband and wife had not seen each other in over 28 years as a result of their own voluntary decision, and that the husband had no plans to reunite with his wife if she were not admitted to the United States. He thus concluded that the existence of a marriage on paper for this extended period of time was insufficient to establish a basis for the approval of this waiver.

On appeal, the applicant contests this decision, asserting that her continued exclusion will result in extreme hardship to her husband in the United States in that he is 60 years old and has serious health problems and that he suffers from hypertension and sinus tachycardia. She claims that her son, now age 35, who lives with her, will soon immigrate to the United States based on a petition filed by the applicant's husband. She asserts that her son is mentally retarded and unable to care for himself, which will exacerbate her husband's condition. She asserts that her forced absence will work a hardship on both her husband, who will have to continue to support two households and will thus be unable to retire, and on her son, who will be deprived of adequate medical care and attention.

A waiver of bar to admission that results from section 212(a)(9) of the Act is dependent first upon a showing that the fact of the bar imposes an extreme hardship on a qualifying family member. Congress provided this waiver but limited its application. By such limitation it is evident that it did not intend that a waiver be granted merely due to the fact that a qualifying relationship existed. The key term in the provision is 'extreme' and thus only in cases of great actual or prospective injury to the United States nation will the bar be removed. Common results of the bar, such as separation, financial difficulties, etc., in themselves are insufficient to warrant approval of an application unless combined with much more extreme impacts. *Matter of W—*, 9 I & N Dec. 1 (BIA 1960); *Matter of Shaughnessy*, 12 I & N Dec. 810 (BIA 1968). The burden of proof in such a proceeding lies with the applicant, and while an analysis of a given application includes a review of all claims put forth in light of the facts and circumstances of a case, such analysis does not extend to discovery of undisclosed negative impacts.

In the matter at bar, many of the applicant's statements regarding the causes and extent of any hardship which would result from her exclusion are refuted by the record. The applicant now claims that her son, age 36, is severely retarded and unable to care for himself. However, the record contains a medical report wherein her son is found to be moderately retarded, able to care for himself, and able to do simple industrial work. It further notes that he has been employed in Hong Kong. The applicant's claim that the separation from her husband causes him financial hardship is refuted by the fact that she is employed in Hong Kong and is in fact self-supporting. The applicant's typification of her husband as a person with severe medical problems with no one other than his wife to look to is refuted both by the description of his medical condition and the fact that he has three adult daughters in the United States. All of these facts, when combined with a 28-year voluntary separation, establish that any hardship that will be imposed on either the applicant's husband or any of her four children, when taken either individually or collectively, falls far short of extreme. Accordingly, the decision of the district director is affirmed and the appeal will be dismissed.

Notes

1. The 1990 Act eliminated the requirement that the applicant show extreme hardship, but added a requirement that the exclusionary acts preceded the application for admission, entry or adjustment by 15 years (except in the case of persons excluded on grounds of prostitution). Like most waivers this waiver is discretionary.

2. In 1981 Congress amended the deportation waiver of section 241(f) and added subsection (2) which provided for a waiver of deportability where the person was convicted of a "single offense of simple possession of 30 grams or less of marihuana," where the applicant is the spouse, parent, or child of a citizen of the United States or of a lawful permanent resident, and there is a showing of extreme hardship. *See* 8 U.S.C. § 1251(f)(2).

3. A marihuana conviction in and of itself is not sufficient to require a waiver, as the conviction must be for "illicit possession." *Lennon v. INS*, 527 F.2d 187 (2d Cir. 1975). However, if not clear from the conviction record, the applicant will bear the burden of proving that her conviction related to "30 grams or less of marihuana," and thereby satisfy one of the prerequisites for section 241(a)(2)(B) relief. *Matter of Grijalva*, Interim Dec. 3075 (BIA 1988).

Index to Appendix

Waiver Provisions

Statutes

Documentary waiver for returning permanent residents.
8 U.S.C. § 1181(b), Sec. 211(b)

Notwithstanding the provisions of section 212(a)(7)(A) of this Act in such cases or in such classes of cases and under such conditions as may by regulations be prescribed, returning resident immigrants, defined in section 101(a)(27)(A), who are otherwise admissible may be readmitted to the United States by the Attorney General in his discretion without being required to obtain a passport, immigrant visa, reentry permit or other documentation.

*   *   *

Requests by aliens previously excluded or deported to reapply for admission.
8 U.S.C. §§ 1182(a)(6), Sec. 212(a)(6)

(A) Any alien who has been excluded from admission and deported and who again seeks admission within one year of the date of such deportation is excludable, unless prior to the alien's reembarkation at a place outside the United States or attempt to be admitted from foreign contiguous territory the Attorney General has consented to the alien's reapplying for admission.

(B) Any alien who—(i) has been arrested and deported, (ii) has fallen into distress and has been removed pursuant to this or any prior Act, (iii) has been removed as an alien enemy, or (iv) has been removed at Government expense in lieu of deportation pursuant to section 242(b), and who seeks admission within 5 years of the date of such deportation or removal (or within 20 years in the case of an alien convicted of an aggravated felony) is excludable, unless before the date of the alien's embarkation or reembarkation at a place outside the United States or attempt to be admitted from foreign contiguous territory the Attorney General has consented to the alien's applying or reapplying for admission.

Waivers for certain nonimmigrants.
8 U.S.C. § 1182(d), Sec. 212(d)

(3) Except as provided in this subsection, an alien (A) who is applying for a nonimmigrant visa and is known or believed by the consular officer to be ineligible for such visa under one or more of the paragraphs enumerated in subsection (a) of this section (other than paragraphs (3)(A), (3)(C) and (3)(D)), after approval by the Attorney General of a recommendation by the Secretary of State or by the consular officer that the alien be admitted temporarily despite his inadmissibility, be granted such a visa and may be admitted into the United States temporarily as a nonimmigrant in the discretion of the Attorney General, or (B) who is inadmissible under one or more of the paragraphs enumerated in subsection (a) of this section (other than paragraphs (3)(A), (3)(C) and (3)(D)), but who is in possession of appropriate documents or is granted a waiver thereof and is seeking admission, may be admitted into the United States temporarily as a nonimmigrant in the discretion of the Attorney General.

(4) Either or both of the requirements of paragraph (7)(B)(i) of subsection (a) of this section may be waived by the Attorney General and the Secretary of State acting jointly (A) on the basis of unforeseen emergency in individual cases, or (B) on the basis of reciprocity with respect to nationals of foreign contiguous territory or of adjacent islands and residents thereof having a common nationality with such nationals, or (C) in the case of aliens proceeding in immediate and continuous transit through the United States under contracts authorized in section 1228(d) of this title.

* * *

(8) Upon a basis of reciprocity accredited officials of foreign governments, their immediate families, attendants, servants, and personal employees may be admitted in immediate and continuous transit through the United States without regard to the provisions of this section except paragraphs (3)(A), (3)(B), (3)(C) and (7)(B) of subsection (a) of this section.

* * *

Parole
8 U.S.C. § 1182(d)(5) and (7), Sec. 212(d)(5) and (7)

(5)(A) The Attorney General may, except as provided in subparagraph (B) or in Section 214(f), in his discretion parole into the United States temporarily under such conditions as he may prescribe for emergent reasons or for reasons deemed strictly in the public interest any alien applying for admission to the United States, but such parole of such alien shall not be regarded as an admission of the alien and when the purposes of such parole shall, in the opinion of the Attorney General, have been served the alien shall forthwith return or be returned to the custody from which he was paroled and thereafter his case shall continue to be dealt with in the same manner as that of any other applicant for admission to the United States.

(B) The Attorney General may not parole into the United States an alien who is a refugee unless the Attorney General determines that compelling reasons in the public interest with respect to that particular alien require that the alien be paroled into the United States rather than be admitted as a refugee under section 207.

(7) The provisions of subsection (a) of this section, other than paragraph (7), of said subsection, shall be applicable to any alien who shall leave Guam, Puerto Rico, or the Virgin Islands of the United States, and who seeks to enter the continental United States or any other place under the jurisdiction of the United States. The Attorney General shall by regulations provide a method and procedure for the temporary admission to the United States of the aliens described in this proviso. Any alien described in this paragraph, who is excluded from admission to the United States, shall be immediately deported in the manner provided by section 1227(a) of this title.

*   *   *

Exchange student (J-1) provision and waiver.
8 U.S.C. § 1182(e), Sec. 212(e)

No person admitted under section 101(a)(15)(J) or acquiring such status after admission (i) whose participation in the program for which he came to the United States was financed in whole or in part, directly or indirectly, by an agency of the Government of the United States or by the government of the country of his nationality or his last residence, (ii) who at the time of admission or acquisition of status under section 101(a)(15)(J) was a national or resident of a country which the Director of the United States Information Agency, pursuant to regulations prescribed by him, had designated as clearly requiring the services of persons engaged in the field of specialized knowledge or skill in which the alien was engaged, or (iii) who came to the United States or acquired such status in order to receive graduate medical education or training, shall be eligible to apply for an immigrant visa, or for permanent residence, or for a nonimmigrant visa under section 101(a)(15)(H) or section 101(a)(15)(L) until it is established that such person has resided and been physically present in the country of his nationality or his last residence for an aggregate of at least two years following departure from the United States: Provided, That upon the favorable recommendation of the Director of the United States Information Agency, pursuant to the request of an interested United States Government agency, or of the Commissioner of Immigration and Naturalization after he has determined that departure from the United States would impose exceptional hardship upon the alien's spouse or child (if such spouse or child is a citizen of the United States or a lawfully resident alien), or that the alien cannot return to the country of his nationality or last residence because he would be subject to persecution on account of race, religion, or political opinion, the Attorney General may waive the requirement of such two-year foreign residence abroad in the case of any alien whose admission to the United States is found by the Attorney General to be in the public interest: And provided further, That, except in the case of an alien described in clause (iii), the Attorney General may, upon the favorable recommendation of the Director of the United States Information Agency, waive such two-year foreign residence requirement in any case in which the foreign country of the alien's nationality or last residence has furnished the Director of the United States Information Agency a statement in writing that it has no objection to such waiver in the case of such alien.

*   *   *

Waivers for aliens excludable for physical or mental disorders or certain communicable diseases.
8 U.S.C. § 1182(g), Sec. 212(g)
The Attorney General may waive the application of—

(1) section (a)(1)(A)(i) in the case of any alien who—

(A) is the spouse or the unmarried son or daughter, or the minor unmarried lawfully adopted child, of a United States citizen, or of an alien lawfully admitted for permanent residence, or of an alien who has been issued an immigrant visa, or

(B) has a son or daughter who is a United States citizen, or an alien lawfully admitted for permanent residence, or an alien who has been issued an immigrant visa, or

(2) subsection (a)(1)(A)(ii) in the case of any alien, in accordance with such terms, conditions, and controls, if any, including the giving of bond, as the Attorney General, in his discretion after consultation with the Secretary of Health and Human Services, may by regulation prescribe.

*   *   *

Waivers for certain criminal convictions and for prostitutes or those engaged in the business of prostitution.
8 U.S.C. § 1182(h), Sec. 212(h)
The Attorney General may, in his discretion, waive the application of subparagraphs (A)(i)(I), (B), (D), and (E) of subsection (a)(2) and subparagraph (A)(i)(II) of such subsection insofar as it relates to a single offense of simple possession of 30 grams or less of marijuana in the case of an immigrant who is the spouse, parent, son, or daughter of a citizen of the United States or alien lawfully admitted for permanent residence if—

(1) it is established to the satisfaction of the Attorney General that—

(A) the alien is excludable only under subparagraph (D)(i) or (D)(ii) of such subsection or the activities for which the alien is excludable occurred more than 15 years before the date of the alien's application for a visa, entry, or adjustment of status, and

(B) the admission to the United States of such alien would not be contrary to the national welfare, safety, or security of the United States, and

(C) the alien has been rehabilitated; and

(2) the Attorney General, in his discretion, and pursuant to such terms, conditions and procedures as he may by regulations prescribe, has consented to the alien's applying or reapplying for a visa, for admission to the United States, or adjustment of status. No waiver shall be provided under this subsection in the case of an alien who has been convicted of (or who has admitted committing acts that constitute) murder or criminal acts involving torture.

* * *

Waivers for aliens who have committed certain fraudulent acts or misrepresentations.
8 U.S.C. § 1182(i), Sec. 212(i)

The Attorney General may, in his discretion, waive application of clause (i) of subsection (a)(6)(C)—

(1) in the case of an alien who is the spouse, parent, or son or daughter of a United States citizen or of an alien lawfully admitted for permanent residence, or

(2) if the fraud or misrepresentation occurred at least 10 years before the date of the alien's application for a visa, entry, or adjustment of status and it is established to the satisfaction of the Attorney General that the admission to the United States of such alien would not be contrary to the national welfare, safety, or security of the United States.

Waivers for certain persons in possession of an immigrant visa.
8 U.S.C. § 1182(k), Sec. 212(k)

Any alien, excludable from the United States under paragraph (5)(A) or (7)(A)(i) of subsection (a), who is in possession of an immigrant visa may, if otherwise admissible, be admitted in the discretion of the Attorney General if the Attorney General is satisfied that exclusion was not known to, and could not have been ascertained by the exercise of reasonable diligence by, the immigrant before the time of departure of the vessel or aircraft from the last port outside the United States and outside foreign contiguous territory or, in the case of an immigrant coming from foreign contiguous territory, before the time of the immigrant's application for admission.

Executive Pardons for crimes and aggravated felonies
8 U.S.C. § 1251(a)(2)(A), Sec. 241(a)(2)(A)

(iv) Waiver Authorized.—Clauses (i), (ii), and (iii) shall not apply in the case of an alien with respect to a criminal conviction if the alien subsequent to the criminal conviction has been granted a full and unconditional pardon by the President of the United States or by the Governor of any of the several States.

Waiver for certain misrepresentations
8 U.S.C. § 1251(a)(1)(H), 241(a)(1)(H)

The provisions of this paragraph relating to the deportation of aliens within the United States on the ground that they were excludable at the time of entry as aliens described in section 212(a)(6)(C)(i), whether willful or innocent, may, in the discretion of the Attorney General, be waived for any alien (other than an alien described in paragraph (6) or (7)) who—

(i) is the spouse, parent, son, or daughter of a citizen of the United States or of an alien lawfully admitted to the United States for permanent residence; and

(ii) was in possession of an immigrant visa or equivalent document and was otherwise admissible to the United States at the time of such entry except for those grounds of inadmissibility specified under paragraphs (5)(A) and (7)(A) of section 212(a) which were a direct result of that fraud or misrepresentation. A waiver of deportation for fraud or misrepresentation granted under this subparagraph shall also operate to waive deportation based on the grounds of inadmissibility at entry directly resulting from such fraud or misrepresentation.

Chapter 13
Naturalization and Citizenship

As immigration law can be viewed as the control of the movement of persons between countries, the law of citizenship can be viewed as controlling membership or participation in the national community. While the laws governing who is or may become a citizen will vary from country to country, its attainment always will bring rights greater than those enjoyed by aliens. Generally citizenship will allow a person the rights of entry and participation.[1] Naturalization is a benefit which grants the equivalent of citizenship as it is the acquisition of citizenship other than through birth.[2]

The subject of naturalization and citizenship is one of the most complex areas of immigration and nationality law. In this chapter we will explore the principles governing citizenship, expatriation, and denaturalization.

Even though there are numerous references in the Constitution to citizenship, the original document never defined the term. Instead of defining citizenship, the Constitution empowered Congress to enact a "uniform rule of naturalization."[3] The fourteenth amendment, which was adopted after the Civil War, contained the first definition of citizenship in the Constitution and provides that:

> All persons born or naturalized in the United States, and subject to the jurisdiction thereof, are citizens of the United States and of the state wherein they reside.

The case which follows was the first major case that dealt with the issue of who was a citizen.

A. Citizenship, a Historical Perspective

Dred Scott v. Sandford
60 U.S. (19 How.) 393 (1856)

[Reporter's Note: Prior to the institution of the present suit, an action was brought by Scott for his freedom in the Circuit Court of St. Louis county (State court), where there was a verdict and judgment in his favor. On a writ of error to the Supreme Court of the State, the judgment below was reversed and the case remanded to the Circuit Court, where it was continued to await the decision of the case now in question.

---

1. In the United States the fundamental rights include the full right of movement, participation, and equal treatment under the law.

2. Whether citizenship is acquired at birth depends upon whether birth was in the U.S. or whether one or both of the parents were U.S. citizens.

3. U.S. Const. art. I, § 8, cl. 4.

The declaration of Scott contained three counts: that Sandford had assaulted the plaintiff; that he had assaulted Harriet Scott, his wife; and that he had assaulted Eliza Scott and Lizzie Scott, his children.]

Chief Justice TANEY delivered the opinion of the Court:

* * *

The question is simply this: Can a [N]egro, whose ancestors were imported into this country, and sold as slaves, become a member of the political community formed and brought into existence by the Constitution of the United States, and as such become entitled to all the rights, and privileges, and immunities guarantied by that instrument to the citizen? One of which rights is the privilege of suing in a court of the United States in the cases specified in the Constitution.

It will be observed, that the plea applies to that class of persons only whose ancestors were [N]egroes of the African race, and imported into this country, and sold and held as slaves. The only matter in issue before the court, therefore, is whether the descendants of such slaves, when they shall be emancipated, or who are born of parents who had become free before their birth, are citizens of a State, in the sense in which the word citizen is used in the Constitution of the United States....

The situation of this population was altogether unlike that of the Indian race. The latter, it is true, formed no part of the colonial communities, and never amalgamated with them in social connections or in government. But although they were uncivilized, they were yet a free and independent people, associated together in nations or tribes, and governed by their own laws. Many of these political communities were situated in territories to which the white race claimed the ultimate right of dominion. But that claim was acknowledged to be subject to the right of the Indians to occupy it as long as they thought proper, and neither the English nor colonial Governments claimed or exercised any dominion over the tribe or nation by whom it was occupied, nor claimed the right to the possession of the territory, until the tribe or nation consented to cede it. These Indian Governments were regarded and treated as foreign Governments, as much so as if an ocean had separated the red man from the white; and their freedom has constantly been acknowledged, from the time of the first emigration to the English colonies to the present day, by the different Governments which succeeded each other. Treaties have been negotiated with them, and their alliance sought for in war; and the people who compose these Indian political communities have always been treated as foreigners not living under our Government....

* * *

The words "people of the United States" and "citizens" are synonymous terms, and mean the same thing. They both describe the political body who, according to our republican institutions, form the sovereignty, and who hold the power and conduct the Government through their representatives. They are what we familiarly call the "sovereign people," and every citizen is one of this people, and a constituent member of this sovereignty. The question before us is whether the class of persons described in the plea in abatement compose a portion of this people, and are constituent members of this sovereignty? We think they are not, and that they are not included, and were not intended to be included, under the word "citizens" in the Constitution, and can therefore claim none of the rights and privileges which that instrument provides for and secures to citizens of the United States. On the contrary, they were at that time considered as a subordinate and inferior class of beings, who had been subjugated by the dominant race, and, whether emancipated or not, yet remained subject to their authority, and had no rights or privileges but such as those who held the power and the Government might choose to grant them.

* * *

In discussing this question, we must not confound the rights of citizenship which a State may confer within its own limits, and the rights of citizenship as a member of the Union. It does not by any means follow, because he has all the rights and privileges of a citizen of a State, that he must be a citizen of the United States. He may have all of the rights and privileges of the citizen of a State, and yet not be entitled to the rights and privileges of a citizen in any other State. For, previous to the adoption of the Constitution of the United States, every State had the undoubted right to confer on whomsoever it pleased the character of citizen, and to endow him with all its rights. But this character of course was confined to the boundaries of the State, and gave him no rights or privileges in other States beyond those secured to him by the laws of nations and the comity of States. Nor have the several States surrendered the power of conferring these rights and privileges by adopting the Constitution of the United States. Each State may still confer them upon an alien, or any one it thinks proper, or upon any class or description of persons; yet he would not be a citizen in the sense in which that word is used in the Constitution of the United States, nor entitled to sue as such in one of its courts, nor to the privileges and immunities of a citizen in the other States. The rights which he would acquire would be restricted to the State which gave them. The Constitution has conferred on Congress the right to establish an uniform rule of naturalization, and this right is evidently exclusive, and has always been held by this court to be so. Consequently, no State, since the adoption of the Constitution, can by naturalizing an alien invest him with the rights and privileges secured to a citizen of a State under the Federal Government, although, so far as the State alone was concerned, he would undoubtedly be entitled to the rights of a citizen, and clothed with all the rights and immunities which the Constitution and laws of the State attached to that character.

It is very clear, therefore, that no State can, by any act or law of its own, passed since the adoption of the Constitution, introduce a new member into the political community created by the Constitution of the United States. It cannot make him a member of this community by making him a member of its own. And for the same reason it cannot introduce any person, or description of persons, who were not intended to be embraced in this new political family, which the Constitution brought into existence, but were intended to be excluded from it.

* * *

It is true, every person, and every class and description of persons, who were at the time of the adoption of the Constitution recognised as citizens in the several States, became also citizens of this new political body; but none other; it was formed by them, and for them and their posterity, but for no one else. And the personal rights and privileges guaranteed to citizens of this new sovereignty were intended to embrace those only who were then members of the several State communities, or who should afterwards by birthright or otherwise become members, according to the provisions of the Constitution and the principles on which it was founded. It was the union of those who were at that time members of distinct and separate political communities into one political family, whose power, for certain specified purposes, was to extend over the whole territory of the United States. And it gave to each citizen rights and privileges outside of his State which he did not before possess, and placed him in every other State upon a perfect equality with its own citizens as to rights of person and rights of property; it made him a citizen of the United States.

*   *   *

In the opinion of the court, the legislation and histories of the times, and the language used in the Declaration of Independence, show, that neither the class of persons who had been imported as slaves, nor their descendants, whether they had become free or not, were then acknowledged as a part of the people, nor intended to be included in the general words used in that memorable instrument.

*   *   *

The language of the Declaration of Independence is equally conclusive: It begins by declaring that, "when in the course of human events it becomes necessary for one people to dissolve the political bands which have connected them with another, and to assume, among the powers of the earth, the separate and equal station to which the laws of nature and nature's God entitle them, a decent respect for the opinions of mankind requires that they should declare the causes which impel them to the separation."

It then proceeds to say: "We hold these truths to be self-evident: that all men are created equal; that they are endowed by their Creator with certain unalienable rights; that among them is life, liberty, and the pursuit of happiness; that to secure these rights, Governments are instituted, deriving their just powers from the consent of the governed."

*   *   *

. . . The brief preamble sets forth by whom it was formed, for what purposes, and for whose benefit and protection. It declares that it is formed by the people of the United States; that is to say, by those who were members of the different political communities in the several States; and its great object is declared to be to secure the blessings of liberty to themselves and their posterity. It speaks in general terms of the people of the United States, and of citizens of the several States, when it is providing for the exercise of the powers granted or the privileges secured to the citizen. It does not define what description of persons are intended to be included under these terms, or who shall be regarded as a citizen and one of the people. It uses them as terms so well understood, that no further description or definition was necessary. But there are two clauses in the Constitution which point directly and specifically to the [N]egro race as a separate class of persons, and show clearly that they were not regarded as a portion of the people or citizens of the Government then formed.

*   *   *

. . . [I]t is said that a person may be a citizen, and entitled to that character, although he does not possess all the rights which may belong to other citizens; as, for example, the right to vote, or to hold particular offices; and that yet, when he goes into another State, he is entitled to be recognised there as a citizen, although the State may measure his rights by the rights which it allows to persons of like character or class resident in the State, and refuse to him the full rights of citizenship.

Undoubtedly, a person may be a citizen, that is, a member of the community who form the sovereignty, although he exercises no share of the political power, and is incapacitated from holding particular offices. Women and minors, who form a part of the political family, cannot vote; and when a property qualification is required to vote or hold a particular office, those who have not the necessary qualification cannot vote or hold the office, yet they are citizens.

So, too, a person may be entitled to vote by the law of the State, who is not a citizen even of the State itself. And in some of the States of the Union foreigners not naturalized are allowed to vote. And the State may give the right to free [N]egroes and mulattoes, but that does not make them citizens of the State, and still less of the United States. And the provision in the Constitution giving privileges and immunities in other States, does not apply to them.

Neither does it apply to a person who, being the citizen of a State, migrates to another State. For then he becomes subject to the laws of the State in which he lives, and he is no longer a citizen of the State from which he removed. And the State in which he resides may then, unquestionably, determine his status or condition, and place him among the class of persons who are not recognised as citizens, but belong to an inferior and subject race; and may deny him the privileges and immunities enjoyed by its citizens.

But so far as mere rights of person are concerned, the provision in question is confined to citizens of a State who are temporarily in another State without taking up their residence there. It gives them no political rights in the State, as to voting or holding office, or in any other respect. For a citizen of one State has no right to participate in the government of another. But if he ranks as a citizen in the State to which he belongs, within the meaning of the Constitution of the United States, then, whenever he goes into another State, the Constitution clothes him, as to the rights of person, with all the privileges and immunities which belong to citizens of the State. And if persons of the African race are citizens of a State, and of the United States, they would be entitled to all of these privileges and immunities in every State, and the State could not restrict them; for they would hold these privileges and immunities under the paramount authority of the Federal Government, and its courts would be bound to maintain and enforce them, the Constitution and laws of the State to the contrary notwithstanding. . . .

Concurring opinion of Justice Daniel.

*   *   *

. . . For who, it may be asked, is a citizen? What do the character and status of citizen import? Without fear of contradiction, it does not import the condition of being private property, the subject of individual power and ownership. Upon a principle of etymology alone, the term citizen, as derived from civitas, conveys the ideas of connection or identification with the State or Government, and a participation of its functions. But beyond this, there is not, it is believed, to be found, in the theories of writers on Government, or in any actual experiment heretofore tried, an exposition of the term citizen, which has not been understood as conferring the actual possession and enjoyment, or the perfect right of acquisition and enjoyment, of an entire equality of privileges, civil and political.

Thus Vattel, in the preliminary chapter to his Treatise on the Law of Nations, says: "Nations or States are bodies politic; societies of men united together for the purpose of promoting their mutual safety and advantage, by the joint efforts of their mutual strength. Such a society has her affairs and her interests; she deliberates and takes resolutions in common; thus becoming a moral person, who possesses an understanding and a will peculiar to herself." Again, in the first chapter of the first book of the Treatise just quoted, the same writer, after repeating his definition of a State, proceeds to remark, that, "from the very design that induces a number of men to form a society, which has its common interests and which is to act in concert, it is necessary that there should be established a public authority, to order and direct what is to be done by each, in relation to the end of the association. This political authority is the sovereignty." Again this writer remarks: "The authority of all over each member essentially belongs to the body politic or the State."

By this same writer it is also said: "The citizens are the members of the civil society; bound to this society by certain duties, and subject to its authority; they equally participate in its advantages. The natives, or natural-born citizens, are those born in the country, of parents who are citizens. As society cannot perpetuate itself otherwise than by the children of the citizens, those children naturally follow the condition of their parents, and succeed to all their rights." Again: "I say, to be of the country, it is necessary to be born of a person who is a citizen; for if he be born there of a foreigner, it will be only the place of his birth, and not his country. The inhabitants, as distinguished from citizens, are foreigners who are permitted to settle and stay in the country." (Vattel, Book 1, cap. 19, p. 101.)

*   *   *

It is difficult to conceive by what magic the mere surcease or renunciation of an interest in a subject of property, by an individual possessing that interest, can alter the essential character of that property with respect to persons or communities un-connected with such renunciation. Can it be pretended that an individual in any State, by his single act, though voluntarily or designedly performed, yet without the cooperation or warrant of the Government, perhaps in opposition to its policy or its guaranties, can create a citizen of that State? Much more emphatically may it be asked, how such a result could be accomplished by means wholly extraneous, and entirely foreign to the Government of the State? The argument thus urged must lead to these extraordinary conclusions. It is regarded at once as wholly untenable, and as unsustained by the direct authority or by the analogies of history.

*   *   *

The proud title of Roman citizen, with the immunities and rights incident thereto, and as contradistinguished alike from the condition of conquered subjects or of the lower grades of native domestic residents, was maintained throughout the duration of the republic, and until a late period of the eastern empire, and at last was in effect destroyed less by an elevation of the inferior classes than by the degradation of the free, and the previous possessors of rights and immunities civil and political, to the indiscriminate abasement incident to absolute and simple despotism.

*   *   *

... [C]itizenship was not conferred by the simple fact of emancipation, but that such a result was deduced therefrom in violation of the fundamental principles of free political association; by the exertion of despotic will to establish, under a false and misapplied denomination, one equal and universal slavery; and to effect this result required the exertions of absolute power—of a power both in theory and practice, being in its most plenary acceptation the sovereignty, the state itself—it could not be produced by a less or inferior authority, much less by the will or the act of one who, with reference to civil and political rights, was himself a slave. The master might abdicate or abandon his interest or ownership in his property, but his act would be a mere abandonment. It seems to involve an absurdity to impute to it the investiture of rights which the sovereignty alone had power to impart. There is not perhaps a community in which slavery is recognised, in which the power of emancipation and the modes of its exercise are not regulated by law—that is, by the sovereign authority; and none can fail to comprehend the necessity for such regulation, for the preservation of order, and even of political and social existence.

* * *

Justice McLean dissenting.

* * *

Being born under our Constitution and laws, no naturalization is required, as one of foreign birth, to make him a citizen. The most general and appropriate definition of the term citizen is 'a freeman.' Being a freeman, and having his domicil in a State different from that of the defendant, he is a citizen within the act of Congress, and the courts of the Union are open to him.

It has often been held, that the jurisdiction, as regards parties, can only be exercised between citizens of different States, and that a mere residence is not sufficient; but this has been said to distinguish a temporary from a permanent residence.

* * *

In *Chirae v. Chirae*, (2 Wheat., 261; 4 Curtis, 99,) this court says: 'That the power of naturalization is exclusively in Congress does not seem to be, and certainly ought not to be, controverted.' No person can legally be made a citizen of a State, and consequently a citizen of the United States, of foreign birth, unless he be naturalized under the acts of Congress. Congress has power 'to establish a uniform rule of naturalization.'

It is a power which belongs exclusively to Congress, as intimately connected with our Federal relations. A State may authorize foreigners to hold real estate within its jurisdiction, but it has no power to naturalize foreigners, and give them the rights of citizens. Such a right is opposed to the acts of Congress on the subject of naturalization, and subversive of the Federal powers. I regret that any countenance should be given from this bench to a practice like this in some of the States, which has no warrant in the Constitution.

In the argument, it was said that a colored citizen would not be an agreeable member of society. This is more a matter of taste than of law. Several of the States have admitted persons of color to the right of suffrage, and in this view have recognised them as citizens; and this has been done in the slave as well as the free States. On the question of citizenship, it must be admitted that we have not been very fastidious. Under the late treaty with Mexico, we have made citizens of all grades, combinations, and colors. The same was done in the admission of Louisiana and Florida. No one ever doubted, and no court ever held, that the people of these Territories did not become citizens under the treaty. They have exercised all the rights of citizens, without being naturalized under the acts of Congress.

*　*　*

As to the locality of slavery. The civil law throughout the Continent of Europe, it is believed, without an exception, is, that slavery can exist only within the territory where it is established; and that, if a slave escapes, or is carried beyond such territory, his master cannot reclaim him, unless by virtue of some express stipulation. (Grotius, lib. 2, chap. 15, 5, 1; lib. 10, chap. 10, 2, 1; Wicqueposts Ambassador, lib. 1, p. 418; 4 Martin, 385; Case of the Creole in the House of Lords, 1842; 1 Phillimore on International Law, 316, 335.)

There is no nation in Europe which considers itself bound to return to his master a fugitive slave, under the civil law or the law of nations. On the contrary, the slave is held to be free where there is no treaty obligation, or compact in some other form, to return him to his master. The Roman law did not allow freedom to be sold. An ambassador or any other public functionary could not take a slave to France, Spain, or any other country of Europe, without emancipating him. A number of slaves escaped from a Florida plantation, and were received on board of ship by Admiral Cochrane; by the King's Bench they were held to be free.

*　*　*

I prefer the lights of Madison, Hamilton, and Jay, as a means of construing the Constitution in all its bearings, rather than to look behind that period, into a traffic which is now declared to be piracy, and punished with death by Christian nations. I do not like to draw the sources of our domestic relations from so dark a ground. Our independence was a great epoch in the history of freedom; and while I admit the Government was not made especially for the colored race, yet many of them were citizens of the New England States, and exercised the rights of suffrage when the Constitution was adopted, and it was not doubted by any intelligent person that its tendencies would greatly ameliorate their condition.

*　*　*

Justice Curtis dissenting.

*　*　*

Of this there can be no doubt. At the time of the ratification of the Articles of Confederation, all free native-born inhabitants of the States of New Hampshire, Massachusetts, New York, New Jersey, and North Carolina, though descended from African slaves, were not only citizens of those States, but such of them as had the other necessary qualifications possessed the franchise of electors, on equal terms with other citizens. The Supreme Court of North Carolina, in the case of the State v. Manuel, (4 Dev. and Bat., 20,) has declared the law of that State on this subject, in terms which I believe to be as sound law in the other States I have enumerated, as it was in North Carolina.

"According to the laws of this State," says Judge Gaston, in delivering the opinion of the court, 'all human beings within it, who are not slaves, fall within one of two classes. Whatever distinctions may have existed in the Roman laws between citizens and free inhabitants, they are unknown to our institutions. Before our Revolution, all free persons born within the dominions of the King of Great Britain, whatever their color or complexion, were native-born British subjects—those born out of his allegiance were aliens. Slavery did not exist in England, but it did in the British colonies. Slaves were not in legal parlance persons, but property. The moment the incapacity, the disqualification of slavery, was removed, they became persons, and were then either British subjects, or not British subjects, according as they were or were not born within the allegiance of the British King. Upon the Revolution, no other change took place in the laws of North Carolina than was consequent on the transition from a colony dependent on a European King, to a free and sovereign State. Slaves remained slaves. British subjects in North Carolina became North Carolina freemen. Foreigners, until made members of the State, remained aliens. Slaves, manumitted here, became freemen, and therefore, if born within North Carolina, are citizens of North Carolina, and all free persons born within the State are born citizens of the State. The Constitution extended the elective franchise to every freeman who had arrived at the age of twenty-one, and paid a public tax; and it is a matter of universal notoriety, that, under it, free persons, without regard to color, claimed and exercised the franchise, until it was taken from free men of color a few years since by our amended Constitution.'

* * *

The Constitution of New York gave the right to vote to 'every male inhabitant, who shall have resided,' &c.; making no discrimination between free colored persons and others. (See Con. of N.Y., Art. 2, Rev. Stats. of N.Y., vol. 1, p. 126.) That of New Jersey, to 'all inhabitants of this colony, of full age, who are worth 50 proclamation money, clear estate.'

* * *

The fact that free persons of color were citizens of some of the several States, and the consequence, that this fourth article of the Confederation would have the effect to confer on such persons the privileges and immunities of general citizenship, were not only known to those who framed and adopted those articles, but the evidence is decisive, that the fourth article was intended to have that effect, and that more restricted language, which would have excluded such persons, was deliberately and purposely rejected.

* * *

Among the powers expressly granted to Congress is "the power to establish a uniform rule of naturalization." It is not doubted that this is a power to prescribe a rule for the removal of the disabilities consequent on foreign birth. To hold that it extends further than this, would do violence to the meaning of the term naturalization, fixed in the common law, (Co. Lit., 8 a, 129 a; 2 Ves., sen., 286; 2 Bl. Com., 293,) and in the minds of those who concurred in framing and adopting the Constitution. It was in this sense of conferring on an alien and his issue the rights and powers of a native-born citizen, that it was employed in the Declaration of Independence. It was in this sense it was expounded in the Federalist, (No. 42,) has been understood by Congress, by the Judiciary, (2 Wheat., 259, 269; 3 Wash. R., 313, 322; 12 Wheat., 277,) and by commentators on the Constitution. (3 Story's Com. on Con., 1-3; 1 Rawle on Con., 84-88; 1 Tucker's Bl. Com. App., 255-259.)

It appears, then, that the only power expressly granted to Congress to legislate concerning citizenship, is confined to the removal of the disabilities of foreign birth.

* * *

Undoubtedly, as has already been said, it is a principle of public law, recognised by the Constitution itself, that birth on the soil of a country both creates the duties and confers the rights of citizenship. But it must be remembered, that though the Constitution was to form a Government, and under it the United States of America were to be one united sovereign nation, to which loyalty and obedience on the one side, and from which protection and privileges on the other, would be due, yet the several sovereign States, whose people were then citizens, were not only to continue in existence, but with powers unimpaired, except so far as they were granted by the people to the National Government.

Among the powers unquestionably possessed by the several States, was that of determining what persons should and what persons should not be citizens. It was practicable to confer on the Government of the Union this entire power. It embraced what may, well enough for the purpose now in view, be divided into three parts. First: The power to remove the disabilities of alienage, either by special acts in reference to each individual case, or by establishing a rule of naturalization to be administered and applied by the courts. Second: Determining what persons should enjoy the privileges of citizenship, in respect to the internal affairs of the several States. Third: What native-born persons should be citizens of the United States.

The first-named power, that of establishing a uniform rule of naturalization, was granted; and here the grant, according to its terms, stopped. Construing a Constitution containing only limited and defined powers of government, the argument derived from this definite and restricted power to establish a rule of naturalization, must be admitted to be exceedingly strong. I do not say it is necessarily decisive. It might be controlled by other parts of the Constitution. But when this particular subject of citizenship was under consideration, and, in the clause specially intended to define the extent of power concerning it, we find a particular part of this entire power separated.

Notes

1. *Dred Scott* is included here for its discussion of citizenship. In addition to deciding the question of slavery, this decision was also important for its implication on the power of the national government to legislate. *See* J. Nowak, R. Rotunda, J. Young, Constitutional Law, § 4.4 (3d ed. 1986).

2. One of the present-day implications of citizenship is the right to vote. In earlier times the right to vote was determined by the states and the qualification for voting did not necessarily include citizenship. As seen in the previous case, the right to vote was limited on the basis of gender, race, and property ownership. For an interesting discussion on this topic, *see* Rosberg, *Aliens and Equal Protection: Why Not the Right to Vote*, 75 Mich. L. Rev. 1092 (1977).

3. Increasingly, citizenship carries with it the advantage of securing certain jobs. *See Ambach v. Norwick*, 441 U.S. 68 (1979) (recognizing the political function exception to deny teaching licenses to non-citizens); *Foley v. Connelie*, 435 U.S. 291 (1978) (upholding New York statute denying employment as state troopers to non-citizens); *also see Cabell v. Chavez-Salido*, 454 U.S. 432 (1982); *Matthews v. Diaz*, 426 U.S. 67 (1976) (upholding denial of Medicare benefits to aliens); *see* Rosberg, *The Protection of Aliens from Discriminatory Treatment by the National Government*, 1977 Sup. Ct. Rev. 275. For additional discussion on this subject, see Chapter 14.

B. U.S. Citizenship and Its Acquisition

As a general matter U.S citizenship enures when a person is born in the United States, subject to its jurisdiction, born outside of the United States to one or more parents who are citizens, or by naturalization in the United States. For example, persons in the United States with diplomatic immunity are not subject to the jurisdiction of the United States and therefore their children are not U.S. citizens. The requirements for citizenship contained in the fourteenth amendment are not subject to change by statute but rather are constitutional guarantees.[4] Since the acquisition of citizenship by birth abroad to a U.S. citizen parent is not covered by the fourteenth amendment, it is necessarily left to the Congress whose powers in such matters is plenary. Similarly, Congress' power to regulate other matters relating to the acquisition of citizenship outside of the fourteenth amendment are plenary.[5]

U.S. laws relating to the acquisition of citizenship derive from both the English common law and Roman law principles of *jus soli* and *jus sanguinis*.[6] The *jus soli* principle was derived from the common law rule that the place of a person's birth determined citizenship. *Jus sanguinis* derives from the Roman law rule that citizenship is conferred by relationship or descent. As will be seen in the following discussion, the United States uses a combination of these two principles.

There are a number of guideposts which are helpful in understanding the acquisition of U.S. citizenship. First, legal questions regarding acquisition of U.S. citizenship at birth are governed by the law in effect at the time of the person's birth.[7] Second, the reference in the fourteenth amendment to birth "in the United States" includes birth in the U.S. Territories of the Virgin Islands, Panama Canal Zone, Puerto Rico, and Guam. Third, citizenship of a parent is not sufficient to confer the same status on the child. The rules regarding acquisition of citizenship in the case of a child born outside of the U.S. where one or both parents are U.S. citizens are outlined below.

1. If both parents are U.S. citizens and at least one of the parents has lived in the U.S., then the child is a U.S. citizen.[8]

2. Where one of the parents is a U.S. citizen and the other a "national" of the U.S., then the child born outside of the U.S. and its possessions is a citizen if the U.S. citizen parent has been physically present in the U.S. for a continuous period of at least one year prior to the child's birth.[9]

---

4. *See Afroyim v. Rusk*, 387 U.S. 253, 263 (1967).

5. *See United States v. Wong Kim Ark*, 169 U.S. 649 (1898).

6. The statutory provisions governing citizenship can be found in the Act at section 301. 8 U.S.C. § 1401. In researching questions of citizenship and naturalization, the INS Operation Instructions (OIs) beginning at section 306 should be consulted.

7. *See Montana v. Kennedy*, 366 U.S. 308 (1961).

8. *See* 8 U.S.C. § 1401(c).

9. *See* 8 U.S.C. § 1401(d). The Constitution makes numerous references to citizens of the United States, but makes no reference to the term "nationals." Nationals describes persons

3. If the child is born in an "outlying possession" of the U.S., then the child will be a U.S. citizen if at least one of the parents is a U.S. citizen and has been physically present in the U.S. or a U.S. possession for a continuous period of not less than one year.[10]

4. If the child is born outside the U.S. and outlying possessions, the child will be a citizen even if only one of the parents is a U.S. citizen if that parent has been physically present in the U.S. (or its possessions) for a period totaling ten years. Five of those ten years must have been after the citizen parent reached the age of 14.[11]

5. A child born outside of the U.S. may also acquire U.S. citizenship derivatively through her parent's naturalization.[12]

Rogers v. Bellei
401 U.S. 815 (1971)

Justice BLACKMUN delivered the opinion of the Court.

Under constitutional challenge here, primarily on Fifth Amendment due process grounds, but also on Fourteenth Amendment grounds, is § 301(b) of the Immigration and Nationality Act of June 27, 1952, 66 Stat. 236, 8 U.S.C. § 1401(b).

Section 301(a) of the Act, 8 U.S.C. § 1401(a), defines those persons who "shall be nationals and citizens of the United States at birth." Paragraph (7) of § 301(a) includes in that definition a person born abroad "of parents one of whom is an alien, and the other a citizen of the United States" who has met specified conditions of residence in this country. Section 301(b), however, provides that one who is a citizen at birth under § 301(a)(7) shall lose his citizenship unless, after age 14 and before age 28, he shall come to the United States and be physically present here continuously for at least five years.

The plan thus adopted by Congress with respect to a person of this classification was to bestow citizenship at birth but to take it away upon the person's failure to comply with a post-age-14 and pre-age-28 residential requirement. It is this deprival of citizenship, once bestowed, that is under attack here.

(including both citizens and non-citizens) who owe permanent allegiance to the United States. *See* 8 U.S.C. § 1101(a)(22); *see also* 8 U.S.C. § 1408. A distinction was made between citizen and non-citizen nationals when the United States had more extensive insular possessions whose inhabitants were considered "nationals" of the United States but were not afforded full citizenship rights. A person born in American Samoa or the Swain Islands is a "non-citizen national" with the unrestricted right to enter the U.S. and may obtain U.S. citizenship through relaxed naturalization procedures. *See* O.I. 325.1(a)(2).

10. 8 U.S.C. § 1401(e). The "outlying possession[s]" are defined as the Swain Islands and American Samoa. 8 U.S.C. § 1101(a)(29). Special provision is made granting citizenship to persons born in Puerto Rico after January 13, 1941 and some of those born in Puerto Rico between April 11, 1899 and January 13, 1941. *See* 8 U.S.C. § 1402. Similar provisions exist for persons born in the Panama Canal Zone, Alaska, Hawaii, the Virgin Islands, and Guam.

11. Certain periods of service in the U.S. government, international organizations, or the armed forces will qualify the person for residence purposes. [*See* 8 U.S.C. § 1401(g).]

12. *See* 8 U.S.C. §§ 1431, 1432.

The facts are stipulated:

1. The appellee, Aldo Mario Bellei (hereinafter the plaintiff), was born in Italy on December 22, 1939. He is now 31 years of age.

2. The plaintiff's father has always been a citizen of Italy and never has acquired United States citizenship. The plaintiff's mother, however, was born in Philadelphia in 1915 and thus was a native-born United States citizen. She has retained that citizenship. Moreover, she has fulfilled the requirement of § 301(a)(7) for physical presence in the United States for 10 years, more than five of which were after she attained the age of 14 years. The mother and father were married in Philadelphia on the mother's 24th birthday, March 14, 1939. Nine days later, on March 23, the newlyweds departed for Italy. They have resided there ever since.

3. By Italian law the plaintiff acquired Italian citizenship upon his birth in Italy. He retains that citizenship. He also acquired United States citizenship at his birth under Rev. Stat. § 1993, as amended by the Act of May 24, 1934, § 1, 48 Stat. 797, then in effect. That version of the statute, as does the present one, contained a residence condition applicable to a child born abroad with one alien parent.

4. The plaintiff resided in Italy from the time of his birth until recently. He currently resides in England, where he has employment as an electronics engineer with an organization engaged in the NATO defense program.

5. The plaintiff has come to the United States five different times. He was physically present here during the following periods:

April 27 to July 31, 1948
July 10 to October 5, 1951
June to October 1955
December 18, 1962 to February 13, 1963
May 26 to June 13, 1965.

On the first two occasions, when the plaintiff was a boy of eight and 11, he entered the country with his mother on her United States passport. On the next two occasions, when he was 15 and just under 23, he entered on his own United States passport and was admitted as a citizen of this country. His passport was first issued on June 27, 1952. His last application approval, in August 1961, contains the notation "Warned abt. 301(b)." The plaintiff's United States passport was periodically approved to and including December 22, 1962, his 23d birthday.

6. On his fifth visit to the United States, in 1965, the plaintiff entered with an Italian passport and as an alien visitor. He had just been married and he came with his bride to visit his maternal grandparents.

7. The plaintiff was warned in writing by United States authorities of the impact of § 301(b) when he was in this country in January 1963 and again in November of that year when he was in Italy. Sometime after February 11, 1964, he was orally advised by the American Embassy at Rome that he had lost his United States citizenship pursuant to § 301(b). In November 1966 he was so notified in writing by the American Consul in Rome when the plaintiff requested another American passport.

8. On March 28, 1960, plaintiff registered under the United States Selective Service laws with the American Consul in Rome. At that time he already was 20 years of age. He took in Italy, and passed, a United States Army physical examination.

On December 11, 1963, he was asked to report for induction in the District of Columbia. This induction, however, was then deferred because of his NATO defense program employment. At the time of deferment he was warned of the danger of losing his United States citizenship if he did not comply with the residence requirement. After February 14, 1964, Selective Service advised him by letter that, due to the loss of his citizenship, he had no further obligation for United States military service.

Plaintiff thus concededly failed to comply with the conditions imposed by § 301(b) of the Act.

* * *

The two cases primarily relied upon by the three-judge District Court are, of course, of particular significance here. *Schneider v. Rusk*, 377 U.S. 163 (1964). Mrs. Schneider, a German national by birth, acquired United States citizenship derivatively through her mother's naturalization in the United States. She came to this country as a small child with her parents and remained here until she finished college. She then went abroad for graduate work, was engaged to a German national, married in Germany, and stayed in residence there. She declared that she had no intention of returning to the United States. In 1959, a passport was denied by the State Department on the ground that she had lost her United States citizenship under the specific provisions of § 352(a)(1) of the Immigration and Nationality Act, 8 U.S.C. § 1484(a)(1), by continuous residence for three years in a foreign state of which she was formerly a national. The Court, by a five-to-three vote, held the statute violative of Fifth Amendment due process because there was no like restriction against foreign residence by native-born citizens.

The dissent (Mr. Justice Clark, joined by Justices Harlan and White) based its position on what it regarded as the long acceptance of expatriating naturalized citizens who voluntarily return to residence in their native lands; possible international complications; past decisions approving the power of Congress to enact statutes of that type; and the Constitution's distinctions between native-born and naturalized citizens.

Afroyim v. Rusk, 387 U.S. 253 (1967). Mr. Afroyim, a Polish national by birth, immigrated to the United States at age 19 and after 14 years here acquired United States citizenship by naturalization. Twenty-four years later he went to Israel and voted in a political election there. In 1960 a passport was denied him by the State Department on the ground that he had lost his United States citizenship under the specific provisions of § 349(a)(5) of the Act, 8 U.S.C. § 1481(a)(5), by his foreign voting. The Court, by a five-to-four vote, held that the Fourteenth Amendment's definition of citizenship was significant; that Congress has no "general power, express or implied, to take away an American citizen's citizenship without his assent," 387 U.S., at 257; that Congress' power is to provide a uniform rule of naturalization and, when once exercised with respect to the individual, is exhausted, citing Mr. Chief Justice Marshall's well-known but not uncontroversial dictum in *Osborn v. Bank of the United States*, 9 Wheat. 738 (1824); and that the "undeniable purpose" of the Fourteenth Amendment was to make the recently conferred "citizenship of Negroes permanent and secure" and "to put citizenship beyond the power of any governmental unit to destroy," 387 U.S., at 263. *Perez v. Brownell*, 356 U.S. 44 (1958), a five-to-four holding within the decade and precisely to the opposite effect, was overruled.

The dissent (Mr. Justice Harlan, joined by Justices Clark, Stewart, and White) took issue with the Court's claim of support in the legislative history, would elucidate the Marshall dictum, and observed that the adoption of the Fourteenth Amendment did not deprive Congress of the power to expatriate on permissible grounds consistent with "other relevant commands" of the Constitution.

It is to be observed that both Mrs. Schneider and Mr. Afroyim had resided in this country for years. Each had acquired United States citizenship here by the naturalization process (in one case derivative and in the other direct) prescribed by the National Legislature. Each, in short, was covered explicitly by the Fourteenth Amendment's very first sentence: "All persons born or naturalized in the United States and subject to the jurisdiction thereof, are citizens of the United States and of the State wherein they reside." This, of course, accounts for the Court's emphasis in *Afroyim* upon "Fourteenth Amendment citizenship." 387 U.S., at 262.

*   *   *

The very first Congress, at its Second Session, proceeded to implement its power, under the Constitution's Art. I, § 8, cl. 4, to "establish an uniform Rule of Naturalization" by producing the Act of March 26, 1790, 1 Stat. 103. That statute, among other things, stated,

> And the children of citizens of the United States, that may be born beyond sea, or out of the limits of the United States, shall be considered as natural born citizens: Provided, That the right of citizenship shall not descend to persons whose fathers have never been resident in the United States....

A like provision, with only minor changes in phrasing and with the same emphasis on paternal residence, was continuously in effect through three succeeding naturalization Acts. Act of January 29, 1795, § 3, 1 Stat. 415; Act of April 14, 1802, § 4, 2 Stat. 155; Act of February 10, 1855, c. 71, § 1, 10 Stat. 604. The only significant difference is that the 1790, 1795, and 1802 Acts read retrospectively, while the 1855 Act reads prospectively as well.

*   *   *

The Act of March 2, 1907, § 6, 34 Stat. 1229, provided that all children born abroad who were citizens under Rev. Stat. § 1993 and who continued to reside elsewhere, in order to receive governmental protection, were to record at age 18 their intention to become residents and remain citizens of the United States and were to take the oath of allegiance upon attaining their majority.

The change in § 1993 effected by the Act of May 24, 1934, is reflected in n. 2, supra. This eliminated the theretofore imposed restriction to the paternal parent and prospectively granted citizenship, subject to a five-year continuous residence requirement and an oath, to the foreign-born child of either a citizen father or a citizen mother. This was the form of the statute at the time of plaintiff's birth on December 22, 1939.

The Nationality Act of 1940, § 201, 54 Stat. 1138, contained a similar condition directed to a total of five years' residence in the United States between the ages of 13 and 21.

The Immigration and Nationality Act, by its § 407, 66 Stat. 281, became law in December 1952. Its § 301(b) contains a five years' continuous residence condition (alleviated, with the 1957 amendment, see n. 1, by an allowance for absences less than 12 months in the aggregate) directed to the period between 14 and 28 years of age.

The statutory pattern, therefore, developed and expanded from (a) one established in 1790 and enduring through the Revised Statutes and until 1934, where citizenship was specifically denied to the child born abroad of a father who never resided in the United States; to (b), in 1907, a governmental protection condition for the child born of an American citizen father and residing abroad, dependent upon a declaration of intent and the oath of allegiance at majority; to (c), in 1934, a condition for the child born abroad of one United States citizen parent and one alien parent, of five years' continuous residence in the United States before age 18 and the oath of allegiance within six months after majority; to (d), in 1940, a condition for that child, of five years' residence here, not necessarily continuous, between ages 13 and 21; to (e), in 1952, a condition for that child, of five years' continuous residence here, with allowance, between ages 14 and 28. The application of these respective statutes to a person in plaintiff Bellei's position produces the following results:

1. Not until 1934 would that person have had any conceivable claim to United States citizenship. For more than a century and a half no statute was of assistance. Maternal citizenship afforded no benefit. One may observe, too, that if Mr. Bellei had been born in 1933, instead of in 1939, he would have no claim even today.

2. Despite the recognition of the maternal root by the 1934 amendment, in effect at the time of plaintiff's birth, and despite the continuing liberalization of the succeeding statutes, the plaintiff still would not be entitled to full citizenship because, although his mother met the condition for her residence in the United States, the plaintiff never did fulfill the residential condition imposed for him by any of the statutes.

3. This is so even though the liberalizing 1940 and 1952 statutes, enacted after the plaintiff's birth, were applicable by their terms to one born abroad subsequent to May 24, 1934, the date of the 1934 Act, and were available to the plaintiff. See nn. 5 and 1, supra.

Thus, in summary, it may be said fairly that, for the most part, each successive statute, as applied to a foreign-born child of one United States citizen parent, moved in a direction of leniency for the child. For plaintiff Bellei the statute changed from complete disqualification to citizenship upon a condition subsequent, with that condition being expanded and made less onerous, and, after his birth, with the succeeding liberalizing provisions made applicable to him in replacement of the stricter statute in effect when he was born. The plaintiff nevertheless failed to satisfy any form of the condition.

* * *

Over 70 years ago the Court, in an opinion by Mr. Justice Gray, reviewed and discussed early English statutes relating to rights of inheritance and of citizenship of persons born abroad of parents who were British subjects, United States v. Wong Kim Ark, 169 U.S. 649, 668-671 (1898). The Court concluded that "naturalization by descent" was not a common-law concept but was dependent, instead, upon statutory enactment. The statutes examined were 25 Edw. 3, Stat. 2 (1350); 29 Car. 2, c. 6 (1677); 7 Anne, c. 5, § 3 (1708); 4 Geo. 2, c. 21 (1731); and 13 Geo. 3, c. 21 (1773). Later Mr. Chief Justice Taft, speaking for a unanimous Court, referred to this "very learned and useful opinion of Mr. Justice Gray" and observed "that birth within the limits of the jurisdiction of the Crown, and of the United States, as the successor of the Crown, fixed nationality, and that there could be no change in this rule of law except by statute...." He referred to the cited English statutes and stated, "These statutes applied to the colonies before the War of Independence."

We thus have an acknowledgment that our law in this area follows English concepts with an acceptance of the *jus soli*, that is, that the place of birth governs citizenship status except as modified by statute.

The Constitution as originally adopted contained no definition of United States citizenship. However, it referred to citizenship in general terms and in varying contexts: Art. I, § 2, House; Art. I, § 3, cl. 3, qualifications for Senators; Art. II, § 1, cl. 5, Art. III, § 2, cl. 1, citizenship of the States. And, as has been noted, Art. Article III, § 2, cl. 1, citizenship as affecting judicial power of the United States. And, as has been noted, Article I, § 8, cl. 4, vested Congress with the power to "establish an uniform Rule of Naturalization." The historical reviews in the Afroyim opinions provide an intimation that the Constitution's lack of definitional specificity may well have been attributable in part to the desire to avoid entanglement in the then existing controversy between concepts of state and national citizenship and with the difficult question of the status of Negro slaves.

In any event, although one might have expected a definition of citizenship in constitutional terms, none was embraced in the original document or, indeed, in any of the amendments adopted prior to the War Between the States.

Apart from the passing reference to the "natural born Citizen" in the Constitution's Art. II, § 1, cl. 5, we have, in the Civil Rights Act of April 9, 1866, 14 Stat. 27, the first statutory recognition and concomitant formal definition of the citizenship status of the native born: "[A]ll persons born in the United States and not subject to any foreign power, excluding Indians not taxed, are hereby declared to be citizens of the United States...." This, of course, found immediate expression in the Fourteenth Amendment, adopted in 1868, with expansion to "[a]ll persons born or naturalized in the United States...." As has been noted above, the amendment's "undeniable purpose" was "to make citizenship of Negroes permanent and secure" and not subject to change by mere statute. *Afroyim v. Rusk*, 387 U.S., at 263. *See* H. Flack, Adoption of the Fourteenth Amendment 88-94 (1908). Mr. Justice Gray has observed that the first sentence of the Fourteenth Amendment was "declaratory of existing rights, and affirmative of existing law," so far as the qualifications of being born in the United States, being naturalized in the United States, and being subject to its jurisdiction are concerned. *United States v. Wong Kim Ark*, 169 U.S., at 688. Then follows a most significant sentence:

> But it (the first sentence of the Fourteenth Amendment) has not touched the acquisition of citizenship by being born abroad of American parents; and has left that subject to be regulated, as it had always been, by Congress, in the exercise of the power conferred by the constitution to establish an uniform rule of naturalization.

Thus, at long last, there emerged an express constitutional definition of citizenship. But it was one restricted to the combination of three factors, each and all significant: birth in the United States, naturalization in the United States, and subjection to the jurisdiction of the United States. The definition obviously did not apply to any acquisition of citizenship by being born abroad of an American parent. That type, and any other not covered by the Fourteenth Amendment, was necessarily left to proper congressional action.

The Court has recognized that existence of this power. It has observed, "No alien has the slightest right to naturalization unless all statutory requirements are complied with...." *United States v. Ginsberg*, 243 U.S. 472 (1917). And the Court has specifically recognized the power of Congress not to grant a United States citizen the right to transmit citizenship by descent. As hereinabove noted, persons born abroad, even of United States citizen fathers who, however, acquired American citizenship after the effective date of the 1802 Act, were aliens. Congress responded to that situation only by enacting the 1855 statute. But more than 50 years had expired during which, because of the withholding of that benefit by Congress, citizenship by such descent was not bestowed. Then, too, the Court has recognized that until the 1934 Act the transmission of citizenship to one born abroad was restricted to the child of a qualifying American father, and withheld completely from the child of a United States citizen mother and an alien father. *Montana v. Kennedy, supra.*

Further, it is conceded here both that Congress may withhold citizenship from persons like plaintiff Bellei and may prescribe a period of residence in the United States as a condition precedent without constitutional question.

Thus we have the presence of congressional power in this area, its exercise, and the Court's specific recognition of that power and of its having been properly withheld or properly used in particular situations.

This takes us, then, to the issue of the constitutionality of the exercise of that congressional power when it is used to impose the condition subsequent that confronted plaintiff Bellei. We conclude that its imposition is not unreasonable, arbitrary, or unlawful, and that it withstands the present constitutional challenge.

The Congress has an appropriate concern with problems attendant on dual nationality. *Savorgnan v. United States*, 338 U.S. 491, 500 (1950).... These problems are particularly acute when it is the father who is the child's alien parent and the father chooses to have his family reside in the country of his own nationality. The child is reared, at best, in an atmosphere of divided loyalty. We cannot say that a concern that the child's own primary allegiance is to the country of his birth and of his father's allegiance is either misplaced or arbitrary.

The duality also creates problems for the governments involved. Mr. Justice Brennan recognized this when, concurring in *Kennedy v. Mendoza-Martinez*, 372 U.S. 144, 187 (1963), a case concerning native-born citizens, he observed: "We have recognized the entanglements which may stem from dual allegiance...." In a famous case Mr. Justice Douglas wrote of the problem of dual citizenship. *Tomoya Kawakita v. United States*, 343 U.S. 717, 723-736 (1952). He noted that "[o]ne who has a dual nationality will be subject to claims from both nations, claims which at times may be competing or conflicting," id., at 733; that one with dual nationality cannot turn that status "into a fair-weather citizenship," id., at 736; and that "[c]ircumstances may compel one who has a dual nationality to do acts which otherwise would not be compatible with the obligations of American citizenship," ibid. The District Court in this very case conceded: "It is a legitimate concern of Congress that those who bear American citizenship and receive its benefits have some nexus to the United States."

There are at least intimations in the decided cases that a dual national constitutionally may be required to make an election. In *Perkins v. Elg* (citation omitted), the Court observed that a native-born citizen who had acquired dual nationality during minority through his parents' foreign naturalization abroad did not lose his United States citizenship "provided that on attaining majority he elects to retain that citizenship and to return to the United States to assume its duties." In *Tomoya Kawakita v. United States*, the Court noted that a dual national "under certain circumstances" can be deprived of his American citizenship through an Act of Congress. In *Mandoli v. Acheson*, 344 U.S. 133, 138 (1952), the Court took pains to observe that there was no statute in existence imposing an election upon that dual nationality litigant.

These cases do not flatly say that a duty to elect may be constitutionally imposed. They surely indicate, however, that this is possible, and in *Mandoli* the holding was based on the very absence of a statute and not on any theory of unconstitutionality. And all three of these cases concerned persons who were born here, that is, persons who possessed Fourteenth Amendment citizenship; they did not concern a person, such as plaintiff Bellei, whose claim to citizenship is wholly, and only statutory.

The statutory development outlined in Part IV above, by itself and without reference to the underlying legislative history, committee reports, and other studies, reveals a careful consideration by the Congress of the problems attendant upon dual nationality of a person born abroad. This was purposeful and not accidental. It was legislation structured with care and in the light of then apparent problems.

The solution to the dual nationality dilemma provided by the Congress by way of required residence surely is not unreasonable. It may not be the best that could be devised, but here, too, we cannot say that it is irrational or arbitrary or unfair. Congress first has imposed a condition precedent in that the citizen parent must have been in the United States or its possessions not less than 10 years, at least five of which are after attaining age 14. It then has imposed, as to the foreign-born child himself, the condition subsequent as to residence here.

* * *

We feel that it does not make good constitutional sense, or comport with logic, to say, on the one hand, that Congress may impose a condition precedent, with no constitutional complication, and yet be powerless to impose precisely the same condition subsequent. Any such distinction, of course, must rest, if it has any basis at all, on the asserted "premise that the rights of citizenship of the native born and of the naturalized person are of the same dignity and are coextensive," *Schneider v. Rusk*, 377 U.S., at 165, and on the announcement that Congress has no "power, express or implied, to take away an American citizen's citizenship without his assent." But, as pointed out above, these were utterances bottomed upon Fourteenth Amendment citizenship and that Amendment's direct reference to "persons born or naturalized in the United States." We do not accept the notion that those utterances are now to be judicially extended to citizenship not based upon the Fourteenth Amendment and to make citizenship an absolute. That it is not an absolute is demonstrated by the fact that even Fourteenth Amendment citizenship by naturalization, when unlawfully procured, may be set aside.

A contrary holding would convert what is congressional generosity into something unanticipated and obviously undesired by the Congress. Our National Legislature indulged the foreign-born child with presumptive citizenship subject to subsequent satisfaction of a reasonable residence requirement, rather than to deny him citizenship outright, as concededly it had the power to do, and relegate the child, if he desired

American citizenship, to the more arduous requirements of the usual naturalization process. The plaintiff here would force the Congress to choose between unconditional conferment of United States citizenship at birth and deferment of citizenship until a condition precedent is fulfilled. We are not convinced that the Constitution requires so rigid a choice. If it does, the congressional response seems obvious.

Neither are we persuaded that a condition subsequent in this area impresses one with "second-class citizenship." That cliche is too handy and too easy, and, like most cliches, can be misleading. That the condition subsequent may be beneficial is apparent in the light of the conceded fact that citizenship to this plaintiff was fully deniable. The proper emphasis is on what the statute permits him to gain from the possible starting point of noncitizenship, not on what he claims to lose from the possible starting point of full citizenship to which he has no constitutional right in the first place. His citizenship, while it although conditional, is not "second-class."

The plaintiff is not stateless. His Italian citizenship remains. He has lived practically all his life in Italy. He has never lived in this country; although he has visited here five times, the stipulated facts contain no indication that he ever will live here. He asserts no claim of ignorance or of mistake or even of hardship. He was warned several times of the provision of the statute and of his need to take up residence in the United States prior to his 23d birthday.

We hold that § 301(b) has no constitutional infirmity in its application to plaintiff Bellei. The judgment of the District Court is reversed. Judgment reversed.

Mr. Justice Black, with whom Mr. Justice Douglas and Mr. Justice Marshall join, dissenting.

Notes

1. The statute requiring residency in the U.S. which was being challenged in the *Bellei* case was repealed by the Immigration and Nationality Amendments of 1978, Pub. L. No. 95-432, 92 Stat. 1046.

2. Following the repeal of the physical presence requirement, several courts have interpreted the requirement as having been met where the person was not aware of her claim to citizenship or where the person did not learn of the *claim* before reaching the age of 28. *See Rucker v. Saxbe*, 552 F.2d 998 (3d Cir. 1977); *Ramos-Hernandez v. INS*, 566 F.2d 638 (9th Cir. 1977); O.I. 349.1(c); 301.1(b)(6)(ix).

3. **Passport and Citizenship Claims.** A U.S. passport is prima facie evidence of U.S. citizenship. An individual may make an application for a passport at a U.S. consulate abroad or at designated courthouses and postal facilities throughout the U.S. In any case the passport application is adjudicated by the Department of State and not the INS. Citizenship questions may arise in three different settings. First, an individual may be excluded at the border and may insist on admission as a citizen. Second, one can apply at a U.S. consulate abroad. Third, one can be an applicant for a passport or certificate of citizenship[13] from within the U.S. In the case of a denial of a U.S. passport, administrative review is through the Board of Appellate Review (BAR), whose procedures are governed by 22 C.F.R. § 7.5, and judicial review

---

13. Certificates of citizenship are issued by the INS and passports are issued by the Department of State.

through the district court under 8 U.S.C. § 1401. *See* James, *The Board of Appellate Review of the Department of State: The Right to Appellate Review of Administrative Determinations of Loss of Nationality,* 23 San Diego L. Rev. 261 (1986).

4. *Bellei* highlights both the extent of the congressional power, as well as the analysis required in resolving citizenship questions. In cases of persons born outside of the U.S. of citizen parents, one must review the law in effect at the time of the child's birth.

C. Citizenship through Naturalization

Naturalization is the procedure through which a foreigner may become a citizen of the United States. The statutory provisions dealing with naturalization are found at 8 U.S.C. §§ 1421-1459 and the applicable federal regulations, at 8 C.F.R. § 306 *et seq.*[14] There are three basic requirements for naturalization. First, the person must be a lawful permanent resident of the United States. Second, the permanent resident must have resided continuously in the U.S. (with certain exceptions)[15] for a period of three years if the naturalization applicant obtained permanent residence through marriage to a U.S. citizen and continues to be married to the U.S. citizen spouse at the time of filing the application for naturalization; otherwise the applicant must establish five years of residence. In either case the residence period begins after the person obtains lawful permanent resident status. Third, the law requires that the person have been physically present in the U.S. for at least half of the five years.[16]

The naturalization applicant must have been a resident in the place where the petition is filed for at least three months[17] prior to its filing. This three month residency is a jurisdictional requirement enabling the Attorney General to naturalize the applicant.[18] The applicant must also continue her residence in the U.S. from the date of filing the petition to the time the Attorney General approves citizenship. The applicant must also be a person of good moral character; adhere to the principles of the Constitution; be willing to take an oath of allegiance to the U.S., including the renunciation of citizenship in her native country; understand the English language; and have a knowledge of the workings of the U.S. government and its history.[19]

---

14. For an excellent discussion of the rules governing many citizenship questions, the INS Operating Instructions should be consulted.

15. For the exceptions, *see* 8 U.S.C. § 1427(b).

16. *See* 8 U.S.C. § 1427(c) for some exceptions to this rule.

17. *See* 8 U.S.C. § 1427(a)(1), Sec. 316(a)(1). This change was made by the 1990 Act. The earlier provision contained a six month residency period.

18. The power to confer naturalization was transferred from the courts to the Attorney General in the 1990 Act. *See* 8 U.S.C. § 1421(a), Sec. 310. *But see In Re Duncan,* 713 F.2d 538 (9th Cir. 1983) where the court construed the requirement of residency within the geographic jurisdiction as a venue and not a subject matter jurisdictional provision.

19. Although the applicant must be at least 18 years old, a minor child will become a citizen upon the naturalization of her parents. The child must be residing in the U.S. as a lawful permanent resident and the parent having legal custody must agree to the naturalization. 8 U.S.C. §§ 1431 and 1432.

The requirements listed above are in conformity with international law. International law requires that in order for the acquisition of nationality to be recognized, the state must make the legal bond of nationality accord with the individual's genuine connection with the state.[20]

The Act contains numerous exceptions to the conditions required in the naturalization provisions noted above. The statutory provisions dealing with these special exceptions are found at 8 U.S.C. §§ 1430(b)-(d), 1433, 1435, 1436, and 1438-1440.

From a procedural standpoint, naturalization is a power delegated to the Attorney General by Congress. In the delegation of the naturalization power to the INS, Congress created a different form of review than is found in other areas of immigration law. The initial review of the Attorney General's denial is before the U.S. district court in a *de novo* hearing where the court makes its own findings of fact and conclusions of law.[21] Prior to the 1990 Act, the naturalization power was in the courts, with the INS having an administrative and investigative role.

D. Loss of Citizenship—Expatriation

Expatriation is the voluntary renunciation of citizenship, whether acquired under the guarantees of the fourteenth amendment or by compliance with the statutory requirements. Early questions of the validity of expatriation statutes turned on the issue of whether this power was part of the necessary and proper grant of foreign affairs authority to the federal government or whether citizenship was itself an inalienable right.[22]

In *Afroyim v. Rusk*,[23] the Supreme Court struck down the statutory provision requiring expatriation for voting in a foreign election. Justice Black based his reasoning on grounds that in the absence of a specific grant of power in the Constitution, Congress lacks the power to deprive a citizen of her citizenship without her assent and the fourteenth amendment protects a citizen against the involuntary destruction of her citizenship. Four years later in *Rogers v. Bellei*,[24] the Court distinguished the expatriation of a citizen who obtained his citizenship derivatively through his American mother but failed to return to the United States within the time required by statute, from persons who obtained their citizenship on other grounds.[25] The Court noted that Bellei's citizenship was not obtained under the fourteenth amendment formula but depended entirely on a statutory grant.[26] Justice Black's dissent argued

---

20. *See Nottebohm Case (Liechtenstein v. Guatemala)*, I.C.J. Rep. 4 (1955).

21. *See* 8 U.S.C. § 1421(c), Sec. 310(c). This provision becomes effective for naturalization applications filed after October 30, 1991.

22. *Perez v. Brownell*, 356 U.S. 44 (1958)

23. 387 U.S. 253 (1967).

24. 401 U.S. 815 (1971).

25. The statutory provisions referred to in *Rogers v. Bellei*, 401 U.S. 815 (1971), are no longer in effect.

26. 401 U.S. at 827.

that the fourteenth amendment protects all citizens, and that the requirement for proof of voluntary intent to relinquish should be uniform.

The statutory grounds for expatriation are found at 8 U.S.C. § 1481. The first provision for expatriation upon naturalization in a foreign state was upheld in *Savorgnan v. U.S.*[27] Such a blanket provision is questionable since it does not address the *Afroyim* requirement of specific voluntary intent to relinquish American citizenship. The foreign naturalization of a parent having legal custody of an American child may result in the child's loss of citizenship if the child does not establish residence in the U.S. prior to her twenty-fifth birthday.[28] Note that this scenario is distinguishable from the *Rogers v. Bellei* situation, as it may result in the involuntary loss of citizenship of one "born in the United States."

The taking of an oath of allegiance to a foreign state may, in some situations, constitute a relinquishment of citizenship. However, a mere oath of allegiance for admission to the bar does not entail the transfer of allegiance.[29] The essential act of relinquishment must be voluntary and meaningful.[30] Service in the armed forces of a foreign state without specific authorization of the Secretary of Defense raises the issue of the voluntary nature of such service. If such service is involuntary, it would probably not be construed as an expatriative act. Even if such service is voluntary, however, it is not clear that such foreign military service by itself would be sufficient to demonstrate an intent to relinquish U.S. citizenship.[31]

Performing duties of employment for the government of a foreign state was narrowly construed as an expatriative act after *Afroyim* in the Attorney General's Statement of Interpretation.[32] It is clear, however, that making a *formal* renunciation of nationality before a diplomatic or consular officer of the United States would meet the requirements of an expatriating act and evidence the required specific intent.

All of the foregoing provisions, with the exception of treason, additionally require that the expatriated American take up residence thereafter outside of the United States and its outlying possessions. 8 U.S.C. § 1483(a).

---

27. 338 U.S. 491 (1950).

28. 8 U.S.C. § 1481(a)(1). However, given the requirements of voluntariness in the relinquishment of citizenship and the Court's decision in *Afroyim*, it is not clear how a case such as this would be decided at this time. Even before *Afroyim* there were some circumstances under which a child would not be construed as having lost her citizenship. *See Perri v. Dulles*, 230 F.2d 259 (3d Cir. 1956) (failure to return was out of person's control due to war); *see also Petition of Acchione*, 213 F.2d 845 (3d Cir. 1954); *Rueff v. Brownell*, 116 F. Supp. 298 (D.N.J. 1953) (misadvice by consular officials).

29. *Baker v. Rusk*, 296 F. Supp. 1246 (9th Cir. 1969).

30. A careful review of the cases reveals that only in extremely rare situations is an act viewed as voluntary and meaningful.

31. *See also Nishikawa v. Dulles*, 356 U.S. 129 (1958).

32. 34 Fed. Reg. 1,079 (1969) (reprinted in these materials at page 618). Committing an act of treason or attempting to overthrow the United States might satisfy the *Afroyim* standard of an act that reasonably manifests an individual's intent to transfer or abandon allegiance to the United States. The constitutionality of this provision has not been tested.

Vance v. Terrazas
444 U.S. 252 (1980)

Justice WHITE delivered the opinion of the Court.

Section 349(a)(2) of the Immigration and Nationality Act (Act), 66 Stat. 267, 8 U.S.C. § 1481(a)(2), provides that "a person who is a national of the United States whether by birth or naturalization, shall lose his nationality by . . . taking an oath or making an affirmation or other formal declaration of allegiance to a foreign state or a political subdivision thereof." The Act also provides that the party claiming that such loss of citizenship occurred must "establish such claim by a preponderance of the evidence" and that the voluntariness of the expatriating conduct is rebuttably presumed. § 349(c), as added, 75 Stat. 656, 8 U.S.C. § 1481(c).[1] The issues in this case are whether, in establishing loss of citizenship under § 1481(a)(2), a party must prove an intent to surrender United States citizenship and whether the United States Constitution permits Congress to legislate with respect to expatriation proceedings by providing the standard of proof and the statutory presumption contained in § 1481(c).

Appellee, Laurence J. Terrazas, was born in this country, the son of a Mexican citizen. He thus acquired at birth both United States and Mexican citizenship. In the fall of 1970, while a student in Monterrey, Mexico, and at the age of 22, appellee executed an application for a certificate of Mexican nationality, swearing "adherence, obedience, and submission to the laws and authorities of the Mexican Republic" and "expressly renounc[ing] United States citizenship, as well as any submission, obedience, and loyalty to any foreign government, especially to that of the United States of America, ..." The certificate, which issued upon this application on April 3, 1971, recited that Terrazas had sworn adherence to the United Mexican States and that he "has expressly renounced all rights inherent to any other nationality, as well as all submission, obedience, and loyalty to any foreign government, especially to those which have recognized him as that national." Terrazas read and understood the certificate upon receipt.

---

1. The relevant statutory provisions are §§ 349(a)(2), (c) of the Act, 66 Stat. 267, as amended, 75 Stat. 656, as set forth in 8 U.S.C. § 1481:

(a) From and after the effective date of this chapter a person who is a national of the United States whether by birth or naturalization, shall lose his nationality by—

*   *   *

(2) taking an oath or making an affirmation or other formal declaration of allegiance to a foreign state or a political subdivision thereof;

*   *   *

(c) Whenever the loss of United States nationality is put in issue in any action or proceeding commenced on or after September 26, 1961 under, or by virtue of, the provisions of this chapter or any other Act, the burden shall be upon the person or party claiming that such loss occurred, to establish such claim by a preponderance of the evidence. Except as otherwise provided in subsection (b) of this section, any person who commits or performs, or who has committed or performed, any act of expatriation under the provisions of this chapter or any other Act shall be presumed to have done so voluntarily, but such presumption may be rebutted upon a showing, by a preponderance of the evidence, that the act or acts committed or performed were not done voluntarily.

A few months later, following a discussion with an officer of the United States Consulate in Monterrey, proceedings were instituted to determine whether appellee had lost his United States citizenship by obtaining the certificate of Mexican nationality. Appellee denied that he had, but in December 1971 the Department of State issued a certificate of loss of nationality. The Board of Appellate Review of the Department of State, after a full hearing, affirmed that appellee had voluntarily renounced his United States citizenship. As permitted by § 360(a) of the Act, 66 Stat. 273, 8 U.S.C. § 1503(a), appellee then brought this suit against the Secretary of State for a declaration of his United States nationality. Trial was de novo.

The District Court recognized that the first sentence of the Fourteenth Amendment, as construed in *Afroyim v. Rusk*, 387 U.S. 253, 268 (1967), "protect[s] every citizen of this Nation against a congressional forcible destruction of his citizenship" and that every citizen has "a constitutional right to remain a citizen . . . unless he voluntarily relinquishes that citizenship." A person of dual nationality, the District Court said, "will be held to have expatriated himself from the United States when it is shown that he voluntarily committed an act whereby he unequivocally renounced his allegiance to the United States." Ibid. Specifically, the District Court found that appellee had taken an oath of allegiance to Mexico, that he had "knowingly and understandingly renounced allegiance to the United States in connection with his Application for a Certificate of Mexican Nationality," and that "[t]he taking of an oath of allegiance to Mexico and renunciation of a foreign country [sic] citizenship is a condition precedent under Mexican law to the issuance of a Certificate of Mexican Nationality." Ibid. The District Court concluded that the United States had "proved by a preponderance of the evidence that Laurence J. Terrazas knowingly, understandingly and voluntarily took an oath of allegiance to Mexico, and concurrently renounced allegiance to the United States," and that he had therefore "voluntarily relinquished United States citizenship pursuant to § 349 (a)(2) of the . . . Act."

* * *

The Secretary first urges that the Court of Appeals erred in holding that a "specific intent to renounce U.S. citizenship" must be proved "before the mere taking of an oath of allegiance could result in an individual's expatriation." His position is that he need prove only the voluntary commission of an act, such as swearing allegiance to a foreign nation, that "is so inherently inconsistent with the continued retention of American citizenship that Congress may accord to it its natural consequences, i.e., loss of nationality." We disagree.

* * *

In *Afroyim v. Rusk*, the Court held that § 401(e) of the Nationality Act of 1940, 54 Stat. 1168-1169, which provided that an American citizen "shall lose his nationality by . . . [v]oting in a political election in a foreign state," contravened the Citizenship Clause of the Fourteenth Amendment. Afroyim was a naturalized American citizen who lived in Israel for 10 years. While in that nation, Afroyim voted in a political election. He in consequence was stripped of his United States citizenship. Consistently with *Perez v. Brownell*, 356 U.S. 44 (1958), which had sustained § 401(e), the District Court affirmed the power of Congress to expatriate for such conduct regardless of the citizen's intent to renounce his citizenship. This Court, however, in overruling *Perez*, "reject[ed] the idea . . . that, aside from the Fourteenth Amendment, Congress has any general power, express or implied, to take away an American citizen's citizenship without his assent." The *Afroyim* opinion continued: § 1 of the Fourteenth Amendment is "most reasonably . . . read as defining a citizenship which a citizen keeps unless he voluntarily relinquishes it." 387 U.S., at 262.

The Secretary argues that *Afroyim* does not stand for the proposition that a specific intent to renounce must be shown before citizenship is relinquished. It is enough, he urges, to establish one of the expatriating acts specified in § 1481(a) because Congress has declared each of those acts to be inherently inconsistent with the retention of citizenship. But *Afroyim* emphasized that loss of citizenship requires the individual's "assent," in addition to his voluntary commission of the expatriating act. It is difficult to understand that "assent" to loss of citizenship would mean anything less than an intent to relinquish citizenship, whether the intent is expressed in words or is found as a fair inference from proved conduct. Perez had sustained congressional power to expatriate without regard to the intent of the citizen to surrender his citizenship. *Afroyim* overturned this proposition. It may be, as the Secretary maintains, that a requirement of intent to relinquish citizenship poses substantial difficulties for the Government in performance of its essential task of determining who is a citizen. Nevertheless, the intent of the Fourteenth Amendment, among other things, was to define citizenship; and as interpreted in *Afroyim*, that definition cannot coexist with a congressional power to specify acts that work a renunciation of citizenship even absent an intent to renounce. In the last analysis, expatriation depends on the will of the citizen rather than on the will of Congress and its assessment of his conduct.

*   *   *

In any event, we are confident that it would be inconsistent with *Afroyim* to treat the expatriating acts specified in § 1481(a) as the equivalent of or as conclusive evidence of the indispensable voluntary assent of the citizen. "Of course," any of the specified acts "may be highly persuasive evidence in the particular case of a purpose to abandon citizenship." *Nishikawa v. Dulles*, 356 U.S. 129, 139 (1958) (Black, J., concurring). But the trier of fact must in the end conclude that the citizen not only voluntarily committed the expatriating act prescribed in the statute, but also intended to relinquish his citizenship.

This understanding of *Afroyim* is little different from that expressed by the Attorney General in his 1969 opinion explaining the impact of that case. 42 Op. Atty. Gen. 397. An "act which does not reasonably manifest an individual's transfer or abandonment of allegiance to the United States," the Attorney General said, "cannot be made a basis for expatriation." Voluntary relinquishment is "not confined to a written renunciation," but "can also be manifested by other actions declared expatriative under the [A]ct, if such actions are in derogation of allegiance to this country." Ibid. Even in these cases, however, the issue of intent was deemed by the Attorney General to be open; and, once raised, the burden of proof on the issue was on the party asserting that expatriation had occurred. Ibid. "In each case," the Attorney General stated, "the administrative authorities must make a judgment, based on all the evidence, whether the individual comes within the terms of an expatriation provision and has in fact voluntarily relinquished his citizenship." Id., at 401. It was under this advice, as the Secretary concedes, that the relevant departments of the Government have applied the statute and the Constitution to require an ultimate finding of an intent to expatriate.

Accordingly, in the case now before us, the Board of Appellate Review of the State Department found that appellee not only swore allegiance to Mexico, but also intended to abandon his United States citizenship: "In consideration of the complete record, we view appellant's declaration of allegiance to Mexico and his concurrent repudiation of any and all submission, obedience, and loyalty to the United States as compelling evidence of a specific intent to relinquish his United States citizenship." This same view—that expatriation depends on the will of a citizen as ascertained from his words and conduct—was also reflected in the United States' response to the petition for certiorari in *United States v. Matheson*, 532 F.2d 809, cert. denied, 429 U.S. 823 (1976). Insofar as we are advised, this view remained the official position of the United States until the appeal in this case.

As we have said, *Afroyim* requires that the record support a finding that the expatriating act was accompanied by an intent to terminate United States citizenship. The submission of the United States is inconsistent with this holding, and we are unprepared to reconsider it.

With respect to the principal issues before it, the Court of Appeals held that Congress was without constitutional authority to prescribe the standard of proof in expatriation proceedings and that the proof in such cases must be by clear and convincing evidence rather than by the preponderance standard prescribed in § 1481(c). We are in fundamental disagreement with these conclusions.

In *Nishikawa v. Dulles*, 356 U.S. 129, 78 S. Ct. 612, 2 L. Ed. 2d 659 (1958), an American-born citizen, temporarily in Japan, was drafted into the Japanese Army. The Government later claimed that, under § 401(c) of the Nationality Act of 1940, 54 Stat. 1169, he had expatriated himself by serving in the armed forces of a foreign nation. The Government agreed that expatriation had not occurred if Nishikawa's army service had been involuntary. Nishikawa contended that the Government had to prove that his service was voluntary, while the Government urged that duress was an affirmative defense that Nishikawa had the burden to prove by overcoming the usual presumption of voluntariness. This Court held the presumption unavailable to the Government and required proof of a voluntary expatriating act by clear and convincing evidence.

Section 1481(c) soon followed; its evident aim was to supplant the evidentiary standards prescribed by Nishikawa. The provision "sets up rules of evidence under which the burden of proof to establish loss of citizenship by preponderance of the evidence would rest upon the Government. The presumption of voluntariness, under the proposed rules of evidence, would be rebuttable—similarly—by preponderance of the evidence, ..." H.R. Rep. No. 1086, 87th Cong., 1st Sess., 41, U.S. Code Cong. & Admin. News, p. 2985 (1961).

We see no basis for invalidating the evidentiary prescriptions contained in § 1481(c). *Nishikawa* was not rooted in the Constitution. The Court noted, moreover, that it was acting in the absence of legislative guidance. Nor do we agree with the Court of Appeals that, because under *Afroyim* Congress is constitutionally devoid of power to impose expatriation on a citizen, it is also without power to prescribe the evidentiary standards to govern expatriation proceedings. Although § 1481(c) had been law since 1961, *Afroyim* did not address or advert to that section; surely the Court would have said so had it intended to construe the Constitution to exclude expatriation proceedings from the traditional powers of Congress to prescribe rules of evidence and standards of proof in the federal courts. This power, rooted in the authority of Congress conferred by Art. 1, § 8, cl. 9, of the Constitution to create inferior federal courts, is undoubted and has been frequently noted and sustained. *See*, e.g., *Usery v. Turner Elkhorn Mining Co.*, 428 U.S. 1, 31 (1976).

We note also that the Court's opinion in *Afroyim* was written by Mr. Justice Black who, in concurring in *Nishikawa*, said that the question whether citizenship has been voluntarily relinquished is to be determined on the facts of each case and that Congress could provide rules of evidence for such proceedings. In this respect, we agree with Mr. Justice Black; and since Congress has the express power to enforce the Fourteenth Amendment, it is untenable to hold that it has no power whatsoever to address itself to the manner or means by which Fourteenth Amendment citizenship may be relinquished.

*   *   *

In sum, we hold that in proving expatriation, an expatriating act and an intent to relinquish citizenship must be proved by a preponderance of the evidence. We also hold that when one of the statutory expatriating acts is proved, it is constitutional to presume it to have been a voluntary act until and unless proved otherwise by the actor. If he succeeds, there can be no expatriation. If he fails, the question remains whether on all the evidence the Government has satisfied its burden of proof that the expatriating act was performed with the necessary intent to relinquish citizenship.

The judgment of the Court of Appeals is reversed, and the case is remanded for further proceedings consistent with this opinion.

So ordered.

Mr. Justice Stewart dissents for the reasons stated in Part II of Mr. Justice Brennan's dissenting opinion, which he joins.

Mr. Justice Marshall, concurring in part and dissenting in part.

Expatriation of United States Citizens:
Attorney General's Statement of Interpretation
34 Fed. Reg. 1,079 (1969)

In *Afroyim v. Rusk*, 387 U.S. 253 (1967), the Supreme Court held unconstitutional section 401(e) of the Nationality Act of 1940, which provided that a citizen of the United States shall lose his citizenship by voting in a foreign political election.

The sweeping language of the *Afroyim* opinion raises questions as to its effect on the validity of expatriation provisions, other than those relating to voting, in the Immigration Service and Nationality Act ("the Act") or in former law preserved in section 405(c) of the Act, 8 U.S.C. 1101. These questions are of importance to the Department of State in the administration of the passport laws and to the Immigration and Naturalization in the administration of the immigration laws.

Of course, the ultimate determination of the effect of *Afroyim* is a matter for the courts. The Act empowers the Attorney General, however, to determine *Afroyim*'s effect on the Act for administrative purposes. This Statement of Interpretation will serve to guide both the Department of State and the Immigration and Naturalization Service in the performance of their functions insofar as they involve questions of loss of citizenship.

1. Section 401(e) of the 1940 Act had been ruled constitutional in the Court's earlier decision in *Perez v. Brownell*, 356 U.S. 44 (1958). The majority opinion in *Perez* rejected the argument that "the power of Congress to terminate citizenship depends upon the citizen's assent." 356 U.S. at 61. *Afroyim* expressly overruled *Perez* and held, in agreement with the Chief Justice's dissent in *Perez*, that the Government is without power to deprive a citizen of his citizenship for voting in a foreign election, 387 U.S. at 267. The rule laid down in *Afroyim* is that a U.S. citizen has a constitutional right to remain a citizen "unless he voluntarily relinquishes that citizenship." 387 U.S. at 268.

Afroyim did not expressly address itself to the question of defining what declarations or other conduct can properly be regarded as a "voluntary relinquishment" of citizenship. As a consequence, it did not provide guidelines of sufficient detail to permit me to pass definitively upon the validity of other expatriating provisions of the Act. It did, however, stress the constitutional mandate that no citizen born or naturalized in the United States can be deprived of his citizenship unless he has "voluntarily relinquished" it.

On the question of what constitutes "voluntary relinquishment," we must look to earlier cases in the Supreme Court. Some guidance may be found in earlier opinions of the Justices who joined in the Court's opinion in *Afroyim*. Particularly relevant are the Chief Justice's dissent in *Perez*, which was cited in *Afroyim* with approval, and the concurring opinion of Justice Black (who wrote the opinion of the court in *Afroyim*) in *Nishikawa v. Dulles*, 356 U.S. 129, 138 (1958), decided the same day as *Perez*.

In *Perez*, the Chief Justice stated (356 U.S. at 68-69)

It has long been recognized that citizenship may not only be voluntarily renounced through exercise of the right of expatriation but also by other actions in derogation of undivided allegiance to this country. While the essential qualities of the citizen-state relationship under our Constitution precludes the exercise of governmental power to divest U.S. citizenship, the establishment of that relationship did not impair the principle that conduct of a citizen showing a voluntary transfer of allegiance is an abandonment of citizenship. Nearly all sovereignties recognize that acquisition of foreign nationality ordinarily shows a renunciation of citizenship. Nor is this the only act by which the citizen may show a voluntary abandonment of his citizenship. Any action by which he manifests allegiance to a foreign state may be so inconsistent with the retention of citizenship as to result in loss of that status. In recognizing the consequences of such action, the Government is not taking away U.S. citizenship to implement its general regulatory powers, for, as previously indicated, in my judgment citizenship is immune from divestment under these powers. Rather, the Government is simply giving formal recognition to the inevitable consequences of the citizen's own voluntary surrender of his citizenship.

In *Nishikawa*, Mr. Justice Black stated (356 U.S. at 139):

Of course a citizen has the right to abandon or renounce his citizenship and Congress can enact measures to regulate and affirm such abjuration. But whether citizenship has been voluntarily relinquished is a question to be determined on the facts of each case after a judicial trial in full conformity with the Bill of Rights. Although Congress may provide rules of evidence for such trials, it cannot declare that such equivocal acts as service in a foreign army, participation in a foreign election or desertion from our armed forces establish a conclusive presumption of intention to throw off American nationality....

The foregoing quotations do not come from majority opinions, and *Afroyim* does not adopt them. Indeed, *Afroyim* does not reach the question of whether it may be possible under some circumstances for allegiance to be transferred or abandoned without constituting a voluntary relinquishment of the status of citizenship. That question must await further court decision. Under any reading of *Afroyim*, however, it is clear that an act which does not reasonably manifest an individual's transfer or abandonment of allegiance to the United States cannot be made a basis for expatriation.

2. For administrative purposes, and until the courts have clarified the scope of *Afroyim*, I have concluded that it is the duty of Executive officials to apply the Act on the following basis. "Voluntary relinquishment" of citizenship is not confined to a written renunciation, as under section 345(a)(6) and (7) of the Act, 8 U.S.C. 1431(a)(6) and (7). It can also be manifested by other actions declared expatriative under the Act, if such actions are in derogation of allegiance to this country. Yet even in those cases, *Afroyim* leaves it open to the individual to raise the issue of intent.

Once the issue of intent is raised, the Act makes it clear that the burden of proof is on the party asserting that expatriation has occurred. *Afroyim* suggests that this burden is not easily satisfied by the Government. In the words of Justice Black quoted above from his concurring opinion in *Nishikawa*, the voluntary performance of some acts can "be highly persuasive evidence in the particular case of a purpose to abandon citizenship." Yet some kinds of conduct, though within the proscription of the statute, simply will not be sufficiently probative to support a finding of voluntary expatriation.

For instance, it is obviously not enough to establish a voluntary relinquishment of citizenship that an individual accepts employment as a public school teacher in a foreign country. This I have already decided in the case of a dual national.... A different case would be presented by an individual's acceptance of an important political post in a foreign government.

A similar approach can be taken with respect to service in a foreign army, depending on the particular circumstances involved. Thus, an individual who enlists in the armed forces of an allied country does not necessarily evidence that by so doing he intends to abandon his U.S. citizenship. But it is highly persuasive evidence, to say the least, of an intent to abandon U.S. citizenship if one enlists voluntarily in the armed forces of a foreign government engaged in hostilities against the United States.

The examples mentioned above are, of course, merely illustrative. In each case the administrative authorities must make a judgment, based on all the evidence, whether the individual comes within the terms of an expatriation provision and has in fact voluntarily relinquished his citizenship. In order to avoid conflicts in interpretation between the Department of State and the Immigration and Naturalization Service, these agencies should undertake the consult with each other; if any substantial difference should arise as to any particular type of situation, it should be referred to the Attorney General for resolution.

3. Finally, note should be made as to the scope of this Statement of Interpretation. I believe the *Afroyim* principles reach, and therefore this Statement covers, all of section 349(a) of the Act, section 350, insofar as it relates to dual nationals born or

naturalized in the United States, and section 405(c) insofar as it purports to continue the effectiveness of individual losses of nationality under the similar provisions of sections 401 and 404 of the Nationality Act of 1940.

There are additional considerations relating to dual nationals born abroad which may affect their acquisition and retention of U.S. citizenship. This matter is currently in litigation. Hence this statement does not necessarily apply to loss of U.S. citizenship acquired as a result of birth abroad to a citizen parent or parents.

This statement has no application to a revocation of naturalization unlawfully procured. See *Afroyim v. Rusk*, 387 U.S. at 267, n.23.

Attorney General,
Ramsey Clark.

E. Loss of Citizenship—Denaturalization

Denaturalization is a legal proceeding to revoke the original judicial decree of naturalization. This is a direct attack on the original decree conferring citizenship. It can therefore be brought only against a person who received her citizenship as a result of a judicial decree of naturalization.

Since deprivation of citizenship is a severe loss, the constitutionality of denaturalization and expatriation have often been challenged. The authority to denaturalize has been upheld as an exercise of Congress' constitutional power to establish a uniform rule of naturalization.[33] Under the "necessary and proper" clause, the authority to revoke citizenship that was fraudulently obtained is viewed as a requisite safeguard to maintaining the integrity of the judicial naturalization proceeding.[34] Both the present statute and the 1906 Act provide for the retroactive revocation of naturalization previously granted under 8 U.S.C. § 1451(a). This revocation aspect of the 1906 Act was upheld against a challenge that it was an *ex post facto* law, because it was not punishment to deprive the alien of something to which he was not entitled.[35]

Grounds for Denaturalization

Naturalization may be revoked if it is illegally procured or procured by concealment of a material fact or by willful misrepresentation. 8 U.S.C. § 1451(a). The person's citizenship is revoked after a hearing before a federal judge who finds that citizenship was improperly obtained. Illegal procurement, when separately charged, most often relates to some failure to meet the statutory requirements for naturalization. Examples would be failure to comply with the residence requirements[36] or to take the required oath of allegiance.[37]

Although denaturalization is a civil, not a criminal, proceeding, the government is required to prove the illegality of the original naturalization by "clear, convincing,

---

33. *Knauer v. U.S.*, 328 U.S. 654 (1945).

34. *Id.*

35. *Johannessen v. U.S.*, 225 U.S. 227, 242 (1912).

36. *U.S. v. Parisi*, 24 F. Supp. 414 (D. Md. 1938).

37. *U.S. v. Sremzuch*, 312 F. Supp. 928 (E.D. Wis. 1970).

and unequivocal" evidence. In at least one case where the government was unable to establish to this high degree of certainty that an active Communist failed to meet the requirements of attachment to the United States, the naturalization decree was held to have been improperly revoked.[38]

The consequences for making a misstatement or concealment of fact are so severe that it is generally conceded that the misstatement or concealment must be material.[39] Examples would be concealment of a criminal record,[40] or prior Nazi party membership.[41]

Facts concealed by an applicant in a naturalization proceeding are considered material if disclosure would have justified a denial of citizenship.[42] This is not the sole test, however; concealed facts are also material if their disclosure would have opened to the government an avenue for investigating other facts relating to the applicant's eligibility for naturalization.[43]

Effect of Denaturalization

The effect of a denaturalization decree is to divest the naturalized person of her status as a citizen and to return her to her alien status. The statute provides that the decree "shall be effective as of the original date of the order granting the naturalization."[44] This "relation back" concept raises the question of the effect of denaturalization on other citizens such as spouses and children who may have derived their citizenship from the improperly naturalized alien. The statutory formula is as follows: (a) all derivative citizenship rights are extinguished if the denaturalization was based on actual concealment or misrepresentation;[45] (b) derivative citizenship rights will be extinguished if the denaturalization was based on presumptive fraud unless the affected citizen is residing in the United States at the time of the denaturalization;[46] and (c) the derivative citizenship rights are not affected if the denaturalization was based on illegality.[47]

Fedorenko v. U.S.
449 U.S. 490 (1981)

*   *   *

Petitioner was born in the Ukraine in 1907. He was drafted into the Russian Army in June 1941, but was captured by the Germans shortly thereafter. After being

---

38. *Schneiderman v. U.S.*, 320 U.S. 118 (1943).

39. *Chaunt v. U.S.*, 364 U.S. 350 (1960).

40. *U.S. v. Oddo*, 314 F.2d 115 (2d Cir. 1963).

41. *Klapprott v. U.S.*, 335 U.S. 601 (1949).

42. *Costello v. U. S.*, 365 U.S. 265 (1961).

43. *U.S. v. Galato*, 171 F. Supp. 169 (D. Pa. 1959); *U.S. v. Chandler*, 152 F. Supp. 169 (D. Md. 1957).

44. 8 U.S.C. § 1451(a).

45. 8 U.S.C. § 1451(f)

46. 8 U.S.C. § 1451(f)

47. O.I. 340.3(a)(3).

held in a series of prisoner-of-war camps, petitioner was selected to go to the German camp at Travnicki in Poland, where he received training as a concentration camp guard. In September 1942, he was assigned to the Nazi concentration camp at Treblinka in Poland, where he was issued a uniform and rifle and where he served as a guard during 1942 and 1943. The infamous Treblinka concentration camp was described by the District Court as a "human abattoir" at which several hundred thousand Jewish civilians were murdered.[1] After an armed uprising by the inmates at Treblinka led to the closure of the camp in August 1943, petitioner was transferred to a German labor camp at Danzig and then to the German prisoner-of-war camp at Poelitz, where he continued to serve as an armed guard. Petitioner was eventually transferred to Hamburg where he served as a warehouse guard. Shortly before the British forces entered that city in 1945, petitioner discarded his uniform and was able to pass as a civilian. For the next four years, he worked in Germany as a laborer.

In 1948, Congress enacted the Displaced Persons Act (DPA or Act), 62 Stat. 1009, to enable European refugees driven from their homelands by the war to emigrate to the United States without regard to traditional immigration quotas. The Act's definition of "displaced persons" eligible for immigration to this country specifically excluded individuals who had "assisted the enemy in persecuting civil[ians]" or had "voluntarily assisted the enemy forces ... in their operations...." Section 10 of the DPA, 62 Stat. 1013, placed the burden of proving eligibility under the Act on the person seeking admission and provided that "[a]ny person who shall willfully make a misrepresentation for the purpose of gaining admission into the United States as an eligible displaced person shall thereafter not be admissible into the United States." The Act established an elaborate system for determining eligibility for displaced person status. Each applicant was first interviewed by representatives of the International Refugee Organization of the United Nations (IRO) who ascertained that the person was a refugee or displaced person. The applicant was then interviewed by an official of the Displaced Persons Commission, who made a preliminary determination about his eligibility under the DPA. The final decision was made by one of several State Department vice consuls, who were specially trained for the task and sent to Europe to administer the Act. Thereafter, the application was reviewed by officials of the Immigration and Naturalization Service (INS) to make sure that the applicant was admissible into the United States under the standard immigration laws.

In October 1949, petitioner applied for admission to the United States as a displaced person. Petitioner falsified his visa application by lying about his wartime activities. He told the investigators from the Displaced Persons Commission that he had been a farmer in Sarny, Poland, from 1937 until March 1942, and that he had then been deported to Germany and forced to work in a factory in Poelitz until the end of the war, when he fled to Hamburg. Petitioner told the same story to the vice consul who reviewed his case and he signed a sworn statement containing these false

---

1. Historians estimate that some 800,000 people were murdered at Treblinka. *See* L. Dawidowicz, The War Against the Jews, 1933-1945, p. 149 (1975); R. Hilberg, The Destruction of the European Jews 572 (1978). The District Court described Treblinka in this manner:

It contained only living facilities for the SS and the persons working there. The thousands who arrived daily on the trains had no need for barracks or mess halls: they would be dead before nightfall. It was operated with a barbarous methodology—brutally efficient—and such camps surely fill one of the darkest chapters in the annals of human existence, certainly the darkest in that which we call Western civilization. 455 F. Supp. 893, 901, n.12 (S.D. Fla.

representations as part of his application for a DPA visa. Petitioner's false statements were not discovered at the time and he was issued a DPA visa, and sailed to the United States where he was admitted for permanent residence. He took up residence in Connecticut and for three decades led an uneventful and law-abiding life as a factory worker.

In 1969, petitioner applied for naturalization at the INS office in Hartford, Conn. Petitioner did not disclose his wartime service as a concentration camp armed guard in his application, and he did not mention it in his sworn testimony to INS naturalization examiners. The INS examiners took petitioner's visa papers at face value and recommended that his citizenship application be granted. On this recommendation, the Superior Court of New Haven County granted his petition for naturalization and he became an American citizen on April 23, 1970.

* * *

Seven years later, after petitioner had moved to Miami Beach and become a resident of Florida, the Government filed this action in the United States District Court for the Southern District of Florida to revoke petitioner's citizenship. The complaint alleged that petitioner should have been deemed ineligible for a DPA visa because he had served as an armed guard at Treblinka and had committed crimes or atrocities against inmates of the camp because they were Jewish. The Government charged that petitioner had willfully concealed this information both in applying for a DPA visa and in applying for citizenship, and that therefore petitioner had procured his naturalization illegally or by willfully misrepresenting material facts.

* * *

On the one hand, our decisions have recognized that the right to acquire American citizenship is a precious one and that once citizenship has been acquired, its loss can have severe and unsettling consequences. *See Costello v. United States*, 365 U.S. 265, 269 (1961); *Chaunt v. United States*, 364 U.S., at 353. For these reasons, we have held that the Government "carries a heavy burden of proof in a proceeding to divest a naturalized citizen of his citizenship." The evidence justifying revocation of citizenship must be "clear, unequivocal, and convincing" and not leave "the issue in doubt." *Schneiderman v. United States*, 320 U.S. at 125 [quoting *Maxwell Land-Grant Case*]. Any less exacting standard would be inconsistent with the importance of the right that is at stake in a denaturalization proceeding. And in reviewing denaturalization cases, we have carefully examined the record ourselves.

At the same time, our cases have also recognized that there must be strict compliance with all the congressionally imposed prerequisites to the acquisition of citizenship. Failure to comply with any of these conditions renders the certificate of citizenship "illegally procured," and naturalization that is unlawfully procured can be set aside. 8 U.S.C. § 1451(a); *Afroyim v. Rusk*, 387 U.S. 253, 267, n.23 (1967). As we explained in one of these prior decisions:

> An alien who seeks political rights as a member of this Nation can rightfully obtain them only upon terms and conditions specified by Congress....

* * *

No alien has the slightest right to naturalization unless all statutory requirements are complied with; and every certificate of citizenship must be treated as granted upon condition that the government may challenge it ... and demand its cancellation unless issued in accordance with such requirements. *United States v. Ginsberg*, supra, at 474-475.

This judicial insistence on strict compliance with the statutory conditions precedent to naturalization is simply an acknowledgment of the fact that Congress alone has the constitutional authority to prescribe rules for naturalization, and the courts' task is to assure compliance with the particular prerequisites to the acquisition of United States citizenship by naturalization legislated to safeguard the integrity of this "priceless treasure." *Johnson v. Eisentrager*, 339 U.S. 763, 791 (1950) (Black, J., dissenting).

Thus, what may at first glance appear to be two inconsistent lines of cases actually reflect our consistent recognition of the importance of the issues that are at stake—for the citizen as well as the Government—in a denaturalization proceeding. With this in mind, we turn to petitioner's contention that the Court of Appeals erred in reversing the judgment of the District Court.

*　　*　　*

Petitioner does not and, indeed, cannot challenge the Government's contention that he willfully misrepresented facts about his wartime activities when he applied for a DPA visa in 1949. Petitioner admitted at trial that he "willingly" gave false information in connection with his application for a DPA visa so as to avoid the possibility of repatriation to the Soviet Union. The District Court specifically noted that there was no dispute that petitioner "lied" in his application. Thus, petitioner falls within the plain language of the DPA's admonition that "[a]ny person who shall willfully make a misrepresentation for the purposes of gaining admission into the United States as an eligible displaced person shall thereafter not be admissible into the United States." 62 Stat. 1013. . . .

At the outset, we must determine the proper standard to be applied in judging whether petitioner's false statements were material. Both petitioner and the Government have assumed, as did the District Court and the Court of Appeals, that materiality under the above-quoted provision of the DPA is governed by the standard announced in *Chaunt v. United States*. But we do not find it so obvious that the *Chaunt* test is applicable here. In that case, the Government charged that Chaunt had procured his citizenship by concealing and misrepresenting his record of arrests in the United States in his application for citizenship, and that the arrest record was a "material" fact within the meaning of the denaturalization statute. Thus, the materiality standard announced in that case pertained to false statements in applications for citizenship, and the arrests that Chaunt failed to disclose all took place after he came to this country. The case presented no question concerning the lawfulness of his initial entry into the United States.

*　　*　　*

Section 2(b) of the DPA, 62 Stat. 1009, by incorporating the definition of "[p]ersons who will not be [considered displaced persons]" contained in the Constitution of the IRO, see n.3, supra, specifically provided that individuals who "assisted the enemy in persecuting civil[ians]" were ineligible for visas under the Act. Jenkins testified that petitioner's service as an armed guard at a concentration camp—whether voluntary or not—made him ineligible for a visa under this provision. Jenkins' testimony was based on his firsthand experience as a vice consul in Germany after the war reviewing DPA visa applications. Jenkins also testified that the practice of the vice consuls was to circulate among the other vice consuls the case files of any visa applicant who was shown to have been a concentration camp armed guard. Thus, Jenkins and the other vice consuls were particularly well informed about the practice concerning the eligibility of former camp guards for DPA visas. The District Court evidently agreed that a literal interpretation of the statute would confirm the accuracy of Jenkins' testimony. But by construing § 2(a) as only excluding individuals who voluntarily assisted in the persecution of civilians, the District Court was able to ignore Jenkins' uncontroverted testimony about how the Act was interpreted by the officials who administered it.

*   *   *

The Court of Appeals evidently accepted the District Court's construction of the Act since it agreed that the Government had failed to show that petitioner was ineligible for a DPA visa. Because we are unable to find any basis for an "involuntary assistance" exception in the language of § 2(a), we conclude that the District Court's construction of the Act was incorrect. The plain language of the Act mandates precisely the literal interpretation that the District Court rejected: an individual's service as a concentration camp armed guard—whether voluntary or involuntary made him ineligible for a visa. That Congress was perfectly capable of adopting a "voluntariness" limitation where it felt that one was necessary is plain from comparing § 2(a) with § 2(b), which excludes only those individuals who "voluntarily assisted the enemy forces . . . in their operations. . . ." Under traditional principles of statutory construction, the deliberate omission of the word "voluntary" from § 2(a) compels the conclusion that the statute made all those who assisted in the persecution of civilians ineligible for visas. *See National Railroad Passenger Corp. v. National Assn. of Railroad Passengers*, 414 U.S. 453, 458 (1974). As this Court has previously stated: "We are not at liberty to imply a condition which is opposed to the explicit terms of the statute. . . . To [so] hold . . . is not to construe the Act but to amend it." *Detroit Trust Co. v. The Thomas Barlum*, 293 U.S. 21, 38 (1934). Thus, the plain language of the statute and Jenkins' uncontradicted and unequivocal testimony leave no room for doubt that if petitioner had disclosed the fact that he had been an armed guard at Treblinka, he would have been found ineligible for a visa under the DPA. This being so, we must conclude that petitioner's false statements about his wartime activities were "willfu[l] [and material] misrepresentation[s] [made] for the purpose of gaining admission into the United States as an eligible displaced person." Under the express terms of the statute, petitioner was "thereafter not . . . admissible into the United States."

Our conclusion that petitioner was, as a matter of law, ineligible for a visa under the DPA makes the resolution of this case fairly straightforward. As noted our cases have established that a naturalized citizen's failure to comply with the statutory prerequisites for naturalization renders his certificate of citizenship revocable as "illegally procured" under 8 U.S.C. § 1451(a).

*   *   *

We agree with the Court of Appeals that district courts lack equitable discretion to refrain from entering a judgment of denaturalization against a naturalized citizen whose citizenship was procured illegally or by willful misrepresentation of material facts. Petitioner is correct in noting that courts necessarily and properly exercise discretion in characterizing certain facts while determining whether an applicant for citizenship meets some of the requirements for naturalization. But that limited discretion does not include the authority to excuse illegal or fraudulent procurement of citizenship. As the Court of Appeals stated: "Once it has been determined that a person does not qualify for citizenship, . . . the district court has no discretion to ignore the defect and grant citizenship." By the same token, once a district court determines that the Government has met its burden of proving that a naturalized citizen obtained his citizenship illegally or by willful misrepresentation, it has no discretion to excuse the conduct. Indeed, contrary to the District Court's suggestion, see supra, at 746, this issue has been settled by prior decisions of this Court. In case after case, we have rejected lower court efforts to moderate or otherwise avoid the statutory mandate of Congress in denaturalization proceedings. For example, in *United States v. Ness*, 245 U.S. 319 (1917), we ordered the denaturalization of an individual who "possessed the personal qualifications which entitled aliens to admission and to citizenship," but who had failed to file a certificate of arrival as required by statute. We explained that there was "no power . . . vested in the naturalization court to dispense with" this requirement. Id., at 324, 38 S. Ct., at 120. We repeat here what we said in one of these earlier cases:

> An alien who seeks political rights as a member of this Nation can rightfully obtain them only upon the terms and conditions specified by Congress. Courts are without authority to sanction changes or modifications; their duty is rigidly to enforce the legislative will in respect of a matter so vital to the public welfare. *United States v. Ginsberg*, 243 U.S., at 474-475.

Notes

1. In *Kungys v. U.S.*, 485 U.S. 759 (1988), the Court elaborated on the meaning of material misrepresentation. *Kungys* involved the denaturalization of Juoazas Kungys, who had been accused of participating in the extermination of 2,000 Lithuanian civilians, mostly Jewish, in 1941. Kungys had applied for and received an immigrant visa as a displaced person which he used for his admission to the U.S. in 1948. He was naturalized in 1954. The Office of Special Investigations instituted denaturalization proceedings in 1982 charging Kungys with particpation in the above described atrocities, and with having misrepresented his date and place of birth, wartime occupation and residences in his applications for his immigrant visa and for naturalization.

Justice Kennedy did not participate in the decision and five separate opinions, including a dissent by Justice White, were filed. Five Justices joined in that portion of the decision adopting a *natural tendency* test, or whether the

> misrepresentation or concealment . . . had a natural tendency to affect the official decision. The official decision in question, of course, is whether the applicant meets the requirements for citizenship. This test must be met, of course, by evidence that is clear, unequivocal, and convincing. 485 U.S. at 771.

The Court held that the test had not been met in this case.

2. The *Kungys* Court also held that 8 U.S.C. § 1101(f)(6) precludes good moral character "one who has given false testimony for the purpose of obtaining any benefits under" the Act, irrespective of the materiality of the statement. As the Court stated, "it denominates a person to be of bad moral character on account of having given

false testimony if he has told even the most immaterial of lies with the subjective intent of obtaining immigration or naturalization benefits." 485 U.S. 780.

3. Ultimately, on remand, the *Kungys* case was settled. Kungys was denaturalized with the condition that he be allowed to remain in the U.S. as a permanent resident for the rest of his life. *See* Prinz, *Kungys and Materiality*, Immigration and Nationality Law 1989 Annual Symposium: Advanced Topics 154 (1989).

References

Abramson, *United States Loss of Citizenship Law After Terrazas: Decisions of the Board of Appellate Review*, N.Y.U. J. Int'l L. & Pol'y 829 (1984)

Citizenship: Denaturalization; Diminished Protection of Naturalized Citizens Citizenship in De-Naturalization Proceedings, 14 Tex Int'l L. J. 453 (1979)

Expatriation—A Concept in Need of Clarification, 8 U.C. Davis L. Rev. 375 (1975)

The Expatriation Act of 1954, 64 Yale L.J. 1164 (1955)

Materiality Standard in Denaturalization Cases: Concealment by Naturalized Citizen of Service as Nazi Death Camp Guard, 12 Law Am. 757 (1980)

Rosberg, *Alien and Equal Protection: Why Not the Right to Vote?*, 75 Mich. L. Rev. 1092 (1977)

P. Schuck & R. Smith, Citizenship Without Consent: Illegal Aliens in the American Polity (1985)

Ulman, *Nationality, Expatriation and Statelessness*, 25 Admin. L. Rev. 113 (1973)

Index to Appendix

Naturalization

CITIZENSHIP

8 U.S.C. § 1503(a) Proceedings for declaration of United States nationality

If any person who is within the United States claims a right or privilege as a national of the United States and is denied such right or privilege by any department or independent agency, or official thereof, upon the ground that he is not a national of the United States, such person may institute an action under the provisions of section 2201 of title 28 against the head of such department or independent agency for a judgment declaring him to be a national of the United States, except that no such action may be instituted in any case if the issue of such person's status as a national of the United States (1) arose by reason of, or in connection with, any exclusion proceeding under the provisions of this chapter or any other act, or (2) is in issue in any such exclusion proceeding. An action under this subsection may be instituted only within five years after the final administrative denial of such right or privilege and shall be filed in the district court of the United States for the district in which such person resides or claims a residence, and jurisdiction over such officials in such cases is conferred upon those courts.

Nationals and citizens of United States at birth
8 U.S.C. § 1401, Sec. 301

The following shall be nationals and citizens of the United States at birth:

(a) a person born in the United States, and subject to the jurisdiction thereof;

(b) a person born in the United States to a member of an Indian, Eskimo, Aleutian, or other aboriginal tribe: Provided, That the granting of citizenship under this subsection shall not in any manner impair or otherwise affect the right of such person to tribal or other property;

(c) a person born outside of the United States and its outlying possessions of parents both of whom are citizens of the United States and one of whom has had a residence in the United States or one of its outlying possessions, prior to the birth of such person;

(d) a person born outside of the United States and its outlying possessions of parents one of whom is a citizen of the United States who has been physically present in the United States or one of its outlying possessions for a continuous period of one year prior to the birth of such person, and the other of whom is a national, but not a citizen of the United States;

(e) a person born in an outlying possession of the United States of parents one of whom is a citizen of the United States who has been physically present in the United States or one of its outlying possessions for a continuous period of one year at any time prior to the birth of such person;

(f) a person of unknown parentage found in the United States while under the age of five years, until shown, prior to his attaining the age of twenty-one years, not to have been born in the United States;

(g) a person born outside the geographical limits of the United States and its outlying possessions of parents one of whom is an alien, and the other a citizen of the United States who, prior to the birth of such person, was physically present in the United States or its outlying possessions for a period or periods totaling not less than five years, at least two of which were after attaining the age of fourteen years: Provided, That any periods of honorable service in the Armed Forces of the United States, or periods of employment with the United States Government or with an international organization as that term is defined in section 288 of title 22 by such citizen parent, or any periods during which such citizen parent is physically present abroad as the dependent unmarried son or daughter and a member of the household of a person (A) honorably serving with the Armed Forces of the United States, or (B) employed by the United States Government or an international organization as defined in section 288 of title 22, may be included in order to satisfy the physical-presence requirement of this paragraph. This proviso shall be applicable to persons born on or after December 24, 1952, to the same extent as if it had become effective in its present form on that date.

Persons born in Puerto Rico on or after April 11, 1899
8 U.S.C. § 1402, Sec. 302

All persons born in Puerto Rico on or after April 11, 1899, and prior to January 13, 1941, subject to the jurisdiction of the United States, residing on January 13, 1941, in Puerto Rico or other territory over which the United States exercises rights of sovereignty and not citizens of the United States under any other Act, are declared to be citizens of the United States as of January 13, 1941. All persons born in Puerto Rico on or after January 13, 1941, and subject to the jurisdiction of the United States, are citizens of the United States at birth.

Persons born in the Canal Zone or Republic of Panama
on or after February 26, 1904
8 U.S.C. § 1403, Sec. 303

(a) Any person born in the Canal Zone on or after February 26, 1904, and whether before or after the effective date of this chapter, whose father or mother or both at the time of the birth of such person was or is a citizen of the United States, is declared to be a citizen of the United States.

(b) Any person born in the Republic of Panama on or after February 26, 1904, and whether before or after the effective date of this chapter, whose father or mother or both at the time of the birth of such person was or is a citizen of the United States employed by the Government of the United States or by the Panama Railroad Company, or its successor in title, is declared to be a citizen of the United States.

Persons born in Alaska on or after March 30, 1867
8 U.S.C. § 1404, Sec. 304

A person born in Alaska on or after March 30, 1867, except a non-citizen Indian, is a citizen of the United States at birth. A non-citizen Indian born in Alaska on or after March 30, 1867, and prior to June 2, 1924, is declared to be a citizen of the United States as of June 2, 1924. An Indian born in Alaska on or after June 2, 1924, is a citizen of the United States at birth.

Persons born in Hawaii
8 U.S.C. § 1405, Sec. 305

A person born in Hawaii on or after August 12, 1898, and before April 30, 1900, is declared to be a citizen of the United States as of April 30, 1900. A person born in Hawaii on or after April 30, 1900, is a citizen of the United States at birth. A person who was a citizen of the Republic of Hawaii on August 12, 1898, is declared to be a citizen of the United States as of April 30, 1900.

Persons living in and born in the Virgin Islands
8 U.S.C. § 1406, Sec. 306

(a) The following persons and their children born subsequent to January 17, 1917, and prior to February 25, 1927, are declared to be citizens of the United States as of February 25, 1927:

(1) All former Danish citizens who, on January 17, 1917, resided in the Virgin Islands of the United States, and were residing in those islands or in the United States or Puerto Rico on February 25, 1927, and who did not make the declaration required to preserve their Danish citizenship by article 6 of the treaty entered into on August 4, 1916, between the United States and Denmark, or who, having made such a declaration have heretofore renounced or may hereafter renounce it by a declaration before a court of record;

(2) All natives of the Virgin Islands of the United States who, on January 17, 1917, resided in those islands, and were residing in those islands or in the United States or Puerto Rico on February 25, 1927, and who were not on February 25, 1927, citizens or subjects of any foreign country;

(3) All natives of the Virgin Islands of the United States who, on January 17, 1917, resided in the United States, and were residing in those islands on February 25, 1927, and who were not on February 25, 1927, citizens or subjects of any foreign country; and

(4) All natives of the Virgin Islands of the United States who, on June 28, 1932, were residing in continental United States, the Virgin Islands of the United States, Puerto Rico, the Canal Zone, or any other insular possession or territory of the United States, and who, on June 28, 1932, were not citizens or subjects of any foreign country, regardless of their place of residence on January 17, 1917.

(b) All persons born in the Virgin Islands of the United States on or after January 17, 1917, and prior to February 25, 1927, and subject to the jurisdiction of the United States are declared to be citizens of the United States as of February 25, 1927; and all persons born in those islands on or after February 25, 1927, and subject to the jurisdiction of the United States, are declared to be citizens of the United States at birth.

Persons living in and born in Guam
8 U.S.C. § 1407, Sec. 307

(a) The following persons, and their children born after April 11, 1899, are declared to be citizens of the United States as of August 1, 1950, if they were residing on August 1, 1950, on the island of Guam or other territory over which the United States exercises rights of sovereignty:

(1) All inhabitants of the island of Guam on April 11, 1899, including those temporarily absent from the island on that date, who were Spanish subjects, who after that date continued to reside in Guam or other territory over which the United States exercises sovereignty, and who have taken no affirmative steps to preserve or acquire foreign nationality; and

(2) All persons born in the island of Guam who resided in Guam on April 11, 1899, including those temporarily absent from the island on that date, who after that date continued to reside in Guam or other territory over which the United States exercises sovereignty, and who have taken no affirmative steps to preserve or acquire foreign nationality.

(b) All persons born in the island of Guam on or after April 11, 1899 (whether before or after August 1, 1950) subject to the jurisdiction of the United States, are declared to be citizens of the United States: Provided, That in the case of any person born before August 1, 1950, he has taken no affirmative steps to preserve or acquire foreign nationality.

(c) Any person hereinbefore described who is a citizen or national of a country other than the United States and desires to retain his present political status shall have made, prior to August 1, 1952, a declaration under oath of such desire, said declaration to be in form and executed in the manner prescribed by regulations. From and after the making of such a declaration any such person shall be held not to be a national of the United States by virtue of this chapter.

Nationals but not citizens of the United States at birth
8 U.S.C. § 1408, Sec. 308

Unless otherwise provided in section 1401 of this title, the following shall be nationals, but not citizens, of the United States at birth:

(1) A person born in an outlying possession of the United States on or after the date of formal acquisition of such possession;

(2) A person born outside the United States and its outlying possessions of parents both of whom are nationals, but not citizens, of the United States, and have had a residence in the United States, or one of its outlying possessions prior to the birth of such person; and

(3) A person of unknown parentage found in an outlying possession of the United States while under the age of five years, until shown, prior to his attaining the age of twenty-one years, not to have been born in such outlying possession.

(4) A person born outside the United States and its outlying possessions of parents one of whom is an alien, and the other a national, but not a citizen, of the United

States who, prior to the birth of such person, was physically present in the United States or its outlying possessions for a period or periods totaling not less than seven years in any continuous period of ten years—

> (A) during which the national parent was not outside the United States or its outlying possessions for a continuous period of more than one year, and

> (B) at least five years of which were after attaining the age of fourteen years.

The proviso of section 1401(g) of this title shall apply to the national parent under this paragraph in the same manner as it applies to the citizen parent under that section.

Children born out of wedlock
8 U.S.C. § 1409, Sec. 309

(a) The provisions of paragraphs (c), (d), (e), and (g) of section 1401 of this title, and of paragraph (2) of section 1408, of this title shall apply as of the date of birth to a child born out of wedlock if a blood relationship between the child and the father is established by clear and convincing evidence, provided the father had the nationality of the United States at the time of the child's birth, the father unless deceased has agreed in writing to provide financial support for the child until such child reaches the age of eighteen years and if, while such child is under the age of eighteen years, (1) such child is legitimated under the law of the child's residence or domicile, or (2) the father acknowledges paternity of the child in writing under oath, or (3) paternity of the child is established by adjudication of a competent court.

(b) Except as otherwise provided in section 405 of this Act, the provisions of section 1401(g) of this title shall apply to a child born out of wedlock on or after January 13, 1941, and prior to the effective date of this chapter, as of the date of birth, if the paternity of such child is established before or after the effective date of this chapter and while such child is under the age of twenty-one years by legitimation.

(c) Notwithstanding the provision of subsection (a) of this section, a person born, on or after the effective date of this chapter, outside the United States and out of wedlock shall be held to have acquired at birth the nationality status of his mother, if the mother had the nationality of the United States at the time of such person's birth, and if the mother had previously been physically present in the United States or one of its outlying possessions for a continuous period of one year.

NATURALIZATION

Jurisdiction to Naturalize
8 U.S.C. § 1421, Sec. 310

(a) The sole authority to naturalize persons as citizens of the United States is conferred upon the Attorney General.

(b) An applicant for naturalization may choose to have the oath of allegiance under section 1448(a) of this title administered by the Attorney General or by any District Court of the United States for any State or by any court of record in any State having a seal, a clerk, and jurisdiction in actions in law or equity, or law and equity, in which the amount in controversy is unlimited. The jurisdiction of all courts in this subsection specified to administer the oath of allegiance shall extend only to persons resident within the respective jurisdiction of such courts.

(c) A person whose application for naturalization under this subchapter is denied, after a hearing before an immigration officer under section 1447(a) of this Title, may seek review of such denial before the United States district court for the district in which such person resides in accordance with chapter 7 of Title 5. Such review shall be de novo, and the court shall make its own findings of fact and conclusions of law and shall, at the request of the petitioner, conduct a hearing de novo on the application.

(d) A person may only be naturalized as a citizen of the United States in the manner and under the conditions prescribed in this subchapter and not otherwise.

Eligibility for naturalization
8 U.S.C. § 1422, Sec. 311

The right of a person to become a naturalized citizen of the United States shall not be denied or abridged because of race or sex or because such person is married. Notwithstanding section 405(b) of this Act, this section shall apply to any person whose petition for naturalization shall hereafter be filed, or shall have been pending on the effective date of this chapter.

Requirements as to understanding the English language, history, principles, and form of government of the United States
8 U.S.C. § 1423, Sec. 312

No person except as otherwise provided in this subchapter shall hereafter be naturalized as a citizen of the United States upon his own petition who cannot demonstrate—

(1) an understanding of the English language, including an ability to read, write, and speak words in ordinary usage in the English language: Provided, That this requirement shall not apply to any person physically unable to comply therewith, if otherwise qualified to be naturalized, or to any person who, on the date of the filing of his petition for naturalization as provided in section 1445 of this title, either (A) is over fifty years of age and has been living in the United States for periods totaling at least twenty years subsequent to a lawful admission for permanent residence or (B) is over fifty-five years of age and has been living in the United States for periods totaling at least fifteen years subsequent to a lawful admission for permanent residence. Provided further, That the requirements of this section relating to ability to read and write shall be met if the applicant can read or write simple words and phrases to the end that a reasonable test of his literacy shall be made and that no extraordinary or unreasonable condition shall be imposed upon the applicant; and

(2) a knowledge and understanding of the fundamentals of the history, and of the principles and form of government, of the United States.

Deserters from the armed forces
8 U.S.C. § 1425, Sec. 314

A person who, at any time during which the United States has been or shall be at war, deserted or shall desert the military, air, or naval forces of the United States, or who, having been duly enrolled, departed, or shall depart from the jurisdiction of the district in which enrolled, or who, whether or not having been duly enrolled, went or shall go beyond the limits of the United States, with intent to avoid any draft into the military, air, or naval service, lawfully ordered, shall, upon conviction thereof by a court martial or a court of competent jurisdiction, be permanently ineligible to become a citizen of the United States; and such deserters and evaders shall be forever incapable of holding any office of trust or of profit under the United States, or of exercising any rights of citizens thereof.

Aliens relieved of service
8 U.S.C. § 1426, Sec. 315

(a) Notwithstanding the provisions of section 405(b) but subject to subsection (C) of this Act, any alien who applies or has applied for exemption or discharge from training or service in the Armed Forces or in the National Security Training Corps of the United States on the ground that he is an alien, and is or was relieved or discharged from such training or service on such ground, shall be permanently ineligible to become a citizen of the United States.

(b) The records of the Selective Service System or of the Department of Defense shall be conclusive as to whether an alien was relieved or discharged from such liability for training or service because he was an alien.

(c) An alien shall not be ineligible for citizenship under this section or otherwise because of an exemption from training or service in the Armed Forces of the United States pursuant to the exercise of rights under a treaty, if before the time of the exercise of such rights the alien served in the Armed Forces of a foreign country of which the alien was a national.

Requirements of naturalization
8 U.S.C. § 1427, Sec. 316[48]

(a) No person, except as otherwise provided in this subchapter, shall be naturalized unless such applicant, (1) immediately preceding the date of filing his application for naturalization has resided continuously, after being lawfully admitted for permanent residence, within the United States for at least five years and during the five years immediately preceding the date of filing his application has been physically present therein for periods totaling at least half of that time, and who has resided within the State or within the district of the Service in the United States in which the applicant filed the application for at least three months, (2) has resided continuously within the United States from the date of the application up to the time of admission to citizenship, and (3) during all the period referred to in this subsection has been and still is a person of good moral character, attached to the principles of the Constitution of the United States, and well disposed to the good order and happiness of the United States.

(b) Absence from the United States of more than six months but less than one year during the period for which continuous residence is required for admission to citizenship, immediately preceding the date of filing the application for naturalization, or during the period between the date of filing the application and the date of any hearing under section 1447(a) of this title, shall break the continuity of such residence, unless the applicant shall establish to the satisfaction of the Attorney General that he did not in fact abandon his residence in the United States during such period.

Absence from the United States for a continuous period of one year or more during the period for which continuous residence is required for admission to citizenship (whether preceding or subsequent to the filing of the application for natu-

---

48. The changes made in this section by the 1990 Act were to conform the language with the fact that the application for naturalization was no longer to be filed with the district court. *See* Sec. 407, Immigration Act of 1990, Pub. L. No. 101-649, 104 Stat. 4978.

ralization) shall break the continuity of such residence, except that in the case of a person who has been physically present and residing in the United States, after being lawfully admitted for permanent residence, for an uninterrupted period of at least one year, and who thereafter is employed by or under contract with the Government of the United States or an American institution of research recognized as such by the Attorney General, or is employed by an American firm or corporation engaged in whole or in part in the development of foreign trade and commerce of the United States, or a subsidiary thereof more than 50 per centum of whose stock is owned by an American firm or corporation, or is employed by a public international organization of which the United States is a member by treaty or statute and by which the alien was not employed until after being lawfully admitted for permanent residence, no period of absence from the United States shall break the continuity of residence if—

(1) prior to the beginning of such period of employment (whether such period begins before or after his departure from the United States), but prior to the expiration of one year of continuous absence from the United States, the person has established to the satisfaction of the Attorney General that his absence from the United States for such period is to be on behalf of such Government, or for the purpose of carrying on scientific research on behalf of such institution, or to be engaged in the development of such foreign trade and commerce or whose residence abroad is necessary to the protection of the property rights in such countries in such firm or corporation, or to be employed by a public international organization of which the United States is a member by treaty or statute and by which the alien was not employed until after being lawfully admitted for permanent residence; and

(2) such person proves to the satisfaction of the Attorney General that his absence from the United States for such period has been for such purpose.

The spouse and dependent unmarried sons and daughters who are members of the household of a person who qualifies for the benefits of this subsection shall also be entitled to such benefits during the period for which they were residing abroad as dependent members of the household of the person.

(c) The granting of the benefits of subsection (b) of this section shall not relieve the applicant from the requirement of physical presence within the United States for the period specified in subsection (a) of this section, except in the case of those persons who are employed by, or under contract with, the Government of the United States. In the case of a person employed by or under contract with Central Intelligence Agency, the requirement in subsection (b) of this section of an uninterrupted period of at least one year of physical presence in the United States may be complied with by such person at any time prior to filing an application for naturalization.

(d) No finding by the Attorney General that the applicant is not deportable shall be accepted as conclusive evidence of good moral character.

(e) In determining whether the applicant has sustained the burden of establishing good moral character and the other qualifications for citizenship specified in subsection (a) of this section, the Attorney General shall not be limited to the applicant's conduct during the five years preceding the filing of the application, but may take into consideration as a basis for such determination the applicant's conduct and acts at any time prior to that period.

(f) (1) Whenever the Director of Central Intelligence, the Attorney General and the Commissioner of Immigration determine that an applicant otherwise eligible for naturalization has made an extraordinary contribution to the national security of the United States or to the conduct of United States intelligence activities, the applicant may be naturalized without regard to the residence and physical presence requirements of this section, or to the prohibitions of section 1424 of this title, and no residence within a particular State or district of the Service in the United States shall be required: Provided, that the applicant has continuously resided in the United States for at least one year prior to naturalization: Provided, further, that the provisions of this subsection shall not apply to any alien described in subparagraphs (A) through (D) of section 1253(h)(2) of this title.

(2) An applicant for naturalization under this subsection may be administered the oath of allegiance under section 1448(a) of this title by any district court of the United States, without regard to the residence of the applicant. Proceedings under this subsection shall be conducted in a manner consistent with the protection of intelligence sources, methods and activities.

(3) The number of aliens naturalized pursuant to this subsection in any fiscal year shall not exceed five. The Director of Central Intelligence shall inform the Select Committee on Intelligence and the Committee on the Judiciary of the Senate and the Permanent Select Committee on Intelligence and the Committee on the Judiciary of the House of Representatives within a reasonable time prior to the filing of each application under the provisions of this subsection.

Revocation of naturalization
8 U.S.C. § 1451, Sec. 340

(a) It shall be the duty of the United States attorneys for the respective districts, upon affidavit showing good cause therefor, to institute proceedings in any District Court of the United States, in the judicial district in which the naturalized citizen may reside at the time of bringing suit, for the purpose of revoking and setting aside the order admitting such person to citizenship and canceling the certificate of naturalization on the ground that such order and certificate of naturalization were illegally procured or were procured by concealment of a material fact or by willful misrepresentation, and such revocation and setting aside of the order admitting such person to citizenship and such canceling of certificate of naturalization shall be effective as of the original date of the order and certificate, respectively: Provided, That refusal on the part of a naturalized citizen within a period of ten years following his naturalization to testify as a witness in any proceeding before a congressional committee concerning his subversive activities, in a case where such person has been convicted of contempt for such refusal, shall be held to constitute a ground for revocation of such person's naturalization under this subsection as having been procured by concealment of a material fact or by willful misrepresentation. If the naturalized citizen does not reside in any judicial district in the United States at the time of bringing such suit, the proceedings may be instituted in the United States District Court for the District of Columbia or in the United States district court in the judicial district in which such person last had his residence.

(b) The party to whom was granted the naturalization alleged to have been illegally procured or procured by concealment of a material fact or by willful misrepresentation shall, in any such proceedings under subsection (a) of this section, have sixty days' personal notice, unless waived by such party, in which to make answers to the petition of the United States; and if such naturalized person be absent from the United States or from the judicial district in which such person last had his residence, such notice shall be given either by personal service upon him or by publication in the manner provided for the service of summons by publication or upon absentees by the laws of the States or the place where such suit is brought.

(c) If a person who shall have been naturalized after the effective date of this chapter shall within five years next following such naturalization become a member of or affiliated with any organization, membership in or affiliation with which at the time of naturalization would have precluded such person from naturalization under the provisions of section 1424 of this title, it shall be considered prima facie evidence that such person was not attached to the principles of the Constitution of the United States and was not well disposed to the good order and happiness of the United States at the time of naturalization, and, in the absence of countervailing evidence, it shall be sufficient in the proper proceeding to authorize the revocation and setting aside of the order admitting such person to citizenship and the cancellation of the certificate of naturalization as having been obtained by concealment of a material fact or by willful misrepresentation, and such revocation and setting aside of the order admitting such person to citizenship and such canceling of certificate of naturalization shall be effective as of the original date of the order and certificate, respectively.

(d) If a person who shall have been naturalized shall, within one year after such naturalization, return to the country of his nativity, or go to any other foreign country, and take permanent residence therein, it shall be considered prima facie evidence of a lack of intention on the part of such person to reside permanently in the United States at the time of filing his petition for naturalization, and, in the absence of countervailing evidence, it shall be sufficient in the proper proceeding to authorize the revocation and setting aside of the order admitting such person to citizenship and the cancellation of the certificate of naturalization as having been obtained by concealment of a material fact or by willful misrepresentation, and such revocation and setting aside of the order admitting such person to citizenship and such canceling of certificate of naturalization shall be effective as of the original date of the order and certificate, respectively. The diplomatic and consular officers of the United States in foreign countries shall from time to time, through the Department of State, furnish the Department of Justice with statements of the names of those persons within their respective jurisdictions who have been so naturalized and who have taken permanent residence in the country of their nativity, or in any other foreign country, and such statements, duly certified, shall be admissible in evidence in all courts in proceedings to revoke and set aside the order admitting to citizenship and to cancel the certificate of naturalization.

(e) Applicability to citizenship through naturalization of parent or spouse. Any person who claims United States citizenship through the naturalization of a parent or spouse in whose case there is a revocation and setting aside of the order admitting such parent or spouse to citizenship under the provisions of subsection (a) of this section on the ground that the order and certificate of naturalization were procured by concealment of a material fact or by willful misrepresentation shall be deemed to have lost and to lose his citizenship and any right or privilege of citizenship which he may have, now has, or may hereafter acquire under and by virtue of such naturalization of such parent or spouse, regardless of whether such person is residing within or without the United States at the time of the revocation and setting aside of the order admitting such parent or spouse to citizenship. Any person who claims

United States citizenship through the naturalization of a parent or spouse in whose case there is a revocation and setting aside of the order admitting such parent or spouse to citizenship and the cancellation of the certificate of naturalization under the provisions of subsections (c) or (d) of this section, or under the provisions of section 1440(c) of this title on any ground other than that the order and certificate of naturalization were procured by concealment of a material fact or by willful misrepresentation, shall be deemed to have lost and to lose his citizenship and any right or privilege of citizenship which would have been enjoyed by such person had there not been a revocation and setting aside of the order admitting such parent or spouse to citizenship and the cancellation of the certificate of naturalization, unless such person is residing in the United States at the time of the revocation and setting aside of the order admitting such parent or spouse to citizenship and the cancellation of the certificate of naturalization.

(f) When a person shall be convicted under section 1425 of title 18 of knowingly procuring naturalization in violation of law, the court in which such conviction is had shall thereupon revoke, set aside, and declare void the final order admitting such person to citizenship, and shall declare the certificate of naturalization of such person to be canceled. Jurisdiction is conferred on the courts having jurisdiction of the trial of such offense to make such adjudication.

(g) Whenever an order admitting an alien to citizenship shall be revoked and set aside or a certificate of naturalization shall be canceled, or both, as provided in this section, the court in which such judgment or decree is rendered shall make an order canceling such certificate and shall send a certified copy of such order to the Attorney General. The clerk of the court shall transmit a copy of such order and judgment to the Attorney General. A person holding a certificate of naturalization or citizenship which has been canceled as provided by this section shall upon notice by the court by which the decree of cancellation was made, or by the Attorney General, surrender the same to the Attorney General.

(h) The provisions of this section shall apply not only to any naturalization granted and to certificates of naturalization and citizenship issued under the provisions of this subchapter, but to any naturalization heretofore granted by any court, and to all certificates of naturalization and citizenship which may have been issued heretofore by any court or by the Commissioner based upon naturalization granted by any court, or by a designated representative of the Commissioner under the provisions of section 702 of the Nationality Act of 1940, as amended, or by such designated representative under any other act.

(i) Nothing contained in this section shall be regarded as limiting, denying, or restricting the power of the Attorney General to correct, reopen, alter, modify, or vacate an order naturalizing the person.

Loss of nationality by native-born or naturalized citizen; voluntary action; burden of proof; presumptions
8 U.S.C. § 1481, Sec. 349

(a) From and after the effective date of this chapter a person who is a national of the United States, whether by birth or naturalization, shall lose his nationality by voluntarily performing any of the following acts with the intention of relinquishing United States nationality:

(1) obtaining naturalization in a foreign state upon his own application, or upon an application filed by a duly authorized agent, after having attained the age of eighteen years; or

(2) taking an oath or making an affirmation or other formal declaration of allegiance to a foreign state or a political subdivision thereof, after having attained the age of eighteen years; or

(3) entering, or serving in, the armed forces of a foreign state if (a) such armed forces are engaged in hostilities against the United States, or (b) such persons serve as a commissioned or noncommissioned officer; or

(4)(A) accepting, serving in, or performing the duties of any office, post, or employment under the government of a foreign state or a political subdivision thereof, after attaining the age of eighteen years if he has or acquires the nationality of such foreign state; or

(B) accepting, serving in, or performing the duties of any office, post, or employment under the government of a foreign state or a political subdivision thereof, after attaining the age of eighteen years for which office, post, or employment an oath, affirmation, or declaration of allegiance is required; or

(5) making a formal renunciation of nationality before a diplomatic or consular officer of the United States in a foreign state, in such form as may be prescribed by the Secretary of State; or

(6) making in the United States a formal written renunciation of nationality in such form as may be prescribed by, and before such officer as may be designated by, the Attorney General, whenever the United States shall be in a state of war and the Attorney General shall approve such renunciation as not contrary to the interests of national defense; or

(7) committing any act of treason against, or attempting by force to overthrow, or bearing arms against, the United States, violating or conspiring to violate any of the provisions of section 2383 of title 18, or willfully performing any act in violation of section 2385 of title 18, or violating section 2384 of title 18 by engaging in a conspiracy to overthrow, put down, or to destroy by force the Government of the United States, or to levy war against them, if and when he is convicted thereof by a court martial or by a court of competent jurisdiction.

(b) Repealed. Pub. L. 99-653, § 19, Nov. 14, 1986, 100 Stat. 3658.

(c) Whenever the loss of United States nationality is put in issue in any action or proceeding commenced on or after September 26, 1961 under, or by virtue of, the provisions of this chapter or any other Act, the burden shall be upon the person or party claiming that such loss occurred, to establish such claim by a preponderance of the evidence. Except as otherwise provided in subsection (b) of this section, any person who commits or performs, or who has committed or performed, any act of expatriation under the provisions of this chapter or any other Act shall be presumed to have done so voluntarily, but such presumption may be rebutted upon a showing, by a preponderance of the evidence, that the act or acts committed or performed were not done voluntarily.

Restrictions on expatriation
8 U.S.C. § 1483, Sec. 351

(a) Except as provided in paragraphs (6) and (7) of section 1481(a) of this title, no national of the United States can expatriate himself, or be expatriated, under this chapter while within the United States or any of its outlying possessions, but expatriation shall result from the performance within the United States or any of its outlying possessions of any of the acts or the fulfillment of any of the conditions specified in this part if and when the national thereafter takes up a residence outside the United States and its outlying possessions.

(b) A national who within six months after attaining the age of eighteen years asserts his claim to United States nationality, in such manner as the Secretary of State shall by regulation prescribe, shall not be deemed to have expatriated himself by the commission, prior to his eighteenth birthday, of any of the acts specified in paragraph (3) and (5) of section 1481(a) of this title.

Chapter 14

Immigrants' Rights in the Social Context

This chapter examines immigrants' rights apart from the formal governmental immigration proceedings to which a large part of this book has been devoted. We will examine the rights of foreigners as they pertain to employment, education, and public entitlements.

A. Employment Discrimination Against Immigrants

Although federal statutes may be invoked to remedy employment discrimination suffered by non-citizens, among the most important developments regarding employment discrimination against immigrants was the enactment of the anti-discrimination provisions contained in the Immigration Reform and Control Act of 1986. This section focuses primarily on IRCA's anti-discrimination provisions and how they relate to other federal statutes prohibiting employment discrimination, such as Title VII of the Civil Rights Act of 1964 ("Title VII")[1] and the Civil Rights Act of 1866 ("Section 1981").[2]

This section is intended only as an overview. The law of employment discrimination is complex, and the relevant federal statutes overlap and interact in ways that are often very complicated, with each of these statutes protecting different classes and each covering different types of employment-related discriminatory activity. Complicating matters further is the fact that employment discrimination law, as a whole, is subject to quite rapid change, either by amendment to applicable statutes or through the decisions of courts. This cautionary note is even more relevant with regard to IRCA's anti-discrimination provision, which is particularly amenable to change because the statute is relatively new. Consequently, few IRCA discrimination cases have been filed as of this writing. Nevertheless, an examination of the materials that are currently available, some of which are set forth in this section, should give the student an overview of employment discrimination law as it relates to immigrants.

Title VII of the Civil Rights Act of 1964

Title VII of the Civil Rights Act of 1964, as amended, is the most comprehensive federal anti-discrimination statute. It prohibits employers of fifteen or more employees

---

1. Codified at 42 U.S.C. § 2000e *et seq.*
2. Codified at 42 U.S.C. § 1981.

from discriminating on the basis of race, color, religion, sex, or national origin. Thus, persons who suffer national origin discrimination by relatively large employers are covered under Title VII.

As will be seen, the law distinguishes between national origin and alienage discrimination. National origin discrimination is the differential treatment of an individual on the basis of "the physical, cultural or linguistic characteristics of a national origin group."[3] Alienage discrimination, on the other hand, entails differential treatment, regardless of national origin or ancestry, because of a person's citizenship status.

Although IRCA applies only to recruiting, hiring, referral for a fee, or discharge, Title VII applies to these and almost all other aspects of employment, including wages or salary, benefits, promotion, working conditions, etc. Title VII is enforced by an administrative agency, the Equal Employment Opportunity Commission ("EEOC").

Title VII, however, does not cover citizenship status or alienage discrimination.[4] Thus, persons who suffer such discrimination must proceed under IRCA, which is the only federal statute that expressly prohibits citizenship status discrimination. Although the regulations implementing IRCA provide for relief from employer retaliation, the statute itself contains no provision expressly corresponding to Title VII's proscription of retaliation against employees who assert their equal employment rights.[5]

Section 1981 and Employment Discrimination

Persons who suffer employment-related discrimination on the basis of race, national origin, and possibly on the basis of alienage may also be protected by 42 U.S.C. §1981 ("Section 1981"). Because of its expansive language in guaranteeing all "persons" the same right "to make and enforce contracts ... as is enjoyed by white citizens," Section 1981 has been recognized as prohibiting discrimination in the employment context.

Although the Supreme Court has revisited the question of whether Section 1981 reaches private action, it is now clear that Section 1981 may be used as a remedy for employment discrimination in the private sector. In *Patterson v. McLean Credit Union,*[6] the Supreme Court reaffirmed the validity of Section 1981's application to, and prohibition of, private racial discrimination, but only as to hiring and discharge. The Court interpreted the statute to exclude from its coverage discrimination related to conditions of employment. Thus, although it is still a very important tool in remedying employment discrimination in the private sector, Section 1981 has been substantially limited in its scope and no longer applies to all aspects of the employment relationship.

Furthermore, for non-citizens who suffer some type of employment discrimination, Section 1981's applicability to alienage discrimination (i.e., in addition to discrimination on the basis of race and color) is still an open question. The Supreme Court denied *certiorari* when the issue was presented in *Bhandari v. First National*

---

3. 29 C.F.R. §1601.1.

4. *Espinoza v. Farah Manufacturing Co.*, 414 U.S. 86 (1973).

5. *See* 28 C.F.R. § 44.201.

6. 491 U.S. ___, 109 S. Ct. 2363 (1989).

Bank of Commerce,[7] declining review of a decision of the Fifth Circuit, which held that Section 1981 was not intended to reach private discrimination on the basis of alienage. Thus, the Supreme Court has yet to decide whether Section 1981 prohibits private alienage discrimination. With respect to alienage discrimination involving state action, however, Section 1981 has been interpreted to include foreigners within its coverage, at least with respect to those lawfully in this country.[8]

Unfair Immigration-Related Employment Practices

As we noted earlier, the immigration laws were amended in 1986, making it unlawful for employers to employ undocumented or "unauthorized" persons.[9] The law imposes a series of escalating fines, potentially leading to criminal sanctions, on employers who violate its mandate. Congress believed that the threat of sanctions created a risk that employers might refuse to hire or otherwise discriminate against persons because they appear to be foreign, have foreign-sounding names, or speak with a foreign accent or in a foreign language. Consequently, Congress included the anti-discrimination provisions in IRCA as a counterbalance to employer sanctions.[10]

These "unfair immigration-related employment practices" provisions create a new cause of action prohibiting discrimination on the basis of citizenship status and, in certain more limited instances, on the basis of national origin.[11] A special administrative process for prosecuting claims under the Act was established. The statute provides that it is an unfair immigration-related employment practice to discriminate with respect to hiring, recruitment, referral for a fee, or discharge because of a person's national origin or citizenship status. Protection against discrimination based on citizenship status extends to all citizens and "intending citizens" (as defined in the statute) as long as the "persons or entities" employ more than three persons.

In addition to creating a new cause of action for citizenship status discrimination, the Act, as mentioned above, also expands the available protection against national origin discrimination by providing that employers (with more than three employees) who are not covered under Title VII of the Civil Rights Act, 42 U.S.C. 2000e *et seq.*, will now be subject to IRCA's prohibition against national origin discrimination. However, because Title VII already prohibits employers with fifteen or more employees from discriminating on the basis of national origin, this expanded protection applies only to claims against employers of between four and fourteen employees.

---

7. 887 F.2d 609 (5th Cir. 1989) (*en banc*) (on remand), *cert. denied,* ___U.S. ___, 110 S. Ct. 22 (1990) (White and O'Connor dissenting to the denial of *certiorari*).

8. *Takahashi v. Fish and Game Commission,* 334 U.S. 410, 419 (1948); *cf.* 42 U.S.C. § 1983.

9. *See* 8 U.S.C. § 1324a.

10. The legislative history of the Act reveals that the antidiscrimination provision was one of the most controversial aspects of the bill and nearly led to its defeat. Opponents of the provision argued that existing federal statutes provided immigrants with sufficient protection against discrimination and that this type of "civil rights legislation" should not be included within an immigration reform law. Proponents, however, argued that the existing federal statutes, none of which unambiguously prohibited private discrimination on the basis of alienage, were clearly insufficient because of their limited coverage and complex enforcement procedures. Carrasco, *The Golden Moment of Legalization,* X In Defense of the Alien 32, 35 (1988).

11. *See* Section 274B, 8 U.S.C. § 1324b.

One source of controversy with regard to claims of employment discrimination brought under the anti-discrimination provisions of IRCA is the proper standard of proof applicable to such cases. The Act itself does not explicitly state what type of showing is required to establish that an employer engaged in unlawful discrimination. However, under long-settled Title VII standards, an individual can prove unlawful discrimination by showing either "disparate treatment" or "disparate impact." Thus, under Title VII a claimant can either prove that an employer intentionally discriminated based upon some unlawful criterion such as national origin or, using disparate impact analysis, that the effect of the employer's activity, even though neutral on its face, was discriminatory.

Although disparate impact analysis is well accepted under Title VII[12] (after which IRCA was modeled), both President Reagan and his Justice Department took the position that IRCA claimants may not use the disparate impact standard to establish unlawful discrimination. When President Reagan signed the bill into law on November 6, 1986, he attempted to create something in the nature of legislative history by including in his signing statement his understanding of what Congress intended by certain of the more important sections of the Act. The President stated that he understood section 274B (the Act's anti-discrimination provisions) to require a " 'discriminatory intent' standard of proof" and that "it would be improper to use the 'disparate impact' theory of recovery."[13] Thus, the President concluded, "a facially neutral employee selection practice that is employed without discriminatory intent will be permissible under the provisions of section 274B."[14]

This view has been criticized and, although the issue is likely to inspire further litigation, at least one district court has already held that both disparate treatment and disparate impact analysis may be used in IRCA cases.[15] In resolving the question, courts will likely focus on the fact that IRCA's "pattern or practice" language, which tracks the language found in Title VII, has not generally been held to require a showing of intentional discrimination in the Title VII context. Thus, such a showing should not be required in the context of 274B anti-discrimination cases.

The following administrative law judge decision is fairly representative of the issues likely to be litigated further in the implementation of the statute's anti-discrimination provisions. Because the following case is an administrative rather than a judicial opinion, undue weight should not be placed on the conclusions reached. In addition, after the case was decided, Congress removed the requirement that the

---

12. *Griggs v. Duke Power Co.*, 401 U.S. 424, 431 (1971); *but see Wards Cove Packing Company, Inc. v. Atonio*, ___U.S. ___, 109 S. Ct. 2115, 2119 (1989).

13. "President's Statement on Signing S. 1200 into Law," 22 *Weekly Comp. Pres. Doc.* 1534 (Nov. 10, 1986).

14. This conclusion, however, is not based on legislative history. Moreover, as a commentary on interpretation of the statute that was not considered by Congress, the presidential signing statement is not a part of the legislative history and, accordingly, should be given little, if any, weight by the courts when interpreting this statute. 2A C. Sands, Sutherland's Statutes and Statutory Construction § 48.05 (N. Singer 4th ed. 1984). Moreover, the sponsor of section 274B has emphatically rejected the President's construction. *See* Frank, *The Anti-Discrimination Amendment*, X In Defense of the Alien 67 (1988).

15. *LULAC v. Pasadena Independent School District*, 662 F. Supp. 443, 449 n. 6, *motion deferred*, 672 F. Supp. 280 (S.D. Tex. 1987).

complainant file a notice of intention to become a citizen in order to seek relief for discrimination.[16] However, the case does explore the more important issues in alienage discrimination.

In Re Charge of Zeki Yeni Komsu v. Mesa Airlines, A Corporation
No. 88-200001, No. 88-200002
(Exec. Off. for Imm. Rev. July 24, 1989)

MORSE, J.

* * *

Background

... [8 U.S.C. § 1324b] was enacted to create new causes of action arising out of any "unfair immigration-related employment practice," 8 U.S.C. § 1324b(a)(1), and to broaden "... the Title VII protections against national origin discrimination ... because of the concern of some Members that people of 'foreign' appearance might be made more vulnerable" to employment discrimination "by the imposition of [employer] sanctions." "Joint Explanatory Statement of the Committee of Conference," Conference Report, Immigration Reform and Control Act of 1986, H.R. Rep. No. 99-1000, 99th Cong., 2d Sess., at 87 (1986).

Practices newly prohibited are those which discriminate against an individual on the basis of that individual's national origin or, in the case of a citizen or national of the United States or an "intending citizen..., because of such individual's citizenship status." 8 U.S.C. § 1324b(a)(1). Section 1324b(a) provides that it is a violation of law, subject to specified exceptions, to discriminate against any individual with respect to hiring, recruitment, referral for a fee, or discharge from employment because of that individual's national origin or citizenship status. The individuals protected against discrimination are U.S. citizens or nationals and those aliens who (1) have been admitted for permanent residence, (2) have been granted the status of aliens lawfully admitted for temporary residence, as applicants for amnesty, (3) have been admitted as refugees, or (4) have been granted asylum provided that each such individual has evidenced "an intention to become a citizen of the United States through completing a declaration of intention to become a citizen...." *Id.* at § 1324b(a)(3).

IRCA directed the President to appoint within the Department of Justice a Special Counsel for Immigration-Related Unfair Employment Practices (Special Counsel, or OSC), responsible for investigating charges, issuing complaints and prosecuting cases before administrative law judges, and authorized to seek judicial enforcement of orders issued by such judges. *Id.* at §§ 1324b(c) and (j)(1).

Remedies provided for breach of the duty not to discriminate, which the administrative law judge may impose upon determining that the respondent has engaged in an unfair immigration-related employment practice include not only relief on behalf of covered individuals but also liability to the United States upon a finding of a

---

16. While the law does not require that the person have filed papers for naturalization, is she fails to file within six months of eligibility to apply for citizenship. *See* 8 U.S.C. 1324b(a)(3)(B)(i), Sec. 274B(a)(3)(B)(i).

"pattern or practice of discriminatory activity." *Id.* at § 1324b(d)(2). The present case raises questions of first impression under 8 U.S.C. § 1324b with respect both to relief on behalf of the individual complainant, Mr. Zeki Yeni Komsu (charging party, or Komsu), and to liability to the government.

Procedural Summary

The United States, by OSC, to vindicate the public interest and on behalf of Komsu filed two complaints with the Office of the Chief Administrative Hearing Officer (OCAHO) on January 12, 1988, against Mesa Airlines (respondent, or Mesa). The Special Counsel, in effect, asserts in Docket 88-200001 that Mesa engaged in a pattern and practice of discrimination in its hiring of airline pilots by promulgating and adhering to a policy of failure to consider for employment those applicants, including Komsu, who are not citizens of the United States. In Docket 88-200002, the Special Counsel contends that Komsu was not hired as a pilot because Mesa, applying its U.S. citizen-only policy, rejected his employment application.

* * *

Jurisdiction Established

There is no claim here arising out of national origin status. Rather, Mesa is charged with breach of its duty not to discriminate against Komsu by rejecting his application for the reason that he was not a U.S. citizen. It is undisputed that he was at all times relevant to this case a citizen of a nation other than the United States, during all of which time Mesa employed more than fourteen individuals.

A preliminary question, not previously addressed judicially, challenges availability of § 1324b relief in cases like the present one where enforcement of employer sanctions is not directly implicated. At least one commentator has suggested that under the view that the antidiscrimination provisions were adopted "solely to counterbalance IRCA's employer sanctions provisions," only discrimination arising in context of employer sanctions would be actionable. Pivec, "Handling Immigration-Related Employment Discrimination Claims," *Immigration Briefings* (April 1988), at 2.

That suggestion is said to have support in the legislative history of IRCA. For example, the Conference Report, H.R. Rep. No. 99-1000, *supra,* at 87, explains that the antidiscrimination provisions of IRCA " . . . are a complement to the sanctions provisions, and must be considered in this context," and notes that if, as provided by IRCA, "the sanctions are repealed by joint resolution, the antidiscrimination provisions will also expire, the justification for them having been removed." As reflected by the Conference Report, *id.* at 87-88, it is a commonplace that § 1324b had its genesis in apprehension that enactment of employer sanctions, 8 U.S.C. § 1324a, might be perceived to generate discrimination. See also House Committee on the Judiciary, Immigration Control and Legalization Amendments Act of 1986, H.R. Rep. No. 99-682, 99th Cong., 2d Sess., pt. 1, at 68 (1986).

Legislative sunsetting of IRCA's employer sanctions program would terminate the antidiscrimination provisions as well. But the conferees pointed out that "[t]he antidiscrimination provisions would also be repealed in the event of a joint resolution approving a GAO finding that the sanctions had resulted in no significant discrimination, or that the administration of the antidiscrimination provisions had resulted in an unreasonable burden on employers." Conference Report, H.R. Rep. No. 99-

1000, *supra*, at 87. In either of such situations, sanctions could continue despite repeal of the causes of action enacted at 8 U.S.C. § 1324b.

*   *   *

Nothing contained in the unusually structured statutory mechanism for legislative inquiry into the continued viability of either employer sanctions or antidiscrimination provisions, 8 U.S.C. §§ 1324a(m) and (n), spells out or necessarily implies a requirement that causes of action arising under section 1324b must proximately result from enactment (or, implementation) of section 1324a. Nothing contained in IRCA limits causes of action under section 1324b to claims arising out of employer responses to the employer sanctions program mandated by section 1324a. Nothing constrains me to look behind a remedial statute for a limitation that would be inconsistent with the plain words of the statute, 8 U.S.C. § 1324b(a)(1), or included within the catalogue of exceptions to its sweep, 8 U.S.C. §§ 1324b(a)(2) and (4). For all the foregoing reasons, I conclude that 8 U.S.C. § 1324b confers jurisdiction upon administrative law judges to adjudicate complaints whether or not the alleged discriminatory practices implicate either the text or the administration of 8 U.S.C. § 1324a.

This conclusion is consistent also with the expressed views of the Department of Justice in the preamble to the rule . . . [that] . . . made clear the Department's understanding in that Congress banned " . . . all intentional discrimination in light of the likely difficulty for a charging party or the Special Counsel to prove that such discrimination stemmed directly from an employer's desire to avoid sanctions." [52 Fed. Reg. 37,405 (1987).]

*   *   *

Standing of the Charging Party as an Intending Citizen

Very few of the material facts developed on the record are undisputed. It is unquestioned, however, that Mr. Komsu, who was born on March 19, 1960, in Turkey, and attended high school and aeronautical college in Denmark, lawfully entered the United States in November 1985, on a tourist visa. In July 1986, Komsu married and was issued a temporary resident permit; he has been a permanent resident alien of the United States since at least November 1986.

As a lawfully admitted permanent alien he was eligible to qualify as an intending citizen as that term is understood under IRCA. The parties disagree as to whether he evidenced his intent to qualify as an intending citizen in time to obtain standing to maintain this citizenship discrimination charge under IRCA.

Mr. Komsu concededly did not formally evidence his intent to become a citizen prior to October 28, 1987, the date he executed an INS Form N-300, "Application to File Declaration of Intention." Previously, in December 1986 he applied to Mesa for employment as a pilot. Late in March 1987 he filed an updated resume.

. . . Section 1324b(a)(3) excludes from the definition of intending citizen an alien who fails to apply for naturalization within six months of the date the alien first becomes eligible to apply for naturalization or within six months after November 6, 1986, whichever is later. Similarly excluded is an alien who applied on a timely basis but who does not obtain naturalization within 2 years after the date of the application subject to exception provided that the alien can establish that he/she is actively pursuing naturalization.

*   *   *

The Department of Justice, in an interim final rule adopted as final, with changes, has subsequently amended its position on the timing of the filing of an I-772. See 53 Fed. Reg. 48248, November 30, 1988. The revised rule to be codified at 28 C.F.R. §44.101(c)(2)(ii) establishes that the declaration of intention filing requirement is satisfied as long as the declaration is completed and filed not later than the filing of the charge with OSC. Contrary to its prior position, the Department no longer requires that a declaration be completed and filed before the occurrence of the alleged discrimination.

* * *

If the Special Counsel fails to file a complaint before an administrative law judge, "...the person making the charge may "file a complaint directly before..." the judge. *Id.* at § 1324b(d)(2). In the instant action, Komsu filed his charge of discrimination with OSC on November 18, 1987. OSC's filing of the two complaints with the OCAHO on January 12, 1988, was clearly within the statutorily prescribed 120-day period from receipt of the charge during which the Special Counsel is to investigate and determine whether or not to file a complaint with respect to the charge.

As Komsu has been found to be an intending citizen with standing to bring a citizenship discrimination claim under IRCA, OSC has standing to file a complaint on Komsu's behalf. In addition, by virtue of its power to "...conduct investigations respecting unfair immigration-related employment practices and, based on such an investigation...file a complaint..." before an administrative law judge, 8 U.S.C. § 1324b(d)(1), Special Counsel has standing to investigate a charge or proceed on its own initiative and, presumptively, to file a complaint alleging a pattern or practice of discrimination by Mesa.

* * *

IRCA provides no definition of the pattern or practice formulation enacted at section 102, 8 U.S.C. §1324b. However, the House Judiciary Committee did discuss its understanding of the term as provided in section 101 with respect both to criminal and civil injunctive liability under 8 U.S.C. §1324a(f) arising out of violations of prohibitions against employment of unauthorized aliens:

> The term "pattern or practice" has received substantial judicial construction, since the term appears in the Voting Right [sic] Act (42 U.S.C. 1971 *et seq.*), the Civil Rights Act of 1964 (42 U.S.C. § 2000 *et seq.*), and the Fair Housing Act of 1968 (42 U.S.C. 3601 *et seq.*). The Committee emphasizes that it intends to follow the judicial construction of that term as set forth in *U.S. v. Mayton*, 335 F.2d 153 (1964), *International Brotherhood of Teamsters v. U.S.*, 431 U.S. 324, and *U.S. v. International Association of Ironworkers Local No. 1*, 438 F.2d 679 (1971). These cases all indicate that *the term "pattern or practice" has its generic meaning and shall apply to* regular, repeated and intentional activities, but does not include isolated, sporadic or accidental acts. The same interpretation of "pattern or practice" shall apply when that term is used in this bill with regard to the injunctive remedy that may be sought by the Attorney General for recruitment, referral or employment violations, as well as for *certain unfair immigration-related employment practices*.

H.R. Rep. No. 99-682, *supra*, at 59 (emphasis added).

... [A] threshold inquiry must be resolved, i.e., whether Special Counsel may properly maintain a pattern or practice cause of action. This inquiry derives from the peculiar positioning in the statute of the sole provision dealing with pattern or practice in discrimination cases:

Private actions—

If the Special Counsel, after receiving such a charge respecting an unfair immigration-related employment practice which alleges knowing and intentional discriminatory activity or a pattern or practice of discriminatory activity, has not filed a complaint before an administrative law judge with respect to such charge within such 120-day period, the person making the charge may (subject to paragraph (3)) file a complaint directly before such a judge.

8 U.S.C. § 1324b(d)(2).

It may be argued that by such placement under the subsection entitled "Private actions," Congress contemplated that a complaint alleging "a pattern or practice of discriminatory activity" might be filed only by "the person making the charge" and not by the Special Counsel. I think otherwise.

Absent some such indication in the legislative history, it would be inconsistent with the thrust of the protections sought by IRCA to conclude that Special Counsel was to be limited to prosecuting only individualized actions before administrative law judges. Nor should it be assumed that Congress intended to clothe individuals to the exclusion of the newly created statutory officer with authority to initiate actions which reflect "regular, repeated and intentional activities" (as defined by the House Judiciary Committee, H.R. Rep. 99-682, *supra*, at 59). Patently, pattern or practice jurisdiction implicates causes of action initiated by or prosecuted to vindicate the public interest in eliminating ongoing discriminatory practices. *See, e.g., EEOC v. United Parcel Service*, 860 F.2d 372 (10th Cir. 1988).

* * *

Considering that filing of any charge with the OSC is a condition precedent to filing with a judge, I am unable to conclude that Congress intended that the charging party but not the Special Counsel might maintain an action for "a pattern or practice of discriminatory activity." Moreover, in the preceding subsection, 8 U.S.C. § 1324b(c)(2), assigning duties to the Special Counsel, IRCA charges OSC with "... investigation of charges and issuance of complaints under this section and in respect of the prosecution of all such complaints before administrative law judges. ... " There are no words of limitation to suggest that "such complaints" exclude the pattern or practice cases contemplated at subsection (d)(2). I do not overlook that (d)(2) is introduced by the catch-line "Private actions," but I am unable to conclude that those words inform the substantive text.

* * *

The Charging Party was Unlawfully Denied Employment on Citizenship Grounds

In an undated prehearing statement, Eric Trigg, promoted to director of operations prior to that statement, candidly expressed Mesa's hiring practices as applied to Zeki Yeni Komsu:

Mr. Komsu was not hired for two reasons. The first reason is that he was not a citizen of the United States and Mesa had more then [sic] enough qualified U.S. citizens applying for those positions that were available. It is the policy of Mesa to hire only U.S. citizens if a sufficient number of qualified citizens is available to fill the positions needed. The second reason Mr. Komsu was not hired is because of his constant and irritating phone calls to me. These numerous phone calls left me with an unfavorable impression of Mr. Komsu.

Exh. 17.

Within a week of Komsu's filing with EEOC, Larry Risley, in his capacity as Mesa's president, on August 27, 1987, in a letter to EEOC, acknowledged that:

It is the policy of Mesa Airlines, Inc., to hire U.S. citizens only unless the available employee pool is not adequate at the time. During the past 12 months we have not experienced any shortage of U.S. citizen applicants from which to hire.

It is our understanding that there are no acts, laws or statutus [sic] that prohibit this policy. We therefore request this charge be dismissed as Mr. Yeni Komsu was not hired due to his non-citizen status and not because of his national origin—Turkish.

Exh. 10.

*   *   *

[M]onths after Mesa became aware of Komsu's charge of discrimination, Gary Risley, asserting that "[t]he Justice Department is attempting to write the U.S. citizen preference out of the statute . . . ," . . . unambiguously described Mesa's practices in a way which I can only understand as reflecting the view that wholesale exclusion of non-U.S. candidates complied with the law so long as any qualified citizen candidates had also applied. Larry L. Risley, president of Mesa since its founding in 1982, conceded as much.

On the witness stand, Gary Risley asserted he had been mistaken as to Mesa's practices, impeaching as erroneous his broadside, omnibus letter as well as documentary and oral evidence of other Mesa officials. I am unpersuaded by his after-the-fact recantations. Mesa both enunciated and practiced invidious discrimination against non-U.S.citizens. Even after Komsu filed his charges, Mesa officials continued to contend that their employment practices were lawful because the U.S. citizens they hired were as qualified as the non-U.S. citizen candidates. Exhibits 10-12, acknowledging Mesa's hiring preference, reflect a discriminatory hiring policy on their face.

. . . Accordingly, I reject as lacking in trustworthiness the testimony of Gary Risley and others that the prior iterations by himself and others of Mesa's employment policy and practices were erroneous. In so deciding, I need not disbelieve Gary Risley's repudiation of his earlier statement that Mesa maintained two physically separate applicant pools. It is sufficient that Mesa implemented its stated policy of preferring U.S. citizen candidates by failing to compare qualifications of non-U.S. citizen candidates with those of citizen candidates.

It follows without question that Mesa's pilot hiring practices fall outside and fail to qualify for the exception provided at 8 U.S.C. §1324b(a)(4):

. . . it is not an unfair immigration-related employment practice for a person or other entity to prefer to hire, recruit, or refer an individual who is a citizen or national of the United States over another individual who is an alien if the two individuals are equally qualified.

* * *

Mesa's commitment to hiring U.S. pilots to the exclusion of non-U.S. citizens so long as the supply of qualified citizens meets the demand in no way satisfies the exception. The plain words of the exception are inescapable: the employer avoids liability for discrimination if, but only if, there has been a comparison of qualifications as the result of which the selected citizen is found to have qualifications not less than equal to the non-selected alleged discriminatee. Here there was no such comparison.

* * *

On the record before me it is a certainty that Komsu was not rejected on the basis of pilot qualifications in head-to-head competition with any one or more of the U.S. citizen candidates who were selected during the pendency of his application from December 1986 to August 1987, or during any interval in between. I conclude from the testimony of Mesa's witnesses that their evaluation of Komsu's qualifications was after the fact, after he was rejected on citizenship grounds, and not before.

* * *

The results reached in the cases first heard under new legislation such as this will by definition establish precedent. To the extent that any one case turns on unique facts, of course, its precedential significance is reduced. This may be one such case because with the passage of time after enactment of IRCA on November 6, 1986, it may be supposed that employers will be less candid than was Mesa in trumpeting to non-U.S. citizen candidates and to public authorities their unwillingness to hire non-U.S. citizens.

* * *

...I find and conclude that Mr. Komsu was knowingly and intentionally denied employment for the sole reason that he was not a citizen of the United States.

* * *

Where as here the discrimination has been proven, it is the teaching of cases involving Title VII that the burden is on the putative employer to persuade that even absent the discrimination it would not have hired the charging party. *See, e.g.,* *McDonnell-Douglas Corp. v. Green*, 411 U.S. 792 (1973); *Int'l Bhd. of Teamsters v. United States*, 431 U.S. 324 (1977); *Texas Dep't of Community Affairs v. Burdine*, 450 U.S. 248 (1981); *Lowe v. City of Monrovia*, 775 F.2d 998 (9th Cir. 1986).[1]

---

1. *See especially*, the explanatory statement by Justice Stevens, dissenting, distinguishing disparate treatment cases from the disparate impact case before the Court, in *Wards Cove Packing Co., Inc. v. Atonio*, 109 S. Ct. 2115, 2131 (1989) (emphasis added):

In a disparate treatment case there is no "discrimination" within the meaning of Title VII unless the employer intentionally treated the employee unfairly because of race. Therefore, the employee retains the burden of proving the existence of intent at all times. If there is direct evidence of intent, the employee may have little difficulty persuading the factfinder that discrimination has occurred. But in the likelier event that intent has to be established by inference, the employee may resort to the *McDonnell/Burdine* inquiry. In either instance, the employer may undermine the employee's evidence but has no *independent* burden of persuasion.

McDonnell-Douglas, supra, is the seminal case that articulated a four part formula to establish a prima facie showing of discriminatory disparate treatment in Title VII causes of action. An individual or class plaintiff must demonstrate: (1) that he/she belongs to a protected class; (2) that he/she applied for and was qualified for a position for which the putative employer was seeking applicants; (3) that despite being qualified, he/she was rejected; and (4) that after such rejection, the position remained available and the employer continued to seek applicants from individuals having the plaintiff's qualifications. 411 U.S. at 802. The burden of proof is divided into three stages. At the first stage, the charging party must make a prima facie showing of discrimination by satisfying the four criteria enumerated above. After that showing is made, the second stage shifts the burden to the employer "to articulate some legitimate, nondiscriminatory reason for the employee's rejection." *Id.* The third stage returns the burden to the plaintiff to disprove the putative employer's explanation as pretextual, *i.e.*, the pretext or gloss designed to conceal an underlying discriminatory motivation.

The Supreme Court recently reversed the D.C. Circuit as having held erroneously that an employer found to have allowed a discriminatory motive to play a part in an employment decision must prove by *clear and convincing evidence* that it would have made the same decision absent discrimination. By a plurality decision, six justices recently instructed that an employer in a mixed motive case who proves by a *preponderance of the evidence* that it would have made the same employment decision if it had not taken the prohibited discriminatory consideration into account may avoid a finding of liability. *Price Waterhouse v. Hopkins,* [___ U.S. ___, 109 S. Ct. 1775 (1989)].

* * *

The plurality noted that *McDonald v. Santa Fe Trail Transportation Co.,* 427 U.S. 273 (1976) "... dealt with the question whether the employer's stated reason for its decision was *the* reason for its action; unlike the case before us today, therefore, *McDonald* did not involve mixed motives. This difference is decisive in distinguishing this case from those involving 'pretext.' " *Hopkins, supra,* 109 S. Ct. at 1785 n.6. While "but for" analysis may be critical to a pretext case, *e.g., McDonald, supra,* "[w]here a decision was the product of a mixture of legitimate and illegitimate motives, however, it simply makes no sense to ask whether the legitimate reason was '*the* true reason' ... for the decision—which is the question asked by *Burdine*." *Hopkins, supra,* at 1788-89.

* * *

Justices White and O'Connor each separately concurred in the judgment of the Court. Justice White agreed that the plurality opinion of Justice Brennan "is not a departure from and does not require a modification of the Court's holdings ... [in *McDonnell Douglas* and *Burdine*] ... ," even though they were pretext cases involving the search for the one "true" motive behind the employment decision. *Id.*, concurring op. at 1795. He disagreed, however, that the employer must carry its burden through objective evidence, suggesting that "where the legitimate motive found would have been ample grounds for the action taken, and the employer credibly testifies that the action would have been taken for the legitimate reasons alone, this should be ample proof." *Id.* at 1796.

Justice O'Connor disagreed with the plurality as to the analysis to be utilized by a court to determine when a claimant's proof warrants shifting the burden of persuasion to the employer. Title VII prohibits employment decisions made "because of" prohibited considerations, i.e., race, color, religion, sex or national origin. Writing that "[b]ased on its misreading of the words 'because of' in the statute . . . the plurality appears to conclude that if a decisional process is 'tainted' by awareness of sex or race in any way, the employer has violated the statute, and Title VII thus *commands* that the burden shift to the employer . . . ," she concluded instead that the burden shifts only when a disparate treatment claimant shows "by direct evidence that an illegitimate criterion was a substantial factor in the decision." *Id.*, concurring op. at 1804. "Only then would the burden of proof shift to the defendant to prove that the decision would have been justified by other, wholly legitimate considerations." *Id.* at 1805.

* * *

Even assuming that the law were as Justices White and O'Connor understand it to be, I am satisfied that the record before me proves that Mesa's motive not to hire non-U.S. pilots "was a *substantial* factor in the adverse employment action." *Hopkins*, *supra*, White, J., concurring op. at 1795.

That the improper motive, the discriminatory animus, was a substantial factor, if not the only one, in Mesa's hiring decisions is established here . . .

Pattern or Practice Applied

* * *

The question to be decided is whether I am authorized to find a pattern or practice of unlawful discrimination on the basis that individuals presumptively eligible for protection of remedial legislation, but not proven to have qualified, may, nevertheless, comprise the universe of individuals on whose behalf it may be found that an employer practiced such a pattern or practice.

An analogy which suggests inclusion in the class to be counted for pattern or practice purposes of individuals ineligible to maintain an action is found in policy guidance recently issued by the EEOC. Discussing IRCA's impact on remedies available to undocumented aliens under Title VII, the Commission has applied the analysis in *Sure-Tan v. NLRB*, 467 U.S. 883 (1984), which held that undocumented workers were employees for the purposes of, and, therefore, had standing to maintain claims under, the National Labor Relations Act.

EEOC explains that Title VII remedies are intended to discourage employment discrimination both (1) by providing disincentives to potential future discrimination and (2) by restoring an individual charging party as nearly as possible to the position that individual would have been in but for the discrimination. As to both, EEOC explains that Title VII protection is applicable to undocumented workers because if it were not:

> . . . a discriminatory atmosphere might be created in the work place which would violate not only the rights of undocumented workers but also the rights of authorized workers.

Therefore, it is essential to the goals of both Title VII and IRCA that undocumented aliens continue to be covered by Title VII.

EEOC Policy Guidance: *Effect of the Immigration Reform and Control Act of 1986 (IRCA) on the Remedies Available to Undocumented Aliens Under Title VII,* at 5, April 26, 1989, *see Interpreter Releases,* Vol. 66, No. 23, June 19, 1989, at 655-56.

OSC relies on a recent opinion of the Tenth Circuit which sustained authority of the EEOC to maintain a pattern or practice action even where it lacked any ascertainable member of the class to be protected. Without concluding here that precedents implicating EEOC standing necessarily inform IRCA jurisdiction, it cannot be doubted that the court's analysis is instructive, especially in this circuit. In *EEOC v. United Parcel Service, supra,* the court reversed the district court for having granted summary judgment dismissing EEOC's suit for racial discrimination where the only identified individual injured by defendant's conduct had settled his claim.

* * *

In my judgment, IRCA prohibits unfair immigration-related employment practices against aliens (other than unauthorized aliens) without regard to whether they qualify as intending citizens. Interpreting and applying this remedial statute, it appears that protection is provided in the sense of traditional remedies to obtain "make whole" relief only for intending citizens; pattern or practice liability is provided in context of any alien (other than an unauthorized alien) perceived to be the victim of unfair immigration-related employment practices.

* * *

It follows that a pattern or practice of discrimination may arise without proof that more than one alien, as to whom the practice in question impacted, qualifies as an intending citizen within the meaning of section 102. Accordingly, the pattern or practice claim, clearly established, is found to have been proven as a matter of law.

Notes

1. While the *1990 Act* removed the requirement that the complainant file a notice of intention to become a U.S. citizen can it truly be said that the "intending citizen" requirement was removed? Read through the statute [8 U.S.C. 1324b(a)(3)(B)] and see if you can define who are the beneficiaries of the statute? Does it include U.S. citizens, ethnic minorities? Is it intended to proscribe national origin discrimination? What would happen if a company discriminated against certain employees because it preferred to hire permanent residents, would this be in violation of the anti-discrimination provisions?

2. Is the administrative law judge's conclusion in *Komsu* that the statute was intended to cover more than anti-discrimination outside of the context of employer sanctions a reasonable interpretation of the statute? Would the courts take a similar approach in analyzing the statute? A petition for review has been filed in the case. *Mesa Airlines v. United States, appeal docketed,* No. 89-9552 (10th Cir. Jan. 26, 1990). Can you describe alienage discrimination that is not related to employer sanctions?

3. Is it an unfair immigration-related employment practice for an employer seeking to avoid sanctions to require more proof of work authorization than is deemed sufficient under Section 274A? *In Re Charge of Valdivia-Sanchez v. LASA Marketing Firms,* No. 88-200061 (Exec. Off. for Imm. Rev. November 27, 1989), held that it was. In that case, the charging party responded to an employment referral agency's

advertisement and presented a driver's license, social security card, and letters indicating her intent to apply for legalization. She was turned away because she did not have further documentation. She subsequently applied for legalization, then returned to the agency. The agency again requested more proof of work authorization even though Ms. Valdivia then had an I-688A (temporary work permit). Although the administrative law judge did not find that LASA had knowingly discriminated against Ms. Valdivia, he nevertheless concluded that Section 274B had been violated based on LASA's uninformed understanding of what kinds of immigration-related employment documents were required to evince employment authorization in accordance with IRCA, "thus resulting in Ms. Valdivia being rejected with respect to employment for an *illegitimate*, statutorily prohibited reason, i.e., disparate treatment on account of citizenship status" (emphasis in original).

As previously mentioned, there have been relatively few Section 274B discrimination cases that have been filed and processed by the Office of the Special Counsel (OSC) and even fewer that have reached the federal courts. The following case is the first ever dealing with the Act's anti-discrimination provision and was actually filed before the administrative structure provided for in the Act was fully established. This lag in implementation of the OSC explains why the district court exercised its jurisdiction and heard the case even though the plaintiffs had not exhausted all of their administrative remedies as is required under the Act. Such exhaustion is a statutory prerequisite of judicial review.

4. *Private actions.* The 1990 Act now requires the Special Counsel to notify the complainant within 120 days after receiving the charge of its intent not to file a complaint before the Administrative Law Judge. The complainant then has 90 days after receiving such notification, to file her complaint directly before the ALJ. During this 90 day period the Special Counsel may continue to investigate the charge and file a complaint before the ALJ.

League of United Latin American Citizens (LULAC) v. Pasadena Independent School District

662 F. Supp. 443 (S.D. Tex. 1987)

McDONALD, District Judge.

* * *

Plaintiff, League of United Latin American Citizens ("LULAC"), is a non-profit corporation organized under the laws of the state of Texas for benevolent, charitable, educational, and patriotic purposes. LULAC is the oldest national organization of persons of Hispanic descent in the United States and was founded for the express purpose of protecting, defending, and preserving the civil rights of Hispanics.

Plaintiffs Maria Olympia Hernandez, Reina Raquel Guillen, Blanca Lopez, and Maria Garza (the "individual Plaintiffs") are undocumented aliens, each of whom entered the United States before January 1, 1982. As undocumented aliens, the individual Plaintiffs are currently unable to obtain valid social security numbers.

The individual Plaintiffs were employed by the Pasadena Independent School District ("PISD") prior to November 6, 1986. At the time they applied for employment, each individual Plaintiff inserted an invalid social security number on her application form.

The individual Plaintiffs are eligible for the legalization program under Section 245A of IRCA. Each testified that she intends to submit an application for legalization once the program is initiated. Applications for this legalization program will not be accepted until May 5, 1987. The continued employment of the Plaintiffs is permitted under the Grandfather Clause of IRCA, Section 101(a)(3). Upon approval of their legalization applications, each individual Plaintiff will be authorized to secure a valid social security number.

On February 18, 1987, each of the individual Plaintiffs was terminated from her employment as a custodial worker by PISD on the ground that she had provided false information on the PISD employment application by giving an invalid social security number. The Defendant maintains a policy that falsifying information on an application constitutes grounds for refusal to hire or termination. This policy, although in operation when Plaintiffs applied for employment, was not stated on the application nor was it communicated to Plaintiffs by school district personnel.

*   *   *

There is a substantial likelihood, however, that Plaintiffs will prevail on their claim that actions taken by PISD in terminating Plaintiffs violate the anti-discrimination provision of IRCA Section 274B(a). Since this is a case of first impression, it is the Court's duty "to find that interpretation which can most fairly be said to be imbedded in the statute, in the sense of being most harmonious with its scheme and with the general purposes that Congress manifested." *C.I.R. v. Engle*, 464 U.S. 206, 217 (1984) *quoting NLRB v. Lion Oil Co.*, 352 U.S. 282, 297 (1957) (Frankfurter, J., concurring in part and dissenting in part).

*   *   *

... When [the anti-discrimination provisions are] applied to those who are qualified for legalization, and who intend to become citizens, a policy of terminating undocumented aliens for no other reason than that they have given employers a false social security number constitutes an unfair immigration-related employment practice under § 274B(a) of the Act. Only because of Plaintiffs' citizenship status have they been unable to secure valid social security numbers.

Further, Defendant's stated practice clearly contravenes the intent of Congress in enacting this law. In reporting the bill favorably to Congress, the House Judiciary Committee said of the anti-discrimination provision:

> The Committee does not believe barriers should be placed in the path of permanent residents and other aliens who are authorized to work and who are seeking employment, particularly when such aliens have evidenced an intent to become U.S. citizens. It makes no sense to admit immigrants and refugees to this country, require them to work and then allow employers to refuse to hire them because of their immigration (non-citizenship) status. Since Title VII does not provide any protection against employment discrimination based on alienage or non-citizen status, the Committee is of the view that the instant legislation must do so.
>
> H.R. Conf. Report No. 99-682(I), at 70, U.S. Code Cong. & Admin. News 1986, p. 5674....

Though not before the Court, it is undoubtedly true that most employers have a policy of terminating employees who falsify their applications. Under ordinary circumstances, such a policy is justifiable and valid. It is an extraordinary circumstance, however, to have so many undocumented aliens working in the United States under false names and with invalid social security numbers. In the coming months and years, the administrative process established under Section 274B of the Act will have to reconcile many current employment practices with the new rights established under IRCA.[1]

* * *

IRCA explicitly authorizes the Attorney General to seek injunctions against employers who engage in a pattern or practice of hiring aliens who are ineligible for legalization under the Act. Section 274A (f)(2). Similarly, an administrative law judge is empowered to issue cease and desist orders should he or she determine that an employer has engaged in an unfair immigration-related employment practice. Section 274B (g)(2)(A). The Court notes that irreparable injury is presumed where an employee, having exhausted all available administrative remedies, seeks a preliminary injunction in an employment discrimination action under Title VII. *Middleton-Keirn v. Stone*, 655 F.2d 609, 611 (5th Cir. 1981). Exhaustion of administrative remedies is not a viable course of action for Plaintiffs since the administrative procedures established under the Act are not yet in place.

* * *

If Defendant's employment practice is allowed to stand, Plaintiffs and many others similarly situated would be placed in the unfortunate and untenable position of deciding between prospective citizenship and present employment. In order to qualify for legalization, they must come forward and reveal their past misdeeds, misstatements, and falsifications. Once made, these revelations will automatically result in the termination of any qualified alien now working with PISD. Other similarly situated individuals run the risk of being fired from their jobs, either for falsifying their employment applications or for having invalid social security numbers.

If the Court gives way to the Defendant's argument that the value of enforcing its employment policy should expressly reign supreme over Congressional legislation designed to cure a problem which affects all persons living in the United States, whether citizens or not, then the Act would be rendered ineffectual. Also many employers—some unabashedly, others with a wink and a nod—have in the past knowingly and unlawfully hired undocumented aliens who were in this country. It would reward hypocrisy to allow such employers now to terminate qualified undocumented

---

1. Although each complaint will be addressed individually, it seems likely that the administrative courts will rely on the present extensive body of discrimination law, and in particular employment discrimination law, when examining allegations of unfair immigration-related employment practices under Section 274B. Under Title VII, facially neutral employment practices, which have a disparate impact on members of protected classes, have been invalidated in the absence of a showing that there is a business necessity for the practice and that less drastic alternatives to the practice are not feasible. *See Connecticut v. Teal*, 457 U.S. 440 (1982). ... A policy designed to promote accurate employment data could likely be justified as a business necessity. In the present case, it also seems likely that measures less drastic than automatically terminating any worker protected by the Act who falsified information could have been found. If nothing else, Defendant could have allowed the Plaintiffs a few additional weeks to apply for proper work authorization under the Act.

aliens for the sole reason they have made false statements by presenting invalid social security cards.

*   *   *

Notes

1. *Komsu v. Mesa* also addressed the issue of equitable tolling and held that the 180-day time limit for filing a charge with the OSC is not a jurisdictional requirement but more in the nature of a statute of limitations that is subject to waiver, estoppel, and equitable tolling. Accordingly, the ALJ held that the filing of a charge with the EEOC tolled the running of the 180-day limitation period for filing a charge with the OSC. The OSC and EEOC have since filed a Memorandum of Understanding that allows individuals to file charges with the EEOC, which are then referred to the OSC if later determined to have been filed with the wrong agency. The 180-day statute of limitations is tolled while the EEOC has the charge. Similarly, the limitations period is tolled if the charge is erroneously filed with the OSC instead of the EEOC. *See* 54 Fed. Reg. 32, 499 (1989).

2. In *Romo v. Todd Corporation*, No. 87-200001 (Exec. Off. for Imm. Rev., August 19, 1988), *aff'd sub nom., United States v. Todd Corporation*, 900 F.2d 164 (9th Cir. 1990), the ALJ acknowledged that the availability of the disparate impact standard in anti-discrimination cases is still in dispute. The ALJ nevertheless stated that the dispute could not be resolved in the case before him in view of the result reached on the record that the complainant failed to qualify as a protected individual under section 102.

3. How the undocumented in the work force will fare under other federal labor legislation is not yet clear. In an earlier case, pre-dating IRCA, the Supreme Court held that the National Labor Relations Act (NLRA) protected undocumented workers. *See Sure-Tan, Inc. v. NLRB*, 467 U.S. 883 (1984). In *Patel v. Quality Inn South*, 846 F.2d 700 (11th Cir. 1988), *cert. denied*, ___U.S. ___, 109 S. Ct. 1120 (1989), a federal circuit court reversed a district court decision that had held that undocumented workers are not protected under the Fair Labor Standards Act (FLSA). The district court had reasoned that to give the protection of the FLSA to undocumented aliens would encourage illegal immigration and thus undermine the policies behind the INA as amended by IRCA. In reversing, the circuit court concluded that extending FLSA's protection to the undocumented is perfectly consistent with the goals of IRCA in that it removes any incentive employers might have in hiring persons unlawfully in this country. The court held that if the undocumented are paid substandard wages, they can sue their employers in an action under the FLSA. The court thus concluded that undocumented aliens should be entitled to the full range of available remedies under the statute without regard to their immigration status. It found that such a result would be consistent with the policies of IRCA and *Sure-Tan, supra*. For additional discussion of *Sure-Tan* in a post-IRCA era, *see* Blum, *Labor Standards Enforcement and the Results of Labor Migration*, 63 N.Y.U. L. Rev. 1342 (1988); Harris, *Conflict or Double Deterrence? FLSA Protection of Illegal Aliens and the Immigration Reform and Control Act*, 72 Minn. L. Rev. 900 (1988); Charnesky, *Protection for Undocumented Workers Under the FLSA: An Evaluation in Light of IRCA*, 25 San Diego L. Rev. 379 (1988). *See also NLRB v. Ashkenazy Property Management Corporation*, 817 F.2d 74 (9th Cir. 1987).

4. The *LULAC* case appears to have been decided on the basis of "disparate impact" theory, otherwise known as the "effects test." This mode of analysis was originally given sanction by the Supreme Court in the landmark case of *Griggs v. Duke Power Co.*, 401 U.S. 424, 431 (1971). However, the validity of this theory of liability, at least as applied in the Title VII context, was placed in question in *Wards Cove Packing Company, Inc. v. Atonio*, — U.S. —, 109 S. Ct. 2115, 2119 (1989). There the Court upset the long-standing distribution of burdens of proof in such cases, limited the use of internal work-force comparisons in the making of a prima facie case of discrimination, and required practice-by-practice statistical proof of causation. Compare *Wards Cove* and *LULAC*. Does *LULAC* survive?

References

Carrasco, *The Golden Moment of Legalization*, X In Defense of the Alien 32 (1988)

Employer Sanctions and Anti-Discrimination Under the Immigration Reform and Control Act of 1986 (IRCA), American Bar Association (1990)

Hogan & Hartson, Immigration-Related Employment Discrimination: A Practical Legal Manual for Evaluating and Pursuing Claims in the Wake of IRCA (1988)

Kobdish, *The Frank Amendment to the Immigration Reform and Control Act of 1986—A Labyrinth for Labor Law Litigators*, 41 SW. L.J. 667 (1987)

Perea, English-Only Rules and the Right to Speak One's Primary Language in the Workplace, 23 U. Mich. J. L. Ref. 265 (1990)

Roberts & Yale-Loehr, *Employers as Junior Immigration Inspectors: The Impact of the 1986 Immigration Reform and Control Act*, 21 Int'l Law. 1013 (1987)

Simpson, *U.S. Immigration Reform: Employer Sanctions and Antidiscrimination Provisions*, 9 U. Ark. L.J. 563 (1986-87)

B. Education

The "American people have always regarded education and [the] acquisition of knowledge as matters of supreme importance."[17] Public schools have served as vehicles by which social, political, and cultural ideals have been disseminated and preserved. In *Brown v. Board of Education*,[18] the Court unanimously recognized that "[c]ompulsory school attendance laws and the great expenditures for education both demonstrate our recognition of the importance of education to our democratic society...." However, the Supreme Court has never held that public education is a "fundamental right." In *San Antonio Independent School Dist. v. Rodriguez*,[19] the Court held that education is not a fundamental right and, furthermore, that poverty, standing alone, does not constitute a suspect classification. These are the two strands upon which violations of the equal protection clause of the fourteenth amendment are predicated.

The Court in *San Antonio* implied that had there been an absolute deprivation of education imposed on a particular group, this might be determined to be an

---

17. *Meyer v. Nebraska*, 262 U.S. 390, 400 (1923).

18. *Brown v. Board of Education*, 347 U.S. 483, 493 (1954).

19. 411 U.S. 1, 35 (1973).

impairment of a fundamental right. The plaintiffs in *San Antonio* had claimed that Texas' system of financing public education violated equal protection because it relied on local property taxes. Districts with high property tax bases, therefore, could spend and did spend more on education than those districts with low property tax bases.

Nevertheless, the Court held that there was no denial of a fundamental right, stating:

> we have no indication that the [low taxation] system fails to provide each child with an opportunity to acquire the basic minimal skills.

411 U.S. at 36-37.

Justice Powell, speaking for the Court in *San Antonio*, went on to define a "suspect class" as a "discrete and insular" minority that has historically suffered from "unequal treatment" or is in a position of "political powerlessness" requiring judicial protection from the majority's political processes. Thus, adult citizens have some political power, but undocumented aliens do not because they are not entitled to vote.

The children of undocumented persons seem particularly to fit within Powell's definition of "suspect class." Similar to illegitimate children, they not only have suffered from unequal treatment but are relegated to a state of helplessness, political and otherwise. As the following case demonstrates, the Court has gone to great lengths to obviate the conclusion that the undocumented constitute a suspect class.

Plyler v. Doe
457 U.S. 202 (1982)

[The United States District Court for the Eastern District of Texas, Judge William Wayne Justice, held for plaintiffs, Mexican undocumented children excluded from Texas public schools. On appeal, the Fifth Circuit affirmed.]

Justice BRENNAN delivered the opinion of the Court.

The question presented by these cases is whether, consistent with the Equal Protection Clause of the Fourteenth Amendment, Texas may deny to undocumented school-age children the free public education that it provides to children who are citizens of the United States or legally admitted aliens.

* * *

In May 1975, the Texas Legislature revised its education laws to withhold from local school districts any state funds for the education of children who were not "legally admitted" into the United States. The 1975 revision also authorized local school districts to deny enrollment in their public schools to children not "legally admitted" to the country. Tex. Educ. Code Ann. §21.031 (Vernon Supp. 1981).

* * *

The Fourteenth Amendment provides that "[n]o State shall . . . deprive any person of life, liberty, or property, without due process of law; nor deny to any person within its jurisdiction the equal protection of the laws." Appellants argue . . . that undocumented aliens because of their immigration status, are not "persons within the jurisdiction" of the State of Texas, and that they therefore have no right to the equal protection of Texas law. We reject this argument. Whatever his status under the immigration laws, an alien is surely a "person" in any ordinary sense of that term. Aliens, even aliens whose presence in this country is unlawful, have long been recognized as "persons" guaranteed due process of law by the Fifth and Fourteenth Amendments. *Shaughnessy v. Mezei*, 345 U.S. 206, 212 (1953)...

Appellants seek to distinguish our prior cases, emphasizing that the Equal Protection Clause directs a State to afford its protection to persons within its jurisdiction while the Due Process Clauses of the Fifth and Fourteenth Amendments contain no such assertedly limiting phrase.

* * *

... We have never suggested that the class of persons who might avail themselves of the equal protection guarantee is less than coextensive with that entitled to due process. To the contrary, we have recognized that both provisions ... protect an identical class of persons, and reach every exercise of state authority.

* * *

There is simply no support for appellants' suggestion that "due process" is somehow of greater stature than "equal protection" and therefore available to a larger class of persons. To the contrary, each aspect of the Fourteenth Amendment reflects an elementary limitation on state power. To permit a State to employ the phrase "within its jurisdiction" in order to identify subclasses of persons whom it would define as beyond its jurisdiction ... would undermine the principal purpose for which the Equal Protection Clause was incorporated in the Fourteenth Amendment. The Equal Protection Clause was intended to work nothing less than the abolition of all caste-based and invidious class-based legislation. That objective is fundamentally at odds with the power the State asserts here....

* * *

In applying the Equal Protection Clause to most forms of state action, we thus seek only the assurance that the classification at issue bears some fair relationship to legitimate public purpose.

But we would not be faithful to our obligations under the Fourteenth Amendment if we applied so deferential a standard to every classification. The Equal Protection Clause was intended as a restriction on state legislative action inconsistent with elemental constitutional premises. Thus we have treated as presumptively invidious those classifications that disadvantage a "suspect class,"[1] or that impinge upon the exercise of a "fundamental right." With respect to such classifications, it is appropriate to enforce the mandate of equal protection by requiring the State to demonstrate that its classification has been precisely tailored to serve a compelling governmental interest. In addition, we have recognized that certain forms of legislative classification, while not facially invidious, nonetheless give rise to recurring constitutional difficul-

---

1. Several formulations might explain our treatment of certain classifications as "suspect." Some classifications are more likely than others to reflect deep-seated prejudice rather than legislative rationality in pursuit of some legitimate objective.... Classifications treated as suspect tend to be irrelevant to any proper legislative goal. *See McLaughlin v. Florida*, 379 U.S. 184, 192 (1964).... Legislation imposing special disabilities upon groups disfavored by virtue of circumstances beyond their control suggests the kind of "class or caste" treatment that the Fourteenth Amendment was designed to abolish.

ties; in these limited circumstances we have sought the assurance that the classification reflects a reasoned judgment consistent with the ideal of equal protection by inquiring whether it may fairly be viewed as furthering a substantial interest of the State. We turn to a consideration of the standard appropriate for the evaluation of §21.031.

*   *   *

... [I]ncapability or lax enforcement of the laws barring entry ... [and] ... failure to establish an effective bar to the employment of undocumented aliens, has resulted in the creation of a substantial "shadow population" ... numbering in the millions. ... The existence of such an underclass presents most difficult problems for a Nation that prides itself on adherence to principles of equality under law.[2]

The children who are plaintiffs in these cases are special members of this underclass. Persuasive arguments support the view that a State may withhold its beneficence from those whose very presence within the United States is the product of their own unlawful conduct. These arguments do not apply with the same force to classifications imposing disabilities on ... minor children. ... [T]he children who are plaintiffs in these cases "can affect neither their parents' conduct nor their own status." *Trimble v. Gordon*, 430 U.S. 762, 770 (1977).

*   *   *

Section 21.031 is directed against children, and imposes its discriminatory burden on the basis of a legal characteristic over which children can have little control. It is thus difficult to conceive of a rational justification for penalizing these children for their presence within the United States. Yet that appears to be precisely the effect of §21.031.

Public education is not a "right" granted ... by the Constitution. *San Antonio Independent School Dist. v. Rodriguez*, 411 U.S. 1, 35 (1973). But neither is it merely some governmental "benefit" indistinguishable from other forms of social welfare legislation. Both the importance of education in maintaining our basic institutions, and the lasting impact of its deprivation on the life of the child, mark the distinction. ... [E]ducation provides the basic tools by which individuals might lead economically productive lives to the benefit of us all. ... We cannot ignore the significant social costs borne by our Nation when select groups are denied the means to absorb the values and skills upon which our social order rests.

... [B]y depriving the children of any disfavored group of an education, we foreclose the means by which that group might raise the level of esteem in which it is held by the majority.

*   *   *

Illiteracy is an enduring disability. The inability to read and write will handicap the individual deprived of a basic education each and every day of his life. ...

*   *   *

... Undocumented aliens cannot be treated as a suspect class because their presence in this country in violation of federal law is not a "constitutional irrelevancy."

---

2. We reject the claim that "illegal aliens" are a "suspect class." ... Unlike most of the classifications that we have recognized as suspect, entry into this class, by virtue of entry into this country, is the product of voluntary action. Indeed, entry into the class is itself a crime. ...

Nor is education a fundamental right; a State need not justify by compelling necessity every variation in the manner in which education is provided to its population.... [M]ore is involved in these cases than the abstract question whether §21.031 discriminates against a suspect class, or whether education is a fundamental right....

In determining the rationality of §21.031, we may appropriately take into account its costs to the Nation and to the innocent children who are its victims. In light of these countervailing costs, the discrimination contained in §21.031 can hardly be considered rational unless it furthers some substantial goal of the State.

... Indeed, in the State's view, Congress' apparent disapproval of the presence of these children within the United States, and the evasion of the federal regulatory program that is the mark of undocumented status, provides authority for its decisions to impose upon them special disabilities. Faced with an equal protection challenge respecting the treatment of aliens, we agree that the courts must be attentive to congressional policy; the exercise of congressional power might well affect the State's prerogatives to afford differential treatment to a particular class of aliens. But we are unable to find in the congressional immigration scheme any statement of policy that might weigh significantly in arriving at an equal protection balance concerning the State's authority to deprive these children of an education.

* * *

... In light of the discretionary federal power to grant relief from deportation, a State cannot realistically determine that any particular undocumented child will in fact be deported until after deportation proceedings have been completed. It would of course be most difficult for the State to justify a denial of education to a child enjoying an inchoate federal permission to remain.

We are reluctant to impute to Congress the intention to withhold from these children, for so long as they are present in this country through no fault of their own, access to a basic education....

Appellants argue that the classification at issue furthers an interest in "preservation of the State's limited resources for the education of its lawful residents." Of course, a concern for the preservation of resources standing alone can hardly justify the classification used in allocating those resources....

... While a State might have an interest in mitigating the potential harsh economic effects of sudden shifts in population, §21.031 hardly offers an effective method of dealing with an urgent demographic or economic problem. There is no evidence in the record suggesting that illegal entrants impose any significant burden on the State's economy.... [E]ven ... assum[ing] that the net impact of illegal aliens on the economy of the State is negative, we think it clear that "[c]harging tuition to undocumented children constitutes a ludicrously ineffectual attempt to stem the tide of illegal immigration."

... Of course, even if improvement in the quality of education were a likely result of barring some number of children from the schools of the State, the State must support its selection of this group as the appropriate target for exclusion. In terms of educational cost and need, however, undocumented children are "basically indistinguishable" from legally resident alien children.

Finally, appellants suggest that undocumented children are appropriately singled out because their unlawful presence [makes] them less likely than other children to remain within the boundaries of the State, and to put their education to productive social or political use within the State.... [T]he record is clear that many of the undocumented children disabled by this classification will remain in this country indefinitely, and that some will become lawful residents or citizens of the United States. It is difficult to understand precisely what the State hopes to achieve by promoting the creation and perpetuation of a subclass of illiterates within our boundaries, surely adding to the problems and costs of unemployment, welfare, and crime....

... Accordingly, the judgment of the Court of Appeals in each of these cases is Affirmed.

Justice Marshall, concurring.

While I join the Court's opinion, I do so without in any way retreating from my opinion in San Antonio Independent School District v. Rodriguez, 411 U.S. 1, 70-133 (1973) (dissenting opinion)....

Justice Blackmun, concurring.

I join the opinion and judgment of the Court.

*   *   *

I joined Justice Powell's opinion for the Court in Rodriguez, and I continue to believe that it provides the appropriate model for resolving most equal protection disputes. Classifications infringing substantive constitutional rights necessarily will be invalid, if not by force of the Equal Protection Clause, then through operation of other provisions of the Constitution. Conversely, classifications bearing on nonconstitutional interests—even those involving "the most basic economic needs of impoverished human beings," *Dandridge v. Williams*, 397 U.S. 471, 485 (1970)—generally are not subject to special treatment under the Equal Protection Clause, because they are not distinguishable in any relevant way from other regulation in "the area of economics and social welfare." Ibid. With all this said, however, I believe the Court's experience has demonstrated that the *Rodriguez* formulation does not settle every issue of "fundamental rights" arising under the Equal Protection Clause.

*   *   *

[D]enial of an education is the analogue of denial of the right to vote: the former relegates the individual to second-class social status; the latter places him at a permanent political disadvantage.

*   *   *

Justice Powell, concurring.

I join the opinion of the Court, and write separately to emphasize the unique character of the cases before us.

The classification in question severely disadvantages children who are the victims of a combination of circumstances.... Perhaps because of the intractability of the problem Congress—vested by the Constitution with the responsibility of protecting our borders and legislating with respect to aliens—has not provided effective leadership in dealing with this problem. Although the analogy is not perfect, our holding today does find support in decisions of this Court with respect to the status of illegitimates....

...The classification at issue deprives a group of children of the opportunity for education afforded all other children... A legislative classification that threatens the creation of an underclass of future citizens and residents cannot be reconciled with one of the fundamental purposes of the Fourteenth Amendment.

* * *

Chief Justice Burger, with whom Justice White, Justice Rehnquist, and Justice O'Connor join, dissenting.

Were it our business to set the Nation's social policy, I would agree without hesitation that it is senseless for an enlightened society to deprive any children—including illegal aliens—of an elementary education. I fully agree that it would be folly—and wrong—to tolerate creation of a segment of society made up of illiterate persons, many having a limited or no command of our language. However, the Constitution does not constitute us as "Platonic Guardians" nor does it vest in this Court the authority to strike down laws because they do not meet our standards of desirable social policy, "wisdom," or "common sense." *See TVA v. Hill*, 437 U.S. 153, 194-195 (1978). We trespass on the assigned function of the political branches under our structure of limited and separated powers when we assume a policymaking role as the Court does today.

* * *

I have no quarrel with the conclusion that the Equal Protection Clause of the Fourteenth Amendment applies to aliens who, after their illegal entry into this country, are indeed physically "within the jurisdiction" of a state. However, as the Court concedes, this "only begins the inquiry."...

The dispositive issue in these cases, simply put, is whether, for purposes of allocating its finite resources, a state has a legitimate reason to differentiate between persons who are lawfully within the state and those who are unlawfully there.

* * *

The Court first suggests that these illegal alien children, although not a suspect class, are entitled to special solicitude under the Equal Protection Clause because they lack "control" over or "responsibility" for their unlawful entry into this country. Similarly, the Court appears to take the position that §21.031 is presumptively "irrational" because it has the effect of imposing "penalties" on "innocent" children.

...Illegality of presence in the United States does not—and need not—depend on some amorphous concept of "guilt" or "innocence" concerning an alien's entry. Similarly, a state's use of federal immigration status as a basis for legislative classification is not necessarily rendered suspect for its failure to take such factors into account.

...This Court has recognized that in allocating governmental benefits to a given class of aliens, one "may take into account the character of the relationship between the alien and this country." *Mathews v. Diaz*, 426 U.S. 67 (1976). When that "relationship" is a federally prohibited one, there can, of course, be no presumption that a state has a constitutional duty to include illegal aliens among the recipients of its governmental benefits.

The second strand of the Court's analysis rests on the premise that, although public education is not a constitutionally guaranteed right, "neither is it merely some governmental 'benefit' indistinguishable from other forms of social welfare legislation."

The importance of education is beyond dispute. Yet we have held repeatedly that the importance of a governmental service does not elevate it to the status of a "fundamental right" for purposes of equal protection analysis.... Moreover, the Court points to no meaningful way to distinguish between education and other governmental benefits in this context. Is the Court suggesting that education is more "fundamental" than food, shelter, or medical care?

The Equal Protection Clause guarantees similar treatment of similarly situated persons, but it does not mandate a constitutional hierarchy of governmental services. The central question in these cases, as in every equal protection case not involving truly fundamental rights "explicitly or implicitly guaranteed by the Constitution," *San Antonio Independent School Dist., supra*, 411 U.S., at 33-34, is whether there is some legitimate basis for legislative distinction between different classes of persons....

The State contends primarily that § 21.031 serves to prevent undue depletion of its limited revenues available for education, and to preserve the fiscal integrity of the State's school-financing system against an ever-increasing flood of illegal aliens— aliens over whose entry or continued presence it has no control. Of course such fiscal concerns alone could not justify discrimination against a suspect class or an arbitrary and irrational denial of benefits to a particular group of persons. Yet I assume no Member of this Court would argue that prudent conservation of finite state revenues is per se an illegitimate goal.... The significant question here is whether the requirement of tuition from illegal aliens who attend the public schools—as well as from residents of other states, for example—is a rational and reasonable means of furthering the State's legitimate fiscal ends.

* * *

...The Court has failed to offer even a plausible explanation why illegality of residence in this country is not a factor that may legitimately bear upon the bona fides of state residence and entitlement to the benefits of lawful residence....

It is significant that the Federal Government has seen fit to exclude illegal aliens from numerous social welfare programs, such as the food stamp program,... the old-age assistance, aid to families with dependent children, aid to the blind, aid to the permanently and totally disabled, and supplemental security income programs, the Medicare hospital insurance benefits program, and the Medicaid hospital insurance benefits for the aged and disabled program....

The Court maintains—as if this were the issue—that "barring undocumented children from local schools would not necessarily improve the quality of education provided in those schools."...However, the legitimacy of barring illegal aliens from programs such as Medicare or Medicaid does not depend on a showing that the barrier would "improve the quality" of medical care given to persons lawfully entitled to participate in such programs.

* * *

The Constitution does not provide a cure for every social ill, nor does it vest judges with a mandate to try to remedy every social problem.... Today's cases... present yet another example of unwarranted judicial action which in the long run tends to contribute to the weakening of our political processes....

While the "specter of a permanent caste" of illegal Mexican residents of the United States is indeed a disturbing one, it is but one segment of a larger problem, which is for the political branches to solve.... Yet instead of allowing the political processes to run their course—albeit with some delay—the Court seeks to do Congress' job for it, compensating for congressional inaction. It is not unreasonable to think that this encourages the political branches to pass their problems to the Judiciary.

Notes

1. The Court determined that undocumented persons were not a "suspect class" for purposes of equal protection analysis. In contrast to the involuntary nature of membership in other suspect classes, the undocumented person committed a voluntary (albeit, illegal) act of entry. The Court asserted that their illegal status was not a constitutional irrelevancy because Congress has the power to exclude persons from the United States. In refusing to recognize undocumented persons as a suspect class, the Court obviated the strict scrutiny analysis.

2. It appears that the Court has combined the two factors in *Plyler*, namely, disadvantaged group (the undocumented) and an important interest (education), to justify its use of intermediate scrutiny. It seems from the majority decision that the Court applied nearly strict scrutiny based on these factors despite particular facts that involved a non-suspect classification and a non-fundamental right. In both the Blackmun and Powell concurrences, the Justices urged that the majority opinion should be read narrowly in that the case possessed these unique characteristics.

3. Did the Court in *Plyler v. Doe* muddy the waters of equal protection analysis?

4. In the principal case, the Court held that undocumented children in Texas could not be statutorily denied an education. Also noteworthy is the unreported 1985 decision in *Leticia A. v. Board of Regents of the University of California*, Action No. 588-982-4 (Alameda County), where the California Constitution was held to prohibit a state institution of higher learning from refusing to provide an education to undocumented persons. *See* Olivas, *Plyler v. Doe, and Postsecondary Admissions: Undocumented Adults and "Enduring Disability,"* 15 J. Law & Educ. 19 (1986).

5. The equal protection clause speaks in terms of "persons." The fifth amendment's due process clause also refers to "persons" and was the basis of the decision in *Bolling v. Sharpe*, 347 U.S. 497 (1954), in which the Court held that African-American students in the District of Columbia could not be denied equal educational opportunity. How, then, can "persons" be denied other "rights" (i.e., entitlements)? *See* e.g., *Mathews v. Diaz*, 426 U.S. 67 (1976).

6. In *Shapiro v. Thompson*, 394 U.S. 614, 618 (1969), the Court stated that "Congress may not authorize the States to violate the Equal Protection Clause." There, the Court invalidated the laws of two states and the District of Columbia that denied welfare benefits to residents who had not resided in the jurisdiction for at least a year because the laws *impinged* on the fundamental right of travel. There the Court applied the strict scrutiny tier of review and found that the interests asserted by the state(s) did not constitute a compelling governmental interest sufficient to support the one-year waiting period that the statutes required. Contrary to *Shapiro v. Thompson*, did the Court in *Plyler* indicate that Congress may, in certain circumstances, authorize states to violate the equal protection clause by sanctioning statutes such as the subject statute in *Plyler*? Or can one reconcile the two decisions?

7. What would have been the result had the federal government prohibited the use of federal funds for education of undocumented children?

8. The Court in *Plyler* places some reliance on the assertion that the undocumented should not be treated as a "suspect class" because "entry into the class is itself a crime." 457 U.S. 202, 219. Is such reliance justified if the misdemeanor of entry without inspection, 8 U.S.C. § 1325, is not a continuing offense? *See U.S. v. Rincon-Jimenez*, 595 F.2d 1192 (9th Cir. 1979) (holding that violation of 8 U.S.C. § 1325 is completed at time of entry, and subsequent to such time the appropriate sanction is deportation through civil proceedings).

C. Access to Public Entitlements

As was noted in previous chapters, paupers, beggars, and vagrants are excludable, as are those who "are likely at any time to become public charges."[20] It is also a ground for deportation "within five years after entry [to] become a public charge from causes not affirmatively shown to have arisen after entry."[21]

Beyond the implications regarding immigration status, as such, however, the law of public benefits as applied to aliens is fraught with nuances. The threshold question of eligibility is often dependent on the immigration status of the applicant for benefits. Although such eligibility requirements are usually determined by immigration status as defined by the Immigration and Nationality Act, in some cases courts have carved out their own eligibility classifications.[22]

The extent to which public entitlements can be based on immigration status is largely a question of whether the benefit in issue was enacted by the federal or state government. As is demonstrated in the case of *Graham v. Richardson*, if a state bases eligibility requirements for public entitlements on citizenship status, such legislation is subject to challenge as a denial to persons of the equal protection of the laws under the fourteenth amendment. Congress, on the other hand, may draw distinctions based on alienage when establishing eligibility requirements for federal benefit programs. As the Supreme Court's decision in *Mathews v. Diaz* illustrates, equal protection takes on quite a different meaning within the terms of the fifth amendment due process clause when the federal sovereign acts.

Graham v. Richardson
403 U.S. 365 (1971)

Mr. Justice BLACKMUN delivered the opinion of the Court.

* * *

---

20. 8 U.S.C. § 1182(a)(8); 8 U.S.C. § 1182 (a)(15).

21. 8 U.S.C. § 1251(a)(8).

22. For example, a determination of whether an applicant is deemed to be in the country "permanently residing under color of law" (PRUCOL) has become the governing criterion in many statutory entitlements programs. *See Holley v. Lavine*, 553 F. 2d 845 (2d Cir. 1977), *cert. denied*, 435 U.S. 947 (1978). Calvo, *Alien Status Restrictions on Eligibility for Federally Funded Assistance Programs*, 16 N.Y.U. Rev. L. & Soc. Change 395 (1988)

...The issue here is whether the Equal Protection Clause of the Fourteenth Amendment prevents a State from conditioning welfare benefits either (a) upon the beneficiary's possession of United States citizenship, or (b) if the beneficiary is an alien, upon his having resided in this country for a specified number of years....

No. 609. This case, from Arizona, concerns the State's participation in federal categorical assistance programs. These programs originate with the Social Security Act of 1935, 49 Stat. 620, as amended, 42 U.S.C., c. 7. They are supported in part by federal grants-in-aid and are administered by the States under federal guidelines. Arizona Rev. Stat. Ann., Tit. 46, Art. 2, as amended, provides for assistance to persons permanently and totally disabled (APTD). See 42 U.S.C. §§ 1351-1355. Arizona Rev. Stat. Ann. § 46-233 (Supp. 1970-1971), as amended in 1962, reads:

"A. No person shall be entitled to general assistance who does not meet and maintain the following requirements:

"1. Is a citizen of the United States, or has resided in the United States a total of fifteen years...."

A like eligibility provision conditioned upon citizenship or durational residence appears in § 46-252(2), providing old-age assistance, and in § 46-272(4), providing assistance to the needy blind. See 42 U.S.C. §§ 1201-1206, 1381-1385.

* * *

The three-judge court upheld Mrs. Richardson's motion for summary judgment on equal protection grounds. *Richardson v. Graham*, 313 F. Supp. 34 (Ariz. 1970). It did so in reliance on this Court's opinions in *Takahashi v. Fish & Game Comm'n*, 334 U.S. 410 (1948), and *Shapiro v. Thompson*, 394 U.S. 618 (1969)....

No. 727. This case, from Pennsylvania, concerns that portion of a general assistance program that is not federally supported. The relevant statute is § 432(2) of the Pennsylvania Public Welfare Code, Pa. Stat. Ann., Tit. 62, § 432(2) (1968) originally enacted in 1939. It provides that those eligible for assistance shall be (1) needy persons who qualify under the federally supported categorical assistance programs and (2) those other needy persons who are citizens of the United States. Assistance to the latter group is funded wholly by the Commonwealth.

* * *

...The Fourteenth Amendment provides, "[N]or shall any State deprive any person of life, liberty, or property, without due process of law; nor deny to any person within its jurisdiction the equal protection of the laws." It has long been settled, and it is not disputed here, that the term "person" in this context encompasses lawfully admitted resident aliens as well as citizens of the United States and entitles both citizens and aliens to the equal protection of the laws of the State in which they reside. *Yick Wo v. Hopkins*, 118 U.S. 356, 369 (1886). Nor is it disputed that the Arizona and Pennsylvania statutes in question create two classes of needy persons, indistinguishable except with respect to whether they are or are not citizens of this country. Otherwise qualified United States citizens living in Arizona are entitled to federally funded categorical assistance benefits without regard to length of national residency, but aliens must have lived in this country for 15 years in order to qualify for aid. United States citizens living in Pennsylvania, unable to meet the requirements for federally funded benefits, may be eligible for state-supported general assistance, but resident aliens as a class are precluded from that assistance. Under traditional equal protection principles, a State retains broad discretion to classify as long as its classification has a reasonable basis. . . . This is so in "the area of economics and social welfare." *Dandridge v. Williams*, 397 U.S. 471, 485 (1970). But the Court's decisions have established that classifications based on alienage, like those based on nationality or race, are inherently suspect and subject to close judicial scrutiny. Aliens as a class are a prime example of a "discrete and insular" minority (see *United States v. Carolene Products Co.*, 304 U.S. 144, 152-153, n.4 (1938)) for whom such heightened judicial solicitude is appropriate. Accordingly, it was said in *Takahashi*, 334 U.S., at 420, that "the power of a state to apply its laws exclusively to its alien inhabitants as a class is confined within narrow limits."

Arizona and Pennsylvania seek to justify their restrictions on the eligibility of aliens for public assistance solely on the basis of a State's 'special public interest' in favoring its own citizens over aliens in the distribution of limited resources such as welfare benefits. It is true that this Court on occasion has upheld state statutes that treat citizens and noncitizens differently, the ground for distinction having been that such laws were necessary to protect special interests of the State or its citizens. Thus, in *Truax v. Raich*, 239 U.S. 33 (1915), the Court, in striking down an Arizona statute restricting the employment of aliens, emphasized that "[t]he discrimination defined by the act does not pertain to the regulation or distribution of the public domain, or of the common property or resources of the people of the state, the enjoyment of which may be limited to its citizens as against both aliens and the citizens of other states." 239 U.S., at 39-40. . . .

Takahashi v. Fish & Game Comm'n, 334 U.S. 410 (1948), however, cast doubt on the continuing validity of the special public-interest doctrine in all contexts. There the Court held that California's purported ownership of fish in the ocean off its shores was not such a special public interest as would justify prohibiting aliens from making a living by fishing in those waters while permitting all others to do so. It was said:

> "The Fourteenth Amendment and the laws adopted under its authority thus embody a general policy that all persons lawfully in this country shall abide 'in any state' on an equality of legal privileges with all citizens under nondiscriminatory laws." 334 U.S., at 420.

Whatever may be the contemporary vitality of the special public-interest doctrine in other contexts after *Takahashi*, we conclude that a State's desire to preserve limited welfare benefits for its own citizens is inadequate to justify Pennsylvania's making noncitizens ineligible for public assistance, and Arizona's restricting benefits to citizens and longtime resident aliens. . . .

[A]s the Court recognized in *Shapiro*:

> "[A] State has a valid interest in preserving the fiscal integrity of its programs. It may legitimately attempt to limit its expenditures, whether for public assistance, public education, or any other program. But a State may not accomplish such a purpose by invidious distinctions between classes of its citizens. . . . The saving of welfare costs cannot justify an otherwise invidious classification." 394 U.S., at 633.

Since an alien as well as a citizen is a "person" for equal protection purposes, a concern for fiscal integrity is no more compelling a justification for the questioned classification in these cases than it was in *Shapiro*.

... It is enough to say that the classification involved in *Shapiro* was subjected to strict scrutiny under the compelling state interest test, not because it was based on any suspect criterion such as race, nationality, or alienage, but because it impinged upon the fundamental right of interstate movement.... The classifications involved in the instant cases, on the other hand, are inherently suspect and are therefore subject to strict judicial scrutiny whether or not a fundamental right is impaired....

We agree with the three-judge court in the Pennsylvania case that the "justification of limiting expenses is particularly inappropriate and unreasonable when the discriminated class consists of aliens. Aliens like citizens pay taxes and may be called into the armed forces. Unlike the short-term residents in *Shapiro*, aliens may live within a state for many years, work in the state and contribute to the economic growth of the state." 321 F. Supp. at 253. See also *Purdy & Fitzpatrick v. California*, 71 Cal. 2d 566, 581-582, 79 Cal. Rptr. 77, 456 P.2d 645, 656 (1969). There can be no "special public interest" in tax revenues to which aliens have contributed on an equal basis with the residents of the State.

Accordingly, we hold that a state statute that denies welfare benefits to resident aliens and one that denies them to aliens who have not resided in the United States for a specified number of years violate the Equal Protection Clause.

An additional reason why the state statutes at issue in these cases do not withstand constitutional scrutiny emerges from the area of federal-state relations. The National Government has "broad constitutional powers in determining what aliens shall be admitted to the United States, the period they may remain, regulation of their conduct before naturalization, and the terms and conditions of their naturalization." *Takahashi v. Fish & Game Comm'n*, 334 U.S., at 419; *Hines v. Davidowitz*, 312 U.S. 52, 66 (1941). Pursuant to that power, Congress has provided, as part of a comprehensive plan for the regulation of immigration and naturalization, that "[a]liens who are paupers, professional beggars, or vagrants" or aliens who "are likely at any time to become public charges" shall be excluded from admission into the United States, 8 U.S.C. §§ 1182(a)(8) and 1182(a)(15), and that any alien lawfully admitted shall be deported who "has within five years after entry become a public charge from causes not affirmatively shown to have arisen after entry...." 8 U.S.C. § 1251(a)(8). Admission of aliens likely to become public charges may be conditioned upon the posting of a bond or cash deposit. 8 U.S.C. § 1183. But Congress has not seen fit to impose any burden or restriction on aliens who become indigent after their entry into the United States. Rather, it has broadly declared: "All persons within the jurisdiction of the United States shall have the same right in every State and Territory ... to the full and equal benefit of all laws and proceedings for the security of persons and property as is enjoyed by white citizens...." 42 U.S.C. § 1981. The protection of this statute has been held to extend to aliens as well as to citizens. *Takahashi*, 334 U.S., at 419 n.7....

State laws that restrict the eligibility of aliens for welfare benefits merely because of their alienage conflict with these overriding national policies in an area constitutionally entrusted to the Federal Government. In *Hines v. Davidowitz*, 312 U.S., at 66-67, where this Court struck down a Pennsylvania alien registration statute (enacted in 1939, as was the statute under challenge in No. 727) on grounds of federal preemption, it was observed that "where the federal government, in the exercise of its superior authority in this field, has enacted a complete scheme of regulation ... states cannot, inconsistently with the purpose of Congress, conflict or interfere with, curtail or complement, the federal law, or enforce additional or auxiliary regulations." And in *Takahashi* it was said that the States

> "can neither add to nor take from the conditions lawfully imposed by Congress upon admission, naturalization and residence of aliens in the United States or the several states. State laws which impose discriminatory burdens upon the entrance or residence of aliens lawfully within the United States conflict with this constitutionally derived federal power to regulate immigration, and have accordingly been held invalid." 334 U.S., at 419.

Congress has broadly declared as federal policy that lawfully admitted resident aliens who become public charges for causes arising after their entry are not subject to deportation, and that as long as they are here they are entitled to the full and equal benefit of all state laws for the security of persons and property. The state statutes at issue in the instant cases impose auxiliary burdens upon the entrance or residence of aliens who suffer the distress, after entry, of economic dependency on public assistance....

In *Truax* the Court considered the "reasonableness" of a state restriction on the employment of aliens in terms of its effect on the right of a lawfully admitted alien to live where he chooses:

> "... The assertion of an authority to deny to aliens the opportunity of earning a livelihood when lawfully admitted to the state would be tantamount to the assertion of the right to deny them entrance and abode, for in ordinary cases they cannot live where they cannot work...." 239 U.S., at 42.

The same is true here, for in the ordinary case an alien, becoming indigent and unable to work, will be unable to live where, because of discriminatory denial of public assistance, he cannot "secure the necessities of life, including food, clothing and shelter." State alien residency requirements that either deny welfare benefits to non-citizens or condition them on longtime residency, equate with the assertion of a right, inconsistent with federal policy, to deny entrance and abode. Since such laws encroach upon exclusive federal power, they are constitutionally impermissible.

Arizona suggests, finally, that its 15-year durational residency requirement for aliens is actually authorized by federal law. Reliance is placed on § 1402(b) of the Social Security Act of 1935, added by the Act of Aug. 28, 1950, § 351, 64 Stat. 556, as amended, 42 U.S.C. § 1352(b). That section provides:

> "The Secretary shall approve any plan which fulfills the conditions specified in subsection (a) of this section, except that he shall not approve any plan which imposes, as a condition of eligibility for aid to the permanently and totally disabled under the plan—

> "(2) Any citizenship requirement which excludes any citizen of the United States."[1]

---

1. Pursuant to his rulemaking power under the Social Security Act, 42 U.S.C. § 1302, the Secretary of Health, Education, and Welfare adopted the following regulations, upon which Arizona also relies:

"3720. *Requirements for State Plans*

"A State plan under titles I, X, XIV, and XVI may not impose, as a condition of eligibility,

* * *

It is apparent from this that Congress' principal concern in 1935 was to prevent the States from distinguishing between native-born American citizens and naturalized citizens in the distribution of welfare benefits. It may be assumed that Congress was motivated by a similar concern in 1950 when it enacted § 1402(b). As for the indication in the 1935 Committee Reports that the States, in their discretion, could withhold benefits from noncitizens, certain members of Congress simply may have been expressing their understanding of the law only insofar as it had then developed, that is, before *Takahashi* was decided. But if § 1402(b), as well as the identical provisions for old-age assistance and aid to the blind, were to be read so as to authorize discriminatory treatment of aliens at the option of the States, *Takahashi* demonstrates that serious constitutional questions are presented. Although the Federal Government admittedly has broad constitutional power to determine what aliens shall be admitted to the United States, the period they may remain, and the terms and conditions of their naturalization, Congress does not have the power to authorize the individual States to violate the Equal Protection Clause. *Shapiro v. Thompson*, 394 U.S., at 641. Under Art. I, § 8, cl. 4, of the Constitution, Congress' power is to "establish an uniform Rule of Naturalization." A congressional enactment construed so as to permit state legislatures to adopt divergent laws on the subject of citizenship requirements for federally supported welfare programs would appear to contravene this explicit constitutional requirement of uniformity. . . .

The judgments appealed from are affirmed.

Mr. Justice Harlan joins in Parts III and IV of the Court's opinion, and in the judgment of the Court.

Mathews v. Diaz
426 U.S. 67 (1976)

Mr. Justice STEVENS delivered the opinion of the Court.

The question presented by the Secretary's appeal is whether Congress may condition an alien's eligibility for participation in a federal medical insurance program on continuous residence in the United States for a five-year period and admission for permanent residence. The District Court held that the first condition was unconstitutional and that it could not be severed from the second. Since we conclude that both conditions are constitutional, we reverse.

---

any citizenship requirement which excludes any citizen of the United States."

"3730. *Interpretation of Requirement*

"State plans need not contain a citizenship requirement. The purpose of IV-3720 is to ensure that where such a requirement is imposed, an otherwise eligible citizen of the United States, regardless of how (by birth or naturalization) or when citizenship was obtained, shall not be disqualified from receiving aid or assistance under titles I, X, XIV, and XVI. Where there is an eligibility requirement applicable to noncitizens, State plans may, as an alternative to excluding all noncitizens, provide for qualifying noncitizens, otherwise eligible, who have resided in the United States for a specific number of years."

HEW Handbook of Public Assistance Administration, pt. IV.

Each of the appellees is a resident alien who was lawfully admitted to the United States less than five years ago. Appellees Diaz and Clara are Cuban refugees who remain in this country at the discretion of the Attorney General; appellee Espinosa has been admitted for permanent residence. All three are over 65 years old and have been denied enrollment in the Medicare Part B supplemental medical insurance program established by § 1831 *et seq.* of the Social Security Act of 1935, 49 Stat. 620, as added, 79 Stat. 301, and as amended, 42 U.S.C. 1395j *et seq.* (1970 ed. and Supp. IV).[1] They brought this action to challenge the statutory basis for that denial. Specifically, they attack 42 U.S.C. § 1395o (2) (1970 ed., Supp. IV), which grants eligibility to resident citizens who are 65 or older but denies eligibility to comparable aliens unless they have been admitted for permanent residence and also have resided in the United States for at least five years.[2] Appellees Diaz and Clara meet neither requirement; appellee Espinosa meets only the first.

* * *

The District Court held that the five-year residence requirement violated the Due Process Clause of the Fifth Amendment[3] and that since it could not be severed from the requirement of admission for permanent residence, the alien-eligibility provisions of § 1395o (2)(B) were entirely unenforceable. *Diaz v. Weinberger,* 361 F. Supp. 1 (1973). The District Court reasoned that "even though fourteenth amendment notions of equal protection are not entirely congruent with fifth amendment concepts of due process," *id.,* at 9, the danger of unjustifiable discrimination against aliens in the enactment of welfare programs is so great, in view of their complete lack of representation in the political process, that this federal statute should be tested under the same pledge of equal protection as a state statute. So tested, the court concluded that the statute was invalid because it was not both rationally based and free from invidious discrimination. It rejected the desire to preserve the fiscal integrity of the program, or to treat some aliens as less deserving than others, as adequate justification for the statute. Accordingly, the court enjoined the Secretary from refusing to enroll members of the class and subclass represented by appellees.

* * *

---

1. The Medicare Part B medical insurance program for the aged covers a part of the cost of certain physicians' services, home health care, outpatient physical therapy, and other medical and health care. 42 U.S.C. § 1395k (1970 ed. and Supp. IV). The program supplements the Medicare Part A hospital insurance plan, § 1811 *et seq.* of the Social Security Act of 1935, 49 Stat. 620, as added, 79 Stat. 291, and as amended, 42 U.S.C. § 1395c *et seq.* (1970 ed. and Supp. IV), and it is financed in equal parts by the United States and by monthly premiums paid by individuals aged 65 or older who choose to enroll. 42 U.S.C. § 1395r(b) (1970 ed., Supp. IV).

2. Title 42 U.S.C. § 1395o (1970 ed. and Supp. IV) provides:

"Every individual who—(1) is entitled to hospital insurance benefits under Part A, or (2) has attained age 65 and is a resident of the United States, and is either (A) a citizen or (B) an alien lawfully admitted for permanent residence who has resided in the United States continuously during the 5 years immediately preceding the month in which he applies for enrollment under this part, is eligible to enroll in the insurance program established by this part."

This case does not raise any issues involving subsection (1).

3. "[N]or shall any person . . . be deprived of life, liberty, or property, without due process of the law. . . . " U.S. Const., Amdt. 5.

There are literally millions of aliens within the jurisdiction of the United States. The Fifth Amendment, as well as the Fourteenth Amendment, protects every one of these persons from deprivation of life, liberty, or property without due process of law. Even one whose presence in this country is unlawful, involuntary, or transitory is entitled to that constitutional protection.

The fact that all persons, aliens and citizens alike, are protected by the Due Process Clause does not lead to the further conclusion that all aliens are entitled to enjoy all the advantages of citizenship or, indeed, to the conclusion that all aliens must be placed in a single homogeneous legal classification. For a host of constitutional and statutory provisions rest on the premise that a legitimate distinction between citizens and aliens may justify attributes and benefits for one class not accorded to the other;[4] and the class of aliens is itself a heterogeneous multitude of persons with a wide-ranging variety of ties to this country.

In the exercise of its broad power over naturalization and immigration, Congress regularly makes rules that would be unacceptable if applied to citizens. The exclusion of aliens and the reservation of the power to deport have no permissible counterpart in the Federal Government's power to regulate the conduct of its own citizenry. The fact that an Act of Congress treats aliens differently from citizens does not in itself imply that such disparate treatment is "invidious."

In particular, the fact that Congress has provided some welfare benefits for citizens does not require it to provide like benefits for *all aliens*. Neither the overnight visitor, the unfriendly agent of a hostile foreign power, the resident diplomat, nor the illegal entrant, can advance even a colorable constitutional claim to a share in the bounty that a conscientious sovereign makes available to its own citizens and *some* of its guests. The decision to share that bounty with our guests may take into account the character of the relationship between the alien and this country: Congress may decide

---

4. The Constitution protects the privileges and immunities only of citizens, Amdt. 14, § 1; see Art. IV, § 2, cel. 1, and the right to vote only of citizens. Amdts. 15, 19, 24, 26. It requires that Representatives have been citizens for seven years, Art. I, § 2, cl. 2, and that Senators citizens for nine, Art. I, § 3, cl. 3, and that the President be a "natural born Citizen." Art. II, § 1, cl. 5.

A multitude of federal statutes distinguish between citizens and aliens. The whole of Title 8 of the United States Code, regulating aliens and nationality, is founded on the legitimacy of distinguishing between citizens and aliens. A variety of other federal statutes provide for disparate treatment of aliens and citizens. These include prohibitions and restrictions upon Government employment of aliens, *e.g.*, 10 U.S.C. § 5571; 22 U.S.C. § 1044 (e) upon private employment of aliens, *e.g.*, 12 U.S.C. § 2279; 12 U.S.C. § 72, and upon investments and businesses of aliens, *e.g.*, 12 U.S.C. § 619; 47 U.S.C. § 17; statutes excluding aliens from benefits available to citizens, *e.g.*, 26 U.S.C. § 931 (1970 ed., Supp. IV); 46 U.S.C. § 1171 (a), and from protections extended to citizens, *e.g.*, 19 U.S.C. § 1526; 29 U.S.C. § 633a (1970 ed., Supp. IV); and statutes imposing added burdens upon aliens, *e.g.*, 26 U.S.C. § 6851 (d); 28 U.S.C. § 1391 (d). Several statutes treat certain aliens more favorably than citizens. *E.g.*, 19 U.S.C § 1586 (e); 50 U.S.C. App. § 453 (1970 ed., Supp. IV). Other statutes, similar to the one at issue in this case, provide for equal treatment of citizens and aliens lawfully admitted for permanent residence. 10 U.S.C. § 8253; 18 U.S.C. § 613 (2)(1970 ed., Supp. IV). Still others equate citizens and aliens who have declared their intention to become citizens. *E.g.*, 43 U.S.C. § 161; 30 U.S.C. § 22. Yet others condition equal treatment of an alien upon reciprocal treatment of United States citizens by the alien's own country. *E.g.*, 10 U.S.C. § 7435 (a); 28 U.S.C. § 2502.

that as the alien's tie grows stronger, so does the strength of his claim to an equal share of that munificence.

The real question presented by this case is not whether discrimination between citizens and aliens is permissible; rather, it is whether the statutory discrimination within the class of aliens—allowing benefits to some aliens but not to others—is permissible. We turn to that question.

For reasons long recognized as valid, the responsibility for regulating the relationship between the United States and our alien visitors has been committed to the political branches of the Federal Government.[5] Since decisions in these matters may implicate our relations with foreign powers, and since a wide variety of classifications must be defined in the light of changing political and economic circumstances, such decisions are frequently of a character more appropriate to either the Legislature or the Executive than to the Judiciary. This very case illustrates the need for flexibility in policy choices rather than the rigidity often characteristic of constitutional adjudication. Appellees Diaz and Clara are but two of over 440,000 Cuban refugees who arrived in the United States between 1961 and 1972. And the Cuban parolees are but one of several categories of aliens who have been admitted in order to make a humane response to a natural catastrophe or an international political situation. Any rule of constitutional law that would inhibit the flexibility of the political branches of government to respond to changing world conditions should be adopted only with the greatest caution. The reasons that preclude judicial review of political questions also dictate a narrow standard of review of decisions made by the Congress or the President in the area of immigration and naturalization. . . .

We may assume that the five-year line drawn by Congress is longer than necessary to protect the fiscal integrity of the program. We may also assume that unnecessary hardship is incurred by persons just short of qualifying. But it remains true that some line is essential, that any line must produce some harsh and apparently arbitrary consequences, and, of greatest importance, that those who qualify under the test Congress has chosen may reasonably be presumed to have a greater affinity with the United States than those who do not. In short, citizens and those who are most like citizens qualify. Those who are less like citizens do not.

The task of classifying persons for medical benefits, like the task of drawing lines for federal tax purposes, inevitably requires that some persons who have an almost equally strong claim to favored treatment be placed on different sides of the line; the differences between the eligible and the ineligible are differences in degree rather than differences in the character of their respective claims. When this kind of policy choice must be made, we are especially reluctant to question the exercise of congressional judgment. In this case, since appellees have not identified a principled basis for prescribing a different standard than the one selected by Congress, they have, in effect, merely invited us to substitute our judgment for that of Congress in deciding which aliens shall be eligible to participate in the supplementary insurance program on the same conditions as citizens. We decline the invitation.

---

5. "[A]ny policy toward aliens is vitally and intricately interwoven with contemporaneous policies in regard to the conduct of foreign relations, the war power, and the maintenance of a republican form of government. Such matters are so exclusively entrusted to the political branches of government as to be largely immune from judicial inquiry or interference." *Harisiades v. Shaughnessy, supra,* 342 U.S., at 588-589. . . .

The cases on which appellees rely are consistent with our conclusion that this statutory classification does not deprive them of liberty or property without due process of law.

Graham v. Richardson, 403 U.S. 365, provides the strongest support for appellees' position. That case holds that state statutes that deny welfare benefits to resident aliens, or to aliens not meeting a requirement of durational residence within the United States, violate the Equal Protection Clause of the Fourteenth Amendment and encroach upon the exclusive federal power over the entrance and residence of aliens. Of course, the latter ground of decision actually supports our holding today that it is the business of the political branches of the Federal Government, rather than that of either the States or the Federal Judiciary, to regulate the conditions of entry and residence of aliens. The equal protection analysis also involves significantly different considerations because it concerns the relationship between aliens and theStates rather than between aliens and the Federal Government.

Insofar as state welfare policy is concerned,[6] there is little, if any, basis for treating persons who are citizens of another State differently from persons who are citizens of another country. Both groups are noncitizens as far as the State's interests in administering its welfare programs are concerned. Thus, a division by a State of the category of persons who are not citizens of that State into subcategories of United States citizens and aliens has no apparent justification, whereas, a comparable classification by the Federal Government is a routine and normally legitimate part of its business. Furthermore, whereas the Constitution inhibits every State's power to restrict travel across its own borders, Congress is explicitly empowered to exercise that type of control over travel across the borders of the United States.

The distinction between the constitutional limits on state power and the constitutional grant of power to the Federal Government also explains why appellees' reliance on *Memorial Hospital v. Maricopa County*, 415 U.S. 250, is misplaced. That case involved Arizona's requirement of durational residence within a county in order to receive nonemergency medical care at the county's expense. No question of alienage was involved. Since the sole basis for the classification between residents impinged on the constitutionally guaranteed right to travel within the United States, the holding in *Shapiro v. Thompson*, 394 U.S. 618, required that it be justified by a compelling state interest.[7] Finding no such justification, we held that the requirement violated the Equal Protection Clause. This case, however, involves no state impairment of the right to travel nor indeed any impairment whatever of the right to travel within the United States; the predicate for the equal protection analysis in those cases is simply

---

6. We have left open the question whether a State may prohibit aliens from holding elective or important nonelective positions or whether a State may, in some circumstances, consider the alien status of an applicant or employee in making an individualized employment decision. . . .

7. In *Shapiro v. Thompson*, we held that state-imposed requirements of durational residence within the State for receipt of welfare benefits denied equal protection because such requirements unconstitutionally burdened the right to travel interstate. Since the requirements applied to aliens and citizens alike, we did not decide whether the right to travel interstate was conferred only upon citizens. However, our holding was predicated expressly on the requirement "that all citizens be free to travel throughout the length and breadth of our land uninhibited by statutes, rules, or regulations which unreasonably burden or restrict this movement." 394 U.S., at 629. . . .

not present. Contrary to appellees' characterization, it is not "political hypocrisy" to recognize that the Fourteenth Amendment's limits on state powers are substantially different from the constitutional provisions applicable to the federal power over immigration and naturalization.

Finally, we reject the suggestion that *U. S. Dept. of Agriculture v. Moreno*, 413 U.S. 528, lends relevant support to appellees' claim. No question involving alienage was presented in that case. Rather, we found that the denial of food stamps to households containing unrelated members was not only unsupported by any rational basis but actually was intended to discriminate against certain politically unpopular groups. This case involves no impairment of the freedom of association of either citizens or aliens.

We hold that § 1395o (2)(B) has not deprived appellees of liberty or property without due process of law.

The judgment of the District Court is Reversed.

Notes

1. Consider the following provision of the Immigration Reform and Control Act of 1986, 8 U.S.C. § 1255a(h)(1), temporarily disqualifying newly legalized aliens from receiving certain public welfare assistance.

> During the five-year period beginning on the date an alien was granted lawful temporary resident status under subsection (a) of this section, and notwithstanding any other provision of law—
>
> (A) except as provided in paragraphs (2) and (3), the alien is not eligible for—
>
> (i) any program of financial assistance furnished under Federal law (whether through grant, loan, guarantee, or otherwise) on the basis of financial need, as such programs are identified by the Attorney General in consultation with other appropriate heads of the various departments and agencies of Government (but in any event including the program of aid to families with dependent children under part A of title IV of the Social Security Act [42 U.S.C. §601 *et seq.*]),
>
> (ii) medical assistance under a State plan approved under title XIX of the Social Security Act [42 U.S.C. §1390 *et seq.*], and
>
> (iii) assistance under the Food Stamp Act of 1977 [7 U.S.C. §2011 *et seq.*]; and
>
> (B) a State or political subdivision therein may, to the extent consistent with subparagraph (A) and paragraphs (2) and (3), provide that the alien is not eligible for the programs of financial assistance described in paragraph (A)(ii) furnished under the law of that State or political subdivision.
>
> Unless otherwise specifically provided by this section or other law, an alien in temporary lawful residence status granted under subsection (a) of this section shall not be considered (for purposes of any law of a State or political subdivision providing for a program of financial assistance) to be permanently residing in the United States under color of law.

2. In light of *Mathews*, is there any doubt whether Congress has power to disqualify lawful temporary and permanent residents from public benefits as specified in subsection A?

3. As to subsection B, can a fifth amendment challenge be made regarding the provision itself? Does this section of the law actually require any action?

4. Is legislation enacted by a state on the authority of subsection B constitutional? Or is Congress here attempting "to authorize the individual States to violate the Equal Protection Clause"? *Graham v. Richardson*, 403 U.S. 365, 382 (1971); *Shapiro v. Thompson*, 394 U.S. 618, 641 (1969).

5. Does Congress have the right to constrict the extent of fourteenth amendment equal protection under its Section 5 "power to enforce, by appropriate legislation"? *See Mississippi University for Women v. Hogan*, 458 U.S. 718, 732-33 (1982) [Section "5 grants Congress no power to restrict, abrogate, or dilute these guarantees" *quoting Katzenbach v. Morgan*, 384 U.S. 641, 651 n.10 (1966)]. This is sometimes referred to as the "one-way ratchet theory." L. Tribe, American Constitutional Law 344-45 (2d ed. 1988).

6. Can Congress delegate its virtually plenary power over immigration to the states? Is there anything remaining of the "non-delegation doctrine"? *See Panama Refining Co. v. Ryan*, 293 U.S. 388 (1935).

7. Is it necessary that a state's disqualification of foreigners from eligibility for public benefits be consistent with federal law or policy? Does it matter whether or not the federal law is preemptive? *See DeCanas v. Bica*, 424 U.S. 351 (1976) (state's restriction of employment of those not lawful residents of United States not preempted by federal law or policy).

8. The Court has carved out a substantial exception to the general rule of *Graham* that alienage is a suspect classification. This "public" or "political" function exception has been applied for the most part to state restrictions based on alienage regarding public employment. *See, e.g., Foley v. Connelie*, 435 U.S. 291 (1978) (state troopers); *Ambach v. Norwick*, 441 U.S. 68 (1979) (public school teachers); *Cabell v. Chavez-Salido*, 454 U.S. 432 (1982) (deputy probation officers); *but see Bernal v. Fainter*, 467 U.S. 216 (1984) (notaries public).

9. As the Court notes in *Mathews*, many provisions of the Constitution refer to "citizens." 426 U.S. at 78 n.12. Yet, the fifth amendment refers to "persons." Can the result in *Mathews* be reconciled with the plain language of the due process clause of the fifth amendment, which has been interpreted to include an equal protection component? *Bolling v. Sharpe*, 347 U.S. 497 (1954).

10. Does it make any sense to consider aliens "persons" for purposes of fourteenth amendment analysis but to change the interpretation of the same term for purposes of fifth amendment equal protection analysis when the challenged action in both instances is identical but for the "perpetrator" (state in one, federal in the other)?

Index to Appendix

Unfair Immigration-Related Employment Practices

8 U.S.C. 1324b, Sec. 274B

(a) Prohibition of Discrimination Based on National Origin or Citizenship Status.

(1) General Rule. It is an unfair immigration-related employment practice for a person or other entity to discriminate against any individual (other than an unauthorized alien, as defined in section 1324a (h)(3) of this section) with respect to the hiring, or recruitment or referral for a fee, of the individual for employment or the discharging of the individual from employment—

(A) because of such individual's national origin, or

(B) in the case of a protected individual[23] (as defined in paragraph (3)), because of such individual's citizenship status.

(2) Exceptions.—Paragraph (1) shall not apply to—

(A) a person or other entity that employs three or fewer employees,

(B) a person's or entity's discrimination because of an individual's national origin if the discrimination with respect to that person or entity and that individual is covered under section 703 of the Civil Rights Act of 1964, or

(C) discrimination because of citizenship status which is otherwise required in order to comply with law, regulation, or executive order, or required by Federal, State, or local government contract, or which the Attorney General determines to be essential for an employer to do business with an agency or department of the Federal, State, or local government.

(3) Definition of Protected Individual. As used in paragraph (1), the term "protected individual" means an individual who—

(A) is a citizen or national of the United States, or

(B) is an alien who is lawfully admitted for permanent residence, is granted the status of an alien lawfully admitted for temporary residence under section 1160(a), 1161(a), or 1255a(a)(1) of this title, is admitted as a refugee under section 1157 of this title, or is granted asylum under section 1158 of this title; but does not include (i) an alien who fails to apply for naturalization within six months of

---

23. The reference to "protected individual" was added by the *1990 Act. See* Sec. 553, Immigration Act of 1990, Pub. L. No. 101-649, 104 Stat. 4978 (1990). This change applies only to complaints filed on or after November 29, 1990.

the date the alien first becomes eligible (by virtue of period of lawful permanent residence) to apply for naturalization or, if later, within six months after November 6, 1986 and (*ii*) an alien who has applied on a timely basis, but has not been naturalized as a citizen within 2 years after the date of the application, unless the alien can establish that the alien is actively pursuing naturalization, except that time consumed in the Service's processing the application shall not be counted toward the 2-year period.

(4) Additional Exception Providing Right to Prefer Equally Qualified Citizens. Notwithstanding any other provision of this section, it is not an unfair immigration-related employment practice for a person or other entity to prefer to hire, recruit, or refer an individual who is a citizen or national of the United States over another individual who is an alien if the two individuals are equally qualified.

(5)[24] Prohibition of intimidation or retaliation. It is also an unfair immigration-related employment practice for a person or other entity to intimidate, threaten, coerce, or retaliate against any individual for the purpose of interfering with any right or privilege secured under this section or because the individual intends to file or has filed a charge or a complaint, testified, assisted, or participated in any manner in an investigation, proceeding, or hearing under this section. An individual so intimidated, threatened, coerced, or retaliated against shall be considered, for purposes of subsections (d) and (g) of this section, to have been discriminated against.

(6) Treatment of certain documentary practices as employment practices. For purposes of paragraph (1), a person's or other entity's request, for purposes of satisfying the requirements of section 1324a(b) of this title, for more or different documents than are required under such section or refusing to honor documents tendered that on their face reasonably appear to be genuine shall be treated as an unfair immigration-related employment practice relating to the hiring of individuals.

(b) Charges of Violations.—

(1) In General.—Except as provided in paragraph (2), any person alleging that the person is adversely affected directly by an unfair immigration-related employment practice (or a person on that person's behalf) or an officer of the Service alleging that an unfair immigration-related employment practice has occurred or is occurring may file a charge respecting such practice or violation with the Special Counsel (appointed under subsection (c) of this section). Charges shall be in writing under oath or affirmation and shall contain such information as the Attorney General requires. The Special Counsel by certified mail shall serve a notice of the charge (including the date, place, and circumstances of the alleged unfair immigration-related employment practice) on the person or entity involved within 10 days.

(2) No Overlap with EEOC Complaints.—No charge may be filed respecting an unfair immigration-related employment practice described in subsection (a)(1)(A) of this section if a charge with respect to that practice based on the same set of facts has been filed with the Equal Employment Opportunity Commission under title VII of the Civil Rights Act of 1964 [42 U.S.C. 2000e *et seq.*], unless the charge is dismissed as being outside the scope of such title. No charge respecting an employment practice may be filed with the Equal Employment Opportunity Commission under such title

---

24. Added by Section 534 and 535, Immigration Act of 1990, Pub. L. No. 101-649, 104 Stat. 4978 (1990). These changes apply to complaints filed on or after November 29, 1990.

if a charge with respect to such practice based on the same set of facts has been filed under this subsection, unless the charge is dismissed under this section as being outside the scope of this section.

(c) Special Counsel.—

(1) Appointment.—The President shall appoint, by and with the advice and consent of the Senate, a Special Counsel for Immigration-Related Unfair Employment Practices (hereinafter in this section referred to as the "Special Counsel") within the Department of Justice to serve for a term of four years. In the case of a vacancy in the office of the Special Counsel the President may designate the officer or employee who shall act as Special Counsel during such vacancy.

(2) Duties.—The Special Counsel shall be responsible for investigation of charges and issuance of complaints under this section and in respect of the prosecution of all such complaints before administrative law judges and the exercise of certain functions under subsection (i)(1) of this section.

(3) Compensation.—The Special Counsel is entitled to receive compensation at a rate not to exceed the rate now or hereafter provided for grade GS-17 of the General Schedule, under section 5332 of Title 5, United States Code.

(4) Regional Offices.—The Special Counsel, in accordance with regulations of the Attorney General, shall establish such regional offices as may be necessary to carry out his duties.

(d) Investigation of Charges.—

(1) By Special Counsel.—The Special Counsel shall investigate each charge received and, within 120 days of the date of the receipt of the charge, determine whether or not there is reasonable cause to believe that the charge is true and whether or not to bring a complaint with respect to the charge before an administrative law judge. The Special Counsel may, on his own initiative, conduct investigations respecting unfair immigration-related employment practices and, based on such an investigation and subject to paragraph (3), file a complaint before such a judge.

(2)[25] Private Actions.—If the Special Counsel, after receiving such a charge respecting unfair immigration-related employment practice which alleges knowing and intentional discriminatory activity or or a pattern or practice of discriminatory activity, has not filed a complaint before an administrative law judge with respect to such charge within such 120 day-period, the Special Counsel shall notify the person making the charge of the determination not to file such a complaint during such period and the person making the charge may (subject to paragraph (3)) file a complaint directly before such a judge within 90 days after the date of receipt of the notice. The Special Counsel's failure to file such a complaint within such 120-day period shall not affect the right of the Special Counsel to investigate the charge or to bring a complaint before an administrative law judge during such 90 day period.

(3) Time Limitations on Complaints.—No complaint may be filed respecting any unfair immigration-related employment practice occurring more than 180 days prior to the date of the filing of the charge with the Special Counsel. This subparagraph shall not prevent the subsequent amending of a charge or complaint under subsection (e)(1).

---

25. Amended by Section 537, Immigration Act of 1990, Pub. L. No. 101-649, 104 Stat. 4978 (1990). These changes apply to complaints filed on or after November 29, 1990.

(e) Hearings.—

(1) Notice.—Whenever a complaint is made that a person or entity has engaged in or is engaging in any such unfair immigration-related employment practice, an administrative law judge shall have power to issue and cause to be served upon such person or entity a copy of the complaint and a notice of hearing before the judge at a place therein fixed, not less than five days after the serving of the complaint. Any such complaint may be amended by the judge conducting the hearing, upon the motion of the party filing the complaint, in the judge's discretion at any time prior to the issuance of an order based thereon. The person or entity so complained of shall have the right to file an answer to the original or amended complaint and to appear in person or otherwise and give testimony at the place and time fixed in the complaint.

(2) Judges Hearing Cases.—Hearings on complaints under this subsection shall be considered before administrative law judges who are specially designated by the Attorney General as having special training respecting employment discrimination and, to the extent practicable, before such judges who only consider cases under this section.

(3) Complainant as Party.—Any person filing a charge with the Special Counsel respecting an unfair immigration-related employment practice shall be considered a party to any complaint before an administrative law judge respecting such practice and any subsequent appeal respecting that complaint. In the discretion of the judge conducting the hearing, any other person may be allowed to intervene in the proceeding and to present testimony.

(f) Testimony and Authority of Hearing Officers.—

(1) Testimony.—The testimony taken by the administrative law judge shall be reduced to writing. Thereafter, the judge, in his discretion, upon notice may provide for the taking of further testimony or hear argument.

(2) Authority of Administrative Law Judges. In conducting investigations and hearings under this subsection and in accordance with regulations of the Attorney General, the Special Counsel and administrative law judges shall have reasonable access to examine evidence of any person or entity being investigated. The administrative law judges by subpoena may compel the attendance of witnesses and the production of evidence at any designated place or hearing. In case of contumacy or refusal to obey a subpoena lawfully issued under this paragraph and upon application of the administrative law judge, an appropriate district court of the United States may issue an order requiring compliance with such subpoena and any failure to obey such order may be punished by such court as a contempt thereof.

(g) Determinations.—

(1) Order.—The administrative law judge shall issue and cause to be served on the parties to the proceeding an order, which shall be final unless appealed as provided under subsection (i).

(2) Orders Finding Violations.—

(A) In General.—If, upon the preponderance of the evidence, an administrative law judge determines that any person or entity named in the complaint has engaged in or is engaging in any such unfair immigration-related employment practice, then the judge shall state his findings of fact and shall issue and cause to be served on such person or entity an order which requires such person or entity to cease and desist from such unfair immigration-related employment practice.

(B) Contents of Order.—Such an order also may require the person or entity—

(i) to comply with the requirements of section 274A(b) with respect to individuals hired (or recruited or referred for employment for a fee) during a period of up to three years;

(ii) to retain for the period referred to in clause (i) and only for purposes consistent with section 274A(b)(5), the name and address of each individual who applies, in person or in writing, for hiring for an existing position, or for recruiting or referring for a fee, for employment in the United States;

(iii) to hire individuals directly and adversely affected, with or without back pay; and

(iv) (I) except as provided in subclauses (II) through (IV), to pay a civil penalty of not less than $250 and not more than $2,000 for each individual discriminated against,

(II) except as provided in subclause (IV), in the case of a person or entity previously subject to a single order under this paragraph, to pay a civil penalty of not less than $2,000 and not more than $5,000 for each individual discriminated against,

(III) except as provided in subclause (IV), in the case of a person or entity previously subject to more than one order under this paragraph, to pay a civil penalty of not less than $3,000 and not more than $10,000 for each individual discriminated against, and

(IV) in the case of an unfair immigration-related employment practice described in subsection (a)(6), to pay a civil penalty of not less than $100 and not more than $1,000 for each individual discriminated against, and

(v) to post notices to employees about their rights under this section and employers' obligations under section 274A,

(vi) to educate all personnel involved in hiring and complying with this section or section 274A about the requirements of this section or such section,

(vii) to order (in an appropriate case) the removal of a false performance review or false warning from an employee's personnel file, and

(viii) to order (in an appropriate case) the lifting of any restrictions on an employee's assignments, work shifts, or movements.

(C) Limitation on Back Pay Remedy.—In providing a remedy under subparagraph (B)(iii), back pay liability shall not accrue from a date more than two years prior to the date of the filing of a charge with an administrative law judge. Interim earnings or amounts earnable with reasonable diligence by the individual or individuals discriminated against shall operate to reduce the back pay otherwise allowable under such subparagraph. No order shall require the hiring of an individual as an employee or the payment to an individual of any back pay, if the individual was refused employment for any reason other than discrimination on account of national origin or citizenship status.

(D) Treatment of Distinct Entities. In applying this subsection in the case of a person or entity composed of distinct, physically separate subdivisions each of which provides separately for the hiring, recruiting, or referring for employment, without reference to the practices of, and not under the control of or common control with, another subdivision, each such subdivision shall be considered a separate person or entity.

(3) Orders Not Finding Violations.—If upon the preponderance of the evidence an administrative law judge determines that the person or entity named in the complaint has not engaged and is not engaging in any such unfair immigration-related employment practice, then the judge shall state his findings of fact and shall issue an order dismissing the complaint.

(h) Awarding of Attorneys' Fees.—In any complaint respecting an unfair immigration-related employment practice, an administrative law judge, in the judge's discretion, may allow a prevailing party, other than the United States, a reasonable attorney's fee, if the losing party's argument is without reasonable foundation in law and fact.

(i) Review of Final Orders.—

(1) In General.—Not later than 60 days after the entry of such final order, any person aggrieved by such final order may seek a review of such order in the United States court of appeals for the circuit in which the violation is alleged to have occurred or in which the employer resides or transacts business.

(2) Further Review.—Upon the filing of the record with the court, the jurisdiction of the court shall be exclusive and its judgment shall be final, except that the same shall be subject to review by the Supreme Court of the United States upon writ of certiorari or certification as provided in section 1254 of Title 28, United States Code.

(j) Court Enforcement of Administrative Orders.—

(1) In General.—If an order of the agency is not appealed under subsection (i)(1), the Special Counsel (or, if the Special Counsel fails to act, the person filing the charge) may petition the United States district court for the district in which a violation of the order is alleged to have occurred, or in which the respondent resides or transacts business, for the enforcement of the order of the administrative law judge, by filing in such court a written petition praying that such order be enforced.

(2) Court Enforcement Order.—Upon the filing of such petition, the court shall have jurisdiction to make and enter a decree enforcing the order of the administrative law judge. In such a proceeding, the order of the administrative law judge shall not be subject to review.

(3) Enforcement Decree in Original Review.—If, upon appeal of an order under subsection (i)(1), the United States court of appeals does not reverse such order, such court shall have the jurisdiction to make and enter a decree enforcing the order of the administrative law judge.

(4) Awarding of Attorney's Fees.—In any judicial proceeding under subsection (i) or this subsection, the court, in its discretion, may allow a prevailing party, other than the United States, a reasonable attorney's fee as part of costs but only if the losing party's argument is without reasonable foundation in law and fact.

(k) Termination Dates.—

(1) This section shall not apply to discrimination in hiring, recruiting, referring, or discharging of individuals occurring after the date of any termination of the provisions of section 274A, under subsection (l) of that section.

(2) The provisions of this section shall terminate 30 calendar days after receipt of the last report required to be transmitted under section 274A(j) if—

(A) the Comptroller General determines, and so reports in such report that—

(i) no significant discrimination has resulted, against citizens or nationals of the United States or against any eligible workers seeking employment, from the implementation of section 274A, or

(ii) such section has created an unreasonable burden on employers hiring such workers; and

(B) there has been enacted, within such period of 30 calendar days, a joint resolution stating in substance that the Congress approves the findings of the Comptroller General contained in such report.

The provisions of subsections (m) and (n) of section 274A shall apply to any joint resolution under subparagraphs (B) in the same manner as they apply to a joint resolution under subsection (l) of such section.

Regulations Governing Prohibited Practices

28 C.F.R. § 44

28 C.F.R. § 44.200 Unfair immigration-related employment practices.

(a) General. It is an unfair immigration-related employment practice for a person or other entity to knowingly and intentionally discriminate or engage in a pattern of [sic] practice of knowing and intentional discrimination against any individual (other than an unauthorized alien) with respect to the hiring, or recruitment or referral for a fee, of the individual for employment or the discharging of the individual from employment—

(1) Because of such individual's national origin; or

(2) In the case of a [protected individual], because of such individual's citizenship status.

(b) Exceptions. (1) Paragraph (a) of this section shall not apply to—

(i) A person or other entity that employs three or fewer employees;

(ii) Discrimination because of an individual's national origin if the discrimination with respect to that person or entity and that individual is covered under 42 U.S.C. 2000e-2; or

(iii) Discrimination because of citizenship which—

(A) Is otherwise required in order to comply with law, regulation, or Executive Order; or

(B) Is required by Federal, State, or local government contract; or

(C) Which the Attorney General determines to be essential for an employer to do business with an agency or department of the Federal, State, or local government.

(2)[26] Notwithstanding any other provision of this part, it is not an unfair immigration-related employment practice for a person or other entity to prefer to hire, recruit or refer for a fee an individual who is a citizen or national of the United States over another individual who is an alien if the two individuals are equally qualified.

---

26. The regulations do not include a 28 C.F.R. § 44.200(b)(iii)(C)(1) designation.

28 C.F.R. § 44.201 Intimidation or retaliation prohibited.

No person or other entity subject to § 44.200(a) shall intimidate, threaten, coerce, or retaliate against any individual for the purpose of interfering with any right or privilege secured by this part or because he or she intends to file or has filed a charge or a complaint, testified, assisted, or participated in any manner in an investigation, proceeding, or hearing under this part.

28 C.F.R. § 44.300 Filing a charge.

(a) Who may file.

(1) Any individual who believes that he or she has been adversely affected directly by an unfair immigration-related employment practice, or any individual or private organization authorized to act on such person's behalf, may file a charge with the Special Counsel.

(2) Any officer of the Immigration and Naturalization Service who believes that an unfair immigration-related employment practice has occurred or is occurring may file a charge with the Special Counsel.

(b) When to file. Charges shall be filed within 180 days of the alleged occurrence of an unfair immigration-related employment practice. For purposes of determining when a charge is timely under this paragraph, a charge mailed to the Special Counsel shall be deemed filed on the date it is postmarked.

(c) How to file. Charges may be (1) mailed to: Office of the Special Counsel for Immigration-Related Unfair Employment Practices, P.O. Box 65490, Washington, DC 20035-5490 or (2) delivered to the Office of the Special Counsel at 1100 Connecticut Avenue, NW., Suite 800, Washington, DC 20036.

(d) No overlap with EEOC complaints. No charge may be filed respecting an unfair immigration-related employment practice described in § 44.200(a)(1) if a charge with respect to that practice based on the same set of facts has been filed with the Equal Employment Opportunity Commission under title VII of the Civil Rights Act of 1964, unless the charge is dismissed as being outside the scope of such title. No charge respecting an employment practice may be filed with the Equal Employment Opportunity Commission under such title if a charge with respect to such practice based on the same set of facts has been filed under this section, unless the charge is dismissed by the Special Counsel as being outside the scope of this part.

28 C.F.R. § 44.303 Determination.

(a) Within 120 days of the receipt of a charge, the Special Counsel shall undertake an investigation of the charge and determine whether a complaint with respect to the charge will be brought before an administrative law judge specially designated by the Attorney General to hear cases under section 102 of the Act.

(b) The Special Counsel may, within the 120-day period, issue a letter of determination notifying the charging party and respondent of the Special Counsel's determination that there is no reasonable cause to believe that the charge is true and that a complaint will not be brought by the Special Counsel before an administrative law judge.

(c)(1) If the Special Counsel does not issue a letter of determination pursuant to § 44.303(b) and fails to bring a complaint before an administrative law judge within 120 days of the date specified in the notice provided under § 44.301(b), the charging party, other than an officer of the Immigration and Naturalization Service, may bring his or her complaint directly before an administrative law judge within 90 days of the end of the 120-day period.

(2) If the Special Counsel issues a letter of determination indicating there is no reasonable cause to believe that the charge is true, pursuant to § 44.303(b), the charging party, other than an officer of the Immigration and Naturalization Service, may immediately, or any time within 90 days of the end of the 120-day period, file a complaint directly before an administrative law judge.

(d) The Special Counsel's failure to bring a complaint before an administrative law judge within 120 days shall not affect the right of the Special Counsel—

(1) At any time during the 90-day period defined in paragraph (c)(1) of this section, but before the charging party files a complaint of his or her own, to bring the complaint before an administrative law judge; or

(2) To seek to intervene at any time in any proceeding before an administrative law judge brought by the charging party.

28 C.F.R. § 44.304 Special Counsel acting on own initiative.

(a) The Special Counsel may, on his or her own initiative, conduct investigations respecting unfair immigration-related employment practices when there is reason to believe that a person or entity has engaged or is engaging in such practices.

(b) The Special Counsel may file a complaint with an administrative law judge where there is reasonable cause to believe that an unfair immigration-related employment practice has occurred within 180 days from the date of the filing of the complaint.

Table of Authorities Cited

STATE PROVISIONS

FORMS

Table of Cases

Cases marked with an asterisk are ones which appear in the text.

Articles and Books Cited

Sources marked with an asterisk are ones which appear in the text.

Abramson, *United States of Citizenship Law After Terrazas: Decisions of the Board of Appellate Review*, N.Y.U. J. Int'l & Pol'y 829 (1984)   660

The Agony and the Exodus: Deporting Salvadorans in Violation of the Fourth Geneva Convention, 18 N.Y.U. J. Int'l L. & Pol. 703 (1986)   561

Aleinikoff, *Aliens, Due Process and Community Ties*, 44 U. Pitt. L. Rev. 237 (1983)   29

Note, *The Alien and the Constitution*, 20 U. Chi. L. Rev. 547, 549-50 (1953)   43

Note, *Alien Students in the U.S.: Statutory Interpretation and the Problems of Control*, 5 Suffolk Transnat'l L.J. 235 (1981)   247

Anker, *Discretionary Asylum: A Protection Remedy for Refugees Under the Refugee Act of 1980*, 28 Va. J. Int'l Law 1 (1987)   152, 168

Anker & Posner, *The Forty-Year Crisis: The Legislative History of the Refugee Act of 1980*, 19 San Diego L. Rev. 9 (1981)   152

Anthony, *Which Agency Interpretations Should Bind Citizens and the Courts*, 7 Yale J. on Reg. 1 (1990)   169

Note, *Asylum Adjudication: No Place for the INS*, 20 Colum. Hum. Rts L. Rev. (1988)   153

Barker, *A Critique of the Establishment of a Specialized Immigration Court*, 18 San Diego L. Rev. 25 (1980)   221

Blacks Law Dictionary 112 (5th Ed. 1968)   55

Blum, *Labor Standards Enforcement and the Results of Labor Migration*, 63 N.Y.U. L. Rev. 1342 (1988)   660

W.R. Bohring, *Studies in International Labour Migration* (1984)   409-410

Borchard, *Discretion to Refuse Jurisdiction of Actions for Declaratory Judgments*, 26 Minn. L. Rev. 677 (1942)   221

Boswell, *Immigration Reform Amendments of 1986: Reform or Rehash*, 14 J. Legis. 23 (1987)   19, 349

Boswell, *Rethinking Exclusion: The Rights of Cuban Refugees Facing Indefinite Detention in the United States*, 17 Vand. J. Transnat'l L. 925 (1984)   26, 29

Bryer, *Judicial Review of Questions of Law*, 38 Admin. L. Rev. 363 (1986)   169

*Burgess, *Actual Minimum Job Requirements in Labor Certifications: Application of Title 20, Section 656.21(b)(6) of the Code of Federal Regulations to Experience or Training Gained with the Employer*, 23 San Diego L. Rev. 375 (1986)   420-421

Burke, Coliver, de la Vega & Rosenbaum, *Application of International Human Rights in State and Federal Courts*, 19 Tex. Int'l L.J. 291 (1983)   152

Calvo, *Alien Status Restrictions on Eligibility for Federally Funded Assistance Programs*, 16 N.Y.U. Rev. L. & Soc. Change 395 (1988)   702

Campbell and Taggert, *The International Business Client and Nonimmigrant Visas*, 11 Colo. Law 2545 (1982)   257

J. Card, *Push and Pull Factors at Origin and Destination as Determinants of Migration*, (Aug. 1980) (Study prepared for the Select Commission on Immigration and Refugee Policy)   70

Carrasco, *The Golden Moment of Legalization*, X In Defense of the Alien 32 (1988)   471, 663

Carrasco, *The Implementation of the American Legalization Experiment in Recent Retrospect*, XI In Defense of the Alien 30 (1988)   471, 677

Carro, *From Constitutional Psychopathic Inferiority to AIDS: What is in the Future for Homosexual Aliens*, 7 Yale L. & Pol'y Rev. 201 (1989)   29, 55

Charnesky, *Protection for Undocumented Workers Under the FLSA: An Evaluation in Light of IRCA*, 25 San Diego L. Rev. 379 (1988)   693

Chiswick, *Guidelines for the Reform of Immigration Policy*, 36 U. Miami L. Rev. 36 (1982)   19

Note, *Citizenship: Denaturalization: Diminished Protection of Naturalized Citizens Citizenship in Denaturalization Proceedings*, 14 Tex. Int'l L.J. 453 (1979)   660

Coles, *Temporary Refuge and the Large Scale Influx of Refugees*, 8 Austl. Y.B. Int'l L. 189 (1983)   561

Note, *Compromising Immigration Reform: The Creation of a Vulnerable Subclass*, 98 Yale L.J. 409 (1988)   74

Note, *The Constitutional Rights of Excluded Aliens: Proposed Limitations on the Indefinite Detention of the Cuban Refugees*, 70 Geo. L.J. 1303 (1982)   29

Study, *Consular Discretion in the Immigrant Visa-Issuing Process*, 16 San Diego L. Rev. 87 (1978)   349

Mary Roberts Coolidge, *Chinese Immigration*, (1909)   11

Corwin, *The Numbers Game: Estimates of Illegal Aliens in the U.S. 1970-1981*, 45 Law & Contemp. Probs. 223 (1982)   19

D'Amato, *The Concept of Human Rights in International Law*, 82 Colum. L. Rev. 1110 (1982)   152

L. Davidowicz, *The War Against the Jews: 1933-1945*, (1975)   654

Deluca, *Immigration Law: Entry of International Business Investors*, 17 Int'l Law 535 (1983)   260

Note, *Developments*, 96 Harv. L. Rev. 1334 (1982)   104

Dictionary of Occupational Titles (4th ed. 1977)   271-274, 431, 437

Note, *Due Process and Deportation: A Critical Examination of the Plenary Power and the Fundamental Fairness Doctrine*, 8 Hastings Const. L.Q. 397 (1981)   74

Effect of the Immigration Reform and Control Act of 1986 (IRCA) on the Remedies Available to Undocumented Aliens Under Title VII, 66 Interpreter Releases 655 (1989)   687

P. Ehrlich, L. Bilderback & A. Ehrlich, *The Golden Door: International Migration, Mexico, and the United States*, (1981)   349

Employer Sanctions and Anti-Discrimination Under the Immigration Reform and Control Act of 1986 (IRCA), American Bar Association (1990)   693

Evans, *Entry Formalities in the European Community*, 6 Eur. L. Rev. (1981)   260

EVD Update, 65 Interpreter Releases 964 (1988)   558

Exclusion or Deportation of Aliens for the Conviction of Crimes Involving Moral Turpitude: The Petty Offense Exception, 14 Cornell Int'l L.J. 135 (1981)   583

Note, *Exclusionary Rule in Deportation Proceedings: A Time for Alternatives*, 14 J. Int'l L. & Econ. 349 (1980) 74

Note, *Expatriation—A Concept in Need of Clarification*, 8 U.C.D. L. Rev. 375 (1975) 660

The Expatriation Act of 1954, 64 Yale L.J. 1164 (1955) 659

Note, *Extended Voluntary Departure: Limiting the Attorney General's Discretion in Immigration Matters*, 85 Mich. L. Rev. 152 (1986) 561

Flores, *The Impact of Undocumented Migration on the U.S. Labor Market*, 5 Hous. J. Int'l. L. 287 (1983) 413

Fogel, *Illegal Aliens: Economic Aspects and Public Policy Alternatives*, 15 San Diego L. Rev. 63 (1977) 19

Fragomen & Del Rey, *The Immigration Selection System: A Proposal for Reform*, 17 San Diego L. Rev. 1 (1979) 349

Fragomen & Robosson, *The Foreign Investor: Current Approaches Toward United States Immigration Law*, 18 Vand. J. Transnat'l L. 335 (1985) 260

Frank, *The Anti-Discrimination Amendment*, X In Defense of the Alien 67 (1988) 678

Fuchs, *Immigration Policy and the Rule of Law*, 44 U. Pitt. L. Rev. 433, 433 (1983) 19, 25

Gibney, *The Huddled Masses Myth*, 3 Geo. Imm. L.J. 361 (1989) 29

G. Goodwin-Gill, *The Refugee in International Law* (1986) 147

C. Gordon & S. Mailman, *Immigration Law & Procedure* (rev. ed. 1990) 27, 56, 147, 165, 580

Gordon, *The Immigration Laws of the U.S. and the Employment of Foreign Personnel*, 9 N.C. J. Int'l L. & Comp. Reg. 397 (1984) 221, 260

Gordon, *The Need to Modernize Our Immigration Laws*, 13 San Diego L. Rev. 1 (1975) 583

A. Grahl-Madsen, *The Status of Refugees in International Law* (1966) 161, 178

Green, *The New F-1 Student Regulations: An Analysis*, 7 Immigr. J. 5 (June 1984) 242

Green, *The New F-1 Student Regulations: An Analysis Part II*, 7 Immigr. J. 13 (Dec. 1984) 260

Green, *INS Issues F-1 Operation Instructions: An Overview*, 9 Immigr. J., March 1986 at 3 260

Leo Grelder, Joan W. Moore, & Ralph C. Guzman, *The Mexican American People* (1970) 15

Griffith, *Exclusion and Deportation, Waivers Under Section 212(c) and Section 244(a)(1) of the Immigration and Nationality Act*, 32 De Paul L. Rev. 523 (1983) 583

Guendelsberger, *Implementing Family Unification Rights in American Immigration Law*, 25 San Diego L. Rev. 227 (1988) 471

Harris, *Conflict or Double Deterrence? FLSA Protection of Illegal Aliens and the Immigration Reform and Control Act*, 72 Minn. L. Rev. 900 (1988) 693

Hart, *The Powers of Congress to Limit the Jurisdiction of Federal Courts: An Exercise in Dialectic*, 66 Harv. L. Rev. 1362 (1953) 26, 44

Helton, *The Proper Role of Discretion in Political Asylum*, 22 San Diego L. Rev. 999 (1985) 152, 168

Henkins, *Essays Commemorating the One Hundredth Anniversary of the Harvard Law Review: The Constitution and United States Sovereignty: A Century of Chinese Exclusion and Its Progeny*, 100 Harv. L. Rev. 853 (1987) 29

*U.N. High Comm'r for Refugees, *Handbook on Procedures and Criteria for Determining Refugee Status* (1979)   175-178

R. Hilberg, *The Destruction of the European Jews* (1978)   654

B. Hing, *Handling Immigration Cases* (Supp. 1988)   558, 588

Hing, *Racial Disparity: The Unaddressed Issue of the Simpson-Mazzoli Bill*, 1 La Raza L.J. 21 (1983)   10, 19, 349

Hofstetter, *Economic Underdevelopment and the Population Explosion: Implications for U.S. Immigration Policy*, 45 Law & Contemp. Probs. 55 (1982)   19, 349

Hogan & Hartson, *Immigration—Related Employment Discrimination: A Practical Legal Manual for Evaluating and Revising Claims in the Wake of IRCA*, (1988)   693

Hopper, *Special Handling Labor Certifications for College and University Teachers*, 12 Imm. J. 77 (1989)   432

E. Hull, *Without Justice for All: The Constitutional Rights of Aliens*, (Greenwood Press, 1985)   29

Hurwitz, *Motions Practice Before the Board of Immigration Appeals*, 20 San Diego L. Rev. 79 (1982)   233-237

Note, *Ideological Exclusions—Closing the Border to Political Dissidents*, 100 Harv. L. Rev. 930 (1987)   29

Note, *INS Factory Raids as Nondetentive Seizures*, 95 Yale L.J. 767 (1986)   74

Note, *Immigration for Investors: A Comparative Analysis of U.S., Canadian and Australian Policies*, 7 B.C. Int'l & Comp. L. Rev. 113 (1984)   260

Note, *The Immigration System: Need to Eliminate Discrimination and Delay*, 8 U.C. Davis L. Rev. 191 (1975)   349

Symposium, Implementation of IRCA, 2 Geo. Immigr. L.J. 447 (1988)   74

67 *Interpreter Releases* 224 (1990) 554   Note, *Intracompany Transferee Visas— The Labyrinth of Mobility for International Executives*, 19 N.Y.U. J. Int'l L. & Pol. 679 (1987)   260

James, *The Board of Appellate Review of the Department of State: The Right to Appellate Review of Administrative Determinations of Loss of Nationality*, 23 San Diego L. Rev. 261 (1986)   642

Note, *Jean v. Nelson, A Stark Pattern of Discrimination*, 36 U. Miami L. Rev. 1005 (1982)   152

Juceam & Jacobs, *Constitutional and Policy Considerations of an Article I Immigration Court*, 18 San Diego L. Rev. 29 (1980)   221

Note, *Judicial Review of "Extreme Hardship" in Suspension of Deportation Cases*, 34 Am. U. L. Rev. 175 (1984)   571

Note, *Jurisdiction to Review Prior Orders and Underlying Statutes in Deportation Appeals*, 65 Va. L. Rev. 403 (1979)   221

D. Kesselbrenner & L. Rosenberg, *Immigration Law and Crimes*, (1989)   583

Kobdish, *The Frank Amendment to the Immigration Reform and Control Act of 1986: A Labyrinth for Labor Law Litigators*, 41 SW. L.J. 667 (1987)   693

S.W. Kung, *Chinese in American Life: Some Aspects of Their History, Status, Problems and Contributions* (1962)   11

3 W. LaFave, *Search and Seizure* (1978)   102

Office of General Counsel, INS, U.S. Dept. of Justice, *The Law of Arrest, Search and Seizure for Immigration Offices* (Jan. 1983)   109

Lawful Domicile Under Section 212(c) of the Immigration and Nationality Act, 47 U. Chi. L. Rev. 771 (1982) 583

E. Lazarus, *"The New Colossus"* (1883) 25

Legomsky, *Forum Choices for the Review of Agency Adjudication: A Study of the Immigration Process*, 71 Iowa L. Rev. 1297 (1986) 221, 457, 490

Levinson, *A Specialized Court for Immigration Hearings and Appeals*, 56 Notre Dame L. Rev. 644 (1981) 221

Lichtman, *The New H-1 Regulations: Profession, Professionals and Prominence in Business*, 12 Immigr. J. 69 (1989) 260

Liebowitz, *The Immigration Challenge and the Congressional Response*, 1 La Raza L.J. 1 (1983) 410

Lillich, *The Role of Domestic Courts in Enforcing International Human Rights Law*, 74 Am. Soc. Int'l Proc. 20 (1980) 152

Lopez, *Undocumented Mexican Migration: In Search of a Just Immigration Law and Policy*, 28 U.C.L.A. L. Rev. 615 (1981) 19, 70

Lopez & Lopez, *The Rights of Aliens in Deportation and Exclusion*, 20 Idaho L. Rev. 731 (1984) 74

*Loue, *What Went Wrong With Wang?: An Examination of INS v. Wang*, 20 San Diego L. Rev. 59 (1982) 567-570

Note, *Maintenance of Nonimmigrant Status Under the Immigration and Nationality Act*, 5 N.Y.L. Sch. J. Int'l Comp. L. 391 (1984) 260

Martin, *Due Process and Membership in the National Community: Political Asylum and Beyond*, 44 U. Pitt. L. Rev. 165 (1983) 26, 29, 152

Martin & Houstoun, *European and American Immigration Policies*, 45 Law & Comtemp. Probs. 29 (1982) 19

Maslow, *Recasting our Deportation Laws: Proposals for Reform*, 56 Colum. L. Rev. 309 (1956) 542

Note, *Materiality Standard in Denaturalization Cases: Concealment by Naturalized Citizen of Service as Nazi Death Camp Guard*, 12 Law Am. 757 (1980) 659

C. McWilliams, *Brothers Under the Skin* (rev. 1951) 11

W. Moquin, *A Documentary History of the Mexican Americans* (1971) 14

Musalo, *Swords to Ploughshares: Why the United States Should Provide Refuge to Young Men Who Refuse to Bear Arms for Reason of Conscience*, 26 San Diego L. Rev. 849 (1989) 152

Musto & Ruffo, *Are the Borders Closing? Errico to Reid: A New Court and An Aging Frontier*, 31 U. Miami L. Rev. 1 (1976) 583

Nafziger, *The General Admission of Aliens Under International Law*, 77 Am. J. Int'l L. 804 (1983) 26, 29

J. Nowak, R. Rotunda & J. Young, *Constitutional Law*, § 4.4 (3d ed. 1986) 632

Olivas, *Plyler v. Doe, Toll v. Moreno, and Postsecondary Admissions: Undocumented Adults and "Enduring Disability"*, 15 J. Law & Educ. 19 (1986) 701

Olivas, *Unaccompanied Refugee Children: Detention, Due Process, and Disgrace*, 2 Stan. L. & Pol'y Rev. 159 (1990) 693

I. Oppenheim, *International* (3rd Ed., Roxburgh, 1920) 33

I. Oppenheim, *International Law* (7th Ed., Lauterpacht, 1948) 33

Pedraza-Bailey, *Political and Economic Migrants in America: Cubans and Mexicans*, 165 (1985) 29

Perea, *English-Only Rules and the Right to Speak One's Primary Language in the Workplace*, 23 U. Mich. J. L. Ref. 265 (1990)   693

Perluss & Hartman, *Temporary Refuge: Emergence of a Customary Norm*, Va. J. Int'l L. 551 (1986)   561

Pivec, *Handling Immigration-Related Employment Discrimination Claims*, Immigration Briefings 2 (April 1988)   680

Prinz, *Kungys and Materiality*, Immigration and Nationality Law 1989 Annual Symposium: Advanced Topics 154 (1989)   659

Note, *The Proverbial Catch-22: Unconstitutionality of Section Five of the Immigration Marriage Fraud Amendments of 1986*, 25 Cal. W. L. Rev. 1 (1988)   471

Note, *Reexamining the Constitutionality of INS Workplace Raids After the Immigration Reform and Control Act of 1986*, 100 Harv. L. Rev. 1979 (1987)   74

Note, *A Refugee by any Other Name: An Examination of the Board of Immigration Appeals' Action in Asylum Claims*, 75 Va. L. Rev. 681 (1989)   152

Comment, *The Right of the Alien to be Informed of Deportation Consequences Before Entering a Plea of Guilty or Nolo Contendre*, 21 San Diego L. Rev. 195 (1983)   583

Roberts, *The Board of Immigration Appeals: A Critical Apparaisal*, 15 San Diego L. Rev. 29 (1979)   221

Roberts, *Proposed: A Specialized Statutory Immigration Court*, 18 San Diego L. Rev. 1 (1980)   221

Roberts & Yale-Loehr, *Employers and Junior Immigration Inspectors: The Impact of the 1986 Immigration Reform and Control Act*, 21 Int'l Law 1013 (1987)   693

Rosberg, *Aliens and Equal Protection: Why Not the Right to Vote*, 75 Mich. L. Rev. 1092 (1977)   632, 660

Rosberg, *The Protection of Aliens From Discriminatory Treatment by the National Government*, 1977 Sup. Ct. L. Rev. 275   632

Rosenzweig, *Functional Equivalents of the Border, Sovereignty, and the Fourth Amendment*, 52 U. Chi. L. Rev. 1119 (1985)   74

Rubin & Mancini, *An Overview of the Labor Certification Requirement for Intending Immigrants*, 14 San Diego L. Rev. 76 (1976)   413

C. Sands, *Sutherland's Statutes and Statutory Construction* (4th Ed. 1984)   678

Sanger, *Immigration Reform and Control Act of 1986: The Undocumented Family*, 2 Geo. Imm. L.J. 295 (1988)   19, 471

Scanlan, *Aliens in the Marketplace of Ideas: The Government, the Academy and the McCarran-Walter Act*, 66 Tex. L. Rev. 1481 (1988)   29

Scanlan, *Immigration Law and the Illusion of Numerical Control*, 36 U. Miami L. Rev. 819 (1982)   349

Scanlan, *Regulating Refugee Flow: Legal Alternatives and Obligations Under the Refugee Act of 1980*, 56 Notre Dame L. Rev. 618 (1981)   152

Scharf & Hess, *What Process is Due? Unaccompanied Minors' Rights to Deportation Hearings*, 1988 Duke L.J. 114   74

Schuck, *The Transformation of Immigration Law*, 84 Colum. L. Rev. 1 (1984)   19, 29

P. Schuck & R. Smith, *Citizenship Without Consent: Illegal Aliens in the American Polity* (1985)   660

Note, *Section 212(c) of the Immigration and Nationality Act*, 47 U. Chi. L. Rev. 771 (1982)   583

Note, *Select Commission on Immigration and Refugee Policy: Development of a Fundamental Legislative Policy*, 17 Williamette L. Rev. 141 (1983)   19

Seller, *Historical Perspectives on American Immigration Policy: Case Studies and Current Implications*, 45 Law & Contemp. Probs. 137 (1982)   19

J. Simon, *The Economic Consequences of Immigration*, (1989)   349, 413

Simpson, *U.S. Immigration Reform: Employer Sanctions and Antidiscrimination Provisions*, 9 U. Ark. L.J. 563 (1986-87)   693

Smith & Mendez, *Employer Sanctions and Other Labor Market Restrictions on Alien Employment: The "Scorched Earth" Approach to Immigration Control*, 6 N.C. J. Int'l L. & Com. Reg. 19 (1980)   74

Steel, *In Defense of the Permanent Resident: Alleged Defects Relating to Alien Labor Certification*, 19 S.D.L. Rev. 119 (1987)   413

Stepick, *Haitian Boat People: Both Political and Economic Refugees*, 45 Law & Contemp. Probs. 173 (1982)   152

Sultan, *Ronald Reagan on Human Rights: The Gulag vs. the Death Squads*, 10 U. Dayton L. Rev. 245 (1985)   561

Note, *Suspension of Deportation: A Revitalized Relief for the Alien*, 18 San Diego L. Rev. 65 (1980)   576

Note, *Suspension of Deportation: Illusory Relief*, 14 San Diego L. Rev. 229 (1976)   576

The Tarnished Door: Civil Rights Issue in Immigration, U.S. Commission on Civil Rights 7-12 (1980)   11-17

Note, *Temporary Safe Haven for DeFacto Refugees from War, Violence and Disasters*, 28 Va. J. Int'l L. 509 (1988)   561

Travis, *Migration, Income Distribution and Welfare Under Alternative International Economic Policies*, 45 Law & Contemp. Probs. 81 (1982)   19

Note, *The Treaty Investor Visa: Cure or Bandaid for the Ills of Foreign Investors?*, 15 J. Legis. 45 (1988)   260

L. Tribe, *American Constitutional Law*, 344-45 (2d ed. 1988)   712

Tucker, *Assimilation to the United States: Study of the Adjustment of Status and the Immigration Marriage Fraud Statutes*, 7 Yale L. & Pol'y Rev. 20 (1989)   471, 477

Ulman, *Nationality, Expatriation and Staleness*, 25 Adm. L. Rev. 113 (1973)   628

Note, *United States, Canadian and International Refugee Law: A Critical Comparison*, 12 Hastings Int'l & Comp. L. Rev. 261 (1988)   152

Vattel, Book 1 *Treatise of the Law of Nations*, Cap. 19   628

Verkuil, *A Study of Immigration Procedures*, 31 U.C.L.A. L. Rev. 1141 (1984)   221

Volgt, *Visa Denials on Ideological Grounds and the First Amendment Right to Receive Information: The Case for Stricter Judicial Scrutiny*, 17 Cumb. L. Rev. 139 (1986)   260

Wasserman, *Immigration Law and Procedure*, 211 (1979)   55

*Wasserman, *Practical Aspects of Representing an Alien at a Deportation Hearing*, 14 San Diego L. Rev. 111 (1976)   75-78

Wasserman, *The Undemocratic, Illogical and Arbitrary Laws of the United States*, 3 Int'l Law 254 (1969) 69

Whelan, *Principles of U.S. Immigration Policy*, 44 U. Pitt. L. Rev. 447 (1983) 20

Whom Shall We Welcome, Report of the President's Commission on Immigration and Naturalization (1953) 542

Wildes, *The Need for a Specialized Immigration Court: A Practical Response*, 18 San Diego L. Rev. 53 (1980) 222

Wildes, *The Nonpriority Program of the Immigration and Naturalization Service Goes Public: The Litigative Use of the Freedom of Information Act*, 14 San Diego L. Rev. 42 (1976) 551, 560

Wolff, *The Non-Reviewability of Consular Visa Decisions: An Unjustified Aberration from American Justice*, 5 N.Y. L. Sch. J. Int'l Comp. L. 341 (1984) 222, 260, 349, 384

Note, *Women as a Social Group: Sex-Based Persecution as Grounds for Asylum*, 20 Colum. Hum. Rts. L. Rev. 203 (1988) 152

10A Wright, Miller & Kane, *Federal Practice & Procedure* (1983) 220-221

Index